MEDICOLEGAL TITLES FROM WILEY LAW PUBLICATIONS

THE RIGHT TO DIE
SECOND EDITION
VOLUME 1

SUBSCRIPTION NOTICE

This Wiley product is updated on a periodic basis with supplements to reflect important changes in the subject matter. If you purchased this product directly from John Wiley & Sons, Inc., we have already recorded your subscription for this update service.

If, however, you purchased this product from a bookstore and wish to receive (1) the current update at no additional charge, and (2) future updates and revised or related volumes billed separately with a 30-day examination review, please send your name, company name (if applicable), address, and the title of the product to:

Supplement Department
John Wiley & Sons, Inc.
One Wiley Drive
Somerset, NJ 08875
1-800-225-5945

For customers outside the United States, please contact the Wiley office nearest you.

Professional and Reference Division
John Wiley & Sons Canada, Ltd.
22 Worcester Road
Rexdale, Ontario M9W 1L1
CANADA
(416) 675-3580
1-800-567-4797
Fax: (416) 675-6599

John Wiley & Sons, Ltd.
Baffins Lane
Chichester
West Sussex, PO19 1UD
UNITED KINGDOM
Phone: (44) (243) 779777

Jacaranda Wiley Ltd.
PRT Division
P.O. Box 174
North Ryde, NSW 2113
AUSTRALIA
Phone: (02) 805-1100
Fax: (02) 805-1597

John Wiley & Sons (SEA)
Pte. Ltd.
37 Jalan Pemimpin
Block B # 05-04
Union Industrial Building
SINGAPORE 2057
Phone: (65) 258-1157

THE RIGHT TO DIE
SECOND EDITION
VOLUME 1

ALAN MEISEL

Dickie, McCamey & Chilcote Professor of Bioethics, Law, and Psychiatry
School of Law and School of Medicine
Director, Center for Medical Ethics
University of Pittsburgh
Pittsburgh, Pennsylvania

Wiley Law Publications
JOHN WILEY & SONS, INC.
New York • Chichester • Brisbane • Toronto • Singapore

This text is printed on acid-free paper.

This publication is designed to provide accurate and authoritative information in regard to the subject matter covered. It is sold with the understanding that the publisher is not engaged in rendering legal, accounting, or other professional services. If legal advice or other expert assistance is required, the services of a competent professional person should be sought.

Library of Congress Cataloging-in-Publication Data

ISBN 0-471-04672-8 (set)
ISBN 0-471-04782-5 (vol. 1)
ISBN 0-471-04674-4 (vol. 2)

Printed in the United States of America

10 9 8 7 6 5 4 3 2 1

To Linda, Matthew, and Julia

FOREWORD

Health care professionals, patients, and families are faced today with a bewildering array of complex, and often contradictory, ethical and legal standards on the right to die. It is hard to conceive how rapidly law and ethics have evolved in this field over the last two decades. But it is also difficult to realize how frequently right-to-die cases occur. Conscious decisions to limit medical treatment and let patients die are made in thousands of cases every day in the United States—decisions as simple as not resuscitating an elderly patient with multi-system organ failure or as complex as stopping artificial nutrition and hydration in a young patient with a profound neurologic impairment.

Advances in medical treatment and technology have been the primary driving force generating these new ethical and legal dilemmas. Many of these advanced technologies—cardiopulmonary resuscitation, dialysis, respirators, transplantation, immunosuppressive therapy, and artificial feeding (for example, total parenteral nutrition and percutaneous endoscopic gastrostomy)—did not even exist a few decades ago. And these advances have produced creatures of modern medical technology: brain death, permanent vegetative state, locked-in syndrome, and profound dementia. Another driving force giving rise to ethical and legal dilemmas has been the significant increase in life expectancy, with all the problems attendant upon the aging process, such as those experienced by the four to six million people afflicted with Alzheimer's dementia.

Two notable areas of rapid and substantial evolution of medical practice, law, and ethics are brain death and artificial feeding. Prior to the 1960s, cases of brain death in clinical practice were essentially nonexistent. Since Kansas became the first state to enact a law recognizing brain death as a form of death in 1970, this syndrome has now become a well-established medical entity, and every state now has statutory or case law recognizing this syndrome as the legal death of a human being. Until approximately 25 years ago, the practice of withdrawing artificial nutrition and hydration from patients in a permanent vegetative state or affected by other syndromes of severe brain damage was extremely rare. Today, removal of feeding tubes from these patients is not uncommon, and there is a large body of law and ethics now recognizing that artificial feeding is a medical procedure that may be withdrawn in appropriate cases.

As the legal right-to-die movement passes its 20th anniversary (the *Quinlan* case in 1975) or 25th anniversary (the Kansas law on brain death), many unanswered and troubling legal and ethical questions remain. But one thing is sure. A great deal of statutory and case law has developed during this time. It is extremely helpful to doctors, nurses, ethics committee members, and other health care professionals who deal with these dilemmas on a daily basis to have some reliable guide to these changes and the current state of the law. For this purpose, the second edition of Professor Alan Meisel's *The Right to Die* stands in a class of its own. This text is, by far, the most comprehensive, organized, and readable analysis of the history of legal developments and current law about the right to die, useful and understandable not only to lawyers but also to health care professionals who are not lawyers. It was a monumental undertaking for Professor Meisel to write the first edition and just as substantial an endeavor to revise his original text and bring us up-to-date on recent developments.

This is not a legal text primarily for lawyers. It is directed at a much wider audience of professionals who have found the first edition to be such a useful guide. It is also not intended to be, nor should it be used as, a cookbook for simple legal solutions to complex problems. This is not a book that should be read in one sitting. It requires a great deal of energy and thought on the part of the reader to carefully read and study the complex legal issues that are exhaustively surveyed in these volumes. Any expert working in the field of medical ethics knows what an extraordinary achievement this work represents.

When confronted with the complexities and inconsistencies of ethical and legal standards, how much weight should health care professionals give to actual medical practice, ethical opinions of medical organizations and multidisciplinary bodies, or legal standards? Do changes in clinical practice pave the way for subsequent ethical and legal changes? Does the law lag a few years—or longer—behind clinical practice? What should doctors do in the face of apparently contradictory advice from the hospital legal counsel and the hospital's ethics committee? The United States is so complex and heterogeneous that states vary widely in their current state of the law and ethics. Professor Meisel gives us a comprehensive overview of contemporary law in the United States, exploring both the similarities and the major differences among the states and between case and statutory law.

Numerous legal and ethical issues are still in a state of flux. For example, are there justifiable medical, moral, and legal distinctions between aggressive palliative care (such as giving large doses of sedative or analgesic medication to control suffering during the dying process) and causing death by giving lethal doses of medication (assisted suicide or euthanasia)? Where is the balance between the right of religious freedom for such groups as Jehovah's Witnesses and Christian Scientists and the right of society to impose its values by preserving the lives of healthy children who may die from treatable diseases? Who will make decisions in the future for the increasingly large population of formerly competent patients such as those with Alzheimer's dementia when there is no readily available surrogate? Should the judgments of friends who know the patient's preferences and values have almost as much weight as those of family members? Should cases involving conflicts among decisionmakers be resolved at the institutional level by ethics committees or other institutional mechanisms, or should they routinely go to court for appointment of a guardian? Given the complexity and highly adversarial nature of judicial proceedings, how often, and under what circumstances, should families, patients, or health care professionals be advised to seek judicial resolution of differences of opinion? In the increasingly common cases of severely impaired newborns, where do we draw the line between the parents' right to make decisions for their children based on the parents' own personal value systems and what they perceive to be in the best interests of their children, and health care professionals' rights to preserve life in the face of uncertain prognostic probabilities? How much should federal law, for example, the so-called Baby Doe laws or the U.S. Supreme Court decision in *Cruzan,* apply to individual states? How does state law interact with federal law? How much moral and legal weight should be given to advance directives in the clinical setting?

Two critical issues that, at the present time, are not only unresolved but are also in the earliest stages of a moral/legal debate are examined in the last section of this book. Professor Meisel addresses the legal aspects of the highly controversial issues of assisted suicide/euthanasia and medical futility. Even though powerful special interest groups have highly charged views on these issues, he attempts in these closing chapters—as he does throughout the entire text—to give us an impartial view of contemporary law.

Whatever one's view on the interface between law, ethics, and medicine, we are at least obligated to be aware of relevant legal standards and compare these to actual clinical practice and ethical standards. Professor Meisel's book gives us one important starting point for these deliberations, that is, the current state of the law in the United States in the mid-1990s.

Minneapolis, Minnesota
April 1995

RONALD E. CRANFORD, MD
Associate Physician in Neurology
Hennepin County Medical Center
Faculty Associate
Center for Biomedical Ethics
University of Minnesota

FOREWORD

Before attending law school, I was a staff nurse on a cancer unit of a major medical center from 1980 to 1985. I knew nothing about the law concerning the right to die. Neither did any of the other people with whom I worked, not the other staff nurses, not the nursing supervisors, not the doctors. We made our own rules as the situations required. We had no formal institutional policy about orders not to resuscitate. I never heard the term "double effect." Informed consent meant patients had to sign a form before going for surgery or another special procedure.

Decisions to stop treatment generally were made by a patient's doctor. While these decisions were ostensibly made in the patients' best interest, the nurses and doctors all knew which doctors' patients were routinely transferred to the intensive care unit when death was imminent, which were discharged to hospice care, and which were given morphine in increasing doses. Nobody I knew felt very comfortable with this method of decisionmaking.

The legal landscape since has changed greatly, and it is clear today that the patient's wishes should be paramount when treatment decisions are being made. In its landmark ruling in the *Cruzan* case in 1990, the Supreme Court announced that there is a constitutional dimension to the right to refuse medical treatment. In addition, every state has enacted some form of advance directive law, either a living will statute or a medical power of attorney statute, or both, which allows individuals to preserve their treatment wishes in the event of incompetence. And the federal Patient Self-Determination Act, which went into effect in 1991, mandates that most health care facilities provide information to their patients concerning the right to refuse medical treatment and complete advance directives.

Yet despite these legal changes, much about medical decisionmaking at the end of life remains unchanged. Health care professionals know generally that patients have a right to make decisions about medical treatment and complete advance directives but are often uncertain about the details. Too often, institutional mythology, rather than the rule of law, governs end-of-life decisionmaking. Consequently, the patient's individual voice is still in danger of going unheard.

The rules governing most end-of-life situations are relatively clear. What is not always clear is where to turn for information when these situations arise. Because end-of-life decisionmaking is an esoteric branch of the law, many lawyers—including those who advise health care facilities—are not familiar with anything more than the Supreme Court's *Cruzan* decision.

Professor Meisel's book is therefore an essential tool for anyone interested in questions about withdrawing or withholding life support. Professor Meisel is a highly regarded expert in this area, familiar with both academic theories and clinical practicalities. At Choice In Dying, we receive questions from around the country every day about various end-of-life situations, and *The Right to Die* is an indispensable reference guide. Whether you are a health care provider, a practicing lawyer, a researcher, or simply curious, this book will guide you to and through the information you need.

This second edition of *The Right to Die* contains much more than a compilation of legal updates to the first edition. Professor Meisel has expanded the text to include an examination of such important topics as the relationship between advance directive statutes and right-to-die case law, surrogate decisionmaking statutes and the case law concerning blood transfusions for Jehovah's Witnesses. An entirely new section explores the issue of whether civil liability may attach to end-of-life decisionmaking, a significant area of right-to-die law that has not been fully developed. All of this makes *The Right to Die* comprehensive and timely.

Because each of us will be affected personally one day by end-of-life medical decisions, Professor Meisel's investigation into the law of this area is of more than professional interest. It provides a fascinating window into the way our society is grappling with profound issues such as life, death, individual autonomy, and professional responsibility in a field in which emotions and technology collide.

New York, New York
April 1995

ANN E. FADE, RN, JD
Associate Executive Director of Program
Choice In Dying

PREFACE

In some respects, little has changed in the law governing end-of-life decisionmaking since the first edition of *The Right to Die* was published in 1989, but in other respects the world has been turned upside-down. The medical knowledge and technology that have improved and extended life for so many are still a source of great fear for so many others—the fear that life-sustaining medical treatment will be administered long beyond the point at which it provides any realistic prospect of providing them with a life whose quality they find acceptable.

For the most part, the law in 1989 was on the side of those who did not want to be "treated to death." The developing case law in about a quarter of the states and the living will legislation in the large majority of states recognized the right of individuals to be free of unwanted medical technology, even if the withholding or withdrawal of treatment would result in death. They had, in other words, recognized a right to die, at least in some circumstances.

One thing that has changed is that these trends have been significantly strengthened since 1989. Appellate courts (or federal trial courts) in about half the states have now recognized this right based on the federal Constitution, the state's constitution, or the common law. In only two states (Missouri and New York) have the courts strayed significantly from this consensus. Although the United States Supreme Court—in its first foray in the *Cruzan* case[1] into the mainstream[2] of right-to-die cases—upheld Missouri's departure from the well-trod path, its opinion probably strengthened the consensus. In fact, the *Cruzan* decision was an impetus to the passage of federal legislation—the Patient Self-Determination Act[3]—and led to a flurry of activity in the state legislatures as well. All states have now enacted some form of advance directive legislation. All but three states have living will statutes. State legislatures have also been extremely active in enacting complementary legislation: first, health care power of attorney statutes, and later, surrogate (or family) decisionmaking statutes, do-not-resuscitate statutes, and more recently, a small number of state legislatures have adopted statutes explicitly recognizing that physicians may provide

---

[1] *See* Cruzan v. Director, 497 U.S. 261 (1990).

[2] *See* Bowen v. American Hosp. Ass'n, 476 U.S. 610 (1986) (invalidating regulations governing forgoing of life-sustaining treatment for handicapped newborn infants).

[3] Pub. L. No. 101-508, §§ 4206, 4751 (OBRA), 104 Stat. 1388-115 to -117, 1388-204 to -206 (1990) (codified at 42 U.S.C.A. § 1395cc(f)(1) & *id.* § 1396a(a) (West Supp. 1994)). See **§ 10.21.**

adequate pain-relief medication to patients even if it might inadvertently cause death—what might be referred to as "double effect" statutes.[4]

Out of this multitude of litigation and legislation, a strong national, legal consensus has emerged about end-of-life decisionmaking, marked by only minor exception. It would take something quite unusual to overturn this consensus, and it is likely that as cases of first impression arise in states not yet having a precedential right-to-die case, the courts will adopt this consensus. This is essentially what has happened in the last half decade as the number of states subscribing to the legal consensus about end-of-life decisionmaking has just about doubled from about one dozen to about two dozen. Although many of the new cases are unique in some small way, for the most part they are "copycat" cases both in their facts and in the judicial opinions explaining their resolution.

Yet, all is not well. First, pronouncement of the law by courts and legislatures does not automatically translate into behavioral changes. Many physicians are still hesitant and sometimes resistant to permitting the forgoing of life-sustaining treatment.[5] Despite the fact that the case law has evolved out of end-of-life decisionmaking in nursing homes as well as hospitals, forgoing life-sustaining treatment in a nursing home, especially if that treatment is artificial nutrition and hydration, can be many degrees of magnitude more difficult than in a hospital.[6]

Second, something quite unusual *has* happened. At the same time that the consensus about forgoing life-sustaining treatment has expanded and strengthened, other events have occurred that have the potential for undermining it. While everyone else was waiting for the United States Supreme Court to issue its decision in *Cruzan,* an obscure Michigan pathologist by the name of Jack Kevorkian shifted the ground of the debate about end-of-life decisionmaking when he provided a lethal dose of medication to a woman in the early stages of Alzheimer's disease and then publicized it. Despite the grotesquely theatrical nature of some of Dr. Kevorkian's behavior, it did have the effect of bringing into the open an issue that had been lurking in the shadows. This—along with other factors such as the increased awareness in the United States of the practice of mercy killing in the Netherlands over the past two decades—has sparked a spirited public debate, three state referenda to legalize physician aid-in-dying, one of which was enacted, a trickle of lawsuits challenging the constitutionality of criminal prohibitions on aid-in-dying, and efforts in the medical profession to provide better palliative care to the terminally ill to diminish the pressure to legalize physician aid-in-dying.

The issue of physician-assisted suicide and the closely related issue of active euthanasia have the potential for seriously dividing the medical profession and the public. If that occurs and if the distinction between forgoing life-sustaining treatment (that is, passive euthanasia) and active euthanasia becomes more

---

[4] See § **9.38.**

[5] Solomon et al., *Decisions Near the End of Life: Professional Views on Life-Sustaining Treatments,* 83 Am. J. Pub. Health 14 (1993).

[6] See § **9.40.**

difficult to defend, it is possible that the result will be a retrenchment by courts and legislatures of the law governing the former rather than a liberalization with respect to the latter.

Something else unusual has happened. Although some physicians have still not learned or accepted the legal consensus about forgoing life-sustaining treatment, many others have, and they have integrated it into their care of the dying. Rather than waiting for families to conclude that further treatment is futile and request that it be stopped as has happened in so many of the litigated cases, it is now accepted practice in many places for physicians to initiate discussions about terminating life support. What they are finding, however, is that not all families come to the same conclusion as the Quinlans,[7] the Cruzans,[8] and so many others. Some families want treatment continued even if the attending physician—indeed, any number of physicians—believes that it will not restore the patient's health or save the patient's life. Futile or not, they want "everything possible done." So far, these so-called futility cases have resulted in very little litigation, probably because most can eventually be resolved in the clinical setting. However, resolution often takes time, and sometimes considerable time measured in weeks, months, or even years. Given the increasing pressures on health care providers to reduce costs and the increasing unwillingness of third-party payers to pay for "unnecessary" treatment, the time needed to resolve these controversies could turn out to be a luxury that no one is willing to pay for. If that is the case, it might provide additional incentives to families to agree to terminate "futile" treatment, but it is also possible that it might lead to increased litigation when families refuse either to pay for treatment (that third-party payers will no longer pay for) or to authorize the termination of life support.

This edition of *The Right to Die* updates the legal developments in the consensus about forgoing life-sustaining treatment. I have reorganized the material from the first edition to better reflect both the logic of the decisionmaking process in the clinical setting and the structure of judicial analyses of forgoing life-sustaining treatment. **Part I** deals with introductory material—what the right to die is (**Chapter 1**) and what its legal foundations are (**Chapter 2**). **Part II** focuses on decisionmaking *procedures.* Most of the attention is directed to incompetent patients, but some of the discussion also applies to competent patients. The main theme of **Part II** is whether or not end-of-life decisions need judicial supervision (**Chapter 5**), but I also examine issues of informed consent (**Chapter 3**) and determination of incompetence (**Chapter 4**). The chapter on ethics committees (**Chapter 6**) has been moved to this part to reflect the role they can play in end-of-life decisionmaking.

The focus of **Part III** is *standards* for decisionmaking for incompetent patients (**Chapter 7**). However, this part also discusses limitations that might exist on implementing end-of-life decisions even if the decisionmaking standard

---

[7] *See In re* Quinlan, 355 A.2d 647 (N.J. 1976).

[8] *See* Cruzan v. Harmon, 760 S.W.2d 408 (Mo. 1988).

is met (**Chapter 8**), such as countervailing state interests and limitations that might be imposed by the nature of the patient's illness or injury or by the treatment in question (**Chapter 9**). **Chapter 9** also includes a thorough discussion of do-not-resuscitate statutes, which state legislatures are enacting in increasing numbers.

Part IV is devoted to *advance directives.* **Chapter 10** is a general overview of the law and, in particular, the common law governing advance directives. **Chapters 11** and **12** examine statutory bases for advance directives, specifically, living will statutes and health care power of attorney statutes, respectively. Practical advice for drafting advance directives—especially advance directives that depart from the statutory forms—and for administering advance directives are the subjects of **Chapter 13.** A new chapter, **Chapter 14,** addresses surrogate decisionmaking statutes that are increasingly important in the absence of an advance directive.

Part V deals with decisionmaking for children. There has been very little development here except for a slowly growing body of law concerning mature minors.

In addition, there are several new topics in **Part VI.** Entire chapters are devoted to civil liability in connection with end-of-life decisionmaking (**Chapter 17**), criminal liability arising from forgoing life-sustaining treatment and from more active interventions to end life, including assisted suicide and active euthanasia (**Chapter 18**), and the demands of patients or their surrogates for "futile" medical treatment (**Chapter 19**).

An effort has been made to avoid gender-specific terminology wherever appropriate. However, when this was not possible and in order to avoid inconvenience or awkward phrasing, I have used the masculine pronouns *he, his,* and *him* in their gender-neutral form to stand as the singular indefinite pronoun. This usage is employed to avoid awkward grammatical situations that would likely occur because of limitations of the English language.

Pittsburgh, Pennsylvania ALAN MEISEL
May 1995

ACKNOWLEDGMENTS

In any work of this scope, an author is of necessity indebted to many people. The intellectual inspiration for this book traces its roots to my studies under Jay Katz at Yale Law School, who was then and is now the preeminent theoretician of medical decisionmaking. When I was studying with Dr. Katz more than a quarter century ago, he was assisted by Alexander M. Capron, who went on to become the Director of the President's Commission for the Study of Ethical Problems in Medicine and Biomedical and Behavioral Research (and who is now the Henry W. Bruce Professor of Law and Medicine at the University of Southern California), and who invited me to serve as the Commission's Assistant Director for legal studies, an experience which brought me in closer contact with the topic of this book.

In researching and writing, I have been aided by a number of law students—on the first edition, Kathy Cerminara, Steven Chernus, Karen A. Fisher, Elaine B. Krasik, Birgit Pedersen, Mary A. Schieve, Edward F. Voelker, Jr., and Joan C. Zangrilli; in the supplements to the first edition, Cathy Boyer, Karen McGoldrick DeBroff, Diane D. Krausert, and Christopher J. Matey. Christopher J. Matey and Laura M. Odwazny provided me with outstanding assistance for this edition of *The Right to Die*. Two others have helped me with research on this edition, Kathleen Boehm, a research assistant at the University of Pittsburgh Center for Medical Ethics, and Joel Kemp, a student at Harvard College studying on a R.K. Mellon/N.E.E.D. Fellowship at the Center for Medical Ethics. The assistance and resourcefulness of William Prip, of Choice In Dying, must also be acknowledged.

My everlasting appreciation goes to Dr. Thomas Detre, Senior Vice-Chancellor for Health Sciences at the University of Pittsburgh, for creating an atmosphere in which multidisciplinary collaboration has flourished and in which I have been fortunate to have participated for more than two decades. I have also been fortunate to have had colleagues in the Law and Psychiatry Program and in the Center for Medical Ethics at the University of Pittsburgh, especially Paul S. Appelbaum, Robert M. Arnold, Joel Frader, Charles W. Lidz, and Loren H. Roth, who have provided a continual source of intellectual stimulation and collaboration relevant to the subject of this treatise. Deans at the University of Pittsburgh School of Law—especially former dean Mark A. Nordenberg and current dean Peter M. Shane—have provided an atmosphere most conducive to reflection and writing.

For manuscript preparation, I am indebted to LuAnn Driscoll, Karen Knochel, Darlene Mocello, Carolyn Rohan, and Barbara Salopek, and for general assistance to Beth Ann Pischke and Pat Szalla. The staff at Wiley Law Publications—especially Carol Gross and Susan Junkin—have provided me with an unparalleled, outstanding level of assistance.

Finally, my love and appreciation go to Linda, Matthew, and Julia for their lovingly tolerating my absences through the lengthy gestation of the second edition of *The Right to Die.*

A.M.

ABOUT THE AUTHOR

Alan Meisel is the Dickie, McCamey & Chilcote Professor of Bioethics, Law, and Psychiatry at the University of Pittsburgh, and a graduate of Yale College and Yale Law School. He is also the founder and director of the University's Center for Medical Ethics.

Professor Meisel served on the Ethics Working Group of the White House Task Force on Health Care Reform in 1993. He also served as Assistant Director for Legal Studies at the President's Commission for the Study of Ethical Problems in Medicine in 1982, where he participated in the authorship of the Commission's studies on informed consent (*Making Health Care Decisions*) and on end-of-life decisionmaking (*Deciding to Forego Life-Sustaining Treatment*). He served as a consultant to the Congressional Office of Technology Assessment on its studies on *Life-Sustaining Technologies* and on *Institutional Protocols for Health Care Decisionmaking*.

Professor Meisel, a Fellow of the Hastings Center, has published widely in the fields of health law and medical ethics. The first edition of *The Right to Die* won the 1989 Association of American Publishers Award for the outstanding book in the legal practice category. He is a frequent speaker before audiences of lawyers, physicians, and other health care professionals.

SUMMARY CONTENTS

Volume 1

Volume 2

DETAILED CONTENTS

Volume 1

SHORT REFERENCE LIST

Short Reference	*Full Reference*
EMTALA	Emergency Medical Treatment and Active Labor Act, 42 U.S.C.A. § 1395dd (West 1992)
Hastings Center Guidelines	Hastings Center, Guidelines on the Termination of Life-Sustaining Treatment and Care of the Dying (1987)
PSDA	Patient Self-Determination Act, Pub. L. No. 101-508, §§ 4206, 4751 (OBRA), 104 Stat. 1388-115 to -117, 1388-204 to -206 (1990) (codified at 42 U.S.C.A. § 1395cc(f)(1) & *id.* § 1396a(a) (West Supp. 1994))
President's Commission, Deciding to Forego Life-Sustaining Treatment	President's Commission for the Study of Ethical Problems in Medicine and Biomedical and Behavioral Research, Deciding to Forego Life-Sustaining Treatment (1983)
President's Commission, Making Health Care Decisions	President's Commission for the Study of Ethical Problems in Medicine and Biomedical and Behavioral Research, Making Health Care Decisions: The Ethical and Legal Implications of Informed Consent in the Patient-Practitioner Relationship (1982)
UHCDA	Uniform Health-Care Decisions Act, 9 U.L.A. pt. I at 93 (West Supp. 1994)
UMHCCA	Uniform Model Health-Care Consent Act, 9 U.L.A. pt. I at 453 (West 1988 & Supp. 1994)
URTIA	Uniform Rights of the Terminally Ill Act, 9B U.L.A. 127 (West Supp. 1994)

PART I

INTRODUCTION

CHAPTER 1

WHAT IS THE RIGHT TO DIE?

§ 1.1 Meaning of the Right to Die

This treatise is an examination of the law governing the topic that has come to be known popularly and by some courts as the "right to die."[1] Others refer to it as "forgoing life-sustaining treatment"[2] or "end-of-life decisionmaking" or

---

[1] **US:** Cruzan v. Director, 497 U.S. 261, 277 (1990) ("[We] have been squarely presented with the issue of whether the United States Constitution grants what is in common parlance referred to as a 'right to die.' ").

CA4: *In re* Baby "K," 832 F. Supp. 1022, 1031 (E.D. Va. 1993) ("right to refuse medical treatment, often called a 'right to die' ").

CA: Bouvia v. Superior Court (Glenchur), 225 Cal. Rptr. 297, 307 (Ct. App. 1986) ("right to die is an integral part of our right to control our own destinies").

MI: Rosebush v. Oakland County Prosecutor, 491 N.W.2d 633, 700 (Mich. Ct. App. 1992) ("so-called 'right to die' ").

[2] President's Comm'n for the Study of Ethical Problems in Medicine & Biomedical & Behavioral Research, Deciding to Forego Life-Sustaining Treatment (1983) [hereinafter President's Comm'n, Deciding to Forego Life-Sustaining Treatment].

"decisionmaking near the end of life."[3] It is a relatively young and undeveloped area of the law, yet it is rapidly growing.

The term *right to die* is increasingly used both popularly and in legal contexts to apply to an individual's right to refuse medical treatment, the refusal of which will cause death. Although not used in all legal cases, the term has had long popular currency and is increasingly being used by courts,[4] sometimes in combination with the phrases "natural death" or "death with dignity."[5] The term *right to die* is sometimes equated with *mercy killing* or *euthanasia.*[6] The former is inaccurate, for it contemplates the active taking of life. The term *euthanasia* (or, more properly, passive euthanasia), when used to refer to the withholding or withdrawal of life-sustaining medical treatment, is an accurate depiction of what the law permits under the banner of the right to die, despite the occasional discomfort of judges with the term.[7] Some think it ironic that there would be any need to establish a legal right to die, given that death is inevitable.[8] However, as Justice Stevens observed in the first and only United States Supreme Court case on this subject, *Cruzan v. Director,* "Medical advances have altered the physiological conditions of death in ways that may be alarming: Highly invasive treatment may perpetuate human existence through a merger of body and machine that some might reasonably regard as an insult to life rather than as its continuation."[9] Thus, in effect, the efforts to establish a legal right to die recognize and originate in a technological imperative that sometimes compels the use of medical technology simply because it is available and is capable of

---

[3] *See, e.g.,* Solomon et al., *Decisions Near the End of Life: Professional Views on Life-Sustaining Treatments,* 83 Am. J. Pub. Health 14 (1993).

[4] **US:** Cruzan v. Director, 497 U.S. 261, 277 (1990).

DRI: Gray v. Romeo, 697 F. Supp. 580 (D.R.I. 1988).

CA: Bouvia v. Superior Court (Glenchur), 225 Cal. Rptr. 297, 307 (Ct. App. 1986).

MA: Brophy v. New Eng. Sinai Hosp., Inc., 497 N.E.2d 626, 628, 642 (Mass. 1986).

NJ: *In re* Jobes, 529 A.2d 434, 452–61 (N.J. 1987) (Handler, J., concurring).

NY: Delio v. Westchester County Medical Ctr., 516 N.Y.S.2d 677, 680 (App. Div. 1987).

WA: *In re* Grant, 747 P.2d 445 (Wash. 1987), *modified,* 757 P.2d 534 (Wash. 1988).

[5] **MA:** Brophy v. New Eng. Sinai Hosp., Inc., 497 N.E.2d 626, 628 (Mass. 1986).

WA: *In re* Grant, 747 P.2d 445, 458 (Wash. 1987).

[6] *See, e.g.,* Delio v. Westchester County Medical Ctr., 510 N.Y.S.2d 415, 415 (Sup. Ct. 1986), *rev'd,* 516 N.Y.S.2d 677 (App. Div. 1987).

[7] Kamisar, *When Is There a Constitutional "Right to Die"? When Is There No Constitutional "Right To Live"?,* 25 Ga. L. Rev. 1203, 1203 (1991) ("The 'right to die' is a euphemism for what almost everybody used to call a form of euthanasia—'passive' or 'negative' or 'indirect' euthanasia."). See **Ch. 18.**

[8] *See, e.g.,* Cruzan v. Harmon, 760 S.W.2d 408, 428 (Mo. 1988) (Blackmar, J., dissenting) ("For most of the world's history, and presently in most parts of the world, such decisions would never arise because the technology would not be available.").

[9] 497 U.S. 261, 339 (1990) (Stevens, J., dissenting).

maintaining biological existence but without regard to the meaning of that existence. Justice Stevens's thoughts are also instructive in this regard: "Life, particularly human life, is not commonly thought of as a merely physiological condition or function. Its sanctity is often thought to derive from the impossibility of any such reduction."[10]

The term *right to die* has some unfortunate connotations. Although to many lawyers the word *right* is an almost sacred one, many in the health care professions have a quite different reaction. The rights of patients are often seen as antithetical to the interests (or perhaps even the rights) of health care professionals. The language of "rights" denotes to many an adversarial relationship between patients and health care professionals and perhaps, consciously or unconsciously, conjures up images of the two most dreaded of all legal phenomena, the criminal prosecution and the malpractice lawsuit.

Many health care professionals and laypersons confuse the word *right* with *duty.* Consequently, when *right* is used with *die,* the phrase connotes to some that death is preferable to life. Worse, perhaps, is the connotation that if patients have a right to die, health care professionals have a duty to let them die, to abandon them, or even to kill them. Thinking of this sort is not entirely rational and is sometimes governed by emotional or political concerns. Nonetheless, it does exist and makes the term *right to die* unnecessarily controversial in what is inherently an already controversial area.

Handy substitutes for the phrase *right to die* do not easily suggest themselves. All of the opinions of the justices in *Cruzan v. Director*[11] used the term "right to refuse treatment" or some other variation such as "right to refuse life-sustaining treatment" in preference to "right to die." The President's Commission for the Study of Ethical Problems in Medicine and Biomedical and Behavioral Research, perhaps taking the lead from its own unwieldy name, chose to use the phrase "forgoing life-sustaining treatment."[12] Although more descriptive of the problem than "right to die," "forgoing life-sustaining treatment" is itself somewhat misleading, for it implies that the problem under consideration is making decisions about terminating or withholding treatment; in other words, this formulation assumes the conclusion. The central problems are the legitimacy of *forgoing* or *administering* treatment, and the procedures by which such decisions should be made. Although the overwhelming proportion of reported right-to-die cases have been initiated because of a desire to forgo treatment, we should not lose sight of the fact that this is only one-half of the larger issue of how decisions should be made about life-sustaining treatment, whether the decision ultimately is to forgo treatment or to administer it.

---

[10] *Id.* at 345–46.

[11] 497 U.S. 261 (1990).

[12] *See* President's Comm'n, Deciding to Forego Life-Sustaining Treatment (1983).

§ 1.2 Purpose of This Treatise

This treatise is intended to assist health care professionals, the administrators and risk managers of health care facilities, their legal counsel, and legal counsel for patients and their families in making decisions about forgoing or continuing life-sustaining medical treatment by explaining the law that governs this decisionmaking process. Whether it is warranted or not, concern about legal liability pervades the end-of-life decisionmaking process. Therefore, another purpose of this treatise is to delineate the boundaries between lawful and unlawful practices in order to dispel unwarranted fears and to demarcate where realistic fears begin. Finally, there are areas of this topic, large and small, that are in the process of developing and changing. Another purpose of this treatise is to suggest ways in which the right to die ought to develop.

There is now a clear legal consensus about the circumstances under which and the procedures by which life-sustaining medical treatment can be withheld or withdrawn based on the request of a competent patient or the family or other surrogate of an incompetent patient, without incurring liability. This consensus parallels, and has been strongly shaped by, the one that has developed in the medical profession.[13] However, there is still no case law in about half the jurisdictions, and in those jurisdictions it is a matter of predicting whether or not the generally accepted consensus will be adopted, modified, or rejected by the appellate courts. Although most jurisdictions without case law have one or more statutes (advance directive and surrogate decisionmaking statutes) related to end-of-life decisionmaking, these statutes do not resolve most of the dilemmas that arise. Therefore, another purpose of this treatise is to assist health care professionals and administrators, in consultation with the lawyers who advise them, in jurisdictions without clear legal guidance, in extrapolating from what law there is in their jurisdiction and from the law of other jurisdictions.

§ 1.3 Scope of the Topic

The primary focus of this treatise is on how the case law and statutes should affect decisionmaking about life-sustaining treatment and, more particularly, about whether such treatment may be forgone or must be administered.

Legal Sources of the Right to Die. The right to die is a part of the larger body of law—tort law, constitutional law, and criminal law—governing the manner in which decisions about medical treatment are to be made. The legal sources of the right to die are discussed in **Part I (Chapter 2).**

---

[13] National Ctr. for State Courts, Guidelines for State Court Decision Making in Life-Sustaining Medical Treatment Cases 143 (2d ed. 1992) (principle E).

Decisionmaking Procedures. Since the beginning of right-to-die litigation, the appropriate procedures for making decisions about life-sustaining treatment have been a source of great uncertainty and consternation to health care professionals. The central procedural issue is at what point or points in the process, if any, must decisionmaking take place under judicial auspices or under what circumstances may such decisions be made in the clinical setting between patients, families, friends, and health care professionals without judicial supervision or review?

These questions are especially vexing when patients lack the capacity to make treatment decisions. At some point in a terminal or critical illness, many patients lose this capacity before death occurs *because* the patient is dying. Thus, many patients are not able to participate in decisionmaking for the very reason that a decision needs to be made—that is, because they are incapacitated by the severity of their illness. Some such patients may be comatose, stuporous, senile, or in toxic states. Whatever the reason, decisionmaking in these situations presents far more difficult issues than when patients are able to participate in making decisions about their own health care. However, these issues have lost the preeminence that they once had in the debate about the right to die. There is now hardly any dissent from the general proposition that end-of-life decisionmaking should generally occur in the privacy of the doctor-patient-family relationship. Nonetheless, questions still arise in particular cases about whether or not a particular patient lacks decisionmaking capacity and about who is authorized to speak for such patients.

Although no cookbook of rules can be prescribed for determining what are legally acceptable situations in which to permit the forgoing of life-sustaining treatment, following accepted legal procedures in end-of-life decisionmaking can go a long way in reassuring the participants that the decision is an appropriate one. **Part II** of this treatise addresses decisionmaking procedures for patients who have decisionmaking capacity **(Chapter 3),** the standards for distinguishing between competent and incompetent patients **(Chapter 4),** and decisionmaking procedures for patients who have lost that capacity permanently or temporarily, or possibly never had it **(Chapter 5).** The use of ethics committees in the decisionmaking process is discussed in **Chapter 6. Part IV (Chapters 10 through 14)** addresses mechanisms, primarily statutory, for aiding decisionmaking for incompetent patients, specifically, advance directives (living wills and health care powers of attorney) and the surrogate decisionmaking statutes.

Decisionmaking Standards. The central substantive issue in the law governing end-of-life decisionmaking is to distinguish between those situations in which it is lawful to forgo life-sustaining treatment and those in which it is not. Although the boundaries of the right to die are inherently fuzzy, they do exist. The problem for law is to assure that patients do not fall victim to the twin evils of neglect and abuse on the one hand—being allowed to die (or even having their lives actively ended) when they should not—or, on the other, being "treated to death"—having treatment imposed when it should not be.[14] Thus, this treatise provides guidance as to what kinds of decisions to forgo life-sustaining treatment might be considered impermissible even if the proper procedures are followed.

In the case of competent patients—patients who possess the capacity to make decisions personally and contemporaneously about their own medical care—the right to refuse treatment is gradually becoming absolute. **Chapter 3** discusses decisionmaking for competent patients, and **Chapter 4** addresses standards for determining who is competent and who is not. For incompetent patients, a complex body of law setting forth substantive standards for and limitations on making decisions about forgoing life-sustaining treatment has developed. These standards are discussed in **Chapter 7. Chapter 8** ("Limitations on the Right to Die,") explains the various approaches the courts have used to distinguish those situations in which refusing life-sustaining treatment is considered legitimate from those in which it is not. Although the courts have not confined the right to forgo life-sustaining treatment to particular illnesses or medical conditions nor to particular treatments, participants in the decisionmaking process may find it reassuring to know their situation is not unprecedented and that the courts have made decisions on whether to permit the forgoing of treatment in such cases. Thus, **Chapter 9** provides discussions of the kinds of illnesses and treatments courts have had occasion to consider. The absence of a particular illness or treatment from this discussion, however, should not be taken as suggesting that the forgoing of treatment in such a situation is impermissible.

End-of-Life Decisionmaking for Children. **Part V** addresses end-of-life decisionmaking for children. The common law, discussed in **Chapter 15,** bears some resemblance to decisionmaking for incompetent adults. However, decisionmaking for newborn infants differs substantially from that for older children, both in terms of the procedures and standards to be used and largely because of federal legislation and regulation in this area, which are discussed in **Chapter 16.**

Liability. Concern about liability has been an important motivating force in the development of the law. In addition to what has been the conventional

---

[14] **NV:** McKay v. Bergstedt, 801 P.2d 617, 637 (Nev. 1990) (Springer, J., dissenting) ("I want to be sure that the reader of this dissent does not get this case mixed up with the 'right-to-die' cases in which there is present either imminent death or permanent unconsciousness. We are not dealing here with 'overtreatment' or unwanted prolongation of the dying process.").

NJ: *In re* Jobes, 529 A.2d 434, 453 (N.J. 1987) (Handler, J., concurring) ("'To err either way—to keep a person alive under circumstances under which he would rather have been allowed to die, or to allow that person to die when he would have chosen to live—would be deeply unfortunate.' The courts must find an approach that confronts both forms of potential abuse, while minimizing the possibility of either.") (quoting *In re* Conroy, 486 A.2d 1209, 1220 (N.J. 1985)).

right-to-die case in which a competent patient or the family of an incompetent patient wishes to forgo life-sustaining medical treatment and the physician objects, or the physician agrees but is concerned about incurring liability for *forgoing* treatment, new concerns are arising, including (1) liability for *providing* treatment when patients or families wish for it to be stopped, (2) liability for not providing treatment when patients or, more likely, the families of incompetent patients wish it continued but health care professionals want it to stop (sometimes referred to as *futility* cases), and (3) liability for actively ending the life of a patient or aiding the patient in doing so (active euthanasia and assisted suicide). **Part VI** examines these issues.

As to the first of these, the principles about the imposition of civil liability for providing unwanted medical treatment are clear, but their *application* in the end-of-life decisionmaking context is not.[15] And there is anything but a clear consensus about the other two kinds of situations. The law governing mercy killing and assisted suicide is generally covered by statute, and it is relatively clear that such practices violate the criminal law.[16] Yet, historically, prosecutions have been exceedingly rare despite the widespread belief that some physicians engage in these practices on a not infrequent basis. Consequently, because of the divergence between the formal law and informal practices, there is a great deal of uncertainty about mercy killing and physician-assisted suicide. As a result of the increasingly open challenges to these prohibitions by individual physicians, the law here, too, is undergoing evolution.

There has been very little litigation of futility cases, and although in all litigated cases to date the courts have not permitted physicians to unilaterally withhold or withdraw treatment without the consent of the patient's surrogate, these are very narrow holdings that could easily be distinguished away in subsequent litigation,[17] or they could be resolved legislatively.

Excluded Topics. It is also important to state what this treatise does not deal with. The forgoing of life-sustaining treatment is sometimes intertwined with questions about the determination of death and the donation of organs for transplantation. These are topics, however, that are largely beyond the scope of this treatise.

§ 1.4 Existing Practices

Despite the growing number of right-to-die cases since 1976, the actual number of litigated cases is relatively small. The first right-to-die case, *Quinlan,*[18] was

---

[15] See **Ch. 17.**

[16] See **Ch. 18.**

[17] See **Ch. 19.**

[18] *In re* Quinlan, 355 A.2d 647 (N.J. 1976).

accompanied by a great deal of publicity in the lay press, and subsequent cases have generally received a great deal of public attention, at least in the state where the case was litigated.[19]

But the vast majority of instances of forgoing life-sustaining treatment occur in the private context of the doctor-patient-family relationship, are conducted with little fanfare, and receive no publicity. Each day, hundreds, if not thousands, of critically ill patients die in hospitals, in nursing homes, in hospices, and while being transported by emergency medical technicians[20]—that is, in situations in which decisions have to be made about withholding, withdrawing, or limiting life-sustaining treatment[21]—without creating publicity or litigation. It has been noted in judicial opinions from the beginning of right-to-die litigation[22] that although decisions to forgo life-sustaining treatment might not have explicit legal sanction, they are frequently made extrajudicially by competent patients or the surrogates of incompetent patients in consultation and agreement with physicians, nurses, and other health care professionals. In the *Cruzan* case, Justice Stevens noted that "'[d]ecisions of this kind are made daily by the patient or relatives, on the basis of medical advice and their conclusion as to what is best. Very few cases reach court, and I doubt whether this case would be before us but for the fact that Nancy lies in a state hospital.'"[23] Other judges have made similar observations.[24] Each of these deaths is a potential legal case,

---

[19] Fort Wayne Journal-Gazette v. Baker, 788 F. Supp. 379, 388 (N.D. Ind. 1992) ("Artificial life support for the terminally ill is a matter of intense public controversy. The media's ability to inform the general public of the role of the courts in providing or withdrawing health care for the terminally ill is clearly in the public interest.").

[20] Amicus Curiae Brief for the Am. Hosp. Ass'n at 3, Cruzan v. Director, 497 U.S. 261 (1990) (citing U.S. Nat'l Ctr. for Health Statistics, 37 Monthly Vital Statistics 6 (1989) (approximately 2.2 million deaths per year in the United States)); *id.* (citing U.S. Nat'l Ctr. for Health Statistics, Vital Statistics of the United States (1986) (Approximately 1.3 million deaths annually occur in hospitals.)).

[21] Amicus Curiae Brief for the Am. Hosp. Ass'n at 3 ("Seventy percent die after a decision to forego life-sustaining treatment has been made."), Cruzan v. Director, 497 U.S. 261 (1990) (citing Lipton et al., *Do-Not-Resuscitate Decisions in a Community Hospital: Incidence, Implications and Outcomes,* 256 JAMA 1164 (1986)).

[22] *See, e.g., In re* Quinlan, 355 A.2d 647, 658–59 (N.J. 1976).

[23] Cruzan v. Director, 497 U.S. 261, 337 (1990) (quoting Cruzan v. Harmon, 760 S.W.2d 408 (Mo. 1988) (Blackmar, J., dissenting)).

[24] **US:** Cruzan v. Director, 497 U.S. 261, 314 n.15 (1990) (Brennan, J., dissenting) ("Such decisions are made every day, without state participation. *See* [Cruzan v. Harmon] 760 S.W.2d, at 428 (Blackmar, J., dissenting)."); *id.* at 336–37 (Stevens, J., dissenting) ("'Decisions of this kind are made daily by the patient or relatives, on the basis of medical advice and their conclusion as to what is best. Very few cases reach court, and I doubt whether this case would be before us but for the fact that Nancy lies in a state hospital.'") (quoting Cruzan v. Harmon, 760 S.W.2d 408 (Mo. 1988) (Blackmar, J., dissenting)).

FL: Browning v. Herbert, 568 So. 2d 4, 15 (Fla. 1990) ("The decision to terminate artificial life-sustaining measures is being made over and over in nursing homes, hospitals, and private homes in this nation. It is being made painfully by loving family members, concerned

but only the tip of the iceberg emerges in the courts or the press. Although there are far more cases litigated in trial courts than in appellate courts,[25] the proportion of all cases that are litigated even in trial courts is insignificant.

Thus, most right-to-die "cases" are resolved in the clinical, rather than the judicial, setting.[26] Just how smooth is the course of decisionmaking is another matter. As evidenced by the establishment of ethics committees in many hospitals,[27] there can be a great deal of consternation, if not conflict, surrounding this heavily emotion-laden process. Even in those jurisdictions in which there has been substantial litigation generating a body of reported opinions recognizing a right to die and prescribing procedures for terminating life support, health care personnel and their legal counsel are often reluctant to abide by a patient's or family's wishes,[28] or are genuinely confused about the proper legal course. Nonetheless, in the overwhelming majority of cases, decisionmaking about

---

guardians, or surrogates, in conjunction with the advice of ethical and caring physicians or other health care providers.").

IL: Estate of Longeway v. Community Convalescent Ctr., 549 N.E.2d 292, 295 (Ill. 1989) ("Frequently, the courts are not consulted at all. There is reliable information that for many years, members of a patient's family, together with doctors and clergy, have made decisions to withdraw life-sustaining equipment from incompetent, hopelessly ill patients without seeking judicial approval.").

MN: *In re* Torres, 357 N.W.2d 332, 341 n.4 (Minn. 1984) ("[O]n an average about 10 life-support systems are disconnected weekly in Minnesota.").

MD: 73 Md. Op. Att'y Gen. 253, 287–88 (Op. No. 88-046, Oct. 17, 1988) ("[E]very day in this state doctors are recommending and families are confirming decisions not to use various means of treatment for terminally ill patients who cannot decide for themselves. . . . In our view, this kind of surrogate decisionmaking is . . . legally proper.").

NY: *In re* Storar, 420 N.E.2d 64, 75 (N.Y. 1981) (Jones, J., dissenting) ("There is reliable information that for many years physicians and members of patients' families, often in consultation with religious counselors, have in actuality been making decisions to withhold or to withdraw life support procedures from incurably ill patients incapable of making the critical decisions for themselves.").

[25] The only known, published estimate is that there have been between 2,900 and 7,000 or more trial court cases during the 15-year period between 1975 and 1989. *See* Hafemeister et al., *The Judicial Role in Life-Sustaining Medical Treatment Decisions,* 7 Issues L. & Med. 53 (1991).

[26] Cruzan v. Director 497 U.S. 261, 302 (1990) (Brennan, J., dissenting):

> Of the approximately 2 million people who die each year, 80% die in hospitals and long-term care institutions [*See* President's Comm'n for the Study of Ethical Problems in Medicine & Biomedical & Behavioral Research, Deciding to Forego Life-Sustaining Treatment 15 n.1, 17–18 (1983)], and perhaps 70% of those after a decision to forgo life-sustaining treatment has been made. [*See* Lipton, *Do-Not-Resuscitate Decisions in a Community Hospital: Incidence, Implications and Outcomes,* 256 JAMA 1164, 1168 (1986).]

[27] See **Ch. 6.**

[28] Solomon et al., *Decisions Near the End of Life: Professional Views on Life-Sustaining Treatments,* 83 Am. J. Pub. Health 14 (1993).

life-sustaining treatment is carried out without the interested parties coming to such a level of conflict that litigation results.[29]

§ 1.5 Public Attitudes

It is only a recent phenomenon that individuals have any choice over the timing of their death. As the American Hospital Association observed in its amicus curiae brief before the United States Supreme Court in the *Cruzan* case, "Until the latter part of this century, medicine had relatively little treatment to offer the dying and the vast majority of persons died at home rather than in the hospital."[30] The attitude of the general public is sympathetic to the right to die, that is, sympathetic to the exercise of the choice by competent individuals or their families to withhold or withdraw life-sustaining medical treatment when they believe it is no longer in their interests for it to be administered.

A poll of the residents of New Jersey, a state with a high level of judicial activity and public awareness about end-of-life decisionmaking, revealed that

> 84% of the 800 [people] interviewed felt that a family should be allowed to discontinue treatment for someone "in a coma with no chance of recovery" who is "being kept alive by machines" if the patient had said he or she did not want such treatment; and 64% said the family should be allowed to discontinue treatment under these circumstances even if the patient had said nothing, but the family members nevertheless believe he or she would not want to be sustained in his or her medical condition.[31]

The high level of public awareness in New Jersey does not appear to make its citizens unrepresentative:

> In a nationwide poll conducted in May and June of 1986, 73% of the 1510 respondents approved "withdrawing life support systems, including food and water, from a hopelessly ill patient if they or their family request it." Even more recently, 70% of the 2000 persons from across the nation who participated via television in a conference on life-sustaining medical treatment . . . "strongly agreed" that family members should decide whether to use life-sustaining medical treatment for patients who are unable to choose for themselves.[32]

---

[29] *See Negotiated Death: An Open Secret,* N.Y. Times, Dec. 16, 1984, at 18 (nat'l ed.); *see also* N.Y. Times, Dec. 16, 1984, at 1; Klemesrud, *A Daughter's Story: Aiding Mother's Suicide,* N.Y. Times, Sept. 9, 1985, at 17 (reviewing Last Wish by Betty Rollin).

[30] Cruzan v. Director, 497 U.S. 261, 339 n.11 (1990) (Stevens, J., dissenting).

[31] *In re* Jobes, 529 A.2d 434, 447 n.11 (N.J. 1987) (citing Newark Star Ledger, Aug. 10, 1986, at 18).

[32] *Id.* ("Every recent survey . . . indicates that society believes that a patient's family members should function as his or her surrogate decisionmakers."). *See also* Times Mirror Ctr. for the People and the Press, Reflections of the Times: The Right to Die (1990) (nationwide survey of 1,213 adults conducted in May 1990 found 79% believed that laws should allow patients to decide about being kept alive by medical treatment); N.Y. Times, Nov. 29, 1986, at 32.

However, a gap between attitudes and behavior may exist in the general public. Although families say they would permit life support to be withdrawn, when it comes time to give permission to do so, they are not always as willing. And although most states have enacted legislation recognizing the validity of living wills and health care powers of attorney, most people have not actually executed them.[33] There also appears to be increasing public support for more active measures to end life.[34]

§ 1.6 Medical Attitudes

The consequences of a refusal of treatment by most patients are often not very serious. Much health care is elective, many illnesses and injuries are self-limiting or self-curing, and in any event most conditions for which people seek treatment are not acutely life-threatening. Reasonable people decline treatment for a variety of reasons that seem important to them (although they may seem irrational or unreasonable to others), such as expense, inconvenience, fear, or a belief that the potential benefits of the treatment are insubstantial in comparison with the certain or possible side effects of the treatment.

However, when the likely consequence of a refusal of treatment is that the patient's death will ensue, a variety of concerns come into play which make it more likely that, at the very least, thought will be given to seeking to compel treatment despite the patient's refusal. A poll of physicians by the American Medical Association found that almost 80 percent favored the withdrawal of life support systems from hopelessly ill or irreversibly comatose patients.[35] What doctors do, however, may be different from what they say they would do. One survey of 687 physicians and 759 nurses in five hospitals reported that 47 percent had acted against their consciences by providing life-sustaining medical treatment to terminally ill patients.[36]

---

[33] Cruzan v. Director, 497 U.S. 261, 323 n.21 (1990) (Brennan, J., dissenting) ("Surveys show that the overwhelming majority of Americans have not executed such written instructions. See Emanuel & Emanuel, The Medical Directive: A New Comprehensive Advance Care Document, 261 JAMA 3288 (1989) (only 9% of Americans execute advance directives about how they would wish treatment decisions to be handled if they became incompetent); American Medical Association Surveys of Physician and Public Opinion on Health Care Issues 29–30 (1988) (only 15% of those surveyed had executed living wills); 2 President's Comm'n for the Study of Ethical Problems in Medicine & Biomedical & Behavioral Research, Making Health Care Decisions 241–242 (1982) (23% of those surveyed said that they had put treatment instructions in writing).").

[34] See **Ch. 18.**

[35] *Most Doctors in Poll Would Let the Dying Die,* N.Y. Times, June 5, 1988, at 14 (nat'l ed.) (citing Am. Med. News, June 3, 1988, at 9).

[36] Solomon et al., *Decisions Near the End of Life: Professional Views on Life-Sustaining Treatments,* 83 Am. J. Pub. Health 14 (1993).

Sometimes patients' refusals are simply ignored,[37] possibly on the assumption that the patient is incompetent, and the patient will be treated on the basis of authorization given by a family member.[38] In other instances—usually, when a patient is clearly competent or when family members also decline to authorize treatment—a message that the treatment must be administered may be conveyed to the patient or family by the attending physician, by a nurse, or by a health care administrator. For example, in a case in which a quadriplegic accident victim requested to remain on a respirator but to have all other medical treatment discontinued and to take only such nourishment as she desired, "her doctor . . . advised [her] that his moral ethics would dictate that, if she were to come into the hospital under his care, he would of necessity be required to provide her with continuing life-saving medical treatment."[39]

Occasionally, so strong is the conviction that a patient should receive treatment, the refusal of which is likely to cause death, it is administered over a competent patient's objection[40] or over the objection of the family of an incompetent patient,[41] thereby placing the burden on the patient or family to stop the treatment. On the other hand, sometimes it is family members who are disturbed by and seek to override a patient's—often questionably competent—refusal of treatment.[42]

Thus, the right to decline treatment may be ignored or side-stepped through a variety of stratagems. At one extreme, if patients remain steadfast in their refusal in the face of strong opposition from health care professionals or family members, they might simply be treated anyway.[43] If that path is not taken—for either ethical or legal reasons—at the other extreme an incompetency proceeding[44] or a lawsuit to authorize or compel treatment might be instituted. If, as is

---

[37] **NY:** *Cf. In re* Eichner, 423 N.Y.S.2d 580, 583 (Sup. Ct. Nassau County 1979) ("The petition indicated that Nassau Hospital had refused to turn off the life-support systems.").

[38] *See, e.g.,* Holmes v. Silver Cross Hosp., 340 F. Supp. 125 (N.D. Ill. 1972) (recounting unsuccessful attempts to obtain consent from a family member). See **Ch. 4.**

[39] A.B. v. C., 477 N.Y.S.2d 281, 283 (Sup. Ct. Schenectady County 1984).

[40] *See, e.g.,* Bouvia v. Superior Court (Glenchur), 225 Cal. Rptr. 297 (1986); Bartling v. Superior Court, 209 Cal. Rptr. 220 (Ct. App. 1984). See **Ch. 17.**

[41] **MA:** *In re* Spring, 399 N.E.2d 493 (Mass. App. Ct. 1979), *rev'd,* 405 N.E.2d 115 (Mass. 1980).

NJ: McVey v. Englewood Hosp. Ass'n, 524 A.2d 450 (N.J. Super. Ct. App. Div.), *cert. denied,* 528 A.2d 12 (N.J. 1987).

OH: Estate of Leach v. Shapiro, 469 N.E.2d 1047 (Ohio Ct. App. 1984).

See **Ch. 17.**

[42] **MA:** Lane v. Candura, 376 N.E.2d 1232 (Mass. App. Ct. 1978).

NY: *In re* Nemser, 273 N.Y.S.2d 624 (Sup. Ct. N.Y. County 1966).

[43] **CA:** Bartling v. Superior Court, 209 Cal. Rptr. 220 (Ct. App. 1984).

OH: Estate of Leach v. Shapiro, 469 N.E.2d 1047 (Ohio Ct. App. 1984).

[44] **MA:** Lane v. Candura, 376 N.E.2d 1232 (Mass. App. Ct. 1978).

NJ: *In re* Quackenbush, 383 A.2d 785 (N.J. Super. Ct. P. Div. 1978).

usually the case with terminally ill patients, the patient is already being treated and seeks to have treatment withdrawn or withheld, the burden then falls on the patient or the patient's family to institute judicial proceedings to stop treatment. Sometimes a compromise can be achieved without judicial proceedings; in other cases, however, it cannot.[45]

The reasons for seeking to avoid a patient's refusal of treatment likely to result in death are varied and complex. Health care professionals or administrators[46] might believe that the ethical codes of their profession would prevent them from acceding to the patient's wish, or a physician's own personal credo[47] may prevent compliance. Health care professionals may be bolstered in their beliefs by family members who oppose the patient's choice.

Physicians' attitudes on the issues of assisted suicide (especially, physician-assisted suicide) and mercy killing are just as complex as the general public's. Although there is some support for these practices in the medical profession,[48] the position of medical organizations is generally in opposition.[49] There is some evidence that a significant number of physicians do help patients to die,[50] but few physicians have been willing to admit to it publicly[51] or openly advocate it.

---

[45] *See, e.g.,* Bartling v. Superior Court, 209 Cal. Rptr. 220, 225 n.7 (Ct. App. 1984) (Hospital and physicians "attempted to strike a compromise between their position and the wishes of Mr. and Mrs. Bartling by trying to locate another hospital which would accept Mr. Bartling as a patient. This effort was unsuccessful.").

[46] **CA:** Bartling v. Superior Court, 209 Cal. Rptr. at 225 ("[D]eclarations were submitted to the effect that Glendale Adventist is a Christian hospital devoted to the preservation of life, and it would be unethical for Glendale Adventist's physicians to disconnect life-support systems from patients whom they viewed as having the potential for cognitive, sapient life.").

[47] **NY:** *See* A.B. v. C., 477 N.Y.S.2d 281, 283 (Sup. Ct. Schenectady County 1984).

See § **17.23.**

[48] *See, e.g.,* Cohen et al., *Attitudes Toward Assisted Suicide and Euthanasia Among Physicians in Washington State,* 331 New Eng. J. Med. 89 (1994) (52% believed euthanasia should be legal in some situations but only 33% would be willing to perform it; 53% believed assisted suicide should be legal in some situations, but only 40% would be willing to provide assistance.). *See also* Emanuel, *Euthanasia—Historical, Ethical, and Empiric Perspectives,* 154 Archives Internal Med. 1890, 1898–99 (1994) (Table 3, collecting results of other studies).

[49] *See, e.g.,* Council on Ethical and Judicial Affairs, American Medical Ass'n, *Decisions Near the End of Life,* 267 JAMA 2229, 2232 (1992); Editorial, *No to Physician-Assisted Suicide,* Am. Med. News, Apr. 25, 1994, at 19 (Physicians should become better educated about techniques for controlling pain rather than advocate physician-assisted suicide.).

[50] *See* Emanuel, *Euthanasia—Historical, Ethical, and Empiric Perspectives,* 154 Archives Internal Med. 1890, 1898–99 (1994) (Table 3, collecting results of other studies); *Poll Shows That 1 in 5 Internists Has Helped a Patient Die,* Am. Med. News, Mar. 16, 1992, at 9 ("non-scientific survey" of members of American Society of Internal Medicine).

[51] *See, e.g.,* Quill, *A Case of Individualized Decision Making,* 324 New Eng. J. Med. 691 (1991).

§ 1.7 Legal Antecedents and Current Status of the Right to Die

The right to die is an evolving concept, not a novel or revolutionary one. It is an outgrowth of the common law of informed decisionmaking and constitutional protections accorded privacy and liberty, limited by the constraints imposed by the criminal law, which recognize the right of competent patients or the surrogates of incompetent patients to refuse medical treatment.

Although the first right-to-die case was not decided until 1975,[52] and the term was not used approvingly in a judicial opinion until several years later,[53] the legal antecedents of the right to die are far more venerable. There are several lines of cases dealing with medical decisionmaking that are important wellsprings of the right, as well as another line working to set limits on the right to die. The right to die has evolved and continues to evolve out of the dialectical tension among these various antecedents. Thus, although the law specifically dealing with the right to die may be relatively new and the number of cases relatively few, many of the gaps can be filled in with intelligent extrapolation from these related areas of the law.

The most fundamental of these lines of cases is the law of battery, protecting individuals from nonconsensual bodily contact, which includes unauthorized medical procedures. This has evolved to protection under both battery and negligence law.[54] Thus, there now exists not only a legal right not to be treated without consent, but also a legal right not to be treated without informed consent.[55] The consent and informed consent cases further evolved into an affirmative right to refuse treatment. In addition, the right to refuse treatment has a more recent but less certain grounding in federal constitutional rights of liberty and privacy.[56] These trends, however, run the risk of conflict with criminal law sanctions when the refusal of treatment is likely or certain to lead to the patient's death.[57]

The work of the courts and the legislatures has been and continues to be a process of defining the boundaries of the right to die. In so doing, law-making institutions have had to walk a delicate line between recognizing the individual's right of autonomy in matters of health care and observing the traditional legal

---

[52] *See In re* Quinlan, 348 A.2d 801 (N.J. Super. Ct. Ch. Div. 1975), *rev'd,* 355 A.2d 647 (N.J. 1976).

[53] *See* John F. Kennedy Memorial Hosp. v. Bludworth, 432 So. 2d 611 (Fla. Dist. Ct. App. 1983) ("We are duty bound to implement . . . the . . . right to die with dignity."). *Cf. In re* Quinlan, 348 A.2d 801, 822 (N.J. Super. Ct. Ch. Div. 1975) ("There is no constitutional right to die that can be asserted by a parent for his incompetent adult child.").

[54] See **Ch. 17.**

[55] See **Ch. 3.**

[56] See **Ch. 2.**

[57] See **Ch. 18.**

and moral prohibitions on suicide and homicide and related crimes. As the New Jersey Supreme Court observed in *Quinlan,*

> it is both possible and necessary for society to have laws and ethical standards which provide freedom for decisions, in accord with the expressed or implied intentions of the patient, to terminate or withhold extraordinary treatment in cases which are judged to be hopeless by competent medical authorities, without at the same time leaving an opening for euthanasia.[58]

Despite the willingness of almost every court confronted with the issue to recognize a right to die, their forays into this area have not always resulted in a simplification of the law and the enunciation of easily understandable and applicable rules, but often in the need for continual new forays to distinguish those cases in which life-sustaining treatment may be withheld or withdrawn from those in which no such right exists.

However, the law governing the right to die has clarified considerably in recent years, to the point where it can now be said with a high level of confidence that a consensus has evolved, at least in those jurisdictions in which there has been appellate or federal trial court litigation.[59] Although about half the American jurisdictions still have no case law on the issue,[60] it is almost uniformly the case that each jurisdiction's case of first impression subscribes to the general outlines of the consensus. Even in states that have not yet had a precedential judicial decision, legislation—dealing with advance directives, surrogate decisionmaking, do-not-resuscitate orders, and assisted suicide—has been enacted that is consistent with and reinforces the consensus. However, despite repeated calls by the courts for legislative resolution of these issues,[61] without exception, the legislation addresses some but not all of the issues raised by end-of-life decisionmaking, leaving substantial questions unresolved.

The first reported appellate right-to-die case, *In re Quinlan,*[62] was decided by the New Jersey Supreme Court in 1976. That year also marked the passage of the first significant legislation on the right to die, the California Natural Death Act.[63] Between 1976 and 1989, when the first edition of this treatise was

---

[58] *In re* Quinlan, 355 A.2d 647, 659–60 (N.J. 1976) (quoting Bishop Casey, a witness at trial).

[59] Thor v. Superior Court, 855 P.2d 375, 380 (Cal. 1993) (There is a "developing interdisciplinary consensus . . . [that] now uniformly recognizes the patient's right of control over bodily integrity as the subsuming essential in determining the relative balance of interests.").

See **§ 2.2.**

[60] See **Table 1–1.**

[61] *See, e.g.,* Barber v. Superior Court, 195 Cal. Rptr. 484, 488 (Ct. App. 1983) ("[T]he only long-term solution to this problem is necessarily legislative in nature. . . . Due to legislative inaction, however, we are forced to evaluate petitioners' conduct within the context of the woefully inadequate framework of the criminal law.").

[62] 355 A.2d 647 (N.J. 1976).

[63] Cal. Health & Safety Code § 85-7195 (West Supp. 1988) (repealed).

published, there had been in the vicinity of 50 reported appellate or federal trial court right-to-die cases in 17 jurisdictions (though the exact number of cases depends in part on what one considers a right-to-die case). Since that time, the number of cases has approximately doubled, and the number of jurisdictions with at least one reported appellate or federal trial court right-to-die case has increased to roughly half.[64] There are probably also large numbers of unreported cases.[65] It is difficult to know with any certainty how many such cases there might be because most states have no system for reporting trial court opinions and, even in those that do, many cases go unreported. See **Table 1–1.**

The process of clarification of the law through litigation is limited to the fact patterns similar to that in the *Quinlan* case and its progeny: a situation in which a competent patient or the family of an incompetent patient seeks to have life-sustaining medical treatment withheld or withdrawn from a terminally ill or hopelessly ill patient. New patterns, however, are beginning to emerge, most notably those in which a competent patient requests aid in dying (generally referred to as *assisted suicide*)[66] or requests to have his life actively ended by another (generally referred to as *mercy killing* or *active euthanasia*).[67] Another emerging pattern is that in which physicians seek to withhold or withdraw life-sustaining medical treatment but meet resistance from the surrogate of an incompetent patient (generally referred to as futility cases).[68] As to the first two—assisted suicide and mercy killing—there is a consensus, and the consensus is that such practices are unlawful, but the continued challenges to the consensus make it appear likely that the consensus will break down either through legislative[69] or judicial action[70] or both. With regard to futility cases, there is currently no established consensus about whether "futile" life-sustaining medical treatment can be withheld or withdrawn without the consent of a competent patient or the surrogate of an incompetent patient. What little precedent there is, however, suggests that it may not.[71]

---

[64] See **Table 1–1.**

[65] *See generally* Hafemeister et al., *The Judicial Role in Life-Sustaining Medical Treatment Decisions,* 7 Issues L. & Med. 53 (1991). See **Table 1–1.**

[66] See §§ **18.18, 18.19, 18.22, 18.23,** and **18.25.**

[67] See §§ **18.18, 18.19,** and **18.25.**

[68] See **Ch. 19.**

[69] See § **18.23.**

[70] *See, e.g.,* Compassion in Dying v. Washington, 850 F. Supp. 1454 (W.D. Wash. 1994). See § **18.22.**

[71] **CA4:** *In re* Baby "K," 16 F.3d 590 (4th Cir. 1994).

GA: *In re* Doe, 418 S.E.2d 3 (Ga. 1992).

MN: *In re* Wanglie, No. PX-91-283 (Minn. 4th Dist. Ct. Hennepin County July 1, 1991).

Table 1–1

Right-to-Die Cases by Jurisdiction

UNITED STATES

Supreme Court

Bowen v. American Hosp. Ass'n, 476 U.S. 610 (1986)
Cruzan v. Director, 497 U.S. 261 (1990)

Federal (Department of the Army)

Tune v. Walter Reed Army Medical Hosp., 602 F. Supp. 1452 (D.D.C. 1985)

Court of Appeals

In re Baby "K," 16 F.3d 590 (4th Cir. 1994), *aff'g In re* Baby "K," 832 F. Supp. 1022 (E.D. Va. 1993), *cert. denied,* 115 S. Ct. 91 (1994)
Compassion in Dying v. Washington, 49 F.3d 586 (9th Cir. 1995), *rev'g* 850 F. Supp. 1454 (W.D. Wash. 1994)
Foster v. Tourtelotte, 704 F.2d 1109 (9th Cir. 1983)

District Court—Reported

Deel v. Syracuse Veterans Admin. Medical Ctr., 729 F. Supp. 231 (N.D.N.Y. 1990)
In re Department of Veteran's Affairs Medical Ctr., 749 F. Supp. 495 (S.D.N.Y.), *aff'd,* 914 F.2d 239 (2d Cir. 1990)
Gray v. Romeo, 709 F. Supp. 325 (D.R.I. 1989)
Gray v. Romeo, 697 F. Supp. 580 (D.R.I. 1988)
Lee v. State, 869 F. Supp. 1491 (D. Or. 1994)
Quill v. Koppell, 870 F. Supp. 78 (S.D.N.Y. 1994)
Ross v. Hilltop Rehabilitation Hosp., 676 F. Supp. 1528 (D. Colo. 1987)
Tune v. Walter Reed Army Medical Hosp., 602 F. Supp. 1452 (D.D.C. 1985)
United States v. University Hosp., 575 F. Supp. 607 (E.D.N.Y. 1983), *aff'd on other grounds,* 729 F.2d 144 (2d Cir. 1984)

District Court—Unreported

Foster v. Tourtelotte, No. CV 81-5046-RMT (C.D. Cal. Nov. 16 and 17, 1981)
Newman v. William Beaumont Army Medical Ctr., No. EP-86-CA-276 (W.D. Tex. Oct. 30, 1986)
Sanchez v. Fairview Developmental Ctr., No. CV 88-0129FFF(Tx) (C.D. Cal. Mar. 30, 1988)

Alabama

Trial—Unreported

In re Salter, No. CV-94-160 (Ala. Cir. Ct. Baldwin County Dec. 30, 1994)

Table 1–1
(continued)

Arizona

Appellate—Reported

Rasmussen v. Fleming, 154 Ariz. 207, 741 P.2d 674 (1987), *aff'g and rev'g* 154 Ariz. 200, 741 P.2d 667 (Ct. App. 1986)

Trial—Unreported

Lurie v. Samaritan Health Serv., No. C510198 (Super. Ct. Maricopa County, Ariz. Mar. 24, 1984)

California

Appellate—Reported

Barber v. Superior Court, 147 Cal. App. 3d 1006, 195 Cal. Rptr. 484 (1983)
Bartling v. Glendale Adventist Medical Ctr., 184 Cal. App. 3d 961, 229 Cal. Rptr. 360 (1986)
Bartling v. Glendale Adventist Medical Ctr., 228 Cal. Rptr. 847 (Ct. App. 1986)
Bartling v. Superior Court, 163 Cal. App. 3d 186, 209 Cal. Rptr. 220 (1984)
Bouvia v. County of L.A., 241 Cal. Rptr. 239 (Ct. App. 1987)
Bouvia v. Superior Court (Glenchur), 179 Cal. App. 3d 1127, 225 Cal. Rptr. 297 (1986)
Donaldson v. Van de Kamp, 2 Cal. App. 4th 1614, 4 Cal. Rptr. 2d 59 (1992)
Drabick v. Drabick, 200 Cal. App. 3d 185, 245 Cal. Rptr. 840, *cert. denied,* 488 U.S. 958 (1988), *reh'g denied,* 488 U.S. 1024 (1989)
Eric B. v. Ted B., 189 Cal. App. 3d 996, 235 Cal. Rptr. 22 (1987)
Foster v. Tourtelotte, 704 F.2d 1109 (9th Cir. 1983)
McMahon v. Lopez, 199 Cal. App. 3d 829, 245 Cal. Rptr. 172 (1988)
Morrison v. Abramovice, 206 Cal. App. 3d 304, 253 Cal. Rptr. 530 (1988)
Thor v. Superior Court, 5 Cal. 4th 725, 855 P.2d 375, 21 Cal. Rptr. 2d 357 (1993)
Westhart v. Mule, 261 Cal. Rptr. 640 (Ct. App. 1989) (ordered not published)

Appellate—Unreported

Gary v. Superior Court, No. D006166 (Cal. Ct. App. 4th Dist. Sept. 25, 1987)

Trial—Unreported

Bouvia v. County of Riverside, No. 159780 (Super. Ct. Riverside County, Cal. Dec. 16, 1983)
Cantor v. Weiss, No. 626163 (Super. Ct. L.A. County, Cal. Dec. 30, 1986)
In re Cruse, No. J914410 (Super. Ct. L.A. County, Cal. Feb. 15, 1979)
Foster v. Tourtelotte, No. CV 81-5046-RMT (C.D. Cal. Nov. 16 and 17, 1981)
Gary v. California (Hirth), No. 576-123 (Super. Ct. San Diego County, Cal. Mar. 5 and 23, 1987), *modified* (Apr. 15, 1987)
Sanchez v. Fairview Developmental Ctr., No. 563-313 (Super. Ct. Orange County, Cal. Sept. 2, 1988)
Sanchez v. Fairview Developmental Ctr., No. CV 88-0129FFF(Tx) (C.D. Cal. Mar. 30, 1988)
In re Young, No. A 100863 (Super. Ct. Orange County, Cal. Sept. 11, 1979)

Colorado

Appellate—Reported

Carothers v. Department of Insts., 845 P.2d 1179 (Colo. 1993), *aff'g* 821 P.2d 891 (Colo. Ct. App. 1991)

Trial—Reported

Ross v. Hilltop Rehabilitation Hosp., 676 F. Supp. 1528 (D. Colo. 1987)

Trial—Unreported

In re Peterson, No. 90-PR-0827 (Colo. Dist. Ct. Div. D El Paso County July 6, 1991)
In re Rodas, No. 86PR129 (Colo. Dist. Ct. Mesa County Jan. 22, 1987), *modified* (Apr. 3, 1987)

Connecticut

Appellate—Reported

Foody v. Manchester Memorial Hosp., 40 Conn. Supp. 127, 482 A.2d 713 (Super. Ct. 1984)
McConnell v. Beverly Enters.-Conn., Inc., 209 Conn. 692, 553 A.2d 596 (1989)

Delaware

Appellate—Reported

Newmark v. Williams, 588 A.2d 1108 (Del. 1991)
Severns v. Wilmington Medical Ctr., Inc., 433 A.2d 1047 (Del. 1981)
Severns v. Wilmington Medical Ctr., Inc., 421 A.2d 1334 (Del.), *opinion after remand,* 425 A.2d 156 (Del. Ch. 1980)

Trial—Unreported

In re Gordy, No. C.M. 7428 (Del. Ch. Dec. 30, 1994)
In re Shumosic, No. 5515 (Del. Ch. Sept. 27, 1988)

District of Columbia

Appellate—Reported

In re A.C., 573 A.2d 1235 (D.C. 1990), *vacating and remanding* 539 A.2d 203 (D.C. Ct. App. 1988), *and rev'g* 533 A.2d 611 (D.C. 1987)

Florida

Appellate—Reported

In re Barry, 445 So. 2d 365 (Fla. Dist. Ct. App. 1984)
Browning v. Herbert, 568 So. 2d 4 (Fla. 1990), *aff'g* 543 So. 2d 258 (Fla. Dist. Ct. App. 1989)

Table 1–1
(continued)

Corbett v. D'Alessandro, 487 So. 2d 368 (Fla. Dist. Ct. App.), *review denied,* 492 So. 2d 1331 (Fla. 1986)
In re Dubreuil, 629 So. 2d 819 (Fla. 1993)
John F. Kennedy Memorial Hosp. v. Bludworth, 452 So. 2d 921 (Fla. 1984), *aff'g* 432 So. 2d 611 (Fla. Dist. Ct. App. 1983)
St. Mary's Hosp. v. Ramsey, 465 So. 2d 666 (Fla. Dist. Ct. App. 1985)
Satz v. Perlmutter, 379 So. 2d 359 (Fla. 1980), *aff'g* 362 So. 2d 160 (Fla. Dist. Ct. App. 1978)
In re T.A.C.P., 609 So. 2d 588 (Fla. 1992)
Wons v. Public Health Trust, 541 So. 2d 96 (Fla. 1989), *aff'g* 500 So. 2d 679 (Fla. Dist. Ct. App. 1987)

Trial—Unreported

In re Axelrod, No. 91-241-CG (S) (Fla. Cir. Ct. Palm Beach County July 3, 1991)
In re Baby Girl Muller, No. 88-1073 (Fla. Cir. Ct. Hillsborough County Feb. 9, 1988)
Helstrom v. Florida Life Care, No. 88-1870-CA-01 (Fla. Cir. Ct. Sarasota County May 10, 1988)
Hoffmeister v. Satz, No. 87-28451 CR (Fla. Cir. Ct. 17th Dist. Broward County Feb. 22, 1988)
In re Ray, No. 91-2202 CA A (Fla. Cir. Ct. Okaloosa County July 29, 1991)
Rekstad v. Florida Life Care, Inc., No. 87-4285-CA-01 (Fla. Cir. Ct. Sarasota County Sept. 18, 1987)
In re Rothblatt, No. 87-4256-41 (Fla. Cir. Ct. Pinellas County Aug. 24, 1987)
In re Stone, No. 90-5867 (Fla. Cir. Ct. 17th Dist. Broward County June 24, 1991)
In re Underwood, No. 85-8107 CA T (Fla. Cir. Ct. Brevard County Aug. 30, 1985)
In re Zahn, No. 85-3723 (Fla. Cir. Ct. Broward County Nov. 20, 1986)

Georgia

Appellate—Reported

In re Doe, 262 Ga. 389, 418 S.E.2d 3 (1992)
In re L.H.R., 253 Ga. 439, 321 S.E.2d 716 (1984)
State v. McAfee, 259 Ga. 579, 385 S.E.2d 651 (1989)

Trial—Unreported

In re Doe, Civ. Action No. D-93064 (Super. Ct. Fulton County, Ga. Oct. 17, 1991)
Young v. Emory Univ., Civ. Action No. 83-6143-5 (Super. Ct. Dekalb County, Ga. Aug. 10 and 29, 1983)
Zodin v. Manor, No. 9010821007 (Super. Ct. Cobb County, Ga. Nov. 21, 1990)

Hawaii

Trial—Unreported

In re Crabtree, No. 86-0031 (Haw. Fam. Ct. 1st Cir. Apr. 26, 1990)
Wilcox v. Hawaii, Civ. No. 860116 (Haw. 5th Cir. Ct. June 16, 1986)

Illinois

Appellate—Reported

In re Austin, 615 N.E.2d 411 (Ill. App. Ct. 1993)

C.A. v. Morgan, 236 Ill. App. 3d 594, 603 N.E.2d 1171 (1992), *review denied,* 148 Ill. 2d 642, 610 N.E.2d 1264 (1993)

In re E.G., 133 Ill. 2d 98, 549 N.E.2d 322 (1989), *aff'g and rev'g* 161 Ill. App. 3d 765, 515 N.E.2d 286 (1987)

In re Estate of Greenspan, 137 Ill. 2d 1, 558 N.E.2d 1194 (1990), *on remand,* No. 88P8726 (Ill. Cir. Ct. Cook County Oct. 3, 1990)

Estate of Longeway v. Community Convalescent Ctr., 133 Ill. 2d 33, 549 N.E.2d 292 (1989)

In re Estate of Prange, 166 Ill. App. 3d 1091, 520 N.E.2d 946, *vacated,* 121 Ill. 2d 570, 527 N.E.2d 303, *cert. denied sub nom.* Murphy v. Benson, 488 U.S. 892 (1988)

Indiana

Appellate—Reported

In re Lawrance, 579 N.E.2d 32 (Ind. 1991)

Appellate—Unreported

In re Infant Doe, No. GU8204-00 (Ind. Cir. Ct. Monroe County Apr. 12, 1982), *writ of mandamus dismissed sub nom.* State *ex rel.* Infant Doe v. Baker, No. 482 S 140 (Ind. May 27, 1982), *cert. denied,* 464 U.S. 961 (1983)

Iowa

Appellate—Reported

Morgan v. Olds, 417 N.W.2d 232 (Iowa Ct. App. 1987)

Kentucky

Appellate—Reported

Degrella v. Elston, 858 S.W.2d 698 (Ky. 1993)

Louisiana

Appellate—Reported

In re P.V.W., 424 So. 2d 1015 (La. 1982)

Maine

Appellate—Reported

In re Gardner, 534 A.2d 947 (Me. 1987)

In re Swan, 569 A.2d 1202 (Me. 1990)

Trial—Unreported

In re Hallock, No. 88381 (P. Ct. Kennebec County, Me. Sept. 26, 1988)

Maine Medical Ctr. v. Houle, Civ. Action No. 74-145 (Super. Ct. Cumberland County, Me. Feb. 14, 1974)

Table 1–1
(continued)

In re Weaver, No. 89-177 (P. Ct. Cumberland County, Me. Feb. 27, 1989), *motion to intervene and for reconsideration denied,* No. 89-177 (P. Ct. Cumberland County, Me. Mar. 28, 1989)

Maryland

Appellate—Reported

Mack v. Mack, 329 Md. 188, 618 A.2d 744 (1993)
Mercy Hosp., Inc. v. Jackson, 62 Md. App. 409, 489 A.2d 1130 (1985), *vacated and remanded as moot,* 306 Md. 556, 510 A.2d 562 (1986)
In re Riddlemoser, 317 Md. 496, 564 A.2d 812 (1989)

Trial—Unreported

In re Sahm, No. 92-T-0043 (Baltimore County, Md. Mar. 30, 1992)

Massachusetts

Appellate—Reported

In re Beth, 412 Mass. 188, 587 N.E.2d 1377 (1992)
Brophy v. New Eng. Sinai Hosp., Inc., 398 Mass. 417, 497 N.E.2d 626 (1986)
Custody of a Minor, 385 Mass. 697, 434 N.E.2d 601 (1982)
Custody of a Minor, 378 Mass. 732, 393 N.E.2d 836 (1979)
Custody of a Minor, 375 Mass. 733, 379 N.E.2d 1053 (1978)
In re Dinnerstein, 6 Mass. App. Ct. 466, 380 N.E.2d 134 (1978)
In re Doe, 411 Mass. 512, 583 N.E.2d 1263, *cert. denied sub nom.* Doe v. Gross, 112 S. Ct. 1512 (1992)
In re Hier, 18 Mass. App. Ct. 200, 464 N.E.2d 959, *review denied,* 392 Mass. 1102, 465 N.E.2d 261 (1984)
In re McCauley, 409 Mass. 134, 565 N.E.2d 411 (1991)
Norwood Hosp. v. Munoz, 409 Mass. 116, 564 N.E.2d 1017 (1991)
In re R.H., 35 Mass. App. Ct. 478, 622 N.E.2d 1071 (1993)
In re Spring, 380 Mass. 629, 405 N.E.2d 115 (1980), *rev'g* 8 Mass. App. Ct. 831, 399 N.E.2d 493 (1979)
Spring v. Geriatric Auth., 394 Mass. 274, 475 N.E.2d 727 (1985)
Superintendent of Belchertown State Sch. v. Saikewicz, 373 Mass. 728, 370 N.E.2d 417 (1977)

Trial—Unreported

In re A., No. 94 CP 24 (Mass. Dist. Ct. Malden Div. Dec. 14, 1994)
Beth Israel Hosp. v. Stockton, No. 91E-6 (P. and Fam. Ct. Suffolk County, Mass. May 30, 1991)
In re Laws, No. 226215 (P. and Fam. Ct. Essex Div. Mass. May 4, 1987)

Michigan

Appellate—Reported

Hobbins v. Attorney Gen., 447 Mich. 436, 527 N.W.2d 714 (Mich.), *rev'g* 518 N.W.2d 487 (Mich. Ct. App. 1994), *cert denied sub nom.* Hobbins v. Kelley, 63 U.S.L.W. 3672 (U.S. Apr. 24, 1995) (No. 94-1473), *and cert. denied sub nom.* Kevorkian v. Michigan, 63 U.S.L.W. 3692 (U.S. Apr. 24, 1995) (No. 94-1490)

Martin v. Martin, 200 Mich. App. 703, 504 N.W.2d 917 (1993), *opinion after remand,* 205 Mich. App. 96, 517 N.W.2d 749, *appeal granted,* 525 N.W.2d 451 (Mich. 1994)

People v. Kevorkian, 447 Mich. 436, 527 N.W.2d 714 (Mich. 1994), *cert denied sub nom.* Hobbins v. Kelley, 63 U.S.L.W. 3672 (U.S. Apr. 24, 1995) (No. 94-1473), *and cert. denied sub nom.* Kevorkian v. Michigan, 63 U.S.L.W. 3692 (U.S. Apr. 24, 1995) (No. 94-1490)

Rosebush v. Oakland County Prosecutor, 195 Mich. App. 675, 491 N.W.2d 633 (1992)

Trial—Unreported

In re Blodgett, No. 83-26514-AZ (Mich. Cir. Ct. Washtenaw County May 25, 1984)

In re Culham, No. 87-340537-AZ (Mich. Cir. Ct. Oakland County Dec. 15, 1987)

In re Hayes, No. 90-113811-GD (Mich. Cir. Ct. Macomb County Aug. 30, 1990)

In re Rivlin, No. 89-369904-AZ (Mich. Cir. Ct. Oakland County July 18, 1987)

In re Yetzke, No. 93-155558 GD (P. Ct. Kent County, Mich. Aug. 12, 1993)

Minnesota

Appellate—Reported

In re Torres, 357 N.W.2d 332 (Minn. 1984)

Trial—Unreported

Butcher v. Fashingbauer, No. C7-94-1717 (Minn. 4th Dist. Ct. Ramsey County 1994)

In re Wanglie, No. PX-91-283 (Minn. 4th Dist. Ct. Hennepin County July 1, 1991), *reported in* 7 Issues L. & Med. 369 (1991)

In re Welfare of Steinhaus (Redwood County Ct. Juv. Div. Minn. Sept. 11, 1986), *amended* (Oct. 13, 1987)

Missouri

Appellate—Reported

In re Busalacchi, No. 59582, 1991 WL 26851, 1991 Mo. App. LEXIS 315 (Mar. 5, 1991), *reh'g and/or transfer denied* (Mo. Ct. App. Mar. 26, 1991), *cause ordered transferred to Mo. Sup. Ct.* (Mo. Ct. App. Apr. 15, 1991), *appealed and remanded,* No. 73677, 1991 Mo. LEXIS 107 (Oct. 16, 1991), *appeal dismissed,* No. 73677, 1993 WL 32356 (Mo. Jan. 26, 1993)

Cruzan v. Harmon, 760 S.W.2d 408 (Mo. 1988), *aff'd,* 497 U.S. 261 (1990)

In re Warren, 858 S.W.2d 263 (Mo. Ct. App. 1993)

Trial—Unreported

Cruzan v. Mouton, Estate No. CV384-9P (Mo. Cir. Ct. Jasper County Dec. 14, 1990), *reported in* 6 Issues L. & Med. 433 (1991)

Sullivan v. St. John's Mercy Medical Ctr., No. 561631 (Mo. Cir. Ct. St. Louis County June 8, 1987)

Nebraska

Trial—Unreported

In re Gregoire, Book 43, 161 (Douglas County Ct. Neb. Mar. 1990)

Table 1–1
(continued)

Nevada

Appellate—Reported

McKay v. Bergstedt, 801 P.2d 617 (Nev. 1990)

New Jersey

Appellate—Reported

In re Clark, 216 N.J. Super. 497, 524 A.2d 448 (App. Div. 1987), *aff'g* 210 N.J. Super. 548, 510 A.2d 136 (Ch. Div. 1986)
In re Conroy, 98 N.J. 321, 486 A.2d 1209 (1985), *rev'g* 190 N.J. Super. 453, 464 A.2d 303 (App. Div.), *rev'g* 188 N.J. Super. 523, 457 A.2d 1232 (Ch. Div. 1983)
In re Farrell, 108 N.J. 335, 529 A.2d 404 (1987), *aff'g* 212 N.J. Super. 294, 514 A.2d 1342 (Ch. Div. 1986)
Gleason v. Abrams, 250 N.J. Super. 265, 593 A.2d 1232 (App. Div. 1991)
In re Hughes, 259 N.J. Super. 193, 611 A.2d 1148 (App. Div. 1992)
In re Jobes, 108 N.J. 394, 529 A.2d 434 (1987), *aff'g* 210 N.J. Super. 543, 510 A.2d 133 (Ch. Div. 1986)
McVey v. Englewood Hosp. Ass'n, 216 N.J. Super. 502, 524 A.2d 450 (App. Div.), *cert. denied,* 109 N.J. 182, 528 A.2d 12 (1987)
In re Moorhouse, 250 N.J. Super. 307, 593 A.2d 1256 (App. Div. 1991)
In re Peter, 108 N.J. 365, 529 A.2d 419 (1987)
In re Quinlan, 70 N.J. 10, 355 A.2d 647, *cert. denied sub nom.* Garger v. New Jersey, 429 U.S. 922 (1976), *modifying and remanding* 137 N.J. Super. 227, 348 A.2d 801 (Ch. Div. 1975)
In re Requena, 213 N.J. Super. 443, 517 A.2d 869 (App. Div.), *aff'g* 517 A.2d 886 (N.J. Super. Ct. Ch. Div. 1986)

Appellate—Unreported

In re Donlan, No. A-3103-89T5F (N.J. Super. Ct. App. Div. Oct. 24, 1990)
In re Smerdon, No. 4-6031-89T1 (N.J. Super. Ct. App. Div. Mar. 19, 1991)

Trial—Reported

In re Visbeck, 210 N.J. Super. 527, 510 A.2d 125 (Ch. Div. 1986)

Trial—Unreported

In re Fields (N.J. Super. Ct. Ch. Div. Salem County Nov. 6, 1986)
Fuhrmann v. Kean, No. 86-1951 (D.N.J. July 13, 1987)
In re Putzer, No. P21-87E (N.J. Super. Ct. Ch. Div. Essex County July 9, 1987)

New Mexico

Appellate—Unreported

New Mexico *ex rel.* Smith v. Fort, No. 14,768 (N.M. 1983)

New York

Appellate—Reported

Delio v. Westchester County Medical Ctr., 129 A.D.2d 1, 516 N.Y.S.2d 677 (1987), *rev'g* 134 Misc. 2d 206, 510 N.Y.S.2d 415 (Sup. Ct. Westchester County 1986)
Eichner v. Dillon, 52 N.Y.2d 363, 420 N.E.2d 64, 438 N.Y.S.2d 266 (1981), *aff'g* 426 N.Y.S.2d 517 (App. Div. 1980), *aff'g* 102 Misc. 2d 184, 423 N.Y.S.2d 580 (Sup. Ct. Nassau County 1979)
Elbaum v. Grace Plaza of Great Neck, Inc., 148 A.D.2d 244, 544 N.Y.S.2d 840 (1989)
Fosmire v. Nicoleau, 75 N.Y.2d 218, 551 N.E.2d 77, 551 N.Y.S.2d 876 (1990)
Grace Plaza of Great Neck, Inc. v. Elbaum, 623 N.E.2d 513, 603 N.Y.S.2d 386 (1993), *aff'g* 588 N.Y.S.2d 853 (App. Div. 1992)
In re Hofbauer, 47 N.Y.2d 648, 393 N.E.2d 1009, 419 N.Y.S.2d 936 (1979)
In re Storar, 52 N.Y.2d 363, 420 N.E.2d 64, 438 N.Y.S.2d 266, *cert. denied,* 454 U.S. 858 (1981), *rev'g* 434 N.Y.S.2d 46 (App. Div.), *aff'g* 433 N.Y.S.2d 388, 393 (Sup. Ct. Monroe County 1980)
Weber v. Stony Brook Hosp., 95 A.D.2d 587, 467 N.Y.S.2d 685 (per curiam), *aff'd,* 60 N.Y.2d 208, 456 N.E.2d 1186, 469 N.Y.S.2d 763, *cert. denied,* 464 U.S. 1026 (1983)
In re Westchester County Medical Ctr. (O'Connor), 72 N.Y.2d 517, 531 N.E.2d 607, 534 N.Y.S.2d 886, *rev'g* 139 A.D.2d 344, 532 N.Y.S.2d 133 (1988).
Wickel v. Spellman, 552 N.Y.S.2d 437 (App. Div. 1990)

Trial—Reported

In re Beth Israel Medical Ctr. (Weinstein), 136 Misc. 2d 931, 519 N.Y.S.2d 511 (Sup. Ct. 1987)
Deel v. Syracuse Veterans Admin. Medical Ctr., 729 F. Supp. 231 (N.D.N.Y. 1990)
In re Department of Veteran's Affairs Medical Ctr., 749 F. Supp. 495 (S.D.N.Y.), *aff'd,* 914 F.2d 239 (2d Cir. 1990)
In re Kerr (O'Brien), 135 Misc. 2d 1076, 517 N.Y.S.2d 346 (Sup. Ct. 1986)
In re Long-Island Jewish Medical Ctr. (Malcolm), 147 Misc. 2d 239, 557 N.Y.S.2d 239 (Sup. Ct. 1990)
In re Lydia E. Hall Hosp., 117 Misc. 2d 1024, 459 N.Y.S.2d 682 (Sup. Ct. 1982)
In re Lydia E. Hall Hosp., 116 Misc. 2d 477, 455 N.Y.S.2d 706 (Sup. Ct. 1982)
In re Richardson, 153 Misc. 2d 376, 581 N.Y.S.2d 708 (Sup. Ct. Monroe County 1992)
Saunders v. State, 129 Misc. 2d 45, 492 N.Y.S.2d 510 (Sup. Ct. 1985)
In re Thomas B., 152 Misc. 2d 96, 574 N.Y.S.2d 659 (Fam. Ct. Cattaraugus County 1991)
United States v. University Hosp., 575 F. Supp. 607 (E.D.N.Y. 1983), *aff'd,* 729 F.2d 144 (2d Cir. 1984)
Vogel v. Forman, 134 Misc. 2d 395, 512 N.Y.S.2d 622 (Sup. Ct. 1986)
Workmen's Circle Home & Infirmary for the Aged v. Fink, 135 Misc. 2d 270, 514 N.Y.S.2d 893 (Sup. Ct. 1987)

Trial—Unreported

In re Alderson (Kimbrough), No. 90193/86 (Sup. Ct. N.Y. County, N.Y. Aug. 3, 1988), *reported in* N.Y. L.J., Aug. 9, 1988, at 18
In re Brooks (Leguerrier) (Sup. Ct. Albany County, N.Y. June 10, 1987)
In re Chetta, No. 1086/87 (Sup. Ct. Nassau County, N.Y. May 1, 1987)
Evans v. Bellevue Hosp. (Wirth), No. 16536/87 (Sup. Ct. N.Y. County, N.Y. July 27, 1987), *reported in* N.Y. L.J., July 28, 1987, at 11
In re Gannon (Coons), RJI No. 0189-017460 (Sup. Ct. Albany County, N.Y. Apr. 3, 1989), *vacated,* No. 0189-017460 (Sup. Ct. Albany County, N.Y. Apr. 11, 1989)

Table 1–1
(continued)

In re Hallahan, No. 16338/1989 (Sup. Ct. Bronx County, N.Y. Aug. 28, 1989)
Halperin v. North Shore Univ. Hosp. Ctr., No. 93-020905 (Sup. Ct. Nassau County, N.Y. Aug. 13, 1993)
Hayner v. Child's Nursing Home, No. 0188 015609 (Sup. Ct. Albany County, N.Y. Dec. 5, 1988)
In re Heath (Finsterbach) (Sup. Ct. Oneida County, N.Y. June 12, 1990)
In re Kerr (Essner), No. 21748/86 (Sup. Ct. Bronx County, N.Y. Dec. 17, 1986)
In re Kruczlnicki (Keyes), No. 26796 (Sup. Ct. Warren County, N.Y. Feb. 16, 1989)
Kurzweil v. Harrison, No. 14810/91 (Sup. Ct. N.Y. County, N.Y. July 30 and Aug. 1, 1991)
In re Licopoli (Akullian), No. 1172-88 (Sup. Ct. Albany County, N.Y. Mar. 10, 1988)
Marie v. Astoria Gen. Hosp., No. 03607/88 (Sup. Ct. Queens County, N.Y. Mar. 23, 1988)
In re Mazzarro, No. 90-14709 (Sup. Ct. Suffolk County, N.Y. Jan. 2, 1991)
In re Moschella, No. 5806/84 (Sup. Ct. Queens County, N.Y. May 10, 1984), *reported in* N.Y. L.J., May 22, 1984, at 12, col. 2
In re Plaza Health & Rehabilitation Ctr. (Sup. Ct. Onondaga County, N.Y. Feb. 2, 1984)
In re Ramos, No. 7715-90 (Sup. Ct. Bronx County, N.Y. Mar. 13, 1990)
In re Strauss, No. 8378/87 (Sup. Ct. Bronx County, N.Y. July 1, 1987)
In re Triarsi, No. 86-14241 (Sup. Ct. Suffolk County, N.Y. Aug. 21, 1986), *reported in* N.Y. L.J., Sept. 18, 1986, at 12, col. 5
In re Weiland (Juchnewicz), No. 89-033 (Sup. Ct. Suffolk County, N.Y. Jan. 19, 1989)

North Carolina

Trial—Unreported

In re Hester, No. 91SP (N.C. Dist. Ct. Lincoln County Apr. 3, 1991)
Rettinger v. Littlejohn, No. 91 CVD 4155 (Super. Ct. Forsyth County, N.C. 1991)

North Dakota

Trial—Unreported

In re Bayer, No. 4131 (Burleigh County Ct. N.D. Feb. 5 and Dec. 11, 1987)

Ohio

Appellate—Reported

Anderson v. St. Francis-St. George Hosp., 1995 WL 109128 (Ohio Ct. App. Mar. 15, 1995)
Anderson v. St. Francis-St. George Hosp., 83 Ohio App. 3d 221, 614 N.E.2d 841 (1992)
Couture v. Couture, 48 Ohio App. 3d 208, 549 N.E.2d 571 (1989)
Estate of Leach v. Shapiro, 13 Ohio App. 3d 393, 469 N.E.2d 1047 (1984)
In re Milton, 29 Ohio St. 3d 20, 505 N.E.2d 255, *cert. denied,* 484 U.S. 820 (1987)

Trial—Reported

In re Crum, 61 Ohio Misc. 2d 596, 580 N.E.2d 876 (P. Ct. Franklin County 1991)
Leach v. Akron Gen. Medical Ctr., 68 Ohio Misc. 1, 426 N.E.2d 809 (C.P. P. Div. Summit County 1980)
In re McInnis, 61 Ohio Misc. 2d 790, 584 N.E.2d 1389 (P. Ct. Stark County 1991)

In re Myers, 62 Ohio Misc. 2d 763, 610 N.E.2d 663 (P. Ct. Summit County 1993)

Trial—Unreported

Bloom v. Grant Hosp., No. 85 CV-02-1081 (C.P. Franklin County, Ohio Feb. 26, 1985), *writ of mandamus dismissed,* No. 85-332 (Dec. 4, 1985)
In re Dial, No. 333119 (C.P. P. Div. Franklin County, Ohio Feb. 26, 1985)
In re Thompson, No. 60553 (C.P. P. Div. Scioto County, Ohio June 16, 1993)

Oregon

Trial—Unreported

Evans v. District Attorney, No. E82-2173 (Or. Cir. Ct. Douglas County Dec. 13, 1982)

Pennsylvania

Appellate—Reported

In re Cabrera, 381 Pa. Super. 100, 552 A.2d 1114 (1989)
In re Estate of Dorone, 517 Pa. 3, 534 A.2d 452 (1987), *aff'g* 349 Pa. Super. 59, 502 A.2d 1271 (1985)
In re Fiori, ____ Pa. Super. ____, 652 A.2d 1350 (1995), *aff'g* 13 Fiduc. Rep. 2d 79, 17 Pa. D. & C.4th 558 (C.P. Bucks County, Pa. 1993), *review granted,* No. 6 E.D. Appeal Docket 1995, ____ Pa. ____, ____ A.2d ____ (1995)

Trial—Reported

In re Doe, 8 Fiduc. Rep. 2d 1, 16 Phila. 229, 45 Pa. D. & C.3d 371 (1987)
In re Dorone, 5 Fiduc. Rep. 2d 117 (C.P. Lehigh County, Pa. 1985)
In re E.L.K., 11 Fiduc. Rep. 2d 78 (C.P. Berks County, Pa. 1991)
Pocono Medical Ctr. v. Harley, 11 Fiduc. Rep. 2d 128 (C.P. Monroe County, Pa. 1990)
Ragona v. Preate, 11 Fiduc. Rep. 2d 1, 6 Pa. D. & C.4th 202 (C.P. Lackawanna County 1990), *reported in* 2 BioLaw U:1875 (Dec. 1990)
In re Yetter, 24 Fiduc. Rep. 1 62 Pa. D. & C.2d 619, (C.P. 1973)

Trial—Unreported

Neumann Medical Ctr., Inc. v. Popowich, No. 5663 (C.P. Phila. County, Pa. Apr. 26, 1990)

Rhode Island

Trial—Reported

Gray v. Romeo, 709 F. Supp. 325 (D.R.I. 1989)
Gray v. Romeo, 697 F. Supp. 580 (D.R.I. 1988)

Tennessee

Appellate—Reported

Dockery v. Dockery, 559 S.W.2d 952 (Tenn. Ct. App. 1977)

Table 1–1
(continued)

In re Hamilton, 657 S.W.2d 425 (Tenn. Ct. App. 1983)
State Dep't of Human Resources v. Northern, 563 S.W.2d 197 (Tenn. Ct. App. 1978)

Trial—Unreported

Doe v. Wilson, No. 90-364-II (Ch. Ct. Davidson County, Tenn. Feb. 16, 1990)

Texas

Trial—Unreported

Newman v. William Beaumont Army Medical Ctr., No. EP-86-CA-276 (W.D. Tex. Oct. 30, 1986)
In re Petersen, No. E117,982 (Tex. Dist. Ct. Jefferson County Aug. 4, 1983)

Virginia

Appellate—Reported

In re Baby "K," 16 F.3d 590 (4th Cir. 1994), *aff'g In re* Baby "K," 832 F. Supp. 1022 (E.D. Va. 1993), *cert. denied,* 115 S. Ct. 91 (1994)

Trial—Unreported

Alexandria Hosp. v. McLellan, No. CH 13009 (Va. Cir. Ct. Jan. 19, 1982)
Hazleton v. Powhatan Nursing Home, Inc., No. CH 98287 (Va. Cir. Ct. Fairfax County Aug. 29 and Sept. 2, 1986), *appeal denied,* 6 Va. Cir. Ct. Op. 414 (Aspen 1987)

Washington

Appellate—Reported

Benoy v. Simons, 66 Wash. App. 56, 831 P.2d 167, *review denied,* 120 Wash. 2d 1014, 844 P.2d 435 (1992)
In re Colyer, 99 Wash. 2d 114, 660 P.2d 738 (1983)
Compassion in Dying v. Washington, 49 F.3d 586 (9th Cir. 1995), *rev'g* 850 F. Supp. 1454 (W.D. Wash. 1994)
In re Grant, 109 Wash. 2d 545, 747 P.2d 445 (1987), *modified,* 757 P.2d 534 (Wash. 1988)
In re Hamlin, 102 Wash. 2d 810, 689 P.2d 1372 (1984)
In re Ingram, 102 Wash. 2d 827, 689 P.2d 1363 (1984)
Strickland v. Deaconess Hosp., 47 Wash. App. 262, 735 P.2d 74 (1987)

West Virginia

Appellate—Reported

Belcher v. Charleston Area Medical Ctr., 188 W. Va. 105, 422 S.E.2d 827 (1992)

Wisconsin

Appellate—Reported

L.W. v. L.E. Phillips Career Dev. Ctr., 167 Wis. 2d 53, 482 N.W.2d 60 (1992)

CANADA

Supreme Court

Rodriguez v. Attorney Gen. of Canada and Attorney Gen. of British Columbia, 107 D.L.R.4th 342 (1993)

British Columbia

Rodriguez v. British Columbia (Attorney Gen.) (1993), 76 B.C.L.R. (2d) 145, 22 B.C.A.C. 266, 38 W.A.C. 266, 14 C.R.R. (2d) 34, 79 C.C.C. (3d) 1, [1993] W.W.R. 553

Ontario

Malette v. Shulman, 72 O.R. (2d) 417, 67 D.L.R. (4th) 321, 20 A.C.W.S. (3d) 301 (1990)

Quebec

Nancy B. v. Hotel-Dieu de Quebec, [1992] R.J.Q. 361 (C.S.), (1992) 86 D.L.R. (4th) 385, (1992) 31 A.C.W.S. (3d) 160

UNITED KINGDOM

Airedale N.H.S. Trust v. Bland, [1993] 1 All E.R. 821, [1993] 2 W.L.R. 316, [1994] 1 F.C.R 501, 12

A number of factors make it likely that end-of-life decisionmaking will continue to present difficult issues for health care professionals, patients, and patients' families, and that some of these cases will eventuate in litigation. First, continued technological advances in medical care create an incentive for physicians to continue to provide treatment to hopelessly ill patients. On the other hand, continually increasing pressures to control the costs of medical care create a strong incentive for physicians to want to limit the amount they provide, and hopelessly ill patients are one area in which this can be expected to occur.[72] When the families of incompetent patients wish for treatment to be continued and physicians want it to stop, clashes are likely to occur, some of which will inevitably result in litigation. Although there is no evidence that the costs of care played a significant role in generating the futility cases that have been litigated to date, that could easily change in future cases.

§ 1.8 Health Care Terminology

Physicians are ultimately legally responsible for a patient's treatment, and generally one physician, usually referred to as the *attending physician,* bears final responsibility.[73] However, end-of-life decisionmaking generally involves many other health care professionals. Nurses are almost always involved, and may include masters-level nurses, bachelors-level nurses, registered nurses (RNs), licensed practical nurses (LPNs), and nurse's aides. Depending on the kind of treatment involved, there may also be other, more specialized health care professionals, such as inhalation therapists and nutritionists. Taken together, these professionals are sometimes referred to as the *health care team.*

In addition, because decisionmaking usually (though not always) occurs in a health care institutional setting,[74] the institution often has an interest in the process and outcome separate from that of the health care professionals who are its employees and of those who are affiliated with it but are not employees (that is, independent contractors), which is usually the status of physicians. Thus, health care administrators are often participants in the decisionmaking process. Sometimes the term *health care personnel* is used to refer to the larger group consisting of health care professionals and health care administrators.

Generally, decisionmaking focuses on a treatment or treatments (sometimes referred to as *therapy* or *therapeutic procedures*), which are intended to save or

---

[72] *But see* Paradis, *Making a Living Off the Dying,* N.Y. Times, Apr. 25, 1992, at 15 (nat'l ed.) (claiming that doctors prolong end-of-life medical care to increase revenues for themselves and hospitals).

[73] *Cf.* N.Y. Pub. Health Law § 2961(2) ("'Attending physician' means the physician selected by or assigned to a patient . . . who has primary responsibility for the treatment and care of the patient.").

[74] See § **7.36.**

extend life, improve health, or relieve suffering. However, sometimes a particular procedure is diagnostic rather than therapeutic, in which case its objective is to ascertain more clearly or precisely the nature of the patient's illness or injury and to assist in making recommendations about what treatments are appropriate to consider administering or forgoing.

Bibliography

Burt, R. *Taking Care of Strangers: The Rule of Law in Doctor-Patient Relations.* New York: Free Press, 1979.

Byrn, R. "Compulsory Lifesaving Treatment for the Competent Adult." Fordham Law Review 44 (1975): 1.

Cantor, N. *Legal Frontiers of Death and Dying.* Bloomington: Indiana University Press, 1987.

Carnerie, F. "Euthanasia and Self-Determinism: Is There a Charter Right to Die in Canada?" *McGill Law Journal* 32 (1987): 299.

"Commissioning Morality: A Critique of the President's Commission for the Study of Ethical Problems in Medicine and Biomedical and Behavioral Research: A Symposium." *Cardozo Law Review* 6 (1984): 223.

Cook, D., et al. "Determinants in Canadian Health Care Workers of the Decision to Withdraw Life Support from the Critically Ill." *JAMA* 273 (1995): 703.

Developments in the Law. "Medical Technology and the Law." *Harvard Law Review* 103 (1990): 1519.

Dworkin, R. *Life's Dominion: An Argument About Abortion, Euthanasia, and Individual Freedom.* New York: Knopf 1993.

Hastings Center. *Guidelines on the Termination of Life-Sustaining Treatment and the Care of the Dying.* Bloomington: Indiana University Press, 1987.

Kelly, D. *Critical Care Ethics: Treatment Decisions in American Hospitals.* Kansas City: Sheed & Ward, 1991.

Law Reform Commission of Canada. *Euthanasia, Aiding Suicide, and Cessation of Treatment.* Ottawa: Law Reform Commission of Canada, 1982 and 1983.

Leahy, R. "Legal Death: A Pathfinder to the Current State of the Law and Its Implications." *Legal Reference Services Quarterly* 9 (1989): 73.

Lidz, C., et al. *The Erosion of Autonomy in Long-Term Care.* New York: Oxford University Press, 1992.

Meisel, A. "The Legal Consensus About Forgoing Life-Sustaining Treatment: Its Status and Its Prospects." *Kennedy Institute of Ethics Journal* 2 (1992): 309.

National Center for State Courts. *Guidelines for State Court Decision Making in Life-Sustaining Medical Treatment Cases.* 2d ed. St. Paul: West Publishing Co., 1992.

New Jersey Commission on Legal and Ethical Problems in the Delivery of Health Care. *Problems and Approaches in Health Care Decisionmaking: The New Jersey Experience.* Trenton: New Jersey Bioethics Commission, 1990.

New York State Task Force on Life and the Law. *Life-Sustaining Treatment: Making Decisions and Appointing a Health Care Agent.* New York: New York State Task Force on Life and the Law, 1987.

Office of Technology Assessment. U.S. Congress. *Life-Sustaining Technologies and the Elderly.* Washington: Government Printing Office, 1987.

President's Commission for the Study of Ethical Problems in Medicine and Biomedical and Behavioral Research. *Deciding to Forego Life-Sustaining Treatment: A Report on the Ethical, Medical, and Legal Issues in Treatment Decisions.* Washington: Government Printing Office, 1983.

Rhoden, N. "Litigating Life and Death." *Harvard Law Review* 102 (1988): 375.

Sherlock, R. *Preserving Life: Public Policy and the Life Not Worth Living.* Chicago: Loyola University Press, 1987.

Weir, R. *Abating Treatment with Critically Ill Patients: Ethical and Legal Limits to the Medical Prolongation of Life.* New York: Oxford University Press, 1989.

Wicclair, M. *Ethics and the Elderly.* New York: Oxford University Press, 1993.

CHAPTER 2

NATURE AND SOURCES OF THE RIGHT TO DIE

§ 2.1 Introduction

The right to die is an aspect of the larger, more general right to refuse medical treatment.[1] Its origins are in the same constitutional and common-law doctrines as the right to refuse medical treatment not leading to the patient's death, supplemented in part by statutory enactments.

Right-to-die cases arise as a consequence of two factors. The first is the development and continual refinement of medical technology allowing biological existence to be maintained, almost indefinitely, for patients on the edge of

[1] **MO:** Cruzan v. Harmon, 760 S.W.2d 408 (Mo. 1988), *aff'd sub nom.* Cruzan v. Director, 497 U.S. 261 (1990).

death. Indeed, many right-to-die cases involve patients who are permanently unconscious;[2] a minimum quantity of cerebral functioning still exists that prevents them from meeting the criteria for "brain death."[3] The second factor—the sometimes overwhelming concern of health care professionals, health care administrators, and the lawyers who counsel them—about potential legal liability[4] results in the transformation of what would otherwise be the clinical management of end-of-life cases to legal cases.

The first reported right-to-die case is the now well-known *Quinlan* case.[5] What distinguishes it and its progeny from prior cases involving the refusal of treatment (both by competent patients or on behalf of incompetent patients) is the fact that even if the treatment in question, a mechanical ventilator, were to have been maintained, the patient's condition was such that she could never be returned to any semblance of health, let alone the status quo ante. Prior to the *Quinlan* case, there was a great reluctance in the case law to permit patients to refuse treatment when that refusal would probably lead to their death. *Quinlan* changed that by making clear to the courts what had long been apparent in the health care professions, namely that there is an increasing range of situations in which treatment will keep patients alive but not restore them to health.

CURRENT STATE OF THE LAW

§ 2.2 The Legal Consensus About Forgoing Life-Sustaining Treatment

Although there is no absolute right to die,[6] there is a growing consensus in both the case law and the statutory law that, under appropriate circumstances, the

---

[2] See § **9.53.**

[3] See § **9.48.**

[4] See **Chs. 17** and **18.**

[5] **NJ:** *In re* Quinlan, 355 A.2d 647 (N.J.), *cert. denied sub nom.* Garger v. New Jersey, 429 U.S. 922 (1976).

[6] **DNY:** Deel v. Syracuse Veterans Admin. Medical Ctr., 729 F. Supp. 231, 233 (N.D.N.Y. 1990).

DRI: Gray v. Romeo, 697 F. Supp. 580 (D.R.I. 1988).

AZ: Rasmussen v. Fleming, 741 P.2d 674, 683 (Ariz. 1987).

CA: Thor v. Superior Court, 855 P.2d 375, 383 (Cal. 1993); Donaldson v. Van de Kamp, 4 Cal. Rptr. 2d 59 (Ct. App. 1992). *But see* Bouvia v. Superior Court (Glenchur), 225 Cal. Rptr. 297, 307 (Ct. App. 1986) (Compton, J., concurring) ("I believe she has an absolute right to" refuse force feeding.).

CT: McConnell v. Beverly Enters.-Conn., Inc., 553 A.2d 596, 608 (Conn. 1989) ("[T]he common law right to refuse medical treatment is not absolute, and, in some cases, may yield to a compelling state interest.").

right exists, even if not denominated as such.[7] Courts in a gradually but continually growing number of jurisdictions (see **Table 1–1**) have recognized the existence of such a right, as have almost all legislatures through "advance directive" legislation.[8] No court has rejected the right to die in a wholesale fashion. Today, as the California Supreme Court has observed, there is a "developing interdisciplinary consensus . . . [that] now uniformly recognizes the patient's right of control over bodily integrity as the subsuming essential in determining the relative balance of interests."[9]

The main points of the judicial consensus[10] (and the chapters in which they are discussed in this treatise) are the following:

1. Competent patients have a constitutional and common-law right to refuse treatment. See **Chapter 2.**
2. Incompetent patients have the same substantive rights as competent patients. See **Chapter 2.**

DE: *In re* Severns, 425 A.2d 156, 158 (Del. Ch. 1980).

DC: *Cf. In re* A.C., 573 A.2d 1235, 1245–46 (D.C. 1990) (right to refuse treatment is not absolute).

IL: *In re* E.G., 549 N.E.2d 322, 328 (Ill. 1989).

MA: *In re* Doe, 583 N.E.2d 1263, 1269 (Mass. 1992); Brophy v. New Eng. Sinai Hosp., Inc., 497 N.E.2d 626, 634 (Mass. 1986). *But see In re* Doe, 583 N.E.2d 1263, 1275 (Mass. 1992) (O'Connor, J., dissenting) (majority has granted absolute right to refuse treatment).

MI: *But see* Martin v. Martin, 504 N.W.2d 917, 922 (Mich. Ct. App. 1993) ("Because a patient's right of self-determination is generally recognized as outweighing any countervailing state interests, where a patient currently has the requisite decision-making capacity, the expressed statements of the patient regarding medical treatment will generally control that patient's care, regardless of the consequences of the decision.").

MN: *In re* Torres, 357 N.W.2d 332, 339 (Minn. 1984).

MO: Cruzan v. Harmon, 760 S.W.2d 408 (Mo. 1988).

NV: McKay v. Bergstedt, 801 P.2d 617, 621 (Nev. 1990).

NJ: *In re* Farrell, 529 A.2d 404, 410 (N.J. 1987); *In re* Conroy, 486 A.2d 1209, 1223 (N.J. 1985).

NY: *In re* Storar, 420 N.E.2d 64 (N.Y.), *cert. denied,* 454 U.S. 858 (1981); Delio v. Westchester County Medical Ctr., 516 N.Y.S.2d 677, 691 (App. Div. 1987).

PA: *In re* Doe, 45 Pa. D. & C.3d 371 (C.P. Phila. County 1987).

[7] *See, e.g.,* Saunders v. State, 492 N.Y.S.2d 510, 512 (Sup. Ct. Nassau County 1985) ("[A]pplicant is not claiming any so-called 'right to die' or any right to commit suicide through this 'Refusal'. Rather, [she] is insisting upon what she describes as her 'right as a competent adult to refuse to submit to medical and surgical procedures although the inevitable consequences of her decision will be [her] death.' ").

[8] See **Chs. 11** and **12.**

[9] Thor v. Superior Court, 855 P.2d 375, 380 (Cal. 1993).

[10] *See also* Meisel, *The Legal Consensus about Forgoing Life-Sustaining Treatment: Its Status and Its Prospects,* 2 Kennedy Inst. Ethics J. 309 (1992); Orentlicher, *The Right to Die After* Cruzan, 264 JAMA 2444 (1990).

3. The interests of the state in opposition to the right to forgo life-sustaining medical treatment are virtually nonexistent in the case of competent patients and very weak in the case of incompetent patients whose prognosis for recovery is dim. See **Chapter 8.**
4. The decisionmaking process should generally occur in the clinical setting without resort to the courts, which are, however, available to assist in decisionmaking when an impasse is reached. See **Chapter 5.**
5. In making decisions for incompetent patients, surrogate decisionmakers should first attempt to effectuate the patient's own preferences expressed before the patient lost decisionmaking capacity; however, if these preferences are not known, the decisions about life-sustaining treatment should be made on the basis of the patient's best interests. See **Chapter 7.**
6. In ascertaining an incompetent patient's preferences, the attending physician and surrogate may rely on the patient's "advance directive." See **Chapters 10** through **13.**
7. Artificial nutrition and hydration is a medical treatment and may be withheld or withdrawn under the same conditions as any other form of medical treatment. See **§§ 9.39** and **9.40.**
8. Active euthanasia and assisted suicide are morally and legally distinct from forgoing life-sustaining treatment. See **Chapter 18.**

This consensus is not without exception. A few states require a very high level of proof of an incompetent patient's wishes in order to forgo life-sustaining treatment.[11] Some courts have more willingly given weight (at least in dictum) to the interest of the state in overriding the treatment refusal even of a competent patient;[12] some have required (at least in certain kinds of cases) that the courts play a more substantial role in the decisionmaking process;[13] and some have been unwilling to treat the forgoing of artificial nutrition and hydration on the same terms as other medical treatments.[14] But the consensus has been so strong

---

[11] **MO:** Cruzan v. Harmon, 760 S.W.2d 408, 425 (Mo. 1988) ("'Given the fact that these patients are irreversibly comatose or in a chronic vegetative state, attributing "rights" to these patients at all is somewhat problematic. . . . To be sure, these patients are not "dead" in most of the increasingly multiple senses of the term, but the task of giving content to the notion that they have rights, in the face of the recognition that they could make no decisions about how to exercise any such rights, remains a difficult one.'" (quoting L. Tribe, American Constitutional Law 1368 n.25 (2d ed. 1988)). *But cf. In re* Warren, 858 S.W.2d 263 (Mo. Ct. App. 1993).

NY: *In re* Westchester County Medical Ctr. (O'Connor), 531 N.E.2d 607 (N.Y. 1988) (life-sustaining treatment may not be forgone for incompetent patient in absence of clear and convincing proof that incompetent left instructions to terminate life-sustaining procedures).

[12] **FL:** Satz v. Perlmutter, 362 So. 2d 160 (Fla. Dist. Ct. App. 1978), *aff'd,* 379 So. 2d 359 (Fla. 1980).

[13] See §§ **5.38** through **5.44.**

[14] **MO:** Cruzan v. Harmon, 760 S.W.2d 408 (Mo. 1988), *distinguished in In re* Warren, 858 S.W.2d 263 (Mo. Ct. App. 1993).

and the trend so clear that it has been reasonably safe to advise, in jurisdictions without case law or without clearly contrary statutory direction, that this trend be assumed to govern.

§ 2.3 —The Supreme Court's *Cruzan* Decision

The legal consensus about forgoing life-sustaining treatment had substantially taken shape by 1990, the year in which the United States Supreme Court heard its first right-to-die case. However, there had been no guidance on any important issue by any federal appellate court, and the Supreme Court had previously denied certiorari in five right-to-die cases[15] and in a larger number of related cases.[16] Thus, when a petition for certiorari was filed in *Cruzan v. Harmon,* there was little reason to believe that the Court would agree to review the case. It did, however, and issued its decision and opinion near the end of the 1989 Term.[17]

The patient in this case, Nancy Cruzan, was a woman in her early thirties at the time of the litigation. She lapsed into a persistent vegetative state as a result of serious injuries suffered in an automobile accident seven years before, a state from which, all parties in the case agreed, she would never emerge. About three years after the accident, her parents, who were her court-appointed guardians, came to the realization that, as far as they were concerned, she was dead and

---

OH: Couture v. Couture, 549 N.E.2d 571 (Ohio Ct. App. 1989), *questioned in In re* Crum, 580 N.E.2d 876 (P. Ct. Franklin County, Ohio 1991) (on ground that legislation on which *Couture* was based had been amended).

WA: *In re* Grant, 747 P.2d 445 (Wash. 1987), *modified,* 757 P.2d 534 (Wash. 1988).

See §§ **9.39** and **9.40.**

[15] **CA:** Drabick v. Drabick, 245 Cal. Rptr. 840 (Ct. App. 1988), *cert. denied,* 488 U.S. 958, *reh'g denied,* 488 U.S. 1024 (1989).

IL: *In re* Estate of Prange, 520 N.E.2d 946 (Ill. App. Ct.), *vacated,* 527 N.E.2d 303 (Ill.), *cert. denied sub nom.* Murphy v. Benson, 488 U.S. 892 (1988).

NJ: *In re* Jobes, 529 A.2d 434 (N.J.), *reconsideration and stay denied,* 531 A.2d 1360 (N.J.), *cert. denied sub nom.* Lincoln Park Nursing & Convalescent Home v. Kahn, 483 U.S. 1036 (1987); *In re* Quinlan, 355 A.2d 647 (N.J. 1976).

NY: *In re* Storar, 420 N.E.2d 64 (N.Y.), *cert. denied,* 454 U.S. 858 (1981).

[16] **CA:** *In re* Phillip B., 156 Cal. Rptr. 48 (Ct. App. 1979), *cert. denied sub nom.* Bothman v. Warren B., 445 U.S. 949 (1980).

IN: *In re* Infant Doe, No. GU8204-00 (Ind. Cir. Ct. Monroe County Apr. 12, 1982), *writ of mandamus dismissed sub nom.* State *ex rel.* Infant Doe v. Baker, No. 482 S 140 (Ind. May 27, 1982), *cert. denied,* 464 U.S. 961 (1983).

NY: Weber v. Stony Brook Hosp., 467 N.Y.S.2d 685 (App. Div.) (*per curiam*), *aff'd,* 456 N.E.2d 1186 (N.Y.), *cert. denied,* 464 U.S. 1026 (1983).

OH: *In re* Milton, 505 N.E.2d 255 (Ohio), *cert. denied,* 484 U.S. 820 (1987).

[17] *See* Cruzan v. Director, 497 U.S. 261 (1990), *aff'g* Cruzan v. Harmon, 760 S.W.2d 408 (Mo. 1988).

that further treatment was unwarranted. (Of course she was not legally dead; persons in a persistent vegetative state do not meet the criteria for "brain death" because the brain stem, controlling basic "vegetative" functions such as respiration, circulation, and body temperature, is still alive.[18]) Her parents therefore requested that the tube-feedings keeping her alive be discontinued, a request for which there was abundant clinical and legal precedent.[19]

The administrator of the state-owned hospital treating Nancy Cruzan insisted that her parents obtain a court order to discontinue tube-feeding, and such an order was issued by the county probate court. The state of Missouri—a party to the case largely because of the patient's hospitalization in a state-owned hospital—appealed the decision, and the Missouri Supreme Court reversed, in what was then and still is a very idiosyncratic opinion. The court held that artificial nutrition and hydration could not be withdrawn from a woman in a persistent vegetative state who was not "terminally ill" unless there was proof by clear and convincing evidence that she had authorized such termination prior to losing decisionmaking capacity. In other words, tube-feeding could be terminated only if Nancy Cruzan, herself, had, prior to her accident, authorized it; the Missouri court did not clarify whether a written living will was necessary or whether an oral statement was required. The United States Supreme Court affirmed, holding that the guarantee of liberty contained in the Fourteenth Amendment to the Constitution did not prohibit Missouri from insisting that "evidence of the incompetent's wishes as to the withdrawal of treatment be proved by clear and convincing evidence" in order for treatment to be withdrawn.[20]

Although many believed that it was poor public policy to insist solely on application of such a standard for the termination of life support, it proved impossible to muster a persuasive argument that such a policy was unconstitutional. Although Justices Brennan and Stevens wrote dissenting opinions in which they attempted to do so—indeed, Justice Brennan's opinion reads somewhat like the draft of a majority opinion—in answering "the question . . . simply and starkly [stated,] whether the United States Constitution prohibits Missouri from choosing the rule of decision which it did,"[21] a five-justice majority held, just as simply and starkly, "that it does not."[22]

The Court's precise holding, grounded in the Fourteenth Amendment's guarantee of liberty, rather than in the right of privacy,[23] is narrow and simple—the

---

[18] See §§ **9.48** and **9.53.**

[19] See §§ **9.39** (**Table 9–1**) and **9.53.**

[20] Cruzan v. Director, 497 U.S. at 280.

[21] *Id.* at 277.

[22] *Id.* at 280.

[23] *Id.* at 279 n.7 ("Although many state courts have held that a right to refuse treatment is encompassed by a generalized constitutional right of privacy, we have never so held. We believe this issue is more properly analyzed in terms of a Fourteenth Amendment liberty interest. *See* Bowers v. Hardwick, 478 U.S. 186, 194–195, 106 S. Ct. 2841, 2846, 92 L. Ed. 2d 140 (1986).").

Constitution permits a state to require the rendition of life-sustaining treatment to an incompetent patient unless there is clear and convincing evidence that the patient authorized the forgoing of the treatment prior to losing decisionmaking capacity.[24] However, the possibilities for a more expansive reading of the opinion are apparent, in part because of the existence of two concurring and two dissenting opinions. Thus, it is essential to clarify what the Court held, what important dicta the opinion contains, what implications can reasonably be drawn, and what is merely speculation.

Holding. It is easy to overlook the fact that this decision merely affirms the Missouri Supreme Court's opinion. It does not directly affect the law in any other state. No other state is required to adopt Missouri's rigorous standard for decisionmaking for incompetent patients. In fact, the only other state clearly to have done so already is New York,[25] and *Cruzan* simply means that New York, like Missouri or any other state that might choose, is constitutionally permitted to do so. Confusion about what the Court said in this regard is very likely. Although several other states also require the use of a clear and convincing evidence standard, as the Supreme Court noted, with the exception of Missouri and New York, they do not require clear and convincing evidence that the patient himself or herself authorized the forgoing of life-sustaining treatment before losing decisionmaking capacity.

What these other states require "clear and convincing evidence" of makes all the difference. In some states, it is clear and convincing evidence that the patient would have decided to forgo treatment—in effect, clear and convincing evidence of the substituted judgment standard.[26] In other states, it is clear and convincing evidence that it is not in the patient's best interests, as determined by the family and doctor, that treatment be continued.[27]

Indeed, Justice Stevens's disagreement with the majority was "unrelated to its endorsement of the clear and convincing standard of proof for cases of this kind."[28] He agreed "that the controlling facts must be established with unmistakable clarity."[29] The point of departure for him was "not how to prove the controlling facts but rather what proven facts should be controlling."[30] Similarly, Justice Brennan wrote that the rule endorsed by the majority—a clear and convincing evidence standard of proof in conjunction with a requirement that the patient's actual intent be proved—"skews the result away from a determination that as accurately as possible reflects the individual's own preferences and

---

24 See §§ **5.62** and **7.4.**

25 *In re* Westchester County Medical Ctr. (O'Connor), 531 N.E.2d 607 (N.Y. 1988). See § **7.4.**

26 See §§ **5.62** and **7.7.**

27 See §§ **5.62** and **7.12.**

28 Cruzan v. Director, 497 U.S. 261, 350 (1990) (Stevens, J., dissenting).

29 *Id.* at 350 (Stevens, J., dissenting).

30 *Id.* (Stevens, J., dissenting).

beliefs. It is a rule that transforms human beings into passive subjects of medical technology."[31]

It must be emphasized not only that the Supreme Court's ruling permits but does not require states to insist on proof of the patient's actual intent, but also that it does not require—though it permits—a clear and convincing evidence standard of proof before life support may be terminated. Each state remains free to set its own substantive and evidentiary standards, at least as far as *Cruzan* is concerned. Because state courts are not obliged to follow the Missouri rule, the reasoning of the dissenters (and Justice O'Connor's concurrence) may prove important in influencing and providing arguments for state court judges to resist adopting such a stringent standard.

In fact, this is what has occurred in the wake of *Cruzan*. Several years after the Supreme Court's decision, it is apparent that the pre-*Cruzan* legal consensus is stronger than ever.[32] Some right-to-die cases decided in the state courts after *Cruzan* do not even mention the Supreme Court's opinion, some merely mention it but otherwise virtually ignore it; and like other landmark cases, *Cruzan* tends to be cited as support for many highly tangential propositions. The application of the underlying rule of law articulated by the Missouri Supreme Court has even been called into question in Missouri—or, at least, an attempt has been made by the Missouri Court of Appeals to seriously limit it.[33]

Ironically, the Supreme Court's *Cruzan* opinion and holding did not even have any significant impact on Nancy Cruzan. The Court's decision did not resolve the underlying issue between the litigants in the case. Merely reading the Supreme Court's opinion might lead one to conclude that Nancy Cruzan's feeding tube was never removed, because the Court held that the Missouri Supreme Court decision forbidding its removal did not violate the United States Constitution. But, in fact, that is not what happened. Several months after the Supreme Court's decision, a hearing was held before the same county probate judge who had originally heard the case to consider new evidence of Nancy Cruzan's wishes, and the court again ordered that the feeding tube could be removed.[34] This time, the state of Missouri did not oppose the Cruzan family's request, and it complied with, rather than appealing, the order.[35] Though a group of protestors tried to enter her room to reconnect her feeding tube,[36] and six lawsuits or appeals were filed by Lawyers for Life, the Center for Christian

---

[31] *Id.* at 325 (Brennan, J., dissenting).

[32] *See* Meisel, *A Retrospective on* Cruzan, 20 L., Med. & Health Care 340 (1992).

[33] *See In re* Warren, 858 S.W.2d 263 (Mo. Ct. App. 1993).

[34] *See* Cruzan v. Mouton, Estate No. CV384-9P (Mo. Cir. Ct. Jasper County Dec. 14, 1990), *reported in* 6 Issues in L. & Med. 433 (1991).

[35] Malcolm, *Missouri Family Renews Battle over Right to Die,* N.Y. Times, Nov. 2, 1990, at A12 (nat'l ed.); Gianelli, *The Last Battle?,* Am. Med. News, Nov. 16, 1990, at 1.

[36] N.Y. Times, Dec. 19, 1990, at A14 (nat'l ed.).

Activism, and others seeking to have the feeding tube reconnected,[37] on December 26, 1990, Nancy Cruzan died, 11 days after judicial permission was granted to terminate her tube-feeding.[38]

Dictum. Other than the holding, the most important aspect of the opinion is the dictum that competent patients have a constitutional right to refuse treatment. Although many state courts (and a few federal trial courts) had reached this conclusion,[39] they almost uniformly predicated the right to refuse treatment on other grounds as well—the common law, state constitutions, and state statutes. The United States Supreme Court had never explicitly addressed this issue. Thus, the majority's statement in *Cruzan* that "[t]he principle that a competent person has a constitutionally protected liberty interest in refusing unwanted medical treatment may be inferred from our prior decision"[40] is a welcome one because it makes more certain what had previously only been assumed, though the assumption was widespread and probably well-founded.

Implications. In addition to the holding and dicta, there are several significant implications in the opinion for a variety of aspects of the right to die.

(1) *The Nature of the Substantive Right of an Incompetent Patient.* Although virtually all courts had agreed that the substantive rights of incompetent patients were the same as those of competent patients,[41] the Supreme Court cast doubt on whether such equality of treatment is required as a matter of constitutional law. "The difficulty with [this] claim," the Court pointed out, "is that in a sense it begs the question: an incompetent person is not able to make an informed and voluntary choice to exercise a hypothetical right to refuse treatment or any other right. Such a 'right' must be exercised for her, if at all, by some sort of surrogate."[42]

(2) *Forgoing Artificial Nutrition and Hydration.* The forgoing of artificial nutrition and hydration has been a highly controversial and sensitive subject at least since the *Barber* decision in 1983,[43] when a nurse told the district attorney

---

[37] Colby, *The Lessons of the* Cruzan *Case,* 39 U. Kan. L. Rev. 519, 520 (1991). *See also Court Firm on* Cruzan *Ruling,* N.Y. Times, Dec. 21, 1990, at A30 (nat'l ed.).

[38] Malcolm, *Burial Is End to Long Goodbye for Nancy Cruzan,* N.Y. Times, Dec. 29, 1990, at 1 (nat'l ed.).

[39] See § **2.4.**

[40] Cruzan v. Director, 497 U.S. 261, 278 (1990).

[41] See § **2.5.**

[42] Cruzan v. Director, 497 U.S. at 280. *But compare id.* at 308 (Brennan, J., dissenting) ("Nor does the fact that Nancy Cruzan is now incompetent deprive her of her fundamental rights. . . . As the majority recognizes, . . . the question is not whether an incompetent has constitutional rights, but how such rights may be exercised.").

[43] Barber v. Superior Court, 195 Cal. Rptr. 484 (Ct. App. 1983).

that doctors had killed a patient by terminating artificial nutrition and hydration procedures. Reams of academic papers on the subject have not settled the issue, nor have the increasingly large number of appellate court opinions. (More right-to-die cases have involved the question of forgoing artificial nutrition and hydration than any other treatment.[44]) The Supreme Court did not settle it in *Cruzan* either because the majority opinion assumed (for the purpose of deciding *Cruzan* alone), without deciding, that feeding tubes are the same as other forms of medical treatment.[45] However, five justices (Justice O'Connor in a concurring opinion and the four dissenting justices) did subscribe to the view that the forgoing of artificial nutrition and hydration should be governed by the same principles as any other medical treatment, which is the position taken by every other appellate court to have considered the matter except the Missouri Supreme Court[46] and possibly the Washington Supreme Court.[47] It would therefore be a fair implication from the opinion that a majority of the Court would find no determinative distinction in the forgoing of artificial nutrition and hydration but for the fact that two of these five justices, Justices Brennan and Marshall, subsequently retired from the Court.

Speculation. In the wake of the Supreme Court's decision, health lawyers' phones rang off the hook, ethics committees called urgent meetings, and medical ethicists glumly predicted a new era of overtreatment of hopelessly ill patients. Pundits of all professional persuasions had a field day commenting on what the Supreme Court decided.[48] Much of the commentary was sheer speculation without any basis, or with only the slimmest grounding, in the Court's opinion.

---

[44] See § **9.39.**

[45] Cruzan v. Director, 497 U.S. at 279.

[46] Cruzan v. Harmon, 760 S.W.2d 408, 423 (Mo. 1988) ("[C]ommon sense tells us that food and water do not treat an illness, they maintain a life.").

[47] *Compare In re* Grant, 757 P.2d 445 (Wash. 1987) (holding 5 to 4 that artificial nutrition and hydration was a form of medical treatment that could be forgone by a surrogate on behalf of an incompetent patient) *with In re* Grant, 757 P.2d 534 (Wash. 1988) (in which one of the justices in the original *Grant* majority announced without any explanation that she had changed her vote).

[48] *See, e.g.,* Bopp & Marzen, Cruzan: *Facing the Inevitable,* 19 L., Med. & Health Care 37, 42 (1991) ("On the whole . . . *Cruzan*'s caution will almost certainly generate a greater degree of caution in state courts as well."); Colburn, *Another Chapter in the Case of Nancy Cruzan,* Wash. Post, Oct. 16, 1990, at A7 ("Physicians who are already nervous about the risk of malpractice lawsuits . . . are even more likely to refuse to withhold extraordinary life-continuing care from irreversibly comatose patients unless they have a living will or signed power of attorney form. It's becoming very hard to terminate treatment on anyone in this country. . . . The *Cruzan* decision is having that horrible effect—of physicians starting to practice law, basically.") (quoting George Annas). *Cf. Bioethicists' Statement on the U.S. Supreme Court's* Cruzan *Decision,* 323 New Eng. J. Med. 686 (1990) (statement of 36 bioethicists with backgrounds in law, medicine, and philosophy, explaining decision to physicians to counter possibility of widespread misinterpretation of *Cruzan* in the medical profession).

The most blatant, though incorrect, message that the *Cruzan* decision conveyed (or more properly, that was sometimes imputed to it) is that the Supreme Court had changed all the rules about the termination of life support. More specific versions of this misunderstanding are that

- it is no longer legal to forgo life-sustaining treatment, at least not unless there is a living will;
- patients in a persistent vegetative state must be treated indefinitely;
- it is impermissible to forgo life-sustaining treatment for a never-competent patient.

None of these claims are true, at least not as far as *Cruzan* ruled. All states are constitutionally free to adopt far less rigorous standards than Missouri's for the forgoing of life-sustaining treatment for patients who lack decisionmaking capacity and who may not technically be terminally ill (including persistent vegetative state patients and other patients such as those with Alzheimer's disease).

The Supreme Court did not decide that living wills are necessary to withhold or withdraw life-sustaining treatment. In fact, the Missouri Supreme Court did not even state that Nancy Cruzan's tube-feeding could be halted only if she had executed a living will. (Just how specific the Missouri court requires a patient to be remains uncertain. As Justice Brennan observed, "The court did not specifically define what kind of evidence it would consider clear and convincing, but its general discussion suggests that only a living will or equivalently formal directive from the patient when competent would meet this standard."[49]) Before *Cruzan,* several state courts readily enforced patients' oral statements, made before the loss of decisionmaking capacity, that they would not want treatment.[50] There is no reason to believe—or certainly none based on the Supreme Court's *Cruzan* opinion—that a written advance directive is the only means by which life support can be terminated in jurisdictions applying a standard as stringent as Missouri's. The only other such jurisdiction, New York, has specifically permitted the termination of life-sustaining medical treatment on the basis of an oral advance directive.[51] What is probably more important than whether the statement is written or oral—in any state that might require an advance directive to terminate life support—is how specific it is, and whether it is a "solemn pronouncement" or a "casual remark."[52]

The Supreme Court also did not pass judgment on the validity of health care powers of attorney[53]—an increasingly popular device by which a person can

---

[49] Cruzan v. Director, 497 U.S. 261, 323 (1990) (Brennan, J., dissenting).

[50] See **§ 10.16.**

[51] *See* Eichner v. Dillon, 420 N.E.2d 64 (N.Y. 1981); Elbaum v. Grace Plaza of Great Neck, Inc., 544 N.Y.S.2d 840 (App. Div. 1989).

[52] *In re* Westchester County Medical Ctr. (O'Connor), 531 N.E.2d 607, 612 (N.Y. 1988).

[53] See **Ch. 12.**

name another to make medical decisions for him if he loses the ability to do so—or whether they would meet the "clear and convincing evidence" standard. However, the views of Justice O'Connor in concurrence and the four dissenting justices, taken together, suggest that if faced with this question, the Supreme Court would conclude that, at the very least, a health care power of attorney that specifically empowers an agent to make decisions about life-sustaining treatment is constitutionally permissible, or, perhaps more precisely, that it would be unconstitutional for a state to prohibit the forgoing of life-sustaining treatment on the basis of such a directive or that such a directive does not per se fail to meet the subjective standard. It is more likely that this question will be settled in state courts and legislatures than in the United States Supreme Court. In the aftermath of *Cruzan,* Congress enacted the Patient Self-Determination Act,[54] and spurred by both of these events, most states adopted or revised health care power of attorney statutes.[55]

Another serious misconception is that *Cruzan* prohibits the termination of life support for a "never-competent" patient such as a seriously mentally retarded adult[56] or an infant[57] or young child.[58] Certainly, if a state subscribes to the subjective standard for surrogate decisionmaking, that would seem to be the result that would be dictated, as is the case in New York.[59] But because *Cruzan* does not mandate the subjective standard, there is no reason to assume that that result is mandated except where state law so requires. Appellate opinions subsequent to *Cruzan* have authorized the termination of life support from adults and children on the basis of evidence that would not satisfy the subjective standard.[60]

---

[54] See **§ 10.21.**

[55] See **Ch. 12.**

[56] See **§ 7.10.**

[57] See **Ch. 15.**

[58] See **Ch. 16.**

[59] **NY:** *In re* Storar, 420 N.E.2d 64 (N.Y. 1981); Elbaum v. Grace Plaza of Great Neck, Inc., 544 N.Y.S.2d 840 (App. Div. 1989).

IN: *But see In re* Lawrance, 579 N.E.2d 32 (Ind. 1991) (permitting forgoing of life-sustaining treatment for never-competent patient on basis of best interests standard).

MA: *But see In re* Doe, 583 N.E.2d 1263 (Mass. 1992) (permitting forgoing of life-sustaining treatment for never-competent patient on basis of substituted judgment standard); *In re* Beth, 587 N.E.2d 1377 (Mass. 1992) (same); Custody of a Minor, 434 N.E.2d 601 (Mass. 1982) (same); Superintendent of Belchertown State Sch. v. Saikewicz, 370 N.E.2d 417 (Mass. 1977) (same).

NJ: *But see In re* Moorhouse, 593 A.2d 1256 (N.J. Super. Ct. App. Div. 1991) (same).

WA: *But see In re* Grant, 747 P.2d 445 (Wash. 1987), *modified,* 757 P.2d 534 (Wash. 1988) (permitting forgoing of life-sustaining treatment for never-competent patient on basis of best interests standard); *In re* Hamlin, 689 P.2d 1372 (Wash. 1984) (same).

WI: *But see* L.W. v. L.E. Phillips Career Dev. Ctr., 482 N.W.2d 60 (Wis. 1992) (same).

[60] See **§§ 7.7, 7.11,** and **15.9.**

The Supreme Court decided nothing that should make a physician or health care facility do anything different from what it was doing before the decision, as long as it was following the general legal consensus. *Cruzan* did not change the law in any jurisdiction. Everything is the same, in every state, as it was the moment before the decision was handed down. However, although the *Cruzan* decision does not impose any new responsibilities on physicians or health care facilities, it does underscore what was always, and continues to be, desirable practice in decisionmaking about life-sustaining treatment—that an ounce of prevention is worth a pound of cure. Under the current state of the law, it is as important after *Cruzan* as it was before that patients, while still in possession of their decisionmaking capacity, make plans for their treatment after they lose their ability to decide for themselves. They should designate someone to speak for them and give that person instructions about their goals, values, preferences, and consequently about what kinds of treatment they would or would not want under certain circumstances. A combination of a health care power of attorney and a living will can best accomplish these objectives, but oral instructions are better than no instructions. However, because the formulation of precise instructions is often impossible—requiring as it often does that patients be able to predict how they will die—and because of the unwillingness of most people to think about, let alone plan for, their deaths, physicians and health care facilities have always had, and continue to have, a crucial role to play in deciding when to forgo life-sustaining treatment for the hopelessly ill. Unfortunately, because of excessive concern about legal liability, health care professionals sometimes forsake playing a central role in these critical clinical decisions.

§ 2.4 —Current State of the Law: Competent Patients

The forgoing of life-sustaining medical treatment by competent patients has presented courts with little difficulty in comparison with the issues posed by forgoing treatment for incompetent patients. Only a very small proportion of the litigated cases have involved competent patients,[61] but the right

---

[61] **DDC:** Tune v. Walter Reed Army Medical Hosp., 602 F. Supp. 1452 (D.D.C. 1985).

DNY: Deel v. Syracuse Veterans Admin. Medical Ctr., 729 F. Supp. 231 (N.D.N.Y. 1990).

CA: Thor v. Superior Court, 855 P.2d 375 (Cal. 1993); Bouvia v. Superior Court (Glenchur), 225 Cal. Rptr. 297 (Ct. App. 1986); Bartling v. Superior Court, 209 Cal. Rptr. 220 (Ct. App. 1984).

FL: *In re* Dubreuil, 629 So. 2d 819 (Fla. 1993); Wons v. Public Health Trust, 500 So. 2d 679 (Fla. Dist. Ct. App. 1987), *aff'd,* 541 So. 2d 96 (Fla. 1989); St. Mary's Hosp. v. Ramsey, 465 So. 2d 666 (Fla. Dist. Ct. App. 1985); Satz v. Perlmutter, 379 So. 2d 359 (Fla. 1980), *aff'g* 362 So. 2d 160 (Fla. Dist. Ct. App. 1978).

GA: State v. McAfee, 385 S.E.2d 651 (Ga. 1989).

MA: Norwood Hosp. v. Munoz, 564 N.E.2d 1017 (Mass. 1991).

of competent patients to forgo life-sustaining treatment has been discussed at length in the cases involving incompetent patients. For example, in *Cruzan* the Supreme Court noted, though it was not called upon to decide, that "[t]he principle that a competent person has a constitutionally protected liberty interest in refusing unwanted medical treatment may be inferred from our prior decisions."[62]

What accounts for the paucity of litigated cases involving competent patients is not entirely clear. What is obvious, but question-begging, is that such cases are being handled in hospitals or nursing homes between physician and patient (and patients' families) with little difficulty. Why there is so little difficulty has a few possible explanations. One is that the right of competent patients to refuse treatment is so well-established that its exercise rarely meets with resistance, and thus rarely leads to litigation,[63] or that compromises are being negotiated without the need to resort to the judicial process.[64] A related explanation is that competent patients rarely seek to forgo life-sustaining treatment, but this seems unlikely.[65]

A different sort of explanation is that patients' efforts to forgo life-sustaining treatment are being ignored or overridden, and there is some evidence that this is the case. First, there is some empirical evidence that some health care professionals are unaware of the legal permissibility of forgoing life-sustaining treatment and, indeed, the legal obligation under some circumstances to forgo

---

NV: McKay v. Bergstedt, 801 P.2d 617 (Nev. 1990).

NJ: *In re* Farrell, 529 A.2d 404 (N.J. 1987); *In re* Hughes, 611 A.2d 1148 (N.J. Super. Ct. App. Div. 1992); *In re* Requena, 517 A.2d 869 (N.J. Super. Ct. App. Div. 1986).

NY: Fosmire v. Nicoleau, 551 N.E.2d 77 (N.Y. 1990); Saunders v. State, 492 N.Y.S.2d 510 (Sup. Ct. Nassau County 1985).

PA: *In re* Doe, 45 Pa. D. & C.3d 371 (C.P. Phila. County 1987).

[62] Cruzan v. Director, 497 U.S. 261, 278 (1990) (citing Jacobson v. Massachusetts, 197 U.S. 11, 24–30 (1905) (compulsory vaccination); Breithaupt v. Abrams, 352 U.S. 432, 439 (1957) (search and seizure); Washington v. Harper, 494 U.S. 210, 110 S. Ct. 1028, 1036 (1990) (administration of antipsychotic medications to prisoners); Vitek v. Jones, 445 U.S. 480, 494 (1980) (transfer from prison to mental hospital); Parham v. J.R., 442 U.S. 584, 600 (1979) (psychiatric hospitalization of children); Union Pac. Ry. Co. v. Botsford, 141 U.S. 250 (1891)).

[63] *See, e.g.,* Camp v. White, 510 So. 2d 166 (Ala. 1987) (when patient who had been weaned from ventilator required reattachment to ventilator to save her life but would be permanently dependent on it, physicians discussed this with her family who discussed it with patient; she decided against it and died).

[64] *See Negotiated Death: An Open Secret,* N.Y. Times, Dec. 16, 1984, at 18 (nat'l ed.); N.Y. Times, Dec. 16, 1984, at 1; *see also* Klemesrud, *A Daughter's Story: Aiding Mother's Suicide,* N.Y. Times, Sept. 9, 1985, at 17 (reviewing Last Wish by Betty Rollin).

[65] *See, e.g.,* Neu & Kjellstrand, *Stopping Long-Term Dialysis,* 314 New Eng. J. Med. 14 (1986) (reporting that in 9% of patients with end-stage renal disease, competent patients, or the family or physician of incompetent patients, initiated decision to terminate treatment).

life-sustaining treatment.[66] Second, although the volume of reported actions for damages arising from decisionmaking about life-sustaining treatment is relatively small, virtually all are based on the refusal of physicians to forgo unwanted treatment rather than on the refusal of physicians to provide desired treatment.[67] Finally, attorneys who practice in this area say that it is not at all unusual to be contacted by competent patients, though more frequently by the families of competent patients (as well as incompetent patients), whose facially legitimate requests to forgo life-sustaining treatment have met with resistance or refusal from physicians and/or health care administrators. (Between January and November 1994, Choice in Dying, a nonprofit organization providing assistance to individuals seeking to refuse medical treatment, received 190 telephone inquiries citing unwanted treatment as the main reason for the call.[68])

When a case involving a patient who is not clearly incompetent is litigated, the threshold judicial inquiry often focuses on whether the patient actually is competent. A small but gradually increasing number of courts are in effect, if not in actual word, taking the position that the right of a competent patient to refuse medical treatment is virtually absolute.[69] While purporting to apply

---

[66] *See* Solomon et al., *Decisions Near the End of Life: Professional Views on Life-Sustaining Treatments,* 83 Am. J. Pub. Health 14 (1993) ("[C]hanges in the care of dying patients may not have kept pace with national recommendations, in part because many physicians and nurses disagreed with and may have been unaware of some key guidelines, such as the permissibility of withdrawing treatments.").

[67] See **Ch. 19.**

[68] Personal communication with Ann Fade, Associate Executive Director of Program, Choice in Dying.

[69] **CA:** Thor v. Superior Court, 855 P.2d 375 (Cal. 1993); Bouvia v. Superior Court (Glenchur), 225 Cal. Rptr. 297 (Ct. App. 1986). *But see* Donaldson v. Van de Kamp, 4 Cal. Rptr. 2d 59 (Ct. App. 1992) (competent individual suffering from brain tumor that will be lethal within a few years has no legal right to be placed in premortem cryogenic suspension, which will cause death, nor to enlist assistance of another in ending his life).

FL: *In re* Dubreuil, 629 So. 2d 819 (Fla. 1993); Wons v. Public Health Trust, 500 So. 2d 679 (Fla. Dist. Ct. App. 1987), *aff'd,* 541 So. 2d 96 (Fla. 1989); St. Mary's Hosp. v. Ramsey, 465 So. 2d 666 (Fla. Dist. Ct. App. 1985).

IL: *In re* E.G., 549 N.E.2d 322, 328 (Ill. 1989) (competent patient who is likely to die within a month without blood transfusions, but who with them and chemotherapy is about 80% likely to achieve remission of the disease, may decline treatment).

MA: Norwood Hosp. v. Munoz, 564 N.E.2d 1017 (Mass. 1991).

MI: *But see* Werth v. Taylor, 475 N.W.2d 426 (Mich. Ct. App. 1991).

NJ: *In re* Peter, 529 A.2d 419, 423 (N.J. 1987) ("The patient's medical condition is generally relevant only to determine whether the patient is or is not competent, and if incompetent, how the patient, in view of that condition, would choose to treat it were she or he competent."); *In re* Conroy, 486 A.2d 1209, 1226 (N.J. 1985) ("[T]he right to self-determination ordinarily outweighs any countervailing state interests, and competent persons generally are permitted to refuse medical treatment, even at the risk of death."). *But see In re* Hughes, 611 A.2d 1148 (N.J. Super. Ct. App. Div. 1992).

essentially the same approach in determining the nature and scope of the right to die for competent patients as they do for incompetent patients,[70] by balancing countervailing state interests against the individual's right to refuse treatment, most courts do so in such a way that the state interests are of essentially no weight.[71]

§ 2.5 —Current State of the Law: Incompetent Patients

Cases involving incompetent patients—that is, patients who clearly lack decisionmaking capacity—were the first to reach the courts, probably because they pose far more complex problems than do those involving decisionmaking for competent patients. Beginning with *Quinlan*[72] in 1975 and 1976, the first right-to-die case, and followed the next year by *Saikewicz,*[73] most courts began to espouse the view that "[a]n incompetent's right to refuse treatment should be equal to a competent's right to do so."[74]

NY: Fosmire v. Nicoleau, 551 N.E.2d 77, 85 (N.Y. 1990) (Simons, J., concurring) (majority defines right of self-determination so broadly that for all practical purposes the right is absolute). See §§ **8.2, 8.9,** and **8.14.**

[70] **DNY:** Deel v. Syracuse Veterans Admin. Medical Ctr., 729 F. Supp. 231 (N.D.N.Y. 1990).

FL: Satz v. Perlmutter, 362 So. 2d 160 (Fla. Dist. Ct. App. 1978).

[71] **CA:** Thor v. Superior Court, 855 P.2d 375 (Cal. 1993) (Nonterminally ill quadriplegic prisoner may refuse surgical implantation of feeding tube even if it results in his death.).

FL: Satz v. Perlmutter, 362 So. 2d 160 (Fla. Dist. Ct. App. 1978).

NJ: *In re* Conroy, 486 A.2d 1209, 1223 (N.J. 1985) ("While both of these state interests in life are certainly strong, in themselves they will usually not foreclose a competent person from declining life-sustaining medical treatment for himself. This is because the life that the state is seeking to protect in such a situation is the life of the same person who has competently decided to forego the medical intervention; it is not some other actual or potential life that cannot adequately protect itself.").

[72] *In re* Quinlan, 355 A.2d 647 (N.J. 1976).

[73] Superintendent of Belchertown State Sch. v. Saikewicz, 370 N.E.2d 417 (Mass. 1977).

[74] **WA:** *In re* Grant, 747 P.2d 445, 449 (Wash. 1987), *modified,* 757 P.2d 534 (Wash. 1988).

DRI: *Accord* Gray v. Romeo, 697 F. Supp. 580 (D.R.I. 1988).

AZ: *Accord* Rasmussen v. Fleming, 741 P.2d 674, 685–86 (Ariz. 1987).

CA: *Accord* Drabick v. Drabick, 245 Cal. Rptr. 840, 852 (Ct. App. 1988) ("[M]ost courts have adopted the formula that a patient's 'right to choose' or 'right to refuse' medical treatment survives incompetence. It would be more accurate to say that incompetent patients retain the right to have appropriate medical decisions made on their behalf."). *Cf.* Barber v. Superior Court, 195 Cal. Rptr. 484 (Ct. App. 1983).

CT: *Accord* Foody v. Manchester Memorial Hosp., 482 A.2d 713, 721 (Conn. Super. Ct. 1984).

DE: *Cf.* Severns v. Wilmington Medical Ctr., Inc., 421 A.2d 1334 (Del. 1980).

DC: *Accord In re* A.C., 573 A.2d 1235, 1247 (D.C. 1990).

Until the mid-1980s, this view was largely an accurate account of the substantive rights of incompetent patients in most jurisdictions (with the notable

---

FL: *Accord* Browning v. Herbert, 568 So. 2d 4, 12 (Fla. 1990) ("no basis for drawing a constitutional line between the protections afforded to competent persons and incompetent persons"); John F. Kennedy Memorial Hosp. v. Bludworth, 452 So. 2d 921, 926 (Fla. 1984); Corbett v. D'Alessandro, 487 So. 2d 368, 370 (Fla. Dist. Ct. App.), *review denied,* 492 So. 2d 1331 (Fla. 1986). *Cf. In re* Barry, 445 So. 2d 365 (Fla. Dist. Ct. App. 1984).

GA: *Cf. In re* L.H.R., 321 S.E.2d 716 (Ga. 1984).

IN: *Accord In re* Lawrance, 579 N.E.2d 32, 39 (Ind. 1991) ("Respect for patient autonomy does not end when the patient becomes incompetent.").

KY: *Contra* DeGrella v. Elston, 858 S.W.2d 698, 714 (Ky. 1993) (Wintersheimer, J., dissenting) ("The right to refuse medical treatment in the case of a nonterminally ill person is a personal decision and is not the type of decision which a guardian appointed under Kentucky statutes may make on behalf of an incompetent.").

LA: *Cf. In re* P.V.W., 424 So. 2d 1015 (La. 1982).

MD: *Accord* Mack v. Mack, 618 A.2d 744, 756 (Md. 1993) ("Patients who are unable to exercise the right to refuse treatment for themselves, nevertheless still enjoy the right.").

MA: *Accord In re* Beth, 587 N.E.2d 1377, 1382 (Mass. 1992) ("[I]ncompetent people are entitled to the same respect, dignity and freedom of choice as competent people."); *In re* Doe, 583 N.E.2d 1263, 1267 (Mass. 1992) ("The fact that a person is incompetent should not result in the denial of that person's right to be free from nonconsensual invasions of bodily integrity."); Brophy v. New Eng. Sinai Hosp., Inc., 497 N.E.2d 626, 633 (Mass. 1986); *In re* Spring, 405 N.E.2d 115, 119 (Mass. 1980). *Cf. In re* Hier, 464 N.E.2d 959 (Mass. App. Ct.), *review denied,* 465 N.E.2d 261 (Mass. 1984); Custody of a Minor, 434 N.E.2d 601 (Mass. 1982).

MI: *Accord* Martin v. Martin, 504 N.W.2d 917, 922 (Mich. Ct. App. 1993) ("[W]here a patient has lost the requisite decision-making capacity, it is still the goal to effectuate the patient's right of self-determination."). *Cf.* Rosebush v. Oakland County Prosecutor, 491 N.W.2d 633, 637 (Mich. Ct. App. 1992) (citing first edition of this treatise) ("[M]inors have the same right to decline life-sustaining treatment as their competent adult counterparts.").

MN: *Cf. In re* Torres, 357 N.W.2d 332 (Minn. 1984).

MO: *Contra* Cruzan v. Harmon, 760 S.W.2d 408, 425 (Mo. 1988) ("The common law right to refuse treatment—founded in personal autonomy—is [not] exercisable by a third party absent formalities.").

NJ: *Accord In re* Jobes, 529 A.2d 434, 451 (N.J. 1987); *In re* Peter, 529 A.2d 419, 423 (N.J. 1987); *In re* Visbeck, 510 A.2d 125, 129 (N.J. Super. Ct. Ch. Div. 1986). *Cf. In re* Clark, 510 A.2d 136 (N.J. Super. Ct. Ch. Div. 1986).

OH: *Accord In re* Crum, 580 N.E.2d 876 (P. Ct. Franklin County, Ohio 1991). *Cf.* Leach v. Akron Gen. Medical Ctr., 426 N.E.2d 809 (C.P. P. Div. Summit County, Ohio 1980).

WA: *Accord In re* Colyer, 660 P.2d 738, 744 (Wash. 1983). *Cf. In re* Ingram, 689 P.2d 1363 (Wash. 1984); *In re* Hamlin, 689 P.2d 1372 (Wash. 1984).

WI: *Cf.* L.W. v. L.E. Phillips Career Dev. Ctr., 482 N.W.2d 60, 67 (Wis. 1992) ("[T]he right to refuse all unwanted life-sustaining medical treatment extends to incompetent as well as competent individuals. . . . An incompetent individual does not relinquish the right to refuse unwanted treatment by virtue of incompetency."). *Contra* L.W. v. L.E. Phillips Career Dev. Ctr., 482 N.W.2d 60, 77 n.50 (Wis. 1992) (Steinmetz, J., dissenting) ("There is a difference, however, between decision making of competent and the incompetent. The former can change their minds as to the treatment or lack of treatment while this choice is not available to the incompetent.").

exception of New York[75]). However, this was the case because the right of *competent* patients to refuse treatment was weaker than it was subsequently to become.[76] As competent patients' rights to refuse treatment have approached the absolute, the validity of the position that the incompetent's right to refuse treatment should be equal to that of a competent patient has become increasingly tenuous. Nonetheless, there is still more than a grain of truth to that view, and its continued enunciation serves important rhetorical purposes. It would be more accurate to say, however, especially after the Supreme Court's *Cruzan* opinion, "that incompetent patients retain the right to have appropriate medical decisions made on their behalf," because "to claim that [the incompetent's] 'right to choose' survives incompetence is a legal fiction at best."[77]

Most obviously, the procedural aspects of decisionmaking for incompetent patients cannot, by definition, be the same as for competent patients. But holding procedural concerns aside reveals that the right of incompetent patients to have decisions to forgo life-sustaining treatment made for them has undergone a similar shift toward the absolute end of the spectrum as has been the case with competent patients. Courts continue to balance the right to refuse treatment against countervailing state interests, as they do with competent patients, but find that these interests are devoid of substance if a patient is terminally ill or in a persistent vegetative state or otherwise has an extremely poor prognosis for recovery.[78]

SOURCES OF THE RIGHT TO DIE

§ 2.6 Sources of the Right to Die

A variety of legal grounds for the right to die have been proposed. They include federal constitutional rights of privacy, liberty, and religious freedom, state constitutional rights (usually of privacy), the common-law right to be free from unwanted bodily touching, and various statutory and even regulatory rights.[79] Sometimes these rights are asserted individually, but sometimes attempts are made to ground the right to die in some or all of these individual bases.

---

[75] *See* Grace Plaza of Great Neck, Inc. v. Elbaum, 623 N.E.2d 513 (N.Y. 1993); *In re* Westchester County Medical Ctr. (O'Connor), 531 N.E.2d 607 (N.Y. 1988); *In re* Storar, 420 N.E.2d 64 (N.Y. 1981). *But compare* Elbaum v. Grace Plaza of Great Neck, Inc., 544 N.Y.S.2d 840 (App. Div. 1989) (Evidence strikingly similar to that found in *O'Connor* not to meet requisite standard for termination of life support was found adequate.).

[76] See **§ 2.4.**

[77] Drabick v. Drabick, 245 Cal. Rptr. 840, 854 (Ct. App. 1988).

[78] See **Ch. 8.**

[79] Rosebush v. Oakland County Prosecutor, 491 N.W.2d 633, 635 (Mich. Ct. App. 1992) (citing first edition of this treatise).

There has been a noticeable shift from the earliest right-to-die cases—roughly the first five years, the beginning marked by the *Quinlan*[80] case in 1976 and the end by the *Storar* and *Eichner*[81] cases in 1981—in the legal basis put forth by the courts. Although some of the earlier decisions alluded to a common-law basis for the right to die, by citation to battery cases resulting from nonconsensual bodily touchings by a physician or by reference to the informed consent doctrine,[82] most of those courts actually grounded their holdings in a constitutional right of privacy. The most prominent early cases—*Quinlan, Satz v. Perlmutter,*[83] *Saikewicz*—all found the basis for the right to die in the federal constitutional right of privacy. In *Eichner,* the New York Court of Appeals abandoned the right of privacy in favor of the common-law right to decline or accept medical treatment, because whether or not the right to refuse treatment "is also guaranteed by the Constitution, as an aspect of the right to privacy . . . is a disputed question . . . , which the Supreme Court has repeatedly declined to consider."[84] The New York court therefore also declined to reach that question "because the relief granted to the petitioner, Eichner, is adequately supported by common-law principles."[85] Since *Eichner,* most courts have grounded the right to die in the common law, though sometimes in combination with a constitutional or other basis.[86]

Most courts have not attempted to provide any justification for the choice of a source. In the context of any particular case, the legal basis for the right to die has not been important because courts have not made the scope of the right depend on whether or not the source is common-law or constitutional.[87] However, a constitutionally-grounded right to die could ultimately prove to be a

---

[80] *In re* Quinlan, 355 A.2d 647 (N.J. 1976).

[81] *In re* Storar, 420 N.E.2d 64 (N.Y. 1981); Eichner v. Dillon, 420 N.E.2d 64 (N.Y. 1981).

[82] *See, e.g.,* Superintendent of Belchertown State Sch. v. Saikewicz, 370 N.E.2d 417, 424 (Mass. 1977).

[83] 362 So. 2d 160 (Fla. Dist. Ct. App. 1978), *aff'd,* 379 So. 2d 359 (Fla. 1980).

[84] 420 N.E.2d at 70.

[85] *Id.*

[86] **CA:** Bouvia v. Superior Court (Glenchur), 225 Cal. Rptr. 297, 300 (Ct. App. 1986) (constitutional); Barber v. Superior Court, 195 Cal. Rptr. 484, 489 (Ct. App. 1983) ("It is clear from the legislative findings and declaration provided in [the Natural Death Act], that the Legislature recognized such a right to control one's medical treatment.").

MO: Cruzan v. Harmon, 760 S.W.2d 408, 420 (Mo. 1988) ("The statute's import here is as an expression of the policy of this State with regard to the sanctity of life. We intend no judgment here as to whether the common law right to refuse medical treatment is broader than the Living Will statute.").

NY: Eichner v. Dillon, 426 N.Y.S.2d 517, 537 (App. Div. 1980) (constitutional); Saunders v. State, 492 N.Y.S.2d 510, 514 (Sup. Ct. Nassau County 1985).

WA: *In re* Colyer, 660 P.2d 738, 742 (Wash. 1983) (constitutional).

[87] Eichner v. Dillon, 420 N.E.2d 64, 70 (N.Y. 1981) ("[U]nder certain circumstances the common-law right may have to yield to superior State interests, as it would even if it were constitutionally based.").

stronger right than one based on common-law principles that are subject to legislative overrule.[88] For example, in *Barber*[89] the state contended that the California living will statute was the exclusive means for terminating life-sustaining treatment. Although this argument failed in that context primarily because of the express provision in the statute stating that it does not constitute the exclusive basis for terminating life support,[90] other statutes, differently worded, might be found to supersede common-law rights.[91]

Regardless of the precise source of law, the right to die springs from the same kinds of concerns and seeks to protect the same values: human dignity, self-determination, and unwanted infringement of bodily integrity.[92]

§ 2.7 Common-Law Basis

Most courts ground the right to die in the common-law right to be free from unwanted intrusion on[93] or invasion of[94] bodily integrity, protected through the legal requirements of consent and informed consent to treatment. The courts variously refer to this right as a right of privacy,[95] a right to self-determination or autonomy,[96] or more concretely as a right to control one's

---

[88] Eichner v. Dillon, 426 N.Y.S.2d 517, 540–41 (App. Div. 1980) ("Common-law rights can be abrogated by statute in the exercise of the State's police powers subject only to due process requirements. . . . Constitutional rights on the other hand cannot be so abrogated."), *modified,* 420 N.E.2d 64 (N.Y. 1981).

[89] Barber v. Superior Court, 195 Cal. Rptr. 484 (Ct. App. 1983).

[90] Cal. Health & Safety Code §§ 7186–7195 (West Supp. 1988) (repealed). See **Ch. 11.**

[91] *See, e.g.,* Cruzan v. Harmon, 760 S.W.2d 408 (Mo. 1988). See **§§ 10.10** through **10.16.**

[92] Superintendent of Belchertown State Sch. v. Saikewicz, 370 N.E.2d 417, 424 (Mass. 1977) (citing *In re* Quinlan, 355 A.2d 647 (N.J. 1976)).

[93] **CA:** Bouvia v. Superior Court (Glenchur), 225 Cal. Rptr. 297, 300 (Ct. App. 1986).

KY: DeGrella v. Elston, 858 S.W.2d 698 (Ky. 1993).

MN: *In re* Torres, 357 N.W.2d 332, 339 (Minn. 1984).

NJ: *In re* Conroy, 486 A.2d 1209, 1222 (N.J. 1985).

[94] **AZ:** Rasmussen v. Fleming, 741 P.2d 674, 682–83 (Ariz. 1987).

MA: *In re* Doe, 583 N.E.2d 1263 (Mass. 1992).

MI: Rosebush v. Oakland County Prosecutor, 491 N.W.2d 633, 635 (Mich. Ct. App. 1992).

WA: *In re* Grant, 747 P.2d 445, 449 (Wash. 1987), *modified,* 757 P.2d 534 (Wash. 1988); *In re* Ingram, 689 P.2d 1363, 1368 (Wash. 1984); *In re* Colyer, 660 P.2d 738, 743 (Wash. 1983).

[95] **CA:** Bouvia v. Superior Court (Glenchur), 225 Cal. Rptr. 297, 300 (Ct. App. 1986).

NJ: *In re* Quinlan, 355 A.2d 647, 662 (N.J. 1976).

[96] **DNY:** Deel v. Syracuse Veterans Admin. Medical Ctr., 729 F. Supp. 231 (N.D.N.Y. 1990).

CA: Thor v. Superior Court, 855 P.2d 375, 380 (Cal. 1993) ("'the long-standing importance in our Anglo-American legal tradition of personal autonomy and the right of self-determination'").

ME: *In re* Gardner, 534 A.2d 947, 950 (Me. 1987).

MA: Brophy v. New Eng. Sinai Hosp., Inc., 497 N.E.2d 626, 633 (Mass. 1986).

own body.[97] "The right to self-determination has been described as an individual's 'strong [ ] personal interest in directing the course of his own life', 'an individual's right to behave and act as he deems fit, provided that such behavior and activity do not conflict with the precepts of society.' "[98]

Historically, remedies for invasions of these various interests have been provided by the legal actions for assault and/or battery,[99] supplemented by the actions for intentional infliction of emotional distress and the tort of invasion of privacy.[100] In more recent times, the right to refuse medical treatment has come to be implemented through the requirement that a physician obtain a patient's informed consent to treatment, and the corollary that without the informed consent of the competent patient[101] or the surrogate of an incompetent patient,[102] treatment ordinarily may not be administered.[103]

NJ: *In re* Jobes, 529 A.2d 434, 436 (N.J. 1987); *In re* Farrell, 529 A.2d 404, 410 (N.J. 1987); *In re* Conroy, 486 A.2d 1209, 1223 (N.J. 1985); *In re* Hughes, 611 A.2d 1148, 1151 (N.J. Super. Ct. App. Div. 1992).

NY: Delio v. Westchester County Medical Ctr., 516 N.Y.S.2d 677, 685–86 (App. Div. 1987).

PA: *In re* Doe, 45 Pa. D. & C.3d 371, 381 (C.P. Phila. County 1987).

[97] **CA:** Bouvia v. Superior Court (Glenchur), 225 Cal. Rptr. 297, 300 (Ct. App. 1986).

MO: *Cf. In re* Busalacchi, No. 59582, slip op. at 8, 1991 WL 26851 (Mo. Ct. App. Mar. 5, 1991) ("If she were competent, Christine would have the right to refuse this life-sustaining medical treatment, based upon the doctrine of informed consent.") (dictum).

NJ: *In re* Farrell, 529 A.2d 404, 410 (N.J. 1987); *In re* Conroy, 486 A.2d 1209, 1221 (N.J. 1985).

NY: Eichner v. Dillon, 420 N.E.2d 64, 70 (N.Y. 1981).

PA: Ragona v. Preate, 11 Fiduc. Rep. 2d 1, 5, 6 Pa. D. & C.4th 202 (C.P. Lackawanna County, Pa. 1990).

[98] *In re* Jobes, 529 A.2d 434, 453 (N.J. 1987) (Handler, J., concurring) (citing *In re* Conroy, 486 A.2d at 1228); Norwood Hosp. v. Munoz, 564 N.E.2d 1017 (Mass. 1991).

[99] Cruzan v. Harmon, 760 S.W.2d 408, 416–17 (Mo. 1988). See §§ **17.2** through **17.4.**

[100] See §§ **17.5** through **17.8.**

[101] See **Ch. 3.**

[102] See § **2.5.**

[103] **US:** Cruzan v. Director, 497 U.S. 261, 271 (1990) ("[M]ost courts have based a right to refuse treatment either solely on the common law right to informed consent or on both the common law right and a constitutional privacy right.").

DDC: Tune v. Walter Reed Army Medical Hosp., 602 F. Supp. 1452, 1455 (D.D.C. 1985).

CA: Thor v. Superior Court, 855 P.2d 375, 381 (Cal. 1993) ("[T]he right to refuse medical treatment is equally 'basic and fundamental' and integral to the concept of informed consent."); Donaldson v. Van de Kamp, 4 Cal. Rptr. 2d 59, 62 (Ct. App. 1992); Bouvia v. Superior Court (Glenchur), 225 Cal. Rptr. 297, 300–01 (Ct. App. 1986) (right to refuse any medical treatment follows from the right to consent); Bartling v. Superior Court, 209 Cal. Rptr. 220, 224 (Ct. App. 1984); Barber v. Superior Court, 195 Cal. Rptr. 484, 489 (Ct. App. 1983) (The "obvious corollary [of the principle of informed consent] . . . is that a competent adult patient has the legal right to refuse medical treatment.").

CT: Foody v. Manchester Memorial Hosp., 482 A.2d 713, 717 (Conn. Super. Ct. 1984).

The right to refuse treatment has always been implicit in the requirement of consent to medical treatment. If the requirement of consent means that a physician must obtain a patient's authorization to treat, on pain of being held liable for battery, then a patient is legally entitled to refuse treatment.[104] Before the litigation of right-to-die cases began, there were a number of successful battery cases brought by patients claiming that they were treated without their

---

DC: *In re* A.C., 573 A.2d 1235, 1243 (D.C. 1990).

GA: *In re* Doe, 418 S.E.2d 3, 6 (Ga. 1992).

IL: Estate of Longeway v. Community Convalescent Ctr., 549 N.E.2d 292, 297 (Ill. 1989) (Common-law right to withhold consent and refuse treatment "incorporates all types of medical treatment, including life-saving or life-sustaining procedures.").

IN: *In re* Lawrance, 579 N.E.2d 32, 38 (Ind. 1991).

ME: *In re* Gardner, 534 A.2d 947 (Me. 1987).

MD: Mack v. Mack, 618 A.2d 744, 756 (Md. 1993).

MA: Norwood Hosp. v. Munoz, 564 N.E.2d 1017 (Mass. 1991).

MI: Rosebush v. Oakland County Prosecutor, 491 N.W.2d 633, 635–36 (Mich. Ct. App. 1992) ("The logical corollary of the doctrine of informed consent is that the patient generally possesses the right not to consent, that is, the right to refuse medical treatment and procedures."); Werth v. Taylor, 475 N.W.2d 426, 428 (Mich. Ct. App. 1991) ("Indeed, the whole concept of informed consent to treatment leads to an inference of its converse—informed refusal of treatment.").

MO: Cruzan v. Harmon, 760 S.W.2d 408, 417 (Mo. 1988) ("The logical corollary of the doctrine of informed consent is that the patient generally possesses the right not to consent, that is, to refuse treatment.").

NV: McKay v. Bergstedt, 801 P.2d 617, 621 (Nev. 1990).

NJ: *In re* Conroy, 486 A.2d 1209, 1222 (N.J. 1985) ("The patient's ability to control his bodily integrity through informed consent is significant only when one recognizes that the right also encompasses a right to informed refusal."); *In re* Hughes, 611 A.2d 1148, 1151 (N.J. Super. Ct. App. Div. 1992) (informed consent protects self-determination and self-determination encompasses right to refuse treatment).

NY: *In re* Storar, 420 N.E.2d 64, 70 (N.Y. 1981).

OH: Estate of Leach v. Shapiro, 469 N.E.2d 1047, 1052 (Ohio Ct. App. 1984) ("We perceive [the patient's right to refuse treatment] as the logical extension of the consent requirement and conclude that a patient may recover for battery if his refusal is ignored.").

PA: Ragona v. Preate, 11 Fiduc. Rep. 2d 1, 5, 6 Pa. D. & C.4th 202 (C.P. Lackawanna County, Pa. 1990).

WA: *In re* Grant, 747 P.2d 445, 449 (Wash. 1987), *modified,* 757 P.2d 534 (Wash. 1988); *In re* Colyer, 660 P.2d 738, 744 (Wash. 1983) ("A competent patient may refuse treatment under the informed consent doctrine.").

WI: L.W. v. L.E. Phillips Career Dev. Ctr., 482 N.W.2d 60 (Wis. 1992).

[104] **MI:** Werth v. Taylor, 475 N.W.2d 426, 428 (Mich. Ct. App. 1991) ("Indeed, the whole concept of informed consent to treatment leads to an inference of its converse—informed refusal of treatment.").

consent.[105] In a significant, though small, number of these cases, the unauthorized treatment was legally actionable even though the patient was not injured[106] or had even benefited from the treatment.[107]

The right to die is an application of the right to refuse treatment under circumstances in which such refusal is likely to lead to the patient's death: "The personal right to refuse life-sustaining treatment is now firmly anchored in the common law doctrine of informed consent, which requires the patient's informed consent to the administration of any medical care."[108] Thus, prima facie, life-sustaining medical treatment may not be administered without the informed consent of a competent patient or the surrogate of an incompetent

---

[105] *See* Cruzan v. Harmon, 760 S.W.2d 408, 416–17 (Mo. 1988) ("The common law recognizes the right of individual autonomy over decisions relating to one's health and welfare. From this root of autonomy, the common law developed the principle that a battery occurs when a physician performs a medical procedure without valid consent."). *See generally* Annotation, *Liability of Physician or Surgeon for Extending Operation or Treatment Beyond That Expressly Authorized,* 56 A.L.R.2d 695 (1957); Annotation, *Consent as Condition of Right to Perform Surgical Operation,* 139 A.L.R. 1370 (1942).

[106] **CA7:** Lloyd v. Kull, 329 F.2d 168 (7th Cir. 1964).

GA: Bailey v. Belinfante, 218 S.E.2d 289 (Ga. Ct. App. 1975).

OK: Rolater v. Strain, 137 P. 96 (Okla. 1913).

[107] **CADC:** *Cf.* Bonner v. Moran, 126 F.2d 121, 122 (D.C. Cir. 1941) ("[A] surgical operation is a technical battery, regardless of its results, and is excusable only when there is express or implied consent.").

MN: Mohr v. Williams, 104 N.W. 12 (Minn. 1905) ($10,000 judgment for beneficial surgery on plaintiff's left ear because patient had consented only to surgery on right ear, though verdict excessive).

NJ: *But see* Bennan v. Parsonnet, 83 A. 948 (N.J. 1912) (plaintiff's verdict and judgment for $1,000 for surgical repair of right groin rupture when plaintiff had consented to left repair).

OH: Anderson v. St. Francis-St. George Hosp., 614 N.E.2d 841 (Ohio Ct. App. 1992).

WI: Throne v. Wandell, 186 N.W. 146 (Wis. 1922) ($2,000 award for "distress and humiliation and pain" arising from nonconsensual extraction of plaintiff's teeth that were "broken-down" and "[i]t was only a question of time" when they would have to be extracted anyway).

[108] **ME:** *In re* Gardner, 534 A.2d 947, 951 (Me. 1987).

CA: *Accord* Donaldson v. Van de Kamp, 4 Cal. Rptr. 2d 59, 62 (Ct. App. 1992).

MA: *Accord* Norwood Hosp. v. Munoz, 564 N.E.2d 1017 (Mass. 1991).

MO: *Accord* Cruzan v. Harmon, 760 S.W.2d 408, 417 (Mo. 1988).

NJ: *Accord In re* Jobes, 529 A.2d 434, 454 (N.J. 1987) (Handler, J., concurring).

NY: *Accord* Fosmire v. Nicoleau, 551 N.E.2d 77, 80–81 (N.Y. 1990); Delio v. Westchester County Medical Ctr., 516 N.Y.S.2d 677, 685–86 (App. Div. 1987) (citing statutory requirement for informed consent).

patient.[109] The right of self-determination also requires that treatment not be forgone without the informed consent of a competent patient,[110] though whether life-sustaining medical treatment may be forgone without the informed consent of—indeed, in the face of an express refusal to accede to the forgoing of life-sustaining treatment by—the surrogate of an *incompetent* patient is far more controversial.[111]

Several important implications flow from this fundamental assumption. First and most important is that "whenever possible, the patient himself should . . . be the ultimate decisionmaker."[112] Second, "[t]he law clearly requires that the consent be informed, based upon all information necessary under the circumstances."[113] The information that must be provided is, in general terms, the same as the information to which all patients are entitled in making decisions about any type of health care: "the various treatment options; and the risks, side

---

[109] **AL:** Camp v. White, 510 So. 2d 166, 168 (Ala. 1987) ("The doctors decided that the time had come to discuss the situation with Mrs. Camp's family. A consultation was arranged and the doctors informed the family of the situation and conveyed to them their recommendation that Mrs. Camp not be put back on the respirator-ventilator. The family in turn consulted with Mrs. Camp. She was informed of her situation and of the doctor's opinion that a return to the breathing machine would be permanent. Mrs. Camp was mentally alert. She made the decision not to return to the respirator-ventilator.").

CA: Thor v. Superior Court, 855 P.2d 375 (Cal. 1993); Bartling v. Superior Court, 209 Cal. Rptr. 220, 224 (Ct. App. 1984); Barber v. Superior Court, 195 Cal. Rptr. 484, 492 (Ct. App. 1983).

CT: Foody v. Manchester Memorial Hosp., 482 A.2d 713, 719–20 (Conn. Super. Ct. 1984).

IN: Payne v. Marion Gen. Hosp., 549 N.E.2d 1043 (Ind. Ct. App. 1990) (Informed consent requires physician to determine if patient has capacity to consent to do-not-resuscitate (DNR) order.).

NJ: *In re* Conroy, 486 A.2d 1209, 1222 (N.J. 1985).

NY: Saunders v. State, 492 N.Y.S.2d 510, 514 (Sup. Ct. Nassau County 1985); *In re* Eichner, 423 N.Y.S.2d 580, 591 (Sup. Ct. Nassau County 1979), *aff'd,* 426 N.Y.S.2d 517 (App. Div. 1980), *modified,* 420 N.E.2d 64 (N.Y. 1981).

WA: *In re* Colyer, 660 P.2d 738, 743–44 (Wash. 1983).

[110] **IN:** Payne v. Marion Gen. Hosp., 549 N.E.2d 1043 (Ind. Ct. App. 1990).

[111] See **Ch. 19.**

[112] **CA:** Barber v. Superior Court, 195 Cal. Rptr. 484, 492 (Ct. App. 1983).

CA: *Accord* Bartling v. Superior Court, 209 Cal. Rptr. 220, 224 (Ct. App. 1984).

CT: *Accord* Foody v. Manchester Memorial Hosp., 482 A.2d 713, 719–20 (Conn. Super. Ct. 1984).

[113] **NY:** *In re* Eichner, 423 N.Y.S.2d 580, 591 (Sup. Ct. Nassau County 1979).

DDC: *Accord* Tune v. Walter Reed Army Medical Hosp., 602 F. Supp. 1452, 1455 (D.D.C. 1985).

OH: *Accord* Estate of Leach v. Shapiro, 469 N.E.2d 1047, 1052 (Ohio Ct. App. 1984).

effects, and benefits of each of these options."[114] Third, as long as the patient is competent, the patient's reasons for refusal are irrelevant.[115]

Like much other medical decisionmaking, making decisions about life-sustaining treatment is rarely an isolated event; rather it is a continuing process in which the patient's condition, and therefore the available options, are continually changing. Thus, in practice it is necessary for the physician to carry on a "therapeutic conversation" with the patient on a continual basis.[116] A patient "has the right to insist that treatment be halted once he is fully informed of the consequences and does not wish to incur them."[117]

§ 2.8 Constitutional Rights of Privacy and Liberty

The constitutional right of privacy was the first source used by courts on which to base the right to die, both for competent[118] and incompetent patients.[119] Drawing upon federal constitutional precedents dealing with reproductive rights and thus with control of one's body, the New Jersey Supreme Court in *Quinlan* concluded:

> Although the Constitution does not explicitly mention a right of privacy, Supreme Court decisions have recognized that a right of personal privacy exists and that

---

[114] **NJ:** *In re* Conroy, 486 A.2d 1209, 1231 (N.J. 1985).

WA: *Accord In re* Colyer, 660 P.2d 738, 754–55 (Wash. 1983) (Dore, J., dissenting).

See § **3.15.**

[115] **FL:** St. Mary's Hosp. v. Ramsey, 465 So. 2d 666, 668 (Fla. Dist. Ct. App. 1985) (A competent adult has the right to refuse a transfusion even if refusal "arises from fear of adverse reaction, religious belief, recalcitrance or cost.").

MA: Norwood Hosp. v. Munoz, 564 N.E.2d 1017, 1021 (Mass. 1991) ("It is for the individual to decide whether a particular medical treatment is in the individual's best interests. As a result, '[t]he law protects [a person's] right to make her own decision to accept or reject treatment, whether that decision is wise or unwise.' Lane v. Candura, 6 Mass. App. Ct. 377, 383, 376 N.E.2d 1232 (1978).").

NY: *In re* Eichner, 423 N.Y.S.2d 580, 593–94 (Sup. Ct. Nassau County 1979) (citing *In re* Melideo, 390 N.Y.S.2d 523 (Sup. Ct. 1976)); Erickson v. Dilgard, 252 N.Y.S.2d 705 (Sup. Ct. Nassau County 1962).

See also National Ctr. for State Courts, Guidelines for State Court Decision Making in Life-Sustaining Medical Treatment Cases 125 *et seq.* (2d ed. 1992) (principle A).

[116] See §§ **3.5** through **3.8.**

[117] Tune v. Walter Reed Army Medical Hosp., 602 F. Supp. 1452, 1455 (D.D.C. 1985).

[118] **FL:** Satz v. Perlmutter, 362 So. 2d 160 (Fla. Dist. Ct. App. 1978).

[119] **MA:** Superintendent of Belchertown State Sch. v. Saikewicz, 370 N.E.2d 417 (Mass. 1977).

NJ: *In re* Quinlan, 355 A.2d 647 (N.J. 1976).

> certain areas of privacy are guaranteed under the Constitution. . . . Presumably this right is broad enough to encompass a patient's decision to decline medical treatment under certain circumstances.[120]

Since that decision, a significant number of other courts have based the right to forgo life-sustaining treatment on a constitutional right of privacy,[121] sometimes in combination with a common-law right.[122] However, in response to scholarly[123]

---

[120] *In re* Quinlan, 355 A.2d at 663.

[121] **DRI:** Gray v. Romeo, 697 F. Supp. 580 (D.R.I. 1988).

AZ: Rasmussen v. Fleming, 741 P.2d 674, 681–82 (Ariz. 1987).

CA: McMahon v. Lopez, 245 Cal. Rptr. 172 (Ct. App. 1988); Bartling v. Superior Court, 209 Cal. Rptr. 220, 225 (Ct. App. 1984).

CT: Foody v. Manchester Memorial Hosp., 482 A.2d 713, 717 (Conn. Super. Ct. 1984).

DE: Severns v. Wilmington Medical Ctr., Inc., 421 A.2d 1334, 1347 (Del. 1980).

FL: John F. Kennedy Memorial Hosp. v. Bludworth, 452 So. 2d 921, 923 (Fla. 1984); Corbett v. D'Alessandro, 487 So. 2d 368, 370 (Fla. Dist. Ct. App. 1986); Satz v. Perlmutter, 362 So. 2d 160, 162 (Fla. Dist. Ct. App. 1978).

GA: *In re* L.H.R., 321 S.E.2d 716, 722 (Ga. 1984); Zant v. Prevatte, 286 S.E.2d 715 (Ga. 1982).

MA: *In re* Spring, 405 N.E.2d 115, 119 (Mass. 1980); Superintendent of Belchertown State Sch. v. Saikewicz, 370 N.E.2d 417, 424 (Mass. 1977).

MN: *In re* Torres, 357 N.W.2d 332, 339 (Minn. 1984).

NJ: *In re* Farrell, 529 A.2d 404, 410 (N.J. 1987).

OH: Leach v. Akron Gen. Medical Ctr., 426 N.E.2d 809, 814 (C.P. P. Ct. Summit County, Ohio 1980).

WA: *In re* Grant, 747 P.2d 445, 449 (Wash. 1987), *modified,* 757 P.2d 534 (Wash. 1988); *In re* Ingram, 689 P.2d 1363, 1368 (Wash. 1984); *In re* Colyer, 660 P.2d 738, 742 (Wash. 1983).

See also National Ctr. for State Courts, Guidelines for State Court Decision Making in Life-Sustaining Medical Treatment Cases 125 *et seq.* (2d ed. 1992) (principle A).

[122] **DNY:** Deel v. Syracuse Veterans Admin. Medical Ctr., 729 F. Supp. 231 (N.D.N.Y. 1990).

CA: Bouvia v. Superior Court (Glenchur), 225 Cal. Rptr. 297, 300–01 (Ct. App. 1986).

CT: McConnell v. Beverly Enters.-Conn., Inc., 553 A.2d 596, 601–02 (Conn. 1989).

IL: C.A. v. Morgan, 603 N.E.2d 1171 (Ill. App. Ct. 1992).

IN: *In re* Lawrance, 579 N.E.2d 32, 39 (Ind. 1991).

MA: Norwood Hosp. v. Munoz, 564 N.E.2d 1017 (Mass. 1991); Brophy v. New Eng. Sinai Hosp., Inc., 497 N.E.2d 626, 633 (Mass. 1986).

NJ: *In re* Farrell, 529 A.2d 404, 410 (N.J. 1987).

NY: Eichner v. Dillon, 426 N.Y.S.2d 517, 536–39 (App. Div. 1980).

PA: *In re* Doe, 45 Pa. D. & C.3d 371, 381–82 (C.P. Phila. County 1987).

WA: *In re* Colyer, 660 P.2d 738, 742 (Wash. 1983).

[123] *See* L. Tribe, American Constitutional Law § 15-11, at 1365 (2d ed. 1988).

and judicial criticism,[124] reliance on the right of privacy as a basis for the right to die is diminishing.[125]

The Supreme Court's decision in *Cruzan v. Director*[126] signaled a shift away from the right of privacy to the Fourteenth Amendment's guarantee of personal liberty as a basis for the right to refuse life-sustaining treatment, a development that parallels and derives from a similar doctrinal shift in other related areas.[127] In first addressing the constitutional basis for the right to die, or the right to refuse treatment as the Court preferred to call it, the Court grounded its holding in the Fourteenth Amendment's guarantee of liberty, rather than in the right of privacy.[128] The Court acknowledged that a long line of cases stood for "[t]he principle that a competent person has a constitutionally protected liberty interest in refusing unwanted medical treatment"[129] but that establishing a violation of a liberty interest under the due process clause of the Fourteenth Amendment requires a balancing "against the relevant state interests."[130] Although not called upon by the facts of the case to determine whether this liberty interest would

---

[124] **MO:** Cruzan v. Harmon, 760 S.W.2d 408, 418 (Mo. 1988) ("Based on our analysis of the right to privacy decisions of the Supreme Court, we carry grave doubts as to the applicability of privacy rights to decisions to terminate the provision of food and water to an incompetent patient.").

NY: Eichner v. Dillon, 420 N.E.2d 64, 70 (N.Y. 1981) ("Although several courts have so held [that the constitutional right of privacy creates a right to control one's course of medical treatment] . . . this is a disputed question . . . which the Supreme Court has repeatedly declined to consider. . . . Neither do we reach that question in this case because the relief granted to the petition[er] . . . is adequately supported by common-law principles."). *Cf.* Delio v. Westchester County Medical Ctr., 516 N.Y.S.2d 677, 686 (App. Div. 1987) (Constitutional issue need not be reached.).

[125] Cruzan v. Director, 497 U.S. 261, 271 (1990) ("After *Quinlan,* however, most courts have based a right to refuse treatment either solely on the common-law right to informed consent or on both the common-law right and a constitutional privacy right. *See* L. Tribe, American Constitutional Law § 15-11, p. 1365 (2d ed. 1988).").

[126] 497 U.S. 261 (1990).

[127] *See, e.g.,* Planned Parenthood v. Casey, 505 U.S. ____, 112 S. Ct. 2791 (1992); Bowers v. Hardwick, 478 U.S. 186 (1986).

[128] Cruzan v. Director, 497 U.S. at 279 n.7 ("Although many state courts have held that a right to refuse treatment is encompassed by a generalized constitutional right of privacy, we have never so held. We believe this issue is more properly analyzed in terms of a fourteenth amendment liberty interest. *See* Bowers v. Hardwick, 478 U.S. 186, 194–195, 106 S. Ct. 2841, 2846, 92 L. Ed. 2d 140 (1986).").

[129] *Id.* at 278 (citing Jacobson v. Massachusetts, 197 U.S. 11, 24–30 (1905) (compulsory vaccination); Breithaupt v. Abrams, 352 U.S. 432, 439 (1957) (search and seizure); Washington v. Harper, 494 U.S. 210 (1990) (administration of antipsychotic medications to prisoners); Vitek v. Jones, 445 U.S. 480, 494 (1980) (transfer from prison to mental hospital); Parham v. J.R., 442 U.S. 584, 600 (1979) (psychiatric hospitalization of children); Union Pac. Ry. v. Botsford, 141 U.S. 250 (1891)).

[130] *Id.* at 262.

permit a *competent* patient to refuse artificial nutrition and hydration, the Court stated that "the logic of the cases [from which the principle of a competent patient's right to refuse treatment is derived] would embrace such a liberty interest, [but] the dramatic consequences involved in refusal of such treatment would inform the inquiry as to whether the deprivation of that interest is constitutionally permissible."[131] Further, while "a State is [not] required to remain neutral in the face of an informed and voluntary decision by a physically-able adult to starve to death . . . a state has more particular interests at stake"[132] when a patient lacks decisionmaking capacity. Because "[t]he choice between life and death is a deeply personal decision of obvious and overwhelming finality [a state] may legitimately seek to safeguard the personal element of this choice through the imposition of heightened evidentiary requirements,"[133] in order to protect against abuse of incompetent patients. This doctrinal shift from privacy to liberty has been followed by some,[134] but not all, state courts.[135]

Even before *Cruzan,* courts were increasingly relying either exclusively on a common-law basis or on a common-law right in conjunction with the constitutional right of privacy. Perhaps the most noteworthy example is the New Jersey Supreme Court's *Conroy* decision. Forsaking the constitutional right of privacy that had been its basis for the *Quinlan* decision, the court declined to employ it again in *Conroy* "since the right to decline medical treatment is, in any event, embraced within the common-law right to self-determination."[136]

Some courts finding a constitutional basis for the right to die have expressly stated that it is a federal constitutional right.[137] However, because the courts often fail to so state, this conclusion must be inferred from citations to leading Supreme Court right-of-privacy cases such as *Griswold v. Connecticut*[138] and

---

[131] *Id.* at 279.

[132] *Id.* at 280.

[133] *Id.* at 281.

[134] **CA:** Donaldson v. Van de Kamp, 4 Cal. Rptr. 2d 59, 62 (Ct. App. 1992) (right to refuse unwanted medical treatment "derives from a liberty interest found in the Fourteenth Amendment").

IL: C.A. v. Morgan, 603 N.E.2d 1171 (Ill. App. Ct. 1992).

IN: *In re* Lawrance, 579 N.E.2d 32, 39 (Ind. 1991).

MA: Norwood Hosp. v. Munoz, 564 N.E.2d 1017 (Mass. 1991).

NV: McKay v. Bergstedt, 801 P.2d 617, 622 (Nev. 1990).

OH: *In re* Crum, 580 N.E.2d 876, 878 (P. Ct. Franklin County, Ohio 1991) ("constitutionally protected liberty interest in refusing unwanted medical treatment").

[135] **FL:** Browning v. Herbert, 568 So. 2d 4 (Fla. 1990) (state constitutional right of privacy).

[136] *In re* Conroy, 486 A.2d 1209, 1223 (N.J. 1985).

[137] **MA:** Superintendent of Belchertown State Sch. v. Saikewicz, 370 N.E.2d 417 (Mass. 1977).

NJ: *In re* Quackenbush, 383 A.2d 785 (N.J. Super. Ct. P. Div. 1978).

OH: Leach v. Akron Gen. Medical Ctr., 426 N.E.2d 809 (C.P. P. Div. Summit County, Ohio 1980).

WA: *In re* Ingram, 689 P.2d 1363 (Wash. 1984).

[138] 381 U.S. 479 (1965), *cited in* Superintendent of Belchertown State Sch. v. Saikewicz, 370 N.E.2d 417, 424 (Mass. 1977).

Roe v. Wade.[139] A few courts have either clearly specified their reliance on state constitutional provisions,[140] though usually in conjunction with federal precedents,[141] or have at least implied that they were relying on a state constitutional provision either alone[142] or in combination with the federal constitution.[143]

---

[139] 410 U.S. 113 (1973), *cited in* Superintendent of Belchertown State Sch. v. Saikewicz, 370 N.E.2d 417, 424 (Mass. 1977).

[140] **AZ:** Rasmussen v. Fleming, 741 P.2d 674, 682 (Ariz. 1987).

CA: Donaldson v. Van de Kamp, 4 Cal. Rptr. 2d 59 (Ct. App. 1992); Bouvia v. Superior Court (Glenchur), 225 Cal. Rptr. 297 (Ct. App. 1986); Bartling v. Superior Court, 209 Cal. Rptr. 220, 225 (Ct. App. 1984).

FL: Browning v. Herbert, 568 So. 2d 4 (Fla. 1990); *In re* Barry, 445 So. 2d 365 (Fla. Dist. Ct. App. 1984) (noting state constitution was amended after Satz v. Perlmutter, 379 So. 2d 359 (Fla. 1980), to recognize a right of privacy in medical treatment decisions).

IL: *Cf.* Estate of Longeway v. Community Convalescent Ctr., 549 N.E.2d 292, 297 (Ill. 1989) ("Lacking a clear expression of intent from the drafters . . . , we . . . abstain from expanding the privacy provision of our State constitution to embrace this right.").

IN: *In re* Lawrance, 579 N.E.2d 32, 39 (Ind. 1991).

KY: DeGrella v. Elston, 858 S.W.2d 698, 702 (Ky. 1993).

MO: *Contra* Cruzan v. Harmon, 760 S.W.2d 408, 417 (Mo. 1988) ("We thus find no unfettered right of privacy under our constitution that would support the right of a person to refuse medical treatment in every circumstance.").

NJ: *In re* Quinlan, 355 A.2d 647 (N.J. 1976).

PA: *Cf. In re* E.L.K., 11 Fiduc. Rep. 2d 78, 82 (C.P. Berks County, Pa. 1991) ("The Pennsylvania Constitution under Article 1, Section 1 has created a right to die.").

WA: *In re* Colyer, 660 P.2d 738, 742 (Wash. 1983).

WI: *Cf.* L.W. v. L.E. Phillips Career Dev. Ctr., 482 N.W.2d 60, 65 (Wis. 1992) (Article 1, § 1 of state constitution creates an "independent right to liberty [which] includes an individual's choice of whether or not to accept medical treatment.").

[141] **AZ:** Rasmussen v. Fleming, 741 P.2d 674, 682 (Ariz. 1987).

CA: Bouvia v. Superior Court (Glenchur), 225 Cal. Rptr. 297, 300 (Ct. App. 1986); Bartling v. Superior Court, 209 Cal. Rptr. 220, 225 (Ct. App. 1984).

FL: *In re* Barry, 445 So. 2d 365 (Fla. Dist. Ct. App. 1984).

PA: Ragona v. Preate, 11 Fiduc. Rep. 2d 1, 10, 6 Pa. D. & C.4th 202 (C.P. Lackawanna County, Pa. 1990) (federal 14th Amendment liberty interest and Pennsylvania Constitution art. 1, § 1).

WA: *In re* Grant, 747 P.2d 445 (Wash. 1987); *In re* Colyer, 660 P.2d 738, 742 (Wash. 1983).

[142] **FL:** John F. Kennedy Memorial Hosp. v. Bludworth, 432 So. 2d 611, 619 (Fla. Dist. Ct. App. 1983) (Florida constitution grants express right of privacy.), *rev'd,* 452 So. 2d 921 (Fla. 1984).

NJ: *In re* Quinlan, 355 A.2d 647 (N.J. 1976).

OH: *Cf. In re* Myers, 610 N.E.2d 663, 669 n.4 (P. Ct. Summit County, Ohio 1993) ("While it is clear from Cruzan that the right of privacy is not applicable to removal cases under the federal Constitution, it has not been determined as to whether such a right exists under the Ohio Constitution.").

See generally Gormley & Hartman, *Privacy and the States,* 65 Temple L. Rev. 1279 (1992); Eaton & Larson, *Experimenting with the "Right to Die" in the Laboratory of the States,* 25 Ga. L. Rev. 1253, 1262–68 (1991).

[143] **CA:** McMahon v. Lopez, 245 Cal. Rptr. 172 (Ct. App. 1988).

FL: Corbett v. D'Alessandro, 487 So. 2d 368, 370 (Fla. Dist. Ct. App. 1986).

NJ: *In re* Quinlan, 355 A.2d 647, 663 (N.J. 1976); *In re* Hughes, 611 A.2d 1148, 1151 (N.J. Super. Ct. App. Div. 1992).

Very few courts have addressed the question of the applicability of constitutional rights in the absence of state action. Those that have done so have stated that state action is necessary for a constitutional basis for the existence of a right to forgo life-sustaining treatment.[144] The Supreme Court of Washington, for example, concluded that there is state action in such cases because

> the presence of the state is manifested by its capability of imposing criminal sanctions on the hospital and its staff . . . by its licensing of physicians . . . by the required involvement of the judiciary in the guardianship appointment process . . . and by the state's *parens patriae* responsibility to supervise the affairs of incompetents. . . . Taken together, these factors show a sufficient nexus between the state and the prohibitions against withholding or discontinuance of life sustaining treatment to call into play the constitutional right of privacy.[145]

However, the presence of state action in most right-to-die cases is to be seriously doubted.[146]

Efforts to assert the Eighth Amendment's protection against cruel and unusual punishment as a basis for forgoing life-sustaining treatment have met with little success.[147]

§ 2.9 Religious Belief

It is occasionally asserted that a patient's religious beliefs and the protection accorded such beliefs by the First Amendment constitute a basis for the right to refuse medical treatment. Such assertions were made long before the first right-to-die case, were repeated in the *Quinlan* case, and continue to be made occasionally to this day in two different, but related, kinds of cases. First, in what will be referred to as "religious-belief cases," patients have been motivated to refuse treatment because it is an article of their religious faith that medical treatment in general is prohibited (for example, Christian Science) or that

---

[144] **AZ:** Rasmussen v. Fleming, 741 P.2d 674, 682 n.9 (Ariz. 1987) (state's authority to license and regulate hospitals, health professions, and health care services, and supervisory authority over guardianship of incapacitated persons establishes state action).

NY: Eichner v. Dillon, 426 N.Y.S.2d 517, 540 (App. Div. 1980).

WA: *In re* Colyer, 660 P.2d 738, 742 (Wash. 1983).

[145] **WA:** *In re* Colyer, 660 P.2d at 742.

MO: *Accord* Cruzan v. Harmon, 760 S.W.2d 408, 418 n.14 (Mo. 1988) ("This is not a matter of forfeiture of a constitutional right because that term implies some state action which deliberately removes or limits a constitutional right.").

NY: *Accord* Eichner v. Dillon, 426 N.Y.S.2d 517, 540 (App. Div. 1980), *rev'g In re* Eichner, 423 N.Y.S.2d 580, 590–91 (Sup. Ct. Nassau County 1979). *See also* Eichner v. Dillon, 420 N.E.2d 64 (N.Y. 1981) (avoiding issue by grounding right to die in common law).

[146] See § **17.20.**

[147] *See, e.g., In re* Quinlan, 355 A.2d 647 (N.J. 1976).

specific forms of medical treatment are prohibited (for example, Jehovah's Witnesses). Religious belief is not merely a legal ground for the refusal of treatment, it is the motivating force.

In conventional right-to-die cases, such as in the *Quinlan* case (as well as some subsequent right-to-die cases), the patient (or the patient's surrogate) is not motivated by religious belief to refuse treatment, but rather refuses treatment entirely, primarily, or partially for some other reason. The only thing that distinguishes the religious-belief cases from other right-to-die cases is that the asserted right is based in part on religious belief. In the conventional right-to-die cases, the refusal of treatment is central to the case, and religious belief is asserted (if at all) as a basis thereof; in the religious-belief cases, religious belief is central to the case because, but for the religious belief, the patient would have accepted treatment.

In other words, the primary distinction between the religious-belief cases and right-to-die cases in which religious belief is asserted as a basis for the right to refuse treatment is the ultimate *goal* of the refusal of treatment. In conventional right-to-die cases, patients (or surrogates of incompetent patients) wish to end their lives because of the hopelessness of their condition. By contrast, in the religious-belief cases, patients do not wish to end their lives. Indeed, they often very much wish to live.[148] Their goal in refusing treatment is to maintain the integrity of their religious beliefs. In only a very small number of religious-belief cases does it seem that treatment might have been refused in the absence of such belief,[149] and in all of them it was not at all clear that the patient would survive even if treatment were administered, as is the case in other religious-belief cases.

Generally, though not always, the patients in religious-belief cases are relatively healthy individuals whose current acute medical crisis could most likely be overcome if they were to accept the treatment in question. These patients are ordinarily *not* terminally, incurably, or hopelessly ill,[150] and the treatment sought to be administered to them is more aptly characterized as lifesaving rather than life-sustaining treatment.[151] That is, the treatment is likely to be able to do more than merely prolong the process of dying. These patients are, however, usually critically ill, for if they were not, it is unlikely that any civil or medical authority would have sought to force the imposition of medical treatment.

---

148 *See, e.g.,* Powell v. Columbian Presbyterian Medical Ctr., 267 N.Y.S.2d 450, 451 (Sup. Ct. 1965) (patient "did not object to receiving the treatment involved—she would not, however, direct its use").

149 **DE:** Newmark v. Williams, 588 A.2d 1108 (Del. 1991).

IL: *In re* E.G., 549 N.E.2d 322 (Ill. 1989).

NY: *In re* Long Island Jewish Medical Ctr. (Malcolm), 557 N.Y.S.2d 239 (Sup. Ct. Queens County 1990).

150 See §§ **8.10** through **8.12.**

151 See § **8.13.**

The reception by appellate courts of the assertion of a religious belief for the right to refuse treatment has been and continues to be mixed. In the pre-*Quinlan* religious-belief cases, a number of courts upheld the right of an adult to refuse treatment on the basis of the free exercise clause of the First Amendment.[152] Other courts recognized the First Amendment as a basis for the right to refuse treatment, but declined to uphold the right on the facts of the specific cases, generally either because the patient was found to be incompetent,[153] there was a strong countervailing state interest (namely the protection of minor children),[154] or both.

The First Amendment's free exercise clause was asserted as one of the bases of the right to refuse treatment in *Quinlan.* However, consistent with prior New Jersey religious-belief cases,[155] the court relied on the well-established principle that "the right to religious beliefs is absolute but conduct in pursuance thereof is not wholly immune from governmental restraint," in rejecting this as a basis for the forgoing of life-sustaining treatment.[156] Thereafter, the First Amendment has been invoked very rarely as a basis for the refusal of treatment in conventional right-to-die cases.[157]

Effect of Religious-Belief Cases on the Development of the Right to Die

Despite a long period during which there were no reported religious-belief cases, they began to reappear in the mid-1980s, and with that reappearance, the

---

[152] **CA2:** Winters v. Miller, 446 F.2d 65 (2d Cir. 1971).

DIL: Holmes v. Silver Cross Hosp., 340 F. Supp. 125 (N.D. Ill. 1972).

DC: *In re* Osborne, 294 A.2d 372 (D.C. 1972).

IL: *In re* Estate of Brooks, 205 N.E.2d 435 (Ill. 1965).

NY: *In re* Melideo, 390 N.Y.S.2d 523 (Sup. Ct. 1976) (decided several months after *Quinlan*). *Cf.* Erickson v. Dilgard, 252 N.Y.S.2d 705 (Sup. Ct. Nassau County 1962) (upholding religious belief-based refusal of treatment without stating basis therefor).

PA: *In re* Green, 292 A.2d 387 (Pa. 1972) (mature minor; non-life-threatening condition).

[153] **CADC:** *In re* President & Directors of Georgetown College, 331 F.2d 1000 (D.C. Cir. 1964).

NJ: *But cf.* John F. Kennedy Memorial Hosp. v. Heston, 279 A.2d 670 (N.J. 1971) (no constitutional right to die).

[154] **CADC:** *In re* President & Directors of Georgetown College, 331 F.2d 1000.

NJ: *Cf.* Raleigh Fitkin-Paul Morgan Memorial Hosp. v. Anderson, 201 A.2d 537 (N.J.), *cert. denied,* 377 U.S. 985 (1964); State v. Perricone, 181 A.2d 751 (N.J. 1962) (discussing "religious conviction" as basis for right to refuse treatment but not explicitly mentioning First Amendment).

[155] John F. Kennedy Memorial Hosp. v. Heston, 279 A.2d 670 (N.J. 1971); Raleigh Fitkin-Paul Morgan Memorial Hosp. v. Anderson, 201 A.2d 537 (N.J. 1964); State v. Perricone, 181 A.2d 751 (N.J. 1962).

[156] *In re* Quinlan, 355 A.2d 647, 661–62 (N.J. 1976).

[157] *See, e.g., In re* E.G., 549 N.E.2d 322 (Ill. 1989) (holding that mature minor has common-law right to refuse life-sustaining treatment and declining to reach First Amendment issue).

history of the development of religious belief as a basis for the right to refuse treatment has taken an interesting twist. Even though the right-to-die cases rejected from the outset religious belief as a basis for the right to forgo life-sustaining medical treatment, the religious-belief cases (along with conventional battery and informed consent cases) were important to the development of the right to die. Although very few cases had actually permitted the refusal of treatment on the basis of religious belief, they contained important dicta recognizing prima facie the right of competent adult patients to refuse medical treatment.

The religious-belief cases also played an important part in structuring the analysis of right-to-die cases. It was from the religious-belief cases that courts appropriated the concept of *countervailing state interests* to be weighed against an individual's right to refuse treatment.[158] However, as the analysis of right-to-die cases itself has matured, the mark left by the religious-belief cases has become increasingly formalistic and decreasingly substantive. Courts still routinely invoke the four countervailing state interests—preservation of life, prevention of suicide, protection of innocent third parties, and protection of the ethical integrity of health care professionals—but accord them little or no weight when the patient is incurably ill.[159]

Effect of Right-to-Die Cases on Religious-Belief Cases

What is even more interesting than the effect the religious-belief cases have had on conventional right-to-die cases is the effect of the latter on the former. As the right to die has itself been incrementally strengthened case by case, beginning about 10 years after the *Quinlan* decision the right-to-die cases began to work important changes in the judicial analysis and outcome of religious-belief cases. Prior to about 1985, courts were exceedingly reluctant to permit the refusal of treatment in the religious-belief cases—that is, in those cases in which the patient's health could most likely be restored. Beginning in the mid-1980s, courts have been far more willing to honor the refusal of treatment by a *competent adult* even when the refusal would lead to death and the administration of treatment would almost certainly save the patient's life.[160]

---

[158] **MA:** *See* Superintendent of Belchertown State Sch. v. Saikewicz, 370 N.E.2d 417, 424 (Mass. 1977).

NJ: *Cf. In re* Quinlan, 355 A.2d 647, 664 (N.J. 1976) ("Ultimately there comes a point at which the individual's rights overcome the State interest.").

[159] See §§ **8.14** through **8.19.**

[160] **DGA:** *But see* Novak v. Cobb County-Kennestone Hosp. Auth., 849 F. Supp. 1559 (N.D. Ga. 1994).

FL: *In re* Dubreuil, 629 So. 2d 819 (Fla. 1993); Wons v. Public Health Trust, 541 So. 2d 96 (Fla. 1989); St. Mary's Hosp. v. Ramsey, 465 So. 2d 666 (Fla. Dist. Ct. App. 1985).

MD: *Cf.* Mercy Hosp. Inc. v. Jackson, 489 A.2d 1130 (Md. Ct. Spec. App. 1985), *vacated and remanded as moot,* 510 A.2d 562 (Md. 1986).

Most, but not all,[161] of such cases have involved the refusal of blood transfusions by Jehovah's Witnesses. But interestingly, even in those cases in which the refusal of treatment has been motivated by religious belief, not all courts have clearly recognized religious belief (that is, the First Amendment's free exercise clause) as the basis for the legal right to refuse treatment. Instead, some courts have grounded their holdings in the common-law right to refuse treatment or the constitutional right of privacy, sometimes in conjunction with religious belief as a basis but sometimes not. The result of those cases grounding the right to refuse treatment on a common-law basis, or on a constitutional basis other than the free exercise of religion, is a much more robust right to refuse treatment than one based on religious belief alone for it applies to all competent adults regardless of what their religious beliefs are or whether they even have any.

Perhaps the clearest example of this is *Fosmire v. Nicoleau* in New York, involving the refusal of a blood transfusion said to have been needed by a pregnant Jehovah's Witness in connection with childbirth, a not uncommon fact pattern. The court upheld the patient's refusal of a blood transfusion despite the fact that if she died, a newborn baby would be motherless, on the basis of the common-law right of bodily integrity rather than on the basis of religious belief.[162] The Massachusetts Supreme Judicial Court came to a similar conclusion in the *Munoz* case, also basing the right of a patient of the Jehovah's Witness faith to refuse a blood transfusion both on the common-law right of bodily integrity and the constitutional right of privacy.[163] The Florida Supreme Court, which considered two such cases between 1985 and 1993, grounded the right of Jehovah's Witnesses to refuse blood transfusions on both the constitutional right of privacy and the constitutional right of religious freedom.[164] In a third Florida case, the court of appeal was unclear about the basis for its holding that the patient had the right to refuse a lifesaving blood transfusion, but it appeared not to limit the holding to cases involving an asserted religious belief.[165]

MA: Norwood Hosp. v. Munoz, 564 N.E.2d 1017 (Mass. 1991).

MI: *But see* Werth v. Taylor, 475 N.W.2d 426 (Mich. Ct. App. 1991).

MS: *In re* Brown, 478 So. 2d 1033 (Miss. 1985).

NJ: *But see In re* Hughes, 611 A.2d 1148 (N.J. Super. Ct. App. Div. 1992).

NY: Fosmire v. Nicoleau, 551 N.E.2d 77 (N.Y. 1990).

OH: *In re* Milton, 505 N.E.2d 255 (Ohio 1987).

PA: *But see In re* Estate of Dorone, 534 A.2d 452 (Pa. 1987).

161 **CA:** Bouvia v. Superior Court (Glenchur), 225 Cal. Rptr. 297 (Ct. App. 1986).

GA: State v. McAfee, 385 S.E.2d 651 (Ga. 1989).

NV: McKay v. Bergstedt, 801 P.2d 617 (Nev. 1990).

162 Fosmire v. Nicoleau, 551 N.E.2d 77 (N.Y. 1990).

163 Norwood Hosp. v. Munoz, 564 N.E.2d 1017 (Mass. 1991).

164 *See In re* Dubreuil, 629 So. 2d 819 (Fla. 1993); Wons v. Public Health Trust, 541 So. 2d 96 (Fla. 1989).

165 *See* St. Mary's Hosp. v. Ramsey, 465 So. 2d 666 (Fla. Dist. Ct. App. 1985).

Today the predominant analysis of religious-belief cases bears the strong imprint of right-to-die litigation. The net result is that before *Quinlan,* the right to refuse treatment motivated by and based on religious belief was honored as much in the breach as in the observance. Today, however, the refusal of medical treatment motivated by religious belief is far more likely to be honored. Ironically, the reason for honoring the refusal, however, is likely to have nothing to do with religious belief as a legal basis for the right to refuse treatment. Although some courts have strengthened the right to refuse treatment based on religious grounds (most notably Florida), others (Massachusetts and New York) have refused to recognize such a right but have honored treatment refusals motivated by religious belief on the basis of more generally applicable rights.

§ 2.10 Statutes and Regulations

The overwhelming majority of states have enacted statutes, referred to generically as living will statutes[166] and health care power of attorney statutes,[167] to provide a means by which individuals may plan for decisionmaking about life-sustaining treatment should they become incompetent. Although most of these statutes explicitly disavow the creation of substantive rights, merely claiming to provide a mechanism through which common-law and/or constitutional rights may be implemented,[168] a few courts have found that the public policy of the state is reflected in its advance directive statute, and in some cases the outcome has been substantially affected by the statute's provisions even though the patient did not have an advance directive.[169] Most courts decline to apply either the letter or the spirit of advance directive statutes to individuals who have not executed an advance directive[170] or whose advance directive does not comply with or even conflicts with the statute's provisions.[171]

Some courts have bootstrapped the constitutional or common-law basis of the right to die with state statutory provisions even when the patient does not have an advance directive. Even in cases in which the requirements for the application of the advance directive statute are not met because, for example, no

---

[166] See **Ch. 11.**

[167] See **Ch. 12.**

[168] See §§ **10.10** through **10.16.**

[169] **IL:** Estate of Longeway v. Community Convalescent Ctr., 549 N.E.2d 292 (Ill. 1989) (holding that living will statute permitting termination of artificial nutrition and hydration permits guardian not acting pursuant to living will also to terminate artificial nutrition and hydration).

MO: Cruzan v. Director, 497 U.S. 261 (1990) (holding that state's public policy is that mere existence must be preserved regardless of quality of life).

[170] See § **10.13.**

[171] See § **10.12.**

directive was signed by the patient, courts may still infer a legislative recognition of the right to die.[172]

In addition to advance directive statutes, courts sometimes rely on other statutory provisions, such as informed consent legislation,[173] provisions governing patient participation in decisions regarding medical care[174] that may be a part of a statutory "bill of rights" for patients,[175] legislation recognizing a durable

---

[172] **CA:** Drabick v. Drabick, 245 Cal. Rptr. 840, 853 (Ct. App. 1988) (guardianship statute); Bouvia v. Superior Court (Glenchur), 225 Cal. Rptr. 297, 302 (Ct. App. 1986); Bartling v. Superior Court, 209 Cal. Rptr. 220, 224 (Ct. App. 1984); Barber v. Superior Court, 195 Cal. Rptr. 484, 489 (Ct. App. 1983).

CT: *Compare* McConnell v. Beverly Enters.-Conn., Inc., 553 A.2d 596, 602 (Conn. 1989) ("When the legislature has attempted to respond to this urgent request for statutory assistance, we have an obligation to pursue the applicability of statutory criteria before resorting to an exploration of residual common law rights, if any such rights indeed remain.") *with id.* at 606 (Healey, J., concurring) ("I believe that such a common law right of self-determination exists. I agree with the majority to the extent that it acknowledges the existence of such a common law right. [Citations omitted.] I believe that the statutory scheme did not entirely displace the common law. 'It is an established rule of statutory construction that statutes are not readily interpreted as abrogating common-law rights.' [Citation omitted.] It is also a rule of statutory construction that statutes in derogation of the common law are to be strictly construed.").

GA: *Cf. In re* L.H.R., 321 S.E.2d 716, 722 (Ga. 1984).

IL: *Cf.* Estate of Longeway v. Community Convalescent Ctr., 549 N.E.2d 292, 297 (Ill. 1989).

IN: *In re* Lawrance, 579 N.E.2d 32, 39 (Ind. 1991) (finding source of right to die in living will, health care power of attorney, and surrogate decisionmaking statutes).

MD: Mack v. Mack, 618 A.2d 744 (Md. 1993).

MN: *In re* Torres, 357 N.W.2d 332, 337–38 (Minn. 1984).

MO: *Cf.* Cruzan v. Harmon, 760 S.W.2d 408, 420 (Mo. 1988) ("We intend no judgment here as to whether the common law right to refuse medical treatment is broader than the Living Will statute.").

NY: Eichner v. Dillon, 420 N.E.2d 64, 70 (N.Y. 1981). *Cf.* Fosmire v. Nicoleau, 551 N.E.2d 77, 80–81 (N.Y. 1990).

WA: *In re* Colyer, 660 P.2d 738, 741 (Wash. 1983) ("[T]he findings of the Legislature and the thrust of the [living will] act are in harmony with our ruling today. . . . [O]ur Legislature has acknowledged both an individual's right to control medical decisions and the right to privacy as grounds for withholding or withdrawing life sustaining treatment.").

WI: *Cf.* L.W. v. L.E. Phillips Career Dev. Ctr., 482 N.W.2d 60 (Wis. 1992).

[173] **NY:** Eichner v. Dillon, 420 N.E.2d 64, 70 (N.Y. 1981); Saunders v. State, 492 N.Y.S.2d 510, 514 (Sup. Ct. Nassau County 1985).

[174] **CA:** Bartling v. Superior Court, 209 Cal. Rptr. 220, 225 (Ct. App. 1984) ("One of those rights [in Title 22 of the California Administrative Code, section 70707] is to '[p]articipate actively in decisions regarding medical care.'").

[175] **MN:** *In re* Torres, 357 N.W.2d 332, 338 (Minn. 1984).

power of attorney for health care,[176] or guardianship legislation.[177] In addition, a number of states have adopted regulations governing the rights of patients in health care institutions (predominantly hospitals and nursing homes) that either expressly or impliedly accord patients a right to decline medical treatment or to forgo life-sustaining treatment in particular.[178]

The attorneys general in some states have issued opinions that serve as the basis for making decisions about forgoing life-sustaining treatment.[179]

§ 2.11 Parens Patriae Power

Most right-to-die cases have involved incompetent patients. The courts have generally reached the conclusion that incompetent patients have a right to forgo life-sustaining treatment by first assuming for argument's sake that the patient is competent and then concluding that, because competent patients have a right to forgo treatment, patients who are incompetent ought not to be denied that right simply because they are incompetent. Thus, the courts have generally premised the right of incompetent patients to forgo treatment on the same bases as for competent patients: the common-law rights of autonomy, privacy, and self-determination,[180] or the constitutional right of privacy or liberty. For example, in *Quinlan,* the New Jersey Supreme Court stated

> Our affirmation of Karen's independent right of choice . . . would ordinarily be based upon her competency to assert it. The sad truth, however, is that she is grossly incompetent and we cannot discern her supposed choice. . . . Nevertheless

---

[176] **CA:** Bouvia v. Superior Court (Glenchur), 225 Cal. Rptr. 297, 303 (Ct. App. 1986).

WI: L.W. v. L.E. Phillips Career Dev. Ctr., 482 N.W.2d 60 (Wis. 1992).

[177] **MD:** Mack v. Mack, 618 A.2d 744, 756 (Md. 1993).

MO: *But see* Cruzan v. Harmon, 760 S.W.2d 408, 424 (Mo. 1988) (Guardianship "statute makes no provision for the termination of medical treatment; to the contrary, it places an express, affirmative duty on guardians to assure that the ward receives medical care and provides the guardian with the power to give consent for that purpose. We thus find no statutory basis for the argument that the guardian possesses authority, as a guardian, to order the termination of medical treatment.").

[178] *See* U.S. Dep't of Health & Human Servs., Medicare and Medicaid Requirements for Long Term Care Facilities, 42 C.F.R. § 483.10(b)(4) (1992) ("The resident has the right to refuse treatment."). *See also* Cohen, *Patients' Rights Laws and the Right to Refuse Life-Sustaining Treatment in Nursing Homes,* 2 Biolaw S:231 (Aug. 1989).

[179] **MD:** 73 Md. Op. Att'y Gen. 253 (Op. No. 88-046, Oct. 17, 1988), *explained in* Mack v. Mack, 618 A.2d 744 (Md. 1993).

TX: Tex. Op. Att'y Gen. No. JM-837 (1988) (LEXIS, AG).

[180] See § **2.5.**

> we have concluded that Karen's right of privacy may be asserted on her behalf by her guardian under the peculiar circumstances here present.
>
> If a putative decision by Karen to permit this non-cognitive, vegetative existence to terminate by natural forces is regarded as a valuable incident of her right of privacy, as we believe it to be, then it should not be discarded solely on the basis that her condition prevents her conscious exercise of the choice.[181]

Although the result may be acceptable,[182] the process by which the result was achieved is strained. At its next opportunity, the New Jersey Supreme Court rejected this reasoning. Instead, it confronted the issue of the source of the right to die for incompetent patients, planting it firmly in the parens patriae power of the state to act in the best interests of incompetents, explaining that

> [w]e hesitate . . . to foreclose the possibility of humane actions, which may involve termination of life-sustaining treatment, for persons who never clearly expressed their desires about life-sustaining treatment but who are now suffering a prolonged and painful death. An incompetent, like a minor child, is a ward of the state, and the state's *parens patriae* power supports the authority of its courts to allow decisions to be made for an incompetent that serve the incompetent's best interests, even if the person's wishes cannot be clearly established.[183]

---

[181] **NJ:** *In re* Quinlan, 355 A.2d 647, 664 (N.J. 1976).

MA: *Accord* Superintendent of Belchertown State Sch. v. Saikewicz, 370 N.E.2d 417, 424 (Mass. 1977).

[182] **MO:** *But see* Cruzan v. Harmon, 760 S.W.2d 408, 425 (Mo. 1988) ("*Quinlan* held, broadly and without precedential support, that the right of privacy and the right to refuse medical treatment may be exercised by surrogates in the event of incompetency. In this manner a rationale was born to reach the end sought. . . . [T]hese rights have been explained as rooted in personal autonomy and self-determination. Autonomy means self law—the ability to decide an issue without reference to or responsibility to any other. It is logically inconsistent to claim that rights which are found lurking in the shadow of the Bill of Rights and which spring from concerns for personal autonomy can be exercised by another absent the most rigid of formalities."); *In re* Westchester County Medical Ctr. (O'Connor), 531 N.E.2d 607 (N.Y. 1988) (rejecting forgoing of life-sustaining treatment on behalf of an incompetent patient who lacked an advance directive).

NY: *In re* Storar, 420 N.E.2d 64 (N.Y. 1981) (same).

[183] **NJ:** *In re* Conroy, 486 A.2d 1209, 1231 (N.J. 1985).

IL: *Cf.* Estate of Longeway v. Community Convalescent Ctr., 549 N.E.2d 292, 301 (Ill. 1989) ("[T]he courts have a *parens patriae* power which enables them to protect the estate and person of incompetents.").

WI: *Accord* L.W. v. L.E. Phillips Career Dev. Ctr., 482 N.W.2d 60, 68 n.9 (Wis. 1992) ("*Parens patriae* literally means 'parent of the country' and refers to the role of the state as guardian of persons under legal disabilities, such as juveniles or incompetent persons. Black's Law Dictionary 1114 (6th ed. 1990). Under the theory of *parens patriae* it is the right and duty of the state to step in and act in what appears to be the best interests of the ward. [Citation omitted.]").

The use of the parens patriae power as the basis for decisionmaking for incompetent patients has been more forcefully adopted by the Missouri Supreme Court in *Cruzan v. Harmon.*[184] In addition, that court has been more overtly critical of the notion of self-determination as the basis for the forgoing of treatment of incompetent patients:

> Autonomy means self law—the ability to decide an issue without reference to or responsibility to any other. It is logically inconsistent to claim that rights which are found lurking in the shadow of the Bill of Rights and which spring from concerns for personal autonomy can be exercised by another absent the most rigid of formalities.
>
> Nor do we believe that the common law right to refuse treatment—founded in personal autonomy—is exercisable by a third party absent formalities. A guardian's power to exercise third party choice arises from the state's authority, not the constitutional rights of the ward.[185]

When a third party does make decisions for an incompetent patient, he does so as the "delegatee of the state's *parens patriae* power,"[186] rather than by virtue of exercising the incompetent patient's own rights. The *Cruzan* court clearly rejected the reasoning and language of *Quinlan,* adopted in numerous cases, that "'[t]he only practical way to prevent destruction of the right is to permit the guardian and family of Karen to render their best judgment . . . as to whether she would exercise it in these circumstances.'"[187] It also issued a stinging condemnation to the corollary notion of substituted judgment,[188] criticizing both the *Quinlan* and *Saikewicz* decisions:

> Cases which relied on the doctrine of substituted judgment to permit guardians to choose termination of life support simply failed to consider the source of the guardian's authority to decide. Instead those decisions assumed, without benefit of legal precedent, that the guardian's power to decide is derivative of the incompetent's right to decide, if competent. *See Quinlan* [citation omitted]. That the doctrine has an historical antecedent, *Saikewicz,* [citation omitted], does not change its raison d'etre or the scope of its reach. To fail to appreciate the legal foundation is to risk permitting the application of the doctrine in an unprincipled manner.[189]

The rights of minors, a class of incompetents, have also been found to be grounded in the parens patriae power of the state.[190]

---

[184] 760 S.W.2d 408 (Mo. 1988).

[185] *Id.* at 425.

[186] *Id.*

[187] *Id.* at 413.

[188] See **§ 7.7.**

[189] Cruzan v. Harmon, 760 S.W.2d at 425–26.

[190] **IL:** *In re* E.G., 549 N.E.2d 322, 327 (Ill. 1989). See **Ch. 15.**

Bibliography

Abraham, H. "Abraham, Isaac and the State: Faith-Healing and Legal Intervention." *University of Richmond Law Review* 27 (1993): 951.

Bopp, J. "An Examination of Proposals for a Human Life Amendment." *Capital University Law Review* 15 (1986): 415.

Bopp, J. and D. Avila. "The Due Process "Right to Life" in *Cruzan* and Its Impact on 'Right-to-Die' Law." *University of Pittsburgh Law Review* 53 (1991): 193.

Byrn, R. "Compulsory Lifesaving Treatment for the Competent Adult." *Fordham Law Review* 44 (1975): 1.

Cantor, N. "*Quinlan,* Privacy, and the Handling of Incompetent Dying Patients." *Rutgers Law Review* 30 (1977): 243.

Carnerie, F. "Euthanasia and Self-Determinism: Is There a Charter Right to Die in Canada?" *McGill Law Journal* 32 (1987): 299.

Destro, R. "Quality-of-Life Ethics and Constitutional Jurisprudence: The Demise of Natural Rights and Equal Protection for the Disabled and Incompetent." *Journal of Contemporary Health Law and Policy* 2 (1986): 71.

Eaton, T. and E. Larson, "Experimenting with the 'Right to Die' in the Laboratory of the States." *Georgia Law Review* 25 (1991): 1253.

Gormley, K. and R. Hartman. "Privacy and the States." *Temple Law Review* 65 (1992): 1279.

Handler, A. "Social Dilemmas, Judicial (Ir)resolutions." *Rutgers Law Review* 40 (1987): 1.

Ingram, J. "State Interference with Religiously Motivated Decisions on Medical Treatment." *Dickinson Law Review* 93 (1988): 41.

Kamisar, Y. "When Is There a Constitutional "Right to Die"? When Is There No Constitutional "Right to Live"? *Georgia Law Review* 25 (1991): 1203.

Kempic, A. "The Right to Refuse Medical Treatment Under the State Constitutions." *Cooley Law Review* 5 (1988): 313.

Louisell, D. "Euthanasia and Biathanasia: On Dying and Killing." *Catholic University Law Review* 22 (1973): 723.

Lyon, E. "The Right to Die: An Exercise of Informed Consent, Not an Extension of the Constitutional Right to Privacy." *University of Cincinnati Law Review* 58 (1990): 1367.

Marks, T. and R. Morgan. "The Right of the Dying to Refuse Life Prolonging Medical Procedures: The Evolving Importance of State Constitutions." *Ohio Northern University Law Review* 18 (1992): 467.

Mayo, T. "Constitutionalizing the 'Right to Die.'" *Maryland Law Review* 49 (1990): 103.

Morgan, R. and B. Harty-Golder. "Constitutional Development of Judicial Criteria in Right-to-Die Cases: From Brain Dead to Persistent Vegetative State." *Wake Forest Law Review* 23 (1988): 721.

Pedrick, W. "Dignified Death and the Law of Torts" *San Diego Law Review* 28 (1991): 387.

Rhoden, N. "Litigating Life and Death." *Harvard Law Review* 102 (1988): 375.

Riga, P. "Compulsory Medical Treatment of Adults." *Catholic University Law Review* 22 (1976): 105.

Robertson, J. "*Cruzan* and the Constitutional Status of Nontreatment Decisions for Incompetent Patients." *Georgia Law Review* 25 (1991): 1139.

Stacy, T. "Death, Privacy, and the Free Exercise of Religion." *Cornell Law Review* 77 (1992): 490.

Stone, A. "The Right to Die: New Problems for Law and Medicine and Psychiatry." *Emory Law Journal* 37 (1988): 627.

Swartz, M. "The Patient Who Refuses Medical Treatment: A Dilemma for Hospitals and Physicians." *American Journal of Law and Medicine* 11 (1985): 147.

"The Right to Die: An Extension of the Right to Privacy." *Journal of Maritime Law and Commerce* 18 (1985): 895.

PART II

DECISIONMAKING PROCEDURES FOR ADULTS

CHAPTER 3

BASIC PRINCIPLES OF MEDICAL DECISIONMAKING

§ 3.1 Scope of Part II

The chapters in **Part II** explain the legally accepted procedures governing decisionmaking about medical treatment. As explained in **Chapter 2,** all patients, whether competent or incompetent, have a right to have life-sustaining treatment forgone, subject to whatever limitations may exist on that right. These substantive limitations are discussed in **Chapters 7** through **9.** However, personal exercise of the right is limited to patients with decisionmaking capacity.

The right to have treatment administered or to have it withheld or withdrawn is exercised through the informed consent doctrine, which is the topic of this chapter. When patients possess decisionmaking capacity (that is, they are competent), they must give informed consent to be treated, and if consent is withheld or revoked, treatment must not be administered or it must be halted, respectively. The administration of treatment to a competent patient without informed consent renders the person administering the treatment subject to liability for a variety of torts, including battery, negligence, and intentional infliction of emotional distress.[1]

If a patient lacks decisionmaking capacity, by definition informed consent cannot be obtained from the patient. Decisionmaking capacity and competence are critical concepts because they determine whether the patient is legally entitled to act on his own behalf or whether someone else must act for him. Thus, the fundamental implication of possessing decisionmaking capacity is that one has the right to exercise the right to control one's body. For patients lacking capacity, exercise of that right must be by a third party. The meaning and effect of incompetence are discussed in **Chapter 4,** and the procedures for determining incompetence are discussed in **Chapter 5.** If a patient is incompetent, someone must be appointed to serve as the patient's surrogate decisionmaker—that is, to receive the information required by the informed consent doctrine and then to make a decision about whether to treat or forgo treating the patient. This subject is also discussed in **Chapter 5.**

---

[1] See **Ch. 16.**

§ 3.2 Introduction to the Doctrine of Informed Consent

The legal doctrine of informed consent prescribes the manner in which decisions are to be made to administer or forgo treatment, including life-sustaining medical treatment. This doctrine has developed primarily, though not entirely, in response to lawsuits brought by injured patients for damages based on two related but distinct theories: a battery theory, claiming that the physician failed to obtain the patient's consent to treatment, and a negligence theory, claiming that the physician failed to disclose adequate information about treatment. This chapter discusses informed consent as the means by which decisions should be made between competent patients and their physicians or by surrogates of incompetent patients and the physicians for such patients. The doctrine of informed consent also creates a basis for liability; this is discussed in **Chapter 17.**

The informed consent doctrine establishes the right of patients to make binding decisions about the kinds of health care they wish to have or wish to forgo. It also participates in establishing limits on the extent of this right and delineates the responsibilities and rights of physicians in this decisionmaking process. Justice Cardozo's dictum that "[e]very human being of adult years and sound mind has a right to determine what shall be done with his own body"[2]—so often repeated it has become as trite as it is true—captures these principles succinctly. This is not merely a recognition that individuals have a right to consent to medical treatment, but that there is a corollary right to refuse to consent; that is, the patient has a right to *make decisions* about medical treatment. This right is variously referred to as the right of self-determination, autonomy, or privacy.[3]

The legal doctrine of informed consent establishes the process by which decisions are to be made for competent patients and by surrogates on behalf of incompetent patients. Most fundamentally, it stands for the proposition that there is to be a decisionmaking process and that when possible the patient is to be a participant in it (and when not possible, informed consent must be obtained from the patient's surrogate unless one of the recognized exceptions to the informed consent requirements applies). Just as war is too important to be left to

---

[2] Schloendorff v. Society of N.Y. Hosp., 105 N.E. 92 (N.Y. 1914). *See also* Union Pac. Ry. v. Botsford, 141 U.S. 250 (1891); Cruzan v. Harmon, 760 S.W.2d 408, 417 (Mo. 1988), *aff'd sub nom.* Cruzan v. Director, 497 U.S. 261 (1990) ("The doctrine of informed consent arose in recognition of the value society places on a person's autonomy and as the primary vehicle by which a person can protect the integrity of his body. If one can consent to treatment, one can also refuse it. Thus, as a necessary corollary to informed consent, the right to refuse treatment arose.").

[3] See §§ **2.7** and **2.8.**

generals, the question of whether a patient is to receive treatment and, if so, what treatment should be administered is too important to be left solely to physicians. The patient is not to be relegated to the position of an object with merely the power to veto decisions made by others but is to be a participant and the final authority in making decisions that affect, first and foremost, his own body and life.

§ 3.3 —Competent Patients

The decisionmaking process for competent patients can be summarized simply: the requirements of the informed consent doctrine need to be met, and it then must be determined whether there are applicable substantive limitations on the patient's right to refuse life-sustaining treatment, such as countervailing state interests adequate to override the patient's interests.[4] Procedurally, informed consent envisions a private process between patient and physician that does not ordinarily require recourse to the courts.[5]

The informed consent doctrine requires that decisions about health care be made in a collaborative manner between physician and patient.[6] At the outset, decisionmaking about forgoing life-sustaining treatment should proceed in the same manner as decisionmaking about any other treatment.[7] The physician should initiate a conversation with the patient to provide the patient with information material for decisionmaking.[8] In the course of fulfilling the obligations imposed by the informed consent doctrine, the physician may begin to suspect that the patient lacks decisionmaking capacity. If this occurs, the process

---

[4] **NJ:** *In re* Farrell, 529 A.2d 404, 413 (N.J. 1987).

WA: *In re* Colyer, 660 P.2d 738, 744 (Wash. 1983) ("A competent patient may refuse treatment under the informed consent doctrine."). See **Ch. 8.**

[5] National Ctr. for State Courts, Guidelines for State Court Decision Making in Life-Sustaining Medical Treatment Cases 44 (2d ed. 1992) (standard 6).

[6] **MD:** 73 Md. Op. Att'y Gen. 253, 289 (Op. No. 88-046, Oct. 17, 1988) (Decisionmaking about forgoing life-sustaining treatment is to be a collaborative process among physicians and family.).

[7] **AL:** Camp v. White, 510 So. 2d 166, 168 (Ala. 1987) ("The doctors decided that the time had come to discuss the situation with Mrs. Camp's family. A consultation was arranged and the doctors informed the family of the situation and conveyed to them their recommendation that Mrs. Camp not be put back on the respirator-ventilator. The family in turn consulted with Mrs. Camp. She was informed of her situation and of the doctor's opinion that a return to the breathing machine would be permanent. Mrs. Camp was mentally alert. She made the decision not to return to the respirator-ventilator.").

NJ: *In re* Farrell, 529 A.2d 404, 414 (N.J. 1987) ("[S]ociety must ensure that a patient who has decided to forego life-sustaining treatment . . . is informed about his or her prognosis, the medical alternatives available, and the risk involved.").

NY: *Cf.* Saunders v. State, 492 N.Y.S.2d 510 (Sup. Ct. Nassau County 1985).

[8] See § **3.15.**

of decisionmaking for competent patients needs to be aborted and further inquiry into the patient's decisionmaking capacity made.[9]

There is ordinarily no need for judicial involvement when competent patients make medical decisions, whether about life-sustaining medical treatment or otherwise,[10] unless there is uncertainty about whether in fact the patient possesses decisionmaking capacity. In that case, a judicial proceeding might, but does not necessarily need to, be instituted.[11] If the patient possesses decisionmaking capacity and, after being provided with adequate information to render an informed decision, refuses treatment, there is ordinarily no need for a judicial proceeding.[12]

§ 3.4 —Incompetent Patients

Personal exercise of the right to make decisions about medical treatment is limited to patients with decisionmaking capacity. However, incompetent patients have a right to have a surrogate make decisions about whether to administer or forgo life-sustaining treatment,[13] consistent with the appropriate standard[14] and subject to whatever other limitations may exist on that right.[15] For patients lacking capacity, exercise of that right must be by a third party. Conversely, when a patient is competent, decisions must not be made by a third party[16] unless the patient waives the right to make the decision personally.[17]

---

[9] **NJ:** *In re* Farrell, 529 A.2d 404, 414 (N.J. 1987) ("[S]ociety must ensure that a patient who has decided to forego life-sustaining treatment is competent.").

[10] **CA:** Thor v. Superior Court, 855 P.2d 375, 389 (Cal. 1993) ("[J]udicial intervention . . . tends to denigrate the principle of personal autonomy, substituting a species of legal paternalism for the medical paternalism the concept of informed consent seeks to eschew. . . . Judicial scrutiny therefore should be considered as a course of last resort."); Bartling v. Superior Court, 209 Cal. Rptr. 220, 226 (Ct. App. 1984).

See **Ch. 5.**

[11] See **§ 5.36.**

[12] **NV:** McKay v. Bergstedt, 801 P.2d 617 (Nev. 1990) (judicial weighing of countervailing state interests required when competent, nonterminally-ill patient rejects life support).

See **§ 5.42.**

[13] See **§ 2.5.**

[14] See **Ch. 7.**

[15] See **Chs. 8** and **9.**

[16] **GA:** Kirby v. Spivey, 307 S.E.2d 538 (Ga. Ct. App. 1983).

IN: Payne v. Marion Gen. Hosp., 549 N.E.2d 1043 (Ind. Ct. App. 1990) (patient's informed consent to entry of do-not-resuscitate order required, and not a surrogate's, if the patient were competent).

WV: Belcher v. Charleston Area Medical Ctr., 422 S.E.2d 827 (W. Va. 1992) (same).

[17] See **§ 3.26.**

When a patient lacks decisionmaking capacity, the physician's duties of providing information and obtaining consent are transferred from the patient to the surrogate. Physicians are not ordinarily authorized to administer treatment merely because the patient lacks decisionmaking capacity; rather, the informed consent of the patient's legally authorized representative is necessary.[18] Only when a patient lacks decisionmaking capacity and there is an emergency requiring the immediate rendition of treatment may the attending physician treat without consent.[19]

INFORMED CONSENT: THEORY AND PRACTICE

§ 3.5 The "Idea" of Informed Consent: Collaborative Decisionmaking

The law of informed consent began and has developed almost exclusively through the common-law process, at least until the mid-1970s, when about half of the state legislatures enacted statutes dealing with informed consent.[20] Even in the aftermath of the enactment of these statutes, however, the bulk of the development of the law continues to be judicial. In addition to the large body of judicial opinions, there has been a substantial body of writing on the subject by scholars in a variety of disciplines, primarily law but also philosophy, medicine, and the social sciences. These writings, in conjunction with the case law, have created a body of thought on informed consent that, in an iterative process, has worked its way back into the judicial discussions of the subject.

Taken together, the judicial opinions and scholarly writings have given rise to what Professor Jay Katz, a leading theorist of informed consent, refers to as the

---

[18] **OH:** Estate of Leach v. Shapiro, 469 N.E.2d 1047, 1053 (Ohio Ct. App. 1984) ("Absent an emergency defendants had an obligation to secure consent for Mrs. Leach's treatment from one authorized to act in her behalf, since Mrs. Leach was not capable of consenting, or by court order.").

Council on Ethical & Judicial Affairs, American Medical Ass'n, Code of Medical Ethics § 2.20, at 36, § 2.215, at 52 (1994).

See §§ **5.15** through **5.24** and **Ch. 14.**

[19] Estate of Leach v. Shapiro, 469 N.E.2d at 1053 (Ohio Ct. App. 1984) ("If an emergency existed . . . when . . . life support systems were first employed, such an emergency would ordinarily give rise to an implied consent."). See § **3.23.**

[20] *See* 3 President's Comm'n for the Study of Ethical Problems in Medicine & Biomedical & Behavioral Research, Making Health Care Decisions: The Ethical and Legal Implications of Informed Consent in the Patient-Practitioner Relationship app. L (1982); Meisel & Kabnick, *Informed Consent to Medical Treatment: An Analysis of Recent Legislation,* 41 U. Pitt. L. Rev. 408 (1980).

idea of informed consent.[21] The core of the idea is that decisions about the medical care a person will receive, if any, are to be made in a collaborative manner between patient and physician. That is, if patients are to "chart their own course understandably,"[22] there must be collaborative, mutual, or shared decisionmaking between physician and patient.[23] Each has an essential role to play. The physician brings to medical decisionmaking experience and expertise in both the science and art of medicine. The patient brings knowledge of his own values, goals, hopes, aspirations, and preferences.[24]

This is not to say that all patients know themselves perfectly, but that it is more likely that they know these things about themselves better than does their physician. But even if that is not so, even if the patient is particularly obtuse and the physician particularly perceptive and sagacious, within broad limits[25] it is the patient's right to make "mistakes" about what is best. Indeed, what is best for a patient, both ethically and legally, is defined as what the patient subjectively believes is best and therefore, by definition, is not a "mistake." Thus, the idea of informed consent asserts that physicians must tolerate patients' decisions that the physicians themselves believe are not best for the patients from a medical perspective.

§ 3.6 Goals of Informed Consent

The fundamental goals of informed consent are twofold. The first and clearly most important is patient autonomy or self-determination in the control of the patient's own body,[26] which protects both bodily and psychic integrity. This goal is effectuated by allowing patients to make their own decisions about health care

---

[21] J. Katz, The Silent World of Doctor and Patient at xvi & passim (1984) ("To distinguish between what judges have done and what they have aspired to, one must draw sharp distinctions between the *legal* doctrine, as promulgated by judges, and the *idea* of informed consent, based on a commitment to individual self-determination.").

[22] Canterbury v. Spence, 464 F.2d 772, 781 (D.C. Cir.), *cert. denied,* 409 U.S. 1064 (1972).

[23] **CA:** *See* Bouvia v. Superior Court (Glenchur), 225 Cal. Rptr. 297, 303 (Ct. App. 1986).

NJ: *See In re* Farrell, 529 A.2d 404, 418 (N.J. 1987) (O'Hern, J., concurring) (citing President's Comm'n for the Study of Ethical Problems in Medicine & Biomedical & Behavorial Research, Deciding to Forego Life-Sustaining Treatment 48 (1983)).

[24] Thor v. Superior Court, 855 P.2d 375, 380 (Cal. 1993) ("[T]he relative balance of benefit and burden must lie within the patient's exclusive estimation: 'That personal weighing of values is the essence of self-determination.'"). *See generally* 1 President's Comm'n for the Study of Ethical Problems in Medicine & Biomedical & Behavioral Research, Making Health Care Decisions: The Ethical and Legal Implications of Informed Consent in the Patient-Practitioner Relationship 41–51 (1982).

[25] See §§ **3.24** and **3.25.**

[26] *In re* Farrell, 529 A.2d 404, 410 (N.J. 1987). See §§ **2.6** through **2.8.**

based on their own values.[27] The core notion is the primacy of individual choice.[28]

The second fundamental goal of informed consent is that patients be enabled to exercise their autonomy rationally and intelligently. In order to do so, patients must be provided the information needed for making rational and intelligent decisions. The aim of informed consent is that patients be enabled to make such decisions. Providing patients with relevant information about treatment does not guarantee that they will make intelligent decisions nor does it even guarantee that they will use the information. But without a requirement that such information be provided, the likelihood of rational decisionmaking diminishes. Whether informed consent *requires* that patients make rational and intelligent decisions is another question.[29]

§ 3.7 Conversation About Therapy: Risks versus Options

Collaborative decisionmaking requires that the physician and patient talk, perhaps more than once,[30] about the therapeutic (and/or diagnostic) options that are relevant to the patient. Often both courts and physicians treat informed consent as if it were merely a duty to warn a patient of the possible risks of treatment[31] so that in the event of a lawsuit the physician will have a defense of assumption of risk.

The *idea* of informed consent, however, does not contemplate that informed consent be akin to a medical Miranda warning. Physicians and patients are not natural adversaries (as are the police and criminal suspects), and the law should not encourage them to be. Whether information is provided orally, embodied in a consent form, or both, the goal is not to warn the patient, but to provide enough information to permit intelligent decisionmaking. Therefore, the conversation between physician and patient should resemble ordinary conversation in which people speak, ask questions, and interrupt each other. The most important element of this conversation (and thus of informed consent) should be the patient's therapeutic options rather than the risks of the proposed treatment.

---

[27] **CA:** Thor v. Superior Court, 855 P.2d 375, 380 (Cal. 1993) ("[T]he relative balance of benefit and burden must lie within the patient's exclusive estimation: 'That personal weighing of values is the essence of self-determination.'"); Drabick v. Drabick, 245 Cal. Rptr. 840, 854 (Ct. App. 1988) ("Medical care decisions must be guided by the individual patient's interests and values.").

[28] *In re* Jobes, 529 A.2d 434, 453–54 (N.J. 1987) (Handler, J., concurring).

[29] See § **3.24.**

[30] See § **3.8.**

[31] *See* J. Katz, The Silent World of Doctor and Patient (1984); Katz, *Informed Consent—A Fairy Tale: Law's Vision,* 39 U. Pitt. L. Rev. 137 (1977).

Besides reducing informed consent to a duty to warn, a focus on risks rather than options is based on the unarticulated assumptions that there is a single best course of action for the patient to take and that the physician knows what this course of action is. Apart from often not being the case, this view relegates the patient to a role of acquiescing in or vetoing the physician's recommendation. Such a view is merely a shell of the right to decide about health care. A genuine right to decide necessitates the disclosure of relevant information about the range of available alternative therapeutic or diagnostic procedures.[32]

Of course, physicians in general do have expertise in deciding what is the best treatment from a medical perspective; however, in many situations there is not even a professional consensus about what is best. Consequently, physicians are not prohibited by the informed consent doctrine from giving advice to patients—indeed, they have the responsibility to do so[33]—and many patients desperately want such advice, sometimes to the exclusion of anything else.[34] It is important that advice giving not shade into coercion.[35] Even when there is a consensus in the medical profession about the most advisable medical course, an emphasis on risks rather than options is more likely to lead to a formalistic implementation of informed consent rather than to a process of decisionmaking in which the patient is permitted to bring to bear his own important, personal, and subjective considerations.

§ 3.8 Decisionmaking as a Process

An important corollary of the view of informed consent as collaborative decisionmaking and of the notion that physicians and patients should engage in a conversation about therapy is that informed consent is a process, not an event. It is rare for the care of a patient to involve only a single decision or for all the needed information to be available when a decision must be made. It is more common that treatment strategies evolve over time as additional information becomes available.[36] In end-of-life decisionmaking, there are a variety of points at which decisions can be made to limit treatment, rather than one dramatic decision to continue treatment or forgo treatment and allow death to ensue.[37]

---

[32] See § **3.15.**

[33] Thor v. Superior Court, 855 P.2d 375, 386 (Cal. 1993) ("Doctors have the responsibility to advise patients fully of those matters relevant and necessary to making a voluntary and intelligent choice.").

[34] See § **3.26.**

[35] See § **3.18.**

[36] *See* P. Appelbaum et al., Informed Consent: Legal Theory and Clinical Practice 151–74 (1987); Lidz et al., *Two Models of Implementing Informed Consent,* 148 Archives Internal Med. 1385 (1988).

[37] *See, e.g.,* Fried & Gillick, *Medical Decision-Making in the Last Six Months of Life: Choices about Limitation of Care,* 42 J. Am. Geriatrics Soc'y 303 (1994) ("[C]are is frequently limited before a patient's final illness in the course of routine practice.").

This is frequently not the vision of medical decisionmaking that is always conveyed by the case law. Rather, the cases are based on an "event model" which assumes that informed consent is an event that is only connected with the therapeutic process at a single point in time.

Treating informed consent as an event does not best facilitate patients' being informed. Information is more effectively assimilated when it is provided repetitively over a sustained period. Furthermore, if information is provided at one point, rather than gradually, and if that point is the culmination of a long diagnostic process, it is likely that the information is being provided when a patient's anxiety is at a peak, thereby further impeding the assimilation of information.

§ 3.9 Informed Consent in Practice

Informed consent in practice has turned out to be considerably different from the theory of informed consent. Although it is easy to understand that physicians may find it difficult to accommodate the way in which they practice medicine to the doctrine—calling as it does for a substantial restructuring of the traditional doctor-patient relationship through a transfer of much authority from physician to patient[38]—the courts have had almost as much difficulty in living up to the promise.

Judicial Practice

Legal scholars and medical ethicists have made the doctrine of informed consent either into something—a right of "thorough-going self-determination"[39]—the courts either never really intended it to be despite their lofty prose or into something they have later realized is difficult to enforce. The same cases proclaiming the right of patient self-determination—whether in the broad patient-oriented formulation of the doctrine[40] or the more restrictive physician-oriented formulation[41]—have devised rules making enforcement of that right particularly difficult.[42] In the dicta of cases, where it mattered least to the litigants, the courts proclaimed in resounding tones a thoroughgoing right of self-determination. But when it came to applying the right, the result was often quite different. The full implications of the informed consent doctrine may well have frightened the courts.

---

[38] *See* J. Katz, The Silent World of Doctor and Patient (1984); Note, *Restructuring Informed Consent: Legal Theory for the Doctor-Patient Relationship,* 79 Yale L.J. 1533 (1970).

[39] Natanson v. Kline, 350 P.2d 1093, 1104 (Kan. 1960).

[40] *See, e.g.,* Canterbury v. Spence, 464 F.2d 772 (D.C. Cir. 1972). See **§ 3.14.**

[41] *See, e.g.,* Natanson v. Kline, 350 P.2d 1093 (Kan. 1960). See **§ 3.14.**

[42] *See* Katz, *Informed Consent—A Fairy Tale: Law's Vision,* 39 U. Pitt. L. Rev. 137 (1977).

Clinical Practice

Informed consent has been greeted with a mixture of skepticism and hostility by the medical profession. The opponents of informed consent insist that, by promoting patient self-determination, it undermines significant competing values and, if taken seriously, would make medical practice virtually impossible. Informed consent has been criticized for wasting valuable time that could be spent in rendering treatment, in part because patients do not understand what they are told and in other part because they do not want to be informed. It is said to undermine the trust patients need to place in their physicians if they are to be successfully treated, and it requires disclosure of information about the possibility of the risks of treatment or the failure of treatment that may harm the patient by leading to a psychologically induced self-fulfilling prophecy. Furthermore, the goal of disclosing information to patients about treatment so they may make their own decisions is said to be illusory because disclosure can and usually will be made by the physician in such a way as to assure that the patient agrees to the physician's recommended treatment. It is also said that patients have their minds made up before they acquire the information the informed consent doctrine requires they receive, and the receipt of this information does not change their decision. For other patients, the disclosure of information may needlessly frighten them, possibly to the extent that they refuse necessary treatment.[43]

In actual clinical practice, the opposition to informed consent manifested in medical writing is not as apparent as is disinterest or apathy. Unless one equates the signing of consent forms with genuine informed consent,[44] it is safe to say that informed consent is honored as much in the breach as in the observance in clinical practice;[45] the *idea* of informed consent is almost exclusively a creature of legal theory.

§ 3.10 Consent Forms and Informed Consent

Among health care professionals, there is a tendency to equate the execution of a consent form with obtaining informed consent. Some honestly believe that as long as a patient has signed a consent form authorizing treatment, and that the form either recites the information about the treatment, and especially about the risks of treatment, or says that the patient has been given this information orally, informed consent has been obtained.

---

[43] *See* Meisel, *The "Exceptions" to the Informed Consent Doctrine: Striking a Balance Between Competing Values in Medical Decisionmaking,* 1979 Wis. L. Rev. 413, 415–16.

[44] See **§ 3.10.**

[45] *See* C. Lidz et al., Informed Consent: A Study of Decisionmaking in Psychiatry (1984); Lidz & Meisel, *Informed Consent and the Structure of Medical Care, in* 2 President's Comm'n for the Study of Ethical Problems in Medicine & Biomedical & Behavioral Research, Making Health Care Decisions: The Ethical and Legal Implications of Informed Consent in the Patient-Practitioner Relationship app. C (1982).

This is not so, either in fact or in law.[46] Empirical studies demonstrate that patients have a great deal of difficulty understanding consent forms. Sometimes this is because the forms are written in complex, formal language and are laden with technical jargon so that even reasonably well-educated people might not understand it. The anxiety that patients frequently experience either from their illness or from the status differential they perceive between themselves and their physicians also contributes to their difficulty in understanding the forms.[47] Finally, education of any sort is difficult to accomplish in a standardized, written manner. Consequently, consent forms frequently do not serve the goal of making patients into informed decisionmakers.

In practice, decisions are made without regard to consent forms. Consent forms are often not given to a patient as an aid to decisionmaking while trying to make the decision, but only after a decision has been made and agreed to by all parties. The information in the forms rarely affects a decision that has already been made. Thus, consent forms are treated by both patients and health care professionals as a ritual for confirming a decision already made, rather than as a step in the decisionmaking process. In effect, consent forms symbolize the patient's agreement to a particular medical procedure, thus providing some evidence of consent. Consent forms do not ensure that patients understand and voluntarily consent to these decisions.[48]

Consent forms are not totally devoid of practical value. They remind physicians that informed consent must be obtained. A consent form signed by the patient serves as evidence that the patient at least had an opportunity to read the form (though not necessarily that the patient did in fact read it) and then authorized treatment. In other words, a consent form may make out a prima facie defense for the physician, but it by no means wins the case.[49] (In some jurisdictions, statutes accord varying kinds of presumptions to properly executed consent forms. However, it is less than certain that these statutes work any substantial change in the common law, either substantively or procedurally.[50]) On the other hand, consent forms can provide physicians and health care administrators with a false sense of security, leading them to believe that a signed form constitutes informed consent, which it clearly does not.

---

[46] See § **3.21.**

[47] Meisel & Roth, *Toward an Informed Discussion of Informed Consent: A Review of the Empirical Studies,* 25 Ariz. L. Rev. 265 (1983), *reprinted in* 3 Bioethics Rep. 361 (Oct. 1983).

[48] C. Lidz et al., Informed Consent: A Study of Decisionmaking in Psychiatry 318 (1984); Lidz & Meisel, *Informed Consent and the Structure of Medical Care, in* 2 President's Comm'n for the Study of Ethical Problems in Medicine & Biomedical & Behavioral Research, Making Health Care Decisions: The Ethical and Legal Implications of Informed Consent in the Patient-Practitioner Relationship app. C (1982).

[49] See § **3.21.**

[50] P. Appelbaum et al., Informed Consent: Legal Theory and Clinical Practice 177–79 (1987); Meisel & Kabnick, *Informed Consent to Medical Treatment: An Analysis of Recent Legislation,* 41 U. Pitt. L. Rev. 408, 477 (1980).

§ 3.11 Treatments Requiring Informed Consent

To many judges and commentators, the paradigm of informed consent envisions a single physician in private practice administering a discrete hospital-based treatment, usually (though not always) a surgical procedure. The battery-law origins of informed consent are probably largely responsible for this prototype. Even historically, however, consent to treatment was required not only for surgical procedures but also for any medical procedure, therapeutic or diagnostic, involving contact with the patient's body, such as physical examination.

With the transformation of the consent requirement into informed consent, the scope of applicability has expanded to account for virtually all therapeutic or diagnostic procedures. Informed consent seeks not merely to protect against nonconsensual touching, but also to permit patients to choose whether to be treated or diagnosed at all. The precise nature of the treatment is irrelevant to whether informed consent must be obtained because it is the right of choice that is at stake.[51] One of the earliest cases in which informed consent was applied involved administering radiation therapy,[52] and there are also cases applying informed consent to medications.[53] Nonetheless, in the very small number of jurisdictions either still treating the failure to obtain informed consent as a battery or confused about the issue, contact with the patient's body may still be required before the duty to disclose information about therapy arises.[54]

THE LAW OF INFORMED CONSENT

§ 3.12 Introduction

The legal requirement to obtain informed consent actually imposes two duties on physicians: the duty to inform and the duty to obtain consent. Though related

---

[51] Shultz, *From Informed Consent to Patient Choice: A New Protected Interest,* 95 Yale L.J. 219 (1985).

[52] **KS:** Natanson v. Kline, 350 P.2d 1093 (Kan. 1960).

VA: *See also* Hunter v. Burroughs, 96 S.E. 360 (Va. 1918) (physician has duty under negligence law to warn patient of the dangers of radiation therapy).

[53] **IA:** Van Iperen v. Van Bramer, 392 N.W.2d 480, 483 (Iowa 1986).

VT: Perkins v. Windsor Hosp. Corp., 455 A.2d 810, 813 (Vt. 1982).

[54] Wu v. Spence, 605 A.2d 395 (Pa. Super. Ct. 1992) (administration of medical treatment does not meet requirements for liability for lack of informed consent because there is no technical battery); Boyer v. Smith, 497 A.2d 646 (Pa. Super. Ct. 1985) (same); Malloy v. Shanahan, 421 A.2d 803 (Pa. Super. Ct. 1980) (same).

to each other, they are actionable as separate legal causes of action, the former usually as negligence and the latter as a battery.[55]

§ 3.13 Duty to Inform

The essence of informed consent—indeed the feature distinguishing it from the predecessor requirement of simple consent to medical treatment—is the duty imposed on physicians to inform patients. The source of this duty is the patient's need to have information as a condition of exercising the right of self-determination in a truly autonomous fashion. In addition, the heavy dependence of patients on physicians for their well-being requires the disclosure of information in this fiduciary relationship that would not be required in an arm's-length transaction.[56]

§ 3.14 —Standard of Care

As in negligence cases generally, the standard of care (or, as it is referred to in informed consent cases, the standard of disclosure) is the standard by which the adequacy of the physician's disclosure is measured, thus allowing the factfinder to evaluate whether the duty of disclosure has been fulfilled. Developed in the context of litigation about what particular physicians should have told particular patients, the standard of care, unfortunately, functions far better as a standard for determining breach of duty and hence liability than it does as a guide to physicians for determining what to tell patients.

In cases of professional liability, the standard of care is generally determined by referring to customary professional practice,[57] the proof of which generally requires expert evidence. However, even in cases of professional negligence, the standard of care may be determined by the trier of fact without expert testimony if the matter is one that is within the knowledge and competency of laypersons.[58]

---

[55] **DC:** *In re* A.C., 573 A.2d 1235, 1243 (D.C. 1990) ("[A] surgeon who performs an operation without the patient's consent may be guilty of a battery . . . or . . . if the surgeon obtains an insufficiently informed consent, he or she may be liable for negligence.").

OH: Anderson v. St. Francis-St. George Hosp., 614 N.E.2d 841 (Ohio Ct. App. 1992) (administration of cardiopulmonary resuscitation after refusal by patient, as documented in do-not-resuscitate order, is actionable as battery).

UT: Lounsbury v. Capel, 836 P.2d 188 (Utah 1992).

[56] *See, e.g.,* Canterbury v. Spence, 464 F.2d 772, 782 (D.C. Cir. 1972) ("The patient's reliance upon the physician is a trust of the kind which traditionally has exacted obligations beyond those associated with arm's-length transactions.").

[57] Restatement (Second) of Torts § 299A (1965); W.P. Keeton et al., Prosser and Keeton on the Law of Torts § 32, at 189 (5th ed. 1984).

[58] W.P. Keeton et al., Prosser and Keeton on the Law of Torts § 32, at 189; 1 D. Louisell & H. Williams, Medical Malpractice para. 8.05, at 8-77 to 8-88 (1993).

Furthermore, it is well established that customary professional practice does not determine the standard of care but is merely evidence of it.[59] In the end, it is for the courts to say what is required to avoid being negligent.[60]

Two distinct approaches have developed articulating the standard of care in informed consent cases: a so-called professional (or customary or "reasonable physician") standard and a legal (or lay or "reasonable person") standard. The earlier informed consent cases adopted the traditional approach that the standard of care should be determined by customary professional practice. As the doctrine of informed consent matured, however, other courts concluded that the standard of care should be determined by law rather than by customary practice. The jurisdictions are now about evenly divided on this issue.[61]

Under the professional standard of care, a physician is required to disclose to a patient that kind and degree of information that a reasonably prudent physician under like circumstances would disclose.[62] Consequently, proof of the standard requires expert evidence. In jurisdictions adopting a legal standard of care, a physician is required to disclose that information that a reasonable patient would find material in deciding about the treatment in question. No expert evidence is required, nor indeed permitted, as to what a reasonable patient would find material; this is a question peculiarly within the competence of the jury.[63]

§ 3.15 —Elements of Disclosure

First the judicial decisions and later the statutory law have specified certain kinds (or "elements") of information that must be disclosed in order for the physician to comply with the duty to disclose. A physician who proposes to administer treatment must, before doing so, provide a patient with information about the risks, benefits, nature, and purpose of the proposed treatment, as well as alternative treatments. The focus in the case law, however, has been almost exclusively on disclosure of risks. This emphasis has been so pronounced that the courts have been accused of transforming the informed consent doctrine into little more than a duty to warn of the adverse risks of treatment, making it into a kind of medical Miranda warning.[64] Virtually all of the case law involves litigation arising from situations in which a physician has failed to disclose to a patient a risk of treatment. From the outset, however, the dicta

---

[59] Canterbury v. Spence, 464 F.2d 772, 784 (D.C. Cir. 1972).

[60] *See* T.J. Hooper, 60 F.2d 737 (2d Cir.), *cert. denied,* 287 U.S. 662 (1932); Helling v. Carey, 519 P.2d 981 (Wash. 1974).

[61] Frantz, Annotation, *Modern Status of Views as to General Measure of Physician's Duty to Inform Patient of Risks of Proposed Treatment,* 88 A.L.R.3d 1008 (1978).

[62] *Id.* at 1023–27, § 4(b).

[63] *Id.* at 1034–43, § 6.

[64] *See* J. Katz, The Silent World of Doctor and Patient (1984); Katz, *Informed Consent—A Fairy Tale: Law's Vision,* 39 U. Pitt. L. Rev. 137 (1977).

of the cases have been clear that physicians are also required to provide patients with information about other relevant aspects of treatment: the nature and purpose of the treatment, the anticipated benefits, and the alternative treatments, including the option of no treatment.[65] More recently, cases have begun to hold that the failure to disclose alternative courses of action may be the basis for liability.[66]

These elements of disclosure, in conjunction with the general standard of care, define the nature and scope of a physician's duty to assure that, when a patient consents to treatment, he does so in light of information relevant to that decision. When combined with the general standard of care, these elements require the physician to disclose a reasonable amount of information about the risks, benefits, nature, and purpose of treatment and treatment alternatives—reasonableness being determined by whether the general standard of care is a professional or legal standard. To illustrate: in a jurisdiction adopting a professional standard, physicians are obligated to inform patients of, among other things, those risks of treatment that a reasonable physician would disclose. On the other hand, in a jurisdiction applying a legal standard of care, physicians must tell patients about, among other things, the alternative treatments that a reasonable patient would find material to making a decision whether to undergo or forgo treatment.

Physicians are obligated to provide patients with information in a manner reasonably calculated to make the patient understand it, which involves the use of nontechnical, lay language: "The discussion need not be a disquisition, and surely the physician is not compelled to give his patient a short medical

---

[65] **AZ:** Rasmussen v. Fleming, 741 P.2d 674, 683 (Ariz. 1987) ("[T]he patient must have a clear understanding of the risks and benefits of the proposed treatment alternatives or nontreatment, along with a full understanding of the nature of the disease and the prognosis.").

CA: Thor v. Superior Court, 855 P.2d 375, 381 (Cal. 1993).

NV: McKay v. Bergstedt, 801 P.2d 617, 628 (Nev. 1990) (necessary to fully inform non-terminally ill person dependent on ventilator of "care alternatives that would have been available to him").

WA: *In re* Colyer, 660 P.2d 738, 743 (Wash. 1983) ("Such information must include the possibility of alternative treatment or no treatment at all.").

[66] **CA4:** *Cf.* Lipscomb v. Memorial Hosp., 733 F.2d 332 (4th Cir. 1984) (Maryland law) (plaintiff's judgment based on nondisclosure of materialized risk, but defendant/doctor also failed to disclose alternatives such as antacids and other "conservative measures short of surgery" in treatment of hiatal hernia).

AZ: McGrady v. Wright, 729 P.2d 338 (Ariz. Ct. App. 1986).

CT: Logan v. Greenwich Hosp. Ass'n, 465 A.2d 294 (Conn. 1983).

MD: Sard v. Hardy, 379 A.2d 1014 (Md. 1977).

OK: Smith v. Karen S. Reisig, M.D., Inc., 686 P.2d 285, 289 (Okla. 1984).

WA: Keogan v. Holy Family Hosp., 622 P.2d 1246 (Wash. 1980).

See generally Derrick, Annotation, *Medical Malpractice: Liability for Failure of Physician to Inform Patient of Alternative Modes of Diagnosis or Treatment,* 38 A.L.R.4th 900 (1985).

education; the disclosure rule summons the physician only to a reasonable explanation. . . . That means generally informing the patient in nontechnical terms as to what is at stake."[67]

§ 3.16 Duty to Obtain Consent

It has long been recognized that a physician has a duty to obtain a patient's consent to treatment and that the failure to do so gives rise to liability for battery.[68] Because the major innovation of the informed consent doctrine is the requirement that physicians inform patients about treatment before undertaking to administer or order it, contemporary discussions and analysis of the duty to obtain consent have taken a back seat to discussions of the duty to disclose. Despite the fact that the duty to obtain consent substantially antedates the duty to disclose, just what constitutes obtaining legally valid consent remains somewhat murky. Ironically, the uncertainty has probably been intensified rather than clarified by the long debate over informed consent.

§ 3.17 —Meaning of Consent

The phrase "informed consent" is unfortunate in one respect because it connotes that the expected result of disclosure to the patient is consent to treatment. This overlooks the fact that the purpose of disclosure is to permit patients to make *decisions* about treatment, and a decision may be a refusal as well as a consent. It would be better to speak of "informed decisionmaking" than "informed consent," but "informed consent" is so embedded in common usage and in the usage of the health care and legal professions that any effort to change it would be a slow process at best. "Informed consent" and "consent" in the discussion that follows should be taken to encompass the broader term "decision," denoting refusal as well as consent.

At the very least, the duty to obtain consent requires that the patient or someone authorized to speak for him[69] grant permission for diagnostic procedures or the administration of therapy. This is what is referred to in law as *assent,*[70] to distinguish it from consent. " '[C]onsent' indicates an 'assent' given under circumstances which make it legally effective."[71] Thus, consent is more than merely giving permission for treatment. What the difference is, however, is not entirely clear in law. Consent, of course, may be implied as well as express,

---

[67] Canterbury v. Spence, 464 F.2d 772, 796 n.27 (D.C. Cir. 1972).

[68] See §§ **17.2** through **17.4.**

[69] See **Ch. 5.**

[70] *See* F. Harper et al., The Law of Torts § 3.10, at 298–309 (1986).

[71] F. Harper & F. James, The Law of Torts § 3.10, at 233 (1956).

but merely failing to object to a physician's statement that he will perform a procedure does not constitute consent.[72]

At least two factors besides permission go into making up a legally valid consent: voluntariness and capacity.[73] There may also be a third: understanding.

§ 3.18 ——Voluntariness

A patient's permission is not legally effective unless it is voluntary[74] and freely given,[75] and without duress,[76] undue influence,[77] or coercion.[78] However, it is far easier to state the requirement than to explain and apply it.[79] Just what constitutes duress[80] or undue influence is not entirely certain. "[S]ome forms of influence by other persons are both normal and positive. But at some point, a point not easy to specify, that influence becomes 'undue,' and is seen as interfering with self-determination."[81]

---

[72] **NY:** Elbaum v. Grace Plaza of Great Neck, Inc., 544 N.Y.S.2d 840, 847 (App. Div. 1989).

[73] *In re* Jobes, 529 A.2d 434, 454 (N.J. 1987) (Handler, J., concurring) ("Self-determination in its purest form thus includes elements of knowledge and volition.").

[74] **CA:** Thor v. Superior Court, 855 P.2d 375, 381 (Cal. 1993) (fact that patient is a prisoner does not necessarily jeopardize voluntariness of his consent).

MO: Cruzan v. Harmon, 760 S.W.2d 408, 417 (Mo. 1988). 1 President's Comm'n for the Study of Ethical Problems in Medicine & Biomedical & Behavioral Research, Making Health Care Decisions: The Ethical and Legal Implications of Informed Consent in the Patient-Practitioner Relationship 63–68 (1982).

See also President's Comm'n for the Study of Ethical Problems in Medicine & Biomedical & Behavioral Research, Deciding to Forego Life-Sustaining Treatment 45–51 (1983) (discussing voluntariness in the context of decisionmaking about life-sustaining treatment) [hereinafter President's Comm'n, Deciding to Forego Life-Sustaining Treatment].

[75] Restatement of Torts § 892, at 486 (1939).

[76] Restatement (Second) of Torts § 892B(3) (1977).

[77] **NJ:** *In re* Jobes, 529 A.2d 434, 454 (N.J. 1987) (Handler, J., concurring).

[78] **AZ:** Rasmussen v. Fleming, 741 P.2d 674, 683 (Ariz. 1987).

CA: Thor v. Superior Court, 855 P.2d 375, 381 (Cal. 1993).

MO: Cruzan v. Harmon, 760 S.W.2d 408, 417 (Mo. 1988).

NJ: *In re* Farrell, 529 A.2d 404, 413 (N.J. 1987).

[79] *In re* Jobes, 529 A.2d at 454 (Handler, J., concurring) ("Voluntariness is . . . a difficult concept. The line between motivations we consider normal and legitimate and those we consider distorting or coercive is not always clear.").

[80] Restatement (Second) of Torts § 892B cmt. j (1977) ("Duress is constraint of another's will by which he is compelled to give consent when he is not in reality willing to do so.").

[81] *In re* Jobes, 529 A.2d at 454 n.5 (Handler, J., concurring).

What case law there is concerning voluntariness has developed mostly outside the context of decisionmaking about medical treatment and within the context of extreme behavior. It is clear that permission extracted by the use, or the threatened or attempted use, of physical force is legally ineffective.[82] Although physical force is easy to describe and identify, it is likely to be virtually nonexistent in the ordinary medical context, with the possible exception of force-feeding.[83]

Duress of this sort is more likely in psychiatric hospitals and in medical situations in prisons. Nonetheless, the mere fact that a patient is incarcerated at the time of making a decision about treatment does not mean that the patient is unable to render a legally voluntary decision.[84] Also, giving consent in the face of a physician's threat to institute legal proceedings if consent is not given does not mean that the consent is freely given.[85] At the other extreme, it is also clear that persuasion of the kind "commonly encountered in daily life [is] without legal effect and [is] not normally characterized as duress."[86]

How far short of physical force behavior may be and still constitute duress is an open question. For instance, although "the threat of a good friend that unless the other consents to particular conduct he will never speak to him again is not a basis for legal relief, even though it does in fact succeed in forcing a reluctant consent,"[87] the same may not be true in the context of a fiduciary relationship such as the physician-patient relationship.[88] Thus, when a physician pressured the family of a patient in a persistent vegetative state to consent to the performance of a gastrostomy—despite the patient's prior expressed wishes not to be kept alive by artificial nutrition and hydration—by repeatedly informing them that legal proceedings would result unless consent was given, the consent was not legally effective.[89]

---

[82] Restatement (Second) of Torts § 892B(3) (1977).

[83] *See, e.g.,* Bouvia v. Superior Court (Glenchur), 225 Cal. Rptr. 297 (Ct. App. 1986) (competent patient force-fed).

[84] **CA:** Thor v. Superior Court, 855 P.2d 375, 390 (Cal. 1993):

> [A]ny individual who suffers a debilitating or life-threatening disease or injury inevitably faces choices in medical decisionmaking affected or even dictated by his or her life circumstances, including resultant depression, limited financial resources, and minimal family or social support systems [citation omitted]. Although in some respects unique, the prison environment is simply one such circumstance in the individual's personal calculus; and we have no basis for assuming it inherently jeopardizes the voluntariness of that process for inmates.

[85] **NY:** Elbaum v. Grace Plaza of Great Neck, Inc., 544 N.Y.S.2d 840, 846 (App. Div. 1989).

[86] Restatement (Second) of Torts § 892B(3) (1977).

[87] *Id.*

[88] *Id.* ("Age, sex, mental capacity, the relation of the parties and antecedent circumstances all may be significant.").

[89] Elbaum v. Grace Plaza of Great Neck, Inc., 544 N.Y.S.2d 840 (App. Div. 1989).

§ 3.19 ——Competence

Consent to treatment is valid only if rendered by one who has the capacity to consent.[90] Although the terms "competence" and "incompetence" are frequently used to refer to this concept, one need not be adjudicated incompetent to lack the capacity to consent to medical treatment.[91] The *Restatement (Second) of Torts* uses "capacity" to describe the concept,[92] and, to avoid confusion, the President's Commission expressly eschewed the use of "competence" and "incompetence" in favor of the more cumbersome but more precise "decisionmaking capacity" and "incapacity."[93] The case law is gradually adopting this usage too.[94] Conversely, one who is adjudicated incompetent does not necessarily lack the capacity to consent, nor does the fact that one is mentally deficient or a child mean that the capacity to consent is necessarily lacking.[95]

What does constitute capacity (and more important, incapacity, since capacity is presumed[96]) to consent to medical treatment is a topic widely debated in the medical literature and almost as widely ignored in law. (Perhaps the latter is the cause of the former.) There appears, however, to be a developing consensus regarding the meaning of capacity in cases dealing with medical decisionmaking, including those concerning life-sustaining treatment. This consensus is toward accepting the meaning of capacity implied in the *Restatement of Torts,* namely the ability to appreciate the nature, extent, or probable consequences of the physician's conduct to which consent is given.[97]

---

[90] **AZ:** Rasmussen v. Fleming, 741 P.2d 674, 683 (Ariz. 1987).

CA: Thor v. Superior Court, 855 P.2d 375, 381 (Cal. 1993).

MO: Cruzan v. Harmon, 760 S.W.2d 408, 417 (Mo. 1988).

Restatement (Second) of Torts §§ 892A(2)(a), 892B(3) (1977).

[91] See **Ch. 4.**

[92] Restatement (Second) of Torts § 892A cmt. b (1977). *But see id.* cmt. a.

[93] 1 President's Comm'n for the Study of Ethical Problems in Medicine & Biomedical & Behavioral Research, Making Health Care Decisions: The Ethical and Legal Implications of Informed Consent in the Patient-Practitioner Relationship 56 (1982). *See also* President's Comm'n, Deciding to Forego Life-Sustaining Treatment 43–45 (1983) (discussing decisionmaking capacity in the context of making decisions about life-sustaining treatment).

[94] **AZ:** Rasmussen v. Fleming, 741 P.2d 674, 683 (Ariz. 1987) ("patient must have the capacity to reason and make judgments").

CA: Thor v. Superior Court, 855 P.2d 375, 381 (Cal. 1993).

MO: Cruzan v. Harmon, 760 S.W.2d 408, 417 (Mo. 1988) (same).

[95] Restatement (Second) of Torts § 892A(2) cmt. b (1977).

See §§ **4.7** and **15.3.**

[96] See § **4.8.**

[97] Restatement (Second) of Torts § 892A cmt. b. *Accord* Restatement (Second) of Contracts § 15 & cmt. b (1982).

CA: Thor v. Superior Court, 855 P.2d 375, 381 (Cal. 1993) ("'patient must have a clear understanding of the risks and benefits of the proposed treatment alternatives or nontreatment, along with a full understanding of the nature of the disease and the prognosis'").

Equally troubling as the meaning of capacity to make medical decisions is the legally appropriate procedure for determining whether or not a patient has such capacity, and specifically whether this should be determined by health care professionals in the clinical setting or by the courts. The question of the appropriate procedures for determining a patient's decisionmaking capacity is discussed in **Chapter 5.**

§ 3.20 ——Understanding

It is not clear whether a physician satisfies the requirements of the informed consent doctrine merely by making adequate disclosure of information to a patient, or if the doctor must also ensure that the patient understands the information before proceeding with treatment. In judicial opinions, the word "inform" is sometimes used in such a way as to suggest that the physician's duty is simply to give the patient certain information; at other times, the suggestion is that the patient must be informed in the sense of actually understanding that information. Even after more than a quarter-century of judicial opinions and legislation on informed consent and a far lengthier record on simple consent to medical treatment, it remains unclear whether the physician has any obligation to make reasonable efforts to ascertain whether the patient understands the expected results (including possible harms) of treatment.

The duty to disclose is breached only by inadequate disclosure and not by failure to obtain the patient's permission. The relevant inquiry is what the physician said, rather than what the patient understood.[98] This does not necessarily mean that an inquiry into what the patient understood—and perhaps the physician's conduct in assisting the patient to understand and/or ascertaining the adequacy of that understanding—is irrelevant. Indeed, this is the central inquiry under the duty to obtain consent.[99]

Although adequate disclosure bars an action in negligence for failure to inform, if the patient does not understand the information[100] and the physician knows this,[101] the patient has merely assented or given permission. Legally effective consent has not been given, and consequently an action for battery may

---

WV: Belcher v. Charleston Area Medical Ctr., 422 S.E.2d 827, 838 (W. Va. 1992) (minor is mature and possesses decisionmaking authority if he possesses capacity to appreciate nature and risks involved in procedure to be performed or withheld).

See § **4.26.**

98 Canterbury v. Spence, 464 F.2d 772, 780 n.15 (D.C. Cir. 1972).

99 **AZ:** Rasmussen v. Fleming, 741 P.2d 674, 683 (Ariz. 1987) ("[T]he patient must have a clear understanding of the risks and benefits of the proposed treatment alternatives or nontreatment, along with a full understanding of the nature of the disease and the prognosis.").

CA: Thor v. Superior Court, 855 P.2d 375, 381 (Cal. 1993) (same).

MO: Cruzan v. Harmon, 760 S.W.2d 408, 417 (Mo. 1988) (same).

100 *See* Restatement (Second) of Torts § 892B(2) (1977).

101 *See* Restatement (Second) of Torts § 892B cmts. c–i (1977).

lie.[102] This is because consent induced by a substantial mistake concerning the nature of the interests invaded or the probable extent of harm, and known to the physician, is not legally effective.[103]

The greatest uncertainty involves situations in which the physician is unaware of the patient's lack of understanding but could have, through the exercise of due care, ascertained this deficiency. Cases in which permission for treatment has been obtained from sedated patients provide perhaps the best support for the position that there is an obligation on the part of physicians to ascertain the extent of the patient's understanding. These cases hold that if the sedative was administered and the patient was thereby disabled from understanding information about treatment, the patient's authorization of treatment is not legally valid.[104] Owing to the fiduciary nature of their relationship, physicians ought to be under a greater obligation to ascertain whether a patient understands than would be required in an arms-length relationship.

The existence of an obligation to ensure an adequate level of patient understanding, or at least not to treat in the absence of such a level, is further supported by the concept of decisionmaking capacity. A decision rendered by one who lacks decisionmaking capacity is legally ineffective. *Decisionmaking capacity* is the ability to appreciate certain information, specifically, the nature, extent, and probable consequences of the conduct consented to.[105] Appreciation, in turn, denotes understanding. Thus, if a physician can be held liable in battery for treating without legally effective consent if the patient lacks the capacity to understand, there is a corollary obligation to determine whether or not a patient has the requisite capacity. This requirement can only be met first by making disclosure and then by ascertaining whether the information disclosed was understood. In some cases, the determination of whether the information was understood will be relatively simple, if not self-evident. It may be more complicated in others.[106]

---

[102] **IA:** Morgan v. Olds, 417 N.W.2d 232, 236 (Iowa Ct. App. 1987) ("When a doctor implements a course of treatment without obtaining the patient's consent, he breaches his duty and is liable to the patient for any resultant damages.").

OH: Estate of Leach v. Shapiro, 469 N.E.2d 1047, 1052 (Ohio Ct. App. 1984) ("Not only must a patient consent to treatment, but a patient's consent must be informed consent. There is no legal defense to battery based on consent if a patient's consent to touching is given without sufficient knowledge and understanding of the nature of the touching.").

See §§ **17.2** through **17.4.**

[103] Restatement (Second) of Torts § 892B(2) (1977).

[104] **NM:** Demers v. Gerety, 515 P.2d 645 (N.M. Ct. App. 1973).

TX: Gravis v. Physicians & Surgeons Hosp., 427 S.W.2d 310 (Tex. 1968).

WA: Grannum v. Berard, 422 P.2d 812 (Wash. 1967).

See generally Lockwood, Annotation, *Mental Competency of Patient to Consent to Surgical Operation or Medical Treatment,* 25 A.L.R.3d 1439 § 4 (1969 & Supp. 1994).

[105] Restatement (Second) of Torts § 892A cmt. b.

[106] See § **4.33.**

§ 3.21 Consent Forms

There is no general common-law or statutory requirement that permission for treatment be obtained in writing, or that the explanation required by the informed consent doctrine be made in writing.[107] (Federal regulatory law requires that consent to biomedical and behavioral research ordinarily be obtained in writing and that there be a written explanation.[108]) More importantly, even when written consent is obtained and/or a written explanation given to the patient, liability may be imposed for failure to obtain consent or to make adequate disclosure if legally adequate consent was not obtained or legally adequate information was in fact not provided.[109] Thus, consent forms are neither the equivalent of nor a substitute for informed consent.

It is, however, increasingly common for health care institutions to require physicians to obtain consent in writing to many forms of treatment. Although this practice grew up around consent to surgical procedures, it has been expanded to cover many other therapeutic and diagnostic procedures. The hallmark of therapies and procedures for which written consent is obtained seems to be that they are invasive and/or entail serious risk to the patient, or are experimental or innovative procedures. It has also become increasingly common for physicians in office practice to use consent forms for these kinds of procedures.

There is nothing improper about using consent forms, and there may be some value in doing so. Such forms serve as *evidence* of the fact that consent was in fact given to the administration of treatment. The forms also serve as evidence that disclosure was made. The strength of the evidence varies with the way the form is constructed. A form which merely recites that disclosure was made is far less satisfactory than one that contains the information given to the patient.

EXCEPTIONS TO INFORMED CONSENT

§ 3.22 Introduction

There are situations in which noncompliance with either or both of the duties imposed by the informed consent doctrine is legally excused. These situations

---

[107] **DKS:** Hernandez v. United States, 465 F. Supp. 1091 (D. Kan. 1979).

CO: Maercklein v. Smith, 266 P.2d 1095 (Colo. 1954).

ID: Idaho Code § 39-4305.

LA: Doss v. Hartford Fire Ins. Co., 448 So. 2d 813 (La. Ct. App. 1984).

[108] 45 C.F.R. § 46.117 (1994).

[109] **LA:** Rogers v. Lumbermen's Mut. Casualty Co., 119 So. 2d 649 (La. Ct. App. 1960).

MD: Sard v. Hardy, 379 A.2d 1014 (Md. 1977).

ND: Wasem v. Laskowski, 274 N.W.2d 219, 226 (N.D. 1977).

are referred to as "exceptions" to the informed consent doctrine, and there are four generally recognized legal exceptions: emergencies, incompetence, waiver, and therapeutic privilege.

These exceptions demonstrate that the law recognizes other societal interests than patient self-determination. Although self-determination is an important, indeed a compelling, value, the state also has an interest in medical decisionmaking situations in general, and in those involving life-sustaining treatment in particular, to assure that other important values are safeguarded.[110] The exceptions to informed consent take into account these other important interests.

The effect that the invocation of each exception should have on the duty to obtain informed consent is not well established. Under the simple consent requirement, the effect of invoking an exception was clear: consent need not be obtained from the patient (though it might be necessary from a surrogate in some situations). The problem is more complex, however, under the informed consent doctrine. Because informed consent also imposes the duty to make disclosure, the invocation of an exception might suspend the duty to disclose, the duty to obtain consent, or both.

The effect that an exception to informed consent has should depend both on the exception and the facts and circumstances of particular cases. Each is discussed below.

§ 3.23 Emergency

It is well accepted that, in an emergency, a physician may render treatment without the informed consent of the patient or anyone authorized to consent on the patient's behalf. In fact, prior to the existence of the informed consent requirement, it was well-established that consent is implied in an emergency[111] because the law encourages the rendition of medical care in order to maintain health or save life in situations in which any delay would substantially imperil either.[112]

---

[110] See §§ **8.14** through **8.19.**

[111] **IL:** Estate of Longeway v. Community Convalescent Ctr., 549 N.E.2d 292, 297 (Ill. 1989).

MI: Werth v. Taylor, 475 N.W.2d 426, 428 (Mich. Ct. App. 1991) ("[C]onsent is implied where an emergency procedure is required and there is no opportunity to obtain actual consent or where the patient seeks treatment or otherwise manifests a willingness to submit to a particular treatment.").

OH: Anderson v. St. Francis-St. George Hosp., 614 N.E.2d 841, 844 (Ohio Ct. App. 1992); Estate of Leach v. Shapiro, 469 N.E.2d 1047, 1052 (Ohio Ct. App. 1984).

UT: Lounsbury v. Capel, 836 P.2d 188, 199 (Utah 1992) (doctor "may not rely on the temporary incapacity of [patient], induced by preoperative medication, as a reason to resort to obtaining consent from [patient's wife]"; "spousal consent is particularly suspect in a case such as this where, taking [patient's] version of the facts as true, [spousal] consent followed on the heels of [patient's] own repeated refusals to consent").

[112] **RI:** Miller v. Rhode Island Hosp., 625 A.2d 778, 783 (R.I. 1993) ("In this sea of competing interests, the case at bar compels us to chart a course between the perils of insufficient emergency medical care and violation of a patient's individual liberty.").

Thus, the urgency of the need for medical care is the prime determinant of whether a particular situation should be classified as an emergency. How urgent a situation is depends primarily on the consequences to the patient of delay. If a patient's condition is such that the time necessary for disclosure and consent would seriously jeopardize health or life, the interests in dispensing with informed consent outweigh those promoted by obtaining it.[113] Also, an insistence on compliance with informed consent requirements when it would cause grave harm to patients would prevent health care professionals from exercising their skills in compliance with the ethical obligations of their professions.

The emergency exception cannot legally be used to circumvent a patient's prior legitimate refusal of treatment.[114] A physician is not privileged to wait until the condition of a patient who has refused treatment deteriorates to the point where there can be said to be an emergency and then administer treatment without consent. The prior refusal of treatment by a patient who has decision-making capacity at the time of the refusal is binding on the physician under substantially similar circumstances in the future unless the patient has subsequently changed his mind.[115] However, some courts show a marked disinclination to honor a prior refusal of treatment if the administration of that treatment is substantially likely to restore the patient to health as opposed to merely prolonging the process of dying.[116]

The Effect of the Emergency Exception. What makes a situation into a medical emergency is that time is of the essence in providing treatment to a patient; if there is any delay at all or any significant delay, the chances of saving the patient's life or restoring health will be lost or seriously reduced. Therefore, in a bona fide emergency, disclosure will probably always need to be eliminated or curtailed.[117] Indeed, if there is time for adequate disclosure to a patient, the situation probably should not be considered an emergency. However, there are

---

[113] *Id.* at 787 ("The doctrine of informed consent must, at times, yield to the practical considerations of emergency medical treatment.").

[114] Fosmire v. Nicoleau, 551 N.E.2d 77, 80 (N.Y. 1990) (emergency doctrine inapplicable when patient clearly stated before admission to hospital and throughout stay that she would not consent to blood transfusions).

[115] **OH:** Estate of Leach v. Shapiro, 469 N.E.2d 1047, 1053 (Ohio Ct. App. 1984). See §§ **9.4** through **9.6** and **10.22.**

[116] **MI:** Werth v. Taylor, 475 N.W.2d 426 (Mich. Ct. App. 1991).

NJ: *In re* Hughes, 611 A.2d 1148 (N.J. Super. Ct. App. Div. 1992).

OH: University of Cincinnati Hosp. v. Edmond, 506 N.E.2d 299 (C.P. Hamilton County, Ohio, 1986).

PA: *In re* Estate of Dorone, 534 A.2d 452 (Pa. 1987).

See §§ **8.9** through **8.13.**

[117] **RI:** *See* Miller v. Rhode Island Hosp., 625 A.2d 778, 784 (R.I. 1993) ("'Even in [emergencies] the physician should, as current law requires, attempt to secure a relative's consent if possible. But if time is too short to accommodate discussion, obviously the physician should proceed with the treatment.'") (quoting Canterbury v. Spence, 464 F.2d 772, 788–89 (D.C. Cir. 1972)).

varying degrees of urgency with which treatment must be administered, so that it would be imprudent to hold that an emergency always suspends the duty to disclose. It is more sensible instead that there be a flexible rule permitting disclosure to be suspended when the circumstances are highly exigent but merely to be abbreviated when circumstances are less urgent.

The requirement of obtaining consent must be suspended completely when irreparable harm would befall the patient on account of the efforts to do so. Under some circumstances, however, patient permission might be obtainable even though the patient's understanding might not be sufficient for a conclusion that consent had been given.[118]

§ 3.24 Incompetence

When a patient lacks decisionmaking capacity, compliance with the obligations imposed by the informed consent doctrine are excused, at least with respect to the patient. Although this is referred to as the incompetence exception, the patient need not have been *adjudicated* incompetent for it properly to be invoked.[119]

The Effect of the Incompetence Exception. The proper invocation of the incompetence exception excuses compliance with both the duty of making disclosure to and the duty to obtain consent from the patient. Ordinarily, however, informed consent must be obtained from someone legally authorized to speak for the patient,[120] except in an emergency when this requirement may sometimes be dispensed with too.[121] The latter situation, however, is really an application of the emergency exception.

In order to determine whether a patient lacks decisionmaking capacity so as to permit the application of the incompetence exception, it will sometimes be necessary at least to commence the process of disclosure. Certain patients—those who are unconscious are the clearest example, but those who are seriously delirious, demented, toxic, or stuporous are others—so clearly lack decisionmaking capacity that no overt process of evaluation of competence is required. This is so despite the legal presumption of competence,[122] which in effect is

---

[118] *Id.* at 784 ("In order for the trier of fact to decide whether an emergency existed, a factual inquiry should be undertaken to determine whether a patient was capable of consenting or objecting to emergency treatment.").

[119] See § **5.11.**

[120] See §§ **5.15** through **5.24** and **Ch. 14.**

[121] **RI:** Miller v. Rhode Island Hosp., 625 A.2d 778, 784 (R.I. 1993) ("'Even in [emergencies] the physician should, as current law requires, attempt to secure a relative's consent if possible. But if time is too short to accommodate discussion, obviously the physician should proceed with the treatment.'") (quoting Canterbury v. Spence, 464 F.2d 772, 788–89 (D.C. Cir. 1972)).

[122] See § **4.8.**

overcome by such medical conditions. Similarly, other patients so clearly possess decisionmaking capacity that no colorable question of incompetence can be raised.

However, there are patients lying between these extremes whose decision-making capacity can only be ascertained by making explicit efforts to do so.[123] Sometimes the best way is to engage in a conversation which includes information that the physician needs to provide in order to satisfy the duty of disclosure. Thus, the attending physician must be alert for signs of a lack of decisionmaking capacity both before the process of informing for decisionmaking begins and in the process of informing.[124]

§ 3.25 Therapeutic Privilege

Another exception to the informed consent doctrine is the therapeutic privilege to withhold information if its disclosure would be harmful to the patient. The general purpose of the therapeutic privilege is to "free physicians from a legal requirement which would force them to violate their 'primary duty' to do what is beneficial for the patient."[125]

The therapeutic privilege has a high potential for abuse. If broadly interpreted, it would permit physicians not to provide patients with information whenever they believe that refusing recommended treatment would harm the patient. In effect, this would allow physicians to substitute their judgment for patients' in virtually all instances of decisionmaking.[126] Consequently, the case law "does not accept the paternalistic notion that the physician may remain silent simply because divulgence might prompt the patient to forego therapy the physician feels the patient really needs."[127] The scope of the privilege, however, is not clear. Although much discussed in dictum and commentary, the therapeutic privilege is the basis for the holding in very few cases.

The only discussion of the therapeutic privilege in the context of decisions about life-sustaining treatment appears to be that in the New York do-not-resuscitate statute which permits an attending physician to issue such an order without the patient's informed consent if the patient "would suffer immediate and severe injury from a discussion of cardiopulmonary resuscitation."[128]

---

[123] *See, e.g.,* Martin v. Martin, 504 N.W.2d 917 (Mich. Ct. App. 1993) (specific findings of fact must be made to determine whether patient with severe brain injury is capable of expressing preferences about treatment).

[124] See **Ch. 4.**

[125] Comment, *Informed Consent: The Illusion of Patient Choice,* 23 Emory L.J. 503, 504 (1974).

[126] Canterbury v. Spence, 464 F.2d 772, 789 (D.C. Cir. 1972) (if scope of the privilege is not carefully circumscribed, "it might devour the disclosure rule itself").

[127] *Id.*

[128] N.Y. Pub. Health Law § 2964(3).

The Effect of the Therapeutic Privilege. The therapeutic privilege does not necessarily contemplate complete withholding of information. Because the purpose of the privilege is to protect the patient against the seriously adverse effects of disclosure, the only information that is properly withheld is information with this potential. This kind of information is most likely to be information about risks. The difficulty with this approach is that it may skew the decisionmaking process, probably in favor of physician-recommended treatment because, if a patient is told only about the benefits of a treatment and not the risks, a strong bias is introduced toward a decision in favor of treatment.

Further, it is not certain whether the therapeutic privilege affects only the duty to disclose, or whether it also suspends the duty to obtain the patient's consent. Obtaining consent from a patient seems unlikely to be harmful in the same way that information disclosure could be. Indeed, the effects of a failure to obtain consent followed by the administration of treatment is just what classic battery law is intended to protect against. Thus, even when the therapeutic privilege is properly invoked to withhold information, consent should still be obtained from the patient.

However, if this consent is given on the basis of incomplete information or, worse, on the basis of information skewed in favor of treatment, it can hardly be said to be a genuine exercise in self-determination. Consequently, when the therapeutic privilege is invoked, consideration should be given to making disclosure to a third party, such as a close relative of the patient.[129] The problem is that such disclosure is an empty gesture if the third party does not also have the authority to make a decision about treatment. If that is the case, then the logical link between disclosure and decisionmaking authority is broken, making both disclosure and consent empty gestures. One solution is to make disclosure to and obtain consent from a legally authorized third party, that is, the same person who would serve as the patient's surrogate if the patient lacked decisionmaking capacity; but there is no clear legal authority for doing so if the patient does not in fact lack decisionmaking capacity.

§ 3.26 Waiver

Patients may waive their right to give an informed consent to treatment.[130] For a waiver to be legally effective, the patient must know of the right to be provided with information about treatment by the attending physician and the right to

---

[129] *Compare* Canterbury v. Spence, 464 F.2d 772, 789 (D.C. Cir. 1972) (disclosure should be made to a close relative with a view to securing consent to the proposed treatment) *with* Nishi v. Hartwell, 473 P.2d 116 (Haw. 1970) (no disclosure necessary to patient's wife because her permission is not necessary to authorize treatment).

[130] **CA:** Cobbs v. Grant, 502 P.2d 1 (Cal. 1972); Putensen v. Clay Adams, Inc., 91 Cal. Rptr. 319 (Ct. App. 1970).

WA: Holt v. Nelson, 523 P.2d 211 (Wash. Ct. App. 1974).

make a decision about treatment, including the right to decline it. In addition, the waiver must be voluntarily given.

Although waiver might seem inconsistent with the goal of self-determination, it can actually be an exercise of that goal. Permitting patients to make decisions about treatment is one way of fostering self-determination. However, compelling them to receive information they do not want or to make decisions they do not wish to make is a paternalistic denial of the right of self-determination. Waiver is the *patient's* counterpart to the therapeutic privilege. If a physician may withhold information from a patient because of the harm it threatens, a fortiori a patient may decide that participation in the decisionmaking process will be harmful and to be avoided.

When a patient expresses hesitancy about participating in the decisionmaking process, the physician should tell the patient that disclosure is not mandatory but that the physician will proceed only if the patient wishes. Because there is a fine line between those situations in which patients express the wish not to participate and those in which physicians subtly suggest that they do not care to have patients participate, this information should not be volunteered by the physician without some initial sign of hesitancy from the patient about participation in the decisionmaking process. Otherwise, patients might easily be misled into believing that they are not entitled to be informed and to decide whether to be treated.

The Effect of Waiver. A patient may waive either or both of the duties imposed on physicians by the informed consent doctrine. A patient may therefore relinquish the right to be informed, but still retain the right to decide. Conversely, a patient may, after having been informed, determine that he does not want to or is unable to decide and relinquish that right either to the physician or to a third party whom the patient designates. A patient may alternatively decide that he wishes neither to be informed nor to decide and that he prefers to permit the physician or the patient's designee to receive information and make decisions on the patient's behalf.

Bibliography

Appelbaum, P., et al. *Informed Consent: Legal Theory and Clinical Practice.* New York: Oxford University Press, 1987.

Brennan, T. "Silent Decisions: Limits of Consent and the Terminally Ill Patient." *Law, Medicine and Health Care* 16 (1988): 204.

Campbell, M. "Breaking Bad News to Patients." *JAMA* 271 (1994): 1052.

Comment. "Informed Consent for the Terminal Patient." *Baylor Law Review* 27 (1975): 111.

Comment. "Critical-Care Nurses—Involved in the Informed Consent Process." *University of Toledo Law Review* 19 (1987): 135.

Faden, R. and T. Beauchamp. *A History and Theory of Informed Consent.* New York: Oxford University Press, 1986.

Katz, J. *The Silent World of Doctor and Patient.* New York: Free Press, 1984.

Note. "Informed Consent and the Dying Patient." *Yale Law Journal* 83 (1974): 1632.

President's Commission for the Study of Ethical Problems in Medicine and Biomedical and Behavioral Research, *Making Health Care Decisions: The Ethical and Legal Implications of Informed Consent in the Patient-Practitioner Relationship.* Washington: Government Printing Office, 1982.

Rouse, F. "Different Viewpoints: Does Autonomy Require Informed and Specific Refusal of Life-Sustaining Medical Treatment?" *Issues in Law and Medicine* 5 (1989): 321.

Rozovsky, F. *Consent to Treatment: A Practical Guide.* Boston: Little, Brown, 1984.

Schultz, M. "From Informed Consent to Patient Choice: A New Protected Interest." *Yale Law Journal* 95 (1985): 219.

Winick, B. "On Autonomy: Legal and Psychologic Perspectives." *Villanova Law Review* 37 (1992):1705.

CHAPTER 4

MEANING AND EFFECT OF INCOMPETENCE

§ 4.1 Introduction

It is well accepted in the law of medical decisionmaking and among health care professionals that a patient who is incompetent cannot render a legally binding consent to or refusal of medical treatment. The terms *competence, incompetence,* and *decisionmaking capacity* and *incapacity* are frequently used in discussions of medical decisionmaking. They are a common part of the discourse of health care professionals, lawyers, and laypersons. Despite their commonplace usage, however, the meaning of these terms and the manner of applying them in clinical and judicial contexts has long been a matter of great confusion. The lack of conceptual precision is further complicated by the difficulty in applying the concepts to particular individuals.[1]

In concert with—yet somewhat apart from—the emerging consensus about decisionmaking about life-sustaining treatment, there has been a parallel emergence first in academic circles and then in the case law of a consensus regarding the meaning of competence and incompetence. Despite the emerging consensus, uncertainty and confusion still exist in many trial courts and among health care professionals. Much of the confusion results from legitimate, reasonable, and good-faith disagreement about the underlying concepts that the terms do or should denote: what does it mean to say that a person is competent or incompetent, or possesses or lacks decisionmaking capacity?

This chapter addresses these questions and, more specifically, (1) the relationship between the terms and related concepts, (2) different ways in which the terms are used, and (3) different approaches to assessing competence and incompetence.

---

[1] Browning v. Herbert, 543 So. 2d 258, 272 n.4 (Fla. Dist. Ct. App. 1989), *aff'd,* 568 So. 2d 4 (Fla. 1990) ("[T]he line between competency and incompetency is imprecise.").

§ 4.2 Terminology: Competence and Incompetence; Decisionmaking Capacity and Incapacity; Related Terms

Traditionally, the term *incompetence* has been used to denote the legal status of an individual who has been determined through judicial proceedings to lack the degree of capacity legally required to do a particular act such that that act is clothed with legal significance.[2] One who is incompetent to manage his financial affairs is not necessarily literally unable, for instance, to buy and sell securities. An individual who is physically unable to do so, of course, is incompetent to manage his financial affairs, but a lesser standard of incapacity will usually also render someone incompetent. Just what that standard should be is the nub of the matter and the main concern of this chapter. The same is true in medical decisionmaking. An individual who is comatose manifestly lacks the capacity to make a medical decision. However, an individual who is moderately demented and still possesses the ability to communicate might lack decisionmaking capacity, but not *manifestly* so. Rather, whether he does lack such capacity depends on how we define, and the standards we adopt for determining, decisionmaking capacity. In sum, competence and incompetence (sometimes referred to as competency and incompetency) are the legal labels we attach to reflect *factual states;* namely, that a person respectively does or does not possess the requisite *capacity* to perform a particular task, whether it is managing financial affairs or making medical decisions.

In common usage, however, the strict distinction between these terms is frequently ignored among lawyers, courts, legislators, and health care professionals. A major source of confusion about the meaning of competence and incompetence is the fact that sometimes different terms are used to refer to the same concept, or the same terms are used to refer to different concepts.[3]

So deeply embedded is this common usage that in this treatise *competence* and *decisionmaking capacity* are used synonymously, as are *incompetence* and *lack of decisionmaking capacity.* Rather than dwelling inordinately on the technical distinctions between these terms, this treatise attempts to address functional questions and provide functional answers, both because that is ultimately more important and because there is little hope of attempting to change such deeply ingrained usage. Furthermore, preferable though the terms *decisionmaking capacity* and *lack of decisionmaking capacity* may be to describe the factual status of individuals who have not been judicially determined to be competent or incompetent, they are more unwieldy terms than the much simpler and more familiar competent and incompetent. Indeed, simplicity is what probably explains more widespread usage of the latter. Insistence on using the terms *decisionmaking capacity* and *lack of decisionmaking capacity* also runs the risk

[2] **DCO:** Ross v. Hilltop Rehabilitation Hosp., 676 F. Supp. 1528, 1530 n.1 (D. Colo. 1987) ("Some cases refer to 'mental competency'. We prefer the issue to be one of 'mental capacity'.").

[3] *See* Hastings Ctr., Guidelines on the Termination of Life-Sustaining Treatment and the Care of the Dying 131–32 (1987) (Part Six, III) [hereinafter Hastings Center Guidelines].

that, because of their unwieldiness, the terms will be shortened to *capacity* and *incapacity,* which can be mistakenly equated with a patient's health status. Because a patient may be physically incapacitated but still possess decisionmaking capacity, a new possibility for confusion could be created.

§ 4.3 —Competence and Incompetence

Competence and incompetence refer to legal statuses. A person may be legally incompetent either as a result of a judicial determination—referred to as an adjudication of incompetence—or by virtue of being a minor.

Although in theory the determination of incompetence requires the official legal act of adjudication[4] (at least in the case of an adult[5]), in practice people who have not been adjudicated incompetent are sometimes referred to as incompetent, deemed incompetent, and treated as if they had been adjudicated incompetent either in general or with regard to a particular task such as medical decisionmaking.

§ 4.4 —De Jure and De Facto Incompetence

One who has been adjudicated incompetent or is a minor is sometimes referred to as *de jure* incompetent. Individuals who are incompetent in fact (that is, they lack decisionmaking capacity), but have not by judicial procedures been determined to be such, are sometimes referred to as *de facto* incompetent.[6]

§ 4.5 —Decisionmaking Capacity and Incapacity

Persons who are de facto incompetent are sometimes said to lack capacity rather than competence, with the former term referring to a factual status and the latter to a legal status.[7] In its reports on informed consent[8] and on life-sustaining treatment,[9] the President's Commission for the Study of Ethical Problems in

---

[4] *In re* Hamlin, 689 P.2d 1372, 1381 (Wash. 1984) (Rosellini, J., dissenting) ("[C]ompetency is a legal determination which must be made by a court.").

[5] See § **15.2.**

[6] Uniform Model Health-Care Consent Act § 3 cmt.

[7] Uniform Model Health-Care Consent Act § 3 cmt.

[8] 1 President's Comm'n for the Study of Ethical Problems in Medicine & Biomedical & Behavioral Research, Making Health Care Decisions: The Ethical and Legal Implications of Informed Consent in the Patient-Practitioner Relationship 169–75 (1982).

[9] President's Comm'n for the Study of Ethical Problems in Medicine & Biomedical & Behavioral Research, Deciding to Forego Life-Sustaining Treatment 119–26 (1983).

Medicine and Biomedical and Behavioral Research made this distinction and employed the terms decisionmaking capacity and incapacity to apply to the factual status of an individual.

§ 4.6 —Other Legal Competences Distinguished

In common usage, in addition to referring to both a factual status and a legal status, incompetence is sometimes used with respect to a particular legal context, such as making a contract or a will, testifying under oath, or performing a variety of acts in criminal proceedings, such as entering a plea, standing trial, being executed, hence the terms contractual incapacity, testamentary incapacity, testimonial incapacity, and other similar terms.

The existence of one of these particular kinds of incompetences (whether it merely exists in fact or has been adjudicated as such by a court) has no necessary bearing on other kinds of legal competences because the characteristics of a person relevant to an adjudication of incompetence in one context is not necessarily relevant to competence in another. However, the fact that one is incompetent to perform some particular task having legal consequences should at least raise concern about one's capacity to perform other such tasks.

§ 4.7 —Other Related Concepts

Incompetence is sometimes confused with a number of other concepts, such as mental illness,[10] mental retardation, involuntary civil commitment, and insanity. Some of these concepts are related to incompetence, but they are not the same. The fact that an individual is or has been mentally ill, mentally retarded, involuntarily civilly committed (or voluntarily hospitalized for the treatment of mental illness), or successfully pleaded an insanity defense is of no necessary consequence for that individual's competence to make decisions about life-sustaining treatment.

Mental Illness and Mental Retardation. At one time, someone who was mentally ill or mentally retarded was viewed as de facto incompetent and would almost automatically have been found to be de jure incompetent if judicial proceedings had been instituted.[11] This may still be the case when a general approach to defining and assessing incompetence is employed.[12] However,

---

[10] Sullivan & Youngner, *Depression, Competence, and the Right to Refuse Lifesaving Medical Treatment,* 151 Am. J. Psychiatry 971 (1994).

[11] *See, e.g.,* Anonymous v. State, 236 N.Y.S.2d 88 (App. Div. 1963). *See generally* 41 Am. Jur. 2d *Incompetent Persons* § 1, at 541 (1968).

[12] See §§ **4.23–4.24.**

under the increasingly favored specific incompetence approach,[13] a person is not incompetent merely because of mental disability.[14] In fact, mental illness does not necessarily even raise a presumption of incompetence.[15] In particular patients and particular situations, mental illness or retardation may be important factors in concluding that someone lacks decisionmaking capacity and is thus incompetent,[16] but the concepts are not equivalents. Under the specific incompetence approach, it is not the fact that a person is mentally ill or mentally retarded that is relevant to assessing incompetence. Rather, it is the effect that mental illness or retardation has on the person's ability to do whatever is required—such as make a decision about treatment—that is relevant.

Civil Commitment. An individual who is civilly committed for psychiatric treatment is not ipso facto incompetent.[17] Although civil commitment formerly resulted in the loss of most civil rights,[18] including the right to make decisions about one's medical care (both psychiatric and nonpsychiatric), this is no longer generally the case unless there is a specific adjudication of incompetence resulting in the loss of those rights.[19]

---

[13] See §§ **4.25–4.26.**

[14] S. Brakel et al., The Mentally Disabled and the Law 370–71 (1985). *See, e.g.,* Thor v. Superior Court, 855 P.2d 375, 379 (Cal. 1993) (Psychiatrists who examined quadriplegic prisoner refusing lifesaving treatment found him to be "depressed about his quadriplegic condition but mentally competent to understand and appreciate his circumstances.").

MA: Superintendent of Belchertown State Sch. v. Saikewicz, 370 N.E.2d 417 (Mass. 1977).

NY: *In re* Storar, 420 N.E.2d 64 (N.Y. 1981); New York City Health & Hosps. Corp. v. Stein, 335 N.Y.S.2d 461 (Sup. Ct. N.Y. County 1972).

OH: *In re* Milton, 505 N.E.2d 255 (Ohio 1987).

WA: *In re* Hamlin, 689 P.2d 1372 (Wash. 1984).

[15] **CA2:** Winters v. Miller, 446 F.2d 65, 68 (2d Cir. 1971) ("[T]he law is quite clear in New York that a finding of 'mental illness' even by a judge or jury, and commitment to a hospital, does not raise even a presumption that the patient is 'incompetent' or unable adequately to manage his own affairs. Absent a specific finding of incompetence, the mental patient retains the right to sue or defend in his own name, to sell or dispose of his property, to marry, draft a will, and, in general to manage his own affairs.").

[16] See § **4.23.**

[17] **OH:** *In re* Milton, 505 N.E.2d 255 (Ohio 1987).

[18] S. Brakel et al., The Mentally Disabled and the Law 251–61 (1985).

[19] **DMA:** *E.g.,* Rogers v. Commissioner, 458 N.E.2d 308, 314 (Mass. 1983).

DNJ: *E.g.,* Rennie v. Klein, 476 F. Supp. 1294 (D.N.J. 1979), *modified and remanded,* 643 F.2d 836 (3d Cir. 1981); Rennie v. Klein, 462 F. Supp. 1131 (D.N.J. 1978).

DOH: *E.g.,* Davis v. Hubbard, 506 F. Supp. 915 (N.D. Ohio 1980).

MN: *E.g.,* Jarvis v. Levine, 403 N.W.2d 298 (Minn. 1987).

NY: *E.g.,* Rivers v. Katz, 495 N.E.2d 337 (N.Y. 1986); New York City Health & Hosps. Corp. v. Stein, 335 N.Y.S.2d 461, 465 (Sup. Ct. N.Y. County 1972).

OK: *E.g., In re* K.K.B., 609 P.2d 747 (Okla. 1980).

Insanity. Insanity is a term long used both in law and in medicine, though often with quite different meanings. (The same is true of some other terms used to refer to mental illness, mental retardation, or both, such as lunacy, idiocy, and feeblemindedness.[20]) Over the years, the term insanity has acquired legal connotations while at the same time losing its usage and meaning in the medical profession. Although at one time insanity denoted incompetence,[21] today the term is generally used in law only to refer to those persons who have been found to lack the capacity for criminal responsibility—that is, in the insanity defense.

§ 4.8 Presumption of Competence

Adults are presumed to be legally competent for purposes of decisionmaking about life-sustaining treatment,[22] as they are for other purposes, medical and nonmedical.[23] Like the presumption of innocence applicable to the criminally accused, the presumption of competence is not a matter of fact: Just as not all persons accused of crime are in fact innocent, not all patients in fact have the

---

PA: *E.g., In re* Yetter, 62 Pa. D. & C.2d 619, 623 (C.P. Northampton County 1973) (psychiatric patient does not lose right to make decisions about nonpsychiatric medical care).

WI: *E.g.,* State *ex rel.* Jones v. Gerhardstein, 416 N.W.2d 883 (Wis. 1987).

See generally Hermann, *Autonomy, Self Determination, the Right of Involuntarily Committed Persons to Refuse Treatment, and the Use of Substituted Judgment in Medication Decisions Involving Incompetent Persons,* 13 Int'l J.L. & Psychiatry 361 (1990).

20 *See generally* S. Brakel et al., The Mentally Disabled and the Law 9–20, 369, 375 (1985).

21 *See* 41 Am. Jur. 2d *Incompetent Persons* § 1, at 541 (1968) ("[T]he phrase 'insane person' contemplates a person with such a degree of mental incapacity as to be unable to understand and deal with the common affairs of life.").

22 **DC:** *In re* A.C., 573 A.2d 1235 (D.C. 1990) (improper to assume patient is incompetent).

MA: *In re* Roe, 421 N.E.2d 40 (Mass. 1981).

MI: Martin v. Martin, 504 N.W.2d 917, 924 (Mich. Ct. App. 1993) ("The proof must be clear and convincing that the patient does not have and will not regain the capability of making the decision for himself.") (by implication).

NJ: *In re* Farrell, 529 A.2d 404, 415 (N.J. 1987); *In re* Conroy, 486 A.2d 1209, 1241 (N.J. 1985) ("'[O]ne cannot simply presume that a patient is incompetent. There must be some sort of due process, and if the patient has not been adjudicated to be incompetent, he must be treated as * * * competent.'") (quoting Veatch, *An Ethical Framework for Terminal Care Decisions: A New Classification of Patients,* 32 J. Am. Geriatrics Soc'y 665, 668 (1984)).

NY: Saunders v. State, 492 N.Y.S.2d 510, 516 (Sup. Ct. Nassau County 1985) ("Competency is presumed as the normal condition of a person until the contrary is shown."). *See also* A.B. v. C., 477 N.Y.S.2d 281 (Sup. Ct. Schenectady County 1984) (by implication).

OK: *In re* K.K.B., 609 P.2d 747 (Okla. 1980) (competency presumed even for psychiatric patients).

WI: State *ex rel.* Jones v. Gerhardstein, 416 N.W.2d 883 (Wis. 1987) (same).

Uniform Health-Care Decisions Act § 11(b).

23 *See, e.g.,* 77 C.J.S. *Sales* § 9 (1952).

capacity to make medical decisions. Rather, the legal presumption is a device for instructing the authorities—whether courts or physicians—about how to proceed in the first instance.

The presumption of competence has both substantive and procedural implications. Most fundamentally it means that individuals are to be dealt with as if they possess decisionmaking capacity. Thus, physicians are to embark upon decisionmaking about treatment as if patients are competent. That means first and foremost that physicians are to deal with the patients and not with third parties (such as the patient's family or proxy), they are to provide patients with such information as is required by the doctrine of informed consent, and they must obtain the patient's consent before administering treatment or respect the patient's refusal of such treatment.[24]

A corollary of the presumption of competence is that physicians need not scrutinize the decisionmaking capacity of each patient. However, neither may a physician blithely assume a patient possesses decisionmaking capacity merely because of the legal presumption of competence in the face of reasonable suspicions that, in fact, such capacity is absent. Because the doctor-patient relationship is not an arm's-length relationship, a physician who suspects a patient lacks decisionmaking capacity is obliged to take appropriate steps to establish that incompetence, rather than requiring patients to take any steps to establish that they have decisionmaking capacity. In many other contexts a suspicion that one with whom one is dealing is de facto incompetent poses no obligation to take such steps or alternatively to avoid dealing with the suspected incompetent; however, because the physician-patient relationship is a fiduciary one, this obligation is stronger than that of, for example, a tradesman dealing with another tradesman (or even with a consumer) at arm's length.

From a procedural perspective, the presumption of competence affects the burdens of proof. The proponent of incompetence must initiate a proper procedure for determining whether the patient possesses decisionmaking capacity[25] and should also bear the burden of presenting evidence of the patient's incompetence and the risk of nonpersuasion.[26] Unless both of those burdens are met, the patient's status cannot be changed from competent to incompetent. Further, there should be evidence that the patient will not regain competence,[27] at least if the decision is to forgo life-sustaining treatment.

---

[24] **IN:** Payne v. Marion Gen. Hosp., 549 N.E.2d 1043 (Ind. Ct. App. 1990) (patient's informed consent to entry of do-not-resuscitate order required, and not a surrogate's, if the patient were competent).

WV: Belcher v. Charleston Area Medical Ctr., 422 S.E.2d 827 (W. Va. 1992) (informed consent to do-not-resuscitate order required from mature minor patient, not from patient's parents).

[25] **DC:** *In re* Harris, 477 A.2d 724, 725–26 (D.C. 1984).

[26] **NJ:** *In re* Conroy, 486 A.2d 1209, 1241 (N.J. 1985) ("The proof must be clear and convincing that the patient does not have . . . the capability of making the decision for himself.").

SC: Rogers v. Nation, 326 S.E.2d 182, 185 (S.C. 1985).

[27] **NJ:** *In re* Conroy, 486 A.2d at 1241 ("The proof must be clear and convincing that the patient . . . will not regain the capability of making the decision for himself.").

§ 4.9 —Triggers to Inquiry into Incompetence

Most patients in fact have the capacity to make medical decisions. When a patient is not clearly incompetent but some uncertainty exists—the line between competence and incompetence is frequently imprecise[28]—the legal presumption of competence should resolve some uncertain cases in favor of regarding the patient as having decisionmaking capacity and honoring his decisions about medical care. Not only is competence presumed in law, it is usually assumed in day-to-day affairs, both medical and nonmedical, and the assumption is ordinarily a correct one.

Thus, the question about whether a patient lacks the capacity to make decisions about life-sustaining treatment does not arise in all cases. Some patients are fully alert and unquestionably competent. At the other end of the spectrum, such as when a patient is comatose, there is also no disagreement about the patient's competence, and the clear and undisputed facts defeat the presumption of competence.

Some event or circumstance must trigger an inquiry into incompetence. A patient's general demeanor, difficulty in communicating, or overall medical condition often serve as such triggering conditions. Clinicians also tend to treat patients who are delirious, demented, intoxicated, obtunded, or stuporous as lacking decisionmaking capacity.[29] These conditions alone are not the same as incompetence.[30] Neither, however, should their existence be ignored; they serve as signs to alert both clinical personnel and family members to the need to go beyond the presumption of competence and inquire about the patient's actual decisionmaking capacity.[31]

End-of-Life Decision. The need to make a decision with life-or-death implications may trigger a more formal process of inquiry into the decisionmaking capacity of a patient whose capacity is dubious. Even if a patient is unquestionably lacking in decisionmaking capacity and decisions were previously made without the formalities of an adjudication of incompetency and judicial appointment of a guardian,[32] when a decision is likely to have life-or-death

---

[28] **FL:** Browning v. Herbert, 543 So. 2d 258, 272 n.24 (Fla. Dist. Ct. App. 1989).

IL: *Cf. In re* E.G., 549 N.E.2d 322 (Ill. 1989) (No "bright line" exists between mature minor who possesses decisionmaking capacity and minor who does not.).

[29] *See, e.g.,* Miller v. Rhode Island Hosp., 625 A.2d 778 (R.I. 1993) (highly intoxicated patient treated by emergency room physician as if he lacked the capacity to decide).

[30] **CO:** Blackman v. Rifkin, 759 P.2d 54 (Colo. Ct. App. 1988).

NY: Oates v. New York Hosp., 517 N.Y.S.2d 6 (App. Div. 1987).

RI: Miller v. Rhode Island Hosp., 625 A.2d 778, 786 (R.I. 1993) ("[T]he effect of intoxication does not render every patient incapable of providing informed consent.").

[31] **DC:** *See In re* A.C., 573 A.2d 1235, 1247 (D.C. 1990) (fact that patient was sedated and unconscious should trigger inquiry into competence).

[32] *See, e.g., In re* McInnis, 584 N.E.2d 1389 (P. Ct. Stark County, Ohio 1991) ("It was initially indicated to the court that the underlying reason for the appointment of the guardian was for the purpose for allowing the guardian to discontinue life-sustaining treatment, if necessary.").

implications for the patient, health care personnel and administrators may feel a greater need to be certain about the surrogate's legal authority to make or ratify such decisions, and one way of doing so is to institute proceedings for the adjudication of incompetency and appointment of a guardian.

Refusal of Treatment. Sometimes the triggering event will be the patient's refusal of a recommended treatment.[33] Although in practice, refusal of life-sustaining medical treatment is often viewed as strong evidence of decisionmaking incapacity,[34] it should not be so equated;[35] it should be an important factor in determining whether to *scrutinize* the patient's decisionmaking capacity. Refusal of a recommended treatment especially raises doubts about decisionmaking capacity if the treatment is one to which most patients consent and, a fortiori, if the treatment is the kind that if forgone will almost certainly lead to the patient's death. It is essential, however, to distinguish refusal of treatment as

---

[33] **DNY:** *Cf. In re* Department of Veterans Affairs Medical Ctr., 749 F. Supp. 495 (S.D.N.Y.), *aff'd,* 914 F.2d 239 (2d Cir. 1990) (refusal of treatment by patient's wife led to concern about her decisionmaking capacity).

FL: *E.g.,* Satz v. Perlmutter, 362 So. 2d 160 (Fla. Dist. Ct. App. 1978), *aff'd,* 379 So. 2d 359 (Fla. 1980).

MA: *E.g.,* Lane v. Candura, 376 N.E.2d 1232, 1235 (Mass. App. Ct. 1978) ("Until she changed her original decision and withdrew her consent to the amputation, her competence was not questioned.").

MI: *Cf.* Rosebush v. Oakland County Prosecutor, 491 N.W.2d 633, 635 (Mich. Ct. App. 1992) (transfer of child in persistent vegetative state from rehabilitation center to hospital was blocked when parents contemplated terminating life support).

NY: *Cf. In re* Storar, 420 N.E.2d 64, 68–69 (N.Y. 1981) (hospital first insisted that patient's mother be judicially appointed guardian before it would rely on her consent and subsequently refused to honor her decision as legal guardian when decision was a refusal); Collins v. Davis, 254 N.Y.S.2d 666, 667 (Sup. Ct. Nassau County 1964) (The court signed an order "permitting and allowing a surgical operation upon a patient . . . on the ground that without such an operation the patient would die within a few hours, that the operation might save his life, that the patient was in a comatose state and could not give his consent, and that [the patient's] wife refused to give her consent for reasons that she felt justified refusal, but were medically unsound.").

[34] Sullivan & Youngner, *Depression, Competence, and the Right to Refuse Lifesaving Medical Treatment,* 151 Am. J. Psychiatry 971 (1994).

[35] **MA:** Norwood Hosp. v. Munoz, 564 N.E.2d 1017, 1021 (Mass. 1991) ("It is for the individual to decide whether a particular medical treatment is in the individual's best interests. As a result, '[t]he law protects [a person's] right to make her own decision to accept or reject treatment, whether that decision is wise or unwise.' *Lane v. Candura,* 6 Mass. App. Ct. 377, 383, 376 N.E.2d 1232 (1978)); *Brophy [v. New England Hosp., Inc.,* 398 Mass. 417, 430–31, 497 N.E.2d 626 (1986).]").

NY: Fosmire v. Nicoleau, 551 N.E.2d 77, 81–82 (N.Y. 1990) ("[M]erely declining medical care, even essential treatment, is not considered . . . [an] indication of incompetence."). *Cf.* A.B. v. C., 477 N.Y.S.2d 281 (Sup. Ct. Schenectady County 1984) (Patient seeking to refuse life-sustaining treatment is competent.).

OH: *In re* Milton, 505 N.E.2d 255 (Ohio 1987) (by implication).

a triggering factor from refusal of treatment as evidence (or worse, the equivalent) of incompetence.[36]

§ 4.10 —Significance of Patient Ambivalence and Vacillation

It is not uncommon for patients faced with important decisions about medical care to be uncertain about how to proceed. Sometimes patients hold mutually inconsistent desires or goals, such as wishing to live but wishing also to forgo the treatment said to be necessary to save their lives. This is commonplace among patients with gangrenous limbs for whom amputation is recommended[37] and among adherents to the Jehovah's Witnesses faith who have no desire to die but refuse lifesaving blood transfusions as a matter of religious belief.[38] Even in more run-of-the-mill cases, as a result of uncertainty about what is the best course of action and of conflicting wishes, patients voice uncertainty, continually change their decision, or make a decision but continue to voice concern about whether it is the proper one. And people also change their minds about what they want in the way of medical care,[39] just as they do about other decisions they make. Such ambivalence and vacillation, especially when extreme, sometimes trigger an inquiry into the patient's competence. Depending on the precise facts, this is probably appropriate.

If the patient's competence is already questionable, ambivalence or vacillation sometimes constitutes one of the factors to be taken into account in assessing a patient's decisionmaking capacity.[40] However, neither uncertainty, vacillation, nor ambivalence is the equivalent of decisionmaking incapacity. Even in combination with a mental illness, they should not be equated with

---

[36] *See, e.g., In re* Harvey "U," 501 N.Y.S.2d 920, 922 (App. Div. 1986). See **§ 4.10.**

[37] **MA:** *E.g.,* Lane v. Candura, 376 N.E.2d 1232 (Mass. App. Ct. 1978).

NJ: *E.g., In re* Quackenbush, 383 A.2d 785 (N.J. Super. Ct. P. Div. 1978); *In re* Schiller, 372 A.2d 360 (N.J. Super. Ct. Ch. Div. 1977).

TN: *E.g.,* State Dep't of Human Resources v. Northern, 563 S.W.2d 197 (Tenn. Ct. App. 1978).

[38] See **§ 9.3.**

[39] *See, e.g.,* Danis et al., *Stability of Choices about Life-Sustaining Treatments,* 120 Annals Internal Med. 568 (1994) (Of 2,536 Medicare beneficiaries who initially stated that they would want life-sustaining treatments, between 18 and 43% maintained that preference two years later.); Lee, *Withdrawing Care,* 271 JAMA 1358 (1994) (patients and families more likely to be ambivalent about forgoing life-sustaining treatment if treatment likely to lead to poor quality of life).

[40] **NJ:** *E.g., In re* Quackenbush, 383 A.2d 785, 787 (N.J. Super. Ct. P. Div. 1978) (patient signed a form consenting to the operation but later that day withdrew consent).

NY: *E.g., In re* Kerr (O'Brien), 517 N.Y.S.2d 346, 347 (Sup. Ct. N.Y. County 1986) ("He clearly answered that he did not want to die and that he found the tube uncomfortable and irritating, but he did not affirmatively indicate that he wished to have it removed.").

incompetence.[41] People are often uncertain about many decisions they need to make, both those that are relatively trivial and those that are more momentous. Indeed, such a "reaction may be readily understandable"[42] in light of the patient's prior experience with treatment and the prospect of undesirable adverse consequences of treatment. That a patient would be ambivalent may be even more expectable when the treatment is keeping the patient alive and its discontinuance would lead to the patient's death.[43]

Those who must deal with patients in this kind of situation, such as friends, family, physicians, and nurses, are often irritated or inconvenienced by this kind of behavior. But such behavior is not sufficient cause for determining that the patient lacks decisionmaking capacity.[44]

Fluctuating Decisionmaking Capacity. Incompetence exists in degrees which can change over time. Vacillation can also signal fluctuation in decisionmaking capacity. A patient's decisionmaking capacity is not necessarily a consistent quality. A variety of factors common to ill people, and especially to seriously ill people, can affect decisionmaking capacity, and these factors can wax and wane, with a varying effect on decisionmaking capacity. Pain, depression or even just extreme unhappiness, and isolation, which are frequently associated with illness, affect individuals' abilities to make decisions. Medications that patients are given can also seriously affect decisionmaking capacity.

Some of these effects on decisionmaking capacity are variable. Consequently, sometimes patients may possess decisionmaking capacity and at other times they may not. Or they may have greater capacity at some times than at others. When it is not necessary to make an immediate decision, decisionmaking should be deferred if the patient's decisionmaking capacity is questionable and there is some reasonable possibility that decisionmaking capacity will improve.[45]

---

[41] **CA9:** Foster v. Tourtellotte, 704 F.2d 1009, 1110 (9th Cir. 1983).

CA: Bartling v. Superior Court, 209 Cal. Rptr. 220, 223–24 (Ct. App. 1984) (fact that patient periodically wavered because of severe depression or for any other reason does not justify the conclusion that his capacity to make such a decision was impaired to the point of legal incompetence).

[42] **MA:** Lane v. Candura, 376 N.E.2d 1232, 1236 (Mass. App. Ct. 1978) (patient originally agreed to amputation of leg but withdrew consent on the morning of operation).

[43] **CA:** *E.g.,* Bartling v. Superior Court, 209 Cal. Rptr. 220, 223–24 (Ct. App. 1984).

NY: *E.g., In re* Kerr (O'Brien), 517 N.Y.S.2d 346, 347 (Sup. Ct. N.Y. County 1986).

[44] **CA:** Bouvia v. Superior Court (Glenchur), 225 Cal. Rptr. 297 (Ct. App. 1986).

MA: Lane v. Candura, 376 N.E.2d 1232, 1236 (Mass. App. Ct. 1978).

[45] **FL:** Browning v. Herbert, 543 So. 2d 258, 272 (Fla. Dist. Ct. App. 1989) ("If there is a reasonable probability that the patient will regain sufficient competence to assist in the decisionmaking process, the decision should be deferred.").

MI: Martin v. Martin, 517 N.W.2d 749, 752 (Mich. Ct. App. 1994) (by implication).

See generally Krynski et al., *How Informed Can Consent Be? New Light on Comprehension Among Elderly People Making Decisions About Enteral Tube Feeding,* 34 Gerontologist 36 (1994) (understanding about feeding tubes among patients in long-term care facilities and in community-dwelling groups can be significantly improved).

LEGAL EFFECT OF INCOMPETENCE

§ 4.11 Legal Effect of Incompetence on Medical Decisionmaking

Competence, or decisionmaking capacity, is a prerequisite to a patient's making a legally binding decision about medical treatment.[46] In the most general sense, the consequence of incompetence or incapacity of any kind is a disenfranchisement, that is, the loss of some right or power to control one's own life. Whatever legal consequences would normally ensue from one's actions in the sphere of conduct under consideration do not if one is incompetent. This is true in all areas of the law in which competence is a relevant concept. For instance, the will of an individual who lacks testamentary capacity at the time of its making is unenforceable. Testimonial incapacity is a bar to giving testimony. Similarly, one who lacks the capacity to make medical decisions loses the authority to make legally binding decisions about treatment.

The gross function of the concept of incompetence is to distinguish between those persons who are entitled to exercise decisionmaking prerogatives and those who are not.[47] The effect of incompetence, however, can be more subtle, proceeding in a number of stages. The first set of effects is on the obligations imposed on physicians by the doctrine of informed consent.

Effect on Obligation to Disclose Information. If a patient is incompetent, it is sometimes said that the physician's duty to disclose information to the patient necessary to obtaining informed consent is suspended. Although true in a general sort of way, this view is also oversimplified because it is sometimes not possible to determine whether a patient lacks decisionmaking capacity until one of the prerequisites of informed decisionmaking—relevant information—is provided to the patient.[48]

---

[46] **MI:** Martin v. Martin, 504 N.W.2d 917, 924 (Mich. Ct. App. 1993) ("When faced with a dispute concerning a decision to withhold or withdraw life-sustaining medical treatment, the first task of the trial court is to determine whether the patient has the requisite capacity to make the decision in question."). See **§ 3.19.**

[47] **IN:** Payne v. Marion Gen. Hosp., 549 N.E.2d 1043 (Ind. Ct. App. 1990) (patient's informed consent to entry of do-not-resuscitate order required, and not a surrogate's, if the patient were competent).

MI: Martin v. Martin, 504 N.W.2d 917 (Mich. Ct. App. 1993) (by implication).

WV: Belcher v. Charleston Area Medical Ctr., 422 S.E.2d 827 (W. Va. 1992) (informed consent to do-not-resuscitate order required from mature minor patient, not from patient's parents).

See generally R. Faden & T. Beauchamp, A History and Theory of Informed Consent 287–88 (1986).

[48] See §§ **3.19** and **4.33.**

Effect on Obligation to Obtain Consent. Whether the obligation to disclose information is suspended or not, there is no doubt that a patient's lack of decisionmaking capacity suspends a physician's obligation to obtain the patient's consent to treatment. If a patient lacks decisionmaking capacity, even if he is capable of communication, his decisions about medical care need not be honored by the physician, and in some cases must not be honored. However, the expressed preferences of an incompetent patient should be accorded some weight in decisionmaking.[49]

Initiation of Process of Designation of a Surrogate. When a patient's decisionmaking prerogatives are lost as a result of decisionmaking incapacity, some other party must be designated and empowered to make decisions on the patient's behalf. Therefore, another function of the concept of incompetence is to alert health care personnel to the need for a surrogate decisionmaker and to put into motion the process for determining whether the patient has appointed a surrogate or, if not, for selecting one.[50]

§ 4.12 Effect of Adjudication of Incompetence

Traditionally, an adjudication of incompetence placed an adult under total legal disability, and a guardian was appointed with complete power over the affairs of the incompetent.[51] In effect, the incompetent person, referred to as a ward, was stripped of all civil rights.

In the last two or three decades of the twentieth century, statutes were enacted in many states, distinguishing between general and specific incompetence or plenary and limited guardianship.[52] A general adjudication of incompetence usually (but not always[53]) renders a person incompetent for all purposes. By contrast, an adjudication of specific incompetence, as the term suggests, renders one incompetent for only those limited purposes specified by statute and/or the court's order. When the adjudication of incompetence is specific or limited, the

---

[49] See **§ 7.45.**

[50] **NJ:** *In re* Conroy, 486 A.2d 1209, 1240–41 (N.J. 1985) ("Substitute decisionmaking by a guardian is not permissible unless the patient has been proven incompetent to make the particular medical treatment decision at issue."). See **Chs. 12** and **14.**

[51] S. Brakel et al., The Mentally Disabled and the Law 375 (1985).

[52] *Id.* at 382 n.142 (Alabama, Arkansas, Connecticut, Florida, Idaho, Illinois, Kentucky, Maine, Maryland, Michigan, Nebraska, New York, North Carolina, South Carolina, South Dakota, Texas, Virginia, Washington, West Virginia, and Wisconsin).

[53] **MI:** *E.g.,* Martin v. Martin, 504 N.W.2d 917, 924 (Mich. Ct. App. 1993) ("The fact that a patient has previously been adjudicated incompetent is not controlling.").

NJ: *E.g., In re* Conroy, 486 A.2d 1209 (N.J. 1985) (prior adjudication of incompetence and appointment of a guardian does not empower guardian to make decisions about life-sustaining medical treatment).

guardian is granted authority only for that aspect of the ward's affairs to which the adjudication applies. For example, the guardianship may be limited to authority over either the person or the estate of the incompetent,[54] or it may be even more narrowly limited to specific functions, such personal living decisions, control of a securities brokerage account, or medical decisionmaking.

§ 4.13 —Appointment of Guardian

When a person is adjudicated incompetent, a guardian is appointed to exercise authority over the incompetent's affairs. If the adjudication relates only to the incompetent's financial affairs, the guardian is referred to as a *guardian of the estate;* if the adjudication affects only the incompetent's personal matters, a *guardian of the person* is appointed. In some jurisdictions a guardian is referred to as a committee, conservator, or surrogate.

The scope of the guardian's powers may be limited in a number of ways. First, there may be statutory limitations. Second, a guardian's powers are limited by whether the ward was adjudicated incompetent to manage all of his affairs or only to manage his estate or person. Finally, the powers may be further restricted by the order appointing the guardian.[55]

§ 4.14 —Minors

Minors do not need to be adjudicated incompetent because they are de jure incompetent by virtue of their age.[56] Unless the child is an orphan, there is no need for the appointment of a guardian because the parents are deemed the child's "natural guardians."[57]

In most jurisdictions today, age no longer renders a child incompetent for all purposes. Statutes exist in many states permitting children to authorize certain limited kinds of medical care (for example, treatment for mental illness, substance abuse, venereal disease, and pregnancy), or the common law may

---

[54] *In re* Quinlan, 355 A.2d 647, 670 (N.J.), *cert. denied sub nom.* Garger v. New Jersey, 429 U.S. 922 (1976) ("[D]ivision of guardianship, as between responsibility for the person and the property of an incompetent person, has roots deep in the common law and was well within the jurisdictional capacity of the trial judge.").

[55] *See* Drabick v. Drabick, 245 Cal. Rptr. 840, 851 n.17 (Ct. App. 1988).

[56] **CO:** Carothers v. Department of Insts., 845 P.2d 1179 (Colo. 1993) (by implication).

OH: *But see In re* Myers, 610 N.E.2d 663 (P. Ct. Summit County, Ohio 1993) (judicial appointment of guardian necessary when patient's parents in disagreement about forgoing life-sustaining treatment).

Uniform Model Health-Care Consent Act § 2(2).

[57] See § **15.2.**

permit "mature" minors validly to consent to medical care.[58] A few health care decisionmaking statutes, such as living will statutes,[59] health care power of attorney statutes,[60] and do-not-resuscitate statutes,[61] permit minors to make anticipatory decisions about life-sustaining medical treatment.

§ 4.15 —Guardian's Authority to Forgo Life-Sustaining Treatment

In decisionmaking about life-sustaining treatment, health care personnel must proceed with far more caution in relying on the authority of a guardian than they would in other kinds of medical decisionmaking. This is especially the case when the guardian was not appointed in the context of medical decisionmaking, such as a guardian of the estate, or even when the guardian was granted powers over the person to care for nonmedical matters. Sometimes, it may not be clear whether a particular guardian was granted authority over the patient's person or estate or both.[62] The guardian may also be unclear about the scope of his authority.[63] The same is true in the case of a child. Although parents may be authorized as natural guardians to make medical decisions for their child, their authority to make decisions about forgoing life-sustaining treatment is less axiomatic.[64]

§ 4.16 ——Guardian of the Estate

A guardian of the estate ought not to be presumed, by virtue of such appointment, to possess the authority to make decisions about the patient's personal (that is, nonfinancial) matters, and certainly not to possess the authority to

---

[58] **IL:** *E.g., In re* E.G., 549 N.E.2d 322 (Ill. 1989).

ME: *E.g., In re* Swan, 569 A.2d 1202 (Me. 1990) (enforcement of minor's oral advance directive).

OH: *E.g., In re* Crum, 580 N.E.2d 876 (P. Ct. Franklin County, Ohio 1991).

WV: *E.g.,* Belcher v. Charleston Area Medical Ctr., 422 S.E.2d 827 (W. Va. 1992).

See § **15.3.**

[59] See **Ch. 11.**

[60] See **Ch. 12.**

[61] See §§ **9.4–9.32.**

[62] *Cf.* Browning v. Herbert, 543 So. 2d 258, 262 (Fla. Dist. Ct. App. 1989) (guardian was originally appointed as guardian of estate but seems to have authority to make decisions about life-sustaining treatment although it is possible she was also appointed guardian of person).

[63] *See, e.g., id.* at 271 n.20 ("It actually appears that the guardian did not believe she was empowered to make the decision and, thus, was asking the trial court to make a decision which she did not believe she could make.").

[64] See §§ **15.7–15.8.**

make decisions about life-sustaining treatment.[65] In such a case, the adjudication of incompetence should merely alert health care professionals responsible for the patient's medical treatment to the possibility of the patient's incapacity to make medical decisions. From a practical perspective, a guardian of the estate who is an officer of a trust company or some other financial organization is unlikely to be willing to make any medical decisions, let alone those involving life-sustaining treatment, regardless of what the guardian's legal authority might be.

§ 4.17 ——Plenary Guardianship

If there has been a plenary adjudication of incompetence without any further specification of the guardian's powers, the guardian should be presumed by health care professionals to have the authority to make medical decisions on behalf of the incompetent.[66] However, this is merely a presumption that should be easily defeated by the terms of the judicial decree if it suggests a contrary conclusion or by the protests of the patient and/or the patient's family. If there is any contrary evidence, further clarification of the guardian's authority must be obtained.

A guardian's authority under a plenary adjudication is less certain than if there is a specifically granted authority to make decisions about medical treatment, and the guardian's authority to make decisions about life-sustaining treatment is even more uncertain in the absence of such a specification.[67] In such situations, if the jurisdiction's case law or statutory law does not require judicial approval

---

[65] **FL:** *But cf.* Browning v. Herbert, 543 So. 2d 258, 270 (Fla. Dist. Ct. App. 1989) ("A legal guardian may exercise the patient's right to forego medical treatment."), *aff'd,* 568 So. 2d 4 (Fla. 1990).

NY: *Cf.* N.Y. Pub. Health Law § 2963(1) ("A lack of capacity shall not be presumed from the fact that a committee of the property . . . has been appointed.").

[66] **FL:** Browning v. Herbert, 543 So. 2d 258, 270 (Fla. Dist. Ct. App. 1989) ("A legal guardian may exercise the patient's right to forego medical treatment.").

[67] **MO:** *See* Cruzan v. Harmon, 760 S.W.2d 408, 424 (Mo. 1988), *aff'd,* Cruzan v. Director, 497 U.S. 261 (1990) (statute that "places an express, affirmative duty on guardians to assure that the ward receives medical care and provides the guardian with the power to give consent for that purpose" does not provide basis for contending that "guardian possesses authority, as a guardian, to order the termination of medical treatment"). *But see In re* Warren, 858 S.W.2d 263, 265 (Mo. Ct. App. 1993).

AZ: *But see* Rasmussen v. Fleming, 741 P.2d 674, 688 (Ariz. 1987) ("[T]the right to consent to or approve the delivery of medical care must necessarily include the right to consent to or approve the delivery of no medical care. To hold otherwise would . . . ignore the fact that oftentimes a patient's interests are best served when medical treatment is withheld or withdrawn. To hold otherwise would also reduce the guardian's control over medical treatment to little more than a mechanistic rubberstamp for the wishes of the medical treatment team. . . . [T]he Public Fiduciary as Rasmussen's guardian had the implied, if not express, statutory authority to exercise Rasmussen's right to refuse medical treatment.").

or review of a decision to forgo life-sustaining treatment,as most states do not,[68] it is advisable to seek consent to forgo life-sustaining treatment both from the judicially appointed guardian and from the clinically designated surrogate decisionmaker.

§ 4.18 ——General Guardian of the Person

Patients for whom decisions about life-sustaining treatment need to be made may already have been adjudicated incompetent and had a general guardian of

---

CA: *But see* Drabick v. Drabick, 245 Cal. Rptr. 840, 850 (Ct. App. 1988) ("[A] common sense point about statutory interpretation [is that] a statute that requires a person to make a decision contemplates a decision either way.").

IL: *But see In re* Estate of Greenspan, 558 N.E.2d 1194 (Ill. 1990); Estate of Longeway v. Community Convalescent Ctr., 549 N.E.2d 292, 298 (Ill. 1989) ("[T]he Probate Act impliedly authorizes a guardian to exercise the right to refuse artificial sustenance on her ward's behalf. Section 11a-17 . . . specifically permits a guardian to make provisions for her ward's 'support, care, comfort, health, education and maintenance.' . . . Moreover, if the patient previously executed a power of attorney under the Powers of Attorney for Health Care Law (Ill. Rev. Stat. 1987, ch. 110-1/2, para. 804-1 et seq.), that act permits her to authorize her agent to terminate the food and water that sustain her (Ill. Rev. Stat. 1987, ch. 110-1/2, par. 804-10).").

IN: *But see In re* Lawrance, 579 N.E.2d 32, 39 (Ind. 1991) (statutorily authorized family member's "right to consent to the patient's course of treatment necessarily includes the right to refuse a course of treatment").

KY: *But see* DeGrella v. Elston, 858 S.W.2d 698, 704 (Ky. 1993) (absence in guardianship statutes of provision authorizing guardian of patient in persistent vegetative state to authorize termination of treatment does not preclude such authority because statutes were remedial rather than exclusive).

MD: *But see In re* Riddlemoser, 564 A.2d 812, 816 n.4 (Md. 1989) (power " 'to give necessary consent or approval for medical or other professional care, counsel, treatment, or service' " necessarily implies "power to withhold or withdraw consent to medical treatment") (quoting Md. Est. & Trusts Code Ann. § 13-708(b)(8) and citing with approval 73 Md. Op. Att'y Gen. 253 (Op. No. 88-046, Oct. 17, 1988)).

MN: *But see In re* Torres, 357 N.W.2d 332, 339 (Minn. 1984) ("[S]imply equating the continued physical existence of [an incompetent patient], who has no chance for recovery, with the [patient's] 'best interests' is contrary to law and medical opinion.").

WA: *But see In re* Colyer, 660 P.2d 738, 747 (Wash. 1983) ("[T]he decision to refuse life sustaining treatment is one that falls under the general powers of the guardian.").

WI: *But see* L.W. v. L.E. Phillips Career Dev. Ctr., 482 N.W.2d 60, 71 (Wis. 1992) ("[A] guardian has identical decisionmaking powers as a health care agent [appointed pursuant to the health care power of attorney statute]. To construe the [guardianship statute] any other way would result in an individual losing his or her expressed right to refuse treatment upon appointment of a guardian.").

[68] See §§ **5.25–5.44.**

the person appointed.[69] This is frequently the case with elderly patients who may have been gradually losing decisionmaking capacity over a longer period of time. It is also often the case with patients who have been critically ill for a long period of time, such as patients in a persistent vegetative state.

If so, the decree adjudicating incompetence must be examined for guidance to determine the scope of the guardian's authority. If the adjudication of incompetence clearly encompasses the ward's personal affairs but does not specifically mention medical decisionmaking, it is unclear whether the guardian possesses the authority to make medical decisions for the incompetent. Health care personnel should be extremely cautious in relying on the decision of the guardian based on such an adjudication. This kind of general adjudication of incompetence renders an individual de jure incompetent, but that does not necessarily grant authority to the guardian to make medical decisions in general or decisions about life-sustaining medical treatment in particular[70] nor does it necessarily affect the ward's authority to make medical decisions.[71]

Because judicial involvement in the process of making decisions about life-sustaining treatment is optional in most jurisdictions,[72] the attending physician should deem a guardian of the person to have the authority to make decisions about medical treatment even in the absence of specific empowerment to do so.[73] As is the case with a patient for whom a plenary guardian has been

---

[69] **MD:** *E.g.,* Mack v. Mack, 618 A.2d 744 (Md. 1993).

NJ: *E.g., In re* Conroy, 486 A.2d 1209 (N.J. 1985).

WI: *E.g.,* L.W. v. L.E. Phillips Career Dev. Ctr., 482 N.W.2d 60, 71 (Wis. 1992) ("[C]ourt appointed guardians fulfill the parens patriae duty of the state to protect the best interests of an incompetent ward.").

[70] **NJ:** *In re* Conroy, 486 A.2d at 1240–41 ("Substitute decisionmaking by a guardian is not permissible unless the patient has been proven incompetent to make the particular medical treatment decision at issue.").

[71] **MI:** Martin v. Martin, 504 N.W.2d 917, 924 (Mich. Ct. App. 1993) ("The fact that a patient has previously been adjudicated incompetent is not controlling.").

[72] See **Ch. 5.**

[73] **FL:** *E.g.,* Browning v. Herbert, 543 So. 2d 258, 270 (Fla. Dist. Ct. App. 1989) ("A legal guardian may exercise the patient's right to forego medical treatment."), *aff'd,* 568 So. 2d 4, 13 (Fla. 1990) (by implication) ("We hold that, because Mrs. Browning was unable to exercise her constitutional right of privacy by reason of her medical condition, her guardian was authorized to exercise it for her."); John F. Kennedy Memorial Hosp. v. Bludworth, 452 So. 2d 921, 926 (Fla. 1984).

MO: *E.g., In re* Warren, 858 S.W.2d 263, 265 (Mo. Ct. App. 1993) ("Pursuant to [Mo. Rev. Stat.] section 475.120, a guardian is empowered and charged to act in the ward's best interest. The guardian is authorized without further court order to consent to medical treatment on behalf of the ward. § 475.120.3(2)-(5)."). *But see* Cruzan v. Harmon, 760 S.W.2d 408, 424 (Mo. 1988) ("The statute [Mo. Rev. Stat. § 475.120.3 (1986)] makes no provision for the termination of medical treatment; to the contrary, it places an express, affirmative duty on guardians

appointed, the guardian should be presumed to have the authority to make decisions about forgoing life-sustaining treatment, but the presumption should be regarded as a weak one. Hence, authorization from the patient's family to administer or to forgo life-sustaining treatment also ought to be sought.

In jurisdictions in which there is substantial uncertainty about the need for judicial involvement in the decisionmaking process, it is still reasonable to indulge the presumption that a plenary guardian has the authority to make decisions about life-sustaining medical treatment unless the guardianship statute clearly states otherwise.

A guardian's authority to forgo life-sustaining treatment should be considered to be weaker if the authority to make medical decisions was conferred before the question of forgoing life-sustaining treatment arose. For example, the New Jersey Supreme Court stated in *Conroy* that a general guardian of the person did not have the inherent authority to make a decision to forgo life-sustaining treatment, and that a guardian must be specifically empowered to make such a decision because "a general appointment does not necessarily mean that the incompetent cannot make an informed judgment regarding a *particular medical* treatment."[74] However, this holding is questionable in light of subsequent New Jersey holdings that the surrogate decisionmaker need not even be a court-appointed guardian.[75]

In effect, this is a reiteration of the idea that incompetence is specific to the decision in question.[76] In many cases there will be no doubt that the patient is incompetent for all purposes, as, for example, when the patient is comatose. In most jurisdictions to have considered the issue, family members have the inherent legal authority in such situations to make decisions about forgoing

---

to assure that the ward receives medical care and provides the guardian with the power to give consent for that purpose. We thus find no statutory basis for the argument that the guardian possess authority, as a guardian, to order the termination of medical treatment.").

NJ: *E.g., In re* Conroy, 486 A.2d 1242 (Court involvement is ordinarily not warranted if "a personal guardian has been previously appointed.").

WA: *E.g., In re* Colyer, 660 P.2d 738, 746–47 (Wash. 1983) ("[D]ecision to refuse life sustaining treatment is one that falls under the general powers of the guardian and does not routinely require a court order.").

[74] **NJ:** *In re* Conroy, 486 A.2d at 1241–42 (emphasis added) (not addressing fact that guardian, who was patient's nephew, had previously made critical health care decision in not consenting to amputation).

MD: *Accord* Mack v. Mack, 618 A.2d 744, 752–53 (Md. 1993) (although statute provides that court can grant guardian power to make medical decisions, including withholding treatment, statute does not permit guardian of a person to withhold or withdraw life-sustaining treatment without specific court authorization if there is "'a substantial risk to the life of a disabled person,'" even though guardian was appointed when patient was already in persistent vegetative state).

[75] *See In re* Peter, 529 A.2d 419 (N.J. 1987) (suggesting that clinical designation of a surrogate is an acceptable practice); *In re* Jobes, 529 A.2d 434 (N.J. 1987) (same). See § **5.14.**

[76] See § **4.25.**

life-sustaining treatment, and it is not necessary for there to be a judicially-appointed guardian to do so. However, when a guardian has already been appointed, it is far less certain that such a guardian does have the authority to make decisions about forgoing life-sustaining treatment. Thus, even when there is no uncertainty about a patient's incompetence, it might be advisable to initiate a judicial proceeding to determine the suitability of a previously-appointed guardian for the new purpose of making decisions about life-sustaining treatment.[77]

A general guardian's role is even more attenuated in Massachusetts. Even when the guardian is specifically appointed as a result of the patient's incompetence to make medical decisions and for the purpose of participating in the medical decisionmaking process, the guardian's role is merely to determine whether the attending physician conforms to the judicial order concerning the withdrawal, limitation, or administration of treatment.[78]

The *Busalacchi* case[79] raised the question of a guardian's authority to transfer his ward to a health care facility in another jurisdiction. This is likely to be an important issue in states where the standards for decisionmaking for incompetent patients are unclear or are particularly stringent, such as New York, or Missouri where *Busalacchi* arose.

Although not previously litigated in a reported case prior to *Busalacchi,* there had been speculation that patients might be transferred from jurisdictions with such standards to those with less stringent standards for the termination of life support. When a New York trial court denied a petition to terminate a patient's tube feedings in *Elbaum v. Grace Plaza of Great Neck, Inc.,*[80] some wondered whether the family would not be better off transferring the patient to neighboring New Jersey, where the law was thought to be more hospitable to this request. Instead, the family appealed and the trial court's ruling was reversed. There was similar speculation about transferring Nancy Cruzan from Missouri to a neighboring state, but again another tack was taken—namely, new evidence was introduced at a new hearing regarding the patient's wishes, evidence that was found by the trial court to meet the substantive and evidentiary standards necessary to terminate tube-feeding.[81]

---

[77] *In re* Conroy, 486 A.2d at 1241–42 ("[I]f the patient already has a general guardian, the court should determine whether that guardian is a suitable person to represent the patient with respect to the medical decision in question.").

[78] *In re* Spring, 405 N.E.2d 115, 121–22 (Mass. 1980) ("Under the 'substituted judgment doctrine' of the *Saikewicz* case, . . . the guardian, like the court, must seek to identify and effectuate the actual values and preferences of the ward.").

[79] *In re* Busalacchi, No. 59582, 1991 WL 26851, 1991 Mo. App. LEXIS 315 (Mar. 5, 1991), *appealed and remanded,* No. 73677 (Mo. Oct. 16, 1991).

[80] 544 N.Y.S.2d 840 (App. Div. 1989).

[81] *See* Cruzan v. Mouton, Estate No. CV384-9P (Mo. Cir. Ct. Jasper County Dec. 14, 1990), *reported in* 6 Issues L. & Med. 433 (1991).

In *Busalacchi,* the patient had suffered severe head injuries in an automobile accident. After lengthy stays in an acute care hospital and a rehabilitation hospital, she was transferred to a state-owned rehabilitation center, with a diagnosis of persistent vegetative state. The rehabilitation center eventually recommended transfer of the patient to a skilled nursing facility, but the patient's father, who had been judicially appointed to serve as her guardian, "[d]espite contacting more than 30 nursing homes in Missouri and in California, . . . was unsuccessful in securing placement."[82]

When the guardian sought to transfer the patient to a hospital in Minnesota, the rehabilitation center staff changed the diagnosis to something less severe than persistent vegetative state, and the state sought an injunction to prevent the transfer, arguing that the guardian's intent "was to remove her gastrostomy tube because Minnesota's requirements for removing the feeding tube were less stringent than the requirements in Missouri."[83] The guardian claimed that his purpose in seeking the transfer was that the rehabilitation center "repeatedly had refused to conduct a neurological evaluation of Christine [and that a]t the facility in Minnesota, a team of physicians and therapists, under the direction and supervision of nationally-renowned neurologists, would conduct a complete neurological evaluation of Christine with her gastrostomy tube in place[, which] . . . would take weeks to complete."[84] The guardian also testified "that the removal of the gastrostomy tube . . . was an option he would consider, if the physicians in Minnesota recommended that course of action based upon the results of their neurological evaluation."[85] The trial court denied the state's motion for an injunction and dissolved the temporary restraining order.

The Missouri Court of Appeals reversed and remanded for a determination of a number of factual issues, contending that "[t]his is not a right-to-die case, as *Cruzan* was, because the issue of the actual termination of Christine's feeding and hydration tube is not before us."[86] Rather, the issue "is whether a guardian properly discharges his duties when he attempts to move his ward from the jurisdiction of the court for the ostensible reason of avoiding litigation in Missouri where the decision to remove the feeding tube from his ward may be subject to heightened legal scrutiny."[87] Because a guardian is statutorily charged with acting in the ward's best interests and because moving the ward might constitute a breach of the guardian's legal duties, the court remanded for additional findings that would shed light on what was in the ward's best interests—specifically, evidence about the patient's "present level of physical, sensory, emotional, and cognitive functioning; the medical care she is receiving

[82] *In re* Busalacchi, No. 59582, slip op. at 3 (Mo. Ct. App. Mar. 5, 1991).

[83] *Id.* at 3.

[84] *Id.* at 4.

[85] *Id.*

[86] *Id.* at 10.

[87] *Id.* at 12–13.

presently; and treatment options for her in the future."[88] The state has the burden of going forward with this evidence, and the burden of establishing "that her medical needs are being met at the present time and can be met adequately in the future within the jurisdiction of the Missouri courts."[89] If the state meets its burden, it is the obligation of the guardian

> to provide a reasonable basis for the need to move Christine to another jurisdiction other than a desire to avoid the laws of Missouri. In that regard, the court should consider several nonexclusive factors; such as, guardian's knowledge and perception of Christine's condition, treatment, and prognosis; any additional health risks to Christine attendant upon the move; the need for diagnostic and/or treatment facilities that are available in another jurisdiction; guardian's motivation in moving Christine; the ability and willingness of a health care facility in Missouri to provide the appropriate level of medical care; and the family support, if any, available in the receiving jurisdiction. Only by weighing all the evidence, can the court determine whether the move from Missouri is in the best interests of Christine.[90]

The court's claim that this was not a "right-to-die case" was disingenuous, unless the court meant that this was not a right-to-die case *at that time,* but would become one once the necessary findings of fact were made on remand. It seems clear that, after the hearing on remand, the court intended to apply the standards enunciated in *Cruzan v. Harmon.*[91] Requiring as those standards do that there be clear and convincing evidence of the patient's actual wish to have life support terminated, expressed prior to losing decisionmaking capacity, they would be impossible to meet, because Ms. Busalacchi never expressed any opinion on this subject.

In dissent, Judge Smith offered a number of reasons for affirmance of the trial court's orders. One of the more significant was the argument that the standards to which judicially appointed guardians ought to be held are different from those for parents acting as natural guardians; because the guardian was the patient's father and because the patient was a minor at the time of incapacitation, the parental standards ought to apply. The judge propounded the well-accepted position that parents have a range of discretion in medical decisionmaking for their children, limited only when the exercise of discretion would constitute neglect. Because there "is no evidence or claim of neglect here [and t]he State did not seek Mr. Busalacchi's removal as guardian,"[92] the guardian's decision to transfer the patient to a health care facility in another state is not unreasonable and does not constitute a " 'failure to supply the minimum quality of care which the community will tolerate.' "[93]

---

[88] *In re* Busalacchi, No. 59582, slip op. at 11 (Mo. Ct. App. Mar. 5, 1991).

[89] *Id.*

[90] *Id.* at 12.

[91] 760 S.W.2d 408 (Mo. 1988).

[92] *In re* Busalacchi, No. 59582, slip op. at 5 (Smith, J., dissenting).

[93] *Id.* at 5.

The dissent also believed that the findings of fact to be made on remand had already been made by the trial court, and that the trial court had also "concluded that the patient would remain in the United States and that she would have the protection of the laws of the United States and the State of Minnesota which are entitled to full faith and credit."[94] Finally, Judge Smith emphasized the guardian's claim that, as a matter of federal constitutional law, "a state cannot prevent its residents from traveling to another state to take advantage of the laws of that state,"[95] and that the state to which they would travel "is not a medical or ethical wasteland."[96]

The case was appealed to the Missouri Supreme Court, which, after hearing argument, remanded for more information, including information on the patient's diagnosis of persistent vegetative state.[97] After the Missouri Supreme Court remanded the case, the probate court reconsidered the matter and again permitted the transfer.[98] The state again appealed. The Missouri Supreme Court heard oral argument, but dismissed the case on motion of the state before issuing a decision.[99] Three days later, on application of a self-described "right-to-life advocate," a St. Louis trial court issued a restraining order barring any transfer.[100] Nonetheless, Christine Busalacchi died on March 7, 1993, after her feeding tube was removed, almost six years after the accident that left her in a persistent vegetative state.[101] The director of the Missouri Department of Health subsequently announced that the state would no longer become involved in decisions by families to forgo life-sustaining treatment.[102]

§ 4.19 ——Limited Guardianship for Medical Decisionmaking

If a guardian was explicitly granted authority to make decisions about the ward's medical care in general, health care personnel should presumptively treat the guardian as the patient's lawful surrogate. Unless the order appointing the guardian specifies that his authority is temporary or limited to a particular medical decision, the attending physician should regard the guardian, rather than the patient, as the appropriate decisionmaker.[103]

---

[94] *Id.* at 7.

[95] *Id.* at 8

[96] *Id.* at 9.

[97] *In re* Busalacchi, No. 73677, 1991 Mo. LEXIS 107 (Oct. 16, 1991).

[98] *See* Lewin, *Man Is Allowed to Let Daughter Die,* N.Y. Times, Jan. 27, 1993, at A7 (nat'l ed.).

[99] Busalacchi v. Busalacchi, No. 73677, 1993 WL 32356 (Mo. Jan. 26, 1993).

[100] *See A Right-to-Die Battle Is Still on in Missouri,* N.Y. Times, Jan. 31, 1993, at 29 (late ed.).

[101] *Comatose Woman, Focus of Court Battle, Dies,* N.Y. Times, Mar. 8, 1993, at A7 (nat'l ed.).

[102] *Mo. Bowing Out of Right-to-Die Cases,* Am. Med. News, Mar. 15, 1993, at 36.

[103] See §§ **7.45–7.46.**

Some guardianship statutes, by their terms, empower guardians to consent to medical treatment for the ward. For instance, Missouri's statute empowers the guardian to "assure that the ward receives medical care and other services that are needed."[104] The Missouri Supreme Court construed this statute as prohibiting a guardian from terminating medical care.[105] By contrast, most courts that have considered this issue have followed the lead of the Washington Supreme Court in *Colyer.* The court construed a guardianship statute that states that a guardian of a person has the power "to care for and maintain the incompetent or disabled person, assert his or her rights and best interests, and provide timely, informed consent to necessary medical procedures"[106] as necessarily empowering the guardian to refuse treatment, including life-sustaining treatment, because he is exercising the patient's legal right to do so.[107] The Arizona Supreme Court explained it this way:

> [T]he right to consent to or approve the delivery of medical care must necessarily include the right to consent to or approve the delivery of no medical care. To hold otherwise would . . . ignore the fact that oftentimes a patient's interests are best served when medical treatment is withheld or withdrawn. To hold otherwise would also reduce the guardian's control over medical treatment to little more than a mechanistic rubberstamp for the wishes of the medical treatment team. . . . [T]he Public Fiduciary as Rasmussen's guardian had the implied, if not express, statutory authority to exercise Rasmussen's right to refuse medical treatment.[108]

---

104 Mo. Rev. Stat. § 475.120.3 (1986).

105 Cruzan v. Harmon, 760 S.W.2d 408, 424 (Mo. 1988).

106 Wash. Rev. Code § 11.92.040(3) (1979).

107 **WA:** *In re* Colyer, 660 P.2d 738, 746 (Wash. 1983).

108 **AZ:** Rasmussen v. Fleming, 741 P.2d 674, 688 (Ariz. 1987).

CA: *Accord* Drabick v. Drabick, 245 Cal. Rptr. 840, 850 (Ct. App. 1988) ("[A] common sense point about statutory interpretation [is that] a statute that requires a person to make a decision contemplates a decision either way.").

IL: *Accord In re* Estate of Greenspan, 558 N.E.2d 1194 (Ill. 1990); Estate of Longeway v. Community Convalescent Ctr., 549 N.E.2d 292, 298 (Ill. 1989) ("[T]he Probate Act impliedly authorizes a guardian to exercise the right to refuse artificial sustenance on her ward's behalf. Section 11a-17 . . . specifically permits a guardian to make provisions for her ward's 'support, care, comfort, health, education and maintenance.' . . . Moreover, if the patient previously executed a power of attorney under the Powers of Attorney for Health Care Law (Ill. Rev. Stat. 1987, ch. 110-1/2, para. 804-1 et seq.), that act permits her to authorize her agent to terminate the food and water that sustain her (Ill. Rev. Stat. 1987, ch. 110-1/2, par. 804-10).").

IN: *Accord In re* Lawrance, 579 N.E.2d 32, 39 (Ind. 1991) (statutorily authorized family member's "right to consent to the patient's course of treatment necessarily includes the right to refuse a course of treatment").

KY: *Accord* DeGrella v. Elston, 858 S.W.2d 698, 704 (Ky. 1993) (absence in guardianship statutes of provision authorizing guardian of patient in persistent vegetative state to authorize termination of treatment does not preclude such authority because statutes were remedial rather than exclusive).

In some jurisdictions, courts have construed statutes authorizing the appointment of a guardian for medical decisionmaking purposes to include making decisions about life-sustaining treatment.[109]

If a patient who is de jure or de facto incompetent is still able to express views about medical care, the guardian and attending physician need to ensure that the guardian's decision is in conformance with the controlling standard.[110] Before permitting a guardian appointed to make medical decisions in general to make decisions about life-sustaining treatment, health care personnel should assure themselves that the guardian meets the substantive qualifications to make end-of-life decisions,[111] and that there is no statutory[112] or common-law[113] authority specifically prohibiting this in the jurisdiction.

§ 4.20 Effect of De Facto Incompetence

Individuals who lack decisionmaking capacity but have not been adjudicated incompetent (that is, they are de facto incompetent) are often treated as if they

---

MD: *Accord In re* Riddlemoser, 564 A.2d 812, 816 n.4 (Md. 1989) (power "'to give necessary consent or approval for medical or other professional care, counsel, treatment, or service'" necessarily implies "power to withhold or withdraw consent to medical treatment") (quoting Md. Est. & Trusts Code Ann. § 13-708(b)(8) and citing with approval 73 Md. Op. Att'y Gen. 253 (Op. No. 88-046, Oct. 17, 1988)).

MN: *Accord In re* Torres, 357 N.W.2d 332, 339 (Minn. 1984) ("[S]imply equating the continued physical existence of [an incompetent patient], who has no chance for recovery, with the [patient's] 'best interests' is contrary to law and medical opinion.").

MO: *Accord In re* Warren, 858 S.W.2d 263, 265 (Mo. Ct. App. 1993).

NY: *Cf.* N.Y. Pub. Health Law § 2963(1) ("A lack of capacity shall not be presumed from the fact that a . . . conservator . . . or . . . a guardian has been appointed.").

WI: *Accord* L.W. v. L.E. Phillips Career Dev. Ctr., 482 N.W.2d 60, 71 (Wis. 1992) ("[A] guardian has identical decisionmaking powers as a health care agent [appointed pursuant to the health care power of attorney statute]. To construe the [guardianship statute] any other way would result in an individual losing his or her expressed right to refuse treatment upon appointment of a guardian.").

[109] **CA:** *E.g.,* Drabick v. Drabick, 245 Cal. Rptr. 840, 849 (Ct. App. 1988) (applying Cal. Prob. Code § 2355).

OH: *E.g., In re* Myers, 610 N.E.2d 663 (P. Ct. Summit County, Ohio 1993) (applying Ohio Rev. Code Ann. § 2111.13(C)).

[110] See **Ch. 7.**

[111] See §§ **5.15–5.24.**

[112] *See, e.g., In re* Torres, 357 N.W.2d 332, 337 (Minn. 1984) (Minnesota's statutory guardianship provision "requires the conservator to have court approval before consenting to more controversial medical procedures on behalf of the conservatee.").

[113] **MO:** *E.g.,* Cruzan v. Harmon, 760 S.W.2d 408, 424 (Mo. 1988) (statute that "places an express, affirmative duty on guardians to assure that the ward receives medical care and provides the guardian with the power to give consent for that purpose" does not provide basis for contending that "guardian possesses authority, as a guardian, to order the *termination* of medical treatment") (emphasis added).

NJ: *E.g., In re* Conroy, 486 A.2d 1209, 1242 (N.J. 1985).

had been adjudicated incompetent. For instance, important decisions about financial, medical, and other personal matters are often made by close family members for people who are extremely senile. These are the same kinds of decisions that a court-appointed guardian might make for an adjudicated incompetent.

The absence of wealth and of complicated financial problems generally militates against invoking so formal (and potentially expensive) a proceeding as an adjudication of incompetence and the appointment of a guardian to manage the incompetent's possibly token estate. Instead, family members often make less formal arrangements for taking care of the incompetent's financial affairs, such as conversion of the individual's checking account to a joint account with a relative or having a relative named as a "representative payee," who can then use Social Security checks for the incompetent's living expenses.[114]

Similarly, relatives often take over making decisions about a de facto incompetent's personal affairs. If, for example, a person can no longer cook meals, dress, or perform other tasks of daily living, relatives may simply move his or her belongings into their house or some type of supervised living arrangement, or into either an intermediate or skilled nursing facility if there are medical problems that require continual attention.

Perhaps the fundamental reason that an adjudication of incompetence is not sought is that ordinarily no one challenges the legitimacy of these informal arrangements for dealing with the financial and/or personal affairs of a de facto incompetent. The incompetent himself is frequently unable to challenge these arrangements. Third parties often have no interest in challenging them either; as long as the incompetent's financial liabilities are satisfied, creditors will not object. Similarly, if the person's needs for food, clothing, shelter, and health care are being met, friends or relatives are not likely to object, and social service agencies that are concerned with such issues will not have reason to learn of these informal arrangements.

§ 4.21 —Effect on Medical Decisionmaking

Only infrequently have patients been adjudicated incompetent *before* the issue of decisionmaking capacity arises in the medical decisionmaking process. When a guardian is appointed before issues about medical decisionmaking arise, it is usually to address issues concerning control of the patient's estate. This guardian is sometimes given authority over the person as well as the estate. Even in those exceptional cases in which an adjudication has occurred, it is not always clear whether the adjudication has any bearing on the patient's competence for purposes of medical decisionmaking.[115] So well accepted is the role of family members in making decisions for patients lacking decisionmaking capacity[116]

---

[114] 42 U.S.C.A. § 405(j) (West Supp. 1994); 42 U.S.C.A. § 1383(a)(2) (West 1992 & Supp. 1994).

[115] See §§ **4.15–4.19.**

[116] **NJ:** *In re* Farrell, 529 A.2d 404, 414 (N.J. 1987). See § **5.10.**

that the question is not why so few cases involving de facto incompetent patients go to court but why any do.

For the vast proportion of patients who have not been adjudicated incompetent but who in fact lack decisionmaking capacity, family members make decisions about treatment as a matter of course. This occurs largely because the participants in the medical decisionmaking process simply do not believe that recourse to the courts for an adjudication of incompetence and the appointment of a guardian is warranted. The issues may not be complex, the cost of legal proceedings can be substantial, delay is almost inevitable (and sometimes considerable), thus adding greatly to the cost of care if the patient is hospitalized, and can be injurious to the patient's health.

For medical decisionmaking purposes, the practical consequence for the patient who is dealt with as de facto incompetent is the same as if there had been an adjudication of incompetence: disenfranchisement for the purpose of making medical decisions and assumption of decisional authority by a surrogate decisionmaker. If the patient retains some ability to communicate and/or comprehend, he may continue to play some role in decisionmaking.[117] However, to the extent that the surrogate is viewed by the patient's attending physician and other clinicians as having legitimate authority over these matters, the role that the patient plays depends not only on the patient's residual abilities but also on the combined sufferance of the surrogate and the attending physician.

MEANING OF INCOMPETENCE

§ 4.22 Introduction

Writing more than a half-century ago, one early and prominent commentator on the concept of competence had this to say about the meaning of the term:

> [I]f one reads the cases critically it will be found that no verbal formulation of a test can be made which will fit the standards laid down by the courts. So diverse is the phraseology of the test by courts in different jurisdictions, and even by various opinions in the same jurisdiction, that no single statement of a rule can be constructed which, if it has meaning, will not exclude a majority of the cases.[118]

More than three decades later, the National Commission for the Protection of Human Subjects was still able to observe that there is no single, accepted definition of incompetence to make decisions about health care.[119] Today this

---

[117] See §§ **7.45–7.46.**

[118] Green, *Judicial Tests of Mental Incompetency,* 6 Mo. L. Rev. 141, 147 (1941).

[119] U.S. Dep't of HEW, *Protection of Human Subjects—Research Involving Those Institutionalized as Mentally Infirm: Report and Recommendations of the Nat'l Comm'n for the Protection of Human Subjects of Biomedical and Behavioral Research,* 43 Fed. Reg. 11,328, 11,345–46 (1978) ("[S]tatutory provisions for the adjudication of competence vary widely. . . . Court definitions of competency also vary.").

observation still holds in the main though there are beginning to be signs of an emerging consensus about the meaning of and standards for determining competence and incompetence, at least in the realm of medical decisionmaking.[120]

Competence is a central concern in medical decisionmaking for it is a sine qua non for the exercise of self-determination. Cases involving lifesaving or life-sustaining treatment, sterilization, and psychiatric care are some of the more important areas of decisionmaking in which the concept of incompetence plays a critical role. Nonetheless, the meaning of this concept is usually taken for granted or dealt with only in a cursory way by courts.[121] Few if any courts have grappled in any comprehensive way with the meanings of the concepts of competence and incompetence or decisionmaking capacity and incapacity.

A reason for this oblique treatment of such a fundamental issue is that, despite the theoretically central nature of competence, only rarely is the question before the court whether the patient is incompetent, though there are some important exceptions.[122] One reason is that in many right-to-die cases, there is no doubt that the patient is incompetent, as, for example, in cases in which the patient is comatose.[123] Also, the aversion to analysis may result from the fact that these concepts are elusive and highly fact-sensitive. For instance, in *Ingram,* the Washington Supreme Court recounted that

> [t]he [trial] court received into evidence . . . a letter by a psychiatrist . . . which stated: "[The patient] is totally incompetent because of organic brain syndrome due to chronic obstructive pulmonary disease. . . . She has carcinoma of the larynx and is unable to comprehend her risks."
>
> The only witness at the hearing was . . . a psychiatrist, who . . . testified that although she was fully alert and could respond directly to questions she suffered from delusions regarding the cause of her illness, believing the main cause of her problems was the bad air in her apartment.[124]

On the basis of this testimony and evidence, she was found incompetent, but neither the trial court nor the appellate court provided a definition of or standards for assessing incompetence.

---

[120] See §§ **4.26–4.27.**

[121] *See, e.g.,* Lane v. Candura, 376 N.E.2d 1232, 1233 (Mass. App. Ct. 1978) (trial court "decision does not include a clear-cut finding that Mrs. Candura lacks the requisite legal competence").

[122] **CA:** *E.g.,* Bartling v. Superior Court, 209 Cal. Rptr. 220 (Ct. App. 1984).

FL: *E.g.,* Satz v. Perlmutter, 362 So. 2d 160 (Fla. Dist. Ct. App. 1978).

NJ: *E.g., In re* Farrell, 529 A.2d 404 (N.J. 1987).

NY: *E.g., In re* Kerr (O'Brien), 517 N.Y.S.2d 346 (Sup. Ct. N.Y. County 1986).

[123] See § **9.53.**

[124] **WA:** *In re* Ingram, 689 P.2d 1363, 1365 (Wash. 1984).

MA: *Accord* Lane v. Candura, 376 N.E.2d 1232, 1233–34 (Mass. App. Ct. 1978).

NJ: *Accord In re* Clark, 510 A.2d 136, 137–38 (N.J. Super. Ct. Ch. Div. 1986).

OH: *Accord In re* Milton, 505 N.E.2d 255 (Ohio 1987) (patient with sincere belief in faith healing not delusional and not incompetent and has right to refuse surgery for cancer).

Courts have not been any more helpful in other right-to-die cases. They have been satisfied merely to conclude that the patient is incompetent. The following are examples of the kinds of statements that courts make about a patient's decisionmaking capacity:

- The patient "was always totally incapable of . . . making a reasoned decision about medical treatment."[125]
- "[H]e lacks ability to understand the information conveyed, to evaluate the options, or to communicate a decision."[126]
- The patient was "incapable of . . . intelligently consenting to care."[127]

Despite the absence of clear judicial guidance—or perhaps because of its absence—a good deal of attention has been given in scholarly writings to the meaning of incompetence. There has been a gradual coalescence around one particular approach, based on the patient's understanding of relevant information about decisionmaking.[128] Nonetheless, it cannot be emphasized too strongly that the case law is unclear on the meaning of incapacity to make medical decisions in general, an unclarity that carries over into right-to-die cases.

There are, however, two well-accepted approaches to assessing (if not actually defining) incompetence: the general incompetence approach and the specific incompetence approach. The former is the traditional approach, which is gradually being replaced in many jurisdictions by the latter.[129]

§ 4.23 General Incompetence

The *general incompetence* approach has long been the dominant approach used by courts. However, it is gradually falling into disfavor, spurred by legislative changes and by litigation aimed at enhancing the rights of the mentally ill and mentally retarded,[130] and by the realization that in fact, although some

---

[125] *In re* Storar, 420 N.E.2d 64, 72 (N.Y. 1981).

[126] *In re* Conroy, 486 A.2d 1209, 1241 (N.J. 1985).

[127] *In re* Hamlin, 689 P.2d 1372, 1374 (Wash. 1984).

[128] See § **4.26.**

[129] S. Brakel et al., The Mentally Disabled and the Law 375 (1985).

[130] **DMA:** *E.g.,* Rogers v. Commissioner, 458 N.E.2d 308, 314 (Mass. 1983).

DNJ: *E.g.,* Rennie v. Klein, 476 F. Supp. 1294 (D.N.J. 1979); Rennie v. Klein, 462 F. Supp. 1131 (D.N.J. 1978).

DOH: *E.g.,* Davis v. Hubbard, 506 F. Supp. 915 (N.D. Ohio 1980).

MI: *E.g.,* Martin v. Martin, 504 N.W.2d 917, 924 (Mich. Ct. App. 1993) ("generalized finding of incompetency" is inadequate to resolve the question of a patient's capacity to decide about treatment).

MN: *E.g.,* Jarvis v. Levine, 403 N.W.2d 298 (Minn. 1987).

individuals are incompetent for all purposes (for example, comatose patients), others lose the capacity to perform certain tasks but not others.

Under the general incompetence approach, incompetence is viewed as a characteristic of a person—in particular, an individual's overall ability to function.[131] In this approach, there are no degrees of incompetence: people are either competent or incompetent, though their status might change over time.[132] An individual who has been adjudicated incompetent is considered incompetent for all purposes. General incompetence has its roots in the legal concept in which an adult is presumed to be competent[133] unless and until adjudicated incompetent, and thereafter is considered incompetent for all purposes.[134]

The general incompetence approach is an inferential approach for two reasons. First, an assessment of incompetence is made primarily from a person's overall ability to function and to accomplish life's daily activities, rather than being measured directly. An excerpt from the testimony of an examining psychiatrist in *In re Clark* illustrates the kind of information on which the assessment is based:

> [A]lthough Clark frequently closed his eyes and was lethargic during the doctor's examination, he was able to respond when spoken to. Clark could whisper "yes" and "no" appropriately at times, and could follow instructions to use other means of communicating, such as nodding or shaking his head, or blinking his eyes. . . . [A]lthough Clark was not physically able to write (his hand went off the page), he was able to attempt a purposeful response to Dr. Wolfson's request that he write. He was able to respond to one-step commands, and to make simple arithmetic calculations by showing numbers with his fingers. However, this activity was not consistent or sustained. At times, Clark appeared confused and could not follow Dr. Wolfson's instructions. In response to Dr. Wolfson's question of whether he was happy, Clark nodded "yes." He was aware that he was in a hospital, although he did not know which hospital he was in.[135]

Second, it is an inferential approach because an inference about specific incapacities is drawn from an individual's overall inability to function. In

---

NY: *E.g.,* Rivers v. Katz, 495 N.E.2d 337 (N.Y. 1986); New York City Health & Hosps. Corp. v. Stein, 335 N.Y.S.2d 461 (Sup. Ct. N.Y. County 1972).

OK: *E.g., In re* K.K.B., 609 P.2d 747 (Okla. 1980).

PA: *E.g., In re* Yetter, 62 Pa. D. & C.2d 619, 623 (C.P. Northampton County 1973).

WI: *E.g.,* State *ex rel.* Jones v. Gerhardstein, 416 N.W.2d 883 (Wis. 1987).

[131] *See, e.g.,* Lane v. Candura, 376 N.E.2d 1232, 1233 (Mass. App. Ct. 1978) ("'ward is mentally ill for all purposes'").

[132] **WA:** *In re* Hamlin, 689 P.2d 1372, 1371 (Wash. 1984) ("[S]ome patients are more incompetent than others.").

[133] See § **4.8.**

[134] See § **4.12.**

[135] **NJ:** *In re* Clark, 510 A.2d 136, 137–38 (N.J. Super. Ct. Ch. Div. 1986).

DNY: *Accord In re* Department of Veterans Affairs Medical Ctr., 749 F. Supp. 495, 498 (S.D.N.Y. 1990).

particular, a lack of decisionmaking capacity is inferred from an individual's general incompetence. In the *Clark* case, based on the above evidence of the patient's general inability to function, the doctor concluded that "Clark is not competent to consent to the medical procedure."[136]

The general incompetence approach focuses on the qualities of the person outside the context of medical decisionmaking rather than exclusively within it, though it may take the latter into account as well. It might take into account how the person actually functions in a number of activities, for example, whether the person is able to provide for food, clothing, and shelter, and whether the inability to do any of these things is impeded by some specific functional deficit, such as the inability to maintain a checking account or to pay bills in a timely fashion.

In evaluating competence by this approach, no single factor is determinative. All impairments to cognitive functioning are considered, for example, mental retardation,[137] mental illness,[138] or alcohol or drug intoxication.[139] In addition to

---

[136] *In re* Clark, 510 A.2d at 138.

[137] **KY:** *Cf.* Strunk v. Strunk, 445 S.W.2d 145 (Ky. 1969) (organ transplantation from mentally retarded individual).

MA: *E.g.,* Superintendent of Belchertown State Sch. v. Saikewicz, 370 N.E.2d 417 (Mass. 1977); *In re* R.H., 622 N.E.2d 1071 (Mass. App. Ct. 1993).

NJ: *E.g., In re* Moorhouse, 593 A.2d 1256 (N.J. Super. Ct. App. Div. 1991).

NY: *E.g., In re* Storar, 420 N.E.2d 64 (N.Y. 1981); *cf. In re* Weberlist, 360 N.Y.S.2d 783 (Sup. Ct. N.Y. County 1974) (nonemergency surgery allowing retarded patient to live on own rather than in custodial care).

WA: *E.g., In re* Hamlin, 689 P.2d 1372 (Wash. 1984).

See generally Trenker, Annotation, *Jurisdiction of Court to Permit Sterilization of Mentally Defective Person in Absence of Specific Statutory Authority,* 74 A.L.R.3d 1210 (1976).

[138] **CA2:** *E.g.,* Winters v. Miller, 446 F.2d 65 (2d Cir. 1971).

CA5: *E.g.,* Lester v. Aetna Casualty & Sur. Co., 240 F.2d 676 (5th Cir. 1957).

KY: *E.g.,* Wilson v. Lehman, 379 S.W.2d 478 (Ky. 1964).

MA: *E.g., In re* Hier, 464 N.E.2d 959 (Mass. App. Ct. 1984).

NY: *E.g.,* New York City Health & Hosps. Corp. v. Stein, 335 N.Y.S.2d 461 (Sup. Ct. N.Y. County 1972).

PA: *E.g., In re* Yetter, 62 Pa. D. & C.2d 619, 623 (C.P. Northampton County, Pa. 1973).

WA: *E.g., In re* Ingram, 689 P.2d 1363 (Wash. 1984).

WI: *E.g.,* L.W. v. L.E. Phillips Career Dev. Ctr., 482 N.W.2d 60 (Wis. 1992).

[139] **MO:** *E.g.,* Moore v. Webb, 345 S.W.2d 239 (Mo. Ct. App. 1961).

NM: *E.g.,* Demers v. Gerety, 515 P.2d 645 (N.M. Ct. App. 1973).

NY: *Cf. In re* Lydia E. Hall Hosp., 455 N.Y.S.2d 706, 712 (Sup. Ct. Nassau County 1982) (When patient made decision, "he was alert, oriented and mentally competent to do so. He was not under the influence of analgesic medication or any other sense-altering substances.").

RI: *E.g.,* Miller v. Rhode Island Hosp., 625 A.2d 778 (R.I. 1993).

TX: *E.g.,* Gravis v. Physicians & Surgeons Hosp., 427 S.W.2d 310 (Tex. 1968).

WA: *E.g.,* Grannum v. Berard, 422 P.2d 812 (Wash. 1967).

See generally Lockwood, Annotation, *Mental Competency of Patient to Consent to Surgical Operation or Medical Treatment,* 25 A.L.R.3d 1439 (1969).

the person's general functioning, appearance, speech, cognitive processes, and affect may also be taken into account.

The major deficiency of this approach is that there can be no assurance of a correspondence between a determination of general incompetence and a person's actual ability to participate in medical decisionmaking. A person who seems to be generally incompetent—perhaps because of an inability to provide for life's basics, or perhaps because of manifest deficiencies in memory, cognition, or affect—may actually be capable of making decisions if a reasonable amount of time and energy is spent by health care professionals in working with the patient.

Despite its drawbacks, the general incompetence approach is not without some usefulness. One value is that it alerts persons caring for, or otherwise dealing with, a patient to the fact that the patient's decisionmaking faculties may be so compromised that decisions about treatment must be made by someone acting on the patient's behalf. In other words, if a person is generally incompetent, this is a signal that further inquiry should be made into specific incompetence.[140]

§ 4.24 —Use in Right-to-Die Cases

Despite its inadequacies, the general incompetence approach is frequently used to assess incompetence in clinical settings, sometimes in conjunction with other approaches, but sometimes alone. However, courts have rarely alluded to or even used this approach in right-to-die cases,[141] except in those cases in which there is no doubt about the patient's incompetence because the patient is unconscious[142] or seriously mentally retarded.[143]

---

[140] See §§ **4.25** and **4.33.**

[141] **DNY:** *But see In re* Department of Veterans Affairs Medical Ctr., 749 F. Supp. 495, 498 (S.D.N.Y. 1990) (patient incompetent because "no meaningful contact could be made with the patient").

MI: *But see* Martin v. Martin, 504 N.W.2d 917, 924 (Mich. Ct. App. 1993) ("[T]he trial court simply stated that he was not competent to decide.").

NY: *But see In re* Kerr (O'Brien), 517 N.Y.S.2d 346 (Sup. Ct. N.Y. County 1986) (no basis articulated for finding of incompetence).

[142] *See, e.g., In re* Eichner, 423 N.Y.S.2d 580, 588 (Sup. Ct. Nassau County 1979) ("There can be no question but that Brother Fox [who is in a persistent vegetative state] is incompetent."), *aff'd sub nom.* Eichner v. Dillon, 426 N.Y.S.2d 517 (App. Div. 1980), *modified sub nom. In re* Storar, 420 N.E.2d 64 (N.Y.), *cert. denied,* 454 U.S. 858 (1981).

[143] **MA:** *E.g.,* Superintendent of Belchertown State Sch. v. Saikewicz, 370 N.E.2d 417, 419 (Mass. 1977) ("a mentally retarded person . . . incapable of giving informed consent").

NY: *E.g., In re* Storar, 420 N.E.2d 64, 69 (N.Y. 1981) ("[H]e had an infant's mentality.").

WA: *E.g., In re* Hamlin, 689 P.2d 1372, 1374 (Wash. 1984) (patient had been severely mentally retarded since birth).

§ 4.25 Specific Incompetence

A consensus is emerging, in medical decisionmaking cases in general and right-to-die cases in particular, that incompetence should be viewed as an inability to perform a specific task; hence the term *specific incompetence.* Specific incompetence approaches reject the idea that incompetence is an all-or-nothing condition and instead focus on a person's ability to perform a particular task.[144] Although a general adjudication of incompetence renders an individual de jure incompetent, under a specific incompetence approach, the adjudication of incompetence does not necessarily affect the person's authority to make medical decisions.[145]

Whether one is incompetent depends upon the particular task in question and the particular context in which that task is to be performed. Indeed, under the specific incompetence approach, it does not even make sense to say that a person is incompetent; the only acceptable statement is one that is followed by an object—that is, a person is competent or incompetent to perform *x*.[146] Thus, a determination of specific incompetence, as the phrase suggests, does not result in a general disenfranchisement of the individual, but merely disqualifies the individual from performing a particular task.[147] Specific incompetence also is based on the recognition that for some (and possibly many) patients, incompetence is not binary but rather exists in degrees.[148] Some people are more or less competent than others;[149] some people are more or less competent at specific tasks;[150] and competency may vary over time.

---

[144] *See* President's Comm'n, Deciding to Forego Life-Sustaining Treatment 123 (Patients may have impaired capacity but not lack capacity.); McCullough, *Medical Care for Elderly Patients with Diminished Competence: An Ethical Analysis,* 32 J. Am. Geriatrics Soc'y 150, 151 (1984) ("There is a temptation to think that one's competence, the ability to perform a task, is an either/or matter. One either is or is not competent. This view, however, overlooks the complexity of competence. One is not broadly competent or incompetent. Instead, one is competent for specific tasks. In addition, one may not be altogether incompetent for specific tasks, but only in some respect or another.").

[145] **MI:** Martin v. Martin, 504 N.W.2d 917, 924 (Mich. Ct. App. 1993) ("The fact that a patient has previously been adjudicated incompetent is not controlling.").

NJ: *In re* Conroy, 486 A.2d 1209, 1241–42 (N.J. 1985) (general guardian of the person did not have the inherent authority to make a decision to forgo life-sustaining treatment).

[146] C. Culver & G. Gert, Philosophy in Medicine 52–61 (1982).

[147] N.Y. Pub. Health Law § 2963(5) (determination of incapacity to make a decision about cardiopulmonary resuscitation is not a determination that patient lacks capacity for any other purpose).

[148] **FL:** Browning v. Herbert, 543 So. 2d 258, 272 n.24 (Fla. Dist. Ct. App. 1989) ("The line between competency and incompetency is imprecise.").

IL: *Cf. In re* E.G., 549 N.E.2d 322 (Ill. 1989) (No "bright line" exists between mature minor who possesses decisionmaking capacity and minor who does not.).

[149] *In re* Hamlin, 689 P.2d 1372, 1371 (Wash. 1984).

[150] *See, e.g.,* N.Y. Pub. Health Law § 2963(5) (determination of incapacity to make a decision about cardiopulmonary resuscitation is not a determination that patient lacks capacity for any other purpose).

§ 4.26 The Emerging Consensus: Incompetence as Lack of Understanding

The approach to assessing specific incompetence based on a patient's understanding is emerging as the predominant one.[151] However, few courts have been explicit in recognizing this approach as authoritative, and sometimes it is not even certain whether a court is using it. Rather, a court's acceptance of this approach to assessing incompetence can sometimes only be inferred from the language that the court uses to describe a patient's decision, such as an "informed, rational and knowing decision,"[152] or to describe the patient as incompetent, such as "unable to express an informed choice,"[153] or from the facts that the court takes into account.[154] Also, the opinions that suggest this approach often do so as only one of a number of ways of assessing incompetence. For instance, in *Conroy,* the court stated that "[a] patient may be incompetent because he lacks the ability to understand the information conveyed, to evaluate the options, or to communicate a decision."[155]

---

[151] *See* Hastings Center Guidelines 131 (Part Six, III) (defining "decisionmaking capacity as: (a) the ability to comprehend information relevant to the decision; (b) the ability to deliberate about the choices in accordance with personal values and goals; and (c) the ability to communicate (verbally or nonverbally) with caregivers"); Saks, *Competency to Refuse Psychotropic Medication: Three Alternatives to the Law's Cognitive Standard,* 47 U. Miami L. Rev. 689, 691 & n.7 (1993) (Twentieth century American judicial cases involving competency to consent to medical treatment held that "a person is competent to make a treatment decision if she comprehends the caregiver's explanation of her condition and the treatment, and forms no patently false beliefs—"delusions"—about her condition and the treatment.").

[152] *In re* Lydia E. Hall Hosp., 455 N.Y.S.2d 706, 712 (Sup. Ct. Nassau County 1982).

[153] **NJ:** *In re* Quinlan, 355 A.2d 647, 663 (N.J. 1976).

NY: *Accord In re* Beth Israel Medical Ctr. (Weinstein), 519 N.Y.S.2d 511, 512–13 (Sup. Ct. N.Y. County 1987).

PA: *Accord In re* Doe, 45 Pa. D. & C.3d 371, 388–89 (C.P. Phila. County 1987).

[154] *See, e.g., In re* Kerr (O'Brien), 517 N.Y.S.2d 346, 347 (Sup. Ct. N.Y. County 1986) ("[H]is degree of alertness varied considerably from moment to moment. . . . He was able to respond to some questions with an affirmative squeeze of the hand, to shake his head negatively as to other questions, and to avert his gaze or not respond at all to the more difficult questions. His eyes would close and his head would nod at several points during the interview. Indeed, he appeared to be on the verge of being semi-comatose.").

[155] **NJ:** *In re* Conroy, 486 A.2d 1209, 1241 (N.J. 1985).

MA: *Accord* Lane v. Candura, 376 N.E.2d 1232, 1236 (Mass. App. Ct. 1978) (patient did not lack "ability to understand that in rejecting the amputation she is, in effect, choosing death over life").

MI: *Accord* Martin v. Martin, 504 N.W.2d 917, 924 (Mich. Ct. App. 1993).

NV: *Accord* McKay v. Bergstedt, 801 P.2d 617, 620 (Nev. 1990) ("able to understand the nature and consequences of his decision").

NJ: *Accord In re* Clark, 510 A.2d 136, 137 (N.J. Super. Ct. Ch. Div. 1986) (test "is whether the patient can reasonably understand the condition, the nature and effect of the proposed treatment, and the attendant risks of not pursuing the treatment") (citing *In re* Conroy, 486 A.2d at 1241); *In re* Quackenbush, 383 A.2d 785 (N.J. Super. Ct. P. Div. 1978) (patient capable of appreciating nature and consequences of forgoing treatment). *Cf. In re* Schiller, 372

There are gradually beginning to be some notable exceptions in which courts more clearly articulate that they are using a specific incompetence approach. For example, in the *A.C.* case, the District of Columbia Court of Appeals explicitly recognized that "competence in a case such as this turns on the patient's ability to function as a decision-maker, acting in accordance with her preferences and values."[156] In deciding cases involving teenage children, courts have also begun to recognize that being a minor is not tantamount to lacking decisionmaking capacity. Rather, "mature" minors are entitled to the same decisionmaking prerogatives as adults, or as the Illinois Supreme Court put it, there is no "'bright line' age restriction" separating adults from children.[157] Similarly, the West Virginia Supreme Court, in holding that a physician must obtain the consent of a mature minor patient to enter a do-not-resuscitate (DNR) order rather than the consent of the patient's parents, stated that "[w]hether a child is a mature minor is a question of fact" and that the factual determination includes "whether the minor has the capacity to appreciate the nature, risks, and consequences of the medical procedure to be performed, or the treatment to be

---

372 A.2d 360, 366 (N.J. Super. Ct. Ch. Div. 1977) (patient must have "sufficient mind to reasonably understand the condition, the nature and effect of the proposed treatment, attendant risks in pursuing the treatment, and not pursuing the treatment").

NY: *Accord In re* Storar, 420 N.E.2d 64, 72 (N.Y. 1981) (incompetence defined as either "incapab[ility] of understanding or making a reasoned decision about medical treatment"); *In re* Harvey "U," 501 N.Y.S.2d 920, 921 (App. Div. 1986) (ability to make "an informed, rational decision on the basis of the risks and benefits of the surgery . . . and comprehending the seriousness of his condition and the consequences of not having the procedure performed"). *Cf.* N.Y. Pub. Health Law § 2961(3) ("'Capacity' means the ability to understand and appreciate the nature and consequences of an order not to resuscitate, including the benefits and disadvantages of such an order, and to reach an informed decision regarding the order.").

RI: *Accord* Miller v. Rhode Island Hosp., 625 A.2d 778, 785–86 (R.I. 1993) ("[T]he test for mental capacity to consent to medical treatment is whether the patient has 'sufficient mind to reasonably understand the condition, the nature and effect of the proposed treatment, [and the] attendant risks in pursuing the treatment, and not pursuing the treatment[.]'" [Citations omitted.]).

TN: *Cf.* State Dep't of Human Resources v. Northern, 563 S.W.2d 197 (Tenn. Ct. App. 1978) (patient did not appreciate the fact that she must make a choice).

WA: *Cf. In re* Hamlin, 689 P.2d 1372, 1374 (Wash. 1984) (petition asserted that Hamlin was "'incapable of understanding his illness or intelligently consenting to care'").

WV: *Accord* Belcher v. Charleston Area Medical Ctr., 422 S.E.2d 827, 838 (W. Va. 1992) (capacity to appreciate nature, risks, and consequences of medical procedure).

[156] **DC:** *In re* A.C., 573 A.2d 1235, 1244 (D.C. 1990).

MD: *Cf. In re* Riddlemoser, 564 A.2d 812, 813 (Md. 1989) (statute authorizes appointment of a guardian upon finding that "person lacks sufficient understanding or capacity to make or communicate responsible decisions concerning his person, including provisions for health care").

MI: *Accord* Martin v. Martin, 504 N.W.2d 917 (Mich. Ct. App. 1993).

[157] *In re* E.G., 549 N.E.2d 322, 326 (Ill. 1989).

administered or withheld."[158] In effect, these courts recognize that incompetence is not a global matter, but is specific to particular tasks.

Under this approach, there is a critical need to specify what it is the patient must be unable to understand in order to be deemed incompetent, but the courts frequently fail to attend to this. For instance, in discussing the patient's incompetence in *Storar,* the court remarked that "[h]e was always totally incapable of understanding."[159] Because the patient was mentally retarded since birth, in this case it was sufficient to imply that because he was incapable of understanding anything (so far as could be discerned), he was also incapable of understanding whatever is specifically necessary to understand in the context of medical decisionmaking. To define incompetence in this way, however, does not go much further than the general incompetence approach.

There are patients who are incapable of understanding some things but capable of understanding others, so it is necessary to be specific about what understanding must be deficient in order to deem the patient incompetent to make medical decisions. Because the issue of the patient's incompetence arises in the context of medical decisionmaking, what the patient should understand is information necessary to make the relevant treatment decision. This has been most clearly set forth by the Michigan Court of Appeals in the *Martin* case:

> The test for determining if a person has the requisite capacity to make a decision concerning the withholding or withdrawal of life-sustaining medical treatment is whether the person (1) has sufficient mind to reasonably understand the condition, (2) is capable of understanding the nature and effect of the treatment choices, (3) is aware of the consequences associated with those choices, and (4) is able to make an informed choice that is voluntary and not coerced.[160]

On remand in *Martin,* the trial court stated that the patient "does not have, nor will he regain, sufficient decision-making capacity with respect to a decision to withdraw life-sustaining medical treatment" because he could "understand only very short and very simple questions and cannot accurately comprehend

---

[158] Belcher v. Charleston Area Medical Ctr., 422 S.E.2d 827, 838 (W. Va. 1992).

[159] *In re* Storar, 420 N.E.2d 64, 72 (N.Y. 1981).

[160] **MI:** Martin v. Martin, 504 N.W.2d 917, 924 (Mich. Ct. App. 1993). *Accord* Martin v. Martin, 517 N.W.2d 749 (Mich. Ct. App. 1994).

DC: *Accord In re* A.C., 573 A.2d 1235, 1247 (D.C. 1990) (patient who "was unable to give an informed consent based on her assessment of the risks and benefits of the contemplated surgery" was incompetent).

NJ: *Accord In re* Farrell, 529 A.2d 404, 413 n.7 (N.J. 1987) (citing *In re* Conroy, 486 A.2d 1209, 1222 (N.J. 1985)) (incompetent patient is one who lacks "a clear understanding of the nature of his or her illness and prognosis, and of the risks and benefits of the proposed treatment, and [lacks] the capacity to reason and make judgments about that information").

WV: *Accord* Belcher v. Charleston Area Medical Ctr., 422 S.E.2d 827, 838 (W. Va. 1992) (capacity to appreciate nature, risks, and consequences of medical procedure).

questions that are lengthy, verbose, or that require the retention of multiple thoughts."[161]

The information that the *Martin* court mentioned, of course, is information of the type a physician is required to give the patient under the informed consent doctrine:[162] material information about the potential risks and benefits of treatment, the nature and purpose of the treatment, and the available alternatives. When the determination of incompetency is made by a court, the court should make specific findings about these elements of incompetence.[163] In right-to-die cases, additional information must also be provided.[164]

Although relatively easy to state, the understanding approach still has potential pitfalls. Some of the more apparent ones are:

1. What level of understanding must the patient fail to achieve to be considered incompetent?
2. By what means is it to be determined that the patient does not understand?
3. What is the extent, if any, of the physician's obligation to probe the patient's understanding, or may the physician merely rely upon the patient's statement that he does understand or the absence of any overt sign that the patient does not understand?

In addition, understanding should probably not be measured solely by reference to cognitive criteria. It may not be adequate that a patient can recall information, repeat it, and intelligently answer questions using it. A patient who can do all of these things but is unable to apply the information to her own situation may still be considered incompetent. In other words, a patient must be able to appreciate the relevance of the information to his own situation.[165] For example, a patient may be incompetent even if he understands that he has cancer, that cancer is life-threatening but can sometimes be cured through treatments, and that there may be a number of therapeutic options, each with its own risks and benefits.

---

[161] Martin v. Martin, 517 N.W.2d at 751.

[162] See §§ **3.13–3.15.**

[163] Martin v. Martin, 504 N.W.2d 917, 924–25 (Mich. Ct. App. 1993) (trial court should "issue specific findings reflecting consideration of the various factors for assessing a person's capacity to decide questions of medical treatment").

[164] See § **4.27.**

[165] **MA:** *In re* Hier, 464 N.E.2d 959, 965 (Mass. App. Ct. 1984) ("The judge could reasonably find that, if she were able to appreciate the prospective benefit, Mrs. Hier would look beyond the minor pain associated with hypodermic injection but that she would feel otherwise with respect to a major surgery of dubious benefit and, to her, substantial burden.").

TN: State Dep't of Human Resources v. Northern, 563 S.W.2d 197, 209 (Tenn. Ct. App. 1978) (capacity includes ability to appreciate all relevant facts).

Such was the situation in the *Ingram* case, in which the patient "suffered from delusions regarding the cause of her illness, believing the main cause of her problems was the bad air in her apartment."[166] Because she was unable to appreciate the import of the information for her own condition, she was properly found to be incompetent.

§ 4.27 —Necessity for Adequate Disclosure

Before a patient should be deemed to lack decisionmaking capacity because of a lack of understanding of the information that should be disclosed in order to obtain informed consent, at least two conditions must have been met. First, the physician's disclosure must have been adequate to permit the patient to understand, and second, the physician must have provided the information to the patient in a manner that was susceptible of being understood.[167]

A patient may appear to be incompetent, but not be under the specific incompetence approach, because he is making a decision on the basis of information that is inadequate or incorrect or both. The same patient, if provided with adequate, accurate information material to the decision in question, might appear quite different. If a component of decisionmaking capacity is the ability to appreciate the significance of information about one's own situation, a patient should not be considered incompetent if his denial of the need for a particular treatment results from his not having been told his diagnosis and/or prognosis.

When decisionmaking about life-sustaining treatment occurs, it is essential that, in addition to the other standard elements of information required by the informed consent doctrine,[168] patients know their diagnosis and their prognosis both with and without the treatment or treatments in question. More specifically, they must be told that they are terminally or incurably ill and that the treatment or treatments in question will possibly prolong life but not restore health, if that is the case. If a particular treatment is not curative, patients should also be told that it will only extend life but not save it and be told the likely duration of that

---

[166] **WA:** *In re* Ingram, 689 P.2d 1363, 1365 (Wash. 1984).

DNY: *Accord In re* Department of Veterans Affairs Medical Ctr., 749 F. Supp. 495, 499 (S.D.N.Y. 1990) (refusal of treatment by wife of incompetent patient would not be respected in part because of wife's denial of severity of husband's condition).

[167] **MI:** Martin v. Martin, 504 N.W.2d 917, 924 (Mich. Ct. App. 1993) ("Special care must be taken to ensure that sufficient information has been provided to enable the patient to make an informed choice.") (citing National Ctr. for State Courts, Guidelines for State Court Decision Making in Life-Sustaining Medical Treatment Cases 55–56 (1991)).

NY: *Cf. In re* Lydia E. Hall Hosp., 455 N.Y.S.2d 706, 712 (Sup. Ct. Nassau County 1982).

[168] See § **3.15.**

extension and the benefits and burdens associated both with undergoing and forgoing the treatment or treatments in question.[169]

§ 4.28 Other Approaches to Specific Incompetence

Although the understanding approach to defining specific incompetence appears to be predominant and is the one most consonant with the informed consent doctrine, several others have been mentioned by commentators[170] and some have found some judicial support.

§ 4.29 —Manifestation of Choice

The simplest approach to defining specific incompetence is the manifestation of choice approach, in which a patient who is unable to manifest a choice is deemed to be incompetent to make medical decisions.[171] All other patients, in accordance with the presumption of competence, are viewed as having the capacity to make medical decisions.

---

[169] **CA:** Bartling v. Superior Court, 209 Cal. Rptr. 220, 223 (Ct. App. 1984) (no question patient who "knew he would die if the ventilator were disconnected but nevertheless preferred death to life sustained by mechanical means" was competent).

NY: *In re* Lydia E. Hall Hosp., 455 N.Y.S.2d at 712 (decision was made "with full knowledge that in the absence of the continuation of extraordinary means, namely, his dialysis, his terminal illness would inexorably lead to his demise").

PA: Pocono Medical Ctr. v. Harley, 11 Fiduc. Rep. 2d 128, 129 (C.P. Monroe County, Pa. 1990) (The patient was found to be competent at the time of her advance directive because she was "alert, coherent, oriented in all spheres and fully cognizant of the terminal nature of her illness and the alternative treatments available. . . . The patient acknowledged that her refusal of these extraordinary means could result in death.").

[170] *See* A. Buchanan & D. Brock, Deciding for Others: The Ethics of Surrogate Decision Making (1989); R. Faden & T. Beauchamp, A History and Theory of Informed Consent 291 (1986); Drane, *Competency to Give an Informed Consent,* 252 JAMA 925 (1984); Schaffner, *Competency: A Triaxial Concept,* in Competency: A Study of Informal Competency Determinations in Primary Care 253 (M. Gardell-Cutter & E. Shelp eds., 1991); Saks, *Competency to Refuse Psychotropic Medication: Three Alternatives to the Law's Cognitive Standard,* 47 U. Miami L. Rev. 689 (1993); Saks, *Competency to Refuse Treatment,* 69 N.C. L. Rev. 945 (1991); Sherlock, *Competency to Consent to Medical Care: Toward a General View,* 6 Comprehensive Psychiatry 71 (1984); Note, *Informed Consent and the Dying Patient,* 83 Yale L.J. 1652, 1656–59 (1980).

[171] Appelbaum & Roth, *Competency to Consent to Research,* 39 Archives Gen. Psychiatry 951, 954 (1982); Meisel, *Assuring Adequate Consent: Special Consideration in Patients of Uncertain Competence, in* Alzheimer's Dementia 217 (V. Melnick & N. Dubler eds., 1985); Roth et al., *Tests of Competency to Consent to Treatment,* 134 Am. J. Psychiatry 279, 280 (1977); Stanley, *Competency to Consent to Research, in* Alzheimer's Dementia 198 (V. Melnick & N. Dubler eds., 1985); Stanley & Stanley, *Psychiatric Patients in Research: Protecting Their Autonomy,* 22 Comprehensive Psychiatry 420, 423 (1981).

This approach has been used only rarely,[172] and there is very little, if any, explicit support for it in the case law. About the only situation in which manifestation of choice is a realistic approach to determining incompetence is in cases involving unconscious patients who are, without question, unable to manifest a choice. A patient need not be unconscious in order to be unable to manifest a choice. Patients who are seriously mentally retarded can also fit into this category,[173] although not all mentally retarded patients will prove to be incompetent under this approach, because it is not the status of being mentally retarded that is determinative, but rather a person's functioning.[174]

A test of competence based on the understanding of information necessary to give informed consent would also find unconscious and seriously mentally ill or mentally retarded patients incompetent. The problem with this test, therefore, is not with whom it finds incompetent, but with those whom it does not. Patients who are able to make a choice either verbally or behaviorally will be found competent under this test, but the question will remain whether they possess sufficient knowledge to make a choice that should be honored. This test places too much emphasis on autonomy to the detriment of an individual's well-being.

In some respects, the manifestation of choice test for assessing competence is the easiest to administer. Whether a particular patient who does not manifest a choice is physically or mentally incapable of doing so can be difficult to determine.[175] However, this distinction, although interesting, is not particularly relevant in the application of this approach. What is ascertainable and relevant is the fact that the patient does not manifest to the outside world that he has made a choice when called upon to do so.

A choice may be manifested verbally or through conduct, including a positive or negative shake of the head,[176] a refusal to cooperate with the administration of a treatment,[177] or a patient's interference with a particular procedure, such as removing a feeding tube.[178] Some patients may be fully mentally competent but may have lost the physical ability to speak and/or write. This is particularly true

---

[172] **NJ:** *Cf. In re* Conroy, 486 A.2d 1209, 1241 (N.J. 1985) ("A patient may be incompetent because he lacks the ability . . . to communicate a decision.").

[173] **MA:** Superintendent of Belchertown State Sch. v. Saikewicz, 370 N.E.2d 417 (Mass. 1977).

NY: *In re* Storar, 420 N.E.2d 64 (N.Y. 1981).

WA: *In re* Grant, 747 P.2d 445 (Wash. 1987), *modified,* 757 P.2d 534 (Wash. 1988); *In re* Hamlin, 689 P.2d 1372 (Wash. 1984).

[174] *See, e.g., In re* R.H., 622 N.E.2d 1071 (Mass. App. Ct. 1993).

[175] *See, e.g., In re* Clark, 510 A.2d 136, 137 (N.J. Super. Ct. Ch. Div. 1986) ("difficult to say how much Clark understands because he cannot communicate to any significant degree").

[176] *See, e.g., id.* at 137–38 (patient could follow instructions to use other means of communicating, such as nodding or shaking head or blinking eyes).

[177] **MA:** *Cf.* Superintendent of Belchertown State Sch. v. Saikewicz, 370 N.E.2d 417, 432 (Mass. 1977) (a factor in deciding to forgo treatment was patient's inability to cooperate with the treatment).

[178] *See, e.g., In re* Hier, 464 N.E.2d 959 (Mass. App. Ct. 1984).

for patients with a paralyzing illness such as amyotrophic lateral sclerosis. They may, however, be able to signify a choice by blinking their eyes in response to questions with a predetermined meaning assigned to different numbers of blinks.[179]

§ 4.30 —Nature of Decisionmaking Process

Another suggested approach to specific incompetence focuses on the manner in which a patient decides about a recommended treatment. It is sometimes said that a patient is incompetent because of an inability to make a "reasoned decision,"[180] or some similar phrase, such as an inability to "intelligently consent,"[181] to "evaluate the options,"[182] or to make an "informed, rational and knowing decision."[183] It is difficult to determine whether any courts actually subscribe to this definitional approach, because no court has specifically endorsed it, and those that suggest it do so in combination with other approaches.[184]

This approach is grounded in the view that if a person is able to make a decision but is unable to make it in a particular manner, the decision does not deserve to be honored. Thus, this approach runs the risk of infringing on the broad legal and ethical basis of the informed consent doctrine, which permits patients to make decisions for their own idiosyncratic reasons if they so choose.[185]

---

[179] **NJ:** *E.g., In re* Clark, 510 A.2d 136 (N.J. Super. Ct. Ch. Div. 1986).

PA: *E.g., In re* Doe, 45 Pa. D. & C.3d 371 (C.P. Phila. County 1987).

[180] *In re* Storar, 420 N.E.2d 64, 72 (N.Y. 1981).

[181] *In re* Hamlin, 689 P.2d 1372, 1374 (Wash. 1984).

[182] *In re* Conroy, 486 A.2d 1209, 1241 (N.J. 1985).

[183] **MA:** *Cf.* Lane v. Candura, 376 N.E.2d 1232, 1233–34 (Mass. App. Ct. 1978) (trial court was not satisfied that patient "arrived at her decision in a rational manner, *i.e.,* 'after careful consideration of the medical alternatives.' ").

NY: *In re* Lydia E. Hall Hosp., 455 N.Y.S.2d 706, 712 (Sup. Ct. Nassau County 1982).

[184] **NJ:** *E.g., In re* Conroy, 486 A.2d 1209, 1241 (N.J. 1985) ("A patient may be incompetent because he lacks the ability to understand the information conveyed, to evaluate the options, or to communicate a decision.").

NY: *E.g., In re* Storar, 420 N.E.2d 64, 72 (N.Y. 1981) (incompetence defined as either "incapab[ility] of understanding or making a reasoned decision about medical treatment"); *In re* Lydia E. Hall Hosp., 455 N.Y.S.2d at 712 (patient made an "informed, rational and knowing decision" and is therefore not incompetent).

WA: *E.g., In re* Hamlin, 689 P.2d 1372, 1374 (Wash. 1984) (petition asserted Hamlin was " 'incapable of understanding his illness or intelligently consenting to care' ").

[185] **CA:** Thor v. Superior Court, 855 P.2d 375, 381 (Cal. 1993) ("Because health care decisions intrinsically concern one's subjective sense of well-being, this right of personal autonomy does not turn on the wisdom, *i.e.,* medical rationality, of the individual's choice.").

FL: St. Mary's Hosp. v. Ramsey, 465 So. 2d 666, 668 (Fla. Dist. Ct. App. 1985) (A competent adult has the right to refuse a transfusion even if his refusal "arises from fear of adverse reaction, religious belief, recalcitrance or cost.").

IL: *In re* Estate of Brooks, 205 N.E.2d 435, 442 (Ill. 1965) (beliefs that are "unwise, foolish or ridiculous" do not render patient incompetent).

The approach would disqualify more people from decisionmaking than an approach based on a lack of understanding because patients who understand the information relevant to informed consent may still not use it, may not use all of it, or may not weigh the various constellations of risks and benefits of each medical option against one another.

There are a number of ways in which additional content might be given to this approach. One is to consider whether in making a decision the patient takes into account the information the physician gives pursuant to the informed consent doctrine. Some patients may use information in a way that is so obviously bizarre as to indicate a serious deficiency in their decisionmaking process.[186] The cause of such a problem might be delirium, dementia, depression, mental retardation, psychosis, intoxication, or stupor. Therefore, this approach can be modified by requiring that a patient engage in a rational manipulation of relevant information to avoid being deemed incompetent.[187]

§ 4.31 —Reasons for Decision

Another approach mentioned by commentators,[188] but finding little if any support in the courts, focuses on the manner in which a patient is able to explain a decision to accept or refuse treatment. Because in practice a patient's competence is far less likely to be questioned when he consents to treatment than when he refuses it, this definitional approach focuses on a patient's reasons for refusal of treatment.

Under this approach, incompetence could be defined as a patient's inability to articulate *rational reasons* for a decision. To the extent that a patient is permitted to make medical decisions for any reason or none at all,[189] this approach has the

---

[186] *See, e.g., In re* Ingram, 689 P.2d 1363, 1365 (Wash. 1984).

[187] Appelbaum & Roth, *Competency to Consent to Research—A Psychiatric Overview,* 39 Archives Gen. Psychiatry 951, 954 (1982).

[188] Appelbaum & Roth, *Competency to Consent to Research,* 39 Archives Gen. Psychiatry 951, 954 (1982); Roth et al., *Tests of Competency to Consent to Treatment,* 134 Am. J. Psychiatry 279, 281 (1977); Stanley & Stanley, *Psychiatric Patients in Research: Protecting Their Autonomy,* 22 Comprehensive Psychiatry 420, 424 (1981).

[189] **CA:** Thor v. Superior Court, 855 P.2d 375, 363 (Cal. 1993) ("Because health care decisions intrinsically concern one's subjective sense of well-being, this right of personal autonomy does not turn on the wisdom, *i.e.,* medical rationality, of the individual's choice.").

FL: St. Mary's Hosp. v. Ramsey, 465 So. 2d 666, 668 (Fla. Dist. Ct. App. 1985) ("adult has the right to refuse a transfusion regardless of whether his refusal to do so arises from fear of adverse reaction, religious belief, recalcitrance or cost").

IL: *In re* Estate of Brooks, 205 N.E.2d 435, 442 (Ill. 1965) (beliefs that are "unwise, foolish or ridiculous" do not render patient incompetent).

NY: *In re* Eichner, 423 N.Y.S.2d 580, 593–94 (Sup. Ct. Nassau County 1979) (citing *In re* Melideo, 390 N.Y.S.2d 523 (Sup. Ct. Suffolk County 1976); Erickson v. Dilgard, 252 N.Y.S.2d 705 (Sup. Ct. Nassau County 1962)).

effect of stripping a patient of his decisional prerogatives and should therefore be disfavored.

A more satisfactory, though still problematic, variant looks to the motivation for the reasons. For instance, patients whose reasons appear to be the product of mental illness, such as delusions[190] or hallucinations, might be considered incompetent, whereas a patient who refuses treatment because of an aversion to accepting a statistically small risk of a relatively minor side effect ought not to be considered incompetent. However, the difficulty and potential arbitrariness in drawing a satisfactory line between acceptable and unacceptable motivations presents a serious obstacle to the use of this approach.

§ 4.32 —Nature of Decision

In another approach, it is the patient's decision that determines whether he has decisionmaking capacity.[191] Under this approach, a patient is considered incompetent if his choice, as opposed to his reasoning process or the reasons articulated in support of the decision, can be characterized as "wrong," "unreasonable," "irrational," or "irresponsible," or something similar.

Although this approach is useful in alerting physicians and courts to the fact that a patient might be incompetent, it is biased in favor of decisions to accept treatment, even when such decisions are made by people who are incapable of understanding relevant information about treatment or applying that information to their own situation. In practice, under this approach the refusal of treatment is equated with incompetence.

Defining incompetence in this manner is paternalistic to an extreme, and is thoroughly inconsistent with the assumptions and goals of the manner in which the law, in accordance with the informed consent doctrine, allocates decisional authority between patient and physician. This approach undermines a patient's decisional authority by honoring its exercise only when it is congruent with societal standards as applied by physicians, and thus the law clearly disfavors it. The refusal of a recommended treatment cannot be equated with incompetence any more than consent to a recommended treatment can be equated

---

[190] **NJ:** *E.g., In re* B., 383 A.2d 760, 762 (N.J. Super. Ct. L. Div. 1977) (psychiatric patient's refusal to take medication reflects delusional thinking). *Cf. In re* Quackenbush, 383 A.2d 785, 788 (N.J. Super. Ct. P. Div. 1978).

PA: *But see In re* Yetter, 62 Pa. D. & C.2d 619, 623 (C.P. Northampton County, Pa. 1973) (patient not incompetent even though her refusal of treatment was based in part on delusional reasons).

[191] Meisel, *Assuring Adequate Consent: Special Considerations in Patients of Uncertain Competence, in* Alzheimer's Dementia 219 (V. Melnick & N. Dubler eds., 1985); Roth et al., *Tests of Competency to Consent to Treatment,* 134 Am. J. Psychiatry 279, 280–81 (1977); Stanley & Stanley, *Psychiatric Patients in Research: Protecting Their Autonomy,* 22 Comprehensive Psychiatry 420, 423 (1981).

with competence.[192] The nature of the treatment is not relevant, and thus the fact that the patient objects to life-sustaining treatment does not render him incompetent.[193]

This approach is probably used more frequently than admitted in clinical settings and, though it is rarely if ever articulated, possibly even in judicial determinations of incompetence. A portion of the opinion in *Lane v. Candura* recites expert testimony that, though disapproved by the court, illustrates how this approach works:

> Dr. Kelley, one of two psychiatrists who testified, . . . state[d] that in his opinion Mrs. Candura was incompetent to make a rational choice. . . . His testimony, read closely, and in the context of the questions put to him, indicates that his opinion is not one of incompetence in the legal sense, but rather that her ability to make a rational choice (*by which he means the medically rational choice*) is impaired. . . . Until she changed her original decision and withdrew her consent . . . , her competence was not questioned. But the irrationality of her decision does not justify a conclusion that Mrs. Candura is incompetent in the legal sense.[194]

§ 4.33 Process Approach

Although representing a substantial improvement over the general incompetence approach and the other specific incompetence approaches, the emerging judicial consensus favoring the understanding approach[195] still leaves something to be desired. The primary problem with the understanding approach is that it derives from an "event model" of informed consent rather than a process model.[196] That is, the understanding approach to incompetence assumes that informed consent is a static event; that on a single occasion, a single

---

[192] **CA:** Thor v. Superior Court, 855 P.2d 375, 381 (Cal. 1993) ("Because health care decisions intrinsically concern one's subjective sense of well-being, this right of personal autonomy does not turn on the wisdom, *i.e.,* medical rationality, of the individual's choice.").

MD: 73 Md. Op. Att'y Gen. 253, 267–68 (Op. No. 88-046, Oct. 17, 1988) (patient not incompetent merely because of disagreement with a physician's suggested treatment plan).

[193] 73 Md. Op. Att'y Gen. 253, 268 (Op. No. 88-046, Oct. 17, 1988) (citing Tune v. Walter Reed Army Medical Hosp., 602 F. Supp. 1452, 1455 (D.D.C. 1985)).

[194] **MA:** Lane v. Candura, 376 N.E.2d 1232, 1235–36 (Mass. App. Ct. 1978) (emphasis added).

IL: *Accord In re* Estate of Brooks, 205 N.E.2d 435, 442 (Ill. 1965) (beliefs that are "unwise, foolish or ridiculous" do not render patient incompetent).

NY: *Accord In re* Eichner, 423 N.Y.S.2d 580, 593–94 (Sup. Ct. Nassau County 1979) (decision of an incompetent patient made before the patient became incompetent should be honored because "the right is raised under such circumstances that its *exercise would be entirely rational and understandable*") (emphasis added). *But cf. In re* Kerr (O'Brien), 517 N.Y.S.2d 346 (Sup. Ct. N.Y. County 1986).

[195] See § **4.26.**

[196] *See* Hastings Center Guidelines 132–33 (Part Six, III). See § **3.8.**

physician provides relevant information to a patient about a recommended therapy.[197] While this may accurately represent many decisionmaking situations between doctors and patients, it also fails to take into account the many and possibly far more important situations in which decisionmaking takes place over a period of time, in which patients obtain information from more than one health care professional, and more than one decision needs to be made, features often characteristic of decisionmaking about life-sustaining treatment.

An approach to determining incompetence consistent with the process model of informed consent is far more preferable because a patient's lack of decisionmaking capacity may become manifest in different ways and because these signs may only become apparent with the passage of time and the efforts necessary to comply with the informed consent doctrine. Questions about decisionmaking capacity can arise at different points in the process: (1) at the threshold of the decisionmaking process, an individual may not even be able to discuss treatment, as contemplated by the informed consent doctrine; (2) a patient who is not incompetent at the threshold may still exhibit signs of incompetence later in the process.

Threshold Incompetence

The informed consent doctrine obligates physicians to make disclosure and obtain consent. However, these duties are suspended if the patient is incompetent.[198] If a patient is incontestably incompetent—for example, an unconscious patient—the physician need not even attempt to provide information to the patient, let alone obtain consent. In such a situation, in effect, a physician (if the determination of incompetence is made clinically) or a court (if the determination is judicial) applies the general incompetence approach.[199] Only slightly less unambiguous are situations involving patients whose cognitive and perhaps affective faculties are seriously compromised by such permanent conditions as mental retardation[200] or senility,[201] or even by more transient conditions

---

[197] Lidz et al., *Two Models of Implementing Informed Consent,* 148 Archives Internal Med. 1385 (1988).

[198] See § **3.24.**

[199] See § **4.23.**

[200] **MA:** Superintendent of Belchertown State Sch. v. Saikewicz, 370 N.E.2d 417 (Mass. 1977).
NY: *In re* Storar, 420 N.E.2d 64 (N.Y. 1981).
WA: *In re* Hamlin, 689 P.2d 1372 (Wash. 1984). *Cf. In re* Grant, 747 P.2d 445 (Wash. 1987).

[201] **MA:** *E.g., In re* Dinnerstein, 380 N.E.2d 134 (Mass. App. Ct. 1978).
NJ: *E.g., In re* Conroy, 486 A.2d 1209 (N.J. 1985).

such as delirium, intoxication, or stupor. Other patients may be less manifestly incompetent, but a reasonable person might still be skeptical about competence, such as when a patient is mentally ill but not patently psychotic,[202] or is mentally retarded but not profoundly so, or is unable to provide for life's basic necessities.

Process Incompetence

If a patient is not clearly incompetent, the physician is obligated to present the patient with the therapeutic or diagnostic options that are available, as well as associated information about risks and benefits, in order to obtain the patient's informed consent (or refusal). The other way in which the question of incompetence can arise is during this process of providing information. For instance, a patient may be unable to understand the information required by the informed consent doctrine. However, if efforts are made to work with the patient about areas of misunderstanding for some hours, days, or even weeks, depending on the nature of the information, the nature of the patient's difficulties in understanding it, and the urgency of the need to make a decision, the patient's understanding may improve to the point where he will be capable of decision-making.[203]

Conversely, a person who seems competent to be informed may indeed not be competent under a specific incompetence approach. The process of explaining treatment options and other material information involves a give-and-take of information, with the physician telling the patient some things, the patient responding both verbally and behaviorally and indicating comprehension or confusion and occasionally asking questions, and the physician asking the patient questions to probe the patient's comprehension. In the course of this conversation, the physician may find that the patient understands little or nothing of what has been explained. Alternatively, although the patient may understand the information in a literal manner, he may be unable to appreciate its significance for his own situation, or the patient may use the information in a highly idiosyncratic fashion. Finally, even if the patient adequately understands the information, he may be unable to use it in making a decision, or he may be unable to make a decision at all, and is therefore to be considered incompetent under one or more of the specific incompetence approaches.

---

[202] *See, e.g., In re* Ingram, 689 P.2d 1363 (Wash. 1984).

[203] *Cf.* Martin v. Martin, 504 N.W.2d 917, 924 (Mich. Ct. App. 1993) ("The record does not indicate that there was ever any concerted effort to specifically inform Michael of the nature and purpose of the proceedings or to ask him specifically what his treatment preferences might be.").

Bibliography

Appelbaum, P., and T. Grisso. "Assessing Patients' Capacities to Consent to Treatment." *New England Journal of Medicine* 319 (1988): 1635.

Appelbaum, P., and L. Roth. "Competency to Consent to Research." *Archives of General Psychiatry* 39 (1982): 951.

Brakel, S., et al. *The Mentally Disabled and the Law.* Chicago: American Bar Foundation, 1985.

Brilmayer, L. "Interstate Preemption: The Right to Travel, the Right to Life, and the Right to Die." *Michigan Law Review* 91 (1993): 873.

Buchanan, A., and D. Brock. *Deciding for Others: The Ethics of Surrogate Decision Making.* New York: Cambridge University Press, 1989.

Comment. "Determining Patient Competency in Treatment Refusal Cases." *Georgia Law Review* 24 (1990): 733.

Deaver, B. "The Competency of Children." *Cooley Law Review* 4 (1987): 522.

Drane, J. "Competency to Give an Informed Consent." *JAMA* 252 (1984): 925.

Federman, A. "Conservatorship: A Viable Alternative to Incompetency." *Fordham Urban Law Journal* (1985–86): 815.

Finkel, N., et al. "Competency, and Other Constructs in Right to Die Cases." *Behavioral Science and the Law* 11 (1993): 135.

Fitten, L., et al. "Assessing Treatment Decision-Making Capacities in Elderly Nursing Home Residents." *Journal of the American Geriatrics Society* 38 (1990): 1097.

Green, L. "Judicial Tests of Mental Incompetency." *Missouri Law Review* 6 (1941): 141.

Lo, B. "Assessing Decision-Making Capacity." *Law, Medicine and Health Care* 18 (1990): 193.

Maciunas, K., and A. Moss. "Learning the Patient's Narrative to Determine Decision-making Capacity: The Role of Ethics Consultation." *Journal of Clinical Ethics* 3 (1992): 287.

Markson, L., et al. "Physician Assessment of Patient Competence." *Journal of the American Geriatrics Society* 42 (1994): 1074.

Meisel, A. "Assuring Adequate Consent: Special Consideration in Patients of Uncertain Competence." In *Alzheimer's Dementia,* edited by V. Melnick and N. Dubler, 217. New York: Humana Press, 1985.

Note. "Informed Consent and the Dying Patient." *Yale Law Journal* 83 (1980): 1652.

Perlin, M. *Mental Disability Law: Civil and Criminal.* Charlottesville, VA: Michie Co., 1989.

Rosoff, A., and G. Gottlieb. "Preserving Personal Autonomy for the Elderly: Competency, Guardianship, and Alzheimer's Disease." *Journal of Legal Medicine* 8 (1987): 1.

Roth, L., et al. "Tests of Competency to Consent to Treatment." *American Journal of Psychiatry* 134 (1977): 279.

Saks, E. "Competency to Refuse Psychotropic Medication: Three Alternatives to the Law's Cognitive Standard." *University of Miami Law Review* 47 (1993): 689.

Saks, E. "Competency to Refuse Treatment." *North Carolina Law Review* 69 (1991): 945.

Schaffner, K. "Competency: A Triaxial Concept." In *When Are Competent Patients Incompetent?: A Study of Informal Competency Determinations in Primary Care,* edited by M. Gardell-Cutter and E. Shelp, 253. Boston: Kluwer Law Book Publishers, Inc., 1991.

Scogin, F. "Guardianship Proceedings with Older Adults: The Role of Functional Assessment and Gerontologists." *Law and Psychology Review* 10 (1986): 123.

Sherlock, R. "Competency to Consent to Medical Care: Toward a General View." *Comprehensive Psychiatry* 6 (1984): 71.

Sullivan, M., and S. Youngner. "Depression, Competence, and the Right to Refuse Lifesaving Medical Treatment." *American Journal of Psychiatry* 151 (1994): 971.

Wolff, K. "Determining Patient Competency in Treatment Refusal Cases." *Georgia Law Review* 24 (1990): 733.

Young, E., et al. "Does Depression Invalidate Competence? Consultants' Ethical, Psychiatric, and Legal Considerations." *Cambridge Quarterly of Healthcare Ethics* 2 (1993): 505.

CHAPTER 5

DETERMINATION OF INCOMPETENCE, DESIGNATION OF A SURROGATE, AND REVIEW OF DECISIONS

THE APPROPRIATE FORUM FOR END-OF-LIFE DECISIONMAKING: COURTS AND CLINICAL SETTINGS

§ 5.1 The General Issue: Going to Court

The fundamental legal question in decisionmaking about life-sustaining treatment is always the same: may treatment be withheld or withdrawn or must it be started or continued? However, this question does not always arise in a straightforward fashion. Rather, it is often posed in procedural, rather than substantive, terms and posed in a variety of ways.

To a significant extent, the early history of the right to die was shaped by concerns about the proper procedures to be followed in end-of-life decisionmaking for incompetent patients. For example, in the *Quinlan* case, the initial question before the court was whether Karen Quinlan's father was a suitable party to act as the guardian of her person.[1] The trial court ruled that neither he nor Karen's mother was qualified, because of their wish to have life-sustaining treatment discontinued, which the court ruled was not in Karen's best interests.

[1] *See In re* Quinlan, 348 A.2d 801 (N.J. Super. Ct. Ch. Div. 1975).

On appeal, the New Jersey Supreme Court held that Mr. Quinlan was qualified to be the guardian. Implicit in this holding was that it was permissible to discontinue life-sustaining treatment, and of course the court explicitly so held.

As the *Quinlan* case illustrates, just below the surface of procedural issues lie important substantive issues, and the two are often inextricably intertwined. Although the ostensible reason for recourse to judicial proceedings was to appoint a guardian, the real reason was that the attending physician and hospital refused to implement the decision that her parents had made to forgo life-sustaining treatment. The invocation of judicial proceedings was to determine whether life-sustaining treatment could be forgone. In working its way toward that question, the courts did consider the propriety of the patient's father serving as guardian, but by that point that issue was so intertwined with the propriety of withdrawing treatment that the resolution of the surrogacy issue flowed from the resolution of the larger question whether treatment could be terminated and whether liability would arise from so doing. Thus, once a clinical case becomes a judicial case, procedural and substantive issues usually merge. Even if the substantive question is squarely raised, antecedent procedural issues of incompetence and surrogacy are sometimes made subject to judicial reexamination.

When questions about the legitimacy of forgoing life-sustaining treatment are posed, they are frequently a variant on the procedural question, Do we have to go to court to withhold or withdraw life-sustaining treatment? After some initial hesitancy, a strong judicial consensus has evolved that decisions about forgoing life-sustaining treatment for incompetent patients—and, a fortiori, for competent patients[2]—generally ought to be made in the clinical setting without routine recourse to the courts to adjudicate the patient's competency, to designate a surrogate decisionmaker, or to pass on the fundamental issue: whether treatment is to be administered or forgone.[3] This conclusion has been most succinctly stated by the California Court of Appeal:

> [C]ourts do not have a general commission to supervise medical treatment decisions. Patients make their own treatment decisions with the advice of their physicians. Family members, and sometimes other persons, participate when the patients cannot. Courts, on the other hand, become involved only when no one is available to make decisions for a patient or when there are disagreements.[4]

The evidence about whether this consensus has had a significant impact in the clinical setting is unclear. The sole study that exists[5] indicates that there is still

[2] National Ctr. for State Courts, Guidelines for State Court Decision Making in Life-Sustaining Medical Treatment Cases 44 (2d ed. 1992) (standard 6).

[3] *Cf. id.* at 36–37 (standard 3).

[4] Drabick v. Drabick, 245 Cal. Rptr. 840, 847 (Ct. App. 1988).

[5] Solomon et al., *Decisions Near the End of Life: Professional Views on Life-Sustaining Treatments,* 83 Am. J. Pub. Health 14 (1993).

a great deal of uncertainty among health care professionals about forgoing life-sustaining treatment and that many times treatment is continued even when their judgment and that of the families of incompetent patients are in agreement that it should be discontinued.

These findings are not inconsistent with the anecdotes that one hears from many health care professionals. This is not to say that practice is uniform. Many doctors have participated in terminating life support on many occasions and have no hesitancy about doing so under proper circumstances. Others in the same jurisdiction, indeed in the same hospital, can be far more reluctant to do so. Sometimes the variation is not so much among doctors as among hospitals. In some hospitals, there is a palpable level of anxiety among health care professionals of all stripes about terminating life support. It is also likely that there is a significant variation in practice between hospitals and long-term care facilities. It is common knowledge that forgoing treatment in a long-term care facility, especially artificial nutrition and hydration, can be extraordinarily difficult to do unless the patient has a clearly applicable advance directive.

Despite the strong consensus, uncertainty and anxiety still exist among health care professionals, health care administrators, and their legal counsel about the propriety of proceeding without a judicial imprimatur of one sort or another, and often more explicitly about whether criminal or civil liability will be imposed without such approval. It is this uncertainty, apprehension, and anxiety that is responsible for transforming a clinical case involving questions about life-sustaining treatment into a legal case.

The fear of legal liability is a prime factor in making physicians and health care administrators reticent about forgoing life-sustaining treatment (despite how unrealistic such fears have turned out to be),[6] and therefore a prime factor in their requiring a court order before they will allow such treatment to be withheld or withdrawn.[7] This fear arises primarily from a surrogate's decision to forgo life-sustaining treatment for an incompetent patient, but it may also arise from a decision made by a competent patient. Concern about the validity of a clinical determination of incompetence and designation of a surrogate, and thus whether liability might result, may also prompt recourse to the courts.[8] However, the most pressing issue in the right-to-die cases that reach the courts is

---

[6] See **Chs. 17** and **18.**

[7] *See, e.g.,* DeGrella v. Elston, 858 S.W.2d 698, 700 (Ky. 1993) ("This case is not in court because there is a dispute between the family members as to the patient's wishes, or between the physicians as to the medical evidence. The case is before our Court because Sue's attending physician and the nursing home fear legal sanctions, administrative, civil or even criminal, should they carry out the wishes of the patient as expressed through her mother and legal guardian. Being thus concerned, they have advised the family they require court authorization before permitting or participating in the removal of the medical device which provides Sue with nourishment and water.").

[8] *See* Hastings Ctr., Guidelines on the Termination of Life-Sustaining Treatment and the Care of the Dying 31 (1987) (Part One, II(8)(a)).

usually what should be done rather than whether the patient is capable of deciding and, if not, who should decide. As a consequence, there is little definitive guidance in most jurisdictions about the validity of the clinical approach to determining incompetence and designating a surrogate. However, with only a few exceptions, a consensus is building in the courts that these issues should be dealt with in the clinical setting in the absence of compelling reasons to the contrary.

In the first 15 years or so of right-to-die litigation roughly spanning the period between *Quinlan* and *Cruzan,* many litigated cases were "me too" cases. That is, similar issues had been litigated in other jurisdictions (and sometimes in the same jurisdiction), but everyone felt better having their own case to rely on. In the last few years, however, there has been a noticeable shift in the nature of the litigated cases. They are now raising new issues, many of them growing out of the existing consensus and attempting to expand its reach. They include the so-called "futility" cases,[9] including the maintenance of brain-dead individuals on life support at their families' insistence,[10] and the issue of physician-assisted suicide,[11] and some other curiosities, such as cryogenic preservation[12] and organ donation from anencephalic infants.[13]

Though less frequent, a surrogate's demand that life-sustaining treatment continue to be administered—"futility" cases—can create a similar concern. One reason for such concern might be the financial costs to the patient's family or to the health care facility of unreimbursed care.[14] Even when the costs of care are fully reimbursed, health care professionals may feel a responsibility for the wise stewardship of societal resources. Another reason for concern might be the demoralizing effect that the inappropriate continuation of treatment can have on health care personnel and on the patient's family.

Although judicial proceedings are usually commenced as a result of concern about liability for the patient's death if life-sustaining treatment is withdrawn or withheld, as previously mentioned, the question is not always framed that way. Sometimes the question posed is whether the person speaking for the patient has the legal authority to do so, and thus a demand is made that that person be judicially appointed as guardian.[15] Less frequently, concern is expressed as to

---

[9] See **Ch. 19.**

[10] *See, e.g., Hospital Fights Parents' Wish to Keep Life Support for a "Brain Dead" Child,* N.Y. Times, Feb. 12, 1994, at 6 (nat'l ed.); *Brain-Dead Florida Girl Will Be Sent Home on Life Support,* N.Y. Times, Feb. 19, 1994, at 7 (nat'l ed.).

[11] See **Ch. 18.**

[12] *See* Donaldson v. Van de Kamp, 4 Cal. Rptr. 2d 59 (Ct. App. 1992).

[13] *See In re* T.A.C.P., 609 So. 2d 588 (Fla. 1992).

[14] *See In re* Spring, 399 N.E.2d 493, 499 (Mass. App. Ct. 1979) ("We intimate no opinion on the weight to be given the factor of cost to the family where that is a relevant consideration."). *Cf.* Uhlman & Pearlman, *Perceived Quality of Life and Preferences for Life-Sustaining Treatment in Older Adults,* 151 Archives Internal Med. 495, 497 (1991) ("[O]lder patients' preferences for the care of life-threatening illness may be influenced primarily by criteria other than quality of life," including costs of care.).

[15] *See, e.g., In re* Quinlan, 355 A.2d 647 (N.J. 1976).

whether the patient is competent or incompetent, and doctors or health care administrators insist that there be a judicial determination of the patient's decisionmaking capacity.[16]

§ 5.2 Specific Procedural Issues

The uncertainty and anxiety that arise from end-of-life decisionmaking and that give rise to the fear of criminal or civil liability, thereby creating an impetus for going to court, manifest themselves in several distinct but related issues.

Decisionmaking Capacity. The first procedural matter for determination in medical decisionmaking generally and end-of-life decisionmaking in particular is whether the patient possesses or lacks decisionmaking capacity.[17] If a patient is competent to make decisions, the remainder of the decisionmaking process is far simpler than if the patient lacks decisionmaking capacity; the question of surrogate designation is avoided entirely because decisional authority remains in the competent patient and it is improper for the physician to utilize a surrogate decisionmaker[18] or ordinarily to seek recourse to the courts.[19] Review, if it occurs at all, is conducted predominantly through informal, clinically-based mechanisms such as ethics committees,[20] as evidenced by the extremely small number of reported cases involving competent patients. However, before a patient's decisionmaking capacity can be assessed, it is necessary to understand what this concept and the related concepts of competence and incompetence mean.[21]

---

[16] *See, e.g.,* Satz v. Perlmutter, 379 So. 2d 359 (Fla. 1980).

[17] **MI:** Martin v. Martin, 504 N.W.2d 917, 924 (Mich. Ct. App. 1993) ("When faced with a dispute concerning a decision to withhold or withdraw life-sustaining medical treatment, the first task of the trial court is to determine whether the patient has the requisite capacity to make the decision in question. *In re* A.C., 573 A.2d 1235, 1247 (D.C.App.1990); *Conroy.*").

NY: *In re* Beth Israel Medical Ctr. (Weinstein), 519 N.Y.S.2d 511, 512 (Sup. Ct. N.Y. County 1987).

[18] **GA:** Kirby v. Spivey, 307 S.E.2d 538 (Ga. Ct. App. 1983).

IN: Payne v. Marion Gen. Hosp., 549 N.E.2d 1043 (Ind. Ct. App. 1990) (patient's informed consent to entry of do-not-resuscitate order required, and not a surrogate's, if patient were competent).

WV: Belcher v. Charleston Area Medical Ctr., 422 S.E.2d 827 (W. Va. 1992) (same).

See **§ 3.3.**

[19] **CA:** Thor v. Superior Court, 855 P.2d 375, 389 (Cal. 1993) ("[J]udicial intercession . . . tends to denigrate the principle of personal autonomy, substituting a species of legal paternalism for the medical paternalism the concept of informed consent seeks to eschew."). *See also* Bartling v. Superior Court, 209 Cal. Rptr. 220, 226 (Ct. App. 1984).

[20] See **Ch. 6.**

[21] See **Ch. 4.**

In many cases, decisionmaking capacity, which is logically the first issue in the decisionmaking process, is not a real issue because the patient is either clearly competent or incompetent. If the patient is comatose, for example, there is no need for an adjudication of incompetence because there can be no doubt that the patient lacks decisionmaking capacity. In fact, even when end-of-life decisions are brought to court, if the patient so clearly lacks decisionmaking capacity, the question of incompetence will be virtually disregarded and attention will be directed to the more practical task of designating a surrogate. By the same token, if the patient is alert, communicative, and appears to comprehend, there is usually no doubt that the patient is competent, at least at the outset. Thus, the first juncture at which the question about going to court might arise is often avoided.

Surrogacy. Closely related to the means for assessing decisionmaking capacity is the method for designating a surrogate decisionmaker for incompetent patients. The central questions are whether a surrogate must be designated through judicial proceedings or if this may be accomplished in the clinical setting, and who the surrogate should be.

Once appointed, surrogates need guidance about how to make decisions for incompetent patients. A number of different but related standards have evolved for the guidance of surrogates.[22] These standards are also those to be applied in the review process, if there is one, in determining whether to implement or modify the surrogate's decision about life-sustaining treatment.

Substantive Decisions About and Review of Decisions to Terminate Life Support. The third juncture at which recourse to the courts might be undertaken is when a decision is made to forgo life-sustaining treatment. Regardless of how it was determined that the patient lacked decisionmaking capacity and regardless of how a surrogate was clothed with authority to act, a requirement of recourse to the courts might be imposed at this point. The court could function in either of two ways. First, it might play a restricted role, merely reviewing the decision that has been made to determine whether it is consistent with the relevant facts and law. Second, the court might play a more expansive role, reviewing the same relevant facts but reserving to itself the authority to make the ultimate decision whether treatment should be forgone.[23]

§ 5.3 General Approaches to Decisionmaking

Two general approaches to decisionmaking procedures have emerged: a clinical approach and a judicial approach. A third combines elements of these two.

---

[22] See **Ch. 7.**

[23] *See, e.g.,* Superintendent of Belchertown State Sch. v. Saikewicz, 370 N.E.2d 417 (Mass. 1977).

§ 5.4 —Clinical Approach

Under the clinical approach, the three components of the decisionmaking process—assessment of capacity to decide, designation of a surrogate, and review of decisions—take place in the clinical setting. The patient's capacity is determined by physicians[24] (perhaps with the assistance of consultants such as neurologists, psychiatrists, or psychologists),[25] a person to act as the patient's surrogate emerges from among the patient's family and friends and is recognized as the patient's legitimate spokesman by the patient's attending physician, and review (if any) occurs through some sort mechanism devised by the health care institution, such as an ethics committee, prognosis committee, or independent experts.

The clinical approach is overwhelmingly (though not without exception) favored by courts for all aspects of end-of-life decisionmaking because even the courts do not regard themselves as "the proper place to resolve the agonizing personal problems that underlie these cases. Our legal system cannot replace the more intimate struggle that must be borne by the patient, those caring for the patient, and those who care about the patient."[26]

§ 5.5 —Judicial Approach

Under the judicial approach, each of the constituent procedural issues in the decisionmaking process—assessment of capacity, designation of a surrogate, and review—occurs in court with the ultimate decisions made by the judge. At the beginning of right-to-die litigation, a strong divergence of opinion arose between the New Jersey and Massachusetts Supreme Courts about the proper role for courts in the decisionmaking process. Despite the intense support by the Massachusetts court for judges playing a central role in end-of-life decisionmaking,

---

[24] *See, e.g.,* Cohen et al., *Do Clinical and Formal Assessments of the Capacity of Patients in the Intensive Care Unit to Make Decisions Agree?,* 153 Archives Internal Med. 2481 (1993) (Intuitive assessments by residents and nurses of patients' competence highly correlate with formal assessments using mental status exams.). *Cf. In re* Estate of Wood, 553 A.2d 772 (Pa. Super. Ct. 1987) (medical testimony unnecessary to prove incompetence; lay testimony will suffice).

[25] *But cf.* Sullivan & Youngner, *Depression, Competence, and the Right to Refuse Lifesaving Medical Treatment,* 151 Am. J. Psychiatry 971, 976–77 (1994) (discussing limitations on use of psychiatrists to assess decisionmaking capacity).

[26] **NJ:** *In re* Jobes, 529 A.2d 434, 451 (N.J. 1987). *Accord In re* Farrell, 529 A.2d 404, 407–08 (N.J. 1987).

CA: *Accord* Morrison v. Abramovice, 253 Cal. Rptr. 530, 535 (Ct. App. 1988).

FL: *Accord* Browning v. Herbert, 543 So. 2d 258, 268–69 (Fla. Dist. Ct. App. 1989), *aff'd,* 568 So. 2d 4 (Fla. 1990).

MA: *Accord In re* Spring, 399 N.E.2d 493, 499 n.9 (Mass. App. Ct. 1979), *rev'd,* 405 N.E.2d 115 (Mass. 1980).

other courts have concurred with this view in rare instances and for extremely limited purposes. In general, there has never been a great deal of judicial enthusiasm for routine recourse to the courts for resolving these issues. See **§ 5.37.**

§ 5.6 —Mixed Approach

Under a third, or "mixed" approach, certain aspects of the decisionmaking process are accomplished clinically and others judicially. Under one variation, the decisionmaking process begins in the clinical setting and only goes to court if serious impediments to decisionmaking arise. Under the other variant, decisionmaking begins under judicial supervision with a determination of incompetence and concomitant designation of a surrogate, and proceeds clinically without judicial review.[27]

§ 5.7 Terminology: Surrogate, Guardian, and Similar Terms

There are a variety of terms used to describe the individuals who make decisions on behalf of another:

Surrogate ordinarily refers to one who, in fact, makes a medical decision on behalf of another. Whether a particular surrogate has the legal authority to make such decisions is one of the topics of this chapter. Sometimes the term *legally authorized representative* is used to refer to a surrogate.

A *guardian* is a surrogate who has been appointed by a court to act in this capacity. (In some jurisdictions, other terms, such as *conservator* or *committee,* are used instead of *guardian.* In jurisdictions with a civil law background, the terms *tutor* or *curator* may be used.) *Natural guardian* refers to one who is the guardian of a minor child by operation of law rather than by judicial appointment.[28] A *proxy* or *proxy decisionmaker* is a person selected by a patient, while in possession of decisionmaking capacity, to act as a surrogate decisionmaker in the event of a later loss of decisionmaking capacity. See **Chapter 12.**

These terminological distinctions are not always precisely observed, thereby interjecting additional confusion into the decisionmaking process for patients

---

[27] *In re* Jobes, 529 A.2d 434, 447 n.12 (N.J. 1987) ("In many cases, an application for the appointment of a medical guardian can be integrated into routine fiduciary guardianship proceedings. When a court considers an application for guardianship, it can also consider whether the proposed guardian will be the appropriate person (*i.e.,* close family member or friend) to make future medical decisions for the ward. Thus, in many cases at the difficult juncture when important medical decisions must be made about an incompetent's medical treatment, no further judicial intervention would be necessary.").

[28] See **§ 15.2.**

who lack decisionmaking capacity. In addition, in any given case there may be more than one potential surrogate. A patient who lacks decisionmaking capacity may have a number of family members who are ready, willing, and able to make decisions on the patient's behalf. Also, a patient who lacks decisionmaking capacity may have previously been adjudicated incompetent for some medical or nonmedical purpose and thus have had a guardian appointed, and/or may have executed an advance directive designating a proxy decisionmaker, and/or may have family members or close friends available to make health care decisions. Sorting out the conflicting claims of each of these potential surrogates to the legal authority to make decisions on the patient's behalf can be a daunting task for health care professionals.

DETERMINATION OF INCOMPETENCE AND DESIGNATION OF A SURROGATE

§ 5.8 Relationship Between Incompetence Determination and Surrogate Designation

Although conceptually distinct, determination of incompetence and designation of a surrogate decisionmaker are inextricably intertwined in practice, whether done in the clinical setting or under judicial auspices. If a patient is adjudicated incompetent to make medical decisions, the court appoints a guardian who is empowered to make decisions about the patient's medical care. Similarly, if a patient is clinically determined to lack decisionmaking capacity, the designation of a surrogate usually, but not always, occurs there as well without recourse to judicial proceedings.

It is usually quite clear in end-of-life decisionmaking whether the patient is competent or incompetent. The task at hand is generally to determine who it is that speaks for the patient thought to lack decisionmaking capacity, rather than to assess whether the patient in fact lacks such capacity. Sometimes the determination of incompetence is made clinically, but the designation of a surrogate requires recourse to the courts because, for example, the patient has no family.[29] Consequently, the determination of incompetence is often a by-product of the designation of a surrogate. For example, in *Quinlan,* because she was comatose, there was no doubt that the patient was incompetent; her incompetence was stipulated at trial.[30] Nonetheless, her father applied for a judicial determination

---

[29] **MA:** *E.g.,* Superintendent of Belchertown State Sch. v. Saikewicz, 370 N.E.2d 417 (Mass. 1977).

NJ: *E.g., In re* Peter, 529 A.2d 419 (N.J. 1987).

WA: *E.g.,* Benoy v. Simons, 831 P.2d 167, 171 n.3 (Wash. 1992); *In re* Hamlin, 689 P.2d 1372 (Wash. 1984).

[30] *In re* Quinlan, 355 A.2d 647, 653 (N.J. 1976).

of incompetence.[31] The true purpose of the action was not to determine incompetence but to clothe himself with clear authority to make decisions about his daughter's care, authority which was questioned by the patient's physicians. Thus, although the form in which judicial proceedings are often begun is an adjudication of incompetence, the real issues are often the designation of the proper person to make medical decisions for the patient and the permissibility of forgoing life-sustaining treatment.[32]

§ 5.9 Choice of Clinical or Judicial Approach to Determining Incompetence and Designating a Surrogate

The need to have someone make a decision about forgoing life-sustaining treatment for incompetent patients is a frequent occurrence[33] and one that can

---

[31] *Id.* at 651.

[32] *See, e.g., In re* McInnis, 584 N.E.2d 1389, 1390 (P. Ct. Stark County, Ohio 1991) ("It was initially indicated to the court that the underlying reason for the appointment of the guardian was for the purpose for allowing the guardian to discontinue life-sustaining treatment, if necessary.").

[33] **US:** Cruzan v. Director, 497 U.S. 261, 314 n.15 (1990) (Brennan, J., dissenting) ("Such decisions are made every day, without state participation. *See* [Cruzan v. Harmon] 760 S.W.2d, at 428 (Blackmar, J., dissenting)."); *id.* at 323 (Stevens, J., dissenting) ("'Decisions of this kind are made daily by the patient or relatives, on the basis of medical advice and their conclusion as to what is best. Very few cases reach court, and I doubt whether this case would be before us but for the fact that Nancy lies in a state hospital.'") (quoting Cruzan v. Harmon, 760 S.W.2d 408 (Mo. 1988) (Blackmar, J., dissenting)).

FL: Browning v. Herbert, 568 So. 2d 4, 15 (Fla. 1990) ("The decision to terminate artificial life-sustaining measures is being made over and over in nursing homes, hospitals, and private homes in this nation. It is being made painfully by loving family members, concerned guardians, or surrogates, in conjunction with the advice of ethical and caring physicians or other health care providers.").

IL: Estate of Longeway v. Community Convalescent Ctr., 549 N.E.2d 292, 295 (Ill. 1989) ("Frequently, the courts are not consulted at all. There is reliable information that for many years, members of a patient's family, together with doctors and clergy, have made decisions to withdraw life-sustaining equipment from incompetent, hopelessly ill patients without seeking judicial approval.").

MD: 73 Md. Op. Att'y Gen. 253, 287–88 (Op. No. 88-046, Oct. 17, 1988) ("[E]very day in this state doctors are recommending and families are confirming decisions not to use various means of treatment for terminally ill patients who cannot decide for themselves. . . . In our view, this kind of surrogate decisionmaking is . . . legally proper.").

MA: *In re* Spring, 399 N.E.2d 493, 499 n.9 (Mass. App. Ct. 1979) ("The importance of the role of the family and the doctor is highlighted by the self-evident fact that the vast majority of treatment decisions relative to persons who are incompetent by reason of senility or retardation are made for them, by their family and the doctor, without court proceedings. This practice is sanctioned not merely by tradition but by the institutional limitations in the ability of courts to make day-to-day treatment decisions, even if restricted to treatments of a potentially life-saving or life-prolonging nature.").

become a major impediment to decisionmaking, having the potential for causing long delays in the decisionmaking process and substantial anxiety among family and health care personnel. This issue can impede decisionmaking for both factual and legal reasons. First, there might be no family or friends to speak for the patient, or, equally troublesome, there might be a surfeit of individuals seeking to speak for the patient and not always with the same voice. Assuming that there is, in fact, someone to speak for the patient, there is often concern about whether this person or persons have the legal authority to make binding decisions on the patient's behalf.

Although both the factual and legal concerns can be eliminated or moderated if the patient has designated a surrogate through a health care power of attorney (see **Chapter 12**) or some less formal means (see **§ 10.16**), or if there is a surrogate decisionmaking statute that identifies the proper party to make decisions (see **Chapter 14**), in fact few patients have appointed surrogates, many states still do not have surrogate decisionmaking statutes, and, even in those that do, the statutes do not always clearly resolve the problem.

Concern about the legitimacy of the clinical approach has long pervaded medical decisionmaking[34] but commanded little judicial attention because its uncertain status did not create problems of the magnitude involved in decisionmaking about life-sustaining treatment. Of so little consequence was this problem prior to *Quinlan* that there is a dearth of case law on the subject.[35] Although the clinical approach has long been used by physicians, until recently about the only generalization that can be made concerning its legitimacy is found in legal treatises, which suggest that when the patient cannot give consent a close family

---

MN: *In re* Torres, 357 N.W.2d 332, 341 n.4 (Minn. 1984) ("At oral argument it was disclosed that on an average about 10 life-support systems are disconnected weekly in Minnesota.").

NY: *In re* Storar, 420 N.E.2d 64, 75 (N.Y.) (Jones, J., dissenting), *cert. denied,* 454 U.S. 858 (1981) ("There is reliable information that for many years physicians and members of patients' families, often in consultation with religious counselors, have in actuality been making decisions to withhold or to withdraw life support procedures from incurably ill patients incapable of making the critical decisions for themselves.") (citing Levisohn, *Voluntary Mercy Deaths,* 8 J. Forensic Med. 57, 68 (survey of the Chicago Medical Convention "revealed that 61% of the physicians present believed that euthanasia was being practiced by members of the profession")); Saunders v. State, 492 N.Y.S.2d 510, 515 (Sup. Ct. Nassau County 1985) ("Every day, and with limited legal guidance, families and doctors are making decisions for patients unable to do so themselves.").

See also Smedira et al., *Withholding and Withdrawal of Life Support from the Critically Ill,* 322 New Eng. J. Med. 309 (1990).

34 *See, e.g.,* E. Kinkead, Torts § 376, at 789 (1903) ("[W]here an operation is to be performed upon . . . [a] person non compos mentis, who is to give consent is not decided.").

35 U.S. Dep't of HEW, *Protection of Human Subjects—Research Involving Those Institutionalized as Mentally Infirm: Report and Recommendations of the National Commission for the Protection of Human Subjects of Biomedical and Behavioral Research,* 43 Fed. Reg. 11,328, 11,352 (1978) (uncertain status of clinical approach characterized as a "consent limbo").

member should do so.[36] However, even the treatise writers hedge their bets. For example, one states that "health care providers should not rely solely on the consent of a patient's spouse or next-of-kin if a legal guardian has or can be appointed to safeguard the patient's interests."[37]

§ 5.10 Customary Medical Practice in Determining Incompetence and Designating a Surrogate

Determination of incompetence and designation of a surrogate—or more specifically, reliance an incompetent patient's close family member to act as surrogate—without going to court occur routinely in clinical practice,[38] and are a deeply embedded and officially approved[39] professional custom. As one commentator has observed, this practice

> is so well known in society at large that any individual [patient] who finds the prospect particularly odious has ample warning to make other arrangements better suited to protecting his own ends or interests.[40]

Customary practices of the medical profession are generally accorded deference by courts.[41] Cases dealing with decisionmaking for incompetent patients

---

[36] *See, e.g., Consent to Medical and Surgical Procedures,* 2 Hosp. L. Manual 163 (Lasky et al. eds., Sept. 1985) ("Whenever possible, a hospital or other provider of health care services contemplating treatment of a person arguably incompetent should try to obtain 'substituted consent' from the person's next of kin or a court order authorizing the proposed treatment."); 2 J. Horty, *Consents-3, in* Hospital Law 9 (Feb. 1981) ("[I]t is usually standard operating procedure when no official guardian has been appointed for an incompetent patient for physicians to seek the consent of the patient's spouse, next-of-kin or others who have been providing for the patient's needs."); J. King, The Law of Medical Malpractice 136 (1986) ("When no judicial determination of incompetency has been made, the consent of the spouse or parent should be obtained when incompetency is reasonably apparent."); Lockwood, Annotation, *Mental Competency of Patient to Consent to Surgical Operation or Medical Treatment,* 25 A.L.R.3d 1439, 1441 (1969) ("The accepted practice is to get the consent of the patient himself if he is a competent adult, or if this is not possible, to obtain the consent of a spouse, parent, relative or someone in a capacity as a guardian.").

[37] 2 J. Horty, *Consents-3, in* Hospital Law 10 (Feb. 1981).

[38] *See* Smedira et al., *Withholding and Withdrawal of Life Support from the Critically Ill,* 322 New Eng. J. Med. 309 (1990) (of decisions to terminate life support among 115 patients, 110 lacked decisionmaking capacity and had families who participated in the decisionmaking process).

[39] Council on Ethical & Judicial Affairs, American Medical Ass'n, Code of Medical Ethics § 2.20, at 36 (1994) ("Without an advance directive that designates a proxy, the patient's family should become the surrogate decisionmaker.").

[40] Capron, *Informed Consent in Catastrophic Disease Research and Treatment,* 123 U. Pa. L. Rev. 340, 424–25 (1974).

[41] *See, e.g.,* Canterbury v. Spence, 464 F.2d 772, 784 (D.C. Cir. 1972). *But see, e.g.,* Gates v. Jensen, 595 P.2d 919 (Wash. 1979); Helling v. Carey, 519 P.2d 981 (Wash. 1974).

often note in passing that consent was sought from the patient's next of kin without so much as even suggesting that there was anything improper in so doing.[42] In landmark companion New York cases, *Storar* and *Eichner,* Judge Jones, writing in partial dissent, noted with regard to this practice that

> [t]here is reliable information that for many years physicians and members of patients' families, often in consultation with religious counselors, have in actuality been making decisions to withhold or to withdraw life support procedures from incurably ill patients incapable of making the critical decisions for themselves. . . . While, of course, there can be no categorical assurance that there have been no erroneous decisions thus reached, or even that in isolated instances death has not been unjustifiably hastened for unacceptable motives, at the same time there is no empirical evidence that either society or its individual members have suffered significantly in consequence of the absence of active judicial oversight. There is no indication that the medical profession whose members are most closely aware of current practices senses the need for or desires judicial intervention.[43]

Another New York judge summed it up more pithily, stating that "[e]very day, and with limited legal guidance, families and doctors are making decisions for patients unable to do so themselves."[44] That is, a clinical determination that a

---

[42] **AL:** *E.g.,* Camp v. White, 510 So. 2d 166 (Ala. 1987) (doctors consulted family of competent patient who then consulted patient).

ID: *E.g.,* Manning v. Twin Falls Clinic & Hosp., Inc., 830 P.2d 1185, 1187 (Idaho 1992) (describing how determination was made not to resuscitate patient suffering from chronic obstructive pulmonary disease: "At the time of his hospitalization . . . , Manning's disease was in its final stage and the treating physician . . . told Manning's family that his death was imminent. Upon his admission, and at the request of the family, the record indicates that Manning was classified as a "no code" patient meaning the hospital and its employees were directed by the family not to place Manning on a respirator or resuscitate him if he were to suddenly expire. The family and Dr. Kassis agreed this was to be Manning's last hospital admission.").

NY: *E.g.,* Erickson v. Dilgard, 252 N.Y.S.2d 705, 706 (Sup. Ct. Nassau County 1962) (Permission was sought by doctors from son as well as patient for blood transfusion: "His son who is a party respondent in this proceeding also refused to give permission for a transfusion, but was willing to authorize the operation without blood transfusion.").

[43] *In re* Storar, 420 N.E.2d 64, 75–76 (N.Y. 1981) (Jones, J., dissenting). *Accord In re* Storar, 434 N.Y.S.2d 46, 47 (App. Div. 1980) (Cardamone, J., dissenting) ("Courts should not decide whether and when to discontinue the medical support system for a dying patient. This dilemma is part of the human condition too personal to extend beyond the decision of the family or guardian guided by the medical advice available.").

[44] **NY:** Saunders v. State, 492 N.Y.S.2d 510, 515 (Sup. Ct. Nassau County 1985).

US: *Accord* Cruzan v. Director, 497 U.S. 261, 314 n.15 (1990) (Brennan, J., dissenting) ("Such decisions are made every day, without state participation. *See* [Cruzan v. Harmon] 760 S.W.2d, at 428 (Blackmar, J., dissenting)."); *id.* at 336 (Stevens, J., dissenting) ("'Decisions of this kind are made daily by the patient or relatives, on the basis of medical advice and their conclusion as to what is best. Very few cases reach court, and I doubt whether this case would be before us but for the fact that Nancy lies in a state hospital.'") (quoting Cruzan v. Harmon, 760 S.W.2d 408 (Mo. 1988) (Blackmar, J., dissenting)).

patient lacks decisionmaking capacity is presumptively legitimate and no formal adjudication of incompetence is ordinarily necessary before a patient is disenfranchised from decisionmaking;[45] and judicial appointment of a guardian is not ordinarily required to clothe a surrogate with legally valid decisionmaking authority.[46]

FL: *Accord* Browning v. Herbert, 568 So. 2d 4, 15 (Fla. 1990).

IL: *Accord* Estate of Longeway v. Community Convalescent Ctr., 549 N.E.2d 292, 295 (Ill. 1989).

MD: *Accord* 73 Md. Op. Att'y Gen. 253, 287–88 (Op. No. 88-046, Oct. 17, 1988).

MN: *Accord In re* Torres, 357 N.W.2d 332, 341 n.4 (Minn. 1984) ("At oral argument it was disclosed that on an average about 10 life support systems are disconnected weekly in Minnesota. This follows consultation between the attending doctor and the family with the approval of the hospital ethics committee.").

NY: *Accord In re* Storar, 420 N.E.2d 64, 75 (N.Y. 1981) (Jones, J., dissenting) ("There is reliable information that for many years physicians and members of patients' families, often in consultation with religious counselors, have in actuality been making decisions to withhold or to withdraw life support procedures from incurably ill patients incapable of making the critical decisions for themselves.").

WI: *Accord* L.W. v. L.E. Phillips Career Dev. Ctr., 482 N.W.2d 60, 72 n.16 (Wis. 1992) ("[T]he Guidelines for State Court Decision Making in Authorizing or Withholding Life-Sustaining Medical Treatment note that the American Hospital Association estimates that 70% of the estimated 6,000 deaths that occur daily in the United States are somehow timed or negotiated with patients, family and doctors quietly agreeing on not using death delaying technology. Guidelines, p. 17 n.40. . . . It is obvious that there is a generalized society sanctioned practice that most of these life-sustaining medical treatment decisions are made without a guardian or any court intervention. Guidelines, p. 18 n.41.").

[45] Uniform Model Health-Care Consent Act, 9 U.L.A. 453, 460–61 (1988) (comment to § 3) ("Custom suggests and necessity dictates that the initial determination that one is incapable of consenting rest with the health-care provider.").

[46] **US:** Cruzan v. Director, 497 U.S. 261, 336 (1990) (Stevens, J., dissenting) ("'Decisions about medical treatment have customarily been made by . . . those closest to the patient if the patient, because of youth or infirmity, is unable to make the decisions. Decisions of this kind are made daily by the patient or relatives, on the basis of medical advice and their conclusion as to what is best.'") (quoting Cruzan v. Harmon, 760 S.W.2d 408, 428 (Mo. 1988) (Blackmar, J., dissenting)).

MA: *In re* Spring, 399 N.E.2d 493, 499 n.9 (Mass. App. Ct. 1979) ("The importance of the role of the family and the doctor is highlighted by the self-evident fact that the vast majority of treatment decisions relative to persons who are incompetent by reason of senility or retardation are made for them, by their family and the doctor, without court proceedings. This practice is sanctioned not merely by tradition but by the institutional limitations in the ability of courts to make day-to-day treatment decisions, even if restricted to treatments of a potentially life-saving or life-prolonging nature.") (citing *In re* Dinnerstein, 380 N.E.2d 134, 137 n.5 (Mass. App. Ct. 1978), *rev'd,* 405 N.E.2d 115 (Mass. 1980)).

NY: *Cf. In re* Beth Israel Medical Ctr. (Weinstein), 519 N.Y.S.2d 511, 515 (Sup. Ct. N.Y. County 1987) ("[I]t would be best if [decisions] were made, as in the past, by the family in consultation with the patient's physician.").

See also Areen, *The Legal Status of Consent Obtained from Families of Adult Patients to Withhold or Withdraw Treatment,* 258 JAMA 229 (1987).

This professional custom usually suffices. It is a natural, almost reflexive, way of making decisions for patients who lack decisionmaking capacity. As the New Jersey Supreme Court observed,

> [o]ur common human experience teaches us that family members and close friends care most and best for a patient. They offer love and support and concern, and have the best interests of the patient at heart. The importance of the family in medical treatment decisions is axiomatic.
>
> [F]amilies commonly exhibit the greatest degree of concern about the welfare of ailing family members. It is they who come to the hospital and involve themselves in the sick person's care and comfort. Competent patients usually actively solicit the advice and counsel of family members in decisionmaking. Family members routinely ask questions of the medical staff about the patient's condition and prognosis; one study found they frequently asked more questions than patients themselves did. Family members, in fact, commonly act as advocates for patients in the hospital, looking out for their comfort, care, and best interests.[47]

Similarly, a Maryland judge has observed that

> [a]nother reason why a patient's loved ones are best able to make the decision that the incompetent patient would want made is that the choice most people would want made, should they become incompetent, would be whatever their loved ones would choose on their behalf. For example, [one poll] found:
>
> "An overwhelming 88 percent of Americans say the family should decide whether to end artificial life support when an individual is in a coma without

---

[47] **NJ:** *In re* Farrell, 529 A.2d 404, 414 (N.J. 1987) (quoting Newman, *Treatment Refusals for the Critically Ill: Proposed Rules for the Family, the Physician and the State,* III N.Y.L.Sch. Hum. Rts. Ann. 35 (1985)). *Accord In re* Jobes, 529 A.2d 434, 445 (N.J. 1987).

US: *Compare* Cruzan v. Director, 497 U.S. 261, 354 (1990) (Stevens, J., dissenting) ("[C]hoices about life and death are profound ones, not susceptible of resolution by recourse to medical or legal rules. It may be that the best we can do is to ensure that these choices are made by those who will care enough about the patient to investigate her interests with particularity and caution.") *with id.* at 286 ("Close family members may have a strong feeling—a feeling not at all ignoble or unworthy, but not entirely disinterested, either—that they do not wish to witness the continuation of the life of a loved one which they regard as hopeless, meaningless, and even degrading. But there is no automatic assurance that the view of close family members will necessarily be the same as the patient's would have been had she been confronted with the prospect of her situation while competent.").

GA: *Accord In re* L.H.R., 321 S.E.2d 716, 723 (Ga. 1984) ("[T]he decision whether to end the dying process is a personal decision for family members or those who bear a legal responsibility for the patient.").

MI: *Accord* Rosebush v. Oakland County Prosecutor, 491 N.W.2d 633, 686–87 (Mich. Ct. App. 1992).

OH: *Accord In re* Myers, 610 N.E.2d 663, 670–71 (P. Ct. Summit County, Ohio 1993) (parents are ones who know teenage daughter "best, who have suffered with her, who have consulted with her doctors, who have watched her deterioration, and who have the natural instinct of parents for her best interest").

> hope of recovery and has left no instructions on personal wishes. Only 8 percent said doctors should make the decision; 1 percent said the courts should decide, and no one selected the state."[48]

What results, in effect, is a presumption that the family of an incompetent patient acts in the patient's best interests,[49] a presumption which can be overcome by evidence that this is not, in fact, the case.[50]

Clinical determinations of incompetence and designations of surrogates are frequently not overt. They are so routinely made in clinical settings that it strains the meaning of the word "determination" to characterize them as such. In practice, when a patient is thought to lack decisionmaking capacity, the attending physician involves family members rather than the patient in the decisionmaking process.[51] From this it can be inferred that the physician deems the patient to be incompetent. Thus, the "determination" of incompetence in effect occurs when the attending physician engages in decisionmaking with the patient's family or some other party the physician considers to represent the patient. This is not to say that formal assessments of decisionmaking capacity never occur. When the patient is not clearly incompetent, for example, when the patient is not unconscious, formal assessments are often used, and standards are beginning to be developed for making such assessments.[52]

Similarly, only in unusual cases can it be said that attending physicians do anything as formal as designate a surrogate decisionmaker. Often, it just happens without anyone giving any formal recognition to the process. One family member or a small group or even a friend of the patient may have

---

[48] Mack v. Mack, 618 A.2d 744, 774 (Md. 1993) (Chasanow, J., concurring and dissenting) (quoting Coyle, *How Americans View High Court,* Nat'l L.J., Feb. 26, 1990, at 1, 36 (citing National Law Journal/LEXIS poll of over 800 people)).

See also Times Mirror Ctr. for the People & the Press, Reflections of the Times: The Right to Die (1990) (nationwide survey of 1,213 adults conducted in May 1990 found 71% wanted closest family member to decide whether to continue medical treatment); Cohen-Mansfield et al., *The Decision to Execute a Durable Power of Attorney for Health Care and Preferences Regarding the Utilization of Life-Sustaining Treatments in Nursing Home Residents,* 151 Archives Internal Med. 289, 290 (1991) (90% of 93 nursing home patients would choose relative to make their health care decisions, with 64% choosing a son or daughter); Gamble et al., *Knowledge, Attitudes, and Behavior of Elderly Persons Regarding Living Wills,* 151 Archives Internal Med. 277 (1991) (of 52% of 75 elderly persons who knew about living wills but had not executed one, 93% wanted family to make decisions for them if they lost decisionmaking capacity).

[49] *See* Michael H. v. Gerald D., 491 U.S. 110 (1989) (upholding constitutionality of California's favored treatment of traditional family relationships); Parham v. J.R., 442 U.S. 584 (1979) (upholding constitutionality of parental decisionmaking for mentally ill minors).

[50] See § **5.35.**

[51] *See, e.g., In re* Department of Veterans Affairs Medical Ctr., 749 F. Supp. 495 (S.D.N.Y.), *aff'd,* 914 F.2d 239 (2d Cir. 1990) ("Both the physicians and the patient's wife are in agreement that Mr. Warren is not at the present time competent to decide the matter for himself.").

[52] *See, e.g.,* T. Grisso, Evaluating Competencies: Forensic Assessments and Instruments (1986); Appelbaum & Grisso, *Assessing Patients' Capacities to Consent to Treatment,* 319 New Eng. J. Med. 1635 (1988).

predominated in caring for the patient, dealing with health care personnel, and expressing concern for the patient's well-being. This person was probably making medical and other decisions for the patient before the patient was admitted to a health care institution and continues to do so when the need for more explicit decisionmaking arises. The allegations of the complaint in *Westhart v. Mule* nicely capture this process:

> George Martin Westhart was admitted to Anaheim Memorial Hospital . . . was suffering from congestive heart failure, pneumonia, chronic organic brain syndrome secondary to previous multiple strokes, and dehydration. He had been ill for eight years, having endured a debilitating stroke in 1977, and as a result "was unable to walk, speak, make decisions for himself regarding his health care, and unable to communicate his wishes, desires, and consent regarding the course and scope of his medical treatment." In light of his deteriorating condition, Barbro Westhart, George's wife of 45 years, "took it upon herself" to make decisions for him. Thus, acting on her husband's behalf and asserting his legal right, Westhart informed defendants no "extraordinary or heroic measures [were to be] taken to prolong [her husband's] deteriorating condition." Westhart "stated that she did not want her husband put on a respirator, that she did not want [cardiopulmonary resuscitation], or any heroic measures taken because her husband was basically a 'vegetable.'" . . .
>
> . . . Nor did [Mrs.] Westhart ever initiate proceedings to be appointed guardian, conservator, or attorney-in-fact; she deemed such action unnecessary because she was already making decisions for him.[53]

When a patient is of dubious decisionmaking capacity (for example, the patient is able to communicate but not always coherently), decisionmaking will sometimes take place as if the patient were competent simply because all concerned parties are satisfied with the decisions being made or because the consequences of the decisions are not particularly troubling. The treatment and decisionmaking process proceeds smoothly as long as the health care team and family members agree on the proper course of treatment. In such circumstances, little if any thought is given to the need for a more formal designation of a surrogate decisionmaker. If a patient begins to lose the capacity for conversation and/or cognition, as many hopelessly ill patients eventually do, the patient's family gradually takes over the patient's decisional authority. Indeed, the family may have shared this role with the patient from the outset, regardless of the patient's decisionmaking capacity.

Occasionally, this custom—in which decisionmaking for incompetent patients naturally falls to ready, willing, and able family members—breaks down. An event that substantially raises the level of discomfort of the attending physician or other members of the health care team in continuing to make treatment decisions in the existing way is usually needed before thought is given to actually designating a surrogate decisionmaker. The primary catalyst for turning to the judicial approach is insoluble disagreement among the participants in the decisionmaking process.[54]

---

[53] 261 Cal. Rptr. 640, 641, 642 (Ct. App. 1989) (ordered not published) (footnotes omitted).

[54] See § **5.29.**

§ 5.11 Legal Status of Clinical Determinations of Incompetence

The customary practice of physicians in making determinations of incompetence in ordinary medical decisionmaking has gradually become the accepted norm in right-to-die cases too. In early right-to-die cases, there was some confusion about whether decisionmaking could proceed without an adjudication of incompetence.[55] This uncertainty probably arose in large part because of the black-letter law that "competency is a legal determination which must be made by a court,"[56] and that what physicians determine is whether or not a patient lacks decisionmaking capacity. But to the extent that the courts accept a clinical determination that a patient lacks decisionmaking capacity as an adequate basis for proceeding with surrogate decisionmaking, they have in effect recognized that a judicial determination of incompetence is not routinely needed.

The uncertainty of the early cases has largely dissipated. Few courts have addressed this issue explicitly, primarily because few litigants ever raise it and because courts assume that the customary practice of physicians determining incompetence is acceptable. The most overt statement to this effect is that of the New Jersey Supreme Court in the *Farrell* case:

> Adults are presumed competent. We trust that two independent physicians' determinations of competency sufficiently bolster that presumption in this context to preclude the need for any court action to establish the competency of the patient. . . . We see no necessity to depart from this general rule when a competent patient refuses life-sustaining treatment.[57]

And when discussion does occur, it is frequently intermingled with the related questions concerning the proper role of courts in designation of a surrogate and review of decisions to forgo life-sustaining treatment.

The fact that physicians or hospital administrators acting at the behest of physicians sometimes seek adjudications of incompetence or urge patients'

---

[55] *See, e.g., In re* Conroy, 486 A.2d 1209, 1240 (N.J. 1985) ("A necessary prerequisite to surrogate decision-making is a judicial determination that the patient is incompetent to make the decision for himself and designation of a guardian for the incompetent patient if he does not already have one.").

[56] *See, e.g., In re* Hamlin, 689 P.2d 1372 (Wash. 1984) (Rosellini, J., dissenting).

[57] **NJ:** *In re* Farrell, 529 A.2d 404, 415 n.8 (N.J. 1987) (citing President's Comm'n for the Study of Ethical Problems in Medicine & Biomedical & Behavioral Research, Deciding to Forego Life-Sustaining Treatment 44 (1983)), *overruling In re* Conroy, 486 A.2d 1209, 1240 (N.J. 1985) (by implication). *Accord* Gleason v. Abrams, 593 A.2d 1232 (N.J. Super. Ct. App. Div. 1991) (holding that regulation permitting patient competency to be determined by attending physician must be modified to require determination by two nonattending physicians).

NY: *Cf.* N.Y. Pub. Health Law § 2963(2) (McKinney Supp. 1994) ("A determination that an adult patient lacks capacity shall be made by the attending physician to a reasonable degree of medical certainty.").

WA: *Accord In re* Hamlin, 689 P.2d 1372 (Wash. 1984).

See also Hastings Center Guidelines 23 (Part One, II(3)(a)).

family members to do so might be thought to cast doubt on the validity of clinical determinations. However, this merely indicates that even physicians do not view the professional custom as the *exclusive* means for making such determinations. These cases are best understood as exceptions to the general rule that the clinical approach is legitimate[58] rather than as establishing a requirement for the judicial approach. Or they may merely have been more factually difficult cases in which it was desirable, though not necessary, for there to be a judicially appointed guardian.[59]

Similarly, the existence of statutory procedures for the judicial determination of incompetence might be thought to imply that these statutes require recourse to the judicial process as the sole legally valid means for determining incompetence to make medical decisions. Despite the black-letter law that "competency is a legal determination which must be made by a court,"[60] the matter is not so simple. The question really is whether there must be an adjudication of incompetence for there to be a transfer of decisional authority or whether an adjudication is merely one means for so doing.

All jurisdictions have statutorily prescribed procedures for adjudicating incompetence and appointing a guardian of the person.[61] It is not always clear from the statutes, however, whether they are intended to be the exclusive means for making decisions about personal matters, especially medical decisionmaking, for individuals unable to do so for themselves. In early right-to-die litigation, there was some uncertainty in the case law about whether there must be an adjudication of incompetence. Some of the leading cases seemed to require it although the issue was never as squarely presented and explicitly discussed as it might have been. However, most of the courts to initially seem to require an adjudication of incompetence later clearly backed away from such a requirement.[62] The only exceptions of any note are an opinion of the District of Columbia Court of Appeals, *In re A.C.*,[63] raising the question of whether to perform a cesarean delivery of a terminally ill patient's baby. The court mandated that in the future

---

[58] See §§ **5.29–5.36.**

[59] *See, e.g.*, Browning v. Herbert, 543 So. 2d 258, 270 (Fla. Dist. Ct. App. 1989), *aff'd*, 568 So. 2d 4 (Fla. 1990) ("We are not holding that a legal guardian must always be appointed to make life-sustaining medical decisions. While a legal guardian is not essential in all cases, it is comforting that such a guardian exists in this case. A guardian who is appointed by a court and who has taken an oath . . . is more likely to give the responsibility the serious attention which it deserves. . . . Especially in difficult cases, we would urge the appointment of a legal guardian.").

[60] *In re* Hamlin, 689 P.2d at 1381 (Rosellini, J., dissenting).

[61] *See generally* S. Brakel et al., The Mentally Disabled and the Law 408–14 tbl. 7.3 (1985).

[62] **NJ:** *Compare In re* Conroy, 486 A.2d 1209 (N.J. 1985) *and In re* Quinlan, 355 A.2d 647 (N.J. 1976) *with In re* Peter, 529 A.2d 419 (N.J. 1987) *and In re* Jobes, 529 A.2d 434 (N.J. 1987) *and In re* Farrell, 529 A.2d 404 (N.J. 1987).

WA: *Compare In re* Colyer, 660 P.2d 738 (Wash. 1983) *with In re* Hamlin, 689 P.2d 1372 (Wash. 1984).

[63] **DC:** 573 A.2d 1235, 1247 (D.C. 1990).

NY: *Cf.* Fosmire v. Nicoleau, 551 N.E.2d 77 (N.Y. 1990) (adversary judicial hearing required before overriding competent patient's refusal of lifesaving blood transfusion).

a trial judge personally determine through observation and questioning of the patient whether the patient possesses the capacity to decide "unless it is impossible to do so" and to use "any available means" to determine the patient's wishes. However, a narrower reading of the holding, consistent with the facts of the case, suggests that the court was requiring a judicial determination of incompetence only if a patient is questionably competent and the patient's decision is unclear. Had the patient been comatose, it is unlikely that a judicial determination of incompetence would have been required.

The most stalwart proponent of the judicial approach for the determination of incompetence and the designation of a surrogate is the Massachusetts Supreme Judicial Court,[64] which is consistent with its holdings in the areas of psychiatric treatment,[65] in which it has been a national leader, and sterilization.[66] However, even this court no longer seems to insist on judicial formalities to the extent that it once did in right-to-die cases.[67]

The consensus position now clearly is that judicial determination of incompetence and appointment of a guardian are not routinely required, but the courts have usually added the observation that they are always available as a forum for determining incompetence, appointing guardians, and reviewing decisions about life-sustaining treatment.[68] Legislatures have also begun to recognize this as a proper role for courts in end-of-life decisionmaking.[69]

---

[64] Superintendent of Belchertown State Sch. v. Saikewicz, 370 N.E.2d 417, 433 (Mass. 1977) ("Probate Court is the proper forum in which to determine the need for the appointment of a guardian or a guardian ad litem.").

[65] **MA:** Rogers v. Commissioner, 458 N.E.2d 308, 314 (Mass. 1983); *In re* Roe, 421 N.E.2d 40 (Mass. 1981).

[66] *In re* Moe, 432 N.E.2d 712 (Mass. 1982).

[67] See § **5.37.**

[68] **CA:** Barber v. Superior Court, 195 Cal. Rptr. 484, 492 (Ct. App. 1983) ("While guardianship proceedings might be used in this context, we are not aware of any authority requiring such a procedure.").

FL: Browning v. Herbert, 568 So. 2d 4, 16 (Fla. 1990); John F. Kennedy Memorial Hosp. v. Bludworth, 452 So. 2d 921, 926 (Fla. 1984); *In re* Barry, 445 So. 2d 365 (Fla. Dist. Ct. App. 1984).

GA: *In re* L.H.R., 321 S.E.2d 716, 723 (Ga. 1984).

KY: DeGrella v. Elston, 858 S.W.2d 698, 704 (Ky. 1993) (guardianship proceedings not required; guardianship statutes are "remedial rather than exclusive").

NY: Fosmire v. Nicoleau, 551 N.E.2d 77, 80 (N.Y. 1990) ("[W]hen there is bona fide question of the patient's competence the doctor or health care facility may seek a court ruling."). *Cf. In re* Storar, 420 N.E.2d 64, 76 (N.Y. 1981) (Jones, J., dissenting) ("I would have hoped that our court . . . would expressly have recognized the availability of, but not the necessity for, judicial approval of surrogate decisions in cases such as these.").

WA: *In re* Hamlin, 689 P.2d 1372, 1378–79 (Wash. 1984).

President's Comm'n, Deciding to Forego Life-Sustaining Treatment 154.

[69] *See, e.g.,* N.J. Stat. Ann. § 26:2H-66.a ("In the event of disagreement among the patient, health care representative, and attending physician concerning the patient's decision making capacity or the appropriate interpretation and application of the terms of an advance directive to the patient's course of treatment, the parties may seek to resolve the disagreement by means

When a judicial determination of incompetence is desired, the question of who can and should initiate judicial proceedings can sometimes cause great confusion and consequent delay in right-to-die cases. In some cases, disinterested third parties have brought actions for the determination of incompetence and appointment of a guardian. The New York courts have twice spoken on this matter, both times condemning the practice.[70]

The burden ought to be on the health care institution to institute judicial proceedings if it wishes to contest a patient's refusal of treatment, rather than requiring the patient to go to court to establish his rights.[71] This appropriately respects the presumption of a patient's right to refuse treatment and avoids unwarranted delay and emotional turmoil for the family, and possibly great tragedy such as occurred in a Chicago hospital when a father, whose pleas to have a ventilator turned off from his infant son were met with the hospital's insistence that he obtain a court order, disconnected the ventilator himself, holding the staff at bay with a gun.[72]

The Florida Supreme Court in the *Dubreuil*[73] case addressed this problem in the context of a competent patient. According to *Dubreuil,* the court's earlier opinion in the *Wons*[74] case left the impression that hospitals are obligated to assert any state interest that might be supported by the facts, and especially the

---

of procedures and practices established by the health care institution, including but not limited to, consultation with an institutional ethics committee, or with a person designated by the health care institution for this purpose or may seek resolution by a court of competent jurisdiction.").

[70] *See* Weber v. Stony Brook Hosp., 456 N.E.2d 1186 (N.Y.), *cert. denied,* 464 U.S. 1026 (1983) (petitioner who had no direct or personal knowledge of the facts relating to the patient's condition, the treatment being administered, or the factors prompting her parents to adopt the course they have has no standing to institute proceedings); *In re* Klein, 538 N.Y.S.2d 274, 276 (App. Div. 1989) ("Ultimately, the record confirms that these absolute strangers to the Klein family, whatever their motivation, have no place in the midst of this family tragedy."). *But cf.* Grace Plaza of Great Neck, Inc. v. Elbaum, 623 N.E.2d 513, 515 (N.Y. 1993) ("burden of instituting legal proceedings [is] on those seeking to discontinue treatment").

[71] **FL:** Wons v. Public Health Trust, 541 So. 2d 96, 98 (Fla. 1989).

NY: *But cf.* Grace Plaza of Great Neck, Inc. v. Elbaum, 623 N.E.2d at 515–16 (placing burden on family not for determination of incompetence but for determination of incompetent patient's wishes).

[72] *See* Symposium, *Family Privacy and Persistent Vegetative State,* 17 Law, Med., & Health Care 295–346 (1989). *See also Comatose Toddler Shot to Death; Heartsick Father Turns Himself In,* N.Y. Times, June 30, 1985, § 1, at 15, 18 (late city final ed.); *Man Forces a Nurse to Let His Father Die,* N.Y. Times, Dec. 24, 1985, at A8 (late city final ed.); *Man Shoots Wife in Hospital,* N.Y. Times, Aug. 9, 1985, at A7 (nat'l ed.); Barron, *Hospital Death Ruled Accidental; Man's Children Won't Be Charged,* N.Y. Times, Jan. 26, 1990, at A13 (nat'l ed.) (district attorney did not prosecute family who turned off critically ill father's ventilator because "'[l]egally, there's no way a criminal charge could be sustained here'").

[73] *In re* Dubreuil, 629 So. 2d 819 (Fla. 1993).

[74] Wons v. Public Health Trust, 541 So. 2d 96 (Fla. 1989).

abandonment of children.[75] But in *Dubreuil,* the court clarified that this is not the case, because, "[u]ntil today, we were not asked to determine whether it is appropriate for a health care provider, as opposed to another party, to assert the state interests in the first instance."[76] When actually faced with the question, the court concluded that it is not proper for the hospital to assert the state's interest, giving several reasons for this conclusion.

First, a health care provider must respect a patient's wishes. The provider's role is to provide medical treatment, and not to act as a "substitute parent." Unless ordered to do so by a court of competent jurisdiction, a health care provider must honor a patient's wishes to decline treatment. (Although the court did not say so, a provider should also be entitled to override a refusal of treatment in an emergency in which the patient, unlike Mrs. Dubreuil, had not made a considered judgment to refuse treatment prior to the emergency.[77]) Second, if the health care provider is to question a competent patient's refusal of treatment, it potentially puts the provider in an awkward position between the patient and family members who may support or oppose the patient's position. Third, the health care provider has a potential conflict of interest. Many times, the provider will be motivated primarily by its own interests—in avoiding adverse publicity, in preventing legal liability, in assuring payment for the services it renders—rather than the patient's. Finally, the health care provider is a private entity, and therefore it is inappropriate for it to shoulder the state's burden of asserting its interests. Taking these factors into consideration, the court concluded that the burden of asserting the state's interests, not surprisingly, is on the state.[78]

If a health care provider intends to override a patient's treatment refusal, it bears the responsibility for notifying the state attorney and interested parties, such as family members, who are known to it. As long as the provider acts in good faith in following a patient's wishes, it "cannot be subjected to civil or criminal liability."[79] The court did not explain what it meant by good faith in this context.[80] However, if the provider has doubts about whether the patient is

---

[75] *In re* Dubreuil, 629 So. 2d at 823 ("[I]t will be necessary for hospitals that wish to contest a patient's refusal of treatment to commence court proceedings and sustain the heavy burden of proof that the state's interest outweighs the patient's constitutional rights.") (citing Wons v. Public Health Trust, 541 So. 2d at 98).

[76] *Id.* at 823.

[77] See §§ **3.23, 10.22,** and **10.23.**

[78] *In re* Dubreuil, 629 So. 2d at 823 ("Therefore, we recede from *Wons* to the extent that it may be read to put any burden of proof on the health care provider with respect to asserting the state interests.").

[79] *Id.* at 823–24 ("When a health care provider, acting in good faith, follows the wishes of a competent and informed patient to refuse medical treatment, the health care provider is acting appropriately and cannot be subjected to civil or criminal liability.").

[80] *But see* Browning v. Herbert, 543 So. 2d 258, 274 (Fla. Dist. Ct. App. 1989) (good faith in the context of surrogate making decision for incompetent patient means that "the decision was made with honesty of intention and in an honest effort to make the decision which the patient, if competent, would make").

competent or doubts about whether the patient has been adequately informed such that his decision meets the standards for informed consent (even though a refusal), following the patient's wishes is probably not acting in good faith. A health care provider should not complacently accept every refusal of treatment. Under some circumstances—such as when the patient's decisionmaking capacity is in question—a health care provider might be obligated to take action and the failure to do so might be the basis for negligence liability. Although the court did not address this issue, the same is true of the refusal of treatment by the surrogate of an incompetent patient. Health care professionals are not obligated to blindly follow surrogates' directions. At the least, they must be satisfied that those directions meet the applicable substantive standard for decisionmaking for incompetent patients.

After being notified by the health care provider of a refusal of treatment—recalling that this is a refusal of treatment the administration of which will almost certainly save the patient's life—the state attorney has discretion in each case to decide whether or not to proceed with litigation in an attempt to override a competent patient's refusal. The court observed that "[t]his procedure should eliminate needless litigation by health care providers while honoring the patient's wishes and giving other interested parties the right to intervene if there is a good faith reason to do so."[81]

In many cases of an urgent nature when competent patients refuse life-saving medical treatment, health care providers seek *ex parte* hearings. The New York Court of Appeals[82] and the District of Columbia Court of Appeals[83] have both roundly condemned this practice. The *Dubreuil* court did not expressly address this practice but cited this aspect of the New York decision approvingly.[84]

§ 5.12 Legal Status of Clinical Designation of a Surrogate

It is common practice among physicians to turn to family members to make decisions about medical care for patients who do not possess decisionmaking

---

[81] *In re* Dubreuil, 629 So. 2d at 824.

[82] *See* Fosmire v. Nicoleau, 551 N.E.2d 77 (N.Y. 1990).

[83] *See In re* A.C., 573 A.2d 1235 (D.C. 1990).

[84] **FL:** *In re* Dubreuil, 629 So. 2d at 828 (citing Fosmire v. Nicoleau, 551 N.E.2d 77 (for proposition that "trial court erred by signing ex parte order compelling blood transfusion without giving patient or her husband notice and the opportunity to be heard even though only three hours lapsed between making the application and signing of the order, and an additional six hours before the order was executed")).

DFL: *But see* McKenzie v. Doctors' Hosp. of Hollywood, Inc., 765 F. Supp. 1504 (S.D. Fla. 1991), *aff'd without opinion*, 974 F.2d 1347 (11th Cir. 1992).

IL: *Cf. In re* Estate of Brooks, 205 N.E.2d 435 (Ill. 1965) (implicitly condemning ex parte application for administration of blood transfusion to Jehovah's Witness).

capacity. Courts, especially in right-to-die cases, have almost universally endorsed this practice, at least as a presumptive rule.

§ 5.13 —In Medical Decisionmaking Generally

There is little authoritative case law on the authority of patients' family members to make general medical decisions for patients when they lose decisionmaking capacity because there has been very little challenge, in cases not involving life-sustaining treatment, leveled at the practice of clinical determination of incompetence and designation of a surrogate. This results largely from the fact that physicians view the decisions that need to be made as routine. This is not to say that the medical procedures in question are without medical risk but rather that, because they are the kinds of decisions that physicians are accustomed to making in conjunction with competent patients, physicians do not become particularly consternated by having to make them with the families of incompetent patients.

The lack of questioning of clinical designation of a surrogate is also explained by the lack of perceived legal risk in such decisionmaking. In cases not raising life-or-death questions, the stakes are rarely high enough to cause health care personnel or families to seriously question the legitimacy of decisionmaking by the patient's family. Thus, the incentive to litigate these issues and obtain clarification is often absent.

Most of the guidance in cases involving ordinary medical decisionmaking is obiter dictum at best, and usually so oblique that it indicates that the court was not addressing the specific question.[85] For example, in discussing whether the court could authorize surgery on an incompetent patient, a New York court stated that it "is fully empowered to grant authorization therefor, *especially where there is no close relative* who is in the position to give consent."[86] However, if the patient is competent or is now incompetent but made a decision about the treatment in question before losing decisionmaking capacity, the decision of the patient governs, not that of a family member.[87]

---

[85] **CA:** *E.g.*, Barber v. Superior Court, 195 Cal. Rptr. 484, 493 (Ct. App. 1983) ("When the patient, himself, is incapable of deciding for himself, because of his medical condition or for other reasons, there is no clear authority on the issue of who and under what procedure is to make the final decision.").

GA: *E.g.*, Kirby v. Spivey, 307 S.E.2d 538 (Ga. Ct. App. 1983) (by implication).

See also Hastings Center Guidelines 24 (Part One, II(3)(b)).

[86] *In re* Strauss, 391 N.Y.S.2d 168, 169 (App. Div. 1977) (emphasis added). *Accord* Long Island Jewish-Hillside Medical Ctr. v. Levitt, 342 N.Y.S.2d 356 (Sup. Ct. Nassau County 1973) (patient's sister would have been proper party to authorize surgery if she had been willing to act as surrogate) (by implication).

[87] *See In re* Dubreuil, 603 So. 2d 538, 541 (Fla. Dist. Ct. App. 1992) (patient's "constitutional right to refuse treatment was [not] in any way dependent upon the consent of her husband"). See **§ 10.14.**

A few cases have addressed this issue in the context of actions for damages after treatment was administered to a patient on the basis of consent by a family member. The precedents are unclear and conflicting. Some suggest but do not hold that the consent of an incompetent patient's spouse is legally valid authorization to provide treatment,[88] unless the patient has personally refused the treatment in question before losing the capacity to do so,[89] but there are virtually no cases concluding that consent of a spouse to *forgo* treatment is valid.[90] There is also contrary authority that spouses are not empowered, in the absence of statute or judicial appointment as a guardian, to make medical decisions for incompetent patients.[91] A number of cases suggest that parents may provide valid authorization for the treatment of their adult offspring,[92] and

---

[88] **CA5:** *E.g.*, Lester v. Aetna Casualty & Sur. Co., 240 F.2d 676 (5th Cir. 1957) (Louisiana law).

DPR: *E.g.*, Aponte v. United States, 582 F. Supp. 65 (D.P.R. 1984) (consent must be obtained from the guardian or next of kin if patient not competent).

HI: *E.g.*, Nishi v. Hartwell, 473 P.2d 116, 122–23 (Haw. 1970).

IL: *E.g.*, Pratt v. Davis, 79 N.E. 562 (Ill. 1906) (physician liable in trespass because husband did not consent to wife's operation).

KY: *E.g.*, Wilson v. Lehman, 379 S.W.2d 478, 479–80 (Ky. 1964).

LA: *E.g.*, Percle v. St. Paul Fire & Marine Ins. Co., 349 So. 2d 1289, 1300 (La. Ct. App. 1960); Rogers v. Lumbermen's Mut. Casualty Co., 119 So. 2d 649, 652–53 (La. Ct. App. 1960).

MI: *E.g.*, Young v. Oakland Gen. Hosp., 437 N.W.2d 321, 325 (Mich. Ct. App. 1989) (per curiam) ("Where a patient is incompetent, the patient's surrogate decisionmaker, usually a member of the patient's family, makes a decision which would have been made by the patient if he or she were still competent.") (citing Morgan v. Olds, 417 N.W.2d 232 (Iowa Ct. App. 1987)).

NJ: *E.g.*, *In re* Conroy, 486 A.2d 1209 (N.J. 1985).

NY: *E.g.*, *In re* Barbara, 474 N.Y.S.2d 799, 801 (App. Div. 1984) (authorization for surgical procedure for incompetent adult may be obtained from patient's spouse, parent, adult child, or a court of competent jurisdiction).

UT: *E.g.*, Lounsbury v. Capel, 836 P.2d 188, 197 (Utah 1992) (statute authorizing spouse to consent to health care applies "only in an emergency or if the spouse is otherwise unable to give his or her own consent").

[89] *See, e.g.*, *In re* Dubreuil, 629 So. 2d 819 (Fla. 1993).

[90] *See, e.g.*, Collins v. Davis, 254 N.Y.S.2d 666 (Sup. Ct. Nassau County 1964).

[91] **CA5:** *E.g.*, Karp v. Cooley, 493 F.2d 408, 421 (5th Cir. 1974) (Texas law) (relationship of husband and wife does not create legal authorization in one to give consent for treatment of the other).

LA: *E.g.*, Beck v. Lovell, 361 So. 2d 245, 250–51 (La. Ct. App. 1978) (spousal consent unacceptable unless there is an emergency).

TX: *E.g.*, Gravis v. Physicians & Surgeons Hosp., 427 S.W.2d 310, 311 (Tex. 1968).

[92] **CA:** *E.g.*, Farber v. Olkin, 254 P.2d 520 (Cal. 1953) (right to consent to treatment resides in the parent who has the legal responsibility to maintain such adult offspring).

FL: *E.g.*, Ritz v. Florida Patient's Compensation Fund, 436 So. 2d 987 (Fla. Dist. Ct. App. 1983).

NY: *E.g.*, Anonymous v. State, 236 N.Y.S.2d 88, 90 (App. Div. 1963) (analogy to rule requiring parental consent for minor child dictates that parent is authorized to speak in behalf

others indicate by way of dictum that the consent of other family members is a legally valid authorization of treatment.[93] This approach is adopted by the several Uniform Acts,[94] none of which, however, has been widely adopted. However, to this proposition, too, there are dissenting views.[95]

Most of the direct challenges to the practice of doctors turning to family members to make decisions for patients who lack the capacity to do so have arisen in cases involving involuntary sterilization and involuntary psychiatric treatment. The modern trend, both in sterilization[96] and psychiatric

---

of a mentally ill adult child for whom no committee of the person has been appointed); McCandless v. State, 162 N.Y.S.2d 570 (App. Div. 1957).

SD: *E.g.,* Dewes v. Indian Health Serv., 504 F. Supp. 203 (D.S.D. 1980) (by implication) (failure to explain the options available and to obtain consent of parents).

[93] **CADC:** *E.g.,* Canterbury v. Spence, 464 F.2d 772, 789 n.92 (D.C. Cir. 1972) ("Where patient is legally or factually incapable of giving consent, the established rule is that, absent an emergency, the physician must obtain the necessary authority from a relative.").

CA: *E.g.,* Cobbs v. Grant, 502 P.2d 1, 10 (Cal. 1972) (if patient is incompetent, authority to consent is transferred to the patient's legal guardian or closest available relative).

MI: *E.g.,* Young v. Oakland Gen. Hosp., 437 N.W.2d 321, 325 (Mich. Ct. App. 1989) (per curiam) (where there was a dispute after treatment was rendered as to whether patient's daughter or grandson, whom patient had raised as if he were a son, was the patient's "legal representative," hospital did not err in treating patient's daughter as legal representative "until a legal guardian was actually appointed").

MO: *E.g.,* Steele v. Woods, 327 S.W.2d 187, 198 (Mo. 1959).

NC: *E.g.,* Kennedy v. Parrott, 90 S.E.2d 754, 758 (N.C. 1956).

NY: *E.g.,* Long Island Jewish-Hillside Medical Ctr. v. Levitt, 342 N.Y.S.2d 356 (Sup. Ct. Nassau County 1973); *In re* Nemser, 273 N.Y.S.2d 624 (Sup. Ct. N.Y. County 1966).

RI: *E.g.,* Miller v. Rhode Island Hosp., 625 A.2d 778 (R.I. 1993) ("'Even in [emergencies] the physician should, as current law requires, attempt to secure a relative's consent if possible'") (quoting Canterbury v. Spence, 464 F.2d 772, 788–89 (D.C. Cir. 1972)).

[94] See §§ **10.17–10.20.**

[95] **CADC:** *E.g.,* Bonner v. Moran, 126 F.2d 121 (D.C. Cir. 1941) (consent of aunt is not legally adequate though possibly because operation was for benefit of another besides minor).

TX: *E.g.,* Rishworth v. Moss, 159 S.W. 122, 123–24 (Tex. Ct. App. 1913) (sister not empowered to authorize treatment for minor).

[96] **DCT:** *E.g.,* Ruby v. Massey, 452 F. Supp. 361, 366 (D. Conn. 1978) (Parents "may neither veto nor give valid consent to the sterilization of their children.").

CO: *E.g., In re* A.W., 637 P.2d 366, 370 (Colo. 1981).

IN: *E.g.,* A.L. v. G.R.H., 325 N.E.2d 501 (Ind. Ct. App. 1975), *cert. denied,* 425 U.S. 936 (1976) (common law does not invest parents with power to have 15-year-old brain-damaged son sterilized despite sincerity of their belief that it is in child's best interests).

KY: *E.g.,* Holmes v. Powers, 439 S.W.2d 579 (Ky. 1969).

MD: *E.g.,* Wentzel v. Montgomery Gen. Hosp., 447 A.2d 1244 (Md. 1982), *cert. denied,* 459 U.S. 1147 (1983).

MA: *E.g., In re* Moe, 432 N.E.2d 712 (Mass. 1982).

treatment,[97] is to require judicial determination of incompetence and designation of a surrogate. Sterilization was distinguished from right-to-die cases by the New Jersey Supreme Court in this way:

> In *Quinlan* we found that the only practical way to preserve the comatose patient's right to discontinue artificial life-support was to allow the guardian and family "to render their best judgment, subject to . . . qualifications . . . , as to whether she would exercise it in these circumstances." . . . But *Quinlan* concerned a very special situation. The alternatives available there were much more clear-cut than those here. The patient could continue to live indefinitely in a coma with the support of artificial apparatus or she could have the apparatus removed and allow natural forces to take over, probably resulting in her death. This choice is not conducive to detached evaluation and resolution by the person exercising it in behalf of the patient. A decision to choose life or death will rely on instinct more than reasoned calculation. Other than considering the medical opinions to determine the chances of the patient's future recovery, there are few factors for a court to weigh in deciding what is in the incompetent's best interest. The Court in *Quinlan* thought it best to defer to the parents' judgment as long as safeguards were observed. Also, the Court was not made aware in that case of any history of abuse in such decisions.
>
> In contrast, sterilization of incompetents, especially the mentally impaired, has been subject to abuse in the past. . . . We must ensure that the law does not allow abuse to continue. Since the sterilization decision involves a variety of factors well suited to rational development in judicial proceedings, a court can take cognizance of these factors and reach a fair decision of what is the incompetent's best interest.[98]

NJ: *E.g., In re* Grady, 426 A.2d 467 (N.J. 1981).

PA: *E.g.,* Terwilliger v. Wands, 450 A.2d 1376 (Pa. Super. Ct. 1982).

TX: *E.g.,* Frazier v. Levi, 440 S.W.2d 393 (Tex. Ct. App. 1969).

WI: *But cf.* L.W. v. L.E. Phillips Career Dev. Ctr., 482 N.W.2d 60, 69 n.11 (Wis. 1992) (distinguishing sterilization from forgoing of life-sustaining treatment in determining substantive standard for decisionmaking for person lacking decisionmaking capacity).

[97] **DNJ:** *E.g.,* Rennie v. Klein, 476 F. Supp. 1294 (D.N.J. 1979), *modified and remanded,* 643 F.2d 836 (3d Cir. 1981); Rennie v. Klein, 462 F. Supp. 1131 (D.N.J. 1978).

DOH: *E.g.,* Davis v. Hubbard, 506 F. Supp. 915 (N.D. Ohio 1980).

MA: *E.g.,* Rogers v. Commissioner, 458 N.E.2d 308, 314 (Mass. 1983).

MN: *E.g.,* Jarvis v. Levine, 403 N.W.2d 298 (Minn. 1987).

NY: *E.g.,* Rivers v. Katz, 495 N.E.2d 337, (N.Y. 1986).

OK: *E.g., In re* K.K.B., 609 P.2d 747 (Okla. 1980).

WI: *E.g.,* State *ex rel.* Jones v. Gerhardstein, 416 N.W.2d 883 (Wis. 1987).

See generally Hermann, *Autonomy, Self Determination, the Right of Involuntarily Committed Persons to Refuse Treatment, and the Use of Substituted Judgment in Medication Decisions Involving Incompetent Persons,* 13 Int'l J.L. & Psychiatry 361 (1990).

[98] *In re* Grady, 426 A.2d 467, 475 (N.J. 1981).

§ 5.14 —In Right-to-Die Cases

A clear trend has emerged in right-to-die cases favoring the legitimacy of the clinical designation of surrogates.[99] This trend, however, has had to overcome an uncertain common-law background.[100] Few right-to-die cases have extensively addressed the question of whether or not there needs to be a judicial appointment of a guardian to serve as surrogate to make decisions about forgoing life-sustaining treatment, though the number is greater and the discussion sometimes more explicit than with the related issue of determination of incompetence.[101]

The uncertainty in early right-to-die cases is exemplified by the contrasting views expressed in *John F. Kennedy Memorial Hospital v. Bludworth.*[102] The majority of the Florida Supreme Court held that "[i]f there are close family members such as the patient's spouse, adult children, or parents, who are willing to exercise this right on behalf of the patient, there is no requirement that a guardian be judicially appointed."[103] In contrast, a concurring justice expressed

---

[99] **CA:** Barber v. Superior Court, 195 Cal. Rptr. 484, 492 (Ct. App. 1983) ("While guardianship proceedings might be used in this context, we are not aware of any authority requiring such procedure.").

CT: Foody v. Manchester Memorial Hosp., 482 A.2d 713, 721 (Conn. Super. Ct. 1984) ("[T]he family lawfully may act as the patient's substitute decision-maker.").

FL: Browning v. Herbert, 543 So. 2d 258, 271 (Fla. Dist. Ct. App. 1989), *aff'd,* 568 So. 2d 4 (Fla. 1990) ("Guardians and other family members regularly make medical decisions for patients on matters less critical than life-sustaining treatment. We do not intend by this opinion to preclude that practice or to require great formalities for those decisions."); John F. Kennedy Memorial Hosp. v. Bludworth, 452 So. 2d 921, 926 (Fla. 1984) (guardian need not be appointed if there are close family members).

IN: *In re* Lawrance, 579 N.E.2d 32, 41, 42 (Ind. 1991) (purpose of surrogate decisionmaking statute is "to resolve health care decisions without a need for court proceedings").

NJ: *In re* Jobes, 529 A.2d 434, 447 (N.J. 1987) (no need to appoint guardian if there are close and caring family members to exercise patient's right of self-determination).

OH: *In re* McInnis, 584 N.E.2d 1389 (P. Ct. Stark County, Ohio 1991) (spouse, without judicial appointment as guardian, has common-law authority to make decisions about life-sustaining treatment, and court "will not appoint guardians for the sole purpose to continue or withhold life-sustaining treatment").

WA: *In re* Hamlin, 689 P.2d 1372 (Wash. 1984) (guardianship proceedings not necessary if family agrees forgoing life-sustaining treatment in best interests of patient).

See generally President's Comm'n, Deciding to Forego Life-Sustaining Treatment 154.

[100] See § **5.13.**

[101] See § **5.11.**

[102] 452 So. 2d 921 (Fla. 1984).

[103] **FL:** John F. Kennedy Memorial Hosp. v. Bludworth, 452 So. 2d 921, 926 (Fla. 1984). *Accord* Browning v. Herbert, 543 So. 2d 258, 271 (Fla. Dist. Ct. App. 1989), *aff'd,* 568 So. 2d 4 (Fla. 1990) ("Guardians and other family members regularly make medical decisions for patients on matters less critical than life-sustaining treatment. We do not intend by this opinion to preclude that practice or to require great formalities for those decisions.").

the view that "[a]n incompetent can act only through a guardian; no one but a [judicially appointed] guardian can substitute his judgment for a ward. Certainly, if an incompetent cannot convey property except through a guardian, an equal safeguard should apply to the cessation of life."[104]

The Florida Supreme Court recognized that "[d]octors, in consultation with close family members are in the best position to make these decisions."[105] The court did state that they should be *close* family members—spouse, adult children, or parents[106]—suggesting that if a patient has no close family, a guardian must be judicially appointed. And it also stated, in what has come to be the widely-accepted judicial position, that although this is the normal way in which decisions should be made, the courts are always open to hear these matters if a request is made by the family, a guardian if there is one, the physician, or the hospital.[107]

The development of the law in two states in particular, Washington and New Jersey, exemplifies the uncertainty and false starts in this area. In Washington, the supreme court held in 1983 in the *Colyer* case that a guardian must be judicially appointed when making decisions about life-sustaining treatment.[108]

IN: *Accord In re* Lawrance, 579 N.E.2d 32, 39 (Ind. 1991) ("In our society, health care decision making for patients typically transfers upon incompetence to the patient's family.").

IA: *Accord* Morgan v. Olds, 417 N.W.2d 232 (Iowa Ct. App. 1987) ("[T]he doctor, as part of his duty to the incompetent patient, must consult with the incompetent patient's surrogate decisionmaker before implementing a course of treatment.").

OH: *Accord In re* McInnis, 584 N.E.2d 1389 (P. Ct. Stark County, Ohio 1991) ("[T]he spouse, individually and without the intervention of the court, without the appointment of a guardian, has such authority under the common law.").

[104] John F. Kennedy Memorial Hosp. v. Bludworth, 452 So. 2d at 927 (McDonald, J., concurring *in result*).

[105] *Id.* at 926.

[106] *Id.*

[107] **FL:** John F. Kennedy Memorial Hosp. v. Bludworth, at 926–27. *Accord* Browning v. Herbert, 568 So. 2d 4, 16 (Fla. 1990); *In re* Barry, 445 So. 2d 365, 372 (Fla. Dist. Ct. App. 1984).

GA: *In re* Doe, 418 S.E.2d 3, 6 (Ga. 1992); *In re* L.H.R., 321 S.E.2d 716, 723 (Ga. 1984).

KY: DeGrella v. Elston, 858 S.W.2d 698, 709–10 (Ky. 1993).

MI: Rosebush v. Oakland County Prosecutor, 491 N.W.2d 633, 638 (Mich. Ct. App. 1992) (citing first edition of this treatise).

NY: Fosmire v. Nicoleau, 551 N.E.2d 77, 80 (N.Y. 1990) ("when there is bona fide question of the patient's competence the doctor or health care facility may seek a court ruling"). *Cf. In re* Storar, 420 N.E.2d 64, 76 (N.Y. 1981) (Jones, J., dissenting in part) ("I would have hoped that our court . . . would expressly have recognized the availability of, but not the necessity for, judicial approval of surrogate decisions in cases such as these."); *In re* Nemser, 273 N.Y.S.2d 624 (Sup. Ct. N.Y. County 1966) (suggesting that resort to the judicial process for such a determination was unwarranted).

WA: *In re* Hamlin, 689 P.2d 1372, 1378–79 (Wash. 1984).

President's Comm'n, Deciding to Forego Life-Sustaining Treatment 154.

[108] *In re* Colyer, 660 P.2d 738, 750–51 (Wash. 1983).

Guardianship procedures, it observed, "serve to protect against too precipitous a decision or the appointment of one with less than proper motives. Moreover, we do not perceive them as being overly burdensome. . . . Thus, judicial participation at this juncture affords minimal intrusion into the personal decision regarding treatment, but nevertheless serves to protect against abuse."[109] However, only 20 months later, the court concluded in *Hamlin* that guardianship proceedings are *not* "a necessary predicate"[110] to making decisions to forgo life-sustaining treatment:

> If the incompetent patient's immediate family, after consultation with the treating physician and the prognosis committee, all agree with the conclusion that the patient's best interests would be advanced by withdrawal of life sustaining treatment, the family may assert the personal right of the incompetent to refuse life sustaining treatment without seeking prior appointment of a guardian.[111]

Because Mr. Hamlin had no family, the court did not need to address this issue. It chose to do so, however, because of the confusion that had arisen from its prior holding and discussion of this matter in *Colyer* in which the patient did have family. Clearly changing its mind in *Hamlin,* the court reflected on "[l]anguage used in *Colyer* [that] can be construed to require appointment of a guardian before any treatment decision can be made concerning an incompetent patient,"[112] and concluded that "[t]his, however, is not the intended result."[113] The court continued by explaining that

> [i]n *Colyer,* we stated that guardianship hearings would not be overly burdensome, but upon reflection, the approach that best accommodates these most fundamental societal decisions is to allow the surrogate decision maker, the family, to make the decision free of the cumbersomeness and costs of legal guardianship proceedings. If all parties, the immediate family, the treating physicians and the prognosis committee, agree as to the course of treatment, a guardian is not necessary.[114]

---

[109] *Id.* at 747.

[110] **WA:** *In re* Hamlin, 689 P.2d 1372, 1377 (Wash. 1984). *Accord In re* Grant, 747 P.2d 445 (Wash. 1987), *modified,* 757 P.2d 534 (Wash. 1988). *But cf. In re* Hamlin, 689 P.2d 1372, 1381 (Wash. 1984) ("circumvent[ion of] court-appointed guardian proceedings negates the safeguards inherent in the guardian statutes") (Rosellini, J., dissenting).

FL: *But cf.* Browning v. Herbert, 543 So. 2d 258, 270 (Fla. Dist. Ct. App. 1989), *aff'd,* 568 So. 2d 4 (Fla. 1990) (not requiring guardianship proceedings, but observing that "[a] guardian who is appointed by a court and who has taken an oath . . . is more likely to give the responsibility the serious attention which it deserves.").

[111] **WA:** *In re* Hamlin, 689 P.2d at 1377 (citing Barber v. Superior Court, 195 Cal. Rptr. 484 (Ct. App. 1983)).

FL: *Accord* John F. Kennedy Memorial Hosp. v. Bludworth, 452 So. 2d 921 (Fla. 1984).

Accord President's Comm'n, Deciding to Forego Life-Sustaining Treatment.

[112] *In re* Hamlin, 689 P.2d at 1377.

[113] *Id.*

[114] *Id.* (citing John F. Kennedy Memorial Hosp. v. Bludworth, 452 So. 2d 921 (Fla. 1984)).

As in the *Bludworth* case, this drew a strong rebuke from a dissenting justice who would have held that only "in cases where family members can demonstrate the patient's intent to vest them with authority to act in this manner, guardianship proceedings might be unnecessary."[115]

The experience in New Jersey parallels that in Washington, and in some respects is even more confusing because of the greater number of cases and substantially longer period of time involved. The 1976 opinion in *Quinlan,*[116] reiterated in the 1985 opinion in *Conroy,*[117] clearly supports judicial designation of a surrogate. However, two 1987 cases, *Peter*[118] and *Jobes,*[119] suggest that the clinical designation of a surrogate is an acceptable practice. In *Peter,* the patient had designated her own surrogate decisionmaker through an advance directive, a practice which the court approved, and in dictum commented that

> [i]n the absence of [a patient-] designated decisionmaker, if there is a close family member, . . . the Ombudsman should defer decisions about life-support to the family member. Thus, the Ombudsman must consult with the health care providers and treating physician, if there is one, to ascertain whether there is a close caring family member who will be able and willing to make such decisions.[120]

When, however, there are no close family members or "the relatives may not be able to adequately represent the patient's interests,"[121] a guardian must be appointed. In *Jobes,* the court clearly stated that when a patient is incompetent, "[i]f there are close and caring family members who are willing to make this decision [to terminate life support for a patient in a persistent vegetative state] there is no need to have a guardian appointed."[122]

Furthermore, the third companion case to *Jobes* and *Peter*—*Farrell*[123]—holds that the closely-related issue of incompetence determination need not be judicially made for a patient at home who has decided to forgo life-sustaining treatment, a holding also "applicable to patients in hospitals and nursing homes."[124] This decision appears to overrule *Conroy*'s requirement that "[a] necessary prerequisite to surrogate decisionmaking is a judicial determination that the patient is incompetent to make the decision for himself and designation of a guardian for the incompetent patient if he does not already have one."[125] Also,

---

115 *Id.* at 1381 (Rosellini, J., dissenting).

116 *In re* Quinlan, 355 A.2d 647 (N.J. 1976).

117 *In re* Conroy, 486 A.2d 1209 (N.J. 1985).

118 *In re* Peter, 529 A.2d 419 (N.J. 1987).

119 *In re* Jobes, 529 A.2d 434 (N.J. 1987).

120 *In re* Peter, 529 A.2d at 428–29.

121 *Id.* at 429.

122 *In re* Jobes, 529 A.2d at 447.

123 *In re* Farrell, 529 A.2d 404 (N.J. 1987).

124 *Id.* at 415 n.8.

125 *In re* Conroy, 486 A.2d 1209, 1240 (N.J. 1985).

Conroy seemed to require a judicial determination of incompetence as a "necessary prerequisite to surrogate decisionmaking . . . [b]ecause of the special vulnerability of mentally and physically impaired, elderly persons in nursing homes and the potential for abuse with unsupervised institutional decision-making in such homes."[126] Therefore, it should not be concluded on the basis of *Conroy* that such a requirement is necessary in the case of patients not in nursing homes.

Many cases address the three distinct aspects of the question of the judicial role in decisionmaking about life-sustaining treatment without distinguishing among them. Most of the cases that do not require routine judicial participation in end-of-life decisionmaking and that do not expressly address the question of whether there must be the judicial appointment of a guardian implicitly hold that there need not be. For example, the Minnesota Supreme Court, although holding that in the particular case before it a court order was necessary to forgo life-sustaining treatment, gave support to the practice of clinical designation of a surrogate when it remarked that "on an average about 10 life-support systems are disconnected weekly in Minnesota. This follows consultation between the attending doctor and the family with the approval of the hospital ethics committee. It is not intended by this opinion that a court order is required in such situations."[127] Although these remarks were directed specifically to the necessity for judicial review of a decision to forgo life-sustaining treatment and not to designation of a surrogate, the court's tacit approval of such decisions made between attending physician and family lends strong support to clinical designation of a surrogate.

A number of cases involving minor children also support the practice of clinical designation of a surrogate in decisionmaking about life-sustaining treatment.[128] In one such case, the Georgia Supreme Court stated that, "[i]n any

---

[126] *Id.; see also id.* at 1242 ("Ordinarily, court involvement will be limited to the determination of incompetency, and the appointment of a guardian, unless a personal guardian has been previously appointed.").

[127] **MN:** *In re* Torres, 357 N.W.2d 332, 341 n.4 (Minn. 1984).

US: *Accord* Cruzan v. Director, 497 U.S. 261, 314 n.15 (1990) (Brennan, J., dissenting); Cruzan v. Director, 497 U.S. 261, 336–37 (1990) (Stevens, J., dissenting).

FL: *Accord* Browning v. Herbert, 568 So. 2d 4, 15 (Fla. 1990).

IL: *Accord* Estate of Longeway v. Community Convalescent Ctr., 549 N.E.2d 292, 295 (Ill. 1989).

MD: *Accord* 73 Md. Op. Att'y Gen. 253, 287–88 (Op. No. 88-046, Oct. 17, 1988).

NY: *Accord In re* Storar, 420 N.E.2d 64, 75 (N.Y. 1981) (Jones, J., dissenting); Saunders v. State, 492 N.Y.S.2d 510, 515 (Sup. Ct. Nassau County 1985) ("Every day, and with limited legal guidance, families and doctors are making decisions for patients unable to do so themselves.").

See also Smedira et al., *Withholding and Withdrawal of Life Support from the Critically Ill,* 322 New Eng. J. Med. 309 (1990).

[128] **FL:** *E.g., In re* Barry, 445 So. 2d 365, 372 (Fla. Dist. Ct. App. 1984).

GA: *E.g., In re* L.H.R., 321 S.E.2d 716, 722 (Ga. 1984).

LA: *E.g., In re* P.V.W., 424 So. 2d 1015, 1019 (La. 1982) (citing statutes).

See **Ch. 15.**

discussion of who will exercise the incompetent patient's constitutional right to refuse treatment, we must recognize the importance of the family in our society. This recognition is particularly crucial when the patient is a child."[129] However, because it is far better accepted in cases not involving the forgoing of life-sustaining treatment that parents are their minor children's natural guardians and thus need not have judicial approval to act on behalf of their children, these cases are of lesser precedential value in instances of the forgoing of life-sustaining treatment on behalf of incompetent adults.

WHO MAY SERVE AS SURROGATE

§ 5.15 Who May Serve as Surrogate When Judicially Appointed

When a surrogate is judicially appointed to make decisions about life-sustaining treatment, courts are usually guided by statutory provisions setting forth the criteria for appointment of a guardian of the person. These statutes set forth general criteria permitting the appointment of any adult who is "competent," "suitable," or "qualified."[130] Some are even more general, permitting any adult to serve.[131] A few specifically disqualify certain types of individuals from serving as guardians, such as providers of health care or social welfare services, convicted felons, judges, suspended or disbarred lawyers, spouses, and guardians ad litem.[132]

In addition to establishing qualifying and disqualifying factors, some statutes also establish priority schemes for the appointment of a guardian. The predominant preference is the ward's nearest relative,[133] followed by the ward's stated preference.[134] However, the paramount consideration in selecting a guardian is the best interests of the ward.[135]

Guardianship statutes grant substantial discretion to the trial court in the designation of a guardian, and appellate courts will rarely overturn these decisions and only for clear abuse.[136] Even when not expressly granted, this broad

---

[129] *In re* L.H.R., 321 S.E.2d 716, 722 (Ga. 1984). See §§ **15.2** and **15.4.**

[130] *See* S. Brakel et al., The Mentally Disabled and the Law 416–24 tbl. 7.4, cols. 12, 13 (1985).

[131] *Id.*

[132] *Id.*

[133] *See, e.g., In re* Quinlan, 355 A.2d 647, 670 (N.J. 1976) ("statute creates an initial presumption of entitlement to guardianship in the next of kin").

[134] **PA:** *See In re* E.L.K., 11 Fiduc. Rep. 2d 78 (C.P. Berks County, Pa. 1991). *See generally* S. Brakel et al., The Mentally Disabled and the Law 416–24 tbl. 7.4, cols. 14, 15 (1985).

[135] Guthrie, Annotation, *Priority and Preference in Appointment of Conservator or Guardian for an Incompetent,* 65 A.L.R.3d 991, 995–96 (1975).

[136] *See* S. Brakel et al., The Mentally Disabled and the Law 385 (1985) (citing 39 Am. Jur. 2d *Guardian and Ward* § 27 (1968)).

discretion is widely recognized. This discretion is so broad as to even permit courts to disregard statutory priority schemes in designating a guardian.[137] Therefore, legislative attempts to assist the courts in choosing a guardian serve merely as guidelines that are subject to judicial discretion.

In determining who is fit to serve as guardian, it can also be difficult for a court (or a physician, in dealing with family members of an incompetent patient) to make this determination independent of what the candidates for guardian would decide about forgoing life-sustaining treatment if appointed. The potential for this is nicely illustrated in a Pennsylvania trial court case,[138] though the court seemed to be able to make the decision on other grounds. The patient was a 76-year-old woman who had a son living out of state and a daughter with whom she resided prior to hospitalization. At the time of the hearing, she had been hospitalized for five months, was "not alert, [was] frequently unconscious," and was totally dependent on mechanical ventilation.[139] A disagreement arose between the son and the daughter as to whether a do-not-resuscitate (DNR) order should be written. There was strong evidence that the son was closer to the patient than the daughter, and that there had been much conflict between daughter and mother. The court observed that

> both children are eminently qualified to serve as guardians . . . ; they are loving, compassionate, and intelligent individuals. . . . [T]hey are not really separated by a great divide over the issuance of a DNR order—what actually divides them is [the daughter's] faith in Mother's ability to recover and her resolve to get Mother well. [The son] wants a DNR order imposed immediately because he wants Mother to die with dignity—he does not believe she would elect to exist in a vegetative state. . . . [Daughter] will permit a DNR order to be placed when she believes all hope is lost.[140]

The court appointed the daughter as guardian, largely on the ground that "[a]lthough [the son] clearly has Mother's best interests in mind and is equally competent as [the daughter] to act as a guardian . . . he is not physically present" and cannot be contacted easily in an emergency. "Therefore, due to practical reasons [the daughter] is better qualified to act as Mother's guardian."[141]

---

[137] **FL:** *E.g.,* Fla. Stat. Ann. § 744.312, *construed in In re* Quindt, 396 So. 2d 1217 (Fla. Dist. Ct. App. 1981) (appointment of long-standing friend upheld against challenge by ward's daughter).

MO: *E.g.,* Mo. Ann. Stat. § 475.055(2), *followed in In re* Tepen, 599 S.W.2d 533 (Mo. Ct. App. 1980) (upholding appointment of stranger as guardian rather than spouse or close relative).

See generally Guthrie, Annotation, *Priority and Preference in Appointment of Conservator or Guardian for an Incompetent,* 65 A.L.R.2d 991 (1975).

[138] *In re* E.L.K., 11 Fiduc. Rep. 2d 78 (C.P. Berks County, Pa. 1991).

[139] *Id.* at 78–79.

[140] *Id.* at 82.

[141] *Id.* at 83.

Most of the case law construing statutory provisions governing the designation of a guardian has arisen in contexts other than medical decisionmaking. Nonetheless, the principles enunciated in those cases are relevant to how courts should proceed in cases that do involve medical decisionmaking.

§ 5.16 —In Right-to-Die Cases

Few right-to-die cases have addressed the issue of the appropriate person to serve as a judicially appointed guardian; however, the courts seem to apply the same general principles as in other cases. It is the responsibility of the court appointing the guardian to "determine whether the guardian is a suitable person to represent the patient with respect to the medical decision in question. Such a determination necessitates an inquiry into the guardian's knowledge of the patient and motivations or possible conflicts of interest."[142]

For instance, the trial court opinion in the *Eichner* case echoed the general rule in guardianship cases preferring "that the next of kin be appointed the committee for an incompetent rather than a stranger"[143] but acknowledged that "in appropriate circumstances an individual other than a relative may be appointed the committee even though surviving relatives can be located. The factor of paramount importance is what the best interests and welfare of the incompetent require."[144] It is noteworthy that the New York statute does not "expressly [accord] a preference to blood relatives or their nominees"[145] and that "[t]here is no positive rule of law compelling the court to appoint a next of kin nor any absolute subordination of strangers to relatives."[146]

---

[142] **MI:** Martin v. Martin, 504 N.W.2d 917, 925 (Mich. Ct. App. 1993).

[143] **NY:** *In re* Eichner, 423 N.Y.S.2d 580, 588 (Sup. Ct. Nassau County 1979).

NJ: *Accord In re* Jobes, 529 A.2d 434, 447 n.12 (appropriate person is a close family member or friend).

NY: *In re* Eichner, 423 N.Y.S.2d at 588 ("We look particularly to a close family relative, a spouse, parent, child, brother, sister or grandchild—in Brother Fox's case, a member of his religious family—as an appropriate person to initiate, as Committee of the incompetent, the process of reaching such a decision.").

[144] **MD:** *Cf.* Mack v. Mack, 618 A.2d 744, 752 (Md. 1993) (holding that it is not appropriate to merge issues of who can best fill duties of guardian and what is in patient's substantive best interests).

[145] *In re* West, 212 N.Y.S.2d 832, 833 (App. Div. 1961).

[146] *Id.* at 834. *But see* Weber v. Stony Brook Hosp., 456 N.E.2d 1186 (N.Y. 1983) (petitioner who had no direct or personal knowledge of the facts relating to the patient's condition, the treatment being administered, or the factors prompting her parents to adopt the course they have has no standing to institute proceedings); *In re* Klein, 538 N.Y.S.2d 274, 276 (App. Div. 1989) ("While there is no statutory provision which grants a preference to the incompetent's next of kin, blood relatives or their nominees for such appointments, nonetheless, the case law in this State has firmly established that 'strangers will not be appointed as committee of the person or property of the incompetent, unless it is impossible to find within the family circle, or their nominees, one who is qualified to serve [citation omitted].' ").

Two important considerations can also be gleaned from the New Jersey cases. First, a general guardian appointed before the question of life-sustaining treatment arose is not empowered to make decisions about such treatment.[147] Rather, the court must determine whether the guardian is a suitable person to represent the patient with respect to the issue now in question. Such a determination requires inquiry into the guardian's knowledge of the patient, motivation, or possible conflicts of interest.[148] In other words, courts should make a new determination of whether one previously appointed to serve as a general guardian of the person would serve the ward's best interest in making a specific medical decision.

Second, the fact that an individual is a close family member is not a disqualifying factor for serving as guardian when the decision to be made involves life-sustaining treatment. In fact, "[i]n most instances, the familial relationship will strengthen, and not undermine, the guardian's best judgment in exercising the personal rights of the incompetent."[149] Similarly, the fact that a close family member may be a beneficiary of the estate of the ward does not per se disqualify him.[150]

§ 5.17 Criteria for Determining Surrogate When Clinically Designated

As the judicial consensus has clarified that there is no routine requirement that judicial proceedings be initiated to adjudicate incompetence and appoint a guardian,[151] the necessity increases for the development of legal guidance as to who should serve as surrogate for a patient who has been determined by a physician to lack decisionmaking capacity. Traditionally, there have been a number of considerations to be taken into account, the primary one being the customary medical practice of using close family members to make decisions

---

[147] *In re* Conroy, 486 A.2d 1209, 1241 (N.J. 1985). See **§ 4.15.**

[148] *Id.*

[149] **WA:** *In re* Colyer, 660 P.2d 738, 747 n.4 (Wash. 1983) (citing 39 C.J.S. *Guardian and Ward* § 98 (1976)).

MI: *Accord* Martin v. Martin, 517 N.W.2d 749, 754 (Mich. Ct. App. 1994).

NJ: *Accord In re* Quinlan, 355 A.2d 647, 670 (N.J. 1976) ("[W]hile Mr. Quinlan feels a natural grief, and understandably sorrows because of the tragedy which has befallen his daughter, his strength of purpose and character far outweighs these sentiments and qualifies him eminently for guardianship of the person as well as the property of his daughter. Hence we discern no valid reason to overrule the statutory intendment of preference to the next of kin.").

[150] **MI:** Martin v. Martin, 517 N.W.2d 749, 754 (Mich. Ct. App. 1994).

WA: *In re* Colyer, 660 P.2d 738, 747 n.4 (Wash. 1983).

See **§ 5.35.**

[151] See **§§ 5.11–5.14.**

for such patients. The strong consensus that has evolved from litigated right-to-die cases strongly supports this practice.[152]

For several decades, a few states have had statutes specifically setting forth who is legally empowered, without recourse to guardianship proceedings, to make medical decisions for a person who lacks decisionmaking capacity. Roughly at about the time of the Supreme Court's *Cruzan* decision in 1990,[153] an increasing number of state legislatures began to realize the importance of providing increased certainty in this area and have enacted such statutes or amended existing ones. (These statutes are discussed in **Chapter 14.**) In the absence of such a statute, or in the absence of a patient-designated surrogate (discussed in **Chapter 12**), a surrogate should be designated in accordance with the criteria set forth by courts.

§ 5.18 —Presumption of Family Member as Surrogate

Unless there is legislation or clear case law to the contrary, the patient's close family members should be presumed to have the legal authority to make medical decisions on behalf of incompetent patients.[154] As Justice Brennan remarked in his dissent in *Cruzan,* "[A] State generally must either repose the choice with the person whom the patient himself would most likely have chosen as proxy or leave the decision to the patient's family."[155]

As long as a family member knows the patient well and can be faithfully guided by the patient's interests rather than his own, he should be presumed to be qualified to serve as surrogate. Health care professionals should turn to close family members for decisionmaking for patients lacking decisionmaking capacity unless there is some special aspect of the situation that suggests otherwise.[156] When family members act as surrogates, they should of course make decisions in consultation with the patient's attending physician or other

---

[152] See § **5.18.**

[153] *See* Cruzan v. Director, 497 U.S. 261 (1990).

[154] **CA:** Barber v. Superior Court, 195 Cal. Rptr. 484, 493 (Ct. App. 1983) (patient's "wife was the proper person to act as a surrogate for the patient with the authority to decide issues regarding further treatment, and would have so qualified had judicial approval been sought").

FL: Browning v. Herbert, 568 So. 2d 4, 13 (Fla. 1990); John F. Kennedy Memorial Hosp. v. Bludworth, 452 So. 2d 921 (Fla. 1984).

GA: *In re* Doe, 418 S.E.2d 3, 6 (Ga. 1992).

NJ: *In re* Jobes, 529 A.2d 434, 444–45 (N.J. 1987).

WA: *In re* Hamlin, 689 P.2d 1372, 1377 (Wash. 1984) (citing *Barber v. Superior Court*)).

President's Comm'n, Deciding to Forego Life-Sustaining Treatment. See §§ **5.15–5.16.**

[155] Cruzan v. Director, 497 U.S. 261, 328 (1990) (Brennan, J., dissenting).

[156] See § **5.35.**

doctors[157] in the same collaborative manner as should operate if the patient were competent.

This presumption is grounded in the importance placed on self-determination even for patients who lack decisionmaking capacity at the time that significant decisions are to be made about their medical treatment. Who is to speak *for* the patient depends on who is best able to satisfy the substantive standards for decisionmaking for incompetent patients. Because of the wish to honor self-determination, these standards require as much knowledge as possible of the patient's actual or assumed wishes about treatment, and, if that is lacking, about the patient's own interests relevant to decisionmaking.[158] Thus, who should be authorized to speak for the patient depends primarily on who best knows what the patient would have spoken.

The courts assume that "the family is best able to decide what the patient would have wanted."[159] The Florida Supreme Court, in *John F. Kennedy Memorial Hospital v. Bludworth,* concisely summed up the consensus that has emerged in the case law as follows:

> If there are *close family members* such as the patient's spouse, adult children, or parents, who are willing to exercise this right on behalf of the patient, there is no requirement that a guardian be judicially appointed. . . . The decision to terminate artificial life supports is a decision that normally should be made in the patient-doctor-family relationship.[160]

---

[157] **MA:** *In re* Spring, 399 N.E.2d 493, 499 (Mass. App. Ct. 1979).

WA: *In re* Hamlin, 689 P.2d 1372, 1377 (Wash. 1984).

See **§ 3.4.**

[158] Hackler & Hiller, *Family Consent to Orders Not to Resuscitate: Reconsidering Hospital Policy,* 254 JAMA 1281, 1282 (1990) ("Surrogacy preserves a measure of patient autonomy beyond a point at which it would otherwise be lost. It succeeds in this purpose to the extent that surrogates choose as the patient would have chosen. When there is no evidence of patient preference, the rationale for family surrogacy is different: promoting patients' best interests by choosing advocates who are most concerned with their welfare, or respecting the integrity of the family as a social unit."). See **Ch. 7.**

[159] **NJ:** *In re* Jobes, 529 A.2d 434, 447 (N.J. 1987). *Accord In re* Farrell, 529 A.2d 404 (N.J. 1987).

US: *Accord* Cruzan v. Director, 497 U.S. 261, 325 (1990) (Brennan, J., dissenting).

FL: *Accord* John F. Kennedy Memorial Hosp. v. Bludworth, 452 So. 2d 921 (Fla. 1984).

IL: *Accord* Estate of Longeway v. Community Convalescent Ctr., 549 N.E.2d 292, 300 (Ill. 1989).

MD: *Accord* Mack v. Mack, 618 A.2d 744, 758 (Md. 1993).

MA: *Accord In re* Spring, 399 N.E.2d 493, 499 n.9 (Mass. App. Ct. 1979).

MI: *But cf.* Werth v. Taylor, 475 N.W.2d 426, 430 (Mich. Ct. App. 1991) (neither patient's prior competent refusal of treatment nor her husband's contemporaneous refusal of treatment on her behalf were binding in a medical emergency).

[160] **FL:** John F. Kennedy Memorial Hosp. v. Bludworth, 452 So. 2d 921, 926 (Fla. 1984) (emphasis added).

CA: *Accord* Barber v. Superior Court, 195 Cal. Rptr. 484, 493 (Ct. App. 1983).

Courts have come to the same conclusion when the patient is a minor.[161] Even when the surrogate is judicially appointed, courts might be willing to confer decisionmaking authority jointly on the guardian and other family members. For instance, in *Quinlan,* the court frequently referred to the "guardian and family" of Karen Quinlan as the persons authorized to make a decision about treatment on her behalf.[162] The evidence about whether, as a general rule, families in fact know what patients wanted is mixed.[163] But even if the assumption that families know what patients want is flawed, it is reasonable to assume, at least absent evidence to the contrary, that patients want family members to speak for them, and there is some evidence that in fact that is the case.[164]

Concern has been expressed about the suitability of next of kin to serve as surrogates when life-sustaining treatment is at issue because of the potential that they will act in their own self-interest rather than the best interests of the patient.

CT: *Accord* Foody v. Manchester Memorial Hosp., 482 A.2d 713, 721 (Conn. Super. Ct. 1984).

NJ: *Accord In re* Peter, 529 A.2d 419, 429 (N.J. 1987).

NY: *Accord* Eichner v. Dillon, 426 N.Y.S.2d 517, 548 (App. Div. 1980).

WA: *Accord In re* Hamlin, 689 P.2d 1372, 1377 (Wash. 1984).

161 **FL:** *E.g., In re* Barry, 445 So. 2d 365, 372 (Fla. Dist. Ct. App. 1984).

MA: *E.g.,* Custody of a Minor, 434 N.E.2d 601 (Mass. 1982) (by implication).

See § **15.2.**

162 *In re* Quinlan, 355 A.2d 647, 664, 671 (N.J. 1976).

163 *Compare* Tomlinson et al., *An Empirical Study of Proxy Consent for Elderly Persons,* 30 Gerontologist 54, 59 (1990) ("Close family members performed slightly better than physicians in reflecting patient's wishes. But . . . the use of family members does not in itself improve protection of the elderly patient's interests unless they are also required to act on the basis of a substituted judgment standard.") *and* Danis et al., *Patients and Families' Preferences for Medical Intensive Care,* 260 JAMA 797, 799 (1988) ("Families' preferences were similar to those of surviving patients.") *with* Zweibel & Cassel, *Treatment Choices at the End of Life: A Comparison of Decisions by Older Patients and Their Physician-Selected Proxies,* 29 Gerontologist 615, 620 (1989) ("[M]iddle-generation family proxies" of widowed elderly patients underestimate patients' preferences for resuscitation and "often choose care . . . that goes against what the patients would choose for themselves."); Uhlmann et al., *Physicians' and Spouses' Predictions of Elderly Patients' Resuscitation Preferences,* 43 J. Gerontology M115 (1988) (empirical evidence that spouses overestimate patients' preferences for CPR).

164 **MO:** *See* Mack v. Mack, 618 A.2d 744, 774 (Md. 1993) (Chasanow, J., concurring and dissenting) (quoting Coyle, *How Americans View High Court,* Nat'l L.J., Feb. 26, 1990, at 1, 36 (citing *National Law Journal*/LEXIS poll of over 800 people that found that "88 percent of Americans say the family should decide whether to end artificial life support when an individual is in a coma without hope of recovery and has left no instructions on personal wishes")). Cohen-Mansfield et al., *The Decision to Execute a Durable Power of Attorney for Health Care and Preferences Regarding the Utilization of Life-Sustaining Treatments in Nursing Home Residents,* 151 Archives Internal Med. 289, 290 (1991) (90% of 93 nursing home patients would choose relative to make their health care decisions, with 64% choosing a son or daughter); Gamble et al., *Knowledge, Attitudes, and Behavior of Elderly Persons Regarding Living Wills,* 151 Archives Internal Med. 277 (1991) (of 52% of 75 elderly persons who knew about living wills but had not executed one, 93% wanted family to make decisions for them if they lost decisionmaking capacity).

Those courts addressing the issue have concluded that a family member serving as surrogate without judicial appointment of a guardian to make decisions about life-sustaining treatment does not per se constitute a conflict of interest, although there may be one in a particular case. For example, in *Quinlan,* the court observed that although "[t]he character and general suitability of Joseph Quinlan as guardian for his daughter, in *ordinary* circumstances, could not be doubted,"[165] the trial court had serious reservations about whether the patient's father was qualified to serve as guardian of the person because of his avowed desire to discontinue life-sustaining treatment.[166] These reservations, at least as a general matter, were put to rest by the New Jersey Supreme Court in the 1987 trilogy of *Peter,*[167] *Jobes,*[168] and, most significantly, *Farrell,* in which the court sounded the praises of familial decisionmaking: "The law has traditionally respected 'the private realm of family life which the state cannot enter.' . . . Accordingly, numerous statutes [dealing with intestate succession and guardianship] presume that family members care about and will care for one another."[169] Doubts about the suitability of family members to act because of potential pecuniary conflict of interest have also been dismissed.[170]

§ 5.19 —Rationale for Family Member as Surrogate

There are a number of reasons why close family members are preferred as surrogate decisionmakers. The President's Commission cited five:

---

165 **NJ:** *In re* Quinlan, 355 A.2d 647, 657 (N.J. 1976) (emphasis added).

US: *Accord* Cruzan v. Director, 497 U.S. 261, 286 (1990) ("No doubt is engendered by anything in this record but that Nancy Cruzan's mother and father are loving and caring parents. If the State were required by the United States Constitution to repose a right of "substituted judgment" with anyone, the Cruzans would surely qualify.").

166 *In re* Quinlan, 355 A.2d at 670.

167 *In re* Peter, 529 A.2d 419, 429 (N.J. 1987) ("[I]f there is a close family member . . . the Ombudsman should defer decisions about life-support to the family member.").

168 *In re* Jobes, 529 A.2d 434, 447 (N.J. 1987) ("Generally in the absence of . . . a close degree of kinship, we would not countenance health care professionals deferring to the relatives of a patient, and a guardian would have to be appointed.").

169 **NJ:** *In re* Farrell, 529 A.2d 404, 414 (N.J. 1987) (citing Prince v. Massachusetts, 321 U.S. 158, 166 (1944)).

MA: *Accord In re* Spring, 399 N.E.2d 493, 499 n.9 (Mass. App. Ct. 1979).

170 **MA:** *See In re* Spring, 399 N.E.2d 493, 499 n.8 (Mass. App. Ct. 1979).

OH: *Cf.* Leach v. Akron Gen. Medical Ctr., 426 N.E.2d 809, 811 (P. Ct. Summit County, Ohio 1980) ("Mrs. Leach's condition is a continuing anxiety to her family. In addition, it constitutes an expense approximating $500 a day to her insurance company.").

WA: *See In re* Colyer, 660 P.2d 738, 747 n.4 (Wash. 1983).

See § **5.35.**

(1) The family is generally most concerned about the good of the patient.
(2) The family will also usually be most knowledgeable about the patient's goals, preferences, and values.
(3) The family deserves recognition as an important social unit that ought to be treated, within limits, as a responsible decisionmaker in matters that intimately affect its members.
(4) Especially in a society in which many other traditional forms of community have eroded, participation in a family is often an important dimension of personal fulfillment.
(5) Since a protected sphere of privacy and autonomy is required for the flourishing of this interpersonal union, institutions and the state should be reluctant to intrude, particularly regarding matters that are personal and on which there is a wide range of opinion in society.[171]

A number of reasons have been offered by courts for favoring family members as decisionmakers, but for each there is often a cogent counterargument in principle though not always in fact. The primary judicial rationale is that "family members and close friends care most and best for a patient . . . and have the best interests of the patient at heart."[172] So strong is this assumption that it has been said that "[t]he importance of the family in medical treatment decisions is axiomatic."[173] While this assumption is probably true in most, if not the overwhelming number of, cases, it is not universally so. The existence of statutes protecting various individuals from abuse at the hands of family members—child abuse, spousal abuse, elder abuse—is not only stark testimony to the fact that not only are all family members not kind and loving but also that the law recognizes that this is the case. Nonetheless, because family decisionmaking is not an ironclad rule but only a legal presumption or starting point, both judges and health care professionals must remain sensitive to the possibility of exceptions in particular cases, which is the reason why courts have not foreclosed the

---

[171] President's Comm'n, Deciding to Forego Life-Sustaining Treatment 128.

[172] **NJ:** *In re* Farrell, 529 A.2d 404, 414 (N.J. 1987).

US: *Accord* Cruzan v. Director, 497 U.S. 261, 325 (1990) (Brennan, J., dissenting).

CA: *Accord* Barber v. Superior Court, 195 Cal. Rptr. 484, 493 (Ct. App. 1983) (family is "concerned for [the patient's] comfort and welfare").

FL: *Accord* John F. Kennedy Memorial Hosp. v. Bludworth, 452 So. 2d 921 (Fla. 1984).

IL: *Accord* Estate of Longeway v. Community Convalescent Ctr., 549 N.E.2d 292, 300 (Ill. 1989).

MD: *Accord* Mack v. Mack, 618 A.2d 744, 758 (Md. 1993).

MA: *Accord In re* Spring, 399 N.E.2d 493, 499 n.9 (Mass. App. Ct. 1979).

OH: *Accord In re* Myers, 610 N.E.2d 663, 670–71 (P. Ct. Summit County, Ohio 1993) (parents are ones who know teenage daughter "best, who have suffered with her, who have consulted with her doctors, who have watched her deterioration, and who have the natural instinct of parents for her best interest").

[173] *In re* Farrell, 529 A.2d 404, 414 (N.J. 1987).

possibility of instituting guardianship proceedings for the designation of a surrogate.

A closely related reason is that family members are said to be "in the best position to know [the patient's] own feelings and desires."[174] Again, while often true, this will not always be the case. Some people may more readily confide their deepest fears, concerns, hopes, and other feelings to persons who are not family members or at least not close family members. Ability to know the patient's own desires is an important criterion for acting as surrogate,[175] but whether close family members are in the best position to know what the patient probably desires varies considerably. Even when family members do not have explicit knowledge of a patient's wishes, it has been said that "the family's knowledge exists nevertheless, intuitively felt by them and available as an important decisionmaking tool."[176]

According to *Barber v. Superior Court,* the most important reason for conferring decisionmaking authority on the patient's family is that "[t]hey [are] the people who would be most affected by the decision."[177] This rationale, however, cuts both ways. The fact that close family members will be affected most by the decision is also cause for concern that their decisions will be motivated by self-interest in addition to, or even instead of, the patient's interest.[178]

The discussion in *Quinlan* points up another difficulty. The standard often used to determine the suitability of a family member to serve as surrogate—that is, the ability to act in the patient's best interests—is one of the standards used to determine the legitimacy of the decisions that a surrogate ultimately makes.[179] That being the case, the process of designating a surrogate can easily become something of a fiction. Rather than attempting to determine whether a potential surrogate is qualified to act, the court or the attending physician might take into consideration the decision that that person would make if acting as surrogate. If the court or attending physician approved of that decision, the person's authority to act as surrogate would be confirmed, and vice versa. This is similar to assessing a patient's competence by looking at the decision he makes rather than the manner in which he makes decisions.[180] It is, in other words, conclusory reasoning, which permits the party who determines who is to serve as surrogate to substitute his judgment for the surrogate's about whether treatment should be administered or forgone.

---

174 Barber v. Superior Court, 195 Cal. Rptr. at 493.

175 See **Ch. 7.**

176 *In re* Jobes, 529 A.2d 434, 445 (N.J. 1987).

177 195 Cal. Rptr. at 493.

178 **WA:** *Cf. In re* Colyer, 660 P.2d 738, 747 (Wash. 1983) ("In giving the guardian the authority to make such a judgment, we are aware of the danger that a guardian might act on the basis of less than worthy motives."). See § **5.35.**

179 See §§ **7.11–7.13.**

180 See § **4.28.**

§ 5.20 —Factors in Selecting Among Family Members

Two factors—the closeness of the relationship between patient and surrogate and the best interests of the patient—should govern when a surrogate is clinically designated, as they do when a guardian is appointed.[181] However, in many cases, these principles of designation may merely narrow the potential group (for example, by excluding more distant relatives from consideration when closer relatives are qualified to serve) without yielding a single decisionmaker.

Closeness of Relationship Between Patient and Surrogate

The closeness of the relationship between the patient and a potential surrogate is an important factor in determining the fitness of that person to serve as surrogate. This can be measured by reference to consanguinity, subjective factors, and/or functional criteria.

Consanguinity. Historically, the designation of a judicially appointed guardian has relied heavily upon marriage or blood relationship.

> "[C]onsanguinity is a factor that may well be given consideration by the chancellor in the appointment of a guardian because nearest of kin are more likely to treat a ward with kindness and affection." [Citations omitted.] Nevertheless, . . . "all the parties here should be reminded that appointment to that position rests solely in the discretion of the equity court." [Citation omitted.] A statutory preference in the appointment of a guardian, although seemingly mandatory and absolute, is always subject to the overriding concern of the best interest of the ward. [Citations omitted.][182]

The clinical designation of a surrogate has been substantially influenced by this judicial practice. Attending physicians are often urged by hospital administrators (who are likely advised by legal counsel) to seek guidance from the order of priority for the appointment of a guardian in the state's guardianship statute.[183] In states in which the guardianship statute does not contain a priority scheme, physicians are sometimes counseled to seek guidance from the state's statutory order of distribution in intestate succession. That is, all other things being equal, the patient's spouse should be preferred over the patient's offspring,

---

[181] See § **5.15.**

[182] Mack v. Mack, 618 A.2d 744, 752 (Md. 1993).

[183] *See, e.g.,* Young v. Oakland Gen. Hosp., 437 N.W.2d 321, 325 (Mich. Ct. App. 1989) (per curiam). *See generally* S. Brakel et al., The Mentally Disabled and the Law 416–24 tbl. 7.4 (1985).

siblings, and parents. Similarly, if there is no spouse, the patient's offspring are preferred over siblings.[184]

These principles of surrogate designation are now reasonably well accepted in cases involving decisionmaking about life-sustaining treatment. Perhaps the most authoritative and useful statement in this regard is that of the New Jersey Supreme Court in *Jobes:*

> Normally those family members close enough to make a substituted judgment would be a spouse, parents, adult children, or siblings. Generally in the absence of such a close degree of kinship, we would not countenance health care professionals deferring to the relatives of a patient, and a guardian would have to be appointed.[185]

The primary reason for this is that close family members are assumed to best know the patient's wishes and interests.[186] Thus, mechanical reliance on the order of intestate succession is inadvisable, at least in the absence of either a statutory basis or judicial precedent for doing so. Although intestate succession statutes may be based on similar assumptions and may have goals similar to those of decisionmaking for incompetent patients, there are also important differences between them. One of the most important goals of decisionmaking for incompetent patients is to protect the patient (possibly against the family). The goal of the statutory scheme for intestate succession is to protect the family possibly from the testator (who is the loose analogue of the incompetent patient). Occasionally, health care personnel make an almost fetishistic search for some family member, no matter how distantly related, to serve as surrogate, a failing to which the courts have also occasionally succumbed.[187]

Although the New Jersey Supreme Court's direction is conventional enough wisdom that it should raise no eyebrows, the court followed it with the further instruction that "if the attending health care professionals determine that another relative, e.g., a cousin, aunt, uncle, niece, or nephew, functions in the role of the patient's nuclear family, then that relative can and should be treated as a close

---

[184] **MD:** Mack v. Mack, 618 A.2d 744, 752 (Md. 1993) ("geographical proximity to [patient does not necessarily] weight [] the best interest scale in favor of appointing the father as guardian").

PA: *In re* E.L.K., 11 Fiduc. Rep. 2d 78, 83 (C.P. Berks County, Pa. 1991) ("Although [son] clearly has Mother's best interests in mind and is equally competent as [daughter] to act as a guardian . . . he is not physically present" and cannot be contacted easily in an emergency. "Therefore, due to practical reasons [daughter] is better qualified to act as Mother's guardian.").

[185] *In re* Jobes, 529 A.2d 434, 447 (N.J. 1987). *Accord In re* Peter, 529 A.2d 419, 429 (N.J. 1987) ("[I]f there is a close family member . . . the Ombudsman should defer decisions about life-support to the family member."). See **§ 5.18.**

[186] See **§ 5.19.**

[187] *See* President's Comm'n for the Study of Ethical Problems in Medicine & Biomedical & Behavioral Research, Making Health Care Decisions 126 (1982) ("In some cases when a guardian is needed, courts have gone to remarkable lengths to identify and appoint even distant family members.") (citing Long Island Jewish-Hillside Medical Ctr. v. Levitt, 342 N.Y.S.2d 356 (Sup. Ct. Nassau County 1973)).

and caring family member."[188] This suggests that consanguinity per se—or at least a close degree of kinship—is not the only consideration in the designation of a surrogate.

Subjective Factors. Courts are increasingly recognizing that kinship per se is not necessarily the best, nor should it be the sole, measure of a surrogate's suitability.[189] It is not blood or marital relationship per se that makes close family members qualified to be surrogate decisionmakers, but the fact that they are "concerned for [the patient's] comfort and welfare."[190] Indeed, in some cases, such as when there is demonstrable evidence that the next of kin are substantially influenced by considerations of self-interest involving inheritance or other factors, kinship ought to be a disqualification.[191]

The closeness of the relationship between the patient and particular family members and/or friends[192] can be measured by reference to subjective factors as well as by consanguinity. Although subjective factors are probably far more important than objective ones, they are sometimes difficult to ascertain. They may not be in evidence, perhaps because the patient is unconscious or because family members do not visit the patient.

Subjective criteria focus on the nature of the past relationship between the patient and the family member, including such matters as whether the two lived together or apart or near or distant, were friends as well as relatives, and maintained frequent contact with each other. Consideration should also be given to current matters, such as whether a particular candidate for surrogate visits the patient and the nature of the interaction, if any, between them.[193] The attending

---

[188] *In re* Jobes, 529 A.2d at 447.

[189] **MN:** *In re* Kowalski, 478 N.W.2d 790 (Minn. 1991) ("Kinship is not a conclusive factor in determining the best interests of the ward.").

NJ: *In re* Jobes, 529 A.2d 434, 453 (N.J. 1987) (Handler, J., concurring) ("[T]here will be difficult cases in which the relationship of family members . . . of the patient may not be close enough for them to be an appropriate source for the awesome decision of whether to discontinue life-perpetuating treatment.").

[190] **CA:** Barber v. Superior Court, 195 Cal. Rptr. 484, 493 (Ct. App. 1983) ("some or all of [the patient's family] were present at the hospital nearly around the clock").

NJ: *Accord In re* Jobes, 529 A.2d 434, 445 (N.J. 1987); *In re* Farrell, 529 A.2d 404, 414 (N.J. 1987) ("[F]amilies commonly exhibit the greatest degree of concern about the welfare of ailing family members.") (citing Newman, *Treatment Refusals for the Critically Ill: Proposed Rules for the Family, the Physician and the State,* III N.Y.L. Sch. Hum. Rts. Annual 35 (1985)).

See also Hardwig, *What About the Family?,* 20 Hastings Center Rep. 5 (Mar.–Apr. 1990).

[191] **NJ:** *In re* Jobes, 529 A.2d 434, 447 (N.J. 1987) ("There will . . . be some unfortunate situations in which family members will not act to protect a patient.").

WA: *But cf. In re* Colyer, 660 P.2d 738, 747 n.4 (Wash. 1983) (being beneficiary of estate should not alone disqualify one from serving as guardian).

See § **5.35.**

[192] See § **5.21.**

[193] *See, e.g.,* Browning v. Herbert, 568 So. 2d 4, 9 (Fla. 1990) (court-appointed guardian, who was patient's second cousin, had also lived with patient for four to five years).

physician can sometimes assess these criteria, but information should also be sought from other members of the health care team (especially nurses and social workers) who sometimes have a better opportunity to become acquainted with the patient and the family and to obtain this kind of information.

Courts have only recently begun to speak to the issue of how closely related family members must be to serve as surrogates. The available guidance is vague. The New Jersey Supreme Court remarked that "[g]enerally in the absence of such a close degree of kinship [as spouse, parents, adult children, or siblings], we would not countenance health care professionals deferring to the relatives of a patient, and a guardian would have to be appointed."[194]

One such instance was *In re Torres,*[195] in which the only known living relatives were a cousin and an aunt living in a distant state. The aunt had raised the patient from infancy. She was unable to attend the conservatorship hearing because of age and health, but sent a letter stating "her belief that he 'would not wish to be sustained by mechanical devices.' "[196] This letter was not entered into evidence, but the trial court took notice of it as part of the file from previous hearings.[197] Although this case did not raise the question of whether either of these relatives could serve as surrogate, it illustrates that what is essential is closeness of a family member in terms of knowledge of the patient, rather than consanguinity. If the aunt had not been in close contact with the patient for some time, neither the fact of blood relationship nor the fact that she had raised him from infancy should necessarily qualify her as a surrogate.

Functional Criteria. Some consideration has been given to employing functional criteria to determine which (if any) family member should serve as a surrogate. The relevant question is whether the particular family member "functions in the role of the patient's nuclear family."[198] If so, then "another relative, e.g., a cousin, aunt, uncle, niece, or nephew . . . can and should be treated as a close and caring family member."[199]

Best Interests

The single most important factor in the designation of a surrogate is the candidate's ability to make decisions that are motivated primarily by a concern for the patient's well-being. A corollary is the absence of any significant motive for the potential surrogate to act in his own interest or the interest of third parties

---

[194] *In re* Jobes, 529 A.2d 434, 447 (N.J. 1987).

[195] 357 N.W.2d 332 (Minn. 1984).

[196] *Id.* at 336.

[197] *Id.*

[198] *In re* Jobes, 529 A.2d at 444.

[199] *Id.*

to the detriment of the patient's welfare. The attending physician should strive to ascertain which family members seem to be acting least out of self-interest and most out of concern for the patient's well-being.[200]

§ 5.21 —Friends

Sometimes patients have no living family members, especially, but not exclusively, elderly patients who may have outlived their spouses and/or children, or who never had either.[201] In other situations, family members may be very distantly related, may live at a great distance from the patient, or may otherwise not have had much or any recent contact with the patient.[202] Family members may be close in terms of blood relationship but distant in their contacts with and knowledge of the patient. In such cases, reliance on, or indeed insistence on, involvement in decisionmaking by such a family member elevates form over substance. Thus, when family members are available to make decisions but do not know the patient well, they should not be regarded as qualified to serve as a surrogate.[203]

---

[200] *See* S. Brakel et al., The Mentally Disabled and the Law 386 (1985). See § **5.35.**

[201] **FL:** *E.g.,* Browning v. Herbert, 568 So. 2d 4 (Fla. 1990).

NJ: *E.g., In re* Peter, 529 A.2d 419, 428–29 (N.J. 1987).

NY: *E.g., In re* Kerr (O'Brien), 517 N.Y.S.2d 346 (Sup. Ct. N.Y. County 1986).

[202] *See, e.g., In re* Torres, 357 N.W.2d 332 (Minn. 1984).

[203] **MN:** *E.g., In re* Kowalski, 478 N.W.2d 790 (Minn. 1991) ("Kinship is not a conclusive factor in determining the best interests of the ward."); *In re* Kowalski, 382 N.W.2d 861, 865 (Minn. Ct. App. 1986) ("Courts generally select someone with family ties or the nominees of such persons when appointing a guardian. However, that requirement is not mandatory and the court will disregard the application of a family member if their interest and those of the ward would conflict.") (quoting Schmidt v. Hebeisen, 347 N.W.2d 62, 64 (Minn. Ct. App. 1984)).

NJ: *E.g., In re* Jobes, 529 A.2d 434, 447 (N.J. 1987) ("If there are no close family members . . . then a guardian must be appointed."); *id.* at 453 (Handler, J., concurring) ("[T]here will be difficult cases in which the relationship of family members or putative friends of the patient may not be close enough for them to be an appropriate source for the awesome decision of whether to discontinue life-perpetuating treatment.").

NY: *E.g.,* N.Y. Pub. Health Law §§ 2961(5), 2965(4)(a)(vii) (in absence of family or patient-designated surrogate, a close friend, defined as a person over 18 years of age "who presents an affidavit to an attending physician stating that he is a close friend of the patient and that he has maintained such regular contact with the patient as to be familiar with the patient's activities, health, and religious or moral beliefs and stating the facts and circumstances that demonstrate such familiarity").

See also President's Comm'n, Deciding to Forego Life-Sustaining Treatment 127 n.20 (describing instance in which friend was preferable surrogate over daughter); Council on Ethical & Judicial Affairs, American Medical Ass'n, Code of Medical Ethics § 2.20, at 36 (1994) ("Family includes persons with whom the patient is closely associated.").

Under such circumstances the designation of a close friend of the patient to act as the surrogate should be considered.[204] This is especially, but not exclusively, so in the case of unmarried domestic partners, whether heterosexual or homosexual.[205] However, there is little in the way of precedent on this point. In *Jobes* the New Jersey Supreme Court held that "the right of a patient in an irreversibly vegetative state to determine whether to refuse life-sustaining medical treatment may be exercised by the patient's family or close friend."[206] Although the statement was prefaced by the phrase "we hold," the patient had close family who were acting as surrogate decisionmakers, and hence the statement with regard to a friend acting as a surrogate is dictum. The court made clear in a companion case, *Peter,* that although a friend could act as surrogate, "a specific designation by the patient that the close friend should make surrogate medical decisions on his or her behalf" is required or else there must be a judicial appointment of a guardian.[207] However, inasmuch as the patient had designated her friend as her surrogate, through a power of attorney, this remark was also dictum. Subsequent to the New Jersey Supreme Court cases, an intermediate appellate court in New Jersey tacitly endorsed decisionmaking by a friend or friends of a patient.[208] The *Browning* case is similar in that although the court recognized that the right to refuse treatment may be "exercised by proxies or surrogates such as close family members or friends,"[209] the patient actually had a court-appointed guardian. The New York "DNR" statute expressly recognizes the legitimacy of consent by a friend to a DNR order for an incompetent patient if close family members are not available.[210]

---

[204] Council on Ethical & Judicial Affairs, American Medical Ass'n, Code of Medical Ethics § 2.20, at 36 (1994) ("[W]hen there is no person closely associated with the patient, but there are persons who both care about the patient and have sufficient relevant knowledge of the patient, such persons may be appropriate surrogates.").

[205] **MN:** *E.g., In re* Kowalski, 478 N.W.2d 790 (Minn. 1991) (ward's lesbian partner should have been named guardian in preference to ward's father).

NY: *E.g.,* Evans v. Bellevue Hosp., No. 16536/87 (N.Y. Sup. Ct. N.Y. County July 27, 1987), *reported in* N.Y. L.J., July 28, 1987, at 11 (petition to terminate life-sustaining medical treatment by patient's friend for 22 years who was designated by patient, a homosexual AIDS patient, in living will and health care power of attorney).

[206] **NJ:** *In re* Jobes, 529 A.2d 434, 447 (N.J. 1987).

FL: *Accord* Browning v. Herbert, 568 So. 2d 4, 13 (Fla. 1990) (constitutional right to refuse treatment may be exercised not only by a legal guardian, but also by a patient's family or friend).

[207] *In re* Peter, 529 A.2d 419, 429 (N.J. 1987).

[208] *See In re* Moorhouse, 593 A.2d 1256, 1262 (N.J. Super. Ct. App. Div. 1991) ("[F]amily member(s) or friend(s) of an institutionalized mentally retarded patient [must concur in decision] to withdraw life support from the patient.").

[209] **FL:** Browning v. Herbert, 568 So. 2d 4, 13 (Fla. 1990).

[210] *See* N.Y. Pub. Health Law § 2965(2)(vi).

In endorsing the clinical designation of a friend of an incompetent patient to serve as surrogate,[211] the President's Commission defined the term *family* to include friends,[212] in part in recognition of the fact that a person other than a family member may be better suited in some circumstances to serve as a surrogate. This reflects the underlying assumption that it is not kinship per se that qualifies one as a surrogate but how well the candidate for surrogate knows the patient's wishes and interests and is able to act primarily on the basis of the patient's interests rather than his own. Thus, when a patient has no family members, or no family members are available, qualified, or willing to serve as surrogate, consideration should be given to using a friend of the patient.

As is the case with the choice of a family member, using a friend of the patient as surrogate is largely within the judgment and discretion of the attending physician in conjunction with others on the health care team who may know the potential candidate(s) for surrogate. The term *friend* is not susceptible of simple definition for this purpose. A situation could easily be imagined in which one might claim friendship with an incompetent patient which the patient would deny if he were able to do so.[213]

The same general criteria should be employed to determine the suitability of a friend of the patient as would be used to determine the suitability of a relative to serve as surrogate: how well the person knows the incompetent patient and how faithfully he can make decisions guided by the patient's interests rather than his own. In addition, health care personnel should consider the following more specific criteria in determining whether a friend should be permitted to serve as surrogate without judicial appointment as guardian:

1. Is the friend the functional equivalent of a spouse? If the patient and the friend are cohabitants, the friend should be considered a surrogate on the same basis as if he were a legal spouse.
2. The length, nature, and quality of the relationship between the friend and the patient.
3. The recentness of the friend's contact with the patient. If not recent, the friend has no better claim to act as a surrogate than a relative who materializes after a considerable separation from the patient.

---

[211] President's Comm'n, Deciding to Forego Life-Sustaining Treatment 127; President's Comm'n, Making Health Care Decisions 182 & n.11.

[212] President's Comm'n, Deciding to Forego Life-Sustaining Treatment 127.

[213] **NJ:** *In re* Jobes, 529 A.2d 434, 453 (N.J. 1987) (Handler, J., concurring) ("[T]here will be difficult cases in which the relationship of . . . putative friends of the patient may not be close enough for them to be an appropriate source for the awesome decision of whether to discontinue life-perpetuating treatment.").

NY: N.Y. Pub. Health Law § 2965(4)(vii) (permits close friend to make decisions about do-not-resuscitate orders if family are not available but does not define close friend).

§ 5.22 —Health Care Professionals; Public Guardians; Corporate Guardians

In some cases of decisionmaking for incompetent patients, both family and friends will be unavailable, unwilling, or unqualified to serve as decisionmakers. Decisionmaking can be stymied by the absence of an obvious surrogate, leaving a hopelessly ill patient to linger for a substantial period of time in a comatose or semicomatose state with the assistance of much life-support apparatus.

When this occurs, petitioning for the judicial appointment of a guardian is one possible solution. Some courts have suggested that if there is literally no family member or friend to serve as a surrogate,[214] or if such people exist but are otherwise disqualified from serving because of conflict of interest or their own incompetence,[215] there should be recourse to the courts for the appointment of a guardian.[216] However, even this might prove unfruitful because of the absence of anyone to serve as guardian. In such a case, the court might appoint the attending physician or some other member of the health care team to serve as surrogate.[217] However, this can present serious difficulties because of the possibility of conflicts of interest between the health care institution and the patient. Furthermore, to the extent that the application of a substituted judgment standard is required to make a decision for an incompetent patient,[218] there is evidence that health care professionals do not accurately divine patients' wishes,[219] and there is no reason to believe either that a person who does not know the patient well will have any information on which to make a decision based on the patient's own interests. (However, the same may also be true of family members.[220])

---

[214] **US:** *E.g.,* Cruzan v. Director, 497 U.S. 261, 328 n.23 (1990) (Brennan, J., dissenting) ("Only in the exceedingly rare case where the State cannot find any family member or friend who can be trusted to endeavor genuinely to make the treatment choice the patient would have made does the State become the legitimate surrogate decisionmaker.").

NY: *E.g., In re* Beth Israel Medical Ctr. (Weinstein), 519 N.Y.S.2d 511 (Sup. Ct. N.Y. County 1987).

WA: *E.g., In re* Hamlin, 689 P.2d 1372 (Wash. 1984).

[215] See §§ **5.35–5.36.**

[216] **NJ:** *In re* Jobes, 529 A.2d 434, 447 (N.J. 1987) (guardian must be appointed if there are no close family members).

WI: L.W. v. L.E. Phillips Career Dev. Ctr., 482 N.W.2d 60 (Wis. 1992).

[217] **DNY:** *E.g., In re* Department of Veterans Affairs Medical Ctr., 749 F. Supp. 495 (S.D.N.Y. 1990).

WI: *E.g.,* L.W. v. L.E. Phillips Career Dev. Ctr., 482 N.W.2d 60 (Wis. 1992).

[218] See § **7.7.**

[219] *See* Uhlman & Pearlman, *Perceived Quality of Life and Preferences for Life-Sustaining Treatment in Older Adults,* 151 Archives Internal Med. 495 (1991); Uhlmann et al., *Physicians' and Spouses' Predictions of Elderly Patients' Resuscitation Preferences,* 43 J. Gerontology M115 (1988).

[220] *Id.*

Another option is for the court to act as surrogate or to directly approve decisions about administering or forgoing life-sustaining treatment.[221] This can be very inconvenient because the attending physician may need to make a large number of therapeutic and diagnostic choices for a long period of time. If taken literally, the physician would have to obtain court approval for each decision unless there were an emergency. Consequently, courts will sometimes appoint the attending physician, another member of the health care team, or a hospital administrator as guardian.

This appears to be the practice in some hospitals even though there is little or no judicial precedent or statutory basis for doing so.[222] From a purely practical perspective, it is understandable that the patient's attending physician would prefer to avoid guardianship proceedings, especially if there is no person who knows the patient well, or knows him at all, to serve as guardian. If the result of the guardianship proceedings is likely to be the appointment of a health care professional to serve as guardian, the attending physician may believe that nothing of a practical nature is to be gained from the formalities, at the same time that they can impose significant costs and inconveniences. Even when undertaken with judicial approval, this is a very problematic practice. Health care professionals may have interests adverse to the patient's, such as the minimization of hospital length of stay or the use of a critical care unit bed for an acutely ill patient instead of a chronically and terminally ill patient.

However, even if little or nothing is gained from the formalities of guardianship when the patient has a loving and caring family or friend to serve as surrogate, it is the fact that the surrogate has this kind of relationship with the patient that provides the assurances we need to permit us to dispense with guardianship proceedings. In the absence of such assurances—not to mention the existence of potential conflicts of interest when a health care professional serves as surrogate—guardianship proceedings are warranted. Even if they do result in the appointment of the very same person to serve as surrogate who would have served had the guardianship proceedings not occurred, the judicial oversight provided by the guardianship process is the necessary substitute for the protection of the patient's interests that would otherwise be afforded by a close family member or friend acting as surrogate. Consequently, the use of a health care professional to serve as surrogate without guardianship proceedings should be avoided.[223]

---

[221] **MA:** *E.g.,* Superintendent of Belchertown State Sch. v. Saikewicz, 370 N.E.2d 417 (Mass. 1977).

NY: *E.g.,* N.Y. Pub. Health Law § 2966(1)(b).

See **§ 5.37.**

[222] *See* Smedira et al., *Withholding and Withdrawal of Life Support from the Critically Ill,* 322 New Eng. J. Med. 309 (1990) (decisions were made by physicians when family members could not be found).

[223] *See* Hastings Center Guidelines 26 (Part One, II(3)(c)(3)). *But see* N.Y. Pub. Health Law § 2966(1) (permitting attending physician, with approval of a second physician, to enter do-not-resuscitate order when there is no one to serve as surrogate).

In some jurisdictions, there are public or private nonprofit agencies that may act as a guardian for an incompetent person without family or close friends to do so.[224] For example, in Illinois a state-appointed public guardian is assigned to each county, and the court may appoint the public guardian as guardian of any disabled adult. The public guardian has the same powers and duties as other personal guardians, including the rights of a surrogate decisionmaker. Bank or trust company officers who are often appointed to act as guardians of the estate are also a possibility but are usually unwilling to act as guardians of the person.[225]

Corporate guardians—generally chartered, nonprofit organizations such as the local branches of the Association for Retarded Citizens or the Foundation for the Handicapped—are able to serve as guardians in most states.[226] Most, however, will decline to serve as surrogates unless judicially appointed, and, because there is no clear legal authority for their serving without judicial appointment, a health care institution that relies on a clinically designated corporate surrogate does so at its peril.

§ 5.23 —Patient-Appointed Surrogate

Before losing decisionmaking capacity, a patient may have designated someone to act as his surrogate.[227] When state statutory formalities have been satisfied, such designations are prima facie valid and there need not be recourse to the judicial process unless there is some reason for believing that the surrogate does not or cannot[228] make decisions based on the patient's wishes or interests.

---

[224] **AZ:** *E.g.,* Ariz. Rev. Stat. Ann. §§ 14-5601 to -5605 (public fiduciary), *cited in* Rasmussen v. Fleming, 741 P.2d 674 (Ariz. 1987).

IL: *E.g.,* Ill. Ann. Stat. ch. 755, §§ 5/13-1 to -5, *cited in In re* Estate of Greenspan, 558 N.E.2d 1194 (Ill. 1990); Estate of Longeway v. Community Convalescent Ctr., 549 N.E.2d 292 (Ill. 1989).

MO: *E.g.,* Mo. Ann. Stat. §§ 473.730–.773 (public administrator), *cited in* Cruzan v. Harmon, 760 S.W.2d 408 (Mo. 1988).

See generally T. Apolloni & T. Cooke, A New Look at Guardianship: Protective Services That Support Personalized Living 136 (1984); W. Schmidt et al., Public Guardianship and the Elderly (1981); Siemon et al., *Public Guardianship: Where Is It and What Does It Need?,* 27 Clearinghouse Rev. 588 (1993); National Ctr. for State Courts, Guidelines for State Court Decision Making in Life-Sustaining Medical Treatment Cases 141 (2d ed. 1992).

[225] See **§ 4.15.**

[226] *See, e.g., In re* Hamlin, 689 P.2d 1372 (Wash. 1984) (approving the use of a nonprofit agency concerned with welfare of mentally retarded persons to serve as a judicially appointed guardian to make a decision about life-sustaining treatment). *See generally* T. Apolloni & T. Cooke, A New Look at Guardianship: Protective Services That Support Personalized Living 136 (1984).

[227] See **Ch. 12.**

[228] See **§ 5.24.**

Even in the absence of compliance with statutory formalities, a surrogate designated by the patient ought to be considered to have the legal authority to make decisions for the patient when the latter loses the capacity to do so and when there is no reasonable doubt that the patient did in fact make such a designation. In practice, however, instances will arise in which the patient did not communicate that designation to any third party or any credible third party before losing decisionmaking capacity, and thus there will be doubt as to whether in fact the appointment did occur. If the attending physician entertains reasonable doubt about this, proceedings for the judicial appointment of a guardian should be commenced.[229]

§ 5.24 Incompetence of the Surrogate

Just as a person must have decisionmaking capacity to make legally binding treatment decisions for himself, one acting for another must also possess decisionmaking capacity. Lack of decisionmaking capacity of a candidate for surrogate, or of an individual already designated to serve as surrogate, should disqualify that person from serving.[230] The same factors that determine whether a *patient* lacks decisionmaking capacity[231] may lead to the suspicion and ultimately to the conclusion that a surrogate lacks decisionmaking capacity.

If a clinically designated surrogate becomes disqualified from further service because of a loss of decisionmaking capacity, a new surrogate should be designated from among available family members[232] or friends.[233] If none are

---

[229] *See, e.g., In re* Peter, 529 A.2d 419, 429 (N.J. 1987) (requiring clear and convincing evidence that patient appointed person in question to serve as surrogate).

[230] **DNY:** *In re* Department of Veterans Affairs Medical Ctr., 749 F. Supp. 495 (S.D.N.Y. 1990) (refusal of treatment by patient's wife based in part on her denial of the severity of patient's condition and in part on her hostility toward the doctors).

DC: *In re* A.C., 573 A.2d 1235, 1251 n.20 (D.C. 1990) ("The family's primacy in aiding the court as surrogate decision-maker may be subject to challenge for a variety of reasons. For example, grieving family members may themselves be unable to make or communicate an informed decision.").

MI: Rosebush v. Oakland County Prosecutor, 491 N.W.2d 633, 637 n.5 (Mich. Ct. App. 1992) (dictum) (citing first edition of this treatise).

NY: N.Y. Pub. Health Law § 2976(1) (surrogate must be competent to agree to do-not-resuscitate order).

WA: *Cf.* Benoy v. Simons, 831 P.2d 167, 171 n.3 (Wash. 1992) (patient's mother was a minor and "there was serious doubt about her ability to . . . make responsible health care decisions for him").

See President's Comm'n, Deciding to Forego Life-Sustaining Treatment 128. *See generally* McCrary et al., *Questionable competency of a surrogate decisionmaker under a durable power of attorney,* 4 J. Clinical Ethics 166 (1993).

[231] See **Ch. 4.**

[232] See **§ 5.20.**

[233] See **§ 5.21.**

available[234] or if the process of removing the surrogate and designating a new one generates substantial conflict among family members and/or health care personnel, serious consideration should be given to the judicial appointment of a guardian.[235]

If the surrogate was initially appointed by judicial process and thereafter becomes incompetent, the guardian can be replaced only through further judicial proceedings.

JUDICIAL REVIEW OF DECISIONS ABOUT LIFE-SUSTAINING TREATMENT

§ 5.25 Introduction

Once a patient is determined to lack decisionmaking capacity and a surrogate has been designated—whether in the clinical setting or through judicial proceedings—the next steps in the decisionmaking process may proceed, namely a particular decision or decisions about starting or withholding treatment or stopping or continuing it must be made. Indeed, determination of incompetency and designation of a surrogate are merely the preliminaries to what is the real issue. (If the patient possesses decisionmaking capacity and the attending physician or family members disagree with the patient's decision to forgo life-sustaining treatment, "[j]udicial scrutiny . . . should be considered as a course of last resort" because "judicial intervention . . . tends to denigrate the principle of personal autonomy, substituting a species of legal paternalism for the medical paternalism the concept of informed consent seeks to eschew."[236])

At this point, the question often arises about whether those decisions—especially if they are to withhold or withdraw treatment—must be subjected to review before it is legally permissible to effectuate them. Even if it is not a legal requirement that there be review, decisions about life-sustaining treatment often entail great uncertainty about the proper course of action and involve serious and possibly irreversible consequences. Those making or participating in making the decisions, whether health care personnel or family members, sometimes prefer not to have the final say in the matter. Health care personnel are

---

[234] See § **5.22.**

[235] Benoy v. Simons, 831 P.2d 167, 171 n.3 (Wash. 1992).

[236] Thor v. Superior Court, 855 P.2d 375, 389 (Cal. 1993). *Accord* Bartling v. Superior Court, 209 Cal. Rptr. 220, 226 (Ct. App. 1984).

sometimes unwilling to implement a decision to forgo life-sustaining treatment, *believing* that it is medically contraindicated, unethical, and/or illegal, whether that is the case or not. On the other hand, health care personnel sometimes believe that treatment should be withheld or withdrawn but the patient's family wants treatment administered. And sometimes there is uncertainty on the part of health care professionals that the surrogate knows the patient's actual or probable wishes about treatment.

Consequently, physicians and health care administrators sometimes wish to obtain outside guidance or approval of their decision from another authority. Indeed, it is just such concern about implementing decisions to forgo life-sustaining treatment that is the instigating force behind most, if not all, right-to-die litigation. In addition, because a life is at stake, the state has a substantial interest in assuring that a decision to forgo life-sustaining treatment is not casually made.

Often there is a more specific concern about whether there must be *judicial* review. Although the primary question debated by the courts and commentators is whether review should be conducted by courts or by some other body—the one most often suggested is an ethics committee,[237] but review may also be provided by a prognosis committee,[238] an administrative agency,[239] or by consultant physicians[240]—the more fundamental question is whether there should or must be any kind of review.

This aspect of decisionmaking for incompetent patients has been one of the most controversial since the earliest right-to-die cases.[241] By comparison, determining incompetence and designating a surrogate occur comparatively smoothly; only rarely is there recourse to the courts simply to adjudicate incompetence or appoint a guardian. What usually brings the process to a grinding halt, if anything does, is the decision per se to forgo life-sustaining treatment. Often, only then does the question, Is it legal? intrude, and who best to decide that question than a court, or so it seems to physicians and health care administrators.

The question of review can also arise in decisionmaking for competent patients, and here the issue most likely to ignite concern initially is whether the patient is in fact competent.[242] But even if a patient's decisionmaking capacity

---

[237] See § **5.57** and **Ch. 6.**

[238] See § **5.58.**

[239] See § **5.60.**

[240] See § **5.59.**

[241] **NJ:** *In re* Conroy, 486 A.2d 1209, 1242 (N.J. 1985). See § **5.27.**

[242] **CA:** *E.g.,* Bartling v. Superior Court, 209 Cal. Rptr. 220 (Ct. App. 1984).

FL: *E.g.,* Satz v. Perlmutter, 362 So. 2d 160 (Fla. Dist. Ct. App. 1978), *aff'd,* 379 So. 2d 359 (Fla. 1980).

is not in doubt, the family or, more likely, health care professionals may still be concerned about the legitimacy of forgoing treatment, especially when some conduct on the part of the health care team is necessary to discontinue treatment[243] or when the treatment in question is particularly controversial, such as artificial nutrition and hydration.[244]

Overall, the courts have been increasingly unreceptive to the idea of routine judicial review. The earliest right-to-die cases generated a heated debate about the necessity of judicial review of decisions to forgo life-sustaining treatment. In the first right-to-die case, *Quinlan,*[245] the New Jersey Supreme Court required that there be review by what it called an "ethics committee" but strongly disavowed the need for routine judicial review.[246] Almost as if *Quinlan* had intended to lay down the gauntlet, the Massachusetts Supreme Judicial Court responded the next year in the second right-to-die case, *Saikewicz,*[247] by requiring full participation by the courts in all three important stages of a right-to-die case (determination of incompetence, designation of a surrogate, and review of decisions). For awhile it appeared as though this position would prevail, if only from the force of the arguments presented by that court. In retrospect, however, it is now clear that this issue was largely spurious. No other court has seen fit to routinely require judicial review of decisions about life-sustaining treatment, and indeed the Massachusetts court seems to have backed off from its original position.[248] Much of the controversy that punctuated the earliest right-to-die cases has faded as the courts are reaching a consensus on this issue.

Because cases have come to the courts, they have decided them, but most courts continually make clear that judicial review is not routinely required[249] and that review should occur, if at all, in the clinical setting. Of course, the courts are available to review decisions about life-sustaining treatment if any of the parties to the decisionmaking process wish.[250]

---

243 See **Ch. 18.**

244 See §§ **9.39–9.40.**

245 *In re* Quinlan, 355 A.2d 647 (N.J. 1976).

246 *Id.* at 669 ("[A] practice of applying to a court to confirm such decisions would generally be inappropriate, not only because that would be a gratuitous encroachment upon the medical profession's field of competence, but because it would be impossibly cumbersome.").

247 *See* Superintendent of Belchertown State Sch. v. Saikewicz, 370 N.E.2d 417 (Mass. 1977).

248 See § **5.37.**

249 *See, e.g.,* Estate of Longeway v. Community Convalescent Ctr., 549 N.E.2d 292, 300 (Ill. 1989) ("The majority of the cases addressing the issue do not specifically require a court order to withdraw artificial life support."). See § **5.26.**

250 See § **5.27.**

§ 5.26 Judicial Review Not Required

A presumption against judicial review of decisions made by properly designated surrogates to forgo life-sustaining treatment began to emerge beginning with the earliest right-to-die cases.[251] Even those courts that required[252] or seemed to require[253] judicial participation in earlier stages of the decisionmaking process—that is, determination of incompetence and/or designation of a surrogate—were unwilling to impose a requirement that the surrogate's decision be approved in yet another judicial proceeding. The only exception to this was Massachusetts, which required judicial participation in all three stages of the decisionmaking process.[254]

That presumption is now well solidified. Most of the courts addressing the issue of judicial review of decisions to forgo life-sustaining treatment have concluded that such review is not required.[255] Beginning in *Quinlan,* the New

---

[251] *See In re* Quinlan, 355 A.2d 647, 669 (N.J. 1976) ("[A] practice of applying to a court to confirm such decisions would generally be inappropriate, not only because that would be a gratuitous encroachment upon the medical profession's field of competence, but because it would be impossibly cumbersome.").

[252] *See, e.g., In re* Colyer, 660 P.2d 738, 746, 750 (Wash. 1983) (requiring that decisions about forgoing life-sustaining treatment be made by a judicially appointed guardian but holding that a requirement of judicial review of the guardian's decision "where physicians agree on the prognosis and a close family member uses his best judgment as a guardian to exercise the rights of the incompetent . . . would be little more than a formality" in light of court's involvement in the appointment of the guardian), *overruled in In re* Hamlin, 689 P.2d 1372 (Wash. 1984) (requiring judicially appointed guardian only when patient has no family to serve as surrogate and not requiring routine judicial review of decisions to forgo life-sustaining treatment).

[253] *See, e.g., In re* Quinlan, 355 A.2d 647 (N.J. 1976).

[254] *See* Superintendent of Belchertown State Sch. v. Saikewicz, 370 N.E.2d 417 (Mass. 1977).

[255] **DNY:** *In re* Deel, 729 F. Supp. 231, 234 (N.D.N.Y. 1990) ("[R]ight to refuse the continuation of life-sustaining medical treatment is well-recognized, and the VA or any other medical facility may grant such a request if it is satisfied that the patient is mentally competent and fully understands the consequences of his or her decision.").

AZ: Rasmussen v. Fleming, 741 P.2d 674, 691 (Ariz. 1987).

CA: Thor v. Superior Court, 855 P.2d 375 (Cal. 1993) (competent patient); Bartling v. Superior Court, 209 Cal. Rptr. 220, 226 (Ct. App. 1984) (competent patient); Barber v. Superior Court, 195 Cal. Rptr. 484, 493 (Ct. App. 1983).

CO: Carothers v. Department of Insts., 845 P.2d 1179 (Colo. 1993) (implicitly approving decision of trial court "that a court order was not required to enable the Center to carry out the request of the petitioner's parents/guardians . . . to place a [do-not-resuscitate] order in the petitioner's file if the Center's physicians were willing to write such an order").

DC: *In re* A.C., 573 A.2d 1235, 1250 n.19 (D.C. 1990).

FL: Browning v. Herbert, 568 So. 2d 4, 15 (Fla. 1990) (decision of surrogate acting pursuant to a living will or a health care power of attorney does not require judicial review); John F. Kennedy Memorial Hosp. v. Bludworth, 452 So. 2d 921, 922, 926–27 (Fla. 1984); *In re* Barry, 445 So. 2d 365, 372 (Fla. Dist. Ct. App. 1984).

Jersey Supreme Court has been the prime opponent of routine judicial review, a position it has repeatedly reaffirmed.[256] The ground for its opposition was that judicial review "would generally be inappropriate . . . because . . . [it is] a gratuitous encroachment upon the medical profession's field of competence . . . [and is] impossibly cumbersome."[257] The fact that judicial review is cumbersome may be a far more compelling argument than the fact that it is an encroachment on the medical profession. Indeed, whether it encroaches on the "competence" of the medical profession is open to serious

---

GA: *In re* Doe, 418 S.E.2d 3, 5 (Ga. 1992); *In re* L.H.R., 321 S.E.2d 716, 723 (Ga. 1984).

IN: *In re* Lawrance, 579 N.E.2d 32, 41, 42 (Ind. 1991) (The purpose of the surrogate decisionmaking statute is "to resolve health care decisions without a need for court proceedings. . . . Decisions concerning withdrawal of treatment are not necessarily better decided by the courts. It would be hubris to think otherwise.").

KY: DeGrella v. Elston, 858 S.W.2d 698 (Ky. 1993).

LA: *In re* P.V.W., 424 So. 2d 1015, 1020 (La. 1982) (by implication).

MI: Martin v. Martin, 504 N.W.2d 917, 924 (Mich. Ct. App. 1993) ("[J]udicial involvement in a decision to withhold or withdraw life-sustaining medical treatment generally is not required where there is no disagreement among the parties directly concerned about treatment."); Rosebush v. Oakland County Prosecutor, 491 N.W.2d 633, 637 (Mich. Ct. App. 1992) (basing conclusion in part on health care power of attorney legislation).

MO: *In re* Warren, 858 S.W.2d 263, 265 (Mo. Ct. App. 1993) ("[A] guardian has statutory authority to make medical decisions and consent to medical treatment or the withholding of medical treatment in the best interests of the ward without specific court authorization."); *In re* Busalacchi, No. 59582, 1991 WL 26851, at *3, 1991 Mo. App. LEXIS 315 (Mar. 5, 1991) ("[I]n the vast majority of cases, the duties of a guardian are discharged absent court approval.").

NJ: *In re* Peter, 529 A.2d 419, 427 (N.J. 1987) ("[J]udicial review of a surrogate's decision to give effect to the patient's preference is unnecessary unless a conflict arises among the surrogate decisionmaker, the family, the physician and the Ombudsman."); *In re* Jobes, 529 A.2d 434, 449 (N.J. 1987) ("[J]udicial review of such decisions is not necessary or appropriate."); *In re* Farrell, 529 A.2d 404, 415 (N.J. 1987) ("[J]udicial review of a competent patient's refusal of life-sustaining medical treatment is generally not appropriate. Only unusual circumstances, such as a conflict among the physicians, or among the family members, or between the physicians and the family or other health care professionals, would necessitate judicial intervention."); *In re* Conroy, 486 A.2d 1209 (N.J. 1985); *In re* Quinlan, 355 A.2d 647, 669 (N.J. 1976).

NY: *In re* Storar, 420 N.E.2d 64, 74 (N.Y. 1981); *id.* at 75 (Jones, J., dissenting).

WA: *In re* Hamlin, 689 P.2d 1372, 1380 (Wash. 1984).

WI: L.W. v. L.E. Phillips Career Dev. Ctr., 482 N.W.2d 60, 75 (Wis. 1992).

[256] *See In re* Jobes, 529 A.2d 434 (N.J. 1987); *In re* Farrell, 529 A.2d 404 (N.J. 1987); *In re* Peter, 529 A.2d 419 (N.J. 1987); *In re* Conroy, 486 A.2d 1209 (N.J. 1985).

[257] *In re* Quinlan, 355 A.2d 647, 669 (N.J. 1976). *Accord* Barber v. Superior Court, 195 Cal. Rptr. 484, 493 (Ct. App. 1983).

doubt.[258] A decision to forgo life-sustaining treatment "depend[s] as it necessarily must not only on medical data, but on theological tenets and perceptions of human values which defy classification and calibration."[259] Although the process of deciding to forgo life-sustaining treatment includes answering questions based on medical expertise, once those questions are answered the decision itself is not exclusively a medical one. The fact that Karen Quinlan's physicians were concerned about legal liability for forgoing life-sustaining treatment is (and many others continue to be) proof enough that such decisions are at root legal and moral—and not exclusively medical—problems.

A better explanation for the lack of necessity for having recourse to the courts for the forgoing of life-sustaining treatment was provided by the Kentucky Supreme Court:

> The right to terminate medical treatment is not a power belonging to the judiciary to grant or withhold. . . . This case came to the trial court because the attending physician and nursing home would not recognize the patient's right to choose to refuse treatment through her surrogate, not because there is any law requiring the court's prior consent to the exercise of the patient's right. Courts are, and must be, open to decide cases where a controversy exists, including a controversy in a case of this nature. Controversy exists only when someone challenges the existence of a right or the facts to support its exercise. Here, the lawfulness of the act of withholding further treatment depends on the existence of the underlying facts that established the patient's condition, her wishes in such condition, and the irreversible nature of the condition. . . . Thus, though the courts are open for such cases, if no one challenges the existence of the underlying facts, legal action is not essential to the exercise of the patient's right.[260]

In the case of competent patients, the fundamental reason for not requiring judicial review is that "judicial intervention . . . tends to denigrate the principle of personal autonomy, substituting a species of legal paternalism for the medical

---

[258] **MA:** Superintendent of Belchertown State Sch. v. Saikewicz, 370 N.E.2d 417, 435 (Mass. 1977) ("We do not view the judicial resolution of this most difficult and awesome question whether potentially life-prolonging treatment should be withheld from a person incapable of making his own decision as constituting a 'gratuitous encroachment' on the domain of medical expertise. Rather, such questions of life and death seem to us to require the process of detached but passionate investigation and decision that forms the ideal on which the judicial branch of government was created.").

WA: *In re* Colyer, 660 P.2d 738, 746 (Wash. 1983) ("[W]e do not accept the *Quinlan* court's view that judicial intervention is an encroachment upon the medical profession."), *overruled in In re* Hamlin, 689 P.2d 1372 (Wash. 1984).

[259] *In re* Storar, 420 N.E.2d 64, 75 (N.Y. 1981) (Jones, J., dissenting).

[260] DeGrella v. Elston, 858 S.W.2d 698, 709–10 (Ky. 1993).

paternalism the concept of informed consent seeks to eschew. . . . Judicial scrutiny therefore should be considered as a course of last resort."[261]

§ 5.27 Judicial Review Not Required but Permissible

Despite the strong judicial consensus that judicial review of decisions to forgo life-sustaining treatment is not required, the courts have usually made it clear that they are available to hear these matters under certain circumstances.[262] Legislatures have also begun to recognize this as a proper role for courts.[263]

---

[261] Thor v. Superior Court, 855 P.2d 375, 390 (Cal. 1993).

[262] **CA:** Barber v. Superior Court, 195 Cal. Rptr. 484, 493 (Ct. App. 1983).

FL: Browning v. Herbert, 543 So. 2d 258, 270 (Fla. Dist. Ct. App. 1989), *aff'd,* 568 So. 2d 4 (Fla. 1990) ("We are not holding that a legal guardian must always be appointed to make life-sustaining medical decisions. While a legal guardian is not essential in all cases, it is comforting that such a guardian exists in this case. A guardian who is appointed by a court and who has taken an oath . . . is more likely to give the responsibility the serious attention which it deserves. . . . Especially in difficult cases, we would urge the appointment of a legal guardian."); John F. Kennedy Memorial Hosp. v. Bludworth, 452 So. 2d 921, 926–27 (Fla. 1984); *In re* Barry, 445 So. 2d 365, 372 (Fla. Dist. Ct. App. 1984).

GA: *In re* Doe, 418 S.E.2d 3, 5 (Ga. 1992); *In re* L.H.R., 321 S.E.2d 716, 723 (Ga. 1984).

LA: *In re* P.V.W., 424 So. 2d 1015, 1020 (La. 1982) (by implication).

MI: Rosebush v. Oakland County Prosecutor, 491 N.W.2d 633, 637 (Mich. Ct. App. 1992) (basing conclusion in part on health care power of attorney legislation).

NJ: *In re* Jobes, 529 A.2d 434, 451 (N.J. 1987) ("[E]ven in those few cases in which the courts may have to intervene, they will not be making the ultimate decision whether to terminate medical treatment. Rather, they will be acting to insure that all the guidelines and procedures that we have set forth are properly followed."); *In re* Quinlan, 355 A.2d 647, 669 (N.J. 1976).

NY: *In re* Storar, 420 N.E.2d 64, 74 (N.Y. 1981); *id.* at 75 (Jones, J., dissenting).

WA: *In re* Hamlin, 689 P.2d 1372, 1380 (Wash. 1984) (by implication); *In re* Colyer, 660 P.2d 738, 746 (Wash. 1983).

WI: L.W. v. L.E. Phillips Career Dev. Ctr., 482 N.W.2d 60, 75 (Wis. 1992).

[263] **NJ:** *E.g.,* N.J. Stat. Ann. § 26:2H-66.a ("In the event of disagreement among the patient, health care representative, and attending physician concerning the patient's decision making capacity or the appropriate interpretation and application of the terms of an advance directive to the patient's course of treatment, the parties may seek to resolve the disagreement by means of procedures and practices established by the health care institution, including but not limited to, consultation with an institutional ethics committee, or with a person designated by the health care institution for this purpose or may seek resolution by a court of competent jurisdiction.").

NY: *E.g.,* N.Y. Pub. Health Law § 2973(1) (Courts are available to review do-not-resuscitate orders.).

However, some courts seem a little less open than others, possibly conditioning access to specific types of situations.[264] This is because of the judicial recognition that courts should leave as much decisionmaking as possible to private ordering and to be available only when the participants in the decisionmaking process are unable to arrive at a mutually agreeable decision. Indeed, the primary indication for judicial review is the existence of irresolvable disagreement or conflict among those participants.[265] Therefore, it is advisable when seeking judicial review at least to allege conflict or "disagreement between decisionmakers,"[266] "a lack of concurrence among the family, physicians, and medical personnel, or the state,"[267] "evidence of wrongful motives or malpractice,"[268] and/or "abuse."[269] However, one court has added a catchall, suggesting that judicial review was appropriate "if an affected party simply desires a judicial order."[270]

---

[264] *See, e.g.,* Browning v. Herbert, 568 So. 2d 4, 16 (Fla. 1990) (when patient has advance directive, only purpose of judicial review is "to adjudicate legitimate questions pertaining to the written or oral instructions" such as determining whether surrogate's decision is in conformity with patient's wishes).

[265] **CA:** Morrison v. Abramovice, 253 Cal. Rptr. 530, 535 (Ct. App. 1988) ("[C]ourts should intervene only if there is disagreement among the conservator and other interested parties and they have exhausted all nonjudicial efforts to resolve the dispute.").

KY: DeGrella v. Elston, 858 S.W.2d 698 (Ky. 1993).

NJ: *In re* Farrell, 529 A.2d 404, 415 (N.J. 1987) ("Only unusual circumstances, such as a conflict among the physicians, or among the family members, or between the physicians and the family or other health care professionals, would necessitate judicial intervention.").

[266] **GA:** *In re* L.H.R., 321 S.E.2d 716, 723 (Ga. 1984).

CA: *Accord* Morrison v. Abramovice, 253 Cal. Rptr. 530, 535 (Ct. App. 1988).

FL: *Accord* John F. Kennedy Memorial Hosp. v. Bludworth, 452 So. 2d 921, 926–27 (Fla. 1984).

NJ: *Accord In re* Farrell, 529 A.2d 404, 415 (N.J. 1987); *In re* Peter, 529 A.2d 419, 427 (N.J. 1987); *In re* Conroy, 486 A.2d 1209, 1227 (N.J. 1985); *In re* Clark, 510 A.2d 136 (N.J. Super. Ct. Ch. Div. 1986).

WA: *Accord In re* Hamlin, 689 P.2d 1372, 1378 (Wash. 1984) ("[I]f there is disagreement among family members . . . the court may be required to intervene.").

See §§ **5.30–5.36.**

[267] **FL:** *In re* Barry, 445 So. 2d 365, 372 (Fla. Dist. Ct. App. 1984).

ME: *Accord In re* Gardner, 534 A.2d 947, 954 (Me. 1987).

NJ: *Cf. In re* Peter, 529 A.2d 419, 427 (N.J. 1987); *In re* Farrell, 529 A.2d 404, 415 (N.J. 1987); *In re* Conroy, 486 A.2d 1209, 1227 (N.J. 1985); *In re* Clark, 510 A.2d 136, 141 (N.J. Super. Ct. Ch. Div. 1986).

WA: *Cf. In re* Colyer, 660 P.2d 738, 750 (Wash. 1983).

See §§ **5.30–5.36.**

[268] **FL:** John F. Kennedy Memorial Hosp. v. Bludworth, 452 So. 2d 921, 926 (Fla. 1984).

WA: *Accord In re* Colyer, 660 P.2d 738, 750 (Wash. 1983).

[269] **GA:** *In re* L.H.R., 321 S.E.2d 716, 723 (Ga. 1984).

[270] **FL:** *In re* Barry, 445 So. 2d 365, 372 (Fla. Dist. Ct. App. 1984).

There are a number of reasons why the courts are available to review decisions. The most important is to assure that the proper decisionmaking process has been followed and that a reasonable and defensible decision has been made, at least when the participants are themselves unsure about its propriety.[271] Also, when there is disagreement, the potential for instigating civil or criminal proceedings against a participant may be higher than when all the participants are in agreement about the proper course of action.[272] Those participating in the decisionmaking process should not have to risk incurring civil or criminal liability.[273] However, judicial review will not always eliminate any chance of liability,[274] and, at least when the courts have spoken clearly in previous cases, there is no necessity of obtaining judicial review in order to preclude liability.[275] The courts are also available for review of a decision about forgoing life-sustaining treatment if the decision is possibly motivated by something other than the best interests of the patient,[276] such as a desire to cover up medical malpractice.[277]

Judicial review may be sought by a participant in the decisionmaking process (such as a physician, surrogate, judicially appointed guardian, a member of the patient's family, or a friend[278]) or by one charged with the care of the incompetent patient[279] (such as a hospital administrator, an "appropriate representative" of the patient,[280] or a law-enforcement official[281]). Even when recourse to the courts is proper, "the trial court's decision need not and should not always be appealed."[282]

---

[271] *See, e.g., In re* P.V.W., 424 So. 2d 1015, 1020 (La. 1982).

[272] *See* Kirsch, *A Death at Kaiser Hospital,* Cal. Mag., Nov. 1982, at 79 (discussing Barber v. Superior Court, 195 Cal. Rptr. 484 (Ct. App. 1983)).

[273] **NY:** *In re* Storar, 420 N.E.2d 64, 74 (N.Y. 1981).

[274] See § **17.24.**

[275] **FL:** John F. Kennedy Memorial Hosp. v. Bludworth, 452 So. 2d 921, 922 (Fla. 1984).

[276] *Id.* at 926.

[277] *Id.* at 926–27. *See, e.g.,* Herbert v. Superior Court, 215 Cal. Rptr. 477 (Ct. App. 1985) (malpractice case arising from same set of facts as those giving rise to Barber v. Superior Court, 195 Cal. Rptr. 484 (Ct. App. 1983)).

[278] **FL:** Browning v. Herbert, 568 So. 2d 4, 16 (Fla. 1990) ("[I]nterested parties may challenge the decision of the proxy or surrogate."); John F. Kennedy Memorial Hosp. v. Bludworth, 452 So. 2d 921, 926–27 (Fla. 1984); *In re* Barry, 445 So. 2d 365, 372 (Fla. Dist. Ct. App. 1984).

WA: *In re* Hamlin, 689 P.2d 1372, 1378–79 (Wash. 1984) ("[A]ny participant in the decision, members of the incompetent's family, the guardian, the physicians, or the hospital may petition for court intervention."); *In re* Colyer, 660 P.2d 738, 750 (Wash. 1983).

[279] **NY:** *In re* Storar, 420 N.E.2d 64, 74 (N.Y. 1981).

[280] **LA:** *In re* P.V.W., 424 So. 2d 1015, 1020 (La. 1982).

[281] **FL:** *In re* Barry, 445 So. 2d 365, 372 (Fl. Dist. Ct. App. 1984).

[282] **CA:** Drabick v. Drabick, 245 Cal. Rptr. 840, 851 n.16 (Ct. App. 1988).

NJ: *In re* Jobes, 529 A.2d 434, 449 n.17 (N.J. 1987).

§ 5.28 Role of Reviewing Court

Few judicial opinions have actually addressed the precise nature of the court's role in reviewing a decision about forgoing life-sustaining treatment. There are at least two theoretical possibilities. First, a more limited role is for a trial court, literally, to *review* what has transpired in the clinical setting. Under this approach, it might first reopen such questions as whether the patient in fact lacks decisionmaking capacity and whether the person acting as surrogate is appropriately qualified to do so. The central focus of its inquiry should be to determine whether the appropriate substantive standard for making decisions for incompetent patients has been identified and applied.[283] It might also review the evidence adduced bearing on this standard to determine whether the decision was supported by the weight of the evidence.[284] Finally, the court should examine whether the surrogate was acting in good faith.[285]

It has also been suggested that the court should conduct an independent review, as a representative of the state, to determine that "the state's interests do not outweigh the individual's right of privacy."[286] This notion of review is primarily procedural in its focus because it does not specifically examine the decision that has been made. It is definitely not the role of the trial court under this approach "to substitute its judgment for that of the surrogate decisionmaker."[287] Instead, the court is to act "to insure that all the guidelines and procedures that we have set forth are properly followed."[288]

A contrasting approach is for the court actually to make the decision about whether or not to forgo life-sustaining treatment. This is the approach originally taken by the Massachusetts Supreme Judicial Court in *Saikewicz* but gradually abandoned in later cases.[289] In addition to ensuring procedural regularity, the court seemed to relegate to itself not merely the authority to review and confirm the decision of a surrogate decisionmaker but also the authority to make that decision.[290]

---

[283] **FL:** Browning v. Herbert, 543 So. 2d 258, 274 (Fla. Dist. Ct. App. 1989), *aff'd and modified,* 568 So. 2d 4 (Fla. 1990).

[284] **FL:** Browning v. Herbert, 543 So. 2d at 274 (but "trial court should not reweigh the evidence").

[285] *Id.*

[286] *Id.*

[287] *Id.*

[288] *In re* Jobes, 529 A.2d 434, 451 (N.J. 1987).

[289] See § **5.37.**

[290] Superintendent of Belchertown State Sch. v. Saikewicz, 370 N.E.2d 417, 435 (Mass. 1977) ("[S]uch questions of life and death seem to us to require the process of detached but passionate investigation and decision that forms the ideal on which the judicial branch of government was created.").

§ 5.29 When Judicial Review Should Be Sought

The strong consensus that all aspects of the decisionmaking process should occur in the clinical setting without routine recourse to the courts unless there is clear judicial or legislative direction to the contrary[291] is based substantially on judicial confidence that decisions made by family members of incompetent patients are likely to produce the best results.[292] Although this is likely to be the case in most situations, there will be others in which, for a number of reasons, judicial involvement is likely to produce a superior decisionmaking process and is therefore desirable or required.[293]

Thus, while decisionmaking in the clinical setting is presumptively appropriate, there are a number of considerations that health care professionals need to take into account in determining whether, in a particular case, there should be recourse to the judicial process at some point in the process of decisionmaking about life-sustaining treatment. In general, the most important signals for a judicial determination of incompetence, for the appointment of a guardian, and/or for judicial review of a decision to forgo life-sustaining treatment are (1) disagreement among participants in the decisionmaking process, (2) conflict of interest, and (3) absence of someone to serve as surrogate. These factors are discussed in §§ **5.30** through **5.36.**

---

[291] See § **5.37.**

[292] **CA:** *E.g.,* Morrison v. Abramovice, 253 Cal. Rptr. 530, 535 (Ct. App. 1988).

NJ: *E.g., In re* Farrell, 529 A.2d 404, 414 (N.J. 1987) ("'[F]amilies commonly exhibit the greatest degree of concern about the welfare of ailing family members. It is they who come to the hospital and involve themselves in the sick person's care and comfort. Competent patients usually actively solicit the advice and counsel of family members in decisionmaking. Family members routinely ask questions of the medical staff about the patient's condition and prognosis. . . . Family members, in fact, commonly act as advocates for patients in the hospital, looking out for their comfort, care, and best interests.'") (quoting Newman, *Treatment Refusals for the Critically Ill: Proposed Rules for the Family, the Physician and the State,* III N.Y.L. Sch. Hum. Rts. Ann. 35 (1985)).

[293] **FL:** John F. Kennedy Memorial Hosp. v. Bludworth, 452 So. 2d 921, 926 (Fla. 1984); *In re* Barry, 445 So. 2d 365, 372 (Fla. Dist. Ct. App. 1984) ("In cases where doubt exists, or there is a lack of concurrence among the family, physicians, and the hospital, or if an affected party simply desires a judicial order, then the court must be available to consider the matter.").

GA: *In re* L.H.R., 321 S.E.2d 716, 723 (Ga. 1984) (Courts are open to involvement if there is a disagreement between decisionmakers.).

WA: *In re* Hamlin, 689 P.2d 1372, 1378–79 (Wash. 1984) ("[A]ny participant in the decision, members of the incompetent's family, the guardian, the physicians, or the hospital may petition for court intervention. Similarly, if there is disagreement between parties involved in the decisionmaking process, court intervention would be appropriate.").

See also President's Comm'n, Deciding to Forego Life-Sustaining Treatment 154 ("The commission concludes that ordinarily a patient's surrogate—whether designated through judicial proceedings or informally—should have the legal authority to make decisions on behalf of an incapacitated patient.").

§ 5.30 —Disagreement Among Participants in the Decisionmaking Process

The single most important feature of decisionmaking about life-sustaining treatment that counsels in favor of recourse to the courts is the existence of a substantial and irresolvable conflict or disagreement among key participants in the decisionmaking process.[294] The disagreement can be about whether the patient possesses or lacks decisionmaking capacity,[295] about who is the appropriate person to serve as the surrogate,[296] or, more likely,[297] the question giving rise to most right-to-die litigation, whether treatment should be forgone or continued.[298] Legislatures have also begun to recognize this as a proper role for courts.[299]

---

[294] **DC:** *See In re* A.C., 573 A.2d 1235, 1250 n.19 (D.C. 1990) (Judicial review will most likely occur "because there is a conflict as to treatment choice among family members, physicians, or both. Were family members and physicians in complete agreement, it is unlikely that a court would be brought into the discussion.").

MI: *Cf.* Rosebush v. Oakland County Prosecutor, 491 N.W.2d 633, 638 (Mich. Ct. App. 1992) (citing first edition of this treatise). Council on Ethical & Judicial Affairs, American Medical Ass'n, Code of Medical Ethics § 2.20, at 37 (1994).

[295] **MA:** *E.g.,* Lane v. Candura, 376 N.E.2d 1232 (Mass. App. Ct. 1978).

NJ: *E.g., In re* Quackenbush, 383 A.2d 785 (N.J. Super. Ct. P. Div. 1978); *In re* Schiller, 372 A.2d 360 (N.J. Super. Ct. Ch. Div. 1977).

NY: *E.g.,* Fosmire v. Nicoleau, 551 N.E.2d 77, 80 (N.Y. 1990) ("[W]hen there is a bona fide question of the patient's competence the doctor or health care facility may seek a court ruling.").

TN: *E.g.,* State Dep't of Human Resources v. Northern, 563 S.W.2d 197 (Tenn. Ct. App. 1978).

[296] **US:** Cruzan v. Director, 497 U.S. 261, 328 (1990) (Brennan, J., dissenting) ("A State may ensure that the person who makes the decision on the patient's behalf is the one whom the patient himself would have selected to make that choice for him.").

MD: Mack v. Mack, 618 A.2d 744 (Md. 1993).

MI: Martin v. Martin, 504 N.W.2d 917 (Mich. Ct. App. 1993).

MN: *In re* Kowalski, 478 N.W.2d 790 (Minn. 1991).

OH: Couture v. Couture, 549 N.E.2d 571 (Ohio Ct. App. 1989); *In re* Myers, 610 N.E.2d 663 (P. Ct. Summit County, Ohio 1993).

PA: *In re* E.L.K., 11 Fiduc. Rep. 2d 78 (C.P. Berks County, Pa. 1991).

[297] *In re* A.C., 573 A.2d 1235, 1250 n.19 (D.C. 1990) (Judicial review will most likely occur "because there is a conflict as to treatment choice among family members, physicians, or both. Were family members and physicians in complete agreement, it is unlikely that a court would be brought into the discussion.").

[298] See §§ **5.25–5.34.**

[299] **IN:** *Cf. In re* Lawrance, 579 N.E.2d 32, 43 (Ind. 1991) ("When a patient's health care provider or some family member disagrees with the course of action preferred by the patient's parents or other health care decisionmaker, Indiana Code § 16-8-12-7 provides a mechanism for challenges, regardless of whether the initial decision involves court action.").

Recourse to the courts should not be the immediate response at the first sign of disagreement. A judicial resolution should be sought only if the disagreement goes to a significant issue and is truly irresolvable by other means.[300] Consistent with the fact that decisionmaking should be a process rather than an event,[301] efforts should first be made to resolve conflict or disagreement through informal means such as discussion, negotiation, and/or counseling. In the case of patients in health care institutions, the participation of nurses and social workers can be especially helpful in this regard, as they often have substantially more contact with the patient's family and friends than does the attending physician. Clergy, patient representatives or ombudsmen, ethics committees,[302] and ethics consultants are present in many health care institutions and can also sometimes facilitate the resolution of serious disagreement and should be employed before seeking a judicial resolution.

Of course, even when all parties in the decisionmaking process are in agreement, this does not necessarily mean that the course of action agreed upon is a legal one. It is not difficult to imagine that the physician and the family of an incompetent patient (indeed, a competent patient) might agree that the most humane course of action would be to administer a lethal injection to the patient, yet it is clear that this is illegal.[303]

§ 5.31 —Disagreement Among Family Members

Irresolvable disagreement among family members—disagreement as to who should make decisions on behalf of the patient or what those decisions should be—is an extremely important factor in considering whether to seek recourse to

---

NJ: *E.g.,* N.J. Stat. Ann. § 26:2H-66.a ("In the event of disagreement among the patient, health care representative, and attending physician concerning the patient's decision making capacity or the appropriate interpretation and application of the terms of an advance directive to the patient's course of treatment, the parties may seek to resolve the disagreement by means of procedures and practices established by the health care institution, including but not limited to, consultation with an institutional ethics committee, or with a person designated by the health care institution for this purpose or may seek resolution by a court of competent jurisdiction.").

OH: *E.g.,* Ohio Rev. Code Ann. § 2133.08(E) (family members who object to decision made by higher priority surrogate are empowered to file complaint for judicial relief).

See § **14.6.**

300 Morrison v. Abramovice, 253 Cal. Rptr. 530, 535 (Ct. App. 1988) (recourse to courts appropriate only after "interested parties . . . have exhausted all nonjudicial efforts to resolve the dispute").

301 See § **3.8.**

302 See **Ch. 6.**

303 See **Ch. 18.**

the courts.[304] Conflicts among family members, especially those of an apparently long-standing nature, should not be papered over by members of the health care team in an effort to reach a consensus, as such conflicts are likely to resurface later when a critical decision about life-sustaining treatment needs to be made.

When it is not possible to resolve intrafamilial disputes, the attending physician is placed in a difficult, if not untenable, position. Not only does he not know

---

[304] **AZ:** Rasmussen v. Fleming, 741 P.2d 674, 691 (Ariz. 1987) ("Once the court resolves the matters of guardianship and incompetency, however, its encroachment into the substantive decisions concerning medical treatment should be limited to resolving disputes among the patient's family, the attending physicians, an independent physician, the health care facility, the guardian, and the guardian ad litem.").

CA: Barber v. Superior Court, 195 Cal. Rptr. 484, 493 (Ct. App. 1983) (in absence of disagreement among patient's wife and children, wife was proper surrogate decisionmaker).

DC: *In re* A.C., 573 A.2d 1235, 1250 n.19 (D.C. 1990) (judicial review will most likely occur "because there is a conflict as to treatment choice among family members").

IN: *In re* Lawrance, 579 N.E.2d 32, 43 (Ind. 1991) ("When a patient's health care provider or some family member disagrees with the course of action preferred by the patient's parents or other health care decisionmaker, Indiana Code § 16-8-12-7 provides a mechanism for challenges, regardless of whether the initial decision involves court action.").

KY: DeGrella v. Elston, 858 S.W.2d 698, 710 (1993) ("If the attending physician, the hospital or nursing home ethics committee where the patient resides, and the legal guardian or next of kin, all agree and document the patient's wishes and the patient's condition, and if no one disputes their decision, no court order is required to proceed to carry out the patient's wishes.").

MD: Mack v. Mack, 618 A.2d 744 (Md. 1993) (McAuliffe, J., dissenting).

MI: Martin v. Martin, 504 N.W.2d 917, 924 (Mich. Ct. App. 1993) ("[J]udicial involvement in a decision to withhold or withdraw life-sustaining medical treatment generally is not required where there is no disagreement among the parties directly concerned about treatment."); Rosebush v. Oakland County Prosecutor, 491 N.W.2d 633, 639 (Mich. Ct. App. 1992) ("[J]udicial involvement . . . need occur only when the parties directly concerned disagree about treatment, or other appropriate reasons are established for the court's involvement.").

NJ: *In re* Peter, 529 A.2d 419, 427 (N.J. 1987) ("[J]udicial review of a surrogate's decision to give effect to the patient's preference is unnecessary unless a conflict arises among the surrogate decisionmaker, the family, the physician and the Ombudsman."); *In re* Jobes, 529 A.2d 434, 449 (N.J. 1987) (dispute among the members of a patient's family); *In re* Farrell, 529 A.2d 404, 415 (N.J. 1987) ("Only unusual circumstances, such as a conflict among the physicians, or among the family members, or between the physicians and the family or other health care professionals, would necessitate judicial intervention."); *In re* Moorhouse, 593 A.2d 1256, 1261 (N.J. Super. Ct. App. Div. 1991) ("[I]if any one of the involved parties, including the Public Advocate, disagrees with the decision to terminate life support, the decision cannot be implemented without a court order."); *In re* Clark, 510 A.2d 136, 141 (N.J. Super. Ct. Ch. Div. 1986) ("[T]here is not a complete concurrence among the family members, the attending physicians and the hospital Ethics Committee. Therefore, . . . it became necessary to resort to the court.").

who speaks for the patient and thus on whom to rely in decisionmaking, but also he risks incurring the anger of some family members no matter what course is followed. Such anger can be an important ingredient in precipitating a civil and/or criminal action, regardless of the ultimate treatment provided.

Thus, recourse to the courts for the appointment of a guardian is advisable when there is serious and insoluble conflict among family members concerning the patient's decisionmaking capacity, whom the surrogate should be, or what medical course to follow.[305] The failure to go to court—depending on the depth with which disputing family members adhere to their convictions and the outcome of the decision about treatment—is an invitation to liability.[306]

§ 5.32 —Disagreement Between Patient and Treatment Team

Some patients who lack decisionmaking capacity are able to express preferences about particular forms of treatment.[307] However, because of the patient's lack of decisionmaking capacity, the attending physician is not legally obligated to honor the patient's preference.[308] Nonetheless, if incompetence has been determined clinically rather than judicially and if it is possible that the patient may regain decisionmaking capacity at some later time, the physician who ignores the incompetent patient's expressed preference is treading on thin ice. A patient who is treated over his objection and who later regains the capacity to make medical decisions may also regain the capacity to institute an action against the

---

[305] **FL:** John F. Kennedy Memorial Hosp. v. Bludworth, 452 So. 2d 921, 926–27 (Fla. 1984).

ME: *In re* Gardner, 534 A.2d 947, 954 (Me. 1987) ("concurrence of all those closest and dearest to [patient]—his family and friends—" is a significant factor).

MI: Martin v. Martin, 504 N.W.2d 917 (Mich. Ct. App. 1993).

MN: *In re* Kowalski, 478 N.W.2d 790 (Minn. 1991); *In re* Kowalski, 382 N.W.2d 861 (Minn. Ct. App. 1986), *review denied* (Minn. Apr. 18, 1986).

NJ: *In re* Jobes, 529 A.2d 434, 451 (N.J. 1987).

NY: *Contra In re* Nemser, 273 N.Y.S.2d 624 (Sup. Ct. N.Y. County 1966) (courts are not the proper forum for resolving familial disputes about appropriate course of treatment).

OH: *In re* Myers, 610 N.E.2d 663 (P. Ct. Summit County, Ohio 1993) (conflict between patient's parents led to application for appointment of guardian).

PA: *In re* E.L.K., 11 Fiduc. Rep. 2d 78 (C.P. Berks County, Pa. 1991).

WA: *In re* Grant, 747 P.2d 445, 456 n.4 (Wash. 1987) ("[A] guardian need not be appointed to make the decision to withhold life-sustaining treatment if the incompetent patient's family members all agree that such treatment should be withheld.").

[306] *See, e.g.,* Belcher v. Charleston Area Medical Ctr., 422 S.E.2d 827 (W. Va. 1992) (wrongful death action for relying on patient's parents' consent to do-not-resuscitate order rather than seeking decision of mature minor; however, physician's good-faith assessment of minor's maturity level provided immunity from liability for failure to obtain parental consent).

[307] *See, e.g., In re* Hier, 464 N.E.2d 959 (Mass. App. Ct. 1984); Lane v. Candura, 376 N.E.2d 1232 (Mass. App. Ct. 1978). See §§ **7.45–7.46.**

[308] See **Ch. 4.**

physician. This is also possible when the patient does not regain competence but another person, such as a family member or friend, brings an action on behalf of the patient or the patient's estate.[309]

Thus, when the patient is able to express a preference and it is in opposition to the course of action selected by the surrogate and/or the attending physician, it is prudent to obtain an adjudication of incompetence and the appointment of a guardian, and possibly judicial approval of the course of treatment or non-treatment itself.[310]

§ 5.33 —Disagreement Between Family and Treatment Team

The family of an incompetent patient may be united in its view about the proper course of treatment but at odds with the views of the attending physician and/or others on the treatment team. If so, serious consideration must be given to seeking the judicial appointment of a guardian.[311]

§ 5.34 —Disagreement Among Treatment Team Members

Even when the attending physician entertains no uncertainty about the patient's decisionmaking capacity, about who should serve as the surrogate, or about the appropriateness of a decision to administer or forgo life-sustaining treatment, that view may not be shared by other members of the treatment team. If other health care professionals are in serious and irresolvable disagreement, it is highly advisable that there be recourse to the courts.

---

[309] See **Ch. 17.**

[310] *See, e.g.*, N.J. Stat. Ann. § 26:2H-66.a ("In the event of disagreement among the patient, health care representative, and attending physician concerning the patient's decision making capacity or the appropriate interpretation and application of the terms of an advance directive to the patient's course of treatment, the parties may seek to resolve the disagreement by means of procedures and practices established by the health care institution, including but not limited to, consultation with an institutional ethics committee, or with a person designated by the health care institution for this purpose or may seek resolution by a court of competent jurisdiction."). *Cf. In re* Clark, 510 A.2d 136, 141 (N.J. Super. Ct. Ch. Div. 1986) (patient incompetent though not comatose; judicial determination necessary because lack of consensus about whether to implant feeding tube).

[311] **DNY:** *In re* Department of Veterans Affairs Medical Ctr., 749 F. Supp. 495 (S.D.N.Y. 1990) (rejection by patient's wife of physician's recommendation was motivating factor in seeking recourse to court).

DC: *In re* A.C., 573 A.2d 1235, 1250 n.19 (D.C. 1990) ([J]udicial review will most likely occur "because there is a conflict as to treatment choice among family members, physicians, or both. Were family members and physicians in complete agreement, it is unlikely that a court would be brought into the discussion.").

At the very least, those holding opposing views should be given a genuine opportunity to present them, to argue in support of them, and to have the attending physician explain the basis for his position. The forum for such discussion might be a regular ward or treatment-team conference or an ethics committee.[312] If a means for expressing dissenting views within the health care setting is not provided, a member of the treatment team may seek another forum for doing so, such as the press or the district attorney.[313]

§ 5.35 —Conflicts of Interest

Members of the health care team must be alert to potential or real conflicts of interest between patients and their surrogates, despite the possible difficulty in so doing,[314] and they must be prepared to initiate judicial proceedings if they believe that they have substantial reason to believe that a surrogate's decision is motivated primarily by improper considerations.[315]

Conflicts of interest will almost always exist in decisionmaking about life-sustaining treatment.[316] The standards for making such decisions for incompetent patients demand that, if at all possible, the surrogate be someone who knows the patient's wishes and interests well. Such a person is likely to be one who personally stands to lose or gain in some way—or lose and gain in different

---

[312] *See* Hastings Center Guidelines 32 (Part One, II(8)(d)). See **Ch. 6.**

[313] *See* Kirsch, *A Death at Kaiser Hospital,* Cal. Mag., Nov. 1982, at 79 (discussing Barber v. Superior Court, 195 Cal. Rptr. 484 (Ct. App. 1983)).

[314] **WA:** *In re* Hamlin, 689 P.2d 1372, 1381 (Wash. 1984) (Rosellini, J., dissenting) ("Doctors are trained to discover and treat disease and trauma, not to discern the truth of factual assertions. Also, a doctor may not, without significant impertinence, inquire as to the family members' financial relationships to the patient. In fact, a doctor may not be able to even ascertain if all family members have been consulted or even notified of the event.").

[315] **US:** Cruzan v. Director, 497 U.S. 261, 328 (1990) (Brennan, J., dissenting) ("[A] State may exclude from consideration anyone having improper motives.").

[316] **US:** Cruzan v. Director, 497 U.S. 261, 286 (1990) ("Close family members may have a strong feeling—a feeling not at all ignoble or unworthy, but not entirely disinterested, either—that they do not wish to witness the continuation of the life of a loved one which they regard as hopeless, meaningless, and even degrading. But there is no automatic assurance that the view of close family members will necessarily be the same as the patient's would have been had she been confronted with the prospect of her situation while competent.").

DC: *In re* A.C., 573 A.2d 1235, 1250 (D.C. 1990) ("[W]hile in the majority of cases family members will have the best interests of the patient in mind, sometimes family members will rely on their own judgments or predilections rather than serving as conduits for expressing the patient's wishes.").

MD: Mack v. Mack, 618 A.2d 744, 770–71 (Md. 1993) (Chasanow, J., concurring and dissenting) ("There is, of course, the danger that uncaring selfish family members will be motivated by a desire to get rid of incompetent relatives who are unwanted and burdensome.").

See generally Lynn, *Conflicts of Interest in Medical Decision-Making,* 36 J. Am. Geriatric Soc'y 945 (1988).

ways—from the patient's death. In other words, there is an inherent conflict of interest in the theory of surrogate decisionmaking.

The only way to avoid conflicts of interest is either to insist that patients make such decisions for themselves before losing decisionmaking capacity[317] or to utilize as surrogates individuals who have no personal stake in the outcome of the decision. Most courts have rejected both approaches as impractical and not consistent with what most patients would want. Consequently, what is essential is not whether there is a conflict of interest but how pervasive it is and what its effect is. Only when a surrogate decision is motivated primarily by something other than concern for what is best for the *patient* should recourse to the courts be sought.[318]

Through continuing conversation with the patient's family members and friends, the health care team should subtly attempt to ascertain whether surrogates are making decisions in good faith. In the context of decisionmaking about forgoing life-sustaining treatment, at least when a subjective or substituted judgment test is applied,[319] *good faith* means that "the decision was made with honesty of intention and in an honest effort to make the decision which the patient, if competent, would make."[320] Special attention must be paid to possible "economic considerations, family pressures, or other factors of undue influence [that] could cloud a surrogate's judgment."[321]

If a conflict of interest threatens to obstruct the surrogate's ability to act in the patient's best interests, that person ought to be disqualified as a surrogate.[322]

---

[317] See §§ **7.4–7.6.**

[318] **CA:** Drabick v. Drabick, 245 Cal. Rptr. 840, 861 n.38 (Ct. App. 1988) (inflexible rule precluding immediate family members, who are likely to have some testamentary or beneficial interest, from serving as conservator to make decisions about life-sustaining treatment would disqualify those most likely to appreciate the conservatee's personal values).

NJ: *In re* Conroy, 486 A.2d 1209, 1218–19 (N.J. 1985) ("[T]here was no question that the nephew had good intentions and had no real conflict of interest due to possible inheritance when he sought permission to remove the tube.").

PA: Pa. Cons. Stat. Ann. tit. 20, § 5511(F) ("Any family relationship to such individual [ward] shall not, by itself, be considered as an interest adverse to the alleged incapacitated person" in determining who may serve as guardian.).

Council on Ethical & Judicial Affairs, American Medical Ass'n, Code of Medical Ethics § 2.20, at 37 (1994).

[319] See **Ch. 7.**

[320] Browning v. Herbert, 543 So. 2d 258, 274 (Fla. Dist. Ct. App. 1989), *aff'd,* 568 So. 2d 4 (Fla. 1990).

[321] Browning v. Herbert, 543 So. 2d at 274.

[322] **CT:** McConnell v. Beverly Enters.-Conn., Inc., 553 A.2d 596, 604 (Conn. 1989) ("[T]he testimony of all four (husband and children) demonstrates positively that they reached their decision out of love and concern for their mother and wife and respect for her wishes. There is not a hint in the trial court testimony of any ulterior motive on the part of any of the plaintiffs. The trial court had no trouble finding the requisite consent of the next of kin and we conclude that it did not err in so finding.").

MI: Martin v. Martin, 517 N.W.2d 749 (Mich. Ct. App. 1994).

See § **5.20.**

If such a disqualification generates hostility on the part of the disqualified person, or if all potential surrogates are also subject to conflicts of interest, recourse to the courts for the appointment of a guardian is especially advisable. In "exceptional" circumstances when "family members will not act to protect a patient,"[323] health care professionals should not permit the termination of treatment without recourse to the courts.[324]

Financial Conflict of Interest

Perhaps the clearest kind of potential conflict of interest exists when the surrogate is an heir of the patient[325] or is financially responsible for the patient's health care costs and stands to gain financially by the patient's death.[326] This is not to say that an heir will always have a conflict of interest and therefore should be barred from acting as a surrogate, but only that a potential conflict exists.[327] Neither is it necessarily illegitimate for a surrogate to consider questions of cost,

---

[323] **DNY:** *In re* Department of Veterans Affairs Medical Ctr., 749 F. Supp. 495 (S.D.N.Y. 1990) (by implication).

NJ: *In re* Jobes, 529 A.2d 434, 447 (N.J. 1987).

[324] Mack v. Mack, 618 A.2d 744, 770–71 (Md. 1993) (Chasanow, J., concurring and dissenting) (The safeguard when family members are motivated by their own interests is "that health care providers probably will not concur and should require court approval if they believe the family is not really acting in good faith and in accord with the patient's probable views.").

[325] *See, e.g., In re* Visbeck, 510 A.2d 125, 132 (N.J. Super. Ct. Ch. Div. 1986) (risk involved in permitting surrogate to take quality of life into account is that action "might be as crude and as potentially sinister as the desire to inherit wealth").

[326] **US:** *Cf.* Cruzan v. Director, 497 U.S. 261, 333 (1990) (Stevens, J., dissenting) (trial court's "findings make it clear that the parents' request had no economic motivation).

MO: *Cf.* Cruzan v. Harmon, 760 S.W.2d 408, 411 (Mo. 1988) ("The court determined that the State is bearing the entire economic cost of Nancy's care.").

NY: *E.g.,* Grace Plaza of Great Neck, Inc. v. Elbaum, 623 N.E.2d 513 (N.Y. 1993) (husband of nursing home patient refused to pay nursing home's bills on ground that treatment was being provided against patient's will).

[327] **DC:** *In re* A.C., 573 A.2d 1235 (D.C. 1990) ("There may . . . be conflicting interests, or family members may be inclined for their own reasons to disregard what the patient herself would want.").

MA: *Cf. In re* Spring, 399 N.E.2d 493, 499 n.8 (Mass. App. Ct. 1979).

MI: Martin v. Martin, 517 N.W.2d 749, 754 (Mich. Ct. App. 1994) (rejecting claim by mother and sister of patient that patient's wife was unsuitable as a guardian because of financial considerations and "her relationships with others").

NJ: *In re* Conroy, 486 A.2d 1209, 1218–19 (N.J. 1985) ("[T]here was no question that the nephew had good intentions and had no real conflict of interest due to possible inheritance when he sought permission to remove the tube.").

OH: Leach v. Akron Gen. Medical Ctr., 426 N.E.2d 809, 810 (P. Ct. Summit County, Ohio 1980) ("Mrs. Leach's condition is a continuing anxiety to her family. In addition, it constitutes an expense approximating $500 a day to her insurance company.").

especially if the patient would have.[328] For instance, the fact that a family refuses to continue to pay for treatment that it has requested be terminated does not mean that the family is motivated solely by economic factors in arriving at its decision.[329] Thus, judicial proceedings need not automatically be instituted.[330]

A classic example of this is illustrated by an unreported Florida case,[331] in which the patient's wife claimed that the patient's son by a previous marriage was trying to terminate life support to inherit his father's estate and to deprive her of an expectancy under an antenuptial agreement. The patient's son claimed (and the trial court found) that he was merely trying to enforce his father's wishes, and that the patient's wife was "only trying to prolong Mr. Stone's life so that she can gain more monies under the anti-nuptial [*sic*] agreement."[332]

However, financial conflicts of interest can take other forms as well. A patient's social security benefits or private retirement benefits or annuities will terminate or inure to some other party on the death of the patient. Thus, some family members can sometimes benefit themselves by insisting on the *prolongation* of treatment rather than its termination.

Emotional Conflict of Interest

A surrogate might also be motivated, perhaps unconsciously, by a wish to put an end to a tremendous emotional strain on his own life caused by the patient's

---

328 **DC:** *In re* A.C., 573 A.2d at 1251 n.20 (D.C. 1990) (court could conclude that a patient might consider needs of her family in making a treatment decision for herself).

329 **NY:** Elbaum v. Grace Plaza of Great Neck, Inc., 544 N.Y.S.2d 840, 846–47 (App. Div. 1989).

330 **FL:** *Contra* Browning v. Herbert, 568 So. 2d 4, 18 (Fla. 1990) (Overton, J., concurring and dissenting) ("I am concerned that, if there is no judicial involvement [in cases where there is no written living will], these decisions could be made by surrogates who would benefit financially from an early termination of the ward's life.").

IL: Estate of Longeway v. Community Convalescent Ctr., 549 N.E.2d 292, 300–01 (Ill. 1989) ("[C]ourt intervention is necessary [when artificial nutrition and hydration is to be terminated] to guard against the remote, yet real possibility that greed may taint the judgment of the surrogate decisionmaker. . . . We can foresee other cases, however, where the surrogate decisionmaker stands to profit from the patient's demise and covets ill-gotten wealth to the point of fatal attraction. Generally, no penetrating investigation will be required. Nevertheless, the judge is free to inquire as to the beneficiaries and the extent of the patient's estate, if it appears necessary to do so.").

MD: Mack v. Mack, 618 A.2d 744, 770–71 (Md. 1993) (Chasanow, J., concurring and dissenting) (The safeguard when family members are motivated by their own interests is "that health care providers probably will not concur and should require court approval if they believe the family is not really acting in good faith and in accord with the patient's probable views.").

WA: *In re* Colyer, 660 P.2d 738, 747 n.4 (Wash. 1983) (dismissing doubts about the suitability of family members to act because of potential *pecuniary* conflict of interest).

See §§ **7.45–7.46.**

331 *In re* Stone, No. 90-5867 (Fla. Cir. Ct. 17th Dist. Broward County June 24, 1991).

332 *Id.,* slip op. at 3.

illness.[333] Again, this may not be simple to discern,[334] but if it does become apparent, caution should be exercised in relying upon that person to act as surrogate. It is also possible that surrogates may be motivated by conscious or unconscious self-interest to err on the side of administering treatment. Family members and friends who decide to prolong a dying patient's life may be motivated by guilt, by denial of the fact that the patient is terminally ill and that death is inevitable, or even by a desire to inflict suffering on the patient through the administration of painful but not particularly beneficial treatment. When such motives are evident, a serious question arises about the surrogate's fitness to serve, and judicial proceedings should be instituted.

§ 5.36 —Uncertainty About Decisionmaking Capacity or Whom to Designate as Surrogate

Recourse to the courts for an adjudication of incompetency is appropriate when there is serious uncertainty about the patient's decisionmaking capacity[335] or about who is to serve as surrogate.[336] Sometimes there is more than one qualified individual who is ready, willing, and able to serve as a surrogate.[337] Although the attending physician customarily decides which family member to deal with in decisionmaking for an incompetent patient,[338] there may be circumstances when it is not apparent who is best qualified to serve as surrogate. Relying on more than one person to serve is not legally prohibited, and in some cases that may be

---

333 **US:** Cruzan v. Director, 497 U.S. 261, 286 (1990) ("Close family members may have a strong feeling—a feeling not at all ignoble or unworthy, but not entirely disinterested, either—that they do not wish to witness the continuation of the life of a loved one which they regard as hopeless, meaningless, and even degrading. But there is no automatic assurance that the view of close family members will necessarily be the same as the patient's would have been had she been confronted with the prospect of her situation while competent.").

DC: *In re* A.C., 573 A.2d 1235, 1250 (D.C. 1990) ("The court should be mindful, however, that while in the majority of cases family members will have the best interests of the patient in mind, sometimes family members will rely on their own judgments or predilections rather than serving as conduits for expressing the patient's wishes.").

NJ: *In re* Visbeck, 510 A.2d 125, 132 (N.J. Super. Ct. Ch. Div. 1986) (risk involved in permitting surrogate to take quality of life into account is that action might be motivated by "frustrations, aggravations and burdens that dealing with a mentally impaired person poses for those around a patient").

334 **WA:** *In re* Hamlin, 689 P.2d 1372, 1381 (Wash. 1984) (Rosellini, J., dissenting).

335 **NY:** Fosmire v. Nicoleau, 551 N.E.2d 77, 80 (N.Y. 1990) ("[W]hen there is a bona fide question of the patient's competence the doctor or health care facility may seek a court ruling.").

336 Council on Ethical & Judicial Affairs, American Medical Ass'n, Code of Medical Ethics § 2.20, at 37 (1994).

337 *See, e.g., In re* Kowalski, 382 N.W.2d 861 (Minn. Ct. App.), *review denied* (Minn. 1986).

338 See §§ **5.12–5.14.**

the best solution. However, there may be too many interested and available family members and/or friends for all to participate in decisionmaking or to achieve a consensus about decisions. Even when there are fewer, it may be logistically difficult for everyone to be available when necessary.[339] The attending physician (or some other member of the health care team at the attending physician's direction) should attempt to orchestrate an agreement among the patient's family (and/or close friends) as to who will speak for the patient and possibly act as spokesman for the family group as well.

In the absence of such an agreement, the attending physician should exercise the prerogative of dealing with one person (or more, if that is logistically feasible) as surrogate if he is confident that that person is in possession of the kind of information necessary to meet the applicable decisionmaking standard (that is, the subjective standard, substituted judgment standard, or best interests standard). This kind of resolution, however, runs the risk of significantly alienating one or more of the people who are excluded. If they continue to voice strong opposition either to the designated surrogate or to the decisions the surrogate makes, the judicial appointment of a guardian should be sought.[340]

§ 5.37 Judicial Review Required as a Matter of Course

The first two right-to-die cases, *Quinlan*[341] and *Saikewicz,*[342] generated a debate about the necessity of judicial review of decisions to forgo life-sustaining treatment. The originator and strongest proponent of the requirement of review was the Massachusetts Supreme Judicial Court, and for a while it appeared as though this position would prevail, if only from the force of the arguments presented by that court.[343] *Saikewicz* held that a decision to forgo life-sustaining treatment must be made by a court.

339 *See, e.g., In re* Clark, 510 A.2d 136, 141 (N.J. Super. Ct. Ch. Div. 1986) ("In this case, there is not a complete concurrence among the family members, the attending physicians and the hospital Ethics Committee. Therefore, . . . it became necessary to resort to the court.").

340 **US:** *See* Cruzan v. Director, 497 U.S. 261, 328 (1990) (Brennan, J., dissenting) ("A State's inability to discern an incompetent patient's choice still need not mean that a State is rendered powerless to protect that choice. . . . A State may ensure that the person who makes the decision on the patient's behalf is the one whom the patient himself would have selected to make that choice for him. And a State may exclude from consideration anyone having improper motives."); Hastings Center Guidelines 32 (Part One, II(8)(b)).

341 *In re* Quinlan, 355 A.2d 647 (N.J. 1976).

342 Superintendent of Belchertown State Sch. v. Saikewicz, 370 N.E.2d 417 (Mass. 1977).

343 *See, e.g.,* Annas, *Reconciling* Quinlan *and* Saikewicz: *Decision Making for the Terminally Ill Incompetent,* 4 Am. J. L. & Med. 367 (1978) (supporting *Saikewicz*); Baron, *Medical Paternalism and the Rule of Law: A Reply to Dr. Relman,* 4 Am. J. L. & Med. 337 (1978) (supporting *Saikewicz*); Buchanan, *Medical Paternalism or Legal Imperialism: Not the Only Alternatives for Handling* Saikewicz-*Type Cases,* 5 Am. J. L. & Med. 97 (1979) (opposing *Saikewicz*).

As previously discussed,[344] the New Jersey Supreme Court had held in *Quinlan* that judicial review "would generally be inappropriate, not only because it would be a gratuitous encroachment upon the medical profession's field of competence, but because it would be impossibly cumbersome."[345] The following year, the Massachusetts Supreme Judicial Court in the *Saikewicz* decision directly responded that it took a "dim view of any attempt to shift the ultimate decision-making responsibility away from the duly established courts of proper jurisdiction to any committee, panel or group, ad hoc or permanent."[346] "[S]uch questions of life and death," the court explained,

> seem to us to require the process of detached but passionate investigation and decision that forms the ideal on which the judicial branch of government was created. Achieving this ideal is our responsibility and that of the lower court, and is not to be entrusted to any other group purporting to represent the "morality and conscience of our society," no matter how highly motivated or impressively constituted.[347]

The purpose of the courts is "not to displace the traditional role of the family and the attending physician in weighing that question, but to protect the rights of the incompetent person by determining, as best it can, what his wish would be, and ensuring that that wish is carried out if it does not violate the policy of the State or the ethics of the medical profession."[348] The court did, however, admit that "the findings and advice of [ethics committees] as well as the testimony of the attending physicians and other medical experts ordinarily would be of great assistance" to trial courts.[349]

In retrospect, this turned out to be a rather short-lived debate. Its highwater mark was the *Saikewicz* case itself. No other court wholeheartedly embraced a requirement of routine judicial review, and even the Massachusetts courts seem to have quietly and gradually abandoned the requirement of judicial review in right-to-die cases. There are a small number of cases in a few other jurisdictions suggesting that judicial review is routinely appropriate. However, these holdings have had very little, if any, practical impact because in each state, subsequent cases have failed to elaborate on this point or have ignored it, or there have been no subsequent cases.

---

[344] See § **5.26.**

[345] **NJ:** *In re* Quinlan, 355 A.2d 647, 669 (N.J. 1976).

CA: *Accord* Barber v. Superior Court, 195 Cal. Rptr. 484, 493 (Ct. App. 1983).

[346] Superintendent of Belchertown State Sch. v. Saikewicz, 370 N.E.2d 417, 434 (Mass. 1977), *reaffirmed in In re* Spring, 405 N.E.2d 115, 120 (Mass. 1980).

[347] Superintendent of Belchertown State Sch. v. Saikewicz, 370 N.E.2d at 434. *Accord In re* Spring, 405 N.E.2d at 120.

[348] *In re* Spring, 399 N.E.2d 493, 502 (Mass. App. Ct. 1979).

[349] Superintendent of Belchertown State Sch. v. Saikewicz, 370 N.E.2d at 434. *Accord In re* Spring, 405 N.E.2d at 120.

Massachusetts

The first crack in the *Saikewicz* requirement occurred the following year. The reaction of Massachusetts physicians was to take the *Saikewicz* opinion at face value and not to permit the forgoing of life-sustaining treatment without judicial approval.[350] Consequently, in *In re Dinnerstein,*[351] the family of an incompetent patient requesting, with the concurrence of the patient's physicians, that a no-code (do-not-resuscitate, or DNR) order be written for the patient,[352] petitioned the probate court for permission not to resuscitate the patient in the event of cardiac arrest, believing on the basis of *Saikewicz* that they lacked the authority to do so without judicial imprimatur.

The Massachusetts Appeals Court held that a judicial order was not necessary. It distinguished *Saikewicz* on the basis that it was a case in which "treatment was available and which therefore presented a substantial question of choice."[353] By contrast,

> [t]hat is not the situation which presents itself in this case, or in the case of any patient in the terminal stages of an unremitting, incurable mortal illness. . . . Attempts to apply resuscitation, if successful, will do nothing to cure or relieve the illnesses which will have brought the patient to the threshold of death.[354]

In cases in which the patient is dying of an incurable illness, resuscitating that patient after a cardiac or respiratory arrest does no more than prolong the dying process. As such,

> [i]t presents a question peculiarly within the competence of the medical profession of what measures are appropriate to ease the imminent passing of an irreversibly, terminally ill patient in light of the patient's history and condition and the wishes of her family. That question is not one for judicial decision, but one for the attending physician, in keeping with the highest traditions of his profession, and subject to court review only to the extent that it may be contended that he has failed to exercise "the degree of care and skill of the average qualified practitioner, taking into account the advances in the profession."[355]

Dinnerstein, then, muddied the waters. Prior court approval was needed in *Saikewicz* to withhold the administration of chemotherapy to a profoundly mentally retarded ward of a state institution. But it was not needed to issue a no-code order for an elderly, terminally ill patient whose family and physicians

---

[350] *See In re* Dinnerstein, 380 N.E.2d 134, 136 (Mass. App. Ct. 1978).

[351] 380 N.E.2d 134 (Mass. App. Ct. 1978).

[352] See §§ **9.4–9.32.**

[353] *In re* Dinnerstein, 380 N.E.2d at 138.

[354] *Id.* at 138–39.

[355] *Id.*

agreed that cardiopulmonary resuscitation was inappropriate. One distinction between the two situations is that the treatment in question in *Saikewicz,* which was not capable of saving the patient's life any more than that in *Dinnerstein,* at least might have provided a remission of the illness, though it was almost certain that the illness would recur and claim the patient's life.

It is now clear in Massachusetts that judicial approval is generally not required for a do-not-resuscitate order, whatever else might be the requirements for judicial review for the forgoing of other treatments.[356] However, if the patient is an infant who is in the custody of the state, judicial approval should be sought.[357]

Dinnerstein was not appealed to the Massachusetts Supreme Judicial Court, but two years later, that court again had an opportunity to address this issue in *In re Spring.*[358] The *Spring* court observed that there are "a variety of circumstances to be taken into account in deciding whether there should be an application for a prior court order with respect to medical treatment of an incompetent patient."[359] It promulgated a list of factors—not intended to be exclusive—to consider when deciding whether prior judicial approval was necessary in general, thus conceding that it was not always necessary to obtain judicial approval in order to forgo life-sustaining treatment.[360]

Furthermore, dialysis for Spring was more like chemotherapy for Saikewicz than resuscitation for Dinnerstein. It would keep him alive for some period of time; in fact, it was more likely to keep him alive for an extended period than chemotherapy would keep Saikewicz alive. However, the quality of his life to himself would be poor. Finally, the court explicitly approved the *Dinnerstein* holding, stating that "[w]ithout approving all that is said in the opinion of the

---

[356] *See In re* Beth, 587 N.E.2d 1377, 1380 (Mass. 1992) (citing *In re* Dinnerstein, 380 N.E.2d 134; Brophy v. New Eng. Sinai Hosp., Inc., 497 N.E.2d 626 (Mass. 1986)).

[357] *In re* Beth, 587 N.E.2d at 1380. *See also* Custody of a Minor, 434 N.E.2d 601 (Mass. 1982).

[358] 405 N.E.2d 115 (Mass. 1980).

[359] *Id.* at 120–21.

[360] *Id.* at 121:

1. The extent of impairment of the patient's mental faculties
2. Whether the patient is in the custody of a State institution
3. The prognosis without the proposed treatment
4. The prognosis with the proposed treatment
5. The complexity, risk, and novelty of the proposed treatment
6. Its possible side effects
7. The patient's level of understanding and probable reaction
8. The urgency of decision
9. The consent of the patient, spouse, or guardian
10. The good faith of those who participate in the decision
11. The clarity of professional opinion as to what is good medical practice
12. The interests of third persons
13. The administrative requirements of any institution involved.

Appeals Court, we think the result reached on the facts shown in that case was consistent with our holding in the *Saikewicz* case."[361]

The court specifically disavowed any attempt to explain what weight should be accorded to each of the enumerated factors and how to strike a balance among them. And it is not clear that it could have easily done so, because "since the scientific underpinnings of medical practice and opinion are in a constant state of development, our opinion as to a particular set of facts may not be a reliable guide to the proper solution of a future medical problem."[362] To confuse matters further, the court added that because "[n]either the present case nor the *Saikewicz* case involved the legality of action taken without judicial authority . . . our opinions should not be taken to establish any requirement of prior judicial approval *that would not otherwise exist.*"[363]

In *Custody of a Minor,*[364] the court clarified the *Spring* guidelines. Judicial review should be sought when "(1) the [patient] is a ward of the State and in the custody of the [state]; (2) [the patient's] mental faculties have not developed to the point where he is competent to make the decision; (3) the parents have failed to exercise their parental responsibilities; (4) the [patient's] condition is incurable and the prognosis for successful treatment is negative; (5) medical opinion on diagnosis and prognosis was clear and unanimous as to the [patient's] condition and future; and (6) attempts to resuscitate would be painful and intrusive."[365]

The determinative issue in *Custody of a Minor* was that the patient was a ward of the state and had no "loving and concerned family." Interestingly, these factors were also present in the *Saikewicz* case. Thus, *Spring* should be seen as a clear retreat from *Saikewicz.* Just as in the situation involving resuscitation of a terminally ill patient, in light of these cases judicial review should not be required when there is no "significant treatment choice or election which, in light of sound medical advice, is to be made by the patient, if competent to do so,"[366] or by the patient's surrogate if the patient is incompetent.

A subsequent Massachusetts case, however, hints that there may still be some vitality to the requirement of judicial review.[367] The attorney for the defendant, who was incompetent to stand trial, sought to enter a guilty plea to a lesser

---

[361] *Id.* at 120.

[362] *Id.*

[363] *Id.* at 120 (emphasis added).

[364] 434 N.E.2d 601 (Mass. 1982).

[365] *Id.* at 608.

[366] *In re* Dinnerstein, 380 N.E.2d 134, 139 (Mass. App. Ct. 1978) ("[I]f read to apply to the natural death of a terminally ill patient by cardiac or respiratory arrest, [*Saikewicz*] would require attempts to resuscitate dying patients in most cases, without exercise of medical judgment, even when the course of action could aptly be characterized as a pointless, even cruel, prolongation of the act of dying.").

[367] Commonwealth v. Del Verde, 496 N.E.2d 1357 (Mass. 1986) (prosecution of mentally retarded defendant for murder and rape).

offense on the basis of substituted judgment. In holding the concept of substituted judgment inapplicable in this context, the court took more than a page of the opinion to explain what substituted judgment in the *medical* context means and requires—including judicial review.[368] One could infer from this totally gratuitous discussion—gratuitous as far as the matter before the court was concerned—that the court wished to breathe some life into the requirement of judicial review. One could just as easily, however, not draw that conclusion, and subsequent Massachusetts cases clearly do not provide that breath.[369]

Minnesota

The Minnesota Supreme Court held in *Torres* that a court order was required to forgo life-sustaining treatment but did not explain why.[370] This is particularly puzzling in light of the fact that the court held that the conservatorship statute[371] permits but does not specifically require a court order. It would seem that in Minnesota, in situations in which there is no family, a court order is required although the court did not state this explicitly.[372] However, there have been no subsequent appellate right-to-die cases in Minnesota.

New York

Early in right-to-die litigation, a New York intermediate appellate court adopted the *Saikewicz* requirement that judicial approval be obtained for the forgoing of life-sustaining treatment.[373] However, the Court of Appeals reversed, holding that judicial review is generally not required.[374] Subsequently, however, another New York trial court required judicial review.[375] For more than a decade there was no discussion of this issue by the New York courts, until the 1992 opinion

---

[368] *Id.* at 1362 ("Finally, the judge must determine whether the countervailing State interests are so substantial as to outweigh the individual's right to make and pursue the decision.").

[369] *See, e.g., In re* Beth, 587 N.E.2d 1263 (Mass. 1992); *In re* Doe, 583 N.E.2d 1263 (Mass.), *cert. denied sub nom.* Doe v. Gross, 112 S. Ct. 1512 (1992); *In re* R.H., 622 N.E.2d 1071 (Mass. App. Ct. 1993).

[370] *In re* Torres, 357 N.W.2d 332, 341 (Minn. 1984).

[371] Minn. Stat. Ann. § 525.56 subd. 3(4)(a).

[372] *In re* Torres, 357 N.W.2d 332, 341 n.4 (Minn. 1984) (Court order not required to discontinue "life-support systems . . . follow[ing] consultation between the attending doctor and the family with the approval of the hospital ethics committee."). *See also id.* at 341 (Kelley, J., specially concurring) ("I am of the view that in all cases when the decision of continued life or likely death is involved there should be a court procedure similar to the procedure followed in this case.").

[373] Eichner v. Dillon, 426 N.Y.S.2d 517, 549–50 (App. Div. 1980).

[374] Eichner v. Dillon, 420 N.E.2d 64, 74 (N.Y. 1981).

[375] *See* A.B. v. C., 477 N.Y.S.2d 281, 284 (Sup. Ct. Schenectady County 1984) (dictum).

of the Appellate Division in *Grace Plaza of Great Neck, Inc. v. Elbaum.*[376] A dissenting justice drew the conclusion that the majority seemed to require "a court order . . . before artificial life support may be discontinued when a patient is in a permanent, irreversible vegetative state."[377] The majority seemed to rest this requirement on the continual use of the term "trier of fact" in an earlier Court of Appeals decision (*O'Connor*) in its discussion of the standard of proof.[378]

However, the Court of Appeals in *O'Connor* never expressly required a court order to forgo life-sustaining treatment. Rather, it appeared to be using the term *trier of fact* as a synonym for *decisionmaker,* which could refer to an attending physician or a court. It is also possible that the *Grace Plaza* court believed this requirement (if there were one) applied only when the treatment in question was tube-feeding and/or when the patient was in a persistent vegetative state because the court discusses judicial review in the context of a "legal obligation to provide adequate nutrition and hydration" to patients in a persistent vegetative state.[379]

Regardless of what the Appellate Division might have meant, there is no hint in the opinion of the Court of Appeals affirming the *Grace Plaza* case decision[380] that judicial review is required either routinely or in a particular category of cases. Indeed, the court seems to have tried to put to rest the notion that judicial approval is routinely needed in New York for the forgoing of life-sustaining treatment:

> We would but add that in many, perhaps most cases, providers will appropriately consider the family's evidence on the matter conclusive and honor requests to terminate treatment of a hopelessly ill patient (*see* [Eichner v. Dillon]). By doing so they not only avoid continued anguish for the family but also avoid imposing on all parties the expense and delay that accompanies legal proceedings to resolve the question.[381]

It would have been more successful in accomplishing this goal but for two factors. First, the Court of Appeals clearly placed the burden on families, not health care providers, to seek a court order if the family and the provider could not agree that treatment should be terminated. Unlike most courts, the *Grace Plaza* court insisted that a health care provider acting in good faith is entitled to continue treatment and place the burden of seeking judicial resolution on the

---

[376] 588 N.Y.S.2d 853 (App. Div. 1992).

[377] *Id.* at 861 (Rosenblatt, J., concurring and dissenting).

[378] *Id.* at 857 & passim (quoting *In re* Westchester County Medical Ctr. (O'Connor), 531 N.E.2d 607 (N.Y. 1988)).

[379] *Id.* at 857.

[380] Grace Plaza of Great Neck, Inc. v. Elbaum, 623 N.E.2d 513 (N.Y. 1993).

[381] *Id.* at 515.

patient's family: "If the provider refuses to act, we find nothing unfair in placing the burden of instituting legal proceedings on those seeking to discontinue treatment."[382] (The court did not consider what should ensue if the provider "in bad faith, refuses to discontinue treatment [because n]one of the courts below found plaintiff acted in bad faith."[383])

The rationale for this requirement flows from the New York standard for terminating life-sustaining medical treatment for incompetent patients. "*O'Connor* instructs decision-makers to 'err on the side of life' and makes clear that the burden of establishing an incompetent patient's desire to die rests squarely with those who are asserting that desire. That burden does not shift simply because a family member has requested termination of life support."[384] Furthermore, "[a]s intimates of the patient, the family members have access to the necessary evidence and are in the best position to submit it to a court for consideration."[385]

But what follows seems to undercut the preference for erring on the side of life. Rather than instructing that when the provider and the family disagree there must be recourse to the courts, the court instructs that "the family may seek another facility for the patient or it may be able to take the patient into a family member's home."[386] This seems to mean that it would then be acceptable for the family to engage a physician and/or provider who will terminate the patient's life-sustaining medical treatment or that it is permissible for the family to do so itself, in either event without judicial resolution. If that is what is intended, it seems that recourse to the courts is not for the purpose of settling a disagreement about the patient's wishes but about making a health care provider feel better about the termination of life support. A family can thus easily evade the *O'Connor* mandate that treatment may be terminated only if there is clear and convincing evidence that the patient, while competent, gave instructions to that effect, and it appears that the court is providing its authorization to do just that.

The other reason that the court failed to fully clarify the question about whether a court order is required to forgo life-sustaining treatment arises from a concurring opinion intimating that criminal liability was still a distinct possibility if no court order was obtained:

> As indicated in [the majority] opinion, a health care facility, when there is any doubt as to what the patient would have intended, cannot be faulted, under the "specific subjective intent" rule for declining "to discontinue treatment until the issue is legally determined" [citation omitted]. This is certainly true in cases where, as here, an Assistant District Attorney had announced that if life support were withdrawn from Mrs. Elbaum without court permission, the facility risked criminal prosecution.[387]

---

[382] *Id.*

[383] *Id.* at 516.

[384] *Id.*

[385] *Id.*

[386] Grace Plaza of Great Neck, Inc. v. Elbaum, 623 N.E.2d at 516.

[387] *Id.* at 517.

In the final analysis, the law in New York appears to be that a court order is not required to withhold or withdraw life-sustaining medical treatment, but there is a possibility of liability if treatment is forgone without one and the requisite standard for decisionmaking for incompetent patients is subsequently found not to have been met. That, however, is true in every jurisdiction.[388]

Ohio

In the *Leach* case in 1984, a division of the court of appeals stated that

> Until such time as the legislature provides some more efficient means of protecting the rights of patients in Mrs. Leach's condition, we join those courts that require judicial authority for the termination of life-prolonging treatment of an incompetent patient.[389]

This requirement, premised on the absence of any alternative legislatively-mandated safeguards,[390] has not been followed in any other Ohio county,[391] perhaps because of the enactment of living will, health care power of attorney, and surrogate decisionmaking legislation, although no court has subsequently specifically addressed the issue of judicial review and thus has not addressed the rationale of *Leach*. Furthermore, the two cases that *Leach* cites as the basis for this requirement have either themselves been eroded (*Saikewicz*[392]) or never held that judicial review is required (*Eichner*[393]).

Washington

The Washington Supreme Court originally seemed to dispense with the need for judicial review on the assumption that decisions about life-sustaining treatment

---

388 See § **17.24.**

389 Estate of Leach v. Shapiro, 469 N.E.2d 1047, 1052–53 (Ohio Ct. App. Summit County 1984).

390 **OH:** Estate of Leach v. Shapiro, 469 N.E.2d at 1052–53 ("In Ohio, at this time, the court system provides the only mechanism which can protect the interest of the doctor, the hospital, the patient, the family and the state. . . . Until such time as the legislature provides some more efficient means of protecting the rights of patients in Mrs. Leach's condition, we join those courts that require judicial authority for the termination of life-prolonging treatment of an incompetent patient.").

AZ: *Accord* Rasmussen v. Fleming, 741 P.2d 674, 692 (Ariz. 1987) (Feldman, V.C.J., concurring).

391 *See In re* Myers, 610 N.E.2d 663 (P. Ct. Summit County, Ohio 1993); Anderson v. St. Francis-St. George Hosp., 614 N.E.2d 841 (Ohio Ct. App. Hamilton County 1992); *In re* McInnis, 584 N.E.2d 1389 (P. Ct. Stark County, Ohio 1991); *In re* Crum, 580 N.E.2d 876 (P. Ct. Franklin County, Ohio 1991); Couture v. Couture, 549 N.E.2d 571 (Ohio Ct. App. Montgomery County 1989).

392 Superintendent of Belchertown State Sch. v. Saikewicz, 370 N.E.2d 417 (Mass. 1977), *cited in* Estate of Leach v. Shapiro, 469 N.E.2d at 1053.

393 *In re* Eichner, 420 N.E.2d 64 (N.Y. 1981), *cited in* Estate of Leach v. Shapiro, 469 N.E.2d at 1053.

would be made by a judicially-appointed guardian. Thus, judicial review would be required only in limited circumstances:

> [I]f there is disagreement among family members as to the incompetent's wishes or among the physicians as to the prognosis, if the patient has always been incompetent so that his wishes cannot be known, if there is evidence of wrongful motives or malpractice, or if there is no family member to serve as guardian, the court may be required to intervene.[394]

However, when later faced with one of the above situations, specifically a patient who had never been competent, the court reconsidered and specifically held that judicial review was not necessary, at least when "the treating physicians, the prognosis committee, and the guardian are all in agreement that the incompetent patient's best interests are served by termination of life sustaining treatment."[395] An important rationale for and potential limitation on the holding was that a court had previously been involved in the appointment of a guardian.[396]

§ 5.38 Judicial Review Required in Specific Types of Cases

Although most courts have eschewed routine judicial review, a few have required routine review in specific types of cases. Of course, judicial review is appropriate in all jurisdictions under certain circumstances, but those are situational[397] rather than the categorical kinds of requirements discussed in this section.

§ 5.39 —District of Columbia: Pregnant Patients

In the case of *In re A.C.,* the patient was terminally ill and pregnant. She had previously agreed that her baby should be delivered through a cesarean section when she was 28 weeks' pregnant. However, at 26½ weeks, her condition took a serious turn for the worse, and the question arose whether a cesarean delivery should be performed at that time. The patient's competence was highly variable and uncertain, as were her wishes about the delivery. The trial court ordered that the delivery be performed; a stay was sought and denied; but a motion for an en banc rehearing was granted, with the court holding that if the patient is incompetent—that is, incapable of giving informed consent—"then the court

---

394 *In re* Colyer, 660 P.2d 738, 750 (Wash. 1983).

395 *In re* Hamlin, 689 P.2d 1372, 1378 (Wash. 1984).

396 *Id.*

397 See §§ **5.29–5.36.**

must make a substituted judgment."[398] In this statement, the court was clearly holding that the proper standard to be followed was substituted judgment.[399] It is far less clear, however, that the court was requiring that this standard be judicially applied in all cases. Rather it seems that the holding was intended to be confined to the facts of the case: namely, that when recourse to the courts *is* sought, the court is to apply the substituted judgment standard.

§ 5.40 —Florida: Blood Transfusions

The Florida courts have issued a series of path-breaking decisions in cases involving the refusal of blood transfusions by competent adult Jehovah's Witnesses who were the parents of minor children.[400] In previous cases, courts had usually been willing to state that in principle such patients had the right to refuse treatment, but sometimes found that in the circumstances of the case, the state's interest, such as the interest in the welfare of these minor children, outweighed the individual's right to decide.[401] The Florida courts, however, have refused to find the existence of dependent minor children to be an obstacle to the refusal of lifesaving treatment.

What has been unclear, however, is whether or not there must be recourse to the courts in such cases. *Wons v. Public Health Trust* seemed to require judicial approval to be obtained when a hospital was seeking to override a patient's refusal of treatment on the ground that the patient was the parent of a minor child. *Wons* also left the impression that the hospital is obligated to assert any state interest that might be supported by the facts, especially the abandonment of children. Finally, *Wons* seemed to place the burden on the hospital to institute judicial proceedings if it wished to contest a patient's refusal of treatment, rather than require the patient to go to court to establish his rights.[402] This appropriately respects the presumption of a patient's right to refuse treatment.

However, in the *Dubreuil* case, when actually faced with the questions about which parties bore what obligations, the court concluded that it is not proper for the hospital to assert the state's interest. The court reasoned, first, that a health care provider must respect a patient's wishes. The provider's role is to provide medical treatment and not to act as a "substitute parent." Unless ordered to do so by a court of competent jurisdiction, a health care provider must honor a

---

398 *In re* A.C., 573 A.2d 1235, 1247 (D.C. 1990).

399 See §§ **7.7–7.10.**

400 *See In re* Dubreuil, 629 So. 2d 819 (Fla. 1993); Wons v. Public Health Trust, 541 So. 2d 96 (Fla. 1989); St. Mary's Hosp. v. Ramsey, 465 So. 2d 666 (Fla. Dist. Ct. App. 1985).

401 See § **9.3.**

402 *See In re* Dubreuil, 629 So. 2d 819, 823 (Fla. 1993) (citing Wons v. Public Health Trust, 541 So. 2d at 98 ("[I]t will be necessary for hospitals that wish to contest a patient's refusal of treatment to commence court proceedings and sustain the heavy burden of proof that the state's interest outweighs the patient's constitutional rights.")).

patient's wishes to decline treatment.[403] (Although the court does not say so, a provider should also be entitled to override a refusal of treatment in an emergency in which the patient, unlike Mrs. Dubreuil, had not made a considered judgment to refuse treatment prior to the emergency.[404])

Second, if the health care provider is to question a competent patient's refusal of treatment, it potentially puts the provider in an awkward position between the patient and family members who may support or oppose the patient's position.[405] Third, the health care provider has a potential conflict of interest. Many times, the provider will be motivated primarily by its own interests—in avoiding adverse publicity, in preventing legal liability, in assuring payment for the services it renders—rather than the patient's.[406] Finally, the health care provider is a private entity, and therefore it is inappropriate for it to shoulder the state's burden of asserting its interests.[407] Taking these factors into consideration, the court concluded that the burden of asserting the state's interests, not surprisingly, is on the state.[408]

If a health care provider intends to override a patient's treatment refusal, it bears the responsibility for notifying the state attorney and interested parties, such as family members, who are known to it.[409] As long as the provider acts in good faith in following a patient's wishes, it "cannot be subjected to civil or criminal liability."[410]

The court did not explain what it meant by good faith in this context.[411] However, if there are doubts about whether the patient is competent or doubts about whether the patient has been adequately informed such that his decision

---

403 **FL:** *In re* Dubreuil, 629 So. 2d at 823.

NY: *Accord* Grace Plaza of Great Neck, Inc. v. Elbaum, 588 N.Y.S.2d 853 (App. Div. 1992) ("If facilities adopted the recalcitrant position that Grace Plaza did, it would, even without the participation of local prosecutors, require every family or patient to initiate suit in order to assert the wishes of the patient. Grace Plaza's position would compel patients and their families to wage courtroom combat as endless as the medical expenses to which such patients and families would be put, in seeking to overcome rigid or unyielding attitudes on the part of providers.").

404 See §§ **3.23, 10.22,** and **10.23.**

405 *In re* Dubreuil, 629 So. 2d at 823.

406 *Id.*

407 *Id.*

408 *Id.* ("Therefore, we recede from *Wons* to the extent that it may be read to put any burden of proof on the health care provider with respect to asserting the state interests.").

409 *Id.* at 824.

410 *Id.* at 823–24 ("When a health care provider, acting in good faith, follows the wishes of a competent and informed patient to refuse medical treatment, the health care provider is acting appropriately and cannot be subjected to civil or criminal liability.").

411 *But see* Browning v. Herbert, 543 So. 2d 258, 274 (Fla. Dist. Ct. App. 1989) (good faith in context of a surrogate making a decision for an incompetent patient means that "the decision was made with honesty of intention and in an honest effort to make the decision which the patient, if competent, would make").

meets the standards for informed consent (even though a refusal), this is probably not acting in good faith. A health care provider should not sit idly by whenever a patient refuses treatment. Under some circumstances—such as when the patient's decisionmaking capacity is in question—a health care provider might be obligated to take action and the failure to do so might be the basis for negligence liability. Furthermore, the patient's decision to refuse treatment must be based on adequate, relevant information.

The state attorney has the discretion in each case to decide whether or not to proceed with litigation in an attempt to override a competent patient's refusal. The court observed that "[t]his procedure should eliminate needless litigation by health care providers while honoring the patient's wishes and giving other interested parties the right to intervene if there is a good faith reason to do so."[412]

In many cases of an urgent nature when competent patients refuse lifesaving medical treatment, health care providers seek ex parte hearings. The New York Court of Appeals[413] and the District of Columbia Court of Appeals[414] have both roundly condemned this practice.[415] The Florida Supreme Court did not expressly address this practice but cited this aspect of the New York decision approvingly.[416]

§ 5.41 —Illinois: Artificial Nutrition and Hydration; Minors

In two successive decisions in less than a year, the Illinois Supreme Court, while not holding that judicial review of decisions to forgo life-sustaining treatment is always required, imposed a requirement of judicial review when the treatment at issue is artificial nutrition and hydration.[417] In *Longeway,* the court explained that judicial "intervention" is necessary for the forgoing of artificial nutrition and hydration for three reasons:

> First, Illinois has a strong public policy of preserving the sanctity of human life, even if in an imperfect state. . . . Because we agree that a presumption exists favoring life, we find that scrutiny by a judge is appropriate in these cases. . . .

---

[412] *In re* Dubreuil, 629 So. 2d 819, 824 (Fla. 1993).

[413] *See* Fosmire v. Nicoleau, 551 N.E.2d 77 (N.Y. 1990).

[414] *See In re* A.C., 573 A.2d 1235 (D.C. 1990).

[415] See **§ 9.3.**

[416] *See In re* Dubreuil, 629 So. 2d at 828 ("trial court erred by signing ex parte order compelling blood transfusion without giving patient or her husband notice and the opportunity to be heard even though only three hours lapsed between making the application and signing of the order, and an additional six hours before the order was executed") (citing Fosmire v. Nicoleau, 551 N.E.2d 77 (N.Y. 1990)).

[417] *See In re* Estate of Greenspan, 558 N.E.2d 1194 (Ill. 1990); Estate of Longeway v. Community Convalescent Ctr., 549 N.E.2d 292 (Ill. 1989).

> Second, court intervention is necessary to guard against the remote, yet real possibility that greed may taint the judgment of the surrogate decisionmaker. . . .
>
> Third, the courts have a *parens patriae* power which enables them to protect the estate and person of incompetents. [Citations omitted.] Moreover, if the surrogate decisionmaker is a court-appointed guardian, procedural due process questions involving deprivation of life may arise. (U.S. Const., amend. XIV; Ill. Const. 1970, art, 1, § 2.) Although it is uncertain whether sufficient State action is present to invoke the protections of procedural due process, utilizing a court to oversee the guardian's decision as to the termination of artificial nutrition and hydration will forestall any potential constitutional infirmities.[418]

For artificial nutrition and hydration to be forgone, the court must find that

> (1) the incompetent is terminally ill as deemed in section 2(h) of the Illinois Living Will Act [citation omitted], *i.e.,* the patient's condition is incurable and irreversible so that death is imminent and the application of death-delaying procedures serves only to prolong the dying process;
>
> (2) the incompetent has been diagnosed as irreversibly comatose or in a persistently vegetative state;
>
> (3) the incompetent's attending physician and at least two other consulting physicians have concurred in the diagnosis;
>
> (4) the incompetent's right outweighs any interests of the State, as it normally does;
>
> (5) it is ascertained, by an appropriate means—e.g., by the procedure of substituted judgment on the basis of clear and convincing evidence as outlined in *Longeway*—what the incompetent presumably would have decided, if competent, in the circumstances; and
>
> (6) a court enters an order allowing the surrogate to exercise the incompetent's right to refuse the treatment.[419]

If artificial nutrition and hydration is the functional equivalent of other forms of life-sustaining treatment as most courts have held that it is[420] and it is permissible to remove them without judicial review, it is difficult to understand why a different rule should pertain to the forgoing of artificial nutrition and hydration. Indeed, if a majority of justices of the Supreme Court believe that artificial nutrition and hydration is no different from other forms of life-sustaining treatment,[421] requiring judicial review for the forgoing of artificial nutrition and hydration might violate equal protection.

---

[418] Estate of Longeway v. Community Convalescent Ctr., 549 N.E.2d at 300.

[419] *In re* Estate of Greenspan, 558 N.E.2d at 1201.

[420] See §§ **9.39–9.40.**

[421] **US:** *See* Cruzan v. Director, 497 U.S. 261 (1990).

Minors

In the case of termination of life support from a minor patient, the Illinois court invoked similar, though more limited rationales for requiring judicial review—namely, the "sanctity of life" and the parens patriae power of the state to protect persons incompetent to protect themselves.[422] These two factors must be weighed by the trial judge against evidence of the minor's maturity—specifically, "that the minor is mature enough to appreciate the consequences of her actions, and that the minor is mature enough to exercise the judgment of an adult."[423] This is a strange weighing process, and it seems clear from the holding that a court is to honor the minor's decision if it finds by clear and convincing evidence that the minor is mature as defined above. The state's interests are not weighed against these factors; rather they are considerations that require judicial review.

§ 5.42 —Nevada: Competent Nonterminally Ill Patients

The Nevada Supreme Court requires judicial review of a decision to forgo life-sustaining treatment by a competent patient if the patient is not terminally ill (that is, will survive in excess of six months with or without treatment).[424] The purpose of the judicial review is to weigh the state's interests against those of the patient. If the trial court rules in favor of the patient's right to refuse treatment, the decision is not appealable, and if the court rules against the patient's right to refuse treatment, the patient is entitled to expedited appellate review.[425] When life support is terminated in this manner, there is civil and criminal immunity for health care providers who act in good faith.[426]

§ 5.43 —New Jersey: Institutionalized Never-Competent Patient

In the case of an institutionalized, never-competent patient, a New Jersey intermediate appellate court held that in order to forgo life-sustaining treatment

---

[422] *In re* E.G., 549 N.E.2d 322, 327 (Ill. 1989).

[423] *Id.* at 327–28.

[424] McKay v. Bergstedt, 801 P.2d 617 (Nev. 1990) (court declined to rule on procedures to be followed in the case of incompetent patients).

[425] *Id.* at 630–31.

[426] *Id.* at 630 n.6.

there must first be concurrence among the patient's family, attending physician, prognosis committee, and two independent neurologists. If they agree that life support should be terminated, the public guardian must be notified. If the public guardian concurs in this determination, judicial review need not be sought. However, if the public guardian or any of the other parties to the decisionmaking process opposes the termination of life support, judicial approval must be obtained.[427]

§ 5.44 —Washington: Amputation

The Washington Supreme Court held that a court-appointed guardian's decision to forgo treatment must be judicially reviewed when the treatment is a laryngectomy, because such an operation is an "amputation" and Washington has a statutory requirement for review in cases of amputations.[428]

PROS AND CONS OF CLINICAL VERSUS JUDICIAL DECISIONMAKING

§ 5.45 In General

The clinical approach takes many forms depending primarily on how decisionmaking capacity is assessed, how surrogates are designated, whether there is any review of decisions about life-sustaining treatment, and if so what form that review takes. Consequently, the advantages and disadvantages of the clinical approach can vary substantially depending on the health care institution and the jurisdiction. For example, in health care institutions with ethics committees, the value of the clinical approach depends heavily on the manner in which the particular committee functions,[429] and some health care institutions (especially long-term care facilities) do not have ethics committees.

The disinterested nature of judicial oversight of the decisionmaking process can theoretically provide important protections against improper decisionmaking, such as the use of incorrect standards for surrogate decisionmaking. It is the business of courts to protect individual rights.

Courts can assure that all viewpoints and alternatives will be aggressively pursued.[430] This will protect the interests of physicians, health care institutions,

---

427 *In re* Moorhouse, 593 A.2d 1256 (N.J. Super. Ct. App. Div. 1991).

428 *In re* Ingram, 689 P.2d 1363, 1369 (Wash. 1984) (citing Wash. Rev. Code Ann. § 11.92.040(3)(c)).

429 See **Ch. 6.**

430 **MA:** Superintendent of Belchertown State Sch. v. Saikewicz, 370 N.E.2d 417, 433–34 (Mass. 1977).

patients, families, and the state.[431] One of the virtues of courts is that they are detached, neutral, and disinterested decisionmakers. This permits them to "objectively weigh the competing interests in an emotionally charged situation."[432] Courts are also able to protect against surrogates who might act on less than worthy motives such as "an interest in the incompetent's estate or a desire to alleviate the financial burden of the life sustaining treatment."[433] Also of great importance is assurance that decisions about life-sustaining treatment, especially decisions to forgo it, are not made precipitously.[434] Both courts and nonjudicial mechanisms should be able to protect against unduly hasty decisions.[435]

Despite the protections provided by courts, most courts have concluded that there should be a presumption in favor of the clinical approach. As a Florida court observed, "Until we see evidence of some abuse by an informal forum, we believe that its advantages outweigh its disadvantages."[436] Judicial review of decisions to forgo life-sustaining treatment is not necessary on a routine basis to protect either the state's or a patient's interests.[437] No court has agreed with the Massachusetts Supreme Judicial Court that

---

[431] **OH:** Estate of Leach v. Shapiro, 469 N.E.2d 1047, 1053–54 (Ohio Ct. App. 1984).

[432] **OH:** Estate of Leach v. Shapiro, 469 N.E.2d at 1053–54.

NY: *Accord* Eichner v. Dillon, 426 N.Y.S.2d 517, 550 (App. Div. 1980), *modified,* 420 N.E.2d 64 (N.Y. 1981).

[433] **WA:** *In re* Colyer, 660 P.2d 738, 747 (Wash. 1983) (recognizing the possibility but nonetheless rejecting judicial review).

MD: *Accord* 73 Md. Op. Att'y Gen. 253, 291 (Op. No. 88-046, Oct. 17, 1988) ("possibility that a family's decision to refuse . . . artificially administered sustenance might be the product of selfish or other wrong motives").

[434] **NJ:** *In re* Farrell, 529 A.2d 404, 415 (N.J. 1987).

WA: *In re* Colyer, 660 P.2d 738, 747 (Wash. 1983).

[435] **FL:** Browning v. Herbert, 543 So. 2d 258 (Fla. Dist. Ct. App. 1989), *aff'd,* 568 So. 2d 4 (Fla. 1990).

NJ: *In re* Farrell, 529 A.2d 404, 415 (N.J. 1987) (two independent confirmations of competence by medical experts can forestall hasty medical decisions).

[436] *See* Browning v. Herbert, 543 So. 2d 258, 271 (Fla. Dist. Ct. App. 1989), *aff'd,* 568 So. 2d 4 (Fla. 1990).

[437] **DNY:** *E.g., In re* Deel, 729 F. Supp. 231, 234 (N.D.N.Y. 1990) (Although the hospital's "concern . . . that proper consideration is given to Mr. Deel's circumstances before his request to have the life-support system removed is granted . . . is commendable, . . . the [hospital] need not obtain a court order to accede to Mr. Deel's wishes. His right to refuse the continuation of life-sustaining medical treatment is well-recognized.").

FL: *E.g.,* John F. Kennedy Memorial Hosp. v. Bludworth, 452 So. 2d 921, 924–25 (Fla. 1984).

GA: *E.g., In re* L.H.R., 321 S.E.2d 716, 723 (Ga. 1984) ("While the state has an interest in the prolongation of life, the state has no interest in the prolongation of dying, and although there is a moral and ethical decision to be made to end the process, that decision can only be made by the surrogate.").

See §§ **5.26–5.27.**

> questions of life and death . . . require the process of detached but passionate investigation and decision that forms the ideal on which the judicial branch of government was created. Achieving this ideal is our responsibility and that of the lower court, and is not to be entrusted to any other group purporting to represent the "morality and conscience of our society," no matter how highly motivated or impressively constituted.[438]

In fact, the Massachusetts court has quietly abandoned a routine requirement of judicial involvement in all three of the legal stages of the decisionmaking process.[439]

Although not speaking directly to the issue of judicial participation in decision-making about life-sustaining treatment, the Supreme Court has recognized that "[a] State is entitled to guard against potential abuses"[440] such as situations in which incompetent patients do not have family members to serve as surrogates. The reason for this is that "[t]he choice between life and death is a deeply personal decision of obvious and overwhelming finality."[441] "And even where family members are present, '[t]here will, of course, be some unfortunate situations in which family members will not act to protect a patient.'"[442] However, as Justice Brennan recognized, "the decision to come forward to request a judicial order to stop treatment represents a slowly and carefully considered resolution by at least one adult and more frequently several adults that discontinuation of treatment is the patient's wish,"[443] and therefore recourse should not be routine.

However, judicial proceedings, especially at the trial level, are sometimes as informal and nonadversarial as decisionmaking in the clinical setting.[444] Another problem is that judges sometimes do not understand the law in their jurisdiction, or there is no law in their jurisdiction and they have difficulty discerning the larger national trends. There are other drawbacks associated with end-of-life decisionmaking in the courts. The most serious are delay and invasion of privacy, which can take an additional toll in emotional and physical burdens on the patient, the family, and the health care team.

---

[438] Superintendent of Belchertown State Sch. v. Saikewicz, 370 N.E.2d 417, 434 (Mass. 1977).

[439] See **§ 5.37.**

[440] Cruzan v. Director, 497 U.S. 261, 281 (1990).

[441] *Id.*

[442] *Id.* (quoting *In re* Jobes, 529 A.2d 434, 477 (N.J. 1987)).

[443] **US:** Cruzan v. Director, 497 U.S. at 318 (Brennan, J., dissenting).

WA: *Accord In re* Colyer, 660 P.2d 738, 746 (Wash. 1983) ("[T]he formalities of a legal determination might chill a guardian's resolve to assert the rights of his ward.").

[444] Cruzan v. Director, 497 U.S. at 262 ("[A] State is entitled to consider that a judicial proceeding to make a determination regarding an incompetent's wishes may very well not be an adversarial one, with the added guarantee of accurate factfinding that the adversary process brings with it."). *But compare id.* at 318 (Brennan, J., dissenting) ("[A]ny concern that those who come forward will present a one-sided view would be better addressed by appointing a guardian ad litem, who could use the State's powers of discovery to gather and present evidence regarding the patient's wishes.").

By contrast, the clinical approach is relatively expeditious and, consequently, imposes lesser burdens on the participants in the decisionmaking process. However, the clinical approach is not entirely cost-free. The major concern about end-of-life decisionmaking in the clinical setting is that in most health care institutions, there is no established structure for review of such decisions by disinterested individuals, even employees of the institution who are not involved in the care of the particular patient. The possibility of tacit collusion to ignore established rules of law—such as whether there is clear and convincing evidence to meet the substantive standard for forgoing life-sustaining treatment—is omnipresent and difficult to discern precisely because of the absence of routine disinterested review.

Until recently, one of the drawbacks of using the clinical approach was uncertainty about its legitimacy. Widespread judicial approval of the clinical tradition of assessing patients' competence and of collaborating with family members of incompetent patients to make decisions for them has caused this uncertainty to diminish or even to disappear. This is certainly the case in those jurisdictions that have definitive appellate right-to-die cases. However, because the consensus is so strong, there should be far greater certainty about the legality of relying on the clinical approach even in those jurisdictions that have no precedential case law.

§ 5.46 Protection Against Abuse

The objectives of the clinical and judicial approaches are in a general way the same: to protect patients from abuse resulting from incorrect decisions. This is accomplished by ensuring that legally accepted standards are employed in the decisionmaking process. A decision is usually thought to be abusive if it results in the improper forgoing of life-sustaining treatment, but abuse can also occur when unwanted treatment *is* provided.[445]

From a substantive perspective, the propriety of a decision about life-sustaining treatment for an *incompetent* patient is dependent, first, on the application of the correct standard for surrogate decisionmaking.[446] Assuming that has occurred, the propriety of a decision then depends on whether there are one or more countervailing state interests strong enough to overcome the decision[447] or whether there is some other consideration determining whether the decision is legitimate, such as whether it involves active or passive means of ending life.[448]

---

[445] **MA:** *In re* Dinnerstein, 380 N.E.2d 134, 137 (Mass. App. Ct. 1978) ("[T]he *Saikewicz* case, if read to apply to the natural death of a terminally ill patient by cardiac or respiratory arrest, would require attempts to resuscitate dying patients in most cases, without exercise of medical judgment, even when that course of action could aptly be characterized as a pointless, even cruel, prolongation of the act of dying.").

[446] See **Ch. 7.**

[447] See **Ch. 8.**

[448] See **Ch. 18.**

Protection from improper decisions about life-sustaining treatment also requires procedural protections.[449] From a procedural perspective, a decision about life-sustaining treatment is proper if adequate safeguards exist to ensure that the decision is substantively appropriate, that the decision is made on the basis of reliable evidence, that the weight of the evidence is sufficient to meet the appropriate standard of proof, that a mechanism for review is available, and that the procedures are adequate to detect improper motives on the part of the participants in the decisionmaking process.[450]

Another important consideration in determining whether a decision about life-sustaining treatment is legitimate is whether each of the three legal stages of the decisionmaking process—determination of incompetency, designation of a surrogate, and review of a decision—has proceeded properly. A decision should be considered improper if any one or more of these stages is inadequate or has not proceeded fairly.

§ 5.47 Speed and Convenience

An important consideration is the speed with which decisions can be made. The judicial approach almost invariably interjects significant delay into the

---

[449] **IN:** *In re* Lawrance, 579 N.E.2d 32, 42 (Ind. 1991) ("We expect the first line of defense against abuses in withdrawal of treatment to be the ethical guidelines of the medical profession. . . . Health care providers involved in withdrawal of treatment decisions are also likely to act very conservatively in light of the external constraints on their professional conduct" such as state and federal licensing regulations, adult and child protective services statutes and regulations, and criminal sanctions.).

MO: *Cf.* Cruzan v. Harmon, 760 S.W.2d 408, 425 (Mo. 1988) ("It is logically inconsistent to claim that rights which are found lurking in the shadow of the Bill of Rights and which spring from concerns for personal autonomy can be exercised by another absent the most rigid of formalities.").

WA: *In re* Hamlin, 689 P.2d 1372, 1378 (Wash. 1984) ("We are convinced that the remaining procedural safeguards surrounding this decision will adequately protect against abuse.").

[450] **MD:** Mack v. Mack, 618 A.2d 744, 770–71 (Md. 1993) (Chasanow, J., concurring and dissenting):

> There is, of course, the danger that uncaring selfish family members will be motivated by a desire to get rid of incompetent relatives who are unwanted and burdensome. The safeguard in this situation will be that health care providers probably will not concur and should require court approval if they believe the family is not really acting in good faith and in accord with the patient's probable views. In addition, Maryland statutes require all hospitals to have Patient Care Advisory Committees, sometimes called "Ethics Committees." Md. Code (1982, 1990 Repl. Vol., 1992 Cum. Supp.), Health-General Art., §§ 19-370 to 19-374. . . . These committees could review a family's request to withdraw life-sustaining medical treatments for a patient if there is any question about whether the request is appropriate or made in bad faith.

NJ: *Cf. In re* Jobes, 529 A.2d 434, 447 (N.J. 1987) (In "exceptional" circumstances when "family members [do] not act to protect a patient," health care professionals should not permit the termination of treatment without the judicial appointment of a guardian.).

WA: *In re* Colyer, 660 P.2d 738, 747 (Wash. 1983).

decisionmaking process.[451] The clinical approach is generally, but not always, more expeditious, and speed is sometimes a mixed blessing.[452]

The clinical approach operates far more simply than the judicial approach. Courts have frequently characterized the judicial approach as cumbersome,[453] involving substantial inconvenience and delay to all parties involved.[454] Even assuming that there may not be appellate review, the delay introduced into decisionmaking by trial court proceedings alone can be considerable.

Although it is important to guard against precipitous decisions,[455] delay can nullify the right of an incompetent patient,[456] for in the meantime the patient

---

451 **IL:** C.A. v. Morgan, 603 N.E.2d 1171, 1184 (Ill. App. Ct. 1992) ("[T]ime is often a major factor. . . . Unfortunately, the proceedings below and the appeals process has already added months of uncertainty to an unfortunate situation.").

NJ: *In re* Farrell, 529 A.2d 404, 415 (N.J. 1987) ("No matter how expedited, judicial intervention in this complex and sensitive area may take too long. . . . The mere prospect of a cumbersome, intrusive, and expensive court proceeding during such an emotional and upsetting period in the lives of a patient and his or her loved ones would undoubtedly deter many persons from deciding to discontinue treatment."); *In re* Jobes, 529 A.2d 434, 449 (N.J. 1987).

NY: *In re* Storar, 420 N.E.2d 64, 75 (N.Y. 1981) (Jones, J., dissenting).

452 **IL:** *See* Estate of Longeway v. Community Convalescent Ctr., 549 N.E.2d 292, 301 (Ill. 1989) ("The slow, deliberate nature of the court system may frustrate the family and loved ones of the patient. Although we feel that the courts can act expeditiously in clear-cut uncontested cases, we acknowledge these objections and the difficulty in reaching a balanced approach to this dilemma.").

453 **AZ:** Rasmussen v. Fleming, 741 P.2d 674, 691 (Ariz. 1987).

CA: Barber v. Superior Court, 195 Cal. Rptr. 484, 493 (Ct. App. 1983).

FL: John F. Kennedy Memorial Hosp. v. Bludworth, 452 So. 2d 921, 924–25 (Fla. 1984). *Contra* Browning v. Herbert, 543 So. 2d 258, 270 (Fla. Dist. Ct. App. 1989), *aff'd,* 568 So. 2d 4, 15 (Fla. 1990) ("In this state, the appointment of a legal guardian for a severely ill individual is neither cumbersome nor overly time-consuming.").

NJ: *In re* Farrell, 529 A.2d 404, 415 (N.J. 1987) ("Too many patients have died before their right to reject treatment was vindicated in court."); *In re* Quinlan, 355 A.2d 647, 669 (N.J. 1976).

NY: *In re* Storar, 420 N.E.2d 64, 75 (N.Y. 1981) (Jones, J., dissenting).

WA: *In re* Grant, 747 P.2d 445 (Wash. 1987), *modified,* 757 P.2d 534 (Wash. 1988); *In re* Hamlin, 689 P.2d 1372, 1377 (Wash. 1984); *In re* Colyer, 660 P.2d 738, 746 (Wash. 1983).

WI: L.W. v. L.E. Phillips Career Dev. Ctr., 482 N.W.2d 60, 75 (Wis. 1992).

454 **NY:** *In re* Storar, 420 N.E.2d 64, 75 (N.Y. 1981) (Jones, J., dissenting) ("The lapse of time necessarily consumed in appellate review before there can be a final judicial determination will almost always be unacceptable and makes recourse to judicial proceedings impractical.").

WA: *In re* Colyer, 660 P.2d 738, 746 (Wash. 1983).

455 **WA:** *In re* Grant, 747 P.2d 445, 458 (Wash. 1987), *modified,* 757 P.2d 534 (Wash. 1988) (Andersen, J., concurring and dissenting) (citing Siegler & Weisbard, *Against the Emerging Stream: Should Fluids and Nutritional Support Be Discontinued?,* 145 Archives Internal Med. 129 (1985)); *In re* Hamlin, 689 P.2d 1372, 1381 (Wash. 1984) (Rosellini, J., dissenting) ("[T]he majority's decision to circumvent court-appointed guardian proceedings negates the safeguards inherent in the guardian statutes."); *In re* Colyer, 660 P.2d 738, 747 (Wash. 1983).

456 **FL:** Browning v. Herbert, 543 So. 2d 258, 269 (Fla. Dist. Ct. App. 1989), *aff'd,* 568 So. 2d 4 (Fla. 1990) ("[I]t is important that the decision be prompt."); John F. Kennedy Memorial Hosp. v. Bludworth, 452 So. 2d 921, 924–25 (Fla. 1984).

might die of natural causes, possibly with added pain, suffering, and expense to the patient and others if the time involved to obtain judicial review is excessive. The New Jersey Supreme Court has observed that "[n]o matter how expedited, judicial intervention in this complex and sensitive area may take too long. Thus, it could infringe the very rights that we want to protect."[457] The Nevada Supreme Court similarly commented that "if the process involved in validating a patient's election to refuse or terminate medical treatment is unduly protracted, the patient's rights become hollow and meaningless, if not entirely ineffectual."[458] And in fact, most reported right-to-die cases have seen the patient die before final adjudication could be obtained.[459]

If decisionmaking capacity could be assessed, a surrogate designated, and review obtained only through the judicial process, participants in the decisionmaking process would have an incentive to evade these burdensome and intrusive requirements or to avoid making decisions that they otherwise would have made, which is ultimately to the detriment of patients and families, health care professionals, and institutions.[460] Because these matters can more conveniently and expeditiously be handled in the clinical setting, it is more likely that they will in fact occur than if recourse must be had to the courts. If resort to the courts is necessary, it may increase the likelihood that treatment will be continued even if patients and families object.

Although the delays involved in judicial decisionmaking in general are legion, there are statutory or customary procedures in most jurisdictions for

---

[457] *In re* Jobes, 529 A.2d 434, 449 (N.J. 1987).

[458] McKay v. Bergstedt, 801 P.2d 617, 629 (Nev. 1990).

[459] **AZ:** *E.g.,* Rasmussen v. Fleming, 741 P.2d 674, 680 (Ariz. 1987).

CA: *E.g.,* Bartling v. Superior Court, 209 Cal. Rptr. 220 (Ct. App. 1984).

FL: *E.g.,* Browning v. Herbert, 543 So. 2d 258, 269 (Fla. Dist. Ct. App. 1989), *aff'd,* 568 So. 2d 4 (Fla. 1990) ("The list of cases in which courts 'grant' a right of privacy only after the patient has expired, grows longer every day."); John F. Kennedy Memorial Hosp. v. Bludworth, 452 So. 2d 921 (Fla. 1984); Satz v. Perlmutter, 362 So. 2d 160 (Fla. Dist. Ct. App. 1978); Corbett v. D'Alessandro, 487 So. 2d 368, 369 (Fla. Dist. Ct. App.), *review denied,* 492 So. 2d 1331 (Fla. 1986).

GA: *E.g., In re* Doe, 418 S.E.2d 3 (Ga. 1992); *In re* L.H.R., 321 S.E.2d 716 (Ga. 1984).

IN: *E.g., In re* Lawrance, 579 N.E.2d 32 (Ind. 1991).

MD: *E.g., In re* Riddlemoser, 564 A.2d 812 (Md. 1989).

MA: *E.g., In re* Spring, 405 N.E.2d 115 (Mass. 1980); Superintendent of Belchertown State Sch. v. Saikewicz, 370 N.E.2d 417, 422 (Mass. 1977).

NJ: *E.g., In re* Jobes, 529 A.2d 434, 449 (N.J. 1987) (citing *In re* Conroy, 486 A.2d 1209 (N.J. 1985)).

NY: *E.g., In re* Storar, 420 N.E.2d 64 (N.Y. 1981).

WA: *E.g., In re* Hamlin, 689 P.2d 1372, 1374 (Wash. 1984).

WI: *E.g.,* L.W. v. L.E. Phillips Career Dev. Ctr., 482 N.W.2d 60 (Wis. 1992).

[460] **NJ:** *In re* Jobes, 529 A.2d 434, 449 (N.J. 1987).

WA: *In re* Colyer, 660 P.2d 738, 746 (Wash. 1983) ("[T]he formalities of a legal determination might chill a [surrogate's] resolve to assert the rights of his ward.").

rapid, emergency access to the courts. However, although they may be useful in preventing an irreversible situation—usually the forgoing of treatment, almost certainly leading to the patient's death—decisionmaking about life-sustaining treatment generally involves questions complex enough that summary judicial procedures are inappropriate and therefore of limited practical usefulness.

§ 5.48 Access to Experts

Certain aspects of the decisionmaking process, such as assessment of decision-making capacity and confirmation of diagnosis and prognosis, usually necessitate the use of experts, such as neurologists, psychiatrists, and psychologists, or others, depending on the patient's condition. Experts are often available in hospitals and are accustomed to performing such evaluations; this is less likely to be the case in nursing homes, although they can usually be obtained from another health care institution with little difficulty.

When the clinical approach is used, the cooperation of both intra- and extra-institutional experts generally poses little difficulty. By contrast, the judicial approach can create a logistical nightmare in the simplest of cases. Consequently, experts might be more reluctant to participate in a judicial proceeding than in an institutionally based process.

§ 5.49 Instituting Litigation

A significant stumbling block to the operation of the judicial approach is finding someone to institute judicial proceedings. Physicians are often reluctant to undertake this task, and health care administrators are often no more willing to do so nor to commit a clinical employee such as a nurse or a social worker to the task. To some extent, this resistance results from the financial costs associated with the judicial proceeding. Additionally, physicians and health care administrators believe that it is their proper role to provide treatment but not to initiate legal proceedings. Some may even view the initiation of such proceedings as creating a conflict of interest for the physician or institution, at least when the patient, though of dubious competence, still has the ability to object to treatment.

The Florida Supreme Court ruled in *In re Dubreuil*[461] that it is not a hospital's responsibility to initiate judicial proceedings to determine the legitimacy of a competent patient's objection to lifesaving treatment. If a competent patient's objection is to be overruled, it must be because of a countervailing state interest. Thus, if it is anyone's responsibility to initiate judicial proceedings, it is the responsibility of the *state,* not the hospital, to do so.

The court asserted four reasons for its conclusion. First, "[p]atients do not lose their right to make decisions affecting their lives simply by entering a health

---

[461] 629 So. 2d 819 (Fla. 1993).

care facility. Despite concededly good intentions, a health care provider's function is to provide medical treatment in accordance with the patient's wishes and best interests, not as a 'substitute parent' supervening the wishes of a competent adult."[462] Second, requiring the hospital to initiate judicial proceedings puts it in the "awkward position of having to argue zealously against the wishes of its own patient, seeking deference to the wishes or interests of nonpatients [such as the patient's family] . . . and the State itself."[463] Third, the hospital may have a conflict between its interest in protecting itself from liability and protection of the patient's right of self-determination. Finally, it is inappropriate to impose a public burden on a private entity.

Consequently, the court concluded that if a health care provider believes that a refusal of treatment should be overridden, its responsibility is to inform the state attorney, who then has the discretion to initiate proceedings. "This procedure should eliminate needless litigation by health care providers while honoring the patient's wishes and giving other interested parties the right to intervene."[464] If the health care provider acts in good faith in honoring a competent patient's decision, it is immune from liability.[465] Although the court's holding applies specifically to competent patients, similar arguments can be applied to incompetent patients, or at least those incompetent patients whose wishes are established. However, an institutional policy, formal or informal, against initiating judicial proceedings could give rise to liability if it were to result in undue delay in the decisionmaking process.[466]

Families are often equally reluctant to initiate judicial proceedings. The primary source of reluctance is the serious burdens the patient's illness has placed on the family, such as the physical and emotional strain of caring for, being concerned about, and visiting a seriously ill loved one. This is further compounded by unfamiliarity with the legal system and the financial cost of litigation.

In cases in which all participants are reluctant to institute judicial proceedings, a great deal of time and energy can be consumed in the attempt by health care personnel, family members, and friends to find someone else willing to do so.

---

[462] *In re* Dubreuil, 629 So. 2d at 823.

[463] *Id.*

[464] *Id.* at 824.

[465] *Id.* at 823–24. See § **17.24.**

[466] **NJ:** *Cf.* Strachan v. John F. Kennedy Memorial Hosp., 538 A.2d 346 (N.J. 1988) (hospital liable for emotional distress resulting from delay in disconnecting life support from brain dead patient); McVey v. Englewood Hosp. Ass'n, 524 A.2d 450 (N.J. Super. Ct. App. Div.), *cert. denied,* 528 A.2d 12 (N.J. 1987) (hospital and physicians not liable for not discontinuing ventilator without expeditiously obtaining judicial appointment of a guardian).

OH: *Cf.* Estate of Leach v. Shapiro, 469 N.E.2d 1047 (Ohio Ct. App. 1984) (complaint states cause of action for unreasonable delay in effectuating judicial order to discontinue life support).

See §§ **17.5–17.7.**

§ 5.50 Financial Costs

The clinical approach entails minimal, if any, financial costs for most of the participants. There may be some out-of-pocket costs such as consultants' fees, though these might be reimbursed by third-party payers, but there are no analogues to the costs ordinarily associated with litigation.

By contrast, judicial proceedings involve sometimes considerable financial expense.[467] Ordinarily, both the petitioner and the respondent need to be represented by counsel. Expert witness fees and court costs are likely to be incurred. Because a court case is likely to involve a delay that would not occur in a clinical approach, other costs can be incurred. To the extent that the delay results in longer hospitalization, there will be additional medical expenses.

§ 5.51 Physical and Emotional Burdens

Delay in the decisionmaking process can impose additional burdens on patients in the form of physical pain,[468] and on patients[469] and/or families[470] in terms of emotional suffering. Health care professionals, too, are not immune from the emotional stress caused by attending patients who are enduring great suffering that will be relieved only by death.[471] Demoralization can also result from not being permitted to treat patients who are being denied treatment by their own or a surrogate's refusal to consent. The relative rapidity of the clinical approach can reduce these burdens.

§ 5.52 Willingness to Participate in Decisionmaking

For the same reasons that families have an aversion to instituting litigation, they may be more willing to serve as a surrogate if they are clinically designated rather than judicially appointed.[472] Court-appointed guardians are more likely to

---

[467] **KY:** DeGrella v. Elston, 858 S.W.2d 698, 710 (Ky. 1993) ("expensive and intrusive").

WA: *In re* Hamlin, 689 P.2d 1372, 1377 (Wash. 1984) ("cumbersomeness and costs of legal guardianship proceedings").

[468] *E.g.,* Bouvia v. Superior Court (Glenchur), 225 Cal. Rptr. 297 (Ct. App. 1986).

[469] **FL:** *E.g.,* Satz v. Perlmutter, 379 So. 2d 359 (Fla. 1980).

GA: *E.g.,* State v. McAfee, 385 S.E.2d 651 (Ga. 1989).

NV: *E.g.,* McKay v. Bergstedt, 801 P.2d 617 (Nev. 1990).

[470] **MA:** *In re* Spring, 405 N.E.2d 115, 123 (Mass. 1980) ("a fearful strain was imposed upon" patient's family and health care professionals).

[471] *See, e.g.,* Warthen v. Toms River Community Memorial Hosp., 488 A.2d 229 (N.J. Super. Ct. App. Div.), *cert. denied,* 501 A.2d 296 (N.J. 1985).

[472] **FL:** Browning v. Herbert, 543 So. 2d 258, 271 (Fla. Dist. Ct. App. 1989), aff'd, 568 So. 2d 4 (Fla. 1990) ("the informal forum may encourage greater openness by doctors, nurses, and family members").

have to account, and to account publicly, for their decisions than clinically designated surrogates, which is one of the virtues of the judicial approach, though it will often not be viewed as such by potential surrogates.

If there is a great deal of difficulty in finding some appropriate person to serve as guardian,[473] there will be delay and its attendant problems. In some cases this may even lead to a stalemate in the decisionmaking process, with clinical personnel insisting on the continuation of treatment that even they do not believe to be medically appropriate without the permission of a guardian or a court order.

§ 5.53 Disruption of Health Care

The routine use of the judicial approach to decisionmaking about life-sustaining treatment could "disrupt the work of doctors in ways that will detrimentally affect the treatment given to patients generally."[474] Certainly, the judicial approach does require the attending physician and possibly health care administrators and other members of the health care team to take time away from their usual functions to participate in judicial proceedings. However, the clinical approach does also. On balance, however, procedures in the clinical context are inherently less disruptive because of their characteristics of convenience, less formality, and speed; and because they are more familiar and less intimidating to health care professionals, they are more likely to elicit their prompt participation.

§ 5.54 Respect for Privacy

Decisionmaking about life-sustaining treatment is a complex and sensitive matter involving very personal considerations.[475] It always occurs during "an emotional and upsetting period in the lives of a patient and his or her loved ones."[476] Consequently, many believe that courts are "unsuited and ill-equipped to solve" these problems,[477] though not all agree.

---

[473] See § **5.22.**

[474] *In re* Colyer, 660 P.2d 738, 745 (Wash. 1983) (citing Relman, *The* Saikewicz *Decision: Judges as Physicians,* 298 New Eng. J. Med. 508 (1978)).

[475] **CA:** Morrison v. Abramovice, 253 Cal. Rptr. 530, 535 (Ct. App. 1988) (referring to decision-making about life-sustaining treatment as an "intimate struggle").

NY: *In re* Storar, 434 N.Y.S.2d 46, 47 (App. Div. 1980) (Cardamone, J., dissenting) (these decisions are "too personal to extend beyond the decision of the family or guardian guided by the medical advice available."), *rev'd,* 420 N.E.2d 64 (N.Y.), *cert. denied,* 454 U.S. 858 (1981).

[476] *In re* Farrell, 529 A.2d 404, 415 (N.J. 1987).

[477] **NY:** *In re* Storar, 420 N.E.2d 64, 75 (N.Y. 1981) (Jones, J., dissenting).

CA: *Accord* Morrison v. Abramovice, 253 Cal. Rptr. 530 (Ct. App. 1988).

FL: *Accord* Browning v. Herbert, 543 So. 2d 258 (Fla. Dist. Ct. App. 1989), *aff'd,* 568 So. 2d 4 (Fla. 1990).

The more that decisionmaking occurs within the confines of the health care institution (or the patient's home[478]), the less likely there will be any publicity and intrusion on the privacy of the patient and family. The clinical approach allows decisionmaking to be conducted as part of the normal flow of medical practice and, consequently, respects the privacy of patients and families to an extent rarely possible when judicial proceedings are instituted.

The judicial approach is quite public by comparison. It occurs outside the health care setting—the hospital, nursing home, hospice, or patient's home. Thus, the case becomes known to persons other than health care professionals, including those who may not be imbued with the same professional commitment to confidentiality and the same sensitivity for critically ill patients and their families. Second, judicial proceedings are ordinarily open to the public,[479] and the press, alert to litigation of more than routine interest, often accords tremendous attention to right-to-die cases. Thus, even courts are taking explicit cognizance of these facts in holding that "[j]udicial intervention in 'right to die' cases should be minimal."[480] A court "is not a forum which always preserves a party's right of privacy."[481] A Florida court, recognizing that because in Florida the right to die is based on the state constitutional right of privacy, concluded that because

> the remedy exists to fulfill a right of privacy . . . the procedures to invoke and enforce this right should be as private as the state's competing interests can permit for such a delicate decision. We obviously do a poor job of protecting Mrs. Browning's right of privacy by discussing the details of her medical condition and the nature of her family structure in a highly publicized decision which will be preserved for posterity. For the Floridians who follow Mrs. Browning, we hope to create a more private decisionmaking process.[482]

§ 5.55 Avoiding Adverse Publicity

Decisions to forgo life-sustaining treatment generate not only public interest but also public controversy. It matters little whether the patient and/or family wishes

---

KY: *Accord* DeGrella v. Elston, 858 S.W.2d 698, 710 (Ky. 1993) ("Judicial intervention into private decision-making of this sort is expensive and intrusive.").

NJ: *Accord In re* Farrell, 529 A.2d 404 (N.J. 1987); *In re* Jobes, 529 A.2d 434 (N.J. 1987); *In re* Peter, 529 A.2d 419 (N.J. 1987).

[478] *E.g., In re* Farrell, 529 A.2d 404 (N.J. 1987).

[479] *Cf.* National Ctr. for State Courts, Guidelines for State Court Decision Making in Life-Sustaining Medical Treatment Cases 53 (2d ed. 1992) (standard 9) ("Although a presumption should exist in favor of open hearings and public records, the court may take steps to protect the privacy and minimize the anguish of the individuals involved in these cases.").

[480] Morrison v. Abramovice, 253 Cal. Rptr. 530, 535 (Ct. App. 1988).

[481] Browning v. Herbert, 543 So. 2d 258, 271 (Fla. Dist. Ct. App. 1989), *aff'd,* 568 So. 2d 4 (Fla. 1990).

[482] Browning v. Herbert, 543 So. 2d at 268–69.

to forgo treatment and the physician and health care institution want to administer it, or vice versa. Such cases are lightning rods for publicity and will inevitably be viewed negatively by some segment of the community.

It is therefore in the interests not only of the patient's and family's privacy but also of the health care institution and individual health care professionals that publicity be avoided. The clinical approach is far better suited to so doing than the judicial approach.

NONJUDICIAL REVIEW

§ 5.56 Nonjudicial Review

The primary alternative to judicial review of decisions about life-sustaining treatment is some form of review in the clinical setting. As a practical matter, there is likely to be one or more formal or informal reviews within the health care institution, by persons including the attending physician, consultant physicians, health care administrators, legal counsel, and/or a committee. A number of courts and commentators have urged the use of committees as an alternative or supplement to judicial review of a surrogate's decisions. These are usually referred to as ethics committees[483] but are sometimes called prognosis committees (or boards),[484] and an increasing number of health care institutions are establishing them to undertake such review.

§ 5.57 —Ethics Committees

The idea of using a committee based in a health care institution to review decisions about life-sustaining treatment had its judicial origins in the *Quinlan* case.[485] The question of review was interjected in the opinion in response to the court's concerns about creating an atmosphere in which physicians could make such decisions without excessive fear of legal liability.

The court was hesitant "in this imperfect world" to quell these fears by providing immunity to physicians for forgoing life-sustaining treatment.[486] Further, it had ruled out routine judicial review as being "impossibly cumbersome."[487] Consequently, it seized on the idea of using a hospital-based committee, an idea borrowed from a law review article written by a physician.[488] The court

---

483 See § **5.57** and **Ch. 6.**

484 See § **5.58.**

485 *In re* Quinlan, 355 A.2d 647 (N.J. 1976).

486 *Id.* at 668.

487 *Id.* at 669.

488 *See* Teel, *The Physician's Dilemma: A Doctor's View: What the Law Should Be,* 27 Baylor L. Rev. 6 (1975).

held that the use of an ethics committee was mandatory. However, the court prescribed its function as being review of the patient's prognosis,[489] rather than the surrogate's decision, thereby making the term *ethics committee* a misnomer.[490]

In prescribing the use of such a committee, the court relied on the article's claim that many hospitals had interdisciplinary ethics committees.[491] In fact, even five years after the *Quinlan* decision, very few hospitals had ethics committees, and a majority of those that did were in New Jersey, largely as a result of the *Quinlan* decision.[492] In other words, the court assumed that an entity that in fact did not exist in most hospitals would play a significant role in the decisionmaking process for incompetent patients. Ironically, this ill-founded assumption was responsible, more than any other single factor, for the creation of ethics committees in a significant number of hospitals today.

Although in the case of nonhospitalized patients, the New Jersey Supreme Court later abandoned the notion of an ethics committee in favor of other forms of review,[493] its opinion has influenced a number of other courts to recommend or tacitly approve of,[494] though not to require,[495] review of a surrogate's decisions by an ethics committee.[496]

---

[489] *In re* Quinlan, 355 A.2d 647, 671–72 (N.J. 1976).

[490] *In re* Peter, 529 A.2d 419, 428 n.12 (N.J. 1987). *Cf. In re* Conroy, 486 A.2d 1209, 1227 (N.J. 1985) (*Quinlan* required approval by "an 'Ethics Committee' (or, more accurately, a prognosis committee)").

[491] *In re* Quinlan, 355 A.2d at 668.

[492] Youngner et al., *A National Survey of Hospital Ethics Committees, in* President's Comm'n, Deciding to Forego Life-Sustaining Treatment 443 (41% of the hospitals with ethics committees were in New Jersey). *See also In re* Jobes, 529 A.2d 434, 448 (N.J. 1987) ("Amicus New Jersey Hospital Association has informed us that since *Quinlan* was decided, approximately eighty-five percent of New Jersey's acute-care hospitals have established prognosis committees that check the attending physician's prognosis when withdrawal of life support from a vegetative patient is under consideration. Thus it appears that the *Quinlan* procedure is functioning in the setting for which it was intended.").

[493] *In re* Peter, 529 A.2d 419 (N.J. 1987) (nursing home patient in persistent vegetative state); *In re* Jobes, 529 A.2d 434 (N.J. 1987) (nonelderly nursing home patient); *In re* Farrell, 529 A.2d 404 (N.J. 1987) (patient in homecare); *In re* Conroy, 486 A.2d 1209 (N.J. 1985) (nursing home patient not in persistent vegetative state).

[494] **KY:** DeGrella v. Elston, 858 S.W.2d 698, 710 (Ky. 1993) ("If the attending physician, the hospital or nursing home ethics committee where the patient resides, and the legal guardian or next of kin, all agree and document the patient's wishes and the patient's condition, and if no one disputes their decision, no court order is required to proceed to carry out the patient's wishes.").

MA: *In re* Beth, 587 N.E.2d 1377, 1380 (Mass. 1992) ("Courts should not be in the business of reviewing uncontroversial "no-code" cases simply because doctors and hospitals seek to shield themselves from liability.").

See also Council on Ethical & Judicial Affairs, American Medical Ass'n, Code of Medical Ethics § 2.20, at 37 (1994).

[495] **WA:** *But cf. In re* Colyer, 660 P.2d 738, 755 (Wash. 1983) (Dore, J., dissenting).

[496] See **Ch. 6.**

§ 5.58 —Prognosis Committees

In some jurisdictions, the right of a patient, whether possessing or lacking decisionmaking capacity, to forgo life-sustaining treatment is heavily dependent upon the patient's prognosis.[497] Determining prognosis is ordinarily the function of the patient's attending physician and of any consultant-physicians the attending physician enlists to assist.[498] However, to safeguard the accuracy of prognostication, the *Quinlan* court prescribed that a committee should confirm the attending physician's prognosis for any incompetent patient for whom life-sustaining treatment was sought to be forgone.[499] Though it used the term *ethics committee,* it is clear that confirmation of prognosis is what the court intended for the committee to do.[500]

Some courts have held that a prognosis committee should not be an interdisciplinary ethics committee, as recommended in *Quinlan,* but a medical professional group, composed of physicians.[501] What is needed is "[c]oncurrence by professional colleagues, who are not attending physicians but who

---

[497] See **Ch. 8.**

[498] *See, e.g., In re* Colyer, 660 P.2d 738, 749 (Wash. 1983) ("prognosis determination is a medical one").

[499] **NJ:** *In re* Quinlan, 355 A.2d 647, 649 (N.J. 1976) ("[P]hysicians should consult with hospital ethics committee and if committee should agree with physicians' prognosis, the life-support systems may be withdrawn.").

WA: *In re* Colyer, 660 P.2d 738, 749 (Wash. 1983) (a need to "protect against erroneous diagnoses as well as questionable motives").

[500] **NJ:** *In re* Peter, 529 A.2d 419, 428 n.12 (N.J. 1987); *In re* Visbeck, 510 A.2d 125, 132–33 (N.J. Super. Ct. Ch. Div. 1986).

NY: Eichner v. Dillon, 426 N.Y.S.2d 517, 550 (App. Div. 1980).

WA: *In re* Hamlin, 689 P.2d 1372, 1377 (Wash. 1984); *In re* Colyer, 660 P.2d 738 (Wash. 1983).

[501] **NJ:** *Cf. In re* Visbeck, 510 A.2d 125, 132–33 (N.J. Super. Ct. Ch. Div. 1986) (recommending prognosis committee but not specifying whether must be composed of physicians).

NY: Eichner v. Dillon, 426 N.Y.S.2d at 550.

WA: *In re* Colyer, 660 P.2d at 749 (because of "its amorphous character . . . its use of nonmedical personnel to reach a medical decision, and . . . its bureaucratic intermeddling") (citing Annas, *Reconciling* Quinlan *and* Saikewicz: *Decision Making for the Terminally Ill Incompetent,* 4 Am. J.L. & Med. 367, 379 (1978); Cantor, Quinlan, *Privacy, and the Handling of Incompetent Dying Patients,* 30 Rutgers L. Rev. 243, 255 (1977); Collester, *Death, Dying and the Law: A Prosecutorial View of the* Quinlan *Case,* 30 Rutgers L. Rev. 304, 320–21 (1977); Hirsh & Donovan, *The Right to Die: Medico-Legal Implications of* In re Quinlan, 30 Rutgers L. Rev. 267, 280–85 (1977)). *Cf. In re* Hamlin, 689 P.2d 1372, 1377 (Wash. 1984) (recommending prognosis committee but not specifying composition).

nonetheless have an understanding of the patient's condition."[502] The prognosis committee should agree there is no reasonable medical probability that the patient will return to a cognitive, sapient state.[503]

It has been recommended that such a committee not be a standing committee and that composition on a case-by-case basis may be preferable because different patients' conditions require different kinds of expertise.[504] Anticipating the problem overlooked by the *Quinlan* court that a particular health care institution may not have such a committee, the Washington Supreme Court stated that the trial court might appoint a committee if none existed.[505]

Washington also requires that the recommendation of the prognosis committee be unanimous.[506] If there is disagreement among physicians on the board, judicial review is then required.[507] A New York intermediate appellate court suggested that review by a prognosis committee be a prerequisite to judicial review,[508] but no such requirement has been imposed by the Court of Appeals.

§ 5.59 —Medical Review

Some courts require that the attending physician's prognosis that the patient is terminally ill or some such equivalent[509] be confirmed by another physician or physicians, as distinguished from a prognosis committee's performing the same function. A physician's review is sometimes required instead of judicial or

---

[502] **WA:** *In re* Colyer, 660 P.2d at 749.

MA: *Accord In re* Spring, 399 N.E.2d 493, 499 n.8 (Mass. App. Ct. 1979), *rev'd,* 405 N.E.2d 115 (Mass. 1980).

OH: *Accord* Leach v. Akron Gen. Medical Ctr., 426 N.E.2d 809, 816 (P. Ct. Summit County, Ohio 1980) (licensed physician and neurologist selected by guardian must examine patient and certify that she is in a persistent vegetative state "and that there is no reasonable medical possibility that she will regain any sapient or cognitive function").

[503] **WA:** *In re* Colyer, 660 P.2d at 749–50.

[504] *Id.* at 749 & n.7.

[505] **WA:** *In re* Colyer, 660 P.2d at 749 n.7; *id.* at 755 (Dore, J., dissenting).

NY: *See also* Eichner v. Dillon, 426 N.Y.S.2d 517, 550 (App. Div. 1980) (if hospital has no standing ethics committee, "hospital's chief administrative office shall appoint" one).

[506] **WA:** *In re* Hamlin, 689 P.2d 1372, 1378 (Wash. 1984); *In re* Colyer, 660 P.2d 738, 749 (Wash. 1983).

NY: *Contra* Eichner v. Dillon, 426 N.Y.S.2d at 550 ("confirmation of prognosis shall be by a majority . . . although lack of unanimity may later be considered by the court").

[507] *In re* Hamlin, 689 P.2d 1372, 1378 (Wash. 1984); *In re* Colyer, 660 P.2d 738, 750 (Wash. 1983).

[508] Eichner v. Dillon, 426 N.Y.S.2d at 550.

[509] See §§ **8.9–8.13.**

committee review[510] and sometimes as an adjunct thereto.[511] Courts often speak of requiring a physician's "certificate" by which they mean "an affidavit, sworn statement, or deposition."[512] In New York, pursuant to statute,[513] "surrogate-decisionmaking committees" are empowered to make decisions about major medical treatment for institutionalized, mentally ill patients who lack the capacity to consent.[514]

Nevada requires a detailed "procedural matrix" for the review of decisions to forgo life-sustaining treatment from competent adult patients, consisting of the following procedures:

Two non-attending physicians must examine the [patient] to determine and certify in writing . . . that

(a) the patient is mentally competent to understand his or her prognosis and was properly informed thereof, and that the patient was apprised of treatment alternatives and the consequences that will or are likely to result from refusing medical treatment or electing to withdraw medical therapy, including life support systems then in use;

---

[510] **CA:** *Cf.* Morrison v. Abramovice, 253 Cal. Rptr. 530, 533 (Ct. App. 1988) (conservator must consult with attending physician before authorizing forgoing of tube-feeding but is not bound by physician's opinion).

CT: Foody v. Manchester Memorial Hosp., 482 A.2d 713, 721 (Conn. Super. Ct. 1984).

FL: John F. Kennedy Memorial Hosp. v. Bludworth, 452 So. 2d 921, 926 (Fla. 1984); *In re* Barry, 445 So. 2d 365, 372 (Fla. Dist. Ct. App. 1984) (at least two physicians).

GA: *In re* L.H.R., 321 S.E.2d 716, 723 (Ga. 1984) ("[t]wo physicians with no interest in the outcome of the case").

IL: Rosebush v. Oakland County Prosecutor, 491 N.W.2d 633, 638 (Mich. Ct. App. 1992) ("The above diagnosis and prognosis must be made by the attending physician. Two physicians with no interest in the outcome of the case must concur in the diagnosis and prognosis.").

NJ: *Cf. In re* Peter, 529 A.2d 419, 429 (N.J. 1987) (two independent medical opinions); *In re* Jobes, 529 A.2d 434, 448 (N.J. 1987) ("at least two independent physicians knowledgeable in neurology"); *In re* Farrell, 529 A.2d 404, 415 (N.J. 1987) (two nonattending physicians must examine patient to confirm that patient is fully informed about prognosis).

NY: *Cf.* N.Y. Pub. Health Law §§ 2963(3), 2966(1) (one other physician must concur with attending physician that patient lacks decisionmaking capacity and that cardiopulmonary resuscitation is futile).

OH: Leach v. Akron Gen. Medical Ctr., 426 N.E.2d 809, 816 (P. Ct. Summit County, Ohio, 1980) (licensed physician and neurologist).

WA: *In re* Grant, 747 P.2d 445, 456 (Wash. 1987).

[511] **IL:** *E.g.,* Estate of Longeway v. Community Convalescent Ctr., 549 N.E.2d 292, 299 (Ill. 1989) ("Finally, the accuracy of the diagnosis must be safeguarded. Consequently, the patient's attending physician along with at least two other consulting physicians must concur in the diagnosis.").

NJ: *E.g., In re* Conroy, 486 A.2d 1209, 1242 (N.J. 1985) (adjunct to administrative review).

[512] Browning v. Herbert, 543 So. 2d 258, 271–72 (Fla. Dist. Ct. App. 1989).

[513] N.Y. Mental Hyg. Law §§ 80.01–.13.

[514] *See In re* Beth Israel Medical Ctr. (Weinstein), 519 N.Y.S.2d 511, 516 (Sup. Ct. N.Y. County 1987).

(b) the patient's condition is irreversible or the extent to which the condition may be improved through medical intervention;

(c) the patient is or reasonably appears to be free of coercion or pressure in making his or her decision;

(d) if the patient is nonterminal *i.e.,* has an estimated life expectancy of six months or more either with or without artificial life support systems, that he or she was apprised of the care options available to the patient through governmental, charitable and private sources with due regard for the value of life, and certify in writing without liability except for fraud, that the aforesaid explanation of care alternatives was given and the patient's response thereto.[515]

After this part of the procedure has been accomplished, if the patient is not terminally ill, there must be judicial review to weigh the state's interests against the patient's right to refuse treatment.[516] If the patient is terminally ill "the patient's constitutional and common law rights of self-determination shall be deemed to prevail over the . . . State interests, and the patient may refuse treatment or elect to have existing therapy, including any life support systems."[517] Immunity from civil or criminal liability is conferred upon "any physician or health care provider who assists the patient in the implementation of his or her decision, including the administration of any sedative or pain medication to ease the patient's pre-death anxieties or pain."[518] This procedure applies only to competent patients; the court has not prescribed any procedures for the termination of life support from incompetent patients.[519] The Nevada Supreme Court described this scheme as "designed to fill a temporary void which we trust will be supplanted by timely legislative action,"[520] but the legislature has not yet taken the cue.

§ 5.60 —Administrative Review

The task of reviewing decisions about life-sustaining treatment might also be assigned to an administrative agency. The New Jersey Supreme Court, in the *Conroy* case, mandated this approach for nursing home patients because of the unlikelihood that nursing homes would have an ethics committee.[521]

The court distinguished the procedures for making decisions about forgoing life-sustaining treatment in nursing homes from those to be used in hospitals, giving five reasons for the distinction:

---

[515] McKay v. Bergstedt, 801 P.2d 617, 630 (Nev. 1990).

[516] *Id.* at 630–31. See **§ 5.30.**

[517] *Id.* at 630.

[518] *Id.*

[519] *Id.* at 631 n.5.

[520] *Id.* at 629.

[521] *In re* Conroy, 486 A.2d 1209, 1238 (N.J. 1985). *See also In re* Peter, 529 A.2d 419 (N.J. 1987); *In re* Jobes, 529 A.2d 434 (N.J. 1987).

1. "[R]esidents of nursing homes are a particularly vulnerable population."
2. "[N]ursing-home residents are often without any surviving family. . . . Thus, the involvement of caring family members that was an integral part of the decision-making process in *Quinlan* may not be a realistic possibility for many nursing-home residents."
3. "[P]hysicians play a much more limited role in nursing homes than in hospitals . . . [and] generally are not chosen by the [nursing home] residents and are not familiar with their personalities and preferences."
4. "[N]ursing homes as institutions suffer from peculiar industry-wide problems to which hospitals are less prone. . . . 'In many cases [nursing home residents] have not even received humane treatment. And in an alarming number of known cases, they have actually encountered abuse and physical danger.'"
5. "[N]ursing homes generally are not faced with the need to make decisions about a patient's medical care with the same speed that is necessary in hospitals."[522]

As a result of these distinctions, the court concluded that when it is determined that the substantive standards for forgoing life-sustaining treatment for patients in nursing homes[523] are met, notification must be given[524] to the Office of the Ombudsman for the Institutionalized Elderly.[525] The Ombudsman is to treat each such notification as a possible instance of abuse within the meaning of the statute and is therefore obligated to investigate the situation and report to appropriate governmental agencies.[526] The Omnbudsman may refer cases of questionable criminal abuse for prosecution.[527] The court recommended that the Ombudsman exercise his discretionary authority to appoint physicians to review the patient's medical condition. If these physicians confirm that the medical circumstances warrant the forgoing of life-sustaining treatment, treatment may be forgone as long as the relevant substantive standard has been met.

An intermediate appellate court in New Jersey modified this procedure in the case of a never-competent patient who resided in a state institution for the

[522] *In re* Conroy, 486 A.2d at 1237–38 (citing Senate Subcomm. on Long-Term Care of the Special Comm. on Aging, Nursing Home Care in the United States: Failure in Public Policy, Introductory Report, S. Rep. No. 1420, 93d Cong., 2d Sess. 16 (1974)). *Accord In re* Peter, 529 A.2d 419, 429 (N.J. 1987) (Nursing home patients are at risk of an "uneven level of care, minimal medical supervision, and frequent lack of family support.").

[523] See **§ 7.32.**

[524] *In re* Conroy, 486 A.2d at 1241. *See also In re* Peter, 529 A.2d 419, 429 (N.J. 1987).

[525] **NJ:** *See* N.J. Stat. Ann §§ 30:13-1 to 30:13-11. *See also* Gleason v. Abrams, 593 A.2d 1232 (N.J. Super. Ct. App. Div. 1991) (holding that regulation permitting patient competency to be determined by attending physician must be modified to require determination by two non-attending physicians).

ME: *See also In re* Gardner, 534 A.2d 947, 949 (Me. 1987) (citing Me. Rev. Stat. Ann. tit. 22, §§ 3470–3476 (Supp. 1986) (requiring State Department of Human Services to intervene to protect against possible abuse)).

[526] *In re* Conroy, 486 A.2d at 1242.

[527] *Id.*

mentally retarded, over whom the Office of Ombudsman had no jurisdiction. The court held that if there was agreement among the patient's family, attending physician, prognosis committee, two independent neurologists, and the state's public guardian, life support could be terminated. However, if any of these parties dissented from the decision, judicial approval would be needed.[528]

Administrative agency review of a surrogate's decision is feasible only where an administrative agency already has jurisdiction over the matter in question. Many states may have no such agency, or its jurisdiction over decisions about life-sustaining treatment may be doubtful. It is one thing for a court to order a nonexistent hospital committee to review a decision; at least the hospital can create such a committee, though possibly with some difficulty. It is quite another for a court to order into existence an administrative agency or even to enlarge the jurisdiction of an existing agency.

Even when such an agency exists, ways will be found to circumvent it if its procedures are unduly cumbersome and slow, just as avoidance of judicial review is sought because of those features. The experience in New Jersey in this regard is not encouraging. Two years after the *Conroy* requirements were laid down by the supreme court, it had occasion to revisit this issue and noted that "[t]hough 'well over 100' persons have inquired with the Office of the Ombudsman for the Institutionalized Elderly regarding the procedures *Conroy* required before medical treatment can be withdrawn from nursing home patients, only one case has been officially brought to the Ombudsman's attention."[529]

OTHER PROCEDURAL CONSIDERATIONS

§ 5.61 Standard of Proof

Many courts have considered the question of what standard of proof is to be applied in right-to-die cases and have almost unanimously concluded that proof by clear and convincing evidence is required.[530]

---

[528] *In re* Moorhouse, 593 A.2d 1256 (N.J. Super. Ct. App. Div. 1991).

[529] *In re* Jobes, 529 A.2d 434, 460 (N.J. 1987) (Handler, J., concurring) (citing *Curbs on Ending Life Supports Are Ignored,* N.Y. Times, Nov. 28, 1986, at B-15).

[530] **AZ:** Rasmussen v. Fleming, 741 P.2d 674, 691 (Ariz. 1987).

CT: McConnell v. Beverly Enters.-Conn., Inc., 553 A.2d 596, 604 (Conn. 1989).

FL: Browning v. Herbert, 568 So. 2d 4, 15 (Fla. 1990); John F. Kennedy Memorial Hosp. v. Bludworth, 432 So. 2d 611, 620 (Fla. Dist. Ct. App. 1983), *rev'd,* 452 So. 2d 921 (Fla. 1984).

ME: *In re* Gardner, 534 A.2d 947, 953 (Me. 1987).

MD: Mack v. Mack, 618 A.2d 744, 758–59 (Md. 1993).

MI: Martin v. Martin, 517 N.W.2d 749 (Mich. Ct. App. 1994); Martin v. Martin, 504 N.W.2d 917 (Mich. Ct. App. 1993).

MO: Cruzan v. Harmon, 760 S.W.2d 408, 425 (Mo. 1988).

Clear and convincing evidence is "proof sufficient to persuade the trier of fact that the patient held a firm and settled commitment to the termination of life supports under the circumstances like those presented,"[531] or is evidence which "produces in the mind of the trier of fact a firm belief or conviction as to the truth of the allegations sought to be established, evidence so clear, direct and weighty and convincing as to enable [the factfinder] to come to a clear conviction, without hesitancy, of the truth of the precise facts in issue."[532] The fact that evidence is contradicted does not mean that it fails to meet the clear-and-convincing standard.[533] Similarly, the fact that evidence is uncontroverted does not necessarily mean that it meets that or any other standard.[534] Whether it satisfies the applicable standard is a matter "left to the sound discretion of the trial court."[535] Nonetheless, an appellate court might overrule a trial court's determination when its own independent review of the evidence causes it to conclude otherwise as it did in the *Elbaum* case, in which it reversed the trial

---

NJ: *In re* Jobes, 529 A.2d 434, 441 (N.J. 1987); *In re* Conroy, 486 A.2d 1209, 1241 (N.J. 1985); *In re* Moorhouse, 593 A.2d 1256 (N.J. Super. Ct. App. Div. 1991).

NY: *In re* Westchester County Medical Ctr. (O'Connor), 531 N.E.2d 607, 612 (N.Y. 1988) ("Nothing less than unequivocal proof will suffice."); Eichner v. Dillon, 420 N.E.2d 64, 72 (N.Y. 1981), *modifying* 426 N.Y.S.2d 517, 545 (App. Div. 1980); Elbaum v. Grace Plaza of Great Neck, Inc., 544 N.Y.S.2d 840 (App. Div. 1989); *In re* Beth Israel Medical Ctr. (Weinstein), 519 N.Y.S.2d 511, 516 (Sup. Ct. N.Y. County 1987); *In re* Lydia E. Hall Hosp., 455 N.Y.S.2d 706, 712 (Sup. Ct. Nassau County 1982).

PA: *In re* E.L.K., 11 Fiduc. Rep. 2d 78 (C.P. Berks County, Pa. 1991) (by implication) (hypothetical discussion prior to becoming ill followed by patient's uncertainty about what she wanted to do when she did become ill); Ragona v. Preate, 11 Fiduc. Rep. 2d 1 (C.P. Lackawanna County, Pa. 1990).

WA: *In re* Colyer, 660 P.2d 738, 750 (Wash. 1983). *Contra In re* Ingram, 689 P.2d 1363, 1371 (Wash. 1984) ("[T]he court need not place on any party any particular burden of proof or persuasion.").

531 **NY:** *In re* Westchester County Medical Ctr. (O'Connor), 531 N.E.2d 607, 613 (N.Y. 1988).

MI: *Accord* Martin v. Martin, 517 N.W.2d 749, 754 (Mich. Ct. App. 1994) (Fact that patient's "preferences were expressed repeatedly, adamantly, and in different contexts, together with the evidence showing that he had similar discussions with others, indicate that [he] was firm and settled in his desire to have life-sustaining medical treatment withheld or withdrawn in the circumstances described.").

532 **NJ:** *In re* Jobes, 529 A.2d 434, 441 (N.J. 1987).

US: *Accord* Cruzan v. Director, 497 U.S. 261, 285 n.11 (1990).

533 **FL:** Browning v. Herbert, 543 So. 2d 258, 273 (Fla. Dist. Ct. App. 1989) ("It is possible for the evidence in such a case to be clear and convincing, even though some evidence may be inconsistent.").

534 **FL:** Browning v. Herbert, 543 So. 2d 258, 273 (Fla. Dist. Ct. App. 1989) ("[I]t is possible for the evidence to be uncontroverted, and yet not be clear and convincing.").

NJ: *In re* Jobes, 529 A.2d 434, 441 (N.J. 1987) (citing *In re* Colyer, 660 P.2d 738, 754–55 (Wash. 1983) (Dore, J., dissenting)).

535 *In re* Torres, 357 N.W.2d 332, 341 (Minn. 1984).

court's finding that the testimony of the patient's husband, sister, son, and daughter about six different occasions on which the patient evidenced a desire not to have life-sustaining treatment did not meet the clear-and-convincing standard.[536]

The rationale for the clear-and-convincing-evidence standard is that because "particularly important personal interests are at stake,"[537] a court "would be remiss if it did not adopt the highest possible civil standard of clear and convincing."[538] Courts "should determine that the surrogate's decision was based upon substantial competent evidence."[539] Such a "standard serves to 'impress the factfinder with the importance of the decision' . . . and it '"forbids relief whenever the evidence is loose, equivocal or contradictory."' "[540]

In the *Cruzan* case before the United States Supreme Court, the constitutionality of requiring a clear-and-convincing-evidence standard of proof (in addition to the constitutionality of requiring a substantive subjective standard, discussed below) was a serious dividing point between the majority and the dissenting justices. The majority observed that the standard of proof "serves as 'a societal judgment about how the risk of error should be distributed between the litigants.' "[541] Because an erroneous decision to terminate life-sustaining treatment is "final and irrevocable" and "not susceptible of

---

[536] **NY:** Elbaum v. Grace Plaza of Great Neck, Inc., 544 N.Y.S.2d 840 (App. Div. 1989). *See also In re* Westchester County Medical Ctr. (O'Connor), 531 N.E.2d 607, 612 n.3 (1988).

[537] **NY:** Eichner v. Dillon, 420 N.E.2d 64, 72 (N.Y. 1981) (citing Addington v. Texas, 441 U.S. 418, 424 (1979)).

US: *Accord* Cruzan v. Director, 497 U.S. 261, 283 (1990) ("interests . . . are more substantial . . . than those involved in a run-of-the-mine civil dispute").

IL: *Accord In re* Estate of Greenspan, 558 N.E.2d 1194 (Ill. 1990) (clear and convincing evidence required because Illinois public policy values sanctity of life); Estate of Longeway v. Community Convalescent Ctr., 549 N.E.2d 292, 300 (Ill. 1989) (same); *In re* E.G., 549 N.E.2d 322 (Ill. 1989) (same).

[538] Leach v. Akron Gen. Medical Ctr., 426 N.E.2d 809, 815 (P. Ct. Summit County, Ohio 1980).

[539] **FL:** Browning v. Herbert, 543 So. 2d 258, 274 (Fla. Dist. Ct. App. 1989), *aff'd,* 568 So. 2d 4 (Fla. 1990).

IL: *Accord In re* Estate of Greenspan, 558 N.E.2d 1194, 1201 (Ill. 1990); Estate of Longeway v. Community Convalescent Ctr., 549 N.E.2d 292, 300 (Ill. 1989); *In re* E.G., 549 N.E.2d 322 (Ill. 1989).

LA: *Accord In re* P.V.W., 424 So. 2d 1015, 1020 (La. 1982).

ME: *Accord In re* Swan, 569 A.2d 1202, 1206 (Me. 1990); *In re* Gardner, 534 A.2d 947, 953 (Me. 1987).

OH: *Accord* Leach v. Akron Gen. Medical Ctr., 426 N.E.2d 809, 815 (P. Ct. Summit County, Ohio 1980).

[540] Eichner v. Dillon, 420 N.E.2d 64, 72 (N.Y. 1981) (quoting Addington v. Texas, 441 U.S. 418, 427 (1979).

[541] Cruzan v. Director, 497 U.S. 261, 283 (1990) (quoting Santosky v. Kramer, 455 U.S. 745, 755 (1982); Addington v. Texas, 441 U.S. at 423.

correction,"[542] a stringent standard of proof is justified because "the more stringent the burden . . . , the more that party bears the risk."[543]

Justice Brennan's dissent cogently distinguished prior cases in which the court required a clear-and-convincing-evidence standard from the case before it on the ground that in the other cases "the imbalance imposed by a heightened evidentiary standard was not only acceptable but required because the standard was deployed to protect an individual's exercise of a fundamental right, as the majority admits."[544] By contrast, the application of a clear-and-convincing-evidence standard to the facts of *Cruzan* imposes an "obstacle to the *exercise* of a fundamental right."[545] The fact that once life-sustaining treatment has been withheld or withdrawn the decision is irrevocable does not mean that we must err on the side of preserving life because

> from the point of view of the patient, an erroneous decision in either direction is irrevocable. An erroneous decision to terminate artificial nutrition and hydration, to be sure, will lead to failure of that last remnant of physiological life, the brain stem, and result in complete brain death. An erroneous decision not to terminate life-support, however, robs a patient of the very qualities protected by the right to avoid unwanted medical treatment. His own degraded existence is perpetuated; his family's suffering is protracted; the memory he leaves behind becomes more and more distorted.[546]

Although Justice Brennan's reasoning and conclusion seem sound, his assumption that the standard of proof is the sole culprit seems incorrect. Rather, the threat to individual interests comes not from the high standard of proof alone, but in conjunction with *what* Missouri required to be proved by clear and convincing evidence, namely, the patient's subjective intent.[547] On one point, however, Justice Brennan is almost certainly correct, and that is that requiring proof by clear and convincing evidence does not always enhance the accuracy of the factfinding process, but, as "[the Court has] always recognized, . . . shifting the risk of error reduces the likelihood of errors in one direction at the cost of increasing the likelihood of errors in the other."[548] Indeed, the application of a high standard of proof to a stringent substantive standard for surrogate decisionmaking may encourage perjury and thus may increase error in favor of *forgoing* treatment. However, it is possible that Justice Brennan is correct in his belief that "a trial court has the means of ferreting out [venal motives],"[549] and therefore that this concern is not as serious as first appears.

---

[542] Cruzan v. Director, 497 U.S. at 283.

[543] *Id.*

[544] *Id.* at 319–20 (Brennan, J., dissenting).

[545] *Id.* (Brennan, J., dissenting) (emphasis added).

[546] *Id.* at 320 (Brennan, J., dissenting).

[547] See §§ **7.4–7.6.**

[548] Cruzan v. Director, 497 U.S. 261, 320 (1990) (Brennan, J., dissenting).

[549] *Id.* at 318 (Brennan, J., dissenting).

Although some litigants have advocated a beyond-a-reasonable-doubt standard of proof,[550] no court has held that this standard should be applied and some have specifically rejected it.[551] An even higher standard of proof, namely, that "all witnesses concur" that life-sustaining treatment should be forgone, is even less appropriate because "such a rule would take the decision processes from the trier of facts and give it to any witness who, for whatever motive, wanted to prevent the relief sought."[552]

The Massachusetts Supreme Judicial Court appears to be the only court to have expressly repudiated a clear-and-convincing-evidence standard of proof. In *In re Doe,* that court approved a trial court's conclusion that "the legal standard to be used as a guide in making his decision was 'a "preponderance of the evidence" with an "extra measure of evidentiary protection" [by reason of] specific findings of fact after a "careful review of the evidence."' "[553] In effect, the court concluded that a standard of proof couched in a more stringent word-formula does not necessarily guarantee adequate protection, for it may be evaded in practice by a trial court, thus leaving as the only option available to an appellate court the task of reweighing the evidence. Thus, the court rejected a formulaic approach in favor of one it believed to be more susceptible to review on appeal, that is, a requirement that trial courts "set forth their findings in 'meticulous detail' [rather] than . . . merely label their findings as meeting a particular standard." The clear-and-convincing-evidence standard, the court observed, should be applicable when the *government* seeks to infringe on an individual's liberty interests. But "[h]ere, by contrast, Doe's guardian (as well as her parents) are attempting to determine Doe's preference in order to vindicate Doe's rights to bodily integrity and privacy."[554]

The question of what standard of proof is to be applied is an issue primarily when the surrogate's decision is subject to judicial or administrative review. When review occurs in the health care institution, questions about the standard of proof are likely to be dormant because nonlegal decisionmakers are less accustomed to thinking in such terms. The Florida District Court of Appeal, however, has stated that evidentiary requirements such as the burden of proof apply to surrogate decisionmaking even when it occurs without judicial

---

550 **US:** Cruzan v. Director, 497 U.S. at 318 (Brennan, J., dissenting).

OH: Leach v. Akron Gen. Medical Ctr., 426 N.E.2d 809 (P. Ct. Summit County, Ohio 1980).

551 **NY:** *E.g.,* Eichner v. Dillon, 420 N.E.2d 64, 72 (N.Y. 1981), *modifying* 426 N.Y.S.2d 517, 545 (App. Div. 1980).

OH: *E.g.,* Leach v. Akron Gen. Medical Ctr., 426 N.E.2d at 815.

552 **OH:** Leach v. Akron Gen. Medical Ctr., 426 N.E.2d at 815.

WA: *But cf. In re* Colyer, 660 P.2d 738, 750 (Wash. 1983) ("Disagreement among the physicians on the prognosis committee may foreclose any action to withhold or withdraw treatment without court intervention. In instances of disagreement, application could be made to the court to resolve the dispute with the aid of expert testimony.").

553 583 N.E.2d 1263, 1271 (Mass. 1992).

554 **MA:** 583 N.E.2d at 1269.

US: *Accord* Cruzan v. Director, 497 U.S. 261, 319–20 (1990) (Brennan, J., dissenting).

involvement in the decisionmaking process (or in what it referred to as an "informal forum").[555]

In situations in which there is no need for judicial review, the standard of proof is less certain. New York has held that "[c]lear and convincing proof should . . . be required in cases where it is claimed that a person, now incompetent, left instructions to terminate life sustaining procedures when there is no hope of recovery."[556] Although this seems to be the standard in New Jersey too when there is an advance directive, ironically when there is no advance directive and the substituted judgment standard applies, "[t]he interested parties need not have clear and convincing evidence of the patient's intentions; they need only 'render their best judgment' as to what medical decision the patient would want them to make."[557] This, however, may merely be an example of confusing the standard of proof with the standard for surrogate decisionmaking, as discussed below.

§ 5.62 —Relationship Between Evidentiary and Substantive Standards

Discussions of the appropriate standard of proof have been thrown into a state of considerable confusion by the habit of courts and commentators of failing to distinguish between the standard of proof and the substantive standard for forgoing life-sustaining treatment. Discussions of these two standards are generally intermingled so that it is not always easy to discern the difference between them.

"Clear and convincing evidence" is a traditional evidentiary standard for proving facts in dispute, well accepted in certain types of litigation long before right-to-die cases.[558] It has become the clearly dominant accepted standard of proof in right-to-die cases.

In right-to-die cases, when a patient lacks decisionmaking capacity, virtually[559] all courts have exhibited a preference for, or have required, the use of

---

[555] Browning v. Herbert, 543 So. 2d 258, 271 (Fla. Dist. Ct. App. 1989), *aff'd,* 568 So. 2d 4 (Fla. 1990).

[556] **NY:** Eichner v. Dillon, 420 N.E.2d 64, 72 (N.Y. 1981). *Accord* Delio v. Westchester County Medical Ctr., 516 N.Y.S.2d 677, 687 (App. Div. 1987); *In re* Lydia E. Hall Hosp., 455 N.Y.S.2d 706, 711, 712 (Sup. Ct. Nassau County 1982) (by implication).

FL: *Accord* Browning v. Herbert, 543 So. 2d 258, 273 (Fla. Dist. Ct. App. 1989), *aff'd,* 568 So. 2d 4 (Fla. 1990) ("Although we permit the guardian to make this decision in an informal forum, we emphasize that the decision must still be made upon clear and convincing evidence.").

NJ: *Accord In re* Conroy, 486 A.2d 1209, 1241 (N.J. 1985).

[557] *In re* Peter, 529 A.2d 419, 425 (N.J. 1987) (quoting *In re* Quinlan, 355 A.2d 647, 664 (N.J. 1976)).

[558] J. Strong et al., McCormick on Evidence § 340, at 442–43 (4th ed. 1992).

[559] **CA:** *But see* Drabick v. Drabick, 245 Cal. Rptr. 840 (Ct. App. 1988).

either a subjective standard or a substituted judgment standard in order to forgo life-sustaining treatment.[560] To meet these standards, there must be evidence, respectively, of the patient's actual or probable wishes about the administration or forgoing of treatment. To satisfy the prevailing standard of proof, there needs to be not just some evidence, or a preponderance of the evidence, but *clear and convincing evidence* of the patient's actual or probable wishes. Or to put it another way, there must either be clear and convincing evidence that the subjective standard is met or there must be clear and convincing evidence that the substituted judgment standard is met, depending on which substantive standard is required.[561] (The standard of proof must be met not only to prove the applicable standard for surrogate decisionmaking, but also in determining whether or not a patient lacks or possesses decisionmaking capacity.[562])

The confusion arises in part from the relative ease of referring to the two concepts together—standard of proof and standard for surrogate decisionmaking—as the "clear and convincing evidence" standard, in comparison with referring to them by some very unartful but more precise phrase, such as the "clear and convincing evidence that the patient expressed the wish to terminate" treatment standard. Thus the label properly applied to the *evidentiary* standard is frequently used as a shorthand expression encompassing both the evidentiary and substantive standards for forgoing life-sustaining treatment.[563] For example, in the *Mack* case, the Maryland Supreme Court clearly insists that there be proof by clear and convincing evidence, but it confuses this evidentiary standard with the substantive standard for decisionmaking for incompetent patients. This is evident from its citation of a long list of cases in other states which it describes as "requir[ing] the proponent of withholding or withdrawing life support to bear the burden of proving by clear and convincing evidence that the ward's decision would have been to forego life support."[564] Although the cited cases do require clear and convincing evidence, most apply a substituted judgment standard, rather than a strict subjective standard, and some even permit the application of a best interests standard when the substituted judgment standard cannot be met. Thus, although the Maryland court's terminology is confused, it actually employs the evidentiary and substantive standards correctly by requiring that there be proof that the substituted judgment standard is met by clear and

---

[560] See § **7.2.**

[561] *See, e.g.,* Mack v. Mack, 618 A.2d 744, 753 (Md. 1993) (trial court "correctly held that the burden was . . . to prove, by clear and convincing evidence, that [incompetent patient's] judgment *was,* or *would be,* that life-sustaining measures should be withdrawn were he to be in a persistent vegetative state." (emphasis added)).

[562] **NY:** *See In re* Harvey "U," 501 N.Y.S.2d 920, 921 (App. Div. 1986).

[563] **KY:** *But see* DeGrella v. Elston, 858 S.W.2d 698, 706 (Ky. 1993) (The court implicitly recognizes the difference between the evidentiary and substantive standard: "Clear and convincing evidence was introduced, of . . . the strength of the patient's commitment to the termination of life in such circumstances.").

[564] Mack v. Mack, 618 A.2d 744 (Md. 1993).

convincing evidence. The confusion could have been easily avoided by recognizing that there are two different kinds of standards, recognizing which evidentiary standard and which substantive standard the court is requiring, and recognizing the relationship between the two—namely, that the evidentiary standard tells us how satisfied we must be that the substantive standard is met; specifically, that there is clear and convincing evidence of what the patient would have decided.

In *Cruzan v. Director,*[565] the Supreme Court was presented with the question of whether it is constitutionally permissible for a state to require clear and convincing evidence that the patient authorized the termination of treatment prior to losing decisionmaking capacity in order for such treatment to be stopped or withheld. The Court concluded that such a standard did not offend the Fourteenth Amendment's guarantee that liberty not be deprived without due process of law.

The Court most definitely did not hold that clear and convincing evidence is constitutionally *required* in order to terminate life support. But more critical for current purposes is that the Court recognized that although a number of state courts had required clear and convincing evidence, very few had required clear and convincing evidence of a patient's subjective intent to terminate life support. The Court understood, as so many others have failed to, that "clear and convincing evidence" answers the question, How much evidence is needed to forgo life-sustaining treatment? and not the question, What kind of evidence is needed to forgo life-sustaining treatment?

Indeed, the *Cruzan* dissenters' disagreement with the majority was "unrelated to its endorsement of the clear and convincing standard of proof for cases of this kind."[566] They agreed "that the controlling facts must be established with unmistakable clarity."[567] The point of disagreement, for them, was "not *how* to prove the controlling facts [standard of proof] but rather *what* proven facts [substantive standard] should be controlling."[568] Thus, there are actually two parts to the holding: first, that a state may require a clear-and-convincing-evidence standard of proof, and second, that it may require that proof to meet the subjective standard for surrogate decisionmaking.

Thus, in effect, the Missouri Supreme Court required, and the United States Supreme Court upheld against constitutional challenge, two separate but related requirements: (1) that there be clear and convincing evidence (the *evidentiary* standard) and (2) that Nancy Cruzan made a decision before losing decisionmaking capacity that she wanted her treatment stopped under circumstances such as these (the *substantive* "subjective standard"). In other words, Missouri requires clear and convincing evidence that the "subjective standard"[569] has

---

565 497 U.S. 261 (1990).

566 *Id.* at 350 (Stevens, J., dissenting).

567 *Id.*

568 *Id.* (emphasis added).

569 See **§§ 7.4–7.6.**

been met.[570] (Other courts requiring that the termination of life support for an incompetent patient occur only if the subjective standard can be met also require clear and convincing evidence to that effect.[571])

The precise degree of specificity required by the Missouri court is unclear.[572] Whether Nancy Cruzan needed to have spoken directly to the treatment (feeding tube) and condition (persistent vegetative state) was, after the Supreme Court's decision, still an open question in Missouri. However, a subsequent decision by the Missouri Court of Appeals,[573] because it holds that the *Cruzan* requirements are applicable only to feeding tubes, suggests that one wishing to forgo that procedure should specify it in an advance directive. It is possible that, should a jurisdiction require too great a level of specificity, the Supreme Court might find that it unduly burdens an individual's Fourteenth Amendment liberty interest. Similarly, if a state were to require an even higher standard of proof than clear and convincing evidence, that too might be found to unduly burden individual interests.

In other jurisdictions in which the clear-and-convincing-evidence standard of proof has been adopted, it must be applied to the accepted substantive standard for decisionmaking by a surrogate in that jurisdiction. In jurisdictions requiring the use of the substituted judgment standard,[574] what must be proved—by clear and convincing evidence—is that the patient would have requested the termination of life support had he considered the question.[575] Similarly, in those jurisdictions in which the best interests standard may be employed,[576] for

---

[570] **MO:** *But see In re* Warren, 858 S.W.2d 263 (Mo. Ct. App. 1993) (limiting applicability of subjective standard to cases of forgoing artificial nutrition and hydration).

[571] **ME:** *Cf. In re* Swan, 569 A.2d 1202 (Me. 1990); *In re* Gardner, 534 A.2d 947 (Me. 1987).

NY: *See In re* Westchester County Medical Ctr. (O'Connor), 531 N.E.2d 607 (N.Y. 1988).

[572] Cruzan v. Director, 497 U.S. 261, 323 (1990) (Brennan, J., dissenting) ("The court did not specifically define what kind of evidence it would consider clear and convincing, but its general discussion suggests that only a living will or equivalently formal directive from the patient when competent would meet this standard. *See* [*Cruzan v. Harmon,*] 760 S.W.2d, at 424–425.").

[573] *In re* Warren, 858 S.W.2d 263 (Mo. Ct. App. 1993).

[574] See §§ **7.7–7.10.**

[575] **KY:** *E.g.,* DeGrella v. Elston, 858 S.W.2d 698 (Ky. 1993); Mack v. Mack, 618 A.2d 744, 757 (Md. 1993) (in absence of living will or health care power of attorney, "inquiry focuses on whether [patient], while competent sufficiently had evidenced his views, one way or the other, to enable the court to determine, by clear and convincing evidence, what [his] decision would be under the present circumstances").

NJ: *But see In re* Jobes, 529 A.2d 434, 451 (N.J. 1987) (when patient is in persistent vegetative state, "[t]he interested parties need not have clear and convincing evidence of the patient's intentions; they need only 'render their best judgment' as to what medical decision the patient would want them to make") (quoting *In re* Quinlan, 355 A.2d 647, 664 (N.J. 1976)).

[576] See §§ **7.11–7.25.**

treatment to be forgone there must be clear and convincing evidence that its continuation is not in the patient's best interests.[577]

§ 5.63 Waiting Period

Whatever the type of review, even the simplest one requiring that another physician review the attending physician's prognosis, decisions to forgo life-sustaining treatment should not be made precipitously.[578] A decision to continue treatment can always be reversed; a decision to forgo ordinarily cannot be reversed unless it does not in fact lead to the patient's death.[579] This is not to say that physicians and other decisionmakers should automatically continue treatment when there is the least doubt but rather that, when there is significant doubt, if there is to be error, it is best that it be on the side of continuing the patient's treatment and life.

No court has mandated a specific period of time that must elapse before a decision to forgo life-sustaining treatment may be implemented.[580] To do so would pose difficult questions, such as when the time period begins to run. Consequently, courts have generally avoided this issue and implicitly deferred to medical standards.

---

[577] **US:** Cruzan v. Director, 497 U.S. 261, 284 (1990) ("We note that many courts which have adopted some sort of substituted judgment procedure in situations like this, whether they limit consideration of evidence to the prior expressed wishes of the incompetent individual, or whether they allow more general proof of what the individual's decision would have been, require a clear and convincing standard of proof of such evidence.").

IL: C.A. v. Morgan, 603 N.E.2d 1171, 1181 (Ill. App. Ct. 1992) (where best interests standard applies, there must be "clear and convincing evidence" of patient's prognosis).

[578] **WA:** *In re* Colyer, 660 P.2d 738, 750 (Wash. 1983).

[579] *See, e.g.,* McFadden, *Quinlan, 31, Dies; Focus of '76 Right to Die Case,* N.Y. Times, June 12, 1985, at A-1.

[580] **WA:** *But see In re* Colyer, 660 P.2d at 755 (Dore, J., dissenting) ("Where the patient is on a life supporting mechanism . . . , is not legally dead, and has not previously requested termination under those conditions, I would require a waiting period of at least 120 days before a prognosis of the patient's future is attempted.").

Bibliography

Annas, G. "Reconciling *Quinlan* and *Saikewicz:* Decision Making for the Terminally Ill Incompetent." *American Journal of Law and Medicine* 4 (1978): 367.

Baron, C. "Assuring 'Detached but Passionate Investigation and Decision': The Role of Guardians Ad Litem in *Saikewicz*-Type Cases." *American Journal of Law and Medicine* 4 (1978): 111.

Baron, C. "Medical Paternalism and the Rule of Law: A Reply to Dr. Relman." *American Journal of Law and Medicine* 4 (1978): 337.

Buchanan, A. "Medical Paternalism or Legal Imperialism: Not the Only Alternatives for Handling *Saikewicz*-Type Cases." *American Journal of Law and Medicine* 5 (1979): 97.

Cantor, N. "*Quinlan,* Privacy, and the Handling of Incompetent Dying Patients." *Rutgers Law Review* 30 (1977): 243.

Francis, L. "The Roles of the Family in Making Health Care Decisions for Incompetent Patients." *Utah Law Review,* 1992: 735.

Glantz, L. "The Case of Earle Spring: Terminating Treatment of the Senile." *Medicolegal News* 8, no. 4 (1980): 14.

Glantz, L. "Post-*Saikewicz* Judicial Actions Clarify the Rights of Patients and Families." *Medicolegal News* 6, no. 4 (1978): 9.

Hafemeister, T., et al. "The Judicial Role in Life-Sustaining Medical Treatment Decisions." *Issues in Law and Medicine* 7 (1991): 53.

Kamisar, Y. "Active v. Passive Euthanasia: Why Keep the Distinction." *Trial* 29 (1993): 32.

Kindregan, M. "Mental Incompetents and the Right to Die: A Symposium. The Court as Forum for Life and Death Decisions: Reflections on Procedures for Substituted Consent." *Suffolk University Law Review* 11 (1977): 919.

Krasik, E. "The Role of the Family in Medical Decisionmaking for Incompetent Adult Patients: A Historical Perspective and Case Analysis." *University of Pittsburgh Law Review* 48 (1987): 539.

Liacos, P. "Dilemmas of Dying." *Medicolegal News* 7, no. 3 (1979): 4.

New York State Task Force on Life and the Law. *Life-Sustaining Treatment: Making Decisions and Appointing a Health Care Agent.* New York: New York State Task Force on Life and the Law, 1987.

New York State Task Force on Life and the Law. *When Others Must Choose: Deciding for Patients Without Capacity.* New York: New York State Task Force on Life and the Law, 1992.

Newman, S. "Treatment Refusals for the Critically Ill: Proposed Rules for the Family, the Physician and the State." *New York Law School Human Rights Annual* 3 (1985): 35.

Pollock, S. "Life and Death Decisions: Who Makes Them and by What Standards?" *Rutgers Law Review* 41 (1989): 505.

Riga, P. "Impersonal Decision Maker: Courts of Equity and the Right-to-Die Cases." *Catholic Law Review* 24 (1979): 301.

Robertson, J. "Legal Criteria for Orders Not to Resuscitate: A Response to Justice Liacos." *Medicolegal News* 8, no. 1 (1980): 4.

Symposium. "Family Privacy and Persistent Vegetative State." *Law, Medicine and Health Care* 17 (1989): 295.

Weinberg, J. "Whose Right Is It Anyway? Individualism, Community and the Right to Die: A Commentary on the New Jersey Experience." *Hastings Law Journal* 40 (1988): 119.

CHAPTER 6

ETHICS COMMITTEES

§ 6.1 Introduction

As discussed in **Chapter 5,** most courts have concluded that end-of-life decisionmaking does not routinely need to be subjected to judicial review at any stage of the decisionmaking process. Nonetheless, these same courts have made it clear that they are available to participants in the decisionmaking process if needed to resolve otherwise insoluble conflicts about the patient's decisionmaking capacity, the appropriate surrogate for an incompetent patient, or what decision should be made about starting, stopping, or limiting life-sustaining medical treatment. Many courts have also suggested, though with virtually no amplification, that "ethics committees" might also serve a useful role in the decisionmaking process prior to, and as a means of avoiding, judicial review, performing the same sorts of roles as a court might play.[1]

The strong judicial bias against routine involvement in end-of-life decisionmaking—as well as the clear, though less strong, explicit judicial support for ethics committees—has created an impetus in favor of their creation in health care institutions. This impetus has been given strong encouragement by the Joint Commission on Accreditation of Healthcare Organizations, which has adopted an accreditation standard requiring health care institutions to have "a mechanism . . . for coordinating and facilitating the family's and/or guardian's involvement in decision making throughout the course of treatment."[2] This mechanism might be an ethics committee or an ethics consultant.[3]

---

[1] See **§ 6.3.**

[2] Joint Comm'n on Accreditation of Healthcare Organizations, Accreditation Manual for Hospitals (1992) (standard R1.1.1.3.2.1 & Intent of R1.1.1.3 Through R1.1.1.3.2.3).

[3] *JCAHO Requires Hospitals to Address Ethical Issues,* 7 Med. Ethics Advisor 121 (Oct. 1991).

There has also been voluminous discussion in the professional and scholarly literature recommending that health care institutions establish ethics committees. These committees have received tremendous praise and adulation in some quarters and have been promoted as panaceas for many of the ethical dilemmas and other difficulties that arise in the process of decisionmaking about life-sustaining treatment, although cautions have also been sounded.[4] In spite of several reasons for caution,[5] the discussion about establishing and using ethics committees for decisionmaking purposes continues to grow. Ethics committees have been proposed as vehicles not only to address questions about end-of-life decisionmaking but also to resolve a variety of other issues about medical decisionmaking.

Before establishing an ethics committee, a health care institution needs to know what such a committee is, what functions it can and cannot perform, what its composition might be, what the scope of its authority is, and what some of its limitations are, including possible liability. Although ethics committees are relatively new, there is substantial experience with some of their fore-runners, specifically the committees that were established in the 1960s to ration kidney dialysis when it was a new and very scarce resource, and the institutional review boards (IRBs) that operate mostly in medical research institutions and are mandated by federal law[6] to review research involving human subjects. The record of these related committees[7] raises serious concerns about ethics committees and should at least give pause to their most enthusiastic proponents.

§ 6.2 The "Consensus Model" of an Ethics Committee

Despite the enthusiasm about ethics committees, there is no clear consensus about what they are, the standards by which they should function,[8] the education

---

[4] *See, e.g.,* Wolf, *Ethics Committees and Due Process: Nesting Rights in a Community of Caring,* 50 Md. L. Rev. 798 (1991).

[5] See §§ **6.5–6.6.**

[6] Protection of Human Subjects, 45 C.F.R. pt. 46 (1993).

[7] *See* R. Fox & J. Swazey, The Courage to Fail 200–01 & passim (1974).

[8] *See, e.g., Virginia Network Debates Standards,* Hosp. Ethics, Nov.–Dec. 1994, at 9 (Virginia Bioethics Network has begun a process of development of guidelines for ethics committees and their activities, including training to be ethics consultants); Fox & Stocking, *Ethics Consultants' Recommendations for Life-Prolonging Treatment of Patients in a Persistent Vegetative State,* 270 JAMA 2578 (1993) (81% of 117 experienced ethics committee members arrived at a clear consensus on only easiest hypothetical case and disagreed considerably on others). *See generally* J. LaPuma & D. Schiedermayer, Ethics Consultation: A Practical Guide (1994).

and training that qualifies one to serve on them,[9] how they should be held accountable, or a number of other important issues. There is not even consensus on what ethics committees should be called. Originally, the simple term *ethics committee* or *hospital ethics committee* was used. The President's Commission, however, referred to them as "institutional ethics committees" in order to imply that they could be established and used in any kind of health care institution and not solely in hospitals, where they had their origin.[10] Ethics committees are sometimes also referred to as *bioethics committees* or *biomedical ethics committees.*

Just how many hospitals have ethics committees today is not clear, in part because of the lack of unanimity about what an ethics committee is. According to a survey undertaken by the American Hospital Association's National Society for Patient Representatives, as of 1985, 59 percent of hospitals had working ethics committees, double the number from 1983.[11] However, the 1992 American Hospital Association survey revealed that only 51 percent of hospitals had ethics committees.[12]

The functions of ethics committees are also quite variable. Individual health care institutions are free to charge ethics committees with certain functions and deny them others. However, ethics committees are generally thought of as having one or more of three functions.[13] The role originally intended by the courts to be played by ethics committees is case consultation, that is, providing advice to participants in the decisionmaking process—patients, families, and members of the health care team—for resolving ethical dilemmas that arise in the process of decisionmaking about life-sustaining treatment.[14] In addition

---

[9] *See, e.g.,* LaPuma & Priest, *Medical Staff Privileges for Ethics Consultants: An Institutional Model,* 18 Quality Rev. Bull. 17 (1991); LaPuma & Schiedermayer, *Ethics Consultation: Skills, Roles, and Training,* 114 Annals Internal Med. 155 (1991).

[10] President's Comm'n for the Study of Ethical Problems in Medicine & Biomedical & Behavioral Research, Deciding to Forego Life-Sustaining Treatment 161–70 & passim (1983).

[11] McCarrick & Adams, *Ethics Committees in Hospitals* at i (National Reference Ctr. for Bioethics Literature, Kennedy Inst. of Ethics, Geo. U. 1987), *updated in* McCarrick, *Ethics Committees in Hospitals,* 2 Kennedy Inst. of Ethics J. 285 (1992). *See also* L.W. v. L.E. Phillips Career Dev. Ctr., 482 N.W.2d 60, 74 & n.18 (Wis. 1992) ("Increasingly, health care facilities such as hospitals and nursing homes are creating bioethics committees. In 1990, the American Hospital Association estimated that over 60 percent of United States hospitals had formed bioethics committees.") (citing Gramelspacher, *Institutional Ethics Committees and Case Consultation: Is There a Role?,* 7 Issues L. & Med. 73 (1991)).

[12] Letter from Donald F. Phillips, American Hospital Ass'n, to author (Feb. 7, 1995).

[13] *See* Hastings Ctr., Guidelines on the Termination of Life-Sustaining Treatment and the Care of the Dying 100 (1987) (Part Five, § A, I) [hereinafter Hastings Center Guidelines]; Hoffman, *Does Legislating Hospital Ethics Committees Make a Difference? A Study of Hospital Ethics Committees in Maryland, the District of Columbia, and Virginia,* 19 Law, Med. & Health Care 105 (1991) (50% of hospitals had ethics committees; 67% of ethics committees draft policies, 61% are involved in education, and 69% review particular cases).

[14] **NJ:** *See In re* Quinlan, 355 A.2d 647 (N.J. 1976). See **§ 6.12.**

ethics committees can engage in policymaking[15] and education.[16] These functions may turn out to be just as important as case consultation. Indeed, because they are less controversial, they may, in the long run, become the more important functions of ethics committees.

There is strength in this uncertainty. Health care institutions establishing an ethics committee are free to experiment. Perhaps from the variety of experiences a consensus will develop about what ethics committees can do best. Alternatively, it is possible that ethics committees will remain flexible so as to better meet the needs of different health care institutions.

Despite the uncertainties about ethics committees, there are also areas of agreement. Although there is no single model of what an ethics committee should do and how it should be composed, a consensus is beginning to evolve based primarily on the scholarly and professional literature, spurred by the President's Commission,[17] and beginning to find some support in case law. This will be referred to as the *consensus model* of an ethics committee. The remainder of the discussion in this chapter is based on the assumption that what is meant when the term *ethics committee* is used is the consensus model.

The following is perhaps the best description of the consensus model from a legal authority:

> A hospital biomedical ethics committee is "a multi-disciplinary group of health care professionals within a health care institution that has been specifically established to address the ethical dilemmas that occur within that institution. At the present time, these dilemmas frequently concern the treatment or non-treatment of patients who lack decision-making capabilities." . . . Comprised of physicians, nurses, therapists, clergy, social workers and attorneys who represent a variety of disciplines, interests and points of view, these committees are uniquely suited to provide guidance to physicians, families and guardians when ethical dilemmas arise.[18]

---

[15] *See, e.g., In re* Jobes, 529 A.2d 434, 463 (N.J. 1987) ("As an aid to physicians and families, hospitals and other health-care facilities, such as nursing homes, should give serious consideration to making available the services of ethicists and institutional ethics committees. Hospitals that cannot afford or attract a bio-ethicist could, nonetheless, authorize the establishment of an ethics committee. Such a committee can not only perform an educational and policy-making role, but also act as an advisor to the patient's family and physician."). See **§§ 6.15–6.16.**

[16] *See, e.g., In re* Jobes, 529 A.2d at 463. See **§ 6.18.**

[17] President's Comm'n, Deciding to Forego Life-Sustaining Treatment 160–70. *See also* Judicial Council, Am. Medical Ass'n, *Guidelines for Ethics Committees in Health Care Institutions,* 253 JAMA 2698 (1985).

[18] **MN:** *In re* Torres, 357 N.W.2d 332, 335 n.2 (Minn. 1984) (quoting Cranford & Doudera, *The Emergence of Institutional Ethics Committees,* 12 Law, Med. & Health Care 13 (Feb. 1984)). *See also* Cranford & Jackson, *Neurologists and the Hospital Ethics Committee,* 4 Seminars in Neurology 15 (1984)).

NJ: *Accord In re* Jobes, 529 A.2d 434, 463–64 (N.J. 1987) (Pollock, J., concurring).

§ 6.3 Legal Status of Ethics Committees

Although "courts appear to be impressed by careful and thoughtful study" by ethics committees,[19] there is no legal duty based either on case law[20] or statute[21] for a health care institution to have an ethics committee. In those jurisdictions in which courts have specifically held that ethics committee review of decisions to forgo life-sustaining treatment is not required,[22] it is especially safe to assume that there is no *legal* mandate for health care institutions to have ethics committees. However, a number of courts have acknowledged their existence and recommended their use or establishment.[23] Even the Massachusetts Supreme

---

[19] Office of Legal & Regulatory Affairs, American Hosp. Ass'n, Report of the Adjunct Legal Task Force on Biomedical Ethics, Legal Issues and Guidance for Hospital Biomedical Ethics Committees 3 (Jan. 1985). *See, e.g.,* Rosebush v. Oakland County Prosecutor, 491 N.W.2d 633 (Mich. Ct. App. 1992).

[20] **GA:** *In re* L.H.R., 321 S.E.2d 716, 723 (Ga. 1984) ("In the narrow case before us no hospital ethics committee need be consulted. This in no way forecloses use of such a committee if this is the choice of the hospital, physician or family.").

WI: L.W. v. L.E. Phillips Career Dev. Ctr., 482 N.W.2d 60 (Wis. 1992) (by implication).

[21] **MD:** *But see* Md. Code Ann., Health-Gen. §§ 19-370 to -374 (requiring hospitals to establish a patient care advisory committee to "offer advice in cases involving individual life-threatening conditions" on request of patient, physician, registered nurse, social worker, family member, guardian, agent under a health care power of attorney, or any other health care practitioner directly involved in care of the patient).

NY: *But cf.* N.Y. Pub. Health Law § 2972 (Hospitals must establish a "mediation system for the purpose of mediating disputes regarding the issuance of orders not to resuscitate.").

[22] **FL:** John F. Kennedy Memorial Hosp. v. Bludworth, 452 So. 2d 921, 926 (Fla. 1984).

GA: *In re* L.H.R., 321 S.E.2d 716 (Ga. 1984).

MA: Superintendent of Belchertown State Sch. v. Saikewicz, 370 N.E.2d 417 (Mass. 1977).

MI: Rosebush v. Oakland County Prosecutor, 491 N.W.2d 633, 638 (Mich. Ct. App. 1992) ("In the narrow case before us no hospital ethics committee need be consulted.").

WA: *In re* Colyer, 660 P.2d 738 (Wash. 1983).

[23] **FL:** Browning v. Herbert, 543 So. 2d 258, 269 n.16, 271 (Fla. Dist. Ct. App. 1989); *In re* Barry, 445 So. 2d 365, 372 & n.5 (Fla. Dist. Ct. App. 1984).

GA: *In re* L.H.R., 321 S.E.2d 716. *Cf.* Ga. Code Ann. § 31-39-4(e)(2) (requiring review of do-not-resuscitate order issued by attending physician for incompetent patient having no surrogate).

IN: *In re* Lawrance, 579 N.E.2d 32, 42 (Ind. 1991).

KY: DeGrella v. Elston, 858 S.W.2d 698 (Ky. 1993).

MD: Mack v. Mack, 618 A.2d 744, 771 (Md. 1993) (Chasanow, J., concurring and dissenting) (ethics "committees could review a family's request to withdraw life-sustaining medical treatments for a patient if there is any question about whether the request is appropriate or made in bad faith").

MI: Rosebush v. Oakland County Prosecutor, 491 N.W.2d at 638.

MN: *In re* Torres, 357 N.W.2d 332 (Minn. 1984).

Judicial Court, although repudiating ethics committees as a substitute for judicial review of decisions to forgo life-sustaining treatment, recognized that "the findings and advice of such groups . . . ordinarily would be of great assistance to a probate judge faced with such a difficult decision . . . [and that] it [is] desirable for a judge to consider such views wherever available and useful to the court."[24]

Despite the enthusiasm with which the courts have sometimes embraced the idea of ethics committees, the New Jersey Supreme Court, which first catapulted the idea of ethics committees into the public arena in the *Quinlan* case,[25] has backed off from its initial enthusiasm. In the *Conroy* case, decided almost a decade after *Quinlan,* the court decided not to rely upon ethics committees to make or review decisions about withdrawing life-sustaining treatment from patients in nursing homes on the ground that few nursing homes have them.[26] In so doing, it implicitly recognized that its assumption in *Quinlan* that hospitals had ethics committees was an erroneous one.

Courts have thus far discussed ethics committees only in the context of their value in the decisionmaking process. None has yet to confront the potential legal liabilities that may be incurred as a result of ethics committee activities, although a lawsuit was filed against an ethics committee[27] arising from the facts in the *Bouvia* case.[28] If civil liability might be incurred for the failure to

---

NJ: *In re* Jobes, 529 A.2d 434, 463 (N.J. 1987); *In re* Farrell, 529 A.2d 404, 418–19 (N.J. 1987) ("such a committee might have provided aid and counsel to a physician and family facing . . . [a] decision to discontinue the life-supporting apparatus"); *In re* Quinlan, 355 A.2d 647 (N.J. 1976).

NY: *In re* Storar, 420 N.E.2d 64 (N.Y.), *cert. denied,* 454 U.S. 858 (1981).

WA: *In re* Hamlin, 689 P.2d 1372, 1373 (Wash. 1984); *In re* Colyer, 660 P.2d at 755 (Dore, J., dissenting).

WI: L.W. v. L.E. Phillips Career Dev. Ctr., 482 N.W.2d 60, 74 (Wis. 1992) (if such a committee is available, guardian should request it to review decision, and should consider its opinion in determining whether it is in patient's best interests to forgo treatment).

24 Superintendent of Belchertown State Sch. v. Saikewicz, 370 N.E.2d 417, 434 (Mass. 1977).

25 *In re* Quinlan, 355 A.2d 647 (N.J. 1976). See **§ 6.4.**

26 **NJ:** *In re* Conroy, 486 A.2d 1209, 1238 (N.J. 1985). *See also In re* Peter, 529 A.2d 419, 428 (N.J. 1987) ("Unfortunately, because Ms. Peter is in a nursing home, there is no prognosis committee.").

DE: *See also* Severns v. Wilmington Medical Ctr., Inc., 421 A.2d 1334, 1338 (Del. 1980) ("The Wilmington Medical Center does not have an Ethics Committee or like body which has as a part of its functions the approval or disapproval of the discontinuance of life support systems.").

But see Olson et al., *Early Experiences of an Ethics Consult Team,* 42 J. Am. Geriatrics Soc'y 437 (1994).

27 Bouvia v. Superior Court (Glenchur), 225 Cal. Rptr. 297 (Ct. App. 1986).

28 *See Bouvia Sues Hospital Ethics Committee,* 3 Hosp. Ethics 13 (Jan.–Feb. 1987) (litigation discontinued by plaintiff on advice of counsel; Griffith D. Thomas, Esq., Personal Communication (Mar. 29, 1990)).

consult an ethics committee, an obligation to do so could implicitly be said to exist. The law on this issue is completely undeveloped, and it is impossible to predict whether such an obligation will evolve. Furthermore, liability might ensue not only for failure to consult an ethics committee when one exists, but also for deviation from (or possibly even compliance with) ethics committee recommendations.[29]

IMPETUS FOR ETHICS COMMITTEES

§ 6.4 Substitute for Judicial Review

The primary judicial (and regulatory[30]) impetus for ethics committees has been for them to serve as a substitute for judicial review of decisions about life-sustaining treatment, or some component of the decisionmaking process, such as determining decisionmaking capacity or designating a surrogate. Although few courts have required judicial review of end-of-life decisions,[31] the absence of such an explicit requirement is uncertain cause for comfort. In the overwhelming majority of jurisdictions in which there is no positive legal requirement to obtain judicial review of a decision to forgo life-sustaining treatment, the silence of the courts and legislatures may stand for nothing more than their failure to have addressed these issues, not their view on their proper resolution. Moreover, only a few courts have expressly approved the use of ethics committees,[32] and only infrequently has express judicial approval been given for substituting them for judicial review,[33] and then only in one aspect of the decisionmaking process: review of the prognosis given by the attending physicians and consultants.[34] Put bluntly, using ethics committees in lieu of courts to review decisions or various aspects of the decisionmaking process might not protect against any liability sought to be imposed as a result of actions taken by health care professionals or surrogates.[35]

---

[29] See §§ **6.23** and **6.31.**

[30] See § **16.22.**

[31] See §§ **5.37–5.44.**

[32] See § **6.3.**

[33] Council on Ethical & Judicial Affairs, American Medical Ass'n, Code of Medical Ethics § 2.20, at 37 (1994) ("[T]he use of ethics committees specifically designed to facilitate sound decisionmaking is recommended before resorting to the courts."), § 2.215, at 52 ("Ethics committees or infant review committees should also be utilized to facilitate parental decisionmaking.").

[34] See § **5.58.**

[35] **NJ:** *But see In re* Quinlan, 355 A.2d 647, 671 (N.J. 1976) ("If that consultative body agrees that there is no reasonable possibility of Karen's ever emerging from her present comatose condition to a cognitive, sapient state, the present life-support system may be withdrawn and said action shall be without any civil or criminal liability therefor on the part of any participant, whether guardian, physician, hospital or others. We herewith specifically so hold.").

On balance, however, the silence of the courts should probably be interpreted neither as support for required judicial review of decisions to forgo life-sustaining treatment nor as disapproval of ethics committees review. Virtually without exception, as right-to-die cases of first impression in a jurisdiction occur, the courts have rather consistently followed both substantive and procedural principles of law set down in earlier cases in other jurisdictions, though there are important exceptions.[36]

Despite the increasingly clear and consistent mandate from appellate courts that recourse to the courts for the resolution of disputes about end-of-life decisionmaking is not required and is often not even desirable,[37] physicians and the health care administrators to whom they usually turn for advice in such matters are often advised by their legal counsel to go to court before permitting the removal of life support.

The advice to go to court is frequently born more of fear than of knowledge of the law. In essence, the advice is that when in doubt it is best to "play it safe," that is, either go to court or continue to provide treatment even if patients or their families object. (This latter course is increasingly less likely to be safe because of the potential for liability for nonconsensual treatment.[38]) Physicians and health care administrators are generally averse to going to court because of the real or supposed difficulties associated with obtaining a judicial resolution of these dilemmas. Furthermore, the costs of providing care to patients, who themselves or whose surrogates object to further treatment, can be high. These costs are not merely financial in nature; they can exact a high emotional toll, too, from patients, families, and health care personnel.

In recognition of the difficulties associated with judicial review, the New Jersey Supreme Court recommended in *Quinlan* instead that a hospital ethics committee be involved in such decisionmaking.[39] The court based its recommendation for the use of an ethics committee on a law review article, and it blindly accepted the author's assertion that "'[m]any hospitals have ethics

---

[36] **MO:** Cruzan v. Harmon, 760 S.W.2d 408 (Mo. 1988) (refusing to permit discontinuation of artificial nutrition and hydration in absence of advance directive).

NY: *In re* Westchester County Medical Ctr. (O'Connor), 531 N.E.2d 607 (N.Y. 1988) (refusing to permit forgoing of any life-sustaining treatment unless there is an advance directive).

[37] *See, e.g., In re* Nemser, 273 N.Y.S.2d 624, 629 (Sup. Ct. N.Y. County 1966) (Presented with the question of whether an 80-year-old woman's gangrenous limb should be amputated at the request of her lawyer/son and over the objection of her physician/son, the court opined against "the current practice of members of the medical profession and their associated hospitals of shifting the burden of their responsibilities to the courts, to determine, in effect, whether doctors should proceed with certain medical procedures . . . [and the] . . . ultra-legalistic maze we have created to the extent that society and the individual have become enmeshed and paralyzed by its unrealistic entanglements!").

[38] See **Ch. 17.**

[39] *In re* Quinlan, 355 A.2d 647, 669 (N.J. 1976) ("We consider that a practice of applying to a court to confirm such decisions would generally be inappropriate, not only because that would be a gratuitous encroachment upon the medical profession's field of competence, but because it would be impossibly cumbersome.").

committees' "[40] when in fact they did not.[41] Furthermore, the term *ethics committee* was somewhat of a misnomer in light of the function that the court assigned to the committee, namely, confirmation of the patient's prognosis.[42]

Quinlan's support for ethics committees was almost immediately challenged by the Massachusetts Supreme Judicial Court, which expressed outright disdain for the use of ethics committees in lieu of judicial review, although acknowledging the potential usefulness of such a committee as an adjunct to judicial decisionmaking.[43] Nonetheless, the idea of using ethics committees instead of courts to make such decisions captured the imagination of many physicians and health care administrators who saw them as a way of avoiding unwanted inconvenience, expense, and perhaps publicity, and who often resented the law's telling them how to practice medicine.[44]

In addition to the fact that the article relied on by the New Jersey Supreme Court in *Quinlan* was surely mistaken about how many hospitals had ethics committees, the court assigned the committee a task different from that contemplated by the article's author. The ethics committee was not to decide whether it was proper to remove life support from Karen Quinlan, because the court had already determined that it was legal to do so if she were in a persistent vegetative state. Instead, the function of the so-called ethics committee (a committee that did not in fact exist in the hospital caring for Karen Quinlan) was to review the attending physicians' prognosis. Then, according to the court, if the committee "agrees that there is no reasonable possibility of Karen's ever emerging from her present comatose condition to a cognitive, sapient state, the . . . life-support system may be withdrawn" and no liability would be incurred.[45]

To characterize such a committee as an ethics committee is to imply that the function of the committee is to decide what is right. In fact, however, the function assigned to the committee, to confirm the patient's prognosis, was not

---

[40] *Id.* at 668 (quoting Teel, *The Physician's Dilemma: A Doctor's View: What the Law Should Be,* 27 Baylor L. Rev. 6, 8 (1975)).

[41] *In re* Jobes, 529 A.2d 434, 448 (N.J. 1987) (According to the New Jersey Hospital Association, "since *Quinlan* was decided, approximately eighty-five percent of New Jersey's acute-care hospitals have established prognosis committees that check the attending physician's prognosis when withdrawal of life support from a vegetative patient is under consideration," but it is possible that these are prognosis committees rather than ethics committees.). See **§ 6.4.**

[42] See **§ 6.4.**

[43] Superintendent of Belchertown State Sch. v. Saikewicz, 370 N.E.2d 417, 434 (Mass. 1977) ("We take a dim view of any attempt to shift the ultimate decisionmaking responsibility away from the duly established courts of proper jurisdiction to any committee, panel or group, ad hoc or permanent.").

[44] *Cf.* Scaria v. St. Paul Fire & Marine Ins. Co., 227 N.W.2d 647 (Wis. 1975) (Hanssen, J., dissenting) ("Children play at the game of being a doctor, but judges and juries ought not to.").

[45] *In re* Quinlan, 355 A.2d 647, 671 (N.J. 1976).

a moral issue but a medical one. Other courts, assisted by commentators,[46] have recognized the distinction between an ethics committee and a prognosis committee. Some, following the lead set by *Quinlan,* have required that the patient's prognosis be confirmed by a group of physicians, though, in recognition that this is a medical function, not by a multidisciplinary group.[47] Others have recommended that ethics committees, usually multidisciplinary in nature, be created in health care institutions to assist in resolving the difficult dilemmas created by decisionmaking about life-sustaining treatment.[48] These committees are intended to assist patients, families, and health care professionals in the decisionmaking process and to avoid recourse to the courts.[49] The New Jersey Supreme Court, the source of the original confusion, has subsequently recognized the distinction between a prognosis committee and an ethics committee, and endorsed genuine ethics committees as useful in the process of decisionmaking about life-sustaining treatment.[50]

Like judicial review, review by an ethics committee assumes that the views of all interested parties have been taken into account in the decisionmaking process.[51] Many if not all of the participants in this process often wish to avoid judicial review for a number of reasons.[52] The informality of ethics committee review can be more acceptable because it "'can be more sensitive, prompt,

---

[46] *See, e.g.,* President's Comm'n, Deciding to Forego Life-Sustaining Treatment 166; Annas, *Reconciling* Quinlan *and* Saikewicz: *Decision Making for the Terminally Ill Incompetent,* 4 Am. J.L. & Med. 367 (1979); Collester, *Death, Dying and the Law: A Prosecutorial View of the* Quinlan *Case,* 30 Rutgers L. Rev. 304, 320–21 (1977); Hirsh & Donovan, *The Right to Die: Medico-Legal Implications of* In re Quinlan, 30 Rutgers L. Rev. 267, 280–85 (1977).

[47] **KY:** *E.g.,* DeGrella v. Elston, 858 S.W.2d 698, 710 (Ky. 1993) ("If the attending physician, the hospital or nursing home ethics committee where the patient resides, and the legal guardian or next of kin, all agree and document the patient's wishes and the patient's condition, and if no one disputes their decision, no court order is required to proceed to carry out the patient's wishes.").

MD: *E.g.,* Mack v. Mack, 681 A.2d 744, 771 (Md. 1993) (Chasanow, J., concurring and dissenting).

See §§ **5.57** and **5.58.**

[48] See § **6.3.**

[49] See §§ **6.4** and **6.12.**

[50] *See In re* Peter, 529 A.2d 419, 428 n.12 (N.J. 1987) ("[W]e refer to the consultative body of a hospital that should confirm an attending physician's diagnosis of persistent vegetation as a 'prognosis,' rather than an 'ethics,' committee."); *In re* Jobes, 529 A.2d 434, 463 (N.J. 1987) (Pollock, J., concurring) ("The kind of committee envisioned by the President's Comm'n is not a prognosis committee, as contemplated by *Quinlan,* but a committee that could 'advise patients, families, and practitioners who are trying to make informed decisions.'") (citing President's Comm'n, Deciding to Forego Life-Sustaining Treatment 166); *In re* Farrell, 529 A.2d 404, 418–19 (N.J. 1987) (O'Hern, J., concurring).

[51] **NJ:** *In re* Jobes, 529 A.2d at 463 (Pollock, J., concurring) (citing President's Comm'n, Deciding to Forego Life-Sustaining Treatment 164).

[52] See §§ **5.45–5.55.**

and discrete.' "[53] Ethics committees can provide support to participants in the process in making difficult decisions,[54] and they can diffuse responsibility for decisions about forgoing life-sustaining treatment.[55] Decisions can then be more easily made, whether they be to forgo or to administer treatment, thus breaking impasses that may arise in the decisionmaking process. Most important, ethics committees achieve these benefits " 'while assuring that decisions involving the life and death of incompetent patients will serve their best interests.' "[56]

Review by ethics committees has its drawbacks too. It is not at all clear that diffusion of responsibility for difficult decisions is socially desirable, however much it may be welcome to participants in the decisionmaking process. The use of a committee might too easily diffuse individual responsibility by permitting individual committee members to hide behind the cloak of anonymity that the collectivity provides. "Deferring the decision to an 'ethics committee,' " one judge has observed, "merely shifts the burden of decision to another unqualified tribunal, further removing it from the family or guardian where it rightfully belongs."[57] Another judge has asserted that, although a multidisciplinary committee may diffuse responsibility, "such a committee may be unable to reach a consensus, or in the alternative, it may use the bureaucratic format, wherein no one is singularly responsible, to treat marginal cases too lightly. Either way, the use of such a committee has many substantive and procedural problems and serves to bureaucratize an essentially personal and private decision."[58]

It is arguable that decisions of the kind that may be the subject of ethics committee review or consultation are the kind that are best made in a forum that is more politically responsible than a committee of a health care institution, that is, a forum whose operations are open to the public and whose members are accountable to the public. The burden of responsibility may not weigh as heavily on members of a committee as it might on a judge whose actions are subject to public scrutiny.[59]

---

[53] *In re* Jobes, 529 A.2d at 463 (Pollock, J., concurring).

[54] **NJ:** *In re* Jobes, 529 A.2d at 464 (Pollock, J., concurring) (" 'affords support for decisions being made within that triad, relying on the courts as a last resort' ") (quoting New Jersey Hospital Ass'n's Ethics Task Force); *In re* Farrell, 529 A.2d 404, 418 (N.J. 1987) (O'Hern, J., concurring) ("[S]uch a committee might have provided aid and counsel to a physician and family facing such a decision.").

[55] **NJ:** *In re* Quinlan, 355 A.2d 647, 669 (N.J. 1976) (Ethics committees " 'diffuse the responsibility for making these judgments. Many physicians, in many circumstances, would welcome this sharing of responsibility.' ") (quoting Teel, *The Physician's Dilemma: A Doctor's View: What the Law Should Be,* 27 Baylor L. Rev. 6, 8–9 (1975)).

WA: *In re* Colyer, 660 P.2d 738, 755 (Wash. 1983) (Dore, J., dissenting) ("lighten[s] somewhat the heavy burden . . . upon . . . physicians").

[56] *In re* Jobes, 529 A.2d 434, 463 (N.J. 1987) (Pollock, J., concurring) (citing brief of New Jersey Public Advocate).

[57] *In re* Storar, 434 N.Y.S.2d 46, 47 (App. Div. 1980) (Cardamone, J., dissenting), *rev'd,* 420 N.E.2d 64 (N.Y. 1981).

[58] *In re* Colyer, 660 P.2d at 749–50 n.8.

[59] Superintendent of Belchertown State Sch. v. Saikewicz, 370 N.E.2d 417 (Mass. 1977).

§ 6.5 Improving the Decisionmaking Process

Ethics committees have the potential for improving the manner in which end-of-life decisions are made in a number of ways. First, they can double-check the attending physician and other members of the health care team to be sure that important facts concerning medical issues or the patient's personal preferences are not overlooked. Second, ethics committees, by providing a forum for the airing of disagreements and for facilitating consensus, can help in resolving disagreements among members of the health care team or among family members. Perhaps the most important benefit of ethics committees, indeed the characteristic without which courts might be less enthusiastic about them as a substitute for judicial review, is the belief that they will identify and counsel against decisions that are substantively impermissible[60] or that are based on improper motivations.[61]

Despite the enthusiasm for ethics committees, they are not likely to be a panacea for problems arising in the decisionmaking process about life-sustaining treatment. Indeed, consultation or review by an ethics committee in individual instances of end-of-life decisionmaking has the potential for causing serious problems. Although it is generally recommended that ethics committees contain lay members,[62] they are primarily a form of peer review. Peer review as a form of professional control has been the subject of substantial, penetrating criticism for a considerable time. In particular, IRBs for biomedical and behavioral research, after which ethics committees have in part been modeled, have received mixed reviews as guardians of the rights of research subjects.[63]

The primary concern about peer review is that the participants are not neutral and detached decisionmakers in the manner of judges. They may have a direct interest in the outcome of a particular issue because its resolution may affect them in similar cases. They may be close friends or colleagues of participants in particular cases or, worse, they may be superiors or subordinates of a participant, and their judgment may be subtly or not-so-subtly influenced by personal or professional considerations wholly unrelated to the merits of the case. For

---

[60] **NJ:** *In re* Jobes, 529 A.2d 434, 463 (N.J. 1987) (Pollock, J., concurring) ("'[T]he committee would seek to ensure that the interests of all parties, especially those of the incapacitated person, have been adequately represented, and that the decision reached lies within the range of permissible alternatives.'") (quoting President's Comm'n, Deciding to Forego Life-Sustaining Treatment 164).

[61] **NJ:** *In re* Quinlan, 355 A.2d 647, 669 (N.J. 1976) ("screening out, so to speak, a case which might be contaminated by less than worthy motivations of family or physician").

WA: *In re* Colyer, 660 P.2d 738, 755 (Wash. 1983) (Dore, J., dissenting).

[62] See **§ 6.7.**

[63] *See* Goldman & Katz, *Inconsistency and Institutional Review Boards,* 248 JAMA 197 (1982). *See also* Levine, *Inconsistency and IRBs: Flaws in the Goldman-Katz Study,* 6 IRB 4 (Jan.–Feb. 1984); Goldman & Katz, *Reply: Compelling Evidence for New Policies,* 6 IRB 6 (Jan.–Feb. 1984).

example, nurses, social workers, and physician house staff may feel pressured to conform or subordinate their views to those of senior physician members of the committee. This is not to suggest that all physician members will hold similar views, or that all nurses and social workers will hold similar views in opposition to those of physicians, but that when in fact this does occur it may interfere with a considered, open, and dispassionate committee review of the decisionmaking process.

§ 6.6 Reducing Liability Exposure

By improving the decisionmaking process, ethics committee review has the potential for reducing the liability exposure of health care institutions and health care professionals.[64] Ethics committee review might, however, be a mixed blessing in terms of liability exposure because it conceivably could lead to liability for its own activities.[65]

The risk of liability surrounding end-of-life decisionmaking might be reduced in a number of ways. First, and most obviously, a deliberative process might help to assure that decisions were made that were lawful and acceptable to all interested parties. A second and less direct, though ultimately more extensive, way in which ethics committee review might reduce the risk of liability is by the reporting by ethics committees of case deliberations to professional staff members of the health care institution, thus providing them with a continuing series of examples of how to approach and resolve end-of-life decisionmaking. When faced with similar problems, they may then be in a better position to resolve these issues properly or they may become more sensitized to the need to seek advice.

Cooperation between the ethics committee and the health care institution's risk management and/or quality assurance officers might serve as another way to reduce the liability exposure of the health care institution. Also, if a pattern of inadequate decisionmaking processes or substantively questionable decisions develops with respect to a particular physician, group, or team of health care professionals, it is then possible to take remedial action, for example, by counseling the professionals and/or reporting to the medical staff privileges authorities, or even by reporting to appropriate state licensing authorities.

---

[64] **NJ:** *In re* Quinlan, 355 A.2d 647, 669 (N.J. 1976) ("such a system would be protective to the hospital as well as the doctor").

WA: *In re* Colyer, 660 P.2d 738, 755 (Wash. 1983) (Dore, J., dissenting).

[65] See §§ **6.24–6.30.**

ORGANIZATIONAL ISSUES

§ 6.7 Multidisciplinary Composition

Multidisciplinary membership is a hallmark of ethics committees.[66] Diversity of membership, whether professional or nonprofessional, brings different points of view to committee functioning and makes the committee more representative of the communities both within and outside the health care institution. Consequently, the committee's actions are more likely to be viewed as legitimate and having the force of moral authority that might be lacking if the committee were more parochially constituted.[67]

The number of committee members should be a function of two variables: first, the number of people necessary to represent the different points of view that the committee believes need to be represented; and second, an overall committee size that will not be so large and unwieldy as to impede committee deliberations and other activities. The latter concern can be ameliorated to some extent by the committee's operating through subcommittees or individual consultants (who might report back to the larger committee) when performing case consultation.[68] Hospitals lacking a particular expertise might band together with other hospitals to form a multi-institutional ethics committee.[69]

The kinds of dilemmas that ethics committees address require expertise in the medical facets of a particular patient's condition, in interpersonal skills in dealing with patients and families, in analyzing ethical dilemmas, in relevant legal considerations, and in knowledge of community standards. Thus, an ethics

---

[66] **NJ:** *In re* Jobes, 529 A.2d 434, 463 (N.J. 1987) (Pollock, J., concurring) ("Such an ethics committee would include a diverse membership drawing upon physicians, clergy, ethicists, nurses, attorneys, and members of the general public."); *In re* Quinlan, 355 A.2d 647, 669 (N.J. 1976) ("In the real world and in relationship to the momentous decision contemplated, the value of additional views and diverse knowledge is apparent.").

WA: *In re* Colyer, 660 P.2d 738, 755 (Wash. 1983) (Dore, J., dissenting).

See generally Hastings Center Guidelines 101–02 (Part Five, § A, II(2)(b)).

[67] *See* Office of Legal & Regulatory Affairs, American Hosp. Ass'n, Report of the Adjunct Legal Task Force on Biomedical Ethics, Legal Issues and Guidance for Hospital Biomedical Ethics Committees 55 (Jan. 1985).

[68] See **§ 6.12.**

[69] **WA:** *E.g., In re* Colyer, 660 P.2d 738, 755 n.2 (Wash. 1983) (Dore, J., dissenting) (suggesting establishing by state medical association of standing committee for benefit of hospitals and medical facilities not having their own ethics committees).

WI: *E.g.,* L.W. v. L.E. Phillips Career Dev. Ctr., 482 N.W.2d 60, 74 (Wis. 1992) (noting use of ethics committee of health system-wide ethics committee).

committee should have members knowledgeable in health care administration, law, various medical specialties, medical ethics, ethics, nursing, social work, and theology.[70] Unlike a prognosis committee, the functions of an ethics committee are not strictly medical in nature, and, consequently, a committee composed exclusively of physicians is unnecessary and undesirable.[71] Physicians, of course, will need to serve on the committee both to provide expertise in relevant medical specialties and to provide legitimacy within the health care institution to the committee's actions.

An ethics committee should also have as a member an attorney knowledgeable about the law concerning life-sustaining treatment. Because one of the attorney's functions should be to provide expertise on a body of law that is complex, subtle, and incipient in its development, it is sometimes said that the attorney member should not be the health care institution's corporate counsel, who may have little understanding of patient care issues and whose foremost objective may be to avoid liability. However, advice intended to protect the institution against liability should not be in conflict with patients' best interests. Perhaps in early right-to-die cases, attorneys acted prudently in advising health care institutions to err strongly on the side of treatment, even over the objection of the patient and/or family. However, it is now clear that liability can be imposed for the nonconsensual administration of, as well as forgoing, life-sustaining treatment.[72] Consequently, what is most important is not whether the attorney member represents the health care institution but rather his degree of expertise in the relevant law.

In addition to professional expertise, a knowledge of the values of the communities that the health care institution serves is necessary for the functioning of the consensus model of an ethics committee.[73] If the diverse views of the community served by the health care institution are to be represented, it is desirable that there be lay representatives from different walks of life. The sine qua non of lay or community members is that they not be employees of the health care institution in which the committee functions. Some might be professionals whose expertise is valuable to the committee, such as a lawyer or a pastor.

§ 6.8 Medical Staff versus Institutional Committee

A health care institution must decide whether its ethics committee should be a medical staff committee, a management committee, or a committee of the board of trustees.[74] A medical staff committee may promote a greater degree of

---

[70] President's Comm'n, Deciding to Forego Life-Sustaining Treatment 166.

[71] **NJ:** *In re* Jobes, 529 A.2d 434, 463 (N.J. 1987) (Pollock, J., concurring).

[72] See **§§ 17.2–17.7.**

[73] President's Comm'n, Deciding to Forego Life-Sustaining Treatment 166.

[74] *See* Hastings Center Guidelines 101 (Part Five, § A, II(1)).

acceptance of the committee among physicians, something that may prove necessary to the viability of the committee, at least in its infancy. A medical staff committee is also more likely to be protected from liability by peer review protection statutes.[75] However, because the administration of a health care institution and the governing board to which it reports are ultimately responsible for overseeing all aspects of patient care, there is a good argument for an ethics committee to be directly responsible to management. Alternatively, an ethics committee can be a committee of the board of trustees, reporting directly to that board rather than to hospital management. Either a board or management committee might also help to avoid physician dominance of the committee and assure that it functions as a truly multidisciplinary committee.

§ 6.9 Confidentiality of Deliberations

Ethics committees need to determine whether and to what extent their operations will be confidential. There are actually three specific issues flowing from this larger one: (1) who may attend meetings and discussions, (2) who may have access to committee records and reports, and (3) whether there is an obligation on the part of ethics committee members to keep information obtained in the course of their business confidential. A related question is whether ethics committees should keep written records at all.[76]

To a large extent, these questions are resolved by the fact that confidentiality of information about patients is subject to a number of existing legal protections. Depending on the jurisdiction, there may be state legislation and/or rules issued by regulatory authorities making patient information confidential.[77] Further, there is a general common-law protection accorded to such information.[78] Thus, ethics committee meetings clearly should not be open to the general public in the same manner that judicial proceedings ordinarily are. Ethics committee records should be accorded the same degree of confidentiality within the health care institution as is given to records of any other institutional committee dealing with patient care issues. Finally, members of ethics committees ought to have the same obligation of confidentiality with regard to information about identifiable patients that they would if they were members of the health care team treating the patient; namely, they may not ordinarily disclose such information to others except as is necessary for the patient's care and treatment.

Issues of confidentiality, however, go beyond information about particular patients. To operate effectively, ethics committees must develop a trusting atmosphere both among committee members and between the committee and those who consult it or who might potentially consult it. Ethics committees do

---

[75] See § **6.32.**

[76] See § **6.10.**

[77] *See* M. Macdonald et al., Health Care Law: A Practical Guide § 19.02(3)(c) (1991).

[78] See § **6.29.**

not merely discuss issues of ethics, law, and medicine, but they are also concerned with equally if not more delicate issues, such as errors in professional judgment, personality clashes, professional misconduct, and quality of care. Without a vow of confidentiality to which all ethics committee members subscribe, the functioning of ethics committees can only suffer. Individuals will be reluctant to serve or to participate fully and health care professionals will be reluctant to bring cases to the committee or to be forthcoming with the committee in the absence of such a trusting atmosphere.

However, ethics committees must take care not to err too far in the other direction. Undue secrecy might promote suspicion about the committee, which could undermine its legitimacy. Efforts to conceal ethics committee operations from patients or family members who are potential litigants may be counterproductive because records might be discoverable anyway[79] and because a more forthcoming posture might help them to understand why certain actions were taken, and consequently fend off litigation. A certain amount of openness might also encourage ethics committee members to take greater care than if their deliberations were not subject to scrutiny. Finally, in cases in which ethics committee deliberations precede judicial review, courts may accord greater weight to ethics committee recommendations when they are able to review the information and discussion that formed the basis of the recommendation.

§ 6.10 Recordkeeping

Ethics committees should have a consistent recordkeeping policy that should be consistently applied. The arguments against excessive ethics committee secrecy also weigh heavily in favor of ethics committees' maintaining written records of their activities. In addition, in cases in which ethics committee deliberations precede judicial review, courts might accord greater weight to ethics committee recommendations when they are able to review the information and discussion that formed the basis of the recommendation.

Ethics committee records should include notes or reports in the medical records of individual patients about whom the committee is consulted, as well as a set of permanent records maintained by those with responsibility for the operation of the committee. The standard practice is for consultants to put a note in the medical record of the patient about whom the consultation was requested in order to minimize any misunderstanding about what the advice was and to make the advice available to all members of the health care team who presumably need to know it in order to treat the patient. Inconsistent procedures—for example, only sometimes writing a note or report in the patient's medical record—can raise suspicions of intentional wrongdoing rather than inadvertence.

---

[79] See § **6.32.**

The note in the patient's medical record should include the information that was presented to the committee, the family members or friends of the patient, and the professional staff who were involved; the significant issues that were considered; and the ethics committee's recommendations.[80] It is also important that the note be written in such a manner as to avoid statements that might be considered defamatory or critical of the patient, the family, and the professional staff, or critical of the manner in which the case has been handled by members of the health care team.[81]

Including this information in the patient's medical record means that committee recommendations in a particular case will be subject to discovery even if the committee's own records are not. However, at least at the present, it seems unlikely that there is much protection against discovery for the committee's records either.[82] Thus, including the information in the patient's own record adds little additional risk. Furthermore, the need for those treating the patient to know the ethics committee's advice probably outweighs any risks associated with including the information in the individual patient's record.

§ 6.11 Committee's Jurisdiction and Authority (Mandatory/Optional)

The jurisdiction and authority of ethics committees are usually described as being optional or mandatory. If a health care institution designates its committee as optional/optional, health care professionals are obligated neither to consult the committee nor to follow its advice if consulted. If the committee is a mandatory/optional one, the committee must be consulted in designated classes of situations, but its conclusions are merely advisory, and the persons seeking them are not bound by them as far as the authorities of the health care institution are concerned. If the committee is designated as mandatory/mandatory, however, not only must the committee be consulted for various designated kinds of cases, but also its advice must be followed. Finally, if a committee is designated as being optional/mandatory, there is no need to consult it, but if it is consulted, its advice is binding. Because ethics committees are creatures exclusively of the institution in which they operate, whether their jurisdiction is mandatory or optional and whether their authority is mandatory or optional depend entirely on the wishes of the institutional authorities (that is, medical staff, management, or board of trustees) responsible for their creation.

---

[80] Office of Legal & Regulatory Affairs, American Hosp. Ass'n, Report of the Adjunct Legal Task Force on Biomedical Ethics, Legal Issues and Guidance for Hospital Biomedical Ethics Committees (Jan. 1985).

[81] See § **6.29.**

[82] See § **6.32.**

In practice, most committees are optional/optional,[83] and mandatory/optional is the second most prevalent type of committee. This testifies to an overwhelming sentiment that, although health care professionals ought to be encouraged or even required to consult ethics committees, ultimately it is their responsibility (and specifically that of the attending physician) to determine the appropriate course of action, and ethics committees ought to be purely advisory. If health care professionals were given the option of seeking advice and then required to follow it, there would be a strong disincentive at the outset even to seek advice. Consequently, the optional/mandatory model is unlikely to see widespread use. The bias toward optional jurisdiction and authority also reflects the overall uncertainty about the value of ethics committees and accounts for the fact that the mandatory/mandatory model has not been widely implemented.

There is, however, a potential pitfall from both the optional/optional and mandatory/optional models, namely, that the physician who fails to consult an existing ethics committee, or consults it but does not follow its advice, might run a risk of liability greater than would exist if there were no committee or if the committee were not consulted.[84]

FUNCTIONS OF ETHICS COMMITTEES

§ 6.12 Case Consultation

The original function intended by courts for ethics committees is *case consultation,* that is, assistance in resolving ethical dilemmas arising from the treatment of particular patients, especially forgoing life-sustaining treatment.[85] Some ethics committees perform case consultation as committees of the whole, while others conduct it through subcommittees or individual consultants. When either of the latter two methods is used, reports should be made back to the full committee at least for advisory purposes, if not for discussion and either revision or ratification of the advice given.

---

[83] **NJ:** *See In re* Jobes, 529 A.2d 434, 464 (N.J. 1987) (Pollock, J., concurring) ("Recourse to an ethics committee need not be mandatory, and the decision to seek ethical guidance is best left to the judgment of the patient or someone who can speak on his or her behalf, such as a family member or physician."). *Cf.* President's Comm'n, Deciding to Forego Life-Sustaining Treatment 162–63 (role of some ethics committees is "primarily consultative").

[84] See § **6.28.**

[85] President's Comm'n, Deciding to Forego Life-Sustaining Treatment 161 n.122 (using term "ethics committee" to refer to "those committees having the potential to become involved in decisionmaking in particular patient's cases"). *See also* Pruzinsky, *Definition and Evaluation of Biomedical Ethics Consultations: An Annotated Bibliography,* 2 BioLaw S:221 (Aug. 1989) (bibliography on case consultation).

As originally envisioned in *Quinlan,* ethics committees are to review decisions already made by the family and attending physician. The committee substitutes for judicial review of the attending physician's prognosis.[86] Although it is now universally recognized that the review of prognosis is not properly the domain of an ethics committee,[87] an important legacy of the original idea remains intact. Ethics committees may be used as a substitute for judicial review of decisions that have been made in the ordinary course of medical decisionmaking.[88] The *Quinlan* court intended for decisionmaking to proceed in an otherwise unaltered manner from that which would ordinarily occur, that is, appointing a guardian, disclosing relevant information by the attending physician to the guardian, and obtaining consent to withdraw treatment. Once that had all been done, the ethics committee would be consulted and, if it agreed with the prognosis of the attending physicians, life support could be withdrawn.[89]

The case consultation envisioned by *Quinlan* was retrospective. However, case consultation can occur concurrent with the ordinary decisionmaking process.[90] In fact, the evolution of ethics committees has been in the direction of concurrent case consultation. Along with this gradual transformation from retrospective to concurrent consultation, the courts have increasingly contemplated a primarily advisory role for ethics committees.[91] This differs in two ways from the function

---

[86] *In re* Quinlan, 355 A.2d 647, 669 (N.J. 1976). See §§ **5.57** and **5.58.**

[87] See § **6.4.**

[88] **NJ:** *In re* Jobes, 529 A.2d 434, 464 (N.J. 1987) (Pollock, J., concurring) ("[A]n ethics committee 'enhances, not replaces, the all important patient/family/ physician relationship and affords support for decisions being made within that triad, relying on the courts as a last resort'") (citing Ethics Task Force, Council on Professional Practice, New Jersey Hospital Ass'n, Considerations and Recommendations for Institutional Ethics Committees 7 (1986)); *In re* Farrell, 529 A.2d 404, 418 (N.J. 1987) (O'Hern, J., concurring) ("[S]uch a committee might have provided aid and counsel to a physician and family facing such a decision.").

[89] **NJ:** *In re* Quinlan, 355 A.2d 647, 671–72 (N.J. 1976).

WA: *See also In re* Colyer, 660 P.2d 738, 749 (Wash. 1983) (unanimous concurrence from prognosis board or committee of no fewer than two physicians is required).

[90] **GA:** *E.g., In re* Doe, 418 S.E.2d 3, 4 (Ga. 1992) (hospital's ethics committee "considered and evaluated Jane's condition and recommended the hospital back Jane's mother's desire to enter a DNR order and deescalate medical treatment").

MA: *E.g., In re* Doe, 583 N.E.2d 1263, 1270 (Mass. 1992).

MI: *E.g.,* Martin v. Martin, 504 N.W.2d 917, 920 (Mich. Ct. App. 1993); Rosebush v. Oakland County Prosecutor, 491 N.W.2d 633, 635 (Mich. Ct. App. 1992).

NJ: *E.g., In re* Moorhouse, 593 A.2d 1256, 1263 (N.J. Super. Ct. App. Div. 1991).

NY: *E.g., In re* Westchester County Medical Ctr. (O'Connor), 531 N.E.2d 607, 609 (N.Y. 1988).

[91] **NJ:** *In re* Jobes, 529 A.2d at 463 (Pollock, J., concurring) ("The kind of committee envisioned by the President's Comm'n is . . . a committee that could 'advise patients, families, and practitioners who are trying to make informed decisions.'") (quoting President's Comm'n, Deciding to Forego Life-Sustaining Treatment 166).

envisioned in *Quinlan.* First, use of an ethics committee is usually optional rather than mandatory. Second, the concurrence of the ethics committee with decisions made in the clinical setting is not required for those decisions to be effectuated.

Thus, in effect, the function of many ethics committees has been transformed from one of review (denoting approval or disapproval) to one that is consultative (denoting an advisory capacity). When providing review, the ethics committee must grant its approval before a decision is permitted to go into effect (specifically, here, a decision to forgo life-sustaining treatment). By contrast, when viewed as a consultative body, an ethics committee is available to advise participants in the decisionmaking process but has no formal authority to approve or disapprove of any aspect of that process or to permit or prohibit a decision about life-sustaining treatment. However, the line between case review and case consultation is not sharp.[92]

Besides providing retrospective review or concurrent case consultation, an ethics committee might itself make decisions about forgoing life-sustaining treatment.[93] It might do so broadly by dictating to physician and patient or surrogate that treatment shall be administered or shall be withheld or terminated. Or it might act more narrowly by assuming the role of surrogate, as, for example, when there is no one else available to serve, and collaborating with the attending physician in the decisionmaking process.

Most of the commentary on ethics committees recommends that a decisionmaking function should be abjured, and certainly courts have not envisioned this function for them. Instead, ethics committees should assist the attending physician and other health care professionals involved in the patient's care to analyze the moral and legal aspects of decisionmaking about life-sustaining treatment for particular patients—perhaps by laying out a range of acceptable actions—and leave primary decisionmaking to competent patients or to the families and physicians of incompetent patients.[94] Regardless of what type of role the committee plays, there are important questions of due process that have only begun to be addressed by commentators,[95] but not yet by courts.

---

[92] *See, e.g., In re* Quinlan, 355 A.2d 647, 671 (N.J. 1976) (although requiring review of patient's prognosis, ethics committee referred to as "consultative body").

[93] *See* President's Comm'n, Deciding to Forego Life-Sustaining Treatment 164 (20 to 30% of committees surveyed engaged in decisionmaking). *See, e.g., In re* Westchester County Medical Ctr. (O'Connor), 531 N.E.2d 607, 609 (N.Y. 1988) ("[T]he matter was brought before the hospital's ethics committee which found that it would be inappropriate to withhold this treatment under the circumstances.").

[94] *See, e.g., In re* Jobes, 529 A.2d 434, 463 (N.J. 1987) (Pollock, J., concurring) ("As envisioned by the President's Comm'n, '[w]hen ethics committees serve [as] reviewers, they do not supplant the principal decisionmaker for incapacitated persons (that is, families and practitioners) but they do provide for efficient review without regularly incurring the liabilities of judicial review,'" quoting President's Comm'n, Deciding to Forego Life-Sustaining Treatment 164).

[95] *See* Fletcher, *Ethics Committees and Due Process,* 20 Law, Med. & Health Care 291 (1992); Hoffman, *Regulating Ethics Committees in Health Care Institutions—Is It Time?,* 50 Md. L. Rev. 746 (1991); Wolf, *Ethics Committees and Due Process: Nesting Rights in a Community of Caring,* 50 Md. L. Rev. 798 (1991).

§ 6.13 —Outcome and Process Consultation

When engaged in case consultation, an ethics committee can provide advice about or review either the outcome of the decisionmaking process ("outcome consultation") or the process itself ("process consultation"). Outcome consultation involves evaluating the appropriateness of a decision, ordinarily a decision about administering or forgoing life-sustaining treatment, but it might include other related questions.[96] When performing outcome consultation, it is the committee's responsibility to review the decision to determine whether it was an acceptable or appropriate one.[97] The committee's conclusions could be binding or advisory, depending on how the committee is constituted in a given health care institution.[98] If advisory, the attending physician and surrogate or competent patient would still be free to act on their view of the matter.[99]

For example, in an institution (or jurisdiction) in which it has become accepted practice to permit the withholding of ventilatory support when requested by a competent patient or the surrogate of an incompetent patient, caregivers might still be uncertain about the permissibility of forgoing other forms of life support, such as artificial nutrition and hydration. The review by an ethics committee of a decision to terminate tube-feeding might make it easier for caregivers to accept its legitimacy; or, by contrast, the committee may determine that such a practice is of questionable enough legitimacy that the committee might advise against it or advise that judicial guidance be sought.

However, there are some decisions that, even if all participants in the decisionmaking process concur, are clearly beyond the pale of moral or legal acceptability, and that fact ought to be evident to the ethics committee and communicated to the participants in the decisionmaking process. If, for example, a competent patient suffering from amyotrophic lateral sclerosis wishes to be permitted to die but is afraid to have the ventilator turned off, even with sedation, and therefore requests the administration of a lethal dose of a pain killing medication, an ethics committee presented with this issue would be remiss for not recognizing that such action constitutes some form of criminal homicide.

Process consultation, by contrast, focuses on the appropriateness of the manner in which decisionmaking or one or more of its constituents occur, including assessment of decisionmaking capacity, designation of a surrogate, the adequacy of disclosure to the surrogate or competent patient (that is,

---

[96] See § **6.14.**

[97] **NJ:** *In re* Jobes, 529 A.2d 434, 463 (N.J. 1987) (Pollock, J., concurring) ("'Through reviewing decisions . . . the committee would seek to ensure . . . that the decision reached lies within the range of permissible alternatives,'" quoting President's Comm'n, Deciding to Forego Life-Sustaining Treatment 164).

WA: *Cf. In re* Colyer, 660 P.2d 738, 755 (Wash. 1983) (Dore, J., dissenting) (screen out cases in which "family or physician motivated by less than worthy considerations").

[98] See § **6.11.**

[99] See § **6.28.**

informed consent), the standards for surrogate decisionmaking, and the use of advance directives. An ethics committee might be able to point out any flaws in the decisionmaking process, whether they have tainted the decision, and how the decisionmaking process or portions of it might be repeated and improved so that there is greater confidence that the ultimate decision is an ethically and legally appropriate one. For instance, an ethics committee might advise in the case of a patient of uncertain decisionmaking capacity that the attending physician obtain a consultation from another health care professional with expertise in the evaluation of decisionmaking capacity.

§ 6.14 —Specific Topics for Case Consultation

When performing case consultation, ethics committees can be especially helpful in providing advice about the same sorts of issues for which recourse to the courts could be sought: assessment of decisionmaking capacity, surrogate designation, adequacy of information provided to the patient or surrogate, standards for surrogate decisionmaking, the use of advance directives, and whether to go to court. However, health care professionals may not know how to formulate these specific questions. Instead, they may formulate their concerns in terms of the simple question, "Do we have to go to court?" and be unable to go much beyond that in terms of specifying why they believe they need guidance. Thus, ethics committees could also be consulted when there are merely amorphous questions about the need for advice, or the appropriateness of forgoing or continuing life-sustaining treatment, or, as it is often put, "going to court."

Assessment of Decisionmaking Capacity

An attending physician might request consultation from an ethics committee when a patient's decisionmaking capacity is in question. The committee could suggest ways to reduce the uncertainty about the patient's decisionmaking capacity, such as advising that a consultation be sought from a psychologist. Or the committee might review the procedures already used to evaluate decisionmaking capacity and advise whether the procedures are adequate.

Only in those jurisdictions in which it is clearly necessary to obtain a judicial declaration of incompetency[100] would the attending physician need to do so if both he and the ethics committee believed the patient lacked decisionmaking capacity. Ethics committee consultation would still be helpful in those jurisdictions by assisting the attending physician in determining that a patient of questionable competence should be treated as competent.

---

[100] See § **5.11.**

Designation of a Surrogate

When it is unclear which family member ought to speak for the patient, when family members or a particular family member may have a conflict of interest with the patient, or when there are no family members,[101] the committee process might prove useful in resolving these issues without resorting to the judicial process.

Adequacy of Information

Probably the most important constituent of the decisionmaking process for committee review is the adequacy and accuracy of information available to all competent patients or surrogates. This involves, at a minimum, determining if the surrogate was provided with all information material to making the decision or decisions in question. Beyond this, however, it is essential to be certain that the attending physician or other health care personnel who imparted this information to the surrogate was fully and correctly informed about all relevant information, especially about the options available. Another aspect of information with which the ethics committee ought to be concerned is opinions (that is, matters of medical judgment rather than medical knowledge) that have been conveyed by health care professionals to the patient or surrogate, such as the diagnosis and especially the prognosis with and without treatment.

Standards for Surrogate Decisionmaking

An ethics committee might perform a task that comes close to reviewing the ultimate decision that the participants made. It might review the standard that the surrogate used in making a decision about life-sustaining treatment, review the information about the patient that the surrogate used, and review the application of the standard to that information.

Standard for Decisionmaking. The ethics committee should attempt to ascertain what standard for surrogate decisionmaking the surrogate used and whether it was appropriate, given the information about the patient that was available or should have been available to the surrogate.[102] It will not always be easy or even possible to ascertain the standard used. Rarely will a surrogate be sophisticated enough to actually know what the standards are, although as health care professionals become more sophisticated about such decisionmaking they should be able to educate surrogates in this regard. Rather, the committee might have to

---

[101] See §§ **5.29–5.36.**

[102] See **Ch. 7.**

ascertain the standard inferentially by asking specific questions of the surrogate (and perhaps of other participants, both lay and professional, in the decisionmaking process), such as "Do you know if [the patient] ever expressed any desire not to be kept alive for a long period in a coma?" and "Did you take that information into consideration when making your decision?" If the response to these and similar questions is along the lines of "We did what [the patient] wanted," the committee can infer that a subjective standard was used, whereas if the response is more along the lines of "We did what we thought was best for [the patient]," it would appear that a best interests standard was used.

Information About the Patient. The ethics committee can attempt to ascertain whether the surrogate and the attending physician were in possession of adequate information about the patient relevant to making a decision about life-sustaining treatment. This includes information about the patient's specific wishes concerning the treatment decision in question, which is necessary to know if a subjective or substituted judgment standard is to be applied, and information about the patient's values, preferences, wishes, goals, personality, and the like necessary for the application of a best interests standard (and also useful in the application of the substituted judgment standard). Also, the committee should inquire about whether the patient, though incompetent, is able to express views about treatment either verbally or behaviorally because they might also be relevant to making a decision about life-sustaining treatment.[103]

Furthermore, the ethics committee should determine what efforts the surrogate and/or health care professionals have made to uncover information about the patient's preferences and interests. If these efforts were inadequate, the committee would have grounds to recommend that implementation of any decision to discontinue treatment be postponed or that a decision to continue treatment be reevaluated after further information is gathered.

Application of the Standard. Decisionmakers might have available all information about the patient relevant to making a decision on his behalf and they might use the correct standard for surrogate decisionmaking, yet they might come up with an inappropriate decision about forgoing or continuing life-sustaining treatment. This could result either from a failure to *use* relevant information or from a misunderstanding of the nature of a particular standard for surrogate decisionmaking and how it is to be applied, or both. Furthermore, the application of the standard depends not just on information about the patient's decisionmaking preferences but also on medical information about the patient's diagnosis, prognosis, the risks and benefits of treatment, and the available therapeutic options.[104] The ethics committee should ascertain whether or not all

---

[103] See §§ **7.45–7.46.**

[104] **NJ:** *In re* Farrell, 529 A.2d 404, 419 (N.J. 1987) (O'Hern, J., concurring) ("[T]he availability of such a review panel would reinforce the ability of a guardian ad litem to present to the court any available medically acceptable alternatives that might assist the court in making a decision.").

of this information was considered by the surrogate. The committee could, by applying the appropriate standard to the relevant information about the patient, determine whether the decision made by the surrogate and attending physician was similar to the one that it would have made had it been clothed with that authority. If there is a great deviation between the two, that should at least be a matter for discussion with the surrogate and/or attending physician, and in some cases should be cause for seeking judicial review.

Use of Advance Directives. An ethics committee can also advise about advance directives. When a written directive is in conflict with the patient's more recent oral wishes, when a proxy's or surrogate's decisions are inconsistent with the instructions in a directive, or when a directive requests an act of questionable legality or ethicality, committee review might prove helpful. In many cases such review might resolve problems, though in others—for example, when there is question about the authenticity of an advance directive—the committee might only be able to recommend that judicial guidance be sought.

§ 6.15 Policymaking

Some of the questions for which ethics committees are consulted arise because of uncertainty among health care professionals about the permissibility of certain courses of conduct in forgoing life-sustaining treatment. In the absence of such law, however, one of the functions that an ethics committee can serve is to formulate policies to guide health care professionals in a particular health care institution. This is especially true in those situations in which a legal, professional, or societal consensus already exists, in which one is emerging, or in which it might be possible to forge one. Committees can draft policies governing the range of topics discussed above that are fit subjects for case-by-case committee consultation. Although such policies will not eliminate the need for all individual case consultations, they can narrow the range of situations in which consultations are needed.

§ 6.16 —Institutional Protocols

Health care institutions are increasingly developing written policies to deal with issues involving decisionmaking about life-sustaining treatment. Although sometimes these policies are general in nature, more specific policies, referred to as *institutional protocols,* are increasingly necessary for the guidance of health care professionals, patients, and families,[105] and are perceived to be

---

[105] Congressional Office of Technology Assessment, Institutional Protocols for Decisions About Life-Sustaining Treatments (1988).

helpful in avoiding litigation.[106] These policies are often developed by the institution's ethics committee, which sometimes also administers them. Institutional protocols are a form of private, interstitial lawmaking that can help to fill in the gaps in the law. Like judicial, statutory, and regulatory law, protocols can be used within a health care institution to establish substantive standards for conduct and rules of procedure for determining the applicability of those standards to particular cases.[107]

Institutional protocols have generally been developed on a piecemeal basis to deal with particular aspects of medical decisionmaking. For example, many hospitals have long had policies for obtaining consent to treatment. More recently, hospitals have also begun to develop protocols for writing do-not-resuscitate orders,[108] a process that has been spurred by the adoption of a requirement by the Joint Commission on Accreditation of Healthcare Organizations that all hospitals have a written policy on the use of resuscitation.[109]

Provisions of the Patient Self-Determination Act[110] require health care institutions, as a condition of participation in Medicare and/or Medicaid programs, to "maintain written policies and procedures" applicable to "all adult individuals receiving medical care" concerning "an individual's rights under State [statutory and case] law . . . to make decisions concerning [their] medical care, including the right to accept or refuse [treatment] . . . and the right to formulate advance directives." In the long run, this requirement is likely to result in the formulation of relatively comprehensive institutional protocols concerning not merely the forgoing of life-sustaining treatment but also related issues concerning informed consent to and the right to refuse non-life-sustaining treatment, the determination of incompetency, and the designation of surrogates. Health care institutions need not reinvent the wheel when seeking to develop institutional protocols or guidelines about forgoing life-sustaining treatment. Many health care institutions have published their guidelines.[111] Some have been collected in other places,[112] and many others have been published in connection with the

---

[106] **NJ:** *See* Strachan v. John F. Kennedy Memorial Hosp., 538 A.2d 346 (N.J. 1988); Cerminara, *Life Sustaining Treatment Policy: Put It in Writing,* Provider, July 1990, at 26.

[107] **NJ:** Strachan v. John F. Kennedy Memorial Hosp., 538 A.2d at 349 ("If 'procedures' are to be viewed as more than mere 'paperwork' and considered indispensable in this area—in the nature of a standard that governs the medical community—then those procedures should be designed and imposed by those most directly involved, the physicians and hospitals themselves. That is the business of the medical community itself, not of this Court.").

[108] See §§ **9.4–9.30.**

[109] Joint Comm'n on Accreditation of Hosp., Accreditation Manual for Hospitals § MA.1.4.11, at 90 (1988).

[110] See § **10.21.**

[111] *See, e.g.,* Meisel et al., *Hospital Guidelines for Deciding About Life-Sustaining Treatment: Dealing with Health Limbo,* 14 Critical Care Med. 239 (1986).

[112] *See, e.g.,* President's Comm'n, Deciding to Forego Life-Sustaining Treatment app. I (policies on cardiopulmonary resuscitation).

implementation of the Patient Self-Determination Act.[113] Furthermore, comprehensive sets of guidelines on forgoing life-sustaining treatment, widely cited in judicial opinions, have been published by private organizations.[114]

Written policies or protocols are useful in assuring a consistent understanding among all health care professionals in a given institution about what the policy and procedures on a particular subject actually are.[115] They are also useful when the law is uncertain, as it often is with respect to particulars about forgoing life-sustaining treatment.[116] This is especially desirable in jurisdictions in which there is no clear law on the right to die. However, when there is clear law, it is likely that there will still be a great number of questions left unaddressed by the cases and statutes.

§ 6.17 —Legal Status of Institutional Protocols

The utility of institutional protocols depends in part on the confidence that health care professionals have in their legitimacy. Unfortunately, their legal status is uncertain because courts have not been presented directly with the question of whether institutional protocols should have the force of law or the requisites that could enhance their legitimacy.

The first factor in determining the legal status and thus the effect of institutional protocols is their consistency with existing law. From the perspective of institutional liability, reliance on a protocol is safest and most certain when the protocol accurately embodies state law. Although the protocol or some of its provisions might perform important educational functions within health care institutions, they have no independent legal effect, for health care professionals who rely on them are in reality relying on existing law. They do, however, provide a convenient means by which health care professionals can become acquainted with legal requirements.

Protocols that go beyond the law—in the sense that they stake out institutional positions on issues that have not been addressed (or have not been thoroughly or clearly addressed) in legislation, regulation, or judicial decision—are more helpful to health care professionals, but their legal effect is less certain.

---

[113] *See, e.g.,* Commission on Legal Problems of the Elderly, Am. Bar Ass'n, Patient Self-Determination Act State Law Guide app. B (1991).

[114] *See* Hastings Center Guidelines; National Ctr. for State Courts, Guidelines for State Court Decision Making in Life-Sustaining Medical Treatment Cases (2d ed. 1992).

[115] **CA3:** Kranson v. Valley Crest Nursing Home, 755 F.2d 46 (3d Cir. 1985).

IN: Payne v. Marion Gen. Hosp., 549 N.E.2d 1043 (Ind. Ct. App. 1990).

[116] **NJ:** *Cf.* Strachan v. John F. Kennedy Memorial Hosp., 538 A.2d 346 (N.J. 1988) (hospital, which lacked policy for removal of brain-dead patients from life support in a state lacking common-law or legislative acceptance of brain death as legal definition of death, liable to family of brain-dead patient for failure to remove life support).

For instance, an institutional protocol might take the position that the health care professionals in the institution should give effect to nonstatutory advance directives,[117] but state law might not have addressed the issue. If life-sustaining treatment were to be terminated in reliance on an advance directive and the institutional protocol endorsing it, the legal validity of that course of conduct would be uncertain. A more radical example would be an institutional protocol recognizing that physicians could provide unlimited self-administered morphine to terminally ill competent patients who requested it with the implicit intent of ending their lives by reducing their respiration from the morphine.

Some reassurance about the desirability of institutional protocols that go beyond settled law is provided by the New Jersey Supreme Court's decision in *Strachan v. John F. Kennedy Memorial Hospital.*[118] The court permitted the imposition of liability on a hospital for the emotional distress caused the parents of a brain-dead patient when the hospital and attending physician engaged in substantial delay in removing the patient from life-support apparatus. Even though New Jersey had not adopted, either through legislation or judicial decision, brain death as the legal definition of death, the court strongly suggested that hospitals ought to develop internal procedures for decisionmaking about the removal of life support from brain-dead patients, adding that "the absence of such procedures may . . . be relevant on the issue of whether these defendants fulfilled the obligation that surely they had: to act reasonably in the face of plaintiffs' request to turn over the body."[119]

More problematic are institutional protocols that conflict with existing state law, especially when the protocol permits the forgoing of life-sustaining treatment more broadly than does state law. Indeed, it can be said with little hesitation that an institutional protocol that clearly and directly conflicts with state law in this manner is an invitation to litigation and that the result of such litigation is almost certain to be adverse to the health care institution, its employees, and any staff physician acting in reliance on the protocol.

An institutional protocol can be in conflict with state law in two general ways. The first is a policy that permits the forgoing of treatment when such an action is not permitted by law. An example is the withholding of artificial nutrition and hydration from a terminally ill patient in reliance on that patient's living will in a state in which the living will statute prohibits withholding of artificial nutrition and hydration.[120] An institutional protocol might also conflict with state law by *prohibiting* the forgoing of treatment, which action is permitted by law, such as a policy prohibiting the forgoing of artificial nutrition and hydration under circumstances in which the case law or legislation has legitimated such a decision.[121]

---

[117] See §§ **10.10–10.16.**

[118] 538 A.2d 346 (N.J. 1988).

[119] 538 A.2d at 349. See § **17.6.**

[120] See § **11.12.**

[121] See §§ **9.39–9.40.**

Less clear, however, is the situation in which an institutional protocol conflicts with the spirit, but not the letter, of existing law. An example would be the withholding of artificial nutrition and hydration at the request of a currently competent, terminally ill patient in a state in which the living will statute prohibits the enforcement of an otherwise valid advance directive requesting the withholding of artificial nutrition and hydration. Although a living will statute probably does not apply to the contemporaneous directive of a *competent* patient,[122] there is at least a colorable argument that the legislative intent is to prohibit the forgoing of artificial nutrition and hydration.[123] On the other hand, in the absence of clear legislative history, it is also reasonable to conclude that the legislature merely meant to prohibit the withholding of artificial nutrition and hydration from patients who lacked the capacity to make a contemporaneous decision about so significant an issue.

In all situations other than those in which the institutional protocol faithfully mirrors settled law, both compliance with and deviation from institutional protocols raise important questions for health care professionals. As a general matter, compliance with or deviation from accepted professional standards is evidence respectively of the exercise of or absence of reasonable care.[124] Institutional protocols are not necessarily the same as accepted professional standards. However, when the standards incorporated in an institutional protocol are consistent with the standards of the larger profession, compliance with them should be considered evidence of the exercise of due care.[125] Protocols that go beyond existing law (but do not clearly conflict with it) in permitting the forgoing of life-sustaining treatment are more likely to be recognized by courts as valid (and therefore to provide protection from liability) if they are consistent with prevailing professional standards of practice.

Although it is not obligatory that institutional procedures be written,[126] they are more likely to be credible to a court, and thus provide a defense in litigation, if embodied in the written, formally adopted form of an institutional protocol. This process evidences serious deliberation, good faith, and reasonableness, which are more likely to be found lacking when a health care institution is unable to provide credible evidence that a policy actually exists, is known throughout the institution, and is consistently applied. For instance, in the *Jobes* case, a nursing home refused to acquiesce in the request of the husband of a patient in a persistent vegetative state to cease artificial nutrition and hydration, and claimed that its policy prohibited such a course of action. The New Jersey

---

[122] See **§ 10.10.**

[123] **MO:** *See* Cruzan v. Harmon, 760 S.W.2d 408 (Mo. 1988).

[124] *See* W.P. Keeton et al., Prosser and Keeton on the Law of Torts § 33, at 193–96 (5th ed. 1984). *See also* Restatement (Second) of Torts §§ 285 (*How Standard of Conduct Is Determined*), 295A (*Custom*), 299A (*Undertaking in Profession or Trade*) (1965).

[125] **NJ:** Strachan v. John F. Kennedy Memorial Hosp., 538 A.2d 346, 349 (N.J. 1988).

[126] *See id.* at 349 ("The imposition of a paperwork duty does little to advance either the mission of health-care providers or the needs of society.").

Supreme Court held that, because the nursing home's policy had never been formalized and because no timely notice of the policy had been given the patient and family, the nursing home could not rely on it as grounds for refusing to comply with an otherwise legal request.[127] In so holding, the court cited another New Jersey case[128] in which the hospital seemed to have had a policy prohibiting the withholding of artificial nutrition and hydration but had failed to communicate it to the patient. Thus, in addition to consistency with existing law and professional standards, there should be adequate notice of institutional policies to patients and families (and probably also to health care professionals[129]), which can best be achieved through a formally adopted policy, and through fidelity and consistency of implementation.

Nonetheless, even these precautions might not suffice when the policy places greater restrictions on the forgoing of life-sustaining treatment than does prevailing law. Thus, a health care institution that adopts a policy prohibiting the withholding of artificial nutrition and hydration in a jurisdiction that recognizes the validity of such a practice under appropriate circumstances cannot necessarily be assured that compliance with such a policy will serve as a protection against liability (in this case, for battery or some other intentional tort[130]), even though appropriate notice has been given.[131]

Institutional protocols, if viewed by courts as a kind of safety code, ought to be admissible as evidence of the standard of care in negligence litigation. Industry-wide health care standards promulgated by the Joint Commission for the Accreditation of Healthcare Organizations (JCAHO) are admissible in many jurisdictions, following the lead set in 1965 in the seminal case of *Darling v. Charleston Memorial Community Hospital,*[132] on the basis that JCAHO standards perform the same function as evidence of custom. Rules and standards of professional associations,[133] licensing standards for hospitals, and bylaws of hospitals and trade organizations[134] have all been admitted as evidence of the

---

[127] *In re* Jobes, 529 A.2d 434, 450 (N.J. 1987).

[128] *In re* Requena, 517 A.2d 869 (N.J. Super. Ct. App. Div. 1986).

[129] See § **17.23.**

[130] See §§ **17.2–17.7.**

[131] **NJ:** *In re* Jobes, 529 A.2d 434, 450 (N.J. 1987) ("We do not decide the case in which a nursing home gave notice of its policy not to participate in the withdrawal or withholding of artificial feeding at the time of a patient's admission. Thus, we do not hold that such a policy is never enforceable. But we are confident in this case that it would be wrong to allow the nursing home to discharge Mrs. Jobes. The evidence indicates that at this point it would be extremely difficult, perhaps impossible, to find another facility that would accept Mrs. Jobes as a patient. Therefore, to allow the nursing home to discharge Mrs. Jobes if her family does not consent to continued artificial feeding would essentially frustrate Mrs. Jobes' right of self-determination.").

[132] 211 N.E.2d 253 (Ill.), *cert. denied,* 383 U.S. 946 (1965).

[133] *See, e.g.,* Stone v. Proctor, 131 S.E.2d 297 (N.C. 1963) (American Psychiatric Association standards for administration of electroconvulsive therapy held admissible as evidence of standard of care).

[134] **IA:** *See* Menzel v. Morse, 362 N.W.2d 465 (Iowa 1985).

standard of care, as have other kinds of safety codes.[135] Defendant's own rules—which is what institutional protocols are likely to be unless they reflect some other external, though extralegal standard—have also been held admissible against hospitals on the issue of the duty of care owed to patients.[136]

§ 6.18 Education

An important function that ethics committees can assume is the education of several constituencies: health care professionals, patients and their families, and the public. Education occurs indirectly when health care professionals learn by either giving or receiving advice, that is, through their service on ethics committees or through consultations that they request as caregivers. By serving as committee members, over time a growing number of health care professionals will learn about the kinds of problems that arise in medical decisionmaking in general and decisionmaking about life-sustaining treatment in particular, and about possible appropriate resolutions of those problems, or appropriate procedures for their resolution, or both. One of an ethics committee's most important educational functions is to inform health care professionals about the kinds of situations in which an ethics consultation is needed. Ethics committees should take into account the lack of sophistication of many health care professionals and aim to educate them about when and how to formulate a request for consultation.

The operation of ethics committees in their consultative and policymaking roles implicitly serves educational functions. Education of patients and families occurs when they come into contact with ethics committees through case consultation. Any publicity given to ethics committee activities serves to educate the general public. The promulgation and dissemination of policies help to alert health care professionals to the existence of certain issues as well as to assist in their resolution.

Committees can more directly educate by sponsoring educational programs to familiarize health care professionals with difficult issues that arise in medical decisionmaking—for example, programs that deal with the assessment of

---

[135] **AR:** *See* HCA Health Serv. of Midwest, Inc. v. National Bank of Commerce, 745 S.W.2d 120 (Ark. 1988). *See generally* Feld, Annotation, *Admissibility in Evidence, on Issue of Negligence, of Codes or Standards of Safety Issued or Sponsored by Governmental Body or by Voluntary Association,* 58 A.L.R.3d 148 (1974).

[136] **NC:** Blanton v. Moses H. Cone Memorial Hosp., Inc., 354 S.E.2d 455 (N.C. 1987).

SD: Fjerstad v. Knutson, 271 N.W.2d 8 (S.D. 1978).

WA: Pedroza v. Bryant, 677 P.2d 166 (Wash. 1984); Pederson v. Dumouchel, 431 P.2d 973 (Wash. 1967).

See also Fed. R. Evid. 803(24) (admissibility of "[a] statement not specifically covered by any of the foregoing exceptions [to the hearsay rule] but having equivalent circumstantial guarantees of trustworthiness"). *Cf.* McCorkle, Annotation, *Admissibility in Evidence of Rules of Defendant in Action for Negligence,* 50 A.L.R.2d 16 (1955).

decisionmaking capacity or the proper use of advance directives—or with routine but important and often neglected matters, such as providing patients or surrogates with information necessary to give informed consent. These programs may take the form of lectures and seminars in which issues can be addressed from a conceptual perspective, or of bedside rounds and clinical conferences in which these issues are considered in the context of actual clinical cases.

Explicit efforts can be made to educate not only health care professionals but also patients (for example, by carrying out the mandates of the Patient Self-Determination Act[137]), families, and the larger public. Standards for accreditation of hospitals issued by the Joint Commission on Accreditation of Healthcare Organizations require that hospitals provide education to patients and families.[138] The committee can assist with writing brochures and other written or audiovisual material for patients and their families to help them understand the kinds of problems that might arise and the roles that they might be called upon to play in decisionmaking about life-sustaining treatment. Public education might take the form of public lectures or conferences, news releases, or public service announcements. Ethics committees can also serve as a forum for community discussion.[139] Whatever form such efforts take, their aim should be to familiarize the public about the kinds of issues that might arise in their own lives or those of their friends or family, and to attempt to prepare them in a general way to participate in them.

The result of these activities could be either to strengthen or weaken the consultative role that committees will play in the future. A highly effective process of educating health care professionals might lead to the resolution of issues they otherwise might have brought to the ethics committee as case consultations. On the other hand, by increasing the familiarity of health care professionals, patients, and families with the kinds of issues that the committee is prepared to address, and by reminding them of the existence of the committee, it is possible that the volume of consultative activity could increase.

LEGAL LIABILITIES

§ 6.19 Legal Liability of Committees

Although ethics committees were originally recommended as a means of removing the fear of liability on the part of physicians taking part in making decisions

---

[137] See § **10.21.**

[138] Joint Comm'n on Accreditation of Healthcare Organizations, 1995 Comprehensive Accreditation Manual for Hospitals 189 *et seq.* (1995).

[139] President's Comm'n, Deciding to Forego Life-Sustaining Treatment 163.

about life-sustaining treatment,[140] the use of ethics committees probably does not actually confer such immunity.[141] Moreover, the use of ethics committees might even engender new liabilities for the health care institution in which they operate as well as for the individuals who serve on them.[142] Because no two ethics committees are alike in terms of authority, composition, functions, and operating procedures, there are no generally recognized standards for committees and thus for the assessment of liability that might be associated with them. Further, because ethics committees are in their infancy, experience with their operation and the legal problems that they might generate is virtually nil, and therefore it is difficult to offer much specific guidance about potential ethics committee liability. Rather than being a source of relief, this uncertainty should be a cause for caution.

Because ethics committees ordinarily have no direct responsibility for patient care, it is likely that any legal proceedings brought against a committee, its members, or the sponsoring institution would also involve charges against a physician or physicians and/or other direct caregivers. In fact, those parties are far more likely to be the object of any lawsuit than ethics committee members. The kinds of activities in which ethics committees are most likely to be involved are so indirectly connected with patient care that the idea of ethics committee liability seems somewhat strained. Nonetheless, the prospect of liability is not completely unrealistic. And, because of the high level of anxiety about liability among health care professionals and health care administrators, regardless of its validity, the fear of liability cannot be cavalierly dismissed.

§ 6.20 Potential Defendants

There are a number of parties who might incur liability as a consequence of the activities of ethics committees. Precisely who, if anyone, will depend upon the circumstances of the particular case: who was involved in some way, the organizational structure of the health care institution, and the particular activity that gave rise to the injury for which compensation is sought or penalties are sought to be imposed.

Health Care Institutions. Under ordinary principles of vicarious liability the health care institution itself should be legally responsible for any civil liability

---

140 **NJ:** *In re* Quinlan, 355 A.2d 647, 669 (N.J. 1976) ("'such an entity could lend itself well to an assumption of a legal status which would allow courses of action not now undertaken because of the concern for liability'") (quoting Teel, *The Physician's Dilemma: A Doctor's View: What the Law Should Be,* 27 Baylor L. Rev. 6, 8–9 (1975)).

141 See § **6.31.**

142 *See generally* Blades & Curreri, *Law, Ethics, and Health Care: An Analysis of the Potential Legal Liability of Institutional Ethics Committees, in* 2 BioLaw S:317 (Dec. 1989); Merritt, *The Tort Liability of Hospital Ethics Committees,* 60 So. Cal. L. Rev. 1239, 1274 (1987). See §§ **6.24–6.30.**

that accrues as a result of its ethics committee's activities. Vicarious criminal liability is also possible but unlikely.[143] When the attending physician is an independent contractor rather than an institutional employee, the operations of an ethics committee might even increase the risk of liability for a health care institution by more directly involving the institution in the process of decision-making about life-sustaining treatment. In the absence of an ethics committee, such decisionmaking will largely be carried out by the attending physician and the competent patient or surrogate of an incompetent patient. However, if the attending physician is not an independent contractor (as increasingly fewer physicians are), this will serve to direct the imposition of liability back onto the health care institution.

In practice, however, the attending physician is unlikely to be the sole professional participant in the decisionmaking process, regardless of whether there is an ethics committee. Other health care professionals—especially nurses and social workers, and sometimes house staff physicians—who are ordinarily employees of the health care institution, are also involved. They may become involved because the attending physician specifically requests their assistance and involvement, because it is in the nature of their professional responsibilities to become involved, or because they are the health care professionals most available to the patient and family and could not avoid involvement even if they wished to. Thus, in practice the existence and operation of an ethics committee is unlikely to create a basis for institutional liability that would not already exist.

Committee Members. Members of ethics committees as individuals are likely targets for liability and should agree to serve only if the health care institution agrees to indemnify them against liability and the costs of defense, preferably through insurance. This is an especially important consideration for members who are not also employees of the sponsoring health care institution, most notably independent contractor physicians and lay members.

Ethics Committees. Unless an ethics committee is a legal entity separate from the health care institution in which it operates, it is unlikely that suit will be brought against the committee as an entity or that it would succeed if brought.

Consultees. The operations of an ethics committee might serve as the basis for liability of the individual health care professionals who seek and rely on its advice.[144] Advice from others, regardless of who they are, will not excuse health care professionals from their ordinary duty to exercise reasonable skill and care in the practice of their profession. Seeking and following ethics committee advice will often be evidence that they did act with due care. However, there could be occasions when the advice is so patently incorrect or unwise that following it might constitute the basis for liability.

---

[143] See § **6.31.**

[144] See § **6.28.**

§ 6.21 Potential Plaintiffs

Family. Most litigated right-to-die cases have arisen from lawsuits filed by family members who were opposed to the course of action taken by the attending physician, and a patient's family members are probably the most likely persons to commence legal proceedings against ethics committee members too. A patient might initiate suit, but as a practical matter most patients in right-to-die cases are not likely to be in any condition to sue, assuming they are still alive.

Health Care Personnel. Patients and their families are not the only ones who might feel aggrieved. Members of the health care team who dissent from the course of action ultimately chosen might also feel aggrieved enough to trigger, if not actually commence, legal proceedings. These are perhaps more likely to be criminal than civil,[145] but civil suits are not outside the realm of possibility. An ethics committee might also be impleaded by a health care professional against whom a civil action was filed.

Strangers. Persons who are total strangers to the patient or family and to the health care institution might also commence civil proceedings or file a criminal or administrative complaint.[146] As a practical matter, they will probably be acting in express or tacit cooperation with some member of the health care team, or some other hospital employee from whom they have obtained information about the existence of the matter in question.

§ 6.22 Liability Related to Committee Authority

Whether liability will arise from the activities of the ethics committee depends in part on the type of authority assigned to an ethics committee within the health care institution.[147] If it is mandatory that the ethics committee be consulted in a particular class of cases or if it is mandatory that the committee's advice be followed, the risk of liability is probably enhanced somewhat over what it would be if either the committee's jurisdiction or advice or both were optional. Certainly this is so when the committee's authority is mandatory, for one who orders or induces another to engage in tortious conduct (including omissions) is liable to the injured party.[148] This is not a form of vicarious liability but liability for the actor's own conduct in ordering another to act tortiously.

---

[145] *See* Kirsch, *A Death at Kaiser Hospital,* Cal. Mag., Nov. 1982, at 79 (discussing Barber v. Superior Court, 195 Cal. Rptr. 484 (Ct. App. 1983)).

[146] *See, e.g.,* Weber v. Stony Brook Hosp., 467 N.Y.S.2d 685 (App. Div., *aff'd per curiam,* 456 N.E.2d 1186 (N.Y.), *cert. denied,* 464 U.S. 1026 (1983) (discussed in § **14.8**).

[147] See § **6.11.**

[148] Restatement (Second) of Torts § 877(a) (1977).

The failure to abide by the advice of an ethics committee, even when institutional rules do not make it mandatory to do so, might be viewed as a lack of due care on the part of the consultee. Furthermore, the presumed moral authority of an ethics committee might be such as to make it quite difficult for a consultee actually to act contrary to the committee's advice. Thus, even when an ethics committee's jurisdiction and/or authority is optional, the existence of the committee and the failure either to consult it or to follow its advice might enhance the risk of liability, not for the committee and its members but for those health care professionals (and possibly surrogates) who have failed to consult or be guided by it.

§ 6.23 Liability Related to Committee Function

The potential liabilities associated with ethics committees also depend upon which activities a particular committee undertakes. Case consultation is most likely to generate liability because this function is most likely to involve the committee in, or bring it to the brink of involvement in, patient care. Acting as decisionmaker[149] is more likely to give rise to liability than any other kind of committee activity, because in effect the committee takes over the role ordinarily occupied by the attending physician. Consequently, the basis and scope of committee liability should be the same as that which the attending physician would have. As a practical matter, however, it is unlikely that many committees function in this manner, and this is another reason why they should not.

The educational[150] and policymaking activities of ethics committees are much more remote sources of liability. They could give rise to liability only to the extent that they create the basis for acts on the part of health care professionals that are themselves grounds for liability, and even then the tenuousness of the connection between them and injury to the patient suggests that liability is highly improbable. Such suits, however, might not be totally groundless if a committee were to adopt a policy concerning decisionmaking about life-sustaining treatment that resulted in the forgoing or administration of such treatment with consequent harm to the patient. The committee might be sued directly by the patient or his representatives. Further, a physician against whom suit was brought might seek to implead the health care institution because of the committee's role in the decisionmaking process.

---

[149] See § **6.12.**

[150] *Cf.* Smith, Annotation, *Tort Liability of Public Schools and Institutions of Higher Learning for Educational Malpractice,* 1 A.L.R. 4th 1139 (1980).

PARTICULAR LIABILITIES

§ 6.24 Conditions Required for Liability

For a health care institution, the ethics committee, and/or its members to incur liability, several conditions must be met. First, the committee as an entity or members of the committee acting for the committee must engage in some legally wrongful conduct in connection with any one of the functions that an ethics committee might perform. In addition, the conduct must be the legal cause of an invasion of some legally protected interest. Depending on the particular interest involved, some kind of physical, emotional, relational, and/or economic harm would have to be incurred by a patient (or his family or estate) as a result of a committee activity. The most plausible bases for the civil liability of ethics committees are the intentional torts of unauthorized treatment and intentional infliction of emotional distress,[151] the tort of professional negligence ("malpractice"),[152] and the relational torts of defamation, invasion of privacy, or breach of confidentiality.[153] In addition, there is a possibility of criminal liability,[154] which though slight cannot be discounted entirely.

One of the most difficult hurdles that a claimant against an ethics committee will have to overcome, regardless of the theory of liability, is the nexus between the committee's activities and the injury to the claimant. In traditional tort-law terminology, this is the problem referred to either as "proximate cause" or "scope of duty."[155] Regardless of the way this problem is viewed, the fact that there are intervening events between the committee's activities and the administration or forgoing of treatment makes the imposition of liability on an ethics committee far more tenuous than it is on the health care professionals attending the patient. As committee involvement becomes more direct, the risk of liability increases. The directness of involvement is related both to the committee's authority and to its functions.[156] Also, the risk of liability is probably greater when the basis for the action against the committee is an intentional tort, assuming the necessary facts can be proved to establish all of the other elements of the cause of action, because the legal requirements for the directness of involvement (that is, legal causation) are far less stringent than they are in negligence.

---

[151] See § **6.25** and **17.2–17.7.**

[152] See §§ **6.26** and **17.9–17.16.**

[153] See § **6.29** and **17.8.**

[154] See § **6.30** and **Ch. 18.**

[155] *See* W.P. Keeton et al., Prosser and Keeton on the Law of Torts § 42, at 272–75 (5th ed. 1984).

[156] See §§ **6.22–6.23.**

§ 6.25 Unauthorized Treatment and Intentional Infliction of Emotional Distress

The unauthorized administration of treatment constitutes the intentional tort of battery. The facts giving rise to a battery will also often support liability for intentional infliction of emotional distress.[157] Although an omission to treat cannot constitute a battery, it too may give rise to liability for intentional infliction of emotional distress as well as provide a basis for negligence.[158]

An ethics committee could become implicated in such liability by advising the attending physician to administer treatment without consent, acquiescing in the physician's actions when it had the authority to take action to prevent it or to inform others who did have such authority, or by otherwise encouraging, approving, or condoning nonconsensual treatment.[159] The best way for an ethics committee to avoid liability for unauthorized treatment, intentional infliction of emotional distress, or aiding others in committing either of those torts is for it to be reasonably respectful of court orders and the conscientiously held views of patients, surrogates, and physicians, and reasonably circumspect about exercising its own authority.

§ 6.26 Negligence

Liability imposed on an ethics committee or its members for negligence arising out of its case consultation, policymaking, or educational activities, although novel in form, would largely be shaped by prevailing principles of negligence law applicable to professional liability in general.[160]

Duty. The threshold problem under a negligence theory is whether the committee owes a legal duty of due care to patients. In situations in which the patient is the consultee, on general principles of tort law it is clear that such a duty is owed. When the consultee is the surrogate, the existence of a duty is somewhat less clear, and when the consultee is a health care professional, the answer is still cloudier because of the uncertainty of whether one owes a duty to refrain from injuring a third party.[161]

The clear trend in the law of torts has been toward an expansion of duties owed third parties. However, this is merely a trend. It is not observed in all jurisdictions, and it is observed only in part in others. Furthermore, even if

---

[157] See §§ **17.2–17.7.**

[158] See § **6.26, 17.5–17.7,** and **17.13–17.15.**

[159] *See* Restatement (Second) of Torts §§ 876(b), 877(a) (1977) (liability for assistance or encouragement to another in breaching duty owed third party ordering or inducing tortious conduct).

[160] See §§ **17.9–17.15.**

[161] Robertson, *Clinical Medical Ethics and the Law: The Rights and Duties of Ethics Consultants, in* J. Fletcher et al., Ethics Consultation in Health Care 165–68 (1989).

general principles of negligence law concerning liability to third parties prove inapposite, an ethics committee might incur negligence liability for aiding and abetting another to commit negligence.[162]

Breach. If an ethics committee owes a duty to patients with whose care it becomes involved, the committee would breach this duty if it failed to meet minimally accepted professional standards in providing advice to those who seek committee guidance. A major difficulty in imposing liability would be to establish the standard of care, and thus a breach of duty. This would be difficult because, as a result of the infancy of ethics committees, there probably is no generally accepted standard of conduct for such committees to follow. On the other hand, this might not prove to be a barrier because the customary standard of professional practice is merely evidence of the legally required standard of care.[163] Negligence might be established if it could be said that the ethics committee failed to act in a reasonably prudent manner as determined by standards of ordinary care even in the absence of any evidence of prevailing custom.[164] Indeed, even conformance with the prevailing professional standard, if one were found to exist, would not insulate the committee from liability for negligence but would merely be evidence of the exercise of reasonable care that the trier of fact would be free to consider or reject.[165]

Causation. For liability to be imposed on an ethics committee, the committee must have contributed to a decision by the patient's attending physician or another health care professional to administer or continue treatment, or to withdraw or withhold treatment. However, legal cause is cut off when there is a superseding cause. The physician's conduct is an intervening act either on the basis that the physician might reject the committee's advice (when it is optional) or that it was the attending physician or someone acting under his direction who actually administered, withheld, or terminated treatment. However, when such intervening conduct is foreseeable to the ethics committee, it will not constitute a superseding cause; that is, it will not cut off the committee's liability.[166] Foreseeability is much more likely to be found to exist when a committee's authority is mandatory than when it is optional. However, even when optional, it might be reasonably foreseeable to an ethics committee, depending on the facts and circumstances of a particular case or depending on the custom in the health care institution as to whether or not physicians follow ethics committee advice, that the consultee will or will not follow the ethics committee's advice.

---

[162] *See* Restatement (Second) of Torts § 876(b) (1977). *See also* Merritt, *The Tort Liability of Hospital Ethics Committees,* 60 So. Cal. L. Rev. 1239, 1274 (1987).

[163] Restatement (Second) of Torts § 295A (1965).

[164] *Id.* § 282.

[165] *Id.* § 295A cmt. c, illus. 2; W.P. Keeton et al., Prosser and Keeton on the Law of Torts § 33, at 193–96 (5th ed. 1984).

[166] Restatement (Second) of Torts § 443.

Damages. An ethics committee's advice could result in bodily harm or death to the patient. It might also have adverse financial consequences for the patient, his estate, or those financially responsible for the patient's care (such as his family, a health insurance company, or a governmental agency). If, as a consequence of committee advice or delays in giving advice, the duration of treatment is negligently lengthened and additional costs are incurred, liability could also be imposed for them.[167] Such facts might also give rise to liability for damages for emotional distress either to the patient's family[168] or to a competent patient.[169]

§ 6.27 —Specific Acts of Negligence

There are many ways in which an ethics committee could fail to exercise reasonable care, all of which would be subsumed under the general standard to which any actor is held accountable. However, there are also several specific ways, based on the kinds of things that ethics committees generally do in case consultation, that are most likely to generate liability, though keeping in mind that, overall, liability for any actions of an ethics committee is likely to be remote.

Inadequate Fact Gathering. A committee ought to verify the information it is given by those who seek its guidance and if possible undertake an independent effort at fact gathering. Otherwise, it might render substandard advice in reliance on inadequate or incorrect information. If the committee renders advice (for example, that it is permissible to withdraw a ventilator) on the basis of a mistaken assumption about the patient (for example, that the patient is in a persistent vegetative state), liability for negligence could be incurred. The feasibility of independent fact gathering or even verification depends on constraints imposed by the facts of a particular case and by institutional policies and practices. The former might include the urgency of the need for action, the time constraints on individual committee members, considerations of patient and/or familial privacy, and the willingness of others to cooperate with the ethics committee.

Defective Communication. Even when a committee acts on the basis of complete and correct information, it might communicate its advice to those who requested it in a confusing or incomplete manner, resulting from the use of technical jargon that the recipients do not understand, mistakenly believing they do, or from a failure to convey the information in writing so that if there is confusion it can be reviewed.

---

[167] *See, e.g.,* Estate of Leach v. Shapiro, 469 N.E.2d 1047 (Ohio Ct. App. 1984). *See also* Restatement (Second) of Torts § 906(c) (1977). See §§ **17.9–17.15.**

[168] See § **17.7.**

[169] See § **17.6.**

Inadequately Informed Patients or Surrogates. A combination of inadequate fact gathering and inadequate communication might lead to ethics committee liability based on a theory of informed consent.[170] Although it is the responsibility of the attending physician to make sure that competent patients or surrogates of incompetent patients receive legally adequate information with which to decide about treatment, an ethics committee might find itself in the position of providing advice on the mistaken assumption that the attending physician adequately informed the patient, surrogate, or family members about the therapeutic options and their risks and benefits. Thus, in situations in which the ethics committee discusses options with these patients, surrogates, and families, it should independently ascertain whether they have previously been adequately informed. Otherwise, any decision made on the basis of such counseling could not be considered an informed decision. If the committee finds that the patient or surrogate is inadequately informed, it should ask the attending physician to provide proper information.

Mistake of Law or Policy. An ethics committee might base its advice on an incorrect understanding of applicable law, institutional policy, ethical principles, or customary medical practice. (Similar mistakes can also occur in the formulation of policy or the conduct of educational activities.) Multidisciplinary composition of the membership of the ethics committee is an important factor in protecting against this possibility.[171] For example, the failure to consult an attorney about applicable law would be strong evidence of negligence, and evidence that an attorney was consulted would be of substantial assistance in establishing that the committee exercised reasonable care in giving advice or formulating policy. Similarly, when rendering advice based on institutional policy, on generally accepted principles of medical ethics, or on religious precepts, it is critical that someone expert in those respective areas be consulted. Finally, it is important that there be adequate medical expertise on the committee in specialties and subspecialties relevant to the kind of case the committee has under consideration, as, for example, a neonatologist if the patient is a newborn infant.

Medical Mistake in Prognosis Review. If the functions of ethics committees are properly understood, the committee should not be assigned the task of confirming a prognosis.[172] Nonetheless, some committees that are designated ethics committees are assigned this function and might be called on to perform it. In addition, some health care institutions have either standing or ad hoc prognosis review committees specifically charged with this function, sometimes to conform with a judicially imposed requirement.[173]

---

[170] See §§ **17.11–17.12.**

[171] See § **6.7.**

[172] See §§ **5.59** and **6.4.**

[173] See § **5.58.**

When performing prognosis review, an ethics committee is acting as a medical consultant, and consequently should be liable for negligence in the same way that an individual physician consultant might be. Consequently, nonphysician members of such a committee are well-advised to play a circumspect role in prognosis review, confining themselves to nonmedical aspects such as asking whether all relevant medical facts are available. Their lack of medical expertise will not serve as a defense to liability if they render medical advice. Indeed, physicians who are not specialists in the area of medicine involved in a particular instance of prognosis review are also in jeopardy in this regard. Thus, for example, an internist or a pediatrician who participates in the review of the prognosis of persistent vegetative state will be held to the standard of care of a specialist (for example, a neurologist) in the performance of that function.[174]

§ 6.28 —Liability of Consultees

The existence and operation of an ethics committee might increase the risk of liability to those who consult an ethics committee. (Ironically, it might also provide a defense in an action brought against those who relied on it.[175]) The most likely bases for such liability would be either for failure to consult a committee or for failure to follow its advice, but it is also possible that liability could arise from following ethics committee advice. The parties most likely to incur this kind of liability are health care professionals who seek committee advice, but it could conceivably accrue to others as well, such as a surrogate.

Failure to Consult Ethics Committee. To serve as a basis for negligence liability, the failure to consult an ethics committee would have to be shown to constitute a failure to use reasonable care. It would have to be established that the standard of care, given the facts of the particular case, was to consult a committee. As long as ethics committees are relatively novel, it is not unreasonable and therefore not a breach of the standard of care to fail to consult one. The more it becomes accepted practice for health care institutions to establish ethics committees and for them to be consulted, the more difficult it will be to assert successfully that it is reasonable not to have consulted an ethics committee. Thus, the existence and use of ethics committees create a kind of self-fulfilling prophecy about their utility, and for legal purposes develop, reinforce, and expand the standard of care.

Failure to Follow Ethics Committee Advice. Once an ethics committee has been consulted, it is more difficult to contend that one is acting reasonably in rejecting its advice than it is to argue that it is reasonable not to have consulted the committee at all. This is especially so if the committee's authority

---

[174] *See* 1 D. Louisell & H. Williams, Medical Malpractice ¶ 8.04(1)(c), at 8-46 (1993).

[175] See § **6.31.**

is mandatory rather than optional.[176] But even if a committee's authority is optional, it might still appear to a trier of fact to be unreasonable first to seek advice from those more knowledgeable about such matters and then to reject it.

Following Ethics Committee Advice. It is also possible that liability might accrue to those who consult an ethics committee for following its advice. This will ordinarily be a very difficult argument to make, if for no other reason than that it is the converse of the foregoing argument, namely that if it is reasonable to seek expert advice then it is reasonable to follow it. However, there is some advice that, even if agreed to by all participants in the decisionmaking process, is clearly beyond the pale of moral or legal acceptability. If the advice is patently bad and the consultee follows it, that bespeaks a failure to use reasonable care. An example is ethics committee endorsement of a request by a competent patient for active euthanasia.[177] In such a situation, the consultee would incur liability if the advice were followed, as might the ethics committee for giving it.

§ 6.29 Defamation, Invasion of Privacy, and Breach of Confidentiality

Other possible, though not particularly likely, torts that might be committed through ethics committee activity are defamation and invasion of privacy or breach of confidentiality.

Defamation. Defamation is probably no more likely to occur through ethics committee activity than it is through the activity of any other committee dealing with patient care matters. The records that a committee keeps about particular cases, and especially the notes that its members might write in a patient's medical record, could be the basis for a libel action by the patient, family, and/or member of the health care team about whom defamatory remarks were made. Similarly, defamatory statements about these people made in committee discussions, deliberations, and consultations could serve as the basis for a slander action. The most likely problems are negative comments about the patient's or family members' attitudes or values. Thus, such comments should be avoided. Because truth is a defense to defamation, it is essential that information that is capable of defamatory meaning be verified if it cannot be eliminated. If this cannot be done, efforts should at least be made to ensure that the information is covered by a common-law privilege, the most likely ones being protection of the interests of the speaker,[178] of the party to

---

[176] See **§ 6.11.**

[177] See **Ch. 18.**

[178] *See* Restatement (Second) of Torts § 594 (1977).

whom the statement is made,[179] of their common interests,[180] or of the public interest.[181]

Invasion of Privacy or Breach of Confidentiality. Slightly more likely than defamation actions are actions for invasion of privacy or breach of confidentiality. However, these too are fairly remote possibilities, especially if the committee acts in good faith and without malice.

Information about a patient's medical condition is considered at common law to be confidential.[182] Unauthorized disclosure of such information by a health care professional is actionable as negligence for violation of professional standards, as a breach of a contract for an implied provision of confidentiality, or as an invasion of privacy.[183] In addition, patient confidentiality is protected by statute or regulation in some jurisdictions,[184] and therefore might be actionable as negligence per se.

The performance of case consultation necessitates access to information about the patient that is subject to these legal protections. However, the disclosure of otherwise confidential information is generally not considered to be the basis for an action if the information is disclosed to other health care professionals for reasonable and bona fide purposes of patient care.[185] Thus, a physician who provides confidential information to a newspaper would be liable for breach of confidence,[186] as would a physician who discloses such information to another physician in a social setting. But when an attending physician or other health care professional discloses confidential information to another physician for purposes of obtaining professional advice about treating the patient, the physician is privileged to do so for the benefit of the patient.

Although less clear, a similar common-law privilege probably also exists for disclosure of confidential patient information to health care administrators and committees of health care institutions for the purpose of determining the appropriate kind of treatment for a particular patient. One possible problem is the presence of noninstitutional employees on some ethics committees. However, for purposes of committee activities, they should be deemed to be agents of the health care institution acting in the interest of the patient. As long as disclosure of confidential information to them is reasonable in nature and scope, made in good faith, and intended to assist them in performance of their committee role, their presence should not negate any privilege that would otherwise exist.

---

[179] *See id.* § 595.

[180] *See id.* § 596.

[181] *See id.* § 598.

[182] M. Macdonald et al., Health Care Law: A Practical Guide § 19.02(1), (3)(a)–(b) (1987).

[183] *See* Restatement (Second) of Torts § 652D (1977).

[184] M. Macdonald et al., Health Care Law: A Practical Guide § 19.02(3)(c) (1987).

[185] 2B Aspen Systems Corp., *Hospital Law Manual,* Medical Records ¶ 3-11, at 58–59 (1994).

[186] **MA:** *Cf.* Spring v. Geriatric Auth., 475 N.E.2d 727 (Mass. 1985) (action properly dismissed under state Fair Information Practices Act for claims based on negligent and intentional invasion of privacy and infliction of emotional distress).

There is probably implied consent, too, for members of the health care team to seek a consultation without the express consent of a competent patient or a surrogate and to provide to ethics committee consultants confidential patient information necessary to perform their tasks. Nonetheless, it is advisable when a consultation with an ethics committee is sought by a health care professional to obtain permission from the patient or surrogate to do so. Although express permission might not be necessary, the failure to at least notify the patient or surrogate that a consultation is being sought might engender serious ill will if they later discover that an ethics committee consultation has been obtained. In addition, this kind of discussion between health care professionals and patients and families can sometimes provide an opportunity for participants in the decisionmaking process to air any disagreements that they might have or possibly to correct misinformation that might exist.

Even when the purpose of disclosing confidential patient information to consultants is clearly for the benefit of health care professionals—for example, when the concern is about avoiding legal liability from treatment decisions—the disclosure ought to be privileged if it is made reasonably and in good faith. In such situations, the ethics committee serves a function analogous to that of an attorney, to whom disclosure for benefit of the professional or institution is clearly privileged.

Another possible basis for an action for invasion of privacy is the disclosure by an ethics committee to others of confidential patient information. Again, if the disclosure is made for purposes of assisting the consultee, the disclosure should be privileged if made reasonably and in good faith. Similarly, if the disclosure is made outside the scope of ordinary committee activities—for example, to the press or as gossip—it should be actionable on the same basis as if it were made by the attending physician or some other health care professional.[187]

One way of guarding against actions for breach of confidentiality is for consultations with ethics committees to be made anonymously, that is, without revelation to the ethics committee of the name of the patient. As a practical matter, however, this is often difficult and will of course be impossible if committee members need to meet the patient, read the medical record, or interview family members. More realistically, health care institutions having an ethics committee with members who are not employees should, at the least, formally adopt rules permitting access to confidential patient information by these members when they are involved in case consultation and when they need to know the information to perform that function. Also, all ethics committee members, whether institutional employees or staff physicians, should be required to provide a pledge of confidentiality when appointed to the committee.

---

[187] *See generally* Cranford et al., *Institutional Ethics Committees: Issues of Confidentiality and Immunity,* 13 Law, Med. & Health Care 52 (Apr. 1985).

§ 6.30 Criminal Liability

The fact that most decisions about life-sustaining treatment are made without recourse to the courts, that only one reported case is a criminal prosecution,[188] and that there are relatively few actions for damages[189] testify to the generally responsible manner in which health care professionals and administrators act in right-to-die cases. However, decisionmaking about life-sustaining treatment contains a potential for criminal liability if health care professionals are not exceedingly careful about the manner in which such decisions are made,[190] and, through case consultation, ethics committees could be implicated in conduct constituting the basis for criminal liability.

As is the case on the civil side, committee activity is most likely to give rise to liability if the committee is acting in a decisionmaking capacity. If the committee is only involved in case consultation, and, a fortiori, if it is engaged in policymaking or education, the indirectness of its connection with any harm to a patient will provide a defense to liability in many, though not all, instances. Furthermore, unlike civil liability, it is an exceedingly remote possibility that the health care institution as a corporate entity could incur criminal liability for the activities of the committee. Because vicarious liability for criminal offenses is ordinarily confined to minor offenses—at common law there was vicarious criminal liability only for criminal nuisance and criminal libel,[191] crimes which are rarely prosecuted today; statutory vicarious liability is narrowly defined and circumscribed to conduct not relevant to ethics committees[192]—it is not likely to be a serious concern.[193] Rather, if criminal liability is incurred at all, the risk is almost exclusively to individual committee members or consultees.

When, as is ordinarily the case, an ethics committee provides advice or review but does not act as the decisionmaker, committee liability should usually depend on the existence of liability on the part of the health care professionals attending the patient. If they have not committed a crime, it is virtually impossible that criminal liability would be found to exist on the part of an ethics committee that had merely provided advice.

---

[188] Barber v. Superior Court, 195 Cal. Rptr. 484 (ct. App. 1983). *Compare* Grace Plaza of Great Neck, Inc. v. Elbaum, 588 N.Y.S.2d 853 (App. Div. 1992) (suggesting criminal liability for forgoing life-sustaining treatment without court order) (dictum) *with id.* (Rosenblatt, J., dissenting) (claiming that majority misreads New York precedents).

[189] See **Ch. 17.**

[190] See **Ch. 18.**

[191] W. LaFave & A. Scott, Criminal Law § 3.9(a), at 251 (2d ed. 1986) ("[E]ven these two exceptions . . . have seldom received recognition in this country.").

[192] *Id.* § 3.9(a), at 251–52 (mentioning as examples the liability of a merchant for fraudulent sales by an employee, liability for the sale of alcoholic beverages to minors, or the liability of owners of motor vehicles for parking offenses).

[193] *See generally id.* § 3.9, at 250–56.

For there even to be ethics committee *accessory* criminal liability, there would still have to be an underlying crime committed by the consultee—the attending physician, other health care professionals, and/or surrogate. The substantive offense could be some form of culpable homicide, criminal battery, or mayhem if the patient died or was injured from the withholding or administration of treatment. In addition, assisting suicide is a crime in many jurisdictions,[194] even though there is no longer any criminal proscription on suicide. The likelihood of such charges being sustained against the health care professionals who actually withheld or administered treatment (apart from active euthanasia) is so unlikely in the typical case that the possibility of ethics committee liability is virtually nil.

Liability for anticipatory offenses might be slightly less remote than for accessory liability because no underlying crime need actually be committed and because the acts necessary to prove either a conspiracy or an attempt are so amorphous. Merely planning (or indeed discussing) or attempting conduct that if it resulted in death or serious bodily harm to the patient would constitute the crimes of murder, manslaughter, battery, or mayhem may satisfy the actus reus requirement for such anticipatory criminal liability.[195] Again, however, if the conduct in question is the forgoing of life-sustaining treatment under appropriate circumstances, as opposed to active euthanasia, the risk of liability is exceedingly low.

IMMUNITIES

§ 6.31 Immunity of Consultees

An important impetus for the first judicial suggestion of the use of an ethics committee, in the *Quinlan* case, was to clothe physicians with immunity from liability for decisions to forgo life-sustaining treatment.[196] Although the court "hesitate[d], in this imperfect world, to propose as to physicians that type of immunity which from the early common law has surrounded judges and grand jurors,"[197] it concluded that "there must be a way to free physicians, in the pursuit of their healing vocation, from possible contamination by self-interest or self-protection concerns which would inhibit their independent medical judgments for the well-being of their dying patients."[198] Although rejecting

---

[194] See **Table 18–1.**

[195] *See generally* W. LaFave & A. Scott, Criminal Law §§ 6.2–6.5, at 495–568 (2d ed. 1986).

[196] *In re* Quinlan, 355 A.2d 647, 668 (N.J. 1976)

[197] *Id.* at 668.

[198] *Id.*

the idea of absolute immunity all but in name, the court implied some form of immunity by concluding that if the ethics committee confirmed the attending physicians' prognosis of persistent vegetative state, life support could be withdrawn "and said action shall be without any civil or criminal liability therefor on the part of any participant, whether guardian, physician, hospital or others."[199]

This is an unfortunate and dangerous implication, for it is not reasonable to believe that other courts, or probably even the New Jersey Supreme Court, would confer either absolute or qualified immunity on consultees who rely on ethics committee guidance.[200] Reliance on the advice of an ethics committee will not provide one who takes action on the basis of that advice—most likely the attending physician or other health care professional, but possibly a surrogate—with immunity from liability.[201] What the court might have intended in *Quinlan* was to confer qualified immunity from liability for negligence in confirming the prognosis, but not from liability for wrongful death or homicide for permitting the discontinuation of life-support if the appropriate standards and procedures were not followed.

However, even that conclusion is probably an overreading of what the result of reliance on the advice of an ethics committee should be. At best, reliance on ethics committee advice tends to demonstrate an exercise of due care, but that is quite different from immunity. Consequently, an ethics committee should warn the consultee that reliance on committee advice is not a guarantee of immunity from legal liability, and that in the final analysis the consultee must exercise his own judgment, perhaps informed by relevant information and advice from others.

When it is mandatory to follow committee advice, the consultee's position is even more difficult, especially if the health care institution could apply sanctions for ignoring the advice. The committee's position is also more difficult. It might inform the consultee that following the advice is required by rules of the health care institution, and the failure to do so could lead to the imposition of sanctions, but that nonetheless the consultee has the choice to either abide by the committee advice or risk the sanctions. In practice, this should not prove to be a serious matter because so few, if any, committees operate in this mandatory fashion, and this is probably one of the reasons why few health care institutions have made it mandatory to follow ethics committee advice.

---

[199] *Id.* at 671.

[200] *See generally* Fleetwood & Unger, *Institutional Ethics Committees and the Shield of Immunity,* 120 Annals Internal Med. 320 (1994). See **§ 17.24.**

[201] **MD:** *But see* Md. Code Ann., Health-Gen. § 5-605(b)(1) (conferring immunity from liability for lack of consent on "a physician who acts in accordance with the recommendation of the [patient care advisory] committee" required by Md. Code Ann., Health-Gen. §§ 19-371 *et seq.*).

§ 6.32 Immunity of Ethics Committees

Statutes in all jurisdictions confer some sort of protection on committees of health care institutions or on medical staffs that perform what is known generally as peer review. Although these statutes have typically been invoked in suits against hospitals by physicians whose staff privileges have been denied, curtailed, or terminated, they have also been used in suits by patients injured by treatment provided within the hospital who have sought to obtain information about the defendant/physician's performance.

Some statutes confer immunity from liability under certain circumstances while others, more limited in the scope of protection they provide, merely create a privilege permitting health care institutions not to disclose certain information generated by the committee in the performance of its functions. To the extent that such a privilege denies crucial evidence to those suing committee members or the sponsoring health care institution, it might have the same practical effect as an immunity. None of these statutes mention ethics committees by name, which is understandable because in most cases they were enacted years before the idea of ethics committees existed.[202] Nonetheless, some are worded in such a way that they might apply to ethics committees depending on the functions that a particular committee undertakes.

On balance, however, it is unlikely that these statutes will apply to ethics committee activities. One commentator has remarked that "[a] careful examination of these statutes . . . suggests that in many states they will be cold comfort to ethics committees."[203] Although there are a number of reasons for this conclusion, the primary one is that the statutes were intended to protect a function differing from those performed by ethics committees, namely, evaluating the quality of medical care provided within the health care institution by physicians to determine whether staff privileges should be terminated or limited. Without statutory protection against disclosure of confidential information, it was believed that physicians who were members of peer review committees or who provided evidence to them would be reluctant to criticize their colleagues' conduct on the record, without which the peer review function could not operate properly.

Peer review protection statutes were enacted to preclude or limit the liability of persons reviewing the quality of treatment already provided but not to protect those actually providing the treatment. To the extent that ethics committees perform an analogous function through retrospective review, there is a better

---

[202] **HI:** *But see* Haw. Rev. Stat. § 663-1.7 (Supp. 1994) (conferring immunity on ethics committees).

NJ: *Cf. In re* Jobes, 529 A.2d 434, 464 (N.J. 1987) (Pollock, J., concurring) ("Creation and implementation of ethics committees raises questions concerning . . . the confidentiality of its records and immunity from suit of its members.").

[203] Merritt, *The Tort Liability of Hospital Ethics Committees,* 60 So. Cal. L. Rev. 1239, 1254 (1987).

argument for the applicability of these statutes than if the committees were engaged in the prospective or concurrent activities performed by some ethics committees, because many of the statutes contemplate protection only for retrospective review.

When, however, ethics committees engage in providing advice similar to the role played by a medical consultant, or when they engage in actual decision-making, their functions cannot be characterized as review, but as concurrent involvement in patient care. Some of the peer review statutes recite that they are not to be construed to protect against liability incurred from patient care.[204] When the statutes are unclear on this issue, however, the courts have been divided on whether there should be a distinction between retrospective and prospective review for purposes of applying the statutory protection.[205] Furthermore, some ethics committees are involved in retrospective review in addition to or in place of prospective or concurrent consultation and the statutes might be held to be applicable in such situations. However, it is the prospective and concurrent functions of ethics committees that are most likely to involve them in or bring them to the brink of involvement in patient care and therefore to create the basis for liability.

There are a number of more specific reasons why peer review protection statutes might be inapplicable. Some statutes are worded in such a way as to clearly exclude the function of ethics committees most likely to give rise to liability[206]—case consultation. Some courts have refused to expand the coverage of such statutes to committees not explicitly named in the statutes.[207] Even when more broadly worded, however, peer review protection statutes are not likely to apply to ethics committee activities because in some jurisdictions the multi-disciplinary composition of the committees will work against their inclusion in the statutory protection.[208]

---

204 **AZ:** *See, e.g.*, Ariz. Rev. Stat. Ann. § 36-445.02(C).

MN: *See, e.g.*, Minn. Stat. Ann. § 145.67.

NM: *See, e.g.*, N.M. Stat. Ann. § 41-9-7.

ND: *See, e.g.*, N.D. Cent. Code § 23-01-02.1.

UT: *See, e.g.*, Utah Code Ann. § 58-12-25.

205 Merritt, *The Tort Liability of Hospital Ethics Committees*, 60 So. Cal. L. Rev. 1239, 1260–63 (1987).

206 *Id.* at 1254.

207 *Id.*

208 *Id.* at 1255.

Bibliography

Annas, G. "Ethics Committees: From Ethical Comfort to Ethical Cover." *Hastings Center Report* 21 (May–June 1991): 18.

Blades, C., and M. Curreri. "Law, Ethics, and Health Care: An Analysis of the Potential Legal Liability of Institutional Ethics Committees." *BioLaw* 2 (1989): S:317.

Brennan, T. "Physicians and Futile Care: Using Ethics Committees to Slow the Momentum." *Law, Medicine and Health Care* 20 (1992): 336.

Capron, A. "Legal Perspectives on Institutional Ethics Committees." *Journal of College and University Law* 11 (1985): 417.

Cohen, C. "Avoiding 'Cloudcuckooland' in Ethics Committee Case Review: Matching Models to Issues and Concerns." *Law, Medicine and Health Care* 20 (1992): 294.

Cohen, C., et al. "Assessing Competency to Address Ethical Issues in Medicine." *Academic Medicine* 66 (1991): 14.

Cranford, R., et al. "Institutional Ethics Committees: Issues of Confidentiality and Immunity." *Law, Medicine and Health Care* 13, no. 2 (1985): 52.

Dubler, N., and L. Marcus. *Mediating Bioethical Disputes: A Practical Guide.* New York: United Hospital Fund, 1994.

Fletcher, J. "Constructiveness Where It Counts." *Cambridge Quarterly of Healthcare Ethics* 2 (1993): 426.

Fletcher, J. "Ethics Committees and Due Process." *Law, Medicine and Health Care* 20 (1992): 291.

Fletcher, J., et al., eds. *Ethics Consultation in Health Care* Ann Arbor: Health Administration Press, 1989.

Frader, J. "Political and Interpersonal Aspects of Ethics Consultation." *Theoretical Medicine* 13 (1992): 31.

Frye-Revere, S. "Some Suggestions for Holding Bioethics Committees and Consultants Accountable." *Cambridge Quarterly of Healthcare Ethics* 2 (1993): 449.

Frye-Revere, S. *The Accountability of Ethics Committees and Consultants.* Frederick, MD: University Publishing Group, 1992.

Hoffman, D. "Does Legislating Hospital Ethics Committees Make a Difference? A Study of Hospital Ethics Committees in Maryland, the District of Columbia, and Virginia." *Law, Medicine and Health Care* 19 (1991): 105.

Hoffman, D. "Mediating Life and Death Decisions." *Arizona Law Review* 36 (1994): 821.

LaPuma, J., and D. Schiedermayer. *Ethics Consultation: A Practical Guide.* Boston: Jones and Bartlett, 1994.

Lilje, C. "Ethics Consultation: A Dangerous, Antidemocratic Charlatanry?" *Cambridge Quarterly of Healthcare Ethics* 2 (1993): 438.

McCarrick, P., and J. Adams. *Ethics Committees in Hospitals,* scope note 3. National Reference Center for Bioethics Literature, Kennedy Institute of Ethics, Georgetown University, 1989. Supplemented in *Kennedy Institute of Ethics Journal* 2 (1992): 285.

Merritt, A. "The Tort Liability of Hospital Ethics Committees." *Southern California Law Review* 60 (1987): 1239.

Office of Technology Assessment, U.S. Congress. *Institutional Protocols for Decisions About Life-Sustaining Treatments.* Washington: Government Printing Office, 1988.

Pruzinsky, T. "Definition and Evaluation of Biomedical Ethics Consultations: An Annotated Bibliography." *BioLaw* 2 (1989): S:221.

Robertson, J. "Ethics Committees in Hospitals: Alternative Structures and Responsibilities." *Issues in Law and Medicine* 7 (1991): 83.

Ross, J., et al. *Health Care Ethics Committees: The Next Generation.* Chicago: American Hospital Publishing, 1993.

Scofield, G. "Ethics Consultation: The Least Dangerous Profession?" *Cambridge Quarterly of Healthcare Ethics* 2 (1993): 403.

Scofield, G. "The Problem of the Impaired Clinical Ethicist." *Quality Review Bulletin* 18 (1992): 26.

Self, D. "Is Ethics Consultation Dangerous?" *Cambridge Quarterly of Healthcare Ethics* 2 (1993): 442.

Skeel, J. "Issues in Clinical Ethics Consultation: An Introduction." *Theoretical Medicine* 12 (1992): 1.

Spielman, B. "Invoking the Law in Ethics Consultation." *Cambridge Quarterly of Healthcare Ethics* 2 (1993): 457.

Swenson, M., and R. Miller. "Ethics Case Review in Health Care Institutions: Committees, Consultants, or Teams?" *Archives of Internal Medicine* 152 (1992): 694.

West, M., and J. Gibson, "Facilitating Medical Ethics Case Review: What Ethics Committees Can Learn from Mediation and Facilitation Techniques." *Cambridge Quarterly of Healthcare Ethics* 1 (1992): 63.

Wolf, S. "Ethics Committees and Due Process: Nesting Rights in a Community of Caring." *Maryland Law Review* 50 (1991): 798.

Wolf, S. "Ethics Committees. Toward a Theory of Process." *Law, Medicine and Health Care* 20 (1992): 278.

PART III

SUBSTANTIVE ASPECTS OF THE RIGHT TO DIE

CHAPTER 7

DECISIONMAKING STANDARDS FOR INCOMPETENT PATIENTS

§ 7.1 Introduction

Once the appointment of a surrogate is accomplished either by the judicial appointment of a guardian or through clinical designation, the standards by which the surrogate is required to make medical decisions must be addressed. This chapter addresses that issue.

These standards constitute the basis for determining the legitimacy of the surrogate's decision, whether it occurs exclusively in the clinical setting or whether there is judicial review. The focal point of this chapter is the different *substantive* standards that courts (and, less frequently, legislatures[1]) have enunciated, approved, and applied in end-of-life decisionmaking for incompetent patients. These standards are related to but must be distinguished from *evidentiary* standards. The two generally work in conjunction with each other but are conceptually distinct.[2]

Although these standards are the *legally* authorized standards for decisionmaking for incompetent patients, there is substantial reason to believe that the *de facto* "standard" most frequently employed in the clinical setting is whether the patient's family and the attending physician are in agreement that life-sustainingmedical treatment should be withheld or withdrawn, in other words, a standard based on "family consent."

OVERVIEW OF STANDARDS

§ 7.2 Hierarchy of Standards for Surrogate Decisionmaking

It is now clear that the central substantive issue in decisionmaking about life-sustaining treatment for incompetent patients is the articulation of the standard by which such decisions are to be made. This was not always so. The early right-to-die cases did not often seem consciously aware of the nature of the enterprise in which they were involved—namely, the formulation of substantive standards. For example, in *Quinlan,* the court phrased the matter this way:

> If a putative decision by Karen to permit this non-cognitive, vegetative existence to terminate by natural forces is regarded as a valuable incident of her right of privacy, as we believe it to be, then it should not be discarded solely on the basis that her condition prevents her conscious exercise of the choice. The only practical way to prevent destruction of the right is to permit the guardian and family of

---

[1] See **Ch. 14.**

[2] See §§ **5.61–5.62.**

> Karen to render their best judgment, subject to the qualifications hereinafter stated, as to whether she would exercise it in these circumstances.[3]

Even when courts were clearer about what they were doing, they tended to frame the issue in terms of a search for the "correct" standard, rather than realizing that there might be a *range* of standards. Thus, the Massachusetts Supreme Judicial Court came to the conclusion that the correct question to be answered was whether the patient himself would have decided to forgo treatment in the circumstances in question had he stopped to consider the matter before losing decisionmaking capacity,[4] and the New York Court of Appeals just as definitively believed that for treatment to be withheld[5] or withdrawn[6] the proper question to be answered was whether the patient had in fact made a decision to do so before losing decisionmaking capacity.

Whether consciously or not, roughly between the *Quinlan* case in 1976 and the *Barber* case in 1983, the groundwork was being laid for the articulation of standards for decisionmaking about life-sustaining treatment for incompetent patients. Two things need to be said about this process. First, the courts increasingly began to realize and consciously articulate what it was in fact that they were doing. Second, it became increasingly clear that most, though by no means all, courts would come to the conclusion that these standards are hierarchical in nature, rather than competing with each other for sole reign. The *Barber* case in 1983 was the first to do so, asserting that a substituted judgment standard should be applied, but "[i]f it is not possible to ascertain the choice the patient would have made, the surrogate ought to be guided in his decision by the patient's best interests."[7] Although claiming that "the authorities are in agreement"[8] about this hierarchy, it cited only two authorities, only one of which was an appellate court (the other was the President's Commission), and that court (the Massachusetts Supreme Judicial Court) in fact had insisted that the standard it set forth was the *sole* acceptable standard.

Within two years of the *Barber* decision, the New Jersey Supreme Court in its second right-to-die decision, *Conroy,*[9] now clearly realized both the nature of the standard-making enterprise and the potential for the creation of a hierarchy of standards. Moreover, it realized that the standards are not only hierarchical, but that they exist on a continuum. However, this decision ultimately proved to be a

---

[3] *In re* Quinlan, 355 A.2d 647, 664 (N.J. 1976).

[4] *See* Superintendent of Belchertown State Sch. v. Saikewicz, 370 N.E.2d 417 (Mass. 1977).

[5] *See In re* Storar, 420 N.E.2d 64 (N.Y. 1981).

[6] *See* Eichner v. Dillon, 420 N.E.2d 64 (N.Y. 1981).

[7] Barber v. Superior Court, 195 Cal. Rptr. 484, 493 (Ct. App. 1983).

[8] *Id.*

[9] *In re* Conroy, 486 A.2d 1209 (N.J. 1985). See §§ **7.15–7.16.**

false start, with the New Jersey court backtracking on the *Conroy* conceptual scheme in the 1987 *Peter*[10] and *Jobes*[11] cases by limiting its application only to patients who fit the "Claire-Conroy pattern."[12]

Nonetheless, other courts have since begun to pick up where the New Jersey Supreme Court left off. The first step in this process was the courts' use of the best interests standard in right-to-die cases[13] when there was inadequate evidence to meet the then-prevailing primary standard, the substituted judgment standard.[14] The next step was the adoption by several courts of a standard more stringent than the substituted judgment standard, a standard most frequently (but inappropriately[15]) referred to as the "clear and convincing evidence" standard and also referred to as an "advance-directive standard." The term preferred for use in this treatise is the "subjective standard," a term borrowed primarily from *Conroy*.[16] For a while, it looked as if most of the courts to employ this stringent standard would require, rather than merely prefer, its use.[17] Some courts appeared to adopt this standard in name while in fact applying the less stringent substituted judgment standard; other courts, in the guise of applying the substituted judgment standard, appeared to adopt the subjective standard in substance.[18]

There should be a hierarchy of standards—and the consensus of the courts is that there is such a hierarchy—in which the subjective standard is the preferred standard, but if there is inadequate evidence to apply it, the substituted judgment standard should be applied, and if there is inadequate evidence to apply that standard, then a best interests standard should be applied.[19] This is consistent

---

[10] *In re* Peter, 529 A.2d 419 (N.J. 1987).

[11] *In re* Jobes, 529 A.2d 434 (N.J. 1987).

[12] See §§ **7.31–7.37.**

[13] See §§ **7.12–7.13.**

[14] See §§ **7.7–7.10.**

[15] See § **5.62.**

[16] **NJ:** *In re* Conroy, 486 A.2d 1209, 1229 (N.J. 1985) ("[L]ife-sustaining treatment may be withheld or withdrawn from an incompetent patient when it is clear that the particular patient would have refused the treatment under the circumstances involved. The standard we are enunciating is a subjective one.").

NY: *See also In re* Westchester County Medical Ctr. (O'Connor), 531 N.E.2d 607 (N.Y. 1988) (Hancock, J., concurring) (referring to the New York standard as the "specific-subjective-intent" standard).

[17] **MO:** *See* Cruzan v. Harmon, 760 S.W.2d 408 (Mo. 1988).

NY: *See In re* Westchester County Medical Ctr. (O'Connor), 531 N.E.2d 607 (N.Y. 1988).

[18] See §§ **7.4–7.6.**

[19] *See* Council on Ethical & Judicial Affairs, American Medical Ass'n, Code of Medical Ethics § 2.20, at 37 (1994).

with the overriding goal of decisionmaking for incompetent patients—effectuation of the patient's right of self-determination.[20] It is an accepted part of the legal consensus that the same moral and legal principles—respect for individual self-determination and bodily integrity—requiring physicians to honor the treatment choices of competent patients should also, insofar as possible, govern decisionmaking for patients who lack decisionmaking capacity. Thus, decisionmaking for incompetent patients, just as with competent patients, must seek to learn what the patient's treatment preferences are:

> In practice, this has come to mean that the goal in decisionmaking for incompetent patients is to approximate as closely as possible the decision about treatment the patient would make if able to do so. This is necessarily a hypothetical exercise. The primary point of divergence among courts subscribing to the consensus is *how* hypothetical an exercise they will permit it to be.[21]

Perhaps the clearest judicial recognition that a consensus has evolved in favor of a hierarchy of standards is a statement of the Michigan Court of Appeals in the *Martin* case:

> [W]here a formerly competent patient lacks the requisite capacity to make a decision regarding the withholding or withdrawal of life-sustaining medical treatment, such treatment may be withheld or withdrawn upon proof by clear and convincing evidence of the patient's previously expressed medical preference to decline the treatment under the circumstances presented. [Footnote omitted] . . . In the absence of clear and convincing evidence of the patient's actual medical preferences under the circumstances, a decision whether to withhold or withdraw consent to life-sustaining medical treatment may be exercised by a surrogate decisionmaker applying the "substituted judgment" or the "best interest" standard.[22]

The Michigan court's frequent references to, quotations from, and citations to *Conroy* bring this debate full circle. For example, *Martin* recognizes that the *Conroy* limited-objective standard[23] is substantially the same as the substituted judgment standard.[24] Similarly, it recognizes that the *Conroy* pure-objective

---

[20] Martin v. Martin, 504 N.W.2d 917, 922 (Mich. Ct. App. 1993) ("[W]here a patient has lost the requisite decision-making capacity, it is still the goal to effectuate the patient's right of self-determination.").

[21] Meisel, *The Legal Consensus About Forgoing Life-Sustaining Treatment: Its Status and Its Prospects,* 2 Kennedy Inst. Ethics J. 309 (1992).

[22] Martin v. Martin, 504 N.W.2d 917, 923 (Mich. Ct. App. 1993).

[23] See § **7.29.**

[24] *Compare* Martin v. Martin, 504 N.W.2d 917, 922 (Mich. Ct. App. 1993) ("Under the substituted judgment standard, a surrogate decision-maker may consent to the withholding or withdrawal of life-sustaining medical treatment where there is some trustworthy evidence that the patient would have refused the treatment at issue and the burdens of prolonged life outweigh the benefits.") *with In re* Conroy, 486 A.2d 1209, 1232 (N.J. 1985) ("Under the limited-objective test, life-sustaining treatment may be withheld or withdrawn . . . when there is some trustworthy evidence that the patient would have refused the treatment, and the decision-maker is satisfied that it is clear that the burdens of the patient's continued life with the treatment outweigh the benefits of that life for him.").

standard is substantially the same as the best interests standard as that standard has been described and used by other courts.[25]

Further support for the recognition of this hierarchy has come from, of all places (given its supreme court's ruling in *Cruzan*), Missouri. In the *Warren* case,[26] involving the withholding of cardiopulmonary resuscitation, the court of appeals applied a best interests standard. It distinguished *Cruzan* and limited its requirement that there be clear and convincing evidence of the patient's prior competent refusal (that is, the subjective standard) to the facts of that case, namely to the forgoing of artificial nutrition and hydration, which it claimed that *Cruzan* characterized not as medical treatment but as basic sustenance, which may not be an accurate characterization.[27] Whether this interpretation of *Cruzan* will prevail depends, of course, on the Missouri Supreme Court, the source of the *Cruzan* opinion and the ultimate judicial authority in Missouri.[28]

§ 7.3 Continuum of Substantive Standards

What seems to have come out of the cases is not only that there is a hierarchy of decisionmaking standards, but also that these standards exist along a continuum of values, marked by self-determination at one end and patient welfare at the other. That is, any given decisionmaking standard for incompetent patients represents a trade-off between these two values. The Michigan Court of Appeals, in explaining that in decisionmaking for incompetent patients, first an effort should be made to apply the subjective standard, then the substituted judgment standard, and finally the best interests standard, stated that

> this sequential analysis is rooted in the fact that, as we progress from one step to the next, we are moving away from deferring to the wishes of the patient to the point where we allow others (fiduciaries, family members, ethics committees, and courts) to decide whether the patient will live or die without reference to the patient's wishes. Our premise is that this should not be permitted except as a last resort, given society's reverence for life and its acknowledgment that patients have an inherent right of self-determination. Nevertheless, we may not eliminate the

---

[25] *Compare* Martin v. Martin, 504 N.W.2d at 922 ("Under the best interest standard, if there is no trustworthy evidence that a formerly competent patient would have declined treatment, then a surrogate decision-maker may still consent to the withholding or withdrawal of life-sustaining medical treatment if doing so would serve the patient's best interests.") *with In re* Conroy, 486 A.2d at 1232 ("In the absence of trustworthy evidence, or indeed any evidence at all, that the patient would have declined the treatment, life-sustaining treatment may still be withheld or withdrawn from a formerly competent person . . . if a third, pure-objective test is satisfied.").

[26] *In re* Warren, 858 S.W.2d 263 (Mo. Ct. App. 1993).

[27] *See* Cruzan v. Harmon, 760 S.W.2d 408, 424 (Mo. 1988) ("The issue is not whether the continued feeding and hydration of Nancy is medical treatment; it is whether feeding and providing liquid to Nancy is a burden to her. *Conroy.* We refuse to succumb to the semantic dilemma created by medical determinations of what is treatment; those distinctions often prove legally irrelevant.").

[28] See § **7.12.**

> third stage because to do so would be to hold that where the patient is incompetent, never expressed a preference, and the court cannot determine what the patient would do under existing circumstances, life support may never be withdrawn. That is not the current state of the law.[29]

Furthermore, the continuum also marks varying degrees of hypotheticality. At one end, the standard for decisionmaking for a competent patient is the least hypothetical; in fact, it requires the patient's *actual* decision, though anticipatory rather than contemporaneous. As one proceeds along the continuum, however, the standard depends increasingly on an *approximation* of the patient's views until at some point any effort to determine the patient's wishes is abandoned. At that point, the standard is based on what the surrogate believes is best for a person in the patient's position.

Further, each of the accepted standards occupies not merely a point on the continuum but a range of points because none of the standards are monolithic. What constitutes, for example, a substituted judgment standard for one court may be more akin to a best interests standard for another. There is the added problem that different courts use different names to refer to similar (if not identical) standards, and other courts use the same name to refer to different standards. Consequently, what we find is that there is actually some significant overlap among the standards.

Informed-Consent Standard. At one end of the continuum of decisionmaking standards is pure self-determination, which exists (if at all) only for competent patients. This value is implemented through what might be referred to as an informed-consent standard, and, of course, because the patient is not incompetent, it is implemented without the use of a surrogate. Decisionmaking through informed consent is contemporaneous, rather than anticipatory as is decisionmaking through an advance directive.

Subjective Standard. Decisionmaking for incompetent patients begins with the subjective standard, slightly to the right of the informed-consent standard. It too seeks to implement self-determination to the highest degree possible for an incompetent patient, by demanding that we have knowledge of the patient's actual ("subjective") wishes. However, because the patient is now incompetent, it is anticipatory, rather than contemporaneous, decisionmaking, and therefore in fact self-determination must be implemented to a somewhat lesser degree than is the case for a competent patient giving informed consent.

As applied by one of the few courts (and perhaps the only one) to insist upon the application of this standard to the exclusion of any other, the New York Court of Appeals, the subjective standard comes very close to the informed-consent

---

[29] **MI:** Martin v. Martin, 504 N.W.2d 917, 923 (Mich. Ct. App. 1993).

KY: *Accord* DeGrella v. Elston, 858 S.W.2d 698, 702 (Ky. 1993) ("as evidence regarding the patient's wishes weakens, the case moves from self-determination towards a quality-of-life test").

standard for competent patients.[30] Interestingly, the New York court describes the standard in a broader fashion than it applies it: the "focus must always be on what the patient *would* say *if* asked today whether the treatment in issue should be terminated."[31] The use of the conditional tense is similar to other courts' formulations of the *substituted judgment* standard. However, the evidence that the New York court requires to satisfy this standard, whatever its name and however formulated, is significantly more demanding than that required by the substituted judgment standard as applied by most other courts. Yet, there are exceptions here too. For example, the Maine Supreme Court, which purports to accept the subjective standard (though not by name), in fact accepts evidence in satisfaction of this standard that would never pass muster in New York. The Maine court, in effect, applies a substituted judgment standard, though rejecting it in name.[32]

Substituted Judgment Standard. The substituted judgment standard occupies a broad, indeed, the broadest, portion of the spectrum of decisionmaking standards. At one end there is the standard as applied in Maine which, as mentioned, rejects the substituted judgment label altogether, yet seems to *apply* that standard. Under this strict version of substituted judgment, the standard is considered to be subjective in nature, seeking to ascertain the patient's actual wishes. The difference between it and the subjective standard is that courts applying this variation on the substituted judgment standard permit the patient's wishes to be *inferred* from the patient's statements and conduct;[33] courts requiring the application of the subjective standard require expressed evidence of the patient's wishes.[34]

The other end of the portion of the spectrum occupied by the substituted judgment standard is marked by a version of the standard that seeks to ascertain not the patient's actual wishes but the patient's probable wishes. An extreme version of this is the standard applied repeatedly by the Massachusetts Supreme

---

[30] See § **7.5.**

[31] *In re* Westchester County Medical Ctr. (O'Connor), 531 N.E.2d 607, 613 (N.Y. 1988) (emphasis added).

[32] *See In re* Swan, 569 A.2d 1202, 1206 (Me. 1990) ("As in *Gardner,* we rest our decision on Chad's own conclusion and not on any theory of substituted judgment."); *In re* Gardner, 534 A.2d 947, 950 (Me. 1987) ("Gardner's case is entirely different from those cases of "substituted judgment" where the patients, now incompetent, have never stated their intent and desire as to being kept alive in an irreversible vegetative state by artificial means. Here we need no substitute for Gardner's own personal judgment. Here Gardner before his terrible accident had made his pertinent wishes well known."). See § **7.5.**

[33] **MA:** Superintendent of Belchertown State Sch. v. Saikewicz, 370 N.E.2d 417, 430 (Mass. 1977) ("we recognize the value of . . . indirect evidence"). See §§ **7.7–7.9.**

[34] *See, e.g.,* Mack v. Mack, 618 A.2d 744, 762 (Md. 1993) (McAuliffe, J., dissenting) (Subjective standard "focuses upon prior statements made by the ward. The substituted judgment approach comes into play when the ward has made no prior statements bearing on the issue, or the statements attributed to the ward do not produce a clear and convincing answer."). See § **7.5.**

Judicial Court to never-competent patients.[35] Although the Massachusetts court proclaims that the substituted judgment standard is a subjective one, it undercuts this in two ways. First, the way in which it describes the meaning of "subjective" opens the door for a broad interpretation of the standard: "the goal is to determine with as much accuracy as possible the wants and *needs* of the individual involved."[36] A standard described in terms of "wants" is a subjective standard. However, the essence of a *best interests* standard is the patient's needs, so that a standard described in terms of "needs" departs significantly, if not entirely, from a standard based on self-determination.

Second, and possibly more important, the continual application of the standard by the Massachusetts court to never-competent patients has the effect of transforming it into an objective standard in fact, if not in name.[37] To ask what a patient would have wanted who never had any capacity to formulate and/or express desires is in fact to apply an objective standard, notwithstanding the court's express rejection of such an approach.[38] The application of the substituted judgment standard to never-competent patients requires that it be stretched so far that, in all but name, it becomes a best interests standard. One might be forgiven for wondering what difference a name makes as long as a defensible result is reached. The appropriate response is that because the application of the substituted judgment standard tends to move that standard toward the best interests standard in cases involving never-competent patients, it can easily begin to do so in cases involving once-competent patients too. In other words, the objectification of the substituted judgment standard works against the goal established by the Massachusetts Supreme Judicial Court of ensuring that decisions made on behalf of once-competent but now incompetent patients are driven by self-determination. The only standard for surrogate decisionmaking that makes any sense for never-competent patients is the best interests standard.

The large middle of the substituted judgment standard portion of the continuum is occupied by classic versions of the standard, all of which draw on the New Jersey Supreme Court's articulation of this standard in *Quinlan*.[39] The substituted judgment standard is so broad that in a single state, it may occupy a significant portion of the continuum of standards. In Florida, for example, the

---

[35] See § **7.10.**

[36] Superintendent of Belchertown State Sch. v. Saikewicz, 370 N.E.2d 417, 430 (Mass. 1977) (emphasis added).

[37] *See generally* Martyn, *Substituted Judgment, Best Interests, and the Need for Best Respect,* 3 Cambridge Q. Healthcare Ethics 195 (1994).

[38] *See* Superintendent of Belchertown State Sch. v. Saikewicz, 370 N.E.2d 417, 430–31 (Mass. 1977) ("[D]etermin[ing] with as much accuracy as possible the wants and needs of the individual involved . . . may or may not conform to what is thought wise or prudent by most people. . . . While it may . . . be necessary to rely to a greater degree on objective criteria [when the patient has never been competent], . . . the effort to bring the substituted judgment into step with the values and desires of the affected individual must not, and need not, be abandoned.").

[39] See §§ **7.7–7.9.**

supreme court has observed that "'it is important for the surrogate decision-maker to fully appreciate that he or she makes the decision which the patient would personally choose,'"[40] thereby suggesting a standard approaching the subjective standard. However, it immediately follows this observation by stating that "'we have adopted a concept of "substituted judgment,"'" which quotes the *Barry* case.[41] *Barry* involved a never-competent patient, suggesting that the substituted judgment standard approaches the best interests standard at the opposite end of the continuum from the subjective standard.

Best Interests Standard. The best interests standard occupies the far end of the continuum marked by the value of patient welfare, rather than self-determination.[42] It is more like the substituted judgment standard than the subjective standard in terms of the width of the range that it occupies, and there is a fair degree of overlap between the substituted judgment and best interests standards.

Versions of the standard at the left end of the best-interests portion of the continuum may actually be more subjective than certain versions of the substituted judgment standard. For example, as previously mentioned, the application of the substituted judgment standard to never-competent patients by the Massachusetts court makes this standard, as applied, an objective one. Because we can never know what the patient would have wanted, we are forced to make decisions on the basis of what we believe to be the patient's best interests. By contrast, in *Conroy,*[43] the New Jersey Supreme Court promulgated two best interests standards, a limited-objective standard and a pure-objective standard.[44] One of the requirements for the application of the limited-objective standard is that "the decision-maker is satisfied that it is clear that the burdens of the patient's continued life with the treatment outweigh the benefits of that life for him."[45] This is the objective part of the standard; it is what permits the court to call it a best interests standard. However, in order for the test to be applied, there must also be "some trustworthy evidence that the patient would have refused the treatment,"[46] which is what makes the test more subjective than the conventional best interests standard and certainly more subjective than *Saikewicz*'s substituted judgment standard.

---

[40] Browning v. Herbert, 568 So. 2d 4, 13 (Fla. 1990) (quoting Browning v. Herbert, 543 So. 2d 258, 269 (Fla. Dist. Ct. App. 1989)).

[41] *Id.* (quoting *In re* Barry, 445 So. 2d 365 (Fla. Dist. Ct. App. 1984)).

[42] **MD:** *See* Mack v. Mack, 618 A.2d 744, 759 (Md. 1993) (best interests standard "presents a complete shift in the substantive legal justification" for decisionmaking because it "is not based on the patient's right of self-determination as to whether treatment should be received or rejected").

[43] *In re* Conroy, 486 A.2d 1209 (N.J. 1985).

[44] See §§ **7.16, 7.29,** and **7.30.**

[45] *In re* Conroy, 486 A.2d at 1232.

[46] *Id.*

The common feature of all the variations on the best interests standard, however, is that this standard seeks primarily, if not exclusively, to implement a person's *best interests* rather than his wishes. It thus reflects and seeks to implement the value of *welfare* or well-being, rather than self-determination or autonomy.

Near the far end of the continuum stands the *Conroy* pure-objective standard. It is even more "objective" than the conventional best interests standard as espoused, for instance, in *Barber*[47] because of the New Jersey Supreme Court's unwillingness to permit it to be used as a basis for forgoing life-sustaining treatment if the patient is incapable of perceiving pain.[48] By contrast, the *Barber* best interests standard, by its willingness to permit life-sustaining medical treatment to be discontinued from a patient in a persistent vegetative state who can perceive no benefits or burdens, takes a different view of what constitutes a patient's welfare.

Perhaps the patient-welfare end of the continuum is marked by the kind of best interests standard used in the *Drabick* case, which reposes full authority in the surrogate to determine what is in a patient's best interests unless the patient has a formal living will.[49]

SUBJECTIVE STANDARD

§ 7.4 Nature of and Rationale for the Subjective Standard

Virtually all courts agree that in making decisions for incompetent patients surrogates should be guided by the incompetent patient's actual wishes—that is, by a "subjective" standard.[50] This standard is frequently (but erroneously[51]) referred to as the "clear and convincing evidence" standard, and it is also sometimes referred to as an "actual intent" standard,[52] a "specific subjective intent" standard,[53] or an "advance directive" standard.

---

[47] Barber v. Superior Court, 195 Cal. Rptr. 484 (Ct. App. 1983). See § **7.12.**

[48] *See In re* Peter, 529 A.2d 419 (N.J. 1987); *In re* Jobes, 529 A.2d 434 (N.J. 1987). See §§ **7.31–7.37.**

[49] Drabick v. Drabick, 245 Cal. Rptr. 840 (Ct. App. 1988). See § **7.25.**

[50] *But see* Drabick v. Drabick, 245 Cal. Rptr. 840 (Ct. App. 1988) (requiring application of best interests standard when there is a statutorily appointed conservator and in the absence of a written advance directive).

[51] *See, e.g., In re* Westchester County Medical Ctr. (O'Connor), 531 N.E.2d 607 passim (N.Y. 1988). See §§ **5.62** and **7.4.**

[52] *See in re* Westchester County Medical Ctr. (O'Connor), 531 N.E.2d at 616 (Hancock, J., concurring) ("[T]he present New York rule . . . requir[es] a factual finding of the patient's actual intent.").

[53] *See id.* ("our specific-subjective-intent rule); Grace Plaza of Great Neck, Inc. v. Elbaum, 623 N.E.2d 513, 516 (N.Y. 1993) (Hancock, J., concurring) ("New York's 'specific subjective intent' rule").

Regardless of the name, the subjective standard requires that any decision about forgoing life-sustaining treatment must be based on instructions the patient *actually gave* before losing decisionmaking capacity. That is, under this standard, life-sustaining treatment may be withdrawn or withheld if the patient himself authorized the forgoing of treatment prior to losing decisionmaking capacity. This standard is distinguished from the substituted judgment standard, at least in theory though not always in application, by its insistence on ascertaining the patient's actual wishes rather than his probable wishes as the substituted judgment standard is willing to do.

The subjective standard is the least hypothetical standard for making decisions about life-sustaining treatment. It requires that we not speculate about what the patient wanted or would have wanted but discover what the patient did in fact want. What makes the standard hypothetical at all is the fact that the patient made the decision about life-sustaining treatment anticipatorily—that is, in advance without knowledge of the precise facts prevailing at the time the decision is to be implemented—rather than contemporaneously or nearly contemporaneously with the implementation of the decision. (Of course, if it were a contemporaneous decision, the patient would have to be in possession of decisionmaking capacity, and we would not need to rely on a surrogate to make decisions for the patient.)

By contrast, the other standards for decisionmaking for incompetent patients require far more speculation about the patient's wishes. The best interests standard is the most hypothetical standard because it relies either not at all or not entirely on the patient's *preferences,* but on what others determine to be his *interests.* The substituted judgment standard is somewhere in between, occupying a rather broad part of the continuum because different courts define and apply it more or less stringently.

Several grounds are given for preferring the subjective standard. First, and most fundamentally, decisionmaking for incompetent patients should be based on the same principles as decisionmaking for competent patients: respect for individual self-determination and bodily integrity. These principles require that physicians honor the treatment choices of competent patients, and therefore, insofar as possible, they should govern decisionmaking for patients who lack decisionmaking capacity. Just as with competent patients, decisionmaking for incompetent patients must seek to learn what the patient's treatment preferences were.

Second, some courts are concerned that unless such a standard is applied, surrogates will make decisions about termination of life support for their own selfish reasons.[54] One basis for this fear is the very broad range of factors that courts have used in describing the primary alternative to the subjective standard,

---

[54] *See, e.g., In re* Department of Veterans Affairs Medical Ctr., 749 F. Supp. 495 (S.D.N.Y.), *aff'd,* 914 F.2d 239 (2d Cir. 1990) (patient's wife's reasons for rejecting treatment were suspect because of her intense hostility toward doctors and because of her denial that patient had gangrene).

the substituted judgment standard.[55] Although most courts construe the substituted judgment standard strictly so as to require evidence of the patient's actual intent—though inferred from statements and conduct rather than expressly stated,[56] as is the case with the subjective standard—other courts will consider far more objective kinds of evidence having little or nothing to do with the particular patient's explicitly stated or inferred preferences. A very strict view of the substituted judgment standard makes it virtually indistinguishable from the subjective standard, and the more expansive view makes it virtually indistinguishable from the best interests standard.

A third reason for preferring the subjective standard is the fear that a patient might have expressed preferences about life-sustaining treatment but changed his mind and not expressed this change, prior to losing decisionmaking capacity.[57] The New York Court of Appeals has been especially plagued by this fear, and consequently, it has insisted upon a subjective standard requiring a "clear expression of a present intention to forego" the treatment in question.[58] In its absence, life-sustaining treatment cannot be withheld or withdrawn. By contrast, the Florida Supreme Court, when confronted with the argument made by the state that a patient may have changed her mind between issuing an advance directive and losing decisionmaking capacity, refused to allow itself to be stymied by this problem and permitted the forgoing of treatment consistent with the wishes the patient had expressed[59] because it was "persuaded that when the patient has taken the time and the trouble to specifically express his or her wishes for future health care in the event of later incapacity, . . . [even] through oral declarations,"[60] there is no need to indulge the hypothetical possibility that the patient may have had a change of mind. As the court aptly noted, in such circumstances, "even the failure to act constitutes a choice. That choice must be the patient's choice whenever possible."[61]

As applied by some courts, the subjective standard can be extraordinarily exacting. For example, in the *O'Connor* case,[62] the New York Court of Appeals refused to find that the patient had authorized the termination of a feeding tube prior to losing decisionmaking capacity despite a record replete with conversations that she had had with friends and family, spanning more than a decade, in

---

55 See § **7.9.**

56 *See* Mack v. Mack, 618 A.2d 744, 762 (Md. 1993) (McAuliffe, J., dissenting) (The subjective standard "focuses upon prior statements made by the ward. The substituted judgment approach comes into play when the ward has made no prior statements bearing on the issue, or the statements attributed to the ward do not produce a clear and convincing answer.").

57 **NY:** *In re* Westchester County Medical Ctr. (O'Connor), 531 N.E.2d 607, 614 (N.Y. 1988).

58 *See id.* at 616 (Hancock, J., concurring); *see also id.* at 619 ("what does the patient desire done") (Simons, J., dissenting).

59 *See* Browning v. Herbert, 568 So. 2d 4 (Fla. 1990). See § **7.6.**

60 Browning v. Herbert, 568 So. 2d at 15.

61 *Id.* at 13.

62 *In re* Westchester County Medical Ctr. (O'Connor), 531 N.E.2d 607 (N.Y. 1988).

which she expressed her views that she abhorred the notion of prolonging the process of dying through medical means. Similarly, the Missouri Supreme Court in *Cruzan*[63] overturned the trial court's findings that Nancy Cruzan would have authorized the discontinuation of treatment, based on substantial testimony of four witnesses on at least four different occasions.[64]

One judge of the New York Court of Appeals has described the standard as unworkable and recommended legislative revision,[65] but this is not quite the proper characterization. It is an eminently workable standard; the problem is with the results that it works. The first is substantive: that people who almost definitely would have wanted life-sustaining medical treatment terminated had they given it any thought will be denied their wish because they did not think to express it in the formal and solemn manner as required in New York, a manner to which only judges and lawyers might be accustomed.[66] The second result that this standard works is that although families are not formally required to obtain judicial ruling on the adequacy of the evidence of the patient's wish to forgo life-sustaining treatment, this will often be the practical result except where the patient has executed a written advance directive.[67] This standard also disadvantages those lacking familiarity with what the law expects, which in this case might be the overwhelming majority.[68] Thus, the "rule is not only unworkable, it is unwise."[69] Finally, a standard this exacting is an invitation to perjury, fabrication, or at least selective recall on the part of family members and to complicity on the part of their legal counsel.

One of the most serious consequences of applying the subjective standard was noted by Justice Brennan in *Cruzan.* This standard results in the expulsion of families from the decisionmaking process. Families are unlikely to be, but conceivably might be, motivated by venal motives,[70] as Justice Brennan observed, but trial courts have means to safeguard against them besides the

---

[63] Cruzan v. Harmon, 760 S.W.2d 408 (Mo. 1988).

[64] *See* Cruzan v. Director, 497 U.S. 261, 321 n.19 (1990) (Brennan J., dissenting).

[65] Grace Plaza of Great Neck, Inc. v. Elbaum, 623 N.E.2d 513, 516 (N.Y. 1993) (Hancock, J., concurring). *See also In re* Westchester County Medical Ctr. (O'Connor), 531 N.E.2d 607, 625 (N.Y. 1988) (Simons, J., dissenting) (rule is "unworkable because it requires humans to exercise foresight they do not possess").

[66] *See* Lindgren, *Death by Default,* 56 Law & Contemp. Probs. 185 (1993).

[67] *See, e.g.,* Elbaum v. Grace Plaza of Great Neck, Inc., 544 N.Y.S.2d 840 (App. Div. 1989).

[68] **US:** Cruzan v. Director, 497 U.S. 261, 323 (1990) (Brennan, J., dissenting) ("Too few people execute living wills or equivalently formal directives for such an evidentiary rule to ensure adequately that the wishes of incompetent persons will be honored.").

[69] *In re* Westchester County Medical Ctr. (O'Connor), 531 N.E.2d 607, 626 (N.Y. 1988) (Simons, J., dissenting).

[70] Cruzan v. Director, 497 U.S. 261, 286 (1990) (majority acknowledged that "[n]o doubt is engendered by anything in this record but that Nancy Cruzan's mother and father are loving and caring parents [and i]f the State were required by the United States Constitution to repose a right of 'substituted judgment' with anyone, the Cruzans would surely qualify"). See **§ 5.35.**

standard of proof—primarily the appointment of a guardian ad litem.[71] Where, as "here, the family members, friends, doctors and guardian ad litem agree, it is not because the process has failed, as the majority suggests. . . . It is because there is no genuine dispute as to Nancy's preference."[72] Another serious objection is that offered by Justice Stevens in *Cruzan,* that the subjective standard

> fails to respect the best interests of the patient. . . . It too, relies on what is tantamount to a waiver rationale: the dying patient's best interests are put to one side and the entire inquiry is focused on her prior expressions of intent. [Footnote omitted.] An innocent person's constitutional right to be free from unwanted medical treatment is thereby categorically limited to those patients who had the foresight to make an unambiguous statement of their wishes while competent.[73]

A California judge expressed a similar view:

> Some courts have taken the position that an incompetent patient's hypothetical desire to forego life-sustaining treatment must be proved by clear and convincing evidence or some other standard and, when so proved, is conclusive. . . . [W]e have found no authority—other than cases on the subject of life-sustaining treatment—to support the idea that a person can exercise (or waive) a fundamental constitutional and common law right unintentionally through informal statements years in advance. It would be a dangerously unpredictable precedent.[74]

§ 7.5 States Requiring Subjective Standard

In order to prevent the abuses that might arise from the application of less exacting standards such as the substituted judgment standard and the best interests standard, some states (though very few in number) require the application of a pure subjective standard. If this standard cannot be met, life-sustaining treatment must be continued. If that occurs, in effect the state "assume[s] the role of deciding for the patient."[75]

New York

New York has been the most unyielding proponent of not merely the priority of the subjective standard but also its exclusivity. Over a period of more than a decade, the court of appeals has reaffirmed that in New York life-sustaining

---

[71] *Id.* at 317 (Brennan, J., dissenting).

[72] *Id.* at 319 (Brennan, J., dissenting).

[73] *Id.* at 338–39 (Stevens, J., dissenting).

[74] Drabick v. Drabick, 245 Cal. Rptr. 840, 856 (Ct. App. 1988).

[75] Cruzan v. Director, 497 U.S. 261, 327 (1990) (Brennan, J., dissenting). *See also* Hastings Ctr., Guidelines on the Termination of Life-Sustaining Treatment and the Care of the Dying 28 (1987) (Part One, II(4)(c)(1)).

treatment may not be forgone unless there is a "clear expression of a present intention to forego" the treatment in question.[76] Only New York unequivocally requires the application of the subjective standard and will not permit the forgoing of life-sustaining treatment unless it is met, and the court construes the standard most strictly.[77]

In its first foray into this matter in 1981 in the companion *Storar* and *Eichner* cases, the court permitted the termination of a ventilator from a man in a persistent vegetative state (*Eichner*) but refused to permit the forgoing of blood transfusions necessary to keep alive a man who was dying from cancer (*Storar*). In *Eichner*, the patient, Brother Fox, was a member of a Catholic religious order, and in the course of discussions of the *Quinlan* case within the order, he had expressed the view "that he would not want any of this 'extraordinary business' done for him under those circumstances."[78] According to the court of appeals, these statements "were obviously solemn pronouncements and not casual remarks made at some social gathering."[79] As Brother Fox was 83 years old and had been a member of the order for 66 years, "nor can it be said that he was too young to realize or feel the consequences of his statements."[80] Brother Fox's view was also a "persistent commitment" because it had been expressed only two months prior to the events in question.[81] Finally, "[t]here was . . . no need to speculate as to whether he would want this particular medical procedure to be discontinued under these circumstances [because w]hat occurred to him was identical to what happened in the Karen Ann Quinlan case, which had originally prompted his decision."[82] Wishing to avoid the question of whether a surrogate could make a decision to forgo life-sustaining treatment on behalf of an incompetent patient, the court found that it was able to do so because this was a situation in which the patient "made the decision for himself before he became incompetent."[83] For this court, Brother Fox's situation was a rather straightforward application to incompetent patients of the long-accepted common-law principles for decisionmaking for competent patients.

---

[76] *See In re* Westchester County Medical Ctr. (O'Connor), 531 N.E.2d 607, 616 (N.Y. 1988) (Hancock, J., concurring); *see also id.* at 619 ("what does the patient desire done") (Simons, J., dissenting).

[77] *See* Grace Plaza of Great Neck, Inc. v. Elbaum, 623 N.E.2d 513 (N.Y. 1993); *In re* Westchester County Medical Ctr. (O'Connor), 531 N.E.2d 607 (N.Y. 1988); *In re* Storar, 420 N.E.2d 64 (N.Y. 1981).

[78] Eichner v. Dillon, 420 N.E.2d 64, 68 (N.Y. 1981).

[79] **NY:** Eichner v. Dillon, 420 N.E.2d at 72.

NJ: *Cf. In re* Conroy, 486 A.2d 1209, 1230 (N.J. 1985) ("an offhand remark about not wanting to live under certain circumstances made by a person when young and in the peak of health would not in itself constitute clear proof twenty years later that he would want life-sustaining treatment withheld under those circumstances").

[80] Eichner v. Dillon, 420 N.E.2d at 72.

[81] *Id.*

[82] *Id.*

[83] *Id.* at 71.

By contrast, because Mr. Storar was profoundly mentally retarded since birth, he never had the capacity to make a decision for himself. Had this been a situation in which there was a choice among reasonable alternative treatments, his mother as his guardian would have been empowered to make that choice. But this was a choice between a single treatment and death, and absent the kind of evidence that was available in *Eichner,* which was logically impossible to provide, treatment must be continued.

Eichner and *Storar* were extreme opposite cases. In one, there could not have been clearer evidence of the patient's wishes; in the other there was not and could not have been any evidence of the patient's wishes. Most cases fall somewhere in between, as did the next case to be considered by the court of appeals, the *O'Connor* case.[84] In *O'Connor,* the court refused to permit the withholding of tube-feeding, at the unanimous request of her family, from a woman who had suffered a series of strokes. Despite the fact that the record was replete with conversations that Mrs. O'Connor had had with friends and family spanning more than a decade in which she expressed her views that she abhorred the notion of prolonging the process of dying through medical means, in the view of the court, the statements were not clear enough statements directed precisely at the situation in question.

The court's characterizations of her statements are particularly helpful in understanding what kind of evidence suffices in New York to meet the subjective standard:

> Although Mrs. O'Connor's statements about her desire to decline life-saving treatments were repeated over a number of years, there is nothing, other than speculation, to persuade the fact finder that her expressions were more than immediate reactions to the unsettling experience of seeing or hearing of another's unnecessarily prolonged death. Her comments—that she would never want to lose her dignity before she passed away, that nature should be permitted to take its course, that it is "monstrous" to use life-support machinery—are, in fact, no different than those that many of us might make after witnessing an agonizing death. Similarly, her statements to the effect that she would not want to be a burden to anyone are the type of statements that older people frequently, almost invariably make. If such statements were routinely held to be clear and convincing proof of a general intent to decline all medical treatment once incompetency sets in, few nursing home patients would ever receive life-sustaining medical treatment in the future. The aged and infirm would be placed at grave risk if the law uniformly but unrealistically treated the expression of such sentiments as a calm and deliberate resolve to decline all life-sustaining medical assistance once the speaker is silenced by mental disability. That Mrs. O'Connor made similar statements over a long period of time, does not, by itself, transform them from the type of comments that are often made casually into the type of statements that demonstrate a seriousness of purpose necessary to satisfy the "clear and convincing evidence" standard.[85]

[84] *In re* Westchester County Medical Ctr. (O'Connor), 531 N.E.2d 607 (N.Y. 1988). *See also* Wickel v. Spellman, 552 N.Y.S.2d 437 (App. Div. 1990) (forbidding removal of feeding tube in absence of clear and convincing evidence that patient authorized it).

[85] *In re* Westchester County Medical Ctr. (O'Connor), 531 N.E.2d at 610–11.

In short, the evidence of the patient's wishes must be directed at the treatment in question;[86] it must be clear and unequivocal rather than general; it must be about one's own situation,[87] rather than commentary on the condition of others; and, like the proof in *Eichner,* it must be made under circumstances of sufficient solemnity. It is not clear, at least in New York, what is more important: that the patient's prior wishes be "specific" (that is, specify the particular condition for which a particular treatment is not wanted) or that they be "solemn pronouncements." Perhaps neither is more important and both conditions must be satisfied.

The insistence on a strict subjective standard by the New York Court of Appeals does not appear to be shared by the appellate division of the supreme court. In *Storar* the court issued a memorandum decision, giving no rationale for its decision other than that an "incompetent and terminally ill adult, has the same right to refuse such treatment, especially here where it is painful and will only prolong his suffering,"[88] and cited the Massachusetts Supreme Judicial Court's *Saikewicz* decision involving almost identical facts.[89] And in *Eichner,* in which the court of appeals affirmed the appellate division, it specifically repudiated that court's use of the substituted judgment standard as the basis for its decision.

The courts in both of these cases might be forgiven for their errors in light of the fact that the court of appeals had not previously spoken on the subject. However, in two subsequent cases, the appellate division, while not challenging the standard itself evaded its harsh effect by finding that the evidence met it. In one of these cases, *O'Connor,* the decision was reversed on appeal.[90] The other case, *Elbaum,*[91] was not appealed. *Elbaum* is especially interesting because the evidence of the patient's wishes was amazingly similar to the evidence in *O'Connor,* which the court of appeals found *not* to satisfy the subjective standard. It consisted of reactions to the treatment of others, for example:

> Mr. Elbaum, who has been married to Mrs. Elbaum for over 36 years, testified that his wife first expressed her views on extraordinary or artificial life-sustaining medical treatment in the context of the Karen Ann Quinlan case. At that time, Mrs. Elbaum remarked "how awful it must be for the parents to sit vigil over a virtually dead and comatose daughter" and she stated that if she were in a similar situation "she would not want to be on any respirator or any other mechanical means, she wanted to die." Mr. Elbaum testified that another conversation with his

---

[86] *Cf.* Martin v. Martin, 517 N.W.2d 749, 753 (Mich. Ct. App. 1994) (although patient did not refer specifically to tube-feeding and colostomy as procedures he did not want, "he did specifically describe circumstances in which he would be unable to feed himself or in which he would be required to wear diapers to continue living, both of which are applicable to his present situation").

[87] *Cf.* Martin v. Martin, 517 N.W.2d at 752 (statements patient made while competent about not wanting to be kept alive in persistent vegetative state are relevant to determining his preferences for treatment even though he is not in persistent vegetative state).

[88] *In re* Storar, 434 N.Y.S.2d 46, 47 (App. Div. 1980).

[89] Superintendent of Belchertown State Sch. v. Saikewicz, 370 N.E.2d 417 (Mass. 1977).

[90] *In re* Westchester County Medical Ctr. (O'Connor), 532 N.Y.S.2d 133 (App. Div. 1988).

[91] Elbaum v. Grace Plaza of Great Neck, Inc., 544 N.Y.S.2d 840 (App. Div. 1989).

> wife on this topic was triggered by the Sunny Von Bulow matter. According to Mr. Elbaum, his wife expressed an inability to comprehend how the Von Bulow family could permit Mrs. Von Bulow to be sustained as a "vegetable" and he quoted his wife as subsequently stating that "I do not want to be sustained as a vegetable, I want to die with some dignity."
>
> Mr. Elbaum also related the circumstances surrounding a third occasion during which Mrs. Elbaum expressed her views with respect to the subject. He stated that in 1982 a family friend suffered a stroke and was rendered unconscious while riding in the Elbaums' car. The Elbaums took the friend to a nearby hospital, at which time they were informed that the friend was comatose. Thereafter, while the Elbaums were returning home from the hospital, Mrs. Elbaum told her husband, "Murray, I want you to tell me now, I am telling you and I want you to tell me that you will not do anything to sustain my life in the event I am a vegetable. I want it to end, I don't want to be sustained." Thereafter, Mr. Elbaum testified, he and his wife again discussed the incident, and she stated "If I am ever in a similar state and it is hopeless, I don't want to be sustained by any tubes or machines or antibiotics."[92]

The evidence consisted of statements made under conditions similar to those in *O'Connor* rather than circumstances of solemnity equivalent to those in *Eichner;* for example:

> Mrs. Elbaum's sister, Mrs. Renee Schutzer, similarly testified to separate conversations with her sister concerning the Karen Ann Quinlan and Sunny Von Bulow cases, and added that on another occasion after Mrs. Elbaum saw the film "Whose Life Is It Anyway," which involved the right of an incapacitated individual to decline medical treatment, Mrs. Elbaum stated that that was a "horrible situation" and "it was very disturbing to her."[93]

Nonetheless, the second department of the appellate division, the same court that had decided *O'Connor* (and *Eichner*), held that this evidence met the very standard adopted in *Eichner* and reiterated in *O'Connor.* This is the way in which it characterized the above evidence:

> Mrs. Elbaum, while competent, repeatedly extracted a series of promises from her husband and family members to be highly significant since it reflects a serious and consistent purpose of mind and an intent to bind others to effectuate her desires *in futuro* [citation omitted]. Although some of these promises were extracted in immediate response to unsettling events, such as the family friend's stroke in 1982 and her observations of her mother being fed by means of a nasogastric tube, the record establishes that Mrs. Elbaum reiterated her views and extracted renewed

---

[92] **NY:** Elbaum v. Grace Plaza of Great Neck, Inc., 544 N.Y.S.2d at 844.

IL: *Accord In re* Estate of Greenspan, 558 N.E.2d 1194 (Ill. 1990) (relying on testimony and stipulations of patient's wife, four children, employee, and rabbi that patient would not have wanted to be kept alive like this).

[93] Elbaum v. Grace Plaza of Great Neck, Inc., 544 N.Y.S.2d at 844.

> promises from those same family members under less emotional circumstances [citation omitted]. [W]e find that the record as a whole in this case establishes that Mrs. Elbaum's statements and reflections on the subject of artificial and extraordinary life-sustaining medical treatments were made with a similar resolve and purpose so as to constitute "solemn pronouncements" [citation omitted].[94]

The New York Court of Appeals's insistence on the subjective standard has resulted in substantial part from its fear that the patient who might have expressed preferences about life-sustaining treatment has suffered a "change of heart" and not expressed this change prior to losing decisionmaking capacity.[95] According to the court, "we can never be completely certain of the answer to our question, since the inquiry assumes that the patient is no longer able to express his or her wishes. Most often, therefore, the inquiry turns on interpretation of statements on the subject made by the patient in the past. This exercise presents inherent problems."[96] What this pat analysis ignores, however, is the fact that requiring the administration of treatment also has inherent problems, especially when there is a substantial amount of evidence, as in *O'Connor,* that the patient did not want to live the kind of life or die the kind of death to which the court's decision would consign her.

The extraordinary difficulty in meeting the strict New York rule is compounded by another court of appeals decision, *Grace Plaza of Great Neck, Inc. v. Elbaum*. In this sequel to the *Elbaum* case, the nursing home in which Mrs. Elbaum resided, which mounted a significant battle to prevent her husband from having the feeding tube removed, and in which she languished for a substantial period of time while her family sought to have treatment stopped (eventually through litigation), sued Mr. Elbaum for the bills that he had refused to pay for her care during this period of time.

The trial court held that he was not responsible for the costs of her care in the nursing home from the time that he requested that life-sustaining treatment be withdrawn until her death, when treatment finally was discontinued pursuant to court order in the prior proceeding. The appellate division reversed, holding that the late patient's husband was responsible for the costs of her care, because to hold otherwise would create a right on the part of a surrogate "to decide when another person should die," a right not recognized in New York law.[97] The court of appeals affirmed, and although acknowledging that there is no obligation to pay for nonconsensual treatment,[98] the court adopted the nursing home's argument and concluded that this was not nonconsensual treatment because the nursing home acted in good faith in its determination that it lacked the kind of

---

[94] *Id.* at 846.

[95] *In re* Westchester County Medical Ctr. (O'Connor), 531 N.E.2d 607, 614 (N.Y. 1988).

[96] *Id.* at 613.

[97] Grace Plaza of Great Neck, Inc. v. Elbaum, 588 N.Y.S.2d 853, 855 (App. Div. 1992).

[98] Grace Plaza of Great Neck, Inc. v. Elbaum, 623 N.E.2d 513, 515 (N.Y. 1993) (citing Shapira v. United Medical Serv., 205 N.E.2d 293 (N.Y. 1965)).

evidence required by New York law to determine that Mrs. Elbaum had objected to the treatment. Although the court firmly disavowed any requirement that a court must always pass on the adequacy of such evidence, that is in fact what is likely to occur because "[i]f a provider harbors some uncertainty on the matter, it acts within the dictates of *O'Connor* if it refuses to discontinue treatment until the issue is legally determined."[99]

Missouri

The Missouri Supreme Court adopted the subjective standard in the *Cruzan* case in 1988. That case is now probably the best known right-to-die case because it is the only one involving an adult[100] to have been reviewed by the United States Supreme Court, despite petitions for review in a number of other right-to-die[101] and related[102] cases. Nancy Cruzan was a woman in her early 30s at the time of the litigation. She was in a persistent vegetative state from which, all parties in the case agreed, she would never emerge. She lapsed into this condition as a result of serious injuries suffered in an automobile accident seven years before. About three years after the accident, her parents, who were her court-appointed guardians, came to the realization that she was dead, as far as they were concerned, and that further treatment was unwarranted. (Of course she was not legally dead; persons in a persistent vegetative state do not meet the criteria for "brain death"[103] because the brain stem, controlling basic "vegetative" functions such as respiration, circulation, and body temperature, is still alive.[104]) Her

---

[99] *Id.* at 515 (citing *In re* Westchester County Medical Ctr. (O'Connor), 531 N.E.2d 607 (N.Y. 1988)).

[100] *See also* Bowen v. American Hosp. Ass'n, 476 U.S. 610 (1986) (involving a handicapped newborn infant). See **Ch. 16.**

[101] **CA:** Drabick v. Drabick, 245 Cal. Rptr. 840 (Ct. App.), *cert. denied,* 488 U.S. 958 (1988), *reh'g denied,* 488 U.S. 1024 (1989); *In re* Phillip B., 156 Cal. Rptr. 48 (Ct. App.), *cert. denied sub nom.* Bothman v. Warren B., 445 U.S. 949 (1979).

IL: *In re* Estate of Prange, 520 N.E.2d 946 (Ill. App. Ct.), *vacated,* 527 N.E.2d 303 (Ill.), *cert. denied sub nom.* Murphy v. Benson, 488 U.S. 892 (1988).

NJ: *In re* Jobes, 529 A.2d 434 (N.J.), *reconsideration and stay denied,* 531 A.2d 1360 (N.J.), *cert. denied sub nom.* Lincoln Park Nursing & Convalescent Home v. Kahn, 483 U.S. 1036 (1987); *In re* Quinlan, 355 A.2d 647 (N.J.), *cert. denied sub nom.* Garger v. New Jersey, 429 U.S. 922 (1976).

NY: *In re* Storar, 420 N.E.2d 64 (N.Y.), *cert. denied,* 454 U.S. 858 (1981).

[102] **IN:** *In re* Infant Doe, No. GU8204-00 (Ind. Cir. Ct. Monroe County Apr. 12, 1982), *writ of mandamus dismissed sub nom.* State *ex rel.* Infant Doe v. Baker, No. 482 S 140 (Ind. May 27, 1982), *cert. denied,* 464 U.S. 961 (1983).

NY: Weber v. Stony Brook Hosp., 467 N.Y.S.2d 685 (App. Div.) (per curiam), *aff'd,* 456 N.E.2d 1186 (N.Y.), *cert. denied,* 464 U.S. 1026 (1983).

OH: *In re* Milton, 505 N.E.2d 255 (Ohio), *cert. denied,* 484 U.S. 820 (1987).

[103] See § **9.48.**

[104] See § **9.53.**

parents therefore requested that the tube-feedings keeping her alive be discontinued, a request for which there was, by that time, abundant clinical and legal precedent.

The administrator of the state-owned hospital treating Nancy Cruzan insisted that her parents obtain a court order to discontinue tube-feeding, and such an order was obtained from the county probate court. The state of Missouri appealed the decision, and the Missouri Supreme Court reversed, holding that in the case of a nonterminally ill, incompetent patient, a "subjective standard" must be met by clear and convincing evidence in order to terminate treatment.[105] In other words, tube-feeding could be terminated only if Nancy Cruzan, herself, had, prior to her accident, authorized it; whether a written living will was necessary or an oral statement would suffice was not clarified by the Missouri court. The United States Supreme Court upheld this requirement against a challenge that it violated the guarantee of liberty contained in the Fourteenth Amendment to the constitution.[106]

The best way to understand how stringent a standard the Missouri court had promulgated is to examine the evidence of the patient's wishes that it had found inadequate:

> The trial court had relied on the testimony of Athena Comer, a long-time friend, co-worker and a housemate for several months, as sufficient to show that Nancy Cruzan would wish to be free of medical treatment under her present circumstances. [Citation omitted.] Ms. Comer described a conversation she and Nancy had while living together, concerning Ms. Comer's sister who had become ill suddenly and died during the night. The Comer family had been told that if she had lived through the night, she would have been in a vegetative state. Nancy had lost a grandmother a few months before. Ms. Comer testified that: "Nancy said she would never want to live [as a person in a vegetative state] because if she couldn't be normal or even, you know, like half way, and do things for yourself, because Nancy always did, that she didn't want to live . . . and we talked about it a lot." [Citation omitted.] She said "several times" that "she wouldn't want to live that way because if she was going to live, she wanted to be able to live, not to just lay in a bed and not be able to move because you can't do anything for yourself." [Citation omitted.] "[S]he said that she hoped that [all the] people in her family knew that she wouldn't want to live [as a vegetable] because she knew it was usually up to the family whether you lived that way or not." [Citation omitted.]
>
> The conversation took place approximately a year before Nancy's accident and was described by Ms. Comer as a "very serious" conversation that continued for approximately half an hour without interruption. [Citation omitted.] The Missouri Supreme Court dismissed Nancy's statement as "unreliable" on the ground that it was an informally expressed reaction to other people's medical conditions. 760 S.W. 2d, at 424.
>
> The Missouri Supreme Court did not refer to other evidence of Nancy's wishes or explain why it was rejected. Nancy's sister Christy, to whom she was very close,

---

105 *See* Cruzan v. Harmon, 760 S.W.2d 408 (Mo. 1988).

106 Cruzan v. Director, 497 U.S. 261 (1990).

> testified that she and Nancy had had two very serious conversations about a year and a half before the accident. A day or two after their niece was stillborn (but would have been badly damaged if she had lived), Nancy had said that maybe it was part of a "greater plan" that the baby was stillborn and did not have to face "the possible life of mere existence." [Citation omitted.] A month later, after their grandmother had died after a long battle with heart problems, Nancy said that "it was better for my grandmother not to be kind of brought back from a critical, near point of death. . . . [citation omitted]."
>
> Nancy's sister Christy, Nancy's mother, and another of Nancy's friends testified that Nancy would want to discontinue the hydration and nutrition. Christy said that "Nancy would be horrified at the state she is in." [Citation omitted]. She would also "want to take that burden away from [her family]." [Citation omitted.] Based on "a lifetime of experience [I know Nancy's wishes] are to discontinue the hydration and the nutrition." [Citation omitted]. Nancy's mother testified: "Nancy would not want to be like she is now. [I]f it were me up there or Christy or any of us, she would be doing for us what we are trying to do for her. I know she would, . . . as her mother." [Citation omitted.][107]

Thus, in Missouri, it seemed all but certain after *Cruzan* that the subjective standard was also required. A more limited reading of *Cruzan,* however, is that it does not hold that life support cannot be terminated if the subjective standard cannot be met. Rather it stands for the proposition that life support cannot be terminated if the subjective standard cannot be met for a patient in a persistent vegetative state because as to such patients, the argument that treatment is burdensome and/or nonbeneficial is unsupportable.[108] This reading of *Cruzan* is supported by the subsequent decision of the Missouri Court of Appeals, holding that *Cruzan* should be limited to the forgoing of tube-feeding, which the supreme court had not considered to be a form of medical treatment, and not applied to cardiopulmonary resuscitation.[109]

Maine

Maine may also have adopted the subjective standard, but whether this is so is very unclear. Although the Maine Supreme Court has repudiated the substituted judgment standard by name and claimed to find "convincing the New York

---

[107] *Id.* at 321 n.19 (Brennan, J., dissenting).

[108] Cruzan v. Harmon, 760 S.W.2d at 424 ("Given the fact that Nancy is alive and that the burdens of her treatment are not excessive for her, we do not believe her right to refuse treatment, whether that right proceeds from a constitutional right of privacy or a common law right to refuse treatment, outweighs the immense, clear fact of life in which the state maintains a vital interest.").

[109] *See In re* Warren, 858 S.W.2d 263 (Mo. Ct. App. 1993). ***But see*** Cruzan v. Harmon, 760 S.W.2d at 424 ("The issue is not whether the continued feeding and hydration of Nancy is medical treatment; it is whether feeding and providing liquid to Nancy is a burden to her. *Conroy.* We refuse to succumb to the semantic dilemma created by medical determinations of what is treatment; those distinctions often prove legally irrelevant.").

court's reasoning on this issue,"[110] the evidence it has found sufficient to meet the standard is far less exacting than that required by the New York Court of Appeals.

In the first Maine case, *Gardner,* the supreme court remarked that it found "convincing the New York court's reasoning on this issue," and it held "that when an individual has clearly and convincingly in advance of treatment expressed his decision not to be maintained by life-sustaining procedures in a persistent vegetative state, health care professionals must respect that decision."[111] When read in context, this statement means that the court held only that there *was* clear and convincing evidence that Mr. Gardner had stated that he did not want such treatment and it was permissible to discontinue it. It did not hold that there *must* be such evidence for it to be permissible to discontinue treatment. That issue was not presented, for the simple reason that such evidence did exist. Thus the situation in Maine after *Gardner* was like that in New York after *Eichner v. Dillon;*[112] that is, we know that the court permitted the forgoing of life-sustaining treatment when there was clear and convincing evidence, but we do not know what it would do if clear and convincing evidence were lacking.

In the second case, *Swan,*[113] the Maine court was almost as unclear on this issue as it was in *Gardner.* Finding that there was clear and convincing evidence that the patient (in a persistent vegetative state) had said before losing decision-making capacity that he would not have wanted to be kept alive like this, the court held that artificial nutrition and hydration could be discontinued. However, the court added that "[a]s in *Gardner,* we rest our decision on Chad's own conclusion and not on any theory of substituted judgment,"[114] thus rejecting the substituted judgment standard and suggesting, but not holding, that the subjective standard must be met.

Finally, to further confuse matters, the kind of evidence that the court considered in determining that it was permissible to terminate life-sustaining treatment is the kind ordinarily associated with the substituted judgment standard rather than the subjective standard, namely:

> The record establishes by clear and convincing evidence that Chad expressed his desire on two separate occasions not to be artificially maintained in his current state. The first occasion took place during a discussion with his mother, Linda Swan, about the *Gardner* case. That case was highly publicized in the Lewiston area, and Joseph Gardner was the stepgrandson of a close friend of Chad's grandmother. Chad, then aged 16, and his mother "discussed what it meant to be a 'vegetable.' She explained that such a person needed total care in someone else's hands; and that someone must do everything for you. Chad wanted to know why

---

[110] *In re* Gardner, 534 A.2d 947, 953 (Me. 1987).

[111] *Id.*

[112] 420 N.E.2d 64 (N.Y. 1981).

[113] *In re* Swan, 569 A.2d 1202 (Me. 1990).

[114] *Id.* at 1206.

> they wouldn't let him [Joseph Gardner] die. His mother remembers him saying: 'If I can't be myself . . . no way . . . let me go to sleep.'"

The second occasion took place in January 1989, only eight days before Chad's accident when, with his older brother Scott, Chad visited Joey Rollins, one of Scott's friends who was comatose in a hospital after a car accident. "Chad saw Joey briefly, after which his brother Scott asked him if he saw Joey. Chad said 'I don't ever want to get like that. . . . I would want somebody to let me leave—to go in peace.'"[115]

Although the court ended its recounting of the evidence with the observation that "[b]oth of Chad's expressions were made in the context of serious discussion with family members about people Chad knew, whose plight he understood," the kind of evidence involved were reactions to the medical treatment of others. In *O'Connor,* the New York Court of Appeals found that such expressions did not meet the subjective standard because they "were [no] more than immediate reactions to the unsettling experience of seeing or hearing of another's unnecessarily prolonged death . . . [which are] no different than those that many of us might make,"[116] and thus are "casual remarks" and not "solemn pronouncements."[117] At least in New York, it is not clear that it is specificity that is required so much as "solemnity," that is, that the patient made the statements in a context in which they should be viewed as solemn pronouncements rather than casual remarks.[118]

§ 7.6 States Preferring but Not Requiring Subjective Standard

After the Supreme Court's decision in *Cruzan,* there was the possibility that the state courts might move away from the substituted judgment standard and begin to require the application of the subjective standard.[119] Although such a move is

---

[115] *Id.* at 1205.

[116] *In re* Westchester County Medical Ctr. (O'Connor), 531 N.E.2d 607, 614 (N.Y. 1988).

[117] *Id.* at 612 (quoting Eichner v. Dillon, 420 N.E.2d 64, 72 (N.Y. 1981)).

[118] **NY:** *In re* Westchester County Medical Ctr. (O'Connor), 531 N.E.2d 607 (N.Y. 1988).

NJ: *Cf. In re* Conroy, 486 A.2d 1209, 1230 (N.J. 1985) ("Another factor that would affect the probative value of a person's prior statements of intent would be their specificity.").

[119] *See, e.g.,* Bopp & Marzen, Cruzan: *Facing the Inevitable,* 19 Law, Med. & Health Care 37, 42 (1991) ("On the whole . . . *Cruzan*'s caution will almost certainly generate a greater degree of caution in state courts as well."); Colburn, *Another Chapter in the Case of Nancy Cruzan,* Wash. Post, Oct. 16, 1990, at 7 ("Physicians who are already nervous about the risk of malpractice lawsuits . . . are even more likely to refuse to withhold extraordinary life-continuing care from irreversibly comatose patients unless they have a living will or signed power of attorney form. It's becoming very hard to terminate treatment on anyone in this country. . . . The *Cruzan* decision is having that horrible effect—of physicians starting to practice law, basically.") (quoting George Annas).

not required by *Cruzan*—the Supreme Court did not rule that the constitution prohibits the use of the substituted judgment standard—this distinction might all too easily be overlooked. (For example, an Ohio trial court stated that "substituted judgment is no longer valid" after *Cruzan* because of the Court's failure to find the constitutional right of privacy to be the basis for the right to have treatment terminated.[120] *Cruzan* does not bar the use of substituted judgment; it merely permits a state to bar its use.) In fact, state courts have not moved to discard the substituted judgment standard and require the use of the subjective standard.[121] However, few courts have actually decided a case in which the evidence was such that the substituted judgment standard could be met but the subjective standard could not.[122] Thus, in practice, with the exception of New York and possibly Missouri, the potentially adverse impact of the subjective standard on forgoing life-sustaining treatment has not materialized.

Most courts simply prefer the clearest proof of the patient's actual wishes if at all possible. About the only specific exception is one California decision, *Drabick,* which held that a conservator must consider the patient's "expressed preferences" but is not bound by them and instead "must act in the conservatee's best interests."[123] A more general exception is the Massachusetts Supreme Judicial Court, which has, in effect, stated that the high level of clarity embodied in the subjective standard has no particular value. It has done this in three ways. First, it has permitted the substituted judgment standard to be used for never-competent patients.[124] Second, it has permitted surrogates, making decisions under the aegis of the substituted judgment standard, to take into account a wide variety of objective factors more closely associated with a best interests standard than with a subjective standard.[125] Finally, it has been unclear about whether or not the surrogate is to make a decision based on the patient's actual or probable wishes or to "substitute" his own decision for the patient's.[126]

Some courts have expressed a preference for using the subjective standard, but, for a number of reasons, have not required its use.[127] First, there is a

---

[120] **OH:** *In re* Myers, 610 N.E.2d 663, 669 (P. Ct. Summit County, Ohio 1993).

PA: *See also* Ragona v. Preate, 11 Fiduc. Rep. 2d 1, 1 (C.P. Lackawanna County, Pa. 1990) (applying a subjective standard, but unclear about whether it believed that standard to be required or whether it merely applied that standard because the evidence met it).

[121] *See* Meisel, *A Retrospective on* Cruzan, 20 Law, Med., & Health Care 340 (1992).

[122] See § **7.3.**

[123] Drabick v. Drabick, 245 Cal. Rptr. 840, 857 (Ct. App. 1988). See § **7.25.**

[124] See § **7.10.**

[125] See § **7.9.**

[126] See § **7.8.**

[127] **IL:** *E.g.,* Estate of Longeway v. Community Convalescent Ctr., 549 N.E.2d 292, 299 (Ill. 1989) ("although actual, specific express intent would be helpful and compelling, the same is not necessary for the exercise of substituted judgment by a surrogate").

KY: *E.g.,* DeGrella v. Elston, 858 S.W.2d 698, 706 (Ky. 1993).

WI: *E.g.,* L.W. v. L.E. Phillips Career Dev. Ctr., 482 N.W.2d 60, 67 (Wis. 1992).

recognition that most people, for a variety of reasons, simply do not talk about their wishes about what kind of life-sustaining medical treatment they would or would not want if they were not able to contemporaneously decide for themselves. This fact was the basis for Justice Brennan's dissent in *Cruzan:*

> Too few people execute living wills or equivalently formal directives for such an evidentiary rule to ensure adequately that the wishes of incompetent persons will be honored.[21] While it might be a wise social policy to encourage people to furnish such instructions, no general conclusion about a patient's choice can be drawn from the absence of formalities. The probability of becoming irreversibly vegetative is so low that many people may not feel an urgency to marshal formal evidence of their preferences. Some may not wish to dwell on their own physical deterioration and mortality. Even someone with a resolute determination to avoid life support under circumstances such as Nancy's would still need to know that such things as living wills exist and how to execute one. Often legal help would be necessary, especially given the majority's apparent willingness to permit States to insist that a person's wishes are not truly known unless the particular medical treatment is specified.
>
> [21] Surveys show that the overwhelming majority of Americans have not executed such written instructions. *See* Emanuel & Emanuel, The Medical Directive: A New Comprehensive Advance Care Document, 261 JAMA 3288 (1989) (only 9% of Americans execute advance directives about how they would wish treatment decisions to be handled if they became incompetent); American Medical Association Surveys of Physician and Public Opinion on Health Care Issues 29–30 (1988) (only 15% of those surveyed had executed living wills); 2 President's Commission for the Study of Ethical Problems in Medicine and Biomedical and Behavioral Research, Making Health Care Decisions 241–242 (1982) (23% of those surveyed said that they had put treatment instructions in writing).[128]

The Wisconsin Supreme Court rejected a requirement of a subjective standard based as much on practical considerations as on jurisprudential ones. Based on the observation that "[r]elatively few individuals provide explicit written or oral instructions concerning their treatment preferences should they become incompetent," the court concluded that a

> failure to act is not a decision to accept all treatment, nor should society's increasing ability to prolong the dying process make it one. To adopt the clear and convincing standard [that is, the subjective standard] would doom many individuals to a prolonged vegetative state sustained in a life form by unwanted, perhaps detrimental, means that are contrary to the person's best interest.[129]

[128] Cruzan v. Director, 497 U.S. 261, 323 (1990) (Brennan, J., dissenting).

[129] **WI:** L.W. v. L.E. Phillips Career Dev. Ctr., 482 N.W.2d at 67–68.

MD: *Accord* Mack v. Mack, 618 A.2d 744, 768 (Md. 1993) (Chasanow, J., concurring and dissenting) ("I doubt that very many healthy, robust young people . . . ever seriously consider that they may someday be in an accident and be reduced to a persistent vegetative state. Even if some did contemplate such a horrible event, how many would have clearly and convincingly formed and evidenced their views that, if in a persistent vegetative state, they would at some point choose to terminate artificial life support or, alternatively, that they would choose to remain in that state until they die of 'old age.'").

Requirements that such discussions be solemn pronouncements and not casual remarks made, possibly, in reaction to the treatment of others,[130] in combination with a high standard of proof,[131] virtually ensures that in few cases will the evidence satisfy the standard and permit life-sustaining treatment to be forgone.

Second, and more fundamentally, the objection has been made that the subjective standard requires an impossibility: "[w]hat the rule literally demands is . . . a factual determination of the incompetent patient's actual desire at the time of the decision."[132] To the extent that decisionmaking for incompetent patients is predicated on self-determination, patients must give informed consent to—or, more precisely, must make an informed decision about—forgoing life-sustaining treatment, or else it may not be forgone.[133] However, informed consent requires that the patient be competent, and because of course an incompetent cannot be competent, carried to its logical conclusion, treatment cannot be forgone. The Missouri Supreme Court put it this way in *Cruzan:*

> A decision as to medical treatment must be informed. There are three basic prerequisites for informed consent: the patient must have the capacity to reason and make judgments, the decision must be made voluntarily and without coercion, and the patient must have a clear understanding of the risks and benefits of the proposed treatment alternatives or nontreatment, along with a full understanding of the nature of the disease and the prognosis. [Citation omitted.] In the absence of these three elements, neither consent nor refusal can be informed. Thus, it is definitionally impossible for a person to make an informed decision—either to consent or to refuse—under hypothetical circumstances; under such circumstances, neither the benefits nor the risks of treatment can be properly weighed or fully appreciated.[134]

This may be a somewhat rhetorical exaggeration, but the type of evidence required by the two prime proponents of requiring the subjective standard, Missouri and New York, made it extremely difficult to meet this standard.[135]

The insistence on informed consent for an incompetent patient to forgo life-sustaining treatment also introduces a serious asymmetry into the law. As the Missouri Supreme Court properly noted, an informed decision by a competent patient is required not only to refuse treatment, but also to consent to it. Thus, logically we should not be able to *administer* treatment to an incompetent patient without informed consent any more than we should be able to withhold or withdraw treatment from an incompetent patient without informed refusal. In fact, however, the Missouri and New York courts indulge a preference in favor of treatment, if the standard cannot be met, to "err on the side of preserving

---

[130] See § **7.5.**

[131] See § **5.62.**

[132] *In re* Westchester County Medical Ctr. (O'Connor), 531 N.E.2d 607, 616 (N.Y. 1988) (Hancock, J., concurring).

[133] **MO:** Cruzan v. Harmon, 760 S.W.2d 408, 416–17 (Mo. 1988).
NY: *In re* Storar, 420 N.E.2d 64, 70 (N.Y. 1981).

[134] Cruzan v. Harmon, 760 S.W.2d 408, 417 (Mo. 1988).

[135] See § **7.5.**

life."[136] That is, perhaps, as it should be,[137] but if it is, the basis for continuing treatment is the patient's best interests, rather than self-determination, which can serve equally well as the basis for forgoing treatment.[138]

Requiring the application of the subjective standard foils patients' intentions when they have not expressed them as fully or as "clearly and convincingly" as the subjective standard requires. Unlike the substituted judgment standard, which seeks to get a complete picture of the patient and is willing to make inferences about wishes based on partially expressed views, the subjective standard takes a more "all or nothing" approach. Insistence on the application of the subjective standard means that courts will "displace [the patient's] own assessment of the processes associated with dying," thereby "discard[ing] evidence of her will, ignor[ing] her values, and depriv[ing] her of the right to a decision as closely approximating her own choice as humanly possible."[139]

Finally, when combined with the requirement that the patient's subjective intent to have treatment forgone be proved by clear and convincing evidence,[140] the subjective standard virtually requires that people be able to predict the manner in which they will die in order for life-sustaining treatment to be withheld or withdrawn. Justice Brennan's observation that "[u]nder fair rules of evidence, it is improbable that a court could not determine what the patient's choice would be"[141] is hard to refute. The failure to acknowledge the acceptability of the substituted judgment standard means that the state will appropriate the patient's choice, and there "[i]s [no] reason to suppose that a State is more likely to make the choice that the patient would have made than someone who knew the patient intimately."[142]

In recognition of the difficulties associated with the subjective standard, although most courts prefer to apply such a standard, they are willing to apply the more objective substituted judgment standard when the evidence does not satisfy the subjective standard.[143] Perhaps the most important difference between the two standards is the respective presumption that exists. Those courts insisting on the application of the subjective standard err on the side of

---

[136] Cruzan v. Harmon, 760 S.W.2d 408, 426 (Mo. 1988).

[137] *But see* Cruzan v. Director, 497 U.S. 261, 311 & passim (1990) (Brennan, J., dissenting); *id.* at 347 & passim (Stevens, J., dissenting).

[138] *See id.* at 311–12 (Brennan, J., dissenting) ("For some, the idea of being remembered in their persistent vegetative states rather than as they were before their illness or accident may be very disturbing."). See § **7.13.**

[139] *Id.* at 330 (Brennan, J., dissenting).

[140] See §§ **5.61–5.62.**

[141] Cruzan v. Director, 497 U.S. at 327 (Brennan, J., dissenting).

[142] *Id.*

[143] *See, e.g.,* Rosebush v. Oakland County Prosecutor, 491 N.W.2d 633, 639 n.7 (Mich. Ct. App. 1992) (requiring use of subjective standard "would always preclude the termination of life-support efforts for minors and other persons who have never been legally competent, in direct contradiction of the right to refuse medical treatment").

administering treatment and maintaining life even if it is only biological existence, whereas those willing to apply the substituted judgment standard err on the side of permitting the termination of life support.

The scheme for employing the subjective standard in those jurisdictions that prefer, but do not require, its use was first set out by the New Jersey Supreme Court in *Conroy,* which, in effect, established the hierarchy of standards.[144] *Conroy* was also the first case to clearly differentiate the subjective standard from the substituted judgment standard. Although this hierarchy of standards has become the consensus position in the courts,[145] in New Jersey the *Conroy* scheme applies only to a very narrow class of patients, and if a particular patient does not meet the criteria for employing *Conroy,* a different scheme must be used.[146]

SUBSTITUTED JUDGMENT STANDARD

§ 7.7 Origins and Application of Substituted Judgment Standard in Right-to-Die Cases

The substituted judgment standard is the predominant standard for making end-of-life decisions for incompetent patients. Like the subjective standard, the substituted judgment standard attempts to ascertain the wishes of an incompetent patient as evidenced prior to the patient's loss of decisionmaking capacity. However, instead of insisting that the patient actually have made the decision in question, the substituted judgment standard relies on the patient's probable wishes if his actual wishes cannot be ascertained. Courts applying this standard are willing to infer, to varying degrees, the patient's decision from direct and indirect evidence of his wishes, expressed while the patient was still competent.

When the issue of forgoing life-sustaining treatment for incompetent patients was first posed to courts, the almost reflexive but unconscious reaction of judges was to attempt to avoid making such difficult decisions by wishing that the patient could do it for himself. One can almost sense that in the following passage from the *Quinlan* opinion:

> We have no doubt, in these unhappy circumstances, that if Karen were herself miraculously lucid for an interval (not altering the existing prognosis of the condition to which she would soon return) and perceptive of her irreversible condition, she could effectively decide upon discontinuance of the life-support apparatus, even if it meant the prospect of natural death.[147]

---

[144] See *In re* Conroy, 486 A.2d 1209 (N.J. 1985). See §§ **7.2** and **7.26–7.30.**

[145] See § **7.2.**

[146] See §§ **7.31–7.36.**

[147] *In re* Quinlan, 355 A.2d 647, 663 (N.J. 1976).

This wish was immediately transformed into a mechanism for deciding such cases by attempting to discover whether Karen had expressed any relevant preferences prior to losing decisionmaking capacity and if so, whether they could be discerned. The evidence on this point, taken by the trial court, was that

> Karen Quinlan is quoted as saying she never wanted to be kept alive by extraordinary means. The statements attributed to her by her mother, sister and a friend are indicated to have been made essentially in relation to instances where close friends or relatives were terminally ill. In one instance an aunt, in great pain, was terminally ill from cancer. In another instance the father of a girl friend was dying under like circumstances. In a third circumstance a close family friend was dying of a brain tumor. Mrs. Quinlan testified that her daughter was very full of life, that she loved life and did not want to be kept alive in any way she would not enjoy life to the fullest.[148]

The trial court rejected this evidence as the basis for its decision because

> [s]he made these statements at the age of 20. In the words of her mother, she was full of life. She made them under circumstances where another person was suffering, suffering in at least one instance from severe pain. While perhaps it is not too significant, there is no evidence she is now in pain. . . .
>
> The conversations with her mother and friends were theoretical ones. She was not personally involved. They were not made under the solemn and sobering fact that death is a distinct choice. [Citation omitted.] Karen Quinlan, while she was in complete control of her mental faculties to reason out the staggering magnitude of the decision not to be 'kept alive,' did not make a decision. This is not the situation of a 'living will' which is based upon a concept of informed consent.[149]

The supreme court also concluded that this testimony was not of "sufficient probative weight" to decide the case.[150]

Nonetheless, had the court been more confident of the probative value of the evidence, it would have permitted the forgoing of treatment based on it. In fact, almost a decade later, in *Conroy* the court reconsidered its evaluation of the evidence in *Quinlan* and concluded it had been wrong to "disregard evidence of statements that Ms. Quinlan made to friends concerning artificial prolongation of the lives of others who were terminally ill."[151] Thus was introduced into right-to-die cases the notion of deciding such cases for incompetent patients by attempting to discern what the patient would have decided about forgoing life-sustaining treatment. While an incompetent patient could not literally be made competent, nonetheless the court could ask, supposing that the patient were competent, what would the patient decide?

---

[148] *In re* Quinlan, 348 A.2d 801, 814 (N.J. Super. Ct. Ch. Div. 1975).

[149] *Id.* at 819.

[150] *In re* Quinlan, 355 A.2d at 664.

[151] *In re* Conroy, 486 A.2d 1209, 1230 (N.J. 1985). *Accord In re* Peter, 529 A.2d 419, 427 n.8 (N.J. 1987).

This approach was also consistent with that of decisionmaking for competent patients because it sought to implement the principle of self-determination. After discussing the nature and basis for the right to die, the court addressed the problem of how that right should be exercised on behalf of a patient in a persistent vegetative state and concluded that "[t]he only practical way to prevent destruction of the right is to permit the guardian and family of Karen to render their best judgment, subject to the qualifications hereinafter stated, as to whether *she would exercise it* in these circumstances."[152]

The New Jersey Supreme Court found a precedent for this approach in the doctrine of "substituted judgment." In exercising their power to protect incompetent patients—the parens patriae power—"[c]ourts . . . have sometimes implemented medical decisions and authorized their carrying out under the doctrine of 'substituted judgment,' "[153] which had grown out of the best interests standard. In administering incompetents' estates, guardians are required to act in the best interests of the ward. The best interests standard had been narrowly interpreted as requiring a guardian to apply the income of the estate only to the direct needs of the ward and as preventing the distribution of any funds to third parties, even those who might be the natural objects of the ward's affection and bounty. In response, some courts developed the substituted judgment standard as an alternative:

> The doctrine of substituted judgment . . . was utilized to authorize a gift from the estate of an incompetent person to an individual when the incompetent owed no duty of support. The English court accomplished this purpose by substituting itself as nearly as possible for the incompetent, and acting on the same motives and considerations as would have moved him. . . . In essence, the doctrine in its original inception called on the court to "don the mental mantle of the incompetent."[154]

---

[152] *In re* Quinlan, 355 A.2d at 664 (emphasis added).

[153] *Id.* at 666.

[154] **NY:** Eichner v. Dillon, 426 N.Y.S.2d 517, 548 (App. Div. 1980), *rev'd,* 420 N.E.2d 64 (N.Y. 1981).

DC: *Accord In re* A.C., 573 A.2d 1235, 1249 (D.C. 1990) ("Under the substituted judgment procedure, the court as decision-maker must 'substitute itself as nearly as may be for the incompetent, and . . . act upon the same motives and considerations as would have moved her. . . .' *City Bank Farmers Trust Co. v. McGowan,* 323 U.S. 594, 599, 65 S. Ct. 496, 498, 89 L. Ed. 483 (1945).").

IL: *Accord* Estate of Longeway v. Community Convalescent Ctr., 549 N.E.2d 292, 299 (Ill. 1989) (Substituted judgment was implicitly adopted by the legislature in a health care power of attorney statute provision stating, "'Your agent will have authority * * * to obtain or terminate any type of health care, including withdrawal of food and water * * * if your agent believes such action would be consistent with your intent and desires.' . . . Ill. Rev. Stat. 1987, ch. 110-1/2, par. 804-10.").

MA: *Accord* Superintendent of Belchertown State Sch. v. Saikewicz, 370 N.E.2d 417, 431 (Mass. 1977).

See generally Harmon, *Falling Off the Vine: Legal Fictions and the Doctrine of Substituted Judgment,* 100 Yale L.J. 1, 16–55 (1990).

Under the substituted judgment standard, courts have permitted the guardian of an incompetent's estate to make decisions that do not necessarily promote the narrow best interests of the ward. A guardian may, without liability for wasting the estate, make distributions from the estate to persons or charities to which the ward himself would have made distributions had he not been incompetent. This has been permitted on the ground that the ward, had he been competent, would not have made exclusively selfish decisions, but would have made certain charitable ones as well.[155]

As in the administration of the estates of incompetent wards, the limits of the best interests standard began to become apparent in the 1950s when kidney transplantations began to occur between living donors. Courts were occasionally called upon to determine whether a minor or a mentally deficient adult could donate a kidney to a close relation, usually a sibling.[156] As they had beginning a century earlier with the administration of incompetents' estates, the courts began to employ the substituted judgment standard. However, outside this limited area prior to right-to-die cases, the substituted judgment standard seems to have played no formal role in the law of medical decisionmaking.

Despite the weak impact of the substituted judgment standard in other medical decisionmaking cases, it quickly came to occupy center stage in right-to-die cases.[157] Although the New Jersey court approved the substituted judgment standard—*Quinlan* actually applied a best interests standard because of the inadequacy of the evidence to meet the substituted judgment standard—it shed little light on its meaning and application in the absence of an advance directive from the patient. This was to be left to a succession of other courts, beginning with the *Saikewicz*[158] decision the year after *Quinlan,* in which the Massachusetts Supreme Judicial Court laid the groundwork for substituted judgment to become the predominant standard for use by surrogates.

Saikewicz raised the question of whether chemotherapy for the treatment of cancer should be administered to a 67-year-old man who was profoundly mentally retarded since birth and had been institutionalized for virtually his entire adult life. Drawing on *Quinlan,* the court concluded that "the central

---

155 *See In re* A.C., 573 A.2d 1235, 1249 (D.C. 1990) (citing Strunk v. Strunk, 445 S.W.2d 145, 147–48 (Ky. 1969)).

156 **CT:** *E.g.,* Hart v. Brown, 289 A.2d 386 (Conn. Super. Ct. 1972).

KY: *E.g.,* Strunk v. Strunk, 445 S.W.2d 145 (Ky. 1969).

WI: *But see In re* Pescinski, 226 N.W.2d 180 (Wis. 1975) (rejecting doctrine).

See generally Annotation, *Transplantation: Power of Parent, Guardian, or Committee to Consent to Surgical Invasion of Ward's Person for Benefit of Another,* 35 A.L.R.3d 683 (1971).

157 *See* National Ctr. for State Courts, Guidelines for State Court Decision Making in Life-Sustaining Medical Treatment Cases 55 (2d ed. 1992) (standard 10(B)(b)).

158 Superintendent of Belchertown State Sch. v. Saikewicz, 370 N.E.2d 417 (Mass. 1977). *See also In re* Doe, 583 N.E.2d 1263 (Mass. 1992).

concern" in decisionmaking for incompetent patients is "that the guardian's decision conform, to the extent possible, to the decision that would have been made by" the patient himself.[159] More specifically, the standard to be applied in making decisions for incompetent patients is one that will yield a "decision . . . which would be made by the incompetent person, if that person were competent, but taking into account the present and future incompetency of the individual as one of the factors which would necessarily enter into the decision-making process of the competent person."[160]

To emphasize what the court stressed as the subjective nature of the inquiry, the court claimed to reject the dictum in *Quinlan* that Karen Quinlan's life need not be prolonged if her prognosis for recovery was virtually nonexistent because "most people in like circumstances would choose a natural death."[161] By contrast, *Saikewicz* recognized that what a particular patient would have wanted may not conform to "what is thought wise or prudent by most people."[162] Despite the avowedly purely subjective nature of the standard, however, its application in *Saikewicz* led, as it often does, to the interjection of considerations other than the intentions of the now incompetent patient.

Within a short time of the *Saikewicz* decision, the three dominant standards for surrogate decisionmaking began to differentiate themselves from each other, and a consensus evolved that the substituted judgment standard is the preferred standard among the three "because of its straightforward respect for the integrity and autonomy of the individual,"[163] and most courts have adopted it in

---

[159] Superintendent of Belchertown State Sch. v. Saikewicz, 370 N.E.2d at 429.

[160] **MA:** Superintendent of Belchertown State Sch. v. Saikewicz, 370 N.E.2d at 431.

DDC: *Accord* Tune v. Walter Reed Army Medical Hosp., 602 F. Supp. 1452, 1454 (D.D.C. 1985).

CT: *Accord* Foody v. Manchester Memorial Hosp., 482 A.2d 713, 721 (Conn. Super. Ct. 1984).

MA: *Accord* Brophy v. New Eng. Sinai Hosp., Inc., 497 N.E.2d 626, 633 (Mass. 1986); Custody of a Minor, 434 N.E.2d 601, 605 (Mass. 1982); *In re* Spring, 405 N.E.2d 119 (Mass. 1980); *In re* Hier, 464 N.E.2d 959, 961 (Mass. App. Ct.), *review denied,* 465 N.E.2d 261 (Mass. 1984).

OH: *Accord In re* Myers, 610 N.E.2d 663, 669 (P. Ct. Summit County, Ohio 1993) ("'Substitute judgment' involves attempting to make the same decision as the ward would have made, if competent, through the use of evidence, mainly statements of the ward prior to incompetency, to determine the ward's state of mind or wishes.").

PA: *Accord In re* Fiori, 13 Fiduc. Rep. 2d 79 (C.P. Bucks County, Pa. 1993).

[161] Superintendent of Belchertown State Sch. v. Saikewicz, 370 N.E.2d at 429 (paraphrasing *In re* Quinlan, 355 A.2d 647, 664 (N.J. 1976)).

[162] **MA:** Superintendent of Belchertown State Sch. v. Saikewicz, 370 N.E.2d at 430. *Accord In re* Spring, 399 N.E.2d 493, 499 (Mass. App. Ct. 1979).

WA: *Accord In re* Ingram, 689 P.2d 1363, 1369 (Wash. 1984).

[163] Superintendent of Belchertown State Sch. v. Saikewicz, 370 N.E.2d at 431.

decisionmaking for incompetent patients.[164] Although the more demanding subjective standard might be preferable, its attempted application is often thwarted by the absence of evidence necessary to meet it. By contrast, the substituted judgment standard strikes a reasonable balance between implementing self-determination for incompetent patients and protecting patients' welfare. The substituted judgment standard is also preferable to the best interests standard because the latter departs from the principle of self-determination, and only when it is impossible to meet the substituted judgment standard should the best interests standard be applied.[165] The acceptance by virtually all courts considering the issue of the principle that incompetent patients must be accorded the same substantive rights as competent patients[166] has been at the root of the widespread judicial acceptance of the substituted judgment standard.

There has, however, been some important criticism of the substituted judgment standard coming, as it were, from both sides though both sides agree that the substituted judgment standard does not adequately protect the interests of incompetent patients. Those who insist on the application of the subjective standard are concerned that the substituted judgment standard does not

---

[164] **CA:** Barber v. Superior Court, 195 Cal. Rptr. 484 (Ct. App. 1983).

CT: Foody v. Manchester Memorial Hosp., 482 A.2d 713 (Conn. Super. Ct. 1984).

DC: *In re* A.C., 573 A.2d 1235, 1247 (D.C. 1990).

FL: Browning v. Herbert, 568 So. 2d 4 (Fla. 1990); John F. Kennedy Memorial Hosp. v. Bludworth, 452 So. 2d 921 (Fla. 1984); Corbett v. D'Alessandro, 487 So. 2d 368 (Fla. Dist. Ct. App.), *review denied,* 492 So. 2d 1331 (Fla. 1986); *In re* Barry, 445 So. 2d 365 (Fla. Dist. Ct. App. 1984).

IL: *In re* Estate of Greenspan, 558 N.E.2d 1194 (Ill. 1990); Estate of Longeway v. Community Convalescent Ctr., 549 N.E.2d 292, 299 (Ill. 1989).

IA: Morgan v. Olds, 417 N.W.2d 232 (Iowa Ct. App. 1987).

LA: *In re* P.V.W., 424 So. 2d 1015 (La. 1982).

MD: Mack v. Mack, 618 A.2d 744 (Md. 1993).

MA: *In re* Beth, 587 N.E.2d 1377 (Mass. 1992); *In re* Doe, 583 N.E.2d 1263 (Mass. 1992).

MI: Rosebush v. Oakland County Prosecutor, 491 N.W.2d 633 (Mich. Ct. App. 1992).

NJ: *In re* Peter, 529 A.2d 419 (N.J. 1987); *In re* Quinlan, 355 A.2d 647 (N.J. 1976).

NY: Eichner v. Dillon, 420 N.E.2d 64 (N.Y. 1981); Delio v. Westchester County Medical Ctr., 516 N.Y.S.2d 677 (App. Div. 1987), *questioned in In re* Westchester County Medical Ctr. (O'Connor), 531 N.E.2d 607 (N.Y. 1988); Workmen's Circle Home & Infirmary for the Aged v. Fink, 514 N.Y.S.2d 893 (Sup. Ct. Bronx County 1987).

OH: Leach v. Akron Gen. Medical Ctr., 426 N.E.2d 809 (P. Ct. Summit County, Ohio 1980). *Cf. In re* McInnis, 584 N.E.2d 1389 (P. Ct. Stark County, Ohio 1991) ("[I]n the absence of advance directives the administration or the withdrawal of life-sustaining treatment should be based upon medical expertise, consistent with the patient's wishes, as they are expressed by the family members.").

WA: *In re* Ingram, 689 P.2d 1363 (Wash. 1984); *In re* Colyer, 660 P.2d 738 (Wash. 1983).

WI: L.W. v. L.E. Phillips Career Dev. Ctr., 482 N.W.2d 60 (Wis. 1992).

[165] See § **7.12.**

[166] See §§ **2.2, 2.3,** and **2.5.**

adequately protect self-determination,[167] and there is certainly truth to that argument in the cases in which courts have interpreted that standard loosely, essentially applying objective criteria rather than attempting to ascertain the patient's probable wishes.[168] On the other hand, other critics contend that the substituted judgment standard should not apply even if there is the clearest evidence of what the patient actually said he wanted in such circumstances. The basis for this critique is that individuals cannot foresee or comprehend the circumstances that they might be in, and thus any opinions they express about how they wish to be treated should those situations arise are hypothetical. Further, their wishes and interests in the new situation might well be quite different than they imagined that they would be, to the extent that we might even consider them to be different persons post-incompetency than when they were competent. Consequently, the only appropriate standard for decisionmaking for incompetent patients is the best interests standard.[169]

§ 7.8 Meaning of "Substituted Judgment": Subjective or Objective?

In explaining the meaning and operation of the substituted judgment standard, courts sometimes speak of the surrogate's substituting his judgment for that of the incompetent patient.[170] It is not always clear whether these courts really mean that the surrogate should exercise his own judgment or whether this is merely imprecise language. Certainly this interpretation is inconsistent with the spirit of the substituted judgment standard, especially as contrasted with the best interests standard. The essential distinction between the two is that under the best interests standard the surrogate is to do what is best for the patient in the surrogate's own judgment,[171] though based on some objective criteria,[172] whereas under the substituted judgment standard the surrogate is to attempt to

---

[167] See § **7.4.**

[168] See §§ **7.8–7.10.**

[169] *See* Dresser & Robertson, *Quality of Life and Non-Treatment Decisions for Incompetent Patients, A Critique of the Orthodox Approach,* 17 Law, Med. & Health Care 234 (1989); Dresser, *Life, Death and Incompetent Patients: Conceptual Infirmities and Hidden Values in the Law,* 28 Ariz. L. Rev. 373, 379–82 (1986); Robertson, Cruzan *and the Constitutional Status of Nontreatment Decisions for Incompetent Patients,* 25 Ga. L. Rev. 1139 (1991).

[170] **DC:** *E.g., In re* A.C., 573 A.2d 1235, 1249 (D.C. 1990) ("Under the substituted judgment procedure, the court as decision-maker must 'substitute itself as nearly as may be for the incompetent, and . . . act upon the same motives and considerations as would have moved her. . . . ' *City Bank Farmers Trust Co. v. McGowan,* 323 U.S. 594, 599, 65 S. Ct. 496, 498, 89 L. Ed. 483 (1945).").

MN: *E.g., In re* Torres, 357 N.W.2d 332, 341 (Minn. 1984) ("[T]he conservator had the right to issue his substituted judgment for that of the comatose conservatee.").

[171] Drabick v. Drabick, 245 Cal. Rptr. 840 (Ct. App. 1988).

[172] See §§ **7.12–7.25.**

replicate what the *patient* would decide if competent to do so.[173] The Florida Supreme Court described the surrogate's role under the substituted judgment standard this way:

> [I]t is important for the surrogate decisionmaker to fully appreciate that he or she makes the decision which the patient would personally choose. In this state, we have adopted a concept of "substituted judgment." [*In re Guardianship of Barry,* 445 So. 2d 365, 370–71 (Fla. 2d DCA 1984)]. One does not exercise another's right of self-determination or fulfill that person's right of privacy by making a decision which the state, the family, or public opinion would prefer. The surrogate decisionmaker must be confident that he or she can and is voicing the patient's decision.[174]

Ironically, however, the *Barry* case, cited for the proposition that Florida adheres to a substituted judgment standard, bears striking similarity to *Saikewicz,* for it too involved a never-competent patient (though an infant, rather than a mentally retarded adult).

The source of this error has been accurately described by the Maryland Court of Appeals as follows:

> From the standpoint of initiating a request to withdraw life-sustaining treatment, the judgment of the guardian or applicant for guardianship is truly substituted for that of the ward. But, from the standpoint of whether the treatment is to be withdrawn, the "substituted judgment" label is a misnomer. The judgment of the guardian is not accepted by the court in lieu of the judgment of the ward. Rather, because the right is one of self-determination, the inquiry focuses on whether the ward had determined, or would determine, that treatment should be withdrawn under the circumstances of the case.[175]

Perhaps this is merely quibbling about words. Nonetheless, the distinction between a surrogate's attempting to replicate a patient's decision based on evidence about what the patient wanted and "substituting his judgment for that of the incompetent patient" is an extremely significant one frequently overlooked by courts.[176]

Ideally the surrogate should be guided by the patient's explicit expressions before becoming incompetent.[177] If, however, that standard is to be strictly

---

[173] **MI:** Rosebush v. Oakland County Prosecutor, 491 N.W.2d 633, 639 (Mich. Ct. App. 1992) (citing first edition of this treatise).

[174] Browning v. Herbert, 568 So. 2d 4, 13 (Fla. 1990).

[175] Mack v. Mack, 618 A.2d 744, 750 (Md. 1993).

[176] **NJ:** *But see In re* Conroy, 486 A.2d 1209 (N.J. 1985). See §§ **7.16, 7.27,** and **7.28.**

[177] **CA:** Barber v. Superior Court, 195 Cal. Rptr. 484, 493 (Ct. App. 1983) ("The authorities are in agreement that any surrogate, court appointed or otherwise, ought to be guided . . . first by his knowledge of the patient's own desires and feelings, to the extent that they were expressed before the patient became incompetent.").

CT: Foody v. Manchester Memorial Hosp., 482 A.2d 713, 720–21 (Conn. Super. Ct. 1984).

applied, it might frequently be impossible because such evidence is often lacking. The substituted judgment standard is particularly difficult—if not impossible—to apply in a situation in which the patient, like Saikewicz, has never been competent.[178] Thus, from the start, most courts have departed from a strict application of the standard—indeed, the subjective standard differentiated itself from the substituted judgment standard for this reason[179]—and permitted surrogate decisionmakers to consider a variety of factors from which the incompetent patient's subjective intent can be inferred. In so doing, the standard has been transformed from one in which the patient's actual subjective intent is the guide to one in which the surrogate can genuinely be said to substitute his judgment for the unknown wishes of the incompetent patient because, although those wishes are unknown, there is adequate evidence from which they can realistically be inferred.[180]

The consequence of using the substituted judgment standard in cases in which evidence of the patient's subjective intent is absent or unclear has been an

---

DC: *In re* A.C., 573 A.2d 1235, 1249 (D.C. 1990) ("[T]he substituted judgment inquiry is primarily a subjective one: as nearly as possible, the court must ascertain what the patient would do if competent.").

FL: Browning v. Herbert, 568 So. 2d 4 (Fla. 1990).

MA: *In re* Spring, 399 N.E.2d 493, 499 (Mass. App. Ct. 1979).

NJ: *In re* Conroy, 486 A.2d 1209, 1229–30 (N.J. 1985).

[178] See **§ 7.10.**

[179] **MD:** *See* Mack v. Mack, 618 A.2d 744, 762 (Md. 1993) (McAuliffe, J., dissenting) (The subjective standard "focuses upon prior statements made by the ward. The substituted judgment approach comes into play when the ward has made no prior statements bearing on the issue, or the statements attributed to the ward do not produce a clear and convincing answer.").

[180] **DE:** Newmark v. Williams, 588 A.2d 1108, 1117 (Del. 1991) ("This Court must . . . substitute its own objective judgment to determine what is in Colin's 'best interests.'").

FL: Browning v. Herbert, 568 So. 2d 4, 13 (Fla. 1990) ("We emphasize and caution that when the patient has left instructions regarding life-sustaining treatment, the surrogate must make the medical choice that the patient, if competent, would have made, and not one that the surrogate might make for himself or herself, or that the surrogate might think is in the patient's best interests.").

MA: *Cf. In re* Doe, 583 N.E.2d 1263, 1268 (Mass. 1992) ("five factors that judges must consider in substituting their judgment for that of incompetent people").

MO: Cruzan v. Harmon, 760 S.W.2d 408, 424–26 (Mo. 1988).

NY: *In re* Westchester County Medical Ctr. (O'Connor), 531 N.E.2d 607, 613 (N.Y. 1988) ("no person or court should substitute his judgment"); Elbaum v. Grace Plaza of Great Neck, Inc., 544 N.Y.S.2d 840, 847 (App. Div. 1989).

WI: L.W. v. L.E. Phillips Career Dev. Ctr., 482 N.W.2d 60, 69 (Wis. 1992) ("A substituted judgment is not conceived to be solely the judgment of the surrogate, but the judgment of the ward exercised by a surrogate who has sufficient information derived from past history of the ward when competent to reasonably ascertain what the decision of the ward would be were he or she presently competent to make the required decision.").

objectification of what was intended to be a subjective standard.[181] At first the *Saikewicz* court appeared to follow to the extreme its injunction that a subjective standard is to be applied, stating that "[e]vidence that most people choose to accept the rigors of chemotherapy has no direct bearing on the likely choice that Joseph Saikewicz would have made."[182] However, in explaining why such evidence has no "direct bearing," the court stated that "[u]nlike most people, Saikewicz has no capacity to understand his present situation or his prognosis."[183]

This statement implies that the court would have paid attention to what most people would have done had Saikewicz himself been like "most people," and further implies that in practice the standard is not a subjective one. This implication is reinforced by the court's discussion of *Quinlan,* suggesting that on those facts, consideration should have been given to what others would want under the same circumstances. The *Saikewicz* court said as much: "[T]hus it is not unreasonable to give weight to a supposed general, and widespread, response to the situation" that Karen Quinlan was in.[184]

Saikewicz further retreated from a subjective standard when it acknowledged that

> [e]vidence that most people would or would not act in a certain way is certainly an important consideration in attempting to ascertain the predilections of any individual, but care must be taken, as in any analogy, to ensure that operative factors are similar or at least to take notice of the dissimilarities.[185]

The court agreed that the fact that most people consent to a particular treatment and the fact that the treatment will extend life are "appropriate indicators" of what an incompetent patient would have wanted.[186]

The result has been, especially but not exclusively in Massachusetts, that the substituted judgment standard has moved from being a point on the continuum of standards for surrogate decisionmaking to occupying a good part of the center of that continuum. The courts that have engaged in a broadening of the substituted judgment standard have tended to do so by moving it toward the best interests standard and by making it barely indistinguishable from the best

---

[181] **MA:** *Cf. In re* Doe, 583 N.E.2d 1263, 1268 (Mass. 1992) ("it may . . . be necessary to rely to a greater degree on objective criteria" in case of never-competent person).

MO: Cruzan v. Harmon, 760 S.W.2d 408, 424–26 (Mo. 1988).

NY: *In re* Westchester County Medical Ctr. (O'Connor), 531 N.E.2d at 613 ("objective factors used in the so-called 'substituted judgment' approach").

[182] **MA:** Superintendent of Belchertown State Sch. v. Saikewicz, 370 N.E.2d 417, 430 (Mass. 1977).

WA: *Accord In re* Ingram, 689 P.2d 1363, 1369 (Wash. 1984).

[183] Superintendent of Belchertown State Sch. v. Saikewicz, 370 N.E.2d at 430.

[184] *Id.*

[185] *Id.* at 429.

[186] *Id.* at 431.

interests standard. For instance, the Illinois Supreme Court, while acknowledging the subjective nature of the substituted judgment inquiry, mandated that "the patient's personal value system must guide the surrogate . . . [w]here no clear intent exists."[187]

However, other courts have employed a loose definition of the subjective standard, causing it to move in the direction of the substituted judgment standard.[188] Consequently, the substituted judgment standard not only occupies the broad middle of the continuum but also tends to overlap with both ends.

A small number of courts seem to explicitly recognize both the objective and subjective aspects of the substituted judgment standard and the potential for its overlap with the subjective standard on the one hand and the best interests standard on the other. One of those courts was the Florida District Court of Appeal in *Browning,*[189] which, commenting on the relationship between the subjective standard and the substituted judgment standard, observed that substituted judgment

> does not allow the guardian to truly substitute the guardian's judgment for that of the patient. The guardian makes the decision which the evidence establishes the patient would have made under these circumstances. The guardian makes the decision which the patient would have made even if that decision is different than the decision which the guardian would make for himself or herself.[190]

---

[187] Estate of Longeway v. Community Convalescent Ctr., 549 N.E.2d 292, 299 (Ill. 1989).

[188] See **§ 7.5.**

[189] Browning v. Herbert, 543 So. 2d 258 (Fla. Dist. Ct. App. 1989).

[190] **FL:** Browning v. Herbert, 543 So. 2d 258, 272–73 (Fla. Dist. Ct. App. 1989) ("We emphasize and caution that when the patient has left instructions regarding life-sustaining treatment, the surrogate must make the medical choice that the patient, if competent, would have made, and not one that the surrogate might make for himself or herself, or that the surrogate might think is in the patient's best interests.").

KY: *Accord* DeGrella v. Elston, 858 S.W.2d 698, 711 (Ky. 1993) (Lambert, J., concurring) ("[A] . . . fundamental objection [to the substituted judgment standard] is that the perceived moral and ethical values of the patient may be lost or significantly influenced by the values of the surrogate. Moreover, there is a substantial danger that 'quality of life' considerations may leak into the analytical process. As it is commonly understood, substituted judgment would likely be so subjective as to undermine any confidence that the patient's wishes were being truly observed.").

MD: *Accord* Mack v. Mack, 618 A.2d 744, 757 (Md. 1993) ("From the standpoint of initiating a request to withdraw life-sustaining treatment, the judgment of the guardian or applicant for guardianship is truly substituted for that of the ward. But, from the standpoint of whether the treatment is to be withdrawn, the 'substituted judgment' label is a misnomer. The judgment of the guardian is not accepted by the court in lieu of the judgment of the ward. Rather, because the right is one of self-determination, the inquiry focuses on whether the ward had determined, or would determine, that treatment should be withdrawn under the circumstances of the case."); *id.* at 762 (McAuliffe, J., dissenting) ("'Substituted judgment' is not a particularly apt term—the very result we wish to avoid is the substitution of someone else's judgment for that of the ward. Rather, the aim is to determine, by reference to all that may be known about the ward, what decision he or she would make if presently competent and possessed of complete information concerning all relevant factors.").

The court most critical of the unclarity of the substituted judgment standard and its potential for being all things to all people is the Missouri Supreme Court. According to that court, the source of a guardian's power to make decisions on behalf of an incompetent patient is not the patient's decisional right, but the state's parens patriae power.[191] Other courts have erred in applying

> the doctrine of substituted judgment . . . in abrogation of the state's *parens patriae* power, not in furtherance of it . . . [thereby] "allow[ing] the truly involuntary to be declared voluntary, thus bypassing constitutional, ethical and moral questions, and avoiding the violation of taboos. Third party consent is a miraculous creation of the law—adroit, flexible, and useful in covering the unseemly reality of conflict with the patina of cooperation."[192]

Further confusion of the substituted judgment and subjective standards has resulted from courts' carelessness with terminology. The primary reason for this confusion is that courts often refer to the subjective standard as the "clear and convincing evidence standard," which is not a substantive standard for decisionmaking for incompetent patients but an evidentiary standard that can be employed in the implementation of any substantive standard.[193] For example, in *Mack v. Mack,*[194] the Maryland Court of Appeals definitely wanted to employ a clear-and-convincing-evidence standard of proof, and it just as definitely wanted to employ a substituted judgment standard. But it confused this evidentiary standard with the substantive standard for decisionmaking for incompetent patients, which is clear from its citation of a long list of cases in other states that it describes as "requir[ing] the proponent of withholding or withdrawing life support to bear the burden of proving by clear and convincing evidence that the ward's decision would have been to forego life support."[195] Although the cited cases do require clear and convincing evidence, most apply a substituted judgment standard, rather than a strict subjective standard, and some even permit the application of a best interests standard when the substituted judgment standard cannot be met. Further, after discussing the standard of proof, the court then described the kind of evidence that is admissible, which clearly describes a substituted judgment standard and not a subjective standard:

---

[191] Cruzan v. Harmon, 760 S.W.2d 408, 425–26 (Mo. 1988).

[192] **MO:** Cruzan v. Harmon, 760 S.W.2d at 426 (quoting Price & Burt, *Sterilization, State Action, and the Concept of Consent,* Law & Psychol. Rev. 58 (Spring 1975)).

ME: *Cf. In re* Swan, 569 A.2d 1202, 1206 (Me. 1990) ("As in *Gardner,* we rest our decision on Chad's own conclusion and not on any theory of substituted judgment."); *In re* Gardner, 534 A.2d 947 (Me. 1987).

NY: *Accord In re* Westchester County Medical Ctr. (O'Connor), 531 N.E.2d 607 (N.Y. 1988).

[193] See § **5.62.**

[194] 618 A.2d 744 (Md. 1993).

[195] *Id.* at 754.

> The scope of the evidence that may be received in the inquiry is as wide as the concepts of relevance and materiality are to the state of mind issue. Oral, as well as written, statements of the ward, made prior to the ward's incompetency, should be considered. Evidence of this character will include any actual, expressed intent or desire to have artificial sustenance withdrawn, *but the evidence is not limited to specific, subjective intent evidence.* The patient's "'philosophical, religious and moral views, life goals, values about the purpose of life and the way it should be lived, and attitudes toward sickness, medical procedures, suffering and death'" should be explored. [Citations omitted.] These guidelines "should aid in ascertaining [the patient's] desires and in reaching a decision" *based upon clear and convincing evidence.* [Citation omitted.][196]

§ 7.9 Factors to Be Considered in Applying Substituted Judgment

The Massachusetts courts and others adopting the substituted judgment standard (as well as some adopting the subjective standard) have provided a list of factors to be considered by the surrogate in applying the substituted judgment standard. In addition, the New Jersey Supreme Court has promulgated a similar list of factors to be taken into account by surrogates in applying its unique standards for surrogate decisionmaking.[197] Of course, the predominant factors in applying the substituted judgment standard, especially the stricter versions of that standard, are written or oral expressions of the patient's wishes.[198]

The Maryland Court of Appeals made the general observation that

> [t]he scope of the evidence that may be received in the inquiry [about substituted judgment] is as wide as the concepts of relevance and materiality are to the state of mind issue. Oral, as well as written, statements of the ward, made prior to the ward's incompetency, should be considered. Evidence of this character will include any actual, expressed intent or desire to have artificial sustenance withdrawn, but the evidence is not limited to specific, subjective intent evidence. . . .
>
> In some cases the evidence will be direct. . . . In other cases, the court must make its findings as a matter of inference from all of the evidence. That inference must be closely connected to the clear evidence presented.[199]

The factors gleaned from *Saikewicz* are:

---

[196] *Id.* at 758 (emphasis added).

[197] See §§ **7.16–7.20.**

[198] National Ctr. for State Courts, Guidelines for State Court Decision Making in Life-Sustaining Medical Treatment Cases 81–87 (2d ed. 1992) (standards 13 and 14).

[199] Mack v. Mack, 618 A.2d 744, 758 (Md. 1993).

1. The patient's age[200]
2. The probable side effects of treatment[201]
3. The chance of producing a temporary or permanent cure[202]
4. The likelihood that treatment will cause suffering, such as a continuing state of pain and disorientation[203]
5. The patient's ability to cooperate with the treatment, because an uncooperative patient would have to be physically restrained to administer treatment, which would compound pain and fear.[204]

This list has been supplemented in subsequent cases with some factors that are more reminiscent of a best interests standard.

6. The patient's reactions to medical treatment of others[205]

---

[200] **MA:** Superintendent of Belchertown State Sch. v. Saikewicz, 370 N.E.2d 417, 432 (Mass. 1977).

NY: *Accord In re* Beth Israel Medical Ctr. (Weinstein), 519 N.Y.S.2d 511, 517 (Sup. Ct. N.Y. County 1987), *overruled by implication, In re* Westchester County Medical Ctr. (O'Connor), 531 N.E.2d 607 (N.Y. 1988).

[201] **MA:** Superintendent of Belchertown State Sch. v. Saikewicz, 370 N.E.2d at 432. *Accord In re* Beth, 587 N.E.2d 1377, 1382 (Mass. 1992) ("the probability of adverse side effects from the treatment"); Brophy v. New Eng. Sinai Hosp., Inc., 497 N.E.2d 626, 631 (Mass. 1986).

MD: *Accord* Mack v. Mack, 618 A.2d 744, 758 (Md. 1993).

NY: *In re* Beth Israel Medical Ctr. (Weinstein), 519 N.Y.S.2d at 517, *overruled by implication, In re* Westchester County Medical Ctr. (O'Connor), 531 N.E.2d 607 (N.Y. 1988).

[202] Superintendent of Belchertown State Sch. v. Saikewicz, 370 N.E.2d at 432.

[203] **MA:** Superintendent of Belchertown State Sch. v. Saikewicz, 370 N.E.2d at 432.

NY: *Accord In re* Beth Israel Medical Ctr. (Weinstein), 519 N.Y.S.2d at 517 (pain or suffering with or without the procedure), *overruled by implication, In re* Westchester County Medical Ctr. (O'Connor), 531 N.E.2d 607 (N.Y. 1988).

See § **9.31.**

[204] Superintendent of Belchertown State Sch. v. Saikewicz, 370 N.E.2d at 432. *Accord In re* Spring, 399 N.E.2d 493, 500 (Mass. App. Ct. 1979.

[205] **CT:** McConnell v. Beverly Enters.-Conn., Inc., 553 A.2d 596, 605 (Conn. 1989) (The patient worked as a registered nurse in an emergency room and "often saw the tragedy that befell those who suffered severe head injuries" and "[s]he had also been adamant that her own mother, when dying of cancer, not be placed on any life support system.").

IL: *In re* Estate of Greenspan, 558 N.E.2d 1194, 1198 (Ill. 1990) (patient's discussion of *Quinlan* case and reaction to discontinuation of treatment of a friend relevant to applying substituted judgment standard).

KY: DeGrella v. Elston, 858 S.W.2d 698, 709 (Ky. 1993) ("reactions the patient voiced regarding particular types of medical treatment").

ME: *In re* Swan, 569 A.2d 1202, 1205 (Me. 1990) (reaction to discussion of *In re* Gardner, 534 A.2d 947 (Me. 1987)).

7. The patient's religious beliefs[206]
8. A consistent pattern of conduct by the patient with respect to prior decisions about his own medical care[207]
9. When there is a "close-knit" family, the decision of the family, particularly when in accord with the recommendation of the attending physician[208]
10. The life expectancy with or without the contemplated procedure[209]

NJ: *In re* Peter, 529 A.2d 419, 427 n.9 (N.J. 1987); *In re* Conroy, 486 A.2d 1209, 1229–30 (N.J. 1985).

NY: *But see In re* Westchester County Medical Ctr. (O'Connor), 531 N.E.2d at 614 (rejecting as relevant consideration); Elbaum v. Grace Plaza of Great Neck, Inc., 544 N.Y.S.2d 840, 845 (App. Div. 1989) (quoting *O'Connor*).

OH: *Cf. In re* Myers, 610 N.E.2d 663, 665 (P. Ct. Summit County, Ohio 1993) (applying best interests standard but noting that patient had said after "visiting a relative in the hospital who was on life support systems due to severe brain injury" that "'she wouldn't want to go through life like that'").

PA: *In re* E.L.K., 11 Fiduc. Rep. 2d 78 (C.P. Berks County, Pa. 1991) (patient's reaction to husband's death too hypothetical).

[206] **FL:** Browning v. Herbert, 543 So. 2d 258, 272 (Fla. Dist. Ct. App. 1989).

KY: DeGrella v. Elston, 858 S.W.2d 698, 709 (Ky. 1993) ("religious beliefs and the tenets of that religion").

MD: Mack v. Mack, 618 A.2d 744, 758 (Md. 1993).

MA: *In re* Beth, 587 N.E.2d 1377, 1382 (Mass. 1992); *In re* Doe, 583 N.E.2d 1263, 1268 (Mass. 1992); Brophy v. New Eng. Sinai Hosp., Inc., 497 N.E.2d 626, 631 (Mass. 1986).

NJ: *In re* Conroy, 486 A.2d 1209, 1230 (N.J. 1985); *In re* Quinlan, 355 A.2d 647, 658 (N.J. 1976). *But cf. In re* Jobes, 529 A.2d 434, 443 (N.J. 1987) (religious affiliation offers no guide when religion neither requires nor forbids treatment).

NY: *In re* Westchester County Medical Ctr. (O'Connor), 531 N.E.2d at 617 (Hancock, J., concurring); *In re* Beth Israel Medical Ctr. (Weinstein), 519 N.Y.S.2d 511, 517 (Sup. Ct. N.Y. County 1987), *overruled by implication, In re* Westchester County Medical Ctr. (O'Connor), 531 N.E.2d 607 (N.Y. 1988).

PA: *Cf. In re* E.L.K., 11 Fiduc. Rep. 2d 78 (C.P. Berks County, Pa. 1991) (discussion of Jewish position on do-not-resuscitate orders).

[207] **DC:** *In re* A.C., 573 A.2d 1235, 1250 (D.C. 1990).

KY: DeGrella v. Elston, 858 S.W.2d 698, 709 (Ky. 1993) ("the patient's consistent pattern of conduct with respect to prior decisions about his own medical care").

NJ: *In re* Conroy, 486 A.2d at 1229–30.

[208] **MA:** *In re* Spring, 399 N.E.2d 493 (Mass. App. Ct. 1979).

NY: *In re* Beth Israel Medical Ctr. (Weinstein), 519 N.Y.S.2d at 517 (views of those close to patient), *overruled by implication, In re* Westchester County Medical Ctr. (O'Connor), 531 N.E.2d 607 (N.Y. 1988).

PA: *Cf. In re* Myers, 610 N.E.2d 663, 670–71 (P. Ct. Summit County, Ohio 1993) (not "close-knit" family, but views of mother, father, and stepmother must be considered because they know patient best).

[209] *In re* Beth Israel Medical Ctr. (Weinstein), 519 N.Y.S.2d at 517, *overruled by implication, In re* Westchester County Medical Ctr. (O'Connor), 531 N.E.2d 607 (N.Y. 1988).

11. The extent of the patient's physical and mental disability and degree of helplessness[210]

12. The patient's statements, if any, which directly or impliedly manifest his views on life-prolonging measures[211]

13. The quality of the patient's life with or without the procedure; that is, the extent, if any, of pleasure, emotional enjoyment, or intellectual satisfaction that the patient will obtain from prolonged life[212]

14. The views of the physician[213]

15. The type of care that will be required if life is prolonged as contrasted with what will be actually available[214]

16. The patient's prognosis, both with and without treatment[215]

---

[210] **NY:** *In re* Westchester County Medical Ctr. (O'Connor), 531 N.E.2d at 617 (Hancock, J., concurring); *In re* Beth Israel Medical Ctr. (Weinstein), 519 N.Y.S.2d at 517, *overruled by implication, In re* Westchester County Medical Ctr. (O'Connor), 531 N.E.2d 607 (N.Y. 1988).

[211] **DC:** *In re* A.C., 573 A.2d 1235, 1250 (D.C. 1990) (prior oral or written statements by the patient "even though the treatment alternatives at hand may not have been addressed").

IL: *In re* Estate of Greenspan, 558 N.E.2d 1194, 1202 (Ill. 1990) ("evidence of the patient's intent, derived either from a patient's explicit expressions of intent or from knowledge of the patient's personal value system").

KY: DeGrella v. Elston, 858 S.W.2d 698, 708–09 (Ky. 1993) ("[t]he oral directives the patient gives to a family member, friend or health care provider").

NY: *In re* Beth Israel Medical Ctr. (Weinstein), 519 N.Y.S.2d at 517, *overruled by implication, In re* Westchester County Medical Ctr. (O'Connor), 531 N.E.2d 607 (N.Y. 1988).

PA: *Cf. In re* Myers, 610 N.E.2d 663, 665 (P. Ct. Summit County, Ohio 1993) (applying best interests standard but noting that patient had said "on several occasions prior to the accident . . . that 'she wouldn't want to go through life like that' ").

See Council on Ethical & Judicial Affairs, American Medical Ass'n, Code of Medical Ethics § 2.20, at 37 (1994).

[212] **MA:** *In re* Beth, 587 N.E.2d 1377, 1382 (Mass. 1992). *But see* Superintendent of Belchertown State Sch. v. Saikewicz, 370 N.E.2d 417, 432 (Mass. 1977) ("[V]ague, and perhaps ill-chosen, term 'quality of life' should be understood as a reference to the continuing state of pain and disorientation precipitated by the chemotherapy treatment"; "To the extent that [the quality of life] equates [with] the value of life . . . , we firmly reject it.").

NY: *In re* Beth Israel Medical Ctr. (Weinstein), 519 N.Y.S.2d at 517, *overruled by implication, In re* Westchester County Medical Ctr. (O'Connor), 531 N.E.2d 607 (N.Y. 1988).

[213] *In re* Westchester County Medical Ctr. (O'Connor), 531 N.E.2d at 617 (Hancock, J., concurring); *In re* Beth Israel Medical Ctr. (Weinstein), 519 N.Y.S.2d at 517, *overruled by implication, In re* Westchester County Medical Ctr. (O'Connor), 531 N.E.2d 607 (N.Y. 1988).

[214] *In re* Beth Israel Medical Ctr. (Weinstein), 519 N.Y.S.2d at 517, *overruled by implication, In re* Westchester County Medical Ctr. (O'Connor), 531 N.E.2d 607 (N.Y. 1988).

[215] **FL:** Browning v. Herbert, 543 So. 2d 258, 272 (Fla. Dist. Ct. App. 1989), *aff'd,* 568 So. 2d 4 (Fla. 1990).

MD: Mack v. Mack, 618 A.2d 744, 758 (Md. 1993).

MA: *In re* Beth, 587 N.E.2d 1377, 1382 (Mass. 1992); *In re* Doe, 583 N.E.2d 1263, 1268 (Mass. 1992); Brophy v. New Eng. Sinai Hosp., Inc., 497 N.E.2d 626, 631 (Mass. 1986).

NY: *In re* Westchester County Medical Ctr. (O'Connor), 531 N.E.2d 607, 617 (N.Y. 1988) (Hancock, J., concurring).

17. The impact on the patient's family[216]
18. The nature of the prescribed medical assistance, including its benefits, risks, invasiveness, painfulness, and side effects[217]
19. The sentiments of the family or intimate friends[218]
20. The patient's "value system"[219]
21. The "context in which prior declarations, treatment decisions, and expressions of personal values were made, including whether statements were made casually or after contemplation, or in accordance with deeply held beliefs"[220]
22. The patient's expressed preferences.[221]

As can be seen, this is a very broad list on its face, and even broader in practice because it is not "intended to be definitive, but only to suggest some of

---

[216] **MD:** Mack v. Mack, 618 A.2d 744, 758 (Md. 1993).

MA: *In re* Beth, 587 N.E.2d 1377, 1382 (Mass. 1992); *In re* Doe, 583 N.E.2d 1263, 1268 (Mass. 1992); Brophy v. New Eng. Sinai Hosp., Inc., 497 N.E.2d 626, 631 (Mass. 1986).

NY: *In re* Westchester County Medical Ctr. (O'Connor), 531 N.E.2d 607, 617 (N.Y. 1988) (Hancock, J., concurring).

[217] **FL:** Browning v. Herbert, 543 So. 2d 258, 272 (Fla. Dist. Ct. App. 1989).

MA: *In re* Doe, 583 N.E.2d 1263, 1268 (Mass. 1992).

NY: *In re* Westchester County Medical Ctr. (O'Connor), 531 N.E.2d 607, 617 (N.Y. 1988) (Hancock, J., concurring).

[218] **MA:** *In re* Beth, 587 N.E.2d 1377, 1382 (Mass. 1992) ("[B]oth the child's mother and father have expressed their desire that extraordinary measures not be used to prolong the child's life.").

NY: *In re* Westchester County Medical Ctr. (O'Connor), 531 N.E.2d 607, 617 (N.Y. 1988) (Hancock, J., concurring).

[219] **DC:** *In re* A.C, 573 A.2d 1235, 1250 (D.C. 1990) (Because "[m]ost people do not foresee what calamities may befall them . . . [t]he court . . . should pay special attention to the known values and goals of the incapacitated patient, and should strive, if possible, to extrapolate from those values and goals what the patient's decision would be.").

MD: *Accord* Mack v. Mack, 618 A.2d 744, 758 (Md. 1993) ("[t]he patient's 'philosophical, religious and moral views, life goals, values about the purpose of life and the way it should be lived, and attitudes toward sickness, medical procedures, suffering and death' ").

MA: *Cf. In re* Beth, 587 N.E.2d 1377, 1382 (Mass. 1992) ("the child's ethical, moral or religious values").

See Council on Ethical & Judicial Affairs, American Medical Ass'n, Code of Medical Ethics § 2.20, at 37 (1994).

[220] **DC:** *In re* A.C., 573 A.2d 1235, 1251 (D.C. 1990).

KY: DeGrella v. Elston, 858 S.W.2d 698, 708 (Ky. 1993).

See Council on Ethical & Judicial Affairs, American Medical Ass'n, Code of Medical Ethics § 2.20, at 37 (1994).

[221] **MD:** Mack v. Mack, 618 A.2d 744, 758 (Md. 1993).

MA: *In re* Doe, 583 N.E.2d 1263, 1268 (Mass. 1992); Brophy v. New Eng. Sinai Hosp., Inc., 497 N.E.2d 626, 631 (Mass. 1986).

See Council on Ethical & Judicial Affairs, American Medical Ass'n, Code of Medical Ethics § 2.20, at 37 (1994).

the considerations which should be taken into account when resolving these issues."[222]

Some of the factors tend to move the substituted judgment standard toward the subjective end of the continuum—for example, the patient's expressed preferences—while others have been specifically rejected as being relevant to the subjective standard—for example, the patient's reactions to the treatment of others.[223] Other factors tend to move the substituted judgment standard toward the objective end of the continuum—for instance, the likelihood that treatment will cause the patient suffering and the patient's quality of life.[224] Yet other factors seem wholly illegitimate under all but the most expansive reading of the best interests standard, such as "the sentiments of the family or intimate friends."[225] Nonetheless, there are limits. Even in those courts that consider a broad array of factors under the aegis of the substituted judgment standard, such as the Massachusetts Supreme Judicial Court, there is an unwillingness to consider the financial cost of the care.[226]

§ 7.10 Application to Never-Competent Patients

Decisionmaking for incompetent patients who have never been competent—primarily children and mentally retarded individuals—poses an especially difficult problem in an already difficult area. Fortunately it is not a frequent problem.[227] Conceptually, decisionmaking for never-competent patients is merely a

---

[222] *In re* Westchester County Medical Ctr. (O'Connor), 531 N.E.2d 607, 617 (N.Y. 1988) (Hancock, J., concurring) ("no exhaustive list can be set forth"); *In re* Beth Israel Medical Ctr. (Weinstein), 519 N.Y.S.2d 511, 517 (Sup. Ct. N.Y. County 1987), *overruled by implication, In re* Westchester County Medical Ctr. (O'Connor), 531 N.E.2d 607 (N.Y. 1988).

[223] *In re* Westchester County Medical Ctr. (O'Connor), 531 N.E.2d at 614 ("reactions to the unsettling experience of seeing or hearing of another's unnecessarily prolonged death" not clear and convincing evidence of patient's own wishes).

[224] See §§ **7.22–7.24.**

[225] See § **7.24.**

[226] *See In re* Doe, 583 N.E.2d 1263, 1269 n.15 (Mass. 1992). *See also In re* Beth, 587 N.E.2d 1377, 1382 (Mass. 1992).

[227] **FL:** *E.g., In re* Barry, 445 So. 2d 365 (Fla. Dist. Ct. App. 1984) (infant).

IN: *E.g., In re* Lawrance, 579 N.E.2d 32 (Ind. 1991).

MA: *E.g., In re* Beth, 587 N.E.2d 1377 (Mass. 1992); *In re* Doe, 583 N.E.2d 1263 (Mass. 1992); Custody of a Minor, 434 N.E.2d 601 (Mass. 1982) (infant); Superintendent of Belchertown State Sch. v. Saikewicz, 370 N.E.2d 417 (Mass. 1977). *Cf. In re* Hier, 464 N.E.2d 959 (Mass. App. Ct. 1984) (elderly woman with long history of mental illness and psychiatric hospitalization).

NJ: *E.g., In re* Moorhouse, 593 A.2d 1256 (N.J. Super. Ct. App. Div. 1991).

NY: *E.g., In re* Storar, 420 N.E.2d 64 (N.Y. 1981).

WA: *E.g., In re* Grant, 747 P.2d 445 (Wash. 1987), *modified,* 757 P.2d 534 (Wash. 1988); *In re* Hamlin, 689 P.2d 1372 (Wash. 1984).

variant of the larger problem of decisionmaking for patients whose preferences about treatment are unknown and unknowable.

Thus, it is logical that in a jurisdiction such as New York, requiring the application of the subjective standard, in which a decision to forgo life-sustaining treatment can be made only on the basis of the patient's expressed wishes, life-sustaining treatment may not be forgone by a surrogate on behalf of a never-competent patient.[228] The Supreme Court's decision in *Cruzan,*[229] that a state may require the application of such a subjective standard without violating the constitution, should have no effect on decisionmaking for never-competent patients in jurisdictions that permit the forgoing of life-sustaining treatment on the basis of other standards such as the best interests standard or the substituted judgment standard.

Most cases of never-competent patients involve children, and a relatively substantial and consistent body of law has developed concerning decisionmaking about life-sustaining treatment for them.[230] Few jurisdictions have ever had to confront this issue with adult patients, and only in Massachusetts has there been more than a single case. This likely results less from the nature of the standard than from the Massachusetts Supreme Judicial Court's dogmatic adherence to the substituted judgment standard (whether the decision involves life-sustaining or other kinds of treatment).[231] The first Massachusetts right-to-die case to have adopted the substituted judgment standard, *Saikewicz,* applied it to a never-competent adult patient. As so applied, it is convoluted and leads to fictional results.[232] It has been described as "an exercise of

---

WI: *E.g.,* L.W. v. L.E. Phillips Career Dev. Ctr., 482 N.W.2d 60, 63 (Wis. 1992) (elderly man with long history of mental illness and psychiatric hospitalization "may never have been competent").

See **Ch. 15.**

[228] *In re* Westchester County Medical Ctr. (O'Connor), 531 N.E.2d 607, 616 (N.Y. 1988) (Hancock, J., concurring) ("there are serious difficulties in *Storar*"); *id.* (Simmons, J., dissenting); *In re* Storar, 420 N.E.2d 64, 72 (N.Y. 1981); *In re* Kerr (O'Brien), 517 N.Y.S.2d 346 (Sup. Ct. N.Y. County 1986) (family, but not a friend, may make a substituted judgment decision for an incompetent patient).

[229] Cruzan v. Director, 497 U.S. 261 (1990).

[230] See **Ch. 15.**

[231] *See In re* Moe, 432 N.E.2d 712 (Mass. 1982) (sterilization); *In re* Roe, 421 N.E.2d 40 (Mass. 1981) (psychiatric medications).

[232] **MA:** *In re* Doe, 583 N.E.2d 1263, 1268 (Mass. 1992) ("We recognize that in situations in which there is an attempt to use substituted judgment for a never-competent person, it is a legal fiction.").

MI: Rosebush v. Oakland County Prosecutor, 491 N.W.2d 633, 639 (Mich. Ct. App. 1992) (substituted judgment standard inappropriate for never-competent patients) (citing first edition of this treatise).

NJ: *In re* Jobes, 529 A.2d 434, 449 (N.J. 1987) (substituted judgment unworkable when patient has always been incompetent) (citing President's Comm'n for the Study of Ethical Problems in Medicine & Biomedical & Behavioral Research, Deciding to Forego Life-Sustaining

imagination"[233] equivalent to asking "if it snowed in summer would it really be winter?"[234]

The Massachusetts courts have been deservedly chastised for using the substituted judgment standard in cases concerning patients who were never competent.[235] Despite the criticism, however, they have reaffirmed their adherence to this standard by its subsequent application in the case of an infant[236] (though at least one other jurisdiction has too[237]), contending that its use has the "theoretical utility" of focusing attention on and giving weight to factors peculiar to the particular incompetent patient, rather than to people generally.[238] It has also been applied to a child in a persistent vegetative state,[239] a mentally retarded adult in a persistent vegetative state,[240] and a mentally retarded adult in need of hemodialysis;[241] however, the Massachusetts Supreme Judicial Court

---

Treatment 132–33 (1983) [hereinafter President's Comm'n, Deciding to Forego Life-Sustaining Treatment]); *In re* Peter, 529 A.2d 419, 424 (N.J. 1987); *In re* Conroy, 486 A.2d 1209, 1219 (N.J. 1985) (limiting holding to patients "who, though formerly competent, [are] now incompetent").

NY: *In re* Storar, 420 N.E.2d at 72–73 (unrealistic to attempt to determine whether never-competent patient would want to continue potentially life-prolonging treatment if he were competent).

OH: *In re* Myers, 610 N.E.2d 663, 670 (P. Ct. Summit County, Ohio 1993) ("application [to never-competent patients] leads to complicated and meaningless variations of the substitute [*sic*] judgment test") (citing this treatise).

See generally Harmon, *Falling Off the Vine: Legal Fictions and the Doctrine of Substituted Judgment,* 100 Yale L.J. 1 (1990).

233 *In re* Jobes, 529 A.2d at 455 (Handler, J., concurring).

234 **NY:** *In re* Storar, 420 N.E.2d at 72–73 (quoting a witness at trial).

MA: *Accord In re* Beth, 587 N.E.2d 1377, 1382 (Mass. 1992) (Nolan, J., dissenting; O'Connor, J., dissenting); *In re* Doe, 583 N.E.2d 1263 (Mass. 1992) (Nolan, J., dissenting; O'Connor, J., dissenting); Brophy v. New Eng. Sinai Hosp., Inc., 497 N.E.2d 626, 643 (Mass. 1986) (Lynch, J., dissenting) ("It would be an error of great magnitude to conflate a substituted judgment with an actual judgment. Such a mistake . . . is paternalism masquerading as the mere ratification of autonomous choice.").

MO: *Accord* Cruzan v. Harmon, 760 S.W.2d 408, 424 n.20 (Mo. 1988) ("*Saikewicz* adopts substituted judgment to a remarkable end.").

235 *See* Baron, *Medical Paternalism and the Rule of Law: A Reply to Dr. Relman,* 4 Am. J. Law & Med. 337 (1978) (supporting *Saikewicz*); *Is Dying Better Than Dialysis for a Woman with Down Syndrome?*, 3 Cambridge Q. Healthcare Ethics 270 (1994); Schwartz, *Commentary on "Is Dying Better Than Dialysis for a Woman with Down Syndrome?",* 3 Cambridge Q. Healthcare Ethics 271 (1994); Leudtke, *Commentary on "Is Dying Better Than Dialysis for a Woman with Down Syndrome?",* 3 Cambridge Q. Healthcare Ethics 274 (1994).

236 *See* Custody of a Minor, 434 N.E.2d 601, 609 (Mass. 1982) (court must "seek to act on the same motives and considerations as would have moved the child").

237 *In re* Barry, 445 So. 2d 365 (Fla. Dist. Ct. App. 1984).

238 *In re* Hier, 464 N.E.2d 959, 965 (Mass. App. Ct. 1984).

239 *In re* Beth, 587 N.E.2d 1377 (Mass. 1992).

240 *In re* Doe, 583 N.E.2d 1263 (Mass. 1992).

241 *In re* R.H., 622 N.E.2d 1071 (Mass. App. Ct. 1993).

appears to have inexplicably abandoned it in favor of a best-interests-type standard in the case of a child needing a blood transfusion.[242]

The most unusual case involving never-competent patients, because of the patient's medical and mental statuses, is *In re R.H.*[243] In all of the other cases involving never-competent patients, the patient was either permanently unconscious or virtually incapable of communication. At the time of the hearing, R.H. was a 33-year-old woman who was a resident of a state-operated institution for the mentally retarded. She had Down's Syndrome and was moderately mentally retarded. "As a result of her mental retardation," according to the court, "she is not and has never been competent to manage her personal and financial affairs or provide informed consent for any medical treatment."[244] However,

> she has a degree of communication and comprehension skills. She can make verbal requests for her wants and needs, answers the telephone correctly, communicates both at Fernald and at work in brief, simple conversations, and uses sign language to express more abstract ideas (e.g., she has been able to inform her program supervisor, who can understand her speech, when she needs more work and whether she wants her work station moved to a warmer location because she is cold). She has participated in a diet workshop program in the course of which she made known her understanding of the basic concepts of dieting and nutrition.[245]

The court took note that she functioned at a fairly high level in other ways too:

> R.H. has led a relatively active life. She is a friendly woman who initiates interactions with Fernald staff and her peers. She enjoys dancing, bowling, listening to music, looking at magazines, and socializing with family members, other Fernald residents, and staff. She helps with her own laundry, can attend to her own personal hygiene and other routine living tasks, and can self-regulate her activities (e.g., she knows when she needs rest). She works four days a week at an Arlington workshop collating, folding, punching out index cards for templates, stuffing envelopes, and performing some disassembling work. She is able to work independently, pays close attention to her tasks and their completeness, and is regarded as a very competent worker. She has been able to adapt successfully to changes in her living conditions, including loss of familiar staff and peers, introduction of new staff and peers, and moving her living quarters.[246]

In fact, there are probably many similar situations that never get litigated, and one can only wonder how they are resolved.

As to her medical status, she was suffering from chronic and terminal kidney failure, a condition, as the court observed, "for which a cure, and not merely a life-prolonging palliative, is theoretically available."[247] Her kidney failure had

---

[242] *See In re* McCauley, 565 N.E.2d 411 (Mass. 1991).

[243] *In re* R.H., 622 N.E.2d 1071 (Mass. App. Ct. 1993).

[244] *Id.* at 1073.

[245] *Id.*

[246] *Id.*

[247] *Id.* at 1079.

progressed to the point where she might die soon (and if not soon, certainly in the next one to three years) if she did not receive either dialysis or a transplanted kidney.[248] The latter was not immediately available, if it would ever become available at all.

The Department of Mental Retardation petitioned to have dialysis administered because the patient's "mother has consistently and vehemently opposed the initiation of any dialysis treatment, expressing concern that R.H. would be unable to tolerate it."[249] The trial court denied the petition, and the petitioner appealed. In a firm rebuke, the appeals court held that trial court decision was "unsupported by the evidence and clearly erroneous,"[250] vacated the judgment, and remanded for further findings of fact. Because the situation was "of such urgency and the risks posed by further delay so imminently life-threatening,"[251] the court also ordered that dialysis be begun.

In light of the Massachusetts Supreme Judicial Court's reaffirmation of the application of the substituted judgment standard to never-competent patients in two recent cases,[252] the appeals court was virtually compelled by stare decisis to do so. Based on the facts of this case, there was at least some information about the patient from which one could colorably infer her wishes, but in all of the previous cases involving never-competent patients, whether in Massachusetts or other jurisdictions, there was little or none.

The trial court's decision was based almost exclusively on the finding that R.H. " 'cannot tolerate dialysis treatment,' " and the appeals court's reversal was based substantially on the fact that there was little if any basis in the record to support that finding. The trial court concluded that "[i]f treatment is ordered, she would not understand the disruption of her daily routine and its replacement with a forced regimen consisting of a three hour session every other day at a hemodialysis unit. . . . She is unable to provide the mental commitment, the understanding, the patience, discipline and desire which is essential to success."[253]

The trial court based its decision primarily on the evidence of expert witnesses, which, however, was hardly unanimous. In fact, of the five physicians who provided recommendations, three concluded that dialysis was appropriate. R.H.'s current and former physicians in the state institution recommended dialysis because they believed she could cooperate with treatment and because it "would give her ten or twenty more years of 'a good quality life,' and that it was their ethical obligation to give her the opportunity to continue to enjoy her life for as long as possible."[254] The evidence provided by "[a] hospital dialysis unit director who examined R.H. and her medical history before trial and had treated mentally retarded patients with more severe mental and behavior

[248] *Id.* at 1074.

[249] *In re* R.H., 622 N.E.2d 1071, 1074 (Mass. App. Ct. 1993).

[250] *Id.* at 1080.

[251] *Id.* at 1079–80.

[252] *See In re* Doe, 583 N.E.2d 1263 (Mass. 1992); *In re* Beth, 587 N.E.2d 1377 (Mass. 1992).

[253] *In re* R.H., 622 N.E.2d at 1075.

[254] *Id.* at 1074.

problems than hers, believed that dialysis would be a medically reasonable form of treatment for her . . . [and] stated without qualification that there was no medical reason not to begin dialysis for her."[255]

Only R.H.'s current nephrologist and another nephrologist felt that she was not a suitable candidate for dialysis. They both had experience treating mentally retarded persons with dialysis and based this recommendation on "their anticipation that she could not be expected to cooperate with or tolerate the treatment, could not understand its purpose, and could not cope with the ensuing pain and discomfort."[256]

What was most puzzling about the trial court's decision and central to the appeals court's reversal was the fact that the trial court only considered in passing and summarily rejected the obvious option of trying hemodialysis before concluding that it would be unsuccessful because R.H. would be unable to cooperate with this therapeutic regimen. The guardian ad litem had called this possibility to the court's attention, but had refrained from recommending it because R.H.'s family "were thoroughly opposed to even a trial" of therapy.[257] The appeals court noted that "[t]o the suggestion of 'let's try it and see if she can handle it,'" the trial court found "'that we would be setting her up to fail, and [that] such an experiment [should] not be undertaken.'"[258]

The *R.H.* case is important for at least two reasons. First, despite the court's lip service to the application of the substituted judgment standard, the previously discussed key evidence in the case clearly bears on the patient's *interests* rather than her actual or probable *preferences* despite her relatively high level of functioning. Second, the case helps to underscore that the phrase "never-competent patient" (or "mentally retarded patient") obscures as much as it elucidates. Such patients cannot be dealt with categorically; there must be an examination of the facts of each case for there will be some, perhaps many, in which it is possible to discern the patient's wishes, and even if not, their interests should not be considered to be monolithic.

Other jurisdictions have recognized the difficulty, if not impossibility, of applying anything other than a best interests standard in the case of never-competent patients, and all[259] but New York have appropriately done so. Other jurisdictions apply a best interests standard in the case of (never-competent)

---

[255] *Id.* at 1075; *see also id.* at 1078 n.5.

[256] *Id.* at 1075.

[257] *Id.*

[258] *Id.*

[259] **IN:** *In re* Lawrance, 579 N.E.2d 32 (Ind. 1991).

MI: Rosebush v. Oakland County Prosecutor, 491 N.W.2d 633 (Mich. Ct. App. 1992) (dictum as to adults).

WA: *In re* Hamlin, 689 P.2d 1372 (Wash. 1984).

WI: *Cf.* L.W. v. L.E. Phillips Career Dev. Ctr., 482 N.W.2d 60 (Wis. 1992) (elderly chronic schizophrenic patient who might once have been competent).

Council on Ethical & Judicial Affairs, American Medical Ass'n, Code of Medical Ethics § 2.20, at 37 (1994) ("[T]he surrogate's decision should not be challenged as long as the decision is based on the decisionmaker's true concern for what would be best for the patient.").

children, where it is more commonly accepted anyway.[260] In Indiana, the supreme court decided a case involving the termination of tube feeding to a patient in a persistent vegetative state by reference to the surrogate decisionmaking statute, holding that the patient's parents had authority under the statute to forgo life-sustaining treatment as long as the attending physician was in agreement, but not specifically applying any particular standard for decisionmaking, other than, perhaps, that the family and attending physician act in "good faith."[261]

If the choice is between using the substituted judgment standard for a never-competent patient and not permitting the forgoing of life-sustaining treatment, it is probably preferable to err on the side of life,[262] which was the approach chosen by the New York Court of Appeals in *Storar.*[263] However, there clearly is a middle ground, suggested by the New Jersey Supreme Court in *Conroy.*[264] If the premise is correct that never-competent patients are merely a species of incompetent patients about whom a surrogate decisionmaker has absolutely no information concerning treatment or nontreatment preferences, a pure-objective standard for surrogate decisionmaking should be applied.[265]

BEST INTERESTS STANDARD

§ 7.11 Origins of Best Interests Standard

In choosing a guardian, courts have almost invariably pointed to the best interests standard as the hallmark of qualification to serve. Under this standard, "[t]he cardinal consideration governing the court in its appointment of a guardian for the person and estate of a ward is how to serve most effectively the

---

[260] See **Ch. 15.**

[261] *See In re* Lawrance, 579 N.E.2d 32, 43 (Ind. 1991).

[262] **FL:** *See* Browning v. Herbert, 543 So. 2d 258, 273 (Fla. Dist. Ct. App. 1989).

[263] **NY:** *In re* Storar, 420 N.E.2d 64 (N.Y. 1981).

FL: *Cf.* Browning v. Herbert, 568 So. 2d 4, 13 (Fla. 1990) ("A critical problem regarding the exercise of an incompetent's choice is sometimes posed by the inability of the incompetent to express his or her immediate wishes. Unfortunately, human limitations preclude absolute knowledge of the wishes of someone in Mrs. Browning's condition. However, we cannot avoid making a decision in these circumstances, for even the failure to act constitutes a choice."); *In re* Barry, 445 So. 2d 365 (Fla. Dist. Ct. App. 1984) (substituted judgment standard applied in case of never-competent infant).

OH: *Cf. In re* Crum, 580 N.E.2d 876 (P. Ct. Franklin County, Ohio 1991) (applying both a substituted judgment standard and a best interests standard).

[264] **NJ:** *In re* Conroy, 486 A.2d 1209 (N.J. 1985).

CA: *See also* Drabick v. Drabick, 245 Cal. Rptr. 840, 849 (Ct. App. 1988) ("When the client is permanently unconscious, however, the attorney must be guided by his own understanding of the client's best interests. There is simply nothing else the attorney can do.") (dictum).

[265] See **§ 7.30.**

best interests and temporal, moral and mental welfare of a living person."[266] The traditional standard for choosing a guardian has thereby become the standard for measuring the acceptability of a guardian's conduct in managing the ward's affairs, based on the implicit assumption that, if the ward's best interests are the paramount consideration in appointing a guardian,[267] the person appointed pursuant to that criterion must act in the ward's best interests.[268]

The application of the best interests standard to medical decisionmaking for incompetent patients is so well accepted outside the end-of-life context that there is barely any judicial discussion of the subject. What discussion exists occurs mostly in the context of parental decisionmaking about medical care for their children, usually when parents have refused the administration of recommended treatment or sought the administration of an unconventional therapy.[269] Most of the older cases involving surrogate decisionmaking for adult incompetent patients involved situations in which the patient's life could probably have been saved if the treatment in question were administered,[270] and thus are not directly on point when an incompetent patient's prognosis, even with treatment, is poor at best.

§ 7.12 Applicability to Right-to-Die Cases

Despite the frequent use of the best interests standard in making medical decisions outside the end-of-life context, the standard has played a decidedly subordinate role in decisionmaking about life-sustaining treatment. One reason

---

[266] Rasmussen v. Fleming, 741 P.2d 674, 688 (Ariz. 1987). *See generally* President's Comm'n, Deciding to Forego Life-Sustaining Treatment 132; S. Brakel et al., The Mentally Disabled and the Law 386 (1985); 39 Am. Jur. 2d *Guardian and Ward* § 31 (1968); 44 C.J.S. *Insane Persons* § 37 (1945).

[267] *Cf.* Couture v. Couture, 549 N.E.2d 571 (Ohio Ct. App. 1989) (patient's father sought to replace patient's mother as guardian "because she expressed a willingness and intention to terminate life support system"). *See generally* 39 Am. Jur. 2d *Guardian and Ward* § 31 (1968); Hackler & Hiller, *Family Consent to Orders Not to Resuscitate: Reconsidering Hospital Policy,* 254 JAMA 1281, 1282 (1990) ("When there is no evidence of patient preference, the rationale for family surrogacy is different: promoting patients' best interests by choosing advocates who are most concerned with their welfare, or respecting the integrity of the family as a social unit."). See **§§ 5.15–5.16.**

[268] **MD:** *Contra* Mack v. Mack, 618 A.2d 744, 752 (Md. 1993) (holding that it is not appropriate to merge issues of who can best fulfill duties of guardian and what is in patient's substantive best interests).

OH: *In re* Myers, 610 N.E.2d 663, 669–70 (P. Ct. Summit County, Ohio 1993) ("The best interest test has been the historic and traditional guardianship standard . . . and the traditional *parens patriae* test in juvenile medical treatment cases in Ohio.").

[269] **DE:** Newmark v. Williams, 588 A.2d 1108, 1117 (Del. 1991) ("The 'best interests' analysis is hardly unique or novel. Federal and State courts have unhesitatingly authorized medical treatment over a parent's religious objection when the treatment is relatively innocuous in comparison to the dangers of withholding medical care."). See **Ch. 15.**

[270] *See* Annotation, *Power of Courts or Other Public Agencies, in the Absence of Statutory Authority, to Order Compulsory Medical Care for Adult,* 9 A.L.R.3d 1391 (1966).

is that because of the grounding of the right to die in self-determination, courts have been reluctant to employ a standard with such tenuous ties to self-determination. Even in its most attenuated form, the substituted judgment standard at least gives lip service to self-determination.[271] Another reason is that the traditional version of the best interests standard—that is, the mere injunction to act in the patient's best interests—is too vague to provide useful guidance either to surrogates or to courts.

Nonetheless, courts are gradually coming to make a place for the best interests standard in end-of-life decisionmaking, in large part based on the realization that self-determination cannot always be achieved because the patient's actual or probable wishes cannot be determined. Furthermore, led by the New Jersey Supreme Court, there is a gradual recognition of the important role of the parens patriae power in decisionmaking for incompetent patients, important both in theory and for practical reasons.[272] The second problem with the best interests standard—its vagueness—has begun to be remedied in large part by the influence of the President's Commission report on life-sustaining treatment,[273] which substantially enhanced the intellectual foundation of this standard and advocated its use when other standards for decisionmaking for incompetent patients cannot be met. Courts are beginning to put meat on the bones of this standard.

There is far more agreement about the meaning of the best interests standard in its general outlines than its specifics. In general terms, the best interests standard is analogous to a "reasonable person" standard.[274] In theory, both standards are purely objective. As applied, however, both standards sometimes incorporate subjective as well as objective elements.[275] Evidence that a patient

---

[271] Brophy v. New Eng. Sinai Hosp., Inc., 497 N.E.2d 626, 633 (Mass. 1986); President's Comm'n, Deciding to Forego Life-Sustaining Treatment 134–36.

[272] See § **7.28.**

[273] President's Comm'n, Deciding to Forego Life-Sustaining Treatment.

CA: *E.g.,* Barber v. Superior Court, 195 Cal. Rptr. 484, 491 (Ct. App. 1983) ("A more rational approach involves the determination of whether the proposed treatment is proportionate or disproportionate in terms of the benefits to be gained versus the burdens caused.").

NJ: *E.g., In re* Conroy, 486 A.2d 1209, 1235 (N.J. 1985) (citing President's Comm'n, Deciding to Forego Life-Sustaining Treatment 84–85 & n.122).

[274] **MD:** *Cf.* Mack v. Mack, 618 A.2d 744, 760–61 (Md. 1993) (rejecting use of best interests standard) ("[I]t is unlikely that the Legislature contemplated that the courts would authorize the withdrawal of artificially administered sustenance to a ward in a persistent vegetative state based on a best interest-reasonable person interpretation of the statute.").

NJ: *In re* Conroy, 486 A.2d at 1229 (by implication from statement that the subjective standard "is not what a reasonable or average person would have chosen to do under the circumstances but what the particular patient would have done if able to choose for himself").

[275] *See* W.P. Keeton et al., Prosser and Keeton on the Law of Torts § 32, at 175 (5th ed. 1985) ("Under the latitude of this phrase [the same or similar circumstances], the courts have made allowance not only for the external facts, but sometimes for certain characteristics of the actor himself, and have applied, in some respects, a more or less subjective standard. Depending on the context, therefore, the reasonable person standard may, in fact, combine in varying measure both objective and subjective ingredients.").

had wished to refuse treatment is not necessary for a decision under the best interests standard, but if such evidence is present, it is generally considered as a relevant (although not dispositive) factor.[276]

This lack of agreement on the specifics may result from the fact that far fewer courts have had occasion to actually apply it and thus have not had to concern themselves with its elaboration in the same way that they have with the substituted judgment standard. In part the inattention to the best interests standard might be explained by the reluctance of the courts to use it because it avowedly is not based on self-determination, and because of the fear that it has the potential for becoming so broad as to permit not merely termination of life support in the absence of actual or implied patient consent, but also termination in the absence of consent of some person close to the patient, and even to permit more active means of ending life.[277] Instead of employing the best interests standard, or instead of even adopting it, some courts have stretched the substituted judgment standard to include objective factors.[278]

Although some courts accept the best interests standard as a valid standard for making decisions about life-sustaining treatment, very few have actually applied it,[279] and a few have rejected it altogether, holding that, in the absence of

---

[276] **CA:** Drabick v. Drabick, 245 Cal. Rptr. 840, 857 (Ct. App. 1988):

> Stated precisely, the apparent role of the conservatee's prior statements under existing law is this: the conservatee's prior statements inform the decision of the conservator, who must vicariously exercise the conservatee's rights. Such statements do not in themselves amount to the exercise of a right. The statute gives the conservator the exclusive authority to exercise the conservatee's rights, and it is the conservator who must make the final treatment decision regardless of how much or how little information about the conservatee's preferences is available.

MN: *In re* Torres, 357 N.W.2d 332, 339 (Minn. 1984) ("At a minimum, any determination of a conservatee's 'best interests' must involve some consideration of the conservatee's wishes.").

WI: L.W. v. L.E. Phillips Career Dev. Ctr., 482 N.W.2d 60, 70 (Wis. 1992) (even if evidence of patient's wishes is present, decision must focus solely on what is in best interests of patient, not necessarily considering patient's past wishes, values, or beliefs).

[277] See §§ **7.22–7.24.**

[278] See §§ **7.8–7.9.**

[279] *See* Cruzan v. Director, 497 U.S. 261, 338–39 (1990) (Stevens, J., dissenting) ("[T]his Court's opinion . . . fails to respect the best interests of the patient. . . . It, too, relies on what is tantamount to a waiver rationale: the dying patient's best interests are put to one side and the entire inquiry is focused on her prior expressions of intent. [Footnote omitted.] An innocent person's constitutional right to be free from unwanted medical treatment is thereby categorically limited to those patients who had the foresight to make an unambiguous statement of their wishes while competent.").

AZ: *E.g.,* Rasmussen v. Fleming, 741 P.2d 674, 688–89 (Ariz. 1987) ("Unfortunately, the record in this case is barren of any evidence that Rasmussen expressed her medical desires in any form prior to becoming incompetent. Where no reliable evidence of a patient's intent exists, as here, the substituted judgment standard provides little, if any, guidance to the surrogate decisionmaker and should be abandoned in favor of the 'best interests' standard.").

CA: *E.g.,* Drabick v. Drabick, 245 Cal. Rptr. 840 (Ct. App. 1988); Barber v. Superior Court, 195 Cal. Rptr. 484 (Ct. App. 1983).

knowledge of an incompetent patient's preferences, life-sustaining treatment may not be forgone.[280] Other courts reject the best interests standard in name, but the manner in which they apply the substituted judgment standard is such as

---

CT: *E.g.,* Foody v. Manchester Memorial Hosp., 482 A.2d 713, 720–21 (Conn. Super. Ct. 1984) ("If the exercise of the right is to be maintained where no expression has been made by an incompetent patient as to treatment, it must take place within the context of an analysis which seeks to implement what is in that person's best interests by reference to objective societally shared criteria.").

DE: *E.g.,* Newmark v. Williams, 588 A.2d 1108 (Del. 1991) (three-year-old patient).

MI: *E.g.,* Martin v. Martin, 504 N.W.2d 917, 922 (Mich. Ct. App. 1993) ("Under the best interest standard, if there is no trustworthy evidence that a formerly competent patient would have declined treatment, then a surrogate decision-maker may still consent to the withholding or withdrawal of life-sustaining medical treatment if doing so would serve the patient's best interests."); Rosebush v. Oakland County Prosecutor, 491 N.W.2d 633, 637 (Mich. Ct. App. 1992) (if incompetent patient's preferences are unknown, "surrogate should make a decision based on the best interests of the patient").

MN: *E.g., In re* Torres, 357 N.W.2d 332, 337 (Minn. 1984) ("[I]f the conservatee's best interests are no longer served by the maintenance of life supports, the probate court may empower the conservator to order their removal despite the absence of a specific [statutory] provision . . . which authorizes the court to do so.").

MO: *E.g., In re* Warren, 858 S.W.2d 263, 265 (Mo. Ct. App. 1993) (guardian has statutory authority to make medical decisions, including withholding of treatment in best interests of ward).

NJ: *E.g., In re* Conroy, 486 A.2d 1209 (N.J. 1985).

NY: *E.g., In re* Beth Israel Medical Ctr. (Weinstein), 519 N.Y.S.2d 511 (Sup. Ct. N.Y. County 1987) (relying on Rivers v. Katz, 495 N.E.2d 337 (N.Y. 1986)), *overruled by implication, In re* Westchester County Medical Ctr. (O'Connor), 531 N.E.2d 607 (N.Y. 1988).

OH: *E.g., In re* Myers, 610 N.E.2d 663, 669 (P. Ct. Summit County, Ohio 1993) (minor patient) (applying best interests standard rather than substituted judgment standard because "substituted judgment is no longer valid" after *Cruzan* because of Court's failure to find the constitutional right of privacy to be basis for right to have treatment terminated, and because required to do so by Ohio Rev. Code § 2111.50(C) in the case of a ward).

PA: *E.g., In re* E.L.K., 11 Fiduc. Rep. 2d 78 (C.P. Berks County, Pa. 1991) (by implication) (in absence of clear evidence of what incompetent patient wanted, patient's daughter would be appointed guardian because she had her patient's best interests at heart).

WA: *E.g., In re* Grant, 747 P.2d 445, 457 (Wash. 1987), *modified,* 757 P.2d 534 (Wash. 1988) ("There will be many situations where it cannot be ascertained what choice the patient would make if competent. In such cases, the guardian must make a good-faith determination of whether the withholding of life-sustaining treatment would serve the incompetent patient's best interests."); *In re* Hamlin, 689 P.2d 1372, 1375, 1377, 1378 (Wash. 1984).

[280] **FL:** Browning v. Herbert, 543 So. 2d 258, 273 (Fla. Dist. Ct. App. 1989) (rejecting objective or best interest approach), *aff'd,* 568 So. 2d 4 (Fla. 1990) (but affirming validity of application of substituted judgment standard to a never-competent patient in *In re* Barry, 445 So. 2d 365 (Fla. Dist. Ct. App. 1984)).

IL: *Cf.* Estate of Longeway v. Community Convalescent Ctr., 549 N.E.2d 292, 299 (Ill. 1989) ("While not passing on the viability of the best-interests theory in Illinois, we decline to adopt it in this case because we believe the record demonstrates the relevancy of the substituted-judgment theory.").

to accept and utilize a best interests standard in practice.[281] It is likely that over time, many courts will come to accept the best interests standard, as societally acceptable objective standards are formulated for the forgoing of life-sustaining treatment.[282] Those courts that have already accepted the best interests standard have often done so out of the realization that few people engage in the kind of

---

KY: *Cf.* DeGrella v. Elston, 858 S.W.2d 698, 702 (Ky. 1993) (Court applied substituted judgment standard because there was adequate evidence to do so, but remarked that "as evidence regarding the patient's wishes weakens, the case moves from self-determination towards a quality-of-life test. At the point where the withdrawal of life-prolonging medical treatment becomes solely another person's decision about the patient's quality of life, the individual's 'inalienable right to life,' as so declared in the United States Declaration of Independence and protected by Section One (1) of our Kentucky Constitution, outweighs any consideration of the quality of the life, or the value of the life, at stake.").

MD: *Compare* Mack v. Mack, 618 A.2d 744, 759 (Md. 1993) (not appropriate to apply best interests standard to patient in persistent vegetative state "who is not in pain, and who is not terminally ill" because requires making quality-of-life judgment "under judicially adopted standards, without any legislative guidelines") *with id.* at 764 (McAuliffe, J., dissenting) ("[I]t is not only permissible, but indeed necessary, to attribute to the ward the inclination or desire of an ordinary, prudent person under the same circumstances, unless and until there is evidence that he or she would not have shared those views.").

MO: Cruzan v. Harmon, 760 S.W.2d 408 (Mo. 1988).

NY: *In re* Westchester County Medical Ctr. (O'Connor), 531 N.E.2d 607 (N.Y. 1988); *In re* Storar, 420 N.E.2d 64 (N.Y. 1981); Grace Plaza of Great Neck, Inc. v. Elbaum, 588 N.Y.S.2d 853 (App. Div. 1992).

281 **FL:** *E.g., In re* Barry, 445 So. 2d 365 (Fla. Dist. Ct. App. 1984) (application of substituted judgment standard to a never-competent patient).

MA: *E.g.,* Custody of a Minor, 434 N.E.2d 601 (Mass. 1982) (application of substituted judgment standard to a never-competent patient).

WA: *E.g., In re* Colyer, 660 P.2d 738, 748 (Wash. 1983) ("There is no evidence that Bertha Colyer explicitly expressed her desire to refuse life-sustaining treatment. Nevertheless, her husband and her sisters agreed that Bertha Colyer was a very independent woman, that she disliked going to doctors, and, if able to express her views, that she would have requested the treatment be withdrawn. Given the unanimity of the opinions expressed by Bertha's closest kin, together with the absence of any evidence of any ill motives, we are satisfied that Bertha's guardian was exercising his best judgment as to Bertha's personal choice when he requested the removal of the life support system.").

See §§ **7.8** and **7.10.**

282 **CT:** *See* Foody v. Manchester Memorial Hosp., 482 A.2d 713, 720–21 (Conn. Super. Ct. 1984) ("If the exercise of the right is to be maintained where no expression has been made by an incompetent patient as to treatment, it must take place within the context of an analysis which seeks to implement what is in that person's best interests by reference to objective societally shared criteria."). *See also* Emanuel & Emanuel, *Decisions at the End of Life: Guided by Communities of Patients,* 23 Hastings Center Rep. 6 (Sep.–Oct. 1993) (recommending that in absence of evidence that would meet subjective or substituted judgment standard, physicians should be guided by "the preferences of their own communities of patients").

advance directive planning that the subjective standard and some versions of the substituted judgment standard require.[283]

§ 7.13 —Treatment Not Always in Best Interests

Outside the realm of right-to-die cases, the application of traditional notions of the best interests standard has often led to the assumption that treatment is always in an incompetent patient's best interests. In right-to-die cases, however, the courts have generally concluded that medical treatment does not always advance a person's interests.[284] This is evidenced by the fact that competent

---

[283] L.W. v. L.E. Phillips Career Dev. Ctr., 482 N.W.2d 60, 67–68, n.8 (Wis. 1992):

> 2 President's Commission for the Study of Ethical Problems in Medicine and Biomedical and Behavioral Research, Making Health Care Decisions 241–242 (1982) (36% of those surveyed gave instructions regarding how they would like to be treated if they ever became too sick to make decisions; 23% put those instructions in writing) (Lou Harris Poll, September 1982); American Medical Association Surveys of Physician and Public Opinion on Health Care Issues 29–30 (1988) (56% of those surveyed had told family members their wishes concerning the use of life-sustaining treatment if they entered an irreversible coma; 15% had filled out a living will specifying those wishes). *Cruzan,* ____ U.S. at ____ n. 1, 110 S.Ct. at 2857 n. 1 (O'Connor, J., concurring). Congress has recognized this problem. Effective December 1, 1991, health care providers receiving federal benefits are required to provide to all adults receiving medical care written information regarding "an individual's rights under State law (whether statutory or as recognized by the courts of the State) to make decisions concerning such medical care, including the right to accept or refuse medical or surgical treatment and the right to formulate advance directives . . . " 42 U.S.C.A. § 1396a(w)(1) (West Supp.1991). In addition, Congress mandated a "Public Education Campaign" concerning advance directives, declaring in part that: The Secretary, no later than 6 months after the date of enactment of this section, shall develop and implement a national campaign to inform the public of the option to execute advance directives and of a patient's right to participate and direct health care decisions. Requirements for Advanced Directives Under State Plans for Medical Assistance, Pub. L. No. 101-508, § 4751.

[284] **CA:** Thor v. Superior Court, 855 P.2d 375 (Cal. 1993) (competent patients determine what is in their own best interests).

KY: DeGrella v. Elston, 858 S.W.2d 698, 705 (Ky. 1993) ("The position of the appellant is that 'a guardian is a fiduciary and it is unthinkable that a fiduciary could properly act so as to bring about the ward's death.' While we recognize that this argument has superficial appeal, the courts in seventeen of our sister states which have pondered the same issue presented here have not found it 'unthinkable.'").

MA: Superintendent of Belchertown State Sch. v. Saikewicz, 370 N.E.2d 417, 428 (Mass. 1977) ("[T]he . . . [parens patriae] power and responsibility has impelled a number of courts to hold that the 'best interests' of such a person mandate an unvarying responsibility by the courts to order necessary medical treatment for an incompetent person facing an immediate and severe danger to life. . . . Whatever the merits of such a policy where life-saving treatment is available . . . a more flexible view of the 'best interests' of the incompetent patient is not precluded under other conditions.").

patients sometimes refuse treatment, even life-sustaining treatment, and, when there are no countervailing state interests of a compelling nature,[285] that refusal is to be accorded the same respect that a patient's consent to treatment is accorded.[286] When competent patients are confronted by the choice of undergoing or forgoing a life-sustaining treatment, no inquiry is ordinarily made into whether that decision serves the patient's best interests. Rather, it is axiomatically assumed to do so; the patient's best interest is implicitly determined by reference to his or her own standards rather than to external standards.[287] A parallel approach for incompetent patients best respects their dignity: "To presume that the incompetent person must always be subjected to what many rational and intelligent persons may decline," remarked the Massachusetts Supreme Judicial Court, "is to downgrade the status of the incompetent person by placing a lesser value on his intrinsic human worth and vitality."[288]

Thus, most courts have construed the best interests standard as not requiring the administration of treatment simply because treatment is available and might prolong the patient's life. As the Arizona Supreme Court explained in *Rasmussen v. Fleming,*

MN: *In re* Torres, 357 N.W.2d 332, 338 (Minn. 1984) (argument has "appealing simplicity" but patient's best interests may not be served by medical treatment).

MO: *Contra* Cruzan v. Harmon, 760 S.W.2d 408 (Mo. 1988) (not in best interests of patient in persistent vegetative state to discontinue artificial nutrition and hydration because such procedure imposes no burdens on her).

OH: *In re* Myers, 610 N.E.2d 663 (P. Ct. Summit County, Ohio 1993) (minor patient).

WA: *In re* Hamlin, 689 P.2d 1372, 1375 (Wash. 1984) (nonintervention may be in ward's best interests).

WI: L.W. v. L.E. Phillips Career Dev. Ctr., 482 N.W.2d 60, 68 (Wis. 1992).

285 See §§ **8.14–8.19.**

286 **WA:** *In re* Ingram, 689 P.2d 1363, 1369 (Wash. 1984).

287 **CA:** Thor v. Superior Court, 855 P.2d 375, 383 (Cal. 1993) ("'[T]he value of life is desecrated not by a decision to refuse medical treatment but "by the failure to allow a competent human being the right of choice."'").

MA: Superintendent of Belchertown State Sch. v. Saikewicz, 370 N.E.2d 417, 428 (Mass. 1977).

WI: L.W. v. L.E. Phillips Career Dev. Ctr., 482 N.W.2d 60, 70 (Wis. 1992) ("If the [patient's] wishes are clear, it is invariable as a matter of law, both common and statutory, that it is in the best interests of the patient to have those wishes honored, for the patient has made the pre-choice of what he or she considers to be the best interests under the circumstances that arise.").

288 **MA:** Superintendent of Belchertown State Sch. v. Saikewicz, 370 N.E.2d at 428. *Accord In re* Spring, 405 N.E.2d 115 (Mass. 1980).

NY: *Accord* Eichner v. Dillon, 426 N.Y.S.2d 517, 548 (App. Div. 1980) (Decisions about life-sustaining treatment "must be based on the assumption that the patient would have wanted it that way. This approach seeks to fulfill what would be deemed to be the dying patient's own wishes, and reaffirms notions of self-determination."), *modified,* 420 N.E.2d 64 (N.Y.), *cert. denied,* 454 U.S. 858 (1981).

> the right [of a surrogate] to consent to or approve the delivery of medical care must necessarily include the right to consent to or approve the delivery of no medical care. To hold otherwise would . . . ignore the fact that oftentimes a patient's interests are best served when medical treatment is withheld or withdrawn. To hold otherwise would also reduce the guardian's control over medical treatment to little more than a mechanistic rubberstamp for the wishes of the medical treatment team. . . . [T]he Public Fiduciary as Rasmussen's guardian had the implied, if not express, statutory authority to exercise Rasmussen's right to refuse medical treatment.[289]

The California Court of Appeal put it somewhat more generally but also more succinctly: "a common sense point about statutory interpretation [is that] a statute that requires a person to make a decision contemplates a decision either way."[290]

Even if the administration of life-sustaining treatment is not always best in a particular case, one must "begin with a presumption that continued life is in the best interests of the ward. Whether that presumption may be overcome depends upon a good faith assessment by the guardian of several objective factors."[291] Those courts that accept the best interests standard limit its use to situations in which there is inadequate evidence to apply either the subjective standard or the

---

[289] 741 P.2d 674, 688 (Ariz. 1987).

[290] **CA:** Drabick v. Drabick, 245 Cal. Rptr. 840, 850 (Ct. App. 1988).

AZ: *Accord* Rasmussen v. Fleming, 741 P.2d at 688.

IL: *Accord In re* Estate of Greenspan, 558 N.E.2d 1194 (Ill. 1990); Estate of Longeway v. Community Convalescent Ctr., 549 N.E.2d 292, 298 (Ill. 1989).

IN: *Accord In re* Lawrance, 579 N.E.2d 32, 39 (Ind. 1991) (statutorily authorized family member's "right to consent to the patient's course of treatment necessarily includes the right to refuse a course of treatment").

KY: *Accord* DeGrella v. Elston, 858 S.W.2d 698, 704 (Ky. 1993) (absence in guardianship statutes of provision authorizing guardian of patient in persistent vegetative state to authorize termination of treatment does not preclude such authority because statutes were remedial rather than exclusive).

MN: *Accord In re* Torres, 357 N.W.2d 332, 339 (Minn. 1984) ("[S]imply equating the continued physical existence of [an incompetent patient], who has no chance for recovery, with the [patient's] 'best interests' is contrary to law and medical opinion.").

MO: *Accord In re* Warren, 858 S.W.2d 263, 265 (Mo. Ct. App. 1993). *But see* Cruzan v. Harmon, 760 S.W.2d 408, 424 (Mo. 1988) (statute that "places an express, affirmative duty on guardians to assure that the ward receives medical care and provides the guardian with the power to give consent for that purpose" does not provide basis for contending that "guardian possesses authority, as a guardian, to order the termination of medical treatment").

WA: *Accord In re* Colyer, 660 P.2d 738, 746 (Wash. 1983), *construing* Wash. Rev. Code § 11.92.040(3) (1979).

WI: *Accord* L.W. v. L.E. Phillips Career Dev. Ctr., 482 N.W.2d 60, 71 (Wis. 1992).

[291] **WI:** L.W. v. L.E. Phillips Career Dev. Ctr., 482 N.W.2d at 72.

MD: *But cf.* Mack v. Mack, 618 A.2d 744, 763 (Md. 1993) (McAuliffe, J., dissenting) (in absence of evidence to contrary, may infer that patient in persistent vegetative state would elect to terminate life-sustaining treatment).

substituted judgment standard.[292] Only when it is impossible to meet the substituted judgment standard should the best interests standard be applied.[293]

Not all courts adhere to the position that a surrogate has the authority under the aegis of a best interests standard to withhold or withdraw life-sustaining medical treatment. Some courts in effect conclude that continued administration of life-sustaining treatment is conclusively in the best interests of an incompetent patient unless that patient has clearly and unequivocally made a decision to forgo such treatment prior to losing decisionmaking capacity. One such court is the Missouri Supreme Court, which, although not applying the best interests standard by name, concluded in *Cruzan*[294] that it was not in the best interests of the patient in a persistent vegetative state to discontinue artificial nutrition and hydration because such treatment imposes no burdens on her. Consequently, the state's "vital" interest in "the immense, clear fact of life" outweighs whatever interest the patient might have—which the court considered to be hypothetical in light of her comatose state—in having treatment terminated.[295] The court rested heavily (though not entirely) on the state guardianship statute as support for this conclusion, a statute which require guardians to "provide for the ward's 'care, treatment, habilitation, education, support and maintenance,' "[296] and empowers them to

> (2) Assure that the ward receives medical care and other services that are needed;
> (3) Promote and protect the care, comfort, safety, health, and welfare of the ward;
> (4) Provide required consents on behalf of the ward; . . .[297]

---

[292] *See also* Hastings Center Guidelines 27–28 (Part One, II(4)(c)).

[293] **DRI:** Gray v. Romeo, 697 F. Supp. 580 (D.R.I. 1988).

AZ: Rasmussen v. Fleming, 741 P.2d 674, 689 (Ariz. 1987).

CA: Barber v. Superior Court, 195 Cal. Rptr. 484, 493 (Ct. App. 1983).

CT: Foody v. Manchester Memorial Hosp., 482 A.2d 713, 720–21 (Conn. Super. Ct. 1984).

KY: *Contra* DeGrella v. Elston, 858 S.W.2d 698, 702 (Ky. 1993) ("We do not approve permitting anyone to decide when another should die on any basis other than clear and convincing evidence that the patient would choose to do so.").

MI: Rosebush v. Oakland County Prosecutor, 491 N.W.2d 633, 637 (Mich. Ct. App. 1992) ("[I]n making decisions for minors or other incompetent patients, surrogate decision makers should make the best approximation of the patient's preference on the basis of available evidence; if such preference was never expressed or is otherwise unknown, the surrogate should make a decision based on the best interests of the patient.").

NJ: *In re* Conroy, 486 A.2d 1209, 1229–30 (N.J. 1985); *In re* Clark, 510 A.2d 136, 145 (N.J. Super. Ct. Ch. Div. 1986) (applying *Conroy*).

PA: *In re* E.L.K., 11 Fiduc. Rep. 2d 78 (C.P. Berks County, Pa. 1991).

WA: *In re* Grant, 747 P.2d 445, 457 (Wash. 1987), *modified,* 757 P.2d 534 (Wash. 1988).

[294] Cruzan v. Harmon, 760 S.W.2d 408 (Mo. 1988). *See also In re* Warren, 858 S.W.2d 263 (Mo. Ct. App. 1993) (applying best interests standard).

[295] Cruzan v. Harmon, 760 S.W.2d at 424.

[296] *Id.* at 425 (quoting Mo. Rev. Stat. § 475.120.3 (1986)).

[297] *Id.*

From these provisions, the court held that the guardianship statute "places an express, affirmative duty on guardians to assure that the ward receives medical care and provides the guardian with the power to give consent for that purpose" and does not provide a basis for contending that the "guardian possesses authority, as a guardian, to order the *termination* of medical treatment."[298] Similarly, the New York Court of Appeals in *Storar* held that because the patient's wishes were unknown and unknowable, it was in his best interests that treatment be continued even though he would soon die of the disease for which treatment was being provided.[299]

Other courts reach the same result: refusing to permit the use of the best interests standard when the substituted judgment or subjective standard cannot be met, for when they cannot, the result is that treatment must be continued. For them, as articulated by the Illinois Supreme Court,

> [t]he problem with the best-interests test is that it lets another make a determination of a patient's quality of life, thereby undermining the foundation of self-determination and inviolability of the person upon which the right to refuse medical treatment stands.[300]

Or, as the Maryland Court of Appeals explained,

> [a]bandoning the anchorage of the patient's right of self-determination sets courts adrift on a sea of conflicting values and of varying weights to be assigned to those values. Where the values themselves are in a state of flux in society, a legislative body is better equipped to determine, within constitutional limits, whether some lives are not worth living and, if so, how to determine which are the lives that are not worth living.[301]

This thinking is quite at odds with the more common approach in right-to-die cases of empowering guardians to refuse treatment, including life-sustaining treatment, because they are exercising the patient's legal right to do so.

At first it might seem paradoxical that the two courts (Missouri and New York) that have insisted on the most stringent substantive standard for forgoing life-sustaining treatment for incompetent patients have employed its polar opposite, the best interests standard. But that is not so. What these cases illustrate is a rigid adherence to the traditional conception of the best interests standard, namely, that the provision of treatment is always in the patient's best interests, and a complete unwillingness to consider the concept of quality of

---

[298] *Id.* at 424 (emphasis added).

[299] *In re* Storar, 420 N.E.2d 64, 73 (N.Y. 1981) ("[A] court should not in the circumstances of this case allow an incompetent patient to bleed to death because someone, even someone as close as a parent or sibling, feels that this is best for one with an incurable disease.").

[300] Estate of Longeway v. Community Convalescent Ctr., 549 N.E.2d 292, 299 (Ill. 1989).

[301] Mack v. Mack, 618 A.2d 744, 759–60 (Md. 1993).

life.[302] In effect, the best interests standard—or their particular conception of the standard—is the default standard: If clear and convincing evidence of the patient's subjective intent is lacking, treatment must be continued because it is in the patient's best interests to do so because mere existence, regardless of quality, is preferable to nonexistence.

§ 7.14 Benefit/Burden Approach to Best Interests

As previously mentioned, one of the objections to the use of the best interests standard in end-of-life decisionmaking is that it is vague and there is little agreement as to its content. In fact, there *is* a mainstream position on the meaning of the best interests standard; it simply is not as well accepted as the substituted judgment standard. It is the benefit/burden approach, and it has antecedents in the analysis that predicates the right to die on whether or not the treatment sought to be forgone is "ordinary" or "extraordinary,"[303] a distinction having its origins in Roman Catholic moral theology.[304] Any precision of meaning that the distinction between ordinary and extraordinary treatments had has since been lost, at least in the secular context. The distinction is now susceptible of a variety of meanings, many of which are unconvincing, ambiguous, or conclusory. Thus, courts using the benefit/burden approach focus on the underlying concepts meant to be captured in the terms *ordinary* and *extraordinary*—namely, the benefits likely to be conferred by the treatment in question, the burdens likely to flow from that treatment, and the proportionality between the two.[305]

§ 7.15 —The Basic Approach: *Barber*

The first serious explication of the best interests standard in a right-to-die case was the *Barber* decision.[306] Faced with the indictment of two doctors who had, with the consent of the patient's family, withdrawn first ventilatory and then

---

302 See §§ **7.22–7.24.**

303 See § **8.8.**

304 *See In re* Conroy, 486 A.2d 1209, 1235 (N.J. 1985) (citing Sacred Congregation for the Doctrine of the Faith, Declaration on Euthanasia (May 5, 1980), *reprinted in* President's Comm'n, Deciding to Forego Life-Sustaining Treatment 300–07); President's Comm'n, Deciding to Forego Life-Sustaining Treatment 82.

305 Barber v. Superior Court, 195 Cal. Rptr. 484, 491 (Ct. App. 1983) ("The use of these terms [*ordinary* and *extraordinary*] begs the question. A more rational approach involves the determination of whether the proposed treatment is proportionate or disproportionate in terms of the benefits to be gained versus the burdens caused.").

306 Barber v. Superior Court, 195 Cal. Rptr. 484 (Ct. App. 1983).

nutritional support from a patient in a persistent vegetative state, the court dismissed the indictment even though there was no evidence of the patient's actual or implied wishes. Based on the state's living will statute, the court found that prior patient consent was not a prerequisite to the forgoing of life-sustaining treatment,[307] and therefore "[i]f it is not possible to ascertain the choice the patient would have made, the surrogate ought to be guided in his decision by the patient's best interests."[308]

The court proceeded to determine whether, in a such a situation, there was a duty to provide treatment. It concluded that there was, but only if the treatment was "proportionate." As the court explained,

> [u]nder this approach, proportionate treatment is that which, in the view of the patient, has at least a reasonable chance of providing benefits to the patient, which benefits outweigh the burdens attendant to the treatment. Thus, even if a proposed course of treatment might be extremely painful or intrusive, it would still be proportionate treatment if the prognosis was for complete cure or significant improvement in the patient's condition. On the other hand, a treatment course which is only minimally painful or intrusive may nonetheless be considered disproportionate to the potential benefits if the prognosis is virtually hopeless for any significant improvement in condition.[309]

Thus, in a general way, treatment is in a patient's best interests if the benefits outweigh the burdens, from the patient's perspective. More specifically, the court specified that the factors to be taken into account are:

1. "the relief of suffering"
2. "the preservation or restoration of functioning"
3. quality of life
4. extent of the life sustained
5. "the impact of the decision on those people closest to the patient."[310]

The position of the American Medical Association is similar:

> In deciding whether the administration of potentially life-prolonging medical treatment is in the best interest of the patient who is incompetent, the surrogate decisionmaker and physician should consider several factors, including: the possibility of extending life under humane and comfortable conditions; the patient's values about life and the way it should be lived; and the patient's attitudes toward sickness, suffering, medical procedures, and death.[311]

---

[307] *Id.* at 490 (Living will statute "does not represent the exclusive basis for terminating life-support equipment in this state.").

[308] *Id.* at 493.

[309] *Id.* at 491. *See also In re* Conroy, 486 A.2d 1209, 1232 (N.J. 1985).

[310] Barber v. Superior Court, 195 Cal. Rptr. at 493 (citing President's Comm'n, Deciding to Forego Life-Sustaining Treatment 134–35).

[311] American Medical Ass'n, Current Opinions of the Council on Ethical and Judicial Affairs § 2.20, at 14 (1992).

Thus, as conceived of by most courts—namely, that a patient's best interests require that life-sustaining treatment be provided only if its benefits to the patient outweigh its burdens—the application of the best interests standard depends heavily on the meaning accorded to the terms *burden*[312] and *benefit.*[313] The closely related concept of *quality of life*[314] also plays an important role in the application of the standard.

§ 7.16 —The *Conroy* Elaboration

Much of the elaboration of the best interests standard has been performed by the New Jersey Supreme Court in *Conroy.*[315] A substantial portion of the opinion is devoted to discussion of the meaning of the best interests standard. It was the first opinion to do so in a comprehensive fashion, and to date remains the most thorough judicial discussion of the subject. The other courts that have discussed this issue are few in number and have largely echoed the *Conroy* opinion, which itself drew heavily on the President's Commission Report.[316] Nonetheless, this aspect of the opinion has not had a great deal of impact on the holdings of subsequent cases because so few actually turn on an application of the best interests standard.

Conroy recognizes two "best interests" standards, what it refers to as the "limited-objective test" and the "pure-objective test."[317] Because the limited-objective standard takes into account evidence of the patient's wishes—evidence, however, that is not sufficient to satisfy the subjective standard—in fact this standard is more closely akin (if not identical) to the substituted judgment standard and is not really a best interests standard as that term is generally used in cases involving either medical decisionmaking generally or the right to die in particular.

Conroy's pure-objective standard applies if neither the subjective standard nor the pure-objective standard can be satisfied; that is, if there is no trustworthy evidence of the patient's preferences.[318] The *Conroy* court did not state whether

---

312 See §§ **7.17–7.30.**

313 See § **7.21.**

314 See §§ **7.22–7.24.**

315 *In re* Conroy, 486 A.2d 1209 (N.J. 1985).

316 **AZ:** *E.g.,* Rasmussen v. Fleming, 741 P.2d 674, 689 (Ariz. 1987).

CT: *E.g.,* Foody v. Manchester Memorial Hosp., 482 A.2d 713, 721 (Conn. Super. Ct. 1984).

DE: *E.g.,* Newmark v. Williams, 588 A.2d 1108, 1117–19 (Del. 1991).

MI: *E.g.,* Martin v. Martin, 504 N.W.2d 917, 922–23 (Mich. Ct. App. 1993); Rosebush v. Oakland County Prosecutor, 491 N.W.2d 633, 640 (Mich. Ct. App. 1992).

MN: *E.g., In re* Torres, 357 N.W.2d 332, 338–39 (Minn. 1984).

WI: *E.g.,* L.W. v. L.E. Phillips Career Dev. Ctr., 482 N.W.2d 60, 72 (Wis. 1992).

317 See §§ **7.28–7.30.**

318 See § **7.30.**

the surrogate may only take into account matters that he believes the patient would have considered, or whether consideration may also be given to what other reasonable persons in the same condition as the patient would have considered. In this regard, the standard resembles the substituted judgment standard as articulated and applied in *Saikewicz.*[319] Although subjective evidence that the patient would not have wanted the treatment is not a necessary condition for the application of the pure-objective standard, when evidence exists that the patient would have wanted "to be kept alive in spite of any pain that he might experience,"[320] treatment may not be forgone.

In order to apply the pure-objective standard there must be evidence that it would be "inhumane" to administer treatment because of "the recurring, unavoidable and severe pain of the patient's life with the treatment."[321] Consequently, in New Jersey, the standard is inapplicable to patients in a persistent vegetative state who are incapable of experiencing pain.[322] If that condition is met, the surrogate must then weigh the burdens of the patient's continued life with the treatment against the benefits likely to be conferred by the treatment.[323] For treatment to be withheld or withdrawn, the burdens must "clearly and markedly outweigh" the benefits.[324] Thus, the application of the pure-objective standard depends heavily upon the meanings of *burden*[325] and *benefit.*[326] (The *Conroy* standards are discussed at greater length in §§ **7.27** through **7.37.**)

§ 7.17 —Burdens

There are a number of ways in which a treatment may be burdensome. Burdens may be imposed directly by the treatment itself. The method of administration may be painful, or the treatment may have unpleasant, painful, or even lethal side effects. Even if not painful, a treatment may be burdensome because it is uncomfortable or even anxiety-producing, as is sometimes the case with ventilators. Burdens may also result more indirectly from the continued life made possible by the treatment. Even if a treatment is not inherently painful,

---

[319] *See* Superintendent of Belchertown State Sch. v. Saikewicz, 370 N.E.2d 417, 429 (Mass. 1977) ("Evidence that most people would or would not act in a certain way is certainly an important consideration in attempting to ascertain the predilections of any individual, but care must be taken, as in any analogy, to ensure that operative factors are similar or at least to take notice of the dissimilarities."). See §§ **7.7–7.10.**

[320] *In re* Conroy, 486 A.2d 1209, 1232 (N.J. 1985).

[321] *Id.*

[322] *See In re* Peter, 529 A.2d 419 (N.J. 1987); *In re* Jobes, 529 A.2d 434 (N.J. 1987).

[323] *In re* Conroy, 486 A.2d at 1232.

[324] *Id. See also In re* Clark, 510 A.2d 136, 146 (N.J. Super. Ct. Ch. Div. 1986) (finding that benefits outweigh burdens of performance of an enterostomy).

[325] See §§ **7.17–7.20.**

[326] See § **7.21.**

uncomfortable, or anxiety-producing, the fact that it keeps a person alive to continue to suffer the preexisting burdens of the illness for which it is being administered, and/or to suffer the burdens imposed by other treatments, may make it burdensome.

The weighing process involved in applying the benefit/burden approach is highly subjective. Even those things susceptible of quantification (however inaccurate such a process may be), such as life expectancy, will be valued to differing degrees by different people. Furthermore, this approach involves the comparison of inherently noncomparable factors.

Whether a treatment is burdensome must be evaluated on a case-by-case basis.[327] Although "it can be difficult or impossible to measure the burdens" of treatment,[328] it is simpler to classify them. The primary types of burdens as elaborated by the courts are (1) pain, (2) indignity, and (3) diminished quality of life.

The New Jersey Supreme Court has refused to apply the *Conroy* standards to patients in a persistent vegetative state[329] because they are incapable of perceiving anything, be it beneficial or burdensome.[330] Critics of the best interests standard in general and the benefit/burden approach in particular contend that courts are actually attempting to end the suffering of family members rather than of unconscious patients.[331] One view holds that patients would not choose to die unless they were suffering, and thus treatment cannot be forgone for patients in persistent vegetative states on the basis that continued existence imposes disproportionate burdens on them. The better view is that individuals in a persistent vegetative state have no interests and therefore it is not necessary to continue to provide medical treatment.[332]

§ 7.18 ——Pain

The *Conroy* majority adopted a narrow definition of *burden,* seemingly equating the concept with physical pain, both the pain the patient is likely to suffer with

---

[327] **WA:** *In re* Grant, 747 P.2d 445, 454 (Wash. 1987), *modified,* 757 P.2d 534 (Wash. 1988).

[328] *In re* Peter, 529 A.2d 419, 425 (N.J. 1987).

[329] *See In re* Jobes, 529 A.2d 434 (N.J. 1987); *In re* Peter, 529 A.2d 419. See §§ **7.34–7.35.**

[330] *In re* Conroy, 486 A.2d 1209, 1233 (N.J. 1985); *In re* Quinlan, 355 A.2d 647, 655 (N.J. 1976) ("The quality of her feeling impulses is unknown.").

[331] **FL:** John F. Kennedy Memorial Hosp. v. Bludworth, 432 So. 2d 611, 618 (Fla. Dist. Ct. App. 1983), *rev'd,* 452 So. 2d 921 (Fla. 1984). *See also* Gelfand, *Euthanasia and the Terminally Ill Patient,* 63 Neb. L. Rev. 741, 773 (1984); Sherlock, *For Everything There Is a Season: The Right to Die in the United States,* B.Y.U. L. Rev. 545, 578 (1982).

[332] *See* A. Buchanan & D. Brock, Deciding for Others: The Ethics of Surrogate Decisionmaking 128 (1989); Dresser, *Life, Death, and Incompetent Patients: Conceptual Infirmities and Hidden Values in the Law,* 28 Ariz. L. Rev. 378 (1986); Rhoden, *Litigating Life and Death,* 102 Harv. L. Rev. 357, 400 (1988); Robertson, Cruzan *and the Constitutional Status of Nontreatment Decisions for Incompetent Patients,* 25 Ga. L. Rev. 1139, 1157 (1991); Stacy, *Death, Privacy, and the Free Exercise of Religion,* 77 Cornell L. Rev. 490 (1992).

and without treatment and the possibility of its amelioration through therapy.[333] *Conroy* has been criticized for placing too much weight on pain as a criterion for decisionmaking. Equating burden with pain requires that treatment be administered even when it accomplishes little or nothing more than prolonging the process of dying, precisely what the *Conroy* court otherwise seemed to have been intent on preventing. Some patients experience no actual pain because they are not suffering from a *painful* terminal illness,[334] are in a persistent vegetative state,[335] or are receiving strong analgesic medications.

Even if a patient is able to experience pain, the judicious use of analgesic medications can usually control the pain to the extent that it is a negligible consideration.[336] In addition, the evaluation of the extent to which a patient perceives pain may be difficult even if the patient is not comatose.[337] Thus, pain should not be the sole, or even the central, criterion in determining the burdens that treatment imposes.[338] To regard it as such, as Justice Handler observed in a separate opinion in *Conroy,* "transmutes the best interests determination into an exercise of avoidance and nullification rather than confrontation and fulfillment. In most cases the pain criterion will dictate that the decision

---

[333] **NJ:** *In re* Conroy, 486 A.2d 1209, 1232 (N.J. 1985). *Contra In re* Visbeck, 510 A.2d 125, 131 (N.J. Super. Ct. Ch. Div. 1986) (criticizing *Conroy*).

WA: *Cf. In re* Grant, 747 P.2d 445, 450–51 (Wash. 1987), *modified,* 757 P.2d 534 (Wash. 1988).

[334] **NJ:** *In re* Visbeck, 510 A.2d at 131. *See also* Deciding to Forego Life-Sustaining Treatment 278 (only a "minority" of patients undergo painful treatments).

[335] **MA:** *In re* Doe, 583 N.E.2d 1263, 1277 (Mass. 1992) (O'Connor, J., dissenting) (The patient in a persistent vegetative state "is not burdened by life. She need not 'go' to be in peace. For all that appears, with food and drink and care she can 'stay' in peace. Any benefit derived from terminating Jane Doe's life is derived by someone else.").

MN: *In re* Torres, 357 N.W.2d 332, 340 (Minn. 1984).

WI: L.W. v. L.E. Phillips Career Dev. Ctr., 482 N.W.2d 60, 72 (Wis. 1992) ("Pain and suffering are absent, as are joy, satisfaction, and pleasure. Disability is total and no return to an even minimal level of social or human functioning is possible. [President's Comm'n,] Deciding to Forego Life-Sustaining Treatment, 181–182. Patients in a persistent vegetative state are on a completely different footing than patients with other disabilities.").

But see McQuillen, *Can People Who Are Unconscious or in the "Vegetative State" Perceive Pain?,* 6 Issues L. & Med. 373 (1991) (because it is not possible to find out from patients in persistent vegetative state whether they perceive pain, it must be assumed that they do). See **§ 9.53.**

[336] President's Comm'n, Deciding to Forego Life-Sustaining Treatment app. B.

[337] **NJ:** *In re* Conroy, 486 A.2d 1209, 1247 (N.J. 1985) (Handler, J., concurring and dissenting) ("[H]ealth care providers frequently encounter difficulty in evaluating the degree of pain experienced by a patient.").

[338] **NJ:** *In re* Conroy, 486 A.2d at 1247 (Handler, J., concurring and dissenting); *In re* Visbeck, 510 A.2d 125, 131 (N.J. Super. Ct. Ch. Div. 1986) ("[M]odern drug therapy often makes it possible to block the pain fully, or at least to the point where it is bearable.").

WA: *In re* Grant, 747 P.2d 445, 453 (Wash. 1987), *modified,* 757 P.2d 534 (Wash. 1988).

President's Comm'n, Deciding to Forego Life-Sustaining Treatment app. B.

be one not to withdraw life-prolonging treatment and not to allow death to occur naturally."[339]

Subsequently, a New Jersey trial court also took issue with the *Conroy* formulation (though entirely in dictum) because "[m]any of our most debilitating illnesses do not involve pain at all":[340]

> Although one always has to speak cautiously in these basic matters, I would suggest that suffering pain, even severe pain, is perhaps not the worst thing that can befall a human being. I would suggest that for most of us it would be far worse to suffer a very great loss of mental capacity, to become non-functioning, to be totally dependent upon others, to have no privacy in the most basic physical sense. These are quality of life considerations. They relate to the burdens that a patient bears and feels—or, at least, would feel if she were capable of feeling. It seems to me that it is essential to take those quality of life considerations into account in making health care decisions. An approach which eliminates them and considers only pain simply fails, in my judgment, to address the full range of human realities confronting a patient.[341]

The New Jersey Supreme Court may have been influenced by these critiques, and may have begun to retreat from the strict equation of burdens with pain when it declined to apply the *Conroy* standards in the 1987 *Jobes* and *Peter* cases. However, rather than broadening or abandoning them, it merely declined to apply a best interests standard to a patient in a persistent vegetative state incapable of experiencing anything "that the *Conroy* balancing tests are intended or able to appraise."[342]

At least one other court, in a decision that was reversed, has implicitly rejected the applicability of the benefit/burden approach to comatose patients on the assumption that for such

> individual[s] there is no pain and suffering (philosophical considerations aside), [and thus] it would seem to follow that the direct beneficiary of the request [to terminate treatment] is the family of the patient and that the benefits are financial savings and cessation of the emotional drain occasioned by awaiting the medico-legal death of a loved one.[343]

Indeed, it is not clear that the concept of burdens and benefits to the patient has any meaning in the case of a patient who is permanently incapable of

---

339 *In re* Conroy, 486 A.2d at 1247 (Handler, J., concurring and dissenting).

340 *In re* Visbeck, 510 A.2d at 131.

341 *Id.*

342 **NJ:** *In re* Peter, 529 A.2d 419, 425 (N.J. 1987).

WI: *Contra* L.W. v. L.E. Phillips Career Dev. Ctr., 482 N.W.2d 60 (Wis. 1992) (applying best interests standard to patient in persistent vegetative state).

See §§ **7.26–7.37.**

343 **FL:** John F. Kennedy Memorial Hosp. v. Bludworth, 432 So. 2d 611, 618 (Fla. Dist. Ct. App. 1983), *rev'd,* 452 So. 2d 921 (Fla. 1984).

perceiving anything.[344] What this means is not that permanently unconscious patients do not have a right to die but that the nature and scope of that right is difficult, if not impossible, to establish by using the benefit/burden approach. The argument that, because such patients cannot perceive pain, life support systems cannot be withdrawn, in the words of the Minnesota Supreme Court, "neglects the possibility that [the patient] might not want his life prolonged without a hope for recovery."[345] In such cases, therefore, other approaches may have to be used alone or in combination with the benefit/burden approach unless, as Justice Handler argued, courts are more willing to consider dignitary factors other than pain as constituting burdens for permanently unconscious patients.[346]

§ 7.19 ——Indignity

There are other undesirable aspects of receiving life-sustaining medical treatment besides pain that a *competent* patient might wish to take into account in decisionmaking about life-sustaining treatment. A surrogate arguably should be able to take these other aspects of treatment into account also. Thus, although pain is a matter to be considered, its absence should not preclude the forgoing of life-sustaining treatment.

The most fundamental other factor is the indignity to the patient of being kept alive in what the New Jersey Supreme Court referred to as "embarrassment, frustration, helplessness, rage, and other emotional pain."[347] The surrogate should be empowered to take these into account, especially under the

---

[344] **DE:** *In re* Severns, 425 A.2d 156, 157 (Del. Ch. 1980) (patient in coma suffering from severe brain damage "does not suffer discomfort and does not feel pain").

MN: *In re* Torres, 357 N.W.2d 332, 338 (Minn. 1984).

[345] *In re* Torres, 357 N.W.2d at 340.

[346] *In re* Conroy, 486 A.2d 1209 (N.J. 1985) (Handler, J., concurring and dissenting). See **§§ 7.33–7.35.**

[347] **NJ:** *In re* Peter, 529 A.2d 419, 425 (N.J. 1987); *In re* Conroy, 486 A.2d 1209, 1248 (N.J. 1985) (Handler, J., concurring and dissenting) (independence, privacy, dignity, and bodily integrity).

CA: *Accord* Bouvia v. Superior Court (Glenchur), 225 Cal. Rptr. 297, 305 (Ct. App. 1986) (ignominy, embarrassment, humiliation, and dehumanizing aspects created by helplessness).

MN: *Accord In re* Torres, 357 N.W.2d 332, 340 (Minn. 1984) ("'ultimate horror [not of] death but the possibility of being maintained in limbo, in a sterile room, by machines controlled by strangers'") (quoting Steel, *The Right to Die: New Options in California,* 93 Christian Century (July–Dec. 1976)).

NV: *Accord* McKay v. Bergstedt, 801 P.2d 617, 622–23 (Nev. 1990) ("Death . . . may end the indignities associated with life bereft of self-determination and cognitive activity. . . . In short, death is a natural aspect of life that is not without value and dignity.").

WA: *Accord In re* Grant, 747 P.2d 445, 450–51 (Wash. 1987), *modified,* 757 P.2d 534 (Wash. 1988) (indignity).

limited-objective standard, if the patient was known to resent such indignities.[348] Rather than focusing almost exclusively on pain, the focus in surrogate decision-making should include dignitary interests of the patient, because

> some people abhor dependence on others as much, or more, than they fear pain. Other individuals value personal privacy and dignity, and prize independence from others when their personal needs and bodily functions are involved. Finally, the ideal of bodily integrity may become more important than simply prolonging life at its most rudimentary level.[349]

Thus other factors that need to be considered are humiliation, dependence, and the loss of dignity associated with the therapy in question.[350]

The problem is, however, that patients in a persistent vegetative state not only do not experience pain, they also do not experience any of these other negative aspects of life-sustaining medical treatment because loss of the capacity to experience is part and parcel of persistent vegetative state. For this reason, the New Jersey Supreme Court,[351] though not all other courts,[352] has refused to apply the best interests standard to patients in a persistent vegetative state.

A way around this problem was suggested in the dissenting opinions of Justices Brennan and Stevens in *Cruzan.* Even patients who are unable to perceive pain or any other negative aspects of treatment may still have a dignitary interest in having treatment terminated. Justice Brennan pointed out that

> [s]uch conditions are, for many, humiliating to contemplate, as is visiting a prolonged and anguished vigil on one's parents, spouse, and children. A long, drawn-out death can have a debilitating effect on family members. See Carnwath & Johnson, Psychiatric Morbidity Among Spouses of Patients With Stroke, 294 Brit. Med. J. 409 (1987); Livingston, Families Who Care, 291 Brit. Med. J. 919

---

[348] **NY:** In re Westchester County Medical Ctr. (O'Connor), 531 N.E.2d 607 (N.Y. 1988) (Hancock, J., concurring); *id.* (Simons, J., dissenting); *id.* (Simmons, J., dissenting).

WA: *In re* Grant, 747 P.2d at 448 (patient's "mother believes [patient] would not want such treatment, based partly on the fact that Barbara has shown a dislike for taking medication, being made to use a cane, and having suction tubes used on her, and also because Barbara has shown a dislike for the medical staff").

[349] *In re* Conroy, 486 A.2d 1209, 1248 (N.J. 1985) (Handler, J., concurring and dissenting) (citing *In re* Torres, 357 N.W.2d at 340).

[350] **NJ:** *In re* Conroy, 486 A.2d at 1231.

OH: *In re* Myers, 610 N.E.2d 663, 670 (P. Ct. Summit County, Ohio 1993) ("To require someone to remain in [a persistent vegetative] state for perhaps decades . . . is inhumane.").

WI: L.W. v. L.E. Phillips Career Dev. Ctr., 482 N.W.2d 60, 74 (Wis. 1992).

See generally Cantor, *The Permanently Unconscious Patient, Non-Feeding and Euthanasia,* 15 Am. J.L. & Med. 381 (1989).

[351] *In re* Peter, 529 A.2d 419 (N.J. 1987); *In re* Jobes, 529 A.2d 434 (N.J. 1987).

[352] **WI:** L.W. v. L.E. Phillips Career Dev. Ctr., 482 N.W.2d 60 (Wis. 1992).

> (1985). For some, the idea of being remembered in their persistent vegetative states rather than as they were before their illness or accident may be very disturbing. . . . An erroneous decision not to terminate life-support, however, robs a patient of the very qualities protected by the right to avoid unwanted medical treatment. His own degraded existence is perpetuated; his family's suffering is protracted; the memory he leaves behind becomes more and more distorted.[353]

Justice Stevens penned similar thoughts: "Insofar as Nancy Cruzan has an interest in being remembered for how she lived rather than how she died, the damage done to those memories by the prolongation of her death is irreversible."[354]

§ 7.20 ——Other Burdensome Factors

According to the President's Commission, factors to be considered when deciding about life-sustaining treatment are "the relief of suffering, the preservation or restoration of functioning, and the quality as well as the extent of life sustained."[355] "Relief of suffering" should pose little problem as a criterion for forgoing treatment because it is closely related to the concept of benefits.[356] A treatment that does not relieve suffering can be said to be burdensome if it introduces physical or emotional pain or discomfort. The same is true of a treatment that does not achieve the "preservation or restoration of functioning."[357] Other burdens that need to be considered are such things as the treatment's invasiveness[358] or intrusiveness.[359] Furthermore, a surrogate should take

---

[353] **US:** Cruzan v. Director, 497 U.S. 261, 311–12, 320 (1990) (Brennan, J., dissenting). *See also id.* at 344 (Stevens, J., dissenting).

MA: *Accord In re* Beth, 587 N.E.2d 1377, 1382 (Mass. 1992) (patients in persistent vegetative state are "entitled to the same respect, dignity and freedom of choice as competent people").

[354] **US:** Cruzan v. Director, 497 U.S. at 353 (Brennan, J., dissenting); *see also id.* at 344 (Stevens, J., dissenting).

MA: *Accord In re* Beth, 587 N.E.2d 1377, 1382 (Mass. 1992) (patients in persistent vegetative state are "entitled to the same respect, dignity and freedom of choice as competent people").

[355] President's Comm'n, Deciding to Forego Life-Sustaining Treatment 135, *cited in In re* Visbeck, 510 A.2d 125, 132 (N.J. Super. Ct. Ch. Div. 1986).

[356] See **§ 7.21.**

[357] **CA:** Barber v. Superior Court, 195 Cal. Rptr. 484, 493 (Ct. App. 1983).

NJ: *Accord In re* Conroy, 486 A.2d 1209, 1248 (N.J. 1985) (Handler, J., concurring and dissenting).

[358] **NJ:** *In re* Conroy, 486 A.2d at 1237.

WA: *In re* Grant, 747 P.2d 445, 451 (Wash. 1987), *modified,* 757 P.2d 534 (Wash. 1988).

[359] **CA:** Barber v. Superior Court, 195 Cal. Rptr. at 491.

into account that information which a competent patient would be provided under the informed consent doctrine if he were making the decision for himself, namely the risks and side effects of the treatment and of other treatment options, if any.[360]

§ 7.21 —Benefits

In determining whether a treatment is in an incompetent patient's best interests, consideration needs to be given to the benefits, if any, that the proposed course of therapy is likely to confer. This is reflected in the patient's prognosis for recovery if the treatment is administered.[361]

Some of the factors that are relevant in determining the burdens of treatment are also relevant in determining the benefits, for benefits and burdens are conceptually opposite sides of the same coin. Thus, a treatment should be considered beneficial if it relieves suffering or preserves or restores functioning,[362] just as it should be considered burdensome when it does not. The benefits of treatment also include enhancement or preservation of such things as a patient's ability to experience "physical pleasure, emotional enjoyment, [and] intellectual satisfaction."[363]

Most courts do not consider the continuation of life per se—mere biological existence—to be a benefit; otherwise treatment would always have to be administered if it imposed no burdens but would at least keep the patient alive, such as a mechanical ventilator or nutrition and hydration.[364] A treatment may not be particularly burdensome to a patient, yet it may still be unlikely to confer any substantial benefit. In such a situation, it should be permissible for a surrogate to forgo it.

---

[360] **NJ:** *In re* Conroy, 486 A.2d at 1231.

WI: L.W. v. L.E. Phillips Career Dev. Ctr., 482 N.W.2d 60, 72 (Wis. 1992).

[361] See §§ **8.9–8.13.**

[362] **WI:** L.W. v. L.E. Phillips Career Dev. Ctr., 482 N.W.2d 60, 72 (Wis. 1992) (citing President's Comm'n, Deciding to Forego Life-Sustaining Treatment).

[363] *In re* Conroy, 486 A.2d 1209, 1232 (N.J. 1985).

[364] **US:** Cruzan v. Director, 497 U.S. 261, 344–45 (1990) (Stevens, J., dissenting) ("Missouri insists, without regard to Nancy Cruzan's own interests, upon equating her life with the biological persistence of her bodily functions. Nancy Cruzan, it must be remembered, is not now simply incompetent.").

CA: Barber v. Superior Court, 195 Cal. Rptr. 484, 492 (Ct. App. 1983) ("'[S]o long as a mere biological existence is not considered the only value, patients may want to take the nature of that additional life into account as well.' (President's Comm'n, ch. 2, at p. 88.)").

NJ: *In re* Quinlan, 355 A.2d 647, 662 (N.J. 1976) (patient in persistent vegetative state is "probably irreversibly doomed to no more than a biologically vegetative remnant of life").

§ 7.22 —Quality of Life

A treatment may be burdensome if it keeps a patient alive but seriously and adversely affects the patient's quality of life.[365] The term *quality of life* is highly controversial, in part because of its different meanings, one of which is sometimes associated with involuntary euthanasia.[366] If, however, the different meanings of the term are properly distinguished, quality of life can and should be an important factor for the surrogate to take into account in applying the best interests standard.[367]

---

[365] **NV:** McKay v. Bergstedt, 801 P.2d 617 (Nev. 1990).

NJ: *In re* Conroy, 486 A.2d 1209 (N.J. 1985) (Handler, J., concurring and dissenting); *In re* Visbeck, 510 A.2d 125, 131 (N.J. Super. Ct. Ch. Div. 1986).

See § **16.25** (quality of life and decisionmaking for handicapped infants).

[366] **MA:** Brophy v. New Eng. Sinai Hosp., Inc., 497 N.E.2d 626, 640 (Mass. 1986) (Nolan, J., dissenting) ("I can think of nothing more degrading to the human person than the balance which the court struck today in favor of death and against life. It is but another triumph for the forces of secular humanism (modern paganism) which have now succeeded in imposing their anti-life principles at both ends of life's spectrum. Pro dolor.").

NY: *In re* Storar, 420 N.E.2d 64, 75 n.2 (N.Y. 1981) (Jones, J., dissenting in part) ("Because 'euthanasia' can have two meanings, to avoid any possible misunderstanding I explicitly disclaim any intention, expressly or by implication, to invite consideration of 'active' euthanasia—the deliberate use of a life shortening agent for the termination of life.").

WA: *In re* Grant, 747 P.2d 445, 458 (Wash. 1987), *modified,* 757 P.2d 534 (Wash. 1988) (Andersen, J., concurring in part and dissenting in part) ("[T]his is pure, unadorned euthanasia. It is a step upon a slippery slope.").

[367] **CA:** Barber v. Superior Court, 195 Cal. Rptr. 484, 491 (Ct. App. 1983) (mentioning quality of life as one factor to be taken into account in application of the benefit/burden approach).

CT: Foody v. Manchester Memorial Hosp., 482 A.2d 713, 720 (Conn. Super. Ct. 1984).

DE: Newmark v. Williams, 588 A.2d 1108, 1112 (Del. 1991) (Statutory "spiritual treatment exemptions reflect, in part, '[t]he policy of this State with respect to the quality of life' a desperately ill child might have in the caring and loving atmosphere of his or her family, versus the sterile hospital environment demanded by physicians seeking to prescribe excruciating, and life threatening, treatments of doubtful efficacy.").

MD: Mack v. Mack, 618 A.2d 744, 759 (Md. 1993) (for patient in persistent vegetative state, court will not make quality-of-life judgments without legislative guidance).

MA: Brophy v. New Eng. Sinai Hosp., Inc., 497 N.E.2d 626, 635 (Mass. 1986); Superintendent of Belchertown State Sch. v. Saikewicz, 370 N.E.2d 417, 432 (Mass. 1977).

MO: *But see* Cruzan v. Harmon, 760 S.W.2d 408, 422 (Mo. 1988) (cases beginning with *Quinlan* have "abandon[ed] 'the common law's prejudice in favor of life' and 'subtly recast[ed] the state's interest in life as an interest in the quality of life (cognitive and sapient).'") (citing Alexander, *Death by Directive,* 28 Santa Clara L. Rev. 67, 82 (1988)).

NJ: *In re* Visbeck, 510 A.2d at 131 (failure to consider quality of life fails to address "full range of human realities" confronting a patient).

See also Council on Ethical & Judicial Affairs, American Medical Ass'n, Code of Medical Ethics § 2.17, at 33, and § 2.215, at 51 (1994); President's Comm'n, Deciding to Forego Life-Sustaining Treatment 135 ("quality as well as the extent of life sustained" is another factor to be taken into account in determining the burdens that a treatment imposes); Robertson, Cruzan *and the Constitutional Status of Nontreatment Decisions for Incompetent Patients,* 25 Ga. L. Rev. 1139 (1991).

Quality of life is used in two different ways, and not all courts using it are careful to distinguish between them. One use of the term is to signify the quality of one's life to oneself; specifically, whether one wishes to live in a state of extremely poor health, perhaps made even more burdensome by the continued administration of therapy. This use will be referred to as the quality-to-self sense of the phrase. The other way in which the term can be understood is to signify the value of one's life to others or to society at large, that is, in a social utility sense.

Most courts that have specifically addressed the matter have agreed that quality of life in the quality-to-self sense is a legitimate factor to consider in deciding the permissibility of forgoing life-sustaining treatment.[368] Other courts, however, have rejected using quality-of-life considerations of any sort because the state's interest in the mere existence of life is such a strong interest that "a State may properly decline to make judgments about the 'quality' of life that a particular individual may enjoy, and simply assert an unqualified interest in the preservation of human life," though one that still must "be weighed against the constitutionally protected interests of the individual."[369] Courts fear that quality-of-life considerations, even in the quality-to-self sense, might be little more than a semantic camouflage for the opinion that the patient's life has little value to others. It is, in the view of these courts, dangerous to use quality-of-life considerations for patients in a persistent vegetative state, with respect to whom these concerns are usually voiced, but the danger extends beyond these patients. These courts fear that the use of quality-of-life considerations for persistent vegetative state patients will inexorably lead down the proverbial slippery slope to those who are not permanently unconscious but who are profoundly demented or retarded.[370]

---

[368] **MA:** Norwood Hosp. v. Munoz, 564 N.E.2d 1017, 1023 (Mass. 1991) ("quality and integrity of this patient's life after a blood transfusion would be diminished in her view").

NV: McKay v. Bergstedt, 801 P.2d 617 (Nev. 1990) (in determining whether competent, but non-terminally ill man has right to forgo life-sustaining treatment, court must consider patient's quality of life as he perceives it).

NY: *Cf.* Fosmire v. Nicoleau, 551 N.E.2d 77, 82–83 (N.Y. 1990) (Advance directives are enforceable "not because the State consider[s declarants'] lives worthless, but because the State value[s] the right of the individual to decide what type of treatment he or she should receive under particular circumstances.").

PA: Ragona v. Preate, 11 Fiduc. Rep. 2d 1, 10 (C.P. Lackawanna County, Pa. 1990) ("the state's duty must encompass a recognition of an individual's right to make decisions regarding the quality of life").

WA: *In re* Ingram, 689 P.2d 1363, 1366 (Wash. 1984) ("Without question, a laryngectomy would be [a physician's] preference because Ingram would have her best chance of survival and some quality of life afterwards.").

[369] Cruzan v. Director, 497 U.S. 261, 282 (1990).

[370] *See, e.g.,* Mack v. Mack, 618 A.2d 744, 760 (Md. 1993):

> "As a logical progression from that precedent [of patients in a persistent vegetative state], cases eventually would be presented submitting that the best interest of the most severely retarded and feebleminded, who require extended care, who have practically no cognition, and who are too disabled to feed themselves, would be to have sustenance

Similarly, courts are virtually united in the view that it is impermissible to consider quality of life in the social utility sense, though there are occasional dicta to the contrary.[371] The concern with the use of quality of life in the social utility sense as an ingredient in decisionmaking about life-sustaining treatment is that it is a step toward voluntary active euthanasia or involuntary euthanasia, either passive or active.[372]

This reasoning, which has been followed by most courts—the only ones to abandon it are those that have *strengthened* the right to refuse treatment by enforcing it even when a competent patient is *not* terminally ill—was criticized by the Missouri Supreme Court in *Cruzan v. Harmon* as abandoning "the common law's prejudice in favor of life" and "subtly recast[ing] the state's interest in life as an interest in the quality of life (cognitive and sapient)."[373] However, as Justice Brennan observed in *Cruzan v. Director,* "[t]he fact that Missouri actively provides for its citizens to choose a natural death under certain circumstances suggests that the State's interest in life is not so unqualified as the court below suggests."[374]

In the case of competent patients, courts are more willing to take the patient's quality of life into account more explicitly.[375] A competent patient may take into

---

withheld." citing Alexander, *Medical Science Under Dictatorship,* 241 New Eng. J. Med. 39, 44 (1949) (describing medical experimentation of Nazi physicians: "Whatever proportions these crimes finally assumed, it became evident to all who investigated them that they had started from small beginnings. The beginnings at first were merely a subtle shift in emphasis in the basic attitude of the physicians. It started with the acceptance of the attitude, basic in the euthanasia movement, that there is such a thing as life not worthy to be lived. This attitude in its early stages concerned itself merely with the severely and chronically sick. Gradually the sphere of those to be included in this category was enlarged to encompass the socially unproductive, the ideologically unwanted, the racially unwanted and finally all non-Germans. *But it is important to realize that the infinitely small wedged-in lever from which this entire trend of mind received its impetus was the attitude toward the nonrehabilitable sick.*"

(Emphasis added.)

[371] See **§ 7.24.**

[372] **MD:** Mack v. Mack, 618 A.2d at 761 (Absent legislative guidelines for doing so, if quality of life were to be taken into account in making decisions about termination of life support from patient in persistent vegetative state, "[a]s a logical progression from that precedent, cases eventually would be presented submitting that the best interest of the most severely retarded and feebleminded, who require extended care, who have practically no cognition, and who are too disabled to feed themselves, would be to have sustenance withheld.").

MO: Cruzan v. Harmon, 760 S.W.2d 408, 420 (Mo. 1988) ("Were quality of life at issue, persons with all manner of handicaps might find the state seeking to terminate their lives.").

See **Ch. 18.**

[373] 760 S.W.2d at 422 (citing Alexander, *Death by Directive,* 28 Santa Clara L. Rev. 67, 92 (1988)).

[374] 497 U.S. 261, 314 n.15 (1990) (Brennan, J., dissenting).

[375] **CA:** *E.g.,* Bouvia v. Superior Court (Glenchur), 225 Cal. Rptr. 297, 305 (Ct. App. 1986) ("[P]etitioner faces 15 to 20 years of a painful existence, endurable only by the constant administrations of morphine.").

account his own quality of life in both senses of the term because "a competent, emotionally stable, but terminally ill adult whose death is imminent . . . is . . . the best, indeed, the only, true judge of how such life as remains to him may best be spent."[376] There is some evidence that quality-to-self is not the only consideration that competent patients—at least, elderly ones with life-threatening illnesses—take into account, nor necessarily even the most important one. They may be more concerned about matters such as life expectancy and cost of care,[377] which are closer to social-utility than quality-to-self considerations.

The Nevada Supreme Court in *McKay v. Bergstedt* erected some strictures to the use of quality-of-life considerations by competent patients. In that case, it was faced with the petition of a 31-year-old, competent quadriplegic man who

---

FL: *E.g.,* Satz v. Perlmutter, 362 So. 2d 160, 162 (Fla. Dist. Ct. App. 1978) ("[T]he patient's situation [is] wretched.").

GA: *E.g.,* State v. McAfee, 385 S.E.2d 651 (Ga. 1989).

NV: McKay v. Bergstedt, 801 P.2d 617 (Nev. 1990).

[376] **DDC:** Tune v. Walter Reed Army Medical Hosp., 602 F. Supp. 1452, 1458–59 (D.D.C. 1985).

CA: *Accord* Thor v. Superior Court, 855 P.2d 375, 383 (Cal. 1993) ("'[T]he value of life is desecrated not by a decision to refuse medical treatment but "by the failure to allow a competent human being the right of choice."'"); Bouvia v. Superior Court (Glenchur), 225 Cal. Rptr. at 304.

ME: *Compare In re* Gardner, 534 A.2d 947, 955 (Me. 1987) (permitting forgoing of life-sustaining treatment for incompetent patient does not rest on a quality-of-life determination by anyone other than patient when patient, through advance directive, "has himself done the balancing of his own values") *with id.* at 958 (majority decision "premised on the unarticulated notion that [patient's] life is not worth maintaining") (Clifford, J., dissenting).

MA: *Accord* Norwood Hosp. v. Munoz, 564 N.E.2d 1017, 1023 (Mass. 1991) ("[F]or this patient, [a fully competent adult,] death without receiving a blood transfusion is preferable to life after receiving the transfusion. The quality and integrity of this patient's life after a blood transfusion would be diminished in her view.").

NJ: *Accord In re* Peter, 529 A.2d 419, 423 (N.J. 1987); *In re* Conroy, 486 A.2d 1209, 1226 (N.J. 1985) ("competent person's common-law and constitutional rights do not depend on the quality or value of his life").

NY: *Accord* Eichner v. Dillon, 426 N.Y.S.2d 517, 539 (App. Div. 1980).

PA: *Accord* Ragona v. Preate, 11 Fiduc. Rep. 2d 1, 10 (C.P. Lackawanna County, Pa. 1990).

See also Hastings Center Guidelines 134 (Part Six, IV); President's Comm'n, Deciding to Forego Life-Sustaining Treatment 88 ("[S]o long as mere biological existence is not considered the *only value, patients may want to take the nature of that additional life into account as well.*").

[377] *See* Uhlman & Pearlman, *Perceived Quality of Life and Preferences for Life-Sustaining Treatment in Older Adults,* 151 Archives Internal Med. 495, 497 (1991); Danis et al., *Patients and Families' Preferences for Medical Intensive Care,* 260 JAMA 797 (1988) (preferences of patients who survived intensive care poorly correlated with functional status, quality of life, and costs). *But see* Cohen et al., *The Decision to Execute a Durable Power of Attorney for Health Care and Preferences Regarding the Utilization of Life-Sustaining Treatments in Nursing Home Residents,* 151 Archives Internal Med. 289, 293 (1991) ("level of future cognitive function and permanency of treatment procedure were the important determinants" of nursing-home residents' preferences about treatment).

had been in this condition since age 10, to have his ventilator turned off and to be allowed to die. He had made this decision because his parents had cared for him and his mother had died and his father was terminally ill. Although holding that disconnecting the ventilator would not be suicide, the court was still concerned that the result would be the same. Further, the court was concerned that Mr. Bergstedt be clearly aware of the medical and social-service options that existed to help him to live without parental assistance. Therefore, when a competent patient is not terminally ill, the court requires judicial review of the patient's request to have life-sustaining treatment terminated, making the patient's quality of life central to the decision because "[t]he State's interest in the preservation of life relates to meaningful life [and] the State has no overriding interest in interfering with the natural processes of dying among citizens whose lives are irreparably devastated by injury or illness to the point where life may be sustained only by contrivance or radical intervention."[378]

§ 7.23 ——Quality-to-Self

Some courts have hesitated to use quality of life as a criterion in decisionmaking about life-sustaining treatment, but have used it nonetheless, sometimes refusing to admit that they have done so. For example, in *Saikewicz,* the trial court had decided that a severely mentally retarded 67-year-old resident of a state institution should not undergo chemotherapy for a fatal form of leukemia. It cited as one of six factors weighing against administering chemotherapy " 'the quality of life possible for him even if the treatment does bring about remission.' "[379] On appeal, the Massachusetts Supreme Judicial Court observed that

> [t]o the extent that this formulation equates the value of life with any measure of the quality of life, we firmly reject it. . . . Rather than reading the judge's formulation in a manner that demeans the value of the life of one who is mentally retarded, the vague, and perhaps ill-chosen, term "quality of life" should be understood as a reference to the continuing state of pain and disorientation precipitated by the chemotherapy treatment.[380]

The court took pains to point out that a decision to forgo treatment of his life-threatening cancer could not be made on the basis of the fact that he was mentally retarded per se. However, in applying a substituted judgment standard to determine the legitimacy of a surrogate's decision to decline this treatment, the court did take into account whether the patient himself, if for a moment he could be made competent, would decline treatment in part on the basis of his own (now suspended) mental retardation that precluded him from understanding why painful medical procedures were being imposed on him.

---

[378] McKay v. Bergstedt, 801 P.2d 617, 626 (Nev. 1990).

[379] Superintendent of Belchertown State Sch. v. Saikewicz, 370 N.E.2d 417, 432 (Mass. 1977).

[380] *Id.*

Despite the court's avowed denial of the propriety of using the social-utility sense of quality of life—or perhaps because of the court's circumlocutions in reaching this conclusion—the *Saikewicz* decision has been subjected to severe criticism.[381] Perhaps as a result of this experience, in *Conroy* the New Jersey court used more care both in describing the two senses of quality of life and in discussing their roles in decisionmaking. Despite the careful distinction, the court nevertheless concluded that even if a treatment adversely affects the patient's quality of life in the quality-to-self sense it does not necessarily follow that it should be withheld, because to do so "would create an intolerable risk for socially isolated and defenseless people suffering from mental and physical handicaps."[382]

Other courts have been less reticent, either directly or implicitly, about using quality of life as a criterion. One of the most thoughtful judicial discussions is the opinion of a New Jersey trial court in *In re Visbeck:*

> The fact that there is a real risk of making bad decisions if we allow quality of life factors to be considered should not lead us to exclude those factors. For most people, those factors are probably the most important factors involved. To exclude even the consideration of them is to misstate the whole problem and to fail to come to grips with the true human reality of what is involved in these cases. If we require treatment decisions to be made without any reference to quality of life factors, we will be creating other kinds of risks of bad decision making. Worse than that, we will be guaranteeing that bad decisions will be made and that large numbers of people will be thoughtlessly and automatically compelled to continue lives of intolerable bleakness.[383]

In addition to the courts that have expressly addressed the meaning of quality of life in the quality-to-self sense and the propriety of using it in decisionmaking for incompetent patients, a number of others have, in a more casual manner, employed the concept by name.[384] Still other courts, under different rubrics,

---

[381] See **§ 7.10.**

[382] **NJ:** *In re* Conroy, 486 A.2d 1209, 1233 (N.J. 1985).

FL: *Accord* Browning v. Herbert, 543 So. 2d 258 (Fla. Dist. Ct. App. 1989) ("While there clearly are cases in which a patient may elect to forego life-sustaining medical care in a 'quality of life' situation, . . . [i]n such cases, the state's interest in life increases sharply. In such cases, the act intuitively seems closer to suicide.").

WA: *Accord In re* Grant, 747 P.2d 445, 458 (Wash. 1987), *modified,* 757 P.2d 534 (Wash. 1988) (Anderson, J., dissenting) (describing quality of life as a "slippery slope").

[383] 510 A.2d 125, 133 (N.J. Super. Ct. Ch. Div. 1986).

[384] **AZ:** *E.g.,* Rasmussen v. Fleming, 741 P.2d 674, 689 n.23 (Ariz. 1987).

CA: *E.g.,* Barber v. Superior Court, 195 Cal. Rptr. 484, 493 (Ct. App. 1983).

CT: *E.g.,* Foody v. Manchester Memorial Hosp., 482 A.2d 713, 720 (Conn. Super. Ct. 1984).

DE: *E.g.,* Newmark v. Williams, 588 A.2d 1108, 1112 (Del. 1991) (statutory "spiritual treatment exemptions reflect, in part, '[t]he policy of this State with respect to the quality of life' a desperately ill child might have in the caring and loving atmosphere of his or her family, versus the sterile hospital environment demanded by physicians seeking to prescribe excruciating, and life threatening, treatments of doubtful efficacy").

have taken into account quality of life in the quality-to-self sense. For example, in *Dinnerstein,* the Massachusetts Appeals Court permitted a do-not-resuscitate order to be written in the patient's medical record because her life would not be any closer to normal after the administration of the treatment at issue (cardiopulmonary resuscitation) than before. Although the court did not use the phrase "quality of life," the concept was implicit in its statement that " '[p]rolongation of life,' . . . contemplates, at the very least, a remission of symptoms enabling a return towards a normal, functioning, integrated existence."[385] Similarly, it was critical to the holding in *Quinlan* that "[a]s nearly as may be determined, [Quinlan] can never be restored to a cognitive or sapient life."[386] Although not using quality-of-life terminology, the court was clearly considering the quality of Karen Ann Quinlan's life on a ventilator.

These examples illustrate the close connection between quality of life and prognosis.[387] Similarly, the cases in which courts view the treatment at issue as merely prolonging the process of dying (that is, "life-sustaining" or some synonymous phrase), rather than saving a life,[388] implicitly take into consideration the patient's quality of life. Because their prognosis is dim even with that treatment, patients for whom a treatment is only life-sustaining can expect a poor quality of life. The distinction between saving life and sustaining life, or prolonging life and prolonging dying, might merely constitute a distinction between different

---

MA: *But see In re* Spring, 405 N.E.2d 115, 123 (Mass. 1980).

NY: *E.g., In re* Storar, 420 N.E.2d 64, 78 (N.Y. 1981) (Jones, J., dissenting); Eichner v. Dillon, 426 N.Y.S.2d 517, 539 (App. Div. 1980) (competent patient); *In re* Beth Israel Medical Ctr. (Weinstein), 519 N.Y.S.2d 511, 517 (Sup. Ct. N.Y. County 1987) ("Life has no meaning for her."), *overruled by implication, In re* Westchester County Medical Ctr. (O'Connor), 531 N.E.2d 607 (N.Y. 1988).

WA: *E.g., In re* Ingram, 689 P.2d 1363, 1366 (Wash. 1984) ("Without question, a laryngectomy would be [a physician's] preference because Ingram would have her best chance of survival and some quality of life afterwards.").

See also Hastings Center Guidelines 134 (Part Six, IV).

385 *In re* Dinnerstein, 380 N.E.2d 134, 138 (Mass. App. Ct. 1978).

386 *In re* Quinlan, 355 A.2d 647, 655 (N.J. 1976).

387 **DE:** *E.g.,* Newmark v. Williams, 588 A.2d 1108 (Del. 1991).

FL: *E.g.,* John F. Kennedy Memorial Hosp. v. Bludworth, 452 So. 2d 921, 926 (Fla. 1984); Satz v. Perlmutter, 362 So. 2d 160, 162 (Fla. Dist. Ct. App. 1978) (if treatment continued, patient's situation will be "wretched"), *aff'd,* 379 So. 2d 359 (Fla. 1980).

NV: *E.g.,* McKay v. Bergstedt, 801 P.2d 617, 624 (Nev. 1990).

NJ: *E.g., In re* Conroy, 486 A.2d 1209, 1232 (N.J. 1985) ("level of functioning"); *In re* Quinlan, 355 A.2d 647, 669 (N.J. 1976) ("[F]ocal point of decision should be the prognosis as to the reasonable possibility of return to cognitive and sapient life, as distinguished from the forced continuance of that biological vegetative existence to which Karen seems to be doomed.").

OH: *E.g.,* Leach v. Akron Gen. Medical Ctr., 426 N.E.2d 809, 814 (P. Ct. Summit County, Ohio 1980) ("minimal life of an incurably ill, seventy-year-old, semi-comatose woman").

388 See § **8.13.**

qualities of life. It is therefore questionable, at least when used in the quality-to-self sense, whether quality of life is not merely a proxy for prognosis.

The strongest and most thorough critique of *Conroy*'s rejection of the use of quality of life in the quality-to-self sense is that provided in Justice Handler's separate opinion in *Conroy*. His argument is grounded in the strong predilection expressed in the majority opinion that decisionmaking for incompetent patients attempt to replicate, as nearly as possible, the decision that the incompetent patient would have made had she been competent. This view is reflected in the hierarchical nature of the standards for surrogate decisionmaking.[389] Indeed, under the majority's view, if the patient had left explicit and unequivocal directions to limit or forgo treatment "when my quality of life is poor"—assuming that adequate content were given that term by the patient—the surrogate would be required to take it into account.

Justice Handler went further, contending that even if the limited-objective standard[390] were applied, quality of life could be taken into account. In applying such a standard, he would rely on the same kind of medical investigation approved by the majority in applying the subjective standard. This medical investigation

> might include evidence about the patient's present level of physical, sensory, emotional, and cognitive functioning, the degree of physical pain resulting from the medical condition, treatment, and termination of treatment, respectively; the degree of humiliation, dependence, and loss of dignity probably resulting from the condition and treatment; the life expectancy and prognosis for recovery with and without treatment; the various treatment options; and the risks, side effects, and benefits of each of those options.[391]

Justice Handler also pointed out that the majority approved using "the same type of evidence" in applying the limited-objective standard, and "thus implicitly concede[d] that a test that does not rely principally on the presence of pain can entail a meticulous medical investigation and verification."[392] Following what he believed to be the clear implication of the majority's reasoning, he concluded "that the standard should consist of an array of factors to be medically established and then evaluated by the decision-maker both singly and collectively to reach a balance that will justify the determination whether to withdraw or to continue life-prolonging treatment."[393] In addition, Justice Handler went beyond the implications of the majority opinion, suggesting that quality-of-life considerations might be relevant in the application of the pure-objective standard as well as the limited-objective standard.[394]

---

[389] See § **7.3.**

[390] See § **7.29.**

[391] *In re* Conroy, 486 A.2d 1209, 1249 (N.J. 1985) (Handler, J., concurring and dissenting).

[392] *Id.*

[393] *Id.*

[394] *Id.* ("[W]ithdrawal of life-prolonging treatment from an unconscious or comatose, terminally ill individual near death, whose personal views concerning life-ending treatment cannot be ascertained, should be governed by such a standard.").

Justice Handler elaborated on the majority's tripartite standard for decision-making for incompetent patients that would permit quality of life (in the quality-to-self sense) to be taken into account. The threshold criteria for the use of a quality-of-life standard are that the patient

> be terminally ill and facing imminent death. There should also be present the permanent loss of conscious thought processes in the form of a comatose state or profound unconsciousness. Further there should be the irreparable failure of at least one major and essential bodily organ or system[395]

such as the respiratory system,[396] the heart,[397] the circulatory system,[398] the cerebral cortex and brainstem,[399] the cerebral cortex alone,[400] or the swallowing reflex (as in the *Conroy* case itself). Once the threshold criteria are met, factors to be taken into account by the surrogate are "the [patient's] general physical condition . . . [and] the presence of progressive, irreversible, extensive, and extreme physical deterioration, such as ulcers, lesions, gangrene, infection, incontinence, and the like which frequently afflict the bed-ridden, terminally ill."[401] This list is merely illustrative; the precise factors to be considered by the surrogate depend upon the patient's particular illness.[402]

Whether or not the majority failed in subsequent cases to adhere to the implications of its opinion, as Justice Handler later claimed, and whether or not his approach is preferable to the majority's, difficulties still remain. Under the applicable pure-objective standard, a treatment yielding even a small benefit must be administered as long as it is not painful to the patient and its administration is not "inhumane."[403] The failure of both opinions to explore the meaning of this critical term is unfortunate. Furthermore, if Justice Handler really meant that his quality-of-life factors may be taken into account when patients have provided no evidence about their wishes, his approach becomes virtually indistinguishable from that of the *Saikewicz* court (though without the fiction of transforming patients' interests into their wishes) and opens it up to the same criticisms leveled against that approach.[404]

---

[395] *Id.*

[396] *Id.* (citing Barber v. Superior Court, 195 Cal. Rptr. 484 (Ct. App. 1983); *In re* Quinlan, 355 A.2d 647 (N.J. 1976)).

[397] *In re* Conroy, 486 A.2d 1209, 1249 (N.J. 1985) (citing *In re* Dinnerstein, 380 N.E.2d 134 (Mass. App. Ct. 1978)).

[398] *Id.* (citing Superintendent of Belchertown State Sch. v. Saikewicz, 370 N.E.2d 417 (Mass. 1977)).

[399] *Id.* (citing *In re* Torres, 357 N.W.2d 332 (Minn. 1984)).

[400] *Id.* (citing *In re* Hamlin, 689 P.2d 1372 (Wash. 1984)).

[401] *Id.*

[402] *Id.* n.4.

[403] See § **7.30.**

[404] See §§ **7.8–7.9.**

The most direct rejection of quality-of-life considerations in decisionmaking about life-sustaining treatment is *Cruzan v. Harmon.*[405] The Missouri Supreme Court took a clear-cut "vitalist" position, holding that in decisionmaking for incompetent patients, at least when a subjective standard could not be met, "[t]he state's interest is not in quality of life. . . . Instead, the state's interest is in life; that interest is unqualified."[406]

§ 7.24 ——Social Utility

One of the most significant questions concerning the use of the best interests standard is from whose vantage point benefits and burdens are to be considered; specifically, whether it is legitimate to consider the burdens that the continuation of treatment imposes on third parties. Conceptually similar, but of less practical importance, are the benefits, if any, conferred on third parties by the continuation of treatment. This problem is merely another way of asking whether it is permissible to consider the quality of a patient's life to others in surrogate decisionmaking.

The emerging black-letter law is that the quality of a patient's life to others or to society in general may not be taken into account in determining whether life-sustaining treatment may be forgone. For instance, *Conroy* emphatically asserted that the weighing process is to occur from the perspective of the incompetent patient. Neither variation of *Conroy*'s best interests standard authorizes the surrogate to consider "assessments of the personal worth or social utility [of the patient's] life or the value of that life to others."[407] A treatment is not to

---

[405] 760 S.W.2d 408 (Mo. 1988).

[406] *Id.* at 420.

[407] **NJ:** *In re* Conroy, 486 A.2d 1209, 1232–33 (N.J. 1985). *Accord In re* Visbeck, 510 A.2d 125, 132 (N.J. Super. Ct. Ch. Div. 1986).

AZ: *Accord* Rasmussen v. Fleming, 741 P.2d 674, 689 n.23 (Ariz. 1987).

FL: *Accord* Browning v. Herbert, 568 So. 2d 4, 13 (Fla. 1990) ("We emphasize and caution that when the patient has left instructions regarding life-sustaining treatment, the surrogate must make the medical choice that the patient, if competent, would have made, and not one that the surrogate might make for himself or herself, or that the surrogate might think is in the patient's best interests.").

MD: *Accord* Mack v. Mack, 618 A.2d 744, 761 (Md. 1993) (suggesting that such matters could be taken into account by legislature).

MA: *Cf.* Superintendent of Belchertown State Sch. v. Saikewicz, 370 N.E.2d 417, 432 (Mass. 1977) ("[V]ague, and perhaps ill-chosen, term 'quality of life' should be understood as a reference to the continuing state of pain and disorientation precipitated by the chemotherapy treatment;" "To the extent that [the quality of life] equates [with] the value of life . . . , we firmly reject it."). *Compare In re* Doe, 583 N.E.2d 1263, 1269 n.15 (Mass. 1992) ("The judge quite properly did not consider whether Doe's continued care would pose a burden of any kind on anyone. The cost of care in human or financial terms is irrelevant to the substituted judgment analysis.") *with id.* at 1277 (O'Connor, J., dissenting) (A patient in a persistent vegetative state "is not burdened by life. . . . Any benefit derived from terminating Jane Doe's life is derived by someone else.").

be considered burdensome because it imposes suffering, financial cost, or other adverse consequences on other people.[408] Likewise, a treatment is not to be considered beneficial if its only value is to continue a patient's life, but without meaningful existence to the patient himself.[409]

Nonetheless, some judicial opinions intimate that quality of life in the social-utility sense is of legitimate concern to surrogates in making decisions for incompetent patients.[410] The general argument is that, because competent patients may take into account the benefits and burdens to others of forgoing or administering life-sustaining treatment for themselves, surrogates should be able to do so for incompetent patients.[411] The difficulty with this analogy is that the surrogate's role of discerning what the patient would have wanted had he been able to express his desires may force the surrogate to engage in fictions at best.[412] Thus, it may only be a semantic distinction to say that although the surrogate may not take into account the interests of others per se, they may be taken into account to the extent that the patient would have had he been competent and making the decision himself.

MO: *Accord In re* Warren, 858 S.W.2d 263, 267 (Mo. Ct. App. 1993) (Smart, P.J., concurring) ("[T]he authority of court-appointed guardians to consent to DNR orders without court approval is far from unlimited. There must be a sufficient medical basis which is not based on the handicap of the patient, the social utility of the patient's life, or the value of that life to others.").

NY: *Accord In re* Beth Israel Medical Ctr. (Weinstein), 519 N.Y.S.2d 511, 514 (Sup. Ct. N.Y. County 1987) (not "appropriate for a court to determine that someone's life is not worth living simply because in its subjective opinion the patient's quality of life or value to society is negligible") (citing *In re* Storar, 420 N.E.2d 64 (N.Y. 1981)).

WI: *Accord* L.W. v. L.E. Phillips Career Dev. Ctr., 482 N.W.2d 60, 72 (Wis. 1992) ("The guardian should not engage in a subjective 'quality of life' determination on behalf of the ward [citation to *Conroy* omitted].").

See also Hastings Center Guidelines 134 (Part Six, IV).

408 **MD:** Mack v. Mack, 618 A.2d 744, 760 (Md. 1993) ("'[I]n considering the best interests of an incompetent minor, the welfare of society or the convenience or peace of mind of the ward's parents or guardian plays no part.'").

409 **MD:** Mack v. Mack, 618 A.2d 744, 760 (Md. 1993) ("From . . . individual standpoint [of patient in persistent vegetative state], his needs are met [by being maintained by a feeding tube], and he may live for decades.").

MO: *But see* Cruzan v. Director, 497 U.S. 261, 262 (1990) ("[A] State may properly decline to make judgments about the 'quality' of life that a particular individual may enjoy, and simply assert an unqualified interest in the preservation of human life.").

See § **7.13.**

410 **WA:** *See In re* Grant, 747 P.2d 445, 463 (Wash. 1987), *modified,* 757 P.2d 534 (Wash. 1988) (Goodloe, J., dissenting) ("The increasing trend of courts to decide that life of 'lesser' quality is not worth living is quite disturbing.").

411 **DC:** *See In re* A.C., 573 A.2d 1235, 1251 n.20 (D.C. 1990) ("[W]e think it proper for the court to conclude that the patient might consider the needs of her family in making a treatment decision. *See In re Roe, supra,* 383 Mass. at 432, 421 N.E.2d at 58.").

412 **WA:** *In re* Grant, 747 P.2d at 463 (Goodloe, J., dissenting).

Permitting consideration of the interests of others may mask self-interested motives of family members (and health care personnel and third party payors) to relieve their own burdens,[413] whether financial,[414] emotional,[415] or both. Under the rubric of benefits and burdens, one court even considered the interests of other patients in the same or other hospitals and other persons for whom decisions to forgo life-sustaining treatment might have to be made at some later time.[416]

It is ironic, in light of the New Jersey Supreme Court's aversion in *Conroy* to permitting the use of quality of life even in the quality-to-self sense, that perhaps the most direct support for considering the burdens to others that the administering of treatment poses is the observation in its later *Jobes* decision that "a surrogate decisionmaker might consider the patient's likely attitude toward the

---

[413] *See, e.g.,* Leach v. Akron Gen. Medical Ctr., 426 N.E.2d 809, 810 (P. Ct. Summit County, Ohio 1980) ("Mrs. Leach's condition is a continuing anxiety to her family. . . . Mr. Leach, observing his wife's condition, contacted Dr. Shapiro and requested that the use of the respirator be terminated.").

[414] **FL:** John F. Kennedy Memorial Hosp. v. Bludworth, 432 So. 2d 611, 618 (Fla. Dist. Ct. App. 1983) (financial savings are a benefit of forgoing life-sustaining treatment of permanently comatose patient).

MD: Mack v. Mack, 618 A.2d 744, 760 (Md. 1993) ("The best interest . . . standard . . . enlarges the concept of best interest beyond the needs of the ward to include consideration of the emotional and financial impact on, and desires of [the] family and of the burden on the limited resources of society.").

MA: *Cf. In re* Spring, 399 N.E.2d 493, 499 n.8 (Mass. App. Ct. 1979) ("We intimate no opinion on the weight to be given the factor of cost to the family where that is a relevant consideration."). This is one reason why judicial review of a surrogate's decision might be needed. *Contra In re* Hier, 464 N.E.2d 959 (Mass. App. Ct. 1984).

NJ: *In re* Conroy, 486 A.2d 1209, 1218 (N.J. 1985) ("[T]here was no question that the nephew had good intentions and had no real conflict of interest due to possible inheritance when he sought permission to remove the tube.").

OH: Leach v. Akron Gen. Medical Ctr., 426 N.E.2d at 810 ("In addition, it constitutes an expense approximating $500 a day to her insurance company.").

WA: *In re* Hamlin, 689 P.2d 1372, 1381 (Wash. 1984) (Rosellini, J., dissenting) ("Where family members all stand to benefit by termination, they would naturally agree and present a unified front.").

See § **5.35.**

[415] **FL:** John F. Kennedy Memorial Hosp. v. Bludworth, 432 So. 2d at 618 (cessation of emotional drain is a benefit of forgoing life-sustaining treatment of permanently comatose patient).

MD: Mack v. Mack, 618 A.2d 744, 760 (Md. 1993) ("The best interest . . . standard . . . enlarges the concept of best interest beyond the needs of the ward to include consideration of the emotional and financial impact on, and desires of [the] family and of the burden on the limited resources of society.").

[416] **CA:** *See* Bouvia v. County of Riverside, No. 159780 (Cal. Super. Ct. Dec. 16, 1983), *reported in* 2 Bioethics Rep. 458 (court considered interests of "other patients within [the hospital] and other physically handicapped persons who are similarly situated in this nation") (discussed in Bouvia v. Superior Court (Glenchur), 225 Cal. Rptr. 297, 300 (Ct. App. 1986)).

impact of his or her choice of medical treatment on his or her loved ones."[417] The court further elaborated by quoting from an opinion of the Massachusetts Supreme Judicial Court involving the refusal of psychiatric treatment:

> Such a factor is likewise to be considered in determining the probable wishes of one who is incapable of formulating or expressing them himself. In any choice between proposed treatments which entail grossly different expenditures of time or money by the incompetent's family, it would be appropriate to consider whether a factor in the incompetent's decision would have been the desire to minimize the burden on his family.[418]

The *Barber* court also made several statements that could be construed as suggesting that the surrogate may consider the effect on third parties of forgoing life-sustaining treatment. The one most on point was made in describing application of the best interests standard. It explained that "since most people are concerned about the well-being of their loved ones, the surrogate may take into account the impact of the decision on those people closest to the patient."[419] However, the court also used language to the effect that the interests of third parties may not be considered, notably in its holding that physicians are obligated to provide a patient in a persistent vegetative state only with that "treatment . . . which, in the view of the patient, has at least a reasonable chance of providing benefits *to the patient,* which benefits outweigh the burdens attendant to the treatment."[420]

Other courts have made equally oblique statements of support for considering the interests of third parties. The Massachusetts Appeals Court, in stating that it "intimate[d] no opinion on the weight to be given the factor of cost to the family where that is a relevant consideration,"[421] might be read to imply that the interests of third parties are a relevant concern and that they should be accorded some weight. The court added that "the decision of the family," by which it seemed to mean the wishes of the family, "is of particular importance . . . as a factor lending added weight to the patient's interest in privacy and personal

---

[417] *In re* Jobes, 529 A.2d 434, 444 n.10 (N.J. 1987).

[418] *Id.* (quoting *In re* Roe, 421 N.E.2d 40, 58 (Mass. 1981)). *See also* Hardwig, *What About the Family?,* 20 Hastings Center Rep. 5 (Mar.–Apr. 1990). *But see* Bluestein, *The Family in Medical Decisionmaking,* 23 Hastings Center Rep. 6 (May–June 1993).

[419] **CA:** Barber v. Superior Court, 195 Cal. Rptr. 484, 493 (Ct. App. 1983). *See also id.* at 490–91 ("The question presented by this modern technology is, once undertaken, at what point does it cease to perform its intended function and who should have the authority to decide that any further prolongation of the dying process is of no benefit to either the patient *or his family?*") (emphasis added).

DC: *Accord In re* A.C., 573 A.2d 1235, 1251 n.20 (D.C. 1990) ("[W]e think it proper for the court to conclude that the patient might consider the needs of her family in making a treatment decision. *See In re Roe, supra,* 383 Mass. at 432, 421 N.E.2d at 58.").

[420] Barber v. Superior Court, 195 Cal. Rptr. at 491 (emphasis added).

[421] *In re* Spring, 399 N.E.2d 493, 499 n.8 (Mass. App. Ct. 1979).

dignity in the face of any countervailing State interests."[422] Similarly, in describing the operation of the substituted judgment standard, the Washington Supreme Court permitted the surrogate to consider all relevant factors, including "the wishes of family and friends, if those wishes would influence the ward's decision."[423]

Most of the attention to this issue has focused on whether *burdens* to others may be taken into account in determining whether a surrogate may forgo a treatment for an incompetent patient. However, it is also important to consider that a treatment may not impose any burdens nor confer any real benefits on a patient, yet may confer benefits on third parties. For instance, a patient's family (and sometimes the physicians and other health care professionals) may find it easier to accept the fact of the patient's incurability and to permit the forgoing of life-sustaining treatment if they believe that all possibly beneficial treatment has been administered. As long as the treatment is not burdening the patient, there may be reasons for its continued administration in some situations, at least for a short period, until all have become acclimated to the inevitability of the patient's death.[424]

§ 7.25 Other Approaches to Best Interests

Justice Stevens's Dissent in *Cruzan*

In *Cruzan v. Director,* the United States Supreme Court held that it is constitutional for a state to require the continuation of life-sustaining treatment in the absence of clear and convincing evidence of the patient's subjective intent to forgo such treatment. In a dissenting opinion, Justice Stevens contended that "[t]he Court . . . permits the State's abstract, undifferentiated interest in the preservation of life to overwhelm the best interests of Nancy Beth Cruzan, interests which would, according to an undisputed finding, be served by allowing her guardians to exercise her constitutional right to discontinue medical treatment," and that in his view "the Constitution requires the State to care for Nancy Cruzan's life in a way that gives appropriate respect to her own best interests."[425]

---

422 *Id.*

423 **WA:** *In re* Ingram, 689 P.2d 1363, 1370 (Wash. 1984).

NY: *Accord In re* Westchester County Medical Ctr. (O'Connor), 531 N.E.2d 607, 617 (N.Y. 1988) (Hancock, J., concurring) (surrogate may take into account sentiments of family or intimate friends); *In re* Lydia E. Hall Hosp., 455 N.Y.S.2d 706, 711 (Sup. Ct. Nassau County 1982) (guardian ad litem informed court that patient had expressed a desire when competent "'to terminate pain, and the pain not only upon himself, but the pain that was inflicted upon his family'").

424 *See* Hardwig, *What About the Family?,* 20 Hastings Center Rep. 5 (Mar.–Apr. 1990). *But see* Bluestein, *The Family in Medical Decisionmaking,* 23 Hastings Center Rep. 6 (May–June 1993). See **Ch. 19.**

425 Cruzan v. Director, 497 U.S. 261, 331 (1990) (Stevens, J., dissenting).

Justice Stevens's opinion never really comes to grips with what factors should be taken into account in determining best interests. On at least two occasions, he explains what is not relevant to best interests. First, it is not in anyone's best interests merely to be maintained in a state of biological existence.[426] Second, it is in one's interests to be "remembered for how she lived rather than how she died, [and] the damage done to those memories by the prolongation of her death is irreversible."[427] From these comments, we can infer that in his view, it is in a patient's best interests to be maintained in a state of life having some meaningful quality to the patient herself and to be remembered as the person she was prior to the accident or illness that robbed her of this state of existence.

Justice Stevens's only real effort to explain what is in a person's best interests in a positive way is somewhat beside the point given Nancy Cruzan's medical condition: "Insofar as Nancy Cruzan has an interest in the cessation of any pain, the continuation of her pain is irreversible."[428] Despite the repeated statements in *Cruzan* that Nancy Cruzan could perceive pain, it is widely agreed by neurologists that patients in a persistent vegetative state do not experience any pain.[429] Thus, the interests of a patient in a persistent vegetative state are more abstract than the avoidance of pain. Nonetheless, in other kinds of situations, pain can very well be a relevant factor.[430]

In the final analysis, Justice Stevens's approach to the application of the best interests standard can best be characterized as a procedural one. One of the reasons that the majority offered for permitting the state to insist on the continuation of treatment when the patient's wishes are unknown is because of "various possible 'abuses' and inaccuracies that may affect procedures authorizing the termination of treatment"[431] because of possible conflicts of interest between the patient and the patient's family, and he agreed that a "State's procedures must guard against the risk that the survivors' interests are not mistaken for the patient's."[432] For Justice Stevens, however, "the appointment of

---

426 **US:** Cruzan v. Director, 497 U.S. at 351 (Stevens, J., dissenting) ("If Nancy Cruzan's life were defined by reference to her own interests, so that her life expired when her biological existence ceased serving any of her own interests, then her constitutionally protected interest in freedom from unwanted treatment would not come into conflict with her constitutionally protected interest in life.").

MN: *See also In re*.Torres, 357 N.W.2d 332, 339 (Minn. 1984) ("[S]imply equating the continued physical existence of [an incompetent patient], who has no chance for recovery, with the [patient's] 'best interests' is contrary to law and medical opinion.").

WI: *See also* L.W. v. L.E. Phillips Career Dev. Ctr., 482 N.W.2d 60, 72 (Wis. 1992) ("If a prognosis of permanent unconsciousness is correct, . . . continued treatment cannot confer . . . benefits.").

427 Cruzan v. Director, 497 U.S. at 353 (Stevens, J., dissenting).

428 *Id.*

429 See § **9.53.**

430 See § **7.18.**

431 Cruzan v. Director, 497 U.S. at 353 (Stevens, J., dissenting) (citing majority opinion).

432 *Id.*

the neutral guardian ad litem, coupled with the searching inquiry conducted by the trial judge and the imposition of the clear and convincing standard of proof, all effectively avoided that risk in this case."[433] He concludes by posing the rhetorical question, "Why such procedural safeguards should not be adequate to avoid a similar risk in other cases is a question the Court simply ignores."[434] Instead of attempting to set forth the factors that surrogates should take into account in determining whether continuation or termination of life-sustaining treatment is in a patient's best interests, he would rely on procedural safeguards because "[c]hoices about life and death are profound ones, not susceptible of resolution by recourse to medical or legal rules."[435] Thus, he concludes, "[i]t may be that the best we can do is to ensure that these choices are made by those who will care enough about the patient to investigate his or her interests with particularity and caution."[436]

Drabick: Best Interests as "Good Faith"

The most unconventional approach taken to describe how the best interests standard should be applied to a particular case is that contained in the opinion of the California Court of Appeals in *Drabick.*[437] In the absence of a formal advance directive, the court held that, at least when there was a statutorily appointed conservator, the conservator is required to apply a best interests standard. The decision about forgoing life-sustaining treatment for a patient "for whom there is no reasonable hope of return to a cognitive life" is to be made by the conservator. The conservator is to be guided by his own conception of what is in the ward's best interests, limited only by the requirement that the conservator act in good faith "'based on medical advice' whether treatment is 'necessary.'"[438] This good-faith standard means that the conservator is not fit to act when there is a "material" conflict of interest, and it requires the conservator to consider all available information, including an oral or nonbinding written advance directive. However, regardless of how clear and convincing the evidence of the incompetent patient's wishes is, as long as those wishes are not contained in a statutorily binding advance directive, they do not compel the conservator's decision.[439]

---

[433] *Id.*

[434] *Id.* at 353–54.

[435] *Id.*

[436] *Id.*

[437] Drabick v. Drabick, 245 Cal. Rptr. 840 (Ct. App. 1988).

[438] **CA:** Drabick v. Drabick, 245 Cal. Rptr. at 849 (quoting Cal. Prob. Code § 2355(a)).

WI: *Accord* L.W. v. L.E. Phillips Career Dev. Ctr., 482 N.W.2d 60, 75 (Wis. 1992) ("Where the guardian's decision is challenged, the presumption is that continued life is in the best interests of the ward, and the burden rests upon the guardian to show . . . that the decision to withhold or withdraw treatment is in the ward's best interests and was made in good faith.").

[439] Drabick v. Drabick, 245 Cal. Rptr. at 860–61.

INTEGRATED STANDARDS: THE NEW JERSEY APPROACH

§ 7.26 Introduction

The first clear judicial recognition of the existence of a hierarchy of standards for making decisions about life-sustaining medical treatment for incompetent patients was the opinion of the New Jersey Supreme Court in *Conroy.* This opinion was heavily influenced by the views of the President's Commission for the Study of Ethical Problems in Medicine and Biomedical and Behavioral Research, called to the court's attention in an amicus curiae brief filed by the former Commissioners and professional staff members of the Commission. Drawing largely on existing case law and commentary, the New Jersey Supreme Court made the first and still the only sweeping judicial attempt to synthesize the substantive standards for decisionmaking for incompetent patients, among standards previously thought to be in competition with each other. In later cases—*Jobes*[440] and *Peter*[441]—the court partially repudiated the implications of the *Conroy* approach, leaving it somewhat less certain whether a true synthesis had indeed been created.[442]

The *Conroy* scheme of decisionmaking for incompetent patients is simple to state: a surrogate must first attempt to apply the subjective standard.[443] If, however, there is inadequate evidence upon which to implement it, the surrogate should apply the best interests standard.[444] However, the court recognized that the best interests standard is not monolithic. Depending on the evidence available in particular cases, the surrogate could approximate the choice that the incompetent patient would have made had he been competent to choose. At one end of the best interests portion of the continuum (referred to as the limited-objective standard), there is some evidence of the patient's wishes but not enough to satisfy the subjective standard, while at the other end there is literally

---

[440] *In re* Jobes, 529 A.2d 434 (N.J. 1987).

[441] *In re* Peter, 529 A.2d 419 (N.J. 1987).

[442] See §§ **7.33–7.36.**

[443] *In re* Conroy, 486 A.2d 1209, 1231–32 (N.J. 1985). *Accord In re* Jobes, 529 A.2d at 444.

[444] *In re* Conroy, 486 A.2d at 1229–30. *Accord In re* Clark, 510 A.2d 136, 145 (N.J. Super. Ct. Ch. Div. 1986) (applying *Conroy*).

AZ: *Accord* Rasmussen v. Fleming, 741 P.2d 674, 688–89 (Ariz. 1987) (best interests standard to be used when not possible to use substituted judgment standard).

CA: *Accord* Barber v. Superior Court, 195 Cal. Rptr. 484, 493 (Ct. App. 1983).

CT: *Accord* Foody v. Manchester Memorial Hosp., 482 A.2d 713, 720–21 (Conn. Super. Ct. 1984).

WA: *Accord In re* Grant, 747 P.2d 445, 457 (Wash. 1987), *modified,* 757 P.2d 534 (Wash. 1988).

no evidence of what the patient would have wanted had he been competent to decide (the so-called pure-objective standard). If there is insufficient evidence to meet the limited-objective standard, the surrogate is to next attempt to apply the pure-objective standard. If there is not enough evidence to meet that standard, the surrogate next must attempt to apply a pure-objective standard. Finally, if there is insufficient evidence to meet the pure-objective standard, life-sustaining treatment must be continued.

Conroy eschewed the use of the term *substituted judgment,* instead using the term *subjective standard* to apply to what some courts meant by substituted judgment. There is an important difference between the two. Under the substituted judgment standard, the surrogate is enjoined to make decisions by attempting to determine what the ward would have decided had he been able to do so. Under the subjective standard, the surrogate is required to determine what the ward actually decided, and if unable to do so the subjective standard cannot be employed. *Conroy* recognized that the substituted judgment standard, applied when satisfactory evidence of the incompetent patient's wishes is absent, is virtually identical to a best interests standard because the surrogate can only approximate the patient's wishes. *Conroy* did not bar surrogates from using this substituted judgment standard; instead it renamed it the *limited-objective standard,* required that it be used only if the subjective standard could not be, and gave it additional content.

In effect, *Conroy* established a single standard with three hierarchical parts. Rather than viewing the subjective and best interests standards as polar opposites, *Conroy* envisioned them as points on a continuum in which the subjective standard is but a particularized application of the best interests standard, the meaning of which comes from the patient's own subjective preferences.[445] However, the standards are ranked in a preferred order, with the patient's wishes the paramount consideration.

Conroy also recognized that the continuum of decisionmaking standards reflects a trade-off between patient self-determination and patient welfare. Decisionmaking even for incompetent patients should be based on self-determination insofar as possible; hence the preference for the subjective standard. However, as evidence of the patient's wishes becomes less trustworthy, *Conroy* shed the pretense indulged by some other courts, most notably the Massachusetts Supreme Judicial Court,[446] that decisionmaking for incompetent patients can be based on self-determination and starkly recognized that it must be based on the

---

[445] **MN:** *In re* Torres, 357 N.W.2d 332, 339 (Minn. 1984) ("At a minimum, any determination of a conservatee's 'best interests' must involve some consideration of the conservatee's wishes.").

WI: L.W. v. L.E. Phillips Career Dev. Ctr., 482 N.W.2d 60, 70 (Wis. 1992) ("If the wishes are clear, it is invariable as a matter of law, both common and statutory, that it is in the best interests of the patient to have those wishes honored, for the patient has made the pre-choice of what he or she considers to be the best interests under the circumstances that arise.").

[446] See §§ **7.7–7.10.**

state's parens patriae power and obligation to act in the best interests of incompetent persons.[447]

A final characteristic of the *Conroy* approach is the recognition of the need for procedural safeguards. Recognizing that ethics committees do not exist in most long-term care facilities, the court had to devise a safeguard to substitute for the protection accorded by ethics committees, a safeguard mandated in *Quinlan.*[448] The safeguard mandated for nursing home patients was an existing state administrative agency, the Office of Ombudsman for the Elderly.[449] In later cases involving patients who did not fall under the jurisdiction of the Ombudsman, the court again fashioned other procedural safeguards,[450] never, however, requiring routine recourse to the courts for decisionmaking about forgoing life-sustaining treatment.

§ 7.27 The *Conroy* Subjective Standard

Under *Conroy,* surrogate decisionmakers must first attempt to effectuate the actual intent of the now-incompetent patient as developed and expressed before becoming incompetent. To do so is to act in the patient's best interests *as the patient conceived of them,*[451] thereby giving maximal effect to the value of self-determination.

What the patient's choice would have been might be gleaned directly from a written document (such as a living will or a durable power of attorney) or from an oral directive, or it might be deduced from the patient's reactions to the administration of medical treatment to others, from a person's religious beliefs (though the mere fact of religious affiliation is not relevant[452]), from the tenets of the patient's religion, or from the patient's prior pattern of conduct concerning decisions about his own medical care.[453] (These are all factors that can be taken into account under the substituted judgment standard as well.[454])

---

447 Dresser, *Missing Persons: Legal Perceptions of Incompetent Patients,* 46 Rutgers L. Rev. 609, 610 (1994) ("it is becoming increasingly obvious that autonomy does not, and probably will never, provide a ready answer in the vast majority of these cases"). See § **7.28.**

448 See § **5.57** and **Ch. 6.**

449 See §§ **7.32** and **7.34.**

450 See § **7.33.**

451 **IL:** *In re* Estate of Greenspan, 558 N.E.2d 1194, 1200 (Ill. 1990) (discussing relationship between best interests standard and patient's own views of treatment).

NJ: *In re* Conroy, 486 A.2d 1209, 1229–30 (N.J. 1985).

452 *In re* Jobes, 529 A.2d 434, 443 (N.J. 1987).

453 **FL:** Browning v. Herbert, 543 So. 2d 258, 272 (Fla. Dist. Ct. App. 1989) ("[R]eligious or ethical beliefs of a patient can play a significant role" in surrogate decisionmaking.).

NJ: *In re* Conroy, 486 A.2d at 1229–30.

454 See § **7.9.**

Conroy recognized that a genuine subjective standard should be—because, realistically, it only could be—applied when the now incompetent patient's wishes could clearly be known:

> [W]e hold that life-sustaining treatment may be withheld or withdrawn from an incompetent patient when it is clear that the particular patient would have refused the treatment under the circumstances involved. The standard we are enunciating is a subjective one, consistent with the notion that the right that we are seeking to effectuate is a very personal right to control one's own life. The question is not what a reasonable or average person would have chosen to do under the circumstances but what the particular patient would have done if able to choose for himself.[455]

Like the subjective standard applied in New York and Missouri,[456] this is an extremely exacting standard. Evidence that is "remote, general, spontaneous, and made in casual circumstances" does not satisfy it.[457] If the evidence does not satisfy the subjective standard, then other standards, which the *Conroy* court prescribed,[458] must be used instead.

§ 7.28 The Parens Patriae Power and Objective Standards

When the kind of evidence necessary for the application of the subjective standard is absent, decisions about the patient's care should not be made through an attempted application of that standard. Any effort to do so results in the kind of strained reasoning used in *Saikewicz,*[459] casting a shadow of suspicion on the legitimacy of the decisionmaking process. Instead, if the patients' interests are to be adequately protected, some other standard for decisionmaking must be used.

In a major departure from the line of cases beginning with *Saikewicz* (or perhaps even with *Quinlan* itself), *Conroy* firmly planted decisionmaking for incompetent patients whose wishes about treatment are not known in the parens

---

455 **NJ:** *In re* Conroy, 486 A.2d at 1229.

FL: *Accord* Browning v. Herbert, 568 So. 2d 4, 13 & passim (Fla. 1990).

MO: Cruzan v. Harmon, 760 S.W.2d 408, 424–26 (Mo. 1988).

456 See §§ **7.4–7.5.**

457 **US:** *Cf.* Cruzan v. Director, 497 U.S. 261 (1990).

NJ: *In re* Jobes, 529 A.2d 434, 443 (N.J. 1987).

NY: *Cf. In re* Westchester County Medical Ctr. (O'Connor), 531 N.E.2d 607 (N.Y. 1988).

See §§ **10.28–10.34.**

458 See §§ **7.28–7.30.**

459 Superintendent of Belchertown State Sch. v. Saikewicz, 370 N.E.2d 417 (Mass. 1977). See § **7.8.**

patriae power of the state.[460] "[I]t is naive to pretend," the *Conroy* court observed, "that the right to self-determination serves as the basis" for decision-making in such cases,[461] and it was this pretense that led the *Saikewicz* court to attempt to implement the supposed choice of a person who never had the capacity to make choices. In other words, in those situations in which the substantive source of the right to die is the patient's own right to make treatment decisions, the right can be effectuated with fidelity only if the patient is able to and does make such a decision. However, when a patient is unable to make and has not made such a decision, just as the substantive basis for the decision shifts from the right of self-determination to the parens patriae power, so must the standard for the surrogate to use in making it.

Thus, rather than using a subjective or substituted judgment standard derived from the right of self-determination, the traditional best interests standard, which is a corollary of the parens patriae power, must be applied. A best interests test is an objective test; that is, it mandates that decisions be made about the incompetent's well-being by reference to factors other than the patient's actual wishes.[462]

§ 7.29 —Limited-Objective Standard

If the kind and weight of evidence necessary for the surrogate to make a decision under the subjective standard is absent, the surrogate should attempt to apply what *Conroy* called a *limited-objective* standard.[463] This is a two-part standard relying both on evidence about the patient's wishes and on evidence about the patient's welfare. It is "objective" in that it considers factors other than the

---

[460] **NJ:** *In re* Conroy, 486 A.2d 1209, 1231 (N.J. 1985).

MO: *See also* Cruzan v. Harmon, 760 S.W.2d 408, 425–26 (Mo. 1988).

See also President's Comm'n, Deciding to Forego Life-Sustaining Treatment 135 ("The best interests standard does not rest on the value of self-determination but solely on protection of patient's welfare."). See § **2.11.**

[461] *In re* Conroy, 486 A.2d at 1231.

[462] **NJ:** *In re* Conroy, 486 A.2d at 1229–30. *Accord In re* Clark, 510 A.2d 136, 145 (N.J. Super. Ct. Ch. Div. 1986) (applying *Conroy*).

AZ: *Accord* Rasmussen v. Fleming, 741 P.2d 674, 689 (Ariz. 1987).

CA: *Accord* Barber v. Superior Court, 195 Cal. Rptr. 484, 493 (Ct. App. 1983).

CT: *Accord* Foody v. Manchester Memorial Hosp., 482 A.2d 713, 720–21 (Conn. Super. Ct. 1984).

MO: Cruzan v. Harmon, 760 S.W.2d 408 (Mo. 1988) (agreeing that parens patriae power is source of decisionmaking for incompetent patients but interpreting it so as always to require provision of life-sustaining treatment in absence of clear and convincing evidence of patient's wishes to the contrary).

WA: *In re* Grant, 747 P.2d 445, 457 (Wash. 1987), *modified,* 757 P.2d 534 (Wash. 1988).

[463] *In re* Conroy, 486 A.2d 1209, 1231–32 (N.J. 1985).

patient's own expressed views. It is "limited" because it does, however, consider those expressed views and depends only in part on supposition about what the patient would have wanted or what reasonable people would want in the same situation. It also closely resembles the substituted judgment standard when the latter is applied to patients whose actual intent is not known, and it takes into account factors similar to those the courts prescribe for applying the substituted judgment standard in such situations.[464]

Threshold Requirement. To apply the limited-objective standard, there must be "some trustworthy evidence" of what the patient's own choice would have been, even though this evidence might not meet the requirements of the subjective test.[465] In making this threshold determination, the surrogate may consider evidence that "would be too vague, casual, or remote to constitute the clear proof of the patient's subjective intent that is necessary to satisfy the subjective test."[466] For example, the fact that Ms. Conroy "feared and avoided doctors"[467] and "informally expressed reactions to other people's medical conditions and treatment"[468] was information that the surrogate could take into account, though it should not be determinative. Other courts, in implementing oral advance directives, have looked at the incompetent patient's lifestyle as further evidence that the patient would have wanted life-sustaining treatment forgone.[469]

---

464 *See* Rosebush v. Oakland County Prosecutor, 491 N.W.2d 633, 639 (Mich. Ct. App. 1992) (equating substituted judgment standard with *Conroy* limited-objective standard). See **§ 7.9.**

465 *In re* Conroy, 486 A.2d at 1232. *See also In re* Jobes, 529 A.2d 434, 443 (N.J. 1987); *In re* Clark, 510 A.2d 136 (N.J. Super. Ct. Ch. Div. 1986) (refusing to apply limited-objective standard).

DC: *See also In re* A.C., 573 A.2d 1235, 1247 (D.C. 1990) (to assure that "right of bodily integrity is not extinguished simply because someone is ill, or even at death's door . . . a court must determine the patient's wishes by any means available").

IL: *See also* Estate of Longeway v. Community Convalescent Ctr., 549 N.E.2d 292, 300 (Ill. 1989) ("On remand, the court should not hesitate to admit any reliable and relevant evidence if it will aid in judging Longeway's intent.").

466 *In re* Conroy, 486 A.2d at 1232.

467 **NJ:** *In re* Conroy, 486 A.2d at 1218.

WA: *Accord In re* Colyer, 660 P.2d 738, 753 (Wash. 1983) (Dore, J., dissenting) (Mrs. Colyer's four sisters and husband "all testified to substantially the same thing . . . she hated doctors and hospitals, and even when she was very sick she wouldn't go to see a doctor. They all speculated that if she was competent she would make the decision under the present circumstances not to continue with the life supporting mechanism.").

468 *In re* Conroy, 486 A.2d at 1232.

469 **CT:** McConnell v. Beverly Enters.-Conn., Inc., 553 A.2d 596, 605 (Conn. 1989) (Although not specifically applying limited-objective standard, court cited as evidence that patient would have wanted treatment terminated facts that she worked as a registered nurse in an emergency room and "often saw the tragedy that befell those who suffered severe head injuries" and that "[s]he had also been adamant that her own mother, when dying of cancer, not be placed on any life support system.").

Balancing Requirement. Once the threshold requirement is met, the surrogate must weigh two variables: "the burdens of the patient's continued life with the treatment," and the benefits likely to be conferred by the treatment. If "it is clear that the burdens of the patient's continued life with the treatment outweigh the benefits of that life for *him,*" life-sustaining treatment may be forgone.[470] Medical evidence is necessary to establish that the burdens of treatment outweigh the benefits.[471] The application of the limited-objective standard depends heavily on what may be considered a burden[472] and a benefit.[473]

One point that the New Jersey Supreme Court was not clear about is what the result should be if there is "some evidence" that the patient would want to receive the treatment in question, but there was agreement that the burdens of treatment outweighed the benefits, thus militating against treatment—or vice versa.

§ 7.30 —Pure-Objective Standard

If neither the subjective standard nor the limited-objective standard can be met, forgoing life-sustaining treatment might still be accomplished by application of a *pure-objective standard.* It is objective because it relies on assumptions about what the patient, as a reasonable person, would have wanted, rather than on his expressed or inferred wishes. It is a "pure" objective standard because it relies solely on such considerations.

The *Conroy* court did not state whether the surrogate may only take into account matters that he believes the patient would have considered, or whether consideration may also be given to what other reasonable persons in the same condition as the patient would have considered. In this regard, the standard resembles the substituted judgment standard as articulated and applied in *Saikewicz.*[474] Although subjective evidence that the patient would not have

---

ME: *In re* Gardner, 534 A.2d 947 (Me. 1987). *Contra In re* Gardner, 534 A.2d at 957 (Clifford, J., dissenting) (evidence of "active life style" inadequate to support decision to forgo treatment that would result in death).

NY: Delio v. Westchester County Medical Ctr., 516 N.Y.S.2d 677 (App. Div. 1987).

See also National Ctr. for State Courts, Guidelines for State Court Decision Making in Life-Sustaining Medical Treatment Cases 83 (2d ed. 1992) (standard 14(B)).

[470] *In re* Conroy, 486 A.2d at 1232 (emphasis added). See §§ **7.20** and **7.24.**

[471] *Id.*

[472] See §§ **7.17–7.19.**

[473] See § **7.21.**

[474] *See* Superintendent of Belchertown State Sch. v. Saikewicz, 370 N.E.2d 417, 429 (Mass. 1977) ("Evidence that most people would or would not act in a certain way is certainly an important consideration in attempting to ascertain the predilections of any individual, but care must be taken, as in any analogy, to ensure that operative factors are similar or at least to take notice of the dissimilarities."). See §§ **7.7–7.10.**

wanted the treatment is not a necessary condition for the application of the pure-objective standard, when evidence exists that the patient would have wanted "to be kept alive in spite of any pain that he might experience,"[475] treatment may not be forgone.

Like the limited-objective standard, the pure-objective standard has two components:

Threshold Requirement. There is a higher threshold for application of the pure-objective standard than of the limited-objective standard: to forgo treatment in the absence of any evidence of the patient's own wishes, "the recurring, unavoidable and severe pain of the patient's life with the treatment should be such that the effect of administering life-sustaining treatment would be inhumane."[476]

Balancing Requirement. The balancing requirement is the same as in the limited-objective standard. The surrogate must weigh the burdens of the patient's continued life with the treatment against the benefits likely to be conferred by the treatment.[477] For treatment to be withheld or withdrawn, the burdens must "clearly and markedly outweigh" the benefits.[478] Like the limited-objective standard, the application of the pure-objective standard depends heavily upon the meanings of burden[479] and benefit.[480]

One problem with the *Conroy* best interests standards is that they ask that the surrogate take into account two somewhat incomparable entities: evidence of the patient's wishes, and burdens and benefits. Under both best interests standards, whether treatment may be forgone depends on the degree to which the burdens of treatment outweigh the benefits. Under the limited-objective standard, it is permissible to forgo treatment if burdens merely exceed benefits because of the existence of some trustworthy evidence that the patient's wishes would be to do so. But under the pure-objective standard, the differential between burdens and benefits must be greater ("clear and marked") and the patient's condition and the treatment must be such that continued treatment would be "inhumane." The net result is that a patient who has failed to express his wishes has to experience inhumane suffering before treatment may be forgone, whereas a patient who has offered "some trustworthy evidence" is entitled to have treatment withheld or withdrawn, being forced to suffer only to the extent that the burdens of treatment exceed its benefits, but not being forced

---

[475] *In re* Conroy, 486 A.2d 1209, 1232 (N.J. 1985).

[476] *Id.*

[477] *Id.*

[478] *Id. See also In re* Clark, 510 A.2d 136, 146 (N.J. Super. Ct. Ch. Div. 1986) (finding that benefits outweigh burdens of performance of an enterostomy).

[479] See §§ **7.17–7.20.**

[480] See § **7.21.**

to suffer inhumanely. The court does not explain why a lack of evidence of one's wishes should force someone to endure a greater degree of suffering. No other court applying a best interests standard appears to impose such a requirement.

§ 7.31 Erosion of the Hierarchy

Only two years after *Conroy,* the New Jersey Supreme Court simultaneously issued opinions addressing questions left unanswered by *Conroy* in three companion cases: *Peter,*[481] *Jobes,*[482] and *Farrell.*[483] In so doing, the court fell somewhat short of extending the synthetic approach it had begun to create in *Conroy.* After this trilogy of cases, the *Conroy* scheme, it seems, is to apply specifically only to other cases involving the same fact pattern as in *Conroy.* Each of these three cases deviated in some way from that fact pattern. In *Peter,* the patient was in a persistent vegetative state. In *Jobes,* the patient was not "elderly" (and also was in a persistent vegetative state); in *Farrell,* the patient was competent and was not in a nursing home. And, finally, the court had occasion to address the status of the effect of *Conroy* on the *Quinlan* decision-making scheme.

Although the court did not exactly back away from the *Conroy* scheme, neither did it make any efforts to extend or reinforce it by applying it or modifying it to apply to patients not meeting the *Conroy* fact pattern. Instead the court attempted to create variations for other fact patterns. Consequently, though *Conroy* is a much-cited case—primarily for its elaboration of the best interests standard—it is also a little-followed case.

§ 7.32 —Scope of Applicability: Nursing Home Patients

The *Conroy* court took pains to stress on more than one occasion that the holding was limited to the particular fact pattern presented: "an elderly nursing-home resident . . . who is suffering from serious and permanent mental and physical impairments, who will probably die within approximately one year even with the treatment, and who, though formerly competent, is now incompetent to make decisions about her life-sustaining treatment and is unlikely to regain such competence."[484] Just how insistent the New Jersey Supreme Court would be about applying this limitation became clear two years later when it refused to

---

[481] *In re* Peter, 529 A.2d 419 (N.J. 1987).

[482] *In re* Jobes, 529 A.2d 434 (N.J. 1987).

[483] *In re* Farrell, 529 A.2d 404 (N.J. 1987).

[484] *In re* Conroy, 486 A.2d 1209, 1219 (N.J. 1985). *See also In re* Peter, 529 A.2d 419, 423 (N.J. 1987).

apply the *Conroy* approach to patients not meeting the *Conroy* fact pattern, especially patients in a persistent vegetative state.[485] Despite this limitation, the substance of the *Conroy* analysis has not been questioned and appears as sound as before those holdings.

In addition to prescribing new substantive standards for surrogate decision-making, *Conroy* established a new procedural safeguard for implementing these standards. Because the patients to whom the *Conroy* standards apply are elderly, incompetent, and in nursing homes, they are considered to be more vulnerable to abuse than hospitalized patients. Thus, before life-sustaining treatment may be forgone, each of these cases must be referred for investigation to the state Office of Ombudsman.[486]

§ 7.33 —Standards for Patients Not Meeting *Conroy* Criteria

The *Conroy* analysis of standards for surrogate decisionmaking seemed to provide the foundation on which further judicial analysis and development would be built. One loose end left untied in *Conroy* was the status of the standards and procedures for decisionmaking enunciated in *Quinlan,* that is, whether they had been overruled sub silentio, whether they were somehow to be used in conjunction with the *Conroy* approach, or whether they maintained an independent life of their own. Two subsequent companion cases, *Jobes*[487] and *Peter,*[488] indicate that the *Conroy* analysis may not turn out to be the predominant scheme for decisionmaking for incompetent patients but may be limited to the fact pattern in *Conroy* itself.[489]

Most significantly, under *Jobes* and *Peter* the *Conroy* hierarchy of standards does not apply to patients in a persistent vegetative state because they are incapable of perceiving either benefits or burdens and because they do not satisfy *Conroy*'s one-year life-expectancy requirement.[490] Rather, the substituted

---

485 *See In re* Jobes, 529 A.2d 434 (N.J. 1987) ; *In re* Peter, 529 A.2d 419; *In re* Farrell, 529 A.2d 404 (N.J. 1987). *But see In re* Visbeck, 510 A.2d 125, 128 (N.J. Super. Ct. Ch. Div. 1986). See **§§ 7.33–7.36.**

486 *See* Gleason v. Abrams, 593 A.2d 1232 (N.J. Super. Ct. App. Div. 1991). See **§§ 5.60** and **7.34.**

487 *In re* Jobes, 529 A.2d 434 (N.J. 1987).

488 *In re* Peter, 529 A.2d 419 (N.J. 1987).

489 *See In re* Conroy, 486 A.2d 1209, 1219 (N.J. 1985). *See also In re* Peter, 529 A.2d at 423; *In re* Moorhouse, 593 A.2d 1256 (N.J. Super. Ct. App. Div. 1991) (judicial approval necessary to terminate life support from never-competent patient in persistent vegetative state residing in a state institution if public guardian does not concur with decision of family, attending physician, prognosis committee, and two independent neurologists). See **§ 7.32.**

490 *See also* Mack v. Mack, 618 A.2d 744, 759 (Md. 1993) (not appropriate for court, without legislative guidelines, to apply a best interests standard to patients in persistent vegetative state because it "requires . . . a quality-of-life judgment"). See **§§ 7.17–7.24, 7.34,** and **7.35.**

judgment standard enunciated in *Quinlan* is probably still good law as to those patients.[491] There is some doubt about this because the New Jersey Supreme Court implied in *Jobes* that a surrogate should still attempt to apply a subjective standard before resorting to a substituted judgment standard.[492] In addition, although "the processes of surrogate decisionmaking should be substantially the same regardless of where the patient is located,"[493] when such patients are not elderly[494] or are not in a nursing home, the procedural protections accorded by the Office of Ombudsman are absent,[495] and others must be fashioned.

In *Hughes,* a case of elective surgery for a patient of the Jehovah's Witness faith, the New Jersey Superior Court held that a refusal of a blood transfusion, made while the patient was competent, should it become necessary during the course of surgery, was unenforceable because it did not meet a "subjective standard."[496] In so doing, the court quoted from the *Peter* opinion[497] to the effect that a subjective standard is "'applicable in every surrogate-refusal-of-treatment case, regardless of the patient's medical condition or life-expectancy.'"[498] However, the New Jersey Supreme Court did not require, in *Peter* or any other case, anything like the specificity that the *Hughes* court demanded.

§ 7.34 —Elderly Nursing Home Patients in Persistent Vegetative State: *Peter*

The *Peter* case involved a 65-year-old nursing home patient in a persistent vegetative state being kept alive by feedings administered through a nasogastric tube. Apart from the severe neurologic impairments she suffered, her physical condition was otherwise good, and the court observed that "[s]he could survive for many years, possibly decades."[499] Thus, although she partially fit the *Conroy* fact pattern—she was elderly (by the statutory standards governing the

---

[491] **NJ:** *In re* Jobes, 529 A.2d at 444; *In re* Conroy, 486 A.2d at 1218–19.

CA: *Cf.* Drabick v. Drabick, 245 Cal. Rptr. 840 (Ct. App. 1988) (applying best interests standard to patient in persistent vegetative state).

OH: *Cf. In re* Myers, 610 N.E.2d 663 (P. Ct. Summit County, Ohio 1993) (applying best interests standard to patient in persistent vegetative state in preference to substituted judgment standard).

[492] *See In re* Jobes, 529 A.2d at 451 ("Where an irreversibly vegetative patient . . . has not clearly expressed her intentions with respect to medical treatment, the *Quinlan* 'substituted judgment' approach best accomplishes the goal of having the patient make her own decision.").

[493] *Id.* at 448.

[494] See § **7.35.**

[495] See §§ **5.60** and **7.34.**

[496] *In re* Hughes, 611 A.2d 1148 (N.J. Super. Ct. App. Div. 1992).

[497] *In re* Peter, 529 A.2d 419 (N.J. 1987).

[498] *In re* Hughes, 611 A.2d at 1152 (quoting *In re* Peter, 529 A.2d 419, 425 (N.J. 1987)).

[499] *In re* Peter, 529 A.2d 419, 422 (N.J. 1987).

jurisdiction of the Ombudsman for the Institutionalized Elderly[500]), a nursing home resident, suffering from serious and permanent mental and physical impairments, formerly competent, and now incompetent and unlikely to regain competence—she deviated from the *Conroy* requirements in one important particular: Ms. Peter was not likely to die within approximately one year.[501]

The court concluded from that difference that the "one-year life-expectancy test and the limited-objective test set forth in *Conroy* are inapplicable"[502] to patients in a persistent vegetative state:

> While a benefits-burdens analysis is difficult with marginally cognitive patients like Claire Conroy, it is essentially impossible with patients in a persistent vegetative state. By definition such patients, like Ms. Peter, do not experience any of the benefits or burdens that the *Conroy* balancing tests are intended or able to appraise. Therefore, we hold that these tests should not be applied to patients in the persistent vegetative state.[503]

Instead of applying *Conroy,* the court "look[ed] . . . primarily to *Quinlan* for guidance":[504]

> Under *Quinlan,* if the guardian and family of a patient in a persistent vegetative state conclude that the patient would not want to be sustained by life-supporting treatment, and the attending physician agrees that the life-support apparatus should be discontinued, and both the attending physician and hospital prognosis committee verify the patient's medical condition, then the guardian can refuse such treatment on the patient's behalf. . . . The interested parties need not have clear and convincing evidence of the patient's intentions; they need only "render their best judgment" as to what medical decision the patient would want them to make.[505]

The court did, however, dispense with *Quinlan*'s prognosis committee requirement because there was no prognosis committee in the nursing home in question.[506] It is not clear whether this is a categorical dispensation or whether, when a prognosis committee exists in a nursing home, it should play the same role a

---

[500] *See* N.J. Stat. Ann. § 52:27G-1 (granting jurisdiction over patients ages 60 and older to Ombudsman), *cited in In re* Peter, 529 A.2d at 423 n.4.

[501] *In re* Peter, 529 A.2d at 424.

[502] *Id.*

[503] **NJ:** *In re* Peter, 529 A.2d at 425.

OH: *Contra In re* Myers, 610 N.E.2d 663, 670 (P. Ct. Summit County, Ohio 1993) ("To require someone to remain in [a persistent vegetative] state for perhaps decades cannot be in the best interest of that individual. Indeed, it can be argued that to keep an individual in that condition, when there is no hope for recovery, is not only against the best interest, but is inhumane."). See §§ **7.17–7.20** and **7.23.**

[504] *Id.*

[505] *Id.*

[506] *In re* Peter, 529 A.2d at 428. *See also In re* Jobes, 529 A.2d 434, 448 (N.J. 1987) (by implication).

hospital prognosis committee would if the patient were hospitalized. Because of the absence of this safeguard and because of the risks to patients in nursing homes generally,[507] the court required that the Ombudsman be notified and play the same role that he would in a *Conroy*-type situation.[508]

Thus, *Peter* amends *Conroy* in the following way when the patient fits the *Conroy* fact pattern in all regards except that he or she is in a persistent vegetative state and not expected to die within one year: (1) if the *Conroy* subjective standard is met, *Conroy* governs, "to insure that patients' medical preferences are respected"[509] (ironically, much of the *Peter* opinion is dictum because Ms. Peter had executed an advance directive which the court found met the clear-and-convincing-evidence standard that would permit the *Conroy* subjective standard to be applied[510]); but (2) if the subjective standard cannot be met, *Quinlan* governs. Substantively, the decision is to be made in accordance with the substituted judgment standard, and procedurally the Office of Ombudsman must be notified of a decision to forgo life-sustaining treatment, at least when the nursing home lacks a prognosis committee.

Outside New Jersey there is also concern about the potential for the abuse of nursing home patients. In the *Greenspan* case,[511] an amicus curiae, Americans United for Life Legal Defense Fund, contended that various Illinois statutes that require nursing homes to provide residents with "personal care, sheltered care or nursing" and prohibit "neglect" of residents incorporate definitions that prohibit the forgoing of artificial nutrition and hydration.[512] The Illinois Supreme Court rejected this argument for a number of reasons, the most significant of which is "that generalized references to providing food, water, and meals should [not] override . . . a resident's specific right to refuse medical treatment."[513]

§ 7.35 —Nonelderly Nursing Home Patients in Persistent Vegetative State: *Jobes*

Jobes involved an incompetent patient who was being kept alive by an artificial feeding device, specifically a jejunostomy tube or "j-tube." Like Conroy and Peter, Jobes was in a nursing home rather than a hospital. Like Peter but unlike Conroy, she was in a persistent vegetative state. Unlike both of them she was not

---

[507] *In re* Peter, 529 A.2d at 428; *In re* Jobes, 529 A.2d at 448. *See* Cohen, *Patients' Rights Laws and the Right to Refuse Life-Sustaining Treatment in Nursing Homes,* 2 Biolaw S:231 (Aug. 1989).

[508] **NJ:** *In re* Peter, 529 A.2d at 429.

ME: *Cf. In re* Gardner, 534 A.2d 947, 949 (Me. 1987) (State Department of Human Services intervention pursuant to statute).

[509] *In re* Peter, 529 A.2d at 425.

[510] *Id.* at 426–27.

[511] *In re* Estate of Greenspan, 558 N.E.2d 1194 (Ill. 1990).

[512] *Id.* at 1204.

[513] *Id.*

elderly, being 31 years old at the time of decision, and thus not within the statutory authority of the Office of Ombudsman.

Because she was in a persistent vegetative state, the court applied the *Peter* rules. This required first that it be determined whether the *Conroy* subjective standard was met,[514] which was found not to be.[515] Consequently, the *Quinlan* standard had to be applied.[516] However, lacking both the protection of a prognosis committee (as would exist in a hospital) and the Ombudsman (as would exist for an elderly patient), the court fashioned a different protective device for nonelderly nursing home patients in a persistent vegetative state. In such cases, because the main risk is of incorrect diagnosis and prognosis, there must be confirmation of the fact that the patient is in a persistent vegetative state by "at least two independent physicians knowledgeable in neurology" secured by the surrogate decisionmaker, and supplemented by the certification of the patient's attending physician if there is one.[517]

§ 7.36 —Patients in Homecare: *Farrell*

Because "[m]any people wish to die at home in familiar surroundings [a]nd, in many cases, hospitals discharge terminally or irreversibly-ill patients . . . medical care in the home, especially for terminally and irreversibly ill patients, is increasing."[518] Consequently, in *Farrell,* the first and still the only case to deal with decisionmaking for patients in homecare settings, the New Jersey Supreme Court acknowledged that "[a] competent patient's right to exercise his or her choice to refuse life-sustaining treatment does not vary depending on whether the patient is in a medical institution or at home."[519]

However, the decisionmaking procedures to be employed for such patients must vary somewhat from those for hospitalized patients. First, there must be a determination about the patient's decisionmaking capacity.[520] This determination is to be made by the attending physician and confirmed by two other physicians. There need not be a judicial determination, in part because patients are, in law, presumed to be competent[521] and in part because of the requirement for independent confirmation.

---

[514] *In re* Jobes, 529 A.2d 434, 443 (N.J. 1987). *See also In re* Peter, 529 A.2d at 423.

[515] *In re* Jobes, 529 A.2d 434, 443 (N.J. 1987).

[516] *Id. See also In re* Peter, 529 A.2d 419, 424 (N.J. 1987).

[517] *In re* Jobes, 529 A.2d at 448. See § **5.59.**

[518] *In re* Farrell, 529 A.2d 404, 414 (N.J. 1987) (citing President's Comm'n, Deciding to Forego Life-Sustaining Treatment 103).

[519] *Id.* at 413–14.

[520] *Id.* at 413. *See also* Gleason v. Abrams, 593 A.2d 1232, 1236 (N.J. Super. Ct. App. Div. 1991) (in determining competency of patient, *Farrell* applies to patients in hospitals and nursing homes as well as to patients in homecare).

[521] *In re* Farrell, 529 A.2d at 415. See § **4.8.**

If the patient is competent, the attending physician must provide the patient with information adequate to permit the patient to render an informed decision about forgoing life-sustaining treatment and must also ensure that the patient's decision is a voluntary and uncoerced one.[522] The two independent physicians must also confirm that the patient's decision is voluntary and informed.[523]

The court did not address the issue of decisionmaking for incompetent patients in homecare settings, and thus the procedures and standards to be used by the surrogates of such patients are unclear. However, in *Jobes,* the patient was in a nursing home, and the court refers on more than one occasion to "non-hospitalized" patients rather than "nursing home" patients. This suggests, though certainly does not hold, that patients in other health care settings such as hospices and homecare are governed by the same (that is, *Quinlan*) standards for surrogate decisionmaking, at least if they are in a persistent vegetative state.[524]

§ 7.37 Critique of the New Jersey Approach

The *Conroy* hierarchy of standards represented a significant advance over the standards for surrogate decisionmaking that had evolved until that time.[525] However, the *Conroy* standards are not without their own difficulties, the major one being the manner in which the court gives content to the two core concepts of "burdens" and "benefits."[526] Recognizing this difficulty in *Peter* and *Jobes,* the New Jersey court took the position that the *Conroy* standards do not apply to patients in a persistent vegetative state because of the inability of such patients to experience either the benefits or burdens of treatment.

This is an unfortunate turn of events because, despite the difficulties posed by the *Conroy* standards, its approach constitutes an innovative, more general scheme for surrogate decisionmaking. The New Jersey court achieved a significant synthesis among standards previously thought to be in competition with each other.

Although the court identified only three points on this continuum, the opportunity exists for further innovation. The court's discussion of these three points suggests a general approach to surrogate decisionmaking: as the quantity, specificity, and trustworthiness of a patient's prior directives diminish, the more determinative become the net benefits to the patient of treatment in relationship to its burdens.

In one sense, the *Conroy* approach is not a particularly revolutionary departure from previous approaches. The limited-objective standard does what the

---

522 *Id.* at 413. See § **3.18.**

523 *In re* Farrell, 529 A.2d at 414–15.

524 See §§ **7.35–7.36.**

525 See §§ **7.7–7.10.**

526 See §§ **7.17–7.21.**

Saikewicz court[527] did under the aegis of a substituted judgment standard but without resorting to legal fictions. However, one of *Conroy*'s major accomplishments was the reconciliation of the subjective and best interests standards. The court came within a hair's breadth of recognizing that the subjective standard is a kind of best interests standard—specifically, a best interests standard in which content is given to the incompetent patient's best interests by reference to his own advance directives.

The *Jobes* and *Peter* opinions undo the synthetic nature of the *Conroy* tripartite standard. By referring the surrogate back to the *Quinlan* approach—that is, to the substituted judgment standard—once it is found that the subjective standard cannot be applied for patients not meeting the *Conroy* fact pattern,[528] the court introduced a disjunction into the *Conroy* continuum of standards. A more straightforward approach would have been to move closer to the position advocated by Justice Handler's separate *Conroy* opinion of permitting consideration of the patient's "quality of life."[529]

Although in *Peter* and *Jobes* the New Jersey court implicitly accepted Justice Handler's position at least with regard to patients in a persistent vegetative state, it was unwilling to expand the *Conroy* standards to permit quality-of-life considerations to be taken into account by surrogates.[530] Thus, although the court seemed to accept Justice Handler's arguments on the facts of the *Peter* and *Jobes* cases, it may also have felt that it could not set limits for future cases.[531]

The court may have had second thoughts about the wisdom of the *Conroy* tripartite standard for another reason: namely, the difficulty of applying it not only to patients in a persistent vegetative state but to patients like Claire Conroy herself, because even for such patients "it can be difficult or impossible to measure the burdens of embarrassment, frustration, helplessness, rage, and other emotional pain, or the benefits of enjoyable feelings like contentment, joy, satisfaction, gratitude, and well-being that the patient experiences as a result of life-sustaining treatment."[532]

In addition to losing or at least postponing the opportunity for further explicating a synthetic set of standards, the *Jobes* and *Peter* standards for use with patients in a persistent vegetative state have their own difficulties. These cases and their standards probably open up more questions than they put to rest, such as:

---

[527] See § **7.9.**

[528] See § **7.34.**

[529] See §§ **7.19** and **7.23.**

[530] See §§ **7.22–7.24.**

[531] *See In re* Peter, 529 A.2d 419, 425 n.6 (N.J. 1987) ("We are aware that many fear that decisions that allow life-sustaining medical treatment to be withdrawn threaten elderly senile patients and victims of Alzheimer's disease. These elderly patients generally will fit within the *Conroy* pattern. Hence, for those patients—unless they left clear evidence of their disinclination for treatment—a one-year life expectancy test would be applied pursuant to the balancing tests before life-sustaining treatment could be withdrawn.").

[532] *Id.*

1. Do the *Quinlan* standards apply to patients who fail to meet the *Conroy* fact pattern in some other way than by not being in a persistent vegetative state, for example being a never-competent patient?[533]
2. If the *Quinlan* standards do not apply to such patients, do the *Conroy* standards apply, or is there to be some further, yet-to-be-articulated modification?
3. Does *Jobes* imply that the surrogate may go "expert-shopping" until the requisite two physicians are found who will confirm that the patient is in a persistent vegetative state, regardless of the number of physicians consulted who may conclude that the patient is not?
4. Under the requirement for confirmation of the diagnosis and prognosis, what does it mean to say that a physician is "independent"[534] and "knowledgeable in neurology?"[535]

ROLE OF THE SURROGATE IN DECISIONMAKING FOR INCOMPETENT PATIENTS

§ 7.38 Introduction

The word *surrogate* literally means a substitute. In the present context, the surrogate acts as a substitute *decisionmaker* about medical treatment for a patient who lacks the capacity to do so for himself. Thus, it is the role of surrogate to make decisions about the patient's medical care, as the patient would if he had the capacity to do so for himself. But of course it is impossible for the surrogate to act precisely as the patient would if able to do so. Thus, the surrogate's role necessarily deviates somewhat from the ideal.

If competent, the patient would possess almost absolute authority to make whatever decisions he wished about medical treatment.[536] This authority imposes a correlative responsibility on the attending physician (and other members of the health care team) to deal with the surrogate as a substitute for the patient. Even when it has been satisfactorily established that a patient lacks decisionmaking capacity and when a surrogate has been designated in a legally permissible manner, it does not follow that any decision that a surrogate makes must be enforced. The decisional authority of a competent patient is not absolute, and the scope of decisional authority of a surrogate is more limited than that of the patient. It is not the role of the surrogate to make whatever decision he wishes

---

[533] See § **7.10.**

[534] *See In re* Peter, 529 A.2d at 429 ("The Ombudsman should secure two independent medical opinions.").

[535] *See id.* at 428.

[536] See §§ **2.4** and **8.2.**

for whatever reasons he wishes, as might nearly be the case for a competent patient. The reach of a surrogate's decisionmaking authority must be guided by standards—specifically, standards for decisionmaking for incompetent patients—that have been developed by the courts and, to a lesser extent, by legislatures.[537]

The surrogate has two general responsibilities: (1) to marshal all available evidence relevant to the prevailing substantive standard for making decisions for incompetent patients—generally speaking, information about the patient's wishes or the patient's interests or both. When this information is available, it is then the surrogate's responsibility (2) to collaborate with the physician or physicians responsible for the patient's treatment in making an *informed decision* about treatment—in a general way, whether to administer it or forgo it. (Of course, decisionmaking is usually a process involving many decisions that are more or less discrete from each other, rather than one global decision to treat or not treat.)

§ 7.39 —Complying with the Substantive Standard

Regardless of which legal standard for decisionmaking for incompetent patients pertains, it is the responsibility of the surrogate to provide information relevant to prove (or disprove) that standard. In a sense, these standards serve as limitations on the surrogate's authority. This is most apparent under the subjective standard, especially a strict version of that standard. In that case, the surrogate's role is to do no more than to act as a conduit for the decision that the patient made before losing decisionmaking capacity.[538] Thus, a surrogate's decision is improper, and judicial review should be sought, when it is "contrary to the wishes of the patient."[539]

§ 7.40 —Providing Informed Consent

When patients are competent, physicians are ordinarily permitted to initiate treatment only with the consent of the patient. One corollary of this basic requirement is that treatment may not be provided in the absence of the patient's consent (or a legally-recognized exception to the requirement). Another is that treatment to which there has previously been consent must be discontinued if the patient withdraws that consent, and withdrawal of consent may be implied.[540]

---

[537] *See, e.g.*, N.Y. Pub. Health Law § 2965(5)(a) (concerning surrogate decisionmaking about cardiopulmonary resuscitation). See **§ 14.8.**

[538] Ragona v. Preate, 11 Fiduc. Rep. 2d 1, 1 (C.P. Lackawanna County, Pa. 1990) ("court does not decide whether to withdraw the life-supporting treatment, rather our role is to determine and effectuate [the patient's] express intent").

[539] Browning v. Herbert, 568 So. 2d 4, 15 (Fla. 1990).

[540] McConnell v. Beverly Enters.-Conn., Inc., 553 A.2d 596, 604 (Conn. 1989) (consent implied from fact that patient's family instituted legal proceedings).

Consent alone is not sufficient to authorize treatment. In addition, the physician must provide patients with information that is material to making the decisions that are before them. When a surrogate stands in for an incompetent patient, the physician's obligation to the patient to provide such information is transferred to the surrogate.[541] The spirit of the informed consent doctrine also requires the attending physician to keep the surrogate informed of the patient's health (including any change in diagnosis), the options that are available or become available as the patient's condition changes, and the patient's prognosis with and without treatment.[542] The physician must also provide honest answers to the surrogate's questions. Thus, for example, if a physician wishes to insert a feeding tube in an incompetent patient and the family objects based on its knowledge of a patient's prior expressed wishes, and the physician tells the family that the procedure is legally required and that he will obtain a court order, the family's failure to further object does not mean that consent has been given.[543]

Surrogates need information about the available therapeutic options to make a decision. Specifically,

> since the goal is to effectuate the patient's right of informed consent, the surrogate decisionmaker must have at least as much medical information upon which to base his decision about what the patient would have chosen as one would expect a competent patient to have before consenting to or rejecting treatment. Such information might include evidence about the patient's present level of physical, sensory, emotional, and cognitive functioning; the degree of physical pain resulting from the medical condition, treatment, and termination of treatment, respectively;

---

[541] **CA:** *Cf.* Drabick v. Drabick, 245 Cal. Rptr. 840, 849 (Ct. App. 1988) (conservator of incompetent patient statutorily required to engage in a "decisional process").

CT: McConnell v. Beverly Enters.-Conn., Inc., 553 A.2d at 604 (state statute requires that attending physician obtain informed consent of patient's next-of-kin before removing life support system).

DC: *In re* A.C., 573 A.2d 1235, 1251 (D.C. 1990) (when court acts as surrogate decisionmaker, "the court should become as informed about the patient's condition, prognosis, and treatment options as one would expect any patient to become before making a treatment decision").

OH: Estate of Leach v. Shapiro, 469 N.E.2d 1047, 1054 (Ohio Ct. App. 1984) ("[P]hysician's fiduciary obligation of full disclosure flows to the person acting in the patient's behalf.").

[542] **GA:** *In re* L.H.R., 321 S.E.2d 716, 719 (Ga. 1984) (by implication).

MI: Rosebush v. Oakland County Prosecutor, 491 N.W.2d 633, 685 (Mich. Ct. App. 1992) (by implication).

NJ: *In re* Conroy, 486 A.2d 1209, 1231 (N.J. 1985) ("Since the goal [of decisionmaking by a surrogate] is to effectuate the patient's right of informed consent, the surrogate decisionmaker must have at least as much medical information upon which to base his decision about what the patient would have chosen as one would expect a competent patient to have before consenting to or rejecting treatment."); *In re* Clark, 510 A.2d 136, 142 (N.J. Super. Ct. Ch. Div. 1986).

[543] **NY:** Elbaum v. Grace Plaza of Great Neck, Inc., 544 N.Y.S.2d 840, 847 (App. Div. 1989).

> the degree of humiliation, dependence, and loss of dignity probably resulting from the condition and treatment; the life expectancy and prognosis for recovery with and without treatment; the various treatment options; and the risks, side effects, and benefits of each of those options. Particular care should be taken not to base a decision on a premature diagnosis or prognosis.[544]

Surrogates, like competent patients, also need information about alternative courses of action that are not strictly therapeutic, such as the possibility that another health care institution or physician may be more amenable to cooperation with the surrogate's wishes and that the law does not clearly require the course of action that they advocate.[545]

The absence of adequate information can easily lead to a surrogate's making a decision on the basis of incorrect assumptions. For example, in the *Storar* case, medical personnel asked the patient's mother to consent to blood transfusions for her son; she refused to do so in part because "no one had ever explained to her what might happen to him if the transfusions were stopped. She also stated that she was not 'sure' whether he might die sooner if the blood was not replaced."[546]

One important difference when dealing with a surrogate is that the physician should be far more restrained in invoking the therapeutic privilege to withhold information from the surrogate than might be the case in dealing directly with a competent patient.[547] Another difference is that the physician and surrogate must take the patient's current views into account when the patient is capable of expressing them.[548]

However, some of the rules of the informed consent doctrine that tend to disenfranchise patients are equally applicable in the context of surrogate decision-making. For example, if a surrogate lacks the capacity to make a particular decision—for example, because he seems unable to appreciate the magnitude of the risks or benefits of a proposed procedure—that surrogate's decision should not be honored, and a new surrogate should be sought.[549] Similarly, in a genuine emergency, there is no need to consult the surrogate if to do so would seriously jeopardize the life or health of the patient. However, an emergency cannot be

---

[544] **NJ:** *In re* Conroy, 486 A.2d 1209, 1231 (N.J. 1985).

FL: *See also* Browning v. Herbert, 543 So. 2d 258, 271–72 (Fla. Dist. Ct. App. 1989) (surrogate must have information about patient's current medical condition, nature of medical treatment to be withheld or withdrawn, including its benefits, risks, invasiveness, painfulness, and side effects, patient's prognosis with and without treatment, including life expectancy, suffering, and the possibility of recovery).

OH: *See also* Estate of Leach v. Shapiro, 469 N.E.2d 1047, 1054 (Ohio Ct. App. 1984).

[545] **NY:** *See* Elbaum v. Grace Plaza of Great Neck, Inc., 544 N.Y.S.2d 840 (App. Div. 1989).

[546] *In re* Storar, 420 N.E.2d 64 (N.Y. 1981).

[547] **NY:** *See* Darrah v. Kite, 301 N.Y.S.2d 286 (App. Div. 1969). See § **3.25.**

[548] See §§ **7.45–7.46.**

[549] **DNY:** *See In re* Department of Veteran's Affairs Medical Ctr., 749 F. Supp. 495 (S.D.N.Y.), *aff'd,* 914 F.2d 239 (2d Cir. 1990). See § **5.24.**

used to override the prior refusal of a competent patient and similarly should not be used to override the legitimate prior refusal of a surrogate.[550]

As a general rule, the surrogate assumes the decisional authority possessed by the competent patient at the point when the patient is determined to lack decisionmaking capacity. In particular, this means that the physician's obligation to obtain informed consent from the patient is transferred to the surrogate.[551] Conversely, if the patient has not lost (or regains) decisionmaking capacity, the patient has the authority act as his own decisionmaker (unless he waives the right to do so[552]); family members are not permitted to contravene patients' decisions.[553]

§ 7.41 Limits on Surrogate's Decisional Authority

As mentioned in **§ 7.39,** one—and probably the most important—limitation on a surrogate's decisional authority is the requirement that decisions about life-sustaining treatment comply with the prevailing standard for decisionmaking for incompetent patients. However, there are a number of other practical and legal[554] limitations.

§ 7.42 —Limits Imposed by Bias in Favor of Treatment

In practice, the traditional bias of physicians in favor of providing treatment when it is possible to do so often takes precedence over the objections of a surrogate, just as it does over the objections of a competent patient. In fact,

---

[550] **OH:** Estate of Leach v. Shapiro, 469 N.E.2d at 1053. See **§§ 3.23, 10.22,** and **10.23.**

[551] **CT:** McConnell v. Beverly Enters.-Conn., Inc., 553 A.2d 596, 604 (Conn. 1989) ("General Statutes § 19a-571(3) requires that the attending physician obtain the informed consent of the patient's next of kin prior to removing a life support system.").

[552] See **§§ 3.26** and **10.14.**

[553] **DC:** *Cf. In re* A.C., 573 A.2d 1235, 1251 (D.C. 1990) (When the court acts as surrogate decisionmaker, "the court should become as informed about the patient's condition, prognosis, and treatment options as one would expect any patient to become before making a treatment decision.").

FL: *In re* Dubreuil, 603 So. 2d 538, 541 (Fla. Dist. Ct. App. 1992) (patient's "constitutional right to refuse treatment was [not] in any way dependent upon the consent of her husband"), *aff'd,* Dubreuil, 629 So. 2d 819, 827 n.13 (Fla. 1993).

IN: *Cf.* Payne v. Marion Gen. Hosp., 549 N.E.2d 1043 (Ind. Ct. App. 1990) (action for lack of informed consent is stated if patient was not incompetent at time consent to do-not-resuscitate order was given by family member).

OH: Estate of Leach v. Shapiro, 469 N.E.2d 1047, 1054 (Ohio Ct. App. 1984) ("physician's fiduciary obligations of full disclosure flow to the person acting in the patient's behalf").

[554] See **Ch. 8.**

physicians' reluctance about forgoing treatment, especially when that treatment is life-sustaining, may be even greater when the patient is unable to speak for himself. Consequently, there may be a bias in actual clinical situations to accept the consent of a surrogate decisionmaker but to balk at implementing a surrogate's refusal of treatment, and even more so when death is likely to result.

The bias in favor of treatment is often reflected and reinforced in law. An example is *Storar*,[555] in which hospital authorities initially sought permission from the mother of a mentally retarded man in his 50s to conduct diagnostic tests. She initially refused but later consented. In reliance on her consent, the tests were performed. They revealed cancer, and radiation therapy was recommended. The hospital then instituted a judicial proceeding to have the mother appointed guardian because the hospital authorities would not "administer the treatment without the consent of a legal guardian,"[556] despite the fact that they previously relied on her consent to diagnostic tests. Thereafter, on the basis of her consent as court-appointed guardian, radiation therapy was administered. Subsequently, Mr. Storar's doctors asked his mother as guardian to consent to the administration of blood transfusions. She initially refused but soon withdrew her objection. However, she later requested that the transfusions be discontinued. The hospital authorities again instituted a judicial proceeding, this time seeking authorization to continue the transfusions despite the guardian's objections, claiming that without them "death would occur within weeks."[557] In sum, the hospital authorities and physicians relied on the mother's decision, whether in her role as clinically designated surrogate or as court-appointed guardian, only when it was consistent with their recommended course of therapy. They viewed Mrs. Storar's legal authority to make decisions about her son's health care as clearly subsidiary to *what* she decided.[558]

---

[555] *In re* Storar, 420 N.E.2d 64 (N.Y. 1981).

[556] *Id.* at 68.

[557] *Id.* at 69.

[558] **AZ:** *Contra* Rasmussen v. Fleming, 741 P.2d 674, 688 (Ariz. 1987) ("[T]the right to consent to or approve the delivery of medical care must necessarily include the right to consent to or approve the delivery of no medical care. To hold otherwise would . . . ignore the fact that oftentimes a patient's interests are best served when medical treatment is withheld or withdrawn. To hold otherwise would also reduce the guardian's control over medical treatment to little more than a mechanistic rubberstamp for the wishes of the medical treatment team. . . . [T]he Public Fiduciary as Rasmussen's guardian had the implied, if not express, statutory authority to exercise Rasmussen's right to refuse medical treatment.").

CA: *Contra* Drabick v. Drabick, 245 Cal. Rptr. 840, 850 (Ct. App. 1988) ("[A] common sense point about statutory interpretation [is that] a statute that requires a person to make a decision contemplates a decision either way.").

IL: *Contra In re* Estate of Greenspan, 558 N.E.2d 1194 (Ill. 1990); Estate of Longeway v. Community Convalescent Ctr., 549 N.E.2d 292, 298 (Ill. 1989) ("[T]he Probate Act impliedly authorizes a guardian to exercise the right to refuse artificial sustenance on her ward's behalf. Section 11a-17 . . . specifically permits a guardian to make provisions for her ward's 'support, care, comfort, health, education and maintenance.' . . . Moreover, if the patient previously executed a power of attorney under the Powers of Attorney for Health Care Law (Ill. Rev

The bias in favor of treatment is beginning to undergo some erosion from two forces. One is external pressures to control health care costs; the other is the realization in particular cases that continued treatment is futile, that is, that it will not achieve either the patient's (presumed) goals or any set of reasonable objective goals.[559]

When considered in relation to the bias in favor of treatment, the wish of physicians to limit care in some end-of-life cases is easier to see for what, perhaps, it really is: a wish to reassert physician dominance and paternalism within the doctor-patient relationship in general and specifically in end-of-life decisionmaking.

§ 7.43 —Limits Imposed by Guardian ad Litem

Many right-to-die cases are initiated by the filing of a petition to be appointed guardian by some interested party, usually a family member of the patient, often for the express purpose of authorizing the forgoing of life-sustaining treatment.

Stat. 1987, ch. 110½, par. 804-1 *et seq.*), that act permits her to authorize her agent to terminate the food and water that sustain her (Ill. Rev. Stat. 1987, ch. 110½, par. 804-10).").

IN: *Contra In re* Lawrance, 579 N.E.2d 32, 39 (Ind. 1991) (statutorily authorized family member's "right to consent to the patient's course of treatment necessarily includes the right to refuse a course of treatment").

KY: *Contra* DeGrella v. Elston, 858 S.W.2d 698, 704 (Ky. 1993) (absence in guardianship statutes of provision authorizing guardian of patient in persistent vegetative state to authorize termination of treatment does not preclude such authority because statutes were remedial rather than exclusive).

MN: *Contra In re* Torres, 357 N.W.2d at 332, 339 (Minn. 1984) ("[S]imply equating the continued physical existence of [an incompetent patient], who has no chance for recovery, with the [patient's] 'best interests' is contrary to law and medical opinion.").

MO: *Cf.* Cruzan v. Harmon, 760 S.W.2d 408, 424 (Mo. 1988) (statute that "places an express, affirmative duty on guardians to assure that the ward receives medical care and provides the guardian with the power to give consent for that purpose" does not provide basis for contending that "guardian possesses authority, as a guardian, to order the *termination* of medical treatment") (emphasis added). *Contra In re* Warren, 858 S.W.2d 263, 265 (Mo. Ct. App. 1993).

WA: *Contra In re* Colyer, 660 P.2d 738, 747 (Wash. 1983) ("[T]he decision to refuse life sustaining treatment is one that falls under the general powers of the guardian.").

WI: *Contra* L.W. v. L.E. Phillips Career Dev. Ctr., 482 N.W.2d 60, 71 (Wis. 1992) ("[A] guardian has identical decisionmaking powers as a health care agent [appointed pursuant to the health care power of attorney statute]. To construe the [guardianship statute] any other way would result in an individual losing his or her expressed [*sic*] right to refuse treatment upon appointment of a guardian"). *Cf.* N.Y. Pub. Health Law § 2963(1) ("A lack of capacity shall not be presumed from the fact that a . . . conservator . . . or . . . a guardian has been appointed.").

[559] See **Ch. 19.**

In such situations, the court is often empowered, either statutorily or on general equitable principles,[560] to appoint a guardian ad litem.[561]

The role of the guardian ad litem is to represent the best interests of the incompetent,[562] and sometimes this role is statutorily prescribed.[563] The general purpose of the guardian ad litem is to protect the patient against the possibility that an erroneous decision will be made either to terminate or continue life-sustaining treatment. In so doing, "[a] guardian ad litem's task is to uncover any conflicts of interest and ensure that each party likely to have relevant evidence is consulted and brought forward—for example, other members of the family, friends, clergy, and doctors."[564] This role need not necessarily be an adversarial one,[565] but the guardian ad litem should not defer to the wishes of the patient's family so much as "effectively to have delegated the treatment decision" to them.[566] The obligation of the guardian ad litem is "diligently to 'present[] to the judge, after as thorough an investigation as time will permit, all reasonable arguments in favor of administering treatment to prolong the life of the individual involved.' "[567]

In early stages of the proceedings, the specific role of the guardian ad litem in right-to-die litigation is to provide the court with a written "evaluation of the appropriateness of the guardian . . . whose appointment is sought."[568] The

---

560 Superintendent of Belchertown State Sch. v. Saikewicz, 370 N.E.2d 417, 433 (Mass. 1977) (inherent power of court).

561 **AZ:** *E.g.,* Rasmussen v. Fleming, 741 P.2d 674, 690 (Ariz. 1987).

MA: *E.g.,* Superintendent of Belchertown State Sch. v. Saikewicz, 370 N.E.2d at 433.

NJ: *E.g., In re* Jobes, 529 A.2d 434, 437 (N.J. 1987).

WA: *E.g., In re* Grant, 747 P.2d 445 (Wash. 1987), *modified,* 757 P.2d 534 (Wash. 1988); *In re* Colyer, 660 P.2d 738, 750 (Wash. 1983).

Cf. National Ctr. for State Courts, Guidelines for State Court Decision Making in Life-Sustaining Medical Treatment Cases 46 (2d ed. 1992) (standard 7).

562 *In re* Colyer, 660 P.2d 738, 750 (Wash. 1983). *See generally* S. Brakel et al., The Mentally Disabled and the Law 388–89 (1985).

563 *See, e.g.,* Wash. Rev. Code § 11.88.090 (1987), *cited in In re* Colyer, 660 P.2d 738. *See generally* S. Brakel et al., The Mentally Disabled and the Law 416–24 tbl. 7.4 (3d ed. 1985).

564 Cruzan v. Director, 497 U.S. 261, 318 (1990) (Brennan, J., dissenting) (citing *In re* Colyer, 660 P.2d at 748–49 (1983)).

565 **AZ:** Rasmussen v. Fleming, 741 P.2d 674, 690 (Ariz. 1987).

CA: Drabick v. Drabick, 245 Cal. Rptr. 840, 849 (Ct. App. 1988).

NY: Delio v. Westchester County Medical Ctr., 516 N.Y.S.2d 677, 685 (App. Div. 1987).

WA: *In re* Colyer, 660 P.2d 738, 748 (Wash. 1983).

566 *In re* R.H., 622 N.E.2d 1071, 1077 (Mass. App. Ct. 1993).

567 *Id.* (quoting Superintendent of Belchertown State Sch. v. Saikewicz, 370 N.E.2d 417, 433 (Mass. 1977).

568 **WA:** Wash. Rev. Code § 11.88.090(3)(b)(ii), *quoted in In re* Colyer, 660 P.2d at 748.

MA: *Accord* Superintendent of Belchertown State Sch. v. Saikewicz, 370 N.E.2d at 433 (represent the interests of the person).

evaluation made by the guardian ad litem "should focus on the closeness of the relationship between the petitioning party and the incompetent, and any evidence of less than salutary motives."[569] During the pendency of a petition to appoint a guardian, the guardian ad litem may have the authority to consent to emergency lifesaving medical services but not to refuse them.[570]

All authority to act on behalf of the incompetent shifts from the guardian ad litem to the guardian once the latter has been appointed.[571] The guardian ad litem should be dismissed at this time if judicial review of substantive decisions about life-sustaining treatment is not required.[572] However, if there is to be judicial review subsequent to the appointment of a guardian, the guardian ad litem may continue to play an investigatory role:

> The guardian ad litem's function in this context would be to discover all the facts relevant to the decision to withdraw life sustaining treatment and present them to the court. Such facts would include, but are not necessarily limited to: (a) facts about the incompetent: *i.e.,* age, cause of incompetency, relationship with family members and other close friends, attitude and prior statements concerning life sustaining treatment; (b) medical facts: *i.e.,* prognosis for recovery, intrusiveness of treatment, medical history; (c) facts concerning the state's interest in preserving life: *i.e.,* the existence of dependents, other third party interests; and (d) facts about the guardian, the family, other people close to the incompetent, and the petitioner: *i.e.,* their familiarity with the incompetent, their perceptions of the incompetent's wishes, any potential for ill motives.[573]

In Massachusetts, the guardian ad litem is specifically charged with the "responsibility of presenting . . . all reasonable arguments *in favor of administering treatment* to prolong the life of the individual involved . . . [to] ensure that all viewpoints and alternatives will be aggressively pursued and examined."[574] (However, a reflexive role for the guardian ad litem has been criticized by other courts.[575]) Thus, when a Massachusetts guardian ad litem deferred so

---

569 *In re* Colyer, 660 P.2d at 750.

570 *See, e.g.,* Wash. Rev. Code § 11.88.090(7).

571 *See id.* § 11.92.040.

572 *See id.* § 11.88.090(6).

573 **WA:** *In re* Colyer, 660 P.2d at 747–49, *partially overruled in In re* Hamlin, 689 P.2d 1372 (Wash. 1984) (dispensing with blanket requirement of judicial review).

AZ: *Accord* Rasmussen v. Fleming, 741 P.2d 674, 690 (Ariz. 1987).

MA: *Accord In re* R.H., 622 N.E.2d 1071, 1077 (Mass. App. Ct. 1993) (obligation of guardian ad litem is "diligently to 'present[ ] to the judge, after as thorough an investigation as time will permit, all reasonable arguments in favor of administering treatment to prolong the life of the individual involved' ") (quoting Superintendent of Belchertown State Sch. v. Saikewicz, 370 N.E.2d 417 (Mass. 1977); *In re* Spring, 405 N.E.2d 115 (Mass. 1980)).

574 Superintendent of Belchertown State Sch. v. Saikewicz, 370 N.E.2d at 433 (emphasis added), *modified in In re* Spring, 405 N.E.2d at 123 (guardian ad litem has no duty to present arguments he does not believe to be meritorious).

575 **CA:** Drabick v. Drabick, 245 Cal. Rptr. 840, 857–59 (Ct. App. 1988).

WA: *In re* Colyer, 660 P.2d at 748.

much to the views of a never-competent patient's mother and family so as "effectively to have delegated the treatment decision" to them, the guardian ad litem did not properly perform his duties.[576] The guardian ad litem must make an independent investigation and determination. In fact, however, the guardian ad litem

> met [the patient] only twice; had never discussed or attempted to communicate with her regarding either her illness or the proposed treatment; could not resolve the conflicting opinions of the several physicians; and had therefore given paramount weight to the preference manifested by her family that she not receive the "unpleasant" dialysis treatment. Although the guardian ad litem observed that it probably made sense to attempt a brief trial of dialysis treatment, he ultimately decided not to recommend it primarily because he felt obliged to defer to the wishes of R.H.'s family, who were thoroughly opposed to even a trial.[577]

The guardian ad litem may also initiate judicial proceedings, such as appeals.[578]

§ 7.44 —Limits Imposed by Substantive Standards for Surrogate Decisionmaking

The most important legal limitation on the authority of surrogates to make decisions are the substantive standards for making decisions about life-sustaining treatment for incompetent patients. They have been developed primarily by courts, but legislatures are increasingly enacting surrogate decisionmaking statutes, some of which contain substantive as well as procedural requirements for decisionmaking for incompetent patients.[579]

The traditional standards for guiding guardians in carrying out their responsibilities[580]—the substituted judgment standard[581] and the best interests standard[582]—originated and developed in areas of the law other than medical decisionmaking, most notably in guardianships of the estates of incompetents and orphans.[583] Further development has taken place in the area of guardianships of the persons of incompetents and orphans and more recently in child custody matters in divorce, separation, and child neglect.[584] In addition to these two traditional standards, a third has developed in the area of decisionmaking

---

[576] *In re* R.H., 622 N.E.2d at 1077.

[577] *Id.* at 1075.

[578] Rasmussen v. Fleming, 741 P.2d 674, 690 (Ariz. 1987).

[579] See **Ch. 14.**

[580] S. Brakel et al., The Mentally Disabled and the Law 387 (1985).

[581] See §§ **7.7–7.9.**

[582] See §§ **7.11–7.25.**

[583] President's Comm'n for the Study of Ethical Problems in Medicine & Biomedical & Behavioral Research, Deciding to Forego Life-Sustaining Treatment 132.

[584] *See generally* 43 C.J.S. *Infants* §§ 13, 19 (1978).

about life-sustaining treatment: the subjective (or actual-intent) standard.[585] Legal limitations other than those imposed by the standards for decisionmaking for incompetent patients are discussed in **Chapter 8.**

§ 7.45 Preferences of Incompetent Patients

Although many patients who lack decisionmaking capacity are unable to communicate, some can express views about their treatment.[586] As a result, conflict may exist between the surrogate's decisions about medical care and the patient's contemporaneous preferences. As a practical matter, the extent to which these will be taken into account depends in the first instance on the sufferance of the attending physician and the surrogate. What effect these views should have is a difficult question.

Some patients who have lost or never had the ability to speak may be able to express views behaviorally. For instance, the patient in *Storar* was a man who was profoundly retarded since birth, and had "no comprehension of what is happening to him . . . [and] no understanding of why people periodically come to insert a needle into him and compel him to lie still for up to four hours with a needle stuck in a vein." Yet, "[u]nquestionably this is upsetting to him and unquestionably, he does not like it."[587] Similarly, the patient in *Hier,* while unable to speak, made clear her aversion to a feeding tube by continually

---

[585] See **§§ 7.4–7.6.**

[586] **MA:** *E.g., In re* R.H., 622 N.E.2d 1071 (Mass. App. Ct. 1993); *In re* Hier, 464 N.E.2d 959 (Mass. App. Ct. 1984); Lane v. Candura, 376 N.E.2d 1232 (Mass. App. Ct. 1978).

MI: *E.g.,* Martin v. Martin, 504 N.W.2d 917 (Mich. Ct. App. 1993).

MN: *E.g., In re* Friedman, 478 N.W.2d 790 (Minn. 1991).

NJ: *E.g., In re* Schiller, 372 A.2d 360 (N.J. Super. Ct. Ch. Div. 1977).

NY: *E.g., In re* Kerr (O'Brien), 517 N.Y.S.2d 346 (Sup. Ct. N.Y. County 1986); Long Island Jewish-Hillside Medical Ctr. v. Levitt, 342 N.Y.S.2d 356 (Sup. Ct. Nassau County 1973).

TN: *E.g.,* State Dep't. of Human Servs. v. Northern, 563 S.W.2d 197 (Tenn. Ct. App. 1978).

WA: *E.g., In re* Grant, 747 P.2d 445, 457 (Wash. 1987), *modified,* 757 P.2d 534 (Wash. 1988) ("Where the patient has clearly expressed his or her wishes regarding the withholding of life sustaining treatment, these wishes must be given strong consideration, even if made while the patient was incompetent."); *In re* Ingram, 689 P.2d 1363, 1371 (Wash. 1984) (though legally incapable of managing affairs or caring for self, patient can communicate with others and, at least to some extent, understand her plight).

[587] **NY:** *In re* Storar, 433 N.Y.S.2d 388, 392 (Sup. Ct. Monroe County), *aff'd,* 434 N.Y.S.2d 46 (App. Div. 1980), *rev'd,* 420 N.E.2d 64 (N.Y. 1981). *Accord In re* Kerr (O'Brien), 517 N.Y.S.2d 346, 347 (Sup. Ct. N.Y. County 1986) (nasogastric tube is "source of great irritation and discomfort").

CA: *Accord* Drabick v. Drabick, 245 Cal. Rptr. 840, 857–58 (Ct. App. 1988) ("When an incompetent conservatee is still able to communicate with his attorney it is unclear whether the attorney must advocate the client's stated preferences—however unreasonable—or independently determine and advocate the client's best interests [citation omitted]."); Pa. Cons. Stat. Ann. tit. 20, § 5155(E) ("In a hearing to determine whether a guardian shall be ordered to consent to a specific act or omission, if the guardian knows or has reason to know of the incapacitated

removing it.[588] Other patients may be incapable of speech but be able to communicate by shaking their head affirmatively or negatively,[589] squeezing someone's hand,[590] or by blinking their eyes.[591]

An incompetent patient's preferences about treatment expressed while the patient is incompetent should not be cavalierly ignored.[592] If the substituted judgment standard may be used in the case of never-competent patients,[593] a fortiori weight should be given to the contemporaneously expressed subjective wishes of an incompetent patient.[594] Indeed, the Massachusetts Appeals Court has held that a trial court must take into account the views of a never-competent

---

person's objection to the action or omission, whether such objection had been expressed prior or subsequent to the determination of incapacity, the guardian shall report to the court such knowledge or information.").

MA: *Accord In re* Spring, 405 N.E.2d 115, 118 (Mass. 1980) (patient kicked nurses, resisted transportation for dialysis, and pulled the dialysis needles out of his arm); Superintendent of Belchertown State Sch. v. Saikewicz, 370 N.E.2d 417, 432 (Mass. 1977) (patient, though never competent and unable to speak, might still object to treatment); *In re* Hier, 464 N.E.2d 959, 965 (Mass. App. Ct. 1984) (patient's "repeated dislodgements of gastric tubes, her resistance to attempts to insert a nasogastric tube, and her opposition to surgery all may be seen as a plea for privacy and personal dignity").

MI: *Accord* Martin v. Martin, 504 N.W.2d 917, 924 (Mich. Ct. App. 1993) (health care power of attorney statute "explicitly recognizes that an incompetent patient may express a current desire not to have life-sustaining medical treatment withheld or withdrawn").

NJ: *Accord In re* Clark, 510 A.2d 136, 137 (N.J. Super. Ct. Ch. Div. 1986) (Patient could "shake his head 'yes' and 'no,' but could not carry on a conversation.").

588 *In re* Hier, 464 N.E.2d 959 (Mass. App. Ct. 1984).

589 *In re* Clark, 510 A.2d 136, 137 (N.J. Super. Ct. Ch. Div. 1986) (patient could "shake his head 'yes' and 'no,' but could not carry on a conversation").

590 *In re* Westchester County Medical Ctr. (O'Connor), 531 N.E.2d 607, 609 (N.Y. 1988).

591 **IN:** *Cf.* Payne v. Marion Gen. Hosp., 549 N.E.2d 1043, 1048 (Ind. Ct. App. 1990) (questioning whether this form of communication is reliable).

NJ: *In re* Clark, 510 A.2d at 137–38 (patient "could follow instructions to use other means of communicating, such as . . . blinking his eyes"); *In re* Requena, 517 A.2d 886, 888 (N.J. Super. Ct. Ch. Div. 1986) (The patient's "most common form of active communication is by eye-blink response to questions. (One blink for 'Yes,' two blinks for 'No.')").

592 **AK:** *In re* C.D.M., 627 P.2d 607 (Alaska 1981).

FL: Browning v. Herbert, 543 So. 2d 258, 272 n.24 (Fla. Dist. Ct. App. 1989).

MA: *In re* Moe, 432 N.E.2d 712 (Mass. 1982); *In re* Roe, 421 N.E.2d 40 (Mass. 1981); Doe v. Doe, 385 N.E.2d 995 (Mass. 1979).

MI: Martin v. Martin, 504 N.W.2d 917, 924 (Mich. Ct. App. 1993).

NY: *Cf.* N.Y. Pub. Health Law § 2967(4) ("A parent or legal guardian of a minor, in making a decision regarding cardiopulmonary resuscitation, shall consider the minor patient's wishes, including a consideration of the minor patient's religious and moral beliefs.").

WA: *In re* Ingram, 689 P.2d 1363, 1370 (Wash. 1984) (ward's expressed wishes must be given "substantial weight") (citing *In re* A.W., 637 P.2d 366 (Colo. 1981)).

593 See **§ 7.10.**

594 *In re* Hier, 464 N.E.2d 959, 965 (Mass. App. Ct. 1984). *See generally* National Center for State Courts, Guidelines for State Court Decision Making in Life-Sustaining Medical Treatment Cases 44 (2d ed. 1992) (standard 6).

patient if the patient is "capable of expressing or manifesting a choice or preference in such situations."[595] Had it been clear, or were it to become clear after a trial of therapy, that the patient's "subjective preferences [were] against initiation or continuation of" treatment, it would then be appropriate to petition to cease the treatment.[596] This, of course, is consistent with the overriding goal of promoting self-determination. Furthermore, if a patient is incompetent but there is a reasonable probability of regaining "sufficient competency to assist in the decisionmaking process," termination or withholding of treatment should be postponed.[597]

Preferences in Conflict with Advance Directive. Conflicts between a patient's wishes made while competent (and expressed in a written or oral advance directive) and views expressed while incompetent provide a particularly difficult problem. The objective of giving effect to the patient's legal and ethical interest in autonomy cannot serve as a useful guidepost in such situations. In effect, in such situations it is unclear "who" the patient is—the incompetent person who is still able to express a preference, or the previously competent person who expressed a different, and possibly diametrically opposed, preference.

Some advance directive statutes contain provisions permitting patients to overrule their advance directives even if the patients are of questionable competency.[598] Such provisions, however, ordinarily do not apply to oral advance directives or to nonstatutory written directives. Nonetheless, they may still provide useful guides as to how to proceed in such circumstances.

Objections to Treatment. If a patient's cooperation is necessary for administering a particular procedure, as a practical matter a patient's objections to such a therapy need to be given substantial deference.[599] If the patient objects to treatment to the point of obstructing it, that the patient is incompetent becomes academic. For example, in *Hier,*[600] an incompetent patient's continual removal of a gastrostomy feeding tube was a significant factor in the court's decision not to order surgery to replace the tube, even though there was no other reasonable alternative for providing her with food and water.

Greater effect should be accorded to an incompetent patient's refusal of treatment when the patient is terminally ill and the treatment will merely prolong the process of dying than in other situations. In the latter case, the state's interest in the preservation of life may outweigh the individual's interests in

---

595 *In re* R.H., 622 N.E.2d 1071, 1077 (Mass. App. Ct. 1993).

596 *Id.* at 1080 n.9.

597 Browning v. Herbert, 543 So. 2d 258, 272 (Fla. Dist. Ct. App. 1989), *aff'd,* 568 So. 2d 4, 16 (Fla. 1990).

598 See §§ **11.14** and **12.38.**

599 Superintendent of Belchertown State Sch. v. Saikewicz, 370 N.E.2d 417, 432 (Mass. 1977).

600 *In re* Hier, 464 N.E.2d 959 (Mass. App. Ct. 1984).

autonomy.[601] To the extent, however, that an incompetent patient must be subjected to physical force for treatment to be administered, the state's interest in administering even lifesaving treatment diminishes, perhaps to the vanishing point.

For the administration of some treatments, patients can be subjected to physical or chemical restraints,[602] but the use of restraints raises legal and ethical issues of its own.[603]

Preferences in Favor of Treatment. Most of the reported cases involving the expression of views about their treatment by incompetent patients have involved opposition to treatment, and the courts have generally accorded such views a measure of respect, sometimes quite strongly. Although perhaps not a very likely occurrence, an incompetent patient could express a preference for treatment that the attending physician and/or the surrogate opposes, or even that the patient himself opposed when competent.

A rule of thumb in these instances is for physicians to err on the side of administering rather than forgoing treatment when the patient expresses a preference for it. Of course, administration of the treatment must not violate professional standards and/or the attending physician's own conscience. If the treatment would be futile, would confer little or no benefit on the patient, or would impose substantial hardship on the patient, the attending physician should not feel absolutely bound to provide it. This is especially so if the surrogate has consented to its withdrawal or withholding. These are the kinds of considerations that should be taken into account by the surrogate in making a decision under virtually any accepted standard for decisionmaking for incompetent patients.[604] However, a factor weighing in favor of treatment in such

---

[601] See § **8.15.**

[602] **MA:** *E.g., In re* Spring, 405 N.E.2d 115, 123 (Mass. 1980) (uncooperative patient "had to be heavily sedated").

NY: *E.g.. In re* Storar, 420 N.E.2d 64, 69 (N.Y. 1981) (patient given sedative to eliminate apprehension and narcotics to alleviate the pain associated with disease).

See Quill, *Utilization of Nasogastric Feeding Tubes in a Group of Chronically Ill, Elderly Patients in a Community Hospital,* 149 Archives Internal Med. 1937, 1940 (1989) (53% of patients with feeding tubes required restraints to prevent them from pulling tubes out).

[603] Lo & Dornbrand, *Understanding the Benefits and Burdens of Tube Feedings,* 149 Archives Internal Med. 1925, 1925 (1989) ("[R]estraints seem undignified, humiliating, or even cruel. Sedation or 'chemical restraints' to prevent patients from pulling out their [feeding] tubes might seem more acceptable aesthetically but are equally undignified and also have significant side effects."). *Cf.* Weiner & Wettstein, *Legal Issues in Mental Health Care* 134–36 (1993).

[604] *See, e.g., In re* Hier, 464 N.E.2d 959, 965 (Mass. App. Ct. 1984) (Expressions of opposition of an incompetent person, although "not to be given legal effect, are nevertheless to be taken into consideration in applying the substituted judgment test because they are indicative of the burden that she feels in being subjected to advanced medical technologies.").

situations is its ability to relieve pain or otherwise improve the patient's quality of life.[605]

§ 7.46 —Weight to Be Accorded Preferences

The weight to be accorded the preferences of an incompetent patient is an issue that has received little attention. On two occasions, however, the Washington Supreme Court has stated that such preferences should be given a great deal of weight.[606] In particular cases, however, the weight given should depend on the degree of the patient's understanding and on the intensity of the patient's preferences.[607] Even if the patient is unable to understand the need for treatment, additional weight should be accorded to the expressed preference if it is "persistent and determined."[608]

---

[605] See **Ch. 19.**

[606] **WA:** *In re* Grant, 747 P.2d 445, 457 (Wash. 1987), *modified,* 757 P.2d 534 (Wash. 1988) ("strong consideration"); *In re* Ingram, 689 P.2d 1363, 1370 (Wash. 1984) ("substantial weight").

MA: *Cf. In re* Roe, 421 N.E.2d 40 (Mass. 1982) (ward's stated preference concerning administration of antipsychotic medication entitled to serious consideration); Doe v. Doe, 385 N.E.2d 995 (Mass. 1979) (incompetent psychiatric patient's stated preference for outpatient treatments must be treated as critical factor in determination of his best interests).

But see Lo & Dornbrand, *Understanding the Benefits and Burdens of Tube Feedings,* 149 Archives Internal Med. 1925, 1925 (1989) ("[R]emoving the [feeding] tube may be a reflex rather than a purposeful action. But . . . pulling out a feeding tube is not an indication for restraints; instead, physicians should reconsider whether tube feedings are appropriate.").

[607] **MN:** *In re* Friedman, 478 N.W.2d 790 (Minn. 1991) ("If the ward has sufficient capacity, the ward's choices may only be denied by the court if found not to be in the ward's best interests.").

WA: *In re* Ingram, 689 P.2d 1363, 1370–71 (Wash. 1984).

[608] **WA:** *In re* Ingram, 689 P.2d at 1371.

MA: *Accord In re* Hier, 464 N.E.2d 959, 964 (Mass. App. Ct. 1984).

Bibliography

Bluestein, J. "The Family in Medical Decisionmaking." *Hastings Center Report,* 23 (May–June 1993): 6.

Bopp, J., and D. Avila. "Perspectives on *Cruzan:* The Sirens' Lure of Invented Consent: A Critique of Autonomy-Based Surrogate Decisionmaking for Legally-Incapacitated Older Persons." *Hastings Law Journal* 42 (1991): 779.

Brant, J. "The Right to Die in Peace: Substituted Consent and the Mentally Incompetent." *Suffolk University Law Review* 11 (1977): 959.

Buchanan, A. "The Limits of Proxy Decisionmaking for Incompetents." *UCLA Law Review* 29 (1981): 386.

Cantor, N. "Prospective Autonomy: On the Limits of Shaping One's Post-competence Medical Fate." *Journal of Contemporary Health Law and Policy* 8 (1992): 13.

Cantor, N. "*Conroy,* Best Interests, and the Handling of Dying Patients." *Rutgers Law Review* 37 (1985): 543.

Cerminara, K. "Refusing Life-Sustaining Treatment for Incompetent Patients: Mere Existence or a Quality Life?" *Medical Trial Techniques Quarterly* 35 (1988): 121.

Developments in the Law. "Medical Technology and the Law." *Harvard Law Review* 103 (1990): 1519.

Dresser, R. "Life, Death, and Incompetent Patients: Conceptual Infirmities and Hidden Values in the Law." *Arizona Law Review* 28 (1986): 378.

Dresser, R. "Missing Persons: Legal Perceptions of Incompetent Patients." *Rutgers Law Review* 46 (1994): 609.

Dresser, R. "Relitigating Life and Death." *Ohio State Law Journal* 51 (1990): 425.

Dresser, R., and J. Robertson. "Quality of Life and Non-Treatment Decisions for Incompetent Patients, A Critique of the Orthodox Approach." *Law, Medicine and Health Care* 17 (1989): 234.

Gostin, L. "A Right to Choose Death: The Judicial Trilogy of *Brophy, Bouvia,* and *Conroy, Law, Medicine and Health Care* 14 (1986): 198.

Hafemeister, T. "Guidelines for State Court Decision Making in Life-Sustaining Medical Treatment Cases." *Issues in Law and Medicine* 7 (1992): 443.

Hardwig, J. "What About the Family?" *Hastings Center Report* 20 (March–April 1990): 50.

Harmon, L. "Falling Off the Vine: Legal Fictions and the Doctrine of Substituted Judgment." *Yale Law Journal* 100 (1990): 1.

Kadish, S. "Letting Patients Die: Legal and Moral Reflections." *California Law Review* 80 (1992): 857.

Kindregan, M. "Mental Incompetents and the Right to Die: A Symposium. The Court as Forum for Life and Death Decisions: Reflections on Procedures for Substituted Consent." *Suffolk University Law Review* 11 (1977): 919.

Krasnik, E. "The Role of the Family in Medical Decisionmaking for Incompetent Adult Patients: A Historical Perspective and Case Analysis." *University of Pittsburgh Law Review* 48 (1987): 539.

Lindgren, J. "Death by Default." *Law and Contemporary Problems* 56 (1993): 185.

Martyn, S. "Substituted Judgment, Best Interests, and the Need for Best Respect." *Cambridge Quarterly of Healthcare Ethics* 3 (1994): 195.

Morgan, R. "How to Decide: Decisions on Life-prolonging Procedures." *Stetson Law Review* 20 (1990): 77.

New York State Task Force on Life and the Law, *When Others Must Choose: Deciding for Patients Without Capacity.* New York: New York State Task Force on Life and the Law, 1992.

Newman, S. "Treatment Refusals for the Critically and Terminally Ill: Proposed Rules for the Family, the Physician, and the State." *Human Rights Annual* 3 (1985): 35.

Pollock, S. "Life and Death Decisions: Who Makes Them and By What Standards?" *Rutgers Law Review* 41 (1989): 505.

Relman, A. "A Response to Allen Buchanan's Views on Decision Making for Terminally Ill Incompetents," *American Journal of Law and Medicine* 5 (1979): 119.

Rhoden, N. "Litigating Life and Death." *Harvard Law Review* 102 (1988): 357.

Richard, S. "Someone Make Up My Mind: The Troubling Right to Die Issues Presented by Incompetent Patients with No Prior Expression of a Treatment Preference." *Notre Dame Law Review* 64 (1989): 394.

Robertson, J. "*Cruzan* and the Constitutional Status of Nontreatment Decisions for Incompetent Patients." *Georgia Law Review* 25 (1991): 1139.

Stacy, T. "Death, Privacy, and the Free Exercise of Religion." *Cornell Law Review* 77 (1992): 490.

Veatch, R. "Limits of Guardian Treatment Refusal: A Reasonableness Standard." *American Journal of Law and Medicine* 9 (1984): 427.

CHAPTER 8

LIMITATIONS ON THE RIGHT TO DIE

§ 8.1 Introduction

Chapter 7 discussed the tests accepted or rejected by various state courts for determining whether life-sustaining treatment recommended by a physician must be administered or may be forgone. However, in particular cases once the accepted standard is applied, there are still other potential barriers to forgoing life-sustaining treatment that courts frequently address before a decision about life-sustaining treatment may be made.[1] Despite a determination that a patient's actual or probable wishes are not to be treated under the circumstances, or that the patient's best interests dictate the same result, there are still other possible limitations on forgoing life-sustaining treatment. This is because "[t]he right of an individual to forego life sustaining treatment has . . . not been considered absolute and [has] been balanced against the right of a state to protect its citizens."[2] This is particularly important when considering incompetent patients. It is less certain that any such limitations apply to competent patients. **Chapters 8** and **9** examine these further limitations.

There has been a slow evolutionary process in the way in which courts have approached this problem. (It is one that has also been confronted by legislatures

---

[1] **DC:** *E.g., In re* A.C., 573 A.2d 1235, 1252 (D.C. 1990) (after court makes a "substituted judgment" for an incompetent patient, court should consider any "conflicting state interest," but cases in which a state interest is "so compelling that the patient's wishes must yield . . . will be extremely rare and truly exceptional").

MA: *E.g., In re* R.H., 622 N.E.2d 1071, 1076 (Mass. App. Ct. 1993) (court should first determine "'what decision would be made by the incompetent person if he or she were competent'" and then "consider any countervailing State interests").

[2] **MN:** *In re* Torres, 357 N.W.2d 332, 339 (Minn. 1984).

DRI: *Accord* Gray v. Romeo, 697 F. Supp. 580 (D.R.I. 1988).

AZ: *Accord* Rasmussen v. Fleming, 741 P.2d 674, 683 (Ariz. 1987).

CA: *Contra* Bouvia v. Superior Court (Glenchur), 225 Cal. Rptr. 297, 307 (Ct. App. 1986) (Compton, J., concurring) ("I believe she has an absolute right to" refuse force feeding.).

CT: *Accord* McConnell v. Beverly Enters.-Conn., Inc., 553 A.2d 596, 608 (Conn. 1989) ("[T]he common law right to refuse medical treatment is not absolute, and, in some cases, may yield to a compelling state interest.").

DE: *Accord In re* Severns, 425 A.2d 156, 158 (Del. Ch. 1980).

MA: *Accord In re* Doe, 583 N.E.2d 1263 (Mass. 1992); Norwood Hosp. v. Munoz, 564 N.E.2d 1017, 1022 (Mass. 1991); Brophy v. New Eng. Sinai Hosp., Inc., 497 N.E.2d 626, 634 (Mass. 1986).

MO: *Accord* Cruzan v. Harmon, 760 S.W.2d 408, 419 (Mo. 1988), *aff'd,* Cruzan v. Director, 497 U.S. 261 (1990).

NJ: *Accord In re* Farrell, 529 A.2d 404, 410 (N.J. 1987); *In re* Conroy, 486 A.2d 1209, 1223 (N.J. 1985).

NY: *Accord In re* Storar, 420 N.E.2d 64, 67 (N.Y.), *cert. denied,* 454 U.S. 858 (1981); Delio v. Westchester County Medical Ctr., 516 N.Y.S.2d 677, 691 (App. Div. 1987).

PA: *Accord In re* Doe, 45 Pa. D. & C.3d 371, 383 (C.P. Phila. County 1987).

in the drafting of advance directive statutes.[3]) Although this process is still under way, several approaches have emerged. They will be referred to as (1) the categorical approach,[4] (2) the prognostic approach,[5] and (3) the balancing approach.[6] There is some conceptual overlap in some of these approaches, and a particular judicial opinion may employ elements of more than one of them.

In the first decade or so of right-to-die litigation, the courts explored a variety of possible ways to impose limitations on the right to die for both competent and incompetent patients. Since about 1985, however, these efforts have been increasingly formalistic, especially for competent patients, and more and more devoid of true substantive restrictions. The New Jersey Supreme Court's statement in the *Conroy* case that year that "[o]n balance, the right to self-determination ordinarily outweighs any countervailing state interests, and competent persons generally are permitted to refuse medical treatment, even at the risk of death,"[7] marked the formal recognition of this process. Since that time, the barriers to forgoing life-sustaining treatment have gradually eroded not just for competent patients but also for incompetent patients. It is increasingly the case that life-sustaining medical treatment may be forgone without regard to the patient's prognosis—that is, even if the patient is not terminally ill or permanently unconscious, or if the patient's condition is not "hopeless" or "incurable"—and regardless of any interests the state might assert in keeping the patient alive.

§ 8.2 Limitations on Decisions of Competent Patients

Prior to the era of right-to-die litigation beginning with the *Quinlan* case in 1976, the courts had encountered the issue of refusal of treatment a relatively small number of times. These refusals were almost uniformly based on religious belief and almost uniformly involved patients of the Jehovah's Witness faith who were refusing blood transfusions, a medical procedure proscribed by this religion. When actually faced with cases in which the refusal of treatment would lead to the patient's death, courts strongly but reluctantly espoused the right to refuse treatment, so reluctantly that in few judicial cases were the patients actually permitted to refuse the treatment.

The means by which courts circumvented the right to refuse treatment was the invocation of a set of interests the state was said to have in not allowing even a competent person to die.[8] When these countervailing state interests were

---

[3] See §§ **11.9** and **12.17.**

[4] See §§ **8.4–8.8.**

[5] See §§ **8.9–8.13.**

[6] See §§ **8.14–8.19.**

[7] *In re* Conroy, 486 A.2d 1209, 1225 (N.J. 1985).

[8] See §§ **8.14–8.19.**

invoked either singly or in combination, they were frequently found to outweigh the patient's interest in the refusal of treatment. Sometimes the right to refuse treatment was overcome by finding the patient incompetent, in no small part because the patient refused treatment rather than because of the patient's actual decisionmaking capacity. Although in these cases the patients' decisionmaking capacity was not always free from doubt, the fact that courts sometimes resolved close cases by finding that the patients lacked decisionmaking capacity is an indication of their unwillingness to honor the refusal of treatment that would lead, it was said, to their deaths.[9] Sometimes patients' refusals were overridden by finding that societal interests in the well-being of the patients' minor children demanded that the patient not be allowed to die,[10] and sometimes by finding that the ethical integrity of the health care professions demanded that the patient not be allowed to die.[11]

Today, however, judicial thinking in cases of this sort has been strongly influenced by the intervening right-to-die decisions—that is, by cases in which courts have permitted the termination of life-sustaining medical treatment because competent patients judge their life not worth living, or the families of incompetent patients determine that the patient would not have wanted to live in this condition or that it is not in the patient's best interests to do so. What is interesting, and probably essential to an understanding of the pre-*Quinlan* cases, is that the administration of the treatment in question almost certainly would not only have saved the patients' lives, but also restored their health. By contrast, in *Quinlan* and its progeny, the patients were hopelessly ill or injured; the treatment in question could not possibly return them to anything approaching the

---

[9] **CADC:** *E.g., In re* President & Directors of Georgetown College, 331 F.2d 1000 (D.C. Cir. 1964).

DIL: *E.g.,* Holmes v. Silver Cross Hosp., 340 F. Supp. 125 (N.D. Ill. 1972).

IL: *But see In re* Estate of Brooks, 205 N.E.2d 435 (Ill. 1965).

NJ: *E.g.,* John F. Kennedy Memorial Hosp. v. Heston, 279 A.2d 670 (N.J. 1971).

NY: *But see* Erickson v. Dilgard, 252 N.Y.S.2d 705 (Sup. Ct. Nassau County 1962).

PA: *But see In re* Green, 292 A.2d 387 (Pa. 1972) (finding 16-year-old patient mature enough to make his own treatment decisions).

[10] **CADC:** *E.g., In re* President & Directors of Georgetown College, 331 F.2d 1000.

NJ: *E.g.,* Raleigh Fitkin-Paul Morgan Memorial Hosp. v. Anderson, 201 A.2d 537 (N.J. 1964); State v. Perricone, 181 A.2d 751 (N.J. 1962).

NY: *E.g.,* Powell v. Columbian Presbyterian Medical Ctr., 267 N.Y.S.2d 450 (Sup. Ct. N.Y. County 1965).

[11] **CADC:** *E.g., In re* President & Directors of Georgetown College, 331 F.2d 1000.

DCT: *E.g.,* United States v. George, 239 F. Supp. 752 (D. Conn. 1965) (patient "stated he would 'in no way' resist the doctors' actions once the Court's order was signed").

NJ: *E.g.,* John F. Kennedy Memorial Hosp. v. Heston, 279 A.2d 670.

NY: *E.g.,* Powell v. Columbian Presbyterian Medical Ctr., 267 N.Y.S.2d at 451 (Sup. Ct. N.Y. County 1965) (patient "did not object to receiving the treatment involved—she would not, however, direct its use").

status quo ante; at most it could prolong the process of dying. Consequently, in these cases the countervailing state interests have been found to be extremely weak, so weak in fact that rarely if ever do they outweigh the individual's interest in forgoing life-sustaining treatment.[12] Furthermore, in the pre-*Quinlan* cases, the patients had no wish to die; they merely sought to refuse a particular treatment.

Despite the distinctions between these two types of cases, the right-to-die cases have had a substantial impact on the pre-*Quinlan* type of right-to-refuse-treatment case. Beginning about 1985—after approximately a decade of right-to-die cases—the courts in a small but slowly growing number of cases have not only recognized, but have also ceased trying to circumvent, the right to refuse treatment by competent patients whose refusals would almost certainly result in their deaths, but for whom treatment was almost certain to restore their health to the status quo ante. Most of these patients, as in the classic pre-*Quinlan* cases, needed a blood transfusion but were prohibited from consenting to it because of their religious beliefs.[13] Some, however, were not of this type. Rather they

---

[12] **CA:** Thor v. Superior Court, 855 P.2d 375 (Cal. 1993); Bouvia v. Superior Court (Glenchur), 225 Cal. Rptr. 297 (Ct. App. 1986).

DC: *In re* Osborne, 294 A.2d 372 (D.C. 1972).

FL: Wons v. Public Health Trust, 541 So. 2d 96 (Fla. 1989); St. Mary's Hosp. v. Ramsey, 465 So. 2d 666 (Fla. Dist. Ct. App. 1985); Satz v. Perlmutter, 362 So. 2d 160 (Fla. Dist. Ct. App. 1978), *aff'd,* 379 So. 2d 359 (Fla. 1980).

GA: State v. McAfee, 385 S.E.2d 651 (Ga. 1989).

IL: *In re* E.G., 549 N.E.2d 322, 328 (Ill. 1989). *Cf. In re* Doe, 632 N.E.2d 326 (Ill. App. Ct. 1994) (interests of fetus need not be considered in decision to permit pregnant woman to refuse caesarean section claimed to be necessary for birth of healthy baby).

MA: Norwood Hosp. v. Munoz, 564 N.E.2d 1017 (Mass. 1991).

NV: *But cf.* McKay v. Bergstedt, 801 P.2d 617 (Nev. 1990) (competent patient's right to refuse treatment is stronger if terminally ill).

NJ: *In re* Farrell, 529 A.2d 404 (N.J. 1987); *In re* Conroy, 486 A.2d 1209, 1225 (N.J. 1985) ("On balance, the right to self-determination ordinarily outweighs any countervailing state interests, and competent persons generally are permitted to refuse medical treatment, even at the risk of death. Most of the cases that have held otherwise, unless they involved the interest in protecting innocent third parties, have concerned the patient's competency to make a rational and considered choice of treatment.").

NY: Fosmire v. Nicoleau, 551 N.E.2d 77 (N.Y. 1990).

National Ctr. for State Courts, Guidelines for State Court Decision Making in Life-Sustaining Medical Treatment Cases 54, 125 (2d ed. 1992) (standard 10; principle A).

[13] **FL:** Wons v. Public Health Trust, 541 So. 2d 96 (Fla. 1989); St. Mary's Hosp. v. Ramsey, 465 So. 2d 666 (Fla. Dist. Ct. App. 1985).

MD: Mercy Hosp. Inc. v. Jackson, 489 A.2d 1130 (Md. Ct. Spec. App. 1985), *vacated and remanded as moot,* 510 A.2d 562 (Md. 1986).

MA: Norwood Hosp. v. Munoz, 564 N.E.2d 1017 (Mass. 1991).

NY: Fosmire v. Nicoleau, 551 N.E.2d 77 (N.Y. 1990).

involved seriously ill[14] or injured[15] patients, whose medical conditions either would not result in death or would do so many years later and who were mentally intact and in touch with their physical and social environments, unlike patients in many right-to-die cases who are in a persistent vegetative state.[16]

In this new generation of right-to-refuse-treatment cases, societal interests in circumventing or overriding the refusal and compelling the administration of treatment have become increasingly less weighty especially when the patient is competent, so that it is not far from the mark to say, as the New Jersey Supreme Court did, that "a competent patient's right to make that decision [to forgo life support] generally will outweigh any countervailing state interests."[17] In other words, although no court has held that the right to refuse treatment is absolute, the outcome of the contemporary cases in the context of the fact patterns of these cases leads to the conclusion that the right of a competent person to refuse medical treatment is virtually absolute.[18] Perhaps the Florida Supreme Court's *Browning* decision comes the closest to finding the right to be absolute in its observation that "the right to make choices about medical treatment . . . encompasses all medical choices. A competent individual has the [state] constitutional right to refuse medical treatment regardless of his or her medical condition."[19]

§ 8.3 Limitations on Decisions for Incompetent Patients

Although the task of imposing limitations on the right to refuse treatment for competent patients has been difficult and probably emotionally wrenching for

---

[14] **CA:** Bouvia v. Superior Court (Glenchur), 225 Cal. Rptr. 297 (Ct. App. 1986).

[15] **GA:** State v. McAfee, 385 S.E.2d 651 (Ga. 1989).

NV: McKay v. Bergstedt, 801 P.2d 617 (Nev. 1990).

[16] See § **9.53.**

[17] *In re* Jobes, 529 A.2d 434, 451 (N.J. 1987).

[18] **CA:** *E.g.,* Thor v. Superior Court, 855 P.2d 375, 387 (Cal. 1993) ("[A] competent, informed adult, in the exercise of self-determination and control of bodily integrity, has the right to direct the withholding or withdrawal of life-sustaining medical treatment, even at the risk of death, which ordinarily outweighs any countervailing state interest."); Bouvia v. Superior Court (Glenchur), 225 Cal. Rptr. 297 (Ct. App. 1986).

FL: *E.g.,* Wons v. Public Health Trust, 541 So. 2d 96 (Fla. 1989); St. Mary's Hosp. v. Ramsey, 465 So. 2d 666 (Fla. Dist. Ct. App. 1985).

GA: *E.g.,* State v. McAfee, 385 S.E.2d 651 (Ga. 1989).

MA: *E.g.,* Norwood Hosp. v. Munoz, 564 N.E.2d 1017 (Mass. 1991).

NV: *E.g.,* McKay v. Bergstedt, 801 P.2d 617 (Nev. 1990).

NJ: *See In re* Conroy, 486 A.2d 1209, 1226 (N.J. 1985).

NY: *See* Fosmire v. Nicoleau, 551 N.E.2d 77, 85 (N.Y. 1990) ("The majority . . . for all practical purposes, leaves the right absolute.").

[19] **FL:** Browning v. Herbert, 568 So. 2d 4, 10 (Fla. 1990).

CA: *Accord* Bouvia v. Superior Court (Glenchur), 225 Cal. Rptr. 297, 301 (Ct. App. 1986) ("exercise [of right to decline life-sustaining medical treatment] requires no one's approval").

judges—for the reasons that the patients *are* competent and otherwise quite healthy apart from the need for the treatment in question—it has not been a terribly difficult intellectual task. Especially as the courts have increasingly found the right to be virtually absolute, the judicial process has consisted more of tearing down limitations than constructing them.

The same cannot be said for cases involving incompetent patients, and especially in the overwhelming proportion of cases in which those patients are near death or permanently unconscious. (Cases in which patients are not "terminally ill" or "permanently unconscious" present even greater difficulties, but to date few have been litigated.[20]) The courts have attempted to devise a variety of formulas to distinguish cases in which patients may forgo treatment that will result in death from those in which they may not. Because of the case-by-case nature of adjudication, the courts have generally not set out with the express purpose of imposing limitations on the right to die. Rather, they have been presented with particular facts and have had to determine whether a particular patient with particular characteristics and a particular illness may forgo treatment that will certainly, or almost certainly, lead to death.

As a result, a few different approaches to imposing limitations on the forgoing of treatment on behalf of incompetent patients have arisen. The dominant one, explicitly mentioned in virtually all cases, is the so-called balancing approach. The other two—the categorical approach and the prognostic approach—have been more implicitly, less clearly, and less successfully articulated.

CATEGORICAL APPROACH

§ 8.4 Categorical Approach: Introduction

Probably the oldest approach to limiting the forgoing of life-sustaining treatment is the *categorical approach.* It is the one most frequently employed in clinical settings by physicians and, as such, plays a significant role in determining whether a clinical case will be transformed into a legal case.

Under this approach, the forgoing or administration of certain therapeutic measures is permitted or forbidden based on categories of distinctions made in law, medical ethics, and theology. These categories are:

- act versus omission
- withholding versus withdrawing treatment

---

[20] **FL:** Browning v. Herbert, 568 So. 2d 4 (Fla. 1990).

MA: *In re* Spring, 405 N.E.2d 115 (Mass. 1980); *In re* Hier, 464 N.E.2d 959 (Mass. App. Ct.), *review denied,* 465 N.E.2d 261 (Mass. 1984). *Cf. In re* Dinnerstein, 380 N.E.2d 134, 135 (Mass. App. Ct. 1978) ("essentially vegetative state").

MI: Martin v. Martin, 517 N.W.2d 749 (Mich. Ct. App. 1994).

WA: *In re* Grant, 747 P.2d 445 (Wash. 1987), *modified,* 757 P.2d 534 (Wash. 1988).

- intended versus unintended consequences
- ordinary versus extraordinary treatment.

Although the categories are intended to aid in analysis, they often are used as a substitute for analysis by serving as accessories in a process of conclusory reasoning. To illustrate by reference to the ordinary/extraordinary distinction, it is sometimes said that a patient may decline extraordinary, but must accept ordinary, life-sustaining treatment. When using this distinction, rather than inquiring into the meaning of these terms, if a decision to decline treatment is acceptable, the treatment is then labeled extraordinary; if the decision is unacceptable, the treatment is denominated ordinary in order to justify the desired result.[21]

The categorical approach predates contemporary right-to-die cases at least in clinical settings, though evidence of its use by courts is hard to come by. Indeed, with the exception of the ordinary/extraordinary distinction,[22] the categorical approach is still used infrequently by courts and is rarely used independently of another approach.

§ 8.5 Act versus Omission (Killing versus "Letting Die")

A distinction sometimes made by courts and commentators is between "acts" and "omissions." (This distinction is sometimes also referred to as "killing" and "letting die.") This is not surprising in light of the role that the distinction often plays in tort and criminal law. Under this distinction, it is sometimes said that a physician may not commit an affirmative act that results in a patient's death, even when authorized by the patient. To do so would be a "killing," and consent is ordinarily ineffective to bar criminal liability[23] and is usually ineffective as a bar to civil liability when the conduct is also criminal.[24] By contrast, a physician is permitted to comply with a patient's request not to administer life-sustaining treatment because that is merely an omission, or a "letting die," which is not culpable.

Although it is true as a general rule of criminal[25] and tort[26] liability that there is no generalized duty to act to benefit others, there are a number of

[21] *See* President's Comm'n for the Study of Ethical Problems in Medicine & Biomedical & Behavioral Research, Deciding to Forego Life-Sustaining Treatment 60–62 (1983) [hereinafter President's Comm'n, Deciding to Forego Life-Sustaining Treatment].

[22] See § **8.8.**

[23] W. LaFave & A. Scott, Criminal Law § 5.11, at 477 (2d ed. 1986).

[24] Restatement (Second) of Torts § 892C(1) (1977).

[25] W. LaFave & A. Scott, Criminal Law § 3.3(a), at 203 ("Generally one has no legal duty to aid another person in peril."); R. Perkins, Perkins on Criminal Law 593 (2d ed. 1969) ("There is no general legal requirement that one must play the part of a Good Samaritan.").

[26] Restatement (Second) of Torts § 314 cmt. a (1963).

sources from which a positive duty to act can nonetheless originate. One such source is a contractual undertaking,[27] which is what a doctor-patient relationship is.[28] Another source of a positive duty to act is a voluntary undertaking to do so,[29] sometimes in combination with the intended beneficiary's reliance upon that voluntary undertaking.[30] A physician may incur a duty to act by having undertaken to do so, even without the knowledge of the patient. Thus, a physician may be legally culpable for an omission when there is a duty to act,[31] just as there may be culpability for an act itself, depending upon the nature and consequences of the act, and possibly upon the physician's state of mind (for example, whether he intended harm or acted with reckless disregard for the consequences, or even merely failed to use reasonable care).

An omission can actually be more culpable than an act when the omission is intentional but the act is merely negligent. For example, if a patient's life is being maintained by intravenous nutrition and hydration, and a health care professional shuts off the IV drip in order to move the patient for an X ray, and forgets to restart the drip when the patient returns, he has arguably engaged in an act—turning off the IV—causing the patient's death. However, if instead of shutting off the drip, he neglects to monitor the bag and fails to replace it when it runs out, his behavior could be characterized as an omission rather than an act. This distinction should not, however, relieve him of the same liability that might have ensued had he shut off the drip. In either case, the physician is subject to liability for negligence. Whether there is liability[32]—and indeed whether the action or inaction is morally licit[33]—depends not on whether the behavior is characterized as an act or an omission but on whether a duty was owed the patient to act or refrain from acting in a particular manner. Thus, the distinction is of little value in understanding when it is and is not legitimate to forgo life-sustaining treatment.[34]

Finally, it has long been recognized in philosophy, theology, medical ethics, and law that the distinction between an act and an omission is often laden with ambiguity.[35] In the above example of turning off the IV in order to move the patient for an X ray, the cause of the patient's death could just as logically be

---

[27] *Id.*

[28] *See, e.g.*, Hurley v. Eddingfield, 59 N.E. 1058 (Ind. 1901) (physician who refused to attend to patient not liable for his death because of absence of contractual undertaking to do so). *See generally* M. McCafferty & S. Meyer, *Medical Malpractice: Bases of Liability* § 102, at 2 (1985).

[29] Restatement (Second) of Torts § 323 (1963).

[30] *Id.* § 324A cmt. e.

[31] **CA:** Barber v. Superior Court, 195 Cal. Rptr. 484, 490 (Ct. App. 1983) ("There is no criminal liability for failure to act unless there is a legal duty to act.").

[32] Rachels, *Active and Passive Euthanasia,* 292 New Eng. J. Med. 78 (1975).

[33] President's Comm'n, Deciding to Forego Life-Sustaining Treatment 67, 72.

[34] **NY:** Delio v. Westchester County Medical Ctr., 516 N.Y.S.2d 677, 689 (App. Div. 1987) (distinction is "of questionable value").

[35] President's Comm'n, Deciding to Forego Life-Sustaining Treatment 62–73.

characterized as an act of forgetting to restart the IV as one of turning off the IV. As the New Jersey Supreme Court observed in *Conroy,*

> [c]haracterizing conduct as active or passive is often an elusive notion, even outside the context of medical decision-making.
>
> "Saint Anselm of Canterbury was fond of citing the trickiness of the distinction between 'to do' (*facere*) and 'not to do' (*non facere*). In answer to the question 'What's he doing?' we say 'He's just sitting there' (positive), really meaning something negative: 'He's not doing anything at all.' "[36]

The court then presented an example of this haziness in the context of forgoing life-sustaining treatment:

> The distinction [between act and omission] is particularly nebulous . . . in the context of decisions whether to withhold or withdraw life-sustaining treatment. In a case like that of Claire Conroy, for example, would a physician who discontinued nasogastric feeding be actively causing her death by removing her primary source of nutrients; or would he merely be omitting to continue the artificial form of treatment, thus passively allowing her medical condition, which includes her inability to swallow, to take its natural course? . . . The ambiguity inherent in this distinction is further heightened when one performs an act within an over-all plan of non-intervention, such as when a doctor writes an order not to resuscitate a patient.[37]

Courts must sometimes go to great lengths to classify behavior as an act or an omission. In *Barber v. Superior Court,*[38] the court was faced with trying to determine whether physicians who had ordered the cessation first of a ventilator and then of nutrition and hydration to a permanently comatose patient had committed culpable homicide. In doing so, the court attempted to determine whether the physicians' behavior was an act or omission, and concluded that

> [e]ven though these life support devices are, to a degree, "self-propelled," each pulsation of the respirator or each drop of fluid introduced in the patient's body by intravenous feeding devices is comparable to a manually administered injection or item of medication. Hence "disconnecting" of the mechanical device is comparable to withholding the manually administered injection or medication.[39]

Having concluded that the behavior was an omission did not, however, resolve the issue of culpability, for the court correctly acknowledged that an omission could be legally culpable if the physicians were under a duty to do what they omitted to do.[40] The same is true of its moral status. As the President's Commission

---

[36] *In re* Conroy, 486 A.2d 1209, 1234 (N.J. 1985) (citing D. Walton, Ethics of Withdrawal of Life-Support Systems 234 (1983)).

[37] *Id.* at 1234 (citing President's Comm'n, Deciding to Forego Life-Sustaining Treatment 65–66).

[38] 195 Cal. Rptr. 484 (Ct. App. 1983).

[39] *Id.* at 490.

[40] *Id.* at 484.

observed, "merely determining whether what was done involved a fatal act or omission does not establish whether it was morally acceptable . . . . Active steps to terminate life-sustaining interventions may be permitted, indeed required, by the patient's authority to forego therapy even when such steps lead to death."[41]

The difficulties with the act/omission analysis—in characterizing conduct as an act or an omission, and in specifying the moral difference that such a characterization should entail—have led to its inconsistent use by courts in right-to-die cases. Although many purport to reject it, in fact they do so only when analyzing the forgoing of life-sustaining treatment. That is, when an affirmative act is required for treatment to be forgone—such as removing a patient from a ventilator[42]—the courts hold that the distinction between act and omission has no legal validity.[43] However, when the issue is whether a patient is to die by the forgoing of life-sustaining treatment versus an affirmative intervention to end the patient's life—such as the administration of a lethal overdose of medication—the distinction is readily employed to permit the former under the aegis of an omission and prohibit the latter as "active" killing.[44]

§ 8.6 Withholding versus Withdrawing Treatment

It is sometimes said that it is permissible to withhold treatment from a dying patient, but that once begun, treatment may not be withdrawn.[45] This distinction is also sometimes referred to as the difference between "not starting" and "stopping" treatment. Regardless of the nomenclature, this distinction is a variation on the distinction between act and omission,[46] and it is no more

---

[41] President's Comm'n, Deciding to Forego Life-Sustaining Treatment 67, 72.

[42] *See, e.g.,* Satz v. Perlmutter, 362 So. 2d 160, 163 (Fla. Dist. Ct. App. 1978) (withdrawing treatment "appears more drastic because affirmatively, a mechanical device must be disconnected, as distinct from mere inaction").

[43] **AZ:** *E.g.,* Rasmussen v. Fleming, 741 P.2d 674, 689 n.24 (Ariz. 1987).

CA: *E.g.,* Barber v. Superior Court, 195 Cal. Rptr. 484 (Ct. App. 1983). *But see* Donaldson v. Van de Kamp, 4 Cal. Rptr. 2d 59, 63 (Ct. App. 1992) (allowing patient to die from refusal of treatment is distinguishable from premortem cryogenic suspension that will cause death).

NJ: *E.g., In re* Conroy, 486 A.2d 1209, 1233–44 (N.J. 1985).

[44] *See* National Ctr. for State Courts, Guidelines for State Court Decision Making in Life-Sustaining Medical Treatment Cases 145 (2d ed. 1992) ("There are significant moral and legal distinctions between letting die . . . and killing."). See **Ch. 18.**

[45] **NJ:** *In re* Conroy, 486 A.2d 1209, 1234 (N.J. 1985) (citing Clouser, *Allowing or Causing: Another Look,* 87 Annals Internal Med. 622, 624 (1977)) (rejecting distinction).

[46] *Id.* ("Discontinuing life-sustaining treatment, to some, is an 'active' taking of life, as opposed to the more 'passive' act of omitting the treatment in the first instance. In the words of one writer, '[T]he difference between taking away that which one has come to count on as normal support for life and not instituting therapy when a new crisis begins . . . fits nicely a basic moral distinction throughout life—we are not morally obligated to help another person, but we are morally obligated not to interfere with his life-sustaining routines.'") (quoting Clouser, *Allowing or Causing: Another Look,* 87 Annals Internal Med. 622, 624 (1977).

satisfactory in making distinctions between permissible and impermissible forgoings of life-sustaining treatment.[47]

There are a number of serious obstacles to the use of the distinction between withholding and withdrawing treatment as a satisfactory means for defining the boundaries of the right to die. First, there is the ambiguity inherent in characterizing conduct either as a "withholding" or a "withdrawing," similar to that which occurs in characterizing behavior as an act or as an omission. Perhaps more fundamentally, however, the distinction ignores the fact that withholding treatment may be culpable when there is a duty to provide it. Although sometimes there is a moral difference between withdrawing and withholding,[48] this is not always the case.

There is a serious practical difficulty with this distinction. It may entail especially pernicious consequences because it may encourage withholding treatment from a patient who may have benefited from it, out of fear that if such benefit does not materialize, the treatment cannot then be discontinued. Contemplating this problem, the New Jersey Supreme Court observed,

> from a policy standpoint, it might well be unwise to forbid persons from discontinuing a treatment under circumstances in which the treatment could permissibly be withheld. Such a rule could discourage families and doctors from even attempting certain types of care and could thereby force them into hasty and premature decisions to allow a patient to die.[49]

---

[47] National Ctr. for State Courts, Guidelines for State Court Decision Making in Life-Sustaining Medical Treatment Cases 143 (2d ed. 1992).

[48] **NJ:** *In re* Conroy, 486 A.2d at 1234.

MA: *Contra* Brophy v. New Eng. Sinai Hosp., Inc., 497 N.E.2d 626, 637–38 (Mass. 1986) ("[T]he distinction between withholding and withdrawing treatment has no moral significance.").

Contra Council on Ethical & Judicial Affairs, American Medical Ass'n, Code of Medical Ethics § 2.20, at 36 (1994).

[49] **NJ:** *In re* Conroy, 486 A.2d at 1234 (citing Lynn & Childress, *Must Patients Always Be Given Food and Water?,* 13 Hastings Center Rep. 17, 19–20 (Oct. 1983)).

US: *Accord* Cruzan v. Director, 497 U.S. 261, 314 (1990) (Brennan, J., dissenting) (rule requiring that life support may only be terminated if there is clear and convincing evidence that patient authorized such termination prior to losing decisionmaking capacity could undercut "[c]urrent medical practice [of using] . . . heroic measures if there is a scintilla of a chance that the patient will recover, on the assumption that the measures will be discontinued should the patient improve"); *In re* Doe, 583 N.E.2d 1263, 1270 (Mass. 1992) ("[I]f the Commonwealth's interest in preserving life could block removal of the tube in cases like this one, then physicians might refrain from using tubes initially in all but the clearest of cases.").

MA: *Accord* Brophy v. New Eng. Sinai Hosp., Inc., 497 N.E.2d 626, 638 (Mass. 1986).

WI: *Accord* L.W. v. L.E. Phillips Career Dev. Ctr., 482 N.W.2d 60, 75 (Wis. 1992) ("In the absence of such a protected right [to refuse life-sustaining treatment], physicians may be discouraged from attempting certain life-sustaining medical procedures in the first place, knowing that once connected they may never be removed.").

See also Hastings Ctr., Guidelines on the Termination of Life-Sustaining Treatment and the Care of the Dying 130 (1987) (Part Six, II) [hereinafter Hastings Center Guidelines]; President's Comm'n, Deciding to Forego Life-Sustaining Treatment 73–77.

This is not merely a hypothetical concern. In *Tune v. Walter Reed Army Medical Hospital,*[50] the patient could not be taken off a ventilator without a court order because a Department of the Army policy "precluded the withdrawal of life support systems once placed in operation."[51] The court observed that if the doctors had known of the patient's malignancy and lung disease, they would not have ordered her put on a respirator in the first place.[52] This would have denied her the opportunity for recovery, a result that in fact did not materialize, but this could not have been known before the fact.

Despite these problems with using the distinction between withholding and withdrawing treatment as a guide for the application of the right to die, there is an undeniable psychological difference between the two. Health care professionals frequently subscribe to the view, expressed in *Satz v. Perlmutter,* "that [withdrawing treatment] appears more drastic because affirmatively, a mechanical device must be disconnected, as distinct from mere inaction."[53] As a result, health care professionals are far more reticent about stopping treatment than withholding it at the outset. As true as this may be, the distinction was still rejected by the *Perlmutter* court, as it has been by others that have considered it.[54] Nonetheless, the courts have generally concluded that the distinction between withholding and withdrawing treatment should not be determinative of whether treatment may be foregone.[55]

---

[50] 602 F. Supp. 1452, 1453 (D.D.C. 1985).

[51] *Id.*

[52] *Id.*

[53] 362 So. 2d 160, 163 (Fla. Dist. Ct. App. 1978).

[54] **MD:** *But cf. In re* Riddlemoser, 564 A.2d 812, 816 n.5 (Md. 1989) (court "note[s] that the power to withhold treatment and the power to withdraw treatment are separate and distinct" but attaches no significance to the distinction).

MA: *In re* Hier, 464 N.E.2d 959, 964 (Mass. App. Ct. 1984).

NV: McKay v. Bergstedt, 801 P.2d 617, 625 (Nev. 1990) ("no difference between the patient who refuses treatment and the one who accepts treatment and later refuses its continuance because of a resulting loss in the quality of life").

OH: *Cf.* Leach v. Akron Gen. Medical Ctr., 426 N.E.2d 809, 814–15 (C.P. P. Div. Summit County, Ohio 1980) ("[N]o state interest, either legal or societal, exists to the degree necessary to outweigh the Constitutional right" to prevent "withdrawal of extraordinary life support system for the terminally ill in an irreversible, vegetative coma.").

[55] **DRI:** *E.g.,* Gray v. Romeo, 697 F. Supp. 580 (D.R.I. 1988).

AZ: *E.g.,* Rasmussen v. Fleming, 741 P.2d 674, 689 n.24 (Ariz. 1987).

CA: *E.g.,* Bartling v. Superior Court, 209 Cal. Rptr. 220, 225–26 n.4 (Ct. App. 1984).

FL: *E.g.,* Satz v. Perlmutter, 362 So. 2d 160, 163 (Fla. Dist. Ct. App. 1978).

ME: *E.g., In re* Swan, 569 A.2d 1202, 1205 n.4 (Me. 1990) (fact that patient's body rejected gastrostomy tube that would need to be reinserted to sustain life does not distinguish it from situation in which authority is sought to end tube feeding).

MA: *E.g.,* Brophy v. New Eng. Sinai Hosp., Inc., 497 N.E.2d 626, 638 (Mass. 1986).

NJ: *E.g., In re* Jobes, 529 A.2d 434, 444 n.9 (N.J. 1987).

§ 8.7 Intended versus Unintended Consequences ("Double Effect")

Another distinction sometimes used by theologians and ethicists, and less frequently by physicians and courts, to distinguish permissible conduct of physicians in the care of dying patients from impermissible conduct is the distinction between "intended" consequences and "unintended but foreseeable" consequences. This distinction is related to the philosophical principle of *double effect,* originating in Roman Catholic moral theology, which states that there are situations in which it is morally justifiable to cause evil in the pursuit of good.[56] In moral terms, the physician causes an evil, the death of the patient, in the pursuit of accomplishing a good, the amelioration of pain.

The classic example of the application of the principle of double effect in the right-to-die context is the administration by a physician of a pain-killing medication to a terminally ill patient suffering from intractable pain, which, though not intended to be lethal, in fact turns out to be lethal. In such a case, the physician's intent is to relieve the patient's suffering, which is a morally and legally (as long as the drug is legal) acceptable practice. (Indeed, one would fault a doctor—and doctors are increasingly being faulted[57]—for not providing adequate pain relief medication to a suffering patient.) The unintended consequence is that the patient dies because the drugs used as analgesics, most notably morphine, also serve to depress respiration.[58] As the pain becomes more intractable, larger doses of morphine are needed, which eventually can depress the patient's respiration to the point where death results.

There are a number of interpretations of the principle of double effect;[59] under some, causing the death of the patient under such circumstances would be

---

NY: *E.g.,* Elbaum v. Grace Plaza of Great Neck, Inc., 544 N.Y.S.2d 840, 846 (App. Div. 1989) ("[T]he fact that the Elbaum family did not object to the initial use of a nasogastric tube and other extraordinary medical procedures . . . is not fatal to the plaintiff's case. The record reflects that at that point in time, Mrs. Elbaum's condition had not been diagnosed as 'hopeless'."). *But cf.* Workmen's Circle Home & Infirmary for the Aged v. Fink, 514 N.Y.S.2d 893, 896 (Sup. Ct. Nassau County 1987) (permitting withholding of gastrostomy but requiring continuation of intravenous feeding).

WA: *E.g., In re* Grant, 747 P.2d 445 (Wash. 1987), *modified,* 757 P.2d 534 (Wash. 1988).

See also Hastings Center Guidelines 130 (Part Six, II).

[56] *See* May, *Double Effect, in* Encyclopedia of Bioethics 316 (W. Reich ed., 1978); D. Kelly, The Emergence of Roman Catholic Medical Ethics in North America: An Historical, Methodological, Bibliographical Study (1979); Barry & Maher, *Indirectly Intended Life-Shortening Analgesia: Clarifying the Principles,* 6 Issues L. & Med. 117 (1990); Symposium, *Doctrine of Double Effect,* 16 J. Med. & Phil. 467–585 (1991).

[57] See § **9.38.**

[58] *See* Schneiderman & Spragg, *Ethical Decisions in Discontinuing Mechanical Ventilation,* 318 New Eng. J. Med. 984, 987 (1988).

[59] *See* May, *Double Effect, in* Encyclopedia of Bioethics 316 (W. Reich ed., 1978).

morally justifiable. If a physician administered a lethal dose of analgesic medication larger than needed to control pain or to a patient not suffering from pain, with the intent to end the patient's life, such conduct might be culpable homicide.[60] When a lethal dose is administered to a patient for the purpose of controlling or eliminating pain and death is the unintended consequence of such act, should it be considered culpable?[61] One problem with the distinction between intended and unintended but foreseeable consequences is that people do not always act with a single intent. The physician who administers a dose large enough to relieve pain might intend not merely to relieve the pain, but to end the patient's life so as to permanently relieve the patient's suffering.[62] Not only is there a mixed intent, but also it is probably usually impossible to know what other intents the physician might have had besides the licit one of providing relief from pain.

Only a few courts have had occasion to consider the principle of double effect, but none have condemned it.[63] Some recognize that a patient's "right to be free from pain at the time the ventilator [or other life support system] is disconnected is inseparable from his right to refuse medical treatment,"[64] and authorize or order the use of appropriate medications. However, recognizing that the use of strong doses of analgesic medications to avoid pain can inadvertently end the patient's life, one court has provided immunity to the physician in

---

[60] See **Ch. 18.**

[61] President's Comm'n, Deciding to Forego Life-Sustaining Treatment 78.

[62] *See, e.g.,* Wilson et al., *Ordering and Administration of Sedatives and Analgesics During the Withholding and Withdrawal of Life Support from Critically Ill Patients,* 267 JAMA 949, 951 (1992) (among physicians who administered medications in the process of forgoing life-sustaining treatment, although 36% stated that one reason for doing so was to hasten death, "[i]n no instance was hastening death cited as the only reason for ordering drugs").

[63] **MA:** *But see* Brophy v. New Eng. Sinai Hosp., Inc., 497 N.E.2d 626, 640 (Mass. 1986) (Nolan, J., dissenting) (The ethical principle of double effect is "totally inapplicable" to the facts because the patient "will not die from the aneurysm which precipitated loss of consciousness, the surgery which was performed, the brain damage that followed or the insertion of the G-tube. He will die as a direct result of the refusal to feed him.") (citing Bannon, *Rx: Death by Dehydration,* 12 Hum. Life Rev. No. 3, at 70 (1986)).

[64] **GA:** State v. McAfee, 385 S.E.2d 651, 652 (Ga. 1989).

FL: *See also* Fla. Stat. Ann. § 458.326(3) ("Physician may prescribe or administer any controlled substance . . . to a person for the treatment of intractable pain" in accordance with generally accepted medical standards.).

MN: *See also* Minn. Stat. Ann. § 609.215(a) (legitimating principle of double effect by providing that administration, prescription, or dispensation of "medications or procedures to relieve another person's pain or discomfort, even if the medication or procedure may hasten or increase the risk of death," is not abetting or aiding suicide "unless the medications or procedures are knowingly administered, prescribed, or dispensed to cause death").

NV: *Accord* McKay v. Bergstedt, 801 P.2d 617 (Nev. 1990).

TN: *See also* Tenn. Code Ann. § 39-13-216(b)(2) (same as Minnesota above).

such circumstances.[65] The American Medical Association officially recognizes the validity of the principle of double effect.[66]

General principles of criminal and tort liability are not necessarily consonant with the principle of double effect. The principle of double effect overlooks the fact that actors are legally required to consider not only the intended consequences of their conduct, but also those consequences that they know are substantially certain to ensue both in criminal[67] and tort[68] law. Also, the failure to consider those consequences that are reasonably foreseeable is a ground for tort liability for negligence[69] and can be the basis for criminal liability for negligent homicide.[70]

There is a great deal of similarity between the principle of double effect and the act/omission distinction.[71] What is troublesome about the administration of a treatment that, in effect, kills pain by killing the patient is that the conduct involves an "active" taking of life. Indeed, it is precisely this kind of conduct—the administration of a lethal dose of a medication—which is usually envisioned by the term *mercy killing*.[72] If such conduct is culpable, it is not because it constitutes an "act," but because the consequences are brought about in conjunction with the intent (actual or constructive) to cause death.

Like the distinctions between act and omission,[73] and withholding and withdrawing,[74] the distinction between intended and unintended consequences employed in the principle of double effect provides an uncertain basis for imposing limitations on the right to die. In some instances, bona fide treatment which

---

[65] **NV:** McKay v. Bergstedt, 801 P.2d at 631 ("In all cases decided by a district court in favor of the patient, the court's order shall specify that any physician or health care provider who assists the patient in receiving the benefits of his or her decision with minimal pain, shall not be subject to civil or criminal liability.").

[66] *See* Council on Ethical & Judicial Affairs, American Medical Ass'n, Code of Medical Ethics § 2.20, at 37 (1994) ("Physicians have an obligation to relieve pain and suffering . . . of dying patients in their care. This includes providing effective palliative treatment even though it may foreseeably hasten death."); American Medical Ass'n, Current Opinions of the Council on Ethical and Judicial Affairs § 2.20, at 18 (1992) ("For humane reasons, with informed consent, a physician may do what is medically necessary to alleviate severe pain, or cease or omit treatment to permit a terminally ill patient to die when death is imminent. However, the physician should not intentionally cause death."); Council on Ethical & Judicial Affairs, American Medical Ass'n, *Decisions Near the End of Life,* 267 JAMA 2229, 2231 (1992) ("'[T]he administration of a drug necessary to ease the pain of a patient who is terminally ill and suffering excruciating pain may be appropriate medical treatment even though the effect of the drug may shorten life.'").

[67] *See* Model Penal Code § 2.02(2)(b).

[68] *See* Restatement (Second) of Torts § 8A (1963).

[69] *Id.* § 284(a).

[70] Model Penal Code § 210.4.

[71] See § **8.5** and **Ch. 18.**

[72] See § **18.19.**

[73] See § **8.5.**

[74] See § **8.6.**

nevertheless causes death might be warranted, and in other instances it might not, and the principle of double effect does not always provide a principled and consistent means for distinguishing between them.

§ 8.8 Ordinary versus Extraordinary Treatment

The fourth set of distinctions on which courts sometimes rely in imposing limitations on the right to die is the distinction between "ordinary" and "extraordinary" treatment. (Extraordinary treatments are sometimes also referred to as "heroic"[75] or "artificial."[76]) At one time, though increasingly less so, conventional wisdom maintained that "[m]edical ethics . . . permit[s] and support[s] the termination of extraordinary means of treatment or life support systems where there is no hope of a cure and where this is the wish of the patient and his family."[77] That is, the ethics of the medical profession permit patients to decline extraordinary treatment even if doing so will lead to their death, but they are required to accept ordinary treatment.[78] Laypersons are also inclined to employ the ordinary/extraordinary distinction in thinking about what kind of medical treatment they might or might not want.[79]

---

[75] **NJ:** *In re* Conroy, 486 A.2d 1209, 1235 (N.J. 1985) (citing President's Comm'n, Deciding to Forego Life-Sustaining Treatment 84).

PA: Ragona v. Preate, 11 Fiduc. Rep. 2d 1, 6 (C.P. Lackawanna County, Pa. 1990).

[76] **NJ:** *In re* Conroy, 486 A.2d 1209, 1235 (N.J. 1985) (citing President's Comm'n, Deciding to Forego Life-Sustaining Treatment 84); *In re* Quinlan, 355 A.2d 647, 652 (N.J. 1976).

NY: Saunders v. State, 492 N.Y.S.2d 510, 515 (Sup. Ct. Nassau County 1985) ("[T]erminally ill comatose patients have the right to refuse or discontinue extraordinary means of artificial life-support devices.").

[77] **NY:** *In re* Storar, 433 N.Y.S.2d 388, 393 (Sup. Ct. Monroe County), *aff'd,* 434 N.Y.S.2d 46 (App. Div. 1980), *rev'd,* 420 N.E.2d 64 (N.Y. 1981). *Cf.* Delio v. Westchester County Medical Ctr., 516 N.Y.S.2d 677, 687 (App. Div. 1987) (hospital argued that artificial nutrition and hydration was extraordinary treatment); Vogel v. Forman, 512 N.Y.S.2d 622 (Sup. Ct. Nassau County 1986); *In re* Lydia E. Hall Hosp., 455 N.Y.S.2d 706, 710 (Sup. Ct. Nassau County 1982).

CT: *Cf.* Foody v. Manchester Memorial Hosp., 482 A.2d 713, 719–20 (Conn. Super. Ct. 1984).

DE: *Accord* Severns v. Wilmington Medical Ctr., Inc., 421 A.2d 1334, 1349 (Del. 1980).

MA: *Accord* Superintendent of Belchertown State Sch. v. Saikewicz, 370 N.E.2d 417, 423–24 (Mass. 1977). *But see* Brophy v. New Eng. Sinai Hosp., Inc., 497 N.E.2d 626, 637 (Mass. 1986) (distinction between ordinary and extraordinary treatment is a "factor to be considered" but should not be sole or major factor).

See generally Lewis, *Machine Medicine and Its Relation to the Fatally Ill,* 206 JAMA 387 (1968), *quoted in* Superintendent of Belchertown State Sch. v. Saikewicz, 370 N.E.2d at 423.

[78] **NJ:** *In re* Conroy, 464 A.2d 303 (N.J. Super. Ct. App. Div. 1983), *rev'd,* 486 A.2d 1209 (N.J. 1985).

[79] *See, e.g.,* DeGrella v. Elston, 858 S.W.2d 698, 703 (Ky. 1993) ("'[S]he expressed explicitly on many occasions her desire that her life not be maintained if she would come to be under conditions which would require extraordinary means to preserve her life.'").

Although it is sometimes said that the *state* may have an interest in compelling patients to accept ordinary treatment but that there is no compelling state interest in forcing patients to submit to extraordinary treatments,[80] courts have almost unanimously rejected[81] this once sacred tenet of medical ethics[82] as providing a useful basis for limiting the forgoing of life-sustaining treatment, in part because distinguishing between ordinary and extraordinary treatments is difficult, and applying the distinction even more so.[83]

---

[80] **OH:** Leach v. Akron Gen. Medical Ctr., 426 N.E.2d 809, 814–15 (C.P. P. Div. Summit County, Ohio 1980).

[81] **DRI:** *Cf.* Gray v. Romeo, 697 F. Supp. 580, 588 (D.R.I. 1988) ("While this is a factor to be considered, recent decisions have criticized the distinction as one without meaning.").

AZ: *E.g.,* Rasmussen v. Fleming, 741 P.2d 674, 689 n.24 (Ariz. 1987).

FL: *E.g.,* Browning v. Herbert, 568 So. 2d 4, 12 n.6 (Fla. 1990).

KY: *E.g.,* DeGrella v. Elston, 858 S.W.2d at 707 n.5 (citing National Ctr. for State Courts, Guidelines for State Court Decision Making in Life-Sustaining Medical Treatment Cases 143–45 (2d ed. 1992)).

MA: *E.g.,* Brophy v. New Eng. Sinai Hosp., Inc., 497 N.E.2d 626, 637 (Mass. 1986) ("[T]he distinction between extraordinary and ordinary treatment obscures the real issue.").

MO: *E.g.,* Cruzan v. Harmon, 760 S.W.2d 408, 421 (Mo. 1988) ("Since *Quinlan,* the medical profession moved to abandon any distinction between extraordinary and ordinary treatment in considering the propriety of withdrawing life-sustaining treatment.").

NY: *But see In re* Beth, 587 N.E.2d 1377, 1383 (Mass. 1992) (Nolan, J., dissenting). *But cf.* Workmen's Circle Home & Infirmary for the Aged v. Fink, 514 N.Y.S.2d 893, 896 (Sup. Ct. Nassau County 1987) (permitting withholding of gastrostomy but requiring continuation of intravenous feeding and antibiotics).

PA: *E.g.,* Ragona v. Preate, 11 Fiduc. Rep. 2d 1, 6 (C.P. Lackawanna County, Pa. 1990).

[82] **FL:** John F. Kennedy Memorial Hosp. v. Bludworth, 452 So. 2d 921, 926 (Fla. 1984) (attending physician must certify patient's "existence is being sustained only through the use of extraordinary life-sustaining treatment measures"); Satz v. Perlmutter, 379 So. 2d 359, 360 (Fla. 1980).

MA: Superintendent of Belchertown State Sch. v. Saikewicz, 370 N.E.2d 417, 423–24 (Mass. 1977).

NY: *In re* Storar, 433 N.Y.S.2d 388, 393 (Sup. Ct. Monroe County 1980) ("Medical ethics currently permit and support the termination of extraordinary means of treatment or life support systems where there is no hope of a cure and where this is the wish of the patient and his family."); Vogel v. Forman, 512 N.Y.S.2d 622, 624 (Sup. Ct. Nassau County 1986) (nasogastric tube cannot be removed because "feeding a patient is ordinary"); Saunders v. State, 492 N.Y.S.2d 510, 515 (Sup. Ct. Nassau County 1985) (patient could forgo administration of oxygen because "[t]he right of a terminally ill competent adult to discontinue extraordinary medical treatment is well established"); *In re* Lydia E. Hall Hosp., 455 N.Y.S.2d 706, 710 (Sup. Ct. Nassau County 1982).

OH: *Cf.* Leach v. Akron Gen. Medical Ctr., 426 N.E.2d 809, 814–15 (C.P. P. Div. Summit County, Ohio 1980).

[83] **MA:** *See* Brophy v. New Eng. Sinai Hosp., Inc., 497 N.E.2d 626, 638 n.34 (Mass. 1986) ("'As with the other terms discussed, defining and applying a distinction between ordinary and extraordinary treatment is both difficult and controversial and can lead to inconsistent results, which makes the terms of questionable value in the formulation of public policy in this area.'") (quoting President's Comm'n, Deciding to Forego Life-Sustaining Treatment 83, 87–88).

The distinction between ordinary and extraordinary treatment and its use to determine when treatment must be accepted and when it might be refused has its origins in Roman Catholic moral theology[84] and, in cases involving Catholic patients, hospitals, and/or physicians, Catholic clergy serving as expert witnesses have characterized the treatment sought to be forgone as either ordinary or extraordinary.[85] When used as originally intended in Catholic moral theology to take into account the benefits and burdens imposed by a particular treatment, the distinction between ordinary and extraordinary treatment can be helpful in distinguishing between acceptable and unacceptable decisions to forgo life-sustaining treatment.[86] However, it is not always used in this precise fashion.

For many, the distinction between ordinary and extraordinary treatments has become a substitute for analysis.[87] In both clinical and judicial practice, the distinction is often used in a conclusory fashion. Adopting the President's Commission's view on this point, the New Jersey Supreme Court observed that

> while the analysis [employing the distinction between ordinary and extraordinary treatment] may be useful in weighing the implications of the specific treatment for the patient, essentially it merely restates the question. . . . As the President's Commission noted: "The claim, then, that the treatment is extraordinary is more of an expression of the conclusion than a justification for it."[88]

Any number of cases applying the distinction between ordinary and extraordinary treatment give evidence to the conclusory manner in which it is often

---

NJ: *Compare In re* Clark, 510 A.2d 136 (N.J. Super. Ct. Ch. Div. 1986) (testimony of expert witness that an enterostomy procedure for artificial nutrition and hydration is extraordinary treatment) *with In re* Conroy, 486 A.2d 1209 (N.J. 1985) (holding that distinction is not helpful).

See also National Ctr. for State Courts, Guidelines for State Court Decision Making in Life-Sustaining Medical Treatment Cases 144 (2d ed. 1992).

84 *See In re* Conroy, 486 A.2d 1209, 1235 (N.J. 1985); President's Comm'n, Deciding to Forego Life-Sustaining Treatment 82.

85 **MA:** *E.g.*, Brophy v. New Eng. Sinai Hosp., Inc., 497 N.E.2d 626 (Mass. 1986).

NJ: *E.g., In re* Quinlan, 355 A.2d 647 (N.J. 1976).

NY: *E.g.*, Delio v. Westchester County Medical Ctr., 516 N.Y.S.2d 677, 683 (App. Div. 1987) (testimony of Jesuit priest and professor of philosophy that Vatican document published in 1980 rejected distinction between ordinary and extraordinary means of life support as a measure of when it would be ethical to discontinue those means and adopted proportionality test); *In re* Lydia E. Hall Hosp., 455 N.Y.S.2d 706, 710 (Sup. Ct. Nassau County 1982) (Catholic clergyman testified dialysis is extraordinary, not ordinary, treatment.).

86 **CT:** Foody v. Manchester Memorial Hosp., 482 A.2d 713, 719–20 (Conn. Super. Ct. 1984).

NJ: *In re* Conroy, 486 A.2d 1209, 1235 (N.J. 1985); *In re* Quinlan, 355 A.2d at 658–59; Eichner v. Dillon, 426 N.Y.S.2d 517, 527 n.5 (App. Div. 1980); *In re* Storar, 433 N.Y.S.2d 388, 392 (Sup. Ct. Monroe County 1980).

87 **CA:** *See* Barber v. Superior Court, 195 Cal. Rptr. 484, 491 (Ct. App. 1983) ("The use of these terms begs the question.").

88 *In re* Conroy, 486 A.2d at 1235 (citing President's Comm'n, Deciding to Forego Life-Sustaining Treatment 88).

used. For instance, in the *Foody* case, involving a woman suffering from multiple sclerosis whose existence was being sustained by a respirator, the court first acknowledged that medical ethics permits the forgoing of extraordinary treatment and then relied on the testimony of her attending physician who "consider[ed] the use of the respirator an extraordinary measure."[89]

Moreover, the distinction between ordinary and extraordinary treatment is hazy,[90] in part because these terms exist along a continuum rather than as discrete entities. Thus, their application to particular treatments is bound to lead to disagreement even among physicians. Any medical concept that physicians cannot give a concrete meaning to is likely to trouble other decisionmakers or reviewing entities. Nonetheless, courts sometimes rely on expert witnesses to make the distinctions for them.[91]

Thus, the use of this distinction to place limits on the forgoing of life-sustaining treatment has rightly been the subject of substantial criticism. Notable is that of the New Jersey Supreme Court in *Conroy,* which observed that in general usage, in medical practice, and in law, "the terms [ordinary and extraordinary] . . . have assumed too many conflicting meanings to remain useful. To draw a line on this basis for determining whether treatment should be given leads to a semantical milieu that does not advance the analysis."[92] This is hardly surprising in light of the varied and imprecise meanings given to the terms.

Another difficulty with the distinction is that "ordinary" and "extraordinary" are relative terms and, as the standards by which they are given content change, the conclusion that a particular treatment is ordinary or extraordinary will also change. What is extraordinary today may be quite common tomorrow.[93] Similarly, what is ordinary treatment for a particular patient under particular circumstances may be extraordinary for the same patient under different circumstances, or for a different patient under the same circumstances.[94] For example, the New

---

[89] Foody v. Manchester Memorial Hosp., 482 A.2d at 720.

[90] **NY:** Eichner v. Dillon, 426 N.Y.S.2d 517, 527 n.5 (App. Div. 1980); *In re* Lydia E. Hall Hosp., 455 N.Y.S.2d 706 (Sup. Ct. Nassau County, 1982).

[91] *See, e.g., In re* Lydia E. Hall Hosp., 455 N.Y.S.2d at 710 (Roman Catholic clergyman testified that "dialysis to the church is an extraordinary, not an ordinary, treatment. An extraordinary means is defined as something beyond which you are called upon to undergo to sustain life.").

[92] **NJ:** *In re* Conroy, 486 A.2d at 1235 (N.J. 1985) (citing President's Comm'n, Deciding to Forego Life-Sustaining Treatment 87).

CT: *Accord* McConnell v. Beverly Enters.-Conn., Inc., 553 A.2d 596, 606 (Conn. 1989) (Healey, J., concurring) (unable to agree with majority analysis based on distinction between "artificial technology to assist nutrition and hydration, and normal procedures to assist in feeding," and characterization of a gastrostomy tube as a "life support system").

NY: *Accord In re* Westchester County Medical Ctr. (O'Connor), 531 N.E.2d 607, 625 (N.Y. 1988) (Simons, J., dissenting) ("[P]hysicians do not even agree on what is 'extraordinary' or 'ordinary' care.").

[93] **MA:** Brophy v. New Eng. Sinai Hosp., Inc., 497 N.E.2d 626, 638 n.33 (Mass. 1986).

[94] **NJ:** *In re* Conroy, 486 A.2d 1209, 1235 (N.J. 1985).

Jersey Supreme Court explained in *Quinlan* that "one would have to think that the use of the same respirator or life support could be considered 'ordinary' in the context of the possibly curable patient but 'extraordinary' in the context of the forced sustaining of an irreversibly doomed patient."[95] In other words, not only is the distinction a hazy one, but it sometimes is nonexistent, at least in the case of incurably ill patients.[96]

Some courts employ the distinction but without any effort to analyze it.[97] However, possibly because of all of the difficulties with this distinction, courts that do employ it do not use it quite so mechanically as its simple wording suggests. Rather, courts that use this approach often do so as one consideration among several to determine whether a particular patient may forgo a treatment. It is used in conjunction with other approaches, most notably the prognostic approach[98] involving considerations of whether the patient is terminally, incurably, or hopelessly ill,[99] or what the quality of the patient's life will be if the treatment is administered.[100]

Ordinary treatments have been defined as those that "'offer a reasonable hope of benefit and which can be obtained without excessive expense, pain, or other inconvenience. Extraordinary means are all medicines, treatments and operations which cannot be obtained or used without excessive expense, pain or other inconvenience, or if used, would not offer a reasonable hope of benefit.'"[101] The

---

[95] **NJ:** *In re* Quinlan, 355 A.2d 647, 668 (N.J. 1976).

DE: *Accord In re* Severns, 425 A.2d 156, 159 (Del. Ch. 1980) (When the patient is in apparently nonreversible state, "distinction between ordinary and extraordinary medical treatment becomes blurred.").

NY: *Cf. In re* Storar, 433 N.Y.S.2d 388, 392 (Sup. Ct. Monroe County 1980) ("Under the circumstances of this case, the blood transfusions are extraordinary treatments.").

[96] **DE:** *In re* Severns, 425 A.2d 156, 159 (Del. Ch. 1980).

[97] **NY:** *E.g.*, Saunders v. State, 492 N.Y.S.2d 510, 515 (Sup. Ct. Nassau County 1985).

OH: *E.g.*, Leach v. Akron Gen. Medical Ctr., 426 N.E.2d 809, 814–15 (C.P. P. Div. Summit County, Ohio 1980).

[98] See §§ **8.9–8.13.**

[99] **CT:** *E.g.*, Foody v. Manchester Memorial Hosp., 482 A.2d 713 (Conn. Super. Ct. 1984).

NJ: *E.g.*, *In re* Conroy, 486 A.2d 1209, 1225 (N.J. 1985) (an "irreversibly doomed" patient) (citing *In re* Quinlan, 355 A.2d 647, 668 (N.J. 1976)).

NY: *E.g.*, *In re* Storar, 433 N.Y.S.2d 388, 393 (Sup. Ct. Monroe County 1980).

See §§ **8.10–8.12.**

[100] **CT:** *E.g.*, Foody v. Manchester Memorial Hosp., 482 A.2d 713, 720 (Conn. Super. Ct. 1984).

MA: *E.g.*, Superintendent of Belchertown State Sch. v. Saikewicz, 370 N.E.2d 417, 423–24 (Mass. 1977).

NY: *E.g.*, Saunders v. State, 492 N.Y.S.2d 510, 515 (Sup. Ct. Nassau County 1985).

See §§ **7.22–7.24.**

[101] Foody v. Manchester Memorial Hosp., 482 A.2d at 719 (quoting Kelly, Medico-Moral Problems 129 (1959)).

distinction is sometimes framed in terms of the benefits and burdens conferred by the treatment,[102] and it has sometimes been analogized to the distinction between simple and complex treatment.[103] In this usage, extraordinary treatment is equated with treatments that are elaborate, artificial, heroic, aggressive, expensive, or highly invasive.[104] Unfortunately such synonyms advance the analysis no more than do the original labels that they are intended to elucidate.

Despite the substantial criticism leveled at the ordinary/extraordinary distinction, some new life has been breathed into it by its transformation into a "benefits/burdens" approach to defining the best interests standard.[105] The advantage of this reformulation is that it is "extremely fact-sensitive"[106] and therefore can be expected to "lead to different classifications of the same treatment in different situations."[107]

PROGNOSTIC APPROACH

§ 8.9 Prognostic Approach: Introduction

Another approach frequently used by courts for imposing limitations on the right to die (often in combination with the balancing approach[108]) is the prognostic

---

[102] **NJ:** *In re* Conroy, 486 A.2d 1209, 1235 (N.J. 1985) (citing President's Comm'n, Deciding to Forego Life-Sustaining Treatment 84–85 n.122 ("If the benefits of the treatment outweigh the burdens it imposes on the patient, it is characterized as ordinary and therefore ethically required; if not, it is characterized as extraordinary and therefore optional.")).

[103] *Id.* at 1235 (citing President's Comm'n, Deciding to Forego Life-Sustaining Treatment 84).

[104] *Id.*

[105] **CT:** Foody v. Manchester Memorial Hosp., 482 A.2d 713, 719 (Conn. Super. Ct. 1984).

NJ: *In re* Conroy, 486 A.2d at 1235.

NY: Eichner v. Dillon, 426 N.Y.S.2d 517, 527 n.5 (App. Div. 1980) ("Ordinary treatments have been defined as all medicines, treatments and operations which offer a reasonable hope of benefit and which can be obtained and used without excessive pain or other inconvenience. Extraordinary treatments, on the other hand, are those which involve excessive expense, pain or other inconvenience or, in the alternative, are those which do not offer a reasonable hope of benefit."); *In re* Storar, 433 N.Y.S.2d 388, 392 (Sup. Ct. Monroe County 1980).

See §§ **7.11–7.25.**

[106] *In re* Conroy, 486 A.2d at 1235.

[107] **NJ:** *In re* Conroy, 486 A.2d at 1235.

CA: *Accord* Barber v. Superior Court, 195 Cal. Rptr. 484, 491–92 (Ct. App. 1983) (quoting *In re* Quinlan, 355 A.2d 647 (N.J. 1976)).

[108] See §§ **8.14–8.19.**

approach. Under this approach, the patient's prognosis is central,[109] although this is not always immediately apparent from the judicial opinions. Courts usually do not refer overtly to prognosis as the central issue, instead, frequently using a variety of labels—such as terminally ill, incurably ill, or hopelessly ill—to distinguish patients who have a right to die from those who do not.

These labels describe the patient's prognosis should the treatment at issue be administered (either alone or in combination with other treatment). Their implicit (or sometimes explicit) meaning is that, even if the treatment were administered, the patient would either die anyway within a relatively brief period of time, remain permanently comatose,[110] or, although able to live indefinitely, exist in a condition "smothered by physical pain and suffering . . . from which there was no hope of release other than death."[111]

Although many courts employ prognostic terminology in discussing limitations on forgoing life-sustaining treatment, the prognostic approach has come under increasing criticism, especially in the case of competent patients or incompetent patients whose wishes are clearly known, as unduly restricting the

---

[109] **DNY:** *E.g., In re* Department of Veterans Affairs Medical Ctr., 749 F. Supp. 495 (S.D.N.Y.), *aff'd,* 914 F.2d 239 (2d Cir. 1990).

CA: *E.g.,* Drabick v. Drabick, 245 Cal. Rptr. 840, 860–61 (Ct. App. 1988); Barber v. Superior Court, 195 Cal. Rptr. 484, 492 (Ct. App. 1983).

CT: *E.g.,* Foody v. Manchester Memorial Hosp., 482 A.2d 713, 718–19 (Conn. Super. Ct. 1984).

NV: *E.g.,* McKay v. Bergstedt, 801 P.2d 617, 625 (Nev. 1990) ("The primary factors that distinguish Kenneth's type of case from that of a person desiring suicide are attitude, physical condition and prognosis.").

NJ: *E.g., In re* Conroy, 486 A.2d 1209, 1219 (N.J. 1985) (patient "suffering from serious and permanent mental and physical impairments . . . will probably die within approximately one year even with the treatment"); *In re* Quinlan, 355 A.2d 647, 669 (N.J. 1976) ("[T]he focal point of decision should be the prognosis as to the reasonable possibility of return to cognitive and sapient life.").

See also Smedira et al., *Withholding and Withdrawal of Life Support from the Critically Ill,* 322 New Eng. J. Med. 309 (1990) (prognosis is key in physicians' decisions to recommend termination of life support).

[110] **MN:** *In re* Torres, 357 N.W.2d 332, 334 (Minn. 1984) ("'[H]e will not recover as a mentating human being and will not recover consciousness nor regain an ability to communicate or respond or regain any ability to use any of his extremities. . . . The prognosis for his recovery is nil.'").

[111] **NV:** McKay v. Bergstedt, 801 P.2d at 624, 626.

CA: *Accord* Thor v. Superior Court, 855 P.2d 375, 384 (Cal. 1993) ("Especially when the prognosis for full recovery from serious illness or incapacitation is dim, the relative balance of benefit and burden must lie within the patient's exclusive estimation: 'That personal weighing of values is the essence of self-determination.'"); Bouvia v. Superior Court (Glenchur), 225 Cal. Rptr. 297 (Ct. App. 1986).

GA: *Accord* State v. McAfee, 385 S.E.2d 651 (Ga. 1989).

individual interest in self-determination.[112] Perhaps the most explicit statement of this position is the opinion of the Florida Supreme Court in *Browning v. Herbert* that

> [r]ecognizing that one has the inherent right to make choices about medical treatment, we necessarily conclude that this right encompasses all medical choices. A competent individual has the constitutional right to refuse medical treatment regardless of his or her medical condition.[113]

This is also true if the patient is not competent. Although many advance directive statutes originally restricted their applicability to patients who were terminally ill, many have been amended to permit the forgoing of life-sustaining treatment if patients are in a persistent vegetative state.[114]

Although prognostic terminology is usually used by courts to limit the situations in which a right to die exists, occasionally courts use such terminology to expand the right. In *Quinlan,* the court noted that, although Karen Quinlan had "no realistic possibility of returning to any semblance of cognitive or sapient life,"[115] and so could be considered terminally or hopelessly ill, its holding "might . . . be applicable in divers other types of terminal medical situations . . . not necessarily involving the hopeless loss of cognitive or sapient life."[116] This statement was later borne out by the court's holding in *Conroy,* not only applying but extending the *Quinlan* principles to patients not necessarily suffering from a "hopeless loss of cognitive or sapient life."[117] It was just this potential for expanding, rather than limiting, the boundaries of the right to die that was the basis for the rejection of this approach by the Missouri Supreme Court in *Cruzan v. Harmon:*

---

[112] **CA:** Thor v. Superior Court, 855 P.2d 375 (Cal. 1993); Bouvia v. Superior Court (Glenchur), 225 Cal. Rptr. 297 (Ct. App. 1986).

DC: *In re* Osborne, 294 A.2d 372 (D.C. 1972).

FL: Wons v. Public Health Trust, 541 So. 2d 96 (Fla. 1989); St. Mary's Hosp. v. Ramsey, 465 So. 2d 666 (Fla. Dist. Ct. App. 1985).

GA: State v. McAfee, 385 S.E.2d 651.

MA: Norwood Hosp. v. Munoz, 564 N.E.2d 1017 (Mass. 1991).

NV: McKay v. Bergstedt, 801 P.2d 617 (Nev. 1990).

NJ: *In re* Conroy, 486 A.2d 1209, 1226 (N.J. 1985) ("[I]f she were competent, Ms. Conroy's right to self-determination would not be affected by her medical condition or prognosis.").

NY: Fosmire v. Nicoleau, 551 N.E.2d 77 (N.Y. 1990).

[113] 568 So. 2d 4, 13 (Fla. 1990).

[114] See **§§ 11.12** and **12.17.**

[115] 355 A.2d 647, 661 (N.J. 1976).

[116] *Id.* at 671 n.10.

[117] *In re* Conroy, 486 A.2d 1209, 1228–29 (N.J. 1985).

> Where the patient is not terminally ill, as here, the profoundly diminished capacity of the patient and the near certainty that that condition will not change leads inevitably to quality of life considerations. That argument . . . that [the patient] will not recover, is but a thinly veiled statement that her life in its present form is not worth living . . . [which] does not support a decision to cause death.[118]

The Michigan Court of Appeals has weakened even further the use of prognosis as a limitation on the right to die, permitting life-sustaining treatment to be forgone from a patient who was neither terminally ill nor in a persistent vegetative state, though severely brain damaged.[119]

The right of self-determination is the primary consideration in decision-making about medical treatment. What is central should be the patient's actual[120] or probable[121] wishes or, if not known or reasonably knowable, the patient's interests,[122] rather than the nature of the patient's condition. The patient's wishes or interests might reasonably take into account the nature of the patient's condition, but the condition alone should not be determinative.

The following sections discuss the prognostic terminology actually or purportedly used by courts to impose limitations on the right to die. **Sections 11.9** and **12.17** present parallel discussions with respect to living will and health care power of attorney legislation, respectively.

§ 8.10 Terminal Illness

Courts frequently purport to limit the right to die to those who are *terminally ill.*[123] Sometimes the term is used in combination with other prognostic terms,

---

[118] 760 S.W.2d 408, 422 (Mo.1988), *aff'd,* Cruzan v. Director, 497 U.S. 261 (1990).

[119] **MI:** Martin v. Martin, 517 N.W.2d 749 (Mich. Ct. App. 1994).

DE: *See also* Newmark v. Williams, 588 A.2d 1108 (Del. 1991).

FL: *See also* Browning v. Herbert, 568 So. 2d 4 (Fla. 1990).

MA: *See also In re* Spring, 405 N.E.2d 115 (Mass. 1980); *In re* Hier, 464 N.E.2d 959 (Mass. App. Ct. 1984). *Cf. In re* Dinnerstein, 380 N.E.2d 134, 135 (Mass. App. Ct. 1978) ("essentially vegetative state").

WA: *See also In re* Grant, 747 P.2d 445 (Wash. 1987), *modified,* 757 P.2d 534 (Wash. 1988).

[120] See §§ **7.4–7.6.**

[121] See §§ **7.7–7.10.**

[122] See §§ **7.11–7.25.**

[123] **DDC:** Tune v. Walter Reed Army Medical Hosp., 602 F. Supp. 1452, 1458–59 (D.D.C. 1985) ("[S]tate's interest in maintaining life must defer to the right to refuse treatment of a competent, emotionally stable, but terminally ill adult whose death is imminent and who is, therefore, the best, indeed, the only, true judge of how such life as remains to him may best be spent.").

FL: Satz v. Perlmutter, 379 So. 2d 359, 360 (Fla. 1980) (patient must be terminally ill).

such as "irreversible"[124] or "incurable."[125] It generally is used as a term of inclusion: patients who are terminally ill are said to have a right to forgo life-sustaining treatment. However, the implication has arisen that it is also a term of exclusion, that is, that patients who are not terminally ill do not have the right to refuse life-sustaining treatment,[126] an implication that is increasingly not the case for competent patients and that is slowly eroding for incompetent patients.[127] It is now clear from the large number of cases permitting

---

IL: *In re* Estate of Greenspan, 558 N.E.2d 1194, 1201 (Ill. 1990) ("surrogate can exercise the right [to forgo life-sustaining treatment] only if: patient is 'terminally ill' as deemed in section 2(h) of the Illinois Living Will Act (Ill. Rev. Stat. 1987, ch. 110-1/2, par. 702(h)), i.e., the patient's condition is incurable and irreversible so that death is imminent and the application of death-delaying procedures serves only to prolong the dying process" even when there is no living will).

ME: *In re* Gardner, 534 A.2d 947 (Me. 1987).

NV: McKay v. Bergstedt, 801 P.2d 617, 630 (Nev. 1990) ("[I]f the patient is terminally ill or injured . . . the patient's constitutional and common law rights of self-determination shall be deemed to prevail over the . . . State interests.").

NY: Eichner v. Dillon, 426 N.Y.S.2d 517, 550 (App. Div. 1980) (applies to patients who are "incurably and terminally ill," who were in a persistent vegetative state, and whose "prospects of regaining cognitive brain function are extremely remote"); *In re* Lydia E. Hall Hosp., 455 N.Y.S.2d 706, 712 (Sup. Ct. Nassau County 1982) (patient's decision to forgo treatment honored where "based on a compelling desire to escape the constant and severe pain caused by his multiple debilitating irreversible and terminal conditions"). *Cf.* Workmen's Circle Home & Infirmary for the Aged v. Fink, 514 N.Y.S.2d 893 (Sup. Ct. Nassau County 1987) (terminally ill patient has right to forgo extraordinary, but not ordinary, treatment).

WA: *In re* Grant, 747 P.2d 445, 450 (Wash. 1987), *modified,* 757 P.2d 534 (Wash. 1988); *In re* Colyer, 660 P.2d 738, 742 (Wash. 1983) ("adult who is incurably and terminally ill" has a right to die).

[124] *In re* Dinnerstein, 380 N.E.2d 134, 139 (Mass. App. Ct. 1978) ("This case does not offer a life-saving or life-prolonging treatment alterative. . . . It presents a question peculiarly within the competence of the medical profession of what measures are appropriate to ease the imminent passing of an irreversibly, terminally ill patient in light of the patient's history and condition and the wishes of her family.").

[125] **NY:** *E.g.,* Delio v. Westchester County Medical Ctr., 510 N.Y.S.2d 415 (Sup. Ct. Westchester County 1986), *rev'd,* 516 N.Y.S.2d 677 (App. Div. 1987).

WA: *E.g., In re* Grant, 747 P.2d at 449–51 (patient variously described as "incurably ill," "terminally ill," "terminal and incurable").

[126] **NV:** *E.g.,* McKay v. Bergstedt, 801 P.2d 617 (Nev. 1990) (competent patient's right to refuse treatment is stronger if terminally ill).

NY: *E.g.,* Delio v. Westchester County Medical Ctr., 510 N.Y.S.2d 415, *rev'd,* 516 N.Y.S.2d 677.

[127] *Compare* Cruzan v. Harmon, 760 S.W.2d 408, 419 (Mo. 1988) ("state's interest in prolonging life is particularly valid" when patient is in a persistent vegetative state and thus not terminally ill) *with* McConnell v. Beverly Enters-Conn., Inc., 553 A.2d 596 (Conn. 1989) (patient in a persistent vegetative state is terminally ill and thus artificial nutrition and hydration may be discontinued).

withdrawing life support from patients in a persistent vegetative state (patients who are not terminally ill) that classification as terminally ill is not a sine qua non for forgoing life-sustaining treatment.[128] Furthermore, other courts have permitted life-sustaining treatment to be withheld or withdrawn when a patient is neither terminally ill nor in a persistent vegetative state, especially if the

---

AZ: *See* Rasmussen v. Fleming, 741 P.2d 674 (Ariz. 1987).

CA: *See* Thor v. Superior Court, 855 P.2d 375, 387 (Cal. 1993) (right to refuse life-sustaining medical treatment "is [not] reserved to those suffering from terminal conditions"); Donaldson v. Van de Kamp, 4 Cal. Rptr. 2d 59, 62 (Ct. App. 1992) ("right to refuse treatment or life-sustaining measures is not limited to those who are terminally ill"); Bouvia v. Superior Court (Glenchur), 225 Cal. Rptr. 297 (Ct. App. 1986); Bartling v. Superior Court, 209 Cal. Rptr. 220 (Ct. App. 1984).

FL: *See* Browning v. Herbert, 568 So. 2d 4, 13 (Fla. 1990); Wons v. Public Health Trust, 541 So. 2d 96 (Fla. 1989); St. Mary's Hosp. v. Ramsey, 465 So. 2d 666 (Fla. Dist. Ct. App. 1985).

GA: *See In re* Doe, 418 S.E.2d 3, 5 & n.4 (Ga. 1992); State v. McAfee, 385 S.E.2d 651 (Ga. 1989).

IL: *See In re* E.G., 549 N.E.2d 322, 328 (Ill. 1989) (competent patient who is likely to die within month without blood transfusions but who with them and chemotherapy is about 80% likely to achieve remission of disease may decline treatment). *But see In re* Estate of Greenspan, 558 N.E.2d 1194, 1201 (Ill. 1990) ("surrogate can exercise the right [to forgo life-sustaining treatment] only if: patient is 'terminally ill' as defined in section 2(h) of the Illinois Living Will Act (Ill. Rev. Stat. 1987, ch 1101/2, para. 702(h)), i.e., the patient's condition is incurable and irreversible so that death is imminent and the application of death-delaying procedures serves only to prolong the dying process" even when there is no living will); Estate of Longeway v. Community Convalescent Ctr., 549 N.E.2d 292, 293 (Ill. 1989) ("incompetent patient must be terminally ill before this right to refuse artificial sustenance may be exercised").

ME: *See In re* Gardner, 534 A.2d 947 (Me. 1987).

MA: *See* Norwood Hosp. v. Munoz, 564 N.E.2d 1017 (Mass. 1991); Brophy v. New Eng. Sinai Hosp., Inc., 497 N.E.2d 626 (Mass. 1986).

NV: *See* McKay v. Bergstedt, 801 P.2d 617 (Nev. 1990).

NJ: *See In re* Farrell, 529 A.2d 404 (N.J. 1987); *In re* Conroy, 486 A.2d 1209, 1225 (N.J. 1985) ("[T]he right to self-determination ordinarily outweighs any countervailing state interests, and competent persons generally are permitted to refuse medical treatment, even at the risk of death.").

NY: *See* Fosmire v. Nicoleau, 551 N.E.2d 77, 82–84 (N.Y. 1990); Delio v. Westchester County Medical Ctr., 516 N.Y.S.2d 677, 691 (App. Div. 1987) ("no practical or logical reason to limit the exercise of the right of self determination with respect to one's body to terminally ill patients").

[128] *Cf.* National Ctr. for State Courts, Guidelines for State Court Decision Making in Life-Sustaining Medical Treatment Cases 143 (2d ed. 1992) ("The use of terms such as 'terminal illness,' 'terminal condition,' and 'imminently dying' often create more confusion than clarity in [life-sustaining medical treatment] decisions.").

patient is competent,[129] but also if the patient is incompetent. In one case a patient was severely brain damaged but not in a persistent vegetative state—specifically, his

> injuries left him totally paralyzed on his left side but with some limited, though mainly nonfunctional, movement of his right limbs. He cannot eat, walk, or talk, and he has no bladder or bowel control. He is dependent on a feeding tube for nutrition and a colostomy for defecation. Although . . . his cognitive abilities were also seriously affected, Michael remains conscious, he has some awareness of his surroundings, and he can communicate to some extent through head nods.[130]

However, the fact that he was not terminally ill was not determinative. Rather, it "would merely be considered as a factor in determining whether the withholding or withdrawal of life-sustaining medical treatment serves the patient's best interests."[131]

The concept of terminal illness can be conceptualized in two quite distinct ways with significantly different results. One is that the patient will die within a relatively short period of time even if the treatment in question is administered.[132] This is a very narrow concept that significantly constricts the class of

---

[129] **CA:** Thor v. Superior Court, 855 P.2d 375 (Cal. 1993); Bouvia v. Superior Court (Glenchur), 225 Cal. Rptr. 297 (Ct. App. 1986).

DC: *In re* Osborne, 294 A.2d 372 (D.C. 1972).

FL: Wons v. Public Health Trust, 541 So. 2d 96 (Fla. 1989); Satz v. Perlmutter, 362 So. 2d 160 (Fla. Dist. Ct. App. 1978), *aff'd,* 379 So. 2d 359 (Fla. 1980); St. Mary's Hosp. v. Ramsey, 465 So. 2d 666 (Fla. Dist. Ct. App. 1985).

GA: State v. McAfee, 385 S.E.2d 651 (Ga. 1989).

IL: *In re* E.G., 549 N.E.2d 322, 328 (Ill. 1989).

MA: Norwood Hosp. v. Munoz, 564 N.E.2d 1017 (Mass. 1991).

NV: *But cf.* McKay v. Bergstedt, 801 P.2d 617 (Nev. 1990) (competent patient's right to refuse treatment is stronger if terminally ill).

NJ: *In re* Farrell, 529 A.2d 404 (N.J. 1987).

NY: Fosmire v. Nicoleau, 551 N.E.2d 77 (N.Y. 1990).

[130] Martin v. Martin, 517 N.W.2d 749, 751 (Mich. Ct. App. 1994).

[131] Martin v. Martin, 504 N.W.2d 917, 923 (Mich. Ct. App. 1993).

[132] **IL:** *But compare In re* Estate of Greenspan, 558 N.E.2d 1194, 1196 (Ill. 1990) (patient in a persistent vegetative state "is terminally ill in the sense that his illness would have been terminal if current means of keeping him alive were unavailable") *with id.* at 1206 (Ward, J., dissenting) ("[U]nder the majority's seeming standard, patients depend[ent] upon artificial nutrition and hydration would qualify as 'terminally ill' within the meaning of the Living Will Act if they have an incurable and irreversible condition. Those patients qualify as 'terminally ill' even if their conditions are not life-threatening. There are conditions which are incurable and irreversible, but do not necessarily produce a condition of imminent death. Exemplary of this are cerebral palsy, many forms of cancer, emphysema, diabetes, cystic fibrosis and multiple sclerosis.").

NY: *In re* Storar, 420 N.E.2d 64, 69 (N.Y. 1981) ("[A]fter using all medical and surgical means then available, the patient would nevertheless die from the disease.").

persons who fit with it. By contrast, some courts (and living will statutes) use the term *terminally ill* to mean that a patient would die in a short period of time if the treatment under consideration were *withdrawn* or *withheld.*[133] Under this meaning, a larger class of persons can be considered to be terminally ill.

Just what constitutes "a relatively short time" is open to a multitude of interpretations. The New Jersey courts use the term to refer to the likelihood of death within a year.[134] Even when a patient's life expectancy is predicted to be greater than a year, that does not necessarily mean that the patient's illness will not be the cause of death. However, in a New York case, an expert witness testified that a patient he believed had a life expectancy with treatment of six months or less was not considered to be terminally ill.[135] Prediction of when death is likely to occur is also not very accurate.[136] Any term as uncertain in meaning as *terminally ill* is a poor criterion in deciding whether treatment may be forgone.[137]

---

[133] **FL:** *E.g.,* Browning v. Herbert, 568 So. 2d 4, 17 (Fla. 1990) (patient suffered from a terminal illness because death was imminent (four to nine days) if the nasogastric tube were removed).

IL: *Compare In re* Estate of Greenspan, 558 N.E.2d at 1196 (patient in a persistent vegetative state "is terminally ill in the sense that his illness would have been terminal if current means of keeping him alive were unavailable") *with id.* at 1206 (Ward, J., dissenting) ("[U]nder the majority's seeming standard, patients depend[ent] upon artificial nutrition and hydration would qualify as 'terminally ill' within the meaning of the Living Will Act if they have an incurable and irreversible condition. Those patients qualify as 'terminally ill' even if their conditions are not life-threatening. There are conditions which are incurable and irreversible, but do not necessarily produce a condition of imminent death. Exemplary of this are cerebral palsy, many forms of cancer, emphysema, diabetes, cystic fibrosis and multiple sclerosis.").

NV: *E.g.,* McKay v. Bergstedt, 801 P.2d 617, 620 (Nev. 1990) ("[A]lthough Kenneth's quadriplegia was irreversible, his affliction was non-terminal so long as he received artificial respiration.").

[134] **NJ:** *In re* Conroy, 486 A.2d 1209, 1231 (N.J. 1985) (holding limited to "elderly, incompetent nursing-home resident[s] with severe and permanent mental and physical impairments and a life expectancy of approximately one year or less"). *See also In re* Jobes, 529 A.2d 434, 456 (N.J. 1987).

NV: *See also* McKay v. Bergstedt, 801 P.2d 617 (Nev. 1990) (patient not terminally ill if he will survive in excess of six months with treatment).

[135] *In re* Lydia E. Hall Hosp., 455 N.Y.S.2d 706, 708 (Sup. Ct. Nassau County 1982).

[136] **FL:** *E.g.,* Browning v. Herbert, 543 So. 2d 258, 268 (Fla. Dist. Ct. App. 1989), *aff'd,* 568 So. 2d 4 (Fla. 1990) ("Predicting that a condition is 'terminal' within any specific time period or opining on the 'imminence' of death has been very difficult for the medical profession. . . . Distinguishing between serious illnesses, life-threatening conditions, and terminal illnesses is frequently difficult for physicians and nearly impossible for the legal community.").

MA: *E.g., In re* Dinnerstein, 380 N.E.2d 134, 135 (Mass. App. Ct. 1978) (patient's condition is "hopeless" but it is difficult to predict exactly when she will die).

[137] Bartling v. Superior Court, 209 Cal. Rptr. 220, 223 (Ct. App. 1984).

§ 8.11 Incurability

Another frequently used prognostic term is "incurably ill."[138] The New Jersey Supreme Court observed in *Quinlan* that "physicians distinguish between curing the ill and comforting and easing the dying; . . . they refuse to treat the curable as if they were dying or ought to die, and . . . have sometimes refused to treat the hopeless and dying as if they were curable."[139] Thus, it is not inconsistent with the sanctity of human life to permit patients to decline medical treatment in a situation of incurable illness even if they are not terminally ill.[140] Not all courts make a fine distinction between incurable illness and terminal illness, and some use them together[141] or with other prognostic terms such as "irreversible."[142]

---

[138] **CA:** *E.g.,* Bouvia v. Superior Court (Glenchur), 225 Cal. Rptr. 297, 305 (Ct. App. 1986).

CT: *E.g.,* Foody v. Manchester Memorial Hosp., 482 A.2d 713, 721 (Conn. Super. Ct. 1984).

FL: *E.g.,* Satz v. Perlmutter, 362 So. 2d 160, 161 (Fla. Dist. Ct. App. 1978); *In re* Barry, 445 So. 2d 365, 372 (Fla. Dist. Ct. App. 1984).

MA: *E.g., In re* Spring, 405 N.E.2d 115, 120 (Mass. 1980).

WA: *E.g., In re* Grant, 747 P.2d 445, 449 (Wash. 1987), *modified,* 757 P.2d 534 (Wash. 1988); *In re* Colyer, 660 P.2d 738, 751 (Wash. 1983).

[139] **NJ:** *In re* Quinlan, 355 A.2d 647, 667 (N.J. 1976).

IL: *Accord In re* Estate of Greenspan, 558 N.E.2d 1194 (Ill. 1990).

See also Council on Ethical & Judicial Affairs, American Medical Ass'n, Code of Medical Ethics § 2.20, at 37 (1994) ("Even if the patient is not terminally ill or permanently unconscious, it is not unethical to discontinue all means of life-sustaining medical treatment in accordance with a proper substituted judgment or best interests analysis."); American Medical Ass'n, Current Opinions of the Council on Ethical and Judicial Affairs § 2.20, at 19 (1992) ("Even if death is not imminent but a patient is beyond doubt permanently unconscious, and there are adequate safeguards to confirm the accuracy of the diagnosis, it is not unethical to discontinue all means of life-prolonging medical treatment.").

[140] **MA:** Superintendent of Belchertown State Sch. v. Saikewicz, 370 N.E.2d 417, 426 (Mass. 1977).

[141] **NY:** *E.g., In re* Storar, 434 N.Y.S.2d 46, 47 (App. Div. 1980); Eichner v. Dillon, 426 N.Y.S.2d 517, 550 (App. Div. 1980) (applies to patients who are "incurably and terminally ill," who were in a persistent vegetative state, and whose "prospects of regaining cognitive brain function are extremely remote").

WA: *E.g., In re* Grant, 747 P.2d 445, 451 (Wash. 1987), *modified,* 757 P.2d 534 (Wash. 1988) ("[A] person has the right to have life sustaining treatment withheld . . . in an advanced stage of a terminal and incurable illness."); *In re* Colyer, 660 P.2d 738, 742 (Wash. 1983).

[142] **CA:** *E.g.,* Thor v. Superior Court, 855 P.2d 375 (Cal. 1993); Bartling v. Superior Court, 209 Cal. Rptr. 220 (Ct. App. 1984). *Contra* Bouvia v. Superior Court (Glenchur), 225 Cal. Rptr. 297 (Ct. App. 1986).

MA: *E.g., In re* Spring, 405 N.E.2d 115 (Mass. 1980); Lane v. Candura, 376 N.E.2d 1232 (Mass. App. Ct. 1978).

NJ: *E.g., In re* Conroy, 486 A.2d 1209 (N.J. 1985).

NY: *E.g.,* Weber v. Stony Brook Hosp. 467 N.Y.S.2d 685 (App. Div.) (per curiam), *aff'd,* 456 N.E.2d 1186 (N.Y.), *cert. denied,* 464 U.S. 1026 (1983); Saunders v. State, 492 N.Y.S.2d 510 (Sup. Ct. Nassau County 1985); *In re* Lydia E. Hall Hosp., 455 N.Y.S.2d 706, 708 (Sup. Ct. Nassau County 1982). *Contra In re* Melideo, 390 N.Y.S.2d 523 (Sup. Ct. Suffolk County 1976); Powell v. Columbian Presbyterian Medical Ctr., 267 N.Y.S.2d 450 (Sup. Ct. N.Y. County 1965).

WA: *E.g., In re* Ingram, 689 P.2d 1363 (Wash. 1984).

Incurably ill may be slightly more expansive than *terminally ill* because it does not denote a time limit within which the patient is expected to die. For example, a patient suffering from emphysema, chronic respiratory failure, an abdominal aneurysm, and a malignant lung tumor who could live for at least a year if he could be weaned from a ventilator was still entitled to have the ventilator disconnected because, even though he was not considered terminally ill, the patient's condition was incurable.[143]

Another example is the *Saikewicz* case, in which the patient was suffering from acute myeloblastic monocytic leukemia, a disease that is ultimately fatal. If treatment is not administered, death will occur within weeks or months, but with treatment there is a 30 to 40 percent chance of temporary remission.[144] A person suffering from this disease and undergoing chemotherapy might reasonably not be considered to be terminally ill. However, it would be appropriate to characterize such a person as incurably ill because the best that can be hoped for is a temporary remission of the illness.

On the other hand, the concept of incurable illness may impose no limits at all because there are any number of illnesses that will ultimately take a patient's life and thus could be called incurable, yet the patient can reasonably expect to live indefinitely, though perhaps with some compromise and progressive degeneration of functioning. The Nevada Supreme Court has provided some guidance in dealing with such cases. In *McKay v. Bergstedt,*[145] it held that when a competent adult patient is not terminally ill, but is "irreversibly sustained or subject to being sustained by artificial life support systems or some form of heroic, radical medical treatment; and [experiences] enduring physical and mental pain and suffering," life support may be forgone because "the individual's right to decide will generally outweigh the State's interest in preserving life."[146]

§ 8.12 Other Prognostic Terms

There are a variety of other prognostic terms used in judicial opinions to attempt to impose some limits on the right to die and to distinguish legitimate from illegitimate behavior in bringing about a patient's death. These terms tend to overlap with each other and with the previously discussed concepts, and are often used in combination with other prognostic terminology.

---

143 **CA:** Bartling v. Superior Court, 209 Cal. Rptr. at 223. *See also* Bouvia v. Superior Court (Glenchur), 225 Cal. Rptr. 297 (Ct. App. 1986) (competent patient suffering from cerebral palsy who is incurably ill but not terminally ill may forgo force feeding).

NV: *See also* McKay v. Bergstedt, 801 P.2d 617 (Nev. 1990) (quadriplegic patient being sustained on a respirator).

144 Superintendent of Belchertown State Sch. v. Saikewicz, 370 N.E.2d 417, 420–21 (Mass. 1977).

145 801 P.2d 617 (Nev. 1990).

146 *Id.* at 624.

Hopelessness. Courts occasionally use the concept of hopelessness of the patient's illness to establish boundaries to the right to die.[147] Under this approach, it is permissible to forgo life-sustaining treatment if an incompetent patient is hopelessly ill but not otherwise. This concept is essentially synonymous with *incurable.*

No Chance of Recovery. Sometimes it is said that treatment may be forgone for patients who have "no chance of recovery," even when the result will be death.[148] Although closely related to the concept of terminal illness, there can be a difference between them, especially if a terminal illness is defined as one that will bring about death in the near future. For instance in the *Spring* case,[149] the patient, suffering from end-stage kidney disease, might have survived for months without hemodialysis, and a life expectancy of five years was conceivable. Although it was possible that death would not ensue for quite some time, "[t]he treatment did not cause a remission of the disease or restore him even temporarily to a normal cognitive, integrated, functioning existence, but simply kept him alive,"[150] but there was no chance for recovery.

Others. Other prognostic terms used by physicians and adopted by courts to place limits on the right to die include "fatally ill,"[151] "no reasonable prospect that the patient will regain cognitive brain function,"[152] "no reasonable medical possibility . . . of regain[ing] any sapient or cognitive function,"[153] "irreversibly ill,"[154]

---

[147] **CT:** *E.g.,* Foody v. Manchester Memorial Hosp., 482 A.2d 713 (Conn. Super. Ct. 1984).

MA: *E.g., In re* Spring, 405 N.E.2d 115, 121 (Mass. 1980).

NJ: *E.g., In re* Conroy, 486 A.2d 1209, 1218 (N.J. 1985) ("'hopelessly ill with no possibility of returning to any sort of cognitive function'").

WA: *E.g., In re* Colyer, 660 P.2d 738, 749 (Wash. 1983).

[148] **MN:** *E.g., In re* Torres, 357 N.W.2d 332, 335 (Minn. 1984).

NY: *E.g.,* Eichner v. Dillon, 420 N.E.2d 64, 72 (N.Y. 1981). *Cf.* Workmen's Circle Home & Infirmary for the Aged v. Fink, 514 N.Y.S.2d 893 (Sup. Ct. Nassau County 1987) (patient with no hope of recovery has right to forgo extraordinary, but not ordinary, treatment).

WA: *E.g., In re* Hamlin, 689 P.2d 1372, 1378 (Wash. 1984).

[149] *In re* Spring, 405 N.E.2d 115 (Mass. 1980).

[150] **MA:** *In re* Spring, 405 N.E.2d at 118.

MN: *Accord In re* Torres, 357 N.W.2d at 335.

[151] Eichner v. Dillon, 420 N.E.2d 64, 66 (N.Y. 1981).

[152] John F. Kennedy Memorial Hosp. v. Bludworth, 452 So. 2d 921, 926 (Fla. 1984).

[153] **OH:** Leach v. Akron Gen. Medical Ctr., 426 N.E.2d 809, 816 (C.P. P. Div. Summit County, Ohio 1980).

GA: *Accord In re* L.H.R., 321 S.E.2d 716, 716 (Ga. 1984).

[154] **CA:** Bouvia v. Superior Court (Glenchur), 225 Cal. Rptr. 297, 305 (Ct. App. 1986).

MA: *In re* Dinnerstein, 380 N.E.2d 134, 139 (Mass. App. Ct. 1978).

NY: *In re* Lydia E. Hall Hosp., 455 N.Y.S.2d 706, 708 (Sup. Ct. Nassau County 1982). *Cf.* Workmen's Circle Home & Infirmary for the Aged v. Fink, 514 N.Y.S.2d 893 (Sup. Ct. Nassau County 1987) (patient with irreversible brain tumor has right to forgo extraordinary, but not ordinary, treatment).

"a very limited natural life expectancy,"[155] and "permanent and irreversible [with] no reasonable return to a cognitive state."[156] These terms are essentially synonymous with other prognostic terms and are often used in conjunction with them.

§ 8.13 Lifesaving versus Life-Sustaining Treatment

Courts sometimes seek to limit the right to forgo treatment by attempting to distinguish between treatments that will save the patient's life and those that will not. There are several phrases for capturing this distinction. Treatments that will save the patient's life—by which it is usually meant that they will return him to the status quo ante, or at least restore a quality of life that the patient, himself, finds acceptable—are referred to as *lifesaving* treatment. In contrast, treatments that will not return the patient to the status quo ante or will not provide the patient with a satisfactory quality of life are referred to in a variety of ways such as "life-sustaining"[157] or "death prolonging." (Confusion is sometimes added by the fact that the same term is sometimes used to apply to totally opposite concepts.[158])

On their face, these terms refer to the effect of the treatment rather than to the patient's prognosis. In substance, they are but proxies for prognostic concepts and terminology. (These distinctions are sometimes used to refer to different qualities of life.[159]) If a treatment is likely to save the patient's life, it is because the patient is not terminally, incurably, or hopelessly ill, or any other like description. By contrast, when patients are terminally, incurably, or hopelessly ill, any treatment that is administered can only be considered to be life-sustaining,[160] or, as courts sometimes say, the treatment would only prolong life,[161]

---

[155] *In re* Beth Israel Medical Ctr. (Weinstein), 519 N.Y.S.2d 511, 517 (Sup. Ct. N.Y. County 1987).

[156] Foody v. Manchester Memorial Hosp., 482 A.2d 713 (Conn. Super. Ct. 1984).

[157] *See* Council on Ethical & Judicial Affairs, American Medical Ass'n, Code of Medical Ethics § 2.20, at 36 (1994) ("Life-sustaining treatment is any treatment that serves to prolong life without reversing the underlying medical condition.").

[158] *Compare In re* Estate of Dorone, 502 A.2d 1271, 1277 (Pa. Super. Ct. 1985), *aff'd,* 534 A.2d 452 (Pa. 1987) (life-preserving is used to mean lifesaving) *with In re* Spring, 405 N.E.2d 115, 121 (Mass. 1980) (life-preserving used synonymously with life-sustaining).

[159] See **§§ 7.22–7.24.**

[160] **NJ:** *E.g., In re* Conroy, 486 A.2d 1209, 1229 & passim (N.J. 1985) ("We hold that life-sustaining treatment may be withheld or withdrawn from an incompetent patient when it is clear that the particular patient would have refused the treatment under the circumstances involved.").

WA: *E.g., In re* Colyer, 660 P.2d 738, 745–56 (Wash. 1983).

[161] **DDC:** *E.g.,* Tune v. Walter Reed Army Medical Hosp., 602 F. Supp. 1452, 1455 (D.D.C. 1985) ("therapy intended merely to prolong life in the face of mortal illness").

AZ: *E.g.,* Rasmussen v. Fleming, 741 P.2d 674, 683–84 (Ariz. 1987).

MA: *E.g., In re* Spring, 405 N.E.2d 115, 120 & passim (Mass. 1980) ("The treatments in question were intrusive and were life-prolonging rather than life-saving; there was no prospect of cure."); *In re* Dinnerstein, 380 N.E.2d 134, 139 (Mass. App. Ct. 1978).

be life-preserving,[162] only prolong the act of dying[163] or the patient's suffering,[164] or postpone death,[165] but would not be lifesaving.[166] In cases such as these, "[t]he problem before the court is not life or death. That question has already been decided."[167] Rather, "the basic question is how long will society require [a patient] to remain on the threshold of certain death suspended and sustained there by artificial life supports."[168] For example, the Massachusetts Appeals Court explained

> that, when the [Massachusetts Supreme Judicial Court] spoke of life-saving or life-prolonging treatments, it referred to treatments administered for the purpose, and with some reasonable expectation, of effecting a permanent or temporary cure of or relief from the illness or condition being treated. "Prolongation of life," as used in the *Saikewicz* case, does not mean a mere suspension of the act of dying, but contemplates, at the very least, a remission of symptoms enabling a return towards a normal, functioning, integrated existence.[169]

NJ: *E.g., In re* Quinlan, 355 A.2d 647, 652 (N.J. 1976) ("prolongation of life through artificial means").

NY: *E.g.,* Eichner v. Dillon, 420 N.E.2d 64, 66 (N.Y. 1981) (question is about "medical treatments or measures to prolong the lives of patients").

162 **PA:** *But see In re* Estate of Dorone, 502 A.2d at 1277, *aff'd,* 534 A.2d 452 (life-preserving used synonymously with lifesaving rather than life-sustaining).

163 **CA:** *E.g.,* Barber v. Superior Court, 195 Cal. Rptr. 484, 490–91 (Ct. App. 1983).

FL: *E.g.,* John F. Kennedy Memorial Hosp. v. Bludworth, 452 So. 2d 921, 924, 926 (Fla. 1984).

GA: *E.g., In re* Doe, 418 S.E.2d 3, 6 (Ga. 1992) (no state interest in maintaining life support when it prolongs death rather than life); *In re* L.H.R., 321 S.E.2d 716, 722 (Ga. 1984).

MA: *E.g., In re* Dinnerstein, 380 N.E.2d 134, 137 (Mass. App. Ct. 1978).

NJ: *E.g., In re* Quinlan, 355 A.2d at 667; *In re* Hughes, 611 A.2d 1148, 1151 (N.J. Super. Ct. App. Div. 1992) (holding that when treatment "can preserve a healthy young woman's life, not prolong a painful and imminent death," there must be "clear, convincing and unequivocal evidence of the incompetent patient's fully informed decision" to forgo treatment).

NY: *E.g., In re* Eichner, 423 N.Y.S.2d 580, 593 (Sup. Ct. Nassau County 1979).

OH: *E.g.,* Leach v. Akron Gen. Medical Ctr., 426 N.E.2d 809, 812 (C.P. P. Div. Summit County, Ohio 1980).

164 **MA:** *E.g.,* Custody of a Minor, 434 N.E.2d 601, 609 (Mass. 1982).

NJ: *E.g., In re* Conroy, 486 A.2d at 1232.

NY: *E.g., In re* Storar, 434 N.Y.S.2d 46, 47 (N.Y. App. Div. 1980); Eichner v. Dillon, 426 N.Y.S.2d 517, 539 (App. Div. 1980).

165 **WA:** *In re* Hamlin, 689 P.2d 1372, 1375–76 (Wash. 1984).

166 **WA:** *In re* Colyer, 660 P.2d 738, 743 (Wash. 1983).

167 Leach v. Akron Gen. Medical Ctr., 426 N.E.2d at 813.

168 **OH:** Leach v. Akron Gen. Medical Ctr., 462 N.E.2d at 812 (patient being kept alive by mechanical ventilator and feeding through nasogastric tube, and no matter how long kept alive, would still eventually succumb to underlying disease process of amyotrophic lateral sclerosis).

FL: *Accord* John F. Kennedy Memorial Hosp. v. Bludworth, 452 So. 2d 921, 924 (Fla. 1984) ("The issue in these cases is not whether a life should be saved. Rather, it is how long and at what cost the dying process should be prolonged.").

169 *In re* Dinnerstein, 380 N.E.2d 134, 137–38 (Mass. App. Ct. 1978).

In other words, in cases of irreversible terminal illness, although there seems to be a choice between life and death, in reality the choice is between immediate death and delayed death possibly accompanied by added suffering.

The common, underlying theme captured in these terms is the patient's *prognosis*—specifically, there is a right to forgo treatment and consequently to die if the prognosis, even with the treatment, is dim. In fact, in such cases "the life-sustaining technology involved . . . is not traditional treatment in that it is not being used to directly cure or even address the pathological condition. It merely sustains biological functions in order to gain time to permit other processes to address the pathology."[170] However, if the treatment can be characterized as lifesaving, it is because the patient's prognosis for recovery if treated is relatively good, and it is therefore less certain that the forgoing of treatment is permissible. The reason for this is that the state has a more substantial interest in compelling treatment to prevent death than it has in compelling treatment merely to postpone the moment of dying.[171]

This approach substitutes labeling for analysis. Attempts to define key terms such as *lifesaving* and *life-sustaining* often result in the use of other terms, some of which are also used to prescribe the boundaries of the right to die, which requires still further definition. For instance, the intermediate appellate court in *John F. Kennedy Memorial Hospital v. Bludworth*[172] defined a life-sustaining procedure as a "medical procedure which utilize[s] mechanical or other artificial means to sustain, restore, or supplant a vital function, which serve[s] only or primarily to prolong the moment of death, and where . . . death is imminent if such procedures are not utilized."[173]

Also, as with other simple distinctions designed to separate those cases in which treatment may be forgone from those in which it may not, the distinction between lifesaving and life-sustaining treatment can be a hazy one. For example, there are a number of reported cases in which patients need the amputation of a limb because of gangrene that will probably lead to death if surgery is not performed.[174] The general condition of these patients is usually very poor unless surgery is performed, and even then they might not survive. Moreover, there is a chance that if the surgery is not performed they might *not*

---

170 Barber v. Superior Court, 195 Cal. Rptr. 484, 490 (Ct. App. 1983).

171 See §§ **8.14–8.19.**

172 432 So. 2d 611 (Fla. Dist. Ct. App. 1983), *rev'd,* 452 So. 2d 921 (Fla. 1984).

173 432 So. 2d at 619.

174 **DNY:** *E.g., In re* Department of Veteran's Affairs Medical Ctr., 749 F. Supp. 495, 495 (S.D.N.Y.), *aff'd,* 914 F.2d 239 (2d Cir. 1990).

MA: *E.g.,* Lane v. Candura, 376 N.E.2d 1232 (Mass. App. Ct. 1978).

NJ: *E.g., In re* Quackenbush, 383 A.2d 785 (N.J. Super. Ct. P. Div. 1978); *In re* Schiller, 372 A.2d 360 (N.J. Super. Ct. Ch. Div. 1977).

NY: *E.g., In re* Beth Israel Medical Ctr. (Weinstein), 519 N.Y.S.2d 511 (Sup. Ct. N.Y. County 1987); *In re* Nemser, 273 N.Y.S.2d 624 (Sup. Ct. N.Y. County 1966).

TN: *E.g.,* State Dep't of Human Resources v. Northern, 563 S.W.2d 197 (Tenn. Ct. App. 1978).

die[175] and might continue to lead life much the same as before with impaired physical and/or mental functioning but not necessarily be bedridden, wheelchair-bound, or comatose. Is the treatment in such cases lifesaving or life-sustaining? Clearly no generalization can be made to any class of cases, and an answer in any particular case can also be very uncertain because of prognostic uncertainty.

In some cases in which a treatment is characterized as lifesaving, the patient's health can be restored to the status quo ante or some close approximation, so that he can be expected to lead a relatively normal life. However, in other cases, restoration to the status quo ante is merely restoration to a state in which the patient can be expected to succumb relatively soon to some other illness from which he is suffering or even to some other aspect of the same illness for which treatment is administered. For example, in the *Storar* case,[176] the administration of blood transfusions would most likely have prevented the patient from bleeding to death, but that would mean that he would soon die from bladder cancer.[177] In this respect, the blood transfusions are like food: "they would not cure the cancer, but they could eliminate the risk of death from another treatable cause."[178] As a consequence, the court saw them as lifesaving, rather than life-sustaining, and required that they be administered even though experts had testified that "at this stage [in the patient's illness], transfusions may only prolong suffering and that treatment could properly be limited to administering pain killers."[179]

Efforts to distinguish permissible from impermissible forgoing of treatment in this manner have undergone significant erosion. The increasing number of cases since *Quinlan* in which courts have permitted the forgoing of life-sustaining treatment by patients who are deemed terminally ill or who otherwise have an extremely dim prognosis for recovery seems to have had an increasing impact on cases not involving such patients, that is, on cases involving patients whose lives could probably be saved and a quality of life acceptable to them sustained if treatment were administered, especially if the patients are competent or are incompetent but have an applicable advance directive. Although most of these

---

[175] *See, e.g., In re* Conroy, 486 A.2d 1209, 1216 (N.J. 1985).

[176] *In re* Storar, 420 N.E.2d 64 (N.Y. 1981).

[177] *Id.* at 73.

[178] *Id.*

[179] **NY:** *In re* Storar, 420 N.E.2d at 70.

IL: *Accord In re* E.G., 549 N.E.2d 322 (Ill. 1989) (competent patient who is likely to die within a month without blood transfusions but who with them and chemotherapy is about 80% likely to achieve remission of the disease may decline treatment).

NV: *Accord* McKay v. Bergstedt, 801 P.2d 617, 637 (Nev. 1990) (Springer, J., dissenting) ("I want to be sure that the reader of this dissent does not get this case mixed up with the 'right-to-die' cases in which there is present either imminent death or permanent unconsciousness. We are not dealing here with 'overtreatment' or unwanted prolongation of the dying process.").

cases involve the refusal of blood transfusions by Jehovah's Witnesses,[180] the basis for upholding the right to refuse treatment is not a religious one. For example, the Massachusetts Supreme Judicial Court held that the mother of a young child, who was the child's primary caretaker and who had a bleeding ulcer, could refuse a blood transfusion even if the refusal would lead to her death. In addressing the legal basis for the holding, the court observed that:

> We do not think it is necessary, however, to decide whether Ms. Munoz has a free exercise right to refuse the administration of blood or blood products, since we have already held that she has a common law and constitutional privacy right to refuse a blood transfusion. Also, we need not decide whether a patient's right is strengthened because the objection to the medical treatment is based on religious principles.[181]

Also, in cases involving nonreligiously motivated refusals of treatment by competent patients, all of the courts, admittedly few in number, have permitted young, nonterminally ill patients whose treatment maintained the status quo to have that treatment discontinued because the patients deemed their quality of life to be intolerable.[182]

---

[180] **FL:** *See In re* Dubreuil, 629 So. 2d 819 (Fla. 1993); Wons v. Public Health Trust, 541 So. 2d 96 (Fla. 1989); St. Mary's Hosp. v. Ramsey, 465 So. 2d 666 (Fla. Dist. Ct. App. 1985).

MA: *See* Norwood Hosp. v. Munoz, 564 N.E.2d 1017 (Mass. 1991).

MI: *But see* Werth v. Taylor, 475 N.W.2d 426 (Mich. Ct. App. 1991).

NJ: *But see In re* Hughes, 611 A.2d 1148 (N.J. Super. Ct. App. Div. 1992).

NY: *See* Fosmire v. Nicoleau, 551 N.E.2d 77 (N.Y. 1990).

OH: *But see* University of Cincinnati Hosp. v. Edmond, 506 N.E.2d 299 (C.P. Hamilton County, Ohio 1986).

PA: *But see In re* Estate of Dorone, 534 A.2d 452 (Pa. 1987).

[181] **MA:** Norwood Hosp. v. Munoz, 564 N.E.2d 1017, 1021–22 (Mass. 1991) (mother of minor child has right to refuse blood transfusion for bleeding ulcer).

NY: *Accord* Fosmire v. Nicoleau, 551 N.E.2d 77 (N.Y. 1990).

See § **9.3.**

[182] **CA:** *See* Thor v. Superior Court, 855 P.2d 375 (Cal. 1993) (quadriplegic patient wishing to discontinue feeding tube); Bouvia v. Superior Court (Glenchur), 225 Cal. Rptr. 297 (Ct. App. 1986) (upholding refusal of tube feeding by nonterminally but irreversibly ill patient with cerebral palsy).

GA: *See* State v. McAfee, 385 S.E.2d 651 (Ga. 1989) (patient being kept alive by ventilator necessitated by quadriplegia has right to discontinue ventilator even though he will not die from his condition).

NV: *See* McKay v. Bergstedt, 801 P.2d 617 (Nev. 1990) (patient being kept alive by ventilator necessitated by quadriplegia has right to discontinue ventilator even though he will not die from his condition).

See § **8.2.**

BALANCING APPROACH

§ 8.14 Balancing Approach: Introduction

The most frequently mentioned approach to limiting the forgoing of life-sustaining treatment, often used in conjunction with other approaches,[183] is an approach that seeks to balance the interests of the patient and the state. The individual interests at stake are autonomy, self-determination, privacy, and bodily integrity.[184] The state interests generally mentioned are the preservation of life, the prevention of suicide, the protection of third parties, and the ethical integrity of the medical profession, but others have been enumerated.[185]

This approach recognizes that the right to refuse medical treatment may sometimes be outweighed by a state interest in administering it.[186] This approach begins with the assumption that there are competing interests at stake in decisionmaking about life-sustaining treatment. These interests are usually referred to as individual or patient interests on the one hand and state or societal interests on the other. That there are two discrete constellations of interests is an oversimplification, for it assumes the individual patient's interests are of no moment to society. This is clearly not the case,[187] and the failure to recognize this may sometimes mean that a patient's wish to decline treatment is given too little weight.

Courts properly begin with the presumption that individual interests must be accorded a higher degree of importance than state interests[188] (though sometimes honoring it more in the dictum than in the holdings). This presumption has both substantive and procedural implications. As a substantive matter, individual interests cannot be subverted merely because the state has some rational

---

[183] **CT:** *E.g.,* Foody v. Manchester Memorial Hosp., 482 A.2d 713 (Conn. Super. Ct. 1984) (in conjunction with benefits/burdens approach).

FL: *E.g.,* Satz v. Perlmutter, 379 So. 2d 359, 360 (Fla. 1980) (in conjunction with categorical approach).

IL: *E.g., In re* Estate of Greenspan, 558 N.E.2d 1194 (Ill. 1990) (in conjunction with prognostic approach); Estate of Longeway v. Community Convalescent Ctr., 549 N.E.2d 292 (Ill. 1989) (in conjunction with prognostic approach).

[184] See **Ch. 2.**

[185] See **§ 8.19.**

[186] *See, e.g.,* Rosebush v. Oakland County Prosecutor, 491 N.W.2d 633, 636 n.2 (Mich. Ct. App. 1992) (citing first edition of this treatise).

[187] *See, e.g.,* Mercy Hosp. Inc. v. Jackson, 489 A.2d 1130, 1135 (Md. Ct. Spec. App. 1985), *vacated and remanded as moot,* 510 A.2d 562 (Md. 1986) (state, as amicus curiae opposing hospital's effort to override competent patient's refusal of potentially lifesaving blood transfusion, asserted that "compelling need to preserve life is itself limited by society's demand for recognition of fundamental individual liberties).

[188] *See, e.g.,* Bartling v. Superior Court, 209 Cal. Rptr. 220, 225 (Ct. App. 1984).

reason for doing so. For the patient's refusal of treatment to be overridden, if at all, a state's interests (either singly or in combination[189]) must be more than merely rational, given the great import of the patient's constitutionally recognized liberty interest in refusing medical treatment. Some courts have held that the state's interests must be compelling,[190] regardless of whether the right to die is based on the constitution[191] or on common-law principles.[192]

The balancing approach was adopted in *Quinlan* and refined in subsequent cases. The New Jersey Supreme Court, in recognizing a right to die, noted that this right must sometimes give way to state interests in the "preservation and sanctity of human life" and "the right of the physician to administer medical treatment according to his best judgment."[193] In so doing, the court obviously had in mind a case it had decided only five years earlier, in which it had approved a trial court's order to administer a lifesaving blood transfusion to a Jehovah's Witness.[194] According to the court, these interests might predominate

---

[189] Tune v. Walter Reed Army Medical Hosp., 602 F. Supp. 1452, 1456 (D.D.C. 1985) ("[T]hese various state interests, viewed singly or in combination as they may be present here, are insufficient to outweigh plaintiff's interest in dying as she chooses.").

[190] **DE:** *See In re* Severns, 425 A.2d 156, 158 (Del. Ch. 1980).

DC: *See In re* A.C., 573 A.2d 1235, 1252 (D.C. 1990) ("We do not quite foreclose the possibility that a conflicting state interest may be so compelling that the patient's wishes must yield, but we anticipate that such cases will be extremely rare and truly exceptional.).

OH: Leach v. Akron Gen. Medical Ctr., 426 N.E.2d 809, 814 (C.P. P. Div. Summit County, Ohio 1980) ("The Constitutional right to privacy is paramount to a state interest unless that interest can be demonstrated to be compelling or outweighs the individual's Constitutional right. . . . On one side of the scale, this court must place a constitutionally protected right; on the other, any potential interest, either societal or legal, that the state might wish to protect.").

[191] **MA:** *See* Superintendent of Belchertown State Sch. v. Saikewicz, 370 N.E.2d 417 (Mass. 1977).

MN: *See In re* Torres, 357 N.W.2d 332, 339 (Minn. 1984) (citing Severns v. Wilmington Medical Ctr., Inc., 421 A.2d 1334 (Del. 1980).

NY: *See In re* Storar, 420 N.E.2d 64 (N.Y. 1981).

OH: *See* Leach v. Akron Gen. Medical Ctr., 426 N.E.2d at 814.

WA: *See In re* Colyer, 660 P.2d 738 (Wash. 1983).

[192] **MO:** *E.g.,* Cruzan v. Harmon, 760 S.W.2d 408, 420 (Mo. 1988) (by implication).

NJ: *E.g., In re* Conroy, 486 A.2d 1209 (N.J. 1985).

NY: *E.g.,* Eichner v. Dillon, 420 N.E.2d 64, 71 (N.Y. 1981) ("Under certain circumstances the common-law right may have to yield to superior State interests, as it would even if it were constitutionally based."); *In re* Storar, 434 N.Y.S.2d 46, 47 (App. Div. 1980) (Cardamone, J., dissenting) ("The use of terms such as 'affirmative' or 'passive', 'ordinary' or 'extraordinary' is a camouflage; they are distinctions without a difference."); Saunders v. State, 492 N.Y.S.2d 510, 514 (Sup. Ct. Nassau County 1985); *In re* Lydia E. Hall Hosp., 455 N.Y.S.2d 706, 711 (Sup. Ct. Nassau County 1982); *In re* Storar, 433 N.Y.S.2d 388, 393 (Sup. Ct. Monroe County 1980).

OH: *E.g.,* Leach v. Akron Gen. Medical Ctr., 426 N.E.2d 809, 814 (C.P. P. Div. Summit County, Ohio 1980).

[193] *In re* Quinlan, 355 A.2d 647, 663 (N.J. 1976).

[194] *See* John F. Kennedy Memorial Hosp. v. Heston, 279 A.2d 670 (N.J. 1971).

in a case in which treatment could save the patient's life, but the state's interest in administering treatment "weakens and the individual's right to privacy grows as the degree of bodily invasion increases and the prognosis dims."[195] The first case involving the right of a competent, terminally ill patient to die used a similar approach.[196]

This approach is buttressed by *Cruzan,* at least to the extent that the right to refuse treatment is based on constitutional, rather than common-law, principles. The United States Supreme Court acknowledged that a long line of cases stood for "[t]he principle that a competent person has a constitutionally protected liberty interest in refusing unwanted medical treatment."[197] However, establishing a violation of a liberty interest under the due process clause of the Fourteenth Amendment requires a balancing "against the relevant state interests."[198] Although not called upon by the facts of the case to determine whether this liberty interest would permit a competent patient to refuse artificial nutrition and hydration, the Court stated that "the logic of the cases [from which the principle of a competent patient's right to refuse treatment is derived] would embrace such a liberty interest, [but] the dramatic consequences involved in refusal of such treatment would inform the inquiry as to whether the deprivation of that interest is constitutionally permissible."[199]

From a common-law perspective, the *Quinlan* court's balancing test did not do justice to the significance of the individual's interests at stake. The problem might only be seen as a procedural one: the court began with the state's interests and claimed that they weaken as the individual's right grows. One would have thought, especially at that time, that standard constitutional analysis would begin with the individual's interest, which is presumed to predominate unless overcome by a sufficient state interest. In other words, there should be a presumption of a right to refuse treatment that countervailing state interests might overcome, rather than a presumption that treatment must be administered that grows weaker as the patient's interests grow stronger.[200]

---

[195] **NJ:** *In re* Quinlan, 355 A.2d 647, 664 (N.J. 1976).

DE: *Accord In re* Severns, 425 A.2d 156, 159 (Del. Ch. 1980).

WA: *Accord In re* Colyer, 660 P.2d 738, 743 (Wash. 1983).

[196] **FL:** *See* Satz v. Perlmutter, 362 So. 2d 160, 162 (Fla. Dist. Ct. App. 1978).

NV: *See also* McKay v. Bergstedt, 801 P.2d 617, 622 (Nev. 1990) ("[A]s the quality of life diminishes because of physical deterioration, the State's interest in preserving life may correspondingly decrease.").

[197] Cruzan v. Director, 497 U.S. 261, 278 (1990).

[198] *Id.* at 279.

[199] *Id.*

[200] **CA:** Bartling v. Superior Court, 209 Cal. Rptr. 220, 225 (Ct. App. 1984) ("[I]f the right of the patient to self-determination as to his own medical treatment is to have any meaning at all, it must be paramount to the interests of the patient's hospital and doctors.").

MO: *Contra* Cruzan v. Harmon, 760 S.W.2d 408, 424 (Mo. 1988) (Regardless of its source, the right to refuse treatment does not outweigh "the immense, clear fact of life in which the state maintains a vital interest.").

The procedural significance should be that the burden is on those who would seek to thwart individual choice to establish the compelling nature of their reason for so doing; failing to do so requires that individual choice must prevail.

However, that line of approach is thrown somewhat into doubt by *Cruzan,* again insofar as the basis for the refusal of treatment is a constitutional one. *Cruzan* held very little, but it clearly did hold that it is constitutionally permissible (though not mandatory) for a state to require that, for life-sustaining treatment to be forgone, there must be clear and convincing evidence of the patient's wish to do so. While in the case of a competent patient "a State is [not] required to remain neutral in the face of an informed and voluntary decision by a physically-able adult to starve to death," when a patient lacks decisionmaking capacity, because "[t]he choice between life and death is a deeply personal decision of obvious and overwhelming finality [a state] may legitimately seek to safeguard the personal element of this choice through the imposition of heightened evidentiary requirements."[201]

Whatever the failings of the *Quinlan* analysis, subsequent cases have placed the presumption back where it belongs. The New Jersey Supreme Court has itself remarked that "a competent patient's right to make that decision [to forgo life support] generally will outweigh any countervailing state interest."[202] In recent years, the courts have given increasingly short shrift to the state's interests when the patient is competent, even if the patient is not terminally ill or hopelessly ill.[203] When the patient is a competent patient, "the state's interest in preserving life must be truly compelling to justify overriding . . . [the] right to

---

NY: Eichner v. Dillon, 420 N.E.2d 64, 71 (N.Y. 1981) ("The current law identifies the patient's right to determine the course of his own medical treatment as paramount to what might otherwise be the doctor's obligation to provide needed medical care.").

201 Cruzan v. Director, 497 U.S. at 262.

202 **NJ:** *In re* Jobes, 529 A.2d 434, 451 (N.J. 1987).

DC: *Accord In re* A.C., 573 A.2d 1235, 1246 (D.C. 1990).

203 **DC:** *E.g., In re* A.C., 573 A.2d 1235; *In re* Osborne, 294 A.2d 372 (D.C. 1972).

FL: *E.g.,* Browning v. Herbert, 568 So. 2d 4 (Fla. 1990); Wons v. Public Health Trust, 541 So. 2d 96 (Fla. 1989); St. Mary's Hosp. v. Ramsey, 465 So. 2d 666 (Fla. Dist. Ct. App. 1985).

GA: *E.g.,* State v. McAfee, 385 S.E.2d 651 (Ga. 1989).

MA: *E.g.,* Norwood Hosp. v. Munoz, 564 N.E.2d 1017 (Mass. 1991).

NY: *E.g.,* Fosmire v. Nicoleau, 551 N.E.2d 77, 84 n.3 (N.Y. 1990) ("Contrary to the suggestion in the concurring opinions, we are not saying that a statute or regulation is necessary to establish or strengthen an identifiable State's interest. A particular State interest in individual, otherwise private, conduct arises by virtue of the shared common goals and needs of the body politic and exists whether or not the Legislature has chosen to take specific action implementing that interest. All we are saying is that on this record none of the interests asserted by the hospital can be said to outweigh the patient's right to make her own medical choices, a right which is recognized at common law and supported by existing statutes and constitutional principles.").

See § **8.2.**

refuse medical treatment."[204] Less accepted, but also growing in strength, is the view that "[t]his is equally true for incompetent patients, who have just as much right as competent patients to have their decisions made while competent respected, even in a substituted judgment framework."[205]

Some courts have just about foreclosed the possibility of any state interest being strong enough to overcome the right to refuse treatment of a competent or incompetent patient.[206] The New York Court of Appeals, in holding in the *Fosmire* case that a purportedly lifesaving blood transfusion should not have been administered to a competent Jehovah's Witness who had refused it, even though she was pregnant, stated that

> an identified State interest which conflicts with a patient's choice will not always prevail. There are many cases where the State's concern is not sufficient to override the individual's right to determine the course of medical treatment as a patient [citation omitted] or as the parent of a patient [citation omitted]. In these and similar cases the courts have to weigh the interests of the individual against the interests asserted on behalf of the State to strike an appropriate balance.[207]

That is not unusual, but what follows is:

---

[204] **DC:** *In re* A.C., 573 A.2d at 1246.

CA: *Accord* Thor v. Superior Court, 855 P.2d 375, 387 (Cal. 1993) ("[A] competent, informed adult, in the exercise of self-determination and control of bodily integrity, has the right to direct the withholding or withdrawal of life-sustaining medical treatment, even at the risk of death, which ordinarily outweighs any countervailing state interest."); Bouvia v. Superior Court (Glenchur), 225 Cal. Rptr. 297 (Ct. App. 1986).

FL: *Accord* Wons v. Public Health Trust, 541 So. 2d 96 (Fla. 1989); St. Mary's Hosp. v. Ramsey, 465 So. 2d 666 (Fla. Dist. Ct. App. 1985).

GA: *Accord* State v. McAfee, 385 S.E.2d 651 (Ga. 1989).

MA: *Accord* Norwood Hosp. v. Munoz, 564 N.E.2d 1017 (Mass. 1991).

NV: *Accord* McKay v. Bergstedt, 801 P.2d 617 (Nev. 1990).

NJ: *Accord In re* Conroy, 486 A.2d 1209, 1226 (N.J. 1985).

NY: *Accord* Fosmire v. Nicoleau, 551 N.E.2d 77, 85 (N.Y. 1990) ("The majority . . . for all practical purposes, leaves the right absolute.").

[205] **DC:** *In re* A.C., 573 A.2d at 1246. See § **8.3.**

[206] **DC:** *E.g., In re* A.C., 573 A.2d at 1252 ("We do not quite foreclose the possibility that a conflicting state interest may be so compelling that the patient's wishes must yield, but we anticipate that such cases will be extremely rare and truly exceptional.").

MA: Brophy v. New Eng. Sinai Hosp., Inc., 497 N.E.2d 626, 642 (Mass. 1986) (Nolan, J., dissenting) ("[T]he *Saikewicz* 'balancing test' is all but chimerical once it has been discerned what the individual's choice would be.").

NJ: *In re* Peter, 529 A.2d 419, 427 (N.J. 1987) ("[W]e find it difficult to conceive of a case in which the state could have an interest strong enough to subordinate a patient's right to choose not to be artificially sustained in a persistent vegetative state.").

NY: *Cf.* Fosmire v. Nicoleau, 551 N.E.2d 77 (N.Y. 1990) (countervailing state interest must be embodied in legislation to overcome competent patient's right to refuse treatment).

[207] Fosmire v. Nicoleau, 551 N.E.2d at 81.

> [T]he extent to which the State has manifested its commitment to that interest through legislation or otherwise is a significant consideration.[208]

In fact, it is so unusual as to provoke the comment of another judge on the same court, Judge Simon, to observe:

> The majority now define the right of self-determination broadly, holding that unless the State has expressed its interest in overriding the individual's right in specific circumstances, no State interest exists. That reasoning ignores a multitude of statutes and judicial decisions evidencing the State's commitment to the sanctity of life and imposes a burden of specificity on the Legislature which, for all practical purposes, leaves the right absolute. . . .
>
> . . . Indeed, it can reasonably be argued that if competent adults, who are presumed to know the natural and probable consequences of their acts, may reject lifesaving treatment without reason the rule condones a method of suicide.[209]

Surely Judge Simon is correct. There has never been any rule that a state interest be expressed in legislation. But Judge Simon also overreads the majority's opinion, which on its face does not require that the state interest be expressed in legislation, but only that a legislative expression give a great deal more weight to the validity and applicability of the particular interest.

Even if countervailing state interests are to be taken into account, they "are 'by no means a bright-line test, capable of resolving every dispute regarding the refusal of medical treatment. Rather, they are intended merely as factors to be considered while reaching the difficult decision of when a compelling state interest may override the basic constitutional right [ ] of privacy.' "[210] Furthermore, "[t]he means to carry out any such compelling state interest must be narrowly tailored in the least intrusive manner possible to safeguard the rights of the individual."[211]

An interesting, through probably aberrational, exception to this trend is *McKay v. Bergstedt,*[212] involving the petition of a competent, nonterminally ill 31-year-old man who was a quadriplegic, to have his respirator turned off. Although specifically disavowing addressing the procedures for termination of life support for incompetent patients, the court held that when a competent patient is not terminally ill, the state's interests in preservation of life are more

---

[208] **NY:** Fosmire v. Nicoleau, 551 N.E.2d at 81.

OH: *Accord* Estate of Leach v. Shapiro, 469 N.E.2d 1047, 1051–52 (Ohio Ct. App. 1984) ("While the patient's right to refuse treatment is qualified because it may be overborn by competing state interests, we believe that, absent legislation to the contrary, the patient's right to refuse treatment is absolute until the quality of the competing interests is weighed in a court proceeding.").

[209] Fosmire v. Nicoleau, 551 N.E.2d at 85 (Simons, J., concurring).

[210] Browning v. Herbert, 568 So. 2d 4, 14 (Fla. 1990).

[211] *Id.*

[212] 801 P.2d 617 (Nev. 1990).

substantial than when such a patient is terminally ill, and therefore "the patient's decision to refuse treatment or to withdraw existing medical therapy, including life-support systems, must be weighed against the aforesaid State interests,"[213] and that the weighing must take place in a judicial proceeding.[214] The holding in this case cannot be squared with the decisions upholding the right of Jehovah's Witnesses to forgo lifesaving blood transfusions. If refusals of lifesaving treatment are permitted to stand when the treatment is extremely limited in duration and virtually certain to restore the patient to health, then a fortiori a person who is seriously and permanently physically compromised and whose treatment entails no possibility of curing the underlying condition for which it is administered has an even more substantial claim to refuse it.

Origins of the Balancing Approach

Although the comprehensive balancing approach set forth by the courts was first enunciated by the Massachusetts Supreme Judicial Court in *Saikewicz,* that court based this approach on a "survey of recent decisions involving the difficult question of the right of an individual to refuse medical intervention or treatment"[215] and concluded that the decisions "indicate that a relatively concise statement of countervailing State interests may be made."[216] The four commonly accepted competing interests the Massachusetts court "distilled from the cases"[217] are (1) preservation of life, (2) prevention of suicide, (3) protection of the interests of innocent third parties, and (4) maintenance of the ethical integrity of the medical profession.[218]

These four state interests have become a catechistic aspect of judicial right-to-die opinions.[219] Despite the fact that virtually every case finds that they do not

---

[213] *Id.* at 630.

[214] *Id.* at 629–31. See § **5.42.**

[215] Superintendent of Belchertown State Sch. v. Saikewicz, 370 N.E.2d 417, 425 (Mass. 1977).

[216] **MA:** Superintendent of Belchertown State Sch. v. Saikewicz, 370 N.E.2d at 425.

FL: *Accord* Satz v. Perlmutter, 362 So. 2d 160, 162 (Fla. Dist. Ct. App. 1978).

[217] Superintendent of Belchertown State Sch. v. Saikewicz, 370 N.E.2d at 425.

[218] See §§ **8.15–8.19.**

[219] **DFL:** *E.g.,* McKenzie v. Doctors' Hosp. of Hollywood, Inc., 765 F. Supp. 1504, 1506–07 (S.D. Fla. 1991).

DNY: *E.g.,* Deel v. Syracuse Veterans Admin. Medical Ctr., 729 F. Supp. 231, 233–34 (N.D.N.Y. 1990).

AZ: *E.g.,* Rasmussen v. Fleming, 741 P.2d 674, 683 (Ariz. 1987).

CA: *E.g.,* Thor v. Superior Court, 855 P.2d 375 (Cal. 1993); Donaldson v. Van de Kamp, 4 Cal. Rptr. 2d 59, 62 (Ct. App. 1992); Bouvia v. Superior Court (Glenchur), 225 Cal. Rptr. 297, 304 (Ct. App. 1986); Bartling v. Superior Court, 209 Cal. Rptr. 220, 225 (Ct. App. 1984).

CT: *E.g.,* Foody v. Manchester Memorial Hosp., 482 A.2d 713, 718–19 (Conn. Super. Ct. 1984).

outweigh the individual's interests either because the patient is competent or because, if incompetent, the patients' interests are so strong because of their dim or nonexistent prognosis for recovery, courts seem compelled to recite, analyze, and occasionally discourse on this list of interests.[220] Most courts, however, have taken a more flexible view of this approach. The Florida Supreme Court views these four state interests "merely as factors to be considered" and "by no means a bright-line test, capable of resolving every dispute regarding the refusal of medical treatment."[221] Other courts have, in the context of particular cases, examined a variety of other state interests.[222]

When all is said and done, the balancing approach turns out to be not so much an alternative to the prognostic approach as a supplement to it. The operation and application of the balancing approach always requires that certain

---

DE: *E.g., In re* Severns, 425 A.2d 156, 158–59 (Del. Ch. 1980).

DC: *E.g., In re* A.C., 573 A.2d 1235, 1246 (D.C. 1990).

FL: *E.g.,* Browning v. Herbert, 568 So. 2d 4, 14 (Fla. 1990); Wons v. Public Health Trust, 541 So. 2d 96, 97 (Fla. 1989); John F. Kennedy Memorial Hosp. v. Bludworth, 452 So. 2d 921, 924 (Fla. 1984).

GA: *E.g.,* State v. McAfee, 385 S.E.2d 651, 652 (Ga. 1989) (competent patient); *In re* L.H.R., 321 S.E.2d 716, 722–23 (Ga. 1984).

IL: *E.g., In re* E.G., 549 N.E.2d 322, 328 (Ill. 1989) (competent patient); Estate of Longeway v. Community Convalescent Ctr., 549 N.E.2d 292, 299 (Ill. 1989).

MD: *E.g.,* Mack v. Mack, 618 A.2d 744, 755 n.7 (Md. 1993).

MA: *E.g., In re* Beth, 587 N.E.2d 1377, 1381–82 (Mass. 1992); *In re* Doe, 583 N.E.2d 1263, 1268 (Mass. 1992); Norwood Hosp. v. Munoz, 564 N.E.2d 1017 (Mass. 1991); Brophy v. New Eng. Sinai Hosp., Inc., 497 N.E.2d 626, 634 (Mass. 1986); *In re* Spring, 405 N.E.2d 115, 119, 123 (Mass. 1980); *In re* Hier, 464 N.E.2d 959, 965 (Mass. App. Ct. 1984) (dismissing almost summarily all four interests as "not of decisive significance in this case").

MI: *E.g., In re* Rosebush, 491 N.W.2d 633, 636 n.2 (Mich. 1992).

MN: *E.g., In re* Torres, 357 N.W.2d 332, 339 (Minn. 1984).

NV: *E.g.,* McKay v. Bergstedt, 801 P.2d 617, 621 (Nev. 1990).

NY: *E.g.,* Fosmire v. Nicoleau, 551 N.E.2d 77, 81 (N.Y. 1990); Elbaum v. Grace Plaza of Great Neck, Inc., 544 N.Y.S.2d 840, 847 (App. Div. 1989); Delio v. Westchester County Medical Ctr., 516 N.Y.S.2d 677, 691 (App. Div. 1987).

OH: *E.g., In re* Crum, 580 N.E.2d 876 (P. Ct. Franklin County, Ohio 1991).

PA: *E.g., In re* Fiori, 13 Fiduc. Rep. 2d 79 (C.P. Bucks County, Pa. 1993); *In re* Doe, 45 Pa. D. & C.3d 371, 383 (C.P. Phila. County 1987).

WA: *E.g., In re* Grant, 747 P.2d 445, 451 (Wash. 1987), *modified,* 757 P.2d 534 (Wash. 1988); *In re* Ingram, 689 P.2d 1363, 1371 (Wash. 1984).

WI: *E.g.,* L.W. v. L.E. Phillips Career Dev. Ctr., 482 N.W.2d 60, 74 (Wis. 1992).

220 **DDC:** *See* Tune v. Walter Reed Army Medical Hosp., 602 F. Supp. 1452, 1455 (D.D.C. 1985) (discussing the interests even though respondent did not assert any state interests in keeping patient alive).

221 Wons v. Public Health Trust, 541 So. 2d 96, 97 (Fla. 1989).

222 See § **8.19.**

assumptions about the patient's prospects for recovery be made, and often these are stated quite explicitly.[223]

§ 8.15 State Interest in Preservation of Life

The state's interest in the preservation of life is the most significant of the four state interests that may potentially override a patient's right to refuse treatment.[224] It is said to be not merely "a laudable goal . . . , it is a compelling one."[225] Yet, when it comes to applying this interest, most courts hold that [t]here is a substantial distinction in the State's insistence that human life be saved where the affliction is curable, as opposed to the State interest where . . . the issue is not whether but when, for how long, and at what cost to the individual that life may be briefly extended."[226] In other words, the

---

[223] *See, e.g., In re* Severns, 425 A.2d 156, 159 (Del. Ch. 1980) ("[I]nterest of the State in the preservation of human life is diminished in importance by the concomitant rise in the right of an individual . . . to decline to be kept alive as a veritable vegetable.").

[224] **AZ:** Rasmussen v. Fleming, 741 P.2d 674, 683 (Ariz. 1987).

DE: *In re* Severns, 425 A.2d 156, 158 (Del. Ch. 1980).

MA: *In re* Spring, 405 N.E.2d 115, 119 (Mass. 1980); Superintendent of Belchertown State Sch. v. Saikewicz, 370 N.E.2d 417, 425 (Mass. 1977).

NJ: *In re* Conroy, 486 A.2d 1209, 1223 (N.J. 1985).

NY: Delio v. Westchester County Medical Ctr., 516 N.Y.S.2d 677, 691–92 (App. Div. 1987) (patient in persistent vegetative state "has no life for the State to protect in the usual sense"). *Contra* Fosmire v. Nicoleau, 551 N.E.2d 77, 81–82 (N.Y. 1990) (The state "rarely acts to protect individuals from themselves, indicating that the State's interest is less substantial when there is little or no risk of direct injury to the public.").

OH: *Contra In re* Crum, 580 N.E.2d 876, 880 (P. Ct. Franklin County, Ohio 1991) (state had "no interest" in preservation of life of patient in persistent vegetative state).

See also President's Comm'n, Deciding to Forego Life-Sustaining Treatment 32.

[225] **DNY:** Deel v. Syracuse Veterans Admin. Medical Ctr., 729 F. Supp. 231, 234 (N.D.N.Y. 1990) ("transcendent goal of any society which values human life").

FL: St. Mary's Hosp. v. Ramsey, 465 So. 2d 666, 668 (Fla. Dist. Ct. App. 1985).

MA: *In re* Spring, 405 N.E.2d 115, 123 (Mass. 1980).

NV: McKay v. Bergstedt, 801 P.2d 617, 622 (Nev. 1990).

[226] **MA:** Superintendent of Belchertown State Sch. v. Saikewicz, 370 N.E.2d at 425–26. *Accord In re* Doe, 583 N.E.2d 1263, 1269 (Mass. 1992) ("The Commonwealth's interest in preserving life is strongest when it is attempting to protect its citizens from abuse or infringement of their rights. Where, however, as here, the appellees are striving to vindicate Doe's right to refuse invasive treatment, Doe's 'right to self determination must prevail over the State's interest in preserving life for all.' "); *In re* McCauley, 565 N.E.2d 411, 414 n.3 (Mass. 1991) ("While we conclude that the State has an interest in preserving Elisha's life, 'we do not decide here that this interest invariably must control in every case where State intervention is sought to order life-saving medical treatment' "); Brophy v. New Eng. Sinai Hosp., Inc., 497 N.E.2d 626, 635 (Mass. 1986).

DE: *Accord In re* Severns, 425 A.2d at 159.

FL: *Accord* Satz v. Perlmutter, 362 So. 2d 160, 162 (Fla. Dist. Ct. App. 1978).

NV: *Accord* McKay v. Bergstedt, 810 P.2d at 623.

patient's prognosis for recovery plays an important part in the application of this interest.[227]

When a patient is suffering from an incurable condition and is near death, rarely will a court find that the state's interest in the preservation of life outweighs the patient's right to die.[228] Indeed, in such situations the *state* has an interest in honoring patient choice,[229] but in any event the state's interest in the preservation of life is subordinate in such cases, whether a patient is competent[230] or incompetent.[231] The state's interest in the preservation of life not only exists in cases involving the choice between treatment and nontreatment,[232]

---

[227] **MO:** *But see* Cruzan v. Harmon, 760 S.W.2d 408, 419 (Mo. 1988) (when patient is in a persistent vegetative state and is not terminally ill, "[t]he state's interest in prolong life is particularly valid"). See §§ **8.9–8.13.**

[228] **MA:** Brophy v. New Eng. Sinai Hosp., Inc., 497 N.E.2d 626, 642 (Mass. 1986) (Nolan, J., dissenting) ("[T]he *Saikewicz* 'balancing test' is all but chimerical once it has been discerned what the individual's choice would be.").

[229] **MD:** Mercy Hosp. Inc. v. Jackson, 489 A.2d 1130 (Md. Ct. Spec. App. 1985), *vacated and remanded as moot,* 510 A.2d 562 (Md. 1986).

MA: Norwood Hosp. v. Munoz, 564 N.E.2d 1017, 1023 (Mass. 1991) ("[T]the right to privacy is an 'expression of the sanctity of individual free choice and self-determination as fundamental constituents of life. The value of life as so perceived is lessened not by a decision to refuse treatment, but by the failure to allow a competent human being the right of choice.'"); *In re* Conroy, 486 A.2d 1209, 1223–24 (N.J. 1985) (citing Superintendent of Belchertown State Sch. v. Saikewicz, 370 N.E.2d 417, 426 (Mass. 1977)).

[230] **DDC:** Tune v. Walter Reed Army Medical Hosp., 602 F. Supp. 1452, 1458–59 (D.D.C. 1985).

CA: Bartling v. Superior Court, 209 Cal. Rptr. 220, 225 (Ct. App. 1984); Bouvia v. Superior Court (Glenchur), 225 Cal. Rptr. 297 (Ct. App. 1986).

DC: *In re* A.C., 573 A.2d 1235, 1246 (D.C. 1990); *In re* Osborne, 294 A.2d 372 (D.C. 1972).

FL: *In re* Dubreuil, 629 So. 2d 819 (Fla. 1993); Wons v. Public Health Trust, 541 So. 2d 96 (Fla. 1989); St. Mary's Hosp. v. Ramsey, 465 So. 2d 666 (Fla. Dist. Ct. App. 1985); Satz v. Perlmutter, 362 So. 2d 160, 161–62 (Fla. Dist. Ct. App. 1978).

GA: State v. McAfee, 385 S.E.2d 651 (Ga. 1989).

MA: Norwood Hosp. v. Munoz, 564 N.E.2d 1017 (Mass. 1991).

NV: McKay v. Bergstedt, 801 P.2d 617, 624 (Nev. 1990) (competent "individual's right to decide will generally outweigh the State's interest in preserving life").

NY: Fosmire v. Nicoleau, 551 N.E.2d 77 (N.Y. 1990).

[231] **CA:** Drabick v. Drabick, 245 Cal. Rptr. 840, 856 (Ct. App. 1988).

CT: Foody v. Manchester Memorial Hosp., 482 A.2d 713, 719 (Conn. Super. Ct. 1984).

DC: *In re* A.C., 573 A.2d at 1246.

FL: Browning v. Herbert, 568 So. 2d 4, 14 (Fla. 1990).

GA: *In re* L.H.R., 321 S.E.2d 716, 723 (Ga. 1984).

MA: *In re* Beth, 587 N.E.2d 1377, 1382 (Mass. 1992) ("[T]he interest of the State in prolonging a life must be reconciled with the interest of an individual to reject the traumatic cost of that prolongation.") (quoting Superintendent of Belchertown State Sch. v. Saikewicz, 370 N.E.2d 417, 426 (Mass. 1977)); *In re* Hier, 464 N.E.2d 959 (Mass. App. Ct. 1984).

NY: *In re* Storar, 433 N.Y.S.2d 388, 393 (Sup. Ct. Monroe County 1980).

WA: *In re* Colyer, 660 P.2d 738, 743 (Wash. 1983).

[232] **DDC:** Tune v. Walter Reed Army Medical Hosp., 602 F. Supp. 1452, 1453 (D.D.C. 1985).

but also may come into play when a patient decides to undergo a treatment offering a substantially smaller probability of cure than another available option.[233]

The manner in which courts apply the balancing approach demonstrates reliance on unarticulated assumptions about prognosis. When the state's interest in the preservation of life is found to be subordinate to the individual's interest in choice, it is usually in the context of a patient whose life is near its natural end.[234] Indeed, it is because there is no hope of recovery that the state's interest in the preservation and sanctity of life is so weak or not implicated at all.[235] In such cases, little or no state interest is served by briefly extending the life of an incurably ill person.[236]

This reasoning, which has been followed by most courts—the ones to abandon it are largely those that have *strengthened* the right to refuse treatment by

---

[233] **NJ:** *Cf.* Suenram v. Society of Valley Hosp., 383 A.2d 143 (N.J. Super. Ct. L. Div. 1977) (right of privacy of patient near death from cancer permits rejection of orthodox therapy in favor of laetrile) (citing *In re* Quinlan, 355 A.2d 647 (N.J. 1976)).

WA: *See In re* Ingram, 689 P.2d 1363, 1371–72 (Wash. 1984) ("A person's right of self-determination includes the power to choose between these two treatments.").

[234] **DDC:** *E.g.,* Tune v. Walter Reed Army Medical Hosp., 602 F. Supp. at 1458–59.

CA: *E.g.,* Bartling v. Superior Court, 209 Cal. Rptr. 220 (Ct. App. 1984).

CT: *E.g.,* Foody v. Manchester Memorial Hosp., 482 A.2d 713, 719 (Conn. Super. Ct. 1984).

FL: *E.g.,* Satz v. Perlmutter, 362 So. 2d at 161, 162.

GA: *E.g., In re* L.H.R., 321 S.E.2d 716 (Ga. 1984).

MA: *E.g., In re* Hier, 464 N.E.2d 959 (Mass. App. Ct. 1984).

NY: *E.g., In re* Storar, 420 N.E.2d 64 (N.Y. 1981).

WA: *E.g., In re* Grant, 747 P.2d 445 (Wash. 1987), *modified,* 757 P.2d 534 (Wash. 1988); *In re* Colyer, 660 P.2d 738 (Wash. 1983).

[235] **CA:** *Contra* Bouvia v. Superior Court (Glenchur), 225 Cal. Rptr. 297 (Ct. App. 1986) (patient who is not terminally ill, but who is irreversibly ill, may decline forced feeding).

FL: *Contra* St. Mary's Hosp. v. Ramsey, 465 So. 2d 666 (Fla. Dist. Ct. App. 1985) (nonterminally ill patient may refuse lifesaving blood transfusion).

DE: *In re* Severns, 425 A.2d 156, 159 (Del. Ch. 1980).

MA: *In re* Hier, 464 N.E.2d at 965.

NY: *In re* Storar, 433 N.Y.S.2d at 393.

WA: *In re* Grant, 747 P.2d at 451 ("This interest weakens considerably . . . if treatment will merely postpone death for a person with a terminal and incurable condition."); *In re* Colyer, 660 P.2d 738, 743 (Wash. 1983) ("This interest weakens . . . in situations where continued treatment serves only to prolong a life inflicted with an incurable condition.") (citing *In re* Quinlan, 355 A.2d 647 (N.J. 1976)).

[236] **CT:** McConnell v. Beverly Enters.-Conn., Inc., 553 A.2d 596, 608 (Conn. 1989) (Healey, J., concurring) (For a patient in a persistent vegetative state, "this interest of the state is, on balance, greatly diminished. Thus, the 'life' she did not wish to live flickers on without the health or hope that the state properly seeks to guard. In this case, given her unchallenged wishes and her current circumstances, the state's interest in protecting her life is not, I believe, weighty in the total mix of the state's interests.").

OH: Leach v. Akron Gen. Medical Ctr., 426 N.E.2d 809, 814 (C.P. P. Div. Summit County, Ohio 1980).

enforcing it even when a competent patient is *not* terminally ill—was criticized by the Missouri Supreme Court in *Cruzan v. Harmon* as abandoning "the common law's prejudice in favor of life" and "subtly recast[ing] the state's interest in life as an interest in the quality of life."[237] However, as Justice Brennan observed in *Cruzan v. Director,* the fact that the Missouri legislature has provided through advance directive legislation "for its citizens to choose a natural death under certain circumstances suggests that the State's interest in life is not so unqualified as the" Missouri Supreme Court suggested.[238] Furthermore, when a patient is permanently unconscious, as has been the case with so many patients in right-to-die cases, it does not even make sense to speak of a state interest in the preservation of the patient's life. As the California Court of Appeal observed in the *Drabick* case,

> to speak of the state's interest in preserving life is really to miss the point. To put it more precisely, the state has an interest in protecting William's right to have appropriate medical treatment decisions made on his behalf. The problem is not to preserve life under all circumstances but to make the right decisions.[239]

Thus, "[a] conclusive presumption in favor of continuing treatment," such as that erected by the Missouri Supreme Court in *Cruzan,* "impermissibly burdens a person's right to make the other choice."[240]

When a patient is competent, the state's interest in the preservation of life is especially weak "because the life that the state is seeking to protect in such a situation is the life of the same person who has competently decided to forego the medical intervention."[241] Indeed, in such situations the value of life may be lessened rather than enhanced by overriding a competent patient's refusal of treatment.[242] The right to forgo treatment is not lost by a patient's becoming incompetent to exercise the right personally,[243] although the manner in which the right to die is to be exercised in the case of an incompetent patient presents added difficulties of both a procedural and substantive nature. For an incompetent patient as well as a competent patient,

---

[237] 760 S.W.2d 408, 422 (Mo. 1988) (citing Alexander, *Death by Directive,* 28 Santa Clara L. Rev. 67, 92 (1988)).

[238] 497 U.S. 261, 314 n.15 (1990) (Brennan, J., dissenting).

[239] Drabick v. Drabick, 245 Cal. Rptr. 840, 855 (Ct. App. 1988).

[240] *Id.*

[241] **NJ:** *In re* Conroy, 486 A.2d 1209, 1223 (N.J. 1985).

MA: *Accord* Norwood Hosp. v. Munoz, 564 N.E.2d 1017, 1023 (Mass. 1991).

NV: *Accord* McKay v. Bergstedt, 801 P.2d 617, 624 (Nev. 1990) ("[W]here the prospects for a life of quality are smothered by physical pain and suffering, only the sufferer can determine the value of continuing mortality.").

[242] **MA:** Norwood Hosp. v. Munoz, 564 N.E.2d at 1023; Brophy v. New Eng. Sinai Hosp., Inc., 497 N.E.2d 626 (Mass. 1986); Superintendent of Belchertown State Sch. v. Saikewicz, 370 N.E.2d 417, 425–26 (Mass. 1977).

NJ: *In re* Conroy, 486 A.2d at 1223–24.

[243] See § **2.5.**

> [t]he constitutional right to privacy . . . is an expression of the sanctity of individual free choice and self-determination as fundamental constituents of life. The value of life as so perceived is lessened not by a decision to refuse treatment, but by the failure to allow a competent human being the right of choice.[244]

The state's interest in the preservation of life "actually embraces two separate but related concerns: an interest in preserving the life of the particular patient and an interest in preserving the sanctity of all life."[245] Although the United States Supreme Court held in *Cruzan* that the latter is such a strong interest that "a State may properly decline to make judgments about the 'quality' of life that a particular individual may enjoy, and simply assert an unqualified interest in the preservation of human life," still it must "be weighed against the constitutionally protected interests of the individual."[246] In addition to protecting the sanctity of life, the state is also entitled to protect "the personal element" of making a choice about life-sustaining treatment.[247] Thus, for an incompetent patient who has no advance directive, a state is constitutionally permitted to require that life-sustaining treatment be maintained.

Whether or not mere biological existence is a sufficiently compelling interest for the state to prohibit the termination of life support has increasingly come to the forefront of the debate about the scope of the right to die. The leading judicial proponent of the view that the sanctity of life is synonymous with mere biological existence is the Missouri Supreme Court.[248] By contrast, most other courts also consider the patient's quality of life.[249]

---

[244] **MA:** Superintendent of Belchertown State Sch. v. Saikewicz, 370 N.E.2d at 425–26; *In re* Doe, 583 N.E.2d 1263, 1269 (Mass. 1992) ("The Commonwealth's interest in preserving life is strongest when it is attempting to protect its citizens from abuse or infringement of their rights. Where, however, as here, the appellees are striving to vindicate Doe's right to refuse invasive treatment, Doe's 'right to self determination must prevail over the State's interest in preserving life for all.'"); *In re* McCauley, 565 N.E.2d 411, 414 n.3 (Mass. 1991) ("While we conclude that the State has an interest in preserving Elisha's life, 'we do not decide here that this interest invariably must control in every case where State intervention is sought to order life-saving medical treatment'"); Brophy v. New Eng. Sinai Hosp., Inc., 497 N.E.2d 626, 635 (Mass. 1986).

DE: *Accord In re* Severns, 425 A.2d 156, 159 (Del. Ch. 1980).

NV: McKay v. Bergstedt, 801 P.2d at 623.

[245] **NJ:** *In re* Conroy, 486 A.2d at 1223 (citing Cantor, Quinlan, *Privacy, and the Handling of Incompetent Dying Patients,* 30 Rutgers L. Rev. 239, 249 (1977); Annas, In re Quinlan: *Legal Comfort for Doctors,* 6 Hastings Center Rep. 29 (June 1976)). *Accord* Rasmussen v. Fleming, 741 P.2d 674, 683 (Ariz. 1987).

CA: *Accord* Thor v. Superior Court, 855 P.2d 375, 383 (Cal. 1993).

MA: *Accord* Norwood Hosp. v. Munoz, 564 N.E.2d 1017, 1023 (Mass. 1991).

MO: *Accord* Cruzan v. Harmon, 760 S.W.2d 408, 419 (Mo. 1988) ("The state's relevant interest is in life, both its preservation and its sanctity.").

[246] Cruzan v. Director, 497 U.S. 261, 282 (1990).

[247] *Id.* at 281.

[248] *See* Cruzan v. Harmon, 760 S.W.2d 408 (Mo. 1988).

[249] **US:** *E.g.,* Cruzan v. Director, 497 U.S. at 345 (Stevens, J., dissenting) ("Life, particularly human life, is not commonly thought of as a merely physiological condition or function. Its sanctity is often thought to derive from the impossibility of any such reduction.").

§ 8.16 State Interest in Prevention of Suicide

Despite the fact that the state's interest in the prevention of suicide is closely related to the state's interest in the preservation of life,[250] as a practical matter it is a relatively insignificant state interest in right-to-die cases, so much so that some courts avoid mention of the issue or dismiss it summarily.[251] The fundamental reason for this is that courts are unwilling to view the forgoing of treatment, which results in death, as suicide,[252] primarily because "[n]o state interest is compromised by allowing [an individual] to experience a dignified

---

CA: *E.g.,* Drabick v. Drabick, 245 Cal. Rptr. 840, 855 (Ct. App. 1988) ("[T]o speak of the state's interest in preserving life is really to miss the point. To put it more precisely, the state has an interest in protecting William's right to have appropriate medical treatment decisions made on his behalf.").

NV: *E.g.,* McKay v. Bergstedt, 801 P.2d 617, 626 (Nev. 1990) ("The State's interest in the preservation of life relates to meaningful life.").

WI: *E.g.,* L.W. v. L.E. Phillips Career Dev. Ctr., 482 N.W.2d 60, 74 (Wis. 1992) ("An unqualified state interest in preserving life irrespective of either a patient's express wishes or of the patient's best interests transforms human beings into unwilling prisoners of medical technology.").

See §§ **7.22–7.23.**

[250] **NJ:** *In re* Conroy, 486 A.2d 1209, 1224 (N.J. 1985) ("questionable whether it is a distinct state interest worthy of independent consideration").

[251] **CT:** Foody v. Manchester Memorial Hosp., 482 A.2d 713, 720 (Conn. Super. Ct. 1984).

MD: *See also* 73 Md. Op. Att'y Gen. 253, 264 (Op. No. 88-046, Oct. 17, 1988).

MA: *In re* Spring, 405 N.E.2d 115, 123 (Mass. 1980); *In re* Hier, 464 N.E.2d 959, 965 (Mass. App. Ct. 1984) (state's interest in preventing suicide not implicated in decision to forgo major surgical intervention). *Contra* Brophy v. New Eng. Sinai Hosp., Inc., 497 N.E.2d 626 (Mass. 1986) (Lynch, J., dissenting; O'Connor, J., dissenting).

[252] **DFL:** *E.g.,* McKenzie v. Doctors' Hosp. of Hollywood, Inc., 765 F. Supp. 1504, 1507 n.5 (S.D. Fla. 1991).

DNY: *E.g.,* Deel v. Syracuse Veterans Admin. Medical Ctr., 729 F. Supp. 231, 234 (N.D.N.Y. 1990).

CA: *Contra* Donaldson v. Van de Kamp, 4 Cal. Rptr. 2d 59 (Ct. App. 1992) (competent individual suffering from brain tumor that will be lethal within a few years has no legal right to be placed in premortem cryogenic suspension, which will cause death, nor to enlist assistance of another in ending his life).

CT: *E.g.,* McConnell v. Beverly Enters.-Conn., Inc., 553 A.2d 596, 608 (Conn. 1989).

FL: *E.g.,* Browning v. Herbert, 568 So. 2d 4, 14 (Fla. 1990); Wons v. Public Health Trust, 541 So. 2d 96, 100 (Fla. 1989).

MA: *E.g.,* Norwood Hosp. v. Munoz, 564 N.E.2d 1017, 1022 n.5 (Mass. 1991) ("There is a clear distinction between respecting the right of individuals to decide for themselves whether to refuse medical treatment and endorsing the idea that it is acceptable for individuals to take their own lives."). *Compare In re* Doe, 583 N.E.2d 1263, 1270 (Mass. 1992) ("It is well settled that withdrawing or refusing life-sustaining medical treatment is not equivalent to attempting suicide.") *with id.,* at 1274 (O'Connor, J., dissenting) ("I protest the court's legal embrace of suicide—and beyond.").

NJ: *E.g., In re* Farrell, 529 A.2d 404, 411 (N.J. 1987) ("[D]eclining life sustaining medical treatment may not properly be viewed as an attempt to commit suicide.") (citing *In re* Conroy, 486 A.2d 1209, 1224 (N.J. 1985)).

death rather than an excruciatingly painful life."[253] Furthermore, this interest is of little or no import because "the state has expressed a limited interest at best since it imposes no criminal or civil sanction for intentional acts of self-destruction."[254] There are a number of other interrelated explanations for courts' refusals to treat forgoing life-sustaining treatment as suicide, which are discussed in **§§ 18.3** through **18.8.** The state does, however, have "an important interest to ensure that people are not *influenced* to kill themselves."[255]

It is important to note that courts employ a different mode of analysis for the state interest in preventing suicide in comparison with the state interest in the preservation of life. With respect to the latter, courts have essentially found that the right of an individual to refuse treatment strongly outweighs the interest in the preservation of life. However, in considering the prevention of suicide, courts deny that the refusal of treatment even constitutes suicide. This differential analysis could have important implications for how courts regard the efforts to legalize "assisted suicide."[256] If, for instance, courts had held that the state's interest in preventing suicide is weak if a patient is terminally ill, it would be simpler to mount a convincing argument that permitting affirmative acts to end life should be considered legal than if the courts permit the forgoing of life-sustaining treatment because it does not even constitute suicide.

§ 8.17 State Interest in Protection of Third Parties

Courts frequently recognize that a decision to forgo treatment without which the patient will die might affect the interests of other individuals as well as the patient and that the state has an interest in protecting the interests of what are often referred to as "innocent third parties."[257] This is said to be an interest

---

NY: *E.g.,* Fosmire v. Nicoleau, 551 N.E.2d 77 (N.Y. 1990).

PA: *E.g.,* Ragona v. Preate, 11 Fiduc. Rep. 2d 1, 11 (C.P. Lackawanna County, Pa. 1990) (removal of patient's feeding tube "permits her to die from the natural progression of her illness").

WI: *E.g.,* L.W. v. L.E. Phillips Career Dev. Ctr., 482 N.W.2d 60, 75 (Wis. 1992) (based on specific provisions of living will and health care power of attorney statutes, "[r]efusing medical treatment is not suicide").

[253] Donaldson v. Van de Kamp, 4 Cal. Rptr. 2d at 63.

[254] **CA:** Thor v. Superior Court, 855 P.2d 375, 385 (Cal. 1993).

DNY: *But cf.* Quill v. Koppell, 870 F. Supp. 78 (S.D.N.Y. 1994).

DOR: *But cf.* Lee v. State, 869 F. Supp. 1491 (D. Or. 1994).

MI: *But cf.* People v. Kevorkian, 527 N.W.2d 714 (Mich. 1994).

[255] Donaldson v. Van de Kamp, 4 Cal. Rptr. 2d 59, 64 (Ct. App. 1992).

[256] See **Ch. 18.**

[257] **MA:** *E.g.,* Norwood Hosp. v. Munoz, 564 N.E.2d 1017 (Mass. 1991).

IL: *But see In re* Doe, 632 N.E.2d 326, 334 (Ill. App. Ct. 1994) (does not include unborn child).

potentially "of considerable magnitude,"[258] and is responsible for more judicial overrulings of refusals of treatment than any other state interest.[259] However, most of these overrulings occurred in cases (and, to be sure, older ones) in which the patient's condition was such that he could probably be returned to the status quo ante if treatment were administered, and consequently what these cases really concerned was the state's interest in preserving life when it could *meaningfully* be preserved.

Although the formulation of this interest usually focuses on the interests of minor children[260] who might incur emotional[261] and/or financial harm as a result of the loss of a parent, it need not be so limited. It is theoretically possible for other close relatives[262]—including adult offspring of the patient[263] and perhaps even persons emotionally close to the patient but not related by blood or marriage[264]—to assert an interest in the patient's continued life. However, the weight of the interests of such persons is likely to be less substantial, especially

---

[258] Superintendent of Belchertown State Sch. v. Saikewicz, 370 N.E.2d 417, 426 (Mass. 1977).

[259] **DC:** *In re* A.C., 573 A.2d 1235, 1246 (D.C. 1990) ("In those rare cases in which a patient's right to decide her own course of treatment has been judicially overridden, courts have usually acted to vindicate the state's interest in protecting third parties, even if in fetal state.").

NJ: *In re* Farrell, 529 A.2d 404, 412 (N.J. 1987).

[260] **CA:** *E.g.,* Thor v. Superior Court, 855 P.2d 375, 387 (Cal. 1993) ("Generally, this concern arises when the refusal of medical treatment endangers public health or implicates the emotional or financial welfare of the patient's minor children.").

MA: *E.g.,* Superintendent of Belchertown State Sch. v. Saikewicz, 370 N.E.2d at 426.

See § **9.55.**

[261] **MA:** *E.g.,* Norwood Hosp. v. Munoz, 564 N.E.2d at 1025 n.11 ("Every child who loses a mother, however, suffers emotionally. Emotional suffering by a child is not sufficient, by itself, to override the rights of a competent adult to refuse medical treatment, at least in cases where there is evidence that the father and other members of the family are willing to take care of the child.").

[262] **FL:** *In re* Dubreuil, 629 So. 2d 819, 826 n.9 (Fla. 1993) (citing first edition of this treatise).

IL: *In re* E.G., 549 N.E.2d 322 (Ill. 1989) (interests of parents of mature minor must be taken into account if child and parents disagree).

NJ: *In re* Farrell, 529 A.2d 404 (N.J. 1987) (state's interest in protecting third parties inapplicable when patient incurably and terminally ill and children are teenagers).

OH: *In re* Crum, 580 N.E.2d 876, 880 (P. Ct. Franklin County, Ohio 1991) (parents, aunt, and cousin will not be injured by termination of life support).

[263] **AZ:** *E.g.,* Rasmussen v. Fleming, 741 P.2d 674 (Ariz. 1987).

CA: *E.g.,* Bartling v. Superior Court, 209 Cal. Rptr. 220 (Ct. App. 1984).

FL: *E.g., In re* Dubreuil, 629 So. 2d 819, 826 n.9 (Fla. 1993) (citing first edition of this treatise); Satz v. Perlmutter, 379 So. 2d 359 (Fla. 1980).

MA: *E.g., In re* Spring, 405 N.E.2d 115 (Mass. 1980).

[264] **FL:** *See, e.g., In re* Dubreuil, 629 So. 2d at 826 n.9 (citing first edition of this treatise).

NJ: *See, e.g., In re* Peter, 529 A.2d 419 (N.J. 1987).

if the intrusion on the person of the patient is significant.[265] In fact, most right-to-die cases have involved elderly patients with no minor children, and the courts have held that this potential interest does not come into play in such cases.[266] Furthermore, when the immediate family members have all concurred, the interests of third parties are, in a sense, waived.[267]

Indeed, even when there are *minor* children, the state's interest in the protection of third parties is extremely weak when the patient cannot be restored to health. In such cases, a competent patient's decision to refuse treatment may be based in part on the realization that the medical condition and treatment have already caused a great deal of harm to the children.[268] In recent years, courts have increasingly been upholding the refusal of treatment even when the patient is not terminally ill and might be restored to relative health.

In some of the earlier cases—especially those involving members of the Jehovah's Witness religious faith—courts were far more reluctant to permit the forgoing of treatment even by a competent patient when there was a reasonable likelihood that the patient could be restored to health if treatment were administered when the patient had minor children. Although proclaiming the right of

---

[265] **CADC:** *Cf.* Bonner v. Moran, 126 F.2d 121, 122 (D.C. Cir. 1941) (parental consent required for skin graft from 15-year-old for benefit of cousin who had been severely burned).

DC: *See In re* A.C., 573 A.2d 1235, 1243–44 (D.C. 1990) ("In the same vein, courts do not compel one person to permit a significant intrusion upon his or her bodily integrity for the benefit of another person's health.").

IL: *In re* Doe, 632 N.E.2d 326 (Ill. App. Ct. 1994).

PA: McFall v. Shimp, 10 Pa. D. & C.3d 90 (Allegheny County Ct. 1978).

[266] **FL:** Satz v. Perlmutter, 362 So. 2d 160, 162 (Fla. Dist. Ct. App. 1978) (inapplicable where patient's children are adults).

AZ: *Accord* Rasmussen v. Fleming, 741 P.2d 674, 685 (Ariz. 1987).

CA: *Accord* Bartling v. Superior Court, 209 Cal. Rptr. 220, 225 n.6 (Ct. App. 1984).

MA: *Accord In re* Spring, 405 N.E.2d 115, 123 (Mass. 1980).

[267] **DNY:** Deel v. Syracuse Veterans Admin. Medical Ctr., 729 F. Supp. 231, 234 (N.D.N.Y. 1990).

DRI: Gray v. Romeo, 697 F. Supp. 580, 589 (D.R.I. 1988).

CT: McConnell v. Beverly Enters.-Conn., Inc., 553 A.2d 596, 606 (Conn. 1989) (Healey, J., concurring).

IL: *In re* E.G., 549 N.E.2d 322, 328 (Ill. 1989) (when patient is a minor, parental opposition to patient's refusal of treatment "would weigh heavily against the minor's right to refuse").

NV: McKay v. Bergstedt, 801 P.2d 617, 627 (Nev. 1990) ("Robert Bergstedt acquiesced in his son's decision given the circumstances Kenneth was facing.").

NY: Delio v. Westchester County Medical Ctr., 516 N.Y.S.2d 677, 693 (App. Div. 1987) (interest in protection of third parties does not exist when only persons whom state may have an interest in protecting are proponents of the request to discontinue treatment).

PA: *Cf. In re* Doe, 45 Pa. D. & C.3d 371, 376 (C.P. Phila. County 1987) (patient's adult children agree with decision and join in petition to court).

WA: *In re* Grant, 747 P.2d 445, 451 (Wash. 1987), *modified,* 757 P.2d 534 (Wash. 1988).

[268] *See, e.g., In re* Farrell, 529 A.2d 404, 413 (N.J. 1987).

every competent person of adult years and sound mind to refuse medical treatment, the courts frequently found ways to honor the principle and save the patient's life, sometimes by the stratagem of finding that the patient's competence was questionable and/or that there was an emergency, but most often by finding the right to be outweighed when there were dependent minor children.[269] Beginning with *Quinlan,* 10 years' worth of decisions upholding the forgoing of treatment by patients who *were* incurably ill began to have an impact on cases involving patients whose conditions *were* curable. In the more recent of these cases, courts have exhibited an increasing inclination to discount the interests of third parties—even minor children—and to translate dicta into holdings.[270]

Since 1985, a small number of courts in a somewhat larger number of cases have embarked on a course of substantially strengthening the rights of competent nonterminally ill patients to refuse treatment. One subcategory of these cases involves competent patients who are irreversibly ill or injured and who are being kept alive by some form of medical treatment. They, however, are not themselves satisfied with their quality of life. Three of these cases have involved quadriplegic accident victims being kept alive by a ventilator,[271] and one, a patient with severe cerebral palsy being kept alive by a feeding tube.[272] None of them involved patients with dependent children.

The trend toward strengthening the right of Jehovah's Witnesses to refuse lifesaving blood transfusions began in 1985 with the *Ramsey* case[273] decided by

---

[269] **CADC:** *E.g., In re* President & Directors of Georgetown College, 331 F.2d 1000 (D.C. Cir. 1964).

DCT: *E.g.,* United States v. George, 239 F. Supp. 752 (D. Conn. 1965).

DC: *But see In re* Osborne, 294 A.2d 372 (D.C. 1972).

See generally Karnezis, Annotation, *Patient's Right to Refuse Treatment Allegedly Necessary to Sustain Life,* 93 A.L.R.3d 67 (1979).

[270] **FL:** *See In re* Dubreuil, 629 So. 2d 819 (Fla. 1993) (no proof that abandonment of patient's minor children would have occurred if married, but separated, mother died); Wons v. Public Health Trust, 541 So. 2d 96, 97 (Fla. 1989) (refusal of blood transfusion that risked death was not abandonment when patient's two children were teenagers who would be cared for by their father; "While we agree that the nurturing and support by two parents is important in the development of any child, it is not sufficient to override fundamental constitutional rights."); St. Mary's Hosp. v. Ramsey, 465 So. 2d 666 (Fla. Dist. Ct. App. 1985) (nonterminally ill patient with young daughter may refuse lifesaving blood transfusion).

MA: *See* Norwood Hosp. v. Munoz, 564 N.E.2d 1017, 1025 (Mass. 1991) ("[T]he State does not have an interest in maintaining a two-parent household in the absence of compelling evidence that the child will be abandoned if he is left under the care of a one-parent household.").

NY: *See* Fosmire v. Nicoleau, 551 N.E.2d 77 (N.Y. 1990) (state's legitimate interest in family unity does not require parent of minor child to submit to life-saving medical treatment).

[271] **CA:** Thor v. Superior Court, 855 P.2d 375 (Cal. 1993).

GA: State v. McAfee, 385 S.E.2d 651 (Ga. 1989).

NV: McKay v. Bergstedt, 801 P.2d 617 (Nev. 1990).

[272] Bouvia v. Superior Court (Glenchur), 225 Cal. Rptr. 297 (Ct. App. 1986).

[273] St. Mary's Hosp. v. Ramsey, 465 So. 2d 666 (Fla. Dist. Ct. App. 1985).

an intermediate appellate court in Florida and reinforced by decisions of the Florida Supreme Court,[274] the Massachusetts Supreme Judicial Court,[275] and the New York Court of Appeals.[276] The leading case is *In re Dubreuil,*[277] which upheld the right of a pregnant woman to refuse a blood transfusion, necessary to save her life, in conjunction with a cesarean delivery. *Dubreuil* and like decisions should not be read merely to establish a strong right of Jehovah's Witnesses to refuse lifesaving blood transfusions, but as strengthening the right of all competent persons to refuse any form of medical treatment, lifesaving or otherwise, for reasons of religious belief or otherwise.

In *Dubreuil,* there was no dispute that without a blood transfusion, the patient would die because of the loss of a significant amount of blood at the time of childbirth and because of a severe blood clotting disorder. The patient was the mother and caretaker of four young children; she was married but was separated from her husband. Although he did not accompany her to the hospital, he was readily available as evidenced by the hospital's ability to find him and seek his permission for an emergency blood transfusion.

When she was admitted to the hospital, Mrs. Dubreuil "signed a standard consent form agreeing to the transfusion of blood if it were to become necessary."[278] She consented to the cesarean section when it came time to deliver the baby, "but notwithstanding the routine consent form she had signed, she withheld consent to the transfusion of blood on the basis of her values and religious convictions as a Jehovah's Witness."[279] At all times prior to the delivery she was in possession of decisionmaking capacity. Her refusal of a blood transfusion at the time of surgery was treated by the hospital as being unambiguous; the hospital viewed her execution of the standard consent form containing a consent to transfusion to be the nonbinding boilerplate that it was.[280]

Because of the severe loss of blood during the operation, a transfusion was necessary or she would imminently die, but she still refused the transfusion. The hospital contacted her husband who gave permission for the administration of the transfusion. Mr. Dubreuil was not a Jehovah's Witness, and his decision was supported by her two brothers who were also not adherents to the faith. However, her mother was a Jehovah's Witness and she supported her daughter's decision.

Because of the possibility of additional transfusions being necessary and "[u]nsure of its legal obligations and responsibilities under these circumstances,"[281]

---

[274] *See In re* Dubreuil, 629 So. 2d 819; Wons v. Public Health Trust, 541 So. 2d 96.

[275] *See* Norwood Hosp. v. Munoz, 564 N.E.2d 1017 (Mass. 1991).

[276] Fosmire v. Nicoleau, 551 N.E.2d 77 (N.Y. 1990).

[277] *In re* Dubreuil, 629 So. 2d 819.

[278] *Id.* at 820.

[279] *Id.*

[280] *Id.* at 821 & n.3.

[281] *Id.* at 821.

the hospital brought an emergency declaratory judgment action. The court conducted a hearing that day. A strange hearing it must have been because the Florida Supreme Court noted that no testimony was taken but that "during the hearing the hospital's counsel received a telephone call advising that [Mrs. Dubreuil], who had been unconscious, had just become conscious, appeared lucid, and was able to communicate."[282] She was again asked whether she would consent to a blood transfusion, and she again refused.

Nonetheless, the trial judge "orally announced judgment in favor of the hospital, allowing it to administer blood as physicians deemed necessary."[283] Several days later, the court issued a written order justifying its decision on the basis that no evidence was introduced as to how the four minor children would be cared for if their mother died. Consequently, the court concluded that the state's interests outweighed the patient's wishes. The court later denied a motion for a rehearing based on the assertion that the patient's "'extended family as well as friends . . . are willing to assist in the rearing of [her] minor children in the event of her demise.'"[284] The court of appeals affirmed in a split decision.[285]

Despite the fact that the case was moot, the Florida Supreme Court granted review for the standard reason in such cases, namely, that "the issue is one of great public importance, is capable of repetition, and otherwise might evade review."[286] The Florida Supreme Court reversed, holding that there is a presumption in such cases of nonabandonment of minor children and that therefore the burden is on the state to establish that abandonment would occur if the patient's refusal of treatment were honored. Moreover, the court clarified that it is not the hospital's obligation to petition for a judicial hearing in such cases. The burden is on the state to do so, not the hospital, and the hospital discharges any responsibility it might have by notifying the state attorney.

Although the substantive aspects of the opinion do not go beyond existing Florida law as enunciated in *Wons*[287] in 1989 and *Browning*[288] in 1990, their reiteration is important especially in light of the intermediate appellate court's opinion distinguishing *Wons. Wons* and *Browning* held, and *Dubreuil* reaffirmed, that competent patients have a right of privacy, based on the Florida constitution, which encompasses the right to refuse treatment. (The court stressed that the holding was grounded in the state constitution and not in the federal constitution.[289]) *Dubreuil* also reaffirmed *Wons*'s holding that this right of privacy

---

282 *Id.* at 820.

283 *In re* Dubreuil, 629 So. 2d at 820.

284 *Id.*

285 *In re* Dubreuil, 603 So. 2d 538 (Fla. Dist. Ct. App. 1992).

286 *In re* Dubreuil, 629 So. 2d at 822.

287 Wons v. Public Health Trust, 541 So. 2d 96 (Fla. 1989).

288 Browning v. Herbert, 568 So. 2d 4 (Fla. 1990).

289 *In re* Dubreuil, 629 So. 2d at 822 n.5 ("We adhere to the doctrine of primacy enunciated in Traylor v. State, 596 So.2d 957, 962–63 (Fla. 1992), deciding this case under express provisions of the state constitution rather than the federal constitution.").

overlaps the state constitutional right of free exercise of religion. Furthermore, "'[t]he state has a duty to assure that a person's wishes regarding medical treatment are respected.'"[290] Only if the state has a compelling interest can the constitutional right to refuse treatment be overridden, and then only "in the least intrusive manner possible to safeguard the rights of the individual."[291] One such compelling interest is the protection of minor children from abandonment by their parents, also previously established in *Wons* and *Browning*.

Although courts repeatedly state that the interest in the protection of minors can override a competent patient's refusal of medical treatment, in reviewing the cases, the Florida Supreme Court found only two courts that had actually done so. It concluded that one case, the famous *Georgetown* decision,[292] was of "little precedential value given that most of the judges on the circuit court disagreed with Judge Wright, albeit for a variety of reasons, when they were asked to rehear the case en banc,"[293] and that the other[294] was undermined by its reliance on the *Georgetown* case and by the much more recent New York Court of Appeals *Fosmire* decision.[295]

The Florida Supreme Court rejected the appellant's claim that this exception to honoring a competent patient's refusal of treatment is "inherently unsound and dangerous and cannot be consistently applied,"[296] because "some case not yet before us may present a compelling interest to prevent abandonment. Therefore, we think the better course is the one we took in *Wons,* where we held that 'these cases demand individual attention' and cannot be covered by a blanket rule."[297] At the same time, the court did see "some merit" in appellant's argument for abandoning the exception altogether:

> Parenthood, in and of itself, does not deprive one of living in accord with one's own beliefs. Society does not, for example, disparage or preclude one from performing an act of bravery resulting in the loss of that person's life simply because that person has parental responsibilities.[298]

This echoes the New York Court of Appeals's statement in *Fosmire* that "[t]he citizens of this State have long had the right to make their own medical care choices without regard to their . . . status as parents."[299]

---

[290] *Id.* at 822 (quoting Browning v. Herbert, 568 So. 2d 4, 13–14 (Fla. 1990)).

[291] *Id.*

[292] *See In re* President & Directors of Georgetown College, 331 F.2d 1000 (D.C. Cir. 1964).

[293] *In re* Dubreuil, 629 So. 2d at 824 n.8.

[294] *In re* Winthrop Univ. Hosp., 490 N.Y.S.2d 996 (Sup. Ct. Nassau County 1985).

[295] Fosmire v. Nicoleau, 551 N.E.2d 77 (N.Y. 1990).

[296] *In re* Dubreuil, 629 So. 2d at 826.

[297] *Id.* at 827 (quoting Wons v. Public Health Trust, 541 So. 2d 96, 98 (Fla. 1989)).

[298] *Id.* at 826 (citing § 4.15 of the first edition of this treatise).

[299] Fosmire v. Nicoleau, 551 N.E.2d 77, 84 (N.Y. 1990).

On the facts of the case, the court found that the state had not carried its burden of proof on abandonment because the courts below had "failed to properly consider the father of the four children."[300] There is a strong legal presumption of nonabandonment, which can only be rebutted by clear and convincing evidence that Mr. Dubreuil "would not properly assume responsibility for the children under the circumstances,"[301] and there was no evidence that no one else would care for the children. In fact, what evidence there was indicated that "extended family and friends were willing to assist in raising the children in the event of [their mother's] death."[302]

In some respects, New York goes even further than Florida. In *Fosmire,* the court noted that some states seemed to apply a "two-parent" rule—that is, a patient who had minor children could not reject lifesaving treatment at all because of the children's need for two parents—while others had adopted a "one-parent" rule—that is, treatment could be refused if the minor child would still have one parent. The *Fosmire* court categorically rejected both of these rules, analogizing to the fact that "[t]he State does not prohibit parents from engaging in dangerous activities because there is a risk that their children will be left orphans,"[303] and thus there is no warrant for insisting that parents accept lifesaving medical treatment for the benefit of their children. In addition, the court held that unless the state has previously expressed the nature of its interest in a *statute* in overriding a refusal of treatment in circumstances such as these, it cannot do so.

Separate dissents in *Dubreuil* by two justices stressed the importance of maternal nurturance in infants and young children. Although the majority had made clear in its opinion that it wished to avoid "perpetuat[ing] the damaging stereotype that a mother's role is one of caregiver, and the father's role is that of an apathetic, irresponsible, or unfit parent,"[304] there is no indication in the dissenting opinions that they intended to perpetuate such stereotypes. Rather, the dissenters adhered to the view, somewhat unpopular currently but certainly not dishonorable, that children are better off being raised by a father and a mother, when possible, than by only one parent. It is not unlikely that if confronted with this issue, other state courts would adhere to the position of the dissenters, though none has yet done so.[305]

At least as important—and perhaps more important—than the substantive aspects of the holding, because they reiterate established law, are the significant

---

[300] *In re* Dubreuil, 629 So. 2d at 827.

[301] *Id.* at 827.

[302] *Id.* at 828.

[303] Fosmire v. Nicoleau, 551 N.E.2d at 84.

[304] *In re* Dubreuil, 629 So. 2d at 828.

[305] **MA:** *See* Norwood Hosp. v. Munoz, 564 N.E.2d 1017 (Mass. 1991).

NY: *See* Fosmire v. Nicoleau, 551 N.E.2d 77.

procedural issues discussed in *Dubreuil,* specifically the responsibilities of health care providers and the state when a competent patient refuses lifesaving treatment.[306]

§ 8.18 State Interest in Protection of Ethical Integrity of Medical Profession

There is undoubtedly a societal interest in assuring that physicians and other health care professionals are free to practice their professions consistent with the prevailing standards of the profession and consistent with their individual moral values. The best example of the latter is that, despite the legal recognition of the right of a woman to terminate a pregnancy, there is no corresponding obligation on the part of physicians to perform abortions. Indeed, to impose such an obligation would be repugnant even to many who support a woman's right to terminate a pregnancy.

Physicians and other health professionals frequently assert that permitting a patient to forgo life-sustaining treatment violates their rights.[307] This assertion misunderstands the nature of a right. As the California Supreme Court has observed,

> a physician has no duty to treat an individual who declines medical intervention after "reasonable disclosure of the available choices with respect to proposed therapy [including nontreatment] and of the dangers inherently and potentially involved in each." [Citation omitted.] The competent adult patient's "informed refusal" supersedes and discharges the obligation to render further treatment.[308]

Thus, when patients place physicians on notice that they object to treatment, physicians do not violate their professional responsibilities if they accede to the

---

[306] See § **8.8.**

[307] **DCT:** *E.g.,* United States v. George, 239 F. Supp. 752 (D. Conn. 1965).

DE: *E.g.,* Severns v. Wilmington Medical Ctr. Inc., 421 A.2d 1334, 1338 (Del. 1980) ("[C]urrent medical standards in the community" require that certain kinds of treatment not be forgone.).

MA: *E.g.,* Superintendent of Belchertown State Sch. v. Saikewicz, 370 N.E.2d 417, 425–26 (Mass. 1977) (citing *In re* President & Directors of Georgetown College, 331 F.2d 1000 (D.C. Cir. 1964).

NJ: *E.g.,* John F. Kennedy Memorial Hosp. v. Heston, 279 A.2d 670 (N.J. 1971).

WA: *But see In re* Hamlin, 689 P.2d 1372, 1374 (Wash. 1984) (attending physician alleged that "it was medically and ethically wrong to continue life support systems").

See § **17.23.**

[308] **CA:** Thor v. Superior Court, 855 P.2d 375, 383 (Cal. 1993).

NY: *Cf.* Eichner v. Dillon, 420 N.E.2d 64, 71 (N.Y. 1981) ("The current law identifies the patient's right to determine the course of his own medical treatment as paramount to what might otherwise be the doctor's obligation to provide needed medical care.").

patient's wishes.[309] The same is true in the case of patients who lack decision-making capacity. As long as someone legally authorized to decline treatment on the patient's behalf does so, no right of the physician is violated.[310] Nonetheless, health care professionals at least have an interest in, if not responsibility for, practicing their profession in such a manner that they are not continually uncertain about the permissible legal scope of their authority.[311]

In some instances, health care professionals assert that it is a violation of personal[312] or professional ethics[313] to permit a patient to forgo treatment. Although recognizing this as an interest worthy of consideration, the *Saikewicz* court observed that

---

[309] **CA:** Thor v. Superior Court, 855 P.2d 375.

NY: Fosmire v. Nicoleau, 551 N.E.2d 77 (N.Y. 1990).

[310] **MA:** Brophy v. New Eng. Sinai Hosp., Inc., 497 N.E.2d 626, 638 (Mass. 1986) ("[S]o long as we decline to force the hospital to participate in removing [the] G-tube, there is no violation of the integrity of the medical profession.").

See § **17.23.**

[311] **DCT:** United States v. George, 239 F. Supp. at 754 ("[T]he doctor's conscience and professional oath must also be respected. In the present case the patient voluntarily submitted himself to and insisted upon medical care. Simultaneously he sought to dictate to treating physicians a course of treatment amounting to medical malpractice. To require these doctors to ignore the mandates of their own conscience, even in the name of free religious exercise, cannot be justified under these circumstances.").

NJ: John F. Kennedy Memorial Hosp. v. Heston, 279 A.2d at 673 ("Hospitals exist to aid the sick and the injured. The medical and nursing professions are consecrated to preserving life. That is their professional creed. To them, a failure to use a simple, established procedure in the circumstances of this case would be malpractice, however the law may characterize that failure because of the patient's private convictions.").

NY: *In re* Long Island Jewish-Hillside Medical Ctr. v. Levitt, 342 N.Y.S.2d 356, 358 (Sup. Ct. Nassau County 1973) ("The Court takes note that once Mr. Levitt became a patient at [the hospital], it was the responsibility of the hospital and doctors to treat him."). *Cf. In re* Strauss, 391 N.Y.S.2d 168 (App. Div. 1977).

[312] **NY:** A.B. v. C., 477 N.Y.S.2d 281, 283 (Sup. Ct. Schenectady County 1984) ("[H]er doctor has advised [the patient] that his moral ethics would dictate that, if she were to come into the hospital under his care, he would of necessity be required to provide her with continuing life-saving medical treatment.").

[313] **CA:** Bartling v. Superior Court, 209 Cal. Rptr. 220, 223 (Ct. App. 1984).

MA: Brophy v. New Eng. Sinai Hosp., Inc., 497 N.E.2d 626.

NJ: *In re* Jobes, 529 A.2d 434 (N.J. 1987); *In re* Requena, 517 A.2d 869 (N.J. Super. Ct. App. Div. 1986).

NY: Elbaum v. Grace Plaza of Great Neck, Inc., 544 N.Y.S.2d 840, 843 (App. Div. 1989) (The nursing home administrator wrote a letter to the husband of the patient that "stated that the withdrawal of the gastrointestinal tube was contrary to the 'dedication, to the law and to the policies and philosophy of Grace Plaza.' . . . '[E]ven if irrefutable evidence' was forthcoming establishing that she would want the gastrointestinal tube removed, the nursing home would not remove it."); Delio v. Westchester County Medical Ctr., 516 N.Y.S.2d 677, 681 (App. Div. 1987).

See § **17.23.**

> [p]revailing medical ethical practice does not, without exception, demand that all efforts toward life prolongation be made in all circumstances. Rather . . . the prevailing ethical practice seems to be to recognize that the dying are more often in need of comfort than treatment. Recognition of the right to refuse necessary treatment in appropriate circumstances is consistent with existing medical mores; such a doctrine does not threaten either the integrity of the medical profession, the proper role of hospitals in caring for such patients or the State's interest in protecting the same.[314]

Although the court did cite some medical authority for its assertion,[315] at the time this observation was made, it is doubtful that it was correct. It was, rather, an aspiration that possibly became a self-fulfilling prophecy. At any rate, the official position of the American Medical Association is that although the "social commitment of the physician is to sustain life and relieve suffering, [w]here the performance of one duty conflicts with the other, the preferences of the patient should prevail."[316]

The Massachusetts Supreme Judicial Court backed off from its initial strong stand about what the ethics of the medical profession are regarding the forgoing of life-sustaining treatment. In contrast to its unabashed—and perhaps incorrect—pronouncement in *Saikewicz* about the ethics of the medical profession, in response to an assertion in a later case by a hospital and its professional staff that the termination of tube-feeding of a patient in a persistent vegetative state violated its ethical standards,[317] the court subsequently recognized that

---

314 **MA:** Superintendent of Belchertown State Sch. v. Saikewicz, 370 N.E.2d 417, 426–27 (Mass. 1977).

DFL: *Accord* McKenzie v. Doctors' Hosp. of Hollywood, Inc., 765 F. Supp. 1504, 1507 (S.D. Fla. 1991).

DNY: *Accord* Deel v. Syracuse Veterans Admin. Medical Ctr., 729 F. Supp. 231, 234 (N.D.N.Y. 1990).

FL: *Accord* Wons v. Public Health Trust, 541 So. 2d 96, 101 (Fla. 1989).

NY: *Accord In re* Storar, 433 N.Y.S.2d 388, 393 (Sup. Ct. Monroe County 1980).

WI: *Accord* L.W. v. L.E. Phillips Career Dev. Ctr., 482 N.W.2d 60, 75 (Wis. 1992) ("[T]he existence of a protected right to refuse treatment for all individuals competent or incompetent may in a sense protect the integrity of the medical profession. In the absence of such a protected right, physicians may be discouraged from attempting certain life-sustaining medical procedures in the first place, knowing that once connected they may never be removed.").

315 **MA:** Superintendent of Belchertown State Sch. v. Saikewicz, 370 N.E.2d at 423–24 ("The current state of medical ethics in this area is expressed by one commentator who states that: 'we should not use *extraordinary* means of prolonging life or its semblance when, after careful consideration, consultation and the application of the most well conceived therapy it becomes apparent that there is no hope for the recovery of the patient.'") (quoting Lewis, *Machine Medicine and Its Relation to the Fatally Ill,* 206 JAMA 387 (1968).

316 Council on Ethical & Judicial Affairs, American Medical Ass'n, Code of Medical Ethics § 2.20, at 36 (1994).

317 Brophy v. New Eng. Sinai Hosp., Inc., 497 N.E.2d 626.

"the State has an interest in maintaining the ethical integrity of the medical profession by giving hospitals and their staffs a full opportunity to assist those in their care."[318] However, in still another case the court concluded that "so long as we decline to force the hospital to participate . . . there is no violation of the integrity of the medical profession."[319]

Nonetheless, the effect of *Saikewicz* and other similar opinions on yet other courts seems to have underscored and strengthened some health professionals' beliefs that compelling treatment of hopelessly ill patients is undesirable both for the patients and for the health professionals and that "the prevailing medical ethical standards . . . do not require medical intervention at all costs."[320] Thus, it is now well accepted in the health professions that a patient's forgoing life-sustaining treatment is not inherently inconsistent with professional ethics, and numerous medical organizations have adopted statements of principle to that effect. Most notable is the American Medical Association's pronouncement entitled "Withholding or Withdrawing Life-Prolonging Medical Treatment," urging that "[i]n treating a terminally ill or irreversibly comatose patient, the physician should determine whether the benefits of treatment outweigh its

---

[318] Norwood Hosp. v. Munoz, 564 N.E.2d 1017, 1023 (Mass. 1991).

[319] Brophy v. New Eng. Sinai Hosp., Inc., 497 N.E.2d at 638.

[320] **NY:** Delio v. Westchester County Medical Ctr., 516 N.Y.S.2d 677, 693 (App. Div. 1987).

DDC: *Accord* Tune v. Walter Reed Army Medical Hosp., 602 F. Supp. 1452, 1455 n.8 (D.D.C. 1985) ("[M]edical ethics incorporates the duties owed the patient, including, among others, administering treatment only with consent in the case of a competent adult.").

AZ: *Accord* Rasmussen v. Fleming, 741 P.2d 674, 684 (Ariz. 1987).

CA: *Accord* Thor v. Superior Court, 855 P.2d 375, 386 (Cal. 1993); Bartling v. Superior Court, 209 Cal. Rptr. 220, 225 (Ct. App. 1984) ("[I]f the right of the patient to self-determination as to his own medical treatment is to have any meaning at all, it must be paramount to the interests of the patient's hospital and doctors.").

CT: *Accord* Foody v. Manchester Memorial Hosp., 482 A.2d 713, 719 (Conn. Super. Ct. 1984) ("[W]ithdrawal of treatment should be ethically permissible where it no longer offers hope of benefit to the patient.").

FL: *Accord* Satz v. Perlmutter, 362 So. 2d 160, 162 (Fla. Dist. Ct. App. 1978).

MA: *Accord In re* Spring, 405 N.E.2d 115, 123 (Mass. 1980).

NV: *Accord* McKay v. Bergstedt, 801 P.2d 617, 628 (Nev. 1990).

OH: *Accord* Couture v. Couture, 549 N.E.2d 571 (Ohio Ct. App. 1989) (medical ethics permits withdrawal of artificial nutrition and hydration when patient is terminally ill even though death might not be imminent); *In re* Crum, 580 N.E.2d 876 (P. Ct. Franklin County, Ohio 1991).

PA: *Accord* Ragona v. Preate, 11 Fiduc. Rep. 2d 1, 11 (C.P. Lackawanna County, Pa. 1990) ("adherence to . . . wishes [of incompetent patient orally expressed prior to her loss of decisionmaking capacity] is consistent with the ethics of the medical profession").

WA: *Accord In re* Colyer, 660 P.2d 738, 743–44 (Wash. 1983) ("state's interest in the maintenance of the ethical integrity of the medical profession is not at odds with" a right to die).

WI: *Accord* L.W. v. L.E. Phillips Career Dev. Ctr., 482 N.W.2d 60, 75 (Wis. 1992).

burdens. At all times, the dignity of the patient should be maintained."[321] Numerous courts have approvingly cited this standard[322] and those of another relevant medical professional group.[323]

The striking difference between the few pre-*Quinlan* treatment-refusal cases and the contemporary right-to-die cases in addressing the protection of professional ethics again underscores the fundamental importance, if not the centrality, of the patient's prognosis. When treatment holds little or no prospect of restoring the patient to a quality of life acceptable to the patient, there is no state interest in protecting the ethical integrity of the health professions for the simple reason that no such interest is at stake. By contrast, when treatment can save a patient's life, it works more of a hardship on professionals to permit patients entrusted to their care to forgo such treatment.[324] However, even in such cases, the degree of

---

[321] American Medical Ass'n, Current Opinions of the Council on Ethical and Judicial Affairs § 2.18, at 13 (Mar. 15, 1986), *superseded by* Council on Ethical & Judicial Affairs, Am. Medical Ass'n, Code of Medical Ethics: Current Opinions with Annotations § 2.20, at 36 (1994).

[322] **DRI:** *E.g.*, Gray v. Romeo, 697 F. Supp. 580 (D.R.I. 1988).

CA: *E.g.*, Bouvia v. Superior Court (Glenchur), 225 Cal. Rptr. 297, 303–04 (Ct. App. 1986).

FL: *E.g.*, Corbett v. D'Alessandro, 487 So. 2d 368, 372 (Fla. Dist. Ct. App.), *review denied*, 492 So. 2d 1331 (Fla. 1986).

ME: *E.g.*, *In re* Gardner, 534 A.2d 947, 954 (Me. 1987).

MA: *E.g.*, *In re* Doe, 583 N.E.2d 1263, 1270 (Mass. 1992); Brophy v. New Eng. Sinai Hosp., Inc., 497 N.E.2d 626, 638 (Mass. 1986).

NJ: *E.g.*, *In re* Farrell, 529 A.2d 404, 411–12 (N.J. 1987) (citing inter alia policies or principles of New Jersey State Board of Medical Examiners, American College of Physicians, American Medical Ass'n, and American Hosp. Ass'n); *In re* Jobes, 529 A.2d 434, 446 (N.J. 1987); *In re* Peter, 529 A.2d 419, 427 (N.J. 1987).

OH: *E.g.*, Couture v. Couture, 549 N.E.2d 571.

PA: *E.g.*, *In re* Doe, 45 Pa. D. & C.3d 371, 386 (C.P. Phila. County 1987).

WA: *E.g.*, *In re* Grant, 747 P.2d 445, 454 (Wash. 1987), *modified*, 757 P.2d 534 (Wash. 1988) (citing American Medical Ass'n, Current Opinions of the Council on Ethical and Judicial Affairs § 2.18, at 13 (Mar. 15, 1986)).

[323] American Thoracic Soc'y, *Withholding and Withdrawing Life-Sustaining Therapy*, 144 Am. Rev. Respiratory Disease 720 (1991), *reprinted in* 115 Annals Internal Med. 478 (1991); American College of Physicians, Ethics Manual 2940 (2d ed. 1989); American Acad. of Neurology, *Position of the American Academy of Neurology on Certain Aspects of the Care and Management of the Persistent Vegetative State Patient*, 39 Neurology 125 (1989); American Nurses' Ass'n, *Guidelines on Withdrawing or Withholding Food and Fluid*, 2 BioLaw U:1123 (Oct. 1988).

[324] **CADC:** *In re* President & Directors of Georgetown College, 331 F.2d 1000 (D.C. Cir. 1964).

DCT: United States v. George, 239 F. Supp. 752 (D. Conn. 1965).

NJ: John F. Kennedy Memorial Hosp. v. Heston, 279 A.2d 670 (N.J. 1971).

NY: *In re* Nemser, 273 N.Y.S.2d 624 (Sup. Ct. N.Y. County 1966).

hardship is often viewed as too insubstantial to override the patient's right to decide.[325]

The weight accorded this state interest should not depend on the degree of acceptance or rejection of the importance of patient self-determination by the medical profession. The Florida Supreme Court observed in *Browning v. Herbert* that "'[g]iven the fundamental nature of the constitutional rights involved, protection of the ethical integrity of the medical profession alone could never override those rights'" and consequently this is the "least significant" of the state's interests.[326] Similarly, the California Supreme Court concluded that the interest of physicians in providing treatment is not at cross-purposes with patients' interests: "Patient autonomy and medical ethics are not reciprocals; one does not come at the expense of the other. The latter is a necessary component and complement of the former and should serve to enhance rather than constrict the individual's ability to resolve a medical decision in his or her best overall interests."[327]

If health care professionals or the health care institution in which they work is opposed in principle to the forgoing of life-sustaining treatment, that principle should be incorporated into a written policy and promulgated prior to the need for its invocation. Failure to do so is far more likely to result in a finding that the patient's or surrogate's wishes, usually to forgo life-sustaining treatment (but possibly to continue it), must be honored despite their conflict with the principles of the health care professionals or health care institution.[328]

---

[325] **CA:** *E.g.,* Bouvia v. Superior Court (Glenchur), 225 Cal. Rptr. 297.

FL: *E.g.,* Wons v. Public Health Trust, 500 So. 2d 679 (Fla. 1989); St. Mary's Hosp. v. Ramsey, 465 So. 2d 666 (Fla. Dist. Ct. App. 1985). *Cf.* Wons v. Public Health Trust, 541 So. 2d at 100 (Ehrlich, C.J., concurring) ("In some circumstances the cost to the individual of the life-prolonging treatment in economic, emotional or as in this case, spiritual terms, may be too high.").

NY: *E.g.,* A.B. v. C., 477 N.Y.S.2d 281, 283 (Sup. Ct. Schenectady County 1984) ("The Court is sympathetic with petitioner's plight and would honor her request if it arose within the context of an actual and real controversy.").

[326] **FL:** Browning v. Herbert 568 So. 2d 4, 14 (Fla. 1990) (quoting Wons v. Public Health Trust, 541 So. 2d at 101 (Ehrlich, C.J. concurring specially)).

CA: *Accord* Bouvia v. Superior Court (Glenchur), 225 Cal. Rptr. at 301 ("The right to refuse medical treatment is basic and fundamental. . . . Its exercise requires no one's approval. It is not merely one vote subject to being overridden by medical opinion.").

[327] Thor v. Superior Court, 855 P.2d 375, 386 (Cal. 1993).

[328] **DRI:** Gray v. Romeo, 697 F. Supp. 580, 589 (D.R.I. 1988).

NJ: *In re* Jobes, 529 A.2d 434, 450–51 (N.J. 1987).

NY: Elbaum v. Grace Plaza of Great Neck, Inc., 544 N.Y.S.2d 840, 847–48 (App. Div. 1989).

§ 8.19 Other State Interests

In addition to the four state interests that are routinely invoked and almost as routinely discounted, a number of other state interests have been articulated.

Prisoners. There is a substantial state interest in a prison in "the preservation of internal order and discipline, the maintenance of institutional security, and the rehabilitation of prisoners."[329] Thus, when the person refusing treatment is a prisoner, this state interest needs to be weighed against the refusal of treatment.[330]

Only two cases involve prisoners who are also *patients*.[331] Most involve prisoners who were not ill but who refused to eat and were ordered to be force-fed.[332] In the first of these cases, *Commissioner v. Myers,* the court compelled the prisoner to accept dialysis and medication because of the interests mentioned above. In so doing, the court also distinguished *Myers* from *Saikewicz* on the ground that Myer's condition was not incurable and that it would offend the ethics of the medical profession to permit a patient in such a condition to refuse treatment.[333]

That this distinction is a weak one was borne out in the second case, *Thor v. Superior Court.* In the decade and a half between the two cases, the ever-strengthening right of competent patients to refuse treatment manifested in a small, but growing, list of cases involving incurably ill, but nonterminally ill patients,[334] virtually dictated the outcome in *Thor.* In this case, the California Supreme Court, in an especially sweeping opinion, permitted a quadriplegic

---

[329] Commissioner v. Myers, 399 N.E.2d 452, 457 (Mass. 1979).

[330] **MA:** Commissioner v. Myers, 399 N.E.2d at 457.

PA: Commonwealth v. Kallinger, 580 A.2d 887 (Pa. 1990).

[331] **CA:** *See* Thor v. Superior Court, 855 P.2d 375 (Cal. 1993).

MA: *See* Commissioner v. Myers, 399 N.E.2d 452.

[332] **GA:** *See* Zant v. Prevatte, 286 S.E.2d 715 (Ga. 1982) (right of privacy permits prisoner to refuse intrusions on his person even if calculated to preserve his life).

NH: *See In re* Caulk, 480 A.2d 93 (N.H. 1984).

NY: *See* Van Holden v. Chapman, 450 N.Y.S.2d 623 (App. Div. 1982)).

PA: *See* Commonwealth v. Kallinger, 580 A.2d 887.

WV: *See* State *ex rel.* White v. Narick, 292 S.E.2d 54 (W. Va. 1982).

[333] **MA:** Commissioner v. Myers, 399 N.E.2d at 457–58.

[334] **CA:** *See* Bouvia v. Superior Court (Glenchur), 225 Cal. Rptr. 297 (Ct. App. 1986) (patient with cerebral palsy may refuse feeding tube).

FL: *See also In re* Dubreuil, 629 So. 2d 819 (Fla. 1993) (blood transfusions case); Wons v. Public Health Trust, 541 So. 2d 96 (Fla. 1989) (same); St. Mary's Hosp. v. Ramsey, 465 So. 2d 666 (Fla. Dist. Ct. App. 1985) (same).

GA: *See* State v. McAfee, 385 S.E.2d 651 (Ga. 1989) (quadriplegic patient being kept alive by ventilator may have it turned off).

man who was a prisoner to refuse to have a feeding tube, necessary to sustain his life, surgically inserted. Beginning about six months after the accident (in prison) that made him a quadriplegic, he intermittently refused to be fed, "causing severe weight loss and threatening his health. He also has refused necessary medication and treatment for his general care. Consequently, he is at substantial risk of death due to possible pulmonary emboli, starvation, infection, and renal failure."[335] The psychiatrists who examined him found him to be "depressed about his quadriplegic condition but mentally competent to understand and appreciate his circumstances."[336]

In upholding his right to refuse treatment, the court did not establish a blanket rule that any prisoner could refuse any medical treatment or nourishment. It recognized the importance of the state's interest in maintaining order and security in prisons, but concluded that when there was no evidence in fact that these interests were threatened by a prisoner's refusal of treatment or nourishment, as there was not in this case, the refusal could not be overridden. Prison officials are permitted to consider the prisoner's "purpose or motive in determining whether the exercise of rights 'is likely to be . . . disruptive . . . or otherwise detrimental to the effective administration of the [state] prison system.' "[337] Furthermore, the Eighth Amendment's prohibition on cruel and unusual punishment "does not render inmates captives of unwanted ministrations."[338] A prisoner's informed refusal of treatment constitutes a waiver that "discharges the duty to treat and negates the possibility of [the] 'deliberate indifference' "[339] that would constitute a violation of the Eighth Amendment. To hold otherwise would "transmute the prisoner's shield into the physician's sword."[340]

In response to the contention that the prison context inherently compromises the voluntariness of the patient's decision to forgo treatment because of "possible inadequacy of medical and related support services for ill or injured inmate patients,"[341] the court observed that "any individual who suffers a debilitating or life-threatening disease or injury inevitably faces choices in medical

---

MA: *See also* Norwood Hosp. v. Munoz, 564 N.E.2d 1017 (Mass. 1991) (blood transfusion case).

NV: *See* McKay v. Bergstedt, 801 P.2d 617 (Nev. 1990) (quadriplegic patient being kept alive by ventilator may have it turned off).

NY: *See also* Fosmire v. Nicoleau, 551 N.E.2d 77 (N.Y. 1990) (blood transfusion case).

[335] Thor v. Superior Court, 855 P.2d at 379.

[336] *Id.*

[337] *Id.*

[338] *Id.*

[339] *Id.*

[340] *Id.*

[341] Thor v. Superior Court, 855 P.2d at 379.

decisionmaking affected or even dictated by his or her life circumstances, including resultant depression, limited financial resources, and minimal family or social support systems."[342] Recognizing that the prison environment is "in some respects unique, [it still] is simply one such circumstance in the individual's personal calculus; and we have no basis for assuming it inherently jeopardizes the voluntariness of that process for inmates."[343]

Charitable and Humane Care. In *McKay v. Bergstedt,* the Nevada Supreme Court took note that the state has an interest "in encouraging the charitable and humane care of those whose lives may be artificially extended under conditions which have the prospect of providing at least a modicum of quality living."[344] In this case, the court was concerned that Mr. Bergstedt—a young man who had been a quadriplegic as the result of an accident at age 10 and who needed a ventilator to breathe for him—wanted to end his life because of his lack of knowledge of alternatives to providing for his care after his father, who had been his constant caretaker for many years, would die. Had he been aware of these options, he might have concluded that his quality of life would not have been as bleak as he forecast it to be.[345]

Right of Confrontation. The state's interest in ensuring a criminal defendant's right to confront his accuser does not outweigh the individual's interest in forgoing life-sustaining treatment. In *People v. Adams,*[346] a criminal prosecution, the court rejected the defendant's contention that the state should not have permitted a shooting victim to terminate life support, or having done so should be barred from using the victim's statements incriminating the defendant on the basis that it violated the latter's right to confront his accuser. To similar effect is *In re Brown,*[347] holding that the state's interest was not sufficient to override the refusal of a blood transfusion on religious grounds by an individual who was the only person who could provide eyewitness evidence in a criminal prosecution for attempted homicide.

---

342 *Id.* at 380.

343 *Id.*

344 801 P.2d 617, 621 (Nev. 1990).

345 *See* Applebome, *An Angry Man Fights to Die, Then Tests Life,* N.Y. Times, Feb. 7, 1990, at 1 (late ed.) (reporting that Larry McAfee, also a young quadriplegic man who had also wanted his life-sustaining respirator turned off (*see* State v. McAfee, 385 S.E.2d 651 (Ga. 1989)), had "made a tentative, though ambivalent, decision to try to live" after a variety of social services, such as a voice-activated computer, had been made available to him in the wake of publicity about his case).

346 265 Cal. Rptr. 568 (Ct. App. 1990).

347 478 So. 2d 1033 (Miss. 1985).

Welfare of Children. When the patient is a child, the state also has an interest in the protection of the patient's welfare, which may outweigh the parents' fundamental constitutionally protected interest "in the religious upbringing of their children."[348] When "'the child's very life is threatened by a parental decision refusing medical treatment, this State interest clearly supersedes parental prerogatives.'"[349] This subject is discussed in **Chapter 15.**

---

[348] *In re* McCauley, 565 N.E.2d 411, 413 (Mass. 1991).

[349] *Id.* at 414 (quoting Custody of a Minor, 379 N.E.2d 1053 (Mass. 1978)).

Bibliography

Davis, S. Note. "Refusal of Life-Saving Medical Treatment vs. The State's Interest in the Preservation of Life: A Clarification of the Interests at Stake." *Washington University Law Quarterly* 58 (1980): 85.

Lomond, K. "An Adult Patient's Right to Refuse Medical Treatment for Religious Reasons: The Limitations Imposed by Parenthood." *University of Louisville Journal of Family Law* 31 (1992–1993): 665.

Maher, F. "Indirectly Intended Life-Shortening Analgesia: Clarifying the Principles," *Issues in Law and Medicine* 6 (1990): 117.

Peterson, G. Comment. "Balancing the Right to Die with Competing Interests: A Socio-Enigma." *Pepperdine Law Review* 13 (1985): 109.

Symposium. "Doctrine of Double Effect." *Journal of Medicine and Philosophy* 16 (1991): 467.

CHAPTER 9

APPLICATION OF RIGHT TO DIE TO PARTICULAR TREATMENTS AND ILLNESSES

§ 9.1 Introduction

In principle, neither the type of treatment or treatments at issue in a right-to-die case nor the patient's diagnosis are determinative of whether treatment may be forgone or must be administered.[1] Nonetheless, the appropriate resolution of questions about forgoing life-sustaining treatment, whether by courts or in the clinical setting without judicial involvement, is very much dependent on the facts of the particular case. As discussed in **Chapter 8,** accurate information about the patient's diagnosis and especially about the patient's prognosis, both with and without the treatment in question, can be important factors in the decisionmaking process. With the exception of only one form of treatment—artificial nutrition and hydration[2]—the holdings of the cases have not been influenced very much by the particular treatment.[3] However, when a court is confronted for the first time with a request for the withdrawal of a particular form of treatment, it is helpful to have precedents involving that treatment.

The first part of this chapter reviews some of the more important therapies involved in decisionmaking about life-sustaining treatment. The second part of the chapter discusses the various kinds of medical conditions for which these or other treatments might be administered, and the role, if any, that prognosis for that condition has played in the outcome of right-to-die cases. This review is based exclusively on legal, rather than medical, authority except to the extent that the case law often relies on the testimony of expert witnesses, treatises, and policy statements of medical professional organizations. There are differences of opinion among the medical authorities, but it can be useful to know the position the courts have taken based on the conflicting medical evidence.

---

[1] **MA:** Brophy v. New Eng. Sinai Hosp., Inc., 497 N.E.2d 626, 637 (Mass. 1986) ("[T]he primary focus should be the patient's desires and experience of pain and enjoyment—not the type of treatment involved.") (quoting *In re* Conroy, 486 A.2d 1209, 1233 (N.J. 1985)).

NJ: *In re* Jobes, 529 A.2d 434, 446 (N.J. 1987) ("[T]he law does not and should not require any particular therapies to be applied or continued.").

See also President's Comm'n for the Study of Ethical Problems in Medicine & Biomedical & Behavioral Research, Deciding to Forego Life-Sustaining Treatment 3 (1983) [hereinafter President's Comm'n, Deciding to Forego Life-Sustaining Treatment] ("Life-sustaining treatment, as used here, encompasses all health care interventions that have the effect of increasing the life span of the patient. Although the term includes respirators, kidney machines, and all the paraphernalia of modern medicine, it also includes home physical therapy, nursing support for activities of daily living, and special feeding procedures, provided that one of the effects of the treatment is to prolong a patient's life."); Council on Ethical & Judicial Affairs, American Medical Ass'n, Code of Medical Ethics § 2.20, at 36 (1994) ("Life-sustaining treatment may include, but is not limited to, mechanical ventilation, renal dialysis, chemotherapy, antibiotics, and artificial nutrition and hydration.").

[2] See § **9.39.**

[3] *See, e.g., In re* Grant, 747 P.2d 445 (Wash. 1987), *modified,* 757 P.2d 534 (Wash. 1988) ("The right to have life sustaining treatment withheld extends to all artificial procedures which serve only to prolong the life of a terminally ill patient.").

FORMS OF TREATMENT

§ 9.2 Supportive Care

When a decision is made to forgo life-sustaining treatment with the knowledge that it almost certainly will lead to the patient's death, basic nursing care must still be provided "to ensure dignified and respectful treatment of the patient."[4] Care must be taken not to abandon, avoid, or neglect the patient or the patient's family.[5] Many advance directive statutes require that when life-sustaining treatment is forgone, until the patient dies, supportive or palliative care must be provided.[6] That a patient may be incapable of perceiving anything does not excuse the continued provision of such care, although in such cases it is arguably as much for the benefit of others, such as the patient's family and the nursing staff, as it is for the dignity of the patient.[7] In addition, patients should be provided with appropriate kinds and levels of analgesic (pain-killing) medications[8] and sedatives when necessary to relieve anxiety.[9]

§ 9.3 Blood Transfusions

There is a substantial amount of litigation about the refusal of blood transfusions largely because it is a tenet of the Jehovah's Witnesses faith that blood transfusions are impermissible. Virtually all this litigation, however, concerns patients whose lives could be saved and health restored to the status quo ante if the blood transfusions were administered. Consequently, the interest of the state is greater than if the treatment would merely prolong the process of dying but

---

[4] **NJ:** *In re* Jobes, 529 A.2d 434, 446 (N.J. 1987) (citing President's Comm'n, Deciding to Forego Life-Sustaining Treatment 4–5). *Accord In re* Farrell, 529 A.2d 404, 419 (N.J. 1987) (O'Hern, J., concurring).

[5] *See* Hastings Ctr., Guidelines on the Termination of Life-Sustaining Treatment and the Care of the Dying 71–73 (1987) (Part Two, § E.I) [hereinafter Hastings Center Guidelines]. *Cf.* N.Y. Pub. Health Law § 2968 ("Consent to the issuance of an order not to resuscitate shall not constitute consent to withholding or withdrawing medical treatment other than cardiopulmonary resuscitation.").

[6] See § **11.12.**

[7] *See, e.g., In re* Doe, 583 N.E.2d 1263, 1271 n.18 (Mass. 1992) (caregivers ordered to "continue all . . . aspects of . . . daily care [of patient in persistent vegetative state from whom tube feeding would be stopped], as well as requiring them to prevent chapped lips, dry skin, and other possible side effects").

[8] **GA:** *See* State v. McAfee, 385 S.E.2d 651, 652 (Ga. 1989) (patient's "right to be free from pain at the time the ventilator is disconnected is inseparable from his right to refuse medical treatment"). See §§ **9.38** and **16.26.**

[9] **GA:** State v. McAfee, 385 S.E.2d 651 (Ga. 1989).

PA: *In re* Doe, 45 Pa. D. & C.3d 371, 387 (C.P. Phila. County 1987).

not otherwise save the patient's life.[10] Prior to *Quinlan,* courts were notoriously reluctant to actually permit a patient to die from the lack of a blood transfusion. Courts willingly honored the principle that such treatment (as well as any other) may be refused but frequently found ways to circumvent it by finding the patient incompetent,[11] by finding that the patient was the parent of minor children,[12] by finding that the patient's refusal of treatment was ambivalent[13] or uncertain,[14] or by some combination of these and other factors.

A process of rethinking of these cases began in the mid-1980s, probably influenced by the long line of post-*Quinlan* cases that not only reaffirm the principle of the right to refuse treatment regardless of the fact that death will ensue but also actually apply it. The Florida courts have led the way in this movement. Between 1985 and 1993, they issued three decisions, more than any other state, reaffirming the right to refuse lifesaving blood transfusions.[15] All of

---

[10] See §§ **8.14–8.19.**

[11] **CADC:** *E.g., In re* President & Directors of Georgetown College, 331 F.2d 1000 (D.C. Cir. 1964).

DIL: *E.g.,* Holmes v. Silver Cross Hosp., 340 F. Supp. 125 (N.D. Ill. 1972).

IL: *But see In re* Estate of Brooks, 205 N.E.2d 435 (Ill. 1965).

NJ: *E.g.,* John F. Kennedy Memorial Hosp. v. Heston, 279 A.2d 670 (N.J. 1971).

NY: *But see* Erickson v. Dilgard, 252 N.Y.S.2d 705 (Sup. Ct. Nassau County 1962).

PA: *But see In re* Green, 292 A.2d 387 (Pa. 1972) (finding 16-year-old patient mature enough to make his own treatment decisions).

[12] **CADC:** *E.g., In re* President & Directors of Georgetown College, 331 F.2d 1000.

DC: *But see In re* Osborne, 294 A.2d 372 (D.C. 1972).

NJ: *E.g.,* Raleigh Fitkin-Paul Morgan Memorial Hosp. v. Anderson, 201 A.2d 537 (N.J. 1964); State v. Perricone, 181 A.2d 751 (N.J. 1962).

NY: *E.g.,* Powell v. Columbian Presbyterian Medical Ctr., 267 N.Y.S.2d 450 (Sup. Ct. N.Y. County 1965).

[13] **CADC:** *E.g., In re* President & Directors of Georgetown College, 331 F.2d 1000.

DCT: *E.g.,* United States v. George, 239 F. Supp. 752 (D. Conn. 1965) (patient "stated he would 'in no way' resist the doctors' actions once the Court's order was signed").

NJ: *E.g.,* John F. Kennedy Memorial Hosp. v. Heston, 279 A.2d 670.

NY: *E.g.,* Powell v. Columbian Presbyterian Medical Ctr., 267 N.Y.S.2d at 451 (patient "did not object to receiving the treatment involved—she would not, however, direct its use").

[14] **MI:** *E.g.,* Werth v. Taylor, 475 N.W.2d 426 (Mich. Ct. App. 1991).

NJ: *E.g., In re* Hughes, 611 A.2d 1148 (N.J. Super. Ct. App. Div. 1992).

PA: *E.g., In re* Estate of Dorone, 534 A.2d 452 (Pa. 1987).

OH: *Cf.* University of Cincinnati Hosp. v. Edmond, 506 N.E.2d 299 (C.P. Hamilton County, Ohio 1986).

[15] *In re* Dubreuil, 629 So. 2d 819 (Fla. 1993) (patient may refuse blood transfusion in conjunction with caesarean birth even though there are four young children and patient is estranged from husband); Wons v. Public Health Trust, 541 So. 2d 96 (Fla. 1989) (patient, with two minor children, suffering from uterine bleeding may refuse blood transfusion); St. Mary's Hosp. v. Ramsey, 465 So. 2d 666 (Fla. Dist. Ct. App. 1985) (patient who was not terminally ill but who was suffering from chronic kidney disease may decline blood transfusion despite fact that it would save his life and that he had a minor child).

the patients were competent when they refused treatment, a fact which made honoring the refusals easier, but all also had minor children, a fact which often tipped the balance in favor of ignoring or overriding the right to refuse treatment in pre-*Quinlan* cases. In *Wons,* for example, the fact that the patient had a child was deemed irrelevant because "[a]bsent evidence that a minor child will be abandoned, the state has no compelling interest sufficient to override the competent patient's right to refuse treatment."[16] Furthermore, since there was no abandonment because of the existence of another loving parent, the court declined to "decide whether evidence of abandonment alone would be sufficient in itself to override the competent patient's constitutional rights."[17] And in the leading cases, the courts have shown an aversion to restricting the right to refuse treatment only to those who oppose treatment on religious grounds.

To the same effect are decisions in Illinois,[18] Maryland,[19] Massachusetts,[20] and New York.[21] In *Norwood Hospital v. Munoz,*[22] the Massachusetts Supreme Judicial Court refused to order a blood transfusion for the treatment of a bleeding ulcer, said to be necessary to save the patient's life, although the patient was the mother of a young child.[23] The New York Court of Appeals held in *Fosmire v. Nicoleau,*[24] that the patient, a pregnant woman, as a competent adult, had the right to determine the course of her own medical treatment, which included the right to decline blood transfusions, and that the state's claimed interest in preserving the patient's life for the benefit of her child did not override her right to refuse treatment. The court carefully avoided grounding the holding on the basis of the right to practice one's religion and instead grounded it on the common-law right of self-determination. The court gave so little weight to the state's interest that one judge, in a concurring opinion, charged that

> [t]he majority now define the right of self-determination [so] broadly, . . . that unless the State has expressed its interest in overriding the individual's right in specific circumstances, no State interest exists. That reasoning ignores a multitude

---

[16] Wons v. Public Health Trust, 541 So. 2d 96, 99 (Fla. 1989).

[17] *Id.* at 99 n.2.

[18] *In re* Doe, 632 N.E.2d 326 (Ill. App. Ct. 1994) (right of pregnant woman to refuse caesarean section based on religious belief is grounded in common-law right to refuse treatment).

[19] Mercy Hosp. Inc. v. Jackson, 489 A.2d 1130 (Md. Ct. Spec. App. 1985), *vacated and remanded as moot,* 510 A.2d 562 (Md. 1986).

[20] Norwood Hosp. v. Munoz, 564 N.E.2d 1017 (Mass. 1991).

[21] Fosmire v. Nicoleau, 551 N.E.2d 77 (N.Y. 1990). *See also In re* Melideo, 390 N.Y.S.2d 523 (Sup. Ct. Suffolk County 1976).

[22] 564 N.E.2d 1017 (Mass. 1991).

[23] *But see In re* McCauley, 565 N.E.2d 411, 413 (Mass. 1991) (rejecting religious basis for parental right to refuse treatment of eight-year-old child who faced certain death from leukemia if untreated and whose life might be saved if treatment were administered; "'likelihood of recovery will not be known until her physicians are able to determine through conducting further tests [requiring blood transfusions] the type of leukemia she has developed'").

[24] 551 N.E.2d 77 (N.Y. 1990).

> of statutes and judicial decisions evidencing the State's commitment to the sanctity of life and imposes a burden of specificity on the Legislature which, for all practical purposes, leaves the right absolute.[25]

There are, however, some cases that have resisted this trend.[26] Each involved an emergency in which it was impossible to secure the patient's informed consent at the time the transfusion needed to be administered, but also in each there was evidence of varying degrees of probative value that the patient had refused the treatment in advance and while competent. In each case, the courts insisted on an "informed" refusal. However, in at least one of these cases,[27] the court overlooked the fact that the patient's refusal arose from the failure of the doctor to provide adequate information to the patient on the basis of which she could have provided an informed refusal. In other words, these courts have turned informed consent from a shield protecting the patient's autonomy and bodily integrity into a sword permitting these interests to be overridden.[28]

Sight should not be lost of the fact, however, that these are *appellate* courts that have permitted the forgoing of lifesaving blood transfusions, and that they have frequently reversed trial court decisions that ordered that the treatment be administered. In fact, in many of the cases, the patient received the transfusion. When an appellate court recognizes a right of refusal in such circumstances, death will not in fact ensue because the case is factually moot. That is usually not the case for trial courts, which are faced with the real possibility that an identifiable person whose life could have been saved and whose health could have been restored to the status quo ante will instead die. These cases must weigh very heavily on trial judges, as the following excerpt from a trial court opinion illustrates:

> Never before had my judicial robe weighed so heavily on my shoulders. Years of legal training, experience and responsibility had added a new dimension to my mental processes—I, almost by reflex action, subjected the papers to the test of justiciability, jurisdiction and legality. I read [the leading precedent] and was convinced of the proper course from a legal standpoint. Yet, ultimately, my decision to act to save this woman's life was rooted in more fundamental precepts.[29]

---

[25] *Id.* at 85 (Simons, J., concurring).

[26] **MI:** *E.g.,* Werth v. Taylor, 475 N.W.2d 426 (Mich. Ct. App. 1991).

NJ: *E.g., In re* Hughes, 611 A.2d 1148 (N.J. Super. Ct. App. Div. 1992).

OH: *Cf.* University of Cincinnati Hosp. v. Edmond, 506 N.E.2d 299 (C.P. Hamilton County, Ohio 1986).

PA: *E.g., In re* Estate of Dorone, 534 A.2d 452 (Pa. 1987).

[27] *In re* Hughes, 611 A.2d 1148.

[28] See **§ 17.12.**

[29] Powell v. Columbian Presbyterian Medical Ctr., 267 N.Y.S.2d 450, 451 (Sup. Ct. N.Y. County 1965).

Consequently, it is not clear that the slowly growing body of appellate opinions will result in a change in outcome at the trial court level.

There is also a slowly growing body of cases in which patients are virtually certain to die even if a blood transfusion is administered. In *Storar,*[30] the administration of blood transfusions would have prevented the patient from bleeding to death, but the patient would soon have died from the bladder cancer that was causing the bleeding. The court likened the blood transfusions to food: "they would not cure the cancer, but they could eliminate the risk of death from another treatable cause."[31] As a consequence, the court saw them as lifesaving, rather than life-sustaining, and required that they be administered. In light of subsequent developments in cases involving artificial nutrition and hydration, both in New York[32] and in other jurisdictions,[33] the force of this analogy may have been undermined. However, the determinative factor in *Storar* was not the nature of the treatment but the insistence of the New York Court of Appeals on an oral or written advance directive for life-sustaining treatment to be forgone.[34] Because the patient in *Storar* had never been competent, this was an impossibility.

Other courts have honored refusals of blood transfusions when it is unlikely that they would return the patient to the status quo ante. In *Newmark v. Williams,*[35] notable because the patient was a young child of Christian Science parents, the Delaware Supreme Court refused to order administration of chemotherapy for "Burkitt's Lymphoma, an aggressive pediatric cancer," because the chemotherapy "involved terrible temporary and potentially permanent side effects, posed an unacceptably low chance of success [40%], and a high risk that the treatment itself would cause his death."[36] In *In re E.G.,* a similar case except for the fact that the patient was found to be a mature minor[37] who had the capacity to make the decision for herself, the Illinois Supreme Court held that the patient was entitled to refuse life-sustaining blood transfusions even though she was likely to die within a month without the transfusions and there was an 80% likelihood that the transfusions, along with chemotherapy, would achieve remission of the disease. However, the long-term prognosis was "not optimistic, as the survival rate for [such] patients . . . is 20–25%."[38]

---

[30] **NY:** *In re* Storar, 420 N.E.2d 64 (N.Y.), *cert. denied,* 454 U.S. 858 (1981).

[31] 420 N.E.2d at 73.

[32] *See* Delio v. Westchester County Medical Ctr., 516 N.Y.S.2d 677 (App. Div. 1987); Elbaum v. Grace Plaza of Great Neck, Inc., 544 N.Y.S.2d 840 (App. Div. 1989).

[33] See § **9.39.**

[34] See §§ **7.4–7.6.**

[35] 588 A.2d 1108 (Del. 1991).

[36] *Id.* at 1118.

[37] See § **15.3.**

[38] **IL:** *In re* E.G., 549 N.E.2d 322, 323 (Ill. 1989).

DGA: *But see* Novak v. Cobb County-Kennestone Hosp. Auth., 849 F. Supp. 1559 (N.D. Ga. 1994).

§ 9.4 Cardiopulmonary Resuscitation and "DNR" Orders

Cardiopulmonary resuscitation (CPR) is the term used to refer to a constellation of procedures administered to patients "to restore cardiac function or to support ventilation in the event of a cardiac or respiratory arrest"[39] and hence to oxygenate the blood supply, especially vital for brain functioning. According to the Massachusetts Appeals Court,

> [m]any of these procedures are . . . highly intrusive, and some are violent in nature. The defibrillator, for example, causes violent (and painful) muscle contractions which, in a patient suffering (as this patient is) from osteoporosis, may cause fracture of vertebrae or other bones. Such fractures, in turn, cause pain, which may be extreme.[40]

Thus, despite its lifesaving potential, CPR is a treatment that some patients wish to avoid. Furthermore, when patients are terminally ill, CPR might be futile[41] in the sense that although it might temporarily restore the patient's circulation and respiration, death will soon ensue anyway either from the patient's underlying condition or from another cardiac or pulmonary arrest. Consequently, *do-not-resuscitate* orders (DNR orders) are frequently written in clinical practice, and when confronted with the issue, courts have also authorized the withholding of CPR.[42]

NY: *But see In re* Long Island Jewish Medical Ctr. (Malcolm), 557 N.Y.S.2d 239 (Sup. Ct. Nassau County 1990) (treatment ordered for patient, a few weeks short of his 18th birthday, who had refused on religious grounds blood transfusion for treatment of cancer in combination with chemotherapy and radiation, which would provide probability of survival of between 20 and 25% and who was certain to die without transfusion).

[39] N.Y. Public Health Law § 2961(4).

[40] **MA:** *In re* Dinnerstein, 380 N.E.2d 134, 135–36 (Mass. App. Ct. 1978) (citing Houts & Houts, Courtroom Medicine Series: Death § 1.01(3)(d) (1976)).

MD: *Accord In re* Riddlemoser, 564 A.2d 812, 814 n.2 (Md. 1989).

[41] **CO:** Carothers v. Department of Insts., 845 P.2d 1179, 1181 (Colo. 1993).

GA: *In re* Doe, 418 S.E.2d 3 (Ga. 1992).

MA: Custody of a Minor, 434 N.E.2d 601, 607 n.9 (Mass. 1982).

MO: *In re* Warren, 858 S.W.2d 263 (Mo. Ct. App. 1993).

NY: N.Y. Public Health Law § 2161(9) ("'Medically futile' means that cardiopulmonary resuscitation will be unsuccessful in restoring cardiac and respiratory function or that the patient will experience repeated arrest in a short time period before death occurs.").

See **Ch. 19.**

[42] **CA4:** *But see In re* Baby "K," 16 F.3d 590 (4th Cir. 1994) (anencephalic baby must be resuscitated if mother requests).

IL: *E.g.,* C.A. v. Morgan, 603 N.E.2d 1171 (Ill. App. Ct. 1992).

MA: *In re* Beth, 587 N.E.2d 1377 (Mass. 1992); Custody of a Minor, 434 N.E.2d 601; *In re* Dinnerstein, 380 N.E.2d 134 (Mass. App. Ct. 1978).

Questions concerning the withholding or administration of CPR frequently arise in hospitals and nursing homes. At one time, withholding CPR was considered to be so controversial that DNR orders were not openly discussed and were often unwritten.[43] This in turn led, in at least one hospital, to procedures so shoddy that a grand jury described them as "shocking procedural abuses."[44] This kind of concern and the need to clarify the procedures for writing DNR orders led to the enactment of detailed statutes in a growing number of states. See **Table 9–1** in **§ 9.8.**

"Code Status." Despite the controversy, the legislation, and the frequency with which this issue arises in the clinical setting—many hospitals require that a "code status" be assigned to all inpatients or at least to all patients in an intensive care unit—there has been relatively little litigation about forgoing CPR.[45] This

---

MO: *In re* Warren, 858 S.W.2d 263.

NY: *In re* Richardson, 581 N.Y.S.2d 708 (Sup. Ct. Monroe County 1992).

WA: *In re* Grant, 747 P.2d 445, 450 (Wash. 1987), *modified,* 757 P.2d 534 (Wash. 1988) ("[T]he AMA has stated that cardiopulmonary resuscitation—one form of life sustaining treatment—may be withheld 'in cases of terminal irreversible illness where death is not unexpected' or where 'prolonged cardiac arrest dictates the futility of resuscitation efforts.'") (citing 244 JAMA 506 (1980) and 227 JAMA 864 (1974)); *In re* Hamlin, 689 P.2d 1372 (Wash. 1984).

See **§ 9.6.**

43 **NJ:** *See In re* Quinlan, 355 A.2d 647, 657 (N.J.), *cert. denied sub nom.* Garger v. New Jersey, 429 U.S. 922 (1976) (An expert witness testified about "the unwritten and unspoken standard of medical practice implied in the foreboding initials DNR (do not resuscitate), as applied to the extraordinary terminal case. . . . No physician that I know personally is going to try and resuscitate a man riddled with cancer and in agony and he stops breathing. They are not going to put him on a respirator. * * * I think that would be the height of misuse of technology."). *See also* Margolick, *Hospital Is Investigated on Life-Support Policy,* N.Y. Times, June 20, 1982, at 34 (investigation of state attorney general into hospital practice of issuing DNR orders).

44 Sullivan, *Queens Hospital Accused of Denial of Care,* N.Y. Times, Nov. 17, 1982, at B-3.

45 **CA3:** *E.g.,* Kranson v. Valley Crest Nursing Home, 755 F.2d 46 (3d Cir. 1985) (dismissal of § 1983 action against municipally owned nursing home for death of patient allegedly caused by nursing home's DNR policy affirmed).

AZ: *Cf.* Rasmussen v. Fleming, 741 P.2d 674, 679 (Ariz. 1987) (do-not-resuscitate and do-not-hospitalize orders had already been written for nursing home patient and were not subject of litigation).

GA: *E.g., In re* Doe, 418 S.E.2d 3 (Ga. 1992).

IN: *E.g.,* Payne v. Marion Gen. Hosp., 549 N.E.2d 1043 (Ind. Ct. App. 1990) (action against physician and hospital for writing DNR order without consent of allegedly competent patient).

MA: *E.g., In re* Doe, 583 N.E.2d 1263 (Mass. 1992); Custody of a Minor, 434 N.E.2d 601 (Mass. 1982); *In re* Dinnerstein, 380 N.E.2d 134 (Mass. App. Ct. 1978).

MO: *E.g., In re* Warren, 858 S.W.2d 263 (Mo. Ct. App. 1993).

NY: *Cf.* Elbaum v. Grace Plaza of Great Neck, Inc., 544 N.Y.S.2d 840, 847 (App. Div. 1989) (discussing N.Y. DNR statute and concluding that it had no effect on patient's advance directive); *In re* Richardson, 581 N.Y.S.2d 708 (Sup. Ct. Monroe County 1992).

might be explained by the fact that CPR is an emergency treatment.[46] There is rarely if ever any possibility of attempting to determine once an arrest occurs whether CPR should or should not be administered. Thus, if any discretion about administering CPR is to be exercised it must be done through advance planning.[47]

Institutional Policies. Since CPR came into widespread use in the 1960s, most hospitals have developed a formal or informal policy that it be administered to any patient who suffers a cardiopulmonary arrest.[48] (Since January 1, 1988, the Joint Commission on Accreditation of Health Care Organizations has required all hospitals to have a policy on the withholding of resuscitation[49] or risk losing their accreditation.) This "standing order" for CPR in effect establishes a presumption in favor of its administration.[50]

Presumption in Favor of CPR: "Standing Orders." Because of the conditions under which CPR must be administered, the presumption in favor of CPR is eminently sensible.[51] First, a patient who suffers an arrest is, at least by virtue

---

OH: *Cf.* Anderson v. St. Francis-St. George Hosp., 614 N.E.2d 841 (Ohio Ct. App. 1992) (action against hospital and its agents for a variety of torts for administration of CPR to patient who had previously refused it).

PA: *Cf. In re* Doe, 45 Pa. D. & C.3d 371 (C.P. Phila. County 1987); *In re* E.L.K., 11 Fiduc. Rep. 2d 78 (C.P. Berks County, Pa. 1991).

WA: *E.g., In re* Grant, 747 P.2d 445 (Wash. 1987), *modified,* 757 P.2d 534 (Wash. 1988). *Cf. In re* Hamlin, 689 P.2d 1372 (Wash. 1984).

WV: *Cf.* Belcher v. Charleston Area Medical Ctr., 422 S.E.2d 827 (W. Va. 1992) (wrongful death action for relying on patient's parents' consent to DNR order rather than seeking decision of mature minor).

46 **MA:** *In re* Dinnerstein, 380 N.E.2d at 135–36.

WA: *In re* Grant, 747 P.2d at 452 ("[I]n the case of cardiac or respiratory arrest, a decision on whether to resort to life sustaining procedures will have to be made immediately; there will be no time to get court authorization to withhold treatment once an emergency arises.").

47 *See* Hastings Center Guidelines 46 (Part Two, § B.I).

48 *See* President's Comm'n, Deciding to Forego Life-Sustaining Treatment app. I (reprinting examples of such policies).

49 Joint Comm'n on Accreditation of Hosps., Accreditation Manual for Hospitals § MA.1.4.11, at 90 (1988), *discussed in* Miller, *Hospital Policies on Resuscitation: The 1986 Joint Commission Standards,* 5 Hosp. L. Newsl. 1 (Jan. 1988). *See also* American Hosp. Ass'n, *Effective DNR Policies: Development, Revision, Implementation* (1990).

50 American College of Physicians, Ethics Manual 36 (2d ed. 1989). *See also* Hastings Center Guidelines 51 (Part Two, § B.II(9)(c)). *Cf.* N.Y. Pub. Health Law § 2962(1) (McKinney Supp. 1988) ("Every person admitted to a hospital shall be presumed to consent to the administration of cardiopulmonary resuscitation in the event of cardiac or respiratory arrest.").

PA: *But cf.* Kranson v. Valley Crest Nursing Home, 755 F.2d 46, 50 (3d Cir. 1985) (nursing home policy on CPR is that it is not to be routinely performed).

51 President's Comm'n, Deciding to Forego Life-Sustaining Treatment 239–40; American College of Physicians, Ethics Manual 36 (2d ed. 1989).

of the arrest, in no position to decide whether CPR should be administered. Second, if CPR is not administered, the patient almost certainly will die. Finally, if permission to administer CPR is sought from a surrogate, as should ordinarily be the case, the delay occasioned thereby could easily result either in death or severe brain damage.[52] Consequently, at the time of an arrest there is no time to seek a decision about the administration of CPR from either the patient or family members. One court has described the process of administering CPR as follows:

> A . . . do-not-resuscitate order directs a hospital and staff not to employ extraordinary resuscitative measures in the event of cardiac or respiratory failure. "The terminology derives from the development . . . in acute care hospitals, of specialized 'teams' of doctors and nurses trained in the administration of cardiopulmonary resuscitative measures. If a patient goes into cardiac or respiratory arrest, the nurse in attendance causes a notice to be broadcast on the hospital's intercommunications system giving a code word and the room number. The members of the code team converge on the room immediately from other parts of the hospital.[53]

Thus, if CPR is to be withheld, it must be prearranged by the attending physician writing an order in the patient's medical record to withhold CPR in case of a cardiopulmonary arrest. Such an order is generally referred to as a *do-not-resuscitate order* (DNR order),[54] an *order not to resuscitate,*[55] or a *no-code order,*[56] though there is a variety of other terminology reflecting the practice of particular hospitals.[57]

---

[52] **MA:** *In re* Dinnerstein, 380 N.E.2d 134, 135 & n.2 (Mass. App. Ct. 1978) ("These procedures, to be effective, must be initiated with a minimum of delay as cerebral anoxia, due to a cutoff of oxygen to the brain, will normally produce irreversible brain damage within three to five minutes and total brain death within fifteen minutes. . . . 'The cells of the cerebral cortex, which control intellectual or cognitive functions, are destroyed in three to five minutes of anoxia; the cells of the midbrain and the brain stem, which control the body's vegetative functions, can survive for an additional few minutes, thus making possible a continued vegetative or comatose existence in some cases where circulation is restored after irreversible destruction of cells highest on the neuraxis.'").

[53] *In re* Beth, 587 N.E.2d 1377, 1378 (Mass. 1992) (quoting *In re* Dinnerstein, 380 N.E.2d at 136 n.3).

[54] **IL:** C.A. v. Morgan, 603 N.E.2d 1171, 1175 (Ill. App. Ct. 1992) ("Do not resuscitate means do not give cardiac compression or intubation.").

[55] N.Y. Pub. Health Law § 2961(13) ("'Order not to resuscitate' means an order not to attempt cardiopulmonary resuscitation in the event a patient suffers a cardiac or respiratory arrest.").

[56] **ID:** *E.g.,* Manning v. Twin Falls Clinic & Hosp., Inc., 830 P.2d 1185, 1187 (Idaho 1992) ("no code").

MA: *E.g., In re* Beth, 587 N.E.2d at 1378 ("'no code' order, also referred to as a 'DNR' or do-not-resuscitate order").

WV: *E.g.,* Belcher v. Charleston Area Medical Ctr., 422 S.E.2d 827, 830 (W. Va. 1992) (DNR order also known as "No 1-2-3" order).

[57] **DE:** *E.g., In re* Severns, 425 A.2d 156, 158 (Del. Ch. 1980) (permission sought to enter "a so-called no code blue order").

OH: *E.g.,* Anderson v. St. Francis-St. George Hosp., 614 N.E.2d 841 (Ohio Ct. App. 1992) ("No Code Blue").

PA: *E.g.,* State Bd. of Nurse Examiners v. Rafferty, 499 A.2d 289, 291 (Pa. 1985) (referring to "code blue").

So-called *slow codes,* in which the attending physician does not write a DNR order but informally makes it known to the nursing staff and inhalation therapists that when the patient suffers a cardiac arrest, resuscitation efforts should be slow and perfunctory so that the patient will not survive, are clearly improper.[58] Such practices reflect the widespread uncertainty in the 1960s, 1970s, and even the 1980s about the legality of not utilizing cardiopulmonary resuscitation whenever a patient suffered an arrest even though it was clearly not considered good medical practice always to employ it.[59] Although slow codes should have disappeared as the writing and implementation of DNR orders have become more accepted by physicians, other health care professionals, courts, and legislatures, slow codes might experience a resurgence as a way to avoid the insistence by a family that CPR be administered even when it violates accepted standards of medical practice to do so.

§ 9.5 —Informed Consent and DNR Orders

There is much debate about whether the informed consent of a competent patient or of the surrogate of an incompetent patient is necessary to write an order to withhold CPR. As this debate has developed, it has become entwined in the larger debate about so-called *futile* medical treatment, what it is, and what the rights and responsibilities of patients, surrogates, and health care professionals are with respect to such treatment.[60]

The question about the necessity to obtain informed consent to CPR would be a relatively simple matter if it were not for the existence of standing order for CPR to be administered to all patients suffering a cardiopulmonary arrest, which can only be avoided by writing a specific order not to resuscitate. There are essentially two points of view on this issue. The more traditional one, strongly grounded in patient self-determination and the authority of surrogates to assert an incompetent patient's interests, holds that the physicians are obligated to obtain informed consent from a competent patient or surrogate to write a DNR order withholding CPR. The more recently articulated competing position is that informed consent is necessary only when a procedure is recommended to a patient or surrogate. Thus, if the attending physician is not recommending CPR, there is no need to obtain informed consent either to perform it or to withhold it. (If the physician does not recommend CPR when, by accepted

---

[58] Hastings Center Guidelines 48 (Part Two, § B.II(1)); American College of Physicians, Ethics Manual 36 (2d ed. 1989); New York State Task Force on Life & the Law, Do Not Resuscitate Orders: Proposed Legislation and Report 6–7 (1986).

[59] **NJ:** *See In re* Quinlan, 355 A.2d 647, 657 (N.J. 1976) (An expert witness testified about "the unwritten and unspoken standard of medical practice implied in the foreboding initials DNR (do not resuscitate), as applied to the extraordinary terminal case. . . . No physician that I know personally is going to try and resuscitate a man riddled with cancer and in agony and he stops breathing. They are not going to put him on a respirator. * * * I think that would be the height of misuse of technology.").

[60] See **Ch. 19.**

medical standards, it is appropriate to do so, this might constitute negligence.[61]) The difficulty with this latter formulation is that it begs the question of when physicians are professionally and legally obligated to *offer* CPR.

(1) *Informed Consent Required to Withhold CPR/Write DNR Order.* The conventional wisdom is that decisionmaking about DNR orders should begin on the same basis as decisionmaking about any other form of treatment.[62] It is the physician's responsibility to initiate a discussion about CPR if the patient's medical condition makes it reasonably foreseeable that the patient might suffer a cardiopulmonary arrest, and it is not the responsibility of the patient or the patient's family to initiate such a discussion.[63] Some believe that there is a broader imperative than with most other treatments that a physician discuss CPR with all competent patients or surrogates, and not merely to raise the issue in the case of patients who, based on their medical condition, are likely to suffer a cardiopulmonary arrest. This is so because patients and families have come to expect that CPR will be performed when an arrest occurs, and because, at least in the case of terminally ill patients on a slow, downward course, an arrest is always more than a remote possibility.

When the physician initiates a discussion about CPR, as about any other treatment, it should be aimed at ensuring that the patient or the surrogate understands what CPR is, the conditions under which it is used, its risks and benefits, and the consequences of not administering it when an arrest occurs. Then the physician should determine whether the patient or surrogate wishes for CPR to be administered or for a DNR order to be written. When the physician believes that CPR is futile in terms of saving the patient's life or returning the patient to a quality of life that the patient would find acceptable, the patient and family should be told this, and they should be advised that, should a cardiac arrest occur, it is the physician's recommendation that CPR be withheld. However, CPR must not in fact be withheld unless there is consent to doing so.

(2) *Informed Consent Not Required to Withhold CPR/Write DNR Order.* A new line of thinking about decisionmaking about CPR has begun to emerge that rejects the notion that a physician must obtain the informed consent of the patient or surrogate to write a DNR order to withhold CPR. It results in part from a reexamination of the obligations imposed by the requirement to obtain informed consent, in part from the purpose of CPR, in part from experience with

---

[61] See §§ **17.13–17.15.**

[62] **CT:** Foody v. Manchester Memorial Hosp., 482 A.2d 713, 719–20 (Conn. Super. Ct. 1984) ("The DNR order is based upon the philosophy that a person capable of giving informed consent has the right to make his own decision regarding medical care.").

[63] **IN:** Payne v. Marion Gen. Hosp., 549 N.E.2d 1043 (Ind. Ct. App. 1990) (physician must obtain informed consent to write DNR order for competent patient) (by implication). *See also* Hastings Center Guidelines 48-49 (Part Two, § B.II(2)). *But see* Gillon, *Deciding Not to Resuscitate,* 15 J. Med. Ethics 171 (1989) (when patients wish not to discuss the matter it is an infringement on their autonomy to compel them to do so).

the conventional position on decisionmaking about CPR, and in part from the logistics of administering CPR in comparison with other treatments.

First, this line of thinking starts with the proposition that the doctrine of informed consent requires physicians to provide patients or their surrogates with information only about treatments appropriate to the patient's medical condition. This information ideally should be offered before the patient makes a decision, but often the patient makes a decision before obtaining fully relevant information either because the physician structures the discussion that way or because the patient decides before the physician completes the disclosure of information or before the physician even begins the process of informing. (In such a case the physician is still obligated to provide relevant information whether the patient's decision is a consent to or refusal[64] of treatment, unless the patient validly waives further disclosure.[65]) The standing order in favor of CPR merely creates a presumption that CPR is to be administered in the case of an arrest but does not require it. Thus, if a physician does not believe that CPR is appropriate for the patient, a DNR order may be written without obtaining permission for the patient or surrogate to withhold CPR[66] although the patient or surrogate should be told that resuscitation will not be performed.[67]

Second, the original intent was that CPR be used for patients who suffered an *unexpected* cardiopulmonary arrest and who stood a reasonable chance of recovery if their breathing and circulation could be promptly restored. However, for it to be used effectively for that class of patients for whose use it was intended, it must be administered immediately without any opportunity to obtain consent from the patient or permission from the patient's family, let alone informed consent. This fact has resulted in hospitals and nursing homes

---

[64] **CA:** Moore v. Preventive Medicine Medical Group, Inc., 223 Cal. Rptr. 859 (Ct. App. 1986); Truman v. Thomas, 611 P.2d 902 (Cal. 1980).

NY: Crisher v. Spak, 471 N.Y.S.2d 741 (Sup. Ct. N.Y. County 1983).

[65] See § **3.26.**

[66] *See* Council on Ethical & Judicial Affairs, American Medical Ass'n, Code of Medical Ethics § 2.22, at 52–53 (1994); American Thoracic Soc'y, *Withholding and Withdrawing Life-Sustaining Therapy,* 144 Am. Rev. Respiratory Disease 720, 728–30 (1991), *reprinted in* 115 Annals Internal Med. 478, 481–83 (1991); Farber, Letter, 318 New Eng. J. Med. 1757 (1988) (position of Am. College of Physicians); President's Comm'n, Deciding to Forego Life-Sustaining Treatment 244–47. *See also* Hackler & Hiller, *Family Consent to Orders Not to Resuscitate: Reconsidering Hospital Policy,* 254 JAMA 1281, 1282 (1990) ("[M]ost families are not accustomed to being offered a treatment with the suggestion that it be refused. Some will assume that if care is offered it must have some benefit and will interpret refusal as giving up or abandoning the patient.").

[67] *See* Council on Ethical & Judicial Affairs, American Medical Ass'n, Code of Medical Ethics § 2.22, at 53 (1994) ("When there is adequate time to do so, the physician must first inform the patient, or the incompetent patient's surrogate, of the content of the DNR order, as well as the basis for its implementation."). *See also* Schade & Muslin, *Do Not Resuscitate Decisions: Discussions with Patients,* 15 J. Med. Ethics 186 (1989) (physician has duty to determine whether patient wishes to have discussion about do-not-resuscitate orders but has no obligation to have such discussion).

adopting policies to administer CPR whenever a cardiopulmonary arrest occurs. As a result, it gradually became, without any forethought, an accepted medical practice for CPR to be administered to *all* patients who suffer an arrest and not merely those whose arrest was unexpected and who stood a reasonable chance of recovery if CPR were administered. A corollary to this practice has developed requiring that a specific order be written to withhold CPR, not just for those patients who might experience substantial benefit from the treatment but also for those patients who are very unlikely to even survive the resuscitation attempt. This corollary does not take into account the accumulating evidence that CPR does not work very well for many classes of patients.[68]

Third, experience has taught some physicians that if they approach a patient or surrogate to discuss withholding CPR when they believe CPR is not appropriate, the patient or surrogate might demand CPR nonetheless. If the physician accedes to the demand, the consequence is that CPR will be administered if the patient suffers a cardiac arrest, despite the fact that the physician believes that CPR will, at best, not work, or at worst not work *and* inflict significant pain on a person who is already close to death and who may have already suffered greatly. The possible alternative is that the patient or surrogate will commence suit against the physician.[69]

It is possible that when a physician recommends the withholding of CPR and the patient or surrogate rejects that advice, the rejection results not so much from a genuine desire to have CPR administered, but of the manner in which the explanation about CPR is made or because the physician provides no or incomplete information about the consequences of performing CPR. If physicians "us[e] misleading euphemisms, such as, 'Would you want us to do everything possible to save your life if your heart stopped beating?,' "[70] it is easy to see that the natural inclination of many patients and their families would be to respond in the affirmative. However, if the physician begins by explaining what CPR entails and providing an estimate of the likely lack of success with this patient,

---

[68] *See* Lantos et al., *Survival After Cardiopulmonary Resuscitation in Babies of Very Low Birth Weight: Is CPR Futile Therapy?,* 318 New Eng. J. Med 91 (1988); Kellerman, *Predicting the Outcome of Unsuccessful Prehospital Advance Cardiac Life Support,* 270 JAMA 1433 (1993); Lombardi et al., *Outcome of Out-of-Hospital Cardiac Arrest in New York City,* 271 JAMA 678 (1994); Longstreth et al., *Does Age Affect Outcomes of Out-of-Hospital Cardiopulmonary Resuscitation?,* 264 JAMA 2109 (1990); McIntyre, *Loosening Criteria for Withholding Prehospital Cardiopulmonary Resuscitation,* 153 Archives Internal Med. 2189 (1993); Murphy, *Do-Not-Resuscitate Orders: Time for Reappraisal in Long-Term-Care Institutions,* 260 JAMA 2098 (1988); Taffet et al., *In-Hospital Cardiopulmonary Resuscitation,* 260 JAMA 2069 (1988); Tucker et al., *Cardiopulmonary Resuscitation,* 154 Archives Internal Med. 2141 (1994).

[69] **CA4:** *E.g., In re* Baby "K," 16 F.3d 590 (4th Cir. 1994).

GA: *E.g., In re* Doe, 418 S.E.2d 3 (Ga. 1992).

MI: *Cf. In re* Wanglie, No. PX-91-283 (Minn. 4th Dist. Ct. Hennepin County July 1, 1991) (suit to compel continuation of ventilation).

[70] Youngner, *Who Defines Futility?,* 260 JAMA 2094, 2095 (1988). *See also* Stell, *Stopping Treatment on Grounds of Futility: A Role for Institutional Policy,* 11 St. Louis U. Pub. L. Rev. 481 (1992).

and then recommends against its administration (that is, by attempting to obtain an informed decision to forgo CPR)—the patient or surrogate might be more likely to agree to a DNR order.[71] If a patient or family says that they want everything possible done, it is important that they know what "everything possible" involves and what its possible consequences are because it is likely that some, if not many, demands for treatment arise from an inadequate understanding of what treatment involves and can accomplish.

Although to some this approach smacks of coercion, the manner in which the physician provides information and makes a recommendation is decisive. Physicians usually make recommendations either implicitly or explicitly, and patients often value such recommendations, and sometimes highly. To do the same with respect to CPR is inherently no different from doing so with respect to other forms of treatment. Neither physicians nor competent patients or the families of incompetent patients should be assumed to be automatons; thus, discussions about treatment should include advice as well as facts. Furthermore, discussion of CPR, even when it is not offered, has the symbolic value of demonstrating to the patient and family that they are not being abandoned and that the health care team *cares* for them. "All too often, patients or families demand futile treatment because of the symbolic message such treatment conveys—they have come to feel truly cared for only when the most modern invasive technologies are applied."[72]

Finally, the logic of CPR and DNR orders alone and in comparison with other treatments also supports this line of thinking. A DNR order, unlike most other medical orders, is an order to *withhold* treatment; ordinarily, doctors write orders only to *administer* treatment. As to most treatments, the presumption is that no diagnostic nor therapeutic interventions will take place without an order, written or oral, from a doctor to do so. There are, of course, many minor exceptions. Nurses perform a broad range of diagnostic and therapeutic regimens without a specific order—such as taking the patient's temperature and blood pressure and administering mild analgesics for the relief of pain. But certainly CPR is many orders of magnitude different.

Also, the consent of a patient or surrogate is ordinarily not required to withhold treatment. As a matter of logic and logistics, physicians do not offer all kinds of treatments to patients. Rather, there is a professional obligation, recognized in and enforced by law, for physicians to inform patients or their surrogates of the existence, risks, and benefits of those treatments that are reasonably likely to improve a patient's well-being.[73] This same professional obligation applies when the treatment in question is CPR, and thus physicians

---

[71] *See* Murphy, *Do-Not-Resuscitate Orders: Time for Reappraisal in Long-Term-Care Insts.,* 260 JAMA 2098–101 (1988) (23 of 24 patients or families given accurate descriptions of patients' medical conditions, poor prognoses, and the unpleasant reality of dying in a critical care unit opposed resuscitation.); Scofield, *Is Consent Useful When Resuscitation Isn't?,* 21 Hastings Center Rep. 28 (Nov.–Dec. 1991).

[72] Schneiderman et al., *Beyond Futility to an Ethic of Care,* 96 Am. J. Med. 110, 113 (1994).

[73] See § **3.15.**

are obligated to offer it only to those patients for whom it is reasonably likely to improve their well-being.

Under this analysis of decisionmaking about CPR, physicians are under no obligation to offer and administer CPR to all patients, but only to those patients for whom it is likely to be a beneficial therapy.[74] This is the official position of the American Medical Association,[75] although the AMA carefully hedges its position.[76] The broad dicta of both right-to-die cases and ordinary informed consent cases that patients have full authority to make decisions about their medical treatment do not apply to CPR[77] because of the absence of any obligation on the part of a physician to offer "futile" medical treatment.[78] Under this view, "futility is a professional judgment that takes precedence over patient autonomy and permits physicians to withhold or withdraw care deemed to be inappropriate without subjecting such a decision to patient approval."[79] Thus, in the case of a hopelessly ill dying patient, the physician should have no more of an obligation to offer CPR than to offer an appendectomy, aspirin, or a heart transplantation just because in some abstract sense those things are medical interventions that happen to be available in the hospital.[80] What triggers the

---

[74] **CA:** *Cf.* Barber v. Superior Court, 195 Cal. Rptr. 484 (Ct. App. 1983).

CO: Carothers v. Department of Insts., 845 P.2d 1179 (Colo. 1993) (by implication).

[75] *See* Council on Ethical & Judicial Affairs, American Medical Ass'n, Code of Medical Ethics § 2.22, at 52–53 (1994). *See also* American Thoracic Soc'y, *Withholding and Withdrawing Life-Sustaining Therapy,* 144 Am. Rev. Respiratory Disease 720, 728 (1991), *reprinted in* 115 Annals Internal Med. 478, 481 (1991) ("A life-sustaining intervention is futile if reasoning and experience indicate that the intervention would be highly unlikely to result in a meaningful survival for the patient. Here, meaningful survival specifically refers to a quality and duration of survival that would have value to that patient as an individual.").

[76] *See* Council on Ethical & Judicial Affairs, American Medical Ass'n, Code of Medical Ethics §§ 2.03, 2.095 (1994).

[77] **CA:** Moore v. Preventive Medicine Medical Group, Inc., 223 Cal. Rptr. 859 (Ct. App. 1986); Truman v. Thomas, 611 P.2d 902 (Cal. 1980).

CT: Foody v. Manchester Memorial Hosp., 482 A.2d 713, 719–20 (Conn. Super. Ct. 1984) (so-called informed refusal cases, holding that a physician may be held liable to a patient for failing to inform about the risks of a treatment that the patient declines, may also have given rise to this misunderstanding).

NY: Crisher v. Spak, 471 N.Y.S.2d 741 (Sup. Ct. N.Y. County 1983).

[78] *See* Council on Ethical & Judicial Affairs, American Med. Ass'n, Code of Medical Ethics: Current Opinions with Annotations § 2.035, at 6–7 (1994) ("Physicians are not ethically obligated to deliver care that, in their best professional judgment, will not have a reasonable chance of benefitting their patients. Patients should not be given treatments simply because they demand them. Denial of treatment should be justified by reliance on openly stated ethical principles and acceptable standards of care . . . not on the concept of 'futility,' which cannot be meaningfully defined.").

[79] Schneiderman et al., *Medical Futility: Its Meaning and Ethical Implications,* 112 Annals Internal Med. 949, 953 (1990).

[80] *See* New York State Task Force on Life & the Law, Do Not Resuscitate Orders: Proposed Legislation and Report 7–8 (1986); Tomlinson & Brody, *Ethics and Communication in Do-Not-Resuscitate Orders,* 318 New Eng. J. Med. 43 (1988).

physician's obligation to offer any treatment is its ability to improve the patient's well-being without imposing disproportionate burdens.[81]

On balance, the provisions of DNR legislation also support this position. There are a number of provisions in DNR statutes that might be used to construct an argument that a patient or surrogate can compel the provision of CPR, such as the provisions permitting patients to revoke directives[82] and the provisions prohibiting discrimination by health care providers against those without DNR orders or directives.[83] However, these provisions and others must be viewed in their historical context and the purpose of DNR statutes, which were enacted because of the uncertainty about whether it was permissible to write a DNR order. The purpose of DNR statutes is to provide physicians with assurances that it *is* permissible, and to provide individuals with a mechanism for implementing the right to refuse treatment—specifically, the right to refuse cardiopulmonary resuscitation. There is no basis in the history and purpose of these statutes, and little if any in their text, that they were intended to create a right to compel the provision of CPR. The decision whether CPR is to be offered is implicitly left to medical judgment.[84]

If this approach is taken, a specific order to withhold CPR is still needed because of an institution's policy or customary practice of always administering CPR when there is a cardiac arrest unless a specific order has been written to the contrary; but the informed consent of the patient or the informed permission of the surrogate is not necessary to write the order. Before writing the order, respect for patients and their families, not to mention ordinary prudence, strongly suggests that physicians should at least inform patients or families that if a cardiopulmonary arrest occurs, no efforts will be made to resuscitate because of the lack of benefit in comparison with the burden the treatment imposes.[85] What is inadvisable is for the attending physicians to tell patients or surrogates that the decision is up to them. Care should be taken to present this information in such a way that it appears neither that permission is being asked to forgo CPR nor that the patient or family is being pressured into forgoing it. However, that the attending physician believes CPR to be unwarranted does not mean that a patient or surrogate will share that view. There may be good nonmedical warrant for the administration of CPR. A dying

---

[81] American Thoracic Soc'y, *Withholding and Withdrawing Life-Sustaining Therapy,* 144 Am. Rev. Respiratory Disease 720, 728 (1991), *reprinted in* 115 Annals Internal Med. 478, 481 (1991) ("the purpose of a life-sustaining intervention should be to restore or maintain a patient's well-being; and it should not have as its sole goal the unqualified prolongation of a patient's biological life").

[82] See § **9.22.**

[83] See § **9.27.**

[84] See § **19.18.**

[85] *See* Scofield, *Is Consent Useful When Resuscitation Isn't?,* 21 Hastings Center Rep. 28 (Nov.–Dec. 1991). *See also* Gregory & Cotler, *The Problem of Futility: III. The Importance of Physician-Patient Communication and a Suggested Guide Through the Minefield,* 3 Cambridge Q. Healthcare Ethics 257 (1994).

patient might wish, for example, to be kept alive until a visit from a relative can occur.[86]

§ 9.6 ——Case Law on Informed Consent and DNR Orders

There is very little case law addressing the issue of whether or not informed consent must be obtained to write a DNR order. Prior to 1991, there was none, and since that time there have been two cases litigated, neither of which, however, is in any sense definitive. These two cases, *In re Baby "K"*[87] and *In re Doe,*[88] hold that a physician may not withhold cardiopulmonary resuscitation unless the surrogate is in agreement with this decision.[89] *Baby K* is by far the more significant of the two because the holding is based on federal legislation and is therefore potentially precedential in all states. By contrast, the *Doe* case is a relatively narrow decision based on the Georgia DNR statute.[90] Consequently, the reasoning is not necessarily persuasive in any other jurisdiction. (It is not even clear that the court's reasoning would apply to any other treatment deemed by the attending physician to be "futile" because the statute governs only decisionmaking about cardiopulmonary resuscitation.)

Given the sparse amount and unsettled state of the law at this time, in the final analysis the decision of the patient and/or surrogate should be sought and deemed determinative. At the very least, it is indefensible for a physician to write a DNR order without consulting the competent patient or surrogate of an incompetent patient. This may be in the process of changing, in part because of the increasing realization that in many cases the administration of CPR imposes far more in the way of burdens than it yields in the way of benefits, and in part because of the high costs associated with providing care to those near death. The physician who strongly believes that the administration of CPR is inappropriate may—and probably should—counsel the patient and family to that effect but can do no more, save attempting to arrange a transfer of the patient's care to another physician whose views are more consonant with those of the patient or surrogate.[91] There is possibly serious legal risk in a physician's unilaterally

---

[86] Youngner, *Who Defines Futility?,* 260 JAMA 2094, 2095 (1988) ("Living for five more days might give some patients the opportunity to say good-byes, to wait for the arrival of a loved one from another city, or to live to see the birth of a grandchild. For one patient, a life with extreme disability and pain might be quite tolerable; for another it might be totally unacceptable. Risk takers might see a 3% chance as worth taking, while others might give more weight to the 97% chance of failure.").

[87] **CA4:** 16 F.3d 590 (4th Cir.), *cert. denied,* 115 S. Ct. 91 (1994).

[88] 418 S.E.2d 3 (Ga. 1992).

[89] See §§ **19.17–19.18.**

[90] Ga. Code Ann. §§ 31-39-1 to -9. See § **19.18.**

[91] See §§ **9.21, 17.14, 17.15,** and **17.23.**

writing a DNR order without consulting the patient or surrogate.[92] However, only if a patient or surrogate does not ultimately acquiesce in this recommendation or strongly disagrees with it should the attending physician accede to their wishes over his medical judgment that CPR is contraindicated. In such a situation, it is probably advisable not to write the order, particularly if the patient is competent.[93]

§ 9.7 —DNR Legislation

A gradually increasing number of states have enacted statutes addressing the withholding of cardiopulmonary resuscitation. The New York statute, which became effective in 1988, was the first,[94] and although it has served as a springboard for subsequent legislation in other states, those states have adopted a variety of different schemes. Who can make a DNR directive, in what setting is it effective, and how stringently is the implementation regulated vary greatly, depending on the jurisdiction. The DNR statutes do not echo one well-accepted scheme, but rather embody diverse and sometimes disjointed provisions.

§ 9.8 ——Purpose

Because CPR is usually administered under exigent circumstances, it can be difficult to determine rapidly whether or not the patient has previously authorized the forgoing of CPR. Thus, the dominant legislative purpose in enacting statutes authorizing and regulating DNR orders is to assure health care

---

[92] *See, e.g.*, Strickland v. Deaconess Hosp., 735 P.2d 74 (Wash. Ct. App. 1987) (liability claimed for entry of DNR allegedly without patient's or surrogate's consent).

[93] *See* American College of Physicians, Ethics Manual 37–38 (2d ed. 1989); President's Comm'n, Deciding to Forego Life-Sustaining Treatment 244–48; Hackler & Hiller, *Family Consent to Orders Not to Resuscitate,* 264 JAMA 1281 (1990). *But see* Council on Ethical & Judicial Affairs, American Medical Ass'n, *Guidelines for the Appropriate Use of Do-Not-Resuscitate Orders,* 265 JAMA 1868 (1991) ("In the unusual circumstance when efforts to resuscitate a patient are judged by the treating physician to be futile, even if previously requested by the patient, CPR may be withheld. In such circumstances, when there is adequate time to do so, the physician should inform the patient or the incompetent patient's surrogate, of the content of the DNR order, as well as the basis for its implementation, prior to entering a DNR order into the patient's record.").

[94] *See* McClung & Kramer, *Legislating Ethics: Implications of New York's Do-Not-Resuscitate Law,* 323 New Eng. J. Med. 270 (1990) (evaluation of operation of New York statute); Letters, 323 New Eng. J. Med. 1838 (1990); Rosenthal, *Rules on Reviving the Dying Bring Undue Suffering, Doctors Contend,* N.Y. Times, Oct. 4, 1990, at 1 (nat'l ed.).

NY: *In re* Richardson, 581 N.Y.S.2d 708 (Sup. Ct. Monroe County 1992) (construing portions of statute).

professionals that in certain situations it is appropriate and legal not to attempt resuscitation.[95]

These statutes are generally drafted in one of two forms: either as a provision of an advance directive statute or as a freestanding statute. See **Table 9–1.**

Table 9–1

DNR Statutes

AZ:	Ariz. Rev. Stat. Ann. § 36-3251[a,1]
AK:	Ark. Code Ann. §§ 20-13-901 to -908[c,2]
CA:	Cal. Health & Safety Code § 1569.74; Cal. Probate Code § 4753
CO:	Colo. Rev. Stat. §§ 15-18.6-101 to -108[a,3]
CT:	Conn. Gen. Stat. Ann. § 17a-23[b]
FL:	Fla. Stat. Ann. § 765.307[a,1]
GA:	Ga. Code Ann. §§ 31-39-1 to -9[b,3]
ID:	Idaho Code §§ 39-151 to -165[b,3]
IL:	Ill. Ann. Stat. ch. 210, § 50/10.3[b,2]
	Ill. Ann. Stat. ch. 210, § 45/2-104.2[b,4]
KS:	1994 Kan. Sess. Laws ch. 143 (H.R. 2103) (Apr. 7, 1994)[c,3]
MD:	Md. Code Ann., Health § 5-608[a,1,*]
MT:	Mont. Code Ann. §§ 50-10-101 to -107[b,3]
NJ:	N.J. Stat. Ann. § 26:2H-68[b,1]
NM:	N.M. Stat. Ann. § 24-10B-4(J)[2]
NY:	N.Y. Pub. Health Law §§ 2960–2979[b,3]
PA:	Pa. Cons. Stat. Ann. tit. 20, § 5413[a,1]
RI:	R.I. Gen. Laws § 23-4.10-4[a,1]
	R.I. Gen. Laws § 23-4.11-14[a,1]
SC:	1994 S.C. Laws, Act 485 (H.R. 3678) (signed July 14, 1994)
TN:	Tenn. Code Ann. § 68-11-224[b]
UT:	Utah Code Ann. § 75-2-1105.5[a,1]
VA:	Va. Code Ann. § 54.1-2987.1[a,1]
WA:	Wash. Rev. Code Ann. § 43.70.480[a]
WV:	W. Va. Code §§ 16-30C-1 to -16[b,3]
WY:	Wyo. Stat. §§ 35-22-201 to -208[a,1]

[a] authorizes individuals to execute directive not to resuscitate

[b] authorizes physicians to issue DNR order

[c] authorizes both individuals to execute directives and physicians to issue orders not to resuscitate

[1] DNR provision in advance directive statute

[2] emergency medical services statute

[3] freestanding DNR statute

[4] applies to nursing home care

[*] interpreted in 79 Md. Op. Att'y Gen. (1994) (Opinion No. 94-023, May 13, 1994)

---

[95] **GA:** *E.g.,* Ga. Code Ann. § 31-39-1 (also recognizes uncertainty in medical and legal professions about legality of implementing DNR orders).

NY: *E.g.,* N.Y. Pub. Health Law § 2960.

WV: *E.g.,* W. Va. Code § 16-30C-1(b) (also ensures that right of self-determination regarding CPR decision is protected).

§ 9.9 ——Who Is Authorized to Execute Directive or Issue DNR Order

There are two general patterns of legislation for withholding CPR. Some statutes authorize an individual (*declarant*) to execute a *directive* informing health care professionals not to resuscitate. Directives are usually (though they need not be) executed in the outpatient setting. Other statutes authorize physicians to write an *order* authorizing the withholding of CPR. DNR orders are issued either in the prehospital or inpatient setting. The New Mexico statute is the only one that is not clear about whether an individual has the authority to issue a directive not to resuscitate or whether a physician has the authority to issue a DNR order.[96]

(1) *DNR Directives.* The first statutory pattern, placing the authority in the hands of a competent person, authorizes the declarant to unilaterally execute a directive to withhold CPR.[97] In a few jurisdictions, if the declarant lacks decisionmaking capacity, a surrogate may execute a directive to withhold CPR.[98]

(2) *DNR Orders.* The second pattern is decidedly different because it places authority to issue a DNR order in the hands of the attending physician rather than the patient or the patient's representative.[99] Some of these statutes explicitly

---

[96] **NM:** N.M. Stat. Ann. § 24-10B-4(J).

[97] **AZ:** Ariz. Rev. Stat. Ann. § 36-3251.

AR: Ark. Code Ann. § 20-13-901(4)(A) (either adult declarant or attending physician may issue).

CO: Colo. Rev. Stat. § 15-18.6-102 (adult 18 or older).

FL: Fla. Stat. Ann. § 765.307.

KS: 1994 Kan. Sess. Laws ch. 143 (H.B. 2103) (Apr. 7, 1994) (allows either declarant-executed directive or physician-issued order).

PA: Pa. Cons. Stat. Ann. tit. 20, § 5413.

RI: R.I. Gen. Laws §§ 23-4.10-4, -4.11-14.

UT: Utah Code Ann. § 75-2-1105.5 (adult 18 or older).

WA: Wash. Rev. Code Ann. § 43.70.480 (person who signed written directive or durable power of attorney that included DNR provision).

WY: Wyo. Stat. § 35-22-202 (adult with decisional capacity).

[98] **AZ:** Ariz. Rev. Stat. Ann. § 36-3251(D) (agent or guardian with authority to make health care decisions).

CO: Colo. Rev. Stat. § 15-18.6-102.

WY: Wyo. Stat. § 35-22-202.

[99] **AR:** Ark. Code Ann. § 20-13-901(4)(B) (either adult patient or attending physician may issue).

CT: Conn. Gen. Stat. Ann. § 17a-238g.

GA: Ga. Code Ann. § 31-39-4(a).

ID: Idaho Code § 39-151 to -165, *added by* 1994 Idaho Sess. Laws ch. 298 (H.R. 881) (Mar. 31, 1994).

require the consent of the patient[100] or surrogate[101] to the issuance of a DNR order. In some circumstances some of these statutes permit the attending physician to issue a DNR order without the consent of the patient or surrogate.[102]

IL: Ill. Ann. Stat. ch. 210, §§ 45/2-104.2, 50/10.3.

KS: 1994 Kan. Sess. Laws ch. 143, § 1(b-c) (H.R. 2103) (Apr. 7, 1994) (allows either physician-issued order or patient-issued directive).

MD: Md. Code Ann., Health-Gen. § 5-608.

MT: Mont. Code Ann. § 50-10-101(4) (licensed physician may issue order).

NJ: N.J. Stat. Ann. § 26:2H-68(a).

NY: N.Y. Pub. Health Law § 2962(2).

TN: Tenn. Code Ann. § 68-11-224(c).

VA: Va. Code Ann. § 54.1-2987.1.

WV: W. Va. Code § 16-30C-6(a).

100 **CT:** Conn. Gen. Stat. Ann. § 17a-238g.

GA: Ga. Code Ann. § 31-39-4(b) (oral or written consent).

ID: Idaho Code § 39-153(2)(a), *added by* 1994 Idaho Sess. Laws ch. 298 (H.R. 881) (Mar. 31, 1994) (patient must request DNR order for it to have operative effect).

KS: 1994 Kan. Sess. Laws ch. 143, § 3 (H.R. 2103) (Apr. 7, 1994) (directive must be signed by declarant).

NY: N.Y. Pub. Health Law §§ 2964(2)(a)–(b) (allows both oral and written informed consent of patient).

WV: W. Va. Code § 16-30C-6(a).

101 **CT:** Conn. Gen. Stat. Ann. § 17a-238g (person authorized by law).

GA: Ga. Code Ann. § 31-39-4(c) (allows oral or written consent, in good faith, by appropriate authorized person).

ID: Idaho Code § 39-153(2)(a), *added by* 1994 Idaho Sess. Laws ch. 298 (H.R. 881) (Mar. 31, 1994) (patient's legal representative can communicate request for DNR order to attending physician).

KS: 1994 Kan. Sess. Laws ch. 143, § 3 (H.B. 2103) (Apr. 7, 1994) (directive can be signed by surrogate in declarant's presence and by declarant's expressed direction).

NY: N.Y. Pub. Health Law § 2965(3)(c)–(4)(a) (oral or written consent of surrogate valid if two physicians concur that patient is terminal, permanently unconscious, resuscitation would be medically futile, or resuscitation would be extraordinary burden).

WV: W. Va. Code § 16-30C-6(a) (representative or surrogate).

102 **GA:** Ga. Code Ann. § 31-39-4(e) (if patient is incapacitated and no surrogate is available for consent, attending physician may issue DNR order if patient meets statutory requirements and ethics committee concurs with this judgment).

NY: N.Y. Pub. Health Law §§ 2964(3), 2966(1)(a) (consent of patient required if competent adult unless patient would suffer immediate and severe injury from discussion of DNR order, in which case physician may issue order only after written concurrence of another physician, ascertaining wishes of patient without injuring patient, documenting reasons for not consulting patient, obtaining consent of surrogate unless surrogate is unavailable and resuscitation would be medically futile).

WV: W. Va. Code § 16-30C-6(e) (attending physician may issue DNR order for incapacitated patient if second physician who has personally examined patient concurs with evaluation of patient's condition and need for DNR status).

§ 9.10 ——Types of DNR Statutes

DNR Provisions Included in Other Statutes. Some DNR provisions are included in advance directive (that is, living will, health care power of attorney, or general advance directive) statutes[103] or other types of statutes.[104] Provisions dealing with withholding of CPR are integrated into the larger statute and are subject to the governing provisions of that statute.

Freestanding DNR Statutes. Freestanding DNR statutes are generally more comprehensive than DNR provisions included in other statutes. They often include specific guidelines governing the issuance, implementation, and effect of DNR orders.[105] However, like the DNR provisions in advance directive statutes, most of the freestanding DNR statutes leave the actual DNR protocol to be formulated by a state agency, which must incorporate the statutory requirements in the DNR policy.[106]

---

[103] **FL:** Fla. Stat. Ann. § 765.307 (general advance directive).

MD: Md. Code Ann., Health-Gen. § 5-608 (general advance directive).

NJ: N.J. Stat. Ann. § 26:2H-68 (general advance directive).

PA: Pa. Cons. Stat. Ann. tit. 20, § 5413 (general advance directive).

RI: R.I. Gen. Laws § 23-4.10-4 (health care power of attorney); R.I. Gen. Laws § 23-4.11-14 (living will).

UT: Utah Code Ann. § 75-2-1105.5(1)(a) (living will).

VA: Va. Code Ann. § 54.1-2987.1 (general advance directive).

WY: Wyo. Stat. §§ 35-22-201 to -208 (living will).

[104] **AR:** Ark. Code Ann. §§ 20-13-901 to -908 (emergency medical services).

CT: Conn. Gen. Stat. Ann. § 17a-238(g) (social and human services).

IL: Ill. Ann. Stat. ch. 210, § 50/10.3 (emergency medical services); Ill. Ann. Stat. ch. 210, § 45/2-104.2 (nursing homes).

NM: N.M. Stat. Ann. § 24-10B-4(J) (emergency medical services).

TN: Tenn. Code Ann. § 68-11-224 (administrative code).

WA: Wash. Rev. Code Ann. § 43.70.480 (statute governing executive branch and Department of Health).

[105] **CO:** Colo. Rev. Stat. §§ 15-18.6-101 to -108.

GA: Ga. Code Ann. §§ 31-39-1 to -9.

ID: Idaho Code § 39-151 to -165, added by 1994 Idaho Sess. Laws ch. 298 (H.R. 881) (Mar. 31, 1994).

KS: 1994 Kan. Sess. Laws ch. 143 (H.R. 2103) (Apr. 7, 1994).

MT: Mont. Code Ann. §§ 50-10-101 to -107.

NY: N.Y. Pub. Health Law §§ 2960–2979.

WV: W. Va. Code §§ 16-30C-1 to -16.

[106] **CO:** Colo. Rev. Stat. §§ 15-18.6-101 to -108 (DNR protocol to be established by state board of health).

ID: Idaho Code §§ 39-151(8), 39-165, *added by* 1994 Idaho Laws ch. 298 (H.R. 881) (Mar. 31, 1994) (DNR protocol to be established by department of health and welfare).

§ 9.11 ——Witnesses

Some statutes require that the execution of a directive not to resuscitate or the issuance of a DNR order must be witnessed.[107] New York requires a DNR order to be witnessed only if the consent of an adult patient, surrogate decisionmaker, or parent or legal guardian of a minor to the DNR order is oral, in which case the physician's order must be dated and signed in the presence of two adult witnesses, one of whom is another physician affiliated with the hospital at which the patient is being treated.[108] If consent to the DNR order is in writing, it must be dated and signed in the presence of two adult witnesses who also sign.[109]

Some witnessing provisions restrict the persons who may serve as witnesses, prohibiting anyone who might have a conflict of interest. For example, Kansas and Utah require a witness to be at least 18 years old, and exclude as a witness (1) the person who signed the directive on behalf of the patient, (2) a person related to the patient, (3) an heir of the patient, or (4) one directly financially responsible for the patient's medical care.[110]

§ 9.12 ——State Plan and Standardized Forms

Some statutes set forth general requirements for the implementation of a DNR protocol and provide for a state agency to create a DNR policy to be followed statewide and a standard form to be used for DNR orders or directives,[111]

KS: 1994 Kan. Sess. Laws ch. 143, § 8 (H.R. 2103) (Apr. 7, 1994) (emergency medical services board may adopt rules and regulations to implement statute).

MT: Mont. Code Ann. §§ 50-10-101 to -107 (state board of medical examiners to develop DNR protocol; department of health and environmental sciences to develop form of DNR identification).

NY: N.Y. Pub. Health Law §§ 2960–2979 (commissioner of health to establish regulations for implementation and prescribe forms and DNR identification for nonhospital DNR orders).

WV: W. Va. Code §§ 16-30C-1 to -16 (secretary of department of health and human resources implements statewide distribution of DNR forms described in statute).

See § **9.12.**

[107] **AZ:** Ariz. Rev. Stat. Ann. § 36-3251(B).

KS: 1994 Kan. Sess. Laws ch. 143, § 3(d) (H.R. 2103) (Apr. 7, 1994).

NY: N.Y. Pub. Health Law §§ 2964(2), 2965(4)(a), 2967(4)(a).

UT: Utah Code Ann. § 75-2-1105.5.

[108] N.Y. Pub. Health Law §§ 2964(2)(a), 2965(4)(a)(ii), 2967(4)(a)(ii).

[109] *Id.* §§ 2964(2)(b), 2965(4)(a)(i), 2967(4)(a)(i).

[110] **KS:** 1994 Kan. Sess. Laws ch. 143, § 3(d) (H.R. 2103) (Apr. 7, 1994).

UT: Utah Code Ann. § 75-2-1105.5.

[111] **AR:** Ark. Code Ann. § 20-13-906 (board of health to adopt DNR protocol; department of health to adopt DNR identification).

CT: Conn. Gen. Stat. Ann. § 17a-238(g) (applies only to persons under authority of commissioner of mental health).

including in some cases a form to be used to issue a prehospital directive. This prescribed form generally requires the signatures of the declarant, a witness, and the attending physician.[112] Other statutes do not include a sample form, instead requiring that a standardized form be created by the state department of health or the equivalent agency. These statutes mandate that the form include specific descriptive characteristics of the declarant: name, date of birth, sex, eye and hair color, race or ethnic background, name, address and telephone number of the attending physician, the date, and signatures of the patient and the attending physician.[113] Montana requires the DNR form to be readily available free or at a

---

CO: Colo. Rev. Stat. § 15-18.6-103 (board of health to adopt CPR directive protocol, including methods of rapid identification of DNR-status patients).

FL: Fla. Stat. Ann. § 765.307(1) (Department of Health and Rehabilitative Services to adopt form for DNR order).

ID: Idaho Code § 39-165(1), *added by* 1994 Idaho Sess. Laws ch. 298 (H.R. 881) (Mar. 31, 1994) (department of health and welfare shall adopt DNR protocol).

IL: Ill. Ann. Stat. ch. 210, § 50/10.3 (Department of Health to adopt rules authorizing prehospital implementation of physician DNR orders); Ill. Ann. Stat. ch. 210, § 45/2-104.2 (nursing homes must establish DNR policy prescribing format, method of documentation, and duration of physician orders limiting resuscitation).

KS: 1994 Kan. Sess. Laws ch. 143, § 8 (H.R. 2103) (Apr. 7, 1994) (board may adopt rules and regulations to implement act).

MD: Md. Code Ann., Health-Gen. § 5-608(a) (state Institute for Emergency Medical Services Systems and State Board of Physician Quality Assurance to establish DNR protocol).

MT: Mont. Code Ann. § 50-10-105 (board of medical examiners adopts DNR protocol, department of health and environmental sciences to adopt DNR identification).

NM: N.M. Stat. Ann. § 24-10B-4(J) (emergency medical services bureau to adopt regulations pertaining to authorization of emergency medical services providers to honor advance directives in prehospital or interfacility settings).

RI: R.I. Gen. Laws § 23-4.11-14 (director of department of health empowered to promulgate rules and regulations to govern issuance of DNR bracelets).

TN: Tenn. Code Ann. § 68-11-224 (state board for licensing health care facilities shall regulate procedure for issuing and implementing DNR order).

UT: Utah Code Ann. § 75-2-1105.5(2)(a) (Department of Health to establish system of DNR identification).

VA: Va. Code Ann. § 54.1-2987.1 (DNR regulations to be promulgated by Board of Health).

WA: Wash. Rev. Code Ann. § 43.70.480 (department of health shall adopt guidelines and protocols).

WY: Wyo. Stat. § 35-22-203 (state department of health shall make protocol for implementation of CPR directives).

[112] **AZ:** Ariz. Rev. Stat. Ann. § 36-3251(B) (prehospital medical care directive).

KS: 1994 Kan. Sess. Laws ch. 143, § 2 (H.R. 2103) (Apr. 7, 1994) (prehospital DNR request form).

WV: W. Va. Code § 16-30C-6(f) (form of DNR order for persons outside health care facilities).

[113] **CO:** Colo. Rev. Stat. § 15-18.6-103.

UT: Utah Code Ann. § 75-2-1105.5(4).

WY: Wyo. Stat. § 35-22-2034(b).

nominal charge,[114] while Wyoming provides for "controlled distribution of the methods of identifying persons" identified as having a DNR directive.[115] Kansas provides for the certification of "entities" that distribute DNR identifiers. The entities must distribute the identifiers only pursuant to a properly executed DNR directive and must also maintain a toll-free, staffed telephone line to answer queries about the identify of the patient.[116]

§ 9.13 ——Identification of Patients Having DNR Orders

To facilitate rapid and simple identification by health care professionals of patients who do not wish to be resuscitated, some statutes authorize that a specific form of DNR identification, such as an identification card, form, necklace, or bracelet, be used.[117] Other statutes do not provide for any type of DNR identification but do provide for the state department responsible for creating a DNR protocol to adopt a uniform type of DNR identification.[118]

§ 9.14 ——Recording Requirements

Many statutes authorizing physicians to issue DNR orders also require that the order be recorded in the patient's medical record.[119]

---

[114] Mont. Code Ann. § 50-10-107.

[115] Wyo. Stat. § 35-22-203(a).

[116] 1994 Kan. Sess. Laws ch. 143, § 6 (H.R. 2103) (Apr. 7, 1994).

[117] **AZ:** Ariz. Rev. Stat. Ann. § 36-3251(C) (bracelet).

AR: Ark. Code Ann. § 20-13-901(4) (identification card, form, necklace, bracelet).

MT: Mont. Code Ann. § 50-10-101(4) (identification card, form, necklace, bracelet).

NY: N.Y. Pub. Health Law § 2977(6) (patient with nonhospital DNR order may, but is not required to, wear identifying bracelet).

RI: R.I. Gen. Laws § 23-4.11-14(a) (department of health shall issue bracelet marked "DNR," bearing name and address of patient and name, address, license number, and signature of physician who affixed bracelet to patient's wrist).

UT: Utah Code Ann. § 75-2-1105.5(2)(b) (identifying bracelets or other means necessary).

[118] **CO:** Colo. Rev. Stat. § 15-18.6-103.

ID: Idaho Code § 39-165(2), *added by* 1994 Idaho Sess. Laws ch. 298 (H.R. 881) (Mar. 31, 1994) (department of health and welfare shall adopt standard statewide form of DNR identification).

[119] **AR:** Ark. Code Ann. § 20-13-901(4)(B) (grounds for order must be documented in patient's medical file).

CT: Conn. Gen. Stat. Ann. § 17a-238g.

GA: Ga. Code Ann. § 31-39-4(a).

ID: Idaho Code § 39-151(6), *added by* 1994 Idaho Sess. Laws ch. 298 (H.R. 881) (Mar. 31, 1994).

MT: Mont. Code Ann. § 50-10-101(4).

§ 9.15 ——Minors

Most of the statutes requiring consent to a DNR order specifically apply only to patients over the age of 18. However, some statutes provide that a minor is authorized to consent to a DNR order if the attending physician determines the minor has adequate decisionmaking capacity. In some states the minor's consent is needed in addition to the consent of the parents.[120] Even in the absence of a statutory provision empowering a mature minor to consent to a DNR order, the common-law trend is toward recognizing the legal validity of minors authorizing the administration or forgoing of medical treatment, life-sustaining or otherwise.[121] In situations in which the minor is clearly not capable of consent, some statutes specifically provide for parental consent to a DNR order for the child.[122] However, these provisions, too, are not necessary because parents, prima facie, have the authority to forgo life-sustaining treatment on behalf of their children.[123] The Colorado statute provides that only after a physician issues a DNR order for a minor child may the parents of the minor (if married and residing together), the custodial parent, or the legal guardian of the minor execute a directive not to resuscitate.[124]

Most statutes are silent with regard to how parental disagreement about DNR orders should be handled. The New York statute requires the attending physician to submit a dispute between parents to the statutorily required dispute mediation system.[125] The Georgia Supreme Court has held that one parent could revoke a DNR order even if the other parent had consented to it, based on a statutory provision stating that "[a]ny parent, may, at any time, revoke his consent to an order not to resuscitate."[126] This interpretation is not entirely consistent with the

---

NJ: N.J. Stat. Ann. § 26:2H-68(a).

NY: N.Y. Pub. Health Law § 2962(2).

TN: Tenn. Code Ann. § 68-11-224(c).

WV: W. Va. Code § 16-30C-6(a) (documented for person not in health care facility; if in facility, DNR order shall be issued according to policy of facility or in accordance with statute).

[120] **GA:** Ga. Code Ann. § 31-39-4(d) (if attending physician thinks minor sufficiently mature, DNR order not valid without minor's consent).

NY: N.Y. Pub. Health Law § 2967(2)(a).

WV: W. Va. Code § 16-30C-6(d) (if attending physician believes minor between ages 16 and 18 to be sufficiently mature, order not valid without minor's consent; minor's wishes prevail in case of conflict between minor and parents).

[121] See **§ 15.3.**

[122] **GA:** Ga. Code Ann. § 31-39-4(d).

NY: N.Y. Pub. Health Law §§ 2967(3), 4(a) (parent must consider minor's wishes, and religious and moral beliefs).

WV: W. Va. Code § 16-30C-6(d).

[123] See **§ 15.3.**

[124] Colo. Rev. Stat. § 15-18.6-102, *amended by* S. 94-142 (May 4, 1994).

[125] N.Y. Pub. Health Law § 2967(4)(c).

[126] *In re* Doe, 418 S.E.2d 3 (Ga. 1992) (citing Ga. Code Ann. § 31-39-6(a)).

language of the provision of the statute that *permits* "[a]ny parent [to] consent . . . to an order not to resuscitate,"[127] because if one parent were to revoke the order, the other could then reinstate it, and so on. It would be preferable for legislatures to address this issue expressly.

§ 9.16 ——When DNR Order Is Effective

Some statutes specifically prescribe when a DNR directive becomes effective,[128] but most are silent and merely imply that a DNR directive is operative upon creation.

§ 9.17 ——Diagnosis Required for Implementation of DNR Order

Some statutes establish eligibility requirements for patients to be classified as DNR. The most common provision requires the patient to be in a terminal condition or permanently unconscious,[129] the same requirement contained in most living will[130] and some health care power of attorney statutes.[131] The West Virginia statute is unusual in specifically providing that all persons, not just those in a terminal condition or persistent vegetative state, have a right to make their own health care decisions, including the decision to refuse CPR.[132] Other statutes do not explicitly provide preconditions for a person to be qualified for

---

[127] Ga. Code Ann. § 31-39-4(d).

[128] **GA:** Ga. Code Ann. § 31-39-4(a)–(b) (upon issuance by attending physician; patient can consent to implementation at a present or future date, regardless of future mental condition).

NY: N.Y. Pub. Health Law § 2962(2) (upon issuance by attending physician).

[129] **CT:** Conn. Gen. Stat. Ann. § 17a-238g (second opinion corroborating attending physician's diagnosis needed; commissioner of mental health must also review).

GA: Ga. Code Ann. § 31-39-2(4) (medical condition expected to result in imminent death, or a noncognitive state with no reasonable possibility of regaining cognitive functions).

ID: Idaho Code § 39-153, *added by* 1994 Idaho Sess. Laws ch. 298 (H.R. 881) (Mar. 31, 1994) (terminal condition).

MT: Mont. Code Ann. § 50-9-102(11) (terminal condition).

NY: N.Y. Pub. Health Law § 2965(3)(c) (surrogate cannot consent to DNR order unless patient in terminal condition or permanently unconscious).

PA: Pa. Cons. Stat. Ann. tit. 20, § 5413(a) (physician must confirm patient is in terminal condition or is permanently unconscious for declaration governing care given by emergency medical services personnel to become operative).

UT: Utah Code Ann. § 75-2-1105.5(1)(a) (terminal condition).

[130] See **§ 11.9.**

[131] See **§ 12.17.**

[132] W. Va. Code § 16-30C-2(a)(3).

DNR status. However, the statutes that are part of a larger advance directive statute are governed by such a requirement. Some statutes also provide that a DNR order may be issued or a directive to withhold CPR may be executed if CPR would be futile[133] or if resuscitation would impose an extraordinary burden on the patient.[134]

§ 9.18 ——Settings in Which DNR Order May Be Implemented

The statutes governing the implementation of DNR orders and directives can be classified by the settings in which they are operative:

(1) *Prehospital Emergencies.* The majority of DNR statutes contain a provision addressing how emergency medical personnel should act when summoned to provide emergency medical services to an individual not in a hospital and for whom a DNR directive or order is in effect.[135] Some of these statutes

---

[133] **GA:** Ga. Code Ann. § 31-39-2(4).

NY: N.Y. Pub. Health Law § 2965(3)(c) (surrogate may consent to DNR order if CPR futile).

WA: Wash. Rev. Code Ann. § 43.70.480 (if person executed directive requesting withholding futile emergency medical treatment).

[134] **NY:** N.Y. Pub. Health Law § 2965(3)(c).

[135] **AZ:** Ariz. Rev. Stat. Ann. § 36-3251.

AR: Ark. Code Ann. § 20-13-901 to -908.

CO: Colo. Rev. Stat. § 15-18.6-104.

FL: Fla. Stat. Ann. § 765.307(1).

ID: Idaho Code § 39-150, *added by* 1994 Idaho Sess. Laws ch. 298 (H.R. 881) (Mar. 31, 1994) (noninstitutional situations).

IL: Ill. Ann. Stat. ch. 210, § 50/10.3 (prehospital care providers).

KS: 1994 Kan. Sess. Laws ch. 143 (H.R. 2103) (Apr. 7, 1994).

MD: Md. Code Ann., Health-Gen. § 5-608.

MT: Mont. Code Ann. § 50-10-102.

NM: N.M. Stat. Ann. § 24-10B-4(J) (emergency medical services licensing commission to adopt regulations for honoring advance directives in prehospital and interfacility settings).

NY: N.Y. Pub. Health Law §§ 2960–2979 (rules nonhospital and in-hospital DNR orders).

PA: Pa. Cons. Stat. Ann. tit. 20, § 5413.

UT: Utah Code Ann. § 75-2-1105.5.

VA: Va. Code Ann. § 54.1-2987.1.

WA: Wash. Rev. Code Ann. § 43.70.480 (department of health to adopt guidelines for emergency medical services personnel responding to patient who signed written directive requesting futile emergency medical treatment be withheld).

WV: W. Va. Code §§ 16-30C-1 to -16.

WY: Wyo. Stat. § 35-22-204(a).

dictate specific requirements that must have been observed by the patient before a general advance directive or a directive to withhold CPR may be given effect by emergency medical services providers.[136] Some statutes addressing the applicability of advance directives to emergency medical situations explicitly mention directives not to resuscitate,[137] but in the absence of such a specific provision, it is still reasonable to assume that advance directive statutes were intended to apply to CPR. Cardiopulmonary resuscitation is a common form of care given by emergency medical services personnel, and as broadly defined by the statutes, it includes most life-sustaining procedures that emergency medical personnel would perform.[138]

---

[136] **AR:** Ark. Code Ann. § 20-13-904(a) (emergency medical services personnel shall comply with DNR protocol when presented with either DNR identification approved by Department of Health, oral DNR order issued directly by physician, or written DNR order entered on form prescribed by Department).

FL: Fla. Stat. Ann. § 765.307(1) (DNR order must be written on Department of Health standard form and form must be presented to emergency medical services personnel to be honored).

ID: Idaho Code § 39-156(1), *added by* 1994 Idaho Sess. Laws ch. 298 (H.R. 881) (Mar. 31, 1994) (emergency medical services personnel shall comply when presented with either DNR identification or written DNR order).

MD: Md. Code Ann., Health-Gen. § 5-608(c) (emergency medical services personnel only authorized to follow DNR orders in form of order in accordance with protocols established by state Institute for Emergency Medical Services Systems and State Board of Physician Quality Assurance, oral DNR order provided by medical command and control physician, or oral DNR order provided by physician physically present at emergency scene).

MT: Mont. Code Ann. §§ 50-10-101 to -107 (emergency medical services personnel shall comply with DNR protocol when presented with either DNR identification approved by Department of Health, oral DNR order issued directly by physician, or written DNR order entered on form prescribed by Department).

NY: *But see* N.Y. Pub. Health Law § 2977(6) (no person may require bracelet identifying patient's DNR status to be worn as a condition for honoring nonhospital DNR order).

PA: Pa. Cons. Stat. Ann. tit. 20, § 5413(a), (b) (advance directive applies to emergency medical services personnel after declaration becomes operative only if original declaration is presented to emergency medical services personnel, who notify command physician, or based on prior notice from other health care provider, command physician directs emergency medical service personnel according to provisions of declaration).

UT: Utah Code Ann. § 75-2-1105.5(3) (emergency medical services provider not bound to follow DNR order unless patient executing directive complies with Department of Health rules).

[137] **NM:** N.M. Stat. Ann. § 24-10B-4(J).

PA: Pa. Cons. Stat. Ann. tit. 20, § 5413.

WA: Wash. Rev. Code Ann. § 43.70.480.

[138] **AZ:** *E.g.,* Ariz. Rev. Stat. Ann. § 36-3251 (bracelet labeled "Do not resuscitate" identifies patient as refusing any or all of the following treatments: chest compressions, defibrillation, assisted ventilation, intubation, or advanced life-support medications).

ID: *E.g.,* Idaho Code § 39-151(2), *added by* 1994 Idaho Sess. Laws ch. 298 (H.R. 881) (Mar. 31, 1994) (CPR means measures to restore cardiac function or to support breathing).

KS: *E.g.* 1994 Kan. Sess. Laws ch. 143 (H.R. 2103) (Apr. 7, 1994) (chest compressions, assisted ventilations, intubation, defibrillation, administration of cardiotonic medications, or other medical procedure intended to restart breathing or heart functioning).

(2) *Inpatient.* Some statutes are limited to regulating the implementation of DNR directives or orders within health care facilities.[139] Others apply to both inpatient and prehospital settings.[140]

(3) *Transfer.* Some statutes contain a provision explicitly making a DNR directive effective during transfer of the patient between health care facilities.[141] Again, the absence of such a provision should not lead to the implication that an otherwise valid DNR order or directive is not effective during transfer, but for logistical reasons, a patient who wishes such a directive to remain effective during transfer is well-advised to explicitly make his wishes known. It is possible, however, that medical transport personnel will refuse to transfer a patient if a DNR order is in effect.

(4) *Undefined.* A few statutes do not specify the setting in which a DNR directive may be implemented.[142]

§ 9.19 ——Consent to CPR Presumed

A few of the statutes explicitly state that consent to CPR is presumed in the absence of a DNR order or directive.[143] In the absence of such a statutory

---

[139] **CT:** Conn. Gen. Stat. Ann. § 17a-238g (applicable only to persons under supervision of commissioner of mental retardation).

GA: Ga. Code Ann. § 31-39-2.

IL: Ill. Ann. Stat. ch. 210, § 45/2-104.2 (nursing homes).

[140] **CO:** Colo. Rev. Stat. § 15-18.6-104.

KS: 1994 Kan. Sess. Laws ch. 143 (H.R. 2103) (Apr. 7, 1994).

MT: Mont. Code Ann. § 50-10-102.

NY: N.Y. Pub. Health Law §§ 2960–2979 (rules nonhospital and in-hospital DNR orders).

WV: W. Va. Code §§ 16-30C-1 to -16.

WY: Wyo. Stat. § 35-22-204(a).

[141] **NY:** N.Y. Pub. Health Law § 2971 (DNR order effective during interinstitutional transfer).

WV: W. Va. Code § 16-30C-7(b) (DNR order to be respected in health care facilities, ambulances, homes, and communities).

[142] **NJ:** N.J. Stat. Ann. § 26:2H-68.

RI: R.I. Gen. Laws §§ 23-4.11-14; -4.10-4.

TN: Tenn. Code Ann. § 68-11-224.

[143] **CO:** Colo. Rev. Stat. § 15-18.6-104(3).

FL: Fla. Stat. Ann. § 765.307(2).

GA: Ga. Code Ann. § 31-39-3(a).

ID: Idaho Code § 39-158, *added by* 1994 Idaho Sess. Laws ch. 298 (H.R. 881) (Mar, 31, 1994).

NY: N.Y. Pub. Health Law § 2962(1).

WV: W. Va. Code § 16-30C-5(a) (consent presumed unless DNR order, living will for patient in terminal or persistent vegetative condition, or medical power of attorney indicating patient does not wish CPR is in effect).

WY: Wyo. Stat. § 35-22-204(c).

presumption, the common-law presumption of consent to any treatment in an emergency should still govern unless the treatment has been specifically refused in advance.[144] Some statutes explicitly provide that the absence of a DNR order or directive creates no presumption about the patient's intent to be resuscitated or not.[145] What such a provision does to the common-law presumption in favor of administering emergency treatment is not clear, especially in light of the provisions in some statutes that the statute is not intended to impair existing legal rights to withhold CPR.[146] In the absence of a DNR order or directive, the appropriate conduct in the case of an arrest ordinarily should be to administer CPR.

Some of the statutes also stipulate that if there is any doubt about the validity of a directive or about the medical situation, emergency medical services personnel are to proceed with resuscitative efforts as otherwise required.[147]

---

[144] **OH:** Estate of Leach v. Shapiro, 469 N.E.2d 1047 (Ohio Ct. App. 1984).

MI: *Cf.* Werth v. Taylor, 475 N.W.2d 426 (Mich. Ct. App. 1991).

NJ: *Cf. In re* Hughes, 611 A.2d 1148 (N.J. Super. Ct. App. Div. 1992).

OH: *But cf.* University of Cincinnati Hosp. v. Edmond, 506 N.E.2d 299 (C.P. Hamilton County, Ohio 1986).

PA: *Cf. In re* Estate of Dorone, 534 A.2d 452 (Pa. 1987).

[145] **AR:** Ark. Code Ann. § 20-13-905(d).

MT: Mont. Code Ann. § 50-10-104(4).

[146] **AR:** Ark. Code Ann. § 20-13-905(c).

CO: Colo. Rev. Stat. § 15-18.6-103(1).

GA: Ga. Code Ann. § 31-39-9 (in addition, statute does not preclude a court from approving the issuance of a DNR order under circumstances other than those prescribed by the DNR statute).

MT: Mont. Code Ann. § 50-10-104(5).

NJ: N.J. Stat. Ann. § 26:2H-68(c).

TN: Tenn. Code Ann. § 68-11-224(d) (does not impair authority of durable power of attorney provisions).

UT: *But see* Utah Code Ann. § 75-2-1105.5 (directive made under DNR section takes precedence over advance directive).

WV: W. Va. Code § 16-30C-12 (statute also does not preclude court from approving issuance of DNR order under circumstances other than those prescribed by DNR statute).

WY: Wyo. Stat. § 35-22-203(a).

[147] **AZ:** Ariz. Rev. Stat. Ann. § 36-3251(F).

ID: Idaho Code § 39-157, *added by* 1994 Idaho Sess. Laws ch. 298 (H.R. 881) (Mar. 31, 1994) (emergency medical services personnel may disregard DNR order if they believe in good faith order has been revoked, to avoid verbal or physical confrontation, or if ordered to do so by attending physician).

NY: N.Y. Pub. Health Law § 2977(10)(a) (emergency medical services personnel may disregard nonhospital order if they believe in good faith consent was revoked or order canceled, or persons on scene object to order and physical confrontation appears likely).

PA: Pa. Cons. Stat. Ann. tit. 20, § 5413(c) (emergency medical services personnel confronted with conflicting information about patient's wishes for treatment shall act according to accepted treatment protocols and standards appropriate to their level of certification).

RI: R.I. Gen. Laws § 23-4.11-14(b) (if DNR identification bracelet appears tampered with or removed, physician or emergency medical personnel shall not follow instructions on bracelet).

Cardiopulmonary resuscitation and DNR orders in emergencies that arise during surgery or among school children are discussed in **§§ 9.31** and **9.32.**

§ 9.20 ——Effect of DNR Directive or Order on Treatment Other Than CPR

Some statutes are expressly limited to the withholding of CPR and prohibit the withholding of other forms of medical treatment.[148] Even in the absence of such a provision, however, consent not to be resuscitated should not be interpreted as meaning that a patient does not want other treatments.

§ 9.21 ——Duty of Physicians and Nonphysicians to Comply or Transfer

Several statutes impose a duty on an attending physician who is unwilling to comply with a DNR directive to take all reasonable steps to transfer the declarant to a physician or a health care facility that will observe the directive.[149] In West Virginia, the attending physician has no duty to transfer the declarant. Rather, the attending physician has a duty to notify the patient or representative of the physician's unwillingness to effectuate a DNR order or directive, and to permit the declarant to obtain another physician.[150]

Not all statutes addressing the duty of the attending physician to comply with the DNR directive expressly allow the physician to transfer the declarant if the physician has qualms about implementing the directive. The Idaho statute requires the attending physician to take all reasonable steps to comply with a DNR directive, without expressly providing the option of transferring the declarant.[151]

---

[148] **AR:** Ark. Code Ann. § 20-13-901(5)(C)(i).

KS: 1994 Kan. Sess. Laws ch. 143, § 2 (H.R. 2103) (Apr. 7, 1994) (prehospital DNR request form states that decision to withhold CPR will not prevent rendering of other prehospital emergency care).

MD: Md. Code Ann., Health-Gen. § 5-608(a) (prohibits withholding of comfort care and pain-alleviating therapy).

NY: N.Y. Pub. Health Law § 2968.

[149] **AR:** Ark. Code Ann. § 20-13-904(b).

GA: Ga. Code Ann. § 31-39-7(d).

MT: Mont. Code Ann. § 50-10-103(2).

NY: N.Y. Pub. Health Law § 2972(b) (transfer mandated only after dispute mediation is completed).

[150] W. Va. Code § 16-30C-9(c). See **§ 17.23.**

[151] Idaho Code § 39-156(e), *added by* 1994 Idaho Sess. Laws ch. 298 (H.R. 881) (Mar. 31, 1994).

Some statutes require health care professionals other than physicians to comply with a DNR order or directive,[152] and some specifically provide that compliance with a DNR order or directive is mandatory under some circumstances.[153]

§ 9.22 ——Revocation

A few DNR statutes authorize a specific method for revoking a DNR order or directive. Those that do provide a number of different means for doing so.

(1) *By Patient.* A commonly recognized method of revocation is for the patient to revoke the DNR directive or order simply by expressing the desire for resuscitation.[154] In the Kansas statute, which contains a sample form of a DNR

---

[152] **AR:** Ark. Code Ann. § 20-13-904(a) (emergency medical services).

CO: Colo. Rev. Stat. § 50-18.6-104(1).

IL: Ill. Ann. Stat. ch. 210, § 50/10.3.

MD: Md. Code Ann., Health-Gen. § 5-608(a).

MT: Mont. Code Ann. § 50-10-103(1) (emergency medical services personnel).

NY: N.Y. Pub. Health Law § 2977 (emergency medical services and hospital personnel).

UT: Utah Code Ann. § 75-2-1105.5.

WV: W. Va. Code § 16-30C-7 (health care providers).

WY: Wyo. Stat. § 35-22-204(a).

[153] **AR:** Ark. Code Ann. § 20-13-904(a) (emergency medical services personnel must comply when presented with either DNR state-approved identification, oral DNR order issued directly by physician, or written DNR order on state-approved form).

CO: Colo. Rev. Stat. § 50-18.6-104(1) (duty to comply with a DNR order if directive is apparent and immediately available).

MT: Mont. Code Ann. § 50-10-103(1) (comply when presented with either DNR state-approved identification, oral DNR order issued directly by physician, or written DNR order on state-approved form).

UT: Utah Code Ann. § 75-2-1105.5 (no duty to comply with DNR order unless patient wears DNR bracelet or other ID to clearly express intent to continue DNR status).

WV: W. Va. Code § 16-30C-7 (all health care providers must comply when presented with physician-issued DNR order, DNR state-approved identification, or DNR order issued in accordance with policy of health care facility).

WY: Wyo. Stat. § 35-22-204(a) (duty to comply with DNR order if directive is apparent and immediately available).

[154] **CO:** Colo. Rev. Stat. § 15-18.6-107 (patient can revoke at any time).

GA: Ga. Code. Ann. § 31-39-6(a) (patient can revoke through written, oral, or any other form of communication made to members of health care staff; if patient regains capacity, patient can revoke consent of surrogate).

ID: Idaho Code § 39-154, *added by* 1994 Idaho Sess. Laws ch. 298 (H.R. 881) (Mar. 31, 1994) (person may revoke through written or oral declaration or any act evidencing the intent to revoke).

directive, a space is included for revocation of the directive by the declarant by signing the form.[155] Even in the absence of express statutory authorization, any DNR order or directive ought to be considered to be revoked if the patient so requests, possibly even if the patient is incompetent or of dubious competency.[156]

(2) *By Surrogate.* Some statutes allow the surrogate of an incompetent patient to revoke a DNR directive or order.[157] The requirements are at times more stringent for the surrogate to revoke than for a patient to do so. Several statutes require that a surrogate's revocation be witnessed.[158]

(3) *By Attending Physician.* Under some statutes, an attending physician who believes a patient is no longer a candidate for DNR status can revoke a DNR order, sometimes even without the patient's or surrogate's consent to the revocation. The attending physician must include the revocation in the patient's medical chart, cancel the DNR order, and notify the medical staff of the change in status.[159] The result of these provisions is that CPR might then be

---

MD: Md. Code Ann., Health-Gen. § 5-608(b) (if DNR patient expressed desire to be resuscitated prior to cardiac arrest, emergency medical services personnel no longer authorized to follow DNR order).

NY: N.Y. Pub. Health Law § 2969(1) (patient can revoke at any time through written, oral, or any other form of communication made to members of health care staff).

VA: Va. Code Ann. § 54.1-2987.1 (if DNR patient expressed desire to be resuscitated prior to cardiac or respiratory arrest, emergency medical services personnel no longer authorized to follow DNR order).

WY: Wyo. Stat. § 35-22-207 (may be revoked at any time by patient).

155 1994 Kan. Sess. Laws ch. 143, § 2 (H.R. 2103) (Apr. 7, 1994).

156 See §§ **7.45–7.46.**

157 **CO:** Colo. Rev. Stat. § 15-18.6-107, *amended by* S. 94-142 (May 4, 1994) (guardian, agent, or proxy may revoke only those directives originally executed by a guardian, agent, or proxy).

GA: Ga. Code Ann. § 13-39-6(b) (surrogate can revoke with signed and dated writing to health care staff).

NY: N.Y. Pub. Health Law § 2969(2) (surrogate can revoke with signed and dated writing to health care staff).

WV: W. Va. Code § 16-30C-8(c) (by written revocation to physician or professional health care staff, or by orally notifying attending physician in presence of witness).

WY: Wyo. Stat. § 35-22-207.

158 **GA:** Ga. Code Ann. § 31-39-6(b).

NY: N.Y. Pub. Health Law § 2969(2) (witness required only for oral revocation).

WV: W. Va. Code § 16-30C-8(c) (witness required only for oral revocation).

159 **GA:** Ga. Code Ann. § 31-39-5(a) (can revoke if physician thinks patient is no longer candidate even if patient or surrogate refuses to consent to revocation).

NY: N.Y. Pub. Health Law § 2970(2)(a), (b) (if patient consented to and refuses to agree to revocation of DNR order, physician must make reasonable efforts to transfer patient or submit matter to dispute mediation system; physician may unilaterally cancel DNR order issued on consent of surrogate but must notify surrogate).

administered without the consent (indeed, over the prior objection) of the patient. In such a case, the possibility of liability for battery or intentional infliction of emotional distress would loom.[160] However, statutory immunity might apply, depending on the type of immunity provision in the jurisdiction in question.[161]

§ 9.23 ——Dispute Resolution

The New York statute includes a provision governing dispute resolution through a hospital-operated mediation committee. Each hospital must establish a mediation system to consider disputes regarding DNR orders, either by using existing hospital resources and offices or by creating a body specifically for this purpose. If a dispute is submitted to the committee, a DNR order will not be effective until the dispute has been resolved or 72 hours have passed, whichever comes first. Thereafter, the attending physician must either issue a DNR order or arrange for the patient's transfer to another physician or hospital.[162] The Tennessee statute mandates that the board for licensing health care facilities create and regulate a mechanism for resolving conflicts in decision-making.[163]

§ 9.24 ——Judicial Review

The New York statute explicitly provides a right of judicial review of a DNR decision, whether the decision is made through the dispute mediation process or otherwise. The patient, attending physician, parent, legal guardian of a minor patient, any person qualified to be a surrogate, or hospital may initiate judicial proceedings challenging a decision to enter a DNR order. However, a decision of a *patient* not to consent to issuance of a DNR order may not be subjected to judicial review.[164] It is doubtful that in other jurisdictions such explicit authorization is necessary to challenge a DNR decision through the judicial system.[165]

---

[160] **OH:** Anderson v. St. Francis-St. George Hosp., 614 N.E.2d 841 (Ohio Ct. App. 1992). See §§ **17.2–17.7.**

[161] See § **9.26.**

[162] N.Y. Pub. Health Law § 2972.

[163] Tenn. Code Ann. § 68-11-224 (b)(2).

[164] N.Y. Pub. Health Law § 2973.

[165] See §§ **5.25–5.38.**

§ 9.25 ——Penalties

In those states in which the DNR statute is part of advance directive legislation, the penalty provisions of the latter apply.[166] However, few of the freestanding DNR statutes create penalties for misconduct with respect to DNR orders. In some states if an attending physician is unwilling to comply with a DNR order and willfully fails to transfer the patient, the physician is guilty of a misdemeanor.[167] In Idaho a physician who willfully or negligently disregards the intent of the DNR identification is subject to penalty.[168] Other penalty provisions address persons concealing or destroying the DNR identification of another, or falsifying the revocation of the DNR directive of another,[169] or for concealing the revocation of a directive.[170]

§ 9.26 ——Immunities

Many freestanding DNR statutes contain immunity provisions, and in other jurisdictions the immunity provisions of advance directive statutes apply.[171]

(1) *Withholding CPR from DNR-Status Patients.* Some DNR statutes confer immunity for the withholding of CPR from a patient pursuant to a DNR order or directive. All of the immunity provisions protect against civil or criminal

---

[166] See §§ **11.19** and **12.48.**

[167] **MT:** Mont. Code Ann. § 50-10-106(1) (misdemeanor punishable by fine of less than $500 or jail term less than one year).

[168] **ID:** Idaho Code § 39-160(1), *added by* 1994 Idaho Sess. Laws ch. 298 (H.R. 881) (Mar. 31, 1994) ("willfully or negligently disregards the intent of the DNR identification"; misdemeanor, fine not more than $500 or imprisonment of not more than six months).

[169] **ID:** Idaho Code § 39-160(2), *added by* 1994 Idaho Sess. Laws ch. 298 (H.R. 881) (Mar. 31, 1994) (concealing or destroying DNR identification or forging revocation is misdemeanor punishable by fine of less than $500 or jail term less than six months, or both).

MT: Mont. Code Ann. § 50-10-106(2-3) (concealing or destroying DNR identification or forging revocation is misdemeanor punishable by fine of less than $500 or jail term less than one year).

[170] **ID:** Idaho Code § 39-160(3), *added by* 1994 Idaho Sess. Laws ch. 298 (H.R. 881) (Mar. 31, 1994) (falsifying or forging DNR identification or concealing a revocation is misdemeanor punishable by fine of less than $500 or jail term less than one year, or both).

MT: Mont. Code Ann. § 50-10-106(2)–(3) (forging identification or withholding information about revocation is misdemeanor punishable by fine of less than $500 or jail term less than one year).

[171] See §§ **11.17, 12.46,** and **12.47.**

liability and regulatory sanctions for unprofessional conduct.[172] The statutes vary as to whom they confer immunity on and under what circumstances. Some provide immunity to health care facilities withholding CPR in accordance with a DNR directive,[173] to persons withholding CPR under the direction of a physician,[174] to emergency medical services personnel withholding CPR,[175] to health care professionals,[176] or to others who in good faith comply with the directive.[177]

(2) *Administering CPR to DNR-Status Patients.* Some statutes confer immunity on those who administer CPR to a patient who has a DNR order or directive. Some require that the health care professional administering CPR act in good faith and be unaware of the DNR order, or that the health care professional reasonably and in good faith believe that consent to the order had been revoked.[178] Other statutes grant immunity to persons who provide CPR pursuant to a contemporaneous request from the patient despite the existence of a DNR order or directive.[179]

---

[172] **CO:** Colo. Rev. Stat. § 15-18.6-104(1).

GA: Ga. Code Ann. § 31-39-7(a).

ID: Idaho Code § 39-159(a), *added by* 1994 Idaho Sess. Laws ch. 298 (H.R. 881) (Mar. 31, 1994).

KS: 1994 Kan. Sess. Laws ch. 143, § 4 (H.R. 2103) (Apr. 7, 1994).

MT: Mont. Code Ann. § 50-10-102(a), (d).

NY: N.Y. Pub. Health Law § 2974(1).

[173] **CO:** Colo. Rev. Stat. § 15-18.6-104(1).

GA: Ga. Code Ann. § 31-39-7(a).

KS: 1994 Kan. Sess. Laws ch. 143 (H.R. 2103) (Apr. 7, 1994).

MT: Mont. Code Ann. § 50-10-102(a), (d).

NY: N.Y. Pub. Health Law § 2974(1).

[174] **ID:** Idaho Code § 39-159(b), *added by* 1994 Idaho Sess. Laws ch. 298 (H.R. 881) (Mar. 31, 1994).

MT: Mont. Code Ann. § 50-10-102(b) (if DNR identification is discovered on person).

[175] **CO:** Colo. Rev. Stat. § 15-18.6-104(1).

ID: Idaho Code § 39-159(c), *added by* 1994 Idaho Sess. Laws ch. 298 (H.R. 881) (Mar. 31, 1994).

MT: Mont. Code Ann. § 50-10-102(c) (if DNR identification is discovered on person).

[176] **CO:** Colo. Rev. Stat. § 15-18.6-104(1).

GA: Ga. Code Ann. § 31-39-7(a).

NY: N.Y. Pub. Health Law § 2974(1).

[177] **CO:** Colo. Rev. Stat. § 15-18.6-104(1).

[178] **GA:** Ga. Code Ann. § 31-39-7(b).

NY: N.Y. Pub. Health Law § 2974(2).

[179] **ID:** Idaho Code § 39-159(d), *added by* 1994 Idaho Sess. Laws ch. 298 (H.R. 881) (Mar. 31, 1994).

MT: Mont. Code Ann. § 50-10-102(e).

(3) *Other Immunities.* Some statutes provide immunity to a person consenting or declining to consent in good faith, on behalf of a patient, to the issuance of a DNR order.[180]

§ 9.27 ——Effect on Insurance

Several freestanding DNR statutes contain provisions mandating that the existence of a DNR order is to have no effect on the patient's obtaining or maintaining a life insurance policy.[181] Some statutes provide that DNR status cannot be used as a condition for obtaining health insurance or health care services, in order to prevent health insurers or providers from requiring that a patient consent to a DNR order or execute a DNR directive in order to obtain insurance or admission to a health care facility.[182] Some statutes also state that death resulting from withholding CPR through a DNR order is not suicide or homicide.[183] Many advance directive statutes contain similar provisions that apply to directives requesting the withholding of CPR and other forms of life-sustaining treatment.[184]

§ 9.28 ——Access to CPR

Some statutes explicitly provide that the enactment of the DNR statute does not create a duty on the part of a health care facility to have the capability to administer CPR.[185]

---

[180] **GA:** Ga. Code Ann. § 31-39-7(c).

NY: N.Y. Pub. Health Law § 2974(3).

[181] **CO:** Colo. Rev. Stat. § 15-18.6-106 (neither directive nor absence of one shall affect life insurance).

GA: Ga. Code Ann. § 31-39-8(a).

ID: Idaho Code § 39-161(2), *added by* 1994 Idaho Sess. Laws ch. 298 (H.R. 881) (Mar. 31, 1994).

MT: Mont. Code Ann. § 50-10-104(2).

NY: N.Y. Pub. Health Law § 2975(1).

[182] **GA:** Ga. Code Ann. § 31-39-8(b).

ID: Idaho Code § 39-161(3), *added by* 1994 Idaho Sess. Laws ch. 298 (H.R. 881) (Mar. 31, 1994).

MT: Mont. Code Ann. § 50-10-104(3).

NY: N.Y. Pub. Health Law § 2975(2).

[183] **ID:** Idaho Code § 39-161(1), *added by* 1994 Idaho Sess. Laws ch. 298 (H.R. 881) (Mar. 31, 1994).

MT: Mont. Code Ann. § 50-10-104(1).

[184] See §§ **11.20** and **12.49.**

[185] **GA:** Ga. Code Ann. § 31-39-3(c).

NY: N.Y. Pub. Health Law § 2962(4).

WV: W. Va. Code § 16-30C-5(b) (policy of hospital not to provide CPR must be given in writing to the patient or decisionmaker).

§ 9.29 ——Portability

Some freestanding statutes contain a provision that DNR orders executed in other states are held to be valid in their state.[186] Such "portability" provisions are also a part of some advance directive statutes, and a DNR directive issued pursuant to such a statute will be governed by its terms.[187]

§ 9.30 ——Miscellaneous Provisions

DNR Directive Is Not Euthanasia. Generally, the DNR statutes include provisions stating the statute does not authorize mercy killing or euthanasia. This means that death resulting from honoring an DNR order or directive is not the basis for the imposition of civil or criminal liability.[188] The same is true of DNR orders issued pursuant to advance directive statutes.

Mass Casualties. The Arizona and Idaho statutes each include a provision that the DNR statute does not apply to situations involving mass casualties.[189]

Publicity and Education. The New York and West Virginia statutes include programs for informing the general population about the possibility of executing or being issued a DNR order. The New York statute provides for a program of signs and other notification prominently posted throughout all hospitals,[190] and the West Virginia statute requires the state Department of Health and Human Resources to develop and implement a statewide educational program to inform the public about DNR orders.[191]

§ 9.31 —DNR Orders and Surgery

DNR orders pose a unique and difficult quandary for surgeons and anesthesiologists. At first glance, contemplating surgery for a patient with a DNR

---

[186] **ID:** Idaho Code § 39-163, *added by* 1994 Idaho Sess. Laws ch. 298 (H.R. 881) (Mar. 31, 1994).

[187] See §§ **11.21** and **12.50.**

[188] **CO:** Colo. Rev. Stat. § 15-18.6-108.

ID: Idaho Code § 39-152, *added by* 1994 Idaho Sess. Laws ch. 298 (H.R. 881) (Mar. 31, 1994).

MT: Mont. Code Ann. § 50-10-104(6).

WV: W. Va. Code § 16-30C-14.

[189] **AZ:** Ariz. Rev. Stat. Ann. § 36-3251(H).

ID: Idaho Code § 39-164, *added by* 1994 Idaho Sess. Laws ch. 298 (H.R. 881) (Mar. 31, 1994).

[190] N.Y. Pub. Health Law § 2979(1)(b).

[191] W. Va. Code § 16-30C-13(d).

order seems paradoxical.[192] If a patient has a DNR order, it is ordinarily because the patient is terminally or incurably and critically ill, is not expected to live very much longer, and is expected to suffer serious encroachments on quality of life from the resuscitation effort itself. The seeming contradiction is that, having refused cardiopulmonary resuscitation, the patient has, however, opted for an invasive, surgical procedure, accompanied by general anesthesia, which entails further risk from the deliberate depression of cardiac and pulmonary functioning followed by their resuscitation.[193]

In some instances, however, surgery for patients with DNR orders is not as contradictory as it may first appear.[194] Terminally ill patients might choose to undergo a surgical procedure to relieve pain. For example, "a person with incurable colon cancer may develop a bowel obstruction which requires surgical palliation."[195] Or surgery might be performed to implant a catheter into a central blood vessel for the purpose of providing nutrition, hydration, and/or medication.[196]

Without a DNR order, efforts will automatically be made to resuscitate a patient should an arrest occur during surgery or in the postsurgical recovery period. But a patient who has consented to anesthesia and surgery, while maintaining a DNR order, would ordinarily seem to have rejected such resuscitation and accepted the risk of death from cardiac arrest during the operative procedure or in the postoperative period.[197] This is not, however, necessarily the case, because a DNR order could be viewed not as a blanket decision not to resuscitate should a cardiopulmonary arrest occur, but as a mechanism for preventing unwanted resuscitation based on certain assumptions and under specific circumstances. These assumptions are that the patient is critically ill and

---

192 *See* Youngner et al., *DNR in the Operating Room—Not Really a Paradox,* 266 JAMA 2433, 2433 (1991) ("The concern that DNR patients who die will be viewed as 'bad outcomes' is understandable but entirely remediable. In our Department of Anesthesiology, all deaths occurring within 48 hours of anesthesia and surgery are reviewed and classified as expected or unexpected deaths. Expected deaths generally are related to the underlying condition of the patient. . . . [T]he quality assurance review focuses not so much on the manner of death but rather on the appropriateness of the classification. Patients with existing DNR orders usually fall into the category of expected deaths. At quality assurance meetings and mortality and morbidity conferences in our Department of Surgery, the 'complication' of intraoperative death in DNR patients is discussed in the context of the validity of the informed refusal of resuscitation and the adequacy of its documentation in the medical record. These issues, not the fact that the patient's death might have been prevented, are relevant in assessing quality of care.").

193 Truog, *"Do-Not-Resuscitate" Orders During Anesthesia and Surgery,* 74 Anesthesiology 606, 606 (1991).

194 American College of Surgeons, *Statement of the American College of Surgeons on Advance Directives by Patients: "Do Not Resuscitate" in the Operating Room,* 79 Bull. Am. C. Surgeons 29, 29 (1994) ("Some patients with DNR status become candidates for surgical procedures that may provide them with significant benefit even though the procedure may not change the natural history of the underlying disease.").

195 Walker, *DNR in the OR—Resuscitation as an Operative Risk,* 266 JAMA 2407, 2407 (1991).

196 *See* Cohen & Cohen, *Do-Not-Resuscitate Orders in the Operating Room,* 325 New Eng. J. Med. 1879, 1880 (1991).

197 Walker, *DNR in the OR—Resuscitation as an Operative Risk,* 266 JAMA 2407, 2408 (1991).

possibly in the process of dying, that the process of performing CPR will impose significant burdens on the patient, that the likelihood of recovery from a cardiopulmonary arrest is (in the patient's view) too slim to warrant the burdens imposed by the treatment, and that CPR will merely prolong the process of dying but not restore the patient to a quality of life that the patient deems acceptable.

However, when surgery is contemplated for the very same patient—a person who is critically and hopelessly ill and for whom there is no chance for recovery—it is on the assumption that the surgery is intended to improve, and holds out a reasonable prospect of improving, the patient's quality of life. The aim of the surgery is not to prolong the process of dying but to contribute to the quality of the patient's life while in the process of dying. "Furthermore, many of the therapeutic actions employed in resuscitation (for example, intubation, mechanical ventilation, and administration of vasoactive drugs) are also an integral part of anesthetic management."[198]

Different assumptions underlie the performance of CPR in conjunction with such surgery. The surgical setting, including the recovery process, is an environment in which the likelihood of successful resuscitation is far greater than that ordinarily contemplated when a DNR order is written:

> One of the most important reasons for a seriously ill patient to choose DNR status is that cardiopulmonary resuscitation outside of the OR often results in additional suffering and a poor outcome. A large number of these patients will not survive, and many of those who do survive will suffer significant neurological impairment. Resuscitation in the OR is different, however. Most causes of respiratory and/or cardiac arrest in the OR are treatable and rapidly reversible. Furthermore, pain is unlikely in the presence of anesthesia.[199]

Given this changed set of assumptions, ordinary DNR orders should not automatically be carried over to the surgical and recovery settings.[200] Rather, the contemplation of surgery for a patient with a preexisting DNR order ought to provide the occasion for rediscussion of the purpose and value of CPR for this particular patient.[201] CPR in the surgical context is, in effect, a different

---

[198] American College of Surgeons, *Statement of the American College of Surgeons on Advance Directives by Patients: "Do Not Resuscitate" in the Operating Room,* 79 Bull. Am. C. Surgeons 29, 29 (1994).

[199] Truog et al., *DNR in the OR,* 267 JAMA 1465, 1466 (1992). *See also* Walker, *DNR in the OR—Resuscitation as an Operative Risk,* 266 JAMA 2407, 2408 (1991) ("[I]n the heavily monitored environs of the OR, there is an increased likelihood of successful resuscitation. Insisting that physicians refrain from resuscitating patients in this circumstance means allowing preventable deaths to occur, not naturally, but as a direct consequence of surgery and anesthesia.").

[200] American College of Surgeons, *Statement of the American College of Surgeons on Advance Directives by Patients: "Do Not Resuscitate" in the Operating Room,* 79 Bull. Am. C. Surgeons 29 (1994).

[201] *See* Cohen & Cohen, *Do-Not-Resuscitate Orders in the Operating Room,* 325 New Eng. J. Med. 1879, 1880 (1991).

treatment from CPR outside the surgical context. Just as one should not infer from a patient's decision to decline kidney transplantation that hemodialysis ought to be forgone (or vice versa), one should not infer from a DNR order that the patient is not to be resuscitated in the course of, or recovery from, surgery. Although both kinds of treatment—CPR outside the surgical context and CPR in the surgical context—have the same name, they are in reality two different treatments.[202]

There are other reasons that DNR orders should not automatically be carried over to the surgical context. First, it has been suggested that anesthesiologists may provide better care to patients who do not have DNR orders. Although perhaps subconsciously motivated, some anesthesiologists may not give as much anesthetic as clinically indicated if they perceive that their hands are tied in regard to treatment of anesthesia's side effects.[203] Second, whether or not it is so as a matter of law, it is the customary practice of surgeons and anesthesiologists to regard consent for anesthesia as implicit consent for resuscitation.[204] Furthermore, death in the operating room can trigger professional scrutiny, criticism, and internal quality assurance audits.[205] Consequently, a DNR order "could prove frustrating to physicians who may feel forced to stand by and allow the patient to expire when they have the knowledge and the skill to perform resuscitation."[206] Consequently, surgeons may be unwilling to operate on patients with DNR orders, thus depriving them of useful palliative therapies.[207]

---

[202] *See id.* ("Apart from cardiopulmonary resuscitation, many interventions ordinarily performed in the operating room would be classified as forms of resuscitation in any other treatment setting. . . . When cardiac arrest occurs during an operation, the only new therapy required is cardiac massage and countershock.").

[203] Truog et al., *DNR in the OR,* 267 JAMA 1465, 1466 (1992). *See also* Truog, *"Do-Not-Resuscitate" Orders During Anesthesia and Surgery,* 74 Anesthesiology 606, 607 (1991) ("Advanced resuscitation techniques are the means anesthesiologists use to rescue patients when the balance [between analgesia and amnesia and cardiovascular collapse] tips toward physiologic instability. Deprived of these skills by a DNR order, the prudent strategy of an anesthesiologist committed to the patient's survival is to favor less anesthesia and greater hemodynamic stability.").

[204] *See* Truog, *"Do-Not-Resuscitate" Orders During Anesthesia and Surgery,* 74 Anesthesiology 606, 607 (1991). *See also* Cohen & Cohen, *Do-Not-Resuscitate Orders in the Operating Room,* 325 New Eng. J. Med. 1879, 1881 (1991) ("many view the withholding of CPR [in the operating room] as tantamount to killing").

[205] Walker, *DNR in the OR—Resuscitation as an Operative Risk,* 266 JAMA 2407, 2408 (1991).

[206] *Id.*

[207] *But see* Youngner et al., *DNR in the Operating Room—Not Really a Paradox,* 266 JAMA 2433, 2433 (1991) ("The concern that DNR patients who die will be viewed as 'bad outcomes' is understandable but entirely remediable. In our Department of Anesthesiology, all deaths occurring within 48 hours of anesthesia and surgery are reviewed and classified as expected or unexpected deaths. Expected deaths generally are related to the underlying condition of the patient. . . . [T]he quality assurance review focuses not so much on the manner of death but rather on the appropriateness of the classification. Patients with existing DNR orders usually fall into the category of expected deaths. At quality assurance meetings and mortality and morbidity conferences in our Department of Surgery, the 'complication' of intraoperative death in DNR patients is discussed in the context of the validity of the informed

Though not decisive considerations, these factors warrant consideration in the resolution of this dilemma.

Although these problems can be mitigated by the suspension of a DNR order during anesthesia and surgery, even then questions can arise regarding precisely when operative care ends on the one hand, and postoperative care begins and consequently the preoperative DNR order resumes. The recovery of hemodynamic stability and respiratory function after surgery depends on the individual patient, the type of anesthesia used, and the surgical procedure performed.[208] Thus, rather than adopting blanket policies either requiring suspension of DNR orders during anesthesia and surgery or requiring their continuation, decisionmaking about postoperative DNR orders should be similar to that of the initial entry of the DNR order. It should take into account the individual preferences, values, and goals of the particular patient, the patient's diagnosis and prognosis, and the recommendations of the patient's physicians and surgeons.[209] Rather, the decisionmaking process about a DNR order should begin anew when surgery is contemplated, what has been referred to as a policy of "required reconsideration."[210]

§ 9.32 —DNR Orders in Schools

Another difficult issue is raised by school children suffering from incurable illness such as cerebral palsy who are not hospitalized and who are likely to

---

refusal of resuscitation and the adequacy of its documentation in the medical record. These issues, not the fact that the patient's death might have been prevented, are relevant in assessing quality of care.").

[208] *See* Truog, *"Do-Not-Resuscitate" Orders During Anesthesia and Surgery,* 74 Anesthesiology 606, 607 (1991) ("The physiologic effects of anesthesia and surgery rarely terminate at the end of the procedure, when the patient leaves the operating room. Their duration depends upon the anesthetic technique used and the surgical procedure performed.").

[209] *See id.* at 608 (1991) ("Policies are designed to promote uniformity and generally are not well suited to situations that depend heavily on individual preferences and values. Rigid policies related to the management of DNR orders during anesthesia and surgery would restrict rather than enhance the options of the patients and physicians in facing this difficult issue. With the increasing recognition of the autonomy of the competent patient in medical decisionmaking, it would be inappropriate not to seek the patient's guidance and provide as much latitude as possible within the constraints of the physician's own ethical standards."). *See also* Walker, *DNR in the OR—Resuscitation as an Operative Risk,* 266 JAMA 2407, 2411 (1991) ("A more desirable and flexible approach to addressing DNR orders in the OR would stress bedside discussion and encourage a process of shared decisionmaking. Decisions about resuscitating terminally ill patients with DNR orders are best made between individual physicians and patients, not dictated in advance by fixed protocols.").

[210] American College of Surgeons, *Statement of the American College of Surgeons on Advance Directives by Patients: "Do Not Resuscitate" in the Operating Room,* 79 Bull. Am. C. Surgeons 29 (1994); American Soc'y of Anesthesiologists House of Delegates, *Ethical Guidelines for the Anesthesia Care of Patients with Do-Not-Resuscitate Orders or Other Directives that Limit Treatment* (Am. Soc'y of Anesthesiologists, Park Ridge, IL, Oct. 13, 1993) (Sections I, II). *See also* Reeder, *Do Not Resuscitate Orders in the Operating Room,* 57 AORN J. 947 (1993).

suffer cardiac arrest, possibly in school. These children have DNR orders, but public school authorities are reluctant to honor them, possibly out of a misplaced concern about possible liability if they do, and in part out of a concern about the purported adverse impact it would have on teachers and other students for a child to die in school. To date, there has been no appellate litigation around this matter, but there are at least two instances reported in the popular and professional literature in which public school authorities have been unwilling to honor a DNR order for a hopelessly ill but still functional student.[211] However, an opinion letter of the Maryland Attorney General concludes that public school officials must abide by DNR orders, and that they "have no legal basis for substituting their medical judgment for that of the parents and the physician."[212] If a student with a DNR order suffers an arrest, school authorities are to call emergency medical services personnel. However, it is unclear whether under Maryland law, emergency medical services personnel are permitted to honor the order.

§ 9.33 Chemotherapy

Chemotherapy literally means treatment in the form of chemical compounds, that is, medications, but it is commonly used by physicians to refer specifically to medications for treating various forms of cancer. These medications often have serious, unpleasant, and even painful side effects, and physicians and patients alike sometimes consider the treatment to be as bad as the disease. Surprisingly few cases have involved forgoing chemotherapy.[213] The holdings in these cases do not turn on the nature of the treatment involved but are based instead on other considerations, such as those discussed in **Chapter 8.**

---

[211] *See* Kuehl et al., *Should a School Honor a Student's DNR Order?: Case History of S. A.,* 2 Kennedy Inst. Ethics J. 1 (1992); Scofield, *A Lawyer Responds: A Student's Right to Forgo CPR,* 2 Kennedy Inst. Ethics J. 4 (1992); Strike, *An Educator Responds: A School's Interests in Denying the Request,* 2 Kennedy Inst. Ethics J. 19 (1992); Youngner, *A Physician/Ethicist Responds: A Student's Rights Are Not So Simple,* 2 Kennedy Inst. Ethics J. 13 (1992); *Board Votes to Honor Request Not to Revive Girl,* N.Y. Times, Nov. 10, 1993, at B8 (nat'l ed.); *Teachers Now Allowed to Resuscitate a Girl,* N.Y. Times, Dec. 16, 1993, at A12 (nat'l ed.).

[212] 79 Md. Op. Att'y Gen. ____ (1994) (Op. No. 94-028, May 13, 1994).

[213] **DE:** *E.g.,* Newmark v. Williams, 588 A.2d 1108 (Del. 1991).

IL: *E.g., In re* E.G., 549 N.E.2d 322 (Ill. 1989).

MA: *E.g., In re* McCauley, 565 N.E.2d 411 (Mass. 1991); Custody of a Minor, 393 N.E.2d 836 (Mass. 1979); Superintendent of Belchertown State Sch. v. Saikewicz, 370 N.E.2d 417 (Mass. 1977).

NJ: *E.g.,* Suenram v. Society of Valley Hosp., 383 A.2d 143 (N.J. Super. Ct. L. Div. 1977).

NY: *E.g., In re* Storar, 420 N.E.2d 64 (N.Y. 1981); *In re* Hofbauer, 393 N.E.2d 1009 (N.Y. 1979); *In re* Long Island Jewish Medical Ctr. (Malcolm), 557 N.Y.S.2d 239 (Sup. Ct. Queens County 1990).

§ 9.34 Kidney Dialysis

Kidney dialysis is a procedure for cleansing the blood of waste products, which is ordinarily the function of the kidneys and which becomes necessary when kidney failure occurs. As its name suggests, end-stage renal (kidney) disease is fatal if untreated. However, either hemodialysis[214] or peritoneal dialysis[215] is able to maintain the lives of most patients indefinitely. Sometimes, however, kidney failure is secondary to other disease, and the patient will die from that disease even if dialysis is continued.[216] In such cases, dialysis does no more than prolong the dying process.

Dialysis frequently has unpleasant side effects that are sometimes so serious that patients terminate treatment with or without the acquiescence of their physician.[217] Hemodialysis patients who do not expressly decide to terminate treatment sometimes become uncooperative with their treatment, and some even become disruptive to the operation of the dialysis program.[218] Kidney transplantation is increasingly becoming a substitute for chronic dialysis, but

---

[214] **MA:** *In re* R.H., 622 N.E.2d 1071, 1074 n.3 (Mass. App. Ct. 1993) ("Hemodialysis (which will be referred to simply as dialysis) involves cleansing the patient's blood of toxins using filtration machinery to substitute for the failed kidneys. It involves removal of the patient's contaminated blood through a needle inserted in the patient's body and tubes running to an artificial kidney machine that removes toxic and waste substances from the blood. The machine then returns the cleansed blood to the body through another inserted needle.").

[215] *Id.* at 1074 n.2 ("The other form of dialysis [is] peritoneal dialysis, which involves cleansing the blood of its toxins through an abdominal tube . . . [has a greater] risk of infection" and is more labor intensive.).

[216] *See In re* Lydia E. Hall Hosp., 455 N.Y.S.2d 706 (Sup. Ct. Nassau County 1982).

[217] Nelson et al., *The Association of Diabetic Status, Age, and Race to Withdrawal from Dialysis,* 4 J. Am. Soc'y Nephrology 1608–14 (1994) (8.5% of end-stage renal patients died from withdrawal from dialysis, making it fourth leading cause of death for end stage renal disease patients); Neu & Kjellstrand, *Stopping Long-Term Dialysis,* 314 New Eng. J. Med. 14 (1986) (reporting that in 9% of patients with end-stage renal disease, competent patients, or the family or physician of incompetent patients, initiated decision to terminate treatment); Roberts & Kjellstrand, *Choosing Death: Withdrawal from Chronic Dialysis Without Medical Reason,* 223 Acta Medica Scandinavica 818 (1988); Rothenberg, *Withholding and Withdrawing Dialysis from Elderly ESRD Patients: Part 2—Ethical and Policy Issues,* 3 Geriatric Nephrology & Urology 23 (1993); Singer et al., *Nephrologists' Experience With and Attitudes Towards Decisions to Forego Dialysis,* J. Am. Soc'y Nephrology 1235 (1992).

CA: *Cf.* Drabick v. Drabick, 245 Cal. Rptr. 840, 843 (Ct. App. 1988) (court recounts that now permanently unconscious patient had said that he would not be "attached to a kidney machine").

NJ: *Cf.* Warthen v. Toms River Community Memorial Hosp., 488 A.2d 229, 230 (N.J. Super. Ct. App. Div. 1985) (nurse refuses to dialyze patient; "the patient was terminally ill and, she contended, the procedure was causing the patient additional complications").

[218] **CA:** *E.g.,* Payton v. Weaver, 182 Cal. Rptr. 225 (Ct. App. 1982) (holding that there was abandonment of patient when physician refused to continue dialysis).

there can be substantial waiting periods before a kidney becomes available for transplantation,[219] and not all patients with kidney failure are suitable candidates for transplantation.

There are few reported cases involving the forgoing of dialysis. This probably results from the fact that competent patients have a longer period of time in which to experience life with dialysis and its concomitant benefits and burdens, and to make considered judgments about continuing or discontinuing it. Consequently, when a decision to discontinue does occur and because such decisions are not infrequent, there is a greater willingness on the part of physicians to acquiesce in the patient's decision.[220]

In the case of incompetent patients, decisionmaking about terminating or withholding dialysis is treated much as any other treatment. In cases in which patients are terminally ill or hopelessly ill, in a persistent vegetative state, and/or subjectively experience a very low quality of life, courts have had little hesitation in permitting the forgoing of dialysis.[221] By contrast, where the patient is incompetent but leading a subjectively acceptable quality of life, the termination of dialysis is unacceptable,[222] unless the patient authorized its termination before losing decisionmaking capacity[223] or would have done so.[224]

MS: *E.g.*, Brown v. Bower, No. J860759(B) (S.D. Miss. Dec. 21, 1987) (receipt of Hill-Burton funds by hospital obligated hospital to make dialysis available, but did not obligate physician to participate in providing it).

See also Orentlicher, *Denying Treatment to the Noncompliant Patient,* 265 JAMA 1579 (1991) (questioning viability of holdings in *Brown* and *Payton* in light of Americans with Disabilities Act, 42 U.S.C. §§ 12,101–12,213). See **§§ 17.15** and **17.22.**

[219] **MA:** *In re* R.H., 622 N.E.2d 1071, 1079 (Mass. App. Ct. 1993).

[220] Moss et al., *Variation in the Attitudes of Dialysis Unit Medical Directors Toward Decisions to Withhold and Withdraw Dialysis,* 4 J. Am. Soc'y Nephrology 229 (1993) (92% of physician medical directors of adult chronic dialysis units would usually honor a competent patient's request to stop dialysis); Neu & Kjellstrand, *Stopping Long-Term Dialysis,* 314 New Eng. J. Med. 14 (1986) (in 9% of patients with end-stage renal disease, competent patients, or the family or physician of incompetent patients, initiated decision to terminate treatment). *See generally* Hastings Center Guidelines 41–42 (Part Two, § A.III) (discussing special considerations in making decisions about forgoing dialysis).

FL: *Cf.* St. Mary's Hosp. v. Ramsey, 465 So. 2d 666 (Fla. Dist. Ct. App. 1985) (patient requiring chronic dialysis permitted to refuse lifesaving blood transfusion).

MA: *But see* Commissioner v. Myers, 399 N.E.2d 452 (Mass. 1979) (otherwise healthy prisoner not permitted to terminate dialysis).

[221] *See, e.g., In re* Spring, 405 N.E.2d 115 (Mass. 1980).

[222] **MA:** *In re* R.H., 622 N.E.2d 1071 (Mass. App. Ct. 1993).

[223] **NY:** *Cf. In re* Lydia E. Hall Hosp., 455 N.Y.S.2d 706 (oral advance directive; patient terminally ill).

[224] **MA:** *In re* R.H., 622 N.E.2d 1071 (applying substituted judgment standard to a patient with Down's syndrome).

§ 9.35 Life-Support Systems

Life-support system, or just life support, is a nontechnical term used to refer to any kind of equipment and procedures used to keep a patient alive.[225] Often, life support includes a mechanical ventilator,[226] but it is not a necessary component. It may also include means for providing artificial nutrition and hydration,[227] dialysis,[228] elimination of bodily waste, or drug infusions.[229]

There are a multitude of cases that refer to the termination of "life support."[230] However, in general, because of the nonspecific meaning of the term, the

---

[225] **CA:** Barber v. Superior Court, 195 Cal. Rptr. 484 (Ct. App. 1983).

DE: Severns v. Wilmington Medical Ctr., Inc., 421 A.2d 1334 (Del. 1980).

GA: *In re* L.H.R., 321 S.E.2d 716 (Ga. 1984).

NY: *In re* Westchester County Medical Ctr. (O'Connor), 531 N.E.2d 607, 625 (N.Y. 1988) (Simons, J., dissenting) (no agreement on meaning of life-support system).

[226] *See, e.g., In re* Colyer, 660 P.2d 738, 740 (Wash. 1983). See § **9.36.**

[227] *See, e.g.,* McConnell v. Beverly Enters.-Conn., Inc., 553 A.2d 596 (Conn. 1989). See § **9.39.**

[228] See § **9.34.**

[229] **OH:** Leach v. Akron Gen. Medical Ctr., 426 N.E.2d 809 (C.P. P. Div. Summit County, Ohio 1980) (respirator, nasogastric tube, and catheter).

[230] **DDC:** *E.g.,* Tune v. Walter Reed Army Medical Hosp., 602 F. Supp. 1452 (D.D.C. 1985) (respirator).

DNY: *E.g.,* Deel v. Syracuse Veterans Admin. Medical Ctr., 729 F. Supp. 231 (N.D.N.Y. 1990) (respirator).

DRI: *E.g.,* Gray v. Romeo, 697 F. Supp. 580 (D.R.I. 1988) (feeding tube and other life support).

AZ: *E.g.,* Rasmussen v. Fleming, 741 P.2d 674 (Ariz. 1987) (feeding tube).

CA: *E.g.,* Drabick v. Drabick, 245 Cal. Rptr. 840 (Ct. App. 1988) (nasogastric tube); Bartling v. Superior Court, 209 Cal. Rptr. 220 (Ct. App. 1984) (ventilator); Barber v. Superior Court, 195 Cal. Rptr. 484 (Ct. App. 1983) (respirator and other life-sustaining equipment).

CT: *E.g.,* McConnell v. Beverly Enters.-Conn., Inc., 553 A.2d 596 (gastrostomy tube).

DE: *E.g.,* Severns v. Wilmington Medical Ctr., Inc., 421 A.2d 1334 (Del. 1980) (respirator and artificial nutrition and hydration).

FL: *E.g.,* Browning v. Herbert, 568 So. 2d 4 (Fla. 1990) (nasogastric tube); John F. Kennedy Memorial Hosp. v. Bludworth, 452 So. 2d 921 (Fla. 1984) (respirator and artificial nutrition and hydration).

IL: *In re* Estate of Greenspan, 558 N.E.2d 1194 (Ill. 1990) (feeding tube); Estate of Longeway v. Community Convalescent Ctr., 549 N.E.2d 292 (Ill. 1989) (feeding tube).

LA: *In re* P.V.W., 424 So. 2d 1015 (La. 1982) (ventilator).

MD: Mack v. Mack, 618 A.2d 744 (Md. 1993) (nasogastric tube).

MA: *In re* Doe, 583 N.E.2d 1263 (Mass. 1992) (nasoduodenal feeding and hydration); Brophy v. New Eng. Sinai Hosp., Inc., 497 N.E.2d 626 (Mass. 1986) (gastrostomy tube).

MI: Martin v. Martin, 504 N.W.2d 917 (Mich. Ct. App. 1993) (artificial nutrition and hydration); Rosebush v. Oakland County Prosecutor, 491 N.W.2d 633 (Mich. Ct. App. 1992) (respirator and other life support).

MN: *In re* Torres, 357 N.W.2d 332 (Minn. 1984) (feeding tube).

holdings of reported cases that use it have not turned on the characterization of the treatments involved as life support. However, the term did play an important role in the interpretation of an advance directive statute, which permitted the forgoing of "life support." The decision in *McConnell v. Beverly Enterprises-Connecticut, Inc.,*[231] turned on whether or not artificial nutrition and hydration was included within the definition of life-support system. The majority concluded that it was. By contrast, a concurring justice concluded that artificial nutrition and hydration was not part of life support because "[t]he majority never explains how a gastrostomy tube qualifies as a 'mechanical or electronic device' and thus never explains how the gastrostomy tube can be considered a 'life support system' in the statutory scheme."[232]

Terminological disputes of this kind do little to advance analytical thinking. Rather than focusing on classification, courts and legislatures should instead direct their attention (and most courts have) to whether or not the procedure in question, however it might be labeled, is consistent with the patient's actual or presumed wishes, and absent knowledge of those wishes whether it provides the patient with any benefit.[233] Because "life-support" has no precise meaning,[234] its use in statutes as an operative phrase in determining what treatment can be forgone under what circumstances is unfortunate, unhelpful, and potentially misleading.

MO: Cruzan v. Harmon, 760 S.W.2d 408 (Mo. 1988), *aff'd sub nom.* Cruzan v. Director, 497 U.S. 261 (1990) (artificial nutrition and hydration).

NV: McKay v. Bergstedt, 801 P.2d 617 (Nev. 1990) (respirator).

NJ: Strachan v. John F. Kennedy Memorial Hosp., 538 A.2d 346 (N.J. 1988) (respirator); *In re* Farrell, 529 A.2d 404 (N.J. 1987) (respirator); *In re* Peter, 529 A.2d 419 (N.J. 1987) (nasogastric tube); *In re* Jobes, 529 A.2d 434 (N.J. 1987) (jejunostomy tube); *In re* Quinlan, 355 A.2d 647 (N.J. 1976) (respirator); *In re* Moorhouse, 593 A.2d 1256 (N.J. Super. Ct. App. Div. 1991) (respirator); *In re* Clark, 510 A.2d 136 (N.J. Super. Ct. Ch. Div. 1986) (enterostomy); *In re* Farrell, 514 A.2d 1342 (N.J. Super. Ct. Ch. Div. 1986) (respirator).

NY: Elbaum v. Grace Plaza of Great Neck, Inc., 544 N.Y.S.2d 840 (App. Div. 1989) (gastrointestinal tube); Eichner v. Dillon, 426 N.Y.S.2d 517 (App. Div. 1980) (respirator); Wickel v. Spellman, 552 N.Y.S.2d 437 (App. Div. 1990) (nasogastric tube); *In re* Kerr (O'Brien), 517 N.Y.S.2d 346 (Sup. Ct. N.Y. County 1986) (feeding tube); Vogel v. Forman, 512 N.Y.S.2d 622 (Sup. Ct. Nassau County 1986) (nasogastric tube).

OH: Couture v. Couture, 549 N.E.2d 571 (Ohio Ct. App. 1989) (respirator and feeding tube); *In re* Myers, 610 N.E.2d 663 (P. Ct. Summit County, Ohio 1993) (nasogastric tube); Leach v. Akron Gen. Medical Ctr., 426 N.E.2d 809 (respirator, nasogastric tube, and catheter).

WA: *In re* Grant, 747 P.2d 445 (Wash. 1987), *modified,* 757 P.2d 534 (Wash. 1988) (artificial nutrition and hydration).

WI: L.W. v. L.E. Phillips Career Dev. Ctr., 482 N.W.2d 60 (Wis. 1992) (medical treatment including artificial nutrition and hydration).

[231] **CT:** 553 A.2d 596 (Conn. 1989).

[232] *Id.* A.2d at 607 (Healey, J., concurring).

[233] **MO:** *See* Cruzan v. Harmon, 760 S.W.2d at 423 ("The temptation here is to allow medical terminology to dictate legal principle. 'Using medical explanations . . . has utility for the courts. It removes the responsibility for decisions that seem harsh when explained in plainer language.'") (citing Alexander, *Death by Directive,* 28 Santa Clara L. Rev. 67, 83 (1988)).

[234] **NY:** *In re* Westchester County Medical Ctr. (O'Connor), 531 N.E.2d 607, 625 (N.Y. 1988).

§ 9.36 Mechanical Ventilators

Mechanical ventilators, frequently referred to as respirators,[235] are devices that assist patients to breathe.[236] The loss of the ability to breathe is sometimes a transitory result of an injury or illness,[237] and it can be a natural concomitant of diseases; but in the reported litigation it is more likely to be used for the treatment of chronic respiratory insufficiency resulting from terminal illness, such as amyotrophic lateral sclerosis,[238] emphysema,[239] chronic obstructive pulmonary disease (COPD),[240] stroke,[241] and a variety of other conditions.[242]

---

[235] Brandstetter & Tamarin, *Artificial Breathing Support Systems: Preferred Nomenclature for Medicine and the Courts,* N.Y. St. J. Med. 589 (Nov. 1987).

[236] National Insts. of Health, *Workshop Summary—Withholding and Withdrawing Mechanical Ventilation,* 134 Am. Rev. Respiratory Disease 1327 (1986).

[237] *See, e.g.,* Cruzan v. Harmon, 760 S.W.2d 408 (Mo. 1988).

[238] **FL:** Satz v. Perlmutter, 362 So. 2d 160 (Fla. Dist. Ct. App. 1978), *aff'd,* 379 So. 2d 359 (Fla. 1980).

OH: *E.g.,* Leach v. Akron Gen. Medical Ctr., 426 N.E.2d 809 (C.P. P. Div. Summit County, Ohio 1980).

PA: *E.g., In re* Doe, 45 Pa. D. & C.3d 371, 371–72 (C.P. Phila. County 1987).

See § **9.44.**

[239] **CA:** Bartling v. Superior Court, 209 Cal. Rptr. 220 (Ct. App. 1984).

NY: Saunders v. State, 492 N.Y.S.2d 510 (Sup. Ct. Nassau County 1985).

[240] **AL:** Camp v. White, 510 So. 2d 166 (Ala. 1987).

[241] **NJ:** McVey v. Englewood Hosp. Ass'n, 524 A.2d 450 (N.J. Super. Ct. App. Div.), *cert. denied,* 528 A.2d 12 (N.J. 1987).

[242] **DDC:** Tune v. Walter Reed Army Medical Hosp., 602 F. Supp. 1452 (D.D.C. 1985) (adult respiratory distress syndrome).

DNY: Deel v. Syracuse Veterans Admin. Medical Ctr., 729 F. Supp. 231 (N.D.N.Y. 1990) (bronchiolitis obliterans, a degenerative respiratory ailment).

CT: Foody v. Manchester Memorial Hosp., 482 A.2d 713 (Conn. Super. Ct. 1984) (multiple sclerosis).

DE: Severns v. Wilmington Medical Ctr., Inc., 421 A.2d 1334 (Del. 1980) (vegetative state).

FL: John F. Kennedy Memorial Hosp. v. Bludworth, 452 So. 2d 921 (Fla. 1984) (acute respiratory failure from chronic interstitial fibrosis); Satz v. Perlmutter, 379 So. 2d 359 (Fla. 1980) (amyotrophic lateral sclerosis).

GA: *In re* Doe, 418 S.E.2d 3 (Ga. 1992) (degenerative neurological disease); State v. McAfee, 385 S.E.2d 651 (Ga. 1989) (quadriplegia).

MI: Rosebush v. Oakland County Prosecutor, 491 N.W.2d 633 (Mich. Ct. App. 1992) (spinal cord injury).

MN: *In re* Torres, 357 N.W.2d 332 (Minn. 1984) (vegetative state).

NV: McKay v. Bergstedt, 801 P.2d 617 (Nev. 1990) (quadriplegia).

NJ: *In re* Farrell, 529 A.2d 404 (N.J. 1987) (amyotrophic lateral sclerosis); *In re* Quinlan, 355 A.2d 647 (N.J. 1976) (persistent vegetative state); *In re* Moorhouse, 593 A.2d 1256 (N.J. Super. Ct. App. Div. 1991); McVey v. Englewood Hosp. Ass'n, 524 A.2d 450 (N.J. Super. Ct. App. Div. 1987) (deep coma).

The withdrawal of ventilatory support has probably been responsible for more right-to-die cases than has any other form of treatment. In general, courts place little or no emphasis on the nature of this treatment in determining whether it may be forgone or must be continued, relying instead on general principles of decisionmaking about life-sustaining treatment. The only significant exception—significant because it is exceptional—is a dissenting opinion in which the judge concluded that after a patient had been dependent on a ventilator for 23 years, it could no longer be considered medical treatment, but

> a new way of life for its user. . . . The "treatment" in any real sense is over; and just as heart pace-makers, artificial venous or arterial shunts, a variety of prosthetic devices and other such medically sponsored and introduced artifacts may begin as a medical treatment modality, the ventilator begins as a form of medical treatment but ends up as an integral part of its dependent user. Even if it is insisted that these things continue indefinitely to be considered as "treatment," they indeed become far, far more than just treatment after years and years of dependency on them.[243]

When a mechanical ventilator is withdrawn, patients can sometimes breathe on their own.[244] If they cannot, they immediately begin to experience respiratory distress, which in alert patients is painful and anxiety-producing.[245] In such cases, analgesics and/or sedatives can be administered, but they frequently have the effect of hastening dying.[246] When this is an unintended and unavoidable side effect of the legitimate goal of relief of suffering, it is generally not considered morally[247] nor legally culpable.[248] Indeed, it has been held to be obligatory on doctors in such a situation to provide a competent and alert patient with adequate medication to avoid physical and mental suffering.[249]

NY: Eichner v. Dillon, 420 N.E.2d 64 (N.Y. 1981) (persistent vegetative state).

OH: Leach v. Akron Gen. Medical Ctr., 426 N.E.2d 809 (C.P. P. Div. Summit County, Ohio 1980) (persistent vegetative state).

PA: *In re* Doe, 45 Pa. D. & C.3d 371 (C.P. Phila. County 1987) (amyotrophic lateral sclerosis).

WA: *In re* Grant, 747 P.2d 445 (Wash. 1987), *modified,* 757 P.2d 534 (Wash. 1988) (Batten's disease); *In re* Hamlin, 689 P.2d 1372 (Wash. 1984) (persistent vegetative state); *In re* Colyer, 660 P.2d 738 (Wash. 1983) (persistent vegetative state).

See also Hastings Center Guidelines 38 (Part Two, § A.I).

243 **NV:** McKay v. Bergstedt, 801 P.2d at 634 (Springer, J., dissenting).

244 *See, e.g., In re* Quinlan, 355 A.2d 647 (N.J. 1976).

245 *See, e.g.,* State v. McAfee, 385 S.E.2d 651 (Ga. 1989).

246 *See* Schneiderman & Spragg, *Ethical Decisions in Discontinuing Mechanical Ventilation,* 318 New Eng. J. Med. 984, 987 (1988).

247 *See id.* See § **8.7.**

248 *See* Hastings Center Guidelines 39–41 (Part Two, § A.II) (discussing special considerations in making decisions about forgoing ventilation). See §§ **4.5** and **18.18.**

249 **GA:** *See* State v. McAfee, 385 S.E.2d 651 (Ga. 1989).

§ 9.37 Medication

The lives of many dying patients are prolonged by the administration of antibiotic medications to ward off infections to which patients often become susceptible as a result of their debilitated state, some invasive life-support procedures, the prevalence of infection in hospitals, or some combination of these factors.[250]

There is nothing about antibiotics that requires any special analysis. Although it is sometimes said that antibiotics are ordinary treatment and as such cannot be forgone,[251] this is clearly an oversimplification,[252] and in any event the usefulness of the purported distinction between ordinary and extraordinary treatments has been generally rejected by courts.[253] Thus, antibiotics may be forgone on the same basis and pursuant to the same standards for decisionmaking as any other therapy. The small amount of litigation about forgoing antibiotics in large part results from the fact that antibiotics are usually administered to critically ill patients in conjunction with other life-sustaining therapies, and the efforts to have antibiotics forgone occur in conjunction with the efforts to forgo other treatments as well, such as artificial nutrition and hydration. Another reason is attributable to psychological factors, namely, the ease with which antibiotics may be withdrawn or withheld, or the fact that they may be administered in low, ineffectual dosages, thus comforting some of the participants in the decisionmaking process while not in fact contributing to the prolongation of an inevitably dying patient's life.

---

[250] **DE:** *See, e.g., In re* Severns, 425 A.2d 156 (Del. Ch. 1980).

MA: *See, e.g., In re* Doe, 583 N.E.2d 1263 (Mass. 1992).

NJ: *See, e.g., In re* Jobes, 529 A.2d 434 (N.J. 1987); *In re* Quinlan, 348 A.2d 801 (N.J. Super. Ct. Ch. Div. 1975); *In re* Clark, 510 A.2d 136 (N.J. Super. Ct. Ch. Div. 1986) (infection from central line).

NY: *See, e.g.,* Elbaum v. Grace Plaza of Great Neck, Inc., 544 N.Y.S.2d 840 (App. Div. 1989).

WA: *See, e.g., In re* Hamlin, 689 P.2d 1372 (Wash. 1984).

[251] **DE:** Severns v. Wilmington Medical Ctr., Inc., 421 A.2d 1334 (Del. 1980) (by implication).

NJ: *In re* Conroy, 464 A.2d 303 (N.J. Super. Ct. App. Div. 1983) ("A code of treatment for severely ill children, drafted by the Nassau (N.Y.) Pediatric Society Committee on Ethics and Survival, provides that 'ordinary measures are food, fluids, oxygen, antibiotics and pain killers.' Waldman, 'Medical Ethics and the Hopelessly Ill Child,' 88 J. Ped. 890, 892 (1976).").

NY: Workmen's Circle Home & Infirmary for the Aged v. Fink, 514 N.Y.S.2d 893 (Sup. Ct. Bronx County 1987) (distinguishing between gastrostomy, which is extraordinary treatment and may be forgone, and antibiotic treatment, which is ordinary and therefore must be continued). *But see In re* Quackenbush, 383 A.2d 785, 787 (N.J. Super. Ct. P. Div. 1978) (doctor described doses of antibiotics as "heroic measures, meaning quantities in highly unusual amounts").

PA: *In re* Doe, 45 Pa. D. & C.3d 371, 375 (C.P. Phila. County 1987) (physicians of patient with amyotrophic lateral sclerosis agreed to withhold antibiotics should they become necessary).

[252] *See generally* Hastings Center Guidelines 65 (Part Two, § D.I).

[253] See § **8.8.**

§ 9.38 —Medication for Pain Relief (Palliative Care)

Drugs other than antibiotics can be involved in decisions about life-sustaining treatment, most notably analgesic medications (painkillers) and sedatives. The controversy that arises from the use of analgesics and sedatives generally is not whether they may be forgone, but with whether they may and are being administered in amounts large enough to control the patient's pain and anxiety.[254] The debate about active euthanasia and physician-assisted suicide[255] has drawn attention to the fact that appropriate medications and other aspects of a palliative care plan, such as hospice care, can often eliminate or dramatically reduce the pain and suffering that are responsible for some people seeking to actively end their lives, and thus the desirable response is not the legalization of active euthanasia and physician-assisted suicide but the prescription of appropriate kinds and amounts of medications for relief of pain.[256] In practice, however, this is hampered by an unfamiliarity of many physicians with such pain control techniques,[257] including patient-controlled analgesia.

---

[254] *See* Hastings Center Guidelines 30, 72, 74 (Part One, II(6)(b); Part Two, §§ E.I, E.II(1)(c)); *In the Hospital: Pain Control—Part 1,* 14 Harv. Med. Sch. Health Letter 1 (1989) (50 to 75% of hospitalized patients inadequately treated for pain).

[255] *See, e.g.,* Battin, *Euthanasia: The Way We Do It, the Way They Do It,* 6 J. Pain & Symptom Mgmt. 298 (1991); Brescia, *Killing The Known Dying: Notes of a Death Watcher,* 6 J. Pain & Symptom Mgmt. 336 (1991); Clouser, *The Challenge for Future Debate on Euthanasia,* 6 J. Pain & Symptom Mgmt. 306 (1991); Jennings, *Active Euthanasia and Forgoing Life-Sustaining Treatment: Can We Hold the Line?,* 6 J. Pain & Symptom Mgmt. 312 (1991); Klagsbrun, *Physician-Assisted Suicide: A Double Dilemma,* 6 J. Pain & Symptom Mgmt. 325 (1991); Latimer, *Ethical Decision-Making in the Care of the Dying and Its Applications to Clinical Practice,* 6 J. Pain & Symptom Mgmt. 329 (1991); O'Rourke, *Assisted Suicide: An Evaluation,* 6 J. Pain & Symptom Mgmt. 317 (1991); Scofield, *Privacy (or Liberty) and Assisted Suicide,* 6 J. Pain & Symptom Mgmt. 280 (1991). See §§ **18.18–18.25.**

[256] *See* Block & Billings, *Patient Requests to Hasten Death—Evaluation and Management in Terminal Care,* 154 Archives Internal Med. 2039 (1994); Conolly, *Alternatives to Euthanasia: Pain Management,* 4 Issues L. & Med. 497 (1989); Foley, *The Relationship of Pain and Symptom Management to Patient Requests for Physician-Assisted Suicide,* 6 J. Pain & Symptom Mgmt. 289 (1991).

[257] *See* Council on Ethical & Judicial Affairs, American Medical Ass'n, *Decisions Near the End of Life,* 267 JAMA 2229, 2231 (1992) ("[M]any physicians are not informed about the appropriate doses, frequency of doses, and alternate modalities of pain control for patients with severe chronic pain.") (citing Rhymes, *Hospice Care in America,* 264 JAMA 369 (1990); Cherny et al., *The Treatment of Suffering When Patients Request Elective Death,* 10 J. Palliative Care 71 (1994); Cleeland et al., *Pain and Its Treatment in Outpatients with Metastatic Cancer,* 330 New Eng. J. Med. 592 (1994) (42% of those with pain given inadequate analgesia); Collins, *Despite Gains, Pain Management Still Not Under Control,* Am. Med. News, Oct. 14, 1991, at 20; Foley, *The Relationship of Pain and Symptom Management to Patient Requests for Physician-Assisted Suicide,* 6 J. Pain & Symptom Mgmt. 289 (1991); Gianelli, *Euthanasia Opponents Urge Pain-Control Education,* Am. Med. News, Jan. 20, 1992, at 9; Jacax et al., *New Clinical-Practice Guidelines for the Management of Pain in*

When using such medications in the care of the dying, physicians become concerned that the increasingly large doses of medication needed to address some patients' pain will cause the patient's death.[258] There are some cases, however, in which pain cannot be relieved,[259] or can be relieved only by doses of medication so large that they do end the patient's life.[260] However, by application of the principle of double effect,[261] as long as the physician's primary purpose in prescribing analgesics is for the treatment of pain, the fact that the unintended result is the patient's death should not expose the physician to criminal liability.[262] Some courts explicitly recognize that a patient's "right to be free from pain . . . is inseparable from his right to refuse medical treatment,"[263] and authorize or order the use of appropriate medications. However,

---

Patients with Cancer, 330 New Eng. J. Med. 651 (1994); Merz, *Will Doctors Hear the Wake-Up Call?,* Am. Med. News, Dec. 9, 1991, at 3. *See generally* President's Comm'n, Deciding to Forego Life-Sustaining Treatment app. B at 277–97 (*Supportive Care for Dying Patients: An Introduction for Health Care Professionals*).

[258] *See, e.g.,* Foster v. Tourtellotte, 704 F.2d 1009 (9th Cir. 1983) (hospital refused to honor competent patient's request to disconnect the respirator and administer requested medication because sedation might hasten patient's death, possibly making the hospital liable for aiding suicide). *But see* Wilson et al., *Ordering and Administration of Sedatives and Analgesics During the Withholding and Withdrawal of Life Support from Critically Ill Patients,* 267 JAMA 949 (1992) (large doses of sedatives and analgesics administered to patients when life support was withdrawn or withheld did not hasten death).

[259] *See* Miller et al., *Regulating Physician-Assisted Death,* 331 New Eng. J. Med. 119 (1994); Truog et al., *Barbiturates in the Care of the Terminally Ill,* 237 New Eng. J. Med. 1678 (1992).

[260] *See, e.g.,* Sussman, *Sometimes There's Only One Way to End a Patient's Pain,* Am. Med. News, Jan. 11, 1993, at 29 (describing author's treatment of terminally ill cancer patient with morphine for unremitting pain, which patient eventually succumbed to the morphine).

[261] See § **8.7.**

[262] **MA:** *But see* Brophy v. New Eng. Sinai Hosp., Inc., 497 N.E.2d 626, 640 (Mass. 1986) (Nolan, J., dissenting) (Ethical principle of double effect "totally inapplicable" to facts because patient "will not die from the aneurysm which precipitated loss of consciousness, the surgery which was performed, the brain damage that followed or the insertion of the G-tube. He will die as a direct result of the refusal to feed him.") (citing Bannon, *Rx: Death by Dehydration,* 12 Hum. Life Rev. No. 3, at 70 (1986)).

See § **18.18.**

[263] **GA:** State v. McAfee, 385 S.E.2d 651, 652 (Ga. 1989).

FL: *See also* Fla. Stat. Ann. § 458.326(3) ("physician may prescribe or administer any controlled substance . . . to a person for the treatment of intractable pain" in accordance with generally accepted medical standards.

MN: *See also* Minn. Stat. Ann. § 609.215(a) (statute legitimates principle of double effect by providing that administration, prescription, or dispensation of "medications or procedures to relieve another person's pain or discomfort, even if the medication or procedure may hasten or increase the risk of death," is not abetting or aiding suicide "unless the medications or procedures are knowingly administered, prescribed, or dispensed to cause death").

NV: *Accord* McKay v. Bergstedt, 801 P.2d 617 (Nev. 1990).

TN: *See also* Tenn. Code Ann. § 39-13-216(b)(2) (legitimating principle of double effect).

TX: *See also* Texas Intractable Pain Act, Tex. Rev. Civ. Stat. Ann. art. 4495(c).

recognizing that the use of strong doses of analgesic medications to achieve this goal may inadvertently end the patient's life, one court has provided immunity to the physician in such circumstances.[264] This is consistent with the position of the American Medical Association.[265] In moral terms, the physician causes an evil, the death of the patient, in the pursuit of accomplishing a good, the amelioration of pain.

A study reports that in a sample of 44 patients from whom life support was withheld or withdrawn, 75 percent were given sedation and analgesia. The reasons for giving the medications were to relieve pain, anxiety, and air hunger from the termination of ventilatory support, to comfort families who witnessed the dying, and to hasten death. However, "[i]n no instance was hastening death cited as the only reason for ordering drugs,"[266] probably because if it were, the chances of criminal prosecution would be significantly increased.[267]

Both the Georgia and Nevada Supreme Courts have authorized or required the administration of analgesics in conjunction with the termination of life support.[268] The Nevada court also held that in such cases, the trial court's order "shall specify that any physician or health care provider who assists the patient in receiving the benefits of his or her decision [to forgo treatment] with minimal pain, shall not be subject to civil or criminal liability."[269] Thus, the fact that a patient has declined life-sustaining treatment does not mean that he has also waived his right to receive adequate relief from pain through medications.

Physicians are also sometimes concerned about patients becoming addicted to analgesic medications such as morphine,[270] a concern characterized by the

---

[264] **NV:** McKay v. Bergstedt, 801 P.2d 617, 631 (Nev. 1990) ("In all cases decided by a district court in favor of the patient, the court's order shall specify that any physician or health care provider who assists the patient in receiving the benefits of his or her decision with minimal pain, shall not be subject to civil or criminal liability.").

[265] Council on Ethical & Judicial Affairs, American Medical Ass'n, Code of Medical Ethics § 2.20, at 37 (1994) ("Physicians have an obligation to relieve pain and suffering . . . of dying patients in their care. This includes providing effective palliative treatment even though it may foreseeably hasten death."); Council on Ethical & Judicial Affairs, American Medical Ass'n, *Decisions Near the End of Life,* 267 JAMA 2229, 2231 (1992) ("'[T]he administration of a drug necessary to ease the pain of a patient who is terminally ill and suffering excruciating pain may be appropriate medical treatment even though the effect of the drug may shorten life.'").

[266] Wilson et al., *Ordering and Administration of Sedatives and Analgesics During the Withholding and Withdrawal of Life Support from Critically Ill Patients,* 267 JAMA 949, 951 (1992).

[267] *See* Brahams, *Euthanasia: Doctor Convicted of Attempted Murder,* 340 The Lancet 782 (1992). See **§ 18.18.**

[268] *See* State v. McAfee, 385 S.E.2d 651, 652 (Ga. 1989) (patient's "right to be free from pain at the time the ventilator is disconnected is inseparable from his right to refuse medical treatment"); McKay v. Bergstedt, 801 P.2d at 631 (same).

[269] McKay v. Bergstedt, 801 P.2d at 631.

[270] *See, e.g.,* Henneberger, *It Pains a Nation of Stoics to Say 'No' to Pain,* N.Y. Times, Apr. 3, 1994, § 4, at 5 (nat'l ed.). *But see* Rosenthal, *Patients in Pain Find Relief, Not Addiction, in Narcotics,* N.Y. Times, Mar. 23, 1993, at A1 (nat'l ed.).

American Medical Association as "inappropriate"[271] in the case of terminally ill patients. As a consequence of this fear, physicians are sometimes prone to undermedicate patients for pain relief.[272] This is so even when it would be possible to improve the quality of life with adequate medications for the relief of pain.[273] Physicians sometimes also express concern that they will be subject to criminal prosecution, suspension or revocation of their license,[274] or loss of their privileges to prescribe controlled substances[275] if they provide narcotics to patients suffering serious pain; but there does not appear to be any basis in fact for these fears,[276] and undermedication for pain may lead to liability for negligence.[277]

§ 9.39 Nutrition and Hydration

Forgoing artificial nutrition and hydration is one of the most controversial aspects of making decisions about life-sustaining treatment. It is also a problem of potentially great magnitude because large numbers of nursing home patients are maintained on artificial nutrition and hydration.[278] Right-to-die litigation

---

[271] Council on Ethical & Judicial Affairs, American Medical Ass'n, *Decisions Near the End of Life,* 267 JAMA 2229, 2231 (1992) ("[I]nappropriate concerns about addiction too often inhibit physicians from providing adequate analgesia to dying patients."). *See also* Conolly, *Alternatives to Euthanasia: Pain Management,* 4 Issues L. & Med. 497 (1989); Weck, *Pain: What Can Be Done When the Pain Won't Go Away,* 23 FDA Consumer 28 (1989).

[272] *See* Hastings Center Guidelines 30, 72 (Part One, II(6)(b); Part Two, § E).

[273] Rhymes, *Clinical Management of the Terminally Ill,* 46 Geriatrics 57 (1991).

[274] **MT:** *E.g.,* Brackman v. Board of Nursing, 851 P.2d 1055 (Mont. 1993) (disciplinary proceedings against hospice nurses for stockpiling narcotics for use by patients when their needs exceeded prescribed amounts), *discussed in* Duignan-Cabrera, *Montana's "Angels of Mercy,"* Newsweek, June 10, 1991, at 24.

OH: *E.g.,* Liss v. State Medical Bd., No. 91Ap-1281, 1992 WL 238884 (Ohio Ct. App. Sept. 24, 1992) (holding state medical board had not exercised its rule-making authority to prohibit use of Schedule II drugs for treatment of chronic pain, and that use of drugs in such situations met professional standards).

[275] *See* 21 U.S.C.A. § 821 (West 1981 & Supp. 1994).

[276] *See* 21 C.F.R. § 1306.07(c) (1994) (Federal law "is not intended to impose any limitations on a physician or authorize hospital staff . . . to administer or dispense narcotic drugs to persons with intractable pain in which no relief or cure is possible or none has been found after reasonable efforts.").

[277] *See* Roark, *How Much Painkiller Is Enough?—Health Care Workers Are Often on Guard Against Giving Too Much Medication; A Landmark Case Against a Nursing Home Has Sent a Warning Not to Provide Too Little,* L.A. Times, Dec. 10, 1991, at a-1 (home ed.) (discussing award of $15 million to estate of patient who was undermedicated for pain from cancer).

[278] **IL:** Estate of Longeway v. Community Convalescent Ctr., 549 N.E.2d 292, 292–303 (Ill. 1989) (Ward, J., dissenting) ("A recent Federal survey reports that 19.4% of all patients in Illinois' 237 intermediate care facilities and 33.8% of all residents in this State's skilled nursing homes receive tube-feeding or need assistance to obtain sustenance. (Health Standards & Quality Bureau, United States Health Care Financing Administration, Medicare/Medicaid Nursing Home Information 87/88, 1 Report on Illinois, 1, 4 (Dec. 1, 1988).").

reflects that fact. Although seven years passed between the *Quinlan* case and the first reported case involving the withdrawal of artificial nutrition and hydration in 1983,[279] it has been repeatedly litigated and fervently discussed in the literature since then.

A number of interrelated arguments are given for distinguishing artificial nutrition and hydration from other life-sustaining medical treatments. One is that artificial nutrition and hydration constitutes "ordinary" care[280] and as such cannot be discontinued.[281] This argument has virtually no legal currency because it is based on the now discredited distinction between ordinary and extraordinary treatment.[282] Indeed, some contend that artificial nutrition and hydration constitutes basic sustenance rather than a medical procedure, and thus cannot be withheld or withdrawn.[283] These objections are interrelated and suggest an even more fundamental objection "based more on the emotional symbolism of providing food and water to those incapable of providing for themselves rather than on any rational difference."[284] Others have objected to the forgoing of artificial nutrition and hydration, at least through a nasogastric tube, because it is "minimally invasive, causing no pain nor any risk of any disease or infection."[285]

KY: DeGrella v. Elston, 858 S.W.2d 698, 715 (Ky. 1993) (Wintersheimer, J., dissenting) ("It is asserted by one of the Amicus that approximately 900 medicaid residents of long-term care facilities in Kentucky receive nourishment and fluids through a feeding tube. Healthcare Financing Administration, U.S. Department of Health & Human Services, User Defined Summary Report for User Selected Criteria: Total Number of Facilities and Residents with Assistance in Feeding, June 27, 1991).

279 **CA:** *See* Barber v. Superior Court, 195 Cal. Rptr. 484 (Ct. App. 1983).

280 Workmen's Circle Home & Infirmary for the Aged v. Fink, 514 N.Y.S.2d 893, 896 (Sup. Ct. Bronx County 1987) (permitting forgoing of gastrostomy but requiring continuation of nasogastric feeding). *See* Hodges et al., *Tube Feedings: Internists' Attitudes Regarding Ethical Obligations,* 154 Archives Internal Med. 1013 (1994) (16% view artificial nutrition and hydration as "basic humane care for a patient who can no longer feed him/herself," but 84% view it as treatment). *But see In re* Clark, 510 A.2d 136, 140–41 (N.J. Super. Ct. Ch. Div. 1986) (testimony of expert witness that tube feeding via enterostomy is "extraordinary means").

281 **MO:** *See* Cruzan v. Harmon, 760 S.W.2d 408, 421 (Mo. 1988) ("Since *Quinlan,* the medical profession moved to abandon any distinction between extraordinary and ordinary treatment in considering the propriety of withdrawing life-sustaining treatment.").

NY: *See* Delio v. Westchester County Medical Ctr., 516 N.Y.S.2d 677, 688 (App. Div. 1987) (citing *In re* Conroy, 486 A.2d 1209 (N.J. 1985)).

282 See § **8.8.**

283 *See, e.g.,* Cruzan v. Harmon, 760 S.W.2d at 423 ("common sense tells us that food and water do not treat an illness, they maintain a life").

284 **CA:** Barber v. Superior Court, 195 Cal. Rptr. 484, 490 (Ct. App. 1983) (citing President's Comm'n, Deciding to Forego Life-Sustaining Treatment 192 n.52).

WA: *In re* Grant, 747 P.2d 445, 453 (Wash. 1987), *modified,* 757 P.2d 534 (Wash. 1988).

285 **ME:** *In re* Gardner, 534 A.2d 947, 958 (Me. 1987) (Clifford, J., dissenting).

MA: Brophy v. New Eng. Sinai Hosp., Inc., 497 N.E.2d 626 (Mass. 1986) (Lynch, J., dissenting, O'Connor, J., dissenting).

NJ: *In re* Visbeck, 510 A.2d 125, 133 (N.J. Super. Ct. Ch. Div. 1986) (insertion of nasogastric tube is a simple procedure probably unaccompanied by significant pain).

Another objection is based on causation; it is said that when artificial nutrition and hydration are forgone, the patient dies from starvation.[286] By contrast, when a ventilator or dialysis is terminated or not started, it is easier to see that the patient has died of the underlying disease process. To some, this appears closer to active euthanasia or, in the case of competent patients or patients with advance directives, suicide.[287] (Indeed, some even view voluntary withdrawal of artificial nutrition and hydration by a competent, terminally ill patient as a preferable alternative to assisted suicide.[288]) This contention is sometimes met, however, with the argument that it is still the disease that ends the patient's life because it prevents the patient from obtaining nutrition and hydration, just as it is the terminal condition that prevents a ventilator-dependent patient from breathing without assistance.[289]

But see Quill, *Utilization of Nasogastric Feeding Tubes in a Group of Chronically Ill, Elderly Patients in a Community Hospital,* 149 Archives Internal Med. 1937, 1940 (1989) (53% of patients with feeding tubes required restraints to prevent them from pulling tubes out).

[286] **MA:** Brophy v. New Eng. Sinai Hosp., Inc., 497 N.E.2d at 641 (Nolan, J., dissenting).

NJ: *But see In re* Conroy, 486 A.2d 1209, 1226 (N.J. 1985) ("[D]eath would result . . . from underlying medical condition, which included her inability to swallow.").

WI: L.W. v. L.E. Phillips Career Dev. Ctr., 482 N.W.2d 60, 66 (Wis. 1992) ("Unlike most medical technological advances of a mechanistic nature, it is difficult to view nourishment as anything but normal and essential human care. It is difficult not to view the withdrawal of artificial feeding as inducing death through starvation and dehydration.").

See also Hastings Center Guidelines 59–60 (Part Two, § C.1) ("Malnutrition and dehydration are conditions determined by chemical tests. They are not the same as the felt states of hunger and thirst.").

[287] **CA:** *Contra* Bouvia v. Superior Court (Glenchur), 225 Cal. Rptr. 297, 306 (Ct. App. 1986) (patient merely resigned herself to accept an earlier death rather than accepted forced feedings).

KY: *See, e.g.,* DeGrella v. Elston, 858 S.W.2d 698, 714 (Ky. 1993) (Wintersheimer, J., dissenting) ("If as a result of this decision Sue DeGrella's death ultimately follows, it will not be from being in a persistent vegetative state, nor from the effects of the vicious beating. She will die or be killed, as you prefer, by the inherently lethal action of withholding food and water.").

MA: *In re* Doe, 583 N.E.2d 1263, 1277 (Mass. 1992) (O'Connor, J., dissenting) ("[B]ut for removal or non-use of the nasoduodenal tube, Jane Doe will live for the indefinite, perhaps considerable, future. Without it she will promptly die. That is proximate causation according to any recognized definition of that term."); Brophy v. New Eng. Sinai Hosp., Inc., 497 N.E.2d 626 (Mass. 1986) (Nolan, J., dissenting; Lynch J., dissenting; O'Connor, J., dissenting).

WA: *In re* Grant, 747 P.2d 445, 458 (Wash. 1987), *modified,* 757 P.2d 534 (Wash. 1988) (Andersen, J., concurring and dissenting).

See also Hall, *Caring for Corpses or Killing Patients?,* Nursing Mgmt., Oct. 1994, at 18. *See generally* Cantor, *The Permanently Unconscious Patient, Non-Feeding and Euthanasia,* 15 Am. J. L. & Med. 381, 427–35 (1989). See §§ **18.18–18.25.**

[288] *See, e.g.,* Bernat et al., *Patient Refusal of Hydration and Nutrition: An Alternative to Physician-Assisted Suicide or Voluntary Active Euthanasia,* 153 Archives Internal Med. 2723 (1993).

[289] **DRI:** Gray v. Romeo, 697 F. Supp. 580 (D.R.I. 1988) (death will result from underlying disease or affliction that prevents her from chewing or swallowing).

CT: McConnell v. Beverly Enters.-Conn., Inc., 553 A.2d 596, 608 (Conn. 1989) (Healey, J., concurring) (Death "will not be the result of suicide, i.e., self-inflicted, but will be the final result of her inability to receive nutrition and hydration by other than extraordinary means.").

Virtually every reported appellate case (see **Table 9–2** at the end of this section) has rejected these objections to forgoing artificial nutrition and hydration and held that it is a medical procedure, that it may be forgone according to the same standards[290] as any other medical treatment, and that the fact that it involves basic sustenance is not relevant to whether it must be administered or may be forgone.[291] In addition to the virtual unanimity among appellate courts permitting the forgoing of artificial nutrition and hydration,[292] Medicare and Medicaid requirements for long-term care facilities recognize that competent residents have an unqualified right to refuse treatment, including artificial nutrition and hydration when state law permits.[293] As previously noted, it is also

---

IL: *In re* Estate of Greenspan, 558 N.E.2d 1194, 1201 (Ill. 1990).

ME: *In re* Gardner, 534 A.2d 947, 956 (Me. 1987) (cause of death "not his refusal of care but rather his accident and his resulting medical condition, including his inability to ingest food and water"). *But see id.* at 958 (Clifford, J., dissenting) ("Gardner is not terminally ill and if the feeding tube is withdrawn, he will starve to death. Drawing a chain of proximate causation from the accident to his death does not lessen the impact of this stark result. The outcome in such a case should not turn on whether the patient has the capacity to swallow, to lift his head, or to sip from a cup.").

NJ: *In re* Peter, 529 A.2d 419, 428 (N.J. 1987) (withdrawal of nasogastric tube "merely acquiesces in the natural cessation of a critical bodily function").

WA: *In re* Grant, 747 P.2d 445 (Wash. 1987), *modified,* 757 P.2d 534 (Wash. 1988) ("She is suffering from a disease which may eventually cause her to lose the ability to swallow if she has not died before the onset of that complication. In other words, a vital bodily function may have to be performed by artificial means. . . . Yet in none of these cases can the withholding of life sustaining devices be deemed the cause of Barbara's death. The cause of her death will be Batten's disease.").

[290] **NJ:** *See, e.g., In re* Visbeck, 510 A.2d 125 (N.J. Super. Ct. Ch. Div. 1986) (feeding tube ordered because none of applicable standards for surrogate decisionmaking for incompetent patients were met).

NY: *In re* Westchester County Medical Ctr. (O'Connor), 531 N.E.2d 607 (N.Y. 1988) (same).

[291] **MO:** *But see* Cruzan v. Harmon, 760 S.W.2d 408, 423 (Mo. 1988) ("There is substantial disagreement on this point among physicians and ethicists").

OH: *See In re* Myers, 610 N.E.2d 663, 667 (P. Ct. Summit County, Ohio 1993) ("removal of nutrition and hydration from a person in a persistent vegetative state is rapidly becoming a legally accepted practice in the United States").

See also National Ctr. for State Courts, Guidelines for State Court Decision Making in Life-Sustaining Medical Treatment Cases 144 (2d ed. 1992).

[292] **MO:** *But see* Cruzan v. Harmon, 760 S.W.2d at 423 ("There is substantial disagreement on this point among physicians and ethicists.").

OH: *See In re* Myers, 610 N.E.2d at 667 (citing first edition of this treatise) ("removal of nutrition and hydration from a person in a persistent vegetative state is rapidly becoming a legally accepted practice in the United States").

[293] *See* Department of Health & Human Servs., Medicare and Medicaid—Requirements for Long Term Care Facilities, 54 Fed. Reg. 5316, 5321 (Feb. 2, 1989) (comment to 42 C.F.R. § 483.10(b)(4)). *See also* Cruzan v. Director, 497 U.S. 261, 308 (1990) (Brennan, J., dissenting) ("The Federal Government permits the cost of the medical devices and formulas used in enteral feeding to be reimbursed under Medicare. *See* Pub.L. 99-509, s 9340, note following

agreed by the courts that when artificial nutrition and hydration are forgone, the cause of death is the patient's inability to eat, brought about by disease or injury, and cannot properly be characterized as starvation. Apart from the Missouri Supreme Court, which expressed the view that "common sense tells us that food and water do not treat an illness, they maintain a life,"[294] only a few dissenting or trial court opinions would hold otherwise.[295]

Furthermore, artificial nutrition and hydration, like other medical procedures, carries with it its own set of risks, discomforts, and drawbacks. Those forms of artificial nutrition and hydration procedures that require a surgical incision may involve serious complications and risks.[296] Many courts view these procedures as highly intrusive,[297] as must the patients who make attempts to remove their

---

42 U.S.C. § 1395u, p. 592 (1982 ed., Supp. V). The formulas are regulated by the federal Food and Drug Administration as "medical foods," *see* 21 U.S.C. § 360ee, and the feeding tubes are regulated as medical devices, 21 CFR § 876.5980 (1989)."); President's Comm'n, Deciding to Forego Life-Sustaining Treatment 3 ("Life-sustaining treatment, as used here, encompasses all health care interventions that have the effect of increasing the life span of the patient. Although the term includes respirators, kidney machines, and all the paraphernalia of modern medicine, it also includes home physical therapy, nursing support for activities of daily living, and special feeding procedures, provided that one of the effects of the treatment is to prolong a patient's life.").

[294] Cruzan v. Harmon, 760 S.W.2d 408, 423 (Mo. 1988).

[295] **KY:** DeGrella v. Elston, 858 S.W.2d 698, 712 (Ky. 1993) (Wintersheimer, J., dissenting) ("There is an enormous difference between the withdrawal of food and water . . . and the withdrawal of medical treatment. . . . Sue DeGrella is not really being treated, she is being maintained through nourishment.").

MA: Brophy v. New Eng. Sinai Hosp., Inc., 497 N.E.2d 626, 640 (Mass. 1986) (Nolan, J., dissenting) ("process of feeding is simply not medical treatment").

NY: Vogel v. Forman, 512 N.Y.S.2d 622 (Sup. Ct. Nassau County 1986).

WA: *In re* Grant, 747 P.2d 445 (Wash. 1987), (Andersen, J., concurring and dissenting) *modified,* 757 P.2d 534 (Wash. 1988).

[296] **MA:** Brophy v. New Eng. Sinai Hosp., Inc., 497 N.E.2d at 631.

NJ: *In re* Peter, 529 A.2d 419, 427 (N.J. 1987) ("Nasogastric tubes may lead to pneumonia, cause irritation and discomfort, and require arm restraints for an incompetent patient. The volume of fluids needed to carry nutrients itself is sometimes harmful."); *In re* Conroy, 486 A.2d 1209, 1236 (N.J. 1985). *Cf. In re* Jobes, 529 A.2d 434, 438 (N.J. 1987) (complications with gastrostomy tube necessitated insertion of a jejunostomy tube). *Contra In re* Clark, 510 A.2d 136, 144 (N.J. Super. Ct. Ch. Div. 1986) (enterostomy is a low risk procedure).

WA: *In re* Grant, 747 P.2d at 453, *modified,* 757 P.2d 534 (discussing complications that can be caused by nasogastric tube).

[297] **US:** Cruzan v. Director, 497 U.S. 261, 288 (1990) (O'Connor, J., concurring) ("Whether or not the techniques used to pass food and water into the patient's alimentary tract are termed 'medical treatment,' it is clear they all involve some degree of intrusion and restraint.").

MA: *In re* Hier, 464 N.E.2d 959, 964 (Mass. App. Ct. 1984). *But compare* Brophy v. New Eng. Sinai Hosp., Inc., 497 N.E.2d at 634 (gastrostomy tube not invasive as a matter of law) *with id.* at 640 (Nolan, J., dissenting) (gastrostomy tube not invasive for patient in persistent vegetative state).

feeding tubes.[298] Artificial nutrition and hydration procedures can also impose serious risks on patients.[299] In addition, some procedures, such as nasogastric tubes, can contribute to the progression of the disease from which the patient is dying.[300] Finally, the continuation of artificial nutrition and hydration procedures to patients in a persistent vegetative state, the largest category of patients on feeding tubes about which litigation has occurred, denies dignity to such patients.[301] As one judge observed, "[h]onoring [the patient's] request not to be fed artificially is not denying her anything. It is not an infliction of harm upon her . . . [but a] recogni[tion of] her dignity and worth as a human being."[302]

MO: *But see* Cruzan v. Harmon, 760 S.W.2d at 422-23 ("The invasion took place when the gastrostomy tube was inserted with consent at a time when hope remained for recovery. Presently, the tube merely provides a conduit for the introduction of food and water. The continuation of feeding through the tube is not heroically invasive.").

WA: *In re* Grant, 747 P.2d at 453, *modified,* 757 P.2d 534 ("the patient is subjected to highly invasive and intrusive procedures").

[298] **US:** *See, e.g.,* Cruzan v. Director, 497 U.S. 261, 289 (1990) (O'Connor, J., concurring) ("Because of the discomfort such a tube causes, '[m]any patients need to be restrained forcibly and their hands put into large mittens to prevent them from removing the tube.' Major, *The Medical Procedures for Providing Food and Water: Indications and Effects,* in By No Extraordinary Means: The Choice to Forgo Life-sustaining Food and Water 25 (J. Lynn ed. 1986)."); Quill, *Utilization of Nasogastric Feeding Tubes in a Group of Chronically Ill, Elderly Patients in a Community Hospital,* 149 Archives Internal Med. 1937, 1940 (1989) (53% of patients with feeding tubes required restraints to prevent them from pulling tube out); Lo & Dornbrand, *Understanding the Benefits and Burdens of Tube Feedings,* 149 Archives Internal Med. 1925, 1925 (1989) ("[P]ulling out a feeding tube is not an indication for restraints; instead, physicians should reconsider whether tube feedings are appropriate. If they are, patients may be less likely to pull out gastrostomy or jejunostomy tubes than nasogastric tubes.").

MA: *In re* Hier, 464 N.E.2d 959 (Mass. App. Ct. 1984).

NY: *In re* Kerr (O'Brien), 517 N.Y.S.2d 346 (Sup. Ct. N.Y. County 1986).

[299] *See* Cruzan v. Director, 497 U.S. at 307 (1990) (Brennan, J., dissenting) ("The tube can cause pneumonia from reflux of the stomach's contents into the lung. *See* Bernard & Forlaw, *Complications and Their Prevention,* in Enteral and Tube Feeding 553 (J. Rombeau & M. Caldwell eds. 1984). Typically, and in this case (*see* Tr. 377), commercially prepared formulas are used, rather than fresh food. *See* Matarese, *Enteral Alimentation,* in Surgical Nutrition 726 (J. Fischer ed. 1983). The type of formula and method of administration must be experimented with to avoid gastrointestinal problems. *Id.,* at 748. The patient must be monitored daily by medical personnel as to weight, fluid intake and fluid output; blood tests must be done weekly. *Id.,* at 749, 751.").

[300] *In re* Estate of Greenspan, 558 N.E.2d 1194, 1197 (Ill. 1990) (in a patient with Alzheimer's disease, " 'not only does [the feeding tube do] nothing to reverse the injury of the brain, [it] actually allows the disease to continue so that the dying out of brain cells is continuing.' ").

[301] *See* Cruzan v. Director, 497 U.S. 261 (1990) (Brennan, J., dissenting; Stevens, J., dissenting). *See generally* Cantor, *The Permanently Unconscious Patient, Non-Feeding and Euthanasia,* 15 Am. J. L. & Med. 381 (1989).

[302] *In re* Requena, 517 A.2d 869, 892 (N.J. Super. Ct. App. Div. 1986).

Although forgoing artificial nutrition and hydration inevitably leads to death from dehydration and/or starvation, it "may not result in more pain than the termination of any other medical treatment."[303] In conscious patients, if adequate analgesic medication is provided, death should be painless.[304] Indeed, there is medical evidence that "[p]atients who are near death and not receiving nourishment may . . . be more comfortable than comparable patients who receive conventional amounts of nutrition and hydration."[305] "Thus, it cannot be assumed that it will always be beneficial for an incompetent patient to receive artificial feeding or harmful for him not to receive it."[306] However, most patients for whom the forgoing of artificial nutrition and hydration is contemplated are in a persistent vegetative state, and for them it will certainly be painless.[307]

---

[303] **NJ:** *In re* Conroy, 486 A.2d 1209, 1236 (N.J. 1985).

OH: *Accord In re* Myers, 610 N.E.2d 663, 665 (P. Ct. Summit County, Ohio 1993) (person in persistent vegetative state unable to perceive pain).

WA: *Accord In re* Grant, 747 P.2d 445, 453 (Wash. 1987), *modified,* 757 P.2d 534 (Wash. 1988).

See also Hastings Center Guidelines 59–60 (Part Two, § C.I); McCann et al., *Comfort Care for Terminally Ill Patients: The Appropriate Use of Nutrition and Hydration,* 272 JAMA 1263 (1994) ("Food and fluid administration beyond the specific requests of patients may play a minimal role in providing comfort to terminally ill patients.").

[304] **KY:** DeGrella v. Elston, 858 S.W.2d 698 (Ky. 1993).

MA: *But see* Brophy v. New Eng. Sinai Hosp., Inc., 497 N.E.2d 626, 641 n.2 (Mass. 1986) (Lynch, J., dissenting) (description of death by dehydration and starvation).

NY: *In re* Westchester County Medical Ctr. (O'Connor), 531 N.E.2d 607, 610 (N.Y. 1988) (physician/proponent of forgoing artificial nutrition and hydration could not be "medically certain" that patient would not suffer).

OH: *In re* Myers, 610 N.E.2d at 671 ("argument that removal of nutrition and hydration is inhumane is . . . without merit"; "discomfort will be minimal and . . . questionable whether any pain will be experienced").

WA: *In re* Grant, 747 P.2d at 453.

President's Comm'n, Deciding to Forego Life-Sustaining Treatment 50–51, 278–86, app. B.

[305] *In re* Grant, 747 P.2d at 453 (citing Lynn & Childress, *Must Patients Always Be Given Food and Water?,* 13 Hastings Center Rep. 17, 19 (Oct. 1983); Dresser & Boisaubin, *Ethics, Law, and Nutritional Support,* 145 Archives Internal Med. 122, 124 (1985); McCann, *Comfort Care for Terminally Ill Patients: The Appropriate Use of Nutrition and Hydration,* 272 JAMA 1263 (1994); Zerwekh, *The Dehydration Question,* 83 Nursing 47, 49–51 (1983)).

[306] *In re* Conroy, 486 A.2d at 1236.

[307] **CA:** Morrison v. Abramovice, 253 Cal. Rptr. 530, 532 (Ct. App. 1988).

MA: Brophy v. New Eng. Sinai Hosp., Inc., 497 N.E.2d at 631 n.20 (patients in persistent vegetative state do not experience pain) (citing inter alia brief of amicus curiae American Academy of Neurology).

MO: Cruzan v. Harmon, 760 S.W.2d 408, 411, 423, 424 (Mo. 1988).

OH: *In re* Myers, 610 N.E.2d at 666–67, 671.

WI: L.W. v. L.E. Phillips Career Dev. Ctr., 482 N.W.2d 60, 73 (Wis. 1992).

The judicial consensus permitting the forgoing of artificial nutrition and hydration both reflects and has been influenced by the official position of the American Medical Association,[308] widely cited in judicial opinions[309] and echoed in the official positions of other medical organizations,[310] which classifies artificial nutrition and hydration as "life-prolonging medical treatment."

---

[308] Council on Ethical & Judicial Affairs, American Medical Ass'n, Code of Medical Ethics: Current Opinions with Annotations § 2.20, at 36 (1994) ("Life-prolonging medical treatment may include . . . artificial nutrition and hydration.").

[309] **US:** *See* Cruzan v. Director, 497 U.S. 261, 288 (1990) (O'Connor, J., concurring).

CA: *See* Drabick v. Drabick, 245 Cal. Rptr. 840 (Ct. App. 1988); Bouvia v. Superior Court (Glenchur), 225 Cal. Rptr. 297 (Ct. App. 1986).

FL: Browning v. Herbert, 568 So. 2d 4, 10–11, 17 (Fla. 1990) ("[T]here is no legal distinction between gastrostomy or nasogastric feeding and any other means of life support."); Corbett v. D'Alessandro, 487 So. 2d 368 (Fla. Dist. Ct. App.), *review denied,* 492 So. 2d 1331 (Fla. 1986).

IL: *In re* Estate of Greenspan, 558 N.E.2d 1194, 1196 (Ill. 1990) (However, "the American Academy of Medical Ethics and various physicians as amici advise us of their view that deciding to withdraw artificial nutrition and hydration is not a matter of peculiarly scientific or medical competence, that there is no clear medical consensus supporting such withdrawal, and that proffered justifications for such withdrawal rest on no principle that could be limited to patients who are in a persistent vegetative state rather than extending to those who suffer from related dementing processes."); Estate of Longeway v. Community Convalescent Ctr., 549 N.E.2d 292, 296 (Ill. 1989) ("[T]he consensus opinion treats artificial nutrition and hydration as a medical treatment and analyzes the problem of its withdrawal accordingly.").

IN: *In re* Lawrance, 579 N.E.2d 32, 40 (Ind. 1991).

ME: *In re* Gardner, 534 A.2d 947 (Me. 1987).

MA: Brophy v. New Eng. Sinai Hosp., Inc., 497 N.E.2d 626.

NV: *But cf.* McKay v. Bergstedt, 801 P.2d 617, 634 (Nev. 1990) (Springer, J., dissenting) (after 23 years of ventilatory support, ventilator can no longer be considered "treatment" for a competent patient, but "a new way of life for its user").

NJ: *In re* Jobes, 529 A.2d 434 (N.J. 1987); *In re* Peter, 529 A.2d 419, 428 (N.J. 1987) ("[T]here is no objective distinction between withdrawal or withholding of artificial feeding and any other medical treatment").

PA: Ragona v. Preate, 11 Fiduc. Rep. 2d 1 (C.P. Lackawanna County, Pa. 1990).

WA: *In re* Grant, 747 P.2d 445 (Wash. 1987), *modified,* 757 P.2d 534 (Wash. 1988).

WI: L.W. v. L.E. Phillips Career Dev. Ctr., 482 N.W.2d at 66.

[310] American Academy of Neurology, *Position of the American Academy of Neurology on Certain Aspects of the Care and Management of the Persistent Vegetative State Patient,* 39 Neurology 125 (1989), *cited in* Couture v. Couture, 549 N.E.2d 571 (Ohio Ct. App. 1989); American College of Physicians, Ethics Manual 38–39 (2d ed. 1989); American Nurses' Ass'n, *Guidelines on Withdrawing or Withholding Food and Fluid, in* 2 BioLaw U: 1123 (Oct. 1988), *excerpted in* 88 Am. J. Nursing 797 (1988); Hastings Center Guidelines 59 (Part Two, § C.I); Task Force on Ethics of the Society of Critical Care Medicine, *Consensus Report on the Ethics of Foregoing Life-Sustaining Treatments in the Critically Ill,* 18 Critical Care Med. 1435, 1436 (1990) (§ I.A.).

For a number of years, a hot debate raged about this categorization,[311] which some believe is determinative of whether artificial nutrition and hydration must be provided to comatose patients with little or no chance of recovery.

The two earliest cases in this area, *Barber v. Superior Court* and *In re Conroy,* addressed these concerns head-on and set the tone for later judicial consideration, and for the now all-but-unanimous judicial consensus that artificial nutrition and hydration is a medical procedure or that whether it is or not is not determinative of whether it may be forgone. The *Barber* court

> view[ed] the use of an IV administration of nourishment and fluid, under the circumstances, as being the same as the use of the respirator or other form of life support equipment. . . . Medical procedures to provide nutrition and hydration are more similar to other medical procedures than to typical human ways of providing nutrition and hydration. Their benefits and burdens ought to be evaluated in the same manner as any other medical procedure.[312]

Conroy acknowledged that "[o]nce one enters the realm of complex, high-technology medical care, it is hard to shed the 'emotional symbolism' of food."[313] "However," the court continued,

> artificial feedings such as nasogastric tubes, gastrostomies, and intravenous infusions are significantly different from bottle-feeding or spoonfeeding—they are medical procedures with inherent risks and possible side effects, instituted by skilled health-care providers to compensate for impaired physical functioning. Analytically, artificial feeding by means of a nasogastric tube or intravenous infusion can be seen as equivalent to artificial breathing by means of a respirator. Both prolong life through mechanical means when the body is no longer able to perform a vital bodily function on its own.[314]

---

[311] *See generally* By No Extraordinary Means (J. Lynn ed., 2d ed. 1989); McCarrick, Withholding or Withdrawing Nutrition or Hydration (National Reference Ctr. for Bioethics Literature, Kennedy Inst. of Ethics, Geo. Univ. Nov. 1986, rev. 1988) (scope note 7).

[312] Barber v. Superior Court, 195 Cal. Rptr. 484, 490 (Ct. App. 1983).

[313] **NJ:** *In re* Conroy, 486 A.2d 1209, 1236 (N.J. 1985). *Accord In re* Peter, 529 A.2d 419, 427 (N.J. 1987).

OH: *Accord In re* Myers, 610 N.E.2d 663, 666–67 (P. Ct. Summit County, Ohio 1993) (Forgoing artificial nutrition and hydration is controversial because it conjures up "images associated with that debilitating process in a normal and healthy body . . . based on a misconception and do not reflect an accurate understanding of the condition of a person in a persistent vegetative state, his ability to feel pain, or the process of dying by dehydration.").

WA: *Accord In re* Grant, 747 P.2d 445 (Wash. 1987), *modified,* 757 P.2d 534 (Wash. 1988).

See also Hastings Center Guidelines 59 (Part Two, § C.I).

[314] **NJ:** *In re* Conroy, 486 A.2d at 1236. *Accord In re* Requena, 517 A.2d 869, 892 (N.J. Super. Ct. App. Div. 1986).

CA: *Accord* Barber v. Superior Court, 195 Cal. Rptr. at 490.

IN: *Accord In re* Lawrance, 579 N.E.2d 32, 40 (Ind. 1991).

Barber applied an unadorned benefit/burden approach, and concluded that the burdens of treatment outweighed the benefits.[315] Simple intravenous hydration procedures are usually not what are at issue[316] because of the inability of intravenous feeding to sustain life for long periods of time.[317] Rather, long-term use of artificial nutrition and hydration requires procedures such as nasogastric tubes (ng-tubes) inserted into the esophagus through the nose,[318] gastrotomy or

---

ME: *Accord In re* Gardner, 534 A.2d 947, 954–55 (Me. 1987) ("The symbolism is lost in the artificial" nature of the procedure.).

WA: *Accord In re* Grant, 747 P.2d 445, *modified,* 757 P.2d 534.

WI: *Accord* L.W. v. L.E. Phillips Career Dev. Ctr., 482 N.W.2d 60, 66 (Wis. 1992).

315 **MO:** *But cf.* Cruzan v. Harmon, 760 S.W.2d 408, 423–24 (Mo. 1988) (feeding tube not burdensome to patient in persistent vegetative state).

NJ: *In re* Visbeck, 510 A.2d 125 (N.J. Super. Ct. Ch. Div. 1986) (applying benefit/burden approach and finding that benefits outweigh burdens and artificial nutrition and hydration must be administered).

See § **7.15.**

316 **CA:** *But see* Barber v. Superior Court, 195 Cal. Rptr. at 486.

WA: *But see In re* Grant, 747 P.2d 445, *modified,* 757 P.2d 534.

317 **MA:** *In re* Hier, 464 N.E.2d 959, 962 (Mass. App. Ct. 1984).

NJ: *In re* Visbeck, 510 A.2d at 127 ("Intravenous feeding is not a long-term solution to the nutritional needs of a patient . . . who is unable to swallow. Enough fluids to prevent serious dehydration can be supplied intravenously. It is, however, impossible to supply enough calories intravenously to meet the minimum daily needs of a patient.").

318 **AZ:** *Cf.* Rasmussen v. Fleming, 741 P.2d 674, 679 n.1 (Ariz. 1987) (attending physician withdrew nasogastric tube while proceedings were pending and patient was able to swallow food on her own).

CA: Morrison v. Abramovice, 253 Cal. Rptr. 530 (Ct. App. 1988); Drabick v. Drabick, 245 Cal. Rptr. 840 (Ct. App. 1988); Bouvia v. Superior Court (Glenchur), 225 Cal. Rptr. 297 (Ct. App. 1986).

DE: *In re* Severns, 425 A.2d 156 (Del. Ch. 1980).

FL: Browning v. Herbert, 568 So. 2d 4 (Fla. 1990).

IL: *In re* Estate of Greenspan, 558 N.E.2d 1194 (Ill. 1990).

ME: *In re* Gardner, 534 A.2d 947.

MA: *In re* Doe, 583 N.E.2d 1263 (Mass. 1992) (nasoduodenal tube).

NJ: *In re* Peter, 529 A.2d 419 (N.J. 1987); *In re* Conroy, 486 A.2d 1209 (N.J. 1985); *In re* Requena, 517 A.2d 886 (N.J. Super. Ct. Ch. Div. 1986) (patient with amyotrophic lateral sclerosis stated that she did not want nasogastric tube or other artificial nutrition and hydration procedures begun when she was no longer able to swallow), *aff'd,* 517 A.2d 869 (N.J. Super Ct. App. Div. 1986).

NY: *In re* Westchester County Medical Ctr. (O'Connor), 531 N.E.2d 607 (N.Y. 1988); Wickel v. Spellman, 552 N.Y.S.2d 437 (App. Div. 1990); Workmen's Circle Home & Infirmary for the Aged v. Fink, 514 N.Y.S.2d 893 (Sup. Ct. Bronx County 1987); Vogel v. Forman, 512 N.Y.S.2d 622 (Sup. Ct. Nassau County 1986).

OH: *In re* Myers, 610 N.E.2d 663 (P. Ct. Summit County, Ohio 1993); Leach v. Akron Gen. Medical Ctr., 426 N.E.2d 809 (C.P. P. Div. Summit County, Ohio 1980).

WA: *In re* Grant, 747 P.2d 445, *modified,* 757 P.2d 534.

gastrostomy tubes (g-tubes) surgically placed into the stomach,[319] jejunostomy tubes (j-tubes) or enterostomies surgically placed in the small intestine,[320] and other procedures.[321]

However, as *Conroy* points out, the matter is both simpler and more complicated, depending on the patient. For competent patients, there should be virtually no limitations on forgoing artificial nutrition and hydration as is true of other life-sustaining treatments. The California courts have issued two of the most far-reaching opinions involving competent patients. In *Thor*, the supreme court permitted a nonterminally ill prisoner to refuse tube-feeding,[322] and *Bouvia v. Superior Court (Glenchur)*[323] held that a patient had the right to refuse to be fed through a nasogastric tube inserted over her objection, and that she might also forgo *spoon*-feeding.[324] Similarly, incompetent patients who meet the subjective

---

319 **DRI:** Gray v. Romeo, 697 F. Supp. 580 (D.R.I. 1988).

CT: McConnell v. Beverly Enters.-Conn., Inc., 553 A.2d 596 (Conn. 1989).

FL: Browning v. Herbert, 568 So. 2d 4.

IL: Estate of Longeway v. Community Convalescent Ctr., 549 N.E.2d 292, 295 (Ill. 1989) ("Food and water are emotionally symbolic in that food and water are basic necessities of life, and the feeding of those who are unable to feed themselves is the most fundamental of all human relationships.").

KY: DeGrella v. Elston, 858 S.W.2d 698 (Ky. 1993).

ME: *In re* Swan, 569 A.2d 1202 (Me. 1990).

MD: Mack v. Mack, 618 A.2d 744 (Md. 1993).

MA: Brophy v. New Eng. Sinai Hosp., Inc., 497 N.E.2d 626, 630–31 (Mass. 1986) (describing feeding through gastrostomy tube).

MO: Cruzan v. Harmon, 760 S.W.2d 408 (Mo. 1988).

NJ: *In re* Jobes, 529 A.2d 434, 438 (N.J. 1987).

NY: Delio v. Westchester County Medical Ctr., 516 N.Y.S.2d 677, 681 (App. Div. 1987); Workmen's Circle Home & Infirmary for the Aged v. Fink, 514 N.Y.S.2d 893 (Sup. Ct. Bronx County 1987); *In re* Kerr (O'Brien), 517 N.Y.S.2d 346 (Sup. Ct. N.Y. County 1986).

320 **CA:** Thor v. Superior Court, 855 P.2d 375 (Cal. 1993).

NJ: *In re* Jobes, 529 A.2d 434, 437 (N.J. 1987); *In re* Clark, 510 A.2d 125, 137 (N.J. Super. Ct. Ch. Div. 1986).

NY: Delio v. Westchester County Medical Ctr., 516 N.Y.S.2d at 681.

321 **US:** *See* Cruzan v. Director, 497 U.S. 261, 288–89 (1990) (O'Connor, J., concurring) (citing Office of Technology Assessment Task Force, Life-Sustaining Technologies and the Elderly 282 (1988)).

MA: *In re* Hier, 464 N.E.2d 959, 961–62 (Mass. App. Ct. 1984) (describing artificial nutrition and hydration procedures).

322 Thor v. Superior Court, 855 P.2d 375 (Cal. 1993).

323 225 Cal. Rptr. 297 (Ct. App. 1986).

324 **CA:** Bouvia v. Superior Court (Glenchur), 225 Cal. Rptr. at 305.

CT: *But cf.* McConnell v. Beverly Enters.-Conn., Inc., 553 A.2d at 602–03 ("[I]t makes sense to recognize a further distinction between artificial technology to assist nutrition and hydration a fortiori included within the definition of a 'life support system,' and normal procedures to assist in feeding. In other words, the act, read in its entirety and giving effect to every

or substituted judgment standard should be treated essentially the same as competent patients for the purpose of forgoing life-sustaining treatment, including artificial nutrition and hydration.[325]

However, if the patient lacks decisionmaking capacity but there is inadequate evidence of the patient's desires, decisionmaking about artificial nutrition and hydration is more difficult, though no more so than with other treatments. In those jurisdictions permitting treatment to be forgone in accordance with a substituted judgment standard,[326] courts have properly allowed for artificial nutrition and hydration to be terminated if the standard could be met. If this standard cannot be met, some courts permit the application of some form of a best interests standard,[327] as did the *Barber* court. However, if the patient is in a persistent vegetative state,[328] as the New Jersey Supreme Court pointed out in *Conroy,* the patient is capable of experiencing neither burdens nor benefits of artificial nutrition and hydration or any other treatment (at least as that court defined the terms *benefit* and *burden*), and thus either the treatment cannot be forgone or the standard itself is inappropriate for patients in a persistent vegetative state.[329]

The sole right-to-die case to reach the United States Supreme Court, *Cruzan v. Director,*[330] involved the forgoing of artificial nutrition and hydration. This case reviewed *Cruzan v. Harmon,*[331] which held that the parents of a patient in a persistent vegetative state, who had been appointed her guardians, could not terminate artificial nutrition and hydration unless there was clear and convincing evidence that she had authorized its termination before she lost decisionmaking capacity. The Missouri court based its decision in large part on the fact that the state's living will statute prohibited the enforcement of a directive to terminate artificial nutrition and hydration,[332] which it regarded "as an expression of the policy of this State with regard to the sanctity of life."[333] However, if the legislature intended to prohibit the termination of artificial nutrition and

---

section . . . [citations omitted] implicitly contemplates the possible removal from a terminally ill patient of artificial technology in the form of a device such as a gastrostomy tube, but it does not, under any circumstances, permit the withholding of normal nutritional aids such as a spoon or a straw.").

325 *See, e.g., In re* Conroy, 486 A.2d 1209 (N.J. 1985).

326 See §§ **7.7–7.10.**

327 See §§ **7.11–7.25.**

328 See § **9.53.**

329 See §§ **7.26–7.37.**

330 Cruzan v. Director, 497 U.S. 261 (1990).

331 760 S.W.2d 408 (Mo. 1988).

332 **MO:** *See* Mo. Ann. Stat. § 459.010(3).

OH: *Cf. In re* Myers, 610 N.E.2d 663, 668 (P. Ct. Summit County, Ohio 1993) ("The statute is non-binding in that there are neither sanctions nor penalties, nor a mandate that its provisions must be followed.").

333 Cruzan v. Harmon, 760 S.W.2d at 420.

hydration through a living will, a fortiori it ought to have been prohibited even if there had been clear and convincing evidence that Nancy Cruzan had wished for artificial nutrition and hydration to be terminated. Thus, if the living will statute governs the outcome, *Cruzan* was properly decided, but for the wrong reason.

Although the Missouri court's opinion can be read more broadly as requiring a written or oral advance directive from a patient before *any* form of treatment can be forgone once that patient loses decisionmaking capacity, the Missouri Court of Appeals rejected that interpretation in the *Warren* case,[334] and held that cardiopulmonary resuscitation could be withheld from an incompetent patient based on a best interests standard. According to the appeals court, the Missouri Supreme Court refused to permit the forgoing of artificial nutrition and hydration without an advance directive because the court had concluded that artificial nutrition and hydration is not a medical procedure, but basic sustenance.[335]

Although the United States Supreme Court affirmed *Cruzan v. Harmon,* it did not squarely address the constitutionality of the termination of artificial nutrition and hydration, assuming "[f]or purposes of this case, . . . that a competent person would have a constitutionally protected right to refuse lifesaving hydration and nutrition."[336] However, it continued, "[t]his does not mean that an incompetent person should possess the same right, since such a person is unable to make an informed and voluntary choice to exercise that hypothetical right or any other right."[337] Because of "the dramatic consequences involved in refusal of such treatment," the consequences would have to be weighed against the individual's liberty interest to determine whether or not "the deprivation of that interest is constitutionally permissible."[338] In even clearer terms, the Court declared that "[w]e do not think a State is required to remain neutral in the face of an informed and voluntary decision by a physically-able adult to starve to death."[339] Thus, the Court's position on the forgoing of artificial nutrition and hydration has been accurately characterized as ambivalent.[340]

Justice O'Connor's concurring opinion is particularly important, for she, along with the four dissenting justices, constituted a majority on the issue of whether or not "the refusal of artificially delivered food and water is encompassed within [the] liberty interest" protected by the Fourteenth Amendment.[341]

---

334 *In re* Warren, 858 S.W.2d 263 (Mo. Ct. App. 1993).

335 *Id.* at 266 (citing Cruzan v. Harmon, 760 S.W.2d at 412).

336 Cruzan v. Director, 497 U.S. 261, 273 (1990).

337 *Id.* at 280.

338 *Id.* at 279.

339 *Id.* at 280.

340 *See* L.W. v. L.E. Phillips Career Dev. Ctr., 482 N.W.2d 60, 67 (Wis. 1992) ("[W]e base our conclusion that artificial nutrition and hydration is medical treatment which may be refused primarily on the fact that it is indistinguishable from other forms of treatment and not on the ambivalence of the *Cruzan* majority.").

341 Cruzan v. Director, 497 U.S. at 287 (O'Connor, J., concurring).

For Justice O'Connor, "[t]he State's artificial provision of nutrition and hydration implicates identical concerns" as the imposition of forced medical treatment because "[w]hether or not the techniques used to pass food and water into the patient's alimentary tract are termed 'medical treatment,' it is clear they all involve some degree of intrusion and restraint."[342] Consequently, legal rules—such as the numerous living will statutes—restricting or prohibiting the forgoing of artificial nutrition and hydration procedures might be thought to be prima facie violations of due process or equal protection.

The Court's holding might have been expected to have had a substantial political impact on the controversy over artificial nutrition and hydration, perhaps inspiring the enactment of new provisions prohibiting them from being withheld or withdrawn. In fact, the opposite has been the case. In the aftermath of *Cruzan,* state legislatures have been particularly active in enacting or revising first advance directive and then surrogate decisionmaking statutes. However, rather than making it more difficult to forgo artificial nutrition and hydration, much of the new legislation has loosened or removed previously existing statutory restrictions.[343]

Cruzan has also had virtually no effect on the case law. The courts have continued to permit the forgoing of artificial nutrition and hydration on the same basis as other treatments.[344] *Cruzan* should have no effect in those jurisdictions in which the basis for the forgoing of life-sustaining treatment, whether artificial nutrition and hydration or other treatment, has been based on common-law or state constitutional rights. This is precisely what has occurred in Florida. In *Browning v. Herbert,*[345] the supreme court held that the Florida constitutional right of privacy permitted a guardian to authorize the withdrawal of artificial nutrition and hydration on the basis of the patient's written and oral advance directives,[346] despite the fact that had the patient executed a statutorily-based advance directive requesting the forgoing of artificial nutrition and hydration, its implementation would have been barred by the state's advance directive statute.[347]

In addition to the *Cruzan* case, much attention has been paid to the opinion of the New York Court of Appeals in the *O'Connor* case,[348] which denied a

---

[342] *Id.* at 288 (O'Connor, J., concurring).

[343] See §§ **11.12** and **12.26.**

[344] **IN:** *See, e.g., In re* Lawrance, 579 N.E.2d 32 (Ind. 1991).

MA: *In re* Doe, 583 N.E.2d 1263 (Mass. 1992).

WI: L.W. v. L.E. Phillips Career Dev. Ctr., 482 N.W.2d 60 (Wis. 1992).

See generally Meisel, *A Retrospective on* Cruzan, 20 Law, Med., & Health Care 340 (1992) (*Cruzan* has had little impact on development of right-to-die case law).

[345] 568 So. 2d 4 (Fla. 1990).

[346] **FL:** *See also* Corbett v. D'Alessandro, 487 So. 2d 368 (Fla. Dist. Ct. App. 1986).

OH: *In re* Myers, 610 N.E.2d 663 (P. Ct. Summit County, Ohio 1993).

PA: Ragona v. Preate, 11 Fiduc. Rep. 2d 1 (C.P. Lackawanna County, Pa. 1990).

[347] *See* Fla. Stat. Ann. § 765.03(3) (West Supp. 1989) (repealed).

[348] *In re* Westchester County Medical Ctr. (O'Connor), 531 N.E.2d 607 (N.Y. 1988).

guardian permission to authorize the removal of artificial nutrition and hydration. However, that decision should be read not as averse to the termination of artificial nutrition and hydration in principle, but merely as affirming prior New York precedents[349] holding that *no* life-sustaining treatment may be forgone unless the patient provided a clear and convincing oral or written advance directive authorizing its termination. Two reported cases have applied the *O'Connor* rule. In *Elbaum,* the court found—on the basis of evidence strikingly similar to the evidence in *O'Connor* that had been found insufficient—that there was clear and convincing evidence that the patient had authorized the termination of her treatment—artificial nutrition and hydration—prior to losing decision-making capacity, and thus the surrogate's petition to terminate treatment was granted.[350] However, *In re Wickel*[351] affirmed the denial of a petition to remove an ng-tube.

The Ohio Court of Appeals in *Couture v. Couture*[352] issued an opinion in some respects quite like the Missouri court's *Cruzan* decision, though not citing it. It held that the Ohio Durable Power of Attorney for Health Care statute[353] barred the withdrawal of a feeding tube, even though the guardian was not acting pursuant to the same, because the statute evidences that "Ohio has adopted and announced a public policy forbidding withdrawal of hydration or nutrition in a case of this kind," namely when the patient is terminally ill but death is not imminent. This holding was questioned in two subsequent trial court decisions on the ground that the legislation on which *Couture* was based had been amended.[354] As in *Cruzan,* the *Couture* holding was based on a statute not factually applicable to the case because the patient had not executed the kind of document in question, but the court held that the statute announced a public policy applicable to the case.

The only other appellate case calling into question the legitimacy of forgoing artificial nutrition and hydration is *In re Grant,*[355] originally decided by the Washington Supreme Court in 1987. The court held in a 5-4 decision that the parents of a terminally ill child had the authority to terminate artificial nutrition and hydration. Approximately seven months later, the court issued an order under the same caption and docket number titled "revision of the listing of concurring justices," stating that the name of Justice Durham was to be removed as a justice who concurred in the majority opinion and was to be appended to the end of the opinion of Justice Andersen who had concurred in part and dissented

---

[349] *See In re* Storar, 420 N.E.2d 64 (N.Y. 1981).

[350] *See* Elbaum v. Grace Plaza of Great Neck, Inc., 544 N.Y.S.2d 840 (App. Div. 1989).

[351] 552 N.Y.S.2d 437 (App. Div. 1990).

[352] 549 N.E.2d 571 (Ohio Ct. App. 1989)

[353] Ohio Rev. Code Ann. §§ 1337.11–.17 (Anderson 1989) (repealed).

[354] *See In re* Myers, 610 N.E.2d 663 (P. Ct. Summit County, Ohio 1993); *In re* Crum, 580 N.E.2d 876 (P. Ct. Franklin County, Ohio 1991).

[355] 747 P.2d 445 (Wash. 1987).

in part.[356] Although Justice Andersen concurred in the result, he disagreed "with the majority's further decision which allows the patient's life to be taken by withholding intravenous nutrition and hydration or, to use less polite phraseology, to let her die of thirst or starvation."[357] Thus, in the final analysis, a majority of the justices agreed that the forgoing of artificial nutrition and hydration was impermissible.[358]

Table 9–2

Artificial Nutrition and Hydration Cases and Attorneys General Opinions

Arizona
Rasmussen v. Fleming, 741 P.2d 674 (Ariz. 1987)

California
Barber v. Superior Court, 195 Cal. Rptr. 484 (Ct. App. 1983)
Bouvia v. Superior Court (Glenchur), 225 Cal. Rptr. 297 (Ct. App. 1986)
Drabick v. Drabick, 245 Cal. Rptr. 840 (Ct. App. 1988)
McMahon v. Lopez, 245 Cal. Rptr. 172 (Ct. App. 1988)
Morrison v. Abramovice, 253 Cal. Rptr. 530 (Ct. App. 1988)

Connecticut
McConnell v. Beverly Enters.-Conn., Inc., 553 A.2d 596 (Conn. 1989)

Florida
Browning v. Herbert, 568 So. 2d 4 (Fla. 1990)
Corbett v. D'Alessandro, 487 So. 2d 368 (Fla. Dist. Ct. App. 1986)

Illinois
In re Estate of Greenspan, 558 N.E.2d 1194 (Ill. 1990)
Estate of Longeway v. Community Convalescent Ctr., 549 N.E.2d 292 (Ill. 1989)

Indiana
In re Lawrance, 579 N.E.2d 32 (Ind. 1991)

Maine
In re Gardner, 534 A.2d 947 (Me. 1987)
In re Swan, 569 A.2d 1202 (Me. 1990)

---

[356] *In re* Grant, 757 P.2d 534 (Wash. 1988). *See also* Farnam v. CRISTA Ministries, 807 P.2d 830, 843 n.2 (Wash. 1991) (Dore, C.J., concurring and dissenting) ("The original *In re Grant* slip opinion presented a 5-justice majority opinion yielding a 5-2-2 decision. The later, mandated decision, however, contained a 4-3-2 tally of justices after Justice Durham altered her stance and joined with Justice Andersen's concurrence/dissent."); Note, In Re Grant: *Where Does Washington Stand on Artificial Nutrition and Hydration?,* 13 U. Puget Sound L. Rev. 197 (1989).

[357] 747 P.2d at 458.

[358] Farnam v. CRISTA Ministries, 807 P.2d at 844 (Dore, C.J., concurring and dissenting) ("Thus in *Grant,* although seven justices held that an incompetent person's family should be allowed to make decisions regarding the removal of life support, a 5-justice majority qualified this holding and agreed that the removal of nutrition and hydration was a particularly cruel method of euthanasia, inapplicable under the Natural Death Act and meriting deferral to the Legislature for a proper evaluation of public policy.").

Maryland
Mack v. Mack, 618 A.2d 744 (Md. 1993)

Massachusetts
Brophy v. New Eng. Sinai Hosp., Inc., 497 N.E.2d 626 (Mass. 1986)
In re Doe, 583 N.E.2d 1263 (Mass. 1992)
In re Hier, 464 N.E.2d 959 (Mass. App. Ct. 1984)

Michigan
Martin v. Martin, 517 N.W.2d 749 (Mich. Ct. App. 1994)
Martin v. Martin, 504 N.W.2d 917 (Mich. Ct. App. 1993)

Missouri
Cruzan v. Harmon, 760 S.W.2d 408 (Mo. 1988)

New Jersey
In re Clark, 510 A.2d 136 (N.J. Super. Ct. Ch. Div. 1986)
In re Conroy, 486 A.2d 1209 (N.J. 1985)
In re Jobes, 529 A.2d 434 (N.J. 1987)
In re Peter, 529 A.2d 419 (N.J. 1987)
In re Requena, 517 A.2d 886 (N.J. Super. Ct. Ch. Div.), *aff'd,* 517 A.2d 869 (N.J. Super. Ct. App. Div. 1986)
In re Visbeck, 510 A.2d 125 (N.J. Super. Ct. Ch. Div. 1986)

New York
Delio v. Westchester County Medical Ctr., 516 N.Y.S.2d 677 (App. Div. 1987)
Elbaum v. Grace Plaza of Great Neck, Inc., 544 N.Y.S.2d 840 (App. Div. 1989)
Grace Plaza of Great Neck, Inc. v. Elbaum, 623 N.E.2d 513 (N.Y. 1993)
In re Kerr (O'Brien), 517 N.Y.S.2d 346 (Sup. Ct. N.Y. County 1986)
In re Westchester County Medical Ctr. (O'Connor), 531 N.E.2d 607 (N.Y. 1988)
In re Wickel, 552 N.Y.S.2d 437 (App. Div. 1990)
Workmen's Circle Home & Infirmary for the Aged v. Fink, 514 N.Y.S.2d 893 (Sup. Ct. Bronx County 1987)
Vogel v. Forman, 512 N.Y.S.2d 622 (Sup. Ct. Nassau County 1986)

Ohio
Couture v. Couture, 549 N.E.2d 571 (Ohio Ct. App. 1989)
In re Crum, 580 N.E.2d 876 (P. Ct. Franklin County, Ohio 1991)

Pennsylvania
In re Fiori, 652 A.2d 1350 (Pa.), *review granted,* 655 A.2d 989 (Pa. 1995)
Ragona v. Preate, 11 Fiduc. Rep. 2d 1 (C.P. Lackawanna County, Pa. 1990)

Rhode Island
Gray v. Romeo, 697 F. Supp. 580 (D.R.I. 1988)

Texas
Tex. Op. Att'y Gen. No. JM-837 (1987) (LEXIS, AG)

Washington
In re Grant, 747 P.2d 445 (Wash. 1987), *modified,* 757 P.2d 534 (Wash. 1988)

Wisconsin
L.W. v. L.E. Phillips Career Development Ctr., 482 N.W.2d 60 (Wis. 1992)

§ 9.40 —Nutrition and Hydration in Nursing Homes

The fact that there is a legal consensus about the propriety of forgoing artificial nutrition and hydration does not mean that it is well accepted in practice. And in no health care setting is it so difficult to withhold or withdraw feeding tubes as in nursing homes (or as they are formally known, "long-term care facilities"). In theory, the forgoing of artificial nutrition and hydration in long-term care facilities is governed by the same substantive principles of law as in other health care settings but there is a heightened reluctance to forgo artificial nutrition and hydration procedures in long-term care facilities, a reluctance which has little or no basis in law.

Judging by the litigated cases involving the termination of tube-feeding in nursing homes, the reason most frequently mentioned in the reported cases for not honoring a request is conscience—sometimes the conscience of those caring for the patient (for example, doctors, nurses, nursing assistants, nutritionists), and sometimes the conscience of the nursing home as expressed by its administrators[359] because those caring for the patient "feel like they are killing someone in these situations."[360] While this might explain the reluctance to permit the forgoing of artificial nutrition and hydration in nursing homes, it does not explain the apparently greater reluctance to do so in nursing homes than in hospitals. Although it is possible that conscience does play a more significant role in nursing homes than in hospitals because there is a greater chance for health care professionals to get to know the patients better than in hospitals[361]—for

---

[359] **DRI:** *See* Gray v. Romeo, 697 F. Supp. 580, 583, 590 (D.R.I. 1988).

CA: McMahon v. Lopez, 245 Cal. Rptr. 172 (Ct. App. 1988).

NJ: *In re* Jobes, 529 A.2d 434, 437 (N.J. 1987).

NY: Elbaum v. Grace Plaza of Great Neck, Inc., 544 N.Y.S.2d 840, 843 (App. Div. 1989).

[360] Letter from Ellen Olson, M.D., Director of Medical Education and Codirector of the Kathy and Alan C. Greenberg Center on Ethics in Geriatrics and Long Term Care of The Jewish Home & Hospital for Aged, New York, N.Y., to author (July 14, 1993) (on file with author).

[361] *See, e.g., In re* Jobes, 529 A.2d at 440:

> Some of the nurses and nurses' aides who work at the nursing home testified that they had observed examples of what they interpreted as cognitive awareness on the part of Mrs. Jobes. They claimed that she moved her head to aid them in washing her hair; smiled at appropriate times; followed people with her eyes; and relaxed when spoken to or touched in a soothing manner.
>
> In addition, several nurses and aides testified that they saw tears in Mrs. Jobes' eyes when her family visited. Nurses pointed out the phenomenon they described as "tears" to Dr. Carlin when he examined her at the nursing home. He characterized it as an unemotional collection of secretions in the corner of Mrs. Jobes' eyes. Dr. Liss also observed these secretions. He explained that they are merely accumulations of liquid that keep the conjunctiva moist and that they are created by rapid, reflexive eye-blinking, rather than emotions.
>
> Other nurses and nurses' aides testified that they had not observed any cognitive awareness in Mrs. Jobes, and that she gave no response to their verbal commands.

many nursing home residents, the emphasis is as much on "home" as it is on "nursing"—there are other explanations for the difficulty of forgoing tube-feeding in nursing homes. These include greater uncertainty about whether the law permits it,[362] more explicit fears about civil and/or criminal liability,[363] fears about harm to the reputation of the institution,[364] and others,[365] although in most of the reported cases, no reason is expressly stated as to why there was an objection to the termination of tube-feeding.[366] Another possible reason, though never mentioned in appellate opinions, is that there are sometimes economic incentives in the form of greater reimbursement for patients who receive tube-feeding. In fact, the reimbursement rate for providing tube-feeding depends on several factors, including whether there is third-party payment, the type of third-party payment if it exists, and the reimbursement rate negotiated by the particular long-term care facility and state Medicaid authorities. However, while there may be a financial incentive to provide tube-feeding in some cases, the financial incentive may work in the reverse in other cases.

Possibly the most significant factor behind the reluctance of nursing home personnel to permit the forgoing of artificial nutrition and hydration is the fact that nursing homes, unlike hospitals, are subject to a special set of federal regulations (adopted under the authority of the federal Medicaid statute)[367] often supplemented by state statutes and regulations,[368] and which are implemented

---

[362] **CA:** *See, e.g.,* Drabick v. Drabick, 245 Cal. Rptr. 840 (Ct. App. 1988).

IL: *In re* Estate of Greenspan, 558 N.E.2d 1194 (Ill. 1990).

[363] **DRI:** Gray v. Romeo, 697 F. Supp. 580, 583 (D.R.I. 1988).

KY: *See, e.g.,* DeGrella v. Elston, 858 S.W.2d 698, 701 (Ky. 1993).

TN: Robinson v. Beverly Enters.-Tenn., Inc., 1992 WL 200968 (Tenn. Ct. App. Aug. 21, 1992) (not reported in S.W.2d) (nursing home administrator told patient's family "that under Tennessee law the nursing home was not permitted to allow a patient to die of starvation and dehydration and if they did not agree to tube feeding of [patient] they must remove him from" the nursing home).

[364] *See, e.g.,* Gray v. Romeo, 697 F. Supp. at 583.

[365] *See, e.g., In re* Peter, 529 A.2d 419 (N.J. 1987) (objection of Ombudsman); *In re* Conroy, 486 A.2d 1209 (N.J. 1985) (nursing home did not object, but deferred to doctor who objected on the ground that it was unacceptable medical practice).

[366] **AZ:** *See, e.g.,* Rasmussen v. Fleming, 741 P.2d 674 (Ariz. 1987).

FL: *In re* Browning, 568 So. 2d 4 (Fla. 1990).

NY: Wickel v. Spellman, 552 N.Y.S.2d 437 (App. Div. 1990); Vogel v. Forman, 512 N.Y.S.2d 622 (Sup. Ct. Nassau County 1986).

OH: *In re* Crum, 580 N.E.2d 876 (P. Ct. Franklin County, Ohio 1991).

[367] Title XIX of the Social Security Act, 42 U.S.C.A. §§ 1396 *et seq.* (West 1992 & Supp. 1994).

[368] *See, e.g.,* California Dep't of Health Servs., *Guidelines Regarding Withdrawal or Withholding of Life-Sustaining Procedure(s) in Long-Term Care Facilities, discussed in* Drabick v. Drabick, 245 Cal. Rptr. 840, 848 (Ct. App. 1988); Florida Dep't of Health & Rehabilitative Servs., PDRL Info. Letter No. 14-190 (Dec. 17, 1990) (citing Florida Administrative Code Rules 10D-29.110(5), (6), and 10D-29.108(5)(b)(3), (15)).

by state regulatory authorities. These regulations, the tragic history of abuses of nursing home residents that prompted their adoption, and the severe consequences that can ensue from a citation for a violation of these regulations are probably the predominant factor responsible for the difficulty in terminating any kind of life-sustaining medical treatment in a nursing home, and feeding tubes in particular. This factor is sometimes mentioned in reported cases,[369] but no more so than the other factors that motivate litigation and usually in combination with one or more of them.

There are a number of provisions of federal and state statutory law that form the basis for the belief that the withholding or withdrawal of artificial nutrition and hydration from residents of long-term care facilities is impermissible, or at the least for the belief that it is governed by law different from that which is applicable in hospitals.[370] The primary basis for this belief is Medicare and Medicaid legislation and regulation, but various provisions of the Older Americans Act and related state statutes, as well as other state legislation, play a supporting role.

In the final analysis, there is no basis in law for believing that any of these statutory or regulatory provisions override the right of competent patients to refuse treatment (including artificial nutrition and hydration) or the right of incompetent patients to have such a decision made for them by a surrogate as long as the appropriate decisionmaking standard is met. What thin judicial precedent there is supports this conclusion.[371]

---

[369] **CA:** *See, e.g.,* McMahon v. Lopez, 245 Cal. Rptr. 172, 175 (Ct. App. 1988) ("The hospital's management group and attorney were concerned about 'doing the right thing by their patient'; they were also concerned about what position would be taken by officials from the county Department of Health Services and health officials from the state. [C]ounsel for the hospital notified [the attorney for the patient's family] that 'appropriate' people in the state Department of Health declined to offer any opinion on the permissibility of removal or clamping of Avis Flott's feeding tube, and would evaluate the situation only 'after the fact.'").

IN: *In re* Lawrance, 579 N.E.2d 32, 36 (Ind. 1991) ("[T]he home's administrator testified that Manor House was taking no position on the parents' petition, and that the home would comply with the decision of the court. Throughout the proceeding, however, Manor House made clear its concern that the home remained subject to state and federal regulation and sanction regardless of the decision of Sue Ann's family and doctors.").

KY: DeGrella v. Elston, 858 S.W.2d 698, 701 (Ky. 1993) ("This case is not in court because there is a dispute between the family members as to the patient's wishes, or between the physicians as to the medical evidence. The case is before our Court because Sue's attending physician and the nursing home fear legal sanctions, administrative, civil or even criminal, should they carry out the wishes of the patient as expressed through her mother and legal guardian. Being thus concerned, they have advised the family they require court authorization before permitting or participating in the removal of the medical device which provides Sue with nourishment and water.").

[370] *See* Kapp, *State of the Law: Nursing Homes,* 18 Law, Med., & Health Care 282 (1990) (general discussion of law applicable to long-term care facilities).

[371] **IL:** *In re* Estate of Greenspan, 558 N.E.2d 1194, 1204 (Ill. 1990).

Conditions of Participation in Medicare and Medicaid Programs

In order for the costs of caring for Medicare and Medicaid recipients in a long-term care facility to be reimbursed by those programs, the facility must be a certified Medicare/Medicaid provider. And in order to be a certified provider, long-term care facilities must comply with "conditions of participation" in the Medicare and Medicaid programs set forth by the federal agency responsible for their administration, the Health Care Financing Administration (HCFA).[372] In addition, many of the federal requirements are embodied in state statutes and regulations, some of which contain additional requirements.[373]

One of the conditions of participation is that long-term care facilities provide adequate nutrition and hydration to residents.[374] The federal statute governing grants to states for Medicaid programs states that "a nursing facility must provide (or arrange for the provision of) . . . dietary services that assure that the meals meet daily nutritional and special dietary needs of each resident."[375] This statute is implemented by the following regulations:

> (i) Nutrition. Based on a resident's comprehensive assessment, the facility must ensure that a resident . . . [m]aintains acceptable parameters of nutritional status, such as body weight and protein levels, unless the resident's clinical condition demonstrates that this is not possible.
>
> (j) Hydration. The facility must provide each resident with sufficient fluid intake to maintain proper hydration and health.[376]

These regulations have their origins in the documented reports of abuse and neglect of residents of nursing homes that were widespread in the 1960s and 1970s.[377] Although the Senate hearings and the legislation and regulations that

---

[372] *See* Conditions of Participation and Requirements for Long Term Care Facilities, 42 C.F.R. Pt. 483 (1994). *See generally* Lazarus et al., *Don't Make Them Leave Their Rights at the Door: A Recommended Model State Statute to Protect the Rights of the Elderly in Nursing Homes,* 4 J. Contemp. Health L. & Pol'y 321 (1988) (describing administration of Medicaid program).

[373] *See* Cohen, *Patients' Rights Laws and the Right to Refuse Life-Sustaining Treatment in Nursing Homes,* 2 BioLaw S:231 (Aug. 1989) (collecting state statutes and regulations).

[374] *See* Conditions of Participation and Requirements for Long Term Care Facilities, 42 C.F.R. § 483.25(i), (j) (1994).

[375] 42 U.S.C.A. § 1396r(b)(4)(A)(iv) (West Supp. 1994).

[376] Conditions of Participation and Requirements for Long Term Care Facilities, 42 C.F.R. § 483.25(i), (j) (1994).

[377] *See, e.g., In re* Conroy, 486 A.2d 1209, 1238 (N.J. 1985) ("In many cases [nursing home residents] have not even received humane treatment. And in an alarming number of known cases, they have actually encountered abuse and physical danger * * *. [S]ubcommittee transcripts are replete with examples of cruelty, negligence, danger from fires, food poisoning, virulent infections, lack of human dignity, callousness and unnecessary regimentation, and kickbacks to nursing home operators from suppliers. The net impact is that far too many

have flowed from them in the past two decades have done much to improve conditions in long-term care facilities, reports of abuse still occur,[378] including inadequate food for residents.[379]

State Medicaid "Surveys." The process by which federal statutory and regulatory standards—and whatever state law may supplement them—are applied to individual long-term care facilities is referred to as a Medicaid "survey," and the state employees who conduct them are referred to as Medicaid "surveyors."[380] These surveys are conducted on an annual basis,[381] using two federally prescribed forms for the review of long-term care facilities for Medicare/Medicaid certification.[382]

Although difficult to document, there is little doubt among those familiar with the operation of long-term care facilities that administrators of even the best-run nursing homes live in fear of Medicaid surveys. They fear that surveyors will cite them for infractions of regulations that, if sufficient in number or severity, will lead to the loss of their Medicaid certification, with the consequence that

---

patients have needlessly sustained injury and, in some cases, death.") (quoting Senate Subcomm. on Long-Term Care of the Special Comm. on Aging, Nursing Home Care in the United States: Failure in Public Policy, Introductory Report, S. Rep. No. 1420, 93d Cong., 2d Sess. 16 (1974). *See also* Senate Subcomm. on Long-Term Care of the Special Comm. on Aging, 93d Cong., 2d Sess., Nursing Home Care in the United States: Failure in Public Policy, Supporting Paper No. 1, The Litany of Nursing Home Abuses and an Examination of the Roots of Controversy 176 (Comm. Print 1974) (complaints of substandard food ran "the gamut from watery soup and small portions, all the way to charges that unwholesome food was served," and that "the uneaten portion of meals was being scraped off one patient's tray and put on a new plate for a second person; that some meals consisted of one-half slice of bread, a little squash and coffee"). *See generally* Institute of Medicine, Improving the Quality of Care in Nursing Homes (1986).

[378] *See, e.g.*, Perl, *Mending the State's Worst Nursing Homes,* Atlanta J. & Const., Oct. 4, 1992, at E-1 (Ga. sanctioned or fined almost 20% of nursing homes in past year for abuse and neglect of residents).

[379] *Id.* ("When state inspectors showed up last year, they found there wasn't enough food to go around and what was there was often served cold."). *See generally* Institute of Medicine, Improving the Quality of Care in Nursing Homes 3 nn. 2–23 (collecting references), 21 ("Despite extensive government regulation for more than 10 years, some nursing homes can be found in every state that provide seriously inadequate quality of care and quality of life.") (1986).

[380] *See* Howard & Maag, *The New Requirements of Participation and Guidelines, in* National Health Lawyers Ass'n, Long Term Care and the Law § F (1990) (discussing how surveys are conducted).

[381] 42 U.S.C.A. § 1396r(g)(2)(A)(iii)(I) (West 1992) ("Each nursing facility shall be subject to a standard survey not later than 15 months after the date of the previous standard survey conducted under this subparagraph. The statewide average interval between standard surveys of a nursing facility shall not exceed 12 months.").

[382] *See* 42 C.F.R. § 488.110(q) (1994); 42 C.F.R. § 488.100 (1994) (Part A used for initial certification); 42 C.F.R. § 488.105 (1994) (Part B used for all types of surveys such as recertification or complaints as well as for initial certification in conjunction with Part A).

they will no longer qualify for Medicare and Medicaid reimbursement, which might mean that they will be shut down until or unless the deficiencies are corrected.[383] (There are two levels of remedies and sanctions, those for violations that "immediately jeopardize the health and safety of its residents,"[384] and those that do not.[385] However, the nature of the remedies and sanctions is virtually the same regardless of whether or not the violation immediately jeopardizes the health and safety of residents.) Lesser sanctions include fines and prohibitions on admitting new residents until deficiencies are corrected.[386] Although some states have receivership programs that allow nursing homes to continue to operate so that residents are not suddenly without a place to live and be cared for,[387] the result for the nursing home owner can be the same because of the loss of financial control of the facility and negative publicity.

Citations for infractions of nutrition and hydration standards are not formally any more serious than a violation of any other standard. But as a practical matter, surveyors are likely to take evidence of inadequate nourishment of residents very seriously, especially if it is widespread, systematic, or seemingly motivated by the desire of the nursing home administration to economize by providing residents with inadequate food.

The net effect is that nursing home administrators have a substantial incentive to bend over backward to satisfy regulatory standards.[388] Of course, that is just what these standards are intended to achieve. And because nursing home administrators are especially concerned about being cited for infractions of regulations requiring the provision of adequate nutrition and hydration if a resident is undernourished, there is a strong incentive to see that the regulations are not violated. It is easy to imagine a nursing home administrator saying, "how can I be faulted for feeding someone," and equally simple to imagine the same administrator thinking how he would be vilified in the press, if not in

---

[383] *See* 42 U.S.C.A. § 1396r(h) (West 1992).

[384] *Id.* § 1396r(h)(1)(A).

[385] *Id.* § 1396r(h)(1)(B).

[386] *See id.* § 1396r(h). *See, e.g.,* Clay County Manor, Inc., v. Tennessee, Dep't of Health & Env't, 1991 WL 261877 (Tenn. Ct. App. Dec. 13, 1991) (not reported in S.W.2d) (case in which admissions to a nursing home were suspended as a result of noncompliance with federal and state standards discovered through a Medicaid survey).

[387] *See* 42 U.S.C.A. § 1396r(h) (West 1992). *See generally* Lazarus et al., *Don't Make Them Leave Their Rights at the Door: A Recommended Model State Statute to Protect the Rights of the Elderly in Nursing Homes,* 4 J. Contemp. Health L. & Pol'y 321, 336–40 (1988).

[388] *See, e.g.,* Robinson v. Beverly Enters.-Tenn., Inc., 1992 WL 200968 (Tenn. Ct. App. Aug. 21, 1992) (not reported in S.W.2d) (nursing home administrator insisted that patient be tube-fed despite family's refusal, and discharged nursing home physician who supported family's decision and order of patient's prior physician who attended him on his prior hospitalization not to insert a feeding tube; nursing home administrator "took the position that as a nursing home it could not allow a patient to die from starvation and dehydration without an attempt to intervene").

administrative and judicial proceedings, by allowing someone to "starve to death." The unintended but very real consequence is that tube-feeding becomes very difficult to forgo even when such a decision is a lawful one.[389]

Regulatory Right to Refuse Treatment. The same regulatory standards for long-term care facilities in the Medicare/Medicaid conditions of participation, and that contain the provisions for adequate nutrition and hydration, also acknowledge the right of nursing home residents to refuse treatment.[390] This right is implemented through the "Residents Rights" portion of the Medicaid survey requiring that surveyors determine whether "[e]ach resident is given an opportunity to refuse treatment."[391] Because there is no statutory provision paralleling the regulatory provision, it is reasonable to conclude that the regulation is acknowledging the existence of a common-law and/or constitutional right to refuse treatment, especially in light of the fact that so many courts have held such a right to exist. The commentary to another subsection, dealing with the capacity of nursing home residents to make decisions, explicitly acknowledges "the variance in State laws concerning resident rights," on this issue, and consequently "defer[s] entirely to State law on this matter."[392] This also suggests that the draftsmen of the regulations assumed the existence of state-law rights to refuse treatment.

In the statement of this right, no distinction is made between competent patients and incompetent patients,[393] and no specific mention is made of artificial nutrition and hydration. However, the commentary issued when the final rule was promulgated does discuss the right to refuse artificial nutrition and hydration.[394] The commentary begins by restating the "requirement . . . that residents receive a nutritious diet and adequate liquids."[395] That statement is immediately followed by the observation that

---

[389] **CA:** *See, e.g.,* McMahon v. Lopez, 245 Cal. Rptr. 172, 174 (Ct. App. 1988) ("Citing various legal and ethical problems, and particularly problems with licensing and inspection agencies run by defendants state and county, the [skilled nursing facility] refused the request to remove the tube.").

IN: *In re* Lawrance, 579 N.E.2d 32, 36 (Ind. 1991) ("Throughout the proceeding, . . . [the nursing home] made clear its concern that the home remained subject to state and federal regulation and sanction regardless of the decision of Sue Ann's family and doctors.").

[390] 42 C.F.R. § 483.10(b)(4) (1994) ("The resident has the right to refuse treatment.").

[391] 42 C.F.R. § 488.100 (1994) (Code F557).

[392] 54 Fed. Reg. 5316, 5320 (Feb. 2, 1989) (discussing 42 C.F.R. § 483.10(a)(3)).

[393] *See* 42 C.F.R. § 483.10(d)(3) (1994) (limiting specifically only right to "participate in planning care and treatment or changes in care and treatment" to competent patients).

[394] *See* Health Care Fin. Admin., Department of Health & Human Serv., Medicare and Medicaid, Requirements for Long Term Care Facilities, 54 Fed. Reg. 5316, 5321 (Feb. 2, 1989) (comment to 42 C.F.R. § 483.10(b)(4)).

[395] *Id.*

> [w]hen invasive procedures are necessary to accomplish this end, however, the courts have generally held that these procedures constitute treatments that residents or their representatives may refuse just as they may refuse any other medical treatment.[396]

This was an accurate portrayal of the case law when the regulations were drafted in 1989, and it is today as well.

The commentary then acknowledges that this is a "controversial issue," and proceeds to summarize the provisions of state living will statutes dealing with forgoing artificial nutrition and hydration. It notes that in 1989, six state statutes permitted the withdrawal of nutrition and hydration, seven explicitly prohibited it, and 14 were silent.[397] The commentary further observes that

> [b]ecause the right to refuse treatment is protected by law, some believe the right to refuse artificial feeding exists even if a State's living will law has restrictive language excluding artificial feeding from the definition of treatment which may be refused. Such State-imposed restrictions are, therefore, subject to judicial challenge. So far, every trial court decision holding that artificial feeding is unlike other treatments and cannot be refused has been reversed upon appeal. Indeed, in 3 of the 7 States with restrictive language, court challenges to such restrictions have been successful.[398]

Thus HCFA takes no stand on the right to refuse artificial nutrition and hydration, leaving this to be decided under state law. However, the conclusions that it draws about state law are curious. On the one hand, it accurately concludes that state common law as of that date was all but unanimous,[399] that artificial nutrition and hydration is a form of medical treatment that may be refused if the circumstances for refusal of treatment in general obtain.

On the other hand, it undercuts this conclusion by reference to the ambivalence of state living will statutes about forgoing artificial nutrition and hydration. However, it fails explicitly to recognize that these statutes are not applicable to patients who have not executed living wills.[400] Nor are they applicable to patients who have executed a living will but who remain competent.[401] In addition, there has been a great deal of revision of state advance directive statutes since 1989, and only one advance directive statute now completely prohibits the forgoing of artificial nutrition and hydration through an advance directive.[402] Finally, HCFA's understanding of advance directive statutes, while

---

[396] *Id.*

[397] *Id.*

[398] *Id.*

[399] See § **9.39.**

[400] See § **10.13.**

[401] See § **10.14.**

[402] See §§ **11.12** and **12.26.**

not unusual, is both cramped and probably incorrect in its failure to acknowledge that enforceable advance directives may be made (either orally or in writing) without adhering to statutory technicalities. Most advance directive statutes state this quite explicitly in one or more ways.[403] In other words, state advance directive statutes do not technically "prohibit" anything, including the forgoing of artificial nutrition and hydration. These statutes merely confer immunity from liability on those who comply with an advance directive drafted in accordance with the statute although in practice, health care providers (both institutions and individuals) may be more reluctant to implement an advance directive not drafted in compliance with the state's statute than to implement one that is.

The HCFA commentary concludes with the curious and confusing, if not contradictory, statement that "[b]ecause of the discrepancies among State laws and the need for a judicial resolution of this issue, we are leaving the wording of this statement concerning the resident's right to refuse treatment unqualified."[404] In any event, HCFA's interpretation of its own regulations imposes no restrictions on forgoing artificial nutrition and hydration.[405]

In contrast with the federal regulations and commentary, the New York Department of Health has issued a memorandum that is a model of clarity.[406] The memorandum was issued in response to "a number of inquiries from nursing home operators concerning the relationship between a patient's right to refuse treatment, including artificial nutrition and hydration, and a facility's obligation to provide a patient with adequate nutrition."[407] According to this memorandum, neither the state regulatory provision requiring long-term care facilities to provide adequate nutrition[408] nor the provision defining patient neglect to include the failure to provide appropriate services to residents, including nutrition,[409] "requires a nursing home operator to provide a patient with adequate nutrients and fluids when there is clear and convincing evidence that the patient wishes to refuse such care and understands the consequences of such refusal."[410] In other words, if a nursing home resident meets the standard for the forgoing of any life-sustaining treatment prescribed by New

---

[403] See §§ **10.12–10.16.**

[404] 54 Fed. Reg. 5316, 5321 (1989).

[405] *See id.* (commentary to regulation states that "a resident's refusal of treatment must be persistent and consistently documented in the resident's record"; however, this is applicable to refusal of any form of treatment, not merely to artificial nutrition and hydration).

[406] *See* State of N.Y., Dep't of Health Memorandum, Health Facilities Series NH-50, HRF-50 (Oct. 20, 1989).

[407] *Id.* at 1.

[408] N.Y. Comp. Codes R. & Regs tit. 10, § 416.3 (1992).

[409] *Id.* § 81.1(c).

[410] State of N.Y., Dep't of Health Memorandum, Health Facilities Series NH-50, at 1 (Oct. 20, 1989).

York law,[411] that treatment, including tube-feeding, may be withheld or withdrawn. Although in practice it might be more difficult to withhold or withdraw nutrition and hydration from nursing home residents in New York than most other states, this is because of that state's standard for forgoing any life-sustaining medical treatment whether the patient is in a hospital or nursing home.

Older Americans Act and State Statutes for Protection of the Elderly

Another source of the belief that artificial nutrition and hydration procedures cannot be withheld or withdrawn from residents in long-term care facilities is state legislation (and implementing regulations) intended to protect the elderly from abuse and neglect. Qualification for the receipt of federal funding under the Older Americans Act for services for the elderly[412] has been an important impetus for the adoption of these statutes.

Unlike the Medicare and Medicaid requirements, the Older Americans Act applies only incidentally to long-term care facilities. Under the Act, each state must establish an "Office of the State Long-Term Care Ombudsman," the duties of which include investigation and resolution of complaints by or on behalf of older individuals who are residents of long-term care facilities,[413] including complaints about the abuse of residents. Although the Act does not specifically state that the failure to provide nutrition and hydration constitutes abuse, the Act's definition of abuse—"the willful . . . infliction of injury . . . or deprivation by a caretaker of goods or services which are necessary to avoid physical harm"[414]—is broad enough to encompass the failure to provide adequate nutrition and hydration. Thus, at least in the case of *elderly* nursing home residents, the Older Americans Act provides another incentive for nursing home administrators to refuse to forgo tube-feeding even in the face of otherwise-lawful requests from competent residents or the families of incompetent residents to do so.

In addition, many states have enacted statutory protections of the rights of nursing home residents.[415] Some of the provisions of these statutes parallel federal law in protecting patients against abuse.[416] Other state statutes or regulations

---

411 *See In re* Westchester County Medical Ctr. (O'Connor), 531 N.E.2d 607 (N.Y. 1988); Elbaum v. Grace Plaza of Great Neck, Inc., 544 N.Y.S.2d 840 (App. Div. 1989).

412 *See* 42 U.S.C.A. § 3027(a) (West Supp. 1994). The Act applies to "older individual[s]," defined as those 60 years of age or older. *Id.* § 3022(9).

413 *Id.* § 3027(a)(12)(A)(i).

414 *Id.* § 3022(14).

415 *See* Lazarus et al., *Don't Make Them Leave Their Rights at the Door: A Recommended Model State Statute to Protect the Rights of the Elderly in Nursing Homes,* 4 J. Contemp. Health L. & Pol'y 321, 326–27 n.38 (1988) (collecting statutes).

416 *See id.* at 330 n.54 (collecting statutes).

adopted pursuant thereto contain specific provisions requiring the provision of adequate nutrition and hydration.[417]

§ 9.41 Surgery

There has been little litigation involving patients who are terminally ill and for whom major surgical procedures would only prolong the process of dying or would hold out very slim chances for recovery.[418] However, minor and sometimes more difficult surgical procedures are necessary for the insertion of some kinds of artificial nutrition and hydration devices.[419] Even when a treatment might be lifesaving as opposed to merely life-sustaining, a court has permitted a patient to refuse it in favor of another treatment with a less optimistic prognosis.[420]

On numerous occasions, courts have been presented with petitions to order amputation.[421] These cases have generally involved patients who could be restored to the status quo ante by the surgery. Although incompetent patients have generally been ordered to undergo it,[422] courts have generally permitted competent patients to forgo such treatment.[423] Both of these results seem correct.

TREATMENT OF PARTICULAR CONDITIONS

§ 9.42 Treatment of Particular Conditions

The remaining sections in this chapter discuss some medical conditions that have been involved in decisionmaking about life-sustaining treatment. The

---

[417] *See, e.g.,* 28 Pa. Code § 211.6 (1987).

[418] **WA:** *In re* Ingram, 689 P.2d 1363 (Wash. 1984).

[419] *See, e.g., In re* Hier, 464 N.E.2d 959 (Mass. App. Ct. 1984) (gastrostomy).

[420] **WA:** *In re* Ingram, 689 P.2d 1363 (surgery for cancer would provide 70 to 80% chance of survival but destroy patient's ability to speak; radiation therapy would provide 40% chance of survival but would preserve ability to speak).

[421] *See generally* Karnezis, Annotation, *Patient's Right to Refuse Treatment Allegedly Necessary to Sustain Life,* 93 A.L.R.3d 67 (1979).

[422] **NJ:** *E.g., In re* Schiller, 372 A.2d 360 (N.J. Super. Ct. Ch. Div. 1977).

NY: *E.g., In re* Harvey "U," 501 N.Y.S.2d 920 (App. Div. 1986); *In re* Strauss, 391 N.Y.S.2d 168 (App. Div. 1977); Long Island Jewish-Hillside Medical Ctr. v. Levitt, 342 N.Y.S.2d 356 (Sup. Ct. Nassau County 1973).

TN: *E.g.,* State Dep't of Human Resources v. Northern, 563 S.W.2d 197 (Tenn. Ct. App. 1978). *But see In re* Nemser, 273 N.Y.S.2d 624 (Sup. Ct. N.Y. County 1966).

[423] **MA:** *E.g.,* Lane v. Candura, 376 N.E.2d 1232 (Mass. App. Ct. 1978).

NJ: *E.g., In re* Quackenbush, 383 A.2d 785 (N.J. Super. Ct. P. Div. 1978).

President's Commission has noted that most deaths now are caused by "heart disease, cancer, and cerebrovascular disease or illness—illnesses that occur later in life and that are ordinarily progressive for some years before death."[424] Medical technology has progressed to such a point that "[f]or almost any life-threatening condition, some intervention can now delay the moment of death,"[425] thus raising the question of when it is appropriate to do so.

§ 9.43 Degenerative Neurological Diseases

There are a number of different degenerative neurological diseases that inevitably lead to death and have figured in right-to-die litigation.

§ 9.44 —Amyotrophic Lateral Sclerosis (Lou Gehrig's Disease)

Amyotrophic lateral sclerosis, sometimes referred to as Lou Gehrig's disease or ALS, "is a progressively deteriorating, disabling disease of the nervous system,"[426] "involv[ing] degeneration and hardening of portions of the spinal cord. It is characterized by progressive loss of control of the muscles of the body and by increasing paralysis."[427] It is a terminal, incurable illness, resulting in death in from three to five years.[428] Patients suffering from ALS eventually lose the ability to breathe and swallow and must be supported by mechanical ventilation and artificial nutrition and hydration for life to be maintained. They are also subject to cardiac failure, and thus the question of do-not-resuscitate orders may arise.[429] Most ALS patients do not lose their mental competence until extremely late in the disease process. Thus, they are generally fully aware of their increasing loss of both involuntary functions, such as breathing, and voluntary ones, such as speech, which they may find to be

---

[424] President's Comm'n, Deciding to Forego Life-Sustaining Treatment 16, *cited in* Brophy v. New Eng. Sinai Hosp., Inc., 497 N.E.2d 626, 627 n.3 (Mass. 1986).

[425] *Id.* at 1, *cited in* Brophy v. New Eng. Sinai Hosp., Inc., 497 N.E.2d at 627 n.3.

[426] Leach v. Akron Gen. Medical Ctr., 426 N.E.2d 809, 810 (C.P. P. Div. Summit County, Ohio 1980).

[427] **NJ:** *In re* Requena, 517 A.2d 886, 887 (N.J. Super. Ct. Ch. Div. 1986).

PA: *Accord In re* Doe, 45 Pa. D. & C.3d 371, 373 (C.P. Phila. County 1987).

[428] **NJ:** *In re* Requena, 517 A.2d at 887.

OH: Leach v. Akron Gen. Medical Ctr., 426 N.E.2d at 810.

PA: *In re* Doe, 45 Pa. D. & C.3d at 373–74.

[429] **OH:** *See, e.g.,* Estate of Leach v. Shapiro, 469 N.E.2d 1047 (Ohio Ct. App. 1984); Leach v. Akron Gen. Medical Ctr., 426 N.E.2d 809.

PA: *See, e.g., In re* Doe, 45 Pa. D. & C.3d at 375.

particularly distressing.[430] Consequently, all of the reported cases have involved competent patients seeking to have ventilator support discontinued[431] or withheld,[432] or to have a do-not-resuscitate order written so that, in the event of a cardiac arrest, cardiopulmonary resuscitation will not be administered.[433]

§ 9.45 —Alzheimer's Disease and Other Senile Dementias

The term *senility* is often used to apply globally to the "general infirmities of very advanced age."[434] Patients who are described as senile vary greatly in physical and mental condition and capability. Consequently, the term can be a misleading one in decisionmaking about life-sustaining treatment if it is assumed that all patients who are described as senile are incapable of expressing their views and of engaging in contact with others. For instance, the trial court judge who decided both the *Conroy* and the *Visbeck* cases made the following observations about senility:

> When I saw Mrs. Visbeck she was flat on her back in a relaxed, supple position. Her body appeared rather well fleshed out, in contrast to the very withered, almost skeletal, appearance of Claire Conroy. . . . Mrs. Visbeck was being fed intravenously through her right leg. Her nurse told me that she could no longer receive feeding through her arms, and my observation of the discolored and deteriorated condition of the skin over the right arm veins corroborated that. A catheter is permanently inserted to draw off urine.
>
> The conclusion I draw from the evidence and from my observations of Elizabeth Visbeck is that her mental processes are very limited, but she does have significant awareness of her surroundings and she has some limited ability to respond to them. She is not presently in pain, but she is capable of feeling pain. In the course of my judicial duties, I have seen hundreds of elderly mentally impaired patients. Mrs. Visbeck's mental condition is much worse than most of them, but it is markedly better than the mental condition I observed in Claire Conroy.[435]

---

430 **FL:** *See, e.g.,* Satz v. Perlmutter, 362 So. 2d 160, 161 (Fla. Dist. Ct. App. 1978) (patient repeatedly stated to his family, "'I'm miserable take it out," and at a bedside hearing, told the obviously concerned trial judge that whatever would be in store for him if the respirator were removed, "it can't be worse than what I'm going through now'").

NJ: *See, e.g., In re* Requena, 517 A.2d at 887–88.

431 **FL:** *See, e.g.,* Satz v. Perlmutter, 362 So. 2d 160.

NJ: *See, e.g., In re* Farrell, 529 A.2d 404 (N.J. 1987).

432 *See, e.g.,* Leach v. Akron Gen. Medical Ctr., 426 N.E.2d 809.

433 *See, e.g., In re* Doe, 45 Pa. D. & C.3d 371.

434 *In re* Visbeck, 510 A.2d 125, 127 (N.J. Super. Ct. Ch. Div. 1986).

435 *Id.* at 130.

Because there are a large number of senile and related degenerative neurological conditions and organic brain syndromes,[436] it is essential to narrow the diagnosis more precisely than the general descriptive term *senility.* One of the more common is Alzheimer's disease, which

> is a degenerative disease of the brain of unknown origin, described as presenile dementia, and results in destruction of brain tissue and, consequently deterioration in brain function. The condition is progressive and unremitting, leading in stages to disorientation, loss of memory, personality disorganization, loss of intellectual function, and ultimate loss of all motor function. The disease typically leads to a vegetative or comatose condition and then to death. The course of the disease may be gradual or precipitous, averaging five to seven years.[437]

Many people, mostly elderly, suffer from the disease, and it can lead to extremely difficult problems in medical decisionmaking. Many patients with Alzheimer's disease are in nursing homes rather than hospitals because they frequently need little if anything in the way of acute medical care. Thus, the questions that arise about forgoing treatment generally involve do-not-resuscitate orders, the use of antibiotic medications to treat infections, kidney dialysis if renal failure develops,[438] and especially artificial nutrition and hydration.[439] Because of the progressively degenerative nature of the disease, patients eventually lose the ability to feed themselves and then to swallow. Many patients can be spoon- and bottle-fed at first, and therefore withholding nutrition and hydration is probably not advisable unless there is an advance directive specifically requesting that even these types of feedings be forgone. However, when spoon- or bottle-feeding are no longer possible, consideration can be given to not starting artificial nutrition and hydration procedures. The case law emphasizes the fact that such feeding procedures are medical procedures rather than ordinary feeding, so that they can legitimately be withheld[440] if the appropriate standard of decisionmaking for incompetent patients can be met.

Another cause of senility is stroke.[441] Stroke can, but does not invariably, lead to a persistent vegetative state. In some cases, patients who have had serious

---

[436] *See* Cranford, *Major Neurologic Syndromes in Life-Sustaining Medical Treatment Decisions,* 7 Med. Ethics Advisor 87 (July 1991) (table listing different aspects of brain death, persistent vegetative state, permanent locked-in state, and dementia).

[437] *In re* Dinnerstein, 380 N.E.2d 134 (Mass. App. Ct. 1978).

[438] **MA:** *E.g., In re* Spring, 405 N.E.2d 115, 118 (Mass. 1980) (end-stage kidney disease and "chronic organic brain syndrome or senility").

[439] **IL:** *E.g., In re* Estate of Greenspan, 558 N.E.2d 1194 (Ill. 1990) (Alzheimer's disease).

NJ: *E.g., In re* Conroy, 486 A.2d 1209 (N.J. 1985) (senile); *In re* Clark, 510 A.2d 136 (N.J. Super. Ct. Ch. Div. 1986); *In re* Visbeck, 510 A.2d 125 (N.J. Super. Ct. Ch. Div. 1986).

[440] See § **9.39.**

[441] **FL:** *See, e.g.,* Browning v. Herbert, 568 So. 2d 4 (Fla. 1990).

NY: *See, e.g., In re* Westchester County Medical Ctr. (O'Connor), 531 N.E.2d 607 (N.Y. 1988); Vogel v. Forman, 512 N.Y.S.2d 622 (Sup. Ct. Nassau County 1986).

strokes or a series of strokes are described as "vegetative."[442] This is an unfortunate use of these terms because it confuses these patients' conditions with the accepted syndrome referred to as persistent vegetative state.[443]

Decisionmaking about the initiation, limitation, or termination of treatment for elderly senile patients presents extremely delicate and difficult issues because of the great—and unfortunately legitimate[444]—fear that treatment might, at least in the absence of a clear indication of the patient's own wishes about treatment, be forgone based on illegitimate considerations, such as the value of the patient's life to society[445] or the burdens to others in providing for the patient's well-being.[446] The New Jersey Supreme Court has sought to deal with the problem of possible abuse of elderly patients by providing additional safeguards to them in decisionmaking about life-sustaining treatment.[447]

§ 9.46 —Batten's Disease

Batten's disease is a genetically-caused degenerative condition of the central nervous system for which there is no known cure. Most victims die in their teens or early 20s. The disease leads to loss of vision, epileptic seizures, loss of motor control (and consequently the ability to walk, talk, and swallow), and severe mental retardation. Damage to the brain leads to a loss of control of circulation and respiration, which initially causes irregular heart rate and breathing and, finally, cardiac or respiratory arrest and death.[448] The course of the disease is relatively predictable and requires a number of decisions about life-sustaining

---

442 *See, e.g.,* Browning v. Herbert, 568 So. 2d at 9 (neurologist testified patient who suffered a series of strokes, who "appeared alert and would follow [a visitor] with her eyes," and who had uttered a few garbled words on a few occasions, but who could not follow any simple commands "was in a persistent vegetative state, which he defined as the absence of cognitive behavior and inability to communicate or interact purposefully with the environment").

443 See § **9.53.**

444 *See, e.g., In re* Conroy, 486 A.2d 1209, 1238 (N.J. 1985) (citing Senate Subcomm. on Long-Term Care of the Special Comm. on Aging, Nursing Home Care in the United States: Failure in Public Policy, Introductory Report, S. Rep. No. 1420, 93d Cong., 2d Sess. 16 (1974). *See also* Senate Subcomm. on Long-Term Care of the Special Comm. on Aging, 93d Cong., 2d Sess., Nursing Home Care in the United States: Failure in Public Policy, Supporting Paper No. 1, The Litany of Nursing Home Abuses and an Examination of the Roots of Controversy 176 (Comm. Print 1974); *In re* Peter, 529 A.2d 419, 425 n.6 (N.J. 1987); *In re* Visbeck, 510 A.2d 125 (N.J. Super. Ct. Ch. Div. 1986).

See generally Institute of Medicine, Improving the Quality of Care in Nursing Homes (1986).

445 See §§ **7.22–7.23.**

446 See § **7.24.**

447 See § **7.32.**

448 *In re* Grant, 747 P.2d 445, 446 (Wash. 1987), *modified,* 757 P.2d 534 (Wash. 1988).

treatment such as the use of mechanical ventilators, CPR, and artificial nutrition and hydration.[449]

In the sole litigated appellate case involving this disease, *In re Grant,* the Washington Supreme Court permitted the family of a young woman in the terminal stages of the disease, who was blind, bedridden, incontinent, had to be tied to her bed to prevent harm from seizures, and who "had, at most, only a fleeting awareness of her environment,"[450] to withhold CPR and defibrillation, a ventilator, intubation, and artificial nutrition and hydration, under a best interests test.

§ 9.47 —Canavan's Disease

Canavan's disease is a genetically-based progressive, degenerative neurological disorder that ultimately results in death. "Its 'salient clinical features are onset in early infancy, atonia of the neck muscles, hyperextension of the legs and flexion of [the] arms, blindness, severe mental defects and [megalocephaly].' "[451] In *In re Doe,*[452] the Massachusetts Supreme Judicial Court affirmed the trial court's decision permitting the parents of a 33-year-old profoundly retarded woman suffering from this disease to terminate artificial nutrition and hydration on the basis of the substituted judgment standard.

§ 9.48 Brain Death

Death is not generally thought of as a medical condition requiring treatment. Nonetheless, the manner in which death is defined can affect the obligations of physicians to continue to administer or to terminate treatment. The fundamental lesson and incentive for the litigation of right-to-die cases is that physicians need not wait until death occurs to terminate treatment. However, if no decision has previously been made to forgo life-sustaining treatment, when death does occur, physicians are no longer obligated to continue treatment and patients are no longer obligated to accept it. The legislative and judicial revision of the definition of death begun in the late 1960s was "intended only to determine when a person receiving life-sustaining treatment has died. It was not intended to prevent the removal of life-support apparatus until a patient has been declared brain dead."[453]

The common-law definition of death is the cessation of circulation and respiration.[454] Contemporary medical technology, however, has rendered that definition obsolete. The ability through medical devices, most notably the

---

[449] *Id.* at 451–52.

[450] *Id.* at 447.

[451] *In re* Doe, 583 N.E.2d 1263, 1266 n.6 (Mass. 1992).

[452] *Id.*

[453] Rosebush v. Oakland County Prosecutor, 491 N.W.2d 633, 640–41 (Mich. Ct. App. 1992).

[454] *See In re* T.A.C.P., 609 So. 2d 588 (Fla. 1992). *See also* Black's Law Dictionary 188 (6th ed. 1990).

mechanical ventilator, to artificially maintain respiration and consequently circulation almost indefinitely, despite massive damage to the brain, has meant the common-law definition of death, in effect, can be evaded. As the Florida Supreme Court has noted,

> modern medical technology has rendered the [common-law] definition of "death" seriously inadequate. With the invention of life-support devices and procedures, human bodies can be made to breathe and blood to circulate even in the utter absence of brain function.
>
> As a result, the ability to withhold or discontinue such life support created distinct legal problems in light of the "cardiopulmonary" definition of death originally used by Black's Dictionary. For example, health care providers might be civilly or criminally liable for removing transplantable organs from a person sustained by life support, or defendants charged with homicide might argue that their victim's death actually was caused when life support was discontinued.[455]

As a result, many jurisdictions have enacted statutes to make the legal definition of death dependent on brain function rather than cardiopulmonary function.[456] In a smaller number of jurisdictions, a similar change has occurred judicially because of the absence of legislative initiative.[457] All 50 states and the District of Columbia accept brain death as a legal definition of death. **Table 9–3** lists the statutory, judicial, and/or regulatory basis in each jurisdiction.

A small majority of jurisdictions has adopted the definition contained in the Uniform Determination of Death Act,[458] which defines *death* disjunctively, accepting either the common-law definition—the cessation of circulation and respiration—or the so-called whole brain formulation, under which a person is considered to be dead if there is "irreversible cessation of all functions of the entire brain, including the brain stem."[459] There are three basic medical criteria for brain death not ordinarily incorporated into the statutory or judicial definition: "(a) unresponsiveness to normally painful stimuli; (b) absence of spontaneous movements or breathing; and, (c) absence of reflexes."[460]

---

455 *In re* T.A.C.P., 609 So. 2d at 591.

456 President's Comm'n for the Study of Ethical Problems in Medicine & Biomedical & Behavioral Research, Defining Death 65 (1981) [hereinafter President's Comm'n, Defining Death]. *See In re* T.A.C.P., 609 So. 2d at 592.

457 *See* Sweet, Annotation, *Homicide by Causing Victim's Brain-Dead Condition,* 42 A.L.R.4th 742 (1985). See **Table 9–2.**

458 Uniform Determination of Death Act, 12 U.L.A. 412, 412 (Supp. 1994) (Arkansas, California, Colorado, Delaware, District of Columbia, Georgia, Idaho, Indiana, Kansas, Maine, Maryland, Michigan, Minnesota, Mississippi, Missouri, Montana, Nevada, New Hampshire, New Mexico, North Dakota, Ohio, Oklahoma, Oregon, Pennsylvania, Rhode Island, South Carolina, South Dakota, Utah, Vermont, West Virginia, and Wyoming).

459 *Id. See also* Delio v. Westchester County Medical Ctr., 516 N.Y.S.2d 677, 684 n.2 (App. Div. 1987) (citing Smith, *Legal Recognition of Neocortical Death,* 71 Cornell L. Rev. 850, 856–57 (1986)); Hastings Center Guidelines 88, 89 (Part Four, II(2), (3)).

460 Brophy v. New Eng. Sinai Hosp., Inc., 497 N.E.2d 626, 630 n.7 (Mass. 1986) (citing Ad Hoc Committee of the Harvard Medical School to Examine the Definition of Brain Death, *A Definition of Irreversible Coma,* 205 JAMA 337 (1968) (so-called "Harvard criteria")).

Table 9–3

Brain Death

State	Legal Basis
Alabama	Ala. Code §§ 22-31-1 to -4
Alaska	Alaska Stat. § 09.65.120
Arizona	State v. Fierro, 603 P.2d 74 (Ariz. 1979)
Arkansas	Ark. Stat. Ann. § 20-17-101
California	Cal. Health & Safety Code §§ 7180–7183
	People v. Mitchell, 183 Cal. Rptr. 166 (Ct. App. 1982)
Colorado	Colo. Rev. Stat. § 12-36-136
Connecticut	Conn. Gen. Stat. Ann. § 19a-278(b), (c)
Delaware	Del. Code tit. 24, § 1760
District of Columbia	D.C. Code Ann. § 6-2401
Florida	Fla. Stat. Ann. § 382.009
	In re T.A.C.P., 609 So. 2d 588 (Fla. 1992) (adopting common-law definition of death to supplement statutory definition)
Georgia	Ga. Code Ann. § 31-10-16
	Clay v. State, 353 S.E.2d 517 (Ga. 1987)
Hawaii	Haw. Rev. Stat. § 327C-1
Idaho	Idaho Code § 54-1819
Illinois	Ill. Ann. Stat. ch. 755, § 50/2
	People v. Driver, 379 N.E.2d 840 (Ill. App. Ct. 1978)
Indiana	Ind. Code Ann. § 1-1-4-3
	Swafford v. State, 421 N.E.2d 596 (Ind. 1981), *overruled on other grounds,* 463 N.E.2d 228 (Ind. 1984)
Iowa	Iowa Code Ann. § 702.8
Kansas	Kan. Stat. Ann. §§ 77.204–.206
	State v. Shaffer, 574 P.2d 205 (Kan. 1977)
Kentucky	Ky. Rev. Stat. § 446.400
Louisiana	La. Rev. Stat. Ann. § 9:111
Maine	Me. Rev. Stat. Ann. tit. 22, §§ 2811–2813
Maryland	Md. Code Ann., Health-Gen. §§ 5-201 to -202
Massachusetts	Commonwealth v. Golston, 366 N.E.2d 744 (Mass. 1977)
Michigan	Mich. Comp. Laws Ann. §§ 333.1021–.1024
Minnesota	Minn. Stat. Ann. § 145.135
Mississippi	Miss. Code Ann. §§ 41-36-1 to -3
Missouri	Mo. Ann. Stat. § 194.005
Montana	Mont. Code Ann. § 50-22-101
Nebraska	State v. Meints, 322 N.W.2d 809, 812 (Neb. 1982)
Nevada	Nev. Rev. Stat. § 451.007
New Hampshire	N.H. Rev. Stat. Ann. §§ 141-D:l to :2
New Jersey	N.J. Stat. Ann. §§ 26:6A-1 to -8
	Strachan v. John F. Kennedy Memorial Hosp., 538 A.2d 346, 351 (N.J. 1988)
New Mexico	N.M. Stat. Ann. § 12-2-4
New York	People v. Eulo, 472 N.E.2d 286 (N.Y. 1984)
	N.Y. State Dep't of Health Regulation, N.Y. Comp. Codes R. & Regs. tit. 10, § 400.16 (1989)
North Carolina	N.C. Gen. Stat. § 90-323
North Dakota	N.D. Cent. Code §§ 23-06.3-01 to .3-02
Ohio	Ohio Rev. Code Ann. § 2108.30
Oklahoma	Okla. Stat. Ann. tit. 63, §§ 3121–3123
Oregon	Or. Rev. Stat. § 432.300
	State v. Brown, 491 P.2d 1193 (Or. Ct. App. 1971)

State	Legal Basis
Pennsylvania	Pa. Stat. Ann. tit. 35, §§ 10,201–10,203
Rhode Island	R.I. Gen. Laws § 23-4-16
South Carolina	S.C. Code 1976, §§ 44-43-450, -460
South Dakota	S.D. Codified Laws Ann. § 34-25-18.1
Tennessee	Tenn. Code Ann. § 68-3-501
Texas	Tex. Health & Safety Code Ann. § 671.001
	Brooks v. State, 643 S.W.2d 440 (Tex. Ct. App. 1982)
Utah	Utah Code Ann. §§ 26-34-1 to -2
Vermont	Vt. Stat. Ann. tit. 18, § 5218
Virginia	Va. Code Ann. § 54.1-2972
Washington	*In re* Bowman, 617 P.2d 731 (Wash. 1980)
West Virginia	W. Va. Code §§ 16-10-1 to -4
Wisconsin	Wis. Stat. Ann. § 146.71
Wyoming	Wyo. Stat. §§ 35-19-101 to -103

Criticisms of the "Whole Brain" Formulation

Despite the long acceptance of brain death as the medical definition of death and the now unanimous recognition accorded this definition in American law, much confusion remains in medical and lay thinking about the subject. For example, a survey of physicians and nurses actively involved in organ transplantation programs, whose work requires that they understand what brain death is since organs may legitimately be harvested only from those who are dead, revealed that only 35 percent correctly identified the criteria for determining death, that 58 percent did not use consistent criteria for determining death, and that 19 percent personally subscribed to a concept of death different from the legal definition—such as a belief that anencephalic patients or patients in a persistent vegetative state were dead.[461] The understanding of brain death among laypersons betrays similar confusion. For example, it is not atypical for newspaper accounts to explain that a person was declared brain dead, life support was removed, and the person then died.[462] The error is that if the individual is declared to be dead by brain-death criteria, then he is legally dead; the removal of life support cannot make one dead again.

[461] Youngner et al., *"Brain Death" and Organ Retrieval,* 261 JAMA 2205 (1989). *See also* Rasmussen v. Fleming, 741 P.2d 674, 680 (Ariz. 1987) (expert witness testified that patient who was able to take nutrition by mouth was brain dead).

[462] *See, e.g.,* Margolick, *Lamenting Lost Lives, Lost Dreams,* N.Y. Times, Mar. 29, 1994, at A10 (nat'l ed.) ("[T]he two friends, who had been declared 'brain dead' earlier that day, were taken off life support and expired."). *See also* Vogel v. Forman, 512 N.Y.S.2d 622, 624 (Sup. Ct. Nassau County 1986) ("A review of the adjudicated cases in this area discloses authority for the removal of life support systems in those circumstances where it is found that the patient is being kept alive by extraordinary means. In those cases the patients are described as brain-dead and are terminally ill with no hope of recovery and are being kept alive solely by artificial means.").

Because patients declared dead by brain-death criteria do not appear dead in the classic sense[463]—the ventilator continues to perfuse their organs with oxygenated blood and hence their color and body temperature remain normal—families sometimes have difficulty accepting that the patient is dead.[464] Thus, they may seek to have life support continued, which poses difficult dilemmas for health care professionals. First, the continuation of such treatment is expensive and provides no benefit whatever to the "patient." Second, it can be frustrating and demoralizing to the health care professionals to continue to provide "treatment" to dead patients when there are live patients whose situations realistically demand their attention. Nonetheless, doctors sometimes authorize the continuation of life support in such situations, at least for short periods of time until the patient's family is able to accept the fact of the patient's death. There are no litigated cases requiring doctors to do so, and it is not likely that such a claim would be upheld, except possibly in a limited number of jurisdictions where the brain-death statute or regulations contain an exemption for religious beliefs.[465]

Some critics have contended that defining death in terms of the whole brain formulation is inadequate.[466] They would instead use a neocortical, or so-called higher brain, formulation that would classify as dead not only persons whose whole brain has ceased to function but also those in whom *only* the higher brain

---

[463] Youngner & O'Toole, *Withdrawing Treatment in the Persistent Vegetative State,* 331 New Eng. J. Med. 1382 (1994).

[464] *See, e.g., Brain-Dead Florida Girl Will Be Sent Home on Life Support,* N.Y. Times, Feb. 19, 1994, at 7 (nat'l ed.) (parents of 13-year-old girl whom doctors diagnosed as dead by brain death criteria insisted that she was alive and that life-sustaining medical treatment be continued; hospital agreed to continue life support at its expense in parents' home because "'the nursing staff is wrung out'"); *Hospital Fights Parents' Wish to Keep Life Support for a "Brain Dead" Child,* N.Y. Times, Feb. 12, 1994, at 6 (nat'l ed.); *Public Hospital to Finance Home Care of Brain-Dead Teenager,* 3 BNA's Health Law Reporter 287 (1994).

[465] **NJ:** *See* N.J. Stat. Ann. § 26:6A-5 (West Supp. 1992)) ("death of an individual shall not be declared upon the basis of neurological criteria when such a declaration would violate the personal religious beliefs of the individual.")

NY: *See* N.Y. Dep't of Health Regulation, N.Y. Comp. Codes R. & Regs. tit. 10, § 400.16(e)(3) (1989).

[466] *In re* Beth, 587 N.E.2d 1377 (Mass. 1992) ("One commentator argues that our understanding of death should undergo another revision: when the upper brain ceases to function ('neocortical death'), the patient ought to be considered dead. According to this commentator, the values underlying the 'total brain death' and 'neocortical death' standard are compatible: the former, like the latter, rests on the view that consciousness is the sine qua non of human existence, since a person who is permanently unconscious will currently be declared dead even though her respiration could be mechanically maintained. K.G. Gervais, Redefining Death (Yale U. Press, 1986). (p. 1379)."); President's Comm'n, Defining Death 38–41. *See also* A. Buchanan & D. Brock, Deciding for Others: The Ethics of Surrogate Decisionmaking 128 (1989); Stacy, *Death, Privacy, and the Free Exercise of Religion,* 77 Cornell L. Rev. 490 (1992); Halevy & Brody, *Brain Death: Reconciling Definitions, Criteria, and Tests,* 119 Annals Internal Med. 519 (1993) (reviewing criticisms); Veatch, *Brain Death and Slippery Slopes,* 3 J. Clinical Ethics 181 (1992).

has ceased to function. Under the higher brain formulation, death occurs "when a patient suffers an irreversible loss of cognition and consciousness, but retains brain stem functions."[467] The reason for advocating this change is that the neocortex or cerebrum is responsible for those functions and attributes unique to human existence, such as perceptual and sensory awareness, mentation, emotions, or voluntary activity.[468] Consequently, some believe that when these higher functions and attributes are ended because of damage to the neocortical portion of the brain, the individual no longer possesses the attributes of personhood and should in law be considered dead, with the result that any life support could then be terminated with impunity.[469]

A persistent vegetative state involves severe damage to the neocortex, so that the higher functions and attributes of personhood are ended. If the higher brain formulation of death were accepted as the legal definition of death, persons in a persistent vegetative state would be considered dead,[470] as would anencephalic newborn babies.[471] As in the 1960s when the whole brain formulation began to be discussed as a new legal standard for the determination of death,

> tremendous advancements in medical technology in the last several years have made it possible to sustain a person who has minimal brain functioning but who

---

[467] **FL:** *In re* T.A.C.P., 609 So. 2d 588 (Fla. 1992) (holding anencephalic infants are not legally dead because hearts are still beating; anencephaly, "'a congenital absence of major portions of the brain, skull, and scalp,'" is most common birth defect in United States; anencephalic infants can sometimes survive for several days after birth).

NY: Delio v. Westchester County Medical Ctr., 516 N.Y.S.2d 677, 684 (App. Div. 1987) (citing Smith, *Legal Recognition of Neocortical Death,* 71 Cornell L. Rev. 850, 856–57 (1986)).

See also President's Comm'n, Defining Death 38 ("If there are parts of the brain which have no role in sponsoring consciousness, the higher brain formulation would regard their continued functioning as compatible with death.").

[468] **NJ:** *See In re* Jobes, 529 A.2d 434, 439 n.5 (N.J. 1987) ("The cerebrum is the main part of the brain, situated in the upper part of the cranium. It controls thinking, sensory perception, and voluntary and conscious activities. 1 Attorney's Dictionary of Medicine C-110 (Bender 1986).").

NY: *See* Delio v. Westchester County Medical Ctr., 516 N.Y.S.2d at 679.

[469] President's Comm'n, Defining Death 38–40. *See generally* Brody, *Special Issues in the Management of PVS Patients,* 20 Law, Med. & Health Care 104, 113 (1992) ("such patients are clearly non-dead non-persons").

[470] **NJ:** *Cf. In re* Conroy, 486 A.2d 1209, 1227 (N.J. 1985) ("Although Ms. Quinlan's cognitive abilities had been irreversibly lost, only the more highly developed part of her brain had been destroyed, and she was therefore not 'brain dead' under any of the criteria established by the Ad Hoc Committee of the Harvard Medical School").

NY: *See* Delio v. Westchester County Medical Ctr., 516 N.Y.S.2d at 679 (patient in persistent vegetative state described as "neocortically dead").

See generally Brody, *Special Issues in the Management of PVS Patients,* 20 Law, Med. & Health Care 104, 113 (1992) ("such patients are clearly non-dead non-persons").

[471] **CA4:** *See, e.g., In re* Baby "K," 16 F.3d 590 (4th Cir. 1994).

FL: *See, e.g., In re* T.A.C.P., 609 So. 2d 588.

> does not meet the definition of "brain death." . . . It is now possible to hold such persons [in a persistent vegetative state] on the threshold of death for an indeterminate period of time.[472]

The same appears to be true for anencephalic babies, who are born without a cerebral cortex. The common practice has been not to provide life support to such babies and to allow them to die because they are born in the equivalent of a persistent vegetative state. However, as the *Baby K* case[473] demonstrates, if aggressive life support is provided, at least some are capable of being kept alive in a vegetative state indefinitely.

At this time, there are two obstacles to acceptance of neocortical death as the legal definition: one technological and the other symbolic. Before the higher brain formulation of death can gain acceptance, a means must exist to determine that the higher functions of the brain have irreversibly ceased, with the same high degree of certainty that can now be obtained in determining that the entire brain has ceased to function. The other factor in the acceptance of neocortical death as the legal definition is a belief among some that as long as there is spontaneous brain function, however minimal, it cannot be said that life has ceased. This symbolic argument may prove to be a stronger obstacle to acceptance than the technological one. At this time, therefore, no American jurisdiction equates the cessation of neocortical function associated with persistent vegetative state with death.[474]

---

[472] John F. Kennedy Memorial Hosp. v. Bludworth, 452 So. 2d 921, 923 (Fla. 1984).

[473] *In re* Baby "K," 16 F.3d 590 (4th Cir. 1994). See § **19.17.**

[474] **FL:** *In re* Barry, 445 So. 2d 365 (Fla. Dist. Ct. App. 1984) (patient does not fully meet criteria because of minimal brain stem function).

MA: Brophy v. New Eng. Sinai Hosp., Inc., 497 N.E.2d 626 (Mass. 1986) (patient not technically brain dead but in a persistent vegetative state, having suffered serious and irreversible brain damage).

MI: *In re* Torres, 357 N.W.2d 332, 334 (Minn. 1984) (comatose patient is not "'brain dead' under the traditional definition (i.e., a cessation of all brain functions) because laboratory studies show a 'poor but definite cerebral (blood) flow' and 'very rudimentary evidence of low medullary brain stem function'").

NJ: *In re* Jobes, 529 A.2d 434, 438 n.3 (N.J. 1987) (because portion of brain that controls vegetative functions was not destroyed, patient was not "brain dead"); *In re* Quinlan, 355 A.2d 647, 654–56 (N.J. 1976) (patient who has "some brain stem function (ineffective for respiration) and has other reactions one normally associates with being alive, such as moving, reacting to light, sound and noxious stimuli, blinking her eyes, and the like," while in a persistent vegetative state is not dead by brain-death standards).

NY: Delio v. Westchester County Medical Ctr., 516 N.Y.S.2d 677 (App. Div. 1987) (although patient was "not technically 'brain dead,' he had suffered neocortical death").

OH: *In re* Myers, 610 N.E.2d 663, 666 n.1 (P. Ct. Summit County, Ohio 1993) (patient whose brain stem still functioning is not dead). *Cf. In re* Spring, 405 N.E.2d 115, 120 (Mass. 1980) (citing *In re* Dinnerstein, 380 N.E.2d 134 (Mass. App. Ct. 1978), which did not involve "brain death" but an irreversible vegetative coma).

Case Law

Most of the litigation involving brain death has arisen in the context of prosecutions for murder in which the defendant has contended that the cause of death was the removal of life-support equipment rather than the defendant's own antecedent conduct that made the life support necessary. All of these efforts have failed and have provided the courts with the occasion to expand the common-law definition of death to include the cessation of all brain activity. If a patient is dead, there can be no criminal or civil liability for terminating treatment, for there is no duty to provide medical treatment to a corpse.[475] Life support should be withdrawn when the criteria for the determination of brain death have been satisfied. Indeed, continuing to provide life support to a patient who is dead, by whatever the prevailing legal standards, can constitute the basis for liability when it is against the will of the surrogate.[476] Consequently, the victims in these prosecutions were legally dead before the removal of life support, and the defendants' convictions for murder have been upheld because they were responsible for the injuries causing the cessation of whole brain function.[477]

WA: *In re* Ingram, 689 P.2d 1363, 1367 (Wash. 1984) (citing *In re* Bowman, 617 P.2d 731 (Wash. 1980), which "made clear . . . that it was not deciding 'the much more difficult question' of whether life support systems may be terminated if a person is in a chronic, persistent vegetative state").

See generally Cranford, *The Persistent Vegetative State: The Medical Reality (Getting the Facts Straight),* 18 Hastings Center Rep. 27 (Feb.–Mar. 1988) (comprehensive discussion of medical aspects of and confusion about brain death and its relationship to persistent vegetative state).

[475] **CA:** Dority v. Superior Court, 193 Cal. Rptr. 288 (Ct. App. 1983).

CO: Lovato v. District Court, 601 P.2d 1072 (Colo. 1979).

IL: *In re* Haymer, 450 N.E.2d 940 (Ill. 1983).

MA: *In re* Spring, 405 N.E.2d 115, 119 (Mass. 1980) ("In the *Golston* case we held that 'brain death,' 'in the opinion of a licensed physician, based on ordinary and accepted standards of medical practice,' was death. . . . There is no legal basis for a duty to administer medical treatment after death." (citations omitted)).

NY: *Cf.* Alvarado v. New York City Health & Hosps. Corp., 547 N.Y.S.2d 190 (Sup. Ct. N.Y. County 1989) (physicians may terminate life support from terminally ill infant over objections of parents), *vacated and dismissed sub nom.* Alvarado v. City of N.Y., 550 N.Y.S.2d 353 (App. Div. 1990) (order vacated upon determination that infant did not meet statutory definition of brain death).

WA: *In re* Bowman, 617 P.2d 731 (Wash. 1980).

[476] **GA:** *Cf.* Gallups v. Carter, 534 So. 2d 585 (Ala. 1988) (upholding summary judgment in favor of physicians alleged to have terminated life support from brain-dead patient in absence of her family's consent).

NJ: *See* Strachan v. John F. Kennedy Memorial Hosp., 538 A.2d 346 (N.J. 1988).

[477] Sweet, Annotation, *Homicide by Causing Victim's Brain-Dead Condition,* 42 A.L.R.4th 742 (1985).

§ 9.49 Cancer

A small number of litigated right-to-die cases have involved patients with cancer. Cancer is treated, depending on the type, by surgery, chemotherapy, or radiation therapy. In some cases the patients have been terminally ill, and consequently the treatment at issue would only prolong the process of dying and could therefore be forgone.[478] However, in others there was a good possibility of a remission if the treatment at issue were administered. Nonetheless, courts have ordinarily allowed for the forgoing of treatment under such circumstances unless the patient is a child.[479]

---

[478] **DDC:** *E.g.,* Tune v. Walter Reed Army Medical Hosp., 602 F. Supp. 1452 (D.D.C. 1985) (malignant adenocarcinoma).

CA: *E.g.,* Bartling v. Superior Court, 209 Cal. Rptr. 220 (Ct. App. 1984) (malignant lung tumor). *But see* Donaldson v. Van de Kamp, 4 Cal. Rptr. 2d 59 (Ct. App. 1992) (addressing question of whether patient terminally ill with cancer could be cryopreserved, which would end life before cancer did).

DC: *Cf. In re* A.C., 573 A.2d 1235 (D.C. 1990) (addressing question of whether pregnant patient terminally ill with cancer should undergo cesarean).

NJ: *E.g.,* Suenram v. Society of Valley Hosp., 383 A.2d 143 ((N.J. Super. Ct. Law Div. 1977) (patient who probably would not live a month more with accepted cancer treatment not required to accept such treatment and entitled to undergo treatment with unproven drug administered by licensed physician).

NY: *But See, e.g., In re* Storar, 420 N.E.2d 64 (N.Y. 1981) (never-competent terminally ill patient with bladder cancer with three to six months to live); Saunders v. State, 492 N.Y.S.2d 510 (Sup. Ct. Nassau County 1985) (progressive lung cancer without known medical cure).

[479] **DE:** *E.g.,* Newmark v. Williams, 588 A.2d 1108 (Del. 1991) (chemotherapy need not be administered to child suffering from deadly Burkitt's lymphoma, an aggressive cancer, whose parents subscribed to Christian Science beliefs, when treatment offered "only" 40% likelihood of cure but also had "terrible temporary and potentially permanent side effects," including risk of death).

IL: *E.g., In re* E.G., 549 N.E.2d 322 (Ill. 1989) (acute nonlymphatic leukemia).

MA: *E.g., In re* McCauley, 565 N.E.2d 411, 413 (Mass. 1991) (rejecting religious basis for parental right to refuse treatment of minor child who faced certain death from leukemia if untreated and whose life might be saved if treatment were administered; "[t]he right to the free exercise of religion, including the interests of parents in the religious upbringing of their children is, of course, a fundamental right protected by the Constitution. . . . However, these fundamental principles do not warrant the view that parents have an absolute right to refuse medical treatment for their children on religious grounds."); Superintendent of Belchertown State Sch. v. Saikewicz, 370 N.E.2d 417 (Mass. 1977) (acute myeloblastic monocytic leukemia is invariably fatal but temporary remission may occur in 30 to 50% of cases for 2 to 13 months or more).

NY: *E.g., In re* Long Island Jewish Medical Ctr. (Malcolm), 557 N.Y.S.2d 239, (Sup. Ct. Queens County 1990) (treatment ordered of patient, a few weeks short of his 18th birthday, who had refused on religious grounds blood transfusion for treatment of cancer in combination with chemotherapy and radiation, which would provide probability of survival of between 20 and 25%, and who was certain to die without transfusion); *In re* Sampson, 279 N.E.2d 918 (N.Y. 1972) (ordering blood transfusions to be administered to 15-year-old patient in conjunction with surgery for cancer); *In re* Richardson, 581 N.Y.S.2d 708 (Sup. Ct. Monroe County 1992) (DNR order could be written for child with cancer with consent of parents).

§ 9.50 Cardiac Arrest

Cardiac arrest stops the circulation of oxygenated blood to all parts of the body and ordinarily quickly results in death. If, through cardiopulmonary resuscitation, cardiac function can be restored, there are sometimes other procedures that can be used to keep a patient with a damaged heart alive temporarily (for example, left-ventricular assist pumps, cardiopulmonary bypass machines) or even indefinitely (for example, cardiac transplantation). If, however, cardiac function is restored but not rapidly, serious and usually irreversible damage to a variety of organs, especially the brain, can occur.

Reported cases permit the forgoing of treatment for cardiac arrest if consent is given by a person authorized to do so.[480]

§ 9.51 Cerebral Palsy

Cerebral palsy, although a chronic, crippling disease that can have devastating effects on the life of the victim,[481] is not a life-threatening disease per se.[482] In the only case to consider a patient with cerebral palsy, in a far-reaching opinion, the court held that the patient could forgo artificial nutrition and hydration, even if it were to result in her death, despite the fact that she was not terminally ill, which is consistent with the trend generally with respect to refusal of treatment by competent patients.[483]

§ 9.52 Gangrene

There are a number of cases in which patients have needed the amputation of a limb because of gangrene that was predicted to lead to death if surgery were not

---

OH: *E.g., In re* Milton, 505 N.E.2d 255 (Ohio 1987) (legally competent adult could not be required to submit to treatment for cancer in derogation of her religious belief in faith healing).

PA: *E.g., In re* Yetter, 62 Pa. D. & C.2d 619 (C.P. Northampton County 1973) (upholding refusal of treatment for breast cancer based on oral advance directive).

WA: *In re* Ingram, 689 P.2d 1363 (Wash. 1984) (not requiring surgery even though it would give patient 70 to 80% chance of survival, compared with a 40% chance with radiation treatment).

480 See §§ **9.4–9.6.**

481 Bouvia v. Superior Court (Glenchur), 225 Cal. Rptr. 297, 300 (Ct. App. 1986) ("Petitioner's physical handicaps of palsy and quadriplegia have progressed to the point where she is completely bedridden. Except for a few fingers of one hand and some slight head and facial movements, she is immobile. She is physically helpless and wholly unable to care for herself. She is totally dependent upon others for all of her needs.").

482 *Id.*

483 *Id.* See §§ **2.4** and **9.3.**

performed.[484] These patients are generally in very poor condition, but some may live without surgery, continuing to lead life much the same as before with impaired physical or mental functioning, but not necessarily bedridden, wheelchair-bound, or comatose.

Although competent patients are legally entitled to refuse amputation for the treatment of gangrene, there is often a significant question about whether the patient is in possession of decisionmaking capacity. This sometimes occurs because severe gangrene can interfere with cognitive processes. In other cases, the patient has had a history of mental illness, including delusions, and the refusal of amputation results from these delusions. In some of these cases, amputation has been ordered over a patient's refusal,[485] although in others it has not.[486] The more recent cases[487] have shown an increased judicial tolerance for refusal of amputation even when the treatment is likely to save the patient's life and return the patient to a relatively healthy state.[488]

§ 9.53 Persistent Vegetative State; Coma; Severe Brain Damage

More reported appellate cases involve patients in persistent vegetative states than any other condition.[489] This is not particularly surprising in light of the substantial management and emotional problems they present to their caregivers and families, the tremendous resources that the care of such patients can

---

[484] *See generally* Karnezis, Annotation, *Patient's Right to Refuse Treatment Allegedly Necessary to Sustain Life,* 93 A.L.R.3d 67 § 3(b) (1979).

[485] **DNY:** *See In re* Department of Veterans Affairs Medical Ctr., 749 F. Supp. 495 (S.D.N.Y.), *aff'd,* 914 F.2d 239 (2d Cir. 1990).

NJ: *See In re* Schiller, 372 A.2d 360 (N.J. Super. Ct. Ch. Div. 1977) (guardian appointed with power to consent to amputation).

NY: *See* Long Island Jewish-Hillside Medical Ctr. v. Levitt, 342 N.Y.S.2d 356 (Sup. Ct. Nassau County 1973).

TN: *See* State Dep't of Human Resources v. Northern, 563 S.W.2d 197 (Tenn. Ct. App. 1978).

[486] **MA:** *See* Lane v. Candura, 376 N.E.2d 1232 (Mass. App. Ct. 1978).

NJ: *See In re* Quackenbush, 383 A.2d 785 (N.J. Super. Ct. P. Div. 1978).

NY: *See In re* Beth Israel Medical Ctr. (Weinstein), 519 N.Y.S.2d 511 (Sup. Ct. N.Y. County 1987); *In re* Nemser, 273 N.Y.S.2d 624 (Sup. Ct. N.Y. County 1966).

[487] **NJ:** *But cf. In re* Conroy, 486 A.2d 1209 (N.J. 1985) (holding that patient's best interests could conceivably require that feeding tube be inserted in patient who suffered from arteriosclerotic heart disease, hypertension, and diabetes mellitus, and whose left leg was gangrenous to her knee).

[488] See § **8.10.**

[489] **DRI:** *See* Gray v. Romeo, 697 F. Supp. 580 (D.R.I. 1988) (persistent vegetative state).

AZ: Rasmussen v. Fleming, 741 P.2d 674 (Ariz. 1987) (persistent vegetative state; chronic vegetative state).

CA: McMahon v. Lopez, 245 Cal. Rptr. 172 (Ct. App. 1988); Morrison v. Abramovice, 253 Cal. Rptr. 530 (Ct. App. 1988) (persistent vegetative state); Drabick v. Drabick, 245 Cal. Rptr. 840 (Ct. App. 1988) (persistent vegetative state); Barber v. Superior Court, 195 Cal. Rptr. 484 (Ct. App. 1983) (permanent vegetative state).

CT: McConnell v. Beverly Enters.-Conn., Inc., 553 A.2d 596 (Conn. 1989) (irreversible persistent vegetative state); Foody v. Manchester Memorial Hosp., 482 A.2d 713 (Conn. Super. Ct. 1984) (permanent and irreversible coma).

DE: Severns v. Wilmington Medical Ctr., Inc., 421 A.2d 1334 (Del. 1980) (coma).

FL: John F. Kennedy Memorial Hosp. v. Bludworth, 452 So. 2d 921 (Fla. 1984) (comatose, terminally ill); Corbett v. D'Alessandro, 487 So. 2d 368 (Fla. Dist. Ct. App. 1986) (persistent vegetative state); *In re* Barry, 445 So. 2d 365 (Fla. Dist. Ct. App. 1984) (chronic permanent vegetative coma).

GA: *In re* L.H.R., 321 S.E.2d 716 (Ga. 1984) (chronic vegetative state).

IL: *In re* Estate of Greenspan, 558 N.E.2d 1194 (Ill. 1990). *Cf.* Estate of Longeway v. Community Convalescent Ctr., 549 N.E.2d 292 (Ill. 1989) (coma, but not persistent vegetative state; "will never regain consciousness"; "cannot communicate, but opens her eyes and responds to verbal commands and painful stimuli.").

IN: *In re* Lawrance, 579 N.E.2d 32 (Ind. 1991).

KY: DeGrella v. Elston, 858 S.W.2d 698 (Ky. 1993) (persistent vegetative state).

LA: *In re* P.V.W., 424 So. 2d 1015 (La. 1982) (severe and irreversible brain damage).

ME: *In re* Swan, 569 A.2d 1202 (Me. 1990); *In re* Gardner, 534 A.2d 947 (Me. 1987).

MD: Mack v. Mack, 618 A.2d 744 (Md. 1993). *Cf. In re* Riddlemoser, 564 A.2d 812 (Md. 1989) (coma, but not persistent vegetative state).

MA: *In re* Beth, 587 N.E.2d 1377 (Mass. 1992); *In re* Doe, 583 N.E.2d 1263 (Mass. 1992); Brophy v. New Eng. Sinai Hosp., Inc., 497 N.E.2d 626 (Mass. 1986) (persistent vegetative state).

MI: Rosebush v. Oakland County Prosecutor, 491 N.W.2d 633 (Mich. Ct. App. 1992).

MN: *In re* Torres, 357 N.W.2d 332 (Minn. 1984) (permanently comatose).

MO: Cruzan v. Harmon, 760 S.W.2d 408 (Mo. 1988) (persistent vegetative state); *In re* Warren, 858 S.W.2d 263 (Mo. Ct. App. 1993)(persistent vegetative state).

NJ: *In re* Jobes, 529 A.2d 434 (N.J. 1987) (persistent vegetative state); *In re* Peter, 529 A.2d 419 (N.J. 1987) (persistent vegetative state); *In re* Quinlan, 355 A.2d 647 (N.J. 1976) (chronic and persistent vegetative state); *In re* Moorhouse, 593 A.2d 1256 (N.J. Super. Ct. App. Div. 1991).

NY: Eichner v. Dillon, 420 N.E.2d 64 (N.Y. 1981) (vegetative coma); Wickel v. Spellman, 552 N.Y.S.2d 437 (App. Div. 1990); Elbaum v. Grace Plaza of Great Neck, Inc., 544 N.Y.S.2d 840 (App. Div. 1989) (persistent vegetative state); Vogel v. Forman, 512 N.Y.S.2d 622 (Sup. Ct. Nassau County 1986) (vegetative state, but described as not irreversible); *In re* Lydia E. Hall Hosp., 455 N.Y.S.2d 706 (Sup. Ct. Nassau County 1982) (coma).

OH: Leach v. Akron Gen. Medical Ctr., 426 N.E.2d 809 (C.P. P. Div. Summit County, Ohio 1980) (semicomatose or chronic vegetative state); Couture v. Couture, 549 N.E.2d 571 (Ohio Ct. App. 1989) (persistent vegetative state); *In re* Myers, 610 N.E.2d 663, 665–66 (P. Ct. Summit County, Ohio 1993) (persistent vegetative state or permanently unconscious state); *In re* Crum, 580 N.E.2d 876 (P. Ct. Franklin County, Ohio 1991) ("chronic vegetative state").

PA: *In re* Fiori, 13 Fiduc. Rep. 2d 79 (C.P. Bucks County, Pa. Feb. 3, 1993) (comatose or persistent vegetative state); Ragona v. Preate, 11 Fiduc. Rep. 2d 1 (C.P. Lackawanna County, Pa. 1990).

WA: *In re* Hamlin, 689 P.2d 1372 (Wash. 1984) (persistent vegetative state); *In re* Colyer, 660 P.2d 738 (Wash. 1983) (persistent vegetative state).

WI: L.W. v. L.E. Phillips Career Dev. Ctr., 482 N.W.2d 60 (Wis. 1992).

command, and the ability to sustain their biological existence for long periods of time. An accurate estimate of the total number of patients in a persistent vegetative state is hard to come by. In 1983, the President's Commission estimated that there were fewer than 5,000 patients in a persistent vegetative state in the United States.[490] Less than 10 years later, the American Medical Association raised this estimate to at least 20 times the earlier figure.[491] However, another estimate places this figure at approximately 15,000 to 20,000, including those who are totally demented from Alzheimer's disease and similar disorders.[492] It is likely that the number of litigated cases is disproportionately high, precisely because of the problems that caring for such patients raise.

There is some confusion in the courts about persistent vegetative state. For example, the Arizona Supreme Court described a patient who was able to be spoon-fed as being "in an irreversible chronic vegetative state"[493] even though PVS patients are ordinarily incapable of even the primitive kinds of voluntary movement that chewing and swallowing entail, and thus require tube-feeding.[494] Some courts refer to PVS patients as being terminally ill,[495] while others just as assuredly assert that they are not.[496] This might reflect the lack of agreement among physicians on what a persistent vegetative state is.[497]

In general, though not without exception, the courts use the term to

---

490 *See* President's Comm'n, Deciding to Forego Life-Sustaining Treatment 176 n.15.

491 *See* Amicus Curiae Brief for the Am. Medical Ass'n at 11–12, Cruzan v. Director, 497 U.S. 261 (1990).

492 *See* Council on Scientific Affairs & Council on Ethical & Judicial Affairs, American Medical Ass'n, *Persistent Vegetative State and the Decision to Withdraw or Withhold Life Support,* 263 JAMA 426, 427 (1990).

493 Rasmussen v. Fleming, 741 P.2d 674, 685 (Ariz. 1987).

494 *But see* Mitchell et al., *Medical Futility, Treatment Withdrawal and the Persistent Vegetative State,* 19 J. Med. Ethics 71, 71 (1993) ("hand-feeding is possible by placing food at the back of the throat, thus activating the involuntary swallow reflex" controlled by the brain stem).

495 **CT:** *See, e.g.,* McConnell v. Beverly Enters.-Conn., Inc., 553 A.2d 596 (Conn. 1989).

IL: *See, e.g.,* Estate of Longeway v. Community Convalescent Ctr., 549 N.E.2d 292 (Ill. 1989).

496 *See* Cruzan v. Harmon, 760 S.W.2d 408 (Mo. 1988).

497 **NJ:** *In re* Conroy, 486 A.2d 1209, 1229 n.4 (N.J. 1985) ("[T]here is no medical consensus as yet as to what constitutes a permanent vegetative state.") (citing Walton, Ethics of Withdrawal of Life-Support Systems: Case Studies on Decision Making in Intensive Care 82 (1983); President's Comm'n, Deciding to Forego Life-Sustaining Treatment 176–77); *accord In re Jobes,* 529 A.2d 434, 438–40 (N.J. 1987) (conflicting evidence of expert witnesses).

AZ: *Accord* Rasmussen v. Fleming, 741 P.2d 674, 685 n.15 (Ariz. 1987).

FL: *Accord* Browning v. Herbert, 568 So. 2d 4 (Fla. 1990) (patient who suffered a series of strokes, who "appeared alert and would follow [a visitor] with her eyes" and who had uttered a few garbled words on a few occasions, but who could not follow any simple commands was described by one neurologist as being in a persistent vegetative state).

describe a body which is functioning entirely in terms of its internal controls. It maintains temperature. It maintains heart beat and pulmonary ventilation. It maintains digestive activity. It maintains reflex activity of muscles and nerves for low level condition responses. But there is no behavioral evidence of either self-awareness or awareness of the surroundings in a learned manner.[498]

See also Council on Scientific Affairs & Council on Ethical & Judicial Affairs, American Medical Ass'n, *Persistent Vegetative State and the Decision to Withdraw or Withhold Life Support,* 263 JAMA 426 (1990); Cranford, *Major Neurologic Syndromes in Life-Sustaining Medical Treatment Decisions,* 7 Med. Ethics Advisor 87 (July 1991) (table listing different aspects of brain death, persistent vegetative state, permanent locked-in state, and dementia); DeGiorgio & Lew, *Consciousness, Coma and the Vegetative State: Physical Basis and Definitional Character,* 6 Issues L. & Med. 361 (1991); The Multi-Society Task Force on PVS, *Medical Aspects of the Persistent Vegetative State,* 330 New Eng. J. Med. 1499, 1499, 1572 (1994). *See generally* Cranford, *The Persistent Vegetative State: The Medical Reality (Getting the Facts Straight),* 18 Hastings Center Rep. 27 (Feb.–Mar. 1988) (comprehensive discussion of medical aspects of and confusion about persistent vegetative state).

[498] **NJ:** *In re* Jobes, 529 A.2d at 438 (quoting testimony of Dr. Fred Plum, a "world renowned expert on the 'persistent vegetative state' who originated the term").

CA: *Accord* Morrison v. Abramovice, 253 Cal. Rptr. 530, 531 (Ct. App. 1988) (quoting Cranford, *The Persistent Vegetative State: The Medical Reality (Getting the Facts Straight),* 18 Hastings Center Rep. 27, 28, 31 (Feb.–Mar. 1988)).

IL: *Accord In re* Estate of Greenspan, 558 N.E.2d 1194, 1205 (Ill. 1990) (describing the nature of persistent vegetative state).

KY: *Accord* DeGrella v. Elston, 858 S.W.2d 698, 702 (Ky. 1993) (patient "reacts only at a reflexive level, meaning she will withdraw from painful stimulus, but does not experience pain by cognitive thought").

MD: *Accord* Mack v. Mack, 618 A.2d 744 (Md. 1993).

MA: *Accord In re* Doe, 583 N.E.2d 1263, 1266–67 & n.10 (Mass. 1992) ("Doe displays no awareness of herself or her surroundings. Doe 'carries out no volitional activity, nor does she show any cognitive response to any type of sensory stimulus'—including stimuli calculated to cause intense pain in a conscious individual.[10] [[10] "Although Doe responds to stimuli to her legs, the report of the examining neurologist states that in his opinion these responses are purely 'reflexive in nature.' Doe does not react at all to 'noxious stimuli applied to her upper limbs.' Finally, the report noted 'total lack of affective (emotional) change accompanying noxious stimuli applied to either the lower limbs or the upper limbs.'] She exhibits no facial expressions and does not speak. She suffers from both cortical blindness and deafness, and she cannot feel or smell. Doe does not experience hunger or thirst; she is without emotion of any sort. Though her functioning brainstem allows Doe to breathe on her own by means of a tracheostomy, she suffers from 'a total loss of cerebral functioning.'"); Brophy v. New Eng. Sinai Hosp., Inc., 497 N.E.2d 626, 628 n.4 (Mass. 1986).

MO: *Accord* Cruzan v. Harmon, 760 S.W.2d 408, 411 (Mo. 1988) (patient is "'oblivious to her environment except for reflexive responses to sound and perhaps painful stimuli"').

OH: *Accord In re* Myers, 610 N.E.2d 663, 665, 670 (P. Ct. Summit County, Ohio 1993) (The patient's "future physical state would deteriorate, . . . the left arm would probably become hypertonic, and . . . the right arm and legs would probably remain in their present, flaccid state, with decreased muscle tone. [The] bones would become more brittle, and atrophy would continue to occur. [The patient] would also sustain more skin breakdown and bed sores . . . [and] remaining brain tissue would deteriorate. . . . [A]ll higher cognitive brain functions or processes of thought and communication are gone. [O]nly those body functions associated

A PVS patient may appear to be awake,[499] because they develop "'sleep-wake' cycles. . . . In the awake cycle [the patient] blinks, cries out and does things of that sort but is still totally unaware of anyone or anything around her."[500] However, the medical consensus is that

> [a] PVS patient has no mental functions. The eyes may be open at times, but the patient is "completely unconscious, *i.e.,* unaware of him(self) or herself or the surrounding environment. Voluntary reactions or behavioral responses reflecting consciousness, volition, or emotion at the cerebral cortical level are absent." . . . The patient is incapable of experiencing pain and suffering.[501]

In persistent vegetative state, the cerebral cortex of the brain, which is responsible for the cognitive and affective qualities characteristic of personhood, suffers such a serious insult from the loss of oxygen that it begins to deteriorate and die, and eventually does so. When this happens, PVS patients are "neocortically dead."[502] However, they are not legally dead by current

---

with the brain stem, that is, basic reflexes, remain. . . . It is a continuing process in which the body becomes deformed and degenerates. The remainder of the upper brain becomes soft, the limbs become rigid, the bones become brittle and break, and the skin breaks down causing continuing bedsores. . . . What remains of the body waits until an infection or other cause defeats the demand of the brain stem, and death occurs. 'Vegetative state' is truly an appropriate and descriptive term for the condition.").

See also President's Comm'n, Deciding to Forego Life-Sustaining Treatment 174–75. See **§§ 11.9** and **12.17.**

[499] *See, e.g., In re* Jobes, 529 A.2d 434, 440 (N.J. 1987):

> Some of the nurses and nurses' aides who work at the nursing home testified that they had observed examples of what they interpreted as cognitive awareness on the part of Mrs. Jobes. They claimed that she moved her head to aid them in washing her hair; smiled at appropriate times; followed people with her eyes; and relaxed when spoken to or touched in a soothing manner.
>
> In addition, several nurses and aides testified that they saw tears in Mrs. Jobes' eyes when her family visited. Nurses pointed out the phenomenon they described as "tears" to Dr. Carlin when he examined her at the nursing home. He characterized it as an unemotional collection of secretions in the corner of Mrs. Jobes' eyes. Dr. Liss also observed these secretions. He explained that they are merely accumulations of liquid that keep the conjunctiva moist and that they are created by rapid, reflexive eye-blinking, rather than emotions.
>
> Other nurses and nurses' aides testified that they had not observed any cognitive awareness in Mrs. Jobes, and that she gave no response to their verbal commands.

[500] *In re* Quinlan, 355 A.2d 647, 654 (N.J. 1976) (quoting Dr. Morse, a neurologist attending Karen Quinlan). *Accord* Cruzan v. Director, 497 U.S. 261, 309–10 (1990) (Brennan, J., dissenting) (persons in a persistent vegetative state are "devoid of thought, emotion and sensation; they are permanently and completely unconscious").

[501] **CA:** Morrison v. Abramovice, 253 Cal. Rptr. 530, 531 (Ct. App. 1988).

NJ: *Accord In re* Jobes, 529 A.2d 434 (N.J. 1987).

[502] **KY:** DeGrella v. Elston, 858 S.W.2d 698, 702 (Ky. 1993) ("Irreversible brain damage has destroyed Sue's higher brain functioning. Only her brain stem continues to function.").

NY: Delio v. Westchester County Medical Ctr., 516 N.Y.S.2d 677, 679 (App. Div. 1987).

"brain-death" criteria,[503] which requires that the entire brain, including the brain stem, be dead.[504] (It is even arguable that they are not "terminally ill,"[505] though they are most certainly "incurably ill.") In PVS patients, the brain stem survives and continues to regulate the so-called vegetative functions such as metabolism, respiration, and circulation.

It also appears that the thalamus, the portion of the brain that is critical for cognition and awareness of one's surroundings, is also severely damaged in PVS patients.[506] Thus PVS patients are not in contact with their surroundings,[507] and the prognosis for emergence from the state varies from slight to nonexistent

---

503 **AZ:** *But cf.* Rasmussen v. Fleming, 741 P.2d 674, 680 (Ariz. 1987) (expert witness testified that patient who was able to take nutrition by mouth was brain dead).

CA: *See, e.g.,* Drabick v. Drabick, 245 Cal. Rptr. 840, 842 (Ct. App. 1988).

MA: *See, e.g.,* Brophy v. New Eng. Sinai Hosp., Inc., 497 N.E.2d 626, 629 (Mass. 1986).

MI: Rosebush v. Oakland County Prosecutor, 491 N.W.2d 633, 635 (Mich. Ct. App. 1992).

MN: *In re* Torres, 357 N.W.2d 332, 334 (Minn. 1984) (patient comatose, but not dead, because laboratory studies show "'poor but definite cerebral (blood) flow'" and "'very rudimentary evidence of low medullary brain stem function'").

MO: Cruzan v. Harmon, 760 S.W.2d 408 (Mo. 1988).

NJ: *In re* Quinlan, 355 A.2d 647, 654, 655 (N.J. 1976) (persistent vegetative state is not the equivalent of brain death because patient has some brain stem function and moves, reacts to light and sound, and blinks).

NY: Elbaum v. Grace Plaza of Great Neck, Inc., 544 N.Y.S.2d 840 (App. Div. 1989).

OH: *In re* Myers, 610 N.E.2d 663, 666 n.1 (P. Ct. Summit County, Ohio 1993) (person in persistent vegetative state unable to experience pain).

See § **9.48.**

504 **FL:** *Cf. In re* T.A.C.P., 609 So. 2d 588, 590 (Fla. 1992) (anencephalic infants are permanently unconscious and thus like persons in a persistent vegetative state, but are not dead).

NY: Delio v. Westchester County Medical Ctr., 516 N.Y.S.2d 677, 684 (App. Div. 1987).

505 **CA:** Morrison v. Abramovice, 253 Cal. Rptr. 530, 532 (Ct. App. 1988).

CT: *But see* McConnell v. Beverly Enters.-Conn., Inc., 553 A.2d 596 (Conn. 1989) (patient in persistent vegetative state is considered to be terminally ill).

ME: *In re* Gardner, 534 A.2d 947, 958 (Me. 1987) (Clifford, J., dissenting).

MA: Brophy v. New Eng. Sinai Hosp., Inc., 497 N.E.2d 626, 635 (Mass. 1986).

MO: Cruzan v. Harmon, 760 S.W.2d 408 (Mo. 1988) (patient in persistent vegetative state not terminally ill).

See §§ **8.10–8.11.**

506 Kinney et al., *Neuropathological Findings in the Brain of Karen Ann Quinlan: The Role of the Thalamus in the Persistent Vegetative State,* 330 New Eng. J. Med. 1469 (1994).

507 **CA:** Morrison v. Abramovice, 253 Cal. Rptr. 530, 531 (Ct. App. 1988) ("A PVS patient has no mental functions. The eyes may be open at times, but the patient is 'completely unconscious, i.e., unaware of him(self) or herself or the surrounding environment. Voluntary reactions or behavioral responses reflecting consciousness, volition, or emotion at the cerebral cortical level are absent.' . . . The patient is incapable of experiencing pain and suffering.") (quoting Cranford, *The Persistent Vegetative State: Medical Reality (Getting the Facts Straight),* 18 Hastings Center Rep. 27, 28, 31 (Feb.–Mar. 1988)).

MA: *In re* Doe, 583 N.E.2d 1263 (Mass. 1992).

depending on how long the condition has been in existence, and if emergence occurs, functioning and cognition will be extremely low.[508] (When a patient is in a persistent vegetative state deemed to be irreversible, it is now considered proper to refer to the condition as "permanent unconsciousness."[509]) Persons in a persistent vegetative state "are permanently and completely unconscious."[510] They are completely unable to experience anything, including pain.[511] Even the

---

WI: L.W. v. L.E. Phillips Career Dev. Ctr., 482 N.W.2d 60, 67, 73 n.17 (Wis. 1992) ("individuals in a persistent vegetative state cannot experience pain or discomfort" (citing *Position of the American Academy of Neurology on Certain Aspects of the Care and Management of the Persistent Vegetative State Patient,* 39 Neurology 125 (1989)). *Contra* L.W. v. L.E. Phillips Career Dev. Ctr., 482 N.W.2d 60, 78 n.11 (Wis. 1992) (Steinmetz, J., dissenting) ("Interestingly, neither the American Academy of Neurology nor the American Medical Association has suggested laboratory tests that can reliably confirm that a patient's vegetative state is irreversible.").

[508] *See* Andrews, *Recovery of Patients after Four Months or More in the Persistent Vegetative State,* 306 Brit. Med. J. 1597 (1993); Cranford, *Neurological Syndromes and Prolonged Survival: When Can Artificial Nutrition and Hydration Be Forgone?,* 19 Law, Med. & Health Care 13 (1991); The Multi-Society Task Force on PVS, *Medical Aspects of the Persistent Vegetative State,* 330 New Eng. J. Med. 1499, 1572 (1994).

[509] The Multi-Society Task Force on PVS, *Medical Aspects of the Persistent Vegetative State,* 330 New Eng. J. Med. 1499, 1499, 1572 (1994).

[510] Cruzan v. Director, 497 U.S. 261, 310 n.9 (1990) (Brennan, J., dissenting):

The American Academy of Neurology offers three independent bases on which the medical profession rests these neurological conclusions:

> "First, direct clinical experience with these patients demonstrates that there is no behavioral indication of any awareness of pain or suffering.
>
> "Second, in all persistent vegetative state patients studied to date, postmortem examination reveals overwhelming bilateral damage to the cerebral hemispheres to a degree incompatible with consciousness. . . ."
>
> "Third, recent data utilizing positron emission tomography indicates that the metabolic rate for glucose in the cerebral cortex is greatly reduced in persistent vegetative state patients, to a degree incompatible with consciousness."

Position of the American Academy of Neurology on Certain Aspects of the Care and Management of the Persistent Vegetative State Patient, 39 Neurology 125 (1989).

[511] **US:** Cruzan v. Director, 497 U.S. 261, 310 n.9 (1990) (Brennan, J., dissenting).

CA: Morrison v. Abramovice, 253 Cal. Rptr. 530, 531 (Ct. App. 1988).

IL: Estate of Longeway v. Community Convalescent Ctr., 549 N.E.2d 292, 295 (Ill. 1989) ("Persistently comatose patients . . . are said to lack the capacity to feel pain and suffering, thus ameliorating concerns of a horrifying death.").

NY: Walsh v. Staten Island Obstetrics & Gynecology Assocs., P.C., 598 N.Y.S.2d 17, 19 (App. Div. 1993) (infant plaintiff in malpractice action "who cried when he received a painful stimuli, and smiled and laughed at pleasurable stimuli," although in a vegetative state, "clearly had some level of awareness").

PA: Wagner v. York Hosp., 608 A.2d 496 (Pa. Super. Ct. 1992) (rejecting evidence that patient in persistent vegetative state had absolutely no awareness of his surroundings).

WI: L.W. v. L.E. Phillips Career Dev. Ctr., 482 N.W.2d 60, 67, 73 n.17 (Wis. 1992). *But see* Gregory v. Carey, 791 P.2d 1329, 1336 (Kan. 1990) (loss of enjoyment of life is an element of disability, pain, and suffering that may be awarded to a plaintiff in a persistent vegetative state).

See generally Tresch et al., *Clinical Characteristics of Patients in the Persistent Vegetative State,* 151 Archives Internal Med. 930 (1991).

Missouri Supreme Court, which refused to permit the forgoing of life-sustaining treatment in the absence of clear and convincing evidence that the patient would have it terminated, concluded that there is no hope of recovery from a persistent vegetative state.[512] However, with adequate medical care, PVS patients can remain in this state indefinitely,[513] "the longest recorded survival by such means extending for thirty-seven years."[514] As a result, some have advocated changing the definition of death to include patients who lack a functioning cerebral cortex, including PVS patients and anencephalic patients.[515] Another, less drastic approach that provides greater deference to the patient's prior wishes or to the family's wishes, is to create a legal presumption that such patients are dead, and thus that life-sustaining treatment can be forgone, unless the patient has an advance directive requesting treatment in a persistent vegetative state or unless the patient's surrogate so requests.[516]

Some courts have made the finding that a patient is in a persistent vegetative state important, if not determinative.[517] This is because if a patient is in a persistent vegetative state, the prognosis for return to a "cognitive and sapient state"[518] has been thought to be virtually nil.[519] However, that view is undergoing revision in the medical profession. Studies show that patients diagnosed as being in a persistent vegetative state occasionally (though rarely) recover to

---

[512] *See* Cruzan v. Harmon, 760 S.W.2d 408, 422 (Mo. 1988) ("[T]he evidence is clear and convincing that Nancy will never interact meaningfully with her environment again. She will remain in a persistent vegetative state until her death.").

[513] **NJ:** *In re* Jobes, 529 A.2d 434, 459 n.13 (N.J. 1987) (Handler, J., concurring).

NY: Delio v. Westchester County Medical Ctr., 516 N.Y.S.2d 677, 683 (App. Div. 1987).

[514] **MA:** Brophy v. New Eng. Sinai Hosp., Inc., 497 N.E.2d 626, 637 (Mass. 1986).

CA: *Accord* Morrison v. Abramovice, 253 Cal. Rptr. 530, 532 (Ct. App. 1988).

MO: *Accord* Cruzan v. Harmon, 760 S.W.2d at 411 ("experts testified that she could live another thirty years").

OH: *Accord In re* Myers, 610 N.E.2d 663 (P. Ct. Summit County, Ohio 1993) (because of patient's "youth and general good health prior to the accident, she could exist in this deteriorating state for years, and . . . the eventual cause of her death would most likely be infection brought on by her continued physical deterioration and increased immunity to antibiotics").

[515] See § **9.48.**

[516] Angell, *After* Quinlan: *The Dilemma of the Persistent Vegetative State,* 330 New Eng. J. Med. 1524 (1994). *See also* Halevy & Brody, *Brain Death: Reconciling Definitions, Criteria, and Tests,* 119 Annals Internal Med. 519 (1993).

[517] **US:** *See, e.g.,* Cruzan v. Director, 497 U.S. 261, 348 (1990) (Stevens, J., dissenting) ("[A]n unbroken stream of cases has authorized procedures for the cessation of treatment of patients in persistent vegetative states.").

NJ: *See, e.g., In re* Quinlan, 355 A.2d 647, 669 (N.J. 1976) ("[T]he focal point of decision should be the prognosis as to the reasonable possibility of return to cognitive and sapient life.").

[518] *See In re* Quinlan, 355 A.2d at 655 & passim.

[519] **NY:** Eichner v. Dillon, 420 N.E.2d 64, 68 (N.Y. 1981) ("no reasonable likelihood that Brother Fox would ever emerge from the vegetative coma or recover his cognitive powers").

WA: *In re* Colyer, 660 P.2d 738, 740 (Wash. 1983) (persistent vegetative state with no possibility of any "meaningful existence").

some level of consciousness and even functionality. Recovery, however, usually occurs within four months and is exceedingly rare after one year. In addition, the extent of recovery is very limited.[520] The likelihood of recovery depends in part on the nature of the cause of the persistent vegetative state.[521]

A determination that a patient is in a persistent vegetative state must be by clear and convincing evidence[522] and such a diagnosis should be accepted only after the patient has been in that condition for a lengthy period of time.[523] Misdiagnosis of persistent vegetative state is not unusual,[524] in part because of the difficulty of diagnosing PVS,[525] and thus the law should insist on a high standard of proof. The concern for legal purposes about accurate diagnosis of persistent vegetative state was largely theoretical until the now-notorious New York case, *Coons v. Albany Memorial Hospital,*[526] involving a patient diagnosed as being in a persistent vegetative state. Shortly after a court order was issued permitting the removal of a gastrostomy tube, and while her family was searching for a nursing home that would accept her as a patient for the purpose of removing the feeding tube, her condition suddenly improved.[527]

---

[520] Andrews, *Recovery of Patients After Four Months or More in the Persistent Vegetative State,* 306 Brit. Med. J. 1597 (1993) ("Eleven of [43] patients regained awareness four months or more after suffering brain damage. The time to the first reported incidence of eye tracking was between four months and three years, and the time to the first response to command was between four and 12 months. Only one patient was eventually unable to communicate, six could use non-verbal methods of indicating at least a yes or no response, and four were able to speak. Six patients remained totally dependent while two became independent in daily activities. Four patients became independent in feeding, three required help, and four remained on gastrostomy feeding."); The Multi-Society Task Force on PVS, *Medical Aspects of the Persistent Vegetative State,* 330 New Eng. J. Med. 1499, 1572 (1994).

[521] The Multi-Society Task Force on PVS, *Medical Aspects of the Persistent Vegetative State,* 330 New Eng. J. Med. 1499, 1499 (1994) ("Recovery of consciousness from a posttraumatic persistent vegetative state is unlikely after 12 months in adults and children. Recovery from a nontraumatic persistent vegetative state after three months is exceedingly rare in both adults and children. Patients with degenerative or metabolic disorders or congenital malformations who remain in a persistent vegetative state for several months are unlikely to recover consciousness. The life span of adults and children in such a state is substantially reduced. For most such patients life expectancy ranges from 2 to 5 years; survival beyond 10 years is unusual.").

[522] **NJ:** *In re* Jobes, 529 A.2d 434, 441 (N.J. 1987). See § **5.61.**

[523] **NJ:** *See, e.g., In re* Jobes, 529 A.2d at 441 n.6 (six years).

WA: *But see In re* Colyer, 660 P.2d 738, 752 (Wash. 1983) (25 days) (Dore, J., dissenting).

See also Andrews, *Recovery of Patients After Four Months or More in the Persistent Vegetative State,* 306 Brit. Med. J. 1597 (1993); The Multi-Society Task Force on PVS, *Medical Aspects of the Persistent Vegetative State,* 330 New Eng. J. Med. 1499, 1499, 1572 (1994).

[524] Childs et al., *Accuracy of Diagnosis of Persistent Vegetative State,* 43 Neurology 1465 (1993).

[525] *See* De Giorgio & Lew, *Consciousness, Coma, and the Vegetative State: Physical Basis and Definitional Character,* 6 Issues L. & Med. 361, 370 (1991) (describing difficulties in diagnosis of persistent vegetative state).

[526] RJI No. 0189-017460 (Sup. Ct. Albany County, N.Y. Apr. 3, 1989).

[527] *See Patient Awakes from Coma After Right-to-Die Order,* 2 BioLaw U:1418 (June 1989); Steinbock, *Recovery from Persistent Vegetative State? The Case of Carrie Coons,* 19 Hastings Center Rep. 14 (July–Aug. 1989).

Other Forms of Brain Damage

There are a variety of other forms of brain damage that fall short of that occasioned by persistent vegetative state to varying degrees. With proper rehabilitative services, there can be some improvement with some patients in some of these types of conditions. Furthermore, unlike permanent unconsciousness, individuals in these states are able to experience, in varying degrees, some contact with their environment.

Most of the cases in this category have involved patients who are severely mentally retarded. However, the question of forgoing life-sustaining treatment did not arise out of their brain damage, but from the existence of some other life-threatening or hopeless medical condition, such as cancer,[528] renal failure,[529] or persistent vegetative state.[530] In these cases, the courts have applied the same process for decisionmaking for other patients lacking decisionmaking capacity, including a best interests standard in jurisdictions in which that is accepted.[531]

To date, there appears to be only one case, *Martin v. Martin,*[532] involving a patient who was formerly competent, unlike individuals with mental retardation, and whose condition fell short, and possibly far short, of persistent vegetative state, and probably of even being life-threatening. Furthermore, the medical condition that was the impetus for the forgoing of life-sustaining treatment was, unlike the cases involving mentally retarded patients, the patient's brain damage. Given the number of severely brain-damaged individuals who, through the advances of contemporary medicine, are able to survive when they would previously have died, this question is likely to be litigated with some frequency and much fervor in the future.

In *Martin,* the patient, an adult, was described as having

> sustained debilitating injuries in an automobile accident, with the most serious being a closed head injury affecting the bilateral hemisphere of his brain. The injuries significantly impaired his physical and cognitive abilities, left him unable to walk or talk, and rendered him dependent on a colostomy for defecation and a gastrostomy tube for nutrition.[533]

---

[528] **MA:** *E.g.,* Superintendent of Belchertown State Sch. v. Saikewicz, 370 N.E.2d 417 (Mass. 1977).

NY: *E.g., In re* Storar, 420 N.E.2d 64 (N.Y. 1981).

[529] **MA:** *See, e.g., In re* R.H., 622 N.E.2d 1071 (Mass. App. Ct. 1993).

[530] **IN:** *E.g., In re* Lawrance, 579 N.E.2d 32 (Ind. 1991).

MA: *E.g., In re* Doe, 583 N.E.2d 1263 (Mass. 1992).

NJ: *E.g., In re* Moorhouse, 593 A.2d 1256 (N.J. Super. Ct. App. Div. 1991).

WA: *E.g., In re* Hamlin, 689 P.2d 1372 (Wash. 1984).

[531] **NJ:** *See In re* Moorhouse, 593 A.2d 1256 (N.J. Super. Ct. App. Div. 1991).

WA: *See In re* Hamlin, 689 P.2d 1372 (Wash. 1984).

[532] 504 N.W.2d 917 (Mich. Ct. App. 1993), *opinion after remand,* 517 N.W.2d 749 (Mich. Ct. App. 1994), *appeal granted,* 525 N.W.2d 451 (Mich. 1994).

[533] Martin v. Martin, 504 N.W.2d at 920.

There was conflicting testimony about his level of physical, sensory, emotional, and cognitive functioning. One physician testified that the patient had "no meaningful interaction with his environment."[534] Another physician testified that the patient was able

> to carry out some voluntary motor commands on his right side, including the ability to pinch and grasp, as well as the ability to recognize faces, respond emotionally, and communicate with others with head nods, . . . [that he] seemed content with his environment and indicated "no" with a head nod when asked whether he has been in any pain or discomfort, and also when asked if there were ever any times when he felt that he did not want to go on living.[535]

Other expert witnesses presented differing opinions about his level of functioning but described it as falling between these two extremes. Some family members and some of his rehabilitation therapists claimed that he had a "limited ability to interact with others and to respond to simple yes or no questions with head nods; their testimony varied, however, with respect to the consistency and appropriateness of the perceived interaction and responses."[536] The trial court judge visited him and stated on the record that the patient had "moved his right arm and right leg on command, and how he had responded with appropriate head nods to a series of yes or no questions. Witnesses also testified that there are times when Michael becomes completely withdrawn and does not respond to any stimuli."[537] However, all the expert witnesses agreed that he was not in a persistent vegetative state nor was he terminally ill. Thus, the appellate court remanded for specific findings to be made as to whether any effort had ever been made to inform the patient of his current condition, its prognosis, and the treatment and nontreatment options, and to elicit his preferences, as well as to make specific findings on his decisionmaking capacity.

On the second appeal after remand, the court held that there was enough evidence, based on testimony from other witnesses, of the patient's views about being kept alive in a condition of this kind, expressed before his injuries occurred, to meet the substituted judgment standard.[538] Consequently, the court was not required to face the most difficult decision posed by a case of this sort, namely, whether or not in the absence of clear and convincing evidence of a person's actual or probable wishes, it was in his best interests for life-sustaining medical treatment (a feeding tube) to be forgone even though he had some limited contact with his environment. However, in its first opinion, the court stated that if there was inadequate evidence to meet the subjective standard or the substituted judgment standard, a best interests standard should be applied,[539]

---

[534] *Id.* at 921.

[535] *Id.*

[536] *Id.*

[537] *Id.*

[538] Martin v. Martin, 517 N.W.2d 749.

[539] Martin v. Martin, 504 N.W.2d at 923.

but it did not, and it did not need to, decide how that standard would be applied to the facts of this case.

§ 9.54 Paralysis

Most of the patients in right-to-die cases who have been permitted to forgo life-sustaining treatment have been incapable of movement. That most often has been because the patient was in a persistent vegetative state[540] or suffering from some other condition that caused the patient to be bedridden, such as cerebral palsy.[541] However, in *State v. McAfee,*[542] the patient, who was competent, was a ventilator-dependent quadriplegic as a result of a motorcycle accident. The fact that he was not terminally ill as a result of this injury did not limit his right to refuse treatment, and the court held not only that he was entitled to be provided with means for turning his ventilator off but also that he was entitled to be provided with adequate medication for relief of pain and anxiety between the time it was turned off and the time he expired. A similar case is *McKay v. Bergstedt,*[543] involving a 31-year-old man who became a quadriplegic at the age of 10 from a swimming accident. The court in *McKay,* however, exhibited more hesitance than the court in *McAfee,* requiring that because the patient was not terminally ill there be a judicial hearing in order to ensure that the patient was well aware of the possible medical and social options available to assist him in living.[544]

§ 9.55 Pregnancy

Although there are a number of cases raising closely related questions, there are no cases raising the question of forgoing life-sustaining treatment for a terminally ill, incompetent, pregnant patient. Most of the existing reported cases involve patients of the Jehovah's Witness religious faith who have refused or wish to refuse a blood transfusion,[545] and thus the patient's condition is such that

---

[540] See § **9.53.**

[541] *See, e.g.,* Bouvia v. Superior Court (Glenchur), 225 Cal. Rptr. 297 (Ct. App. 1986).

[542] **GA:** 385 S.E.2d 651 (Ga. 1989).

[543] **NV:** 801 P.2d 617 (Nev. 1990).

[544] *See* Patterson et al., *When Life Support Is Questioned Early in the Care of Patients with Cervical-Level Quadriplegia,* 328 New Eng. J. Med. 506 (1993).

[545] **MD:** *See, e.g.,* Mercy Hosp. Inc. v. Jackson, 489 A.2d 1130 (Md. Ct. Spec. App. 1985), *vacated and remanded as moot,* 510 A.2d 562 (Md. 1986).

MA: Norwood Hosp. v. Munoz, 564 N.E.2d 1017 (Mass. 1991).

NJ: Raleigh Fitkin-Paul Morgan Memorial Hosp. v. Anderson, 201 A.2d 537 (N.J.), *cert. denied,* 377 U.S. 985 (1964).

NY: Fosmire v. Nicoleau, 551 N.E.2d 77 (N.Y. 1990); *In re* Jamaica Hosp., 491 N.Y.S.2d 898 (Sup. Ct. Queens County 1985).

the treatment in question will almost certainly return her either to the status quo ante or to a quality of life that she would consider acceptable. In the older cases, courts exhibited an extreme reluctance to permit the forgoing of treatment by or on behalf of a pregnant patient, but that is probably because most of these cases involved patients who were not hopelessly ill. Only rarely has the patient been terminally ill[546] or in a persistent vegetative state;[547] and in one unreported case the mother was brain dead.[548]

In many of the cases raising the question of the involuntary administration of treatment to a pregnant woman, the treatment is for the benefit of the health or life of the fetus rather than the mother.[549] However, in some cases, there is a necessity to treat both the mother and the fetus, although the mother's treatment is sometimes necessitated only by the fact that treatment is ordered for the fetus.[550] When only the health or life of the fetus is in question, the mother's right to die is not involved, and the courts have readily ordered treatment of the fetus or the mother for the benefit of the fetus.[551] This practice has received a great deal of criticism from both legal and medical quarters.[552]

As yet, there has been no really clear test of the right of a pregnant woman to forgo life-sustaining treatment necessary to keep the fetus alive. However, a number of cases are concerned with the authority of competent pregnant women or the surrogates of incompetent pregnant women to make decisions about their medical treatment that will have an adverse impact on the health or life of the

---

546 *See, e.g., In re* A.C., 573 A.2d 1235 (D.C. 1990).

547 *See, e.g., In re* Klein, 538 N.Y.S.2d 274 (App. Div. 1989).

548 *See, e.g.,* University Health Servs., Inc. v. Piazzi, Civ. Action No. CV86-RCCV-464 (Super. Ct. Richmond County, Ga. Aug. 4, 1986), *reprinted in* 2 Issues L. & Med. 415 (1987).

549 **DC:** *See, e.g., In re* A.C., 533 A.2d 611 (D.C. 1987).

GA: *See, e.g.,* Jefferson v. Griffin Spalding County Hosp. Auth., 274 S.E.2d 457 (Ga. 1981); University Health Servs., Inc. v. Piazzi, Civ. Action No. CV86-RCCV-464 (Super. Ct. Richmond County, Ga. Aug. 4, 1986).

MD: *See, e.g.,* Mercy Hosp. Inc. v. Jackson, 489 A.2d 1130 (Md. 1986).

MA: *See, e.g.,* Taft v. Taft, 446 N.E.2d 395 (Mass. 1983).

NJ: *See, e.g.,* Raleigh Fitkin-Paul Morgan Memorial Hosp. v. Anderson, 201 A.2d 537 (N.J. 1964).

NY: *See, e.g., In re* Jamaica Hosp., 491 N.Y.S.2d 898 (Sup. Ct. Queens County 1985).

550 *See, e.g.,* Crouse Irving Memorial Hosp. v. Paddock, 485 N.Y.S.2d 443 (Sup. Ct. Onondaga County 1985) (woman ordered to receive blood transfusions to protect well-being of fetus to be delivered prematurely by cesarean section); *In re* Jamaica Hosp., 491 N.Y.S.2d 898.

551 *But see* Taft v. Taft, 446 N.E.2d at 397 (reversing order that mother undergo surgery to prevent possible miscarriage on ground that "[a]ny interest the State may have in requiring a competent, adult woman to submit to the operation is not established").

552 *See, e.g.,* Board of Trustees, American Medical Ass'n, *Legal Interventions During Pregnancy: Court-Ordered Medical Treatments and Legal Penalties for Potentially Harmful Behavior by Pregnant Women,* 264 JAMA 2663 (1990). *See generally* Coutts, Maternal-Fetal Conflict: Legal and Ethical Issues (National Reference Ctr. for Bioethics Literature, Kennedy Inst. of Ethics, Geo. Univ. 1990) (scope note 15).

fetus. The leading case, *In re A.C.*,[553] involves the right not to be subjected involuntarily to a cesarean section. However, the court's standards for decision-making are clearly relevant to forgoing life-sustaining treatment as well. In *A.C.*, a single judge of the motions division of the District of Columbia Court of Appeals upheld a trial court order that a cesarean delivery be performed on a terminally ill mother, who "had, at best, two days left of sedated life."[554] The court concluded that, in such a case, the mother's right of privacy does not outweigh the interests of the fetus.

Thereafter, the full court issued a sweeping opinion that vacated and remanded the judgment of the single judge, holding that a decision about whether to administer or withhold treatment must be based on the patient's own wishes if the patient is competent, and on the basis of substituted judgment if the patient is incompetent.[555] After the patient's wishes are clarified, a determination must be made by a judge about whether or not the state's interests outweigh the patient's. This will be so only if the state's interests are very substantial. Thus, the patient's "wishes will control in virtually all cases."[556] Indeed, the court took pains to demonstrate just how stringent this standard is by pointing out that it is possible that the state's interests might never be substantial enough to override the patient's decision on any set of facts: "We do not quite foreclose the possibility that a conflicting state interest may be so compelling that the patient's wishes must yield, but we anticipate that such cases will be extremely rare and truly exceptional."[557] Thus, the court's formulation of the test of determining whether or not the patient's actual or probable decision is to be honored is consistent with the judicial consensus about how decisions are to be made for any incompetent patient.[558]

Because the patient had died, the court was unable to remand for a finding on the patient's wishes. It did, however, indicate what kinds of considerations are relevant to making a substituted judgment:

> [I]t would be highly relevant that A.C. had consented to intrusive and dangerous surgeries in the past, and that she chose to become pregnant and to protect her pregnancy by seeking treatment at the hospital's high-risk pregnancy clinic. It would also be relevant that she accepted a plan of treatment which contemplated caesarean intervention at the twenty-eighth week of pregnancy, even though the possibility of a caesarean during the twenty-sixth week was apparently unforeseen. On the other hand, A.C. agreed to a plan of palliative treatment which posed a greater danger to the fetus than would have been necessary if she were

---

[553] 573 A.2d 1235 (D.C. 1990) (en banc).

[554] *In re A.C.*, 533 A.2d 611, 617 (D.C. 1987), *vacated and remanded*, 573 A.2d 1235 (D.C. 1990).

[555] 573 A.2d at 1237.

[556] *Id.* at 1252.

[557] *Id.*

[558] See §§ **7.4–7.10.**

> unconcerned about her own continuing care. Further, when A.C. was informed of the fatal nature of her illness, she was equivocal about her desire to have the baby.[559]

Apart from the facts of the particular case, the court observed that any patient "might consider the needs of her family in making a treatment decision,"[560] and that especially a pregnant patient "may not be concerned exclusively with her own welfare."[561] "Thus it is proper for the court, in a case such as this, to weigh (along with all the other factors) the mother's prognosis, the viability of the fetus, the probable result of treatment or non-treatment for both mother and fetus, and the mother's likely interest in avoiding impairment for her child together with her own instincts for survival."[562]

Finally, the court took the opportunity "to reiterate and emphasize a point that the motions division made in its opinion: 'that this case is not about abortion' . . . [because] the record makes clear that A.C. sought to become pregnant, that she wanted to bear her child as close to term as possible, and that neither she nor anyone associated with her at any time sought to terminate her pregnancy." Rather, the issue "is not *whether* A.C. (or any woman) should have a child but, rather, *who should decide* how that child should be delivered. That decision involves the right of A.C. (or any woman) to accept or forego medical treatment."[563] But the court's further observation that "[t]he Supreme Court has not yet focused on this question in the context of a pregnancy, and we are not so adept at reading tea leaves as to predict how it might rule,"[564] belied its uncertainty on this point. It is a possibility that for many courts, including the Supreme Court, the two issues will be inextricably linked.

Subsequent to the handing down of the court of appeals opinion, the patient's family instituted a malpractice suit against George Washington University Medical Center (GWUMC) where the patient had been treated. This suit was terminated by a consent agreement.[565] The consent agreement provided for an undisclosed amount of damages, but more importantly, set forth a policy that GWUMC adopted for future disposition of such cases, and which might serve as a model for other hospitals,

> recognizing the right of a pregnant patient to determine the course of medical treatment on behalf of herself and her fetus and to refuse medical recommendations and emphasizing that it will rarely be appropriate to seek judicial intervention to resolve ethical issues relating to a patient's decision or to assess or override a pregnant patient's decision.[566]

---

[559] 573 A.2d at 1250.

[560] *Id.* at 1251 (citing *In re* Roe, 421 N.E.2d 40, 57 (Mass. 1981)).

[561] *Id.*

[562] *Id.*

[563] *Id.* at 1245 n.9 (emphasis added).

[564] *Id.*

[565] *See* 2 BioLaw S:607 (July 1991) [hereinafter Settlement Agreement]. *See also* Greenhouse, *Hospital Policy Sets Out Pregnant Patient Rights,* N.Y. Times, Nov. 29, 1990, at 15 (nat'l ed.).

[566] Settlement Agreement, Nov. 21, 1990, § 2, at 3.

Among numerous other provisions, the agreement provides that GWUMC will inform patients at the time of admission about the use of a durable power of attorney to designate a surrogate, and provide forms for that purpose,[567] something that is now required nationwide by the Patient Self-Determination Act.[568] An 11-page appendix, entitled "Policy on Decision-Making by Pregnant Patients at the George Washington University Hospital" acknowledges that health care decisionmaking is a "joint enterprise" between the patient (or surrogate if the patient is incompetent) and the health care team, in which informed consent or informed refusal is required.[569] The policy provides that "great care should be taken to verify that [a pregnant patient's] decision is both informed and authentic" when it "appears unnecessarily to disserve her own or fetal welfare."[570] It spells out how this is to be done, and concludes that "[w]hen a fully informed and competent pregnant patient persists in a decision which may disserve her own or fetal welfare, this hospital's policy is to accede to the pregnant patient's preference whenever possible."[571]

The policy also provides for conscientious objection by health care professionals, who may withdraw from participation in the treatment of a pregnant patient when compliance with the patient's wishes "would cause [the] care-giver to violate his/her professional standards . . . [and] where that patient is given adequate notice and assistance in obtaining competent substitute care."[572] In "remote case[s]" the patient's decision may be "so ethically unsettling" as to "justify an institutional decision to withdraw from the case. Such justification normally would exist when there was unanimity or overwhelming consensus among the attending physician and assisting members of the health care team" of (1) "near certainty of substantial and imminent harm to the [fetus]," (2) "the proposed procedure has a very high possibility of reversing or preventing the anticipated harm to the fetus," (3) "[r]isk to the pregnant patient is minimal," and (4) "[w]ithdrawal from the case is not likely to cause the pregnant patient to abandon medical care for herself and her fetus or otherwise to cause harm to herself."[573] Finally, the procedure states that "[c]ourts are an inappropriate forum for resolving ethical issues . . . and should rarely occur."[574] This final provision directly contradicts the holding of *A.C.* requiring recourse to the courts to determine the patient's wishes and to weigh the state's interests.

Another important case is *In re Doe,*[575] decided by the Appellate Court of Illinois, involving a woman's refusal to submit to a cesarean section claimed by

---

[567] *Id.* § 4(a), at 4.

[568] See § **10.21.**

[569] Settlement Agreement, Nov. 21, 1990, app. A at 1.

[570] *Id.* at 5.

[571] *Id.* at 6.

[572] *Id.* at 8. See § **17.23.**

[573] *Id.* at 8–9.

[574] *Id.* at 9.

[575] 632 N.E.2d 326 (Ill. App. Ct. 1994).

her physician to be immediately necessary to ensure the fetus's live and healthy birth. (In fact, the baby was delivered alive and healthy without a cesarean section.[576]) The patient rejected the recommendation based on "her personal religious beliefs," preferring to await natural childbirth because of "her abiding faith in God's healing powers," a decision with which her husband concurred.[577] The doctor and the hospital administration informed the state's attorney, who filed a petition to have the fetus made a ward of the court. After some procedural skirmishing about whether the juvenile court had jurisdiction over a fetus, the court declined to order the patient to submit to the operation. An appeal was taken by the state's attorney and the public guardian, asserting that the trial court should have balanced the interests of the fetus against those of the mother. The appeals court also rejected this argument and affirmed.

It based its decision primarily on the common-law right to refuse treatment, and to some extent on federal constitutional grounds. The thrust of the holding is that although a fetus "has the legal right to begin life with a sound mind and body," this right is assertable only against third persons, and not against the mother.[578] To hold otherwise would require one person to undergo medical treatment for the benefit of another, a claim that the Illinois Supreme Court had recently rejected in a case of an individual seeking to require another to be tested for compatibility for bone marrow donation,[579] and which the court noted had been rejected by other courts, including the *In re A.C.* court.[580] Thus, there was no need to balance the interests of the fetus against those of the mother. However, the court was careful to distinguish cases in which pregnant women had been ordered to submit to a blood transfusion for the benefit of their fetus on the ground that the risk of a blood transfusion is insubstantial, stating that whether this is permissible in Illinois must be left to a future case.[581]

The court also found support for its holding that the interests of the fetus did not need to be taken into account in three Supreme Court abortion cases, *Roe v. Wade,*[582] *Thornburgh,*[583] and *Casey.*[584] It rejected the argument that because the state may prohibit abortions post-viability it may require women to submit to medical treatment for the benefit of the fetus, explaining that such state power

---

[576] **IL:** 632 N.E.2d at 329.

GA: *See also* Jefferson v. Griffin Spalding County Hosp. Auth., 274 S.E.2d 457 (Ga. 1981) (mother delivered healthy baby without harm to self despite physician's prediction of almost certain death to mother and fetus).

[577] *In re* Doe, 632 N.E.2d at 327.

[578] *Id.* at 332.

[579] *See* Curran v. Bosze, 566 N.E.2d 1319 (Ill. 1990).

[580] **DC:** *See In re* A.C., 573 A.2d 1235 (D.C. 1990). *But see In re* Madyun, 114 Daily Wash. L. Rptr. 2233 (D.C. Super. Ct. July 26, 1986), *reprinted as app. to In re* A.C., 573 A.2d at 1259.

GA: *But see* Jefferson v. Griffin Spalding County Hosp. Auth., 274 S.E.2d 457.

[581] *In re* Doe, 632 N.E.2d at 333.

[582] 410 U.S. 113 (1973).

[583] Thornburgh v. American College of Obstetricians & Gynecologists, 476 U.S. 747 (1986).

[584] Planned Parenthood of Southeastern Pa. v. Casey, 505 U.S. ____, 112 S. Ct. 2791 (1992).

"does not translate into the proposition that the state may intrude upon the woman's right to remain free from unwanted physical invasion of her person when she chooses to carry her pregnancy to term." Further, "*Roe* and its progeny . . . make it clear that, even in the context of abortion, the state's compelling interest in the potential life of the fetus is insufficient to override the woman's interest in preserving her health."[585]

Another difficulty the court foresaw was how an order to submit to a cesarean would be carried out. Both the state's attorney and the public guardian opposed the issuance of an order that would permit the use of force to perform the surgery. For a competent patient,

> "[e]nforcement could be accomplished only through physical force or its equivalent. A.C. would have to be fastened with restraints to the operating table, or perhaps rendered unconscious by forcibly injecting her with an anesthetic, and then subjected to unwanted major surgery. Such actions would surely give one pause in a civilized society, especially when A.C. had done no wrong."[586]

Another relevant case that is also not directly on point is *In re Klein,*[587] which also bespeaks a judicial willingness to place the interests of the patient over that of the fetus. The patient was in an automobile accident that rendered her unconscious. Her husband brought an action to have himself appointed guardian to authorize an abortion if her doctors deemed it necessary to preserve her life. At the time of the writing of the opinion, the patient was approximately 17 weeks' pregnant. The court refused to appoint a guardian of the fetus because "[t]he State has no compelling interest in the protection of the fetus prior to viability, since the mother's constitutional right to privacy, which includes the right to terminate her pregnancy, is paramount at that stage."[588] It also affirmed the appointment of the patient's husband as guardian (and refused to appoint a stranger as guardian who, presumably, would not have authorized the abortion), thereby sanctioning the termination of the pregnancy if medically necessary for the well-being of the patient.[589]

---

[585] *In re* Doe, 632 N.E.2d at 334.

[586] *Id.* at 335 (quoting *In re* A.C., 573 A.2d 1235, 1244 n.8 (D.C. 1990)) ("An even more graphic description of what actually happened when a forced cesarean section was carried out may be found in Gallagher, *Prenatal Invasions & Interventions: What's Wrong With Fetal Rights,* 10 Harvard Women's L.J. 9, 9–10 (1987).").

[587] 538 N.Y.S.2d 274 (App. Div. 1989).

[588] *Id.* at 275.

[589] **DGA:** Bendiburg v. Dempsey, 707 F. Supp. 1318 (N.D. Ga. 1989) (in absence of clear emergency, ex parte orders for medical treatment of minors over objection of parent do not provide adequate due process).

DNY: *Cf. In re* Department of Veterans Affairs Medical Ctr., 749 F. Supp. 495 (S.D.N.Y. 1990) (court refused to hear ex parte application of hospital for authorization to perform amputation without first hearing testimony of incompetent patient's wife).

PA: *But see In re* Estate of Dorone, 534 A.2d 452, 455 (Pa. 1987) (ex parte order permissible when situation was urgent, there was no time to conduct more expansive hearings, and it was beyond dispute that judge knew gist of appellant's testimony).

A few other cases are relevant but also not directly on point. The closest to being on point is an unreported case, *University Health Services, Inc. v. Piazzi,*[590] in which the patient was a brain-dead pregnant woman in the second trimester of pregnancy whose circulation was being maintained by a life-support system. The court denied the petition of the patient's husband to discontinue the life support. (Another man, claiming to be the father of the fetus, requested that life support be continued.) In so ruling, the court relied in part on the Georgia living will statute,[591] which prohibits (as many advance directive statutes do[592]) an otherwise valid advance directive from becoming effective if the declarant is pregnant,[593] despite the fact that the patient did not have an advance directive. Regardless of the validity of the decision itself, its basis leaves much to be desired.[594] Advance directive statutes are intended to apply to persons who have executed an advance directive, which this patient had not, and not to others.[595] Furthermore, they are intended to apply to persons and not to corpses.

The applicability of an advance directive statute was also at issue in *DiNino v. State ex rel. Gorton,* a declaratory judgment action brought by a nonpregnant, nonterminally ill woman to invalidate the portion of the optional provision in the sample living will contained in the Washington advance directive statute[596] that prohibits the enforcement of otherwise valid directives for pregnant women. The state conceded that the provision could be deleted and the living will would still be valid.[597] However, it still contended that a directive requiring termination of a pregnancy prior to removal of life support from the mother would be invalid because it ignores the state's potential interest in the life of the fetus. There was no definitive ruling on this issue because the court held that the action was nonjusticiable.

Ex Parte Hearings

When hospitals initiate actions to override the decision of a pregnant patient or her surrogate, they sometimes do so by filing an ex parte proceeding because

---

590 Civ. Action No. CV86-RCCV-464 (Super. Ct. Richmond County, Ga. Aug. 4, 1986). *See also Doctors Fighting to Save the Fetus of a Brain-Dead Woman,* N.Y. Times, Apr. 25, 1993, § 1, at 14; Fost & Purdy, *The Baby in the Body—Keeping a Comatose Patient on Life Support until Her Child Can Be Born,* 24 Hastings Center Rep. 31 (Jan.–Feb. 1994); Wilson, *Custody of "Miracle Baby" Awarded to Child's Cousin,* S.F. Chron., Oct. 20, 1993, at D3 (baby born of brain-dead mother on life support for last 105 days of pregnancy).

591 Ga. Code Ann. §§ 31-32-1 to 31-32-12.

592 See **§§ 11.11** and **12.27.**

593 Ga. Code Ann. § 31-32-3.

594 *See* Frader, *Have We Lost Our Senses?—Problems with Maintaining Brain-Dead Bodies Carrying Fetuses,* 4 J. Clinical Ethics 347 (1993).

595 *See* Ga. Code Ann. § 31-32-11(a), (c). See **§ 10.13.**

596 *See* Wash. Rev. Code Ann. § 70.122.030 (Supp. 1987) (revised).

597 DiNino v. State *ex rel.* Gorton, 684 P.2d 1297 (Wash. 1984).

judicial review is frequently sought on an emergency basis. Thus, courts are often faced with an urgent application for an order authorizing the patient's attending physicians to administer treatment or perform a cesarean section without the benefit of parties being present to adequately develop the issues before the court.[598] Recognizing that not all of these cases are inherently emergencies but that many gradually become urgent with some forewarning to the physicians that the patient will not accept a particular treatment should it become medically indicated, the New York Court of Appeals—taking into account that on the facts of the case before it there was "a long-standing unequivocal personal decision to decline transfusions"[599]—held that "[a]pplications for court-ordered medical treatment . . . should generally comply with due process requirements of notice and the right to be heard before the order is signed [citation omitted]."[600] Because due process is a "flexible concept," when it is not feasible to accord prior notice and the right to be heard, "the court should make some effort to communicate with the patient or responsible relatives if only to give prompt notice that the order has been signed."[601] However, there were no such exigent circumstances, and further, the court pointed out, "[a]pparently three hours elapsed between the time the application was made and the time the order was signed and an additional six hours passed before it was executed. Thus there was ample time to provide notice and an opportunity for a hearing, however informal."[602] Holding an ex parte hearing and failing to allow representation of respondent's interests has been held to violate due process and give rise to a federal civil rights action for damages.[603]

---

598 *See, e.g.*, Jefferson v. Griffin Spalding County Hosp. Auth., 274 S.E.2d 457 (Ga. 1981).

599 Fosmire v. Nicoleau, 551 N.E.2d 77, 80 (N.Y. 1990).

600 *Id.*

601 *Id.*

602 **NY:** Fosmire v. Nicoleau, 551 N.E.2d at 80.

CA: *Accord* Thor v. Superior Court, 855 P.2d 375, 379 n.2 (Cal. 1993) (disapproving of ex parte and summary proceedings in absence of "actual emergency"; patient not pregnant).

DC: *Cf. In re* A.C., 573 A.2d 1235 (D.C. 1990) (holding that for cesarean section to be ordered for incompetent patient, *court* must determine that patient would have wanted it).

FL: *Accord In re* Dubreuil, 629 So. 2d 819 (Fla. 1993) (reiterating holding of Wons v. Public Health Trust, 541 So. 2d 96 (Fla. 1989), that hospitals cannot override pregnant patients' refusals of treatment without court hearing, and additionally holding that burden of proof is on hospital).

603 *See, e.g.*, Bendiburg v. Dempsey, 909 F.2d 463 (11th Cir. 1990). See § **17.20.**

Bibliography

Alzheimer's Disease and Other Senile Dementias

Cranford, R. "Major Neurologic Syndromes in Life-Sustaining Medical Treatment Decisions." *Medical Ethics Advisor* 7 (July 1991): 87.

Rosoff, A., and G. Gottlieb. "Preserving Personal Autonomy for the Elderly: Competency, Guardianship, and Alzheimer's Disease." *Journal of Legal Medicine* 8 (1987): 1.

Artificial Nutrition and Hydration

Bopp, J. "Nutrition and Hydration for Patients: The Constitutional Aspects." *Issues in Law and Medicine* 4 (1988): 3.

Burt, R. "Withholding Nutrition and Mistrusting Nurturance: The Vocabulary of *In re Conroy.*" *Issues in Law and Medicine* 2 (1987): 317.

Cantor, N. "The Permanently Unconscious Patient, Non-Feeding and Euthanasia." *American Journal of Law and Medicine* 15 (1989): 381.

Dresser R., and E. Boisaubin. "Ethics, Law, and Nutritional Support." *Archives of Internal Medicine* 145 (1985): 122.

Lynn, J., ed. *By No Extraordinary Means: The Choice to Forgo Life-Sustaining Food and Water.* Bloomington, IN: Indiana University Press, 1986.

Peters, P., et al. "Physician Willingness to Withhold Tube Feeding After *Cruzan.*" *Missouri Law Review* 57 (1992): 831.

Brain Death

Grodin, M. "Religious Exemptions: Brain Death and Jewish Law." *Journal of Church and State* 36 (1994): 357.

Guthrie, L. "Brain Death and Criminal Liability." *Criminal Law Bulletin* 15 (1979): 40.

Halevy, A., and B. Brody. "Brain Death: Reconciling Definitions, Criteria, and Tests." *Annals of Internal Medicine* 119 (1993): 519.

New Jersey Commission on Legal and Ethical Problems in the Delivery of Health Care. *The New Jersey Advance Directives for Health Care and*

Declaration of Death Acts: Statutes, Commentaries and Analyses. Trenton: New Jersey Bioethics Commission, 1991.

Olick, R. "Brain Death, Religious Freedom, and Public Policy: New Jersey's Landmark Legislative Initiative." *Kennedy Institute of Ethics Journal* 4 (1991): 275.

Smith, D. "Legal Recognition of Neocortical Death." *Cornell Law Review* 71 (1986): 850.

Cardiopulmonary Resuscitation and DNR Orders

Blackhall, L. "Must We Always Use CPR?" *New England Journal of Medicine* 317 (1987): 1281.

Brett, A., and L. McCullough. "When Patients Request Specific Interventions—Defining the Limits of the Physician's Obligation." *New England Journal of Medicine* 315 (1986): 1347.

Cohen, C., and P. Cohen. "Do-Not-Resuscitate Orders in the Operating Room." *New England Journal of Medicine* 325 (1991): 1879.

Kuehl, K., et al. "Should a School Honor a Student's DNR Order?: Case History of S.A." *Kennedy Institute of Ethics Journal* 2 (1992): 1.

Lantos, J., et al. "The Illusion of Futility in Clinical Practice." *American Journal of Medicine* 87 (1989): 81.

Lantos, J., et al. "Survival After Cardiopulmonary Resuscitation in Babies of Very Low Birthweight: Is CPR Futile Therapy?" *New England Journal of Medicine* 318 (1988): 91.

Lieberson, A. *Advance Medical Directives*. Deerfield, IL: Clark Boardman Callaghan, 1992.

Moss, A. "Informing the Patient About Cardiopulmonary Resuscitation: When the Risks Outweigh the Benefits." *Journal of General Internal Medicine* 4 (1989): 349.

Murphy, D. "Do-Not-Resuscitate Orders: Time for Reappraisal in Long-Term-Care Institutions." *JAMA* 260 (1988): 2098.

Murphy D., and D. Matchar. "Life-Sustaining Therapy: A Model for Appropriate Use." *JAMA* 264 (1990): 2103.

New York State Task Force on Life and the Law. *Do Not Resuscitate Orders*. 2d ed. Albany, NY: New York State Task Force on Life and the Law, 1988.

Scofield, G. "A Lawyer Responds: A Student's Right to Forgo CPR." *Kennedy Institute of Ethics Journal* 2 (1992): 4.

Scofield, G. "Is Consent Useful When Resuscitation Isn't?" *Hastings Center Report* 21 (November–December 1991): 28.

Stell, L. "Stopping Treatment on Grounds of Futility: A Role for Institutional Policy." *St. Louis University Public Law Review* 11 (1992): 481.

Strike, K. "An Educator Responds: A School's Interests in Denying the Request." *Kennedy Institute of Ethics Journal* 2 (1992): 19.

Tomlinson T., and H. Brody. "Ethics and Communications in Do-Not-Resuscitate Orders." *New England Journal of Medicine* 318 (1988): 43.

Tomlinson T., and H. Brody. "Futility and the Ethics of Resuscitation." *JAMA* 264 (1990):1276.

Truog, R. "'Do-Not-Resuscitate' Orders During Anesthesia and Surgery." *Anesthesiology* 74 (1991): 606.

Walker, R. "DNR in the OR—Resuscitation as an Operative Risk." *JAMA* 266 (1991): 2407.

Youngner, S. "A Physician/Ethicist Responds: A Student's Rights Are Not So Simple." *Kennedy Institute of Ethics Journal* 2 (1992): 13.

Youngner, S. "Futility in Context." *JAMA* 264 (1990): 1295.

Youngner, S. "Who Defines Futility?" *JAMA* 260 (1988): 2094.

Youngner, S. et al. "DNR in the Operating Room—Not Really a Paradox." *JAMA* 266 (1991): 2433.

Pain Management

Barry, R., and J. Maher. "Indirectly Intended Life-Shortening Analgesia: Clarifying the Principles." *Issues in Law and Medicine* 6 (1990): 117.

Battin, M. "Euthanasia: The Way We Do It, the Way They Do It." *Journal of Pain and Symptom Management* 6 (1991): 298.

Block, S., and J. Billings. "Patient Requests to Hasten Death—Evaluation and Management in Terminal Care." *Archives of Internal Medicine* 154 (1994): 2039.

Brena, S. "Management of Pain in the Terminally Ill Patient." *Issues in Law and Medicine* 2 (1987): 379.

Brescia, F. "Killing the Known Dying: Notes of a Death Watcher." *Journal of Pain and Symptom Management* 6 (1991): 336.

Cherny, N., et al. "The Treatment of Suffering when Patients Request Elective Death." *Journal of Palliative Care* 10 (1994): 71.

Clouser, K. "The Challenge for Future Debate on Euthanasia." *Journal of Pain and Symptom Management* 6 (1991): 306.

Conolly, M. "Alternatives to Euthanasia: Pain Management." *Issues in Law and Medicine* 4 (1989): 497.

Foley, K. "The Relationship of Pain and Symptom Management to Patient Requests for Physician-Assisted Suicide." *Journal of Pain and Symptom Management* 6 (1991): 289.

Jacox, A., et al. "New Clinical-Practice Guidelines for the Management of Pain in Patients with Cancer." *New England Journal of Medicine* 330 (1994): 651.

Jennings, B. "Active Euthanasia and Forgoing Life-Sustaining Treatment: Can We Hold the Line?" *Journal of Pain and Symptom Management* 6 (1991): 312.

Klagsbrun, S. "Physician-Assisted Suicide: A Double Dilemma." *Journal of Pain and Symptom Management* 6 (1991): 325.

Latimer, E. "Ethical Decision-Making in the Care of the Dying and Its Applications to Clinical Practice." *Journal of Pain and Symptom Management* 6 (1991): 329.

Miller, F., et al. "Regulating Physician-Assisted Death." *New England Journal of Medicine* 331 (1994): 119.

O'Rourke, K. "Assisted Suicide: An Evaluation." *Journal of Pain and Symptom Management* 6 (1991): 317.

Rhymes, J. "Hospice Care in America." *JAMA* 264 (1990): 369.

Scofield, G. "Privacy (or Liberty) and Assisted Suicide." *Journal of Pain and Symptom Management* 6 (1991): 280.

Truog, R. et al. "Barbiturates in the Care of the Terminally Ill." *New England Journal of Medicine* 237 (1992): 1678.

Persistent Vegetative State and Other Forms of Coma

Andrews, K. "Recovery of Patients After Four Months or More in the Persistent Vegetative State." *British Medical Journal* 306 (1993): 1597.

Angell, M. "After *Quinlan:* The Dilemma of the Persistent Vegetative State." *New England Journal of Medicine* 330 (1994): 1524.

Cranford, R., "Major Neurologic Syndromes in Life-Sustaining Medical Treatment Decisions." *Medical Ethics Advisor* 7 (July 1991): 87.

Cranford, R., "The Persistent Vegetative State: The Medical Reality (Getting the Facts Straight)." *Hastings Center Report* 18 (February–March 1988): 27.

DeGiorgio, C., and M. Lew, "Consciousness, Coma and the Vegetative State: Physical Basis and Definitional Character." *Issues in Law and Medicine* 6 (1991): 361.

The Multi-Society Task Force on PVS. "Medical Aspects of the Persistent Vegetative State." *New England Journal of Medicine* 330 (1994): 1499.

Skegg, S. "Irreversibly Comatose Individuals: 'Alive' or 'Dead'?" *Cambridge Law Journal* 33 (1974): 130.

Pregnancy

Coutts, M. *Maternal-Fetal Conflict: Legal and Ethical Issues,* scope note 15. National Reference Center for Bioethics Literature, Kennedy Institute of Ethics, Georgetown University, 1990.

Diamond, M. "Echoes from Darkness: The Case of Angela C." *University of Pittsburgh Law Review* 51 (1990): 1061.

Gallagher, J. "Prenatal Invasions & Interventions: What's Wrong with Fetal Rights." *Harvard Women's Law Journal* 10 (1987): 9.

Goldberg, S. "Medical Choices During Pregnancy: Whose Decision Is It Anyway?" *Rutgers Law Review* 41 (1989): 591.

Johnsen, D. Note. "The Creation of Fetal Rights: Conflicts with Women's Constitutional Rights to Liberty, Privacy, and Equal Protection." *Yale Law Journal* 95 (1986): 599.

Mahoney, J. "Death with Dignity: Is There an Exception for Pregnant Women?" *UMKC Law Review* 57 (1989): 221.

Nelson L., et al. "Forced Medical Treatment of Pregnant Women: Compelling Each to Live As Seems Good to the Rest." *Hastings Law Journal* 37 (1986): 703.

Rhoden, N. "The Judge in the Delivery Room: The Emergence of Court-ordered Caesareans." *California Law Review* 74 (1986): 1951.

Scott, C. "Resisting the Temptation to Turn Medical Recommendations into Judicial Orders: A Reconsideration of Court-Ordered Surgery for Pregnant Women." *Georgia State University Law Review* 10 (1994): 615.

Supportive Care

Crowley, M. "The Hospice Movement: A Renewed View of the Death Process." *Journal of Contemporary Health Law and Policy* 4 (1988): 295.

Hagerman, A. "Hospice: An Alternative Treatment of Care for the Terminally Ill." *Pace Law Review* 8 (1988): 115.